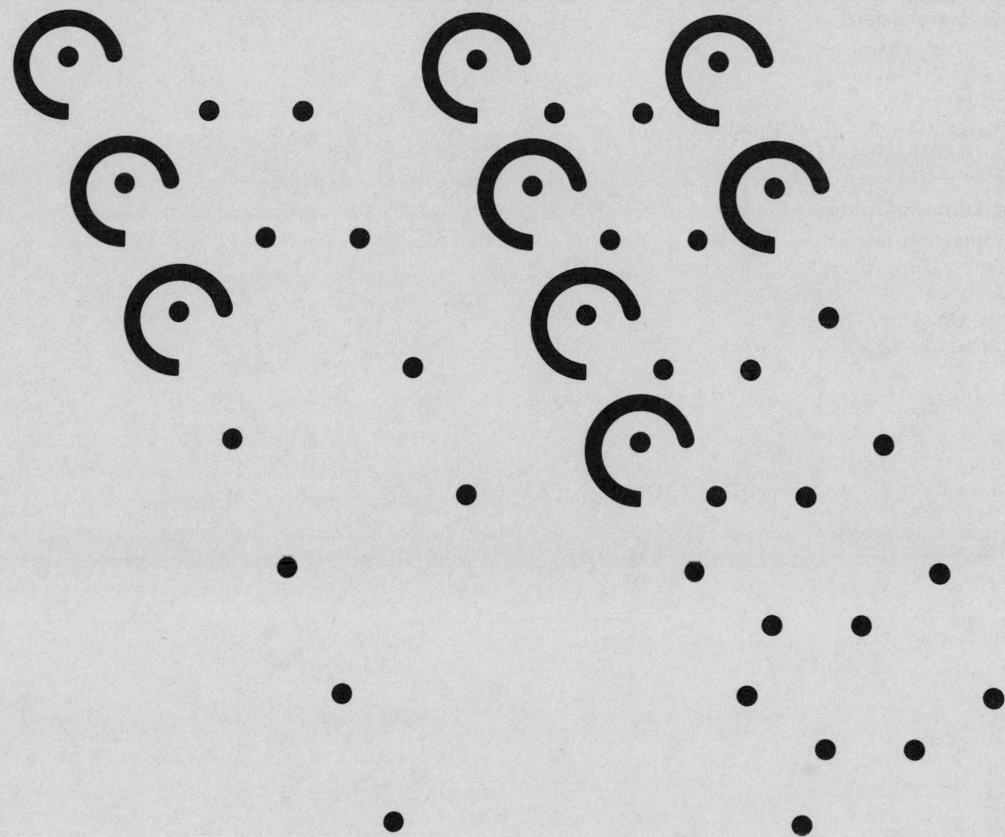

Hermeneia
—A Critical
and Historical
Commentary
on the Bible

Ezekiel 2

A Commentary on the
Book of the Prophet Ezekiel
Chapters 25–48

by Walther Zimmerli

Translated by
James D. Martin

Edited by
Paul D. Hanson
with
Leonard Jay Greenspoon

Fortress
Press

Philadelphia

Translated from the German *Ezekiel 2, II. Teilband* by Walther Zimmerli. Biblischer Kommentar Altes Testament, Band XIII/2. © 1969 Neukirchener Verlag des Erziehungsvereins GmbH, Neukirchen-Vluyn.

Library of Congress Catalog Card Number 75-21540
ISBN 0-8006-6010-2

Printed in the United States of America
Design by Kenneth Hiebert
Type set on an Ibycus System at Polebridge Press
9774C83 20-6010

Contents
Ezekiel 2

The name *Hermeneia,* Greek ἑρμηνεία, has been chosen as the title of the commentary series to which this volume belongs. The word *Hermeneia* has a rich background in the history of biblical interpretation as a term used in the ancient Greek-speaking world for the detailed, systematic exposition of a scriptural work. It is hoped that the series, like its name, will carry forward this old and venerable tradition. A second entirely practical reason for selecting the name lies in the desire to avoid a long descriptive title and its inevitable acronym, or worse, an unpronounceable abbreviation.

The series is designed to be a critical and historical commentary to the Bible without arbitrary limits in size or scope. It will utilize the full range of philological and historical tools, including textual criticism (often slighted in modern commentaries), the methods of the history of tradition (including genre and prosodic analysis), and the history of religion.

Hermeneia is designed for the serious student of the Bible. It will make full use of ancient Semitic and classical languages; at the same time, English translations of all comparative materials—Greek, Latin, Canaanite, or Akkadian—will be supplied alongside the citation of the source in its original language. Insofar as possible, the aim is to provide the student or scholar with full critical discussion of each problem of interpretation and with the primary data upon which the discussion is based.

Hermeneia is designed to be international and interconfessional in the selection of authors; its editorial boards were formed with this end in view. Occasionally the series will offer translations of distinguished commentaries which originally appeared in languages other than English. Published volumes of the series will be revised continually, and eventually, new commentaries will replace older works in order to preserve the currency of the series. Commentaries are also being assigned for important literary works in the categories of apocryphal and pseudepigraphical works relating to the Old and New Testaments, including some of Essene or Gnostic authorship.

The editors of *Hermeneia* impose no systematic-theological perspective upon the series (directly, or indirectly by selection of authors). It is expected that authors will struggle to lay bare the ancient meaning of a biblical work or pericope. In this way the text's human relevance should become transparent, as is always the case in competent historical discourse. However, the series eschews for itself homiletical translation of the Bible.

The editors are heavily indebted to Fortress Press for its energy and courage in taking up an expensive, long-term project, the rewards of which will accrue chiefly to the field of biblical scholarship.

The translator of this volume is Dr. James D. Martin of the University of St. Andrews. The preface to the second German edition was translated by Carl Ehrlich, a graduate student at Harvard University. Professor Leonard Jay Greenspoon of Clemson University provided valuable assistance in copy editing the volume, in preparing bibliographic data, and in searching out errors in references and translations.

The editor responsible for this volume is Paul D. Hanson of Harvard University.

April 1983	*Frank Moore Cross*	*Helmut Koester*
	For the Old Testament	For the New Testament
	Editorial Board	Editorial Board

Since the fascicles of the first German edition of the present commentary appeared (1955–1969), research on the book of Ezekiel has not stood still. Although one still cannot speak of an "hour of Ezekiel" having arrived, as until recently there had been an "hour of Amos," and as presently the "hour of the Deuteronomist(s)" seems to have come, a not insignificant amount of effort has been devoted to Ezekiel during the course of the last few years. In this preface a number of the more significant recent works can be described, with attention to the methodologies they use.

By means of a penetrating form-critical analysis, Hermann Schulz has isolated a certain corpus of "capital-punishment formulas" from OT legal texts and has assigned to them a definite *Sitz im Leben.*[1] Especially the formulations of the Holiness Code appeared to him to point to a certain legal process in capital cases. The author then applies the conclusions drawn from there to the capital-punishment formulations in the book of Ezekiel. This leads him to postulate a "Deuteroezekielian" stratum in Ezekiel. This would include mainly Ezek 18:1–20 (vss 21–32 do not originate from the author of 1–20, rather they could "derive from a scholastic tradition").[2] Yet it is also clearly recognizable in 14:1–11; 33:1–20; and 3:17–21. Also 5:6–9, (10? 11?); 11:12, 17–20, 21; 12:15, (16?), 21–28; 13:22ff; 16:16–21, 26ff; 20:1–31, (32ff); 21:5–10, 29f; 23:28–30, (31), 35, (36ff); 24:13f, (19–24), 25–27; 33; 34 are to be attributed to it.[3] Since at the core of this stratum is to be found not legal literature, but rather "theological legal interpretation" of the legal literature contained in Leviticus 18–20, i.e., a later theological thematization and secondary utilization, this stratum, whose unity is by all means questionable, in any case belongs to a later post-exilic phase.[4]

To assume activity of the prophet Ezekiel with a new emphasis after the fateful year 587 appears to the author already at the outset impossible: "to reckon with different creative periods in Ezekiel's life renders literary-criticism impossible through a preconceived prophetic understanding [Trans.]."[5] The methodological questions that are raised by this view are to be formulated in the following manner: first, whether one can simply reject the historically locatable elements, which can be found in the introductions to the speech units in Ezekiel 18 that are central for Schulz (chapter 18 in my opinion has been ripped into two parts in an inadmissible manner), namely in 18:2, as well as in 33:10; and secondly, whether one can postulate historical sequences through a purely literary-critical and tradition-historical inquiry. In my article "Deutero-Ezechiel?" I have attempted to formulate the methodologically questionable aspect of such an isolation of methods, and of the

1 *Das Todesrecht im Alten Testament. Studien zur Rechtsform der Mot-Jumat-Sätze,* BZAW 114 (Berlin: Töpelmann, 1969).

2 P. 178.

3 P. 184.

4 For a discussion of the whole work and the questions raised by its basic thesis of a definable "capital-punishment law," see my review of it in *ThLZ* 95 (1970): 891–897.

5 P. 166.

construction of historical sequences on the basis of pure form- and tradition-historical postulates.[6]

The redaction-historical method of inquiry, which recently has been the subject of steadily increasing interest in the investigation of other prophetic books, is dominant in the dissertation of Jörg Garscha, written in the school of Otto Kaiser.[7] Once again, the first thing that should be stated is that the redaction-historical problem is rightly being addressed today with new urgency to the prophetic books. The question in what manner a prophetic book, which without doubt did not leave the hands of the prophet in the form in which it lies before us today, achieved its final form is of help. The continuing critical work on Ezekiel will not be able to dispense with it. It is also significant that Garscha begins his study with the complex Ezekiel 17–19, and that he pursues the observations which point to the subsequent insertion of Ezekiel 18.[8] Thereafter Garscha investigates the complexes 22:1–24:14; 21 and 24:15ff; 4–7 and 12; 20 and 21:1–10; 25–28; 29–32; 33–39; 1–3; 8–11; 13–16, all according to an analogous method of inquiry. On the basis of this analysis, far-reaching conclusions are then drawn concerning the redaction-history of the book. The outcome is that at best all that can be claimed for the prophet Ezekiel is an antecedent form of a fable about a vine that forsakes its natural habitat, deduced indirectly from 17:1–10, and the rudiments of the parable of the two women in Ezekiel 23.

Moreover in the dirge over the kingdom of Judah (19:1–9), in the working song that forms the basis of 24:1–14, in the parable of the cypress or cedar that underlies Ezekiel 31, in the date of the beginning of the siege of Jerusalem in 24:1f (and in the cup parable of 23:31–34), foreign material has been taken up from a later "redactor of the prophetic book" (=REzek). The REzek, who is responsible for the basic structure of the book, is to be placed around 485 (first revolt against the Persians) or 460 (revolt of Inaros). He began the book with a call-narrative, which is to be found in 1:1aα, 3a; 2:3–3:9. He frames his first part, which goes until the capture of Jerusalem, with 3:25–27 and 24:25–27. In this framework he encloses the symbolic actions of 4:1–4, 7, 9–12; 5:1–2; 12:1–14; 21:23–27; 24:1–24, which extend from the beginning of the siege until the capture of the city, as well as the original material of 17; 19; 23. On this he appends three prophecies against the Pharaoh in 29:2–5, 31:2a–12, and 32:2–6, 16aα; four similarly constructed prophecies against Ammon, Moab, Tyre; and an only fragmentarily recognizable prophecy against the mountains of Seir, which ends as a prophecy of salvation over the mountains of Israel (the basis of 35:1–36:15). A "symbolic action" in 37:15ff promises a new Davidic empire. The description of the threat from Gog of Magog brings to an end the prophetic book redacted by REzek, which is characterized by its historical interest and a pronounced animosity toward Egypt. The restoration of the Davidic empire is his salvific perspective. Therein an analogous way of thinking betrays itself, that views the future period of salvation as a restitution of the past. Thus the campaign of Gog forms the analogy to the campaign of Nebuchadnezzar, which the first part of the book describes.

The "Deuteroezekielian redaction" (=DEzek) that then follows is, in opposition to Schulz's "Deutero-Ezekiel," an especially extensive further reworking. This distinguishes itself, first of all, by means of a sharp polemic against "the inhabitants of

6 *ZAW* 84 (1972): 501–516.

7 *Studien zum Ezekielbuch. Eine redaktionskritische Untersuchung von Ez 1–39*, Europäische Hochschulschriften 23 (Bern: Lang, 1974).

8 See 1, 391 and 397 in the present commentary.

these ruins" (33:24) and a defense of the claim of the Golah to the land. Secondly, it emphasizes that through the events which Yahweh will cause to happen knowledge of Yahweh will be brought about. Thus the knowledge formulations are to be ascribed to this stratum, although their echo can also be heard in later strata. DEzek is to be dated in the time between 400 and 350.

Around 300, or even a little bit earlier, comes the "sacral-law stratum" (= SEzek), which finally corresponds to the "Deutero-Ezekiel" of Schulz. According to Garscha it comprises 3:17–21; 13:22–23; 14:1–23;[9] 18:1–20 (which is tied into the context of chapters 17–19 by means of the parenthetical verses 17:13aβ, bα, 14b, 15b, 16, 18–19); and 33:1–10. Probably 16:45–48 and 23:36–49 should also be attributed to this stratum. This stratum exhibits a strong individualizing tendency that leads Garscha to ascribe some additional pieces, which are allotted by Schulz to the range of his "Deutero-Ezekiel," not to SEzek, but rather to his DEzek.

After the time of the capture of Tyre by Alexander the Great, the dirges over Tyre and its king in 26:15–18; 27:1–35; 28:11–19 were added; even later the texts with the motif of the descent to hell in 26:19–21; 28:2, 6a, 7–10; 30:10–12; 31:2b, 14b–18; 32:11–14 (?), 17–28. Insertions by a redactor belonging to the wisdom school in chapters 27f and 30 form an additional individual stratum. And finally a not insignificant number of remnants, in all 32 additional elements out of nearly all chapters of Ezekiel 1–39, remain, which cannot definitely be attributed to any of the characteristic strata. To these belong *inter alia* the description of the appearance of God in chapters 1 and 10, and the redemptive conclusion of 17:22–24. Since Sirach presupposes the book of Ezekiel, the latter must have been available in completed form by about 200 B. C., after it had required a period of approximately 370 years for its genesis.[10]

Once again in the case of this analysis of Ezekiel, which does not take into account the complex Ezekiel 40–48 (in my opinion these chapters do play a not insignificant role in the process of dating), one cannot avoid the impression of an exaggerated one-sidedness in an otherwise significant method of inquiry. The passing over from legitimate literary-critical observations *per se* to the identification of pervading uncoverable growth strata, especially in decisions of dating, simply ignores a number of legitimate historical considerations and causes the result reached to appear unconvincing. The ease with which dates are disposed of—they can be found in great number in the component collection of the Egypt prophecies in chapters 29–32 and point mainly to the tenth to twelfth years, i.e., to the time around the fall of Jerusalem[11] —disregards the necessary caution that an appropriate redaction-critical investigation would have had to confer upon an indigenous complex of this type, which has unmistakably had its own history of development. While he prematurely seeks more far-reaching strata in the book, the author misses the special character of exactly this unit, which contains in a striking manner about half of all dates in the whole book of Ezekiel.

Prudent redaction-historical work, which from a methodological viewpoint is urgently needed, will also have to consider a great deal more painstakingly the claim of the dates themselves. The axiom first formulated by Kaiser "to view each text as a redactional creation until the contrary is proven [Trans],"[12] which stands in opposition to the "general axiom to regard a text as original until the contrary is proven

9 In opposition to Schulz, 14:21–23 is not separated from 14:12–20.

10 Pp. 208f.

11 The latest dated prophecy of the book 29:17–20 (21) has then clearly been inserted at a later time.

12 P. 25.

[Trans],"[13] this regards the principle *in dubio pro reo.* This repudiation of general forensic procedure leads to few convincing conclusions. The basis of all literary-critical work, to which the redaction-historical method also belongs, must be an openness to, and not a fundamental distrust of, the very claim of the text itself. The traditional text, which must certainly then be subjected to further thoughtful and critical examination using and combining various courses of inquiry, happens to be the basis of all judgment.

In this age of paying close attention to the Deuteronomic-Deuteronomistic components of OT literature, it is natural to search for Deuteronomistic elements also in the book of Ezekiel. In his work *Die prophetischen Heilserwartungen im Alten Testament. Ursprung und Gestaltwandel* (*The Prophetic Expectations of Salvation in the Old Testament: Origin and Metamorposis*),[14] Siegfried Herrmann, at the end of his thorough investigation of Jeremiah, has also applied this question to the book of Ezekiel. In doing so, the whole of Ezekiel's prophecy of salvation appeared to him to bear the Deuteronomistic stamp.

Following this view in his Bochum dissertation *Überlieferungsgeschichtliche Probleme des Ezechielbuches. Eine Studie zu postezechielischen Interpretationen und Komposition* (*Tradition-historical Problems in the Book of Ezekiel: A Study of Post-Ezekielian Interpretations and Compositions),* Rüdiger Liwak has especially attempted to trace the Deuteronomistic influence in Ezekiel. After painstaking methodological consideration of the question of the possible literary dependence of the book of Ezekiel on the Holiness Code (H), the Priestly source, Deuteronomy, and the book of Jeremiah, he subjected the superscription of the book in Ezek 1:2f and the complexes 2:2b–3:11; 5:4b–17; and 6; 11:14–21; 20 to an exemplary examination, in that he analyzed every complex from a literary-critical, form-critical, tradition-critical, and redaction-critical viewpoint.

As the result of this analysis the author concludes that the pieces dealt with reveal two different styles of Deuteronomistic revision of previous material that originated in the priestly realm. On the one hand, the expansion of previous material through Deuteronomistic insertions can be identified in the book's superscription, in 2:2b–3:11, and in 5:4b–17. On the other hand, one can also find larger independent constructions in chapters 6 and 20 which, like 11:14–21, are also inserted into the original material as in some measure complete and set-off complexes. Thus, according to the author, two styles of historical understanding can be identified in the book of Ezekiel, both of which have their counterpart in the Deuteronomistic history. Ezekiel 20 evidences a cyclical view of early history in its account of the exodus from Egypt, which brings to mind the cyclical understanding of the period of the judges in the Deuteronomistic book of Judges. At the same time, however, in a different passage the simpler sequence of Yahweh's fixing of salvation, disobedience of the people, and Yahweh's judgement—which conforms to 2 Kgs 17:17ff, a piece reflecting Deuteronomistic thought—can be identified. In opposition to Winfried Theil's analysis of the Deuteronomistic revision of Jeremiah,[15] which also comes from the school of S. Herrmann and to which reference is often made for purposes of comparison, Ezekiel does not recognize the demand of obedience as a precondition of salvation, since the activity of Yahweh is here depicted with great rigor as unpredictable. Thus the historical systematization in Ezekiel displays the following

13 P. 22.

14 *BWANT* 85 (Stuttgart: Kohlhammer, 1965).

15 *Die deuteronomistische Redaktion von Jeremiah 1–25,* WMANT 41 (Neukirchen-Vluyn: Neukirchener, 1973).

design (according to its linear aspect): a) Yahweh's fixing of salvation, b) the people's disobedience, c) Yahweh's judgement, d) the people's repentance. Such repentance, however, is not the precondition to e) a (new) fixing of salvation by Yahweh; f) obedience of the people; g) integral relationship, Yahweh-people. In addition to Theil's analysis of Jeremiah, his investigation of H[16] also plays an important role in Liwak's investigation, since a parallel process of a later revision of priestly material in a Deuteronomistic manner is to be found here.

Against this analysis of Ezekiel (in comparison with Garscha, disproportionately more careful), the general preliminary question already raises itself whether the singling out of a limited group of texts, chosen at random, allows a general verdict. More important is the factual question with regard to the contents whether Ezekiel's own words, which were handed down and commented on in his "school" (or in more general terms, the tradition circle that followed him), did not already contain a number of the views which are here claimed as specifically Deuteronomistic. The Deuteronomist would then possibly not even have to be bothered with, since among the contemporary priest-prophet Ezekiel and his school, or in other words his tradition circle whose priestly character is completely accepted by Liwak, something comparable existed which was completely original. Thus Liwak's strongly emphasized thesis that Deuteronomistic thought speaks of the early and fundamental corruption of Israel, from which certain statements in Ezekiel 2f are then judged to be Deuteronomistic, loses all impact in the face of the observation that exactly this view of the nation's history is brought to expression with unsurpassing harshness in Ezekiel 16 and 23, pieces which are impossible to deny to Ezekiel. One even will have to come to the conclusion that here Ezekiel surpasses the Deuteronomistic testimony.

The question comes to mind whether the fact that the author has singled out only isolated texts from the whole book and has apparently not considered the rest in their peculiarity does not backfire on him. In this connection I mean that the linguistic observations listed in the introduction to the present commentary retain their weight in spite of the criticism of their terse summary "in 15½ lines."[17] They pose a genuine question regarding the "Deuteronomicity" of the book of Ezekiel—a question which does not seem to me to have been answered in full by Liwak's work. However, it appears to me as clear as ever that, as for the rest, the studies of S. Herrmann, W. Thiel, and R. Liwak, concerning Jeremiah, Ezekiel, and H, and their linguistic peculiarities, have kept awake the question of Deuteronomistic influence on Ezekiel and make it imperative to continue to examine the question into what depth such influence has penetrated the book.

From another aspect, the postulates contained in Wolfgang Richter's 1971 prospectus, *Exegese als Literaturwissenschaft. Entwurf einer alttestamentlichen Literaturtheorie und Methodologie* (*Exegesis as Literary Science: An Outline of an OT Literary Theory and Methodology*), and the linguistic analysis required by it have stimulated recent investigations. The works of Horacio Simian[18] must be mentioned in this connec-

16 "Erwägungen zum Alter des Heiligkeitsgesetzes," *ZAW* 81 (1969): 40–71.

17 Rüdiger Liwak, *Überlieferungsgeschichtliche Probleme des Ezechielbuches. Eine Studie zu postezechielischen Interpretation und Kompositionen*, Unpub. Diss. (Bochum, 1976), 327 note 19.

18 *Die theologische Nachgeschichte der Prophetie Ezechiels. Form- und traditionskritische Untersuchungen zu Ez 6; 35; 36*, Forschung zur Bibel 14 (Würzburg: Echter, 1974).

tion. While Simian limits his analysis to chapters 6 and 35f, Hossfeld attempts to gain a broader basis, in that he investigates eight varied units: 17:11–24; 22:1–16; 28:1–10; 30:1–19; 34:1–31; 36:16–38 (with an excursus on exodus terminology); 37:1–14 (with an excursus on *nb'* in Ezekiel); 38:1–39:29. On the whole, the methodology of these two works is very much the same. After the "smaller units" have been defined, they are syntactically and stylistically analyzed through a textual-linguistic method of inquiry, and semantically scrutinized; their structure is distinguished, and their "horizon" is determined (thus Simian, in place of which Hossfeld speaks of "composition- and redaction-criticism"). While Simian limits himself to the guidelines that Richter developed through a study of narrative texts, Hossfeld advances to the question of how one is to delineate the "small unit" in prophetic texts, in distinction to narrative ones. In this connection, he treats the formulaic material that constitutes the characteristic feature of prophetic texts. This is without doubt a more adequate approach to the genre of prophetic speech, and it signifies an advance beyond Simian. Thus, on account of its broader design and more appropriate criteria, Hossfeld's investigation is disproportionately more productive than the work of Simian, which, although it is quite careful in its textual-linguistic analysis, is not capable of convincing either through its tradition-critical investigation or especially through its crossing over to historical conclusions.

From the very beginning, Hossfeld gives full weight to the pervading characteristic of Ezekiel's prophetic speech as a report in the first person. Unlike Garscha, the individual aspect of the exilic priest-prophet Ezekiel is not obliterated, even though his analysis leads him to five, at times six redactional strata, evidence of later work on the prophetic book. At the same time, Hossfeld explicitly maintains that the analysis of eight selected macro-texts does not by any means allow an all-inclusive verdict concerning the whole book. With regard to the characterization of the individual redaction strata, which he still places quite close to the prophet himself, he does not yet venture any general characterizing statements concerning the first two mentioned, on account of the paucity of material associated with them. In the third stratum, the theme of the "new exodus" has greater stress laid upon it. The fourth evidences a closer connection to Deuteronomistic literature, while the fifth orients itself linguistically and theologically toward the basic stratum of P and H. The sixth stratum, with its editorial interest in the formulation of conclusions to chapters 28; 34; 36; 39, evidences a linguistic connection to Deutero-Isaiah, the Psalms, and later (post-Deuteronomistic) sections of Jeremiah. According to Hossfeld, the actual prophecy of the prophet Ezekiel is characterized by a double two-phasedness: diachronically through the phases of prophecy of both calamity and salvation, and synchronically through the sermons to the exiles on the one hand and to those remaining in the land on the other. With regard to the content it should be mentioned that in the Gog pericope, i.e., in the original text which he has worked out of 38:1–3a; 39:1b–5, Hossfeld detects a one stanza oracle against a foreign nation, against Gog of Meshech and Tubal, who is in no case to be understood as a "cryptic power" and a "legendary representative of all enemies from the north," but rather as a contemporary ruler. The original Gog oracle thus falls in with the other oracles against foreign nations in the book of Ezekiel. However, the disciples of Ezekiel then felt that they had to "shift the oracle, which had originally alluded to the near future, into a second phase: the distant future" on account of the failure to appear of that which their master had prophesized, since a simple non-appearance did not seem possible to them. Thus 38:3b–9 (minus a few glosses) was added as the first expansion, and 39:7–10 as the second. In this manner, then, the oracle of three stanzas, which in the present commentary is treated as the original basis of the Gog prophecy, came into being. Concerning the expansions which have been joined to this oracle of three stanzas, Hossfeld more or less follows the views advocated in this commentary. A more detailed discussion of the works of Simian and Hossfeld can be found in my reviews in *ThLZ.*[19]

The text-linguistic method used in both works is without doubt here and there capable of elucidating characteristic features of both the original and the redacted book of Ezekiel. To this extent it is able to provide the exegete with useful help and must be taken into account in any attempts at interpretation. To be sure, it must guard itself from its own peculiar inherent danger, in that it does not seek to press the true flexibility of a living, spoken, as well as written language into too rigid structural outlines. The amount of control that one has over one's own personal speaking and writing will always warn against this danger. In this regard, Liwak's work, which explicitly removes itself from Richter's strict method according to which "everything (is) asserted as reliable, which has been understood as a genre, formula, or preconceived pattern [Trans.],"[20] has been consciously held more flexible.

Othmar Keel's work, *Jahwe-Visionen und Siegelkunst. Eine neue Deutung der Majestätsschilderungen in Jes 6, Ez 1 und 10, und Sach 4*[21] (*Visions of Yahweh and Glyptic Art: A New Interpretation of the Appearances of the Majesty in Isa 6, Ezek 1 and 10, and Zech 4*), yields a valuable enrichment for an understanding of the visions of the appearance of the Glory of Yahweh. In its third section,[22] it presents an abundance of depictions of ancient Near Eastern glyptic art, which definitely advances our understanding of the two descriptions of the Glory in Ezekiel 1 and 10. A rich source of ancient Near Eastern depictions of four-winged gods and genies, of four-winged divine bearers, of four-faced divine beings, of throned divinities, and of multi-eyed figures (representations of Bes from Egypt) is made accessible here, to some extent for the first time. Henceforth this work will be indispensible for a deeper understanding of the Ezekielian description of the Glory. However, whether the theological assertion will endure that, according to the self awareness of the prophet, Ezekiel 1 attempted to make Yahweh appear "as the omnipresent God of heaven, close to the exiles [Trans.],"[23] while only Ezekiel 10 had the one enthroned in Jerusalem before his eyes (substitution of the "creatures" by cherubs), requires still more discussion.

David J. Halperin seeks to understand in a completely different manner the deviation of the description of the Glory in Ezekiel 10 from that of Ezekiel 1.[24] In Ezekiel 10 he finds the beginning of an angelological understanding of the *'ôpannîm,* which then comes into common use in later Judaism.

The continuing work on the book of Ezekiel, sketched by means of a few especially characteristic examples and their various methodologies, and the continuing inquiry that can be found in them concerning the unrevealed secrets of

19 For Simian see *ThLZ* 102 (1977); 719–723; for Hossfeld, *ThLZ* 104 (1979): 730–733.

20 Liwak, *Überlieferungsgeschichtliche Probleme,* 327 note 16.

21 Stuttgarter Bibel-Studien 84/85 (Stuttgart: Katholisches Bibelwerk, 1977).

22 Pp. 125–273.

23 P. 272.

24 "The exegetical character of Ezek X 9–17," *VT* 26 (1976): 129–141.

Ezekiel, make clear that the statement found in the preface to the first edition of this commentary remains valid: "for those who follow in the task of expounding this book there is still much new work that remains to be done."[25] The works sketched above in brief mean, each in its own way, an enrichment of the collection of important tools for the exegete of Ezekiel. They must be seriously considered in their methodological assessment, even when the conclusions presented are not always convincing.

Göttingen
March 18, 1978

Walther Zimmerli

25 See 1, xiii.

1. Sources and Abbreviations

Abbreviations used in this volume for sources and literature from antiquity are the same as those used in the *Theological Dictionary of the New Testament,* ed. Gerhard Kittel, tr. Geoffrey W. Bromiley, vol. 1 (Grand Rapids, Michigan, and London: Eerdmans, 1964), xvi–xl. Some abbreviations are adapted from that list and can be easily identified.

In addition, the following abbreviations have been used:

Acts	Acts of the Apostles
AfO	*Archiv für Orientforschung* (Berlin, 1926ff)
AJSL	*American Journal of Semitic Languages and Literatures* (Chicago, 1895–1941)
ALBO	Analecta lovanensia biblica et orientalia
ANEP	*The Ancient Near East in Pictures Relating to the Old Testament,* ed. J. B. Pritchard (Princeton: Princeton Univ. Press, 1954)
ANET	*Ancient Near Eastern Texts Relating to the Old Testaments,* ed. J. B. Pritchard (Princeton: Princeton Univ. Press, 1955)
AO	Der Alte Orient (Leipzig, 1900ff)
AOBAT	*Altorientalische Bilder zum Alten Testament,* ed. H. Gressmann (Tübingen, ^{2}1926)
AOT	*Altorientalische Texte zum Alten Testament,* ed. H. Gressmann (Tübingen, ^{2}1926)
ARAB	*Ancient Records of Assyria and Babylonia,* ed. D. D. Luckenbill (Chicago: University of Chicago Press, 1926–1927 = Westport, CT: Greenwood Press, 1975)
ARE	*Ancient Records of Egypt,* ed. James Henry Breasted (Chicago: University of Chicago Press, ^{2}1920–1923)
ARW	*Archiv für Religionswissenschaft* (Freiburg, Leipzig, Tübingen, 1898–1941)
ATANT	Abhandlungen zur Theologie des Alten und Neuen Testaments
ATD	Das Alte Testament Deutsch
BA	*The Biblical Archaeologist*
Bar	Baruch
BASOR	*Bulletin of the American Schools of Oriental Research*
BBB	Bonner Biblische Beiträge
BEvTh	Beiträge zur evangelischen Theologie (München)
BFChrTh	Beiträge zur Förderung Christlicher Theologie
BH	*Biblia Hebraica,* ed. Rudolf Kittel. "Ezechiel" in BH^2 (1913) prepared by J. W. Rothstein. "Ezechiel" in BH^3 (1937) prepared by Julius A. Bewer
BhEvTh	Beihefte zur evangelischen Theologie (München)
BHTh	Beiträge zur historischen Theologie (Tübingen, 1929ff)
Bibl	*Biblica* (Rome)
BK	Biblischer Kommentar. Altes Testament, eds. Martin Noth, H. W. Wolff, S. Herrmann (Neukirchen)
BM	British Museum
BRA	Beiträge zur Religionsgeschichte des Altertums
BRL	*Biblisches Reallexikon,* ed. Kurt Galling (Tübingen, 1937)
BSF	Biblische Studien (Freiburg)
BWA(N)T	Beiträge zur Wissenschaft vom Alten (und Neuen) Testament
BZ	*Biblische Zeitschrift*
BZAW	Beihefte zur Zeitschrift für die alttestamentliche Wissenschaft
BZNW	Beihefte zur Zeitschrift für die neutestamentliche Wissenschaft
CAD	*The Assyrian Dictionary of the Oriental Institute of the Univeristy of Chicago*
CBQ	*Catholic Biblical Quarterly*
Cent-B	The Century Bible (London)
cf.	Confer, compare with
Chr	Chronicles
CIS	*Corpus inscriptionum semiticarum*
cj.	Conjecture
Cor	Corinthians
COT	Commentar op het Oude Testament, ed. G. Charles Aalders (Kampen)
CQR	*Church Quarterly Review*
CSS	Cursus scripturae (Paris)
CT	*Collectanea theologica*
CultBibl	*Cultura biblica* (Segovia)
DalmanWB	Dalman, Gustaf: *Aramäisch-neuhebräisches Handwörterbuch* (^{2}1922)
Dan	Daniel
Dtn	Deuteronomy
Eccl	Ecclesiastes
Echter-B	Die Heilige Schrift in deutscher Übersetzung (Würzburg: Echter Verlag)

ed.	Editor; edited by
[Ed.]	Editor of this volume of Hermenia
Est	Esther
ET	*The Expository Times*
EThL	*Ephemerides theologicae lovanienses*
EvTh	*Evangelische Theologie*
Ex	Exodus
Ezek	Ezekiel
Ezr	Ezra
f	Designates one verse or page following the verse or page cited
FRLANT	Forschungen zur Religion und Literatur des Alten und Neuen Testaments (Göttingen)
FuF	*Forschungen und Fortschritte* (Berlin)
Gen	Genesis
H	Holiness Code (Leviticus 17–26)
Hab	Habakkuk
Hag	Haggai
HAT	Handbuch zum Alten Testament, ed. Otto Eissfeldt
HBNT	Handbuch zum Neuen Testament
Heb	Hebrews
HKAT	Handkommentar zum Alten Testament, ed. W. Nowack (Göttingen)
HO	*Handbuch der Orientalistik,* ed. B. Spuler (Berlin, 1948ff)
Hos	Hosea
HSAT	Die Heilige Schrift der Alten Testaments, ed. E. Kautzsch (Tübingen)
HTR	*Harvard Theological Review*
HUCA	*Hebrew Union College Annual* (Cincinnati, 1924ff)
IB	*Interpreter's Bible*
Ibid.	In the same place
ICC	The International Critical Commentary of the Holy Scriptures of the Old and New Testament (Edinburgh)
idem.	The same (person)
IEJ	*Israel Exploration Journal* (Jerusalem)
Is	Isaiah
JAOS	*Journal of the American Oriental Society* (New Haven, 1843ff)
JBL	*Journal of Biblical Literature*
JBR	*Journal of Bible and Religion*
Jer	Jeremiah
Jn	John
JNES	*Journal of Near Eastern Studies*
Jon	Jonah
Josh	Joshua
JPOS	*Journal of the Palestine Oriental Society* (Jerusalem, 1920–48)
JPTh	*Jahrbücher für protestantische Theologie* (Leipzig)
JSS	*Journal of Semitic Studies*
JTS	*Journal of Theological Studies*
Ju	Judges
KAT	Kommentar zum Alten Testament, ed. E. Sellin
KeH	Kurzgefasstes exegetisches Handbuch zum Alten Testament (Leipzig)
Kgs	Kings
KHC	Kurzer Hand-Commentar zum Alten Testament, ed. K. Marti
Lam	Lamentations
Lev	Leviticus
LidzEph	Lidzbarski, Mark: *Ephemeris für semitische Epigraphik* (Giessen, 1901–1911)
Lk	Luke
Mal	Malachi
MGWJ	*Monatsschrift für Geschichte und Wissenschaft des Judentums* (Breslau)
Mic	Micah
Mk	Mark
MPL	Migne, J. P.: *Patrologiae cursus completus.* Series latina.
Mt	Matthew
Museon	*Le Museon.* Revue d'études orientales (Louvain)
MVÄG	Mitteilungen der Vorderasiatisch-Ägyptischen Gesellschaft
Na	Nahum
NC	*La Nouvelle Clio* (Brussels)
Neh	Nehemiah
NKZ	*Neue kirchliche Zeitschrift* (Erlangen)
NTS	*New Testament Studies* (Cambridge)
Nu	Numbers
Ob	Obadiah
OIP	The Oriental Institute Publications (Chicago)
OLZ	*Orientalistische Literaturzeitung*
Or	*Orientalia.* Commentarii periodici Pontificii Instituti Biblici (Rome)
OTS	*Oudtestamentische Studiën* (Leiden)
p.(pp.)	Page(s)
PEQ	*Palestine Exploration Quarterly* (London, 1869ff)
PJ	*Palästinajahrbuch*
PrincTR	*Princeton Theological Review*
Prv	Proverbs
Ps	Psalms
PW	Pauly-Wissowa: *Real-Encyclopädie der classichen Altertumswissenschaft*
RB	*Revue biblique*
RES	*Revue des études semitiques* (Paris)
RGG	*Die Religion in Geschichte und Gegenwart*
RGL	*Religionsgeschichtliches Lesebuch,* ed. Alfred Bertholet (Tübingen, 1926ff)
RHPhR	*Revue d'histoire et de philosophie religieuses* (Strasbourg)
RLA	*Reallexikon der Assyriologie,* ed. Erich Ebeling and Bruno Meissner (Berlin, 1928ff)
RLV	*Reallexikon der Vorgeschichte,* ed. Max Ebert (Berlin, 1924–32)
RQ	*Revue de Qumran* (Paris)
Sam	Samuel
SBOT	The Sacred Books of the Old Testa-

	ment, ed. Paul Haupt
Sir	Jesus Sirach (Ecclesiasticus)
Song	Song of Solomon
S.P.C.K.	Society for Promoting Christian Knowledge
StOr	Studia orientalia (Helsinki)
StTh	*Studia theologica.* Cura ordinum theologorum scandinavicorum edita (Lund)
Sumer	*Sumer* (Bagdad)
Syria	*Syria.* Revue d'art oriental et archéologie (Paris)
TDNT	*Theological Dictionary of the New Testament,* ed. Gerhard Kittel (Grand Rapids, Michigan, and London: Eerdmans, 1964ff)
TeU	Tekst en Uitleg (Den Haag, Groningen)
ThB	Theologische Bücherei (München)
ThGl	*Theologie und Glaube*
ThLZ	*Theologische Literaturzeitung*
ThEx	Theologische Existenz Heute (München)
ThR	*Theologische Rundschau*
ThSt	Theologische Studien
ThStKr	*Theologische Studien und Kritiken*
ThT	*Theologische Tijdschrift*
TWNT	*Theologisches Wörterbuch Zum Neuen Testament.* Begun by G. Kittel
ThZ	*Theologische Zeitschrift* (Basel)
tr.	Translator, translated by
[Trans.]	Translator of this volume of Hermeneia
[Trans. by Ed.]	Translated by editor of this volume of Hermeneia
UUÅ	Uppsala universitetsårsskrift (Uppsala)
v(v)	Verse(s)
VAB	Vorderasiatische Bibliothek (Leipzig, 1907–1916)
vol(s)	Volume(s)
VT	*Vetus Testamentum*
VT Suppl	Supplements to Vetus Testamentum (Leiden)
WMANT	Wissenschaftliche Mongraphien zum Alten und Neuen Testament (Neukirchen)
WO	Die Welt des Orients. Wissenschaftliche Beiträge zur Kunde des Morgenlandes (Göttingen)
WuD	*Wort und Dienst*
WVDOG	Wissenschaftliche Veröffentlichungen der Deutschen Orientgesellschaft
WZ	*Wissenschaftliche Zeitschrift*
WZKM	*Wiener Zeitschrift für die Kunde des Morgenlandes* (Vienna, 1886–1940)
ZAW	*Zeitschrift für die alttestamentliche Wissenschaft*
ZB	*Zürcher Bibel*
ZDMG	*Zeitschrift der Deutschen Morgenländischen Gesellschaft*
ZDPV	*Zeitschrift des deutschen Palaestina-Vereins*
Zech	Zechariah
Zeph	Zephaniah
ZKTh	*Zeitschrift für katholische Theologie*
ZLThK	*Zeitschrift für lutherische Theologie und Kirche*
ZS	*Zeitschrift für Semistik und verwandte Gebiete*
ZThK	*Zeitschrift für Theologie und Kirche*
ZWTh	*Zeitschrift für wissenschaftliche Theologie*

2. Short titles of Commentaries, Studies, and Articles Often Cited

Works also contained in the Bibliography of *Ezekiel* 1 are marked with an asterisk (*). Where a "short title" was assigned to an article or book in the earlier volume, the same designation is retained here. With the exception of commentaries, however, works from *Ezekiel* 1 are not listed in the Bibliography of the present volume, i.e., the Bibliography is limited to works cited for the first time in this volume. Commentaries on Ezekiel as well as a few other works are cited by author's name only.

*Aalders
Gerhard Charles Aalders, *Ezechiel,* 2 volumes, COT (Kampen: Kok, 1955 and 1957).

Aalders, *Gog en Magog*
J. G. Aalders, *Gog en Magog in Ezechiël* (Kampen: Kok, 1951).

Abraham, *Schiffsterminologie*
A. Abraham, *Die Schiffsterminologie des Alten Testaments kulturgeschichtlich und etymologisch untersucht,* Unpub. Diss. (Bern, 1914).

*Albrecht, "Geschlecht"
Karl Albrecht, "Das Geschlecht der hebräischen Hauptwörter," *ZAW* 16 (1896): 41–121.

*Albright, *Archaeology*
W. F. Albright, *Archaeology and the Religion of Israel* (Baltimore: Johns Hopkins University Press, 1956).

Albright, "Babylonian Temple-Tower"
W. F. Albright, "The Babylonian Temple-Tower and the Altar of Burnt-Offering" *JBL* 39 (1920): 137–142.

Albright, "Dedan"
W. F. Albright, "Dedan" in *Geschichte und Altes Testament; Festschrift für A. Alt* (Tübingen: Mohr, 1953), 1–12.

Albright, "High Place"
W. F. Albright, "The High Place in Ancient Israel" in *Volume du Congrès, Strasbourg 1956,* VT Suppl 4 (Leiden, 1957), 242–258.

*Albright, "Seal of Eliakim"
W. R. Albright, "The Seal of Eliakim and the Latest Preëxilic History of Judah, with Some Observations on Ezekiel," *JBL* 51 (1932): 77–106.

Alt, "Deltaresidenz"
Albrecht Alt, "Die Deltaresidenz der Ramessiden" in *Kleine Schriften zur Geschichte des Volkes Israel* 3 (München: Beck, 1959), 176–185.

*Alt, "Judas Gaue"
Albrecht Alt, "Judas Gaue unter Josia," *PJ* 21 (1925: 100–116; reprinted in *idem, Kleine Schriften zur Geschichte des Volkes Israel* 2 (München: Beck, 1953), 276–288.

*Alt, *Kleine Schriften*
Albrecht Alt, *Kleine Schriften zur Geschichte des Volkes Israel,* 3 volumes (München: Beck, 1953–59).

*Alt, "Sanheribs Eingriff"
Albrecht Alt, "Die territorialgeschichtliche Bedeutung von Sanheribs Eingriff in Palästina," *PJ* 25 (1929 [1930]): 80–88; reprinted in *idem, Kleine Schriften zur Geschichte des Volkes Israel* 2 (München: Beck, 1953), 242–249.

Alt, "Staatenbildung"
Albrecht Alt, "Die Staatenbildung der Israeliten in Palästina" in *Kleine Schriften zur Geschichte des Volkes Israel* 2 (München: Beck, 1953), 1–65.

Alt, "Taphnaein und Taphnas"
Albrecht Alt, "Taphnaein und Taphnas," *ZDPV* 66 (1943): 64–68.

Anderson, *Alexander's Gate*
Andrew Runni Anderson, *Alexander's Gate, Gog and Magog, and the inclosed Nations* (Cambridge, Mass.: The Mediaeval Academy of America, 1932).

*Auvray
P. Auvray, *Ezéchiel,* Témoins de Dieu, (1947).

Bach, "Bauen und Pflanzen"
Robert Bach, "Bauen und Pflanzen" in *Studien zur Theologie der alttestamentlichen Überlieferungen,* ed. R. Rendtorff and K. Koch (Neukirchen-Vluyn: Neukirchener, 1961), 7–32.

Baedeker, *Egypt*
Karl Baedeker, *Egypt and the Sûdân; Handbook for Travellers* (New York: C. Schribner's Sons, [7]1914).

*Bardtke, "Erweckungsgedanke"
Hans Bardtke, "Der Erweckungsgedanke in der exilisch-nachexilischen Literatur des Alten Testaments" in *Von Ugarit nach Qumran,* BZAW 77 (Berlin, 1958), 9–24.

*Barrois, *Manuel*
A. G. Barrois, *Manuel d'archéologie biblique,* 2 volumes (Paris: Picard, 1939 and 1953).

C. Barth, *Errettung vom Tode*
Christoph Barth, *Die Errettung vom Tode in den individuellen Klage- und Dankliedern des Alten Testaments* (Zollikon: Evangelischer, 1947).

Baudissin, *Geschichte*
Wolf Wilhelm Graf Baudissin, *Die Geschichte des alttestamentlichen Priesterthums* (Leipzig: Hirzel, 1889).

*Baumann, "שוב שבות"
Eberhard Baumann, "שוב שבות Eine exegetische Untersuchung," *ZAW* 47 (1929): 17–44.

*Baumgärtel, "Formel"
Friedrich Baumgärtel, "Die Formel *nᵉʾum jahwe,*" *ZAW* 73 (1961): 277–290.

Baumgärtel, "Gottesnamen"
Friedrich Baumgärtel, "Zu den Gottesnamen in den Büchern Jeremia und Ezechiel" in *Verbannung und Heimkehr. Beiträge zur Geschichte und Theologie Israels im 6. und 5. Jahrhundert v. Chr., Wilhelm Rudolph zum 70. Geburtstage dargebracht* (Tübingen: Mohr [Siebeck], 1961), 1–29.

von Beckerath, *Tanis und Theben*
Jürgen von Beckerath, *Tanis und Theben; historische*

Grundlagen der Ramessidenzeit in Ägypten, Ägyptologische Forschungen 16 (Glückstadt, New York: Augustin, 1951).

*Begrich, *Chronologie*
Joachim Begrich, *Die Chronologie der Könige von Israel und Juda und die Quellen des Rahmens der Königsbücher* (Tübingen: Mohr [Siebeck], 1929).

*Begrich, *Studien*
Joachim Begrich, *Studien zu Deuterojesaja,* BWANT 4:25 (Stuttgart, 1938).

*Begrich, "Tora"
Joachim Begrich, "Die priesterliche Tora" in *BZAW* 66 (Berlin, 1936), 63–88; reprinted in *idem, Gesammelte Studien zum AT,* ThB 21 (München: Kaiser, 1964), 232–260.

Begrich, "Messiasbild"
Karl Begrich, "Das Messiasbild des Ezechiel," *ZWTh* 47 (1904): 433–461.

Bentzen, "Priesterschaft"
Aage Bentzen, "Priesterschaft und Laien in der jüdischen Gemeinde des fünften Jahrhunderts," *AfO* 6 (1930/31): 280–286.

*Bertholet
Alfred Bertholet, *Das Buch Hesekiel erklärt,* KHC 12 (Freiburg: Mohr, 1897).

*Bertholet, *Stellung*
Alfred Bertholet, *Die Stellung der Israeliten und der Juden zu den Fremden* (Freiburg, 1896).

*Bertholet-Galling
Alfred Bertholet and Kurt Galling, *Hesekiel,* HAT 13 (Tübingen: Mohr [Siebeck], 1936).

*Bewer, "Exegese"
Julius A. Bewer, "Beiträge zur Exegese des Buches Ezechiel," *ZAW* 63 (1951): 193–201.

*Bewer, "Textual Notes"
Julius A. Bewer, "Textual and Exegetical Notes on the Book of Ezekiel," *JBL* 72 (1953): 158–168.

Bieling, *Sagen*
Hugo Bieling, *Zu den Sagen von Gog und Magog,* Wissenschaftliche Beilage zum Programm der Sophien-Realschule. Ostern 1882 (Berlin: Weidmannsch Buchhandlung, 1882).

Bietenhard, *tausendjährige Reich*
Hans Bietenhard, *Das tausendjährige Reich; eine biblische-theologische Studie* (Bern: Graf-Lehmann, 1944).

Bilabel, *Geschichte*
Friedrich Bilabel, *Geschichte Vorderasiens und Ägyptens vom 16.-11. Jahrhundert v. Chr.* (Heidelberg: Winter, 1927).

*Blau, "Gebrauch"
Josia Blau, "Zum angeblichen Gebrauch von את vor dem Nominativ," *VT* 4 (1954): 7–22.

Blome, *Opfermaterie*
Friedrich Blome, *Die Opfermaterie in Babylonien und Israel* 1 (Rome: Pontifical Biblical Institute, 1934).

Boettcher, *Neue Aehrenlese*
Julius Friedrich Boettcher, *Neue exegetisch-kritische Aehrenlese zum Alten Testament,* 2. Abtheilung ed. F. Mühlau (1864), 183–191.

Boettcher, *Proben*
Julius Friedrich Boettcher, *Proben alttestamentlicher Schrifterklärung nach wissenschaftlicher Sprachforschung mit kritischen Versuchen über bisherige Exegese und Beiträgen zu Grammatik und Lexicon* (1833), 218–365 (XII. "Exegetisch-kritischer Versuch über die ideale Beschreibung der Tempelgebäude Ezech. C. 40–42; 46:19–24").

*Bonnet, *Reallexikon*
H. Bonnet, *Reallexikon der ägyptischen Religionsgeschichte* (Berlin: 1952).

Borger, *Inschriften Asarhaddons*
Riekele Borger, *Die Inschriften Asarhaddons, Königs von Assyrien,* Archiv für Orientforschung beiheft 9 (Graz: Im Selbstverlag des Herausgebers, 1956).

van den Born, "Ezek 26:2"
A. van den Born, "'De deur (?) der volken' in Ezek 26:2," *StC* 26 (1951): 320–322.

van den Born, 'pays du Magog'
A. van den Born, "Études sur quelques toponymes bibliques," *OTS* 10 (1954): 197–214 (1. 'Le pays du Magog,' 197–201).

*Bousset-Gressmann
Wilhelm Bousset and Hugo Gressmann, *Die Religion des Judentums im späthellenistischen Zeitalter,* HBNT 21 (Tübingen: Mohr [Siebeck], ³1926).

Breasted, *History*
James Henry Breasted, *A History of Egypt from the Earliest Times to the Persian Conquest* (New York: C. Scribner's Sons, ²1920).

*Breuer
Joseph Breuer, *Das Buch Jecheskel übersetzt und erläutert* (Frankfurt: Sänger and Friedberg, 1921).

*Brockelmann
C. Brockelmann, *Hebräische Syntax* (Neukirchen-Vluyn: Neukirchen, 1956).

Brock-Utne, *Gottesgarten*
Albert Brock-Utne, *Der Gottesgarten; eine vergleichende religionsgeschichtliche Studie* (Oslo: Dybwad, 1936).

Brown, "Note"
Theo. Brown, "A Note on Gog," *Folk-lore* (London) 61 (1950): 98–103.

*Browne, *Ezekiel and Alexander*
Laurence Edward Browne, *Ezekiel and Alexander* (London: S.P.C.K., 1952).

*Buber, *Israel*
Martin Buber, *Israel and Palestine: the History of an Idea* (London: East and West Library, 1952).

*C. Budde, "Klagelied"
C. Budde, "Das hebräische Klagelied," *ZAW* 2 (1882): 1–52.

*Bultmann, *History*
Rudolf Karl Bultmann, *The History of the Synoptic Tradition,* tr. John Marsh (Oxford: Basil Blackwell, ²1968).

Chajes, "Ez. 27:4"
H. P. Chajes, "Ex. 27:4," *ZAW* 21 (1901): 79.

Cheminant, *prophéties*
P. Cheminant, *Les prophéties d'Ezéchiel contre Tyr (26–28:19),* 1912.
Childs, "Enemy"
Brevard S. Childs, "The Enemy From the North and the Chaos Tradition," *JBL* 78 (1959): 187–198.
*Cohen, "Studies"
A. Cohen, "Studies in Hebrew Lexicography," *AJSL* 40 (1924): 153–185.
*Cooke
G. A. Cooke, *A Critical and Exegetical Commentary on the Book of Ezekiel,* ICC (Edinburgh: Clark, 1936).
*Cornill
Carl Heinrich Cornill, *Das Buch des Propheten Ezechiel* (Leipzig, 1886).
*Cowley, *Papyri*
Arthur Ernest Cowley, *Aramaic Papyri discovered at Assuan* (London: Moring, 1906).
*Cross, "Tabernacle"
Frank M. Cross, Jr., "The Tabernacle: A Study from an Archaelogical and Historical Approach," *BA* 10 (1947): 45–68.
*Dalman, *Arbeit*
Gustaf Dalman, *Arbeit und Sitte in Palästina,* 7 volumes (Gütersloh: Bertelsmann, 1928–1942).
Dalman, "Wasserversorgung"
Gustaf Dalman, "Die Wasserversorgung des ältesten Jerusalem," *PJ* 14 (1918): 47–72.
Dalman, "zweite Tempel"
Gustaf Dalman, "Der zweite Tempel zu Jerusalem," *PJ* 5 (1909): 29–57.
*Delitzsch, *Schreibfehler*
Friedrich Delitzsch, *Die Lese- und Schreibfehler im Alten Testament* (Berlin, 1920).
*Diehl, *Pronomen*
W. Diehl, *Das Pronomen personale suffixum 2. und 3. pers. plur. des Hebräischen in der alttestamentlichen Überlieferung,* Unpub. Diss. (Giessen, 1895).
*E. L. Dietrich, שוב שבות
Ernst Ludwig Dietrich, שוב שבות. *Die endzeitliche Wiederherstellung bei den Propheten,* BZAW 40 (Giessen: Töpelmann, 1925).
Díez-Macho, "Targum Palestinense"
A. Díez-Macho, "Un segundo fragmento del Targum Palestinense a los Profetas," *Bibl* 39 (1958): 198–205.
*Driver, *Aramaic Documents*
G. R. Driver, *Aramaic Documents of the Fifth Century B.C.* (Oxford: Clarendon, 1954).
*Driver, *Canaanite Myths*
G. R. Driver, *Canaanite Myths and Legends* (Edinburgh: Clark, 1956).
*Driver, "Difficult"
G. R. Driver, "Difficult Words in the Hebrew Prophets" in *Studies in Old Testament Prophecy,* ed. H. H. Rowley (Edinburgh: Clark, 1950), 52–72.
*Driver, "Ezekiel"
G. R. Driver, "Ezekiel: Linguistic and Textual Problems," *Bibl* 35 (1954): 145–159, 299–312.
Driver, *Hebrew Verbal System*
G. R. Driver, *Problems of the Hebrew Verbal System* (Edinburgh: Clark, 1936).
*Driver, "Linguistic Problems"
G. R. Driver, "Linguistic and Textual Problems: Ezekiel," *Bibl* 19 (1938): 60–69, 175–187.
*Driver, "Studies. 8"
G. R. Driver, "Studies in the Vocabulary of the Old Testament. 8," *JTS* 36 (1935): 293–301.
Driver, S. R.
A Treatise on the Use of the Tenses in Hebrew and Some Other Syntactical Questions (Oxford: At the Clarendon Press, 1874, [2]1892).
*Dupont-Sommer, *Essene*
A. Dupont-Sommer, *The Essene Writings from Qumran,* tr. G. Vermes (Cleveland: World, 1962).
*Dürr, *Apokalyptik*
L. Dürr, *Die Stellung des Proppheten Ezechiel in der israelitisch-jüdischen Apokalyptik,* AA IX 1 (Münster: Aschendorff, 1923).
Dürr, *Ursprung*
L. Dürr, *Ursprung und Ausbau der israelitisch-jüdischen Heilandserwartung; ein Beitrag zur Theologie des Alten Testamentes* (Berlin: Schwetschke, 1925).
Dussaud, "Phéniciens au Négeb"
R. Dussaud, "Les Phéniciens au Négeb et en Arabie d'après un texte de Ras Shamra," *Revue de l'histoire des religions* 108 (1933): 5–49.
*Ehrlich, *Randglossen*
Arnold B. Ehrlich, *Randglossen zur Hebräischen Bibel* 5 (Leipzig: Hinrichs, 1912).
*Eichrodt
Walther Eichrodt, *Der Prophet Hesekiel,* ATD, 1970.
Eissfeldt, "Datum"
Otto Eissfeldt, "Das Datum der Belagerung von Tyrus durch Nebukadnezar," *FuF* 9 (1933): 421f.
*Eissfeldt, "El and Yahweh"
Otto Eissfeldt, "El and Yahweh," *JSS* 1 (1956): 25–37.
Eissfeldt, *Erstlinge*
Otto Eissfeldt, *Erstlinge und Zehnten im Alten Testament; Ein Beitrag zur Geschichte des israelitisch-jüdischen Kultus,* BWAT 22 (Leipzig: Hinrichs, 1917).
*Eissfeldt, *OT Introduction*
Otto Eissfeldt, *The Old Testament; An Introduction,* tr. Peter R. Ackroyd (New York: Harper and Row, 1965).
*Eissfeldt, "safatenischen Inschriften"
Otto Eissfeldt, "Das Alte Testament im Lichte der safatenischen Inschriften," *ZDMG* NF 29/104 (1954): 88–118.
*Eissfeldt, "Schwerterschlagene"
Otte Eissfeldt, "Schwerterschlagene bei Hesekiel" in *Studies in Old Testament Prophecy presented to T. H. Robinson,* ed. H. H. Rowley (Edinburgh: Clark,

1950), 73-81.

Elliger, "grossen Tempelsakristeien"
K. Elliger, "Die grossen Tempelsakristeien im Verfasungsentwurf des Ezechiel (42:1ff)" in *Festschrift für A. Alt* (Tübingen: Mohr, 1953), 79–103.

*Elliger, *Leviticus*
K. Elliger, *Leviticus,* HAT 4 (Tübingen: Mohr [Siebeck], 1966).

Elliger, "Nordgrenze"
K. Elliger, "Die Nordgrenze des Reiches Davids," *PJ* 32 (1936): 34–73.

Erman, *Literatur*
Adolf Erman, *Die Literatur der Aegypter* (Leipzig: Hinrichs, 1923).

Erman-Grapow
Adolf Erman and Hermann Grapow, *Wörterbuch der aegyptischen Sprache,* 7 volumes (Leipzig: Hinrichs, 1926–1963.

*Erman-Ranke
Adolf Erman and Hermann Ranke, *Ägypten und aegyptisches Leben im Altertum* (Tübingen: Mohr [Siebeck], 1922–23).

*Ewald
Heinrich Ewald, *Die Propheten des Alten Bundes erklärt,* volume 2, "Jeremja und Hezeqiel" (Göttingen, [2]1868).

*Falkenstein-von Soden
A. Falkenstein and W. von Soden, *Sumerische und akkadische Hymnen und Gebete* (Zürich: Artemis, 1953).

Fensham, "Thunder-Stones"
F. Charles Fensham, "Thunder-Stones in Ugaritic," *JNES* 18 (1959): 273f.

*Filson, "Omission"
Floyd V. Filson, "The Omission of Ezek. 12:26–28 and 36:23b–38 in Codex 967," *JBL* 62 (1943): 27–32.

Fleming, *History of Tyre*
Wallace B. Fleming, *The History of Tyre,* Columbia University Oriental Studies 10 (New York: Columbia University Press, 1915).

*Fohrer-Galling
Georg Fohrer and Kurt Galling, *Ezechiel,* HAT 13 (Tübingen: Mohr [Siebeck], [2]1955).

Forrer, *Provinzeinteilung*
Emil Forrer, *Die Provinzeinteilung des assyrischen Reiches* (Leipzig: Hinrichs, 1920).

Frankfort, *Kingship and the Gods*
H. Frankfort, *Kingship and the Gods* (Chicago: University of Chicago Press, 1948).

*Fredriksson, *Jahwe als Krieger*
Henning Fredriksson, *Jahwe als Krieger* (Lund: Gleerups, 1945).

*Galling, *Altar*
Kurt Galling, *Der Altar in den Kulturen des alten Orients* (Berlin: Curtius, 1925).

*Galling, "Ehrenname"
Kurt Galling, "Der Ehrenname Elisas und die Entrückung Elias," *ZThK* 53 (1956): 129–148.

Galling, "Serubbabel und der Hohepriester"
Kurt Galling, "Serubbabel und der Hohepriester beim Wiederaufbau des Tempels in Jerusalem" in *Studien zur Geschichte Israels im persischen Zeitalter* (Tübingen: Mohr, 1964), 127–148.

Galling, "Serubbabel und der Wiederaufbau"
Kurt Galling, "Serubbabel und der Wiederaufbau des Tempels in Jerusalem" in *Verbannung und Heimkehr. Beiträge zur Geschichte und Theologie Israels im 6. und 5. Jahrhundert v. Chr., Wilhelm Rudolph zum 70. Geburtstage dargebracht* (Tübingen: Mohr [Siebeck], 1961), 67–96.

T. Gaster, "Ezekiel 28:17"
Theodore Gaster, "Ezekiel 28:17," *ET* 62 (1950/51): 124.

Gese
Hartmut Gese, *Der Verfassungsentwurf des Ezechiel (Kap. 40–48) traditionsgeschichtlich untersucht,* BHTh 25 (Tübingen: Mohr, 1957).

*Gesenius-Buhl
Wilhelm Gesenius and F. Buhl, *Hebräisches und aramäisches Handwörterbuch zum AT* (Leipzig, [16]1915).

*Gesenius-Kautzsch
W. Gesenius, *Hebrew Grammer,* E. Kautzsch (ed.) and A. E. Cowley (tr. and reviser) (Oxford: Clarendon, [2]1910).

Glueck, "Explorations"
Nelson Glueck, "Explorations in Eastern Palestine, II," *Annual of the American Schools of Oriental Research* 15 (1935) and "IV," 25–28 (1951).

de Goeje, *muur*
M. J. de Goeje, *De muur van Gog en Magog,* 1888.

*Goetze, *Kleinasien*
Albrecht Goetze, *Kleinasien,* Kulturgeschichte des Alten Orients 3 (München: Beck, [2]1957).

Gordon, *Ugaritic Handbook*
Cyrus H. Gordon, *Ugaritic Handbook* (Rome: Pontifical Biblical Institute, 1947 [1948]).

*Gordon, *Ugaritic Literature*
Cyrus H. Gordon, *Ugaritic Literature* (Rome: Pontifical Biblical Institute, 1949).

Gray, *Sacrifice*
George Buchanan Gray, *Sacrifice in the Old Testament, its Theory and Practice* (Oxford: Clarendon, 1925).

*Gressmann, *Messias*
Hugo Gressmann, *Der Messias,* FRLANT 26 (Göttingen, 1929).

*Gressmann, *Ursprung*
Hugo Gressmann, *Der Ursprung der israelitisch-jüdischen Eschatologie,* FRLANT 6 (Göttingen, 1905).

*Grether, *Name*
Oskar Grether, *Name und Wort Gottes im Alten Testament,* BZAW 64 (Giessen: Töpelmann, 1934).

Grill, "Schlachttag Jahwes"
Severin Grill, "Der Schlachttag Jahwes," *BZ* 2 (1958): 278–283.

*de Groot, *Altäre*
J. de Groot, *Die Altäre des Salomonischen Tempelhofes,* BWAT NF 6 (Stuttgart: Kohlhammer, 1924).
Gunkel, *Märchen*
Hermann Gunkel, *Das Märchen im Alten Testament* (Tübingen: Mohr, 1917).
*Gunkel, *Schöpfung*
Hermann Gunkel, *Schöpfung und Chaos in Urzeit und Endzeit* (Göttingen, ^{2}1921).
Gunneweg, *Leviten*
Antonius H. J. Gunneweg, *Leviten und Priester,* FRLANT 89 (Göttingen: Vandenhoeck & Ruprecht, 1965).
Guthe, *Bibelatlas*
Hermann Guthe, *Bibelatlas* (Leipzig: Wagner & Debes, ^{2}1926).
*Haag, *Untersuchung*
Herbert Haag, *Was lehrt die literarische Untersuchung des Ezechiel-Textes?* (Freiburg in der Schweiz: Paulusdruckerei, 1943).
*Haevernick
H. A. C. Haevernick, *Commentar über den Propheten Ezechiel,* 1843.
Haran, "Studies"
Menaḥem Haran, "Studies in the Account of the Levitical Cities," *JBL* 89 (1961): 45–54, 156–165.
*Harford, *Studies*
John Battersby Harford, *Studies in the Book of Ezekiel* (Cambridge: Cambridge University Press, 1935).
*Heinisch
Paul Heinisch, *Das Buch Ezechiel übersetzt und erklärt,* HSAT 8 (Bonn: Hanstein, 1923).
Heller, "Gog und Magog"
Bernhard Heller, "Gog und Magog im jüdischen Schriftum" in *Jewish Studies in Memory of George A. Kohut,* ed. Salo W. Baron and Alexander Marx (New York: The Alexander Kohut Memorial Foundation, 1935), 350–358.
*Hempel, *Heilung*
Johannes Hempel, *Heilung als Symbol und Wirklichkeit im biblischen Schrifttum* (Göttingen: Vandenhoeck & Ruprecht, ^{2}1965).
*Hempel, *Literatur*
Johannes Hempel, *Die althebräische Literatur und ihr hellenistisch-jüdisches Nachleben* (Wildpark-Potsdam: Akademische Verlagsgesellschaft Athenaion, 1930).
Hermisson, *Sprache*
Hans Jürgen Hermisson, *Sprache und Ritus im altisraelitischen Kult; zur "Spiritualisierung" der Kultbegriffe im Alten Testament,* WMANT 19 (Neukirchen-Vluyn: Neukirchener, 1965).
*Herntrich, *Ezechielprobleme*
Volkmar Herntrich, *Ezechielprobleme,* BZAW 61 (Giessen: Töpelmann, 1933).
*J. Herrmann
Johannes Herrmann, *Ezechiel, übersetzt und erklärt,* KAT (Leipzig: Keichert, 1924).
*J. Herrmann, *Ezechielstudien*
Johannes Herrmann, *Ezechielstudien,* BWAT 2 (Leipzig, 1908).
*Hitzig
F. Hitzig, *Der Prophet Ezechiel erklärt,* KeH 8 (Leipzig, 1847).
Holmberg, *Baum*
U. Holmberg, *Der Baum des Lebens,* Annales Academiae Scientiarum Fennicae 16 (Helsinki, 1922/23).
Hölscher, *Drei Erdkarten*
Gustav Hölscher, *Drei Erdkarten; ein Beitrag zur Erdkenntnis des hebräischen Altertums* (Heidelberg: Winter, 1949).
*Hölscher, *Hesekiel*
Gustav Hölscher, *Hesekiel, der Dichter und das Buch,* BZAW 39 (Giessen: Töpelmann, 1924).
Horst, "Zwei Begriffe"
Friedrich Horst, "Zwei Begriffe für Eigentum (Besitz): נַחֲלָה und אֲחֻזָּה" in *Verbannung und Heimkehr. Beiträge zur Geschichte und Theologie Israels im 6. und 5. Jahrhundert v. Chr., Wilhelm Rudolph zum 70. Geburtstage dargebracht* (Tübingen: Mohr [Siebeck], 1961), 135–156.
*Horst-Robinson, *kleinen Propheten*
Friedrich Horst and Theodore H. Robinson, *Die zwölf kleinen Propheten,* HAT 14 (Tübingen: Mohr [Siebeck], ^{3}1964).
*Howie
Carl Gordon Howie, *The Book of Ezekiel; The Book of Daniel,* The Layman's Bible Commentary 13 (Richmond, Va: John Knox, 1961).
*Howie, *Date*
Carl Gordon Howie, *The Date and Composition of Ezekiel,* Journal of Biblical Literature Monograph Series 4 (Philadelphia: Society of Biblical Literature, 1950).
Howie, "East Gate"
Carl Gordon Howie, "The East Gate of Ezekiel's Temple Enclosure and the Solomonic Gateway of Megiddo," *BASOR* 117 (1950): 13–19.
*Humbert, "bârâ"
Paul Humbert, "Emploi et portée du verbe bârâ (créer) dans l'Ancien Testament," *ThZ* 3 (1947): 401–422.
Humbert, "Démesure"
Paul Humbert, "Démesure et chute dans l'Ancien Testament" in *maqqél shâqédh. La branche d'amandier. Hommage à Wilhelm Vischer* (Montpellier, 1960), 63–82.
*Humbert, "'hinnenî êlékâ'"
Paul Humbert, "Die Herausforderungsformel 'hinnenî êlékâ,'" *ZAW* 51 (1933): 101–108.
*Irwin, *Problem*
William A. Irwin, *The Problem of Ezechiel* (Chicago: The University of Chicago Press, 1943).
*Jahn, *Buch*
Gustav Jahn, *Das Buch Ezechiel auf Grund der Sep-*

tuaginta hergestellt, übersetzt und kritisch erklärt (Leipzig: Pfeiffer, 1905).

*Jahnow, *Leichenlied*
Hedwig Jahnow, *Das hebräische Leichenlied im Rahmen der Völkerdichtung,* BZAW 36 (Giessen: Töpelmann, 1923).

Jean-Hoftijzer
Charles F. Jean and Jacob Hoftijzer, *Dictionnaire des inscriptions sémitiques de l'ouest* (Leiden: Brill, 1960–65).

*Jenni, "Das Wort ʿōlām"
Ernst Jenni, "Das Wort ʿōlām im Alten Testament," *ZAW* 64 (1952 [1953]): 197-248; 65 (1953 [1954]): 1–35.

*Jeremias, *Heiligengräber*
Joachim Jeremias, *Heiligengräber in Jesu Umwelt (Mt. 23, 29; Lk. 11, 47)* (Göttingen: Vandenhoeck & Ruprecht, 1958).

*Jirku, *Materialien*
Anton Jirku, *Materialien zur Volksreligion Israels* (Leipzig: Deichert, 1914).

*Johnson-Gehman-Kase, *Ezekiel*
Allan Chester Johnson, Henry Snyder Gehman, and Edmund Harris Kase, *The John H. Scheide Biblical Papyri, Ezekiel* (Princeton: Princeton University Press, 1938).

Johnson, *Sacral Kingship*
Aubrey R. Johnson, *Sacral Kingship in Ancient Israel* (Cardiff: University of Wales Press, 1955).

*Johnson, *Vitality*
Aubrey R. Johnson, *The Vitality of the Individual in the Thought of Ancient Israel* (Cardiff: University of Wales Press, 1949).

Joüon, "Notes"
Paul Joüon, "Notes philologiques sur le texte hébreu d'Ezéchiel," *Bibl* 10 (1929): 304–312.

*Kautzsch, *Aramaismen*
Emil Kautzsch, *Die Armaismen im Alten Testament untersucht. I. Lexikalischer Teil* (Halle: Niemeyer, 1902).

Kees, "Ägypten"
Hermann Kees, "Ägypten," *RGL.*

Kees, *Ägypten*
Hermann Kees, *Ägypten* (München: Beck, 1933).

Kees, *alte Ägypten*
Hermann Kees, *Das alte Ägypten; eine kleine Landeskunde* (Berlin: Akademie, 1955).

Kees, *Götterglaube*
Hermann Kees, *Der Götterglaube im alten Ägypten,* MVÄG 45 (Leipzig: Hinrichs, 1941).

*Keil
Karl Friedrich Keil, *Biblical Commentary on the Prophecies of Ezekiel,* 2 volumes, tr. James Martin. Biblical Commentaries in the Old Testament (Grand Rapids, Mich.: Eerdmans, 1950).

*Keller, *OTH*
Carl A. Keller, *Das Wort OTH als "Offenbarungszeichen Gottes"* (Basel: Hoenen, 1946).

Kienitz, *Geschichte Aegyptens*
Friedrich Karl Kienitz, *Die politische Geschichte Aegyptens vom 7. bis zum 4. Jahrhundert vor der Zeitwende* (Berlin: Akademie, 1953).

*Klein, "Klima"
Hugo Klein, "Das Klima Palästinas auf Grund der alten hebräischen Quellen," *ZDPV* 37 (1914): 297–327.

*Kliefoth
Th. Kliefoth, *Das Buch Ezechiels übersetzt und erklärt* (Rostock, 1864/65).

*Knabenbauer
Joseph Knabenbauer, *Commentarius in Ezechielem prophetam,* CSS (Paris, 1890).

Knobel, *Völkertafel*
A. Knobel, *Die Völkertafel der Genesis. Ethnographische Untersuchungen* (Giessen: Ricker, 1850).

*Knudtzon, *Amarna*
Jørgen Alexander Knudtzon, *Die El-Amarna-Tafeln,* 2 volumes (1915 = Aalen: Zeller, 1964).

*Koch, "Geschichte"
Klaus Koch, "Zur Geschichte der Erwählungsvorstellung in Israel," *ZAW* 67 (1955 [1956]): 205–226.

Koch, *Priesterschrift*
Klaus Koch, *Die Priesterschrift von Exodus 25 bis Leviticus 16; eine überlieferungsgeschichtliche und literarkritische Untersuchung,* FRLANT 53 (Göttingen: Vandenhoeck & Ruprecht, 1959).

Koch, "Sühne"
Klaus Koch, "Sühne und Sündenvergebung um die Wende von der exilischen zur nachexilischen Zeit," *EvTh 26 (1966):* 217–239.

*Koehler, "Hebräische Vokabeln II"
Ludwig Koehler, "Hebräische Vokabeln II," *ZAW* 55 (1937): 161–174.

*Koehler, *Lichter*
Ludwig Koehler, *Kleine Lichter: fünfzig Bibelstellen erklärt,* Zwingli-Bücherei 47 (Zürich: Zwingli, 1945).

*Koehler-Baumgartner
Ludwig Koehler and Walter Baumgartner, *Lexicon in Veteris Testamenti libros* (Leiden: Brill, 1953).

König, "Vorgeschichte"
E. König, "Zur Vorgeschichte des Namens Russen," ZDMG 70 (1916): 92–96.

*Kopf, "Etymologien"
L. Kopf, "Arabische Etymologien und Parallelen zum Bibelwörterbuch," *VT* 8 (1958): 161–215.

Köster, *Seewesen*
August Köster, *Das antike Seewesen* (Berlin, 1923).

*Kraetzschmar
Richard Kraetzschmar, *Das Buch Ezechiel,* HKAT (Göttingen: Vandenhoeck & Ruprecht, 1900).

*Kraus, *Psalmen*
Hans-Joachim Kraus, *Psalmen,* 2 volumes, BK 15 (Neukirchen-Vluyn: Neukirchener, 1960).

*Kraus, *Worship*
Hans-Joachim Kraus, *Worship in Israel; a Cultic History of the Old Testament,* tr. Geoffrey Buswell

(Richmond, Va.: John Knox, 1966).
Kroll, *Gott und Hölle*
Josef Kroll, *Gott und Hölle, der Mythus vom Descensuskampfe* (Berlin: Teubner, 1932).
*Kuhl, *Prophets*
Curt Kuhl, *The Prophets of Israel,* tr. Rudolf J. Ehrlich and J. P. Smith (Richmond, Va.: John Knox, 1960).
*Kuhl, "'Wiederaufnahme'"
Curt Kuhl, "Die 'Wiederaufnahme'—ein literarkritisches Prinzip?" *ZAW* 64 (1952): 1–11.
Kuhn, "Γὼγ καὶ Μαγώγ"
K. G. Kuhn, "Γὼγ καὶ Μαγώγ," *TDNT* 1, 789–791.
Kuschke, "Jeremia 48:1–8"
Arnulf Kuschke, "Jeremia 48-1–8. Zugleich ein Beitrag zur historischen Topographie Moabs" in *Verbannung und Heimkehr. Beiträge zur Geschichte und Theologie Israels im 6. und 5. Jahrhundert v. Chr., Wilhelm Rudolph zum 70. Geburtstage dargebracht* (Tübingen: Mohr [Siebeck], 1961), 181–196.
Kuschke, "*ḳrjtn*"
Arnulf Kuschke, "Das Deutsche Evangelische Institut für Altertumswissenschaft des Heiligen Landes. Lehrkursus 1960," *ZDPV* 77 (1961): 1–37 ('Zweimal *ḳrjtn* a) Das *ḳrjtn* der Mesa-Stele,' 24–31).
*Kuschke, "Lagervorstellung"
Arnulf Kuschke, "Die Lagervorstellung der priesterschriftlichen Erzählung. Eine überlieferungsgeschichtliche Studie," *ZAW* 63 (1951): 74–105.
Kutsch, "Chronologie"
Ernst Kutsch, "Zur Chronologie der letzten judäischen Könige (Josia bis Zedekia)," *ZAW* 71 (1959): 270–274.
Lasch, "Pfeifen"
R. Lasch, "Das Pfeifen und seine Beziehung zu Dämonenglauben und Zauberei," *ARW* 18 (1915): 589–592.
*Lauha, *ZAPHON*
Aarre Lauha, *ZAPHON, Der Norden und die Nordvölker im Alten Testament* (Helsinki: Der Finnischen Literaturgesellschaft, 1943).
van der Leeuw, *Phänomenologie*
Gerardus van der Leeuw, *Phänomenologie der Religion* (Tübingen: Mohr, [2]1956).
*Levy, *Wörterbuch*
Jacob Levy, *Wörterbuch über die Talmudim und Midraschim,* 5 volumes (Berlin: Harz, 1924).
Maisler, "Lebo-Hamath"
B. Maisler, "Lebo-Hamath and the Northern Boundary of Canaan," *Bulletin of the Jewish Palestine Exploration Society* 12 (1946): 91–102 (Hebrew, with English summary).
Manchot, "Weissagung"
Carl Hermann Manchot, "Ezechiel's Weissagung wider Tyrus. Capitel 26.27.28," *JPTh* 14 (1888): 423–480.
*Matthews
I. G. Matthews, *Ezekiel. An American Commentary on the Old Testament* (Philadelphia: Judson, 1939).
*May
Herbert Gordon May, "The Book of Ezekiel" in *The Interpreter's Bible* 6 (Nashville: Abingdon, 1956), 41–338.
Mazar-Dothan-Dunayevsky, *En-Gedi*
B. Mazar, Trude Dothan, and I. Dunayevsky, *En-Gedi. The First and Second Seasons of Excavations, 1961–62,* *ʿAtiqot* English series 5 (Jerusalem, 1966).
*Meissner, *Achikar*
Bruno Meissner, *Das Märchen vom weisen Achikar,* AO 16,2 (Leipzig: Hinrichs, 1917).
*Messel
Nils Messel, *Ezechielfragen* (Oslo: Dybwad, 1945).
Milik, "Notes"
J. T. Milik, "Notes d'épigraphie et de topographie palestiniennes," *RB* 66 (1959): 550–575.
*Miller, *Verhältnis*
John Wolf Miller, *Das Verhältnis Jeremias und Hesekiels sprachlich und theologisch untersucht* (Assen: Van Gorcum, 1955).
Möhlenbrink, *Tempel*
Kurt Möhlenbrink, *Der Tempel Salomos; eine Untersuchung seiner Stellung in der Sakralarchitektur des Alten Orients,* BWANT 4 (Stuttgart: Kohlhammer, 1932).
Montet, *Géographie*
Pierre Montet, *Géographie de l'Égypte ancienne. Première Partie: To-Mehou, La Basse Égypte* (Paris: Imprimerie Nationale, 1957).
*Moortgat, *Tammuz*
Anton Moortgat, *Tammuz* (Berlin: de Gruyter, 1949).
Morgenstern, "Chapter"
Julian Morgenstern, "A Chapter in the History of the High-Priesthood," *AJSL* 55 (1938): 1–24, 183–197, 360–377.
*Morgenstern, "Jerusalem"
Julian Morgenstern, "Jerusalem—485 B.C.," *HUCA* 27 (1956): 101–179.
Morgenstern, "King-God"
Julian Morgenstern, "The King-God among the Western Semites and the meaning of Epiphanes," *VT* 10 (1960): 138–197.
*Mowinckel, *He That Cometh*
Sigmund Mowinckel, *He That Cometh,* tr. G. W. Anderson (Nashville, Abingdon, 1956).
*Mowinckel, "metrische Aufbau"
Sigmund Mowinckel, "Der metrische Aufbau von Jes 62:1–12 and die neuen sog. 'Kurzverse,'" *ZAW* 65 (1953): 167–187.
*Mowinckel, *Psalmenstudien. II*
Sigmund Mowinckel, *Psalmenstudien. II. Das Thronbesteigungsfest Jahwäs und der Ursprung der Eschatologie* (Kristiania: Dybwad, 1922).

*Müller, *Ezechiel-studien*
David Heinrich Müller, *Ezechiel-studien* (Berlin: Reuther & Reichard, 1895); reprinted as *idem, Biblische Studien* 1 (Wien: Hölder, 1904).

Dieter Müller, "gute Hirte"
Dieter Müller, "Der gute Hirte; Ein Beitrag zur Gesichichte ägyptischer Bildrede," *Zeitschrift für ägyptische Sprache und Altertumskunde* 86 (1961): 126–144.

*Neuss, *Buch*
Wilhelm Neuss, *Das Buch Ezechiel in Theologie und Kunst bis zum Ende des XII. Jahrhunderts,* Beiträge zur Geschichte des Alten Mönchtums und des Benediktinerordens 1–2 (Münster: Aschendorff, 1912).

Noth, "Ammon und Moab"
Martin Noth, "Beiträge zur Geschichte des Ostjordanlandes: III 3. Ammon und Moab," *ZDPV* 68 (1945–51): 36–50.

Noth, *Exodus*
Martin Noth, *Exodus; a Commentary,* tr. J. S. Bowden. The Old Testament Library (Philadelphia: Westminster, 1962).

*Noth, *History of Israel*
Martin Noth, *The History of Israel,* tr. Stanley Godman (New York: Harper & Row, [2]1960).

*Noth, *israelitischen Personennamen*
Martin Noth, *Die israelitischen Personennamen im Rahmen der gemeinsemitischen Namengebung,* BWANT 3, 10 (Stuttgart: Kohlhammer, 1928).

*Noth, "Jerusalem Catastrophe"
Martin Noth, "The Jerusalem Catastrophe of 587 B.C., and its significance for Israel" in *The Laws in the Pentateuch and Other Studies,* tr. D. R. Ap-Thomas (Philadelphia: Fortress, 1967), 260–280.

Noth, *Josua*
Martin Noth, *Das Buch Josua,* HAT 7 (Tübingen: Mohr, [2]1953).

Noth, *Könige*
Martin Noth, *Könige,* BK 9 (Neukirchen-Vluyn: Neukirchener, 1964–1968).

Noth, "Krongut"
Martin Noth, "Das Krongut der israelitischen Könige und seine Verwaltung," *ZDPV* 50 (1927): 211–244.

*Noth, "Noah"
Martin Noth, "Noah, Daniel und Hiob in Ezechiel xiv," *VT* 1 (1951): 251–260.

*Noth, "Office"
Martin Noth, "Office and Vocation in the Old Testament" in *The Laws in the Pentateuch and Other Studies,* tr. D.R. Ap-Thomas (Philadelphia: Fortress, 1967), 229–249.

*Noth, *OT World*
Martin Noth, *The Old Testament World,* tr. Victor I. Gruhn (Philadelphia: Fortress, 1966).

Noth, "Studien"
Martin Noth, "Studien zu den historisch-geographischen Dokumenten des Josuabuches," *ZDPV* 58 (1935): 185–255.

*Noth, *System*
Martin Noth, *Das System der zwölf Stämme Israels,* BWANT 4, 1 (Stuttgart: Kohlhammer, 1930).

*von Orelli
Conrad von Orelli, *Das Buch Ezechiel und die zwölf kleinen Propheten,* Kurzgefasster Kommentar zu den Schriften des Alten und Neuen Testaments (Nördlingen, [2]1896).

von Orelli, "Gog und Magog"
Conrad von Orelli, "Gog und Magog," *Realencyklopädie für protestantische Theologie und Kirche* [3] 6, 761–763.

*Östborn, *Tora*
Gunnar Östborn, *Tora in the Old Testament; a Semantic Study* (Lund: Ohlsson, 1945).

*Parker-Dubberstein
Richard Anthony Parker and Waldo H. Dubberstein, *Babylonian Chronology 626 B.C.–A.D. 75,* Brown University Studies 19 (Providence: Brown University Press, 1956).

*Parrot, *Babylon*
André Parrot, *Babylon and the Old Testament,* tr. B. E. Hooke. Studies in Biblical Archaelogy 8 (London: SCM, 1958).

Pedersen, *Eid*
J. Pedersen, *Der Eid bei den Semiten,* Studien zur Geschichte und Kultur des islamischen Orients 3 (Strassburg: Trübner, 1914).

Piotrowicz, "L'invasion"
Louis Piotrowicz, "L'invasion des Scythes en Asie Antérieure au VIIe siècle av. J.-C.," *Eos* 32 (1929): 473–508.

van der Ploeg, "chefs du peuple"
J. van der Ploeg, "Les chefs du peuple d'Israël et leurs titres," *RB* 57 (1950): 40–61.

Pope, *El*
Marvin H. Pope, *El in the Ugaritic Texts,* VT Suppl 2 (Leiden: Brill, 1955).

Posener, *Dictionary*
Georges Posener, *Dictionary of Egyptian Civilization,* tr. Alix McFarlane (New York: Tudor, 1962).

Procksch, "Fürst"
O. Procksch, "Fürst und Priester bei Hesekiel," *ZAW* 58 (1940/41): 99–133.

*Quell, *Propheten*
Gottfried Quell, *Wahre und falsche Propheten,* BFChrTh 46, 1 (Gütersloh: Bertelsmann, 1952).

Quiring, "Edelsteine"
H. Quiring, "Die Edelsteine im Amtsschild des jüdischen Hohenpriesters und die Herkunft ihrer Namen," *Sudhoffs Archiv für Geschichte der Medizin und der Naturwissenschaften* 38 (1954): 193–213.

*von Rabenau, "Zukunftswort"
Konrad von Rabenau, "Das prophetische Zukunftswort im Buch Hesekiel" in *Studien zur Theologie der alttestamentlichen Überlieferungen,* ed. R. Rendtorff and K. Koch (Neukirchen-Vluyn: Neukirchener, 1961), 61–80.

*von Rad, *Krieg*
Gerhard von Rad, *Der heilige Krieg im alten Israel,* ATANT 20 (Göttingen: Vandenhoeck & Ruprecht, ^{5}1969).
*von Rad, *OT Theology*
Gerhard von Rad, *Old Testament Theology,* 2 volumes, tr. D. M. G. Stalker (New York: Harper and Row, 1962 and 1965).
*von Rad, *Priesterschrift*
Gerhard von Rad, *Die Priesterschrift im Hexateuch literarisch untersucht und theologisch gewertet,* BWANT 4, 13 (Stuttgart: Kohlhammer, 1934).
*von Rad, "Promised Land"
Gerhard von Rad, "The Promised Land and Yahweh's Land in the Hexateuch" in *The Problem of the Hexateuch and Other Essays,* tr. E. W. Trueman Dicken (New York: McGraw-Hill, 1966), 79–93.
Rautenberg, "Zukunftsthora"
Willy Rautenberg, "Zur Zukunftsthora des Hesekiel," *ZAW* 33 (1913): 92–115.
*Reider, "Contributions"
Joseph Reider, "Contributions to the Scriptural Text," *HUCA* 24 (1952/3): 85–106.
*Reider, "Etymological Studies"
Joseph Reider, "Etymological Studies in Biblical Hebrew," *VT* 2 (1952): 113–130.
*Reider, "Studies"
Joseph Reider, "Etymological Studies in Biblical Hebrew," *VT* 4 (1954): 276–295.
*Rendtorff, *Gesetze*
Rolf Rendtorff, *Die Gesetze in der Priesterschrift,* FRLANT NF 44 (Göttingen: Vandenhoeck & Ruprecht, 1954).
Rendtorff, *Studien*
Rolf Rendtorff, *Studien zur Geschichte des Opfers im alten Israel,* WMANT 24 (Neukirchen-Vluyn: Neukirchener, 1967).
Reventlow, "Blut"
Henning Graf Reventlow, "Sein Blut komme über sein Haupt," *VT* 10 (1960): 311–327.
*Reventlow, "Die Völker"
Henning Graf Reventlow, "Die Völker als Jahwes Zeugen bei Ezechiel," *ZAW* 71 (1959): 33–43.
Richter, *ezechielische Tempel*
Georg Richter, *Die ezechielische Tempel; eine exegetische Studie über Ezechiel 40ff,* BFChrTh 16, 2 (Gütersloh, 1912).
Riesenfeld, *Resurrection*
Harald Riesenfeld, *The Resurrection in Ezekiel XXXVII and in the Dura-Europos Paintings,* UUÅ (Uppsala: Lundequists, 1948).
Robinson, *Biblical Researches*
Edward Robinson, *Biblical Researches in Palestine, Mount Sinai and Arabia Petraea* 3 (Boston: Crocker & Brewster, 1841).
*Rohland, *Erwählungstraditionen*
Edzard Rohland, *Die Bedeutung der Erwählungstraditionen Israels für die Eschatologie der alttestamentlichen Propheten,* Unpub. Diss (Heidelberg, 1956).
Roscher, *Omphalosgedanke*
W. H. Roscher, *Der Omphalosgedanke bei verschiedenen Völkern, besonders den semitischen. Ein Beitrag zur vergleichenden Religionswissenschaft, Volkskunde und Archäologie,* 1918.
Rosenau, "Harel"
W. Rosenau, "Harel und Ha-Ariel; Ezechiel 43:15–16," *MGWJ* 65 (1921): 350–356.
*L. Rost, "Bezeichnungen"
Leonhard Rost, "Die Bezeichnungen für Land und Volk im Alten Testament" in *Festschrift Otto Procksch,* ed. A. Alt, J. Herrmann, M. Noth, G. von Rad, E. Sellin (Leipzig: Deichert, 1934), 125–148.
*L. Rost, *Israel*
Leonhard Rost, *Israel bei den Propheten,* BWANT 4, 19 (Stuttgart: Kohlhammer, 1937).
*P. Rost, "Miscellen"
Paul Rost, "Miscellen I," *OLZ* 7 (1904): 390–393, 479–483.
*Rothstein
J. W. Rothstein, *Das Buch Ezechiel,* HSAT (Tübingen, ^{4}1922).
Rowley, "Zadok"
H. H. Rowley, "Zadok and Nehustan," *JBL* 58 (1939): 113–141.
Rudolph, *Chronikbücher*
Wilhelm Rudolph, *Chronikbücher,* HAT 21 (Tübingen: Mohr, 1955).
*Rudolph, *Jeremia*
Wilhelm Rudolph, *Jeremia,* HAT 1, 12 (Tübingen: Mohr [Siebeck], ^{3}1968).
Rüger, *Tyrusorakel*
Hans Peter Rüger, *Das Tyrusorakel Ezek 27,* Unpub. Diss. (Tübingen, 1961).
Sarsowsky, "Notizen"
A. Sarsowsky, "Notizen zu einigen biblischen geographischen und ethnographischen Namen," *ZAW* 32 (1912): 146–151 (II. גַּמָּדִים, חֵילֵךְ, 147f; V. סַבְרַיִם, 149f).
*Scharff-Moortgat
Alexander Scharff and Anton Moortgat, *Ägypten und Vorderasien im Altertum* (Müchen: Bruckmann, 1950).
Schmid, "Jahwe"
Herbert Schmid, "Jahwe und die Kulttraditionen von Jerusalem," *ZAW* 67 (1955): 168–197.
Schmid, *Bundesopfer*
Rudolf Schmid, *Das Bundesopfer in Israel; Wesen, Ursprung und Bedeutung der alttestamentlichen Schelamim* (München: Kosel, 1964).
Schmidt, *heilige Fels*
H. Schmidt, *Der heilige Fels in Jerusalem,* (Tübingen: J. C. B. Mohr [Paul Siebeck], 1933).
Schmökel, *Geschichte*
Hartmut Schmökel, *Geschichte des alten Vorderasien,* HO II, 3 (Leiden: Brill, 1957).
Schott, *Vergleiche*
Albert Schott, *Die Vergleiche in den akkadischen*

Königsinschriften, MVÄG 30 (Leipzig: Hinrichs, 1925).

Schötz, *Sündopfer*
Dionys Schötz, *Schuld- und Sündopfer im Alten Testament,* Breslauer Studien zur historischen Theologie 18 (Breslau: Müller & Seiffert, 1930).

*Schumpp
Meinrad Schumpp, *Das Buch Ezechiel übersetzt und erklärt,* Herders Bibelkommentar (Freiburg: Herder, 1942).

*Schwarzenbach, *Terminologie*
Armin Schwarzenbach, *Die geographische Terminologie im Hebräischen des Alten Testamentes* (Leiden: Brill, 1954).

*Scott, "Phenomena"
R. B. Y. Scott, "Meteorological Phenomena and Terminology in the Old Testament," *ZAW* 64 (1952): 11–25.

Simons, *Geographical and Topographical Texts*
Jan Jozef Simons, *The Geographical and Topographical Texts of the Old Testament* (Leiden: Brill, 1959).

*Simons, *Jerusalem*
Jan Jozef Simons, *Jerusalem in the Old Testament; researches and theories* (Leiden: Brill, 1952).

*Smend
Rudolf Smend, *Der Prophet Ezechiel,* KeH (Leipzig, [2]1880).

Smend, *Weisheit*
Rudolf Smend, *Die Weisheit des Jesus Sirach* (Berlin: Reimer, 1906).

*J. Smith, *Book*
James Smith, *The Book of the Prophet Ezekiel; a new interpretation* (London: S.P.C.K., 1931).

Snaith, "Sacrifices"
N. H. Snaith, "Sacrifices in the Old Testament," *VT* 7 (1957): 308–317.

von Soden, *Akkadisches Handwörterbuch*
Wolfram von Soden, *Akkadisches Handwörterbuch* (Wiesbaden: Harrassowitz, 1959–1979).

von Soden, "Raumbezeichnungen"
Wolfram von Soden, "Akkadisch *ta'û* und hebräisch *tā'* als Raumbezeichnungen," *WO* 1, 5 (1950): 356–361.

Speiser, "*nāśī'*"
E. A. Speiser, "Background and Function of the Biblical *nāśī'*," *CBQ* 25 (1963): 111–117.

*Spiegel, "Ezekiel"
Shalom Spiegel, "Ezekiel or Pseudo-Ezekiel?" *HTR* 24 (1931): 245–321.

*Sprank, *Studien*
Siegfried Sprank and Kurt Wiese, *Studien zu Ezechiel und dem Buch der Richter,* BWANT 3, 4 (Stuttgart: Kohlhammer, 1926).

Staerk, "Gebrauch"
W. Staerk, "Der Gebrauch der Wendung באחרית הימים im at. Kanon," *ZAW* 11 (1891): 247–253.

Staudigel, *Begriffe*
H. Staudigel, *Die Begriffe Gerechtigkeit und Leben und das Problem der Gerechtigkeit Gottes bei Ezechiel,* Unpub. Diss. (Rostock, 1957).

*Steinmann, *Le prophète Ézéchiel*
Jean Steinmann, *Le prophète Ézéchiel et les débuts de l'exil,* Lectio Divina 13 (Paris: Cerf, 1953).

*Steuernagel, "Jahwe"
Carl Steuernagel, "Jahwe, der Gott Israels" in *Studien zur semitischen Philologie und Religionsgeschichte Julius Wellhausen zum siebzigsten Geburtstag,* ed. Karl Marti, BZAW 27 (Giessen: Töpelmann, 1914), 329–349.

*Steuernagel, *Lehrbuch*
Carl Steuernagel, *Lehrbuch der Einleitung in das Alte Testament* (Tübingen: Mohr [Siebeck], 1912).

Stevenson, "ʿOlah"
W. B. Stevenson, "Hebrew ʿOlah and Zebach Sacrifices" in *Festschrift Alfred Bertholet* (Tübingen: Mohr [Siebeck], 1950), 488–497.

*Strack-Billerbeck
Hermann L. Strack and Paul Billerbeck, *Kommentar zum Neuen Testament aus Talmud und Midrasch,* 6 volumes (München: Beck, [2]1956–1961).

*Tallquist, *Himmelsgegenden*
Knut Tallquist, *Himmelsgegenden und Winde,* StOr 2 (Helsinki, 1928).

Torrey, "Alexander the Great"
C. C. Torrey, "Alexander the Great in the Old Testament Prophecies" in *Vom Alten Testament. Karl Marti zum 70. Geburtstage,* BZAW 41 (Giessen: Töpelmann, 1925), 281–286.

*Torrey, *Pseudo-Ezekiel*
C. C. Torrey, *Pseudo-Ezekiel and the Original Prophecy* (New Haven: Yale University Press, 1930 = New York: KTAV Publishing House, 1970).

*Toy
C. H. Toy, *The Book of the Prophet Ezekiel,* SBOT 23 (New York: Dodd, Mead, 1899).

*Troelstra
A. Troelstra, *Ezechiel,* 2 volumes, TeU (Groningen: Wolters, 1931).

Uhlemann, "Gog und Magog"
Max Uhlemann, "Ueber Gog und Magog," *ZWTh* 5 (1862): 265–286.

Unger, *Babylon*
Eckhard Unger, *Babylon, die heilige Stadt nach der Beschreibung der Babylonier* (Berlin and Leipzig: deGruyter, 1931).

Unger, "Namen"
Eckhard Unger, "Namen im Hofstaate Nebukadnezars II," *ThLZ* 50 (1925): 481–486.

Unger, "Nebukadnezar II"
Eckhard Unger, "Nebukadnezar II. und sein Šandabakku (Oberkommissar) in Tyrus," *ZAW* 44 (1926): 314–317.

Unger, "Staatskalender"
Eckhard Unger, "Der älteste Hof- und Staatskalender der Welt," *FuF* 3 (1927): 1f.

de Vaux, *Ancient Israel*
Roland de Vaux, *Ancient Israel, its Life and Institu-*

tions, tr. John McHugh (New York: McGraw-Hill, 1961).

de Vaux, *Studies*
Roland de Vaux, *Studies in Old Testament Sacrifice* (Cardiff: University of Wales Press, 1964).

* Vincent, *Religion*
Albert Vincent, *La Religion des Judéo-Araméens d'Éléphantine* (Paris: Geuthner, 1937).

Vogelstein, "Nebuchadnezzar's Reconquest"
M. Vogelstein, "Nebuchadnezzar's Reconquest of Phoenicia and Palestine and the Oracles of Ezekiel," *HUCA* 23 (1950/51): 197–220.

* Vriezen, "'*Ehje*"
Theodorus Christiaan Vriezen," *'Ehje '^{a}šer 'ehje*" in *Festschrift A. Bertholet* (Tübingen: Mohr [Siebeck], 1950), 498–512.

* Watzinger, *Denkmäler*
Carl Watzinger, *Denkmäler Palästinas,* 2 volumes (Leipzig: Hinrichs, 1933–35).

Weill, "mots"
"Les mots תֻּפֶּיךָ וּנְקָבֶיךָ dans la complainte d'Ezéchiel sur le roi de Tyr (28:11–19)," *Revue des études juives* 42 (1901): 7–13.

Weissbach, *Hauptheiligtum*
Franz Heinrich Weissbach, *Das Hauptheiligtum des Marduk in Babylon, Esagila und Etemenanki,* Wissenschaftliche Veröffentlichungen der Deutschen Orientgesellschaft 59 (Leipzig: Hinrichs, 1938).

Wellhausen, *Prolegomena*
Julius Wellhausen, *Prolegomena to the History of Ancient Israel* (Edinburgh: Black, 1885).

* Wellhausen, *Reste*
Julius Wellhausen, *Reste arabischen Heidentums gesammelt und erläutert* (Berlin: Reimer, ^{2}1897).

* Wevers
John W. Wevers, *Ezekiel,* Cent-B (London: Nelson, 1969).

* Wevers, "Septuaginta-Forschungen"
John W. Wevers, "Septuaginta-Forschungen," *ThR* 22 (1954): 85–138.

Widengren, *Ascension*
Geo Widengren, *The Ascension of the Apostle and the Heavenly Book: King and Saviour III,* UUÅ (Uppsala: Lundequists, 1950).

Widengren, *King and Tree of Life*
Geo Widengren, *The King and the Tree of Life in Ancient Near Eastern Religion: King and Saviour IV,* UUÅ (Uppsala: Lundequists, 1951).

* Wildberger, "Israel"
Hans Wildberger, "Israel und sein Land," *EvTh* 16 (1956): 404–422.

Wilke, "Neumondfest"
F. Wilke, "Das Neumondfest im israelitisch-jüdischen Altertum," *Jahrbuch der Gesellschaft für die Geschichte des Protestantismus in Österreich* 67 (Festschrift für Josef Bohatec) (1951): 171–185.

Wischnitzer-Bernstein, "Conception"
Rachel Wischnitzer-Bernstein, "The Conception of the Resurrection in the Ezekiel Panel of the Dura Synagogue," *JBL* 60 (1941): 43–55.

* Wiseman, *Chronicles*
Donald John Wiseman, *Chronicles of Chaldaean Kings (626–556 B.C.) in the British Museum* (London: The British Museum, 1956).

von Wissmann, "Geographische Grundlagen"
Hermann von Wissmann, "Geographische Grundlagen und Frühzeit der Geschichte Südarabiens," *Saeculum* 4 (1953): 61–114.

* Wolff, *Hosea*
Hans Walter Wolff, *Hosea: A Commentary on the Book of the Prophet Hosea,* tr. Gary Stansell. Hermeneia (Philadelphia: Fortress, 1974).

Wolff, *Joel and Amos*
Hans Walter Wolff, *Joel and Amos,* tr. Waldemar Janzen, S. Dean McBride, Jr., and Charles A. Muenchow, ed. S. Dean McBride, Jr. Hermeneia (Philadelphia: Fortress, 1977).

* Wolff, "'Umkehr'"
Hans Walter Wolff, "Das Thema 'Umkehr' in der alttestamentlichen Prophetie," *ZThK* 48 (1951): 129–148; reprinted in *idem, Ges. Stud. zum AT,* ThB 22 (München: Kaiser, 1964), 130–150.

* Würthwein, *ʿamm*
Ernst Würthwein, *Der ʿamm haʾarez im Alten Testament,* BWANT 4, 17 (Stuttgart: Kohlhammer, 1936).

* Ziegler
Joseph Ziegler, *Ezechiel,* Echter-B (Würzburg: Echter, 1948).

* Ziegler, *Ezechiel*
Joseph Ziegler, *Ezechiel,* Septuaginta. Vetus Testamentum graecum 16, 1 (Göttingen: Vandenhoeck & Ruprecht, 1952).

* Ziegler, "Papyrus 967"
Joseph Ziegler, "Die Bedeutung des Chester Beatty-Scheide Papyrus 967 für die Textüberlieferung der Ezechiel-Septuaginta," *ZAW* 61 (1945/48): 76–94.

* Ziegler, *Susanna*
Joseph Ziegler, *Susanna, Daniel, Bel et Draco,* Septuaginta. Vetus Testamentum graecum 16, 2 (Göttingen: Vandenhoeck & Ruprecht, 1954).

* Zimmerli, *Erkenntnis*
Walther Zimmerli, *Erkenntnis Gottes nach dem Buche Ezechiel,* ATANT 27 (Zürich: Zwingli, 1954); reprinted in *idem, Gottes Offenbarung,* ThB 19 (München: Kaiser, 1963), 41–119.

Zimmerli, "Ezechieltempel"
Walther Zimmerli, "Ezechieltempel und Salomostadt" in *Hebräische Wortforschung; Festschrift zum. 80. Geburtstag von Walter Baumgartner,* VT Suppl 16 (Leiden: Brill, 1967), 389–414; reprinted in *idem, Studien zur alttestamentlichen Theologie und Prophetie. Gesammelte Aufsätze II,* ThB 51 (München: Kaiser, 1974), 148–164.

Zimmerli, "Israel"
Walther Zimmerli, "Israel im Buche Ezechiel," *VT* 8 (1958): 75–90.

*Zimmerli, "Jahwe"
Walther Zimmerli, "Ich bin Jahwe" in *Festschrift für A. Alt* (Tübingen: Mohr [Siebeck], 1953), 179–209; reprinted in *idem, Gottes Offenbarung,* ThB 19 (München: Kaiser, 1963), 11–40.

*Zimmerli, "'Leben' und 'Tod'"
Walther Zimmerli, "'Leben' und 'Tod' im Buche des Propheten Ezechiel," *ThZ* 13 (1957): 494–508; reprinted in *idem, Gottes Offenbarung,* ThB 19 (München: Kaiser, 1963), 178–191.

Zimmerli, "Struktur"
Walther Zimmerli, "Zur Struktur der alttestamentlichen Weisheit," *ZAW* 51 (1933): 177–204.

Zimmerli, "Wahrheitserweis Jahwes"
Walther Zimmerli, "Der Wahrheitserweis Jahwes nach der Botschaft der beiden Exilspropheten" in *Tradition und Situation. Studien zur alttestamentlichen Prophetie Artur Weiser zum 70. Geburtstag dargebracht* (1963), 133–151; reprinted in *idem, Studien zur alttestamentlichen Theologie und Prophetie. Gesammelte Aufsätze II,* ThB 51 (München: Kaiser, 1974), 192–212.

*Zimmerli, "Wort"
Walther Zimmerli, "Das Wort des göttlichen Selbsterweises" in *Mélanges bibliques rédigés en l'honneur d'André Robert,* Travaux de l'Institut Catholique de Paris 4 (Paris, 1957), 154–164; reprinted in *idem, Gottes Offenbarung,* ThB 19 (München: Kaiser, 1963), 120–132.

Zimmerli-Jeremias
Walther Zimmerli and Joachim Jeremias, "παῖς θεοῦ," *TDNT* 5, 654–717 (Zimmerli, 654–677; Jeremias, 677–717).

*Zorell
Franciscus Zorell, *Lexicon hebraicum et aramaicum Veteris Testamenti* (Rome: Pontifical Biblical Institute, 1946–1954).

van Zyl, *Moabites*
A. H. van Zyl, *The Moabites,* Pretoria Oriental Series 3 (Leiden: Brill, 1960).

Editor's Note

The English translation of the Book of Ezekiel printed in this volume is new, based on the ancient texts and following the exegetical decisions of the commentator. Within that translation words within brackets [ ] are regarded by the commentator as interpolations, words within parentheses ( ) amplify the sense implied but not expressly stated by the Hebrew text, words within angle brackets < > represent a textual emendation which is discussed in the textual notes.

Cross references are given as follows: References to pages within this volume follow the form "see above p. 000," whereas references to volume one follow the form "see 1,000."

Pictured on the endpapers is a fragment of the Book of Ezekiel from Cave Four, Qumrān (4AEz^{a}) dating from the first century B.C. The text includes portions of Ezekiel 10:17–11.

Ezekiel 2

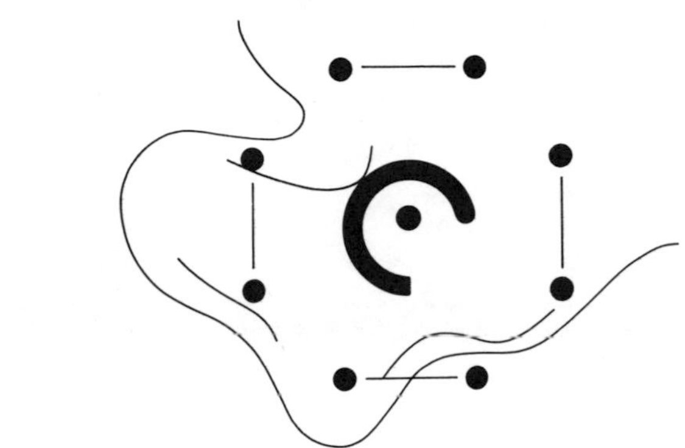

Ezekiel 25–32, in which oracles against Ammon (25:1–7), Moab (25:8–11), Edom (25:12–14), and the Philistines (25:15–17), Tyre (26:1–28:19), Sidon (28:20–23) and Egypt (29:1–32:32) are gathered together, is undoubtedly intended, within the book as a whole, to be a homogeneous compositional unit.[1] As in the layout of Isaiah, Jeremiah (according to 𝔊) and Zephaniah, the final redactor of the book intended it to provide the link between the prophet's proclamation of doom and his proclamation of salvation. That it has been placed in this position only editorially is clear from the fact that two utterances which belong closely together, namely the proclamation of the impending fall of Jerusalem (24:15ff, see especially the addition in vv 25–27) and the report of that fall (33:21–22), have now clearly been separated by the oracles against the nations in 25–32.[2] The oracle against Edom in 35:1ff reveals, of course, that not all oracles against foreign nations have been collected in 25–32. The addition in 21:33–37, which is surely directed against Babylon, should also be recalled in this connection.

If the arrangement in the books of Isaiah and Jeremiah (𝔊), as far as we can see, emerges from the proclamation itself (judgment—oracles against nations—salvation), there is linked with this in the book of Ezekiel a chronological element. If the proclamation of judgment belongs basically, according to the dates given in 1:1f; 8:1; 20:1; 24:1, to the period between the fifth and the ninth years of Jehoiachin, then the proclamation concerning foreign nations belongs, according to the numerous dates in 26:1; 29:1; 30:20; 31:1; 32:1, 17, to the period between the tenth and the twelfth years, i.e. close in time to the final fall of Jerusalem. Only the additional oracle in 29:17ff falls outside these limits. The concluding section (33–48), which follows and which is primarily concerned with the proclamation of salvation, belongs exclusively, according to the dates in 33:21; 40:1, to the period after the fall of the city. According to this, the inner progression of the proclamation is identical with the historical progression.

From the point of view of form, however, Ezekiel 25–32 was not conceived as a unit from the first; it is, rather, a collection of individual oracles. This is clear not only from the addition in 29:17–21 and from the frequent new beginnings with the formula for the coming of a message, but also from the unequal length and number of the oracles with which the individual addressees are provided. Thus we find, for example, alongside the short incomplete oracles against the Philistines in 25:15–17, six, and with the inclusion of the addition in 29:17–21, actually seven independent units in four full chapters (29–32) against Egypt. The question can still be asked whether, apart from the theme of "oracles against the nations," the number seven for the addressees in this collection was not also intended by the redactor. Thus, for example, Amos 1f, in the penultimate stage of its formation (before the addition of the strophe about Judah), seems to provide a consciously formed series of seven oracles. The collection of oracles against foreign nations in Jer 46:1–49:33, dated in the year of the battle of Carchemish, reveals seven addressees (Rudolph). Here in Ezekiel are we to see the counterpart of the 'seven nations' (Dtn 7:1) of Canaan that had first to be defeated before Israel could enter the promised land at the beginning of her history?[3] But this is best regarded as a deliberate intention on the part of the final redactor who is certainly not to be identified with Ezekiel.

It is remarkable that in the list of the seven nations, as is also the case in Jer 46:1–49:33, there is no mention of Babylon. If Jeremiah 46–49, as the tradition of 𝔊 suggests, had its original position in Jeremiah 25 (according to Rudolph, against 𝔊, after the vision of the cup), then the omission of Babylon there is completely understandable, for the seven nations represent the territory which Yahweh has given into the hand of the king of Babylon. In Ezekiel 25–32, in the oracles against Tyre and Egypt, mention is likewise made of their being given into the power of the king of Babylon (26:7ff; 29:17ff; 30:10–

1 On 28:24–26 see below.

2 On 33:1–20 see below.

3 On the authority of the first exodus as the prototype of the future reconstruction of Israel see 20:32ff and Walther Zimmerli. "Le nouvel 'exode' dans le Message des deux grands Prophètes de l'Exil" in *maqqêl shâqédh. La branche d'amandier. Hommage à Wilhelm Vischer* (Montpellier, 1960), 216–227.

12). In the oracle against the other five nations and cities a statement of a similar kind is lacking, though not entirely so, insofar as in 25:4f, 10, 14 a quite different point of view is represented which excludes Babylon because it is the instrument of judgment. The fact that Babylon is not among those to whom is addressed the divine judgment passed on the nations in Ezekiel 25–32 makes it highly probable that this complex was put together by a redactor before the end of the exile. The proclamation of Deutero-Isaiah (e.g. Is 46:1f; 47:1–15) and of Zechariah (2:10–13; 5:11), but also the expansion of Jeremiah's oracles against the nations which is found in Jeremiah 50f and the placing of Is 13:1–14:23 at the head of Isaiah's oracles against the nations, all show that as soon as the impending fall of Babylon was becoming obvious, reticence towards her was replaced in the prophetic oracles against the nations by sharp attack. In the book of Ezekiel such an attack can be glimpsed, but only vaguely, behind the addition contained in 21:33–37.[4] The realization that there is a total lack of polemic against Babylon even in the later expansions in Ezekiel 25–32 is of considerable importance for the problem of the dating of the book of Ezekiel.

The element of addressing foreign nations is itself deeply rooted in the prophetic tradition, as can be seen from Amos 1f. In comparison with Amos's other oracles, the style of address in Amos 1f is remarkably strongly schematized, in that not only the introduction ("For three transgressions of . . . and for four, I will not revoke it"), but also the actual threat reveal a stereotyped manner of expression ("I will send fire . . ." 1:4, 7, 10, 12 [14]; 2:2, 5; "I will cut off the inhabitants from . . ." 1:5, 8; cf. 2:3). This surely indicates that precisely in the oracles against foreign nations even an Amos is influenced by forms already to hand more strongly than he otherwise is. Bentzen's reference to the phenomenon of execration scenes in Egypt would seem to suggest the possibility that in Israel, too, the ritual cursing or prophetic threatening of enemies may have had a definite place in the cult, alongside actual prophetic utterances in the context of a battle (1 Kgs 20:13, 28).[5] Amos 1f seems to indicate just such an occasion of comprehensive threatening of the surrounding enemies.

At the same time, however, the threat against the individual enemy has quite clearly been able to free itself from the context of a cultic setting and establish itself as an independent form. In Ezekiel's oracles against the nations both types are clearly to be found side by side: the threat, metrical in form, which (as is shown by the comparison with 1 Kgs 20) uses, in the form of the proof-oracle, an old type of oracle against an enemy expressed in stereotyped language, together with the individual oracle of judgment against an enemy, possibly made up of figurative motifs. The question posed by Amos 1f concerning the linking together of the metrical threats can be asked only with regard to Ezekiel 25.[6] It certainly does not follow from this that the threat, based on the proof-oracle, is to be categorically separated as non-genuine from the more originally formed figurative oracles simply on account of its typically formal character (Hölscher). Even in his oracles against foreign nations Ezekiel proves to be a figure of synthesis. He makes use of different possibilities of form.

An examination of the dates in Ezekiel 25–32 shows that not only is the exact chronological order interrupted by the obvious addition in 29:17–21, but also the oracles against Egypt begin in 29:1 with a date which antedates that of the oracle against Tyre in 26ff. This disharmony is not to be resolved, as was already attempted in the ancient versions, by manipulating the text of the dates.[7] It points, rather, to the conclusion that the oracles against Egypt in Ezekiel 29–32 represent an editorial entity that was then joined as a whole to Ezekiel 25–28, which is likewise to be regarded as an editorially conceived entity. It is, therefore, valid to examine Ezekiel 25–28 and Ezekiel 29–32 independently.

4 See further the detailed commentary on Ezekiel 38f.

5 Aage Bentzen, "The Ritual Background of Amos 1:2–2:16," *OTS* 8 (1950): 85–99.

6 See below.

7 See the notes on 26:1; 29:1.

A. Oracles against Israel's Palestinian Neighbors

Ezekiel 25–28 is introduced by a comprehensive section (25) consisting of five oracles against four nations (Ammonites, Moabites, Edomites, Philistines). This is followed by three sections directed against Tyre (26; 27; 28:1–19), each of which ends with a similar concluding line (26:21: 27:36b; 28:19b), and by an oracle against Sidon (28:20–23). This group of oracles is concluded in the first instance in 28:24 by means of a summarizing sentence which looks back on all the neighboring nations who despise Israel and which, therefore, unmistakably envisages that section which began with Ezekiel 25. This is followed in 28:25f, after a new introduction, by an even more extensive concluding note which has its counterpart to some extent in 3a:25–29. This mentions specifically the restoration of Israel and the ensuing peace and mentions again in v 26b, using the terminology of v 24, the contempt of the neighboring nations.

On the basis of stylistic observations, Messel thought that he could discern in 25:1–26:6; 28:20–26 a partial collection made by the redactor into which had been inserted only subsequently the still later oracles against Tyre (26:7–28:19) which originated partly before and partly immediately after the fall of Tyre in the time of Alexander (332).[1] Since, however, this severe dissection of Ezekiel 26 appears extremely questionable and since, on the other hand, Ezekiel 26, in view of its closing lines, is not to be separated from 27 and 28, it is best to adhere to the view that in 28:24–26 we have the editorial conclusion of the total collection which comprises 25–28 and which, from the start, included different sections.

In particular, the editorial unit 25–28, if attention is also paid to the introductory formulae for the coming of a message and to the dates, falls into the following subdivisions: (1) a group of oracles, similar in form, against Judah's immediate neighbors (25); (2) the collection of three oracles, held together by their similar concluding lines, against Tyre and its princes (26:1–28:19); a collection which is characterized by an introductory date; and (3) a quite colorless oracle against Sidon (28:20–23), to which are added the summary remark about "their neighbors" (סביבתם) in 28:24 and a comprehensive oracle, introduced by the messenger formula, concerning the peace which awaits Israel after her restoration and after the judgment on her hostile neighbors (28:25–26).

1 Messel, 94f.

1. Five Oracles against Ammon, Moab, Edom and the Philistines

Bibliography

W. F. Albright
"Dedan" in *Geschichte und Altes Testament; Festschrift für A. Alt* (Tübingen: Mohr, 1953), 1–12.

W. F. Albright
"Notes on Ammonite History" in *Miscellanea biblica B. Ubach* (Montserrat, 1954), 131–136.

Frants Peter William Buhl
Geschichte der Edomiter (Leipzig: Edelmann, 1893).

Otto Eissfeldt
"Das Alte Testament im Lichte der safatenischen Inschriften," *ZDMG* 104 (1954): 88–118.

Nelson Glueck
"Explorations in Eastern Palestine, II," *Annual of the American Schools of Oriental Research* 15 (1935) and "IV," 25–28 (1951).

Arnulf Kuschke
"Jeremia 48:1–8. Zugleich ein Beitrag zur historischen Topographie Moabs" in *Verbannung und Heimkehr. Beiträge zur Geschichte und Theologie Israels im 6. und 5. Jahrhundert v. Chr., Wilhelm Rudolph zum 70. Geburtstage dargebracht* (Tübingen: Mohr [Siebeck], 1961), 181–196.

Arnulf Kuschke
"Zweimal *ḳrjtn* a) Das *ḳrjtn* der Mesa-Stele," *ZDPV* 77 (1961): 24–31.

David Heinrich Müller
Biblische Studien 3: Komposition und Strophenbau (Wien: Holder, 1907) ('Die Komposition von Ezechiel Kap. 25,' 40–45).

Martin Noth
"Beiträge zur Geschichte des Ostjordanlandes: III 3. Ammon und Moab," *ZDPV* 68 (1946–51): 36–50.

A. H. van Zyl
The Moabites, Pretoria Oriental Series 3 (Leiden: Brill, 1960).

25

1 [a]And the word of Yahweh came to me: 2/
Son of man, set your face towards the
Ammonites and prophesy against them
3/ and say to the Ammonites: Hear the
word of [the Lord][a] Yahweh. Thus has
[the Lord][a] Yahweh said: Because you
say[b] 'Aha' (jeeringly) over[c] my sanctuary
since it is desecrated[d] and over the land
of Israel since it is laid waste and over[c]
the house of Judah since they have gone
into exile, 4/ see, therefore, I shall hand
you[a] over to the people of the East, and

25: 1a 𝔖 adds the superscription על בני עמון, as it does
1 later before vv 8, 12, 15; 26:1, 28:1, 20; 29:1.
3 3a אדני is lacking in 𝔊 𝔏^{CS} (Ziegler, *Ezechiel,* erroneously, 𝔏^{SW}) 𝔎^{Bo}, see Appendix 1.
b 𝔊, more freely, *ἐπεχάρητε*, 𝔏^{CS} *exultastis.* 𝔊 𝔏^{CS} 𝔖
(על דאמרתון אחן) at this point, and 𝔊 𝔏^{CS} also in v
4a*α*, put the address, in dependence on v 3a, in the
plural. Since, however, even in 𝔊. 𝔏^{CS}, the singular
address can be found in what follows, 𝔐, which in v
3 is also supported by 𝔊^{967} 𝔄, is to be preferred.
c על–אל cf. 1:17 note a.
d On the form נִחַל cf. Gesenius-Kautzsch §67u,
and 22:16.
4 4a 𝔐 נֹתְנָךְ; for the form of the suffix cf. 23:28
note b. 𝔊 (𝔏^{CS}) *παραδίδωμι ὑμᾶς*, on this cf. 25:3 note
b.

they will set up[b] their encampments in
your midst and make their dwellings
among you. They will eat your fruit, and
they will drink your milk[c]. 5/ And I shall
make Rabbah[a] into a camel pasture and
the (settlements of the) Ammonites[b] into
an encampment[c] for flocks of sheep, and
you will know that I am Yahweh.
6 **For thus has [the Lord][a] Yahweh said: Be-**
cause you have clapped your hands[b] and
stamped your feet and have rejoiced
from the heart[c] with all your contempt[d]
over[e] the land of Israel, 7/ see[a], there-

b 𝔐 וְיָשְּׁבוּ is already presumed, in its consonantal form, by 𝔊 𝔏^{CS} 𝔖, but has obviously been understood as a qal (וְיָשְׁבוּ): *καὶ κατασκηνώσουσιν* (𝔏^{CS} *habitabunt*) *ἐν τῇ ἀπαρτίᾳ αὐτῶν* (𝔏^{CS}, echoing 𝔊: *in apparatu suo*) *ἐν σοί*. Similarly 𝔖 ונעמר בכי חילהון. The piel of ישב is otherwise attested in later Hebrew (see Levy, *Wörterbuch*), but nowhere else in 𝔐. The ישבני of the Eshmunazar inscription (1. 17), which G. Hoffmann ("Über einige phönikische Inschriften," *Abhandlungen der Akademie der Wissenschaften in Göttingen* 36 [1889]: 47) wanted to connect with Ezek 25:4, is, according to Johannes Friedrich, *Phönizisch-punische Grammatik* (Rome: Pontifical Biblical Institute, 1951) § 158, 161, 187, to be understood as a suffixed yip'il. So then Ehrlich, *Randglossen*, and others would accept an obvious scribal error for ושמו or וישימו. שים ב occurs also in 17:4; 24:17; 39:21 (שים בתוך 5:5; 11:7; 26:12). There can be no doubt that it must be a synonym for נתן.

c 𝔗 is remarkably different ואינון יבזון ניכסך.

5 5a 𝔊 (𝔏^{C}) has a free paraphrase *τὴν πόλιν τοῦ Αμμων*.

b The simple בני עמון in 𝔐 is explained by the division of the full designation רבת בני עמון (21:25) between the two parallel halves of the statement. An ערי is therefore (against Bertholet, Fohrer) not to be inserted. From the point of view of content, here too, of course, corresponding to the parallel passage, the settlements of the Ammonites are intended.

c 𝔐 מִרְבַּץ, a *hapax legomenon* in the OT, with which may be compared מַרְבֵּץ which is attested only in Zeph 2:15.

6 6a אדני is lacking in 𝔊 𝔏^{C} 𝔎^{Bo}, see Appendix 1.

b According to Kautzsch, *Aramaismen*, 54f, "to slap one's hand on one's knee." While 𝔐 goes over to a second person masculine singular address in vv 6f, 𝔖, as in vv 3–5, consistently has second person feminine singular.

c 𝔐 בנפש, which appears in v 15, is not to be altered, on the basis of 36:5, to a simple נפש.

d In the rendering of 𝔐 ותשמח בכל שאטך בנפש by 𝔊 (𝔏^{C}) *Καὶ ἐπέχαρας ἐκ ψυχῆς σου* and by 𝔖 וחדיתי בנפשכי, the words בכל שאטך do not appear to be attested. Thus Cornill, Fohrer would delete the words as a gloss. Since, however, the parallel passage in v 15 translates the simple בשאט בנפש also with *ἐπιχαίροντες ἐκ ψυχῆς*, the suspicion is aroused that 𝔊 simply interpreted the בכל שאטך, which it did not understand, on the basis of the ותשמח. In the *σου*, which in v 6 is added to the *ἐκ ψυχῆς*, it may be that the suffix of the שאטך of 𝔐 is preserved (cf., however, the free translation of יד by *τὴν χεῖρά σου* and of ברגל by *τῷ ποδί σου*). The root שאט has been misunderstood by the translator again in 16:57. The translator of 28:24, 26; 36:5 is the first to understand it. On the idea of more than one translator of 𝔊 see the Introduction.

e על–אל cf. 1:17 note a

fore, I shall stretch out my hand against you and give you as (spoil)[b] to the peoples and destroy you from among the nations and blot you out from the countries [I will blot you out][c], and you will know that I am Yahweh.

8 **Thus has [the Lord][a] Yahweh said: Because Moab [and Seir][b] say: See, the house of Judah[c] has become like other nations, 9/ see, therefore, I shall expose[a] the slope[b] of Moab from the cities, all its cities[c]—the glory of the land, Beth-jeshimoth,**

7 7a 𝔐 הנני is not attested by 𝔊 𝔏^{C}. Since the verb following הנני is otherwise normally in the participial form (cf. vv 4,9,16) and the continuation with the first person singular perfect has no parallel in Ezek and is paralleled in the OT as a whole only in Jer 44:26, it may well be asked whether the הנני in v 7 has been introduced only at a later stage by assimilation to the adjacent proof-oracles. In v 13 it is missing alongside the consecutive perfect ונטתי. After לכן 𝔖 provides another introduction formula for a message-type oracle.

b Instead of K לבג, the Q לבז is to be read. נתן לבז occurs also in 7:21; 23:46, cf. also היה לבז 26:5; 34:8, 22, 28; 36:4.

c The אשמידך of 𝔐 was obviously already found by 𝔊 (ἀπωλείᾳ) and 𝔏^{C} (*perditione*). By adding the copula 𝔅 𝔖 accommodate it better, but by its lack of syntactical connection and by the fact that it does not fit into the parallelism it reveals itself to be a secondary addition (Cornill, Herrmann, Fohrer).

8 8a אדני is lacking in 𝔊 𝔏^{C} 𝔊^{Bo} 𝔎^{Bo}, see Appendix 1.

b 𝔐 ושעיר is not attested by 𝔊 𝔏^{C} 𝔎^{Bo} 𝔄. Since, from the point of view of content, it is not taken up in vv 8–10 and since it anticipates the oracle against Edom (on the connection between Edom and Seir cf. 35:15) it is to be considered, with the majority of commentators (even Aalders), as a secondary, inept expansion. Is the gloss a sign of the increasing hatred against Edom?

c 𝔊 (𝔏^{C} 𝔄) οἶκος Ισραηλ καὶ Ιουδα. The insertion of Israel has been occasioned here, as in the reading attested by Or Var^{G} (cf. BHK^{3}) in which 𝔐's יהודה has been simply replaced by ישראל, by a desire for greater theological accuracy. The political term בית יהודה, which in the mouth of foreign enemies is particularly appropriate here, is to be replaced or else expanded by the honorific name of the people of God. See Appendix 2. As *lectio difficilior,* 𝔐 here deserves priority.

9 9a 𝔐 פתח literally: "I open"; Jer 13:19, of the capture of a city.

b 𝔐 כתף really "shoulder." The word is often used figuratively as a designation of territory. Schwarzenbach, *Terminologie,* 18f, would refer it to the "mountain ridge which borders a territory," whereas it is normally understood as "mountain slope"; cf., e.g., Karl Heinz Bernhardt, "Beobachtungen zur Identifizierung moabitischer Ortslagen," *ZDPV* 76 (1960): 143 note 26, and Kuschke, "*Ḳrjtn,*" 25. On this point see Josh 15:8, 10f; 18:12f, 16, 18f; Is 11:14. What would be meant here, then, would be the rugged western slope of the Transjordanian plateau, facing both the Jordan valley and also, therefore, Judah. 𝔖 retains the human picture: 'Behold I will crush the power (תקוף) of Moab.'

c 𝔐 מהערים מעריו, which is attested by 𝔖 𝔗 𝔅, is undoubtedly difficult. 𝔊 (𝔏^{C}) ἀπὸ τῶν πόλεων (ἀκρωτηρίων αὐτοῦ corresponds to 𝔐 מקצהו) attests only מהערים which can, therefore, with Ehrlich,

Baal-meon and Kiriathaim[d]. 10/ (And I
shall give it)[a] to the peoples of the East,
to the Ammonites, as a possession so
that the Ammonites be no more
remembered among the nations[b], 11/
and on Moab shall I execute judgment,
and they will know that I am Yahweh.
12 **Thus has [the Lord][a] Yahweh said: Because**
Edom has acted against the house of
Judah in bitter revenge[b] and has acted
very wrongly in taking vengeance on
them[c], 13/ therefore [the Lord][a] Yahweh
has said this: So I shall[b] stretch out my

scarcely simply be deleted. Some would like to correct this to מערים (Cornill and others). Bewer, "Textual Notes," 163f, deletes מהערים, reads מְעָרָה instead of מעריו and links this with v 9bα. On no account is it, with Kraetzschmar, Cooke, to be emended to מערער.

d 𝔐 קריתמה is to be read as קריתימה with Q, according to 𝔊 (𝔏[C]), which wrongly divides πόλεως παραθαλασσίας, and 𝔖 𝔗 𝔙. 𝔐 בעל מעון has been misread by 𝔊 ἐπάνω πηγῆς as מעל מעין.

10 10a 𝔐 ונתתיה would make the new sentence begin only with v 10aβ. V 10aα must then be taken with what precedes, but this makes of vv 9–10aα a clumsy construction and of v 10aβ an intolerably short sentence. The simple נתתיה, attested by 𝔊 𝔏[C] 𝔖 and accepted by most as the original reading, is not satisfactory as a perfect (cf. אעשה v 11). We must, therefore, accept that ונתתיה has been erroneously removed from its original place at the beginning of v 10. Cf. also the parallels in v 4.

b 𝔐 בגוים is not attested by 𝔊 𝔏[C]. The third person feminine singular תזכר at first sight seems to be connected to the third feminine singular suffix referring to the land of Moab. This makes the following בני עמון, which surprisingly appears as subject, seem suspect. The fuller reading of 𝔖 רבת דבני עמון, supported by no other branch of the tradition, must be intended to counteract this difficulty. Reider, "Contributions," 91f, understands בני עמון here in the sense of ארץ בני עמון. See too Driver, *Aramaic Documents,* 19 note 1. Hermann, Bertholet, Fohrer delete בני עמון as a gloss and also delete the mention of the Ammonites in v 10aα as a secondary element. Admittedly, the emphatically positioned ובמואב in v 11a is then unusual. See the exposition.

12 12a אדני is lacking in 𝔊 𝔏[C] 𝔎[Bo], see Appendix 1.

b 𝔐 בנקם נקם. The simple פורענא of 𝔖 seems not to presuppose the cognate accusative נקם. Cornill, therefore, would like to delete נקם, while Bertholet, Fohrer understand בנקם as a variant reading. However, in view of the testimony of 𝔊 𝔏[C] 𝔗 (בתקוף פורענו) 𝔙 (*fecit ultionem ut se vindicaret*) and the parallels 24:8 (25:15 nip'al) it is preferable to adhere to 𝔐.

c 𝔐 ונקמו בהם. 𝔊 (𝔏[C]) καὶ ἐξεδίκησαν δίκην seems to point to וינקמו, so Herrmann, Bertholet, Fohrer. Yet 𝔐's consecutive perfect is surely to be regarded hypotactically as a description of the nearer circumstances of guilt. Gesenius-Kautzsch §112f speaks of immediate dependence on a consecutive imperfect and of the frequentative significance of the consecutive perfect. This paratactic understanding of it as a consecutive imperfect leads to an inelegant mere repetition of the immediately preceding נקם. In 𝔊's δίκην (𝔏[C]) בהם seems to have been misread as נקום. Against BHK[3], Bertholet, it is best to retain 𝔐.

13 13a אדני is lacking in 𝔊 𝔏 𝔎[Bo], see Appendix 1.

b 𝔐, ונטתי. For this kind of continuation with consecutive perfects after the introductory formula, cf.

hand against Edom and shall blot out of it
men and cattle and make it desolate.
From Teman to Dedan[c] they will fall by
the sword, 14/ and I shall execute my
vengeance on Edom by the hand of my
people Israel[a]. And they will deal with
Edom according to my anger and according to my wrath and will know my vengeance, says [the Lord][b] Yahweh.
15 Thus has [the Lord][a] Yahweh said: Because
the Philistines acted full of vengeance[b]
and have taken bitter revenge[c] with contempt of heart[d] to destroy in
longstanding enmity[e], 16/ therefore [the
Lord][a] Yahweh has said this: See, I shall
stretch out my hand against the Philistines and shall root out the Cretans[b] and
destroy the rest (of the inhabitants) of
the sea coast. 17/ And I shall execute
against them great acts of vengeance [in
fierce chastisements][a], and they will
know that I am Yahweh when I execute
my vengeance against them.

35:11 ועשיתי.

c According to the accents in 𝔐, מתימן is to be taken with what precedes it. So, too, 𝔙 𝔗 (𝔗 מדרומא misunderstands 𝔐 here as a point of the compass). The sense, however, demands that it should be taken with ודדנה, which has been wrongly understood by 𝔊 διωκόμενοι as a derivation from נדד (or רדף?). On the dissimilation of the vowel of the ה-locale cf. אָנָה 1 Kgs 2:36,42; and, after an o-sound, נֹבָה 1 Sam 21:2; 22:9 (Gesenius-Kautzsch §90i). The copula here replaces, in a rather careless formulation, an עד which is, in any case, rendered superfluous by the ה-locale. Driver, "Ezekiel," 156, refers to the analogous מעקרון וימה of Josh 15:46. 𝔖 takes the place names with what precedes and introduces the last two words, which Fohrer would like to delete entirely as a "gloss on the formation of a new sentence," as an independent sentence by means of the copula.

14 14a On purely grammatical grounds, the translation: 'I will give my vengeance . . . into the hands of my people Israel' would also be possible. But the use of the expression נתן נקמה in v 17bβ argues for the translation given in the text.

b אדני is lacking in 𝔊 𝔎[Bo], see Appendix 1.

15 15a אדני is lacking in 𝔊 𝔎[Bo], see Appendix 1.

b 𝔐 בנקמה . . . עשות is, on the basis of 𝔊 𝔗 and the parallel in v 12a, to be retained, cf. Driver, "Ezekiel," 156. The simple accusative construction in 𝔖 פורענא. . . עבדו and 𝔙 *fecerunt . . . vindictam* is here, as in v 12, to be regarded as a smoothing of a difficulty.

c Cf. 25:12 note b; The nip'al of נקם, also Ju 16:28.

d On בשאט בנפש cf. v 6 note d.

e 𝔖 "to destroy the old friendship" (רחמותא דעלם), cf. Am 1:11. The expression איבת עולם, which 𝔊 renders with the simple *ἕως αἰῶνος*, is, however, defended by 35:5.

16 16a אדני is lacking in 𝔊 𝔎[Bo], see Appendix 1.

b 𝔙 *et interficiam interfectores,* 𝔗 ואשצי ית עמא דארע חייבין לאישתיצאה elucidate the word play in והכרתי את כרתים.

17 17a 𝔐 בתוכחות חמה is not attested by 𝔊 (otherwise in 5:15). Since, however, תכחות in 5:15 has been rendered by *ἐκδίκησις*, just as has נקמות in 25:17, an abbreviation by the translator cannot definitely be excluded.

Form

The formula for the coming of a message—an address to the prophet and the summons to a prophetic word accompanied by a symbolic gesture—all this in 25:1–3a introduces the unit 25:1–17. The latter is then divided into five fully developed proof-oracles, each of them in three parts and each introduced afresh by the introductory formula for a message-type oracle (vv 3b–5, 6–7, 8–11, 12–14, 15–17). In the last two the formula for a message type oracle has penetrated the proof-oracle itself and in vv 13 and 15 introduces a second element, the threatening word of judgment.

The first impression leads us to suppose that in this context we are dealing with a "series," consciously composed as a unit, of the same type as the series of oracles against the nations in Amos 1f. D. H. Miller speaks of five pairs of strophes. Even if one can scarcely accept for this prophet of the exile a cultic occasion for the "execration of (the) enemies" such as the cultic background supposed by Bentzen for Amos 1f, one might still be inclined to suppose the influence of a formula of this kind.

A closer look, however, warns us against accepting that the whole chapter is a unit. It begins with the commission to the prophet to challenge the Ammonites. This challenge passes quickly from a plural address to the second person feminine singular. Only with the recognition-formula in v 5b is there a return to the second plural. The second proof-oracle (vv 6f), which does not repeat the name of the recipient but simply presupposes it and which can, therefore, not be regarded as an independent oracle, is confined, on the other hand, for no apparent reason, to the second masculine singular. It must be regarded as an expansion of the first oracle against Ammon added at a somewhat later date (Hölscher). The following oracle against Moab (vv 8–11), which, strictly speaking, no longer fits the introduction in vv 1–3a since the latter envisaged only Ammon, switches to an impersonal third person. Since this oracle is clearly dependent, not as far as its form is concerned but certainly as far as its contents go, on the first oracle against Ammon and since it makes specific references to the fate of the Ammonites (v 4), one cannot see in it an independent oracle of a series such as Amos 1f. It will have to be regarded, just as were vv 6f, as an expansion added to the basic Ammonite oracle. The oracles against Edom and the Philistines reveal the same impersonal style. Since they are similar to each other (cf. the repetition of the formula for a message-type oracle, but also the words of threat which resemble those of the expansion in vv 6f), the question may be asked as to whether they were added at the same time as the oracle against Moab or only in a second stage (perhaps at the same time as vv 6f?). Thus, with regard to the whole of 25:1–17, one must reckon with a continuous process of growth. In view of the expansion by the addition of oracles related as to form, one can consider the influence of the model of the series of oracles against foreign nations in Amos 1f as, at the most, fairly remote.

The statements in these strictly constructed proof-oracles are described by Hölscher as "bereft of ideas, stereotyped, devoid of poetic warmth and grace" and are judged as "very poor, purely literary products."[1] But would observations of a similar nature not also have to be made about the oracles in Amos 1f? The evidence of 1 Kgs 20:13, 28 has shown, however, that the basically very rigid schema of the proof-oracle, a schema whose formulae nevertheless recur, had already found its fixed form in the prophetic words of the prophets of the northern kingdom against the Aramaean enemy.[2] From this point of view it is surely more than coincidence that in the case of Ezekiel too the finest examples of the tripartite proof-oracle are to be found precisely among the oracles against foreign nations. The true home of the proof-oracle must surely lie in the language of the national prophets of salvation of the earlier period, language which was aimed at Israel's victory over her enemies. By contrast, an innovation is provided by its extension to the proclamation of doom for Israel and by the additional inclusion of the free, eschatological language of salvation which follows on the proclamation of doom and in which the element of "justification" disappears in the face of the operation of Yahweh's free grace (cf. on 36:22f).

The "archaic character" of many of the elements of form in Ezekiel's language and their proximity to certain traditions of pre-writing prophecy is immediately clear, too, in the use of this type of language, which is often lightly dismissed as the work of a redactor. It is not, however, to be separated from the connection with the formulae of Yahweh's self-revelation which probably have their cultic roots in the solemn proclamation of the law in the decalogue (Pss 50;81—here, it is true, in the form אנכי יהוה).

Setting

All of the oracles against the nations that are brought together in chapter 25 presuppose the final catastrophe of Jerusalem and the consequent signs of enmity on the

1 Hölscher, *Hesekiel*, 132.
2 Zimmerli, "Wort."

part of the surrounding nations. They are all, therefore, to be dated after 587 and certainly later than the dated oracles against Tyre and Egypt. The dating of them around 594 is just as improbable as the dating of them after a hypothetical second destruction of Jerusalem in 486.[3] One should note in this connection that the oracle against Ammon is emphasized amongst the oracles against neighboring peoples by being placed first (also by the fact that there are two of them). This is obviously in keeping with the position immediately after the collapse of 587. Ezek 21:23ff has already been concerned with Ammon. In what follows it is Edom who is emphasized as the real enemy among Israel's neighbors and the one who derives most profit from the catastrophe of 587.[4]

Since Ezekiel certainly lived far from Jerusalem, as is shown for the period after 587 by the polemical oracle against "the inhabitants of these waste places" in 33:24, the oracles all originated in the exile. The topographical details for these neighboring peoples, scanty in comparison with Jeremiah's oracles against foreign nations, are entirely in keeping with this idea.[5]

Interpretation

a. The First Oracle against the Ammonites (25:1–5)

■ **25:1–3** In contrast to the oracle against Tyre which follows in 26:1, the composite oracle against Israel's four immediate neighbors in Palestine, ranged as it is under a single formula for the coming of a message, remains undated.[6] The prophet is addressed as son of man and is bidden in the first instance to turn his face towards the Ammonites and prophesy against them.[7] He is to call them to pay attention and address them directly through the message formula.[8] When the prophet turns to address Moab (vv 8–11), Edom (vv 12–14) and the Philistines (vv 15–17), there is no corresponding summons to a symbolic action accompanying the prophet's turning of himself. This is bound up with the fact that in v 8 the direct address in the second person singular breaks off, and what follows is the impersonal address of the third person plural.
The Ammonites, who in the summons to pay attention were addressed in the plural, are addressed in the oracle itself, by a startling change of address, as an individual female figure (as nation or as city-state?) personified in the second feminine singular. This might raise the question as to whether the introduction in vv 1–3a was prefixed only at a later stage. However, the easy reversal of the recognition statement in v 5b to an address in the second plural cautions against drawing overhasty conclusions at this point.

The Ammonites were recognized by Israel, through their descent from Lot, Abraham's nephew, as a closely related people (Gen 19:38) and, like Israel, they reached their territory about the period of transition to the Iron Age. The heart of their territory was at the hill town of Rabba (see at 21:25). It stretched from there northwest into the fruitful low ground *el-buḳē'a* to the north of *eṣ-ṣuwēleḥ*.[9] As they expanded, the Ammonites came into conflict as early as the period of the Judges and of the early monarchy (Ju 10:17f; 11:1ff; 1 Sam 11) with those Israelite groups which were settled in the southern part of Gilead south of the Jabbok. Then David added their kingdom in personal union to his crown (2 Sam 12:26ff).

The division of the kingdom after Solomon must have released Ammon again from this union. Under her own kings, who came perhaps from Aramaean Beth-Rehob, she once more forged her own history, which again and again led to tensions with Israel-Judah. 2 Chr 20:1ff knows of an attack on Judah in the time of Jehoshaphat; 26:8 and 27:5, of tribute paid to Uzziah and Jotham; Jer 49:1, of encroachments on the tribal territory of Gad. Like Israel, Ammon then found herself within the sphere of Assyrian power. Along with Ahab of Israel, Ba'sa, son of Ruhubi, of Ammon makes a stand at *ḳarḳara* in 853 against Shalmaneser III; king Sanipu of Ammon appears among those paying tribute to Tiglath-pileser III; king Paduil, as vassal of Esarhaddon.[10] Ashurbanipal comes to

3 Kuhl, *Prophets*, suggests the former date; Morgenstern, "Jerusalem," the latter.
4 Cf. on chapter 35.
5 See the list for Moab in Rudolph, *Jeremia*², 263–265.
6 See 1, 144–145.
7 See 1, 131; 1, 182–183 on 6:2f.
8 See 1, 346 on 16:35; 1, 133 on 2:4.
9 See Noth, "Ammon und Moab," 36–44.
10 *AOT* 341, *ANET* 279; *AOT* 348, *ANET* 282; *AOT* 357, *ANET* 291.

fight against Arab intruders in Ammon.[11]

After the battle of Carchemish in 605, Ammon, like Judah, will have passed into the sphere of Nebuchadnezzar's power. Immediately prior to the campaign of 598, we find Ammon (according to 2 Kgs 24:2) entrusted with the task of being Nebuchadnezzar's instrument of punishment against Judah and her refractory king Jehoiakim. According to Jer 27:3 she is then, at least in the early years of Zedekiah's reign, to be found among those powers who, along with Jerusalem, conferred about the possibility of shaking off the Babylonian yoke.[12] The subsequent revolt seems to have been realized in Ammon's case too. According to Ezek 21:23ff Ammon is in the camp of Nebuchadnezzar's enemies. The fact, too, that the murderer of Gedaliah (according to Jer 40:14; 41:1f) finds refuge with the Ammonite king Baalis reveals Ammon's anti-Babylonian stance.

In Ezekiel's prophetic oracle, however, something different emerges. No disagreement with the above mentioned political factors must be constructed out of the fact that what is referred to here is the Ammonites' mockery of captured Jerusalem. In the history of nations, the defeated have consistently been in the wrong. Ammon must have speedily accommodated herself to the new balance of power after 587. So it is not surprising if, against the background of earlier hostility towards Israel and of the periods of Ammon's ignominious subjection to Israel, sounds of malicious joy were heard from Ammon too, sounds which subsequently reached the ears of the exiles.[13] There is, of course, no question of active hostility towards Jerusalem, nor of the appropriation of territory.[14]

However, it is not only anger at the humanly odious attitude towards the defeated that finds expression in the exposition of the proof-oracle. In the threefold description of the defeated, Yahweh names his sanctuary as the first object of the Ammonites' scorn. Thus, what is odious from the human point of view becomes abuse of the sanctuary. Instead of being terrified at the unheard-of fact of the profanation of the holy place in Jerusalem and recognizing in that fact Yahweh's burning righteous anger, Ammon laughs, thereby despising the holy one himself, as she does also in her mockery over the devastated "land of Israel" and the exiled "house of Judah," the latter mentioned by its political name as the representative of "Israel."[15]

■ **25:4** It is for this reason that divine judgment bursts upon Ammon. In the description of this the verb נתן ("hand . . . over") not only appears at the beginning, but appears twice more in what follows, and in this linguistic usage the echo of the old prophetic address in the holy war can still be heard. Only, in keeping with the different historical situation, it is no longer "I give them into your hand."[16] Now Yahweh summons foreigners as instruments of his judgments.[17]

In the case of the בני קדם, O. Eissfeldt thinks particularly of Aramaean groups coming from the southeastern hinterland of Damascus, on whose pre-history some light has been shed by the Safatenite inscriptions.[18] The figure of Job is, in Job 1:3, located in this region.[19] 1 Kgs 5:10 (EVV 4:30) mentions the wisdom of these "people of the east" from the desert. The book of Judges (6:3, 33; 7:12; 8:10) is able to report for the period of the Judges their threatening attacks right into the territory west of the Jordan. Isa 11:14 mentions them as eastern counterparts to the western Philistine oppressors. And Jer 49:28 speaks of an expedition by Nebuchadnezzar against these obviously hostile tribes. The Wiseman Chronicle has confirmed this assertion.[20] The prophet Ezekiel now threatens Ammon, settled on the

11 *ANET* 298.
12 On 27:1 see Rudolph, *Jeremia.*
13 See too Zeph 2:8.
14 For mockery on the part of enemies after the fall of Jerusalem see also Lam 2:15f.
15 On "land of Israel" see 1, 203 on 7:2; see also Appendix 2.
16 von Rad, *Krieg,* 7f.
17 See, however, also the expression in v 14.
18 Eissfeldt, "safatenischen Inschriften," 97–99. See also H. Donner, "Neue Quellen zur Geschichte des Staates Moab in der 2. Hälfte des 8. Jahrh. v. Chr.," Mitteilungen des Instituts für Orientforschung 5 (1957), 175.
19 On this passage see Friedrich Horst, *Hiob,* BK 16 (Neukirchen-Vluyn: Neukirchener, 1968).
20 See Rudolph, *Jeremia.*

edge of the desert, with being overrun by these desert groups who are not designated by any tribal names. The effect of this invasion is described in each of two parallel double sentences: Ammonite territory will become the site of the cattle pens (surrounded by a stone wall) or of the circular encampments (טירות),[21] and tents (משכנים) of these desert groups. And the fruits of the soil (פרי) and of the herds (חלב, milk yield) of the defeated inhabitants will be their booty.

■ **25:5** Thus the desert breaks into the settled land and pushes back the frontiers of the area settled. רבת בני עמון ("the great one of the Ammonites"), the proud center of Ammonite settlement, itself becomes pasture for the camels and flocks of the conquerors, thereby losing its honor.[22] In such judgment Yahweh reveals himself in the mystery of his person.

b. A Second Oracle against the Ammonites (25:6–7)

■ **25:6** A second oracle against Ammon is introduced by a new formula for a message-type oracle, linked to the preceding one by כי (which is then missing in vv 8, 12, 15). It is, like the first, delivered in direct address, but for no apparent reason passes to the masculine form. In its formal structure as a tripartite proof-oracle, as also in its direction of thought, it has the closest of links with the preceding oracle. Only everything is formulated in more general terms and at a greater remove; the concrete aspects have disappeared.

It is true that here too the reason for the divine punishment is given as the malicious joy of the neighboring people. This is described, however, simply by the expressive actions of hand-clapping and foot-stamping. The Aramaism מחא ("to clap") is otherwise found in the OT only in the hymnic expressions in Ps 98:8 and Is 55:12, in both of which passages it describes, in association with כף ("hand"), the breaking out of joy.[23] The gesture described here is not to be separated from the expressions in 6:11 and 21:19, 22.[24] The object of the mockery, of the malicious joy and the contempt directed towards the land of Israel is not developed any further—it is clear from the preceding oracle.

■ **25:7** Even the announcement of the judgment in which Yahweh reveals himself as he is to his enemies remains in more general terms.[25] The graphic description of the people of the East, of their tents and their plunder, gives place here to a more indeterminate description of their being given over as plunder to the nations (גוים). Are we to think more definitely of a punishment inflicted by the king of the nations such as Josephus maintains?[26] The announcement of complete extermination from among the nations, an expression not otherwise found in these words in the book of Ezekiel, has an analogy from the point of view of content possibly only in v 16.

If one were to ask, finally, about the particular aim of this second oracle against Ammon, then one can perhaps point to the more pronouncedly theological expression, which depicts Yahweh himself as acting on his own behalf, and also to the intensification of the threat.

c. An Oracle against the Moabites (25:8–11)

■ **25:8** With the oracle against Moab, introduced once again by the formula for a message-type oracle, the style of the direct address is abandoned. From the point of view of content, of course, the Moab oracle, in contrast to the subsequent oracles against Edom and the Philistines, remains quite closely linked to the original Ammon oracle (vv 2–5). Not only are the same instruments of Yahweh's judgment mentioned as assisted there against Ammon, but twice in v 10 quite specific reference is made to the punishment inflicted on Ammon. Vv 8–11 are thereby characterized as a continuation of vv 2–5, to which verses the Moab oracle (omitting vv 6–7, which are proved by this too to be a later addition) is directly connected.

Israel was aware of standing in the same relationship of kinship to Moab as to Ammon and regarded it as a

21 On this see Dalman, *Arbeit,* 6. 28, 41.
22 See note b to v 5; see 1, 442 on 21:25.
23 Besides this, there is only מחה in Nu 34:11 in an irregular usage. On the subject matter see 1, 184 on 6:11 and 1, 433-434 on 21:19, 22.
24 *Pace* Kautzsch, *Aramaismen;* see 25:6 note b.
25 On the "stretching out of the hand," which is announced here (otherwise than in vv 13, 16) by means of the simple perfect, see 1, 294 on 13:9.
26 *Antiquities* X 9, 7.

"brother" of Ammon (Gen 19:37). Moab, too, became settled about the time of transition to the Iron Age and then obviously became a state before Israel did. The heart of its territory lies between the *wādi el-ḥesa* in the south and the *sēl el-mōdschib* (Arnon) in the north. The territory north of the Arnon was disputed between Israel and Moab.[27]

Although in the time of David, when Moab was made to pay tribute, Israel gained control of it, it was again lost in the ninth century in the time of Mesha, and Moab was able once more to push forward to the plateau at the north end of the Dead Sea.[28] Assyrian records mention payments of tribute to Tiglath-pileser III by Salamanu of Moab; a conspiracy against Sargon II; payment of tribute again under Sennacherib by Kammusunadbi, to Esarhaddon by Musuri, king of Moab, and to Ashurbanipal, whose Arabian campaign took him also to Moab.[29] Like Ammon, Moab too must have passed into the dominion of the neo-Babylonian king in 605. At the time of Jehoiakim's revolt, Moabite troops are mentioned alongside the Ammonites as helping the Babylonians (2 Kgs 24:2). Jer 27:3 mentions Moab together with Ammon as present at the negotiations in Jerusalem in preparation for rebellion against Babylon. After the fall of Jerusalem, however, they are again on the side of the victors and revile the defeated. Apart from Ezek 25:8, this reviling is mentioned also in Zeph 2:8 and Jer 48:27.

The reviling by Ammon in vv 3, 6 was depicted simply as a mocking, malicious delight at the fall of Judah and her temple, but in the words of Moab a different note is to be heard: "See the house of Judah has become like other nations." In the mouth of the enemy, the political designation "house of Judah" is once again used for the people of Yahweh. However, while the similarity of Judah's fate to that of all nations is affirmed, Israel's election and her particular history are touched upon. Becoming like other nations—which in 1 Sam 8:5, in the desire for a king, appears as Israel's great sin and which in Ezek 20:32, according to a word of resignation on the part of the exiles, seems to be inflicted as an inevitable outcome of judgment—is heard here in mocking tones in the mouth of the enemy. In place of terror at the holy judgment of a God who cannot make an exception in favor of his own people, here too, as already in the case of the Ammonites, the cynical mocking reversal of the truth is represented. The judgment of God becomes a refutation of God's dealings with his people.

■ **25:9** Judgment must be passed on the untruth of such blasphemy. Moab is given into the hands of the same people of the east as were summoned against Ammon. The usually well-guarded frontier—what is described here in an imprecise, but psychologically easily explicable, turn of phrase is the frontier opposite Judah—is "opened," i.e. burst open. The unusual expression (cf. note a) may be explained as due to the desire for a play on words in which פתח כתף ("to open the shoulder") here is as much a word play as והכרתי את כרתים ("I shall rout out the Cretans") in v 16. According to the wording, which from the textual point of view is not entirely beyond suspicion (cf. note c), what is actually meant by this "bursting open" is the destruction of the most important cities. Three of these in particular are singled out as "the glory of the land."[30] They seem to lie in a direct line, perhaps even on a trade route, which is a direct link between the southern end of the Arboth (plains of Moab) and the central *belqa* (Kuschke). בית הישימות ("Beth-jeshimoth") is mentioned also in Nu 33:49; Josh 12:3; 13:20 as a Reubenite locality. On archaeological grounds it is surely not, as the name might suggest, to be located beside *khirbet suwēme,* but on the site of *tell el-'azēme,* on the south bank of the *wādi el-'adēme,* about four kilometers above the point where it enters the Dead Sea.[31] While this place still lies in the "plains of Moab," on the floor of the Jordan valley, the second name בעל מעון ("Baal-meon") takes us up to the actual highlands of Moab. According to Josh 13:17, this place, called by its fuller name בית בעל מעון ("Beth-baal-meon"), lies also within Reubenite tribal territory. See

27 See Noth, "Ammon und Moab," 46–50.

28 *AOT* 440–442, *ANET* 320–321; on this see 2 Kgs 3:4–27.

29 *AOT* 348, *ANET* 282; *AOT* 351, *ANET* 287; *AOT* 352, *ANET* 287; *AOT* 357, *ANET* 291; *ANET* 294, 301; *ANET* 298.

30 In 20:6, 15 Canaan is described as the "glory" of all lands; see 1, 408.

31 B. C. Schick, "Bericht über eine Reise nach Moab," *ZDPV* 2 (1879), p. 11 and the map after p. 112. Cf. Kuschke, "*krjtn,*" 25, and the exact description by Glueck, "Explorations, IV," 398–404.

also Nu 32:38; Jer 48:23; and the Mesha Stele line 7. The name of the old settlement has been preserved in present-day *mā'īn* eight kilometers southwest of *mādeba.* The third city קריתים ("Kiriathaim") can be looked for not far away, since on the Mesha Stele too (lines 9f), בעל מען ("Baal-meon") and קריתן (*sic*) are mentioned one after the other as places which Mesha had built "in the land of *mādeba*" (lines 7f: ארץ מהדבא). Otherwise קריתים ("Kiriathaim") is mentioned in Nu 32:37; in Josh 13:19 as a Reubenite city; and in Jer 48:1, 23 as a Moabite city. Eusebius knew that the place is to be located "ten miles west of *mādeba.*"[32] Although Burckhardt sought to locate it at *khirbet et-tēm* east-northeast of *mā'īn,* and Musil, Dhorme and others had thought of *khirbet el-qurējāt* north of *sēl hēdān,* Kuschke has proved that the place is to be located on the site of *khirbet el-qurēje* on the north side of *wādi 'ajūn eḏ-ḏīb,* ten kilometers as the crow flies, fifteen kilometers by road (= the ten miles of Eusebius) west of *mādeba.*[33] The route indicated by the three places leads, therefore, from the floor of the Jordan valley via קריתים ("Kiriathaim") on the ascent to the plateau to בעל מעון ("Baal-meon") which lies on the plateau itself.

The three places mentioned do not all belong to Moabite territory proper, in which quite different cities could have been mentioned.[34] They belong to that territory which in the course of history was disputed between Israel and Moab and which obviously lay in a particular fashion within a Judaean's field of vision. Yet it is remarkable that there is not the slightest mention of these territories being won back for Israel. Are we to see in this already the general renunciation of territory east of the Jordan which is unambiguously intimated in 47:13–48:29?

■ **25:10** In what follows, Ammon is again quite specifically mentioned in the announcement of the judgment which is to be brought about through the agency of the people of the East. Moab stands in the shadow of Ammon, which in Ezekiel's time was unmistakably the leading power east of the Jordan. If Josephus is correct in stating that Nebuchadnezzar, in the fifth year after the destruction of Jerusalem (i.e., in the twenty-third year of his reign) (582/81), overran the Ammonites and the Moabites, then in actual fact a common judgment will have befallen the two states—although from the opposite direction to the one expected in Ezek 25.[35] Yet there are several reservations in connection with Josephus's data, which link this event with a victorious expedition by Nebuchadnezzar against Egypt. The expression that Ammon will be remembered no more has its counterpart in 21:37, an appendix to an oracle against the Ammonites which ought to be directed against Babylon.

■ **25:11** The judgment on Moab itself is expressed in a general formula (cf. 5:10, 15; 11:9; 16:41; 28:22, 26; 30:14, 19). Thus, in his judgment on Moab too, Yahweh reveals himself in the mystery of his person.

d. An Oracle against the Edomites (25:12–14)

■ **25:12–14** If the earlier oracles against Ammon and Moab formed a clearly linked double oracle, the same must be said of the oracles against Edom and the Philistines, although in this pair the second oracle is not subordinated to the first in the manner of the oracle against Moab. However, both in form and in the phraseology of the content, there are such homogeneous elements that is seems justifiable to speak of a pair of oracles. Thus, in both oracles, the introductory formula for a message-type oracle not only stands at the beginning of the oracle, but is repeated in both cases in the final clause after לכן. In both cases the contents are dominated by the catchword נקם ("[take] vengeance"), in the statements both of invective and of threat. It even returns at the end of the second oracle in a concluding expansion of the proof-oracle or its recognition-formula. In both cases the threat begins with the proclamation of the stretching out of the divine hand followed by a והכרתי ("I shall blot out . . .").[36]

Edom, too, to whom Israel feels more closely related than to Ammon and Moab (witness Israel's recognition

32 *Onomastikon* 112, 14ff.

33 For the earlier suggestions see van Zyl, *Moabites,* 87, 83; for Kuschke, see his "*ḳrjtn*" and "Jeremia 48:1–8," 191–194.

34 Cf. the list of names in Jer 48 (Rudolph, *Jeremia*).

35 *Antiquities* X 9, 7.

36 Cf. Amos 1:5, 8; 2:3.

of the Edomite ancestor Esau as the brother of her own ancestor Jacob), is one of the peoples who became settled and formed a state at the beginning of the Iron Age. According to Gen 36:31–39, eight kings, in non-dynastic succession, had already ruled in Edom before Israel achieved the monarchy. Edom's territory originally lay on the east side of the *'araba,* where it stretched from the *wādi el-ḥesa* at the southern end of the Dead Sea southwards, bordering on Moabite territory. David subjected Edom in order to secure for himself the trade route to the Red Sea and the mineral deposits of the *'araba,* and appointed governors in the country (2 Sam 8:13f). Subsequently, with varying success, Edom tried to free herself from Judah (1 Kgs 11:14ff; 22:48; 2 Kgs 3; 8:20–22; 14:7, 22; 16:6).

Edom appears among the vassals of Assyria under Adadnirari III, Tiglath-pileser III who mentions a king Qaušmalaka of Edom, Sargon II, Sennacherib who mentions an Aiarammu, and Esarhaddon who mentions a Quašgabri, as well as under Ashurbanipal who again mentions the same Quašgabri.[37] Jer 27:3 mentions Edom among the powers plotting against Nebuchadnezzar in Jerusalem. At the destruction of Jerusalem in 587, however, Edom too is to be found wholly on the side of the Babylonians assisting in the completion of the work of destruction (Ps 137:7; Ob vv 11, 13f). Is the pressure from the Arabian desert already so strong at this period that Edom, which from of old had been closely related to the southern Israelite tribes,[38] had been thrust in some groups across the *'araba* into the Negeb and from there occupied even the southern part of the Judaean hill country? The fact that in Nehemiah's time a certain Geshem the Arabian is mentioned as the southern neighbor of the Jewish religious state would lead one to suppose that the process of this Edomite-Arabian pressure was already well under way in the sixth century (cf. indeed v 13 too).[39]

■ **25:12** So it is to be understood that, in the present oracle, Edom is accused not only of being a sneering witness of the fall of Jerusalem (35:15), but of active hostility—just as is the case later with the Philistines too. Edom had taken a harsh revenge on Judah, behind which may lie the effect of unforgotten hatred (already Amos 1:11f) produced by the memory of earlier oppressions on the part of the Judaean kings (cf., e.g. 1 Kgs 11:15f). This will of course immediately remind one of their participation in the "day of Jerusalem" when they said, "Raze it, raze it! Down to its foundations!" (Ps 137:7). This revenge is designated, by the forceful expression **אשם**, as a "sin."[40] In this there is the reference to the particularly iniquitous offense of breaking a covenant between brothers. (Dtn 23:8 designates the Edomite as **אחיך**. In another context, Amos 1:9 speaks of a **ברית אחים**.)

■ **25:13** But Yahweh will stretch out his hand,[41] pass a judgment of destruction (14:13, 17, 19) and lay waste by the sword the country from Teman to Dedan. N. Glueck would like to locate **תימן** ("Teman"), which is mentioned in the OT also in Gen 36:15, 42; Jer 49:7, 20; Ob v 9; Amos 1:12 (cf. also Hab 3:3) as the designation of an Edomite locality (district, tribal group, city), in *ṭawilān,* just outside Petra northeast of *el-jī,* a place with unusually marked traces of settlement from Edomite times.[42] **דדן** ("Dedan") is also mentioned in Jer 49:8 as a second name alongside **תימן** ("Teman") to designate Edom. Dedan is reckoned in Gen 10:7 as the brother of Sheba and belonging to the tribe of Ham and in Gen 25:3, in the same combination, as belonging, along with other Arabian tribes, to the posterity of Abraham from his

37 *AOT* 344, *ANET* 281; *AOT* 348, *ANET* 282; *AOT* 351, *ANET* 287; *ANET* 287: Aiarammu, *AOT* 352: Malik(?)rammu; *AOT* 357, *ANET* 291; *ANET* 294, 298, 301.

38 See, for example, Eduard Meyer, *Die Israeliten und ihre Nachbarstämme* (Halle a. S.: Niemeyer, 1906), especially 442–446: "Gesamtergebnis. Juda und die Edomiter."

39 Albrecht Alt, "Judas Nachbarn zur Zeit Nehemias" in *Kleine Schriften zur Geschichte des Volkes Israel* 2 (München: Beck, 1953), 338–345.

40 See 1, 456 on 22:4.

41 See 1, 294 on 13:9.

42 See Glueck, "Explorations, II," 82f, and W. J. Pythian-Adams, "Israel in the Arabah (II)," *Palestine Exploration Fund, Quarterly Statement* (1934): 186; see also Felix Marie Abel, *Géographie de la Palestine* 1 (Paris: Gabalda, ²1933), 284f.

concubine Keturah. The name is to be linked with the oasis *el-'Ulā* in the *ḥijāz,* whether it is originally the name of an ethnic group or the name of the oasis itself.[43] As Albright points out, Dedan, in spite of Jer 49:8, is itself no longer to be reckoned as part of Edom, but as a territory lying beyond the southern frontier of Edom.[44] The formula "from Teman to Dedan," therefore, does not represent a territorial description in the manner of the Israelite "from Dan to Beersheba" (1 Sam 3:20 and elsewhere) or of the Egyptian "from Migdol to Syene" (Ezek 29:10; 30:6), but links in an imprecise way a place in the middle of Edomite territory with one in the far south beyond its frontiers. Does this imprecision once again betray the distance of the prophetic speaker from the localities in question?

■ **25:14** The announcement that Yahweh will summon his people Israel to participate in the judgment against Edom is remarkable. That this is said precisely in Edom's case is surely connected with the fact that, already in the pre-exilic period, Edom belonged in a quite particular way to the sphere of influence of the state of Judah and had already begun to force her way into the territory of the house of Israel. At any rate, this statement can be connected only with difficulty with the rest of Ezekiel's preaching. It is not taken up in Ezek 35f, where there is once again a very detailed passage about judgment on Edom. Since v 14a, from the point of view of content, gives the impression of being a repetition of v 13, which has already described the process of judgment to the bitter end, it must be seriously asked whether v 14a is not a secondary expansion. J. Herrmann finds in the whole of v 14 a gloss from the Maccabean period.[45] If the half-verse is retained in the text, then the oracle against the Edomites and also the following one against the Philistines (and the related second oracle against the Ammonites?) must be attributed to a later hand. On the other hand, however, it is clear that the author is not yet aware of the pressure from the people of the East which, historically speaking, is already in operation. A later hand might, however, also be indicated by the transformation of the recognition-formula, in which the place of the recognition formulation כי אני יהוה ("[Know] that I am the Lord") has been taken by the mention of the act of revenge in which the presentation of Yahweh in the sphere of his historical activity is effected.

e. An Oracle against the Philistines (25:15–17)

■ **25:15–17** As mentioned already, the oracle against the Philistines is so closely linked to the oracle aganst Edom that one must speak of a consciously formed double oracle.

The Philistines reached Palestine from the Aegean as a group of the sea peoples.[46] At the end of the period of the Judges and the beginning of the monarchical period they gave Israel a great deal of trouble and, as a result of this pressure, actually brought about the founding of the Israelite state. The united impetus of five city-states, formed by treaty as a national unit, was no longer able, after having been broken by David (2 Sam 5), to recover completely its earlier strength. It is true that we still hear of isolated battles with Israel and Judah (1 Kgs 15:27; 16:15), but here too the incursion of the Assyrians alters the situation. The Philistine cities, now as confederates now as rebellious enemies of the Assyrians, become Judah's enemies or her seducers. The preaching of Isaiah gives us some hint of this (see e.g., Is 14:28–32; 20; also 9:11). After the catastrophe of Sennacherib's campaign of 701 and according to Sennacherib's own account, Mitinti king of Ashdod, Padi king of Ekron whom Hezekiah had previously held prisoner in Jerusalem, and Ṣilbēl king of Gaza are the ones who profit from the defeat of Judah.[47] Something similar must have happened after Jehoiakim's revolt and the deportation of Jehoiachin, when (according to Jer 13:19) the southern part of Judah was separated and undoubtedly added, in part at least, to the sphere of Philistine power.[48] Is there a connection here with the fact that the Philistines are

43 Albright, "Dedan."
44 Albright, "Dedan," 8.
45 J. Herrmann, *Ezechielstudien,* 28, following Jahn.
46 On this see Friedrich Bilabel, *Geschichte Vorderasiens und Ägyptens vom 16.–11. Jahrhundert v. Chr.* (Heidelberg: Winter, 1927), 231–244.
47 See Alt, "Sanheribs Eingriff."
48 On Jer 13:19 see Alt, "Judas Gaue."

not among the ambassadors of the neighboring nations who, according to Jer 27:3, gathered in Jerusalem to conspire against Nebuchadnezzar? The supposition of Yoyotte that the absence of the Philistine cities is due to the fact that they were vassals of Egypt, which at that very time under Psammetichus II would want no complications with Nebuchadnezzar, is scarcely tenable now on the basis of the new information from the Wiseman Chronicle.[49]

■ **25:15** The participation of the Philistines in the rape of territory makes it readily understandable that the Philistines were charged not only with mocking abuse but, like the Edomites, with having been actively engaged in revenge. This evil, inimical action, stemming from their despising of Israel, is derived, as is the murder of the Edomites in 35:5, from an eternal enmity (איבת עולם).

■ **25:16** Here too, however, Yahweh's outstretched hand (vv 7, 13) will have to punish and destroy. The והכרתי ("I shall root out . . .") (also in vv 7, 13), which, as in v 7, is continued with the parallel והאבדתי ("and destroy"), permits a play on words with the name כרתים ("Cretans"), the Philistine group from which David recruited his mercenaries (והכרתי והפלתי "the Cretans and the Philistines" 2 Sam 8:18; 15:18; 20:7, 23; 1 Kgs 1:38, 44) and after whom part of the southern frontier territory was given the name נגב הכרתי ("the Negeb of the Cretans") 1 Sam 30:14.[50] The name might contain a reminiscence of the immigration route of the Philistines, who, amongst others, came by the sea route from Crete.[51] Zeph 2:5 also describes the גוי כרתים ("nation of the Cretans") as inhabitants of the sea coast (חבל הים). The fact that "the rest of (those living by) the sea coast" (חוף הים Jer 47:7) is mentioned here is to be regarded as an intensification of the pronouncement of annihilation. Already in his oracles against the nations, Amos could speak of the annihilation of the "remnant of the Philistines" (Amos 1:8).[52] There is no sign here of any human agent of Yahweh's judgment.

■ **25:17** Then, however, the catchword נקם ("vengeance"), which dominates this double oracle against Edom and the Philistines, is heard twice more in Yahweh's own mouth, in the pronouncement of divine judgment and in the extension of the normally worded recognition-formula. The arrogant demand for justice on the part of Judah's two neighbors is countered by Yahweh with his own holy demand for justice. In נקם ("vengeance") there is not only the psychologically subjective "relishing of a thirst for revenge," but a strong forensic emphasis. In his vengeance Yahweh makes himself known as the one who does not suffer men to take from him what is his kingly right. Paul too, according to Rom 12:19, knows that "vengeance" is one of God's rights.

Aim

God has sat in judgment on his people. In the fact that he has let the house over which his name was called go up in flames, he has made known that where he comes near, his holy will and wrath also come near. In the fact that the nation which was called by his name (עם יהוה "the people of Yahweh" 36:20) was robbed of all the security of this mercy and was slain by the sword, he has made known that his mercy demands a nation which seeks him. His judgment of his people is meant to testify to his holy mercy.

Ezekiel 25 speaks of men and nations who have become witnesses of this judgment. With impeccable clarity it illuminates the error of those who think that they can remain spectators here and fail to see that they too are victims who, in the face of such judgment, must realize that they themselves are being addressed by God. Instead, they indulge, all unsuspecting, in evil mockery at the disaster that has overtaken the defeated (vv 3, 6). Here there is uncovered that deeper layer of human self-righteousness which finds its justification in the judgment passed on those who have experienced an encounter with God insofar as this encounter has obviously been to no avail, and those who have been blessed have fared no better than those who have not been blessed (v 8). In the mocking words of Israel's neighbors there is unmasked the man who thinks that in the judgment of God he himself is invited to judge and believes that he can give free rein to all the hatred in his own heart.

But God's judgment is directed precisely against such a misunderstanding of the divine will and against all

49 J. Yoyotte, "Sur le Voyage Asiatique de Psammétique II," *VT* 1 (1951): 143.

50 See Y. Aharoni, "The Negeb of Judah," *IEJ* 8 (1958): 28ff.

51 See on this Amos 9:7.

52 See further on 36:3-5.

impenitent self-righteousness and hardness of heart. God has not pronounced judgment against his own so that the scornful triumph of the world should have the last word. This too is part of God's self-revelation, that he opposes such self-righteousness on the part of the world as well as all arrogant "taking of justice into one's own hands" (נקם). God's judgment achieves its objective only when all mocking laughter and, still more, all eager, vindictive assistance for his holiness has come to naught. Only then can the way become clear for a genuine awareness of the holy and merciful self-revelation of God.

2. Three Oracles against Tyre and its Princes

Bibliography

W. Emery Barnes
"Ezekiel's Denunciation of Tyre (Ezek 26–28)," *JTS* 35 (1934): 50–54.

P. Cheminant
Les prophéties d'Ezéchiel contre Tyr (26–28:19), 1912.

R. Dussaud
"Les Phéniciens au Négeb et en Arabie d'après un texte de Ras Shamra," *Revue de l'histoire des religions* 108 (1933): 5–49 (especially 40–49).

Otto Eissfeldt
"Das Datum der Belagerung von Tyrus durch Nebukadnezar," *FuF* 9 (1933): 421f.

Otto Eissfeldt
"Tyros," *PW* NB 2nd Series 7 (1948), 1876–1908.

Wallace B. Fleming
The History of Tyre, Columbia University Oriental Studies 10 (New York: Columbia University Press, 1915).

F. Jeremias
Tyrus bis zur Zeit Nebukadnezars. Geschichtliche Skizze mit besonderer Berücksichtigung der keilschriftlichen Quellen, Unpub. Diss. (Leipzig, 1891).

Carl Hermann Manchot
"Ezechiel's Weissagung wider Tyrus. Capitel 26.27.28," *JPTh* 14 (1888): 423–480.

Teófilo de Orbiso
"El oráculo contra Tiro en Isaías 23 y Ezequiel 26–28," *Estudios biblicos* 1 (1941): 597–625.

C. C. Torrey
"Alexander the Great in the Old Testament Prophecies" in *Vom Alten Testament. Karl Marti zum 70. Geburtstage,* BZAW 41 (Giessen: Töpelmann, 1925), 281–286.

Eckhard Unger
"Der älteste Hof- und Staatskalender der Welt," *FuF* 3 (1927): 1f.

Eckard Unger
Babylon, die heilige Stadt nach der Beschreibung der Babylonier (Berlin and Leipzig: deGruyter, 1931).

Eckhard Unger
"Namen im Hofstaate Nebukadnezars II," *ThLZ* 50 (1925): 481–486.

Eckhard Unger
"Nebukadnezar II. und sein Šandabakku (Oberkommissar) in Tyrus," *ZAW* 44 (1926): 314–317.

M. Vogelstein
"Nebuchadnezzar's Reconquest of Phoenicia and Palestine and the Oracles of Ezekiel," *HUCA* 23 (1950/51): 197–220.

Harold M. Viener
"Ezekiel's Prophecy against Tyre," *Nieuwe theologische studien* 6 (1923): 7f.

Among the oracles against the Palestinian neighbors (chaps. 25–28) the present ones against Tyre and its princes are the most extensive. This complex, dated at the beginning (26:1), seems to be divided up into four entities by the four occurrences of the formula for the coming of a message (26:1; 27:1; 28:1, 11). Corresponding to this, however, is the further observation that in 27:21; 27:36b; 28:19b there occurs in each case a similar concluding verse (slightly expanded in 27:21), which in the manner of a refrain concludes a literary unit. The redactor who inserted these concluding verses must therefore have intended only three units and have regarded the two oracles 28:1–10 and 28:11–19 as a unified whole. In the context of the exposition we shall have to see how these two constituent parts of 28:1–19 fit together from the point of view both of content and of form.

In contrast to the ethnic groups addressed in chapter 25, Tyre refers only to a single Canaanite city-state. While all the nations dealt with in chapter 25 were groups which became indigenous in Palestine about the same time as Israel, we are here dealing with a long-established Canaanite-Phoenician colony which (and this, too, differentiates it from the groups in chapter 25) is entirely geared to trade with the Mediterranean world.

Tyre, called צוֹר (צֹר) "rock" after its position on a rocky island in the sea, is definitely to be located on the site of modern *ṣūr,* about 55 kilometers north of Carmel.[1] If G. Posener is correct in his identification of the "princes of *Dwꜣwj*" mentioned in the execration texts with the princes of Tyre, then the oldest mention of the city, so far attested, would go back to the period of the 12th dynasty of Egypt (19th–18th century).[2] J. A. Wilson also considers as probable the identification of the *Iuatji* (so *ANET*) of the Berlin execration texts with the name of the mainland colony referred to by the Greeks as παλαιὰ Τύρος and known in cuneiform by the name *ušu.*[3]

Subsequently this city—originally situated on two islands and, with its two harbors (one Egyptian and the other Sidonian), predestined for seafaring—appears unequivocally in the conquest lists of Amenhotep III, where a king Abimilki of Tyre figures as the sender of no fewer than ten letters.[4] Thus, according to Papyrus Anastasi I, it is part of the knowledge of a proper Egyptian scribe to know about Tyre: "They say another town is in the sea, named Tyre-the-Port (?). Water is taken to it by the boats, and it is richer in fish than in sand."[5] In the journal of an Egyptian frontier official of the time of Merneptah there is recorded the crossing of the frontier by a messenger who has a letter for the prince of Tyre.[6] David initiated friendly relations with Hiram of Tyre (2 Sam 5:11). That an initial phase of tension may have lain behind that is suggested by 1 Kgs 9:10–14, where Solomon, in the course of a complete overhaul of relationships with Tyre (see also 1 Kgs 5:15–32), restores to the latter its hinterland, which had obviously been taken from it by David. That the Phoenicians are called, both in the OT and in Homer, the "Sidonians" (Dtn 3:9; Ju 3:3; and elsewhere) suggests that Sidon was originally the principal city.[7] In the periods of David, Solomon and then of the Omrids, in whom the northern kingdom Israel is linked even by ties of kinship with the royal house of Tyre (1 Kgs 16:31), it is Tyre that has taken the lead, having become comparatively free of Egypt as a result of the sudden incursion of the sea peoples and having grown into the great colonial power of the Mediterranean.

Nor did the Assyrian invasions pass by Tyre. Ashurnasirpal II (883–859) mentions Tyre among his vassals; Shalmaneser III (858–824) mentions, with regard to his eighteenth and twenty-first years, tribute from Tyre and Sidon; Adad-nirari III (810–783) also mentions Tyre and Sidon among his vassals; and in the case of Tiglath-pileser III, Metenna and Hiram (*Ḫirummu*) of Tyre feature as providers of tribute.[8] Metenna had to hand over to the *rab*- SAG who was sent to Tyre the large sum of one hundred and fifty talents of gold. The harsh treatment of this commercial city, which according to all

1 On the rendering of "Tyre" in 𝔊 see 26:2 note a.

2 Georges Posener, *Princes et pays d'Asie et de Nubie* (Bruxelles: Fondation égyptologique Reine Elisabeth, 1940), 82.

3 See *ANET* 329, note 11; Posener (see preceding fn.), 96, does not identify the *'Iwꜣtji* of the Brussels texts at all.

4 Knudtzon, *Amarna,* 146–155.

5 Adolf Erman, *Die Literatur der Aegypter* (Leipzig: Hinrichs, 1923), 288; *AOT* 103; *ANET* 477.

6 *AOT* 96, *ANET* 258.

7 See below on 28:20–23.

8 *AOT* 340, *ANET* 276; *AOT* 343, *ANET* 280; *AOT* 344, *ANET* 281; *ANET* 282; *AOT* 346, *ANET* 283.

the older records was bent on peace, may have been the reason for the fact that from then on a distinct change of policy on the part of Tyre may be noticed. From the last quarter of the eighth century Tyre joins the rebels. Sennacherib's response to the rebellion of the Phoenician cities was to conquer the mainland colony of *ušu* and inflict harsh revenge on Sidon (see below), while the island city of Tyre is not mentioned and obviously somehow escaped.[9] Esarhaddon, on the other hand, makes specific mention of the conquest of rebellious Tyre: "I conquered Tyre which lies in the middle of the sea (*ša qabal tamtim*); from its king Baal, who trusted in Tirhakah king of Cush, I took away all his cities and his possessions."[10] In spite of this strong statement it would appear, however, that it was never really a question of the conquest of the island fortress. A fragmentary text is more restrained: "In the course of my campaign I threw up earthworks against Baal king of Tyre who had put his trust in his friend Tirhakah king of Cush, had thrown off the yoke of Ashur my lord and had answered me insolently; I cut off bread and water, their means of subsistence."[11] Without its having come to a military conquest, Baal surrenders: "The splendor of my lordship overwhelmed him . . . and he bowed down and implored me as his lord . . . heavy tribute, his daughters with dowries and all the tributes which he had omitted to send. He kissed my feet. I took away from him those of his towns which are situated on the mainland."[12] Thus, once again, Tyre lost its hinterland, which had previously been increased by the addition of sections of Sidonian territory by Esarhaddon after his destruction of Sidon.[13] Under Ashurbanipal, however, Tyre is found once more among the rebels, but again suffers the same fate: "In my third campaign I marched against Baal, king of Tyre . . . I surrounded him with redoubts, seized his communications on sea and land. I (thus) intercepted and made scarce their food supply and forced them to submit to my yoke."[14] Daughters and brother's daughters, even a son, had to be handed over to the Assyrian king, although by an act of mercy the son was sent back again.

With the shifting of the balance of power in the year 605 Tyre, too, must have been among the states of "Ḫattiland" which first submitted to the Babylonian yoke (Wiseman Chronicle). At any rate, in the time of Zedekiah we find Tyre, along with Sidon, among the neighbors of Judah gathered in Jerusalem plotting the rebellion (Jer 27:3). It appears that the rest of Judah's neighbors subsequently withdrew from these plans or at least desisted from them on the arrival of the Babylonians.[15] This time also Tyre remained firm, no doubt relying on its island position. Josephus, drawing on Philostratus's Indian and Phoenician history, gives the additional information that Nebuchadnezzar besieged Tyre for thirteen years during the reign of its king Ithobaal.[16] This siege will have to be dated in the period after the fall of Jerusalem. There is no justification for the supposition that there were two sieges of Tyre (598–586 unsuccessful and 572 successful).[17] Behind Tyre's stubborn resistance we must suppose Egyptian backing, as already in the time of Esarhaddon.[18]

So far, unfortunately, there is no direct information about the precise circumstances in which the end of the siege came about after thirteen years. This time, too, it does not appear to have come to an actual military conquest. If, however, there then appears in Nebuchadnezzar's "court calendar" a "king of Tyre," then it may be presumed that Tyre had once again become subject.[19] This is also indicated by information in texts from the time of Nebuchadnezzar which refer to Tyre and to which Unger has drawn attention.[20] The first text

9 *AOT* 352, *ANET* 287.

10 Riekele Borger, *Die Inschriften Asarhaddons, Königs von Assyrien*, Archiv für Orientforschung Beiheft 9 (Graz: Im Selbstverlag des Herausgebers, 1956), 86.

11 Borger, *Inschriften Asarhaddons*, 112; *AOT* 358; *ANET* 292.

12 *ANET* 291; cf. Borger, *Inschriften Asarhaddons*, 110.

13 Borger, *Inschriften Asarhaddons*, 49.

14 *ANET* 295, also 297.

15 See above on Ezek 25.

16 *Antiquities* X 11, 1.

17 So Vogelstein, "Nebuchadnezzar's Reconquest," 199–207.

18 See above.

19 Unger, "Staatskalender," and *Babylon*, 293; *ANET* 308.

20 Unger, "Nebukadnezar II"; see also Unger, *Babylon*, 36f.

contains a receipt for provisions for "the king and the soldiers who went with him to the land of Tyre" and is probably to be dated in the period of the siege. The remaining four fall in the thirty-fifth, fortieth, forty-first and forty-second years of Nebuchadnezzar. The last three appear to have been written in Tyre itself. It is particularly significant that in the text from Nebuchadnezzar's forty-first year (564/63) a Babylonian *šandabakku,* i.e. chief commissioner, appears as a witness. Thus, after the end of the siege of Tyre, there seems to have been in the city a Babylonian chief commissioner as "keeper of the seal" alongside the king Baal who replaced the rebel Ithobaal.[21]

Tyre was first conquered by the troops of Alexander the Great, who in the course of his siege of the island had a causeway built out from the mainland to enable him to reach the city, although in the end he captured the city with his fleet from the sea. As a result of the causeway which, in the course of time, became a neck of land through further alluvial deposits, Tyre lost its position as an island. The modern *ṣūr* lies on a peninsula which is permanently linked to the mainland.

The question arises as to why Ezekiel, in his oracles against the nations, comes to speak so fully about Tyre in particular. The latter is of course also mentioned in Amos 1:9f; Is 23; Joel 4:4–8 and Zech 9:2–4 in the context of prophetic oracles against foreign nations. However, in none of these places is it mentioned with the emphasis which it has in Ezekiel.

By way of explanation of this remarkable fact, one has to bear in mind not only the actual contemporary historical situation, but also the prophetic tradition in which Ezekiel stands. Behind Ezekiel's proclamation—even his proclamation to the nations—there stands unmistakably Jeremiah's message that Yahweh has given his people over to judgment and has appointed the Babylonian power as the instrument of that judgment. Any resistance to this decree would be equivalent to resistance to the divine plan. Only in this way can it also be understood why Babylon is always absent from those powers which are threatened by the prophet with judgment.[22] In 587, however, apart from Jerusalem, only Egypt and Tyre were in a state of rebellion against Nebuchadnezzar. In the case of both of these the rebellion continued for some years. It thus follows inevitably that the prophetic message must be concerned in a quite special way with Yahweh's judgment on these two powers. The most extensive proclamation concerns Egypt (Ezekiel 29–32). Besides Egypt, there remained only Tyre, the proud city on its island, confident in her naval prestige. It is therefore also quite natural that the late addition in 29:18–21, the very latest dated word of the prophet, is still concerned precisely with judgment on the two powers Egypt and Tyre. From the point of view both of the proclamation and of the contemporary historical situation this fact inspires complete confidence.

To what extent also particular relationships between Jerusalem and Tyre (from as early as the time of Solomon?) have to be taken into consideration remains completely obscure. Mention might be made, however, of Mazar's supposition (communicated orally) that possibly a geographical proximity of those departed from Judah to groups of exiles from Tyre[23] may have contributed to the particularly specific formulation of the oracles against Tyre and also, possibly, to the use of Tyrian traditions.

With regard to details it will become apparent that even the oracles against Tyre are not all from the same mold, but bear obvious signs of reworking—an indication of the continued, intensive preoccupation precisely with the pronouncement of judgment on the nations.

If the question has been raised again and again as to whether in the Tyre oracles it is not the fate of Tyre under Alexander the Great that is described,[24] this assumption creates a host of additional difficulties, which would be better avoided in view of the relatively clearly discernible political relationships in the first half of the sixth century and in view of the possibilities afforded by these relationships for the elucidation of the Tyre oracles.

That the Tyre oracles are characterized in places by an aloofness in their manner of description, which reveals little of the direct breath of an impassioned polemic, is neither new nor unheard of within the framework of Ezekiel's oracles.

21 See further on 29:17ff.

22 See above pp. 3–4.

23 Cf. the place name *bīt-ṣurraia, RLA* 2, 52.

24 Torrey; Messel; Brown, *Ezekiel and Alexander,* and others.

As far as the arrangement of the individual sections within the complex 26:1–28:19 is concerned, one should note that the only proof-oracle, 26:1–6, comes right at the beginning.[25] The concluding formula (כי אני (יהוה) דברתי ("for I [Yahweh] have spoken [it]") is found, apart from 26:5, 14, also in 28:10. Conscious arranging can be seen here in the fact that the proclamation of judgment against Tyre in chapter 26 is followed by the קינה ("lament") in chapter 27 and that the same sequence can be seen in 28:1–19 in its two sections vv 1–10 and vv 11–19, which are directed against the princes of Tyre.

25 See also the similar observations with regard to the complex of the Egypt oracles, chapters 29–32.

a. The Fall of Tyre

Bibliography

A. van den Born
"'De deur (?) der volken' in Ezek 26:2," *StC* 26 (1951): 320–322.

F. Wilke
"Das Neumondfest im israelitisch-jüdischen Altertum," *Jahrbuch der Gesellschaft für die Geschichte des Protestantismus in Österreich* 67 (Festschrift für Josef Bohatec) (1951): 171–185.

26

1 **In the eleventh[a] year, . . .[b], on the first day**
of the month, the word of Yahweh came
to me: 2/ Son of man, because Tyre[a] says
of Jerusalem "Aha! 'the gate[b] of the

26:1 1a 𝔐 בעשתי עשרה. So, too, 𝔊 𝔖 𝔗 𝔙. 𝔊[A] δωδεκατῳ is a branch of the 𝔊 tradition δεκατῳ, which is attested in Origen and in the Catenae. The observation that the numeral "eleven" in the year numbers in Ezekiel is elsewhere (30:20; 31:1) אחת עשרה (שׁנה) might suggest, apart from chronological considerations, that an original בשתי עשרה had been wrongly written as בעשתי עשרה. The same error occurs in 40:49. But see the exposition.

b For the first time in a date the reference to the month is missing. See also 32:17; 40:1. 𝔊[A,410] add to the following μηνός the words τοῦ πρώτου. Since, however, elsewhere in Ezekiel the number of the month always precedes the number of the day, this must be seen as a secondary attempt to fill the existing gap.

2 2a The צר (צור) of 𝔐 is represented in 𝔊 in 26:2, 3, 4, 7, 15; 27, 2, 3 (twice), 8, 32 by Σορ, while then in 28:2, 12; 29:28 (twice) (see also the secondary reproduction of 27:32b by 𝔊[AQ], note c) the name is transcribed as Τυρος. It is difficult to avoid the conclusion that between 27:32 and 28:2 in 𝔊 another translator took over. See the Introduction.

b The plural דלתות is strange alongside the singular verbal form נשברה. 𝔖 𝔙 make the verb plural. 𝔊, whose ἀπόλωλε (τὰ ἔθνη) Cornill would explain as due to an internal Greek scribal error for αἱ πύλαι or ἡ πύλη, offers no help. 𝔗 דהות מספקא סחורא לעממיא ("who supplies much merchandise to the nations round about") recurs in 27:3 as a rendering of 𝔐 רכלת העמים. Thus one may ask whether the translator of 𝔗 had also in 26:2 in his copy the words רכלת העמים, which are not, admittedly, attested by any other textual witness (so Messel, 98). Since, however, the phrase שבר דלת[ות] occurs in Gen 19:19; Is 45:2; Ps 107:16 (here the bursting open of closed doors), it will be a free explanation, in the usual style of 𝔗, of the not entirely clear expression דלתות העמים. An alteration of דלתות to the singular דלת (Cheminant, *prophéties;* Herrmann; Bertholet) would make the sentence grammatically

peoples' is broken, it falls to me[c]. <She who was (once) full> is now laid waste,"[d] 3/ therefore thus says [the Lord][a] Yahweh: Behold, I am against you, O Tyre,[b] and will make many nations surge against you as the sea surges with its waves.[c] 4/ And they will destroy the walls of Tyre and bring down her[a] towers, and I shall wash away her soil from her and make her a bare rock. 5/ She will be a drying place[a] for nets in the middle of the sea, for I have spoken (it), says [the Lord][b] Yahweh, and she will become the prey of the nations. 6/ And her daughters, who[a] are in the land, will be killed by the sword, and they will know that I am Yahweh.

7 **For thus says [the Lord][a] Yahweh: Behold, I shall bring against[b] Tyre [Nebuchadnezzar,[c] king of Babylon][d]**

easier; however, it is by no means essential, especially if in דלתות העמים an already existing catchphrase has been adopted (see the exposition), since as the unexpressed subject of נשברה in any case the name of Jerusalem is in the writer's mind. Such a *constructio ad sensum* is grammatically by no means unusual, see Gesenius-Kautzsch §145h. The suggestion of van den Born, "Ezek 26:2," and Messel that דלתות העמים, read as רכלת העמים, should be deleted as a gloss on Tyre, which is determined by 27:3 and has found its way into the wrong place in the text, is not to be commended either, since in the quotation a mention of the subject of the sentence would be expected. דלתות refers to the two parts of the double gate of a city or the double door of a stately building. This is expressed in 38:11 by means of the dual, in 41:23f, however, by the plural form שתים דלתות.

c On the form נסבה see Gesensius-Kautzsch §67t. On the meaning "to be given into someone's possession" cf. the נסב ל of Jer 6:12.

d 𝔐 אמלאה החרבה "I become full, she has been laid waste" is attested by 𝔙. 𝔊 ἡ πλήρης ἠρήμωται and 𝔗 דהית מליא חרובת, on the other hand, try to find in the derivation from מלא the subject of the sentence. Thus המלאה החרבה should be read.

3 3a אדני is lacking in 𝔊 𝔎^Bo^, see Appendix 1.

b צר is missing in 𝔖.

c The hip'il form כהעלות of 𝔐 does not appear to be attested by 𝔊 ὡς ἀναβαίνει, 𝔖 איך דסלק, 𝔗 כמיסק, 𝔙 *sicut ascendit.* Thus, Cornill, Herrmann and others emend to כעלות. But in the hip'il, which corresponds to the preceding hip'il והעליתי, there seems to have been implicit the mysterious driving force which sets the sea in motion. Cf. also v 19. Grammatically it would also be possible to see in הים the subject and in לגליו the object, introduced as in Aramaic by ל.

4 4a 𝔊 τοὺς πύργους σου here endeavors to maintain the direct address, but in what follows it, too, drops into the third person.

5 5a 𝔐 משטח in vv 5,14 can, according to Bauer-Leander §69x, be understood as the construct of משטוח (47:10). The literal meaning "place for spreading out" is correctly interpreted already by 𝔊 ψυγμὸς (σαγηνῶν), V *siccatio* (*sagenarum*).

b אדני is lacking in 𝔊 𝔎^Bo^, see Appendix 1.

6 6a The אשר of 𝔐, which is omitted by 𝔊, verifies the sense of שדה as the place where the daughters (= daughter villages) live. 𝔗 interprets correctly יתבי כפרנהא דבחקלא "the inhabitants of her villages on the mainland" and prevents the direct connection of בשדה with the verb תהרגנה.

7 7a אדני is lacking in 𝔊, 𝔎^Bo^, see Appendix 1.

b על–אל cf. 1:17 note a. 𝔊 introduces the direct address here too, ἐπὶ σέ.

c 𝔐 נבוכדראצר. 𝔊 Ναβουχοδονοσορ. The form with ר, which corresponds to the Babylonian *nabû-kudurri-uṣur* "May Nabu protect the son" (Johann

from the north the king of kings, with horses and chariots and riders and a levy and many people.[e] 8/ He will slay your daughters in the land with the sword. And he will set up siege works[a] against you and will throw up a mound against you and raise up protective shields against you,[b] 9/ and he will direct the impact of his battering rams[a] against your walls and will tear down your towers with his iron tools.[b] 10/ Because there will be so many of them, the dust of his horses will cover you.[a] At the noise of the horses and wheels and chariots[b] your walls will shake when he enters your gates as one enters[c] a city full of

Jakob Stamm, *Die akkadische Namengebung,* MVÄG 44 [Leipzig: Hinrichs, 1939], 41[3], 43, 158), is found in the OT only in Ezek (26:7; 29:18f; 30:10) and within Jer 21:2–25:9; 29:21–52:30 (in 49:28 נבוכדראצור). Elsewhere in the OT the ר has changed to נ by regressive dissimilation. On this see Rudolf Růžička, *Konsonantische Dissimilation in den semitischen Sprachen,* Beiträge zur Assyriologie und semitischen Sprachwissenschaft 6,4 (Leipzig: Hinrichs, 1909), 24.

d The remarkable phenomenon that Nebuchadnezzar's second title is separated from the first by מצפון would suggest that the words נבוכדראצר מלך בבל, which one would moreover prefer to see introduced by את, have been added as a secondary elucidation. An original reference to Alexander the Great (Torrey, *Pseudo-Ezekiel,* 94, and "Alexander the Great," 284f) is for that reason, moreover, quite unnecessary.

e 𝔐 וקהל ועם רב. 𝔊 *καὶ συναγωγῆς ἐθνῶν πολλῶν σφόδρα* is a free rendering and does not necessitate (in spite of 32:3, see there) an emendation to ובקהל עמים רבים (Cornill, Toy) or to ובקהל עם רב (Bertholet, Fohrer). Cf., e.g., the absolute use of קהל in 16:40, as well as the double expression קהל גדול וחיל רב in 38:15. 𝔖 𝔗 𝔙 also translate as if there were a ב preceding these last two expressions.

8 8a 𝔐 נתן דיק; elsewhere in Ezek the expression is בנה דיק, cf. 4:2; 17:17; 21:27. So 𝔗 here too.

b On the text of 𝔊 in vv 8–9 see Cornill.

9 9a 𝔐 קָבָלוֹ, according to Bauer-Leander §72u' a suffixed form of קֹבָל (Gesenius-Buhl, Koehler-Baumgartner: קְבֹל), which provides as alternative readings either קָבֳלוֹ and קְבָלוֹ, is understood by 𝔊 *ἀπέναντί σου,* on the basis of Aramaic, as a preposition. The *hapax legomenon* (2 Kgs 15:10 is a textual error) must, however, with 𝔙 *arietes,* be understood as a noun describing a siege instrument which breaks down walls with its blows (cf. מחי). Cf. Θ (*προσκροῦσμα*) *ἐνσεισμοῦ.* 𝔐 ומחי seems to have been misread by 𝔊 *τὰς λόγχας* as רמחי, and 𝔖 ושננא דניזכוהי ("and the points of her lances") seems to have followed this.

b חרב cannot here be translated by "sword." 𝔙 more loosely *in armatura sua,* 𝔗 באבני ברזליה. Cf. also Ex 20:25.

10 10a Literally: "On account of the abundance of his horses their dust covers you."

b In dependence on v 10a, 𝔊 (𝔖 𝔏[W]) divides as follows: *καὶ απὸ τῆς φωνῆς τῶν ἱππέων αὐτοῦ καὶ τῶν τροχῶν τῶν ἁρμάτων αὐτοῦ.* The construct form פָּרַשׁ in 𝔐 is to be explained on the basis of the close relationship of the three-fold enumeration. See Gesenius-Kautzsch §130b. On פרש as "team of a war chariot" see Galling, "Ehrenname," 132f, note 2.

c The plural מבואי in 𝔐, which 𝔊 𝔖 𝔗 paraphrase and 𝔙 renders with a singular *quasi per introitum,* is defended by the analogous use of מוצא in 12:4 (see 12:4 note c). The singular forms מבוא and מוצא occur in 2 Sam 3:25. In Ezek 43:11 there must be a

**breaches.[d] 11/ With the hoofs of his
horses he will trample all your streets. He
will kill your people with the sword, and
the pillars in which you stubbornly
trusted[a] will collapse to the ground.[b] 12/
And they will steal[a] your wealth, plunder[a] what you have won by your trade,
tear down[a] your walls, destroy[a] your
luxurious houses and throw[b] your stones,
your timber and your rubble into the
middle of the <sea>,[c] 13/ And I shall[a]
make an end of the noise of your songs,
and the sound of your lyres will be heard
no more. 14/ And I shall make you a bare
rock: you shall become[a] a drying place for
nets, you shall never be rebuilt,[a], for I,
[Yahweh][b], have spoken (it), says [the
Lord][c] Yahweh.**

**15 Thus says [the Lord][a] Yahweh to Tyre: Will
not the islands shake at the crash of your
fall, at the groaning of the wounded and
at the fury of the slaughter[b] in your**

number of entrances.

d 𝔐 מִבְקָעָה read by 𝔊 ἐκ πεδίου (𝔏^{W} *de rampo*) as מִבִּקְעָה. The enemy will take the sea fortress of Tyre by storm, as if it were a city he could take directly from the plain.

11 11a So with *ZB*. 𝔐 מצבות עזך is not fully understood by 𝔊 τὴν ὑπόστασιν τῆς ἰσχύος σου or by 𝔏^{CW} *substantiam virtutis tuae*. Only in Θ στήλας. 𝔖 עלותא "altars."

b On the singular תרד after the plural מצבות see Gesenius-Kautzsch §145k. 𝔐 is attested by 𝔙 *statuae tuae nobiles in terram corruent*, while 𝔊 κατάξει, 𝔖 נסחוף, 𝔗 ימגר are an adaptation of sense to fit the context. The consequent emendation made by most commentators to יוריד is to be rejected.

12 12a The change to a plural subject is strange. Yet the text of 𝔊 𝔏^{W}, which here continues the singular subject of the preceding verses (𝔏^{C} alternates in a remarkable double change within v 12), must surely, against Cornill, Herrmann, Bertholet, represent a secondary harmonization.

b 𝔐 ישימו (𝔗 ישוון, 𝔙 *ponent*) is remarkably colorless. 𝔊 ἐμβαλεῖ, 𝔏^{C} *iactabit*, 𝔏^{W} *immittet* might suggest a reading ישליכו (see also note a), but might equally represent a free translation. The verb שים is often used in Ezek.

c 𝔗 בגו מיא, 𝔙 *in medio aquarum* confirm the מים of 𝔐. 𝔊 𝔏^{CW} 𝔖 suggest the possibility of a scribal error for an original הים.

13 13a 𝔊 (𝔏^{CW}) καὶ καταλύσει (𝔊^{967,V} καταλύσω) adapts this verse, too, to the preceding one. See 26:12 note a.

14 14a There are three possible ways of interpreting the strange forms תהיה and תבנה: 1) The second person masculine singular form is used here for the second feminine. So Herrmann, Aalders. The other passages cited for this phenomenon by Gesenius-Kautzsch §47k, Ezek 22:4; 23:32; Jer 3:5; Is 57:8 are, on account of the textual uncertainty of some of them, not really cogent proofs for this possibility. 2) The assumption of a scribal error for תהיי and תבני. So Cornill, Bertholet, Fohrer. That such a mistake should happen to occur twice is scarcely probable. 3) The reading of them as third person feminine singular in line with vv 4f. But why, then, is not the first part of the verse (in line with v 4) also constructed in this way?

b 𝔐 יהוה is lacking in MSS, Var^{P}, Ed, 𝔊^{967,A} (not, however, in 𝔊^{B}), 𝔏^{CW}, 𝔗 and may be a secondary addition.

c אדני is lacking in 𝔊 𝔏^{CW} 𝔎^{Bo}, see Appendix 1.

15 15a אדני is lacking in 𝔊 (𝔊^{B} κύριος κύριος, 𝔊^{A} ἀδωναι κύριος, in 𝔊^{967,V} v 15a is missing through homoioteleuton), 𝔏^{CW}, 𝔎^{Bo}, see Appendix 1.

b 𝔐 בהרג הרג is mostly emended, with reference to 𝔊 ἐν τῷ σπάσαι μάχαιραν, 𝔏^{C} *in evaginatione gladii*, to בהרג חרב (Cornill, Herrmann, Jahnow, and others). Since, however, 𝔖 𝔗 𝔙 confirm 𝔐 and the expression הרג בחרב is rendered by 𝔊 in vv 6, 8, 11

midst? 16/ And all the princes of the sea[a] will descend from their thrones and will take off their outer robes[b] and remove their colorful garments. They will clothe themselves in terror[c] and will sit on the ground and will tremble in agitation[d] and will be horrified at you. 17/ And they will utter a lament over[a] you and say to you:[b]

How you have [perished,][c]
'disappeared' from the seas,[d]
you famous[e] city [who were strong on

by ἀναιρεῖ or ἀνελεῖν μαχαίρᾳ, it is probable that v 15 in 𝔊 is a free paraphrase. An emendation to בגהר הרג "when the slain man collapses" (Driver, "Linguistic Problems," 176) or to בערג הרג "at the groaning of the wounded" (Ehrlich, *Randglossen*) does not commend itself. For the use of הֶרֶג as the cognate accusative of הרג, Is 27:7 is a good example. At most, instead of בֵּהָרֵג (on the syncope of the ה see Gesenius-Kautzsch §51 1), the reading בֵּהָרֹג might be considered.

16 16a What are referred to are the princes of the coastlands and islands This is made clear by 𝔊 (𝔏^C) οἱ ἄρχοντες ἐκ τῶν ἐθνῶν τῆς θαλάσσης.

b Misunderstood by 𝔊 (𝔏^W) τὰς μίτρας ἀπὸ τῶν κεφαλῶν αὐτῶν.

c𝔐 חרדות ילבשו is interpreted by 𝔊 in substance ἐκστάσει ἐκστήσονται. 𝔏^C attaches the equivalent of חרדות to what precedes and inserts a copula: *in stupore mentis et stupebunt.* 𝔏^W corrects this more in line with 𝔐: *in stupore mentis et dementia induentur.* The favorite adaption since Kraetzschmar, Ehrlich to Is 50:3, with the alteration of חרדות to קדרות "grief," has no support in the tradition. The metaphorical use of לבש is attested for the book of Ezek by 7:27 לבש שממה. But שמם is clearly used in v 16bβ as a synonym for חרד.

d See M. D. Goldmann, "The Meaning of 'רגע,'" *Australian Biblical Review* 4 (1954/55): 15, for this understanding of לרגעים, which is generally translated unsatisfactorily by "unceasingly" (Smend, Kraetzschmar), "once more" (Hermann), "ceaselessly" (Bertholet), "continually" (Fohrer), "every now and then" (*ZB*).

17 17a נשא קינה is constructed with אל in 19:1; 27:32 and with על in 27:2; 28:12; 32:2 (cf. v 16). On על–אל cf. 1:17 note a.

b לך is not attested by 𝔊 (see however, Ziegler, *Ezechiel,* 40, and 𝔏^CW). On the basis of 19:1f it could be dispensed with. See in addition, however, 28:12 (32:2).

c 𝔐 אבדת is unattested by 𝔊 𝔏^CW. Its insertion is a consequence of the misinterpretation of the following נושבת, see note d. Metrical considerations, too, point to the secondary character of אבדת.

d 𝔐 נושבת מימים corresponds to 𝔊 κατελύθης (𝔏^CW *destructa es*) ἐκ θαλάσσης. On this see the translation in v 13 of והשבתי by 𝔊 καὶ καταλύσει (on the third person see above v 13 note a). 𝔊 had before it a reading נִשְׁבַּתְּ, following which even the separative מן becomes meaningful. This was then wrongly derived from ישב, possibly on the basis of 27:3 and written *plene* as a nip'al participle. This then necessitated the insertion of the אבדת. On ימים as a plural of intensity cf. 27:4, 25–27, 33, 34; 28:2, 8; 32:2. An emendation to מים (Cornill, Toy), מאיים (Ehrlich, *Randglossen*) or ממים (Bertholet) is not at all necessary.

e According to Gesenius-Kautzsch §138k and §52s, 𝔐 ההללה is to be understood, though against

the sea, you and your inhabitants],[f]
who <spread>[g] terror before you
among all her inhabitants.[h]
18/ Now (however) the islands[a] tremble
on the day of your fall[b] [and the islands
which are in the sea are terrified at
your end].[c]
19 **For thus says [the Lord][a] Yahweh: When I**
make you a desolate city like the cities
which are no longer inhabited—when
<I>[b] make the flood sweep over you and
when the many waters cover you, 20/
then I shall make you go down to the
people of old with[a] those who go down to

the accentuation of 𝔐, as a pu'al participle without prefix. Bauer-Leander §32e takes it, on the basis of 𝔐, as a pu'al perfect with the article as a substitute for the relative pronoun.

f 𝔐 אשר . . . וישביה is not attested by 𝔊 𝔏^{CW}. The passage could have been accidentally overlooked by homoioarchton alongside v 17bβ. But the meter and the ugly doubling of the relative clauses argue for the originality of the reading of 𝔊. The addition contributes an explanatory comment, in the first half with regard to what has preceded, in the second with regard to the following lines.

g 𝔐 אשר נתנו חתיתם has been syntactically linked with the ישביה of the insertion (see note f). Behind 𝔊 (𝔏^{C}) ἡ δοῦσα τὸν φόβον αὐτῆς we can still see the original אשר נתנה חתיתה.

h 𝔐 לכל יושביה elucidates the subject which arouses the fear. The sphere in which fear is aroused is, in 32:23–26(27), 32, where the phrase נתן חתית recurs, universally introduced by ב. So here, against the majority (see, e.g., Cornill; Cheminant, *prophéties;* Cooke), there is no thought of the inhabitants of the sea (with emendation to יושביו or ישביהם). This is the way it has been understood and explained by the interpretative addition in v 17bα (note f). Already 𝔊, however, no longer seems to have understood 𝔐, which it reproduces exactly. 𝔖 obviously refers the expression to the objects of Tyre's power and reads בכלהון עמוריה דארעא, which would correspond to an original לכל ישבי הארץ. For graphic reasons, Bertholet suggests, instead of this, לכל היבשה.

18 18a 𝔐 איין is an Aramaic plural; see 4:9 note a. It has been misinterpreted as אניות by 𝔙 *naves.*

b The adverbial attribute יום מפלתך has been understood by 𝔖 ביומא דמפולתכי, 𝔙 *in die pavoris tui,* 𝔗 ביום מפלת קטילך in purely temporal terms, by 𝔊 (𝔏^{CW}) ἀφ᾽ ἡμέρας πτώσεώς σου with a subsidiary causal emphasis. The grammatically correct 𝔐 (Brockelmann §100b) should not be emended.

c The "intolerable tautology" (Cornill), the fact that it is not attested by 𝔊 𝔏^{CW}, the absence of metric form reveal v 18b as a prosaic gloss on v 18a. Note also the difference between איין in v 18a and איים in v 18b. מצאתך is unexceptionable (in spite of Cornill's "inexplicable") and corresponds to יום מפלתך in v 18a (interpreted causally, see note b; 𝔖 here interprets מצאתך in temporal terms). 𝔗 is fuller במיפק גלוותיך, 𝔙 *eo quod nullus egrediatur ex te.* 𝔖 ביומא דמפולתכי makes the expression identical to the corresponding one in v 18a.

19 19a אדני is lacking in 𝔊 𝔏^{CW} 𝔎^{Bo}, see Appendix 1.

b 𝔐 בהעלות. 𝔊 (L^{CW}) ἐν τῷ ἀναγαγεῖν με, 𝔗 באסקותי (cf. 𝔖 מסק אנא), 𝔙 *et adduxero* suggest that 𝔐 has arisen through an accidental transposition of the two final consonants (cf. 14:1 note a) and should be corrected to בהעלתי.

20 20a 𝔐 את (יורדי בור) is not, in contrast to most recent commentators, to be emended to אל on the

the pit and will make you dwell, like[b] the ancient ruins in the land, in the depths[c] with those who have gone down to the pit, so that you will not <rise[d] again>[e] in the land of the living.

21 I shall make you an object of (great) terror[a], and you will be no more, [you will be looked for but not found,][b] for ever,[c] says [the Lord][d] Yahweh.

basis of 𝔊 (𝔏CW) πρὸς (τοὺς καταβαίνοντας εἰς βόθρον). The related passages 31:16; 32:18, 24, 25, 29, 30 unanimously support 𝔐, i.e, the thought of the destiny shared with (את) those who go down to the pit.

b 𝔐 כחרבות מעולם is attested by 𝔊 (𝔏CW 𝔙) ὡς ἔρημον αἰώνιον and should not, as is suggested by many recent commentators, be emended on the basis of 𝔖 𝔗 to בחרבות מעולם.

c 𝔐 ארץ תחתיות. 𝔊 βάθη τῆς γῆς, 𝔙 *terra novissima.* In a surprising change, the construct formation of 𝔐, which recurs in 32:18, 24, is in contrast to the appositional expression ארץ תחתית in 31:14, 16, 18. Since 𝔊 reproduces the plural תחתיות only here, and in 32:18 has the singular βάθος τῆς γῆς, it may be asked whether the difference is original or appeared only in a later stage of the tradition. See further the exposition.

d 𝔐 ונתתי צבי "and I give glory (𝔙 *gloriam*) (in the land of the living)" makes no sense and should be emended, on the basis of 𝔊 μηδὲ ἀνασταθῇς, 𝔏CW *neque resusciteris* (cf. also 𝔖 ולא אעבר קימכי), to ותתיצבי or ותתנצבי (Driver, "Linguistic Problems," 176). 𝔗 interprets 𝔐 in a bold paraphrase: "And I give joy (חידוא) in the land of Israel."

e 𝔐 תשבי is attested by all the versions. On ישב "to be inhabited" see also 29:11; 36:35 as well as 35:9. For complete clarity, however, one would prefer to read עוד as well. The revocalization proposed by many, תָּשֻׁבִי is impressive. This would then need to be connected (as in 8:6, 13, 15) with the following verb (see note d).

21 21a בלהה (again in 27:36; 28;19 as well as in Is 17:14; Ps 73:19; Job 18:11 and frequently), which is to be derived from בלה "terrify" (Ezra 4:4), seems to have been understood by 𝔙 *in nihilum,* 𝔗 כדלא הוית in terms of the root בָּלָה and the negative particle בְּלִי. 𝔖 אבדנא is different.

b 𝔐 ותבקשי ולא תמצאי is not attested by 𝔊 𝔏CW and since 26:21 recurs in this same shorter form in 𝔐 in 27:36; 28:19, is to be regarded as a secondary expansion (Cornill, Bertholet, Fohrer).

c The simple עד עולם of the formula in 27:36; 28:19 had, on the evidence of 𝔊 ἔτι εἰς τὸν αἰῶνα, 𝔏CW *amplius in aeternum,* already been altered to עוד לעולם before the intrusion of the expansion (note b).

d אדני is lacking in 𝔊 𝔏C 𝔎, see Appendix 1.

Form

The section 26:1–21, which is placed under a single formula for receiving a message and an introductory address to the prophet, falls into four sections. Each of these sections is introduced afresh with the formula for a message-type oracle (v 3, with the justification for the word of judgment already preceding in v 2, and vv 7, 15, 17). In the third and fourth sections, there is in addition, by way of transition, a כי of motivation. The sections comprising vv 7–14 and vv 19–21 are also concluded by the formula for a divine oracle, while the first section, vv 2–6, has this formula already at the end of v 5a, followed by an expansion in vv 5b–6 which ends in the recognition formula.

If one asks further about the formal structure of these individual sections and about the context in which they now stand joined, then it is clear, in the first instance, that the juxtaposition of vv 2–6 and vv 7–14 is the juxtaposition of two parallels (Kraetzschmar, following Manchot, "Weissagung": mutually exclusive parallels; see also Bertholet). Vv 2–6 are delivered as a tripartite proof-oracle in the style of the oracles of chapter 25. Following on a motivation introduced by יען, which accuses Tyre by quoting her own words, there is in vv 3–5aα the announcement of judgment, which is concluded first in v 5aβγ with כי אני דברתי ("for I have spoken [it]") and the formula for a divine oracle and then in v 6b after a further repetition of the threat of judgment (vv 5b–6a) with the recognition formula.

From the point of view of form, vv 7–14 are constructed more simply in that here only the threat of judgment is expounded and the whole is rounded off concisely in v 14b with כי אני (יהוה)דברתי ("for I [Yahweh] have spoken [it]") and the formula for a divine oracle. From the point of view of content, vv 7–14 prove to be an elucidation of the somewhat obscure threat of judgment in vv 2–6, in that not only is Yahweh's instrument of judgment named, but also the process of destruction is itself described in detail. In vv 8a, 12, 14 the expressions of vv 3–5 are, in part, verbally repeated. Instead of two independent parallels, we have, rather, to do here with a process of expository amplification. The oracle of vv 2–6, which in form is clearly connected with the forms of speech in chapter 25, has, in vv 7–14, in a secondary process of further interpretation and from the point of view of content, been more sharply developed and expounded in a form in which the "text" of this exposition is echoed verbally in vv 8a, 12, 14.

Vv 15–18 contain the lament of the surrounding lands over the fall of Tyre. One is surprised to notice a great similarity between the expressions here and the concluding part of the great poem about the "ship Tyre" in Ezekiel 27, more especially with regard to 27:28–36, a similarity which far surpasses any mere closeness of motifs. 27:28–36 is on no account to be removed from the context of chapter 27. Since, on the other hand, the transition to the new theme in 26:15–18 is completely harmonious but shows no verbal affiliations with what precedes, the conclusion can scarcely be avoided that 26:15–18 has been added to 26:1–14 as an expansion in the light of 27:28–36.

The same process, however, is repeated once more in the final section, vv 19–21, where Tyre's journey to the underworld is described in the vocabulary of the great description of Egypt's journey to the underworld in 32:17–32, which, in its turn, must be regarded as an independent unit.

Thus in chapter 26 the following process of growth can be discerned: to a proof-oracle with an expanded conclusion (vv 2–6) there has been added an exposition, likewise in elevated language (vv 7–14). This word of judgment over Tyre has then been further expanded, with reference to 27:28–36 and 32:17–32 and in clear verbal dependence on these oracles, by the motifs of a lament over the fallen power (vv 15–18) and the journey of that power to the underworld (vv 19–21).

The questions of the origin and date of this group of oracles is best discussed in the context of the detailed exposition.

Interpretation

■ **26:1-6** *a The Sin of Tyre and the Judgment.*

■ **26:1** The formula for the coming of a divine message is in this first oracle against Tyre linked with a date.[1] In the latter, the lack of specification of the month as well as the unusual form, as far as Ezek is concerned, of the year number (note a) is striking. The suspicion of editorial manipulations with regard to the number cannot be entirely suppressed. On the other hand, the quotation of the words of Tyre, which seem to reflect directly the very recent fall of Jerusalem, would suggest a date not too far removed from 587. Yet it will have to remain open whether, in fact, the oracle is to be dated as early as the actual year of the fall of the city. It would, in that case, have to be in one of the last months of the year, after the news of the fall had already reached the exiles.[2] Thus, W. F. Albright proposed to supplement the text with the eleventh (or twelfth) month.[3] According to

1 See 1, 144–145.
2 See also on 33:21.
3 Albright, "Seal of Eliakim," 93.

Parker-Dubberstein, the beginning of the eleventh year of Jehoiachin, i.e. of the eighteenth year of Nebuchadnezzar, fell on April 23, 587. The first day of eleventh month of that year would fall on February 13, 586; the first day of the twelfth month of the same year, on March 15, 586. Regarding the dating on the first of the month (which occurs also in 29:17; 31:1; 32:1), Wilke, pointing to 2 Kgs 4:23, has raised the question whether the day of the new moon might not have been a favorite day for the receiving and the giving of God's word through the prophets.[4] One would then be led to think of a proclamation of the prophetic oracle within a cultic festival.[5]

■ **26:2** The prophet ("son of man") receives from Yahweh the commission to address Tyre directly on account of her utterances in connection with the fall of Jerusalem.[6] This recalls, from the point of view both of form (address in the second feminine singular) and of content (the quotation of the words of the person addressed), the oracle against the Ammonites in 25:3–5 (cf. also the quotation in the Moab oracle in 25:8). While, however, the oracle against the Ammonites contained only the expression of mockery at the fall of Jerusalem, which was made stronger in the words of the Moabites by a thrust at Judah's awareness of her election, 26:2 accentuates the mockery (האח "Aha!" as in 25:3) from the point of view of the rich trading city of Tyre (so, too, then chapter 27): the rich possessions of Jerusalem will now accrue to Tyre. Here, too, as (in a different way) in 11:15; 33:24, a beneficiary of the divine judgment speaks of the way in which the judgment on Jerusalem benefits him.

The person affected by the judgment is here designated (otherwise than in 25:8) not by her everyday name, but by a figure of speech. The mysterious דלתות העמים ("the gate of the peoples") is generally understood by the commentators as a description coined *ad hoc* by Tyre, one which understands the trading rival Jerusalem as "a necessary transit point for traders" (Bertholet). Fohrer modifies this to the extent that "since Solomon, the transit trade between Asia Minor and Mesopotamia on the one hand and Egypt on the other was to a great extent an Israelite monopoly." Smend, on the other hand, interpreted the "door" as a barrier which "checks the flow of peoples to Tyre."

The lack of syntactical agreement of plural דלתות ("gates") (note b) could also, however, suggest that the description דלתות העמים ("the gate of the peoples"), quite apart from its present use, represents an already current title which was conceived of as a "name" in the singular. In that case there was no need for the expression basically to refer to any significance on Jerusalem's part for the opening or closing of trade routes, a suggestion which seems in any case highly doubtful for Jerusalem which lay relatively off the beaten track. It could simply indicate the political significance of this city within Palestine. If one is disinclined to go back to the period of David and Solomon or to the significance of Hezekiah for the anti-Assyrian coalition against Sennacherib, one can think of the history of the period immediately prior to that of Ezekiel, when in the time of Josiah a focal point formed in Jerusalem that tried to assert itself against both Assyria and Egypt.[7] One can point to the fact that, according to the Wiseman Chronicle, after the destruction of Ashkelon in 605 (B. M. 21946, obv. lines 18-20) within Ḫatti-land only "the city of Judah" is explicitly mentioned as the object of a Babylonian attack (B. M. 21946, rev. lines 12–13). One can think of Jeremiah 27, where (obviously in the wake of the rebellion in Babylon of 595/94, see B. M. 21946, rev. lines 21–22) again there was discussion of the possibility of a new rising, and, alongside Edom, Moab and Ammon, Tyre and Sidon too sent their ambassadors to Jerusalem.

Jerusalem (Judah) was particularly to be commended, through her sheltered and yet central and elevated situation, as a center or even as the "door" of the nations and could, through this position of honor, achieve particular wealth. And now Tyre, after the collapse of Jerusalem (nip'al of שבר in 27:34, the qal in 27:26 of the shipwreck; 30:8 of the Pharaoh's relief troops; nip'al in 30:22, the qal in 30:18, 21, 24 of Pharaoh's arm), hopes to fall heir to this position and to the possibilities for profit (nip'al of מלא) inherent in it. The oracle is interpreted by Rabbi Yishaq (*b. Meg.* 6a) in terms of the conflict between Jerusalem and Caesarea.[8]

■ **26:3** On this calculating and selfish mockery, however, there is passed the sentence of judgment, emphatically introduced by the formula for receiving a message-type

4 Wilke, "Neumondfest," 174.

5 On the lamentation of the exiles in worship see 1, 115–116 on 1:1 and 1, 262 on 11:16.

6 See 1, 131.

7 See, e.g., Noth, *History of Israel*, 269–280.

8 A different application is to be found in *b. Pesah* 42b.

oracle.[9] It begins with the challenge formula, which reveals Yahweh himself as the challenger,[10] but then turns at once to political threat with the forces of the "great nations" (גוים רבים 31:6; 38:23; 39:27; see also עמים רבים "many peoples" 3:6; 27:33; 32:3, 9f; 38:6, 8f, 15, 22) that will surge forward like the waves of the sea, an instantly obvious image for the island city of Tyre. One certainly can not, however (with Manchot, who removes the words גוים רבים כהעלות "many nations, as surges" from the text), make it into an actual statement and see in it the announcement of a great spring tide. Rather one might think of a threatening counterpart to Yahweh's "leading up" of the people of Israel from Egypt.[11]

■ **26:4** Those who will assist Yahweh in his judgment will take over the destruction of walls and towers. In the radical completion of the decree of judgment, in which along with rubble and soil from the rocky island all remembrance of the city will be swept away, it is again Yahweh himself who is seen in his action against this place.

■ **26:5** When the fishermen then use what has now become a quite uninhabitable reef as a drying place for their nets, the end of this island settlement will be sealed in the eyes of all. The image of the drying place for nets appears again in 47:10 in the context of an oracle of salvation. In an oracle of doom it can be heard in the "Prophecies of a Potter" from the Hellenistic period in the city of Alexandria: "The city by the sea will become a place where fishermen dry (their nets)."[12] The description of the city of Tyre "in the middle of the sea" was to be heard already in Papyrus Anastasi I and in Esarhaddon (see above).

The oracle would originally have ended with v 5a, the emphatic underlining of the fact that it is Yahweh himself who has spoken. It was then, however, expanded in terms of a more precise actualization. Going back beyond the description of the complete destruction in vv 4–5a, v 5b adds a reference to the plundering of the city.

■ **26:6** When v 6 then goes on to speak of the killing of the "daughters" by the sword, this is not meant in the literal sense,[13] but (as in Josh 15:45; 17:11, 16 and elsewhere) with 𝔗 (note a), refers to the daughter-settlements on the mainland (שדה). Amongst those, *ušu* (Παλαὶα Τύρος) is particularly prominent in the Assyrian inscriptions. That these places, as distinct from Tyre secure on her island site, were particularly exposed to attack from foreign conquerors, is specifically attested by this very information. The recognition formula finally rounds off the divine oracle in the form of a full proof-oracle and gives expression to the fact that through this judgment Yahweh not only speaks but also makes himself known to men.

■ **26:7–14** *β The king from the north and his army as instruments of judgment.*

The basic oracle in vv 1–6 answered the question of who would carry out Yahweh's judgment with a general reference to a horde of nations (גוים רבים). The expansion oracle in vv 7–14 makes this precise, no doubt already aware of the beginning of the siege of Tyre. One may here recall the analogous situation of Jeremiah, who in his early prophecies spoke generally of the foe from the north, but who after 605 quite openly referred to the Babylonians as the enemy. The passage speaks first of Tyre in the third person (v 7), but then, in dependence on the direct speech of the basic oracle, also resorts to direct address to the city (vv 8ff).

■ **26:7** In v 7 two different stages in the elucidation can be recognized. The original text (note d) speaks of the "king of kings" who comes from the north with his forces. The title "king of kings" has a long history.[14] In Egypt it is found as a title of the king in the eighteenth dynasty; it disappears in the following period, however, to reappear only in the Hellenistic period. In Assyria it is first found in the thirteenth century, later however in connection with Ashurnasirpal II, Esarhaddon and Ashurbanipal. Among the neo-Babylonians it has hitherto been found

9 See 1, 133 on 2:4.
10 See 1, 175 on 5:8.
11 See Fredriksson, *Jahwe als Krieger*, 24.
12 *AOT* 50. See also, e.g., the appropriately varied image for a judgment passed on an island settlement in Is 7:25.
13 By way of a curse on the family and descendants of the enemy, see Josef Scharbert, *Solidarität in Segen und Fluch im Alten Testament und in seiner Umwelt*, BBB 14 (Bonn, Hanstein, 1958), 132–135.
14 See Bilabel, *Geschichte*, 207–214.

only as a title of Marduk, but then plays a considerable role in the Persian empire and its successor states. Thus it cannot be decided with certainty whether Nebuchadnezzar himself held the title officially or whether the prophetic oracle simply bestowed it on him in line with older Assyrian nomenclature which might still have been in current use. In view of the long prehistory of this title in the Assyrian period, there is no need to conclude from its occurrence in Ezek 26:7 that vv 7–14 originated in the Persian period or later (as does, e.g. Manchot).

There can be no doubt of the fact that by "king of kings" is meant the ruler of the Babylonian empire. There is certainly no thought here of Gog (as is considered by van den Born). That the arrival of the king is expected from the "north" is quite in line with Jeremiah's statements.[15] A later hand (note d) then felt that further elucidation was necessary and added the name Nebuchadnezzar (note c) with the title "king of Babylon," a title which is already known from 17:12; 19:9; 21:24, 26; 24:2 (further 29:18f; 30:10, 24f; 32:11) and is found also in Nebuchadnezzar's own inscriptions.[16]

A fuller exposition of what is said in vv 1–6 is to be seen also in that the "many nations" of v 3 are described more exactly in v 7, according as they are composed of chariot forces, cavalry and infantry, in no fewer that five expressions.[17] The subsequent description of the hostilities against Tyre is remarkable, in contrast to the basic oracle in vv 1–6, by virtue not only of the fuller description of the individual stages of the process, but also of the correct order in which these are placed.

■ **26:8** Thus, right at the beginning, the mention of the battle against the mainland towns, which in v 6 was added as a secondary expansion, is more correctly placed at the head of the description. The mainland settlements must endure the first blow of the enemy. Only then can the attack against the island fortress follow. Vv 3f had first mentioned the onslaught of the enemies, but had then passed over the actual actions of the battle and had gone right on to the depiction of the destruction that took place after the battle had been won. In the "exposition" this gap is filled out. Vv 8b–11 describe in detail the battle and the penetration of the city. Not until v 12 is the connection with v 4f reached once more. Admittedly this description betrays a remarkable inability to conceive of the actual process of the taking of an island fortress. The basic oracle, with its images of surging sea (v 3) and of washing away (v 4b), had at least kept firmly in mind the particular situation of Tyre. The "exposition" in vv 8b–11, which seeks to present the actual historical process of events without the use of images, falls imperceptibly into the style of the description of the siege of a mainland city. As at the siege of Jerusalem according to 4:2, siege works are constructed and an encircling wall is thrown up.[18] There can be no thought here of the causeway built by Alexander the Great linking the mainland with the island. A roof of shields is constructed over the battering ram to protect the attackers when the ram is brought up to city walls. G. R. Driver compares צנה ("protective shields") with the Latin *testudo.*[19]

■ **26:9** Going beyond 4:2, the impact of the battering rams against the city wall is then described. There follows the description of how the bulwarks, which have become cracked and partly broken down by this battering, are then demolished with iron implements and how it is possible for the chariot forces (or riders?) to break into the city.

■ **26:10–11** The raising of clouds of dust by the mass onslaught of the horses, the rumbling of the war chariots driving with deafening roar through the breaches into the city whose walls tremble at the noise, the clatter of horses' hoofs in the streets of the city, the slaughter of the troops making their last stand in the city, the crash of the splendid pillars at the collapse of the magnificent buildings–all this is described in detail. In connection with מצבות עזך ("the pillars in which you stubbornly trusted") reference is often made to Herodotus's report of the Heracles (=Melkart) temple in Tyre: "There I saw

15 See further on chapters 38f.

16 Stephen Herbert Langdon, *Die neubabylonischen Königsinschriften* (Leipzig: Hinrichs, 1912), 71, 79, and elsewhere.

17 On this see, e.g., 17:15; 23:6, 12, 23; 38:4, 15. On the vacillation in the understanding of פרש, which is mentioned once again in v 10 (singular), see 1, 485 on 23:6.

18 See 1, 162.

19 Driver, "Ezekiel," 156.

it . . . besides that in it there were two pillars, one of refined gold, one of emerald, a great pillar that shone in the nighttime" (2:44). Since, however, the description here is clearly of a typical nature, too much in the way of actual knowledge of details about Tyre should not be expected. The mention of the fall of the strong pillars should be understood as a symbol intended to express the end of all resistance.

■ **26:12** Again it can be seen here how the amplification of vv 1–6 rearranges the components of these verses. While there the plundering of the city was mentioned only in the expansion in v 5b, *post festum* as it were, the description of the plundering in v 12 occurs in the right place, immediately after the taking of the city. Here too, in addition, reference is made to the valuable property (חיל in this sense only here, Manchot) and the merchandise which will be referred to in greater detail with regard to Tyre in chapter 27. Only after the plundering comes the demolition of the walls (v 4aα); in place of the towers of v 4a, whose collapse has already been mentioned in v 9 (feminine plural מגדלתיך instead of the masculine מגדליה in the basic text of v 4), the fine houses are mentioned in the parallel passage. And while v 4aβ, in a magnificent image, spoke of the washing away of the soil from the island of Tyre by Yahweh, doubtless by a huge wave sent by him, this too in v 12b has been made into a human action. The Babylonian troops now set about throwing into the water not only stones and timber, but even the rubble (and the soil?). The שים ("to put, place") of 𝔐 (note b), if it is original, makes the fine image of v 4 rather plainly prosaic.

■ **26:13** The desolation which spreads over the site of Tyre as the result of this judgment is described in this "exposition" first of all (in verbal dependence on Amos 5:23) by the silencing of songs and instruments.

■ **26:14** Only then follow the closing words about the bare, rocky reef and the drying place for the nets, expanded by the remark that Tyre shall never again be rebuilt, for Yahweh has spoken it (on this see vv 4b and 5a).

The Targum-like expository character of vv 7–14 cannot be overlooked. One might in fact even speak in this instance of a classically clear example of such exposition. Alongside the elements of simple exposition and of the translation of unusual expressions into more usual ones, there is also here the borrowing of older, available material. This latter is clear in the relationship of v 13 to Amos 5:23. Van den Born has suggested with regard to vv 9–11 that it is a battle song (*strijdlied*) which refers to the capture of Tyre by Alexander. This observation is correct to the extent that the present description is dependent on an already existing prototype for the descriptions of the conquest of a city. In view of the obvious relationship to the capture of a city on the mainland, the original reference will not have been to Tyre. However, in view of the rectifying divine oracle in 29:17–21, one is forced to the conclusion that 26:7–14 was added certainly after the beginning but also before the end of the siege of Tyre by Nebuchadnezzar, a siege which ended quite differently.

The infiltration of characteristics typical of a description of a mainland siege into the description of the siege of the island city of Tyre can already be observed in the Assyrian royal inscriptions, when Esarhaddon there reports of the construction of trenches (*ḫalṣē*) against Tyre.[20]

■ **26:15–18** γ *The Lament of the Neighboring Princes.* The form of the funeral lament has already been encountered in chapter 19.[21] There the lament stood quite independently. In other places it can be more fully embedded in the report of the events which lead to the situation of the lament. This is the case in 27:26–36. In 26:15–18 an intermediate position can be discerned. The lament in vv 17f is here introduced with a succinct description of the situation, which does not describe how the situation of need came to exist but simply points to its existence. This presupposes that a description of Tyre's collapse has already been given. It will probably have already been the combined complex of vv 1–14 to which vv 15–18 were joined, although there is no specific allusion in the vocabulary to phrases from these verses. The situation and the lament are furnished with typical features which are only lightly slanted towards the particular situation of Tyre.

From the metrical point of view, the קינה ("lament")—rhythm seems to appear (in contrast to BH³) for the first

20 This also disposes of Wiener's theory that this passage deals solely with the conquest of the mainland city of old Tyre.

21 See 1,391–392.

time not just in the lament itself, but already in the introduction in vv 15f. V 16aβ then contains the phenomenon of enjambement, and v 16b then passes into the rhythm that is frequent in Ezekiel, 2+2. The whole is a direct address to Tyre (second person feminine).

■ **26:15** The introduction, which as in 24:25[22] and 38:14 is linked to the previous section by means of a question, takes up the situation of the fall of Tyre in phrases which recur very similarly in 31:16. מפלת ("fall") is a particularly favorite word in Ezekiel's oracles against the nations (see v 18, 27:27; 31:13 "the fallen body," 16; 32:10). It occurs otherwise in the OT only in Ju 14:8, in the same sense as Ezek 31:13, and in Prv 29:16. The "shaking" (רעש), used in v 10 of the city walls, belongs likewise to the motifs of the process of judgment (again in 27:28; 31:16; 38:20). The groans and the deaths in Tyre make the distant coasts shake. Is this thought of as a cosmic process as in 38:20, or does it remain within the sphere of neighborly sympathy?

■ **26:16** The human terror is depicted in greater detail. The princes of the coasts of the maritime world climb down from their thrones that are raised on steps (1 Kgs 10:18–20).This ירד ("descend") too belongs, as 27:29 shows, to the motifs of the description of terror. In the coming "down" of the witnesses of the judgment there is reflected the great "Come down" with which God commands those who are judged (ירד in 26:11; 30:6; especially 26:20; 31:15ff; 32:18f and elsewhere). Along with this coming down in the face of the invasion of death—the antitheses of the unrepentant behavior of 25:3, 6, 8; 26:2—there belongs normally also the submission to all the usual mourning customs.[23] Thus the princes of the coastal regions lay aside their proud attire as well as their gaily colored garments and sit down upon the ground (Job 2:12f). As in 7:27, however, in place of mourning clothes, they are said to put on terror, which envelops them like a garment and will not leave them.[24]

■ **26:17** Above all, however, there belongs to the mourning customs the singing of the קינה ("lament"). It is reproduced here. In it the devastated city is addressed directly. It begins with the plaintive איך ("how"), which elsewhere too, like the fuller form איכה (Is 1:21; Lam 1:1; 2:1; 4:1), can introduce the lament (Is 14:4, 12; cf. Jer 50:23; 51:41). As in Is 14:4 the verb שבת ("'disappeared'") serves to express the end which has come (note d). Then, in accordance with the usual scheme of contrast "once—now," the present death is compared with the former glory. In words which, in the description of the underworld in 32:23ff, are part of a fixed terminology but which occur otherwise neither in Ezek nor in the rest of the OT, the terror is described which the once powerful Tyre has spread over the earth (נתן חתית "spread terror"). Here Tyre is presented in a way which can hardly have corresponded to the historical nature of this commercial city, as a feared conqueror and despotic power similar to Egypt, which is described thus in 32:17ff. The addition which is missing in 𝔊 (note f) sets the statement right: Tyre is strong "on the sea."

■ **26:18** With this former glory there is now contrasted the dismal present (עתה "now") in which, it is true, terror lies over the coasts of the sea, but terror at the fall or, as the interpretative addition in v 18b says, at the "end" of the mighty power.

The lament as a whole, vv 15–18, is made without any specific theological emphasis. Only the introductory formula, by which Tyre is confronted with all the terror and lamentation which occur among the nations by the sea as a question from Yahweh, reminds us that in this event Yahweh speaks (vv 6, 14). See also on chapter 19.

■ **26:19–21** *Tyre's Descent to the Underworld.* While vv 15–18 dealt, from a purely historical point of view, with the terror caused by the fall of Tyre, vv 19–21, which again open with the formula for receiving a message-type oracle and are then formed quite independently, come back to a full theological motivation. This comes about with the help of the motif of the journey to the underworld, which recurs in 28:8; 31:14, 15–18, but especially, in considerable detail, in 32:17ff. Even if the beginning is clearly directed at Tyre, one cannot fail to be aware that the phraseology is dependent on the fuller description of Egypt's fall to the underworld.[25] Here, too, the whole is in the form of direct address.

■ **26:19** What happens to Tyre is here described as being wholly an act of Yahweh's. This act is first of all illustrated by means of two different groups of images. When Yahweh makes Tyre an uninhabited city like (other)

22 See 1,508.

23 On this see 1,506 on 24:16f.

24 וחרדו לרגעים occurs again in 32:10. שמם is used here as in 7:27.

25 See further on 32:17ff.

uninhabited cities, one thinks in the first instance of devastation brought about by the events of war.[26] Should one see also in this an allusion to those stock examples of uninhabited cities, Sodom and Gomorrah? Alongside this, however, there is a second statement, one which is colored by the nature myth and which once more must have the island site of Tyre specifically in mind. The waves of the deep, the "great waters," surely an allusion to the chaotic primeval waters (see also on 31:4), will cover Tyre. What could be dimly sensed in the image of v 3 and in the completion of the destruction by Yahweh according to v 4b is here stated directly in a powerful climax: Tyre will be engulfed by the flood. In the gloss to 31:15 (note b) an allusion is made (incorrectly) to this occurence in a threat against Egypt. The myth of the cosmic flood, which in the OT in Gen 6–8 has been used to give expression to Yahweh's total judgment, is here used as a medium for the proclamation of total judgment on an individual city.

■ **26:20** Then, however, this fact of destruction is described from within, by means of a completely new series of images, as the bringing down of Tyre, now understood in personal terms, to the dark realm of death, which at the same time can be described with the vocabulary of the grave (יורדי בור "those who go down to the pit") and of the "nether world." In the phrase ארץ תחתיות ("the depths") we have once more an expression specially coined by Ezekiel.[27] While in the related expressions תחתיות הארץ (Ps 63:10) and תחתיות ארץ (Is 44:23; Ps 139:15) ארץ seems to mean either the surface of the world inhabited by men, below which lie the mysterious nether regions, or else a total world arranged in various layers, in ארץ תחתיות ("the depths") the mysterious nether world is regarded as a complete and self-contained "country." In ארץ תחתיות ("the depths"), the בור תחתיות of Ps 88:7 and Lam 3:55 is expanded, and the תחתית/שאול תחתיה of Ps 86:13 and Dtn 32:22 is made more concrete in terms of a dwelling place similar to earthly countries. In 32:17ff this region is then populated with individual figures. The present passage, on the other hand, is content with the general information that it is the place of those people who already in the early periods of human history were banished there by death.[28] The expression כחרבות מעולם ("like the ancient ruins in the land"), however, seems to want to say that "they, together with their cities, are to be found in Sheol," and this "must serve as examples of a particularly conclusive destruction of the life force."[29] It is the land of a people who will never again achieve a reversal of their destiny and a return to life.[30] Thus expression is given here to the irrevocable nature of the judgment on Tyre, which can expect no new settlement and no restoration in the "land of the living." The expression ארץ חיים ("land of the living") recurs in 32:23–27, 32. It is found also in Is 53:8; Jer 11:19; Ps 27:13; 52:7 (as ארץ החיים in Is 38:11; Ps 142:6; Job 28:13; in the plural in Ps 116:9).

■ **26:21** In the final verse, however, which recurs in 27:36b and in 28:19b, it is made clear that this non-existence (אינך "you will be no more") is not only a vacuum, but also terror intensified to the highest degree. The addition by which the refrain at this point is further expanded (note b) says that she is sought for, signifying surely a continuing restlessness which prevents us from misunderstanding the non-existence as peace and rest.[31]

Setting

As the detailed examination has shown, Ezekiel 26 is not from a single mold. Rather, to an original oracle 26:1–5a, which has first been expanded to vv 1–6, a supplementary exposition in vv 7–14 has been added. To this have been added two sections, the lament of the nations in vv 15–18 and Tyre's journey to the underworld in vv 19–21, sections whose wording has evidently been nourished by motifs and phrases from the other oracles against Tyre and, above all, from the oracle against Egypt.

The basic oracle in vv 1–6 seems to have been formu-

26 On the phraseology one can compare 29:12 and 30:7.
27 On this see also note c.
28 On עם עולם ("the people of old") see Jenni, "Das Wort 'ōlām," 31, 33.
29 Jenni, "Das Wort 'ōlām," 30.
30 On the world of the dead see also Christoph Barth, *Die Errettung vom Tode in den individuellen Klage-und Dankliedern des Alten Testaments* (Zollikon: Evangelischer, 1947), 76–91.
31 Jenni, "Das Wort 'ōlām," 14: "עולם underlines . . . the irrevocable nature and the finality of the destruction."

lated in fairly close proximity to the fall of Jerusalem in 587, and this is also suggested by the date. On the basis of the general nature of the threat, it has been supposed that in historical terms no actual threat to Tyre had as yet appeared. The situation with regard to the exposition in vv 7–14 is different. Here the avengers summoned by Yahweh are more clearly named. This oracle, which speaks so clearly of the great king and his troops, has been most often located in the period when the siege of Tyre was still in progress. The lower limit for this and for the following two sections must be the date of the oracle in 29:17ff, which admits in veiled terms that the expectations of complete victory and of the plundering (26:12) of Tyre have come to nothing. On this basis, chapter 26 will have achieved its final form before the New Year's day of Jehoiachin's twenty-seventh year, that is before April 26, 571.

The attribution to the prophet Ezekiel himself is certainly to be accepted for the basic oracle in vv 1–6. It is certainly possible that in exile he could have heard of specific utterances in Tyre or of sentiments (possibly via *bīt ṣurraia*) which he himself could then have fitted into an oracle.[32]

It is more difficult to attribute to Ezekiel himself vv 7–14, with their quotation and rearrangement of the elements of vv 1–6 and their quotation from Amos. It is easier to see in this "exposition" and then also in the addition of the motif-type oracles of the lament of the nations (vv 15–18) and of Tyre's descent to the underworld (vv 19–21) the work of the school or tradition-circle which, on this evidence, was already engaged in the continuing exposition of the oracles before Ezekiel himself had uttered his last oracle (29:17–21).

Aim

The prophetic word speaks against the commercial city of Tyre. Tyre is not reproached for being a commercial city. But trade becomes highly questionable at the point where it cannot rise above itself even in the face of God's judgments.

God has judged his people. This judgment did not happen within the sphere of an incorporeal inwardness, but happened to Jerusalem in her full historical reality. In the burning of Jerusalem assets were burned, political and commercial contacts were destroyed. A whole structure of influences on the Palestinan world was destroyed. But in this catastrophe God was speaking and wanted to be recognized in that speaking by his people and by others besides.

Tyre, however, remained commercially calculating, even in the face of this act of God. She noted in this judgment of God the disappearance of an important political center to which she herself had once had to send ambassadors (Jer 27), and the heart of the calculating merchant rejoiced at this. She calculated coolly that what was written off there could now be credited to her. And in all this she failed to hear the voice of God in his condemnatory holiness. Thus God's judgment, which takes place in the depths of the everyday, can be misunderstood when men have their hearts directed only to their own ends.

For this reason, God's judgment must now be proclaimed against Tyre. His voice will echo throughout the world, so that now the terror reaches to the furthest islands, and kings humble themselves before his power. Thus does God tear up men's godless account books, he who is the Lord.

Those who were calculating in Tyre thought that they could calculate their future and their life. But the judgment of God will make it clear that precisely at this point life does not flourish, but rather everything journeys towards death, irrevocably and inevitably. Life, then, can be won only when men cast aside all calculating and, terror-struck before his holy judgments, give to God all the glory.

32 See above p. 24.

b. The Ship Tyre and its Sinking

Bibliography

A. Abraham
Die Schiffsterminologie des Alten Testaments kulturgeschichtlich und etymologisch untersucht, Unpub. Diss. (Bern, 1914).

H. P. Chajes
"Ez. 27:4," *ZAW* 21 (1901): 79.

J. -G. Février
"L'ancienne marine phénicienne et les découvertes récentes," *NC* 1 (1949): 128–143.

J. Garrett
"A Geographical Commentary on Ezekiel XXVII," *Geography* 24 (1939): 240–249.

Gustav Hölscher
Drei Erdkarten; ein Beitrag zur Erdkenntnis des hebräischen Altertums (Heidelberg: Winter, 1949).

Hedwig Jahnow
Das hebräische Leichenlied im Rahmen der Völkerdichtung, BZAW 36 (Giessen: Töpelmann, 1923), especially 213–218.

August Köster
Das antike Seewesen (Berlin, 1923).

R. Lasch
"Das Pfeifen und seine Beziehung zu Dämonenglauben und Zauberei," *ARW* 18 (1915): 589–592.

Hans Peter Rüger
Das Tyrusorakel Ezek 27, Unpub. Diss. (Tübingen, 1961).

Wilfred Harvey Schoff
The Ship "Tyre"; a Symbol of the Fate of Conquerors as prophesied by Isaiah, Ezekiel and John and fulfilled at Nineveh, Babylon and Rome; a study in the Commerce of the Bible (New York: Longmans, Green, 1920).

Jan Jozef Simons
The Geographical and Topographical Texts of the Old Testament (Leiden: Brill, 1959).

Sidney Smith
"The Ship Tyre," *PEQ* 85 (1953): 97–110.

Hermann von Wissmann
"Geographische Grundlagen und Frühzeit der Geschichte Südarabiens," *Saeculum* 4 (1953): 61–114.

See further above p. 21.

27

1 **And the word of Yahweh came to me:**
2/Now[a] you, son of man, raise a lament
over Tyre 3/ and say to Tyre[a], who
dwells[b] <at the entrance to the sea>[c],

27: 2a 𝔐 ואתה is not attested by 𝔊 𝔏[W] 𝔄 Arm (𝔊[B] and
2 𝔏[C] are different; on this see Ziegler, *Ezechiel,* 40f).
See also 7:2 note a.
3 3a 𝔏[W] here still preserves the original predicate to
Tyre: *terrae domus* which, however, has no support
in the rest of the textual tradition.
b Against the assumption that the direct address
to Tyre begins already with הישבתי (on the

merchant[d] of the peoples (,who carries on trade) to many coasts, this is what [the Lord][e] Yahweh says:

3bβ **O Tyre, you <> are <a ship>[f] of perfect beauty.**

4/In the midst of the sea <they have formed you>[a] ['they

י-*compaginis* of the *ketib* see Gesenius-Kautzsch §90 l, m; otherwise Beer-Meyer §45 3d) (so Ewald, Fohrer, *ZB*, BH^3), there is the fact that the address to Tyre by name occurs first in v 3bβ with the quotation of the words of Tyre. Such quotations usually open speeches in Ezekiel. See further, however, on "Form."

c 𝔐 על מבואת ים. 𝔊 (𝔏^{CW}) ἐπὶ τῆς εἰσόδου τῆς θαλλάσσης 𝔙 *in introitu maris,* 𝔖 במעלנא דימא would suggest a reading על מבוא הים. Since ים without the article is unusual in this context (cf., e.g., the הים in 25:16; 26:5,16; 27:29) and since 26:10 attests a masculine plural form of מבוא, 𝔐 must have arisen through a miswriting of ה as ת and subsequent wrong word division.

d 𝔐 רכלת must have been read as רְכֻלַּת by 𝔊 τῷ ἐμπορίῳ 𝔖 תאגורתא and 𝔙 *negotiationi.*

e אדני is lacking in MS^{Ken} 𝔊 𝔏^{CW} 𝔎 𝔄, see Appendix 1.

f 𝔐 צור את אמרת אני כלילת יפי "Tyre, you have said: I am of perfect beauty" is attested more or less identically by the Versions (𝔊 links צור with what precedes: τῇ Σορ, hence 𝔏^{C} *ad sor* which 𝔏^{W} expands to *ad te Sor,* and misunderstands כלילת as a verb περιέθηκα ἐμαυτῇ). The present text, however, in view of the קינה-meter (see below) which is adhered to in what follows, presents considerable difficulties, since it cannot be read otherwise than as a 3 + 3. In addition, there is the difficulty of content, namely that Ezekiel, who otherwise likes to introduce his figures of speech very directly (19:2 אמך לביא; 28:12 אתה חותם; 32:2 אתה כתנים; see also 31:2b,3a), seems in this passage, which goes on to give a full description of the image of the stately vessel, to introduce the comparison only indirectly, through the back door, as it were. Thus there is everything to be said for Wellhausen's ingenious supposition (quoted in Smend) that behind the אני there could be concealed the meaning "ship." One need not read אני אניה, but one can happily leave אני with the vocalization אֳנִי (the emendation to the *nomen unitatis* אניה BH^3, Fohrer, is not absolutely necessary). On אני see 1 Kgs 9:26f; 10:11,22; Is 33:21; the feminine gender is attested in 1 Kgs 10:22; Is 33:21. The word is already attested in the Canaanite Amarna gloss 245:28, where Akkadian *eleppi* (a single ship) is glossed by *a-na-ji* which corresponds to אני (not אניה). The preceding אמרת in 𝔐 does not represent a scribal error. Rather it has been intentionally added to the text as an interpretive element after the original אֳנִי was misread as אֲנִי in order to interpret it along the lines of 28:2(9).

4 4a 𝔐 גבוליך. Plural גבולים "territory" in 1 Sam 5:6; 2 Kgs 15:16; 18:8; Jer 15:13; 17:3; Is 60:18. 𝔐 seems not always to have been understood by the translators but is unanimously attested by them. On the reading of 𝔊 Γωβελιν see Ziegler, *Ezekiel,* with reference to Max L. Margolis, "Hes 27:4," *ZAW* 31 (1911): 313f, and A. Vaccari, "Le Versioni arabe dei

have built you'][b]**,**
have made perfect your beauty.
5/ With junipers[a] **from Senir they built for you**
(on both sides) all your planks.[b]
(The) cedars[c] **of Lebanon they took**
to make a mast.
<From (the) tallest>[d] **6/ oaks of Bashan**
they made your oars.[a]
Your deck(?)[b] **they made from <>**[c]

Profeti," *Bibl* 2 (1921): 417. This has been miswritten in 𝔏^{W} as *Dobelin* and in 𝔏^{C} as *beelim.* 𝔙 *finitimi tui,* understood correctly by 𝔖 תחומיכי and 𝔗 תחומך. From the point of view of content, difficulties have been created by the fact that the reference to the ship has been abandoned in 𝔐 in favor of a reference to the city (with its "territory"). Thus Cornill ("with great reservations") suggested emending to זבולך "your position." Chajes, "Ez. 27:4," vocalized גְּבָלִים and understood the whole of v 4 as: "In the midst of the sea, the men of Byblos (Gebal), your builders, made your beauty perfect." Ziegler; Rüger, *Tyrusorakel,* prefer to follow Driver, "Linguistic Problems," 177, and read גבלוך. This emendation has been adopted above. Hölscher, Bertholet, Fohrer propose reading גדלוך "they made you big."

b 𝔐 בניך "your builders" is an analogous interpretation, which however not only disturbs the meter, but also anticipates the בנו לך which follows in v 5a. With Hölscher and others it should be deleted. Rüger, *Tyrusorakel,* may be right in supposing that originally, in the form בנוך, it was meant as a gloss on the unusual גבלוך.

5 5a 𝔐 ברושים. 𝔊 (𝔏^{CW}) here has *κέδρος* (cf. also 2 Chr 3:5 *κέδρινος*) and in 31:8 *πίτυες* (𝔏^{S} *pinus*). 𝔙 has *abietes* (also in 31:8), 𝔗 בירוון (in 31:8 with an explanatory paraphrase). 𝔖 ערקא "box tree" (also in 31:8). According to Gesenius-Buhl, "cypress"; Koehler-Baumgartner, "Phoenician juniper." So, too, the Accakian *burāšu,* see Wolfgang von Soden, *Akkadisches Handwörterbuch* (Wiesbaden: Harrassowitz, 1959–1979), 139.

b 𝔐 לחתים, read by 𝔙 as two words *cum tabulatis maris,* rendered by 𝔗 with a suffix גישרך. Since, however, the possession is already expressed by the לך, 𝔐 must be the original reading; see also the parallel in v 5b where Cooke; Fohrer; Rüger, *Tyrusorakel,* wish, as a result, to emend תרן to תרנך. On the form לחתים see Bauer-Leander §63q. The dual doubtless refers to the two sides of the ship.

c 𝔐 ארז. 𝔊 (𝔏^{C}) *κυπαρίσσου*; in 17:3, 22f *κέδρος* and in 31:3, 8 *κυπάρισσος*. See 1,361.

d Since in 𝔐 there is one word too many from the metrical point of view and since in v 6a there is one too few to achieve the קינה -meter, עליך should be transferred to v 6. One would then best regard it as a closer definition of אלונים. The alteration to עֶלְיֹנֵי (Cooke; Fohrer; Rüger, *Tyrusorakel*) would, from the graphical point of view, be the most likely.

6 6a 𝔐 מִשּׁוֹט alongside the form מָשׁוֹט in v 29, see Bauer-Leander §68 i.

b קרש in Ex 26:15ff and elsewhere in the description of the Tent of Meeting means "a plank." But alongside לחתים here (v 5) it must have a more specialized meaning. John Gray, *The Legacy of Canaan,* VT Suppl 5 (Leiden: Brill, ^{2}1965), 80, interprets the *qrš* which occurs in Ugaritic, on the basis of Ezek 27:6, as "that which is firm" and refers it to El's throne. Driver, *Canaanite Myths,* 97: "pavil-

<cypresses>(?)[d]
from the coasts of the Kittim.[e]
7/ Brightly embroidered linen[a] from Egypt was your sail[b]
[to serve you as a sign].[c]
Of blue [and red][d] purple from the coasts of Elisha
was your (cabin-) covering.[e]
8/ The <princes>[a] of Sidon and Arvad were your oarsmen.

lion." See also Marvin H. Pope, *El in the Ugaritic Texts*, VT Suppl 2 (Leiden: Brill, 1955), 67f. Rüger, *Tyrusorakel*, on the other hand, assumes with Joseph Aistleitner, *Die mythologischen und kultischen Texte aus Ras Schamra* (Budapest: Akadémie Kaidó, 1959), 138, a meaning "Temenos, district." See the exposition. 𝔊 (𝔏C) misreads קרשך as קדשך: τὰ ἱερά σου. 𝔙 *transtra* "crossbeams," 𝔗 תירומי תרעך "your door beams."

c 𝔐 שן is certainly unanimously attested by the versions. In spite, however, of the involved attempt of 𝔗 to make sense of the statement ("your door beams are made of boxwood planks which are inlaid with ivory בשין דפיל"), it can hardly be original. It should be deleted as an erroneous dittography of the preceding [ע]שו. Metrical considerations also favor the deletion.

d 𝔐 בת אשרים puzzled the versions. 𝔊 οἴκους ἀλσώδεις; 𝔏C *domos hirsutas;* 𝔙 *praetoriola;* 𝔖 simply passes over an expression which it did not understand. It is, as obviously only 𝔗 realized (אשכרעין), to be read as a single word: בתאשרים. The preposition ב could very well have been added as an adjustment after the insertion of the שן (note c). תאשור occurs also in Is 41:19; 60:13; probably also in Ezek 31:3 (which see). Gesenius-Buhl finds in תאשור the *šerbīn;* Koehler-Baumgartner, the cypress.

e Alongside 𝔐 כתים there occurs in KOr the form corresponding to Q, כתיים. 𝔙 interprets *de insulis Italiae,* 𝔗 ממדינת אפוליא.

7 7a 𝔗 breaks 𝔐 שש ברקמה up into the double expression בוץ וצייורין.

b 𝔐 מפרש means literally "spreading out." 𝔊 renders στρωμνή, 𝔏C *stratum.* It is used again in Job 36:29 of the clouds. But most probably, with 𝔙 *velum,* the word means "sail." After the mast has just been mentioned it would be very strange if the sail were not mentioned. Even the "spreading out" (פרש is used in 16:8 of a garment; Nu 4:6ff of a cover; Ju 8:25 of a cloak; Dtn 22:17 of a bed cover) is easily understood (in spite of Is 33:23) of a sail. See further the exposition.

c 𝔐 להיות לך לנס not only disturbs the meter but also destroys the unmistakable parallelism between v 7a and v 7b. It must therefore be a gloss. 𝔊 τοῦ περιθεῖναί σοι δόξαν and 𝔏C *ad circumdandam tibi gloriam* interpret the sign as "distinction" (cf. v 10), while 𝔗, 𝔖 reproduce the נס with the simple את "sign." On אות see Keller, OTH.

d Since the first line is metrically overloaded, it is possible to regard ארגמן as a secondary expansion. The same secondary expansion is found in v 24 in 𝔊A.

e Instead of the participle מְכַסֵּךְ one would, in view of the parallelism, rather see a noun, e.g. מִכְסֵךְ (Gen 8:13; Ex 26:14 and elsewhere). Cf. 𝔊 περιβόλαια, 𝔙 *operimentum,* 𝔗 כסות, 𝔖 תכסית.

8 8a 𝔐 ישבי can, in the first instance, be understood without difficulty: "the inhabitants." It is, however,

Your wise men, O Tyre,[b] were in you,
they were your seamen.
9/ The elders of Byblos[a] [and her wise
men][b] were in you
as your ship's carpenters.[c]
9b **All[d] the ships of the sea and their sailors**
were in you in order to barter[e] for your
wares.
10/ (Men from) Paras and Lud and Put
were in your army as your soldiers.[a]
They hung up shield and helmet in you,
they[a] formed your splendor.[b]

odd that 𝔊 should prefix *οἱ κατοικοῦντες Σιδῶνα* with an additional *καὶ οἱ ἄρχοντές σου*. The reconstruction of an additional נשיאי (Cornill, Fohrer) is, graphically, not easy. But one can probably see in this an original ושריך. For the rendering of שר by *ἄρχων* see 𝔊 in Ezek 17:12; 22:27. Behind ושריך, however, there may lie an original ושרי or, in the event that the addition of the copula should still be attributable to 𝔊 (see v 9 note d), שרי. Since in (v 8b and) v 9a two highly trained population groups (חכמים and זקנים) from two other cities neighboring on Tyre are mentioned as fulfilling menial service in the ship Tyre, the reading which mentions a particular group in Sidon can be commended on the grounds of content as well. In the ישבי of 𝔐, on the other hand, can be discerned a rather colorless correction of the original text which can still be discerned in 𝔊. This correction has then also secondarily found its way into 𝔊.

b Betwen the mention of the groups of foreigners from Sidon and Arvad (v 8a) on the one hand and from Gebal-Byblos on the other (v 9a), groups which are in service in Tyre in menial positions, one is surprised by the mention of the Tyrian "wise men" introduced along with a vocative address to Tyre itself. One is best helped here by the assumption that in צור we have a scribal error for the name of a neighboring city. The most likely candidate for this from the graphical point of view is צמר, which is mentioned immediately after Arvad in the list of Phoenician cities in Gen 10:15ff. According to K. Elliger, "Ein Zeugnis aus der jüdischen Gemeinde im Alexanderjahr 332 v. Chr. Eine territorialgeschichtliche Studie zu Sach 9:1–8," *ZAW* 62 (1950): 71f, the same error occurs also in Zech 9:2. On the corruption of חכמי to חכמיך, the שריך attested by 𝔊 (note a) could serve as an exact analogy. But see below on "Form."

9 9a 𝔊 Βυβλίων has been misunderstood in 𝔏^{C}: *librorum*.

b The וחכמיה, which inelegantly repeats the aristocratic class which has just been mentioned in v 8b and which also appears to be metrically superfluous, is surely to be regarded as a secondary expansion.

c Literallly: "who (re-)fortify what is dilapidated in you," where one would rather read pi'el מחזקי than 𝔐 hip'il מחזיקי. 𝔊 (𝔏^{C}) *ἐνίσχυον τὴν βουλήν σου* has not understood the phrase and simply guesses at an activity of the "wise men."

d 𝔊 𝔏^{C} add the copula, cf. 1:4 note a.

e Contrary to the usual point of view, which tries to interpret מערב from the meaning "give a pledge." Driver, "Difficult," 64–66, has pointed out a root ערב "to give" which is attested in Old South Arabian and in Syriac. In the present passage he would read a pi'el לְעָרֵב "to cause to give."

10 10a 𝔐 אנשי מלחמתך is metrically superfluous and is deleted by Fohrer, Rüger, *Tyrusorakel* (Cheminant,

11 **The men of Arvad and your army(?)[a] were on your walls [round about],[b] and the Gammadites(?)[c] were on your towers. They hung their round shields[d] on your walls[e] round about. They made your beauty perfect.**
12 **Tarshish[a] was your buyer because of the abundance of wealth.[b] For silver,[c] iron,**

prophéties, deletes היו בחילך). It has also been suggested that המה (Cheminant, *prophéties,* נתנו) should be deleted *metri causa.* Echo of v 8b?

b With נתן הדר Rüger, *Tyrusorakel,* compares the antonym לקח הדר, Mic 2:9.

11 11a 𝔐 וחילך could be understood along the lines of 𝔙 *cum exercitu tuo.* Equally well, however, there could lie behind וחילך a geographical reference which we can no longer recognize. Cornill thought of חתלן (47:15; 48:1) in the neighborhood of Hamath; A. Sarsowsky, "Notizen zu einigen biblischen geographischen und ethnographischen Namen," *ZAW* 32 (1912): 146, of Cilicia. Neither is satisfactory.

b 𝔐 סביב is not attested in 𝔊 𝔏^{C} 𝔖 and could be a secondary addition in dependence on v 11b.

c 𝔐 וגמדים seems to have been understood by 𝔊 φύλακες, 𝔏^{C} *custodes,* 𝔖 נטרין as שמרים "watchers." 𝔙 ('A) *pygmaei,* cf. post-biblical Hebrew גַּמָּד "dwarf." 𝔗, which reads קפוטקאי here, is certainly nearer the mark in thinking of the name of a people, however far short it falls with "Cappadocians" of having found the right name. Sarsowsky, "Notizen," 146f, suggests an Aramaean tribe *gamâdu,* which, from a geographical point of view, goes outside the expected range in the neighborhood of Arvad. B. Maisler, *Untersuchungen zur alten Geschichte und Ethnographie Syriens und Palästinas* 1, Arbeiten aus dem Orientalischen Seminar der Universität Giessen 2 (Giessen: Töpelmann, 1930), 8, note 2, considers the *kumidi* of Amarna 116,72ff, which is to be located in north Syria. Martin Noth, "Die Wege der Pharaonenheere in Palästina und Syrien," *ZDPV* 60 (1937): 221f, points to the *ḳmd* of the Karnak lists of Sethos I, but this cannot be located with any precision.

d 𝔐 שלטיהם. 𝔊 (𝔏^{C}) φαρέτρας "quiver" (𝔊 is different in 2 Sam 8:7; 2 Kgs 11:10; Song 4:4; 1 Chr 18:7; 2 Chr 23:9).

e 𝔐 על חומותיך. 𝔊, surprisingly, has ἐπὶ τῶν ὅρμων ("anchorage"), which has been misread by 𝔏^{C} as ὀρέων: *in montibus.*

12 12a 𝔊 (𝔏^{C}) Καρχηδόνιοι; 𝔙, correspondingly, *Chartaginenses.*

b 𝔐 מרב כל הון. 𝔊 (𝔏^{C} 𝔖) πάσης ἰσχύος σου seems to point to a suffixed form. Thus, most modern commentators read הונך with a reference to v 27. Since, howver, the same expression reappears in v 18 without the suffix and since 𝔊 𝔏^{C} 𝔖 also add the suffix there, it is preferable to retain 𝔐 as *lectio difficilior* and to regard 𝔊 𝔏^{C} 𝔖 as a harmonizing translation. Paul Joüon, "Notes philologiques sur le text hébreu d'Ezéchiel," *Bibl* 10 (1929): 304–306, reads הונך כסף and finds, in the secondary scribal error in this introductory verse of the description of the trading, the cause of all subsequent scribal errors, according to which (except in v 14), incorrectly, the goods given to Tyre are introduced by ב, while, *vice versa,* in a large number of passages the ב

tin and lead they handed over your wares. 13/ Javan, Tubal and Meshech[a] were your traders. For slaves[b] and bronze vessels they handed over your merchandise.[c] 14/ From Beth-togarmah: (for)[a] draught-horses and saddle-horses[b] and mules[c] they handed over your wares. 15/ <The men of Rhodes>[a] were your traders. Many coastlands are <the merchants> at your side.[b] They brought ivory tusks[c] and ebony[d] to you as your due. 16/ <Edom>[a] was your buyer in view of the vast number of your products. For

in front of Tyre's barter merchandise has been suppressed. See further below pp. 64–65.

c 𝔊 (𝔏^{C}) adds *καὶ χρυσίον*.

13 13a The last two names have not been understood by 𝔊 (𝔏^{C}): *καὶ ἡ σύμπασα* (תֵּבֵל cf. 𝔊 Na 1:15) *καὶ τὰ παρατείνοντα*.

b Literally "human souls."

c 𝔐 נתנו מערבך. This has been rendered by 𝔙 quite freely *advexerunt populo tuo* and omittted entirely by 𝔖.

14 14a According to the pattern of vv 12f one would expect a ב here before the mention of the goods. Has the simple accusative here taken its place? The variation of the pattern is connected unmistakably with the variation in the introductory information. In place of the naming of the buyers (v 12) or traders (v 13) in a nominal sentence, there occurs here a simple adverbial indication of origin with מן and the name of the country. See also the מאוזל of v 19, after which likewise the goods are listed without the introductory ב. 𝔊 (𝔏^{C}) undoubtedly confirms the reading of 𝔐 in v 14. 𝔙 𝔗 𝔖 display free corrections of the end of the sentence.

b 𝔐 פרשים can in no circumstances (in spite of 𝔊 𝔏^{C} 𝔙) mean "riders" here, but, no doubt originally vocalized as פָּרָשִׁים, refers to the war-horses. See Galling, "Ehrenname," 131–135.

c 𝔐 ופרדים is missing in 𝔊 𝔏^{C}.

15 15a 𝔐 דדן is remarkable in that it recurs in v 20, there in a quite irreproachable context with other Arabian groups. Thus 𝔊 *υἱοὶ Ῥοδίων* 𝔏^{C} *filii Rhodiorum* are probably along the right lines here and suggest a reading רדן. Rhodes is part of the island world which is mentioned immediately after. According to Joüon, "Notes," 306, n. 1, after רכליך a list of goods has fallen out of the text.

b 𝔐 סחרת ידך. In 𝔊 (𝔏^{C}) 𝔗 the יד is unattested. Since it recurs in 𝔐 v 21 in the combination סחרי ידך, it is not simply to be regarded as an error for סחרותיך (Cornill, Fohrer). Erlich, *Randglossen*, renders as "your favorite business connection." Koehler-Baumgartner proposes a complete assimilation to v 21 with the reading סחרי ידך. Joüon, "Notes," 305f, would prefer to read תחת ידך, since אשכר refers to a payment of tribute. In v 21, on the other hand, instead of סחרי ידך, which has wrongly been assimilated to v 15, an original סחריך should be read.

c 𝔐 says literally "ivory horns." 𝔗 finds two elements in that: "ibex horns, elephant tusks." 𝔖 has קרנתא דמשחא "horns for anointing."

d 𝔐 הובנים is a loan-word from Egyptian *hbnj* (according to Koehler-Baumgartner, perhaps of African origin). It has been miunderstood by 𝔗 as טווסין "peacocks" and by 𝔖 לבונתא "incense." 𝔊 (𝔏^{C}) *τοῖς εἰσαγομένοις* has misread the word (as הבאים?).

16 16a 𝔐 ארם, so too 𝔗 𝔙 (*Syrus*). 𝔊 (𝔏^{C}) *ἀνθρώπους* (i.e. אדם), 𝔖 אדום. Since Aram is represented in v 18 by Damascus, 𝔖 (𝔊 𝔏^{C}) has probably preserved the original reading, אֱדֹם.

garnets,[b] red purple and colored cloth and linen[c] and corals(?)[d] and rubies(?)[d] they handed over [for] your merchandise.[e] 17/ Judah and the land of Israel,[a] they were your traders. For *minnith*-wheat[b] and *pannag*[c] and honey and oil and mastic-resin they handed over your merchandise. 18/ Damascus was your buyer in view of the vast number of your products because of the abundance of wealth.[a] For wine from Helbon[b] and wool

b 𝔐 בנפך, 𝔊 στακτήν "Drop, precious stone"; 𝔙 *gummam.* 𝔖 omits the word, while 𝔗 connects it with what follows: בתכיכין דארגוון "for purple garments." This connection is also favored by Driver," Ezekiel," 156, who thinks of a dark red garnet. נפך occurs also in 28:13; Ex 28:18; 39:11. According to Koehler-Baumgartner, it is a loan-word from Egyptian *mfkꜣ.t* "a green semi-precious stone found at Sinai" (Erman-Grapow, 2.56). According to Quiring (see bibliography 28:1–19), however, it is more probably a (ruby-red) garnet; see below 28:13 note b.

c On the basis of an isolated reading of 𝔊[967], Wevers, "Septuaginta-Forschungen," 123f, proposes, as a continuation of a conjecture by Gehman, to read רקמה מתרשיש ובוץ, in place of רקמה ובוץ.

d 𝔐 ראמת occurs again in Job 28:18. The reading of Prv 24:7 is uncertain. In 𝔊 it is simply transliterated and left untranslated. 𝔙 has *sericum* "silk." 𝔐 כדכד, again in Is 54:12, seems to indicate a reddish precious stone. In 𝔊 𝔏[C] 𝔙 it is merely transliterated. After בוץ, 𝔗 has three other items: וצייורין ואבנין טבן ומרגליין "embroideries and precious stones and (unknown) precious stones." 𝔖, on the other hand, has four items, among which נפך and רקמה, which were previously left untranslated, are also taken into account: ופתכא ותכלתא ושאריא ופתותכא "brightly colored clothes and blue purple and silk fabrics and gold-embroidered clothes."

e The double ב in בנפך and בעזבוניך disturbs the structure of the sentence. If one is unwilling to accept a new beginning in the middle of the sentence—preferably then continuing with ארגמן in asyndeton—then the ב must be deleted in one of the words. The end of the sentence has been formed very freely in 𝔙 𝔗 𝔖.

17 17a 𝔐 ארץ ישראל is linguistically unusual for the normal mode of expression in the book of Ezekiel. It occurs otherwise only in 40:2; 47:18. On the usual אדמת ישראל see 1,203. 𝔊 (𝔏[C]) translates οἱ υἱοὶ τοῦ Ισραηλ. See further the exposition.

b 𝔐 בחטי מנית is interpreted by the versions in different ways. 𝔊 ἐν σίτου πράσει, 𝔏[C] *in emptione tritici,* 𝔙 *in frumento primo,* 𝔗 בחיטי ריחוש (ריחוש according to Dalman, *Wörterbuch,* 382, means "balsam oil[?]"), 𝔖 חטא ורוזן ("wheat and rice").

c The *hapax legomenon* פנג must, within the framework of the present list, also indicate an agricultural product. 𝔊 (𝔏[C]) here offers two expressions: μύρων καὶ κασίας "consecrated oil and laurel (cinnamon)." 𝔗 קלוויא, according to Dalman, *Wörterbuch,* 361, is a Greek loan-word κόλβια, κόλλυβα "dainties." Or should one think of קליא "roast corn"? 𝔖 דוחנא "millet" (see 1,168 on 4:9), 𝔙 *balsamum.*

18 18a The combination of ברב מעשיך (cf. v 16) with מרב כל הון (v 12) is awkward, especially since both have virtually the same meaning. 𝔊 (𝔏[C]) attests only one of the two clauses. Did it have only one of them before it, or is it harmonizing?

from Zachar[b] 19/ <> <and wine>[a] they exchanged [for][a] your merchandise. <From Usal>[a] worked[b] iron, cinnamon and spices[c] were exchanged[d] for your merchandise. 20/ Dedan was your trader with stuff for saddle-cloths.[a] 21/ Arabia and all the princes of Kedar, they were the buyers at your side. For lambs[a] and rams and goats—for them they were your buyers.[b] 22/ The traders of [a] Sheba[b] and

b On 𝔐 חלבון and צחר see the exposition. While 𝔊 (𝔏^C) still recognizes חלבון as a place name, 𝔙 *pingui* and 𝔖 שמינא both try to see in it an adjective descriptive of the quality of the wine. 𝔗 combines both חמר חילת מבשל "ripe (fermented?) wine from חילת." The situation is identical in the case of צחר, which 𝔊 (𝔏^C) renders as ἐκ Μιλήτου; 𝔙 *coloris optimi* and 𝔖 חורא both take it as "white," while 𝔗 has מילת כבינא "wrapped up wool (?)" (see *DalmanWB,* 182, 228).

19 19a In 𝔐, the end of v 18 is missing. The conclusion of the verse in 𝔊 (𝔏^C) καὶ οἶνον εἰς τὴν ἀγοράν σου ἔδωκαν, which obviously includes elements from 𝔐 of v 19, shows the way towards a reparation of the damage. In v 19a, מאוזל (to be vocalized as מְאוּזָּל) belongs as a place-name with the list of goods which follows in v 19b. The remainder, whose introductory ודן is an erroneous dittography of the following ויון, which, in turn, is an error for ויין or יין (according to Rüger, *Tyrusorakel,* it is the דדן of v 20 transferred to here), belongs to v 18. The repetition of the י(ו)ין, as well as the misplacement of the words בעזבוניך נתנו (on this see v 16 note e), may already be a result of the textual entanglement. In addition, 𝔊 has made the verb into a second person (ἔδωκας). What remains of v 19 corresponds in its construction to v 14, with its introductory indication of the origin of the goods cited in the second part of the verse. See v 14 note a.

b The *hapax legomenon* עשות is correctly rendered by 𝔊 εἰργασμένος, 𝔏^C *fabricatum,* 𝔙 *fabrefactum,* 𝔖 דתפלחין.

c 𝔐 קדה occurs also in Ex 30:24. קנה, according to Koehler-Baumgartner an abbreviation for קנה טוב (Jer 6:20), occurs also in Is 43:24; Song 4:14. For the double expression 𝔊 offers as an equivalent simply τροχίας; 𝔏^C *cautus* ("wheel"); 𝔙 *stacte et calamus;* 𝔗 קדה וקני בסם, which according to 𝔗 are brought to the market "in iron boxes" (cf. the preceding ברזל). 𝔖 קסיא וקניא.

d The usual נתנו of the pattern (vv 12–14, 16, 17, 19a, 22) is here varied by היה. There is no need to emend.

20 20a 𝔐 בגדי חפש לרכבה. The *hapax legomenon* חפש seems to be a loan-word connected with Accadian *ḫipšu* (*ḫibšu*) and to refer to a kind of material whose use is here more closely defined by לרכבה. 𝔊 understands the word to refer to the horses that pulled the chariots (κτηνῶν ἐκλεκτῶν εἰς ἅρματα), 𝔙 to carpets for sitting on (*tapetibus ad sedendum*). 𝔖 takes vv 20 and 21 closely together.

21 21a 𝔐 כרים is upgraded by 𝔊 καμήλους (but see also Is 60:6) and 𝔗 תורין; while 𝔖, omitting v 21a, connects the statement, rephrased fairly freely, directly with v 20a.

b 𝔐 סחריך. Driver, "Ezekiel," 147, suggests reading סְחֹרָךְ "your trade."

22 22a Since usually each new section begins with the name of the trading partner, 𝔐 רכלי שבא is odd

Raamah, they were your traders. For the finest balsam[c] and for precious stones of every kind[d] and gold they handed over your wares. 23/ Haran and Canneh[a] and Eden,[b] [the traders of Sheba,][c] [Asshur, <the whole of Media>[d] were your traders,][c] 24/ they were your traders. For

and, stylistically, not particularly good in view of the final clause המה רכליך. Thus some commentators look for a graphically similar name (Cornill and others חוילה), while others (Toy, BH^3) delete רכלי as a gloss. The versions (with the exception of 𝔊^{46,86} Arm where the word is missing) confirm 𝔐. In view of the stylistically rather inelegant character of this trading list, which has fairly loosely been turned into a narrative (see below), and in view of the observation that in v 25a and to a lesser extent also in vv 14 and 19 (v 14 note a) there are variations from the normal pattern, the arguments against 𝔐 here are not forceful.

b 𝔐 שְׁבָא. Driver, "Ezekiel," 157, finds here the סבא of Gen 10:7.

c Literally "the best of all balsam." כל is unattested by 𝔊 and 𝔖, but this may be only a simplification. Bertholet, Fohrer, BH^3 delete כל, but see note d.

d כל (in בכל) is unattested by 𝔊 𝔖 𝔅, but is quite unobjectionable (even Bertholet, Fohrer, BH^3 take exception only to the ב).

23 23a According to 𝔗 נציבין, Nisibis. According to A. Mez, *Geschichte der Stadt Ḥarrān in Mesopotamien bis zum Einfall der Araber,* Unpub. Diss. (Strassburg, 1892), 33f note 3, 𝔐 וכנה owes its origin to a corruption of (חרן) ובני (עדן).

b According to 𝔗 חדייב, Adiabene. It is missing in 𝔊.

c After Χαννα (= כנה) there stands in 𝔊 *οὗτοι ἔμποροί σου*, behind which can be discerned the stock phrase המה רכליך (vv 13, 17, 22, 24) that in vv 13, 17, 22 concludes the lists of names. Instead of this, there follows in 𝔐 first רכלי שבא, which repeats here, in a context in which it does not fit at all, the expression which occurs in v 22 in its right place alongside רעמה. Here it must be a gloss which has found its way in here by mistake. Two more names, arranged asyndetically, then follow in 𝔐, rounded off by רכלתך (is this, in line with the סחרת [ידך] of v 15, to be vocalized רְכֻלָּתֵךְ "your merchants" [abstract noun] or to be emended to רֹכְלֹתַיִךְ "your traders" [feminine plural] or, better still, to רֹכְלַיִךְ "your traders" [masculine plural] ?). But this רכלתך clashes intolerably with the המה רכליך which follows at the beginning of v 24. It is likely, then, that the group of names linked with the copula in v 23a*α*, which finds its natural continuation in v 24, has been secondarily disrupted not only by the gloss רכלי שבא, but also by the insertion of the asyndetically arranged short list of names in v 23b with its concluding רכלתך. 𝔊 𝔅 𝔗 all simplify by the insertion of the copula before כלמד, see note d.

d 𝔐 כלמד. 𝔊 *καὶ* Χαρμαν, 𝔅 *et Melmad.* It is not attested by 𝔖. As A. Mez, *loc. cit.* (note a) already supposed, 𝔗 (with ומדי) must be along the right lines. 𝔏 כל מדי. Bewer, "Textual Notes," 164, however, finds in כלמד an erroneous dittography of רכלתך. P. Rost, "Miscellen," 482, finds the corruption of a

fine clothes,[a] for garments of blue
purple[b] and colored cloth and for fabric of
two colors,[c] for firm, twisted ropes[d]—
<for them they were your traders>.[e] 25/
Ships of Tarshish[a] were your caravans
with your merchandise.[b] And you grew
rich[c] and splendid in the midst of the sea.
26 Over mighty waters your oarsmen led you,[a]

marginal note כ׳ למר (= כתב לאמר), according to which the אשור in the text of v 22a should be placed after שבא. He also regards v 23aβb as secondary.

24 24a 𝔐 מכללים is a *hapax legomenon,* but cf. לבשי מכלול in 23:12; 38:4. It is omitted by 𝔊 𝔖 and is understood by 𝔙 *multifariorum* to refer to plurality. For 𝔗 see note c.

b 𝔐 (תכלת) גלומי is a *hapax legomenon.* 𝔊 abbreviates to simple ὑάκινθον, 𝔙 *involucris hyacinthi* (*et polymitorum*) "with dark-blue (and bright) covers," 𝔖 מאני דתכלתא, 𝔗 בגוזין דתכלתא "with sections of blue purple."

c 𝔐 (ברמים) גנזי, to be differentiated from the homonym in Est 3:9; 4:7 "treasures," as a *hapax legomenon* to be interpreted, according to 𝔗 Est 1:3, as גנזי מילתא. ברמים, too, is a *hapax legomenon,* to be understood, however, on the basis of Arabic. It has been understood by 𝔊 καί θησαυροὺς ἐκλεκτούς, 𝔙 *gazarumque pretiosarum,* 𝔖 וסימתא טבתא on the basis of the other meaning of גנזים.

d 𝔊 δεδεμένους σχοινίοις. 𝔙 *quae obvolutae et astrictae erant funibus.* In 𝔖 כד חזיקן בחבלא the first two words still refer to the "treasures" found in the earlier part of the verse and their wrappings, while they confuse the *hapax legomenon* ארוו (ארזים), whose meaning should be understood on the basis of Arabic, with the noun ארז and see in it a final article of trade. 𝔊 καί κυπαρίσσινα, 𝔙 *cedros quoque,* 𝔖 באלפא דערקא "with ships of box-wood."

e 𝔐 במרכלתך is, on the pattern of v 21, to be read as two words בם רכלתך. 𝔗 has greatly expanded the text of v 24.

25 25a The awkwardness of the idea that ships of Tarshish should be the caravans of Tyre has led 𝔊 to paraphrase as follows: πλοῖα, ἐν αὐτοῖς καρχηδόνιοι ἔμποροί σου. 𝔖, too, speaks of בני תרשיש, while 𝔗, also paraphrasing תרשיש, has the expression: בספיני ימא הוו שייטין.

b Dalman, *Arbeit,* 6.160, in dependence on the post-biblical שְׁיָרָה, would prefer to read 𝔐 שרות as שְׁיָרוֹת. The image "ships of Tarshish are your caravans" appears unusual in this otherwise very sober context. Thus Howie, *Date,* 60f, would prefer to read שכיותיך מערבך "thy ships of merchandise." The remarkable combination of the two suffixed expressions שרותיך מערבך can, according to Eugen Täubler, *Biblische Studien; die Epoche der Richter* (Tübingen: Mohr, 1958), 206 note 4 (who besides adheres to the שרותיך of 𝔐), be left, and the second word must be understood, on the basis of Gesenius-Kautzsch §128 d, as a more precise definition in apposition to the first: "Your ships of Tarshish—your caravans with goods." Herrmann, Rüger, *Tyrusorakel,* on the basis of 𝔊 ἐν τῷ συμμείκτῳ σου, 𝔙 *in negotiatione tua,* emend to במערבך.

c Literally "full."

26 26a 𝔗 already understands v 26a in terms of the foundering of the ship which is attributed to the coming of a king strong as a storm. In this connec-

a storm from the east[b] shattered you in the midst of the sea.

27 Your wealth and your wares, your merchandise, your sailors and your seamen, your ship's carpenters[a] and those who trade in your merchandise, and all your soldiers who are in you,[b] and <all>[c] your levy that is in your midst fall into the midst of the sea on the day of your fall.[d]

28 At the loud cry of your seamen the pastures(?)[a] tremble,

29/ and all those who rowed are leaving their ships, the sailors, all the seamen on the sea are going ashore[a]

30/ and wail aloud over you and cry bitterly and throw earth on their heads and roll in the dust

31/ and shave their heads on your account[a] and put on mourning garments and weep over you[a] in bitterness of heart and with a bitter lament[b]

32/ and raise over you[a] [in <their dirge>][b] a lament and lament over you: Who <was like>[c] Tyre in the midst of the sea!

tion, השטים has apparently been read as השסים: עלו עלך דבזו יתך.

b 𝔊 speaks of the south wind (*νότος*), thereby making the incident conform (as Sigfried Morenz, "Joseph in Ägypten," *ThLZ* 84 [1959]: 407, has established in another context) to the Egyptian climate with its baleful south wind. See also *RGG* 1. 120.

27 27a See v 9 note c.

b 𝔐 אשר בך is unattested by 𝔖.

c In place of 𝔐 ובכל, בכל should be read, see the versions.

d In v 27 Hölscher regards as original only the words הונך ועזבוניך יפלו בלב ימים.

28 28a The precise meaning of 𝔐 מגרשות remains uncertain. מגרש otherwise means "pasture" (see also 45:2; 48:17). 26:15, in a similar phrase, speaks of the איים. Cornill, in a *figura etymologica,* wanted to read מרעשות, on which see 𝔊 *φόβῳ φοβηθήσονται.* Toy suggests במצריך, and Fohrer considers הקרשים. 𝔙 advises *classes.* 𝔗 פרוריא "regions." 𝔖, very generally, דחדריכי "which surrounds you." Rüger, *Tyrusorakel,* following Driver, "Ezekiel," 157, renders "waves," but this hardly commends itself from the point of view of content.

29 29a על־אל cf. 1:17 note a. Literally "step on to land."

31 31a על־אל cf. 1:17 note a.

b The whole of v 31 is lacking in 𝔊 𝔎 𝔄.

32 32a על־אל cf. 1:17 note a.

b 𝔐 בְּנִיהֶם, understood by 𝔊 *οἱ υἱοὶ αὐτῶν*, 𝔖 בניהון as בְּנֵיהֶם, following from which, with reference to 32:16; Jer 9:19, the emendation of בנותיהם has already been considered (Erlich, *Randglossen*). 𝔗 בעיניהון is difficult to understand. 𝔐 probably intends ני to be understood as an abbreviation of נהי "lament." 𝔙 *carmen lugubre* points in this direction. Joüon, "Notes," 306, reads בבכיהם and deletes עליך. In any event, the word is to be deleted *metri causa* as an explanatory supplement to the original text (Cornill and others).

c 𝔐 כדמה ("like a silence" ?, "like something destroyed" ?) is scarcely correct. 𝔊 offers no help since it suppresses completely the quotation of the song in v 32b and reproduces v 32aβ(b) only by *καὶ θρήνημα Σορ* (so 𝔊[967] 𝔎 𝔄 Tyc Jerome[test]; only 𝔊[A Q] then = 𝔐; on *Τυρος* see 26:2 note a). Θ *κατασιγηθεῖσα* points, like 𝔙 *quae obmutuit,* to a reading נִדְמָה "brought to silence." Thus Hölscher איך צור נדמה "O how Tyre is destroyed." With 𝔗 דדמי לה however, this form (in the vocalization נִדְמָה?) could also be understood as "made equal, comparable," and in the context this is perhaps most likely. See also Joüon, "Notes," 306f, who then wants to read לצור. See 19:10 note a and Rev 18:18 *τίς ὁμοία τῇ πόλει τῇ μεγάλῃ*, where this interpretation of Ezek 27:32 seems to be presupposed. The assumption of a verb "to be in bonds, be captive" (Reider, "Studies," 279) does not commend itself.

33 **When your wares came from the seas,[a] you satisfied many[b] peoples. By the abundance <of your wealth>[c] and your merchandise you have made (the) kings of the earth rich.**

34 **<Now you are shattered>[a] on the seas[b] in the depths of the water. Your merchandise and all your levy have gone down inside you.**

35/ All the inhabitants of the coastlands are terror-struck on your account, and their kings' hair stands on end, their faces are haggard.[a]

36/ The merchants among the peoples howl at you. You have become an object of terror, and you will be no more for ever[a].

33 33a Literally "came out from the seas." 𝔐 בצאת has been misunderstood by 𝔊 *εὗρες* as מצאת.

b 𝔐 רבים is not attested by 𝔊, but is scarcely superfluous.

c 𝔐 הוניך. Since the plural is not otherwise attested in the OT, the singular הונך should be read here as in all the other passages.

34 34a 𝔐 עת נִשְׁבֶּרֶת "at the time of the breaking" should be read, with 𝔊 𝔙 𝔗, as עַתָּה נִשְׁבַּרְתְּ. Only 𝔖 בזבנא attests עת, but it too, with דאתתברתי, immediately goes over to the finite verbal form.

b Literally "away from the seas."

35 35a 𝔐 רעמו פנים has been misunderstood by 𝔊 *καὶ ἐδάκρυσε τὸ πρόσωπον αὐτῶν* and 𝔖 ודמעי אפיהון as "their faces ran with tears (דמעו)." But in that case one would have expected עיניהם as subject. 𝔙 *mutaverunt vultus* and 𝔗 איתרשימו אפיהון are surely closer to what is meant by רעם. What are meant are the signs of destruction and oppression. See the hip'il of רעם in 1 Sam 1:6. Reider, "Etymological Studies," 120, points to a parallel usage in Arabic.

36 36a 𝔖 adds a final editorial observation: שלמת פלגותא קדמית דעל צור.

Form

Ezekiel 27 is described in its introduction as a קינה ("lament").[1] This is confirmed by the form and content of the chapter. From the point of view of form, from v 3bβ onwards the halting meter of the lament, already familiar from chapter 19, predominates. From the point of view of content, Ezekiel 27 describes the tragic situation of the fall of Tyre. After a lengthy description of the glorious past of the city, which is described in terms of a stately ship, there follows the account of the shipwreck, a disaster which awakens all around the echo of the lament. In an actual doubling of the motif, there is cited in v 32, within the framework of the קינה ("lament") as a whole, the funeral song of those who have been eyewitnesses of the great downfall.

However, in the course of the chapter this image is blurred on a number of occasions. The *qīnah*-rhythm, which could be recognized in vv 3bβ–9a without much difficulty in spite of slight dislocations, is abandoned in v 9b and still more clearly so from v 11 onwards. A list of Tyre's trading relationships in vv 12–24 is in pure prose. Only in v 25b does there appear to be a return to the meter of the beginning, and this is maintained, with slight dislocations, almost to the end of the chapter. In addition, there is a remarkable internal discrepancy, which is parallel to the imbalance in the form. The prose sections are completely unaware of the fact that Tyre was depicted as a stately ship. They are a dispassionate account of the city herself and of her trade. The fact that the city is actually addressed in the second person feminine cannot mislead us on this score. The refrain of "perfect beauty," which occurred like a theme at the head of the whole description of the magnificent construction of the ship and of her splendid fittings and crew, moves completely into the background in the prosaic middle section behind the description of the commercial activities which has a vocabulary all of its own.

These observations, which Manchot (1888) was the first to bring to light, lead in the first instance to an analysis of the present text of 𝔐, which proves, like so many passages in Ezekiel, to have been secondarily expanded. This insight cannot be altered even by the recent attempts to prove the unity of the chapter on grounds of content (Dussaud, Smith) or of form (Bruno).

The introduction in vv 1–3bα, which tells of the

1 On the קינה see 1, 391–392 on chapter 19.

command to the prophet to deliver the קינה ("lament"), has its parallels in 19:1; 28:11–12bα; 32:1–2aα. In comparison with these passages, however, one is struck in 27:1–3 by the lengthy description of the addressee to whom the prophet is to direct his word. Tyre is described here as the great trader among the nations. Since the participle (ת)רכל ("merchant, trader") (masculine and feminine) occurs in the prose insertion in vv 12–24 no fewer than nine times but is otherwise attested in the book of Ezekiel only in 17:4 and since איים רבים ("many coast[land]s") is otherwise attested in Ezekiel only in 27:15, the descriptions of Tyre in v 3a will have to be regarded as a secondary expansion, the aim of which is to announce already in the address the theme of vv 12–24. Also the לצור ("to Tyre") is redundant after the preceding על צור ("over Tyre") of v 2. As in 28:12 it could be replaced by לו ("to it") or (as in 32:2) by אליה ("to it") or (as in 19:2) be simply omitted.

The lament begins in v 3bβ in קינה ("lament")-rhythm. Apparent deviations can be shown, or with great probability supposed, to be secondary textual corruptions.[2] It may further be noted that invariably two five-stress lines are combined to form a distich. This too may be used with great caution as an aid to the critical working out of the original form of the oracle against Tyre. Thus vv 3bβ + 4, 5a + 5b, 6a + 6b, 7aα + 7b each form a pair of five-stress lines. In vv 8–9a this order seems to be disturbed in that here, unmistakably, three similar five-stress lines of related content occur together. But v 8b stands out with its surprising reference to the people of Tyre herself between Tyre's subservient neighboring cities. Attempts have been made to overcome this difficulty by text-critical means.[3] But one can observe further that the first halves of each of the five-stress lines, vv 8b and 9a, correspond closely to each other in construction and choice of words in a way that has not been the case in these pairs of lines hitherto. Thus one begins to suspect that v 8b represents an expansion in the style of the קינה ("lament"), which says that through her own wise men Tyre has the helm in her own hands. With regard to חבליך ("your seamen"), one can recall that "wisdom" in, e.g., Prov 1:5; 12:5 can be described precisely as תחבלות ("the art of steering").[4] The mention of the חבלים in vv 28f could have led to the addition of them in the introductory description. If v 8b is deleted as an expansion, then vv 8a and 9a, which refer to "princes" and "elders" who are at Tyre's disposal for ancillary services, form together a perfect distich.

V 9b stands outside the original context, by reason of its rhythm (3+3?), of the use of the commercial terminology of vv 12–24 and, above all, of the conception of Tyre as the harbor in which ships lie, a conception in which the image of the ship Tyre is abandoned. In the case of v 10, however, it is difficult to be certain. By the deletion of אנשי מלחמתך ("your soldiers") or, better still, of היו בחילך ("were in your army") (Cheminant) and of המה ("they") (note a), one can arrive at a pure קינה double-line. With regard to content one can ask, in spite of Smith's comment that at that time merchant ships and war-ships were certainly not easily distinguished, whether the reference to warriors originally belonged to the peaceful image of the stately ship, especially since this reference does not recur in the continuation in vv 26, 28–32.[5] Thus it is very possible that v 10 too represents an element of expansion of the original image (from a different hand than vv 12–24). In any event, v 10 is then presupposed by the purely prosaic v 11, which is an exegetical expansion of v 10 in which the Arvadites, who have already been mentioned in v 8, are cited once again and where it is the city of Tyre and not the ship which is clearly envisaged.

In vv 12–24 there follows the great prose list of Tyre's commercial relationships, with its own problems of form which must now be specifically discussed. With regard to the working out of the basic text of the קינה ("lament"), there arises the question of how far the insertion extends and where the re-connection with the lament occurs. There is widespread agreement that v 25a—with its מערב ("merchandise"), derived from the vocabulary of vv 12–24, its ships of Tarshish which recall the Tarshish trade of the commercial list (v 12) and the closeness of its concepts to those of v 9b—is still part of the insertion. On the other hand, v 25b, on account of its metrical structure as a five-stress line, is mostly unhesitatingly regarded as part of the lament. In this respect, no attention is paid to the fact that from the point of view of

2 See above v 3 note f, v 4 note b, v 5 note d, v 6 notes c and d, v 7 notes c and d, v 9 note b.

3 See v 8 note b.

4 See Walther Zimmerli, "Zur Struktur der alttestamentlichen Weisheit," *ZAW* 51 (1933): 183.

5 On v 27 see below.

content v 25b still quite clearly looks back to the abundance of goods with which the ship is obviously filled, i.e. to vv 12–24, and that in its final two words it rather inelegantly anticipates the final words of v 26 and, above all, that it lacks a corresponding five-stress line which would make it into a distich. For in v 26 there is a new pair of five-stress lines which clearly belong together. Thus one is forced either to assume before v 25b a textual loss, which is then made intelligible by means of the prose insertion,[6] or else to accept that v 25b is still a transitional verse, which is intended to make the transition from the commercial list to the lament over the stately ship Tyre and equally from the prose to the קינה ("lament")-rhythm.

The continuation of the lament is to be found in the five-stress distich v 26a,b, which forms a seamless join with the distich vv 8a, 9a.[7] In v 27 there again follows a statement which is wholly influenced by the vocabulary of the prose commercial list, but which ends in v 27b in a correct five-stress line. This observation with regard to form might again lead to the search for a corresponding first half. Hölscher reconstructs from v 27ab an original הונך ועזבוניך יפלו בלב ימים. Rüger finds it in the words חבליך מחזקי בדקך וכל אנשי מלחמתך. Here, however, just as little as in v 25b, one will not be deceived by the *qīnah*-meter as to the secondary character of the whole verse, precisely in fact in its refrain-like closing words ביום מפלתך ("on the day of your fall") (26:18; cf. 26:15; 31:16; see also the inelegant repetition of בלב ימים "in the midst of the sea" from v 26).

V 28 connects directly with v 26 (so too Fohrer). In the pairs of five-stress lines in vv 28–29a and 29b–30a a chiastic structure can be observed in the two distichs. Vv 28 and 30a refer to loud crying, while vv 29a and 29b speak of the "going ashore" of the seamen. The five-stress distich vv 30b–31a then describes the mourning customs; vv 31b–32a, the striking up of the mourning song which is then cited. The two five-stress lines which form it, vv 32b and 34a, are however separated in 𝔐 by a pair of double threes, the vocabulary of which is also clearly influenced by the commercial list. V 34b is also an insertion, where again the idea of the ship has been abandoned in favor of that of the city and where מערבך ("your merchandise") comes from the commercial list. The five-stress distich v 35a,b must have closed the original lament. What follows (two double twos) falls metrically outside the lament. The mocking of the merchants is, from the point of view of content, an anticlimax after the terror of the kings, and it also recalls the theme of the traders (vv 12–24). Together with concluding refrain verse (cf. 26:21; 28:19), it is a secondary expansion. Accordingly, the lament in its purified form is as follows:

> O Tyre, you are a ship of perfect beauty. In the midst of the sea they have formed you, have made perfect your beauty.
> With junipers from Senir they built for you (on both sides) all your planks. (The) cedars of Lebanon they took to make a mast.
> From the tallest oaks of Bashan they made your oars. Your deck (?) they made from cypresses (?) from the coasts of Kittim.
> Brightly embroidered linen from Egypt was your sail. Of blue purple from the coasts of Elisha was your (cabin-)covering.
> The princes of Sidon and Arvad were your oarsmen. The elders of Byblos were in you as your ship's carpenters.
> (? Paras and Lud and Put were your soldiers. They hung up shield and helmet in you, they formed your splendor.)
> Over mighty waters your oarsmen led you, a storm from the east shattered you in the midst of the sea.
> At the loud cry of your seamen the pastures (?) tremble, and all those who rowed are leaving their ships.
> The sailors, all the seamen on the sea are going ashore and wail aloud over you and cry bitterly
> and throw earth on their heads and roll in the dust and shave their heads on your account and put on mourning garments
> and weep over you in bitterness of heart and with a bitter lament and raise over you a lament and lament over you:
> "Who was like Tyre in the midst of the sea! Now you are shattered on the seas in the depths of the water."
> All the inhabitants of the coastlands are terror-struck on your account, and their kings' hair stands on end, their faces are haggard.

The lament comprises a total of 12 (if v 10 is original, 13) distichs. It reveals in its layout a simple structure in two parts. Distichs 1–5 (or 6) describe the former glory

6 Fohrer. Rüger's (*Tyrusorakel*) arrangement of strophes—vv 8/9a, 10a/10b, 25b/26—is not very convincing, in spite of the reference to "a kind of enjambement."

7 Or with v 10, see above.

of the ship and its rich fittings. In distich 6 (or 7) there occurs the disaster with the sinking (not depicted in detail) of the ship, over which then in the second part the universal lament is raised (distichs 7–12, or 8–13). In the figurative description of the ship and its crew elements of historical reality are interwoven. The catastrophe can be regarded as artificial only in the reflection of the extent to which the surrounding world joins in the lament.

Setting

The basic form of the lament can be dated with some probability. In it the fall of Tyre is anticipated in a way in which historically it did not subsequently happen. Tyre seems to be already besieged, but the events which are presupposed in the oracle of 29:17–21, which is to be dated at the beginning of the twenty-seventh year of Jehoiachin's deportation (April 26, 571), have not yet taken place. The fate of Jerusalem, which in 26:2 provided the occasion for the word of judgment against Tyre, is not mentioned anywhere in chapter 27. That first excitement has died away. Thus the Tyre oracle in chapter 27 must not be brought too close to the year 587. In it the fate of the city of Tyre is referred to with a remarkable "realism" in which one might discern a trace of personal sympathy.

There are no particular indications in the lament as to the prophet's place of exile.

Interpretation

■ **27:1,2** The original lament is introduced in few words: the formula for the receiving of God's word, address to the prophet (son of man), and the command to raise a קינה ("lament"), which is characterized here (differently from 19:1 and 32:1–2 but similarly to 28:12) by the introductory messenger formula as a word of Yahweh.[8]

■ **27:3** Although the address to Tyre is then maintained throughout the entire oracle, there is no hint anywhere in the text of the קינה ("lament") itself that it is Yahweh who is speaking, far less who is acting. Everything remains, devoid of any theological accent, in the sphere of an event on earth, with earthly characteristics.

The polemical accent, which is achieved in 𝔐 by an alteration of style in terms of a speech by Tyre (v 3bβ, see note f), is alien to the original text of the introduction to the lament. As in the laments in 19:1ff; 28:12ff; 32:2f, the person addressed is directly described by means of a figure of speech. Tyre is comparable to a ship of perfect beauty.[9] This simile is suggested not only by the thought that Tyre is a great commercial port, but equally by its island position, which we find already mentioned in Egyptian and Assyrian accounts.[10]

■ **27:4** The outstanding beauty of Tyre (in Lam 2:15 of Jerusalem) is described by means of the resumption of כלילת יפי ("of perfect beauty," v 3) in כללו יפיך ("they . . . have made perfect your beauty," v 4) words which are specifically Ezekiel's (see also 16:14; 28:12). The verb כלל ("to make perfect") occurs only in Ezek 27:4,11. Of the total of nineteen OT occurrences of the noun יפי ("beauty"), no fewer than ten occur in the book of Ezekiel (16:14f, 25; 27:3f, 11; 28:7, 12, 17; 31:8). The splendor of this beauty (v 10 הדר) is dealt with in what follows. One should not inquire further about the "builders" from whose hands the splendor of this stately ship comes and who are mentioned secondarily in v 4 of 𝔐 (but see note b). Here, in contrast to the beauty of the woman in chapter 16, there is not the slightest suggestion of a divine creator or provider.

■ **27:5f** Two further distichs describe, in the form of a building narrative, the wooden components of the ship. לוח (here "plank") refers in Is 30:8 to a wooden writing tablet, in Song 8:9 to a cedar plank with which one bars a door, in Ex 27:8 to a plank for the building of the altar, in Ex 24:12 (and elsewhere) to the stone tablet on which the decalogue is written, in 1 Kgs 7:36 to a metal plate on the movable bronze stands in the temple. In the present passage the reference must be to the planks of the side of the ship.[11] תרן (here "mast") in Is 30:17 refers to a signal post on a hill, but is also found with the meaning "mast" in Is 33:23 where the "support" (כן) of the mast is also mentioned (by which is meant not only the mast-socket fixed to the deck but, after the manner of Egyptian shipbuilding, the post to which the mast "is lashed" [חזק] by ropes).[12] The ship is equipped with oars (מִשּׁוֹט in v 6 alongside מָשׁוֹט in v 29), a fact which implies no lessening of its dignity. Is 33:21 varies אני שיט ("ship with oars") in the parallel with צי אדיר ("stately ship").[13]

8 See 1, 144–145; 1, 131–132.

9 On shipbuilding in the ancient world see Köster, *Seewesen:* also *BRL*, s.v. "Schiff"; Barrois, *Manuel,* 2.241–243.

10 See above p. 22.

11 Abraham, *Schiffsterminologie*, 36f.

The least clear expression is קרש (here "deck") mentioned in fourth place. The word is attested otherwise only in the description in the P-narrative of the wooden construction of the משכן (about fifty times, especially in Ex 26 and 36) and refers there to the long (according to 26:16, ten cubits by one and a half) accacia planks of which it is made. In the present passage it is used in the singular of a particularly prominent "plank." Gesenius-Buhl supposes that it refers to the deck, Rüger to the deck and deck superstructures;[14] Koehler-Baumgartner has "prow?." This latter, however, is scarcely likely, since the illustrations on the palace gates of *balawāt*[15] as well as the information in Herodotus both suggest that the stem of Phoenician ships was in the form of a horse's head.[16]

The detailed description of the wooden components of the ship is intended to show the extent to which Tyre is able to dispose of the very best materials for each part. One must recall the lack of wood in Egypt, a lack which definitely determined the form of the ships built there (Köster), in order fully to appreciate what it means that "the ship Tyre" can be built so skillfully of the woods appropriate to each part. The woods of her hinterland, the export of which lay entirely in her hands (1 Kgs 5:20ff), are at Tyre's disposal: Phoenician junipers, which, with their tall trunks, provide good building wood and wood for planks, it can fell on Senir. The name שניר ("Senir") is mentioned in the OT also in Dtn 3:9 as the name of Mt. Hermon, the projection at the south-southeast end of the Antilebanon (*jebel eš-šeikh*): "The Sidonians (Phoenicians) call Hermon Sirion, but the Amonites call it Senir." The cedars of Lebanon provide the material for the towering mast.[17] For the oars, however, which, on account of the continuous strain put upon them, had to be made of particularly strong wood, there were the "strong trees" (אלונים), i.e. most probably oaks[18] from Bashan, the hinterland of the Sea of Gennesaret, the modern *en-nuqra*, famous for its rams and bulls (Dtn 32:14; Am 4:1), its rich pasturage (Mic 7:14) and its oak forests (Is 2:13; Zech 11:2). The cypress wood for the deck (?), however, is brought across the sea from the coasts of Kittim.[19] Kittim, descended from Japhet according to Gen 10:4, refers originally to the city of Kition, which can perhaps be identified with Larnaka on Cyprus.[20] The name was then extended to the southern region of Cyprus which was under Phoenician control.[21] It is to be understood in this extended sense in the present passage as a term for the southern part of Cyprus. Subsequently the name was extended still further and became a term for the Macedonians and Seleucids from the Greek world (1 Macc 1:1; 8:5) and finally even for the Romans (Dan 11:30).[22]

■ **27:7** Also imported are the materials which, according to distich 4, are used for the further fitting out of the stately ship. From Egypt comes colored linen. שש ("linen") in Hebrew is an Egyptian loan-word.[23] In Egyptian *šs* refers to the linen which is used for clothes, binding mummies and bed sheets.[24] While the Egyptian, by way of contrast to his neighbors, set great store in his dress by the wearing of the finest white linen,[25] one can observe that great pleasure is taken on the luxury ships (temple barges) of the New Kingdom in colored sails: "The sails consist . . . of the richest and most brightly-colored materials."[26] Such a sail could then also become a sign of recognition for the ship. Is this what the gloss in v 7a is explicitly trying to say? In Is 33:23, directly after the setting up (the making firm) of the mast, the "stretching out" (פרש) of the נס ("sign") is referred to. The question then arises whether נס ("sign") could not then simply be a word for the sail. The illustrations of Phoenician (and Egyptian) ships do not reveal anything of

12 Köster, *Seewesen*, 26.
13 See, e.g., Köster, *Seewesen*, figures 7 and 17.
14 So too Abraham, *Schiffsterminologie*, 38.
15 Adolf Billerbeck and Friedrich Delitzsch, *Die Palasttore Salmanassars II. von Balawat*, Beiträge zur Assyriologie und semitischen Sprachwissenschaft 6, 1 (Leipzig: Hinrichs, 1908).
16 Köster, *Seewesen*, 5af. On Ugaritic *qrš* see note b.
17 On these see 1,361 on 17:4.
18 According to Loew, *quercus aegilops* (= *macrolepis*) "Valonia oak."
19 There is an illustration of timber trade across the sea in Köster, *Seewesen*, plate 13.
20 Phoenician *kt* and *ktj*; see Johannes Friedrich, *Phönizisch-punische Grammatik* (Rome: Pontifical Biblical Institute, 1951) 102.
21 R. Dussaud, "Ile ou rivage dans l'Ancien Testament," *Anatolian Studies* 6 (1956): 63.
22 See also the כתיאים of the Qumran texts and Josephus, *Antiquities* I 6, 1.
23 See 1,341 on 16:10.
24 Erman-Grapow, 4. 539f.
25 Erman-Ranke, 244, 535.
26 Erman-Ranke, 580.

pennants as such (Köster).

Alongside this, imported material is mentioned which is used for the "covering." The reference here is to the screening of the cabins (awnings), which in Egypt as early as the Old Kingdom were constructed behind the mast "of elegantly woven mats or of white linen."[27] Here, too, in the New Kingdom, everything becomes more luxurious and more brightly colored.[28] The stately ship Tyre is in no way inferior to the Egyptian ships in luxurious fittings when she embellishes her cabin with blue (violet) purple cloth from the coasts of Elisha.[29] The name Elisha—which Halévy wished to identify with Elis-Peloponnese, Stade with Carthage, Jensen with somewhere in northwest Africa and Hennig with somewhere on the Canary Islands[30] —probably also points to Cyprus. Amarna letters Nos. 34–40 are from a king of *alašia* to the king of Egypt. The reference to the exporting of copper suggests the connection with Cyprus from which, via Latin, the very word "copper" comes. Further references from Mari, Nuzi and Ugarit are cited by Rüger. More particularly, C. F. A. Schaeffer, wanted to equate *alašia* with the place Enkomi on the east coast of Cyprus.[31] Thus the Enkomi region, inhabited first by the Achaeans and later by the Greeks, would stand opposite the territory round Larnaka, occupied and ruled by the Phoenicians (Rüger). However, the export of purple (cloth) from this region has not so far been attested. That Tyre, the center of the purple-dye industry, of which Pliny (*Hist. nat.* V 76) and Strabo (16.2–23) report in detail, should have imported purple cloth is the most remarkable statement of this whole complex.[32]

■ **27:8f** The crew, however, also contribute to the splendor of the stately ship Tyre. The aristocracy of Tyre's neighbor cities provide the personnel for duties on board this ship. In this can clearly be seen the supremacy of the city of Tyre, which has also been observed in the list in Nebuchadnezzar's Court Calendar.[33] In that earlier period which gave to the Phoenicians the name "Sidonians," Sidon, which is here mentioned first among the helpers of Tyre, acquired this position of preeminence. Sidon is to be found in the modern *ṣaidā* halfway between Beirut and Tyre.[34] Arvad was likewise an island city[35] and is to be located at modern *ruād,* opposite the coastal town of *tartūs* (Antaradus) sixty-four kilometers by road north of Syrian Tripolis. Even in the Amarna letters *arwada* appears as an opponent of Byblos and Tyre,[36] and it appears again and again in the Assyrian campaign reports since Tiglath-pileser I.[37] In the neo-Babylonian period, however, there appears in the court list discussed by Unger, alongside the kings of Tyre and Sidon, also a king of Arvad as member of Nebuchadnezzar's court.[38] The rations lists for the prisoners[39] mention allowances for three carpenters from Arvad.[40] Finally Gebal—the seaport of Byblos, put into by Egyptian ships as early as the third millenium and frequently mentioned in Egyptian and Assyrian annals—[41] beside modern *jebēl*, forty-one kilometers by road north of Beirut, has certainly the most notable history of all the Phoenician ports. The more recent excavations of Montet and Dunand have brought their evidence to light in the most impressive way.[42] The nobles of these cities perform the most menial duties on the stately ship Tyre. The rowing and the responsibility for the correct caulking of the ship are incumbent upon them. In 2 Kgs 12:6–9, 13; 22:5 בדק (here "what is dilapidated") refers to the dilapidated parts of the temple buildings, while in 2 Chr 34:10 the verb בדק refers to the repairing of the cracks. In the case of the ship it means the coating with pitch and the supervision of the dowelling of the planks.

27 Erman-Ranke, 576.
28 Erman-Ranke, 580.
29 A later hand has added a reference to red purple (see note d).
30 See Koehler-Baumgartner.
31 C. F. A. Schaeffer, *Enkomi-Alasia; nouvelles missions en Chypre, 1946–1950,* Publications de la Mission archéologique francaise 1 (Paris: Klincksieck, 1952), 2–8.
32 Fleming, *History of Tyre,* 144f.
33 See above pp. 23f.
34 See further on 28:20–23.
35 *ANET* 276, *AOT* 340, in a report by Ashurnasirpal II: "Arvad in the midst of the sea."
36 101:13ff; 105:12ff; 149:59.
37 1114–1076 B.C.; *ANET* 275, see further the Index in *ANET* 510.
38 Unger, "Namen."
39 See 1, 114–115.
40 *ANET* 308.
41 Index of *ANET* 511.
42 See, e.g., Herbert Haag, *Bibel-Lexikon* (Einsiedeln, ²1964), and *RGG*. On the (infrequent) references to Byblos and its inhabitants in the OT see R. Dussaud,

A later hand has missed in this list any reference to the "seamen" (חֹבֵל cannot be dissociated from חֶבֶל "cord, rope") busy with sail and rudder. This activity, which demands special skill, he has attributed to the "wise men" of Tyre herself in wording which is modeled on v 9a.[43] Later still, a second hand, who also regarded the maintenance of the ship as demanding a special skilled craftsmanship, associated with the elders of Byblos also her "wise men."[44]

■ **27:10** The whole description hitherto has painted a colorful picture of a peaceful display of splendor. This picture, perhaps not till somewhat later, has been enriched by a new element in v 10, which is then in turn interpreted prosaically in v 11. The fact that Tyre was at war with Nebuchadnezzar may have suggested the addition of warlike elements. While the citation of the nobles of Sidon, Arvad and Byblos as oarsmen and ship's carpenters in the stately vessel Tyre was still meant figuratively, the mercenary troops appear entirely in their proper functions.

Paras, Lud and Put (in the last two names a rhyme resembling that in [Pekod] Shoa and Koa in 23:23) is a thoroughly typical group of names of mercenary nations. In the combination "Cush, Put and Lud" (30:5; also Jer 46:9 with the substitution of לודים "men of Lud" for the third element) the rhyme, with which the mercenary names כרתי ופלתי ("Cretans and Philistines") of the Davidic period may be compared,[45] links all three elements. In 38:5 there occurs the combination "Paras, Cush and Put." The oldest form of this series is surely to be found in the combination "Cush, Put and Lud." It points the series in the direction of the Egyptian vassal nations, and in fact this combination occurs both times in oracles against Egypt.[46] In the case of Put, it used to be identified with the Egyptian incense land Punt on the Somali coast.[47] But there are difficulties in the philological equation of Put with Punt. 𝔊 Λίβυες and 𝔅 *Libyes* both point to Libya, as does Josephus' commentary on Gen 10:6, where Put appears alongside Egypt, Cush and Canaan as a son of Ham.[48] If in the Persian royal inscriptions after 518, the time when the Persian satrap in Egypt Aryandes conquered Barka and Cyrene "to subdue the Libyans,"[49] the name *mat puṭu* (which does not appear in the Behustan inscription of Darius I [518]) makes a sudden appearance, this too is an argument in favor of identifying Put with the Lybians, in particular[50] those Libyans from Cyrene and Barka bordering directly on Egypt.[51] Nubian and Lybian mercenaries are already mentioned as important helpers of Pharaoh in the Unis inscription from the Old Kingdom, the period of Phiops I.[52] Both however are also mentioned in identical terms in the New Kingdom as significant mercenary groups.[53]

Lud appears in Gen 10:22 alongside Elam, Asshur and others as a son of Shem and is there certainly to be equated with the Lydians of Asia Minor. 𝔊 and 𝔅 make this equation also in the present passage. But how can Lydians, as is presupposed by 30:5, appear in the Egyptian orbit? The ancient near eastern annals explain this with some clarity. After Ashurbanipal has mentioned for the year 676 (?) that king Gyges of Lydia, "whose name the kings, my fathers, had never heard," had requested help against the Cimmerians and that this king had paid homage, he has to record for the year 665 (?) that no more ambassadors with tribute have come from Lydia and that, further, Gyges "sent his troops to support Psammetichus, the king of Egypt, who had thrown off the yoke of my sovereignty."[54] The appearance of Lydian mercenaries in the Egyptian army need therefore cause no surprise after the middle of the seventh century.[55]

"Byblos et la mention des Giblites dans l'Ancien Testament," *Syria* 4 (1923): 300–315; 5 (1924): 388.

43 See also v 8 note b and above p. 54.

44 See on v 9 note b.

45 See above on 25:16.

46 On Cush, Egypt's neighbor to the south, see below on 30:5.

47 And still is by Friedrich Wilhelm Freiherr von Bissing, "Pyrene (Punt) und die Seefahrten der Ägypter," in *Die Welt des Orients. Wissenschaftliche Beiträge zur Kunde des Morgenlandes,* ed. Ernst Michel (Wuppertal: Hans Putty Verlag, 1948): 148.

48 *Antiquities* I 6,2.

49 Herodotus 4, 167.

50 On the basis of Herodotus 3, 91.

51 See also Rüger, *Tyrusorakel.*

52 Erman-Ranke, 623.

53 Erman-Ranke, 651, 652.

54 The Rassam Cylinder II, 95f; 111–115.

55 For further references see below on 30:5.

This "Cush, Put and Lud" group, which has its origins in Egyptian circumstances, has been changed in 27:10 and 38:5 by the prefixing of Paras. It is instructive to see that the force of the triple grouping still continues to operate. Paras is not added as a fourth name to the three already existing names, but suppresses one of these three names. In 38:5 "Lud" is rejected from the older group. In 27:10, Paras takes the place of the first member of the group (Cush), and the two other members change places. In Ezr 1:1–3 and the first chapter of Esther, פרס means the Persian empire. It is difficult, however, to find this as early as Ezekiel. Therefore Herrmann believes that one can think of the Pharusii mentioned by Pliny, Strabo and Ptolemy. However, the fact that this people had its home on the Atlantic coast south of Morocco does not arouse much confidence in this identification. Halévy, on the other hand, suggested emending פרס to פתרוס (29:14; 30:14).[56] In view of the recurrence of פרס in 38:5 this is unlikely. Thus Rüger would postulate alongside the form "Pathros," which goes back to Egyptian *p3.t3.rśj* (land of the south), a variant "paras," corresponding to Egyptian *p3.rśj*.[57] Yet it is scarcely likely that within the framework of one tradition two forms of the name of the same country stand side by side. Thus one must assume either that behind פרס there is concealed the name of a people hitherto unknown to us or else that in fact the Persians are meant here. In view of the fact that פרס comes first both in 27:10 and in 38:5, suggesting that the name refers to an important group, the second of these assumptions is the more likely. That the Persians were known to their neighbors even before 539 can be deduced from several sources (Rüger). In view of the probability that 27:10 is a later expansion, it is quite possible that its phraseology takes us down to the time when Persian strength began to be obvious to all, i.e. to about the middle of the sixth century.[58]

V 10 states that Tyre wielded military power over all these. Unlike vv 8f this says nothing about the actual conception of Tyre's position, but is using a cliché-type idea which belongs fundamentally to Egypt and can have been easily accommodated to the contemporary situation only by the insertion of Persia. Thus, it is futile to ask precisely how Lydians and Lybians and even Persian warriors reached Tyre. In this connection it is not quite clear whether the idea of the stately ship as the representation of Tyre is still present in v 10 or whether the verse is already thinking of the city and her army.[59] It is true that the hanging up of shields as decoration can still be easily associated with the image of the ship. The various representations of ships from the palace of Sennacherib[60] but also coins from the period of Alexander the Great depict the custom of hanging shields on the upper rail. This custom subsequently spread to the Greeks and is represented on an ivory relief from Sparta. But since it can be shown that this custom was taken over from its use in fortifications and towers, of which v 11 then goes on to speak, it cannot conclusively be maintained that v 10 is still thinking in terms of the ship.[61]

■ **27:11** The cliché-type v 10 is paraphrased once again in v 11 in a purely prose addition and is at the same time brought closer to the historical reality of Tyre. In place of the foreign mercenaries, it is the men of Arvad, already referred to in v 8, who are mentioned as giving military assistance on the walls of Tyre. Did this island fortress in fact provide particularly active help to her sister city in the south when the latter was besieged by Nebuchadnezzar?[62] Whether there are also names concealed in חילך ("your army") and גמדים ("the Gammadites") can no longer be determined with certainty (notes a and c). The image of the ship has been completely abandoned and the idea, as in Song 4:4, is of decoration by means of weapons on the parapets of walls and towers. In this there is found confirmation of the thematic statement (vv 3f) of the perfected beauty of the city.[63]

Alongside the secondary expansion of the image by features drawn from military defense, there stands, in vv 12–25, the expansion by the description of widespread

56 J. Halévy, "Notes de M. J. Halévy," *Journal asiatique* 8e série 19 (1892), 371.

57 The suggestion comes from H. Brunner (see Erman-Grapow, 2. 453).

58 On 38:5 see below.

59 As probably then in חילך; see v 10 note a and above p. 54.

60 Köster, *Seewesen*, figures 7f, pp. 52f, and plate 17.

61 See also the golden shields in Solomon's House of the Forest of Lebanon (in 1 Kgs 10:16; 14:26) and see above all Song 4:4. The combination of shield and helmet recalls 23:24 (קובע) and 38:5 (כובע as in the present passage).

62 See then the king of Arvad in Nebuchadnezzar's Court Calendar (above pp. 23–24).

63 Illustrations in *ANEP* 372f; *AOBAT* 141.

trade, which is again led back by means of v 25b to the original image of the stately ship.[64]

■ **27:26** The text of the original lament had referred in its fifth distich (vv 8a, 9a) to the crew of the ship, her oarsmen and sailors. With the sixth (if v 10 is original, the seventh) distich in v 26 there occurs for the first time an element of movement in the hitherto purely descriptive picture of the magnificent vessel. The ship, propelled by the power of her oarsmen, puts to sea. H. G. May tries to see a reminiscence of the cosmic primeval ocean in מים רבים.[65] But on the sea the ship is caught by a storm from the east and shattered. Palestine knows the east wind as the scorching and destructive hamsin from the desert (Jer 13:24 רוח מדבר "wind from the desert"; see also Jer 4:11 רוח צח שפיים (בא ממדבר) "a hot wind from the bare heights <comes from> the desert"), withering every living thing. Such a wind from the wilderness is at the same time powerful enough to overturn a house and kill those who are inside (Job 1:19). Thus a storm from the east is a dangerous enemy on the sea too, by means of which Yahweh himself destroys ships of Tarshish (Ps 48:8).[66] That the storm "from the east" also refers to the king of Babylon (so Heinisch) is unlikely in view of מצפון ("from the north") of 26:7.

It is remarkable how the account of the actual occurrence of departure and shipwreck is compressed into such a small space, into the two five-stress lines of a single distich. The whole remaining compass of the extensive lament is now given over to the description of the impression created by that event on the world round about. Here again it becomes clear that in this lament there is no development of a dramatic effect for its own sake, but that the main concern is with an event which has a message for the world round about. However fully the visible features are developed initially, the whole clearly aims at an audible challenge intended to terrify men and bring them to humble submission. An echo of this scene can be heard in Rev 18:18 in the apocalyptic event of the fall of Babylon the great.

■ **27:28** Only with the mention of the crying of the drowning seamen does there obtrude into this description of the appalled grief of the surrounding world a vivid feature of the great catastrophe.[67] Does v 28, in the first instance, refer to the terror experienced by the coasts? In view of the uncertainty of the meaning of מגרשות ("pastures"[?]) (note a) it is unfortunately impossible to say with certainty.

■ **27:29ff** The motif of "coming down" (ירד) in view of the great "bringing down" is here referred in a special way to the sailors.[68] The oarsmen abandon their ships and in this way bring them to a standstill. Rabbi Eleazar concludes from this, "In days to come all craftsmen will turn to agriculture."[69] All the sailors go ashore, and in this can be seen the terror at the serious threat to all proud sea journeys (see also Is 2:16). With their cries they answer the cries of the drowning men (the זעק "cry" in v 30 corresponds to that in v 28).

The ninth to the eleventh (or tenth to twelfth) distichs describe how the mourning finds its ritual expression.[70] The mourner scatters earth on his head (Josh 7:6; Job 2:12), he rolls in the dust (Mic 1:10; Jer 6:26), cuts his hair for the dead man (7:18; Lev 21:5; Mic 1:16; Jer 16:6), puts on the mourning garment (7:18).[71] In addition there is the "loud weeping" (בכה) "of the ritual lament" (מספד) (cf. 24:16,23). מר ("bitter") which has already occurred in v 30, is repeated twice in v 31 in order to emphasize the bitter anguish of the lament.

■ **27:32** Everything is concentrated finally in the mourning song which, in the two five-stress lines vv 32b and 34a, contains simply the two basic motifs of the *genre*, the description of the former glory and of the present distress. The former glory is expressed in the form of a hymnic question, "Who is like . . . ."[72] By the addition of בתוך הים ("in the midst of the sea") the question is referred to Tyre's prestige on the sea.

64 On this see below pp. 63ff.

65 Herbert Gordon May, "Some Cosmic Connotations of *Mayim Rabbîm*, 'Many Waters,'" *JBL* 74 (1955): 18.

66 See Klein, "Klima," 322–325.

67 חבליך ("your seamen") summarizes the various categories of vv 8a, 9a; the secondary addition in v 27 enumerates everything in detail again.

68 See above p. 38 on 26:16.

69 According to *b. Yebam.* 63a.

70 See also 1,506 on 24:17.

71 See 1,208.

72 On this see, e.g., the names מיכאל and מיכיהו, and Noth, *Israelitischen Personennamen,* 144, as well as 31:2 and Is 44:7.

■ **27:34** Corresponding to this and introduced by עתה ("now") (note a) is the picture of the present destruction. The shipwreck (שבר "to shatter" resumes the key word of v 26b) hurls proud Tyre into the watery depths. In 𝔐 in vv 33, 34b both parts of the קינה ("lament") have had added to them comments from the standpoint (and with the vocabulary) of the commercial list.[73]

Rüger draws attention to a fine Ugaritic parallel to the description of the lament. Text 67 VI 12–16, 22–25 of the Baal cycle describes the lament of *ltpn* for Baal: "He came down (*yrd*) from his throne, he sat on a stool, and coming down from the stool he sat on the ground; he strewed straw of mourning on his head, dust in which a man wallows on his pate . . . He lifted up his voice and cried: 'Baal is dead. What will become of the people of Dagon's son, what of the multitudes belonging to Baal?'"[74]

■ **27:35** A final twelfth (or thirteenth) distich sums up by way of conclusion and in fairly general language the whole shock which has been caused far and wide by the fall of Tyre. All the inhabitants of the coastlands including even their kings are paralyzed and full of horror in the face of what has happened.

Aim

Like the conclusion of Jesus's miracles, the closing words here reveal the ultimate, hidden orientation of the lament as a whole. While the accounts of Jesus's healing miracles conclude with the astonishment and fear of the crowd who give the glory to God,[75] the description in the lament concludes, in considerable detail, with the depiction of the grief and indescribable horror of the eyewitnesses to the fall of Tyre, which is presented as the shipwreck of the stately ship Tyre. The exception is that in the present description, as has already been mentioned, there is no specific reference to God, and the storm from the east, as opposed to Ps 48:8 (and Ex 14:21), is not described as an instrument sent by God. Only the introduction to the קינה ("lament"), with which the prophet is commissioned on the call of God and which, on the basis of the introductory messenger formula (v 3), is to be transmitted to the listeners as a message with divine authority, makes it clear that this catastrophe, even if it has happened entirely in the earthly sphere as a result of an earthly storm, nevertheless contains a message from another world to all the eyewitnesses of it.

At the same time, however, the fact that the lament anticipates the occurrence of the historical events which it laments (this differentiates chapter 27 from chapter 19) signifies, as in Am 5:1f, a mysterious jolt for the one who is still at rest. In the prophetic funeral lament, which like the petrel announces the coming storm, the occurrence of the great demise has already begun.

It is remarkable how the whole event is described in such an unpolemical way, indeed almost with a gentle sorrow for Tyre, coupled with respect. Only with the secondary insertion of אמרת ("you have said") in v 3 (note f) is any emphasis placed on Tyre's self-esteem, something which was alien to the basic text. There Tyre is described as a splendid, richly adorned creature, a precious flower of human achievement.

One should not overlook the situation in which the lament is spoken. Tyre is besieged and, for the moment, is still able to withstand the enemy. Even in Ezekiel's circle there may have been no lack of secret sympathy for the resistance of this city. Is there not perhaps here a city which can stand firm against the wicked conqueror who reduced Jerusalem to rubble and ashes? Is there not perhaps here a particularly precious flower of human achievement which can assert itself against the Babylonians?

Over and above all such faint emotions and hopes, however, the lament proclaims the shipwreck of the stately ship Tyre. And it dwells so long—for half the poem—on the shock experienced by the world at this collapse, precisely because it wishes to arouse and keep alive this profound horror at what must be proclaimed from the secret counsel of the one who guides history about this noble city of Tyre and her consummate beauty.

Man does not participate in the truth when he basks in the beauty of that which has grown up and been built up among men, nor when he secretly sets his trust and innermost faith on such a product of human nature and human politics, but only when he acknowledges over and

73 On these see below.

74 Driver, *Canaanite Myths,* 108f.

75 Bultmann, *History,* 225f.

above this beauty the hidden judge of all human beauty, the one who does not renounce here either his rights as lord. Before the face of this judge and king of all the world the lament, and the proclamation it contains of the death of Tyre the magnificent, calls to those who hear it, even if in all its description of the past and the present it never explicitly mentions the name of God.

Interpretation

■ **27:12–24** *The commercial list.* Into the middle of the lament over Tyre of perfect beauty there has been inserted secondarily in vv 12–24(25) a long list of her trading relationships, which, by a series of additions and parentheses, has been dovetailed further into the context.

■ **27:3** Thus already in v 3 the description of the addressee to whom the prophet is directed has been expanded by the reference to Tyre's trade. Her position is described with reference to this trade. She sits at the entrance to the maritime world: "מבוא ('entrance') refers to the point at which one can enter something."[76] Many towns lie by the sea. Tyre, the island city with her double harbor, lies where the doors open on to the world of the seacoasts. Her profession too, however, is described with reference to her trading. She is the international trader who journeys forth to the nations on all the coasts of the wide sea.

■ **27:9b** The addition in v 9b disrupts the image of the stately ship Tyre and speaks of foreign ships which put into the harbor of Tyre in order to participate there in the great trade fair.

Form

■ **27:12–24(25)** The great complex vv 12–24(25) is linked to the קִינָה ("lament") from a quite specific point of view, and to fail to notice this is prejudicial to the understanding of it. Directly preceding it in vv 8–11 there has been the reference to the helpers at Tyre's disposal. The basic text (vv 8a, 9a) adheres to the image of the stately ship and speaks of the crew which is at Tyre's service in the persons of the élite of her immediate Phoenician neighbors. In v 10, which was probably added later, and in its prose interpretation in v 11, the image has been expanded by the addition of the military helpers. Vv 12–24 are directly connected to this in that they now speak of Tyre's commercial helpers, and these point worldwide to Tyre's various trading posts.

Vv 12–24 themselves, however, present a second point of emphasis. The section not only aims to be a list of Tyre's commercial helpers, but, over and above, also aims to present a compilation of the goods which can be procured from the individual countries. Behind its present form, one can clearly recognize a straightforward technical trade list of places and goods, which no doubt originally existed simply in the form of a list and has only secondarily been accommodated to the overall theme of the present context. This is already clear from the prevailing formal structure. As rich and varied as is the list of countries and goods, so monotonous and only slightly varied, on the other hand, is the vocabulary of the connecting sections in which the data of the list is now enclosed.

More precisely, the section vv 12–24 is constructed in the following way. In a nominal sentence first of all a city, a nation or an ethnic group is described as assisting Tyre in her commercial dealings. This relationship is expressed in the suffix (סחרתך "*your* buyer" v 12 and elsewhere). The possibilities for variation in the description of the helper are few. Alongside סחרת ("buyer") (vv 12, 16, 18)—concerning which one may ask whether it is intended to be understood as a feminine singular participle "your buyer," or in a neuter sense "buying" or whether it should be understood as analogous to the forms קהלת (Eccl 1:1), ספרת (Ezr 2:55) and פכרת הצביים (Ezr 2:57) as a kind of description of office—there occurs in v 15 סֹחֲרַת יָדֵךְ ("<merchants> at your side") (note b), which is expressed in personal terms in v 21 סחרי ידך ("buyers at your side"). The ידך ("at your side") gives full expression to the idea that the assistance given by the person named is dependent on Tyre, as well as to the

76 Schwarzenbach, *Terminologie,* 79.

point of view which is important for the arrangement of the list, namely, that they are "at Tyre's disposal." Alongside the root סחר ("to buy") there occurs also the root רכל ("to trade"). In this case the wording is usually in personal terms: רכליך ("your traders") (vv 13, 15, 17, 22, 24), mostly with the addition of a strengthening המה ("they") (vv 13, 17, 22, 24). The feminine רכלתך occurs in v 20.[77] In the three passages where סחרתך ("your buyer") occurs, the expression is augmented by מרב כל הון ("because of the abundance of wealth") (v 12), מרב מעשיך ("in view of the vast number of your products") (v 16) or by a combination of both phrases ברב מעשיך מרב כל הון ("in view of the vast number of your products because of the abundance of wealth") (v 18). This scheme of phraseology is broken in only two places, in vv 14 and 19 (note a). There, in place of the nominal sentence there occurs a designation of origin introduced by מן ("from"). This could be the original form of the list showing through. The process of its incorporation might then be reconstructed as follows. From a list which presented its data in the form "From the place X the goods Y," the redactor first of all removed the place names. Following the pattern of vv 8–11 of the (expanded) קינה ("lament"), he listed these places or their inhabitants in an independent nominal sentence as assistants to Tyre in her commercial dealings. In this process only in vv 15, 19 did elements of the original style of the list survive.

In a second independent verbal sentence reference is then made to the goods which are traded, and here the second element of the original list has been incorporated. Here the vocabulary of the "setting" of this rich abundance of names of goods is once more extremely poor. For the goods which are supplied through the trade helpers the word עזבון ("wares, merchandise") is used (vv 12, 14, 16, 19, 22). It means "That which one leaves behind." Rüger has collected a number of impressive references from Old Babylonian business letters which illuminate the sense of this *ezēbu* (עזב). For example VAB VI 147,18–20: "The female slave whom I let you have (*ša te-zi-ba*) I have sold for one mina of silver." According to this, Tyre has "deposited" (עזב) goods with those who assist her in her trade, as it were in her "branches," and these goods are then exchanged by the helpers for the products of the various countries. Other terms are used to vary עזבון, at first alternately. In vv 13, 17, 19 there occurs מערב ("merchandise"), which, with Gesenius-Buhl, Koehler-Baumgartner, Rüger and others, is to be derived from ערב "pledge, bind oneself with a pledge, barter" and is to be rendered as "goods for barter(ing)." Here too the reference is to goods originating from Tyre.

With both of these terms the verbal construction first of all runs as follows: בכסף ... נתנו עזבוניך ("for silver ... they handed over your wares") (v 12) and ... בנפש אדם נתנו מערבך ("for slaves ... they handed over your merchandise") (v 13). The trade or branch representatives of Tyre hand over the Tyrian goods deposited with them for the goods brought to them from their own lands, "for silver" (בכסף) or "for slaves" (בנפש אדם). An emendation of the text to כסף ... נתנו בעזבוניך ("they handed over silver ... for your wares") (so, e.g. Bertholet, Fohrer, Rüger), which, in the transition from v 12a to v 12b, makes the trade partner, instead of the helper (coworker), the subject of the statement, is not advisable. Some have clearly been led into such an emendation of the text by the continuation of the list, which reveals in what follows in its verbal second sentence a fairly marked variation and as a result betrays an obscure blurring of the modes of expression. While the pure wording of vv 12, 13 can still be observed in vv 17, 22, already in v 14 the slight dislocation shows the ב ("for") falling away before the description of the goods (to be replaced by an accusative?). In v 14 this is obviously connected with the preservation of the old wording of the list in the first half of the statement (see above).

V 15, probably with the intention of breaking the monotony of expression, changes over to the quite different wording השיבו אשכרך ("they brought ... as your due"). The noun אשכר (here "due") is to be found in the OT also in Ps 72:10: "The kings of Tarshish and the coasts 'bring tribute' (מנחה ישיבו), the kings of שבא and סבא 'bring a gift' (אשכר יקריבו)." אשכר, which is a loanword in Hebrew from Sumerian *ešgar* via Akkadian *iškāru,* cannot be understood in the present passage in the strict sense of "tribute," since that would imply a

77 On v 23 see note c.

political dependence (against Smend, Jahn; van den Born: *schatting*). Thus it is mostly taken in the looser sense of "payment" (Kraetzschmar, Herrmann, Bertholet, Ziegler, Fohrer). Since this meaning is not attested for the Akkadian *iškāru,* Rüger would prefer to interpret the word in closer association with meanings which are attested in Akkadian, namely as referring to finished products which have been made out of raw materials previously delivered and now "put back" (השיב) on the market. In any case, however, the direction of the statement has changed here in that in v 15b the ethnic group mentioned in v 15a no longer appears as trading helper but as trading partner.

This altered perspective has no doubt then been the cause of the obscurity of v 16 where, after the correct introduction of the list of goods with the ב*-pretii,* the final עזבון ("merchandise") is also introduced by ב (see note e). The same thing has happened in the final part of v 18, which has been misplaced after v 19 (v 19 notes a and b). On the other hand, the neutral wording of v 19b (במערבך היה "were exchanged for your merchandise") is quite correct. V 20 has remained in an abridged form with no concluding verbal element. Finally, in vv 21 and 24 (note e), which begin correctly, the noun clause of the first part of the sentence has been used, with slight variation, also as the conclusion of the second part.

Interpretation

In what follows the data of the trade helpers and the lists of goods have to be gone through in detail before, by way of conclusion, some remarks can be made as to the character, origin and age of the list which has been used in vv 12–24. For the detailed discussion of the places and goods listed here, reference must be made to Gesenius-Buhl, Koehler-Baumgartner, Rüger and the specialized literature cited there. The list contains twelve groups of places and goods.

■ **27:12** 1) Tarshish (תרשיש), whose name W. F. Albright (in the wake of Haupt) thought should be understood as an original appellative "smelting plant, refinery," is introduced in the OT alongside Elishah (see above on v 7) as a son of Javan (Gen 10:4; 1 Chr 1:7).[78] It is known, as Joh 1:3 can show, as a place far from Palestine, a place which is reached by ship (ships of Tarshish are long-distance ships 1 Kgs 10:22; 22:49 and elsewhere) and which obviously lies in precisely the opposite direction from Nineveh from which Jonah is fleeing. Contrary to the suggestion of Albright, who would locate it in Sardinia,[79] and to other suggestions for its localization (see also 𝔊 and 𝔙, note a), it is surely to be found in southern Spain near the mouth of Guadalquivir. After it first belonged to the Phoenician commercial empire (Jer 23:6) (in this connection it even appears in an inscription of Esarhaddon),[80] it also entered, from the seventh century onwards, into the horizon of the Greeks under the name Ταρτησσός. Already Pausanias once mentions in passing "Tartesian ore" and attests the place as a supplier of metal.[81] Jer 10:9 mentions "beaten silver from Tarshish." And Pliny says of Spain in general: "*Metallis plumbi ferri aeris argenti auri tota ferme Hispania scatet.*"[82]

■ **27:13** 2) In Javan (יון), who in Gen 10:2 (1 Chr 1:5) appears as a son of Japheth and in Gen 10:4 (1 Chr 1:7) as the father of Elishah and Tarshish, the name of the Ionians (Akkadian *jāmanu, jāwanu*) can be recognized. This became the collective name in the OT for the Greeks. This is evidence for the fact that the eastern Mediterranean world had its first contact with the Greeks via the Ionian colonies in Asia Minor. This explains why two groups from Asia Minor are connected with Javan. Tubal (תבל) is to be connected with Akkadian *tabal* and Greek Τιβαρηνοί; Meshech (משך), with Akkadian *musku* (*mušku*), Greek Μόσχοι. According to Gen 10:2 (1 Chr 1:5) both are considered, like Javan, to be sons of Japheth. Tubal has his settlements in Cilicia; Meshech, in Phrygia. At the time of the onslaught of the

78 W. F. Albright, "New Light on the Early History of Phoenican Colonization," *BASOR* 83 (1941): 21.

79 Albright (see preceding fn.), 17–22.

80 Borger, *Inschriften Asarhaddons,* 86: "all the kings who dwell in the midst of the sea, from Cyprus and Javan as far as Tarshish, threw themselves at my feet."

81 VI 19, 2.

82 On the metals see also 22:18.

Cimmerians, both were forced away northwards in the direction of the Black Sea. Both appear linked also in 32:26; 38:2f; 39:1. According to Herodotus, they both belong to the nineteenth satrapy of Darius I.[83] The mention of bronze vessels as trading goods can be connected with a report of Sargon II that he had taken as booty "bowls of the land of *tabal* with gold handles" and one of Asshurnasirpal II that he had taken as booty in *musku* "bronze vessels, oxen, sheep and wine."[84] The slave-trade would have been carried on in particular by the Greeks, as seems to be suggested by Joel 4:6.

■ **27:14** 3) Togarmah (בית תוגרמה), according to Gen 10:3 (1 Chr 1:6) a son of Gomer the brother of Javan, is mentioned again in 38:6. It corresponds to Hittite *tegarama* and Akkadian *til garimmu.* While it appears in Hittite texts as a country, it occurs with Sargon and Sennacherib as a city and lies east of Tubal.[85] Horse trading with Asia Minor is also recorded in 1 Kgs 10:28f; 2 Chr 1:16f. Relationships with neighboring *tabal* on the one hand and with Armenia on the other can be seen in the fact that Asshurbanipal speaks of a tribute of "large horses" from king Mugallu of *tabal* and that, on the other hand, Armenia is famed as the land of horses: "Sargon reports that horses there are so numerous that they could not all be broken in."[86]

■ **27:15** 4) The inhabitants of Rhodes (בני רדן, see note a) appear in Gen 10:4 (וורדנים should be read as in 1 Chr 1:7) along with Kittim (see v 6), Elishah (see v 7) and Tarshish as sons of Javan. The connections of the Phoenicians with Rhodes are mentioned by Diodorus and Athenaeus and are revealed in a different way by the pottery found in excavations in Syria and Palestine (Rüger, following Barrois).[87] Tyre cannot have obtained ivory and ebony-wood from Rhodes as raw materials found on the island itself, but at the most as finished products.

■ **27:16** 5) On Edom (note a) see above.[88] In the enumeration of the products coming from there, what is remarkable is the transition from the mention of a precious stone to the listing of textiles and the subsequent return to a reference to precious stones. ארגמן ("red purple") can scarcely, with Driver and Rüger, be connected with נפך ("garnets") and understood simply as the name of a color. It otherwise always describes colored material as can be seen from 𝔗, which first takes the words in a construct relationship (see note b). The understanding of נפך ("garnets") as the name of a precious stone is assured by Ezek 28:13; Ex 28:18; 39:11, the only other places where the word occurs in the OT. In v 7 (note d) ארגמן ("red purple") has been secondarily added after the blue purple from Cyprus. It is strange that Tyre, herself a center of the purple cloth industry, should import purple from Edom. בוץ ("linen") is otherwise attested in the OT only in Esther and Chronicles.[89] According to v 7, שש ברקמה ("brightly embroidered linen") was imported from Egypt.[90] Does Edom here feature as a middleman with regard to the materials mentioned here? ראמת ("corals" [?]) and כדכד ("rubies" [?]) cannot be interpreted with certainty (see note d). J. Wellhausen compares ראמת with the Arabic *ra'ma* "mussel."[91] Rüger further points to Ugaritic *rimt,* the meaning of which, however, is uncertain.

■ **27:17** 6) In the double expression "Judah and the land of Israel," ארץ ישראל ("land of Israel") refers in completely non-theological terms, as in the case also in 40:2 and 47:18 (see note a), to the territory ruled "by a state called Israel."[92] According to 40:2, Jerusalem is located within that territory; according to 47:18, the reference is to the whole of the territory west of the Jordan. On this basis, then, and with this wide concept of the name "Israel," is Judah too to be thought of as included in the ארץ ישראל ("land of Israel")? Or is the description to be taken more narrowly to refer only to the territory of the former northern kingdom? The Chronistic History, in the juxtaposition of 1 Chr 22:2; 2 Chr 2:16 on the one hand and of 2 Chr 30:25; 34:7 on the other, attests the juxtaposition of both possibilities and shows, at the same time, that the territory of the former northern kingdom

83 3, 94.
84 *ARAB* 2, 95; *ARAB* 1, 144.
85 According to Goetze, *Kleinasien,* 46: *gürün.*
86 *ARAB* 2, 297, 325, 352; Goetze, *Kleinasien,* 196.
87 Diodorus V, 58; Athenaeus VIII, 360.
88 Pp. 16f on 25:12–14.
89 On בוץ "Byssus," Akkadian *buṣu* (which, according to von Soden, *Akkadisches Handwörterbuch,* 143 can also describe "an artifical stone, enamel"), see Koehler, *Lichter,* 48–51, who takes the word to mean "linen" on the basis of Akkadian *pūṣu.*
90 On רקמה ("colored stuff") see 1, 340 on 16:10.
91 Wellhausen, *Reste,* 163.
92 L. Rost, *Israel,* 78.

of Israel, even after its fragmentation into a number of Assyrian provinces, could still be described in an archaizing fashion as ארץ ישראל ("land of Israel"). In view of the completely non-theological character of this list, one will be inclined to follow Rüger and regard the addition of Judah not as inclusive but as exclusive. ארץ ישראל ("land of Israel") and יהודה ("Judah") then, leaving aside the contemporary political situation, describe the territories of Judah and the northern kingdom of Israel.

Wheat, honey and oil are mentioned also in Dtn 8:8 and Jer 41:8 as products of land. If the word "*minnith*" (מנית), by which the wheat is more closely defined, is to be associated with the trans-Jordanian place מנית ("Minnith") in Ju 11:33 (which Josephus identifies with Μανιάθη in Ammonite territory),[93] then this seems to lead us out of the Israelite area again. In that case one will need to think of מנית ("minnith") not as a place of origin but as a description of quality, just as in 1 Kgs 22:49, in a somewhat different way, there is a reference to the ships of Tarshish that ply on the Red Sea. With regard to the obscure פנג ("*pannag*"), reference has already been made to Akkadian *akal punigu* (=*pannigu*), with which then Hittite *punniki* has to be associated, which describes something baked.[94] דבש (here "honey") could possibly also mean "grape honey." צרי ("mastic resin") is mentioned again in Gen 37:25; 43:11; Jer 8:22; 46:11; 51:8. According to Gen 37:25; Jer 8:22; 46:11, it is a product of Gilead. Thus either ארץ ישראל ("land of Israel") (contrary to 47:18) must be extended to include Gilead, or else we must again reckon with intermediate trade.

■ **27:18** 7) By "Damascus" is meant the territory of the former Aramaean state of Damascus. The wine of Helbon, even if it is not mentioned anywhere else in the OT, must have been particularly famous. According to VAB IV 9 Col. I, 22–28 and 19A Col. IV, 50–57, Nebuchadnezzar offers to Marduk "wine from the land of . . . ḫilbuni." Strabo and Athenaeus report that the Persians kings drank Halybonian wine, "of which Poseidonius says that it also grows in Damascus in Syria after the Persians planted the vines there."[95] The place is to be located at *ḥelbūn,* 18 kilometers north of Damascus. This same area is also indicated by the information given in the Genesis Apocryphon, which replaces the חובה ("Hobah") of Gen 14:15 by חלבון ("Helbon") (די שימא על שמאל דדמשק "which lies to the north of Damascus").[96] On the other hand, the meaning of צחר (here "from Zachar"), by which the wool imported from Damascus is more closely defined (doubtless again by means of a place name), can no longer be determined. Rüger wonders whether it might not be found in the desert plateau *eṣ-ṣaḥra* northwest of Damascus. This is certainly to be preferred to the suggestion of Driver to equate it with *ṣuḥār* in the Yemen.[97]

■ **27:19** 8) Usal (אוזל, see note a), listed in the Yahwistic table of nations in Gen 10:27 among the Arabian Joktanite clans, is usually equated with *ṣanʿa* in the Yemen. Iron is found in that region.[98] According to the term עשות ("worked") (note b) it was also processed at the place where it was mined. "Cinnamon and spices" (קדה וקנה, see note c) could be imports from Asia and Africa which were then transported along the "incense route" to Tyre. W. Baumgartner (in a letter) would prefer to equate Usal with I/Aṣalla (*i-zal-li*/*a, i-za-al-lu*), attested in cuneiform and lying between Haran and the Tigris. The name survives in Ἰζαλάς in the Greek period and in *jebel el-izal* (*ṭūr ʿabdīn*) in modern times. Etymology and geographical location are much more on the side of this equation than of that with *ṣanʿa.* But difficulties are created by the goods procured from there. In Assyrian and neo-Babylonian annals Isalla is known as a wine region.[99]

93 *Antiquities* V 7, 10; according to Alt, *Kleine Schriften,* 1. 159 n. 3.

94 Ebeling, Otten, *RLA* 3, 156.

95 Strabo XV, 735; Athenaeus I, 28.

96 See N. Avigad and Y. Yadin, *A Genesis Apocryphon* (Jerusalem: Magnes, 1956), plate XXII, line 10, and Dupont-Sommer, *Essene,* 292.

97 Driver, "Ezekiel," 156f.

98 Robert James Forbes, *Metallurgy in Antiquity; a Notebook for Archaelogists and Technologists* (Leiden: Brill, 1950), 385.

99 On this see Franz Heinrich Weissbach, "Izala," *PW* NB 1st series 10 (1919), 1390; *idem, AfO* 7 (1930/31): 43b; Emil Forrer, *Die Provinzeinteilung des assyrischen Reiches* (Leipzig: Hinrichs, 1920), 22f and elsewhere (Izalla); Ernst Honigmann, "Azalla," *RLA*

■ **27:20** 9) 27:20 mentions Dedan (דדן)—*el-'öla*; also בגדי חפש לרכבה ("stuff for saddle-cloths").[100]

■ **27:21** 10) In "Arabia and all the princes of Kedar" (ערב וכל נשיאי קדר) we have a very general reference to the territory of the Beduin of the Arabian-Syrian desert to the east of Syria-Palestine. In Jer 25:23f too, "all the kings of ערב ('Arabia') . . . who live in the desert" are placed alongside the inhabitants of the named oases. קדר ("Kedar"), which appears in P Gen 25:13 (1 Chr 1:29) as the name of an Ishmaelite group, is used in the OT without any fixed location to describe the wandering, semi-nomadic groups of the eastern desert (Is 42:11; 60:7; Jer 49:28f).[101] As was the case with the Kittim who lived far away on the other side of the sea (Jer 2:10), people had only very general ideas about them. Kedar and the Arabs, then are mentioned in Assyrian annals[102] and in the Aramaic dedicatory inscription of the fifth century from *tell el-mašūṭa*[103] and appear sometimes alone, sometimes alternately. Kedar alone occurs in Old South Arabian texts. Pliny mentions the Cedrei as a part of the Arabs.[104] Their wealth in cattle is attested not only in the OT (e.g., Is 60:7) but also in the Assyrian annals.[105]

■ **27:22** 11) Sheba (שבא; there occurs also סבא which represents originally an orthographic variant, but was then misunderstood as the name of an independent group) is reckoned by P Gen 10:7 (1 Chr 1:9), in the form סבא, along with Raamah (רעמה), as a son of the Hamite Cush. In the form שבא, still in Gen 10:7 (1 Chr 1:9), he becomes a son of Raamah. It is to be equated with the Old South Arabian kingdom of Sheba (capital *mārib*), whose history can be traced in inscriptional annals from the eighth to the first centuries B.C. The Yahwist (Gen 10:28, cf. 1 Chr 1:22) more correctly places it along with Usal among the Arabian Joktanite clans descended from Shem (see also Gen 25:3 [1 Chr 1:32] where it appears with Dedan as a son of Jokshan and grandson of Abraham and Keturah). The annals of Assyrian kings mention it from Tiglath-pileser III to Sennacherib. As a trading partner of Israel, it became famous as a result of the visit of the queen of Sheba to Solomon (1 Kgs 10:1ff). It appears also in Ezek 38:13 among the qualified trading groups. As its trading goods, gold is mentioned in Ps 72:15, incense with the term לבונה in Jer 6:20, and both together in Is 60:6. 1 Kgs 10:2 describes all three goods which the queen of Sheba brings with exactly the same terms as in Ezek 27:22: . . . בשמים וזהב ואבן יקרה ("balsam and gold . . . and precious stones").[106] רעמה (Raamah), linked with Sheba and attested in the OT only in the places already mentioned, also appears in Old South Arabian inscriptions. It refers to a place which is probably to be found near the ruin *uhdūd*, a little south of *wādi nejrān*.[107]

■ **27:23f** 12) The three names Haran (חרן), Canneh (כנה) and Eden (עדן) should not be assessed in the light of the gloss רכלי שבא (note c) and looked for in south Arabia.[108] Rather, by Haran (as in Gen 11:31f; 12:5; 27:43 and elsewhere) is meant the great crossroads (Akkadian *ḫarrānu* means "road") at *baliḫ* in upper Mesopotamia. Its modern name is *aski ḫarrān*.[109] Canneh is associated by Simons with the north-Syrian כלנה ("Calneh") (Am 6:2; Is 10:9), the capital of the Assyrian province of Kullani.[110] But a more likely equation is with *kannu'*, attested in late Assyrian private documents and to be located in Mesopotamian Aramaean territory, even if a precise location has not yet been achieved.[111] Finally, the name Eden is mentioned alongside Haran in 2 Kgs 19:12 (Is 37:12). It is probably the Aramaean state *bīt adini*, which was conquered by Shalmaneser III in 856 and made an Assyrian province.[112] From this North-

1, 325a, speaks of a "place in the Palmyrenian steppe-land between Jarki and Damascus."

100 See above pp. 17f on 25:13; see note a.

101 On the latter see Rudolph, *Jeremia*.

102 Borger, *Inschriften Asarhaddons,* 53; for Asshurbanipal *ANET* 298–300.

103 Published in Elizabeth Riefstahl, "Two Hairdressers of the Eleventh Dynasty," *JNES* 15 (1956): 16f.

104 V 12, 65.

105 See also the אלים כרים ועתודים ("Rams, lambs, and goats") of 39:18.

106 See also *Aristeas* 114.

107 See the full documentation in Rüger, *Tyrusorakel.*

108 So, for example, Dussaud, "Phéniciens au Négeb," 47; von Wissmann, "Geographische Grundlagen"; Fohrer.

109 See A. Mez, *Geschichte der Stadt Ḥarrān in Mesopotamien bis zum Einfall der Araber,* Unpub. Diss. (Strassburg, 1892).

110 Simons, *Geographical and Topographical Texts,* 457.

111 See Gesenius-Buhl; Koehler-Baumgartner; Rüger, *Tyrusorakel.*

112 See *RLA* 2, 33f.

Syrian Mesopotamian region are obtained, above all, elaborately embroidered materials and garments made from these (see notes a–c). In addition, reference is made to ropes, and in this respect one might wonder whether these were used for technical operations or also as parts of the clothing (headband, girdle).

The mention of "Assyria and the whole of Media," on the other hand (v 23 note d), must owe its origin to a later tendency towards an attempted completion of the list. It is, however, unable to destroy completely the fragmentary nature of the list. An attempt to salvage אשור at least and to refer it to the city of Asshur (as opposed to the country Assyria; so Rüger) is unlikely in view of the remarkably secondary impression given by the name and especially if the meaning attributed here to כלמד (here "the whole of Media") is correct.

■ **27:25** Finally, v 25 forms the bridge from the list in vv 12–24 back to the text of the קינה ("lament"). While the early part of the insertion was determined by the point of view of the commercial assistance provided by the ethnic groups cited in the list, the conclusion in v 25 is determined by the second focal point of the list, the enumeration of the goods. In an allusion to the beginning of the list in v 12, reference is made to the ships of Tarshish, which like caravans transport the goods to and fro. V 25b takes a further step along the road back to the text of the קינה ("lament") in that now the image of the stately ship Tyre is taken up again. The plurality of ships (v 25a) recedes. Tyre herself is the ship that is laden with all the merchandise. From the rhythmic point of view also, v 25b—which in its בלב ימים ("in the midst of the sea"), in an overhasty "resumption"[113] or better anticipation, is already borrowing from v 26 of the original קינה ("lament")—connects up again with the basic text.

■ **27:27** Then in v 27 there has occurred a further amplification, which looks back to the total entity formed out of the basic text plus the insertion. The closing, formula-like ביום מפלתך ("on the day of your fall") (26:18; cf 26:15; 31:16; 32:10), which in the context of the lively קינה-narrative would not have been necessary, reveals the purpose behind the attaching of the insertion. The latter has the aim of remedying the original reticence of the text, which left the actual process of the catastrophe unexpressed. All the goods (those first!) affected by the catastrophe and then the people affected are listed in full and their plunge into the sea is described. In the enumeration of the goods the vocabulary of the list is used (הון "wealth," עזבון "wares," מערב "merchandise"). The enumeration of the persons keeps partly to the expressions of the קינה ("lament"), but in its summary כל קהלך ("all your levy") goes beyond them.

■ **27:33** The lament of the eyewitnesses of the fall has also been subject to further exposition. It, too, is characterized by its reference to the vocabulary of the trade list. V 33 looks back once again to Tyre's rich trade, and here again the three terms used for the description of the goods in v 27a recur. The word בצאת ("when . . . came out") is strange. According to it, the goods leave the sea and enter the harbor. Essentially the word corresponds to the מבוא הים ("entrance to the sea") of v 3, which strictly speaking designates the place where one "comes into" the sea. By the present "coming out" of the goods from the sea, nations have become satisfied and kings rich in that they acquired their income in this way. So it was once before the fall. Accordingly, v 34b then comments on the present. Goods and people (again the order as in v 27) have come to grief.

■ **27:36** One may wonder whether the concluding v 36 is to be attributed to the redactor who inserted the list. From the linguistic point of view סחר ("to buy"), which in Ezekiel (apart from 38:13) occurs only in the list in vv 12–24 (five times), might suggest so. Over against the profound terror of the world round about, which has found expression in the original קינה ("lament"), here only a faint trace of mockery can be noticed. Just as Tyre, according to 26:2, rejoiced over the fall of her rival Jerusalem, so now Tyre's rivals rejoice over her fall. It must remain open whether the howling contains an element of magic reinforcement of the disaster which has befallen Tyre, a whistling for a storm such as can be established in religio-historical terms.[114] The conclusion in v 36b, however, which takes up 26:21 again, comes from the redactor who assembled chapters 26–28 as a trilogy of oracles against Tyre.[115]

113 Kuhl, "'Wiederaufnahme.'"
114 Lasch, "Pfeifen."
115 See above p. 22.

Setting

The literary critical analysis has shown that the קינה ("lament") in Ezekiel 27 has been subject to a reworking which is different in style and content and which can be separated from it. The form-critical examination has then further shown that the central part of this second stratum consists of a trade list, which, converted to some extent into a narrative, has been joined to the motif of the קינה ("lament") from a particular point of view (trade-helpers). The style of simple enumeration, however, could still be clearly grasped behind the narrative conversion.

Thus, finally, the question arises whether anything further can be said about the origins of this list. The list itself is purely a list of imports. In no sense does it have the aim of giving a full picture of Tyrian trade in all its comings and goings, but describes alone—and this, indeed, in the greatest detail—what Tyre purchases through her trading agents. On the other hand, what the deposited barter merchandise which Tyre offers consists of remains, however much one may regret this, totally obscure. This confirms internally that the list has in no sense been conceived primarily with an eye to the motif of the קינה ("lament"), but basically had its own purpose. The most likely is that this is a matter-of-fact enumeration stemming from a great commercial house or from a government agency.

Fohrer, on the basis of the observation that in the list there is no mention of Egypt as a trading partner, has suggested that the list is originally of Egyptian origin. In the enumeration in vv 9b, 12–21 "there is a great semicircle in the center of which lies Egypt." In vv 22–24, however, we find places on the great "incense route" which leads from South Arabia to Egypt and, on another branch, to Assyria and Media. In v 22a Fohrer reads "Khawilah, Sheba and Ra'imah" and seeks to locate the three places of v 23a in south Arabia.[116] According to Fohrer, the list is to be dated in the time of Amasis (Amoses III, 569–525) because at that time Egypt abandoned a plan to conquer Syria-Palestine and turned towards maritime trade.

It must, however, be seriously considered whether the admittedly remarkable fact that Egypt does not appear as one of Tyre's trading partners has not been evaluated rather one-sidely. In this list other trading partners are also missing, ones which lie closer to Tyre, such as Cyprus, which one would certainly expect after the explicit statements of v 6b. On the other hand, it is also remarkable how noticeably any overlapping of the names in the trade list with those in the קינה ("lament") is avoided. Thus, not only are the names of the other Phoenician cities missing; that would still be understandable in a list such as this which is dealing with foreign trade. Cyprus too is missing, although it is mentioned, with in fact a double expression, in v 6b as an important source of imports. And Egypt too is missing, although it is also mentioned in v 7 as a source of imports. This is scarcely chance, but reveals the coordination of the insertion with the basic text. Names mentioned earlier are not repeated. The conclusion made on the basis of the absence of Egypt and Cyprus from the original thus loses its compelling force.

The idea that behind the list there can be discerned a system of trade routes is then taken up by Rüger and considered in a fairly discriminating way in a careful comparison with the information available from inscriptions. Rüger finds behind the list a system of four or five trade routes.

1) In 27:(12)13–14(15) one can recognize the Persian royal route, of which Herodotus speaks;[117]

2) Vv 16–18 describe the great road along the main watershed of the west-Jordan mountains in its two branches: a) the west-Jordanian (v 17), b) the east-Jordanian דרך המלך ("the King's Highway") (Nu 20:17; 21:22);

3) Vv 19–22, the incense route from South Arabia;

4) V 23, the *ḥarrān šarri,* the road from Asshur to Carchemish.[118]

116 With von Wissmann, "Geographische Grundlagen," 98f, 103.

117 Herodotus 5, 53; see also Kurt Galling, "Von Naboned zu Darius. Studien zur chaldäischen und persischen Geschichte," *ZDPV* 70 (1954): 16.

118 On this see E. Dhorme, "Abraham dans le Cadre de l'Histoire" in *Recueil Édouard Dhorme; Études bibliques et orientales* (Paris: Imprimerie nationale, 1951), 205.

To the question of the age of the list Rüger replies by fixing it in the period after the Egyptian and Babylonian revolts against Xerxes in 484 and 482. At the time the economy of the two countries was so weakened that the absence of both Egypt and Babylon from among Tyre's trading partners could be explained on these grounds. According to Rüger, the list must have been composed by a Jew, since only thus can it be explained how it came into the hands of the redactor of Ezek 27. A participation by Jews in foreign trade is possible in that period.

Rüger's reasoning is not really convincing. If the author of the list really had trade routes in his mind, would one not expect a much more concise mention of specific places? Instead, place names interchange with names of countries (Judah, not Jerusalem; land of Israel) and with the designations of territories conceived often in very broad terms (Arabia and all the princes of Kedar). Also, if it really were trade routes that were being described, one would expect a properly ordered sequence of places (but see, on the other hand, vv 16–18 or vv 19–22). Certainly among the Arabian places, stations on the spice route ought to have been mentioned.

But the intention to visualize specific trade routes can nowhere be clearly perceived in the list. So with Simons, it is better to speak of geographical (trade) areas which are being enumerated here.[119] In vv 12–15 there is the region which, in P's table of nations in Gen 10, to which the beginning of the list is remarkably close, is combined under the name of Japhet; in vv 16–18 (19?) there is the region of Syria-Palestine with its most important trade partners; in (19?) 20–22 there is Arabia. The observation that שבא–רעמה ("Sheba-Raamah") in Gen 10:7 are assigned to Cush (Ham) raises the question whether vv 19–21 should be differentiated as a more closely related group from the more distant (Hamitic) Kush and Raamah. And finally, in vv 23f, there is the region of Mesopotamia. From the traditio-historical point of view, Ezek 27:12ff cannot be separated from Genesis 10. The problems raised by this relationship cannot be pursued further in this context.

As far as the dating of the list is concerned, the data for a positive decision are lacking. The way the expression ארץ ישראל ("land of Israel") is used in Chronicles prevents us from concluding that we have here a list from the period when the northern kingdom still existed. Rather, before 722 one would have expected alongside יהודה ("Judah"), a simple ישראל ("Israel"). The express mention of יהודה ("Judah") alongside ארץ ישראל ("land of Israel"), on the other hand, leads to the supposition that Judah exists as a political entity alongside the politically vague "land" of Israel. Thus one would rather not date the list from the period of the exile. The list could have reached the circles in which the book of Ezekiel was handed down through Tyrian exiles as a document from the period before 587. Every supposition here, however, remains very uncertain.

Aim

It may seem surprising if we are still inquiring about the significance of this bare list for the meaning of the chapter as a whole. And yet the fact cannot be overlooked that the redactor who inserted the section into the קינה ("lament") did not simply intend to enrich the picture of this city threatened by divine judgment with antiquarian notes, but wanted to add to that picture a further significant feature. To the beauty of the stately ship he adds the fully elaborated reference to the commercial wealth and the profusion of the worldwide relationships of the city, which by her trade "has satisfied many peoples and made kings rich" (v 33). Even this superior playing on the keyboard of trade relationships does not remove from wealthy Tyre the need to experience her "day of Yahweh" (the expression is used explicitly of Egypt in 30:3) as a day of judgment and, with all hands and with all her wealth (v 27), to come under the verdict of that day and to become contemptible in the eyes of those traders who were once her commercial assistants (v 36).

119 Simons, *Geographical and Topographical Texts,* 456f.

c. Against the Prince of Tyre

Bibliography

A. A. Bevan
"The King of Tyre in Ezekiel 28," *JTS* 4 (1903): 500–505.

G. A. Cooke
"The Paradise Story of Ezekiel 28," *Old Testament Essays* (London: Charles Griffin and Co., Ltd., 1927), 37–45.

Jan Dus
"Melek Ṣōr-Melqart? (Zur Interpretation von Ez 28:11–19)," *Archiv Orientální* 26 (1948): 179–185.

F. Charles Fensham
"Thunder-Stones in Ugaritic," *JNES* 18 (1959): 273f.

Theodore Gaster
"Ezekiel 28:17," *ET* 62 (1950/51): 124.

Hugo Gressman
Der Messias, FRLANT 26 (Göttingen, 1929), 166–168.

Hedwig Jahnow
Das hebräische Leichenlied im Rahmen der Völkerdictung, BZAW 36 (Giessen: Töpelmann, 1923), 221–228.

Cameron M. Mackay
"The King of Tyre," *CQR* 117 (1934): 239–258.

Julien Morgenstern
"The King-God among the Western Semites and the Meaning of Epiphanes," *VT* 10 (1960): 138–197, especially 152–155.

Marvin H. Pope
El in the Ugaritic Texts, VTSuppl 2 (Leiden: Brill, 1955), especially 97–102.

H. Quiring
"Die Edelsteine im Amtsschild des jüdischen Hohenpriesters und die Herkunft ihrer Namen," *Sudhoffs Archiv für Geschichte der Medizin und der Naturwissenschaften* 38 (1954): 193–213.

Theodorus Christiaan Vriezen
Onderzoek naar de paradijsvoorstelling bij de oude semietische volken (Wageningen: Veenman, 1937), especially 219–223.

Julien Weill
"Les mots תֻּפֶּיךָ וּנְקָבֶיךָ dans la complainte d'Ezéchiel sur le roi de Tyr (28:11–19)," *Revue des études juives* 42 (1901): 7–13.

Geo Widengren
The Ascension of the Apostle and the Heavenly Book: King and Savior III, UUÅ (Uppsala: Lundequists, 1950), especially 94–97.

Geo Widengren
"Early Hebrew Myths and their Interpretation" in *Myth, Ritual, and Kingship,* ed. S. H. Hooke (Oxford: Clarendon, 1958), 149–203, especially 165–169.

As has already been pointed out, the complex 28:1–19 is proved by the closing v 19b to be an independent unit alongside the units 26:1–21 and 27:1–36, which close with the same refrain. But, as is shown by the twofold occurrence of the formula for the receiving of God's word in vv 1 and 11, it again consists of the two self-contained units vv 1–10 and vv 11–19. The redactor who brought them together and concluded them with the refrain in v 19b wished them to be understood as a pair of oracles belonging together.

This association can be understood on the basis of the identity of the addressee who is, however, described in vv 2 and 12 with different titles. If here too the oracle of judgment (vv 1–10) is followed by a קינה ("lament") (vv 11–19), this recalls the sequence in the two independent units chapters 26 and 27, in each of which a small קינה follows an oracle of judgment (26:17f; 27:32-34). This sequence will be repeated on a larger scale in the arrangement of the oracles against Egypt (32:1ff, 17ff as a conclusion to chapters 29-31).

An examination of the contents shows that vv 11–19 contain an oracle which operates to an unusual degree with material of a mythical nature. Vv 1–10, on the other hand, in spite of v 2, produce a more strongly formulaic impression. This need not lead us, with Hölscher, to suggest that vv 1–10 are not genuine. But one can ask the question whether vv 1–10 have not perhaps been prefixed secondarily to the קינה ("lament") (vv 11–19) as its obvious justification. The different ways of addressing the recipient in vv 2 and 12 suggest that the two oracles were not composed at the same time. From the point of view of subject matter one could find a certain parallel to the juxtaposition of vv 1–10 and vv 11–19 in the juxtaposition of 21:1–5 and 21:6–12. There, however, the mysterious image (vv 1–5) which begins with a formula for the receiving of God's word is *followed* by the interpretation (vv 6–12) with a fresh formula for the receiving of God's word. Here, on the other hand, the figurative address in the form of a קינה ("lament") has been *preceded* by an oracle in the form of a judgment which speaks plainly of the prince of Tyre. That a קינה ("lament") can originally stand on its own is proved by chapters 27 and 32.

a A Judgment Oracle on the Prince of Tyre

Bibliography

See above p. 21 and p. 72.

28

1 [a]And the word of Yahweh came to me: 2/
Son of man[a], say to the Prince of Tyre:
Thus has [the Lord][b] Yahweh said: Because your heart has been presumptuous
and you have said: "I am a god[c], I sit on
the seat of the gods in the midst of the
sea," whereas you are a man and not a
god, but in your mind you have thought
that you were like a god[d]—
3 See[a], you are wiser than Daniel[b], nothing
secret can perplex you[c]; 4/ through your

28:1 1a 𝔖 again prefixes a superscription תוב על מלכא, see 25:1 note a.

2 2a 𝔊 ($\mathfrak{L}^{C}$) prefixes καὶ σύ to the address.

b אדני is lacking in 𝔊 $\mathfrak{L}^{C}$ $\mathfrak{K}^{Sa}$, see Appendix 1.

c 𝔗 tones down the blasphemous statement here and in v 9 with the expression דחלא אנא (even the אלהים of 𝔐 vv 2b, 6 is rendered by דחלא); the "seat of the gods" is rendered by מותב תקיפין; לא אל in vv 2b, 9, by לות בך צרוך. The presumptuous statements must not be uttered in their dreadful offensiveness in the course of reading in the context of worship.

d Literally, "You have made your heart like the heart of god."

3 3a 𝔐 הנה is surely to be retained in spite of 𝔊 μή, $\mathfrak{L}^{C}$ *numquid,* 𝔖 דלמא which could all suggest הלא.

b On the orthography דנאל, see 1,315 on 14:14.

c 𝔐 כל סתום לא עממוך is difficult, first of all from the point of view of form, on account of the singular subject and plural predicate, and secondly from the point of view of content, on account of the actual relationship of עמם to סתם. סתם means "to stop up" (2 Kgs 3:19, 25), "keep closed, secret" (Dan 8:26; 12:4, 9) and refers to the secrets and mysteries hidden from ordinary men and accessible only to superior wisdom (Solomon in 1 Kgs 10:1ff; Daniel according to Dan 2). עמם means "to rival" in Ezek 31:8; the hop'al in Lam 4:1 means "to be darkened." 𝔊 ($\mathfrak{L}^{C}$) *ἢ σοφοὶ οὐκ ἐπαίδευσάν σε τῇ ἐπιστήμῃ αὐτῶν* presupposes an additional בחכמתם, which must have fallen out by haplography before the following בחכמתך in v 4 (attested by 𝔊), and, instead of סתום seems to have read חכמים. With the odd *ἐπαίδευσαν* one can always compare the rendering of (על) העמים in 2 Chr 10:11. 𝔙 *secretum* and 𝔗 רז both, on the other hand, read the סתום of 𝔐. 𝔐 עממוך is rendered respectively by *absconditum est a te* and לא יתכסא מיניך. 𝔖 too או כסיתא חזית בחכימותך, which takes over unaltered the first word of v 4 (it is then missing in v 4) and renders 𝔐 עממוך very freely, points to the same sense. The solution of 𝔊 might at first seem impressive (so Toy, Herrmann, Fohrer). It is suspect, however, on account of the frequency of occurrence of the root חכם in vv 3–4a. כל סתום (altered by Cornill "with great reservations" to חרטמים) is to be retained. In the case of עמם, on the other hand, it might be considered whether "rival" might not also bear the variant "be equal, checkmate, make (helplessly) bewildered." Driver, "Linguistic Problems," 177, comes to this very sense via

wisdom and your insight you have gained wealth for yourself and have gathered gold and silver into your treasure-vaults; 5/ in the greatness of your wisdom you have increased your wealth by your trade. But your heart grew presumptuous through your wealth.][a]
6/ therefore thus has [the Lord][a] Yahweh said: [Because you have thought in your mind that you were like a god, 7/ therefore][a] see, I shall bring strangers against you, the most brutal nations, and they will draw their swords <against you> [against the beauty of your wisdom][b] and will desecrate your glory[c]. 8/ They will make you journey down into the pit, and you will die the death of the slain[a] in the midst of the sea. 9/ Will you then say, "I am a god" in the face of <your murderers>[a], whereas you are (then) a man and not a god in the hands of those who <pierce>[b] you? 10/ You will

Jewish Aramaic עמם "to be dark" (cf. Lam 4:1) and Arabic *ġamma* "to be covered, be kept secret." While he, on account of the כל סתום, suggests the singular עִמְמָךְ, it could also nevertheless be considered whether כל סתום, even from the sense point of view ("all hidden questions"), could not be construed as a plural.

5 5a Vv 3–5, which present a fairly extensive comment on the pride of Tyre and its cause, destroy the sentence structure—in which the יען-clause of v 2 is continued in the final clause with לכן in vv 6ff—in an intolerable way and are to be left out of the basic text as a secondary comment.

6 6a אדני is lacking in 𝔊 𝔏^C 𝔎^Sa, see Appendix 1.

7 7a The second יען–לכן of vv 6b/7a, which recapitulates the justification for the judgment oracle and further overloads the sentence, has become necessary as a result of the insertion in vv 3–5, which has caused the statements of v 2 to be forgotten. That this is secondary is clear from the linguistic point of view in that the לבך of v 2 is automatically harmonized with the לבבך of the insertion (v 5), while כלב is taken over unaltered from v 2, and in that the sign of the accusative (את) is added.

b 𝔐 על יפי חכמתך is a remarkable turn of phrase. On its possible sense see Sigmund Mowinckel, *Psalmenstudien. V. Segen und Fluch in Israels Kult und Psalmdichtung* (Kristiania: Dybwad, 1924), 26. The text of 𝔐 is attested by 𝔊 𝔏^C 𝔅 𝔗 𝔖; by 𝔊 𝔏^C, however, it is typically expanded to ἐπὶ σὲ καὶ τὸ κάλλος τῆς ἐπιστήμης σου. The original text is surely to be found in the עליך presupposed there. Only secondarily will this have been expanded by [ו]על יפי חכמתך. In 𝔐 the then apparently superfluous עליך has fallen out. The expansion is essentially connected with the expansion in vv 3–5, insofar as here too the additional reference to חכמה has occurred in a context which previously said nothing about wisdom. The remarkable expression יפי חכמתך can then be explained with reference to the יפעה of the parallel passage, with which the expansion is connected in terms both of sense and of verbal reminiscence (cf. 𝔐 of v 17 with its parallelism of יפיך and יפעתך [on this however see below p. 94 *ad loc.*]). Joüon, "Notes," 307, reads פרי in place of יפי.

c 𝔐 יפעה occurs again in v 17. According to Driver, "Ezekiel," 158, יפעה, on the basis of Arabic *jafaʿa* "to climb up, grow up" and *wafʿun* "high building," contains above all a reference to Tyre's commanding position. Her position on the rock becomes in the broader sense an image of her imposing position.

8 8a (חלל) ממותי occurs again only in Jer 16:4. On this cf. Arabic *mamāt*[un], always plural as in the following מותי in v 10.

9 9a 𝔐 הרגך should, on the basis of 𝔊 𝔖 𝔅, be read as הרגיך.

b 𝔐 מְחַלְלֶיךָ "who desecrate you" should be read, more correctly, with Var^G (𝔅 𝔗 𝔖) as מְחֹלְלֶיךָ. 𝔐

die the death[a] of the uncircumcised at the hands of strangers; for I have spoken, says [the Lord][b] Yahweh.

ביד מחלליך is unattested in 𝔊 𝔏C.
10 10a Plural of intensity, see v 8 note a.
b אדני is lacking in 𝔊 𝔏C 𝔎, see Appendix 1.

Form

The critical review of the text has shown that a fairly succinct basic text has been secondarily enriched and had its content expanded by the motif of the wisdom of the king of Tyre. The antecedent of the total oracle (vv 2–5) has been massively expanded and syntactically destroyed. The transition to the final clause, on the other hand, (vv 6f) had been formally overloaded by an ugly repetition which tries to recall the beginning of the antecedent.

The original oracle, after the removal of these additions, reveals a clear construction which has its close parallel in 26:1–5a.[1] The oracle begins with a reprimand which justifies (יען "because"-clause) the judgment oracle. This not only describes the character of the king of Tyre but, by quoting his words, lets him speak himself. The refutation of the king's empty assertion which follows immediately in v 2b is unique. It has no parallel in 26:1–5a and is therefore deleted by Cheminant, Fohrer (Bertholet: "perhaps . . . a secondary anticipation of vv 6, 9"). There then follows, however, introduced as in 26:3 by לכן ("therefore") and the messenger formula and a following הנני ("see, I . . ."), a judgment oracle which, in v 9 in the form of a question, refers back explicitly to the wording of the reprimand. As a third element, there is in addition the emphatic כי אני דברתי ("for I have spoken"). There is here no expansion by means of a reiteration of the pronouncement of judgment and a recognition formula such as has been added (secondarily) in 26:5b, 6 with the aim of making the unit into a proof-saying.

The addition in vv 3–5 is in the form of a simple description introduced by הנה ("see"), which takes no account of its insertion into a causal clause. From the point of view of content it goes back, in v 5b, to the statement of the basic text in v 2.

It is impossible to recognize a consistent metrical form. Cheminant's reconstruction of a consistent קינה ("lament")-rhythm, which extends C. Budde's supposition that at least in vv 9–10a an echo of the קינה ("lament")-meter of chapter 27 can be perceived,[2] succeeds only by means of repeated changes of word order. In reality there is a free alternating of three- and two-foot lines combined into units of five, six or eight lines.

Setting

It is impossible to discover any further clues as to the determination of the time and place of this undated oracle. However, since the king of Tyre is expected to come to a bad end, the most likely date is during the time while the city was still being besieged, i.e. before the period of the oracle in 29:17–20 (April 26, 571). In addition, it should be noted that the king of Tyre is depicted not with individual characteristics but with typical ones. No conclusions can therefore be made about the special features of his personality. There is nothing, therefore, against the passage's having been composed far off in exile.

Interpretation

■ **28:1-2** The narrative formula for the receiving of God's word is followed by the commision to the prophet to address the prince of Tyre.[3] the latter is described only here in Ezekiel as נגיד צר ("prince of Tyre"). נגיד ("prince") is found in the older texts always in connection with the charismatic (1 Sam 9:16; 10:1, and elsewhere) or dynastic (1Kgs 1:35) designation of the Israelite king and, with the exception of 2 Kgs 20:5 (the expression is missing in the parallel in Is 38:5), is always constructed with a following על ("over") (such as נגיד על עמי "prince over my people"). It is used absolutely in Is 55:4 with reference to David. In Jer 20:1 it appears as a more precise (intensifying?) definition of another title: פקיד נגיד "chief overseer" (see also Dan 9:25 משיח נגיד). Alongside the scant references in Psalms (once), Proverbs (twice), Job (twice) and Daniel (three times), there are 22 occurrences in the Chronistic History. They offer an unevenly spread picture from the point of view of language (construction with על; with ל e.g. הנגיד לבית יהודה, הנגיד לאהרון; and the construct relationship, נגיד

1 See also the proof-sayings in 25:1–5, 8–11, and elsewhere.

2 C. Budde, "Klagelied," 20.

3 See 1, 144–145; on "son of man" see 1, 131–132.

הבית, נגיד בית האלהים) and of content (king, temple supervisor, head of the family, superintendent of the temple treasures, superintendent of a section, leading tribe, commander of the fortifications, army leader, and the like). As far as the etymology of נגיד ("prince") is concerned, Alt thinks, on the basic of the older occurrences, of a primarily religious meaning for the title נגיד ("prince"): "The one designated (by Yahweh)."[4] The broad spread of meaning in later writings might, rather, point to a more broadly conceived beginning.[5] J. van der Ploeg compares Arabic *nağada* I *superavit, manifestus fuit;* IV *elatus fuit.*[6] According to this, נגיד ("prince") would be "L'homme éminent, le prince." In the present passage the title of מלך ("king") has to be avoided. The word is used of a foreign prince, outside the present passage, only in Dan 9:26 and Ps 76:13 where נגידים ("princes") is parallel to מלכי ארץ ("kings of the earth"). Alongside the more matter-of-fact title מלך ("king"), which is used in v 12, the word seems to have a more solemn ring.

The king of Tyre is addressed in respect of his presumptuous pride. That גבה לב ("presumptuousness of heart") is an abomination to Yahweh is known also to the wisdom literature, Prv 16:5. Alongside this there is the reference also to גבה עינים ("presumptuousness of eyes") (Ps 101:5) and גבה רוח ("presumptuousness of spirit") (Eccl 7:8). In Ezekiel the statement that Yahweh exalts the humble but humiliates the proud has already been heard in 17:22–24; 21:31.[7] In the case of this reproach one must not think that it is an attack on specific character traits of the then reigning king (Ithobaal?) of Tyre, of whose personality Ezekiel might have heard. Rather, in the person of the king, here it is the nature of the city of Tyre and her political attitude that is being described. Is the thought then chiefly of the military self-confidence of the island fortress which dares to defy Nebuchadnezzar? Or is the center of interest her commercial potential, by which she knows that she is a power far above all normal human powers? The insertion of vv 3–5 undertakes to be a bit more precise on this point. The basic text leaves all the details open and mentions only the basic attitude of the pride.[8]

By means of a bold quotation of the words of the king of Tyre this attitude is illustrated. The presumptuous assumption of divine dignity, which has a distant parallel in the statement of Pharaoh in 29:3, 9, is expressed in two parallel clauses, which are not however in the same metrical equilibrium. While the אל אני ("I am a god") abruptly affirms the equality with God of the human king of Tyre, a claim in which the Yahwist (Gen 3:5) recognizes man's basic falsehood and his original sin (see also note c), the second clause is somewhat more expansive and at the same time shows how such a blasphemous assertion could be made: "I sit on the seat of the gods in the midst of the sea." The daring island site of Tyre ought to make such a claim understandable.

It is remarkable, in the first instance, that 28:2,9 are the only passages in the book of Ezekiel which use the independent divine designation אל. In 10:5 אל שדי ("El Shaddai") (as a resumption of the simple שדי of 1:24) is also to be found. Now, it has become clear from the Ugaritic texts that אל is basically not an appellative, but the proper name of the chief god in the pantheon. Thus, O. Eissfeldt finds here (as in Is 14:13, also an utterance from the mouth of a heathen king) a reference to this chief god, to whose relationship with Yahweh no further thought is given. He translates, "El I am."[9] More cautiously, M. H. Pope speaks of the intentional ambiguity of the passage, which suggests in the first place that El is to be understood in its appellative sense ("I am *'ēl*"), but behind this, in the mouth of this heathen king, reveals also the allusion to the Ugaritic El.[10] It is necessary to underline even more strongly than Pope does that the text itself undoubtedly means אל to be taken in the first instance as an appellative. Only in this way is it possible to understand the ease with which, in the repetition (v 9), the אלהים ("gods") of the parallel in v 2 is taken over into the first clause and expressed as אלהים אני ("I am a god"). The choice of אל as a parallel to the immediately fol-

4 Albrecht Alt, "Die Staatenbildung der Israeliten in Palästina" in *Kleine Schriften zur Geschichte des Volkes Israel* 2 (München: Beck, 1953), 23.

5 See, e.g., Gesenius-Buhl: "Exalted."

6 J. van der Ploeg, "Les chefs du peuple d'Israël et leur titres," *RB* 57 (1950): 45–47.

7 See 1,446f. See also the addition in 19:11 (1,398) and chapter 31.

8 On the vocabulary of pride see Paul Humbert, "Démesure et chute dans l'Ancien Testament" in *maqqél shâqédh. La branche d'amandier. Hommage à Wilhelm Vischer* (Montpellier, 1960), 63–82.

9 Eissfeldt, "El and Yahweh," especially 29.

10 Pope, *El,* 98f.

lowing אלהים can of course be explained as due to the fact that the proper name Yahweh could scarcely be used in the mouth of a heathen king and that an attempt was being made to impart some local heathen color to the king's words. Alongside this, however, the further observation must not be underrated that אל may have been suggested by the antithesis אל ("god")-אדם ("man") (see below) which was coined much earlier than Ezekiel. In this way one avoids the difficulty, which was in any case not sufficiently appreciated by either Eissfeldt or Pope, that El is certainly attested as the head of the Ugaritic pantheon, but not as city god of Tyre, a position held by Baal Shamen or Melkart.[11]

The introductory clause of the quotation is, in addition, cast in the form of the majestic self-presentation, which in ancient Near Eastern royal inscriptions, certainly in connection with hymns to the gods, could become a hymn of self-praise.[12] Deutero-Isaiah shows how this formula then becomes a form of speech in which Yahweh, the creator of the world, reveals his own uniqueness (41:4; 42:6; 43:11; and elsewhere; in 45:22 in a justificatory clause כי אני אל "for I am God," as, too, in 46:9 זכרו . . . כי אנכי אל "remember . . . for I am God"). Thus from the point of view of form, the king of Tyre usurps the manner of speech which is appropriate only to the creator.

The second statement with which the king of Tyre justifies his claim to divinity uses the mythical concept of a particular dwelling place of the gods, which recurs in v 13 in the concrete idea of a divine garden and in v 14 with a reference to the mountain of the gods (cf. Is 14:13). Was there also the idea of an island seat of the gods "in the midst of sea"? With Pope one would suppose that in the בלב ימים ("in the midst of the sea") of v 2 the proud position of the island city of Tyre is responsible for the coloring of the language. That at the same time there is an allusion here to the place of exile of the Ugaritic El in the underworld is scarcely likely, at any rate in view of the unambiguous emphasis on boasting in v 2.[13] The world around Israel knows of a magnificent dwelling place of the gods, which is described (if one confines oneself to the sphere of mythology) as a mountain (Ps 48:2f) and as a garden (Gen 2:8ff).[14] The king of Tyre, who lives on an island in the midst of the sea, describes in his self-glorification the city in which he, the god, dwells, as this dwelling place of the gods. It is not advisable to think here of "the empty throne in the Melkart temple in Tyre . . . which the god-king was claiming for himself" (Fohrer).

What lies behind this presumptuous self-glorification on the part of the king of Tyre? Research in recent years has paid much attention to kingship in the world around Israel and to its understanding of itself as divine kingship.[15] To an increasing extent also, however, scholars have learned to differentiate the uniform "pattern" of a consistent average concept of kingship and to recognize the differences which exist in statements about the divinity of the king between, for example, Egypt and Babylon, not to mention Israel.[16] In the case of Ezekiel one need presuppose no very close study of these differentiations in the world around him. When, however, he gives expression in his oracles against foreign nations, in particular in the cases of the king of Tyre and the Pharaoh of Egypt, to such statements with which a human creature bursts into the domain of God, the domain from which he has nevertheless received his being, there is revealed there the genuine sense of the crossing of frontiers, which in the court theology of the surrounding world, especially the world surrounding Israel as influenced by Egypt, are a fixed pattern

11 Morgenstern, "King-God," 141f.

12 On this see Sigmund Mowinckel, "Die vorderasiatischen Königs- und Fürsteninschriften. Eine stilistische Studie" in *Eucharisterion für H. Gunkel,* FRLANT 19 (Göttingen, 1923), 278–322, especially 315f.

13 See further below on v 8.

14 On this see, e.g., Hermann Gunkel, *Genesis übersetzt und erklärt* (Göttingen: Vandenhoeck & Ruprecht, 1922).

15 See, e.g., S. H. Hooke, *Myth, Ritual, and Kingship* (Oxford: Clarendon, 1958); Ivan Engnell, *Studies in Divine Kingship in the Ancient Near East* (Uppsala: Almquist & Wiksell, 1943).

16 See, e.g., H. Frankfort, *Kingship and the Gods* (Chicago: University of Chicago Press, 1948): Jean de Fraine, *L'aspect religieux de la royauté israélite; l'institution monarchique dans l'Ancien Testament et dans les textes mésopotamiens,* Analecta biblica 3 (Rome: Pontifical Biblical Institute, 1954); Mowinckel, *He That Cometh.*

precisely in the ritual and myth of kingship.

Thus, out of this sense of the "immoderateness"[17] of the royal action and still within the reprimand, the genuine testimony of Israel is contrasted with the formulations of the surrounding nations. Since in 5:1f, e.g., it became quite clear that Ezekiel must have know the words of Isaiah, here too, in ואתה אדם ולא אל ("whereas you are a man and not a god") one can assume the echo of the pregnant expression used in Is 31:3 against the Egyptians: ומצרים אדם ולא אל ("the Egyptians are men and not God"). This is known to biblical faith, which does not allow the sharp contrast to be assailed even in the sphere of the most elevated human power. The bold arrogance of the creature, which is developed graphically in Is 14:13f in the plan of the titanic assault on heaven, is upbraided in Ezekiel in a more restrained way as a blasphemous condition of the heart, i.e. not only a frame of mind but also an attitude of will.[18]

■ **28:6f** The judgment speech, which is introduced by a new messenger formula, proclaims the divine response (לכן "therefore").[19] In stereotyped language (6:3; 26:7; 29:8, but also Jer 5:15 and elsewhere) Yahweh says in the first person that he will bring the avenger "as the commander-in-chief of foreign nations."[20] "Strangers" (זרים as in 7:21; 11:9; 28:10; 30:12; 31:12), characterized more closely as in 31:12 (30:11) by their brutality, will as sword-wielding warriors implement the divine vengeance. The threat against Egypt in 31:11, expressed in similar terms, makes it explicit that by the "brutal nations" are meant the troops of Nebuchadnezzar. The present statement should be understood in precisely the same way.

■ **28:8-10** When, however, the end is described, with an allusion to the motif of the journey to the underworld (cf. 26:20 and see below on 32:17-32), as a journey to the "pit" (שַׁחת in Ezekiel only otherwise in 19:4, 8, in the sense of a "trap"), one can scarcely combine this with the following בלב ימים ("in the midst of the sea") as a graphic presentation of the underworld in the depths of the sea and find there, with Pope, the Ugaritic idea of the dwelling place of the god El, banished in his old age by Baal, a dwelling place on the mountains of the underworld in direct proximity to the cosmic waters under the earth.[21] There is no thought here either of the particular god El. The fate in the underworld of the one who has fallen in the island fortress "in the midst of the sea" and who comes to lie with the uncircumcised corresponds to the fate of the forces of Pharaoh according to 32:17-21. In this judgment, however, the pitiful lie of the king who thought he was like a god and yet was a mortal creature is plainly revealed.

In the concluding formula, however, which characterizes this whole judgment as an event arising out of the word and command of Yahweh, it is underlined once again which "I" proves in the end to be the real moving force behind history.

■ **28:3-5** The oracle has then been subject to further expansion. As is clear from the ending in v 5a, the aim of this is to explain the origin of the "pride of heart." Instead of the two-fold לבך ("your heart") in v 2, v 5 uses the form לבבך ("your heart") (see also v 7 note a). Already general proverbial wisdom knows that the possessor of wisdom is exposed in a particular way to the danger of pride and self-glorification (thus Prv 3:7; 26:12 and subsequently Is 5:21; Jer 9:22 and the whole polemic of Ecclesiastes).[22] When, in addition, Daniel is cited as a particular representative of lofty wisdom, the question has been raised ever since the discovery of the Daniel of Ugaritic mythology, whether this is not another instance of the conscious employment of local coloring from the Canaanite cities on the Syrian coast.[23] To be sure, the Ugaritic texts known to us speak only of the just ruler Daniel, but (as the figure of Solomon in 1 Kgs 3 shows) right judgment and wisdom belong closely together. Thus there may also have been traditions about wisdom of that Daniel of old. In any event, the present mention of Daniel cannot be explained by an

17 See above Humbert, "Démesure."
18 See 1, 189 on 6:9.
19 See 1, 133 on 2:4.
20 Fredriksson, *Jahwe als Krieger,* 23f.
21 Pope, *El,* 98.
22 See the introduction to Ecclesiastes in Helmer Ringgren and Walther Zimmerli, *Sprüche, Prediger,* ATD 16, 1 (Göttingen: Vandenhoeck & Ruprecht, 1962).
23 So Pope, *El,* 99; Noth, "Noah"; see 1, 315 on 14:14.

appeal to the wise Daniel of the period of the exile in the book of Daniel.[24]

In Solomon it may further be seen how a man's wisdom becomes apparent in the way in which he can illumine what is hidden, not only in an involved legal case (1 Kgs 3:16ff) but equally in the less serious wisdom context of riddles (1 Kgs 10:1ff).[25] Since wisdom in the ancient Near East is never merely theoretical intellectual power, but the art of mastering life, it is quite in line with the understanding of wisdom that the wise man also acquires wealth and that the wise ruler knows how to increase his fortune of gold and silver in his treasure-vaults (see 1 Kings 10; Eccl 2:4ff).[26] In particular, the wisdom of the ruler of Tyre has shown itself in his widespread trading relationships, which brought wealth into his country. This has been fully illustrated by Ezekiel 27, but see also the case of Solomon in 1 Kgs 10:14–22.

While the thought in the basic text of vv 1–10 may have been that of the heathen king's self-deification and the consequent presumptuous confidence of the king of Tyre, the expansion in vv 3–5 extends the picture by means of the more firmly sketched and the psychologically more perceptive traits of clever aptitude and wordly success which can lead to pride. The expansion in v 7, however, adds the thought that wisdom is also "beauty," that means also a blessing through success, but that God in his judgment will also annihilate this "beautiful" wisdom.[27]

Aim

The address of this oracle, as opposed to the Tyre oracles of chapters 26f which envisage Tyre as a political entity, is towards a person whose accountability and threatened state are made plain through God's judgment. This shows that even when God calls nations to account and sits in judgment on the fate of nations, it is not a question of impersonal movements on a vast historical scale in which man is swept along and affected like a growing tree-trunk, but of personal accountability and a personal encounter in the judgment.

In the king Tyre and his words there are revealed the heights of human achievement and success. The basic oracle spoke of the temptation of raising the political head of a successful political body to the sphere of the divine. Where such happens, a two-fold consequence is revealed. God is no longer properly recognized in promise and command by this usurped divinity as the lord that he is. The other consequence follows hard on the heels of the first. Man—ordinary, individual, everyday man—is no longer treated by this usurped divinity as a brother but as a "creature."

The expansion added to the oracle (vv 3–5) affirms first of all, with a certain sincere admiration, that in the head of the body politic of Tyre in fact the gift of wisdom found itself united in a quite special power and fullness. At the same time, however, it affirms with secret horror how, out of this good gift, which to begin with led to rich success and the wonderful expansion of the potentiality of human life, there has grown the bitter fruit of pride that makes men forget the only lord and giver of all created things.

But over and against such pride God will restore his right and thereby reveal what the true reality is in which man, even a king of Tyre, lives. Whoever has arrogated importance to himself will be thrown down into the depths. Where the human representative of the greatest economic and political power claimed for himself divinity and thereby eternal life, he will learn the taste of death, the most abysmal dishonorable death. God will act thus, not apart, but in the midst of human history and will summon foreigners as the severe and merciless instruments which will prove his truth.

The whole, however, is not understood if it is evaluated simply as a historical drama and perhaps marveled at in horror. It is understood only when it is heard as proclamation from the mouth of God himself, and as his own words brought to men's hearing in history. "For I have spoken."

24 On the orthography of the name, which here too differs from that in the book of Daniel, see 1,315.

25 On this see the story of the wise Ahikar, Meissner, *Achikar*. See also the statement of the woman of Tekoa in 2 Sam 14:20.

26 Zimmerli, "Struktur."

27 Sigmund Mowinckel, *Psalmenstudien. V. Segen und Fluch in Israels Kult und Psalmdichtung* (Kristiania: Dybwad, 1924). See v 7 note b.

β The Lament over the King of Tyre

Bibliography

See above p. 21 and p. 72. In addition:

Albert Brock-Utne
Der Gottesgarten; eine vergleichende religionsgeschichtliche Studie (Oslo: Dybwad, 1936), especially 107–120.

28

11 **And the word of Yahweh came to me: 12/**
Son of man, raise a lament over the king
of Tyre and say to him: Thus has [the
Lord][a] Yahweh said[b]: You were a com-
pleted <signet>[c] [full of wisdom][d] [and]

28: 12a אדני is lacking in 𝔊, see Appendix 1.
12 b The whole messenger formula is missing in 𝔏[C] 𝔎.

c 𝔐 חוֹתֵם (תכנית) "sealing" would seem to point to a figure who goes about with the seal. See, e.g., Gressmann, *Messias,* 166: "keeper of the seal of the *Tabnit*" (emended text תבנית; why Gressmann would then like to see חוֹתֵם changed to חוֹתַם is not entirely clear). In another direction van den Born, following a suggestion of Widengren, *Ascension,* 26 note 18, would render "who kept that which had been sealed (die het welverzegelde bewaarde)." He is thinking of the superhuman power which in paradise seals and keeps the tablets of fate (*ṭup šīmāti*) (cf. *Enuma Eliš* 5, 121). The versions, however, point to a reading חוֹתָם or construct חוֹתַם. 𝔊 *ἀποσφράγισμα ὁμοιώσεως.* The expression *ἀποσφράγισμα* is attested in 𝔊 only otherwise in Jer 22:24 as a rendering of חוֹתָם. *ὁμοιώσεως* usually renders דמות (see e.g., 1:10; 10:22). In 8:10, however, in Θ 𝔊[O] it is the translation of תבנית, which is therefore presupposed by 𝔊 in this passage too. In 𝔖 אנת טבעא אנת דדמותא the same misunderstanding seems to obtain (in 𝔐 of 1 Chr 28:11 תבנית is rendered in 𝔖 by דמותא) as also in 𝔙 *signaculum similitudinis.* Is this also the case with the paraphrase of 𝔗 את דמי למנא דצורתא ("you resemble a container with a picture on it")? The תכנית of 𝔐 appears again in 43:10 in an uncertain textual context (see below). On תכן nip'al see e.g., 18:25, 29 "to be right"; pi'el Is 40:13 "to put right"; Is 40:12; Job 28:25 "to determine the measure"; qal Prv 16:27; 21:2; 24:12 "to test." Thus in תכנית there must lie the idea of correctness. On this basis Koehler-Baumgartner: "pattern." Driver, "Ezekiel," 158f, finds in it a particular suggestion of Akkadian *taknū, taknītu* "careful preparation, completion." On the other hand, חותם does not contain the idea of reproduction or stamping (Hermann "stamp of the image"; Ziegler "impression of the original"; Fohrer "copy of a model"). A more ambitious alteration of the text is not to be commended. Thus, e.g., Smith, 75, חתן תנית "bridegroom of Tanith"; Joüon, "Notes," 308, תמים תבונה: Cooke, חכם לתכלית "perfectly wise"; Cheminant, *prophéties,* תמים תבנית "perfect in form."

d 𝔐 מלא חכמה is not attested in 𝔊 𝔏[C] and belongs

of perfect beauty[e]. 13/ You were in Eden, the garden of God. Of precious stones of every kind was your garment[a] [sardin, topaz and moonstone (?), gold topaz, carnelian and jasper, lapis lazuli, garnet and emerald,][b] and of gold was <it

with the insertions in chapter 28, which in particular add the thought of the great wisdom of the king of Tyre (see v 5 note a and v 7 note b).

e 𝔊 (𝔏^{C}) makes it concrete *καὶ στέφανος κάλλους* (see also Lam 2:15). The copula in front of the following כליל will not have been part of the basic text. On 𝔊 see 1:4 note a. In 𝔐 it became necessary as a result of the insertion of the expansion (note d).

13 13a 𝔐 מְסֻכָּתֶךָ is, on the basis of 𝔙 *operimentum tuum,* mostly understood as "your covering" (Gesenius-Buhl, Koehler-Baumgartner), which leads to the thought of a precious garment (a pectoral?) similar to that of the high priest (see below note b). 𝔊 (𝔏^{C}) *ἐνδέδεσαι*, Σ *περιέφραξέ σε* (which is rendered by Jerome as *vinctum atque constrictum;* see Ziegler, *Ezechiel,* 64) and 𝔖 אתחזקת (Brockelmann, *Lexicon Syriacum: se cinxit*) all point in another direction. They derive מסכה from סכך in the sense of "to fence in, enclose." Gesenius-Buhl still reckons with a root סוך, from which מסכה without dagesh would be directly derived. Thus it would also be possible to think that what is being talked of here is, along the lines of v 14b*β*, the protective guarding of the celestial being, the description of which is now continued without the image of the seal, by means of shining precious stones (= stones of fire). In מסכה, however one may understand it, there can also already be a preparation, like a motto, for the following כרוב הסוכך (vv 14, 16).

b The nine names of the precious stones which are found in 𝔐 correspond, with minor rearrangements in sequence (in place of the sequence 1–6, 10–12 in Exodus, here the sequence is 1–2, 6, 10–12, 3–5), to the stones of the first two and the fourth rows of jewels on the high priest's breastplate in Ex 28:17–20. Since the enumeration of them destroys the parallelism between the two parts of 𝔐 (but see below notes c and d) כל אבן יקרה מסכתך // זהב מלאכת תפיך, it should be removed as a secondary insertion. In 𝔊 there are twelve jewel names. Between the sixth and the seventh there are also inserted there the precious metals gold and silver. The sequence in 𝔊 28:13 corresponds exactly to that in 𝔊 Ex 28:17–20. 𝔗 and 𝔙, like 𝔐, offer only nine names. Compared with Ex 28:17–20, 𝔙 lists them in the order 1–2, 6, 10–12, 5,4,3. In 𝔖 there are only eight names, of which only three have any correspondence in 𝔖 Ex 28:17–20. It follows from that that the translation of 𝔖 was made without any reference to the text of P in Ex 28, while the other versions pay heed to the parallelism. On the relationship of the insertion in 𝔊 and 𝔐, see further Cooke, *ad loc.*

Individually, the following remarks may be made about the names. For the arguments, reference may be made in particular to Quiring, "Edelsteine." 1) אדם contains in the name the reference to the red color of the stone. Gesenius-Buhl: carnelian or ruby; Koehler-Baumgartner: ruby or spind. The "sardin" (𝔊 σάρδιον) suggested by Quiring is a more transparent variety of the dark-red carnelian. Rubies did not appear in the Mediterranean world until the second half of the first millennium and are rarely found in the ancient world. The spind, which, like the ruby, comes from Indo-China and Ceylon (the spind also from India), did not reach the near East and the Mediterranean before the Ptolemaic period. 2) פטדה, according to Job 28:19, comes from Cush. Koehler, "Hebräische Vokabeln II," 168f, associates the name with Sanskrit *pīta* "yellow" and finds here the (olive-) chrysolite with the chemical formula $(MgFe_2) SiO_2$ which is found in great quantities at *jezīret zabarjad,* fifty five kilometers east of *rās benāsan* on the Egyptian coast of the Red Sea. According to Quiring, it is correct to adhere to the meaning "topaz" already found in 𝔊 τοπάζιον and 𝔅 *topazius.* Chrysolite in the ancient world (Agatharchides, Pliny) was regarded simply as a slightly less hard variety of the topaz. 3) יהלם, a *hapax legomenon,* is linguistically obscure. 𝔊 and 𝔅 *jaspis.* Quiring wonders whether it is not to be regarded as the milk-white, opalescent moonstone and to see in it a connection with the *ḫulālu*-stone, which in Amarna Letter 25 figures among the gifts of Tušratta to the Pharaoh. Amarna Letter 25, col. 2, 7 mentions at any rate "a new-moon crescent of beautiful *ḫulālu* stones." 4) תרשיש, see 1,129 on 1:16 (10:9). It occurs also in Song 5:14; Dtn 10:6. It is so called from its provenance from Spanish Tartessus (see above p. 65 on 27:12). Spain was noted above all for the supply of two gems, the black jet and the golden yellow "Spanish topaz" (gold topaz). According to Quiring, it is the latter which is meant here. 𝔊 ἄνθραξ; 𝔅 *chrysolithus.* 5) שהם is mentioned in Gen 2:12; Job 28:16; and elsewhere. The name is to be connected with Akkadian *sāmu* "dark red"; *sāmtu* in Akkadian also describes a precious stone. According to Koehler-Baumgartner, it is the carnelian. Carnelians were already found in the jewellery of Queen Šubad of Ur and in Mohenjodaro (third millennium), they formed part of the dowry of the daughter of Tušratta in the Amarna age (Amarna Letters 21f, 25) and have been found in profusion in the harbors of Alexandria (from the Ptolemaic period). 6) ישפה was already described in Akkadian as *jašpu* (or *ašpu*) with the name which has continued on into our "jasper." From the Sumerian period there exist cylinder seals of jasper. Pliny knows of the origin of the finest jasper in India. The purple-colored jasper is considered to be the finest variety. Nabonidus can actually describe the jasper as the "royal stone." 7) The name ספיר "sapphire" has also survived. What is meant here, as already in 1:26 (see 1,122), is the (blue) lapis lazuli, which is somewhat softer than the sapphire (which is difficult to polish) and which was the most valuable precious stone in the ancient near east between the fourth and the second millennia. 8) נפך was mentioned in 27:16

woven>[c], your . . .[d] and your . . .[e] were on you on the day when you were created

(see note b) as a commodity which reached Tyre via Edom. According to Koehler-Baumgartner, "turquoise" or "malachite"; according to Quiring, the garnet, more precisely the ruby-red garnet (almandine). In the excavations in Babylon garnets were found repeatedly, but not rubies (which are first found in the Ptolemaic period). 9) ברקת Akkadian *barraqtu,* Sanskrit *marakatam,* has entered German (via Greek *σμάραγδος*) as "Smaragd" (emerald). The word is connected with the root ברק "lightning" and with the Akkadian *barāqu* "to flash, shine." The emerald appeared late among precious stones. To the fourth and third millennia it was still unknown. It is found in Egypt in the second millennium, and by the first millennium it is among the gems of the first rank. A dark green beryl, it comes from India or from "emerald mountain" *jebel zabāra* in Nubia (east-northeast of Aswan) and from the *wādi sakēt* twenty-two kilometers to the southwest (see Karl Baedeker, *Ägypten und der Sûdan; Handbuch für Reisende* [Leipzig: K. Baedeker [8]1938], 392; idem, *Egypt and the Sûdân; Handbook for Travellers* [New York: C. Scribner's Sons, [7]1914], 377).

c Against the accentuation of 𝔐, וזהב is to be taken with what follows. 𝔊 (𝔏[C]) *καὶ χρυσίου ἐνέπλησας τοὺς θησαυρούς σου* and 𝔖 ודהבא מלית בית גזיך have read מלאכת as מלאת and have simply guessed the meaning of תפיך. 𝔙 *aurum opus decoris tui* tries to find a יפי behind תפיך (cf. v 12). 𝔗 משקען בדהב ("set in gold") connects זהב with what precedes it. Metrical reasons (see below on "Form") suggest closing the stichos with the מלאכת of 𝔐, in which then either a textually corrupt parallel to the מסכתך of v 13a is to be found or to which a suffix pointing to מסכתך must be added. For the above translation מלאכתה has been read.

d 𝔐 תפיך, with which the new stichos begins, remains completely obscure. A derivation from the well-known word תֹּף "tambourine, hand-drum" (see Σ *ἔργον τοῦ τυμπάνου σου*; cf. Fohrer "your hand-drum") is scarcely to be considered. It must be a technical term from the industrial arts, as must also be the case with the immediately following נקביך. G. R. Driver, "Uncertain Hebrew Words," *JTS* 45 (1944): 13f, suggests "earrings, pendant jewel." See also the conjecture פתוחיך (W. Frankenberg, "Review of H. Gunkel, *Genesis übersetzt und erklärt,*" *Göttingische gelehrte Anzeigen* 163 [1901]: 682; Jahnow, *Leichenlied*) "your engravings." Weill, "mots," as a modification of the assumption of Ewald, who found here the אורים and תמים of the high priest, prefers to think of the tablets of fate (Akkadian *ṭuppu*).

e 𝔐 ונקביך. 𝔊 (𝔏[C]) *καὶ τὰς ἀποθήκας σου ἐν σοί* guessed along the lines of the preceding. 𝔖 וכפא טבתא בית חמליך expands to the point of a complete parallel. 𝔙 *et foramina tua* and 'A *καὶ τρήσεων σου* attest 𝔐 without, however, helping towards a clear

[,they had been fixed][f]. 14/ <I associated you with>[a] <the> . . . guardian[b] cherub, on the [holy][c] mountain of God you were, in the midst of stones of fire. You

understanding. Again it must be a technical term. On the basis of the root נקב one would prefer to think of the engraving or cutting of a jewel. Thus Driver (note d), "plaques of metal hollowed so as to hold precious stones" or "pierced beads." On no account should we follow H. Schmidt, *Die Erzählung von Paradies und Sündenfall* (Tübingen: J. C. B. Mohr [Paul Siebeck], 1931), 41, and find here (כוננה. . .) ונקבתך and, on the basis of Gen 2, refer it to the creation of woman. Even the connection with the tunnels of a mine (W. F. Albright, "The Early Alphabetic Inscriptions from Sinai and Their Decipherment," *BASOR* 110 [1948]: 13f note 39: "and thy mines were established when thou wast created" (on this basis Koehler-Baumgartner) leads in a direction which lies far from the text.

f The concluding כוננו of 𝔐 is not attested by 𝔊 𝔏^{C} 𝔖 and is seen, from the metrical point of view also, to be a secondary expansion.

14 14a 𝔊 (𝔏^{C}) *μετὰ τοῦ χερουβ ἔθηκά σε* attests a substantially shorter text. Instead of אַתְּ, which as a second person feminine singular does not accord with the masculine continuation, אֶת (cf. 𝔖 עם) should be read. Instead of the equally puzzling *waw*-consecutive perfect ונתתיך, which, although connected with what follows by 𝔐's accentuation, jars intolerably with the following היית, the simple נתתיך should be read and taken with what precedes.

b 𝔐 ממשח הסוכך is unattested by 𝔊 (𝔏^{C}). 𝔙 *extentus et protegens* (cf. Σ *καταμετρημένος*) seems to understand the difficult ממשח on the basis of a root משח "to measure out" (Aramaic, Syriac), while 𝔖 דמשיח ומטל, with 𝔊^{O} Θ, *κεχρισμένου τοῦ κατασκηνοῦντος*, thinks of the usual משח "to anoint." 𝔗 paraphrases quite freely מרבא למלכו (את מלך). The word recalls the description of the temple cherubs over the ark: סככים על ארון ברית יהוה 1 Chr 28:18; cf. Ex 25:20; 37:9; 1 Kgs 8:7. ממשח is still unexplained. Widengren's explanation (*Ascension,* 96) of the מְ as an interrogative particle ("Oh, what an anointed") convinces as little as the understanding of סוכך as "shadower," which is supposed to be a reference to the idea that the deity protects him with his wings (Ps 17:8; 57:2; and elsewhere) or, in the form of the great tree, shades him with its branches (Hos 14:9; Ezek 31:2–9). See S. H. Hooke, *Myth, Ritual, and Kingship* (Oxford: Clarendon, 1958), 166. It is strange that כרוב is without the article. Since it recurs in v 16, it is not an easy decision simply to add the article. Does כרוב here have the quality of a proper name?

c Since 𝔐 קדש is metrically superfluous and also appears redundant alongside the simpler הר אלהים of v 16, it was doubtless not part of the original text, although it is well attested. It is to be considered as a secondary (but correct) theological interpretation (cf. Ehrlich, *Randglossen,* Hölscher).

d 𝔐 התהלכת is unattested in 𝔊 𝔏^{C}, but it may simply have been omitted because the preceding

walked[d] 15/ blameless [(were) you][a] on your way from the day when you were created—until wickedness[b] was found[c] in you. 16/ Through the abundance of your trade <you filled>[a] your heart with violence and sinned. Then I thrust you away from the mountain of God into uncleanness, and the guardian[b] cherub <drove you into destruction>[c] out of the midst of the stones of fire. 17/ Your heart became proud on account of your beauty, you destroyed your wisdom for the sake of your splendor[a]. I[b] have thrown you to the ground, I have given you into the hands of kings[c] so that they may look their fill at you. 18/ Through the abundance of <your guilt>[a] in[b] your unrighteous trade you have desecrated your sanctuaries. Thus I have made fire go out from the midst of you[c]; it destroyed you, and I have made you dust on the ground in the eyes of all who see you. 19/ All who know you among the nations have become terror-struck at you. You have become an object of terror, and you will be no more for ever.

words were taken with היית. But, with 𝔖, it is to be taken at the beginning of v 15. For this connection there is also the evidence of the remark of Origen (II 115) cited by Ziegler, *Ezechiel*, 223: *ὃς κατὰ τὸν ιεζεκιηλ περιεπάτησεν ἄμωμος ἐν πάσαις ταῖς ὁδοῖς αὐτοῦ ἕως εὑρέθη ἀνομία ἐν αὐτῷ* and V 74 *immaculatus ambulasse describitur.* Against Driver, "Ezekiel," 159, the idea of "proud strutting, swaggering" is not to be read into the statement.

15 15a With 𝔖 (𝔙?) the אתה, which became necessary only after the false division between vv 14 and 15, should be deleted. See also below on "Form."

b On the form עולתה see Gesenius-Kautzsch §90g.

c On the masculine verbal form alongside the feminine subject see Gesenius-Kautzsch §145o.

16 16a 𝔐 מלו (on the form see Rudolf Meyer, "Zur Sprache von 'Ain Feschcha," *ThLZ* 75 [1950]: 721f, against Bauer-Leander §54f, g) necessitates understanding the following תוכך in a plural sense: "all who are in you." But 𝔊 (𝔏[C]) *ἔπλησας* and 𝔖 מלית suggest an original reading מלאת (מלית?) whose ת has fallen out through haplography. See also the continuation with ותחטא.

b The original 𝔊 (see Wevers, "Septuaginta-Forschungen," 124, against Ziegler, "Papyrus 967," 85f) found here, on the evidence of 𝔊[967] *τὸ χερουβ τὸ σεχ* (𝔏[C] *cherubin sech*), a transcribed הסכ[ך], which on that basis should be retained.

c 𝔐 ואבדך is, according to Bauer-Leander §53m, to be understood as an abbreviation of ואאבדך. According to this, the king of Tyre, as in v 14, is himself addressed as a cherub. This is how 𝔐 takes it. 𝔊 *καὶ ἤγαγέ σε* (corresponding to a ויובילך?) makes the distinction here too and sees in the cherub the instrument of punishment. Thus ויאבדך should be read. וְאִבַּדְךָ, suggested by Cornill, Herrmann and others, would have to be understood as a more precise explanation of the *waw*-consecutive imperfect ואחללך by means of a *waw*-consecutive perfect.

17 17a T. Gaster, "Ezekiel 28:17," on the basis of Ugaritic parallels, would like to find in יפעה the idea of bold boasting ("through thine upstart conduct"). See already v 7.

b 𝔊 prefixes *διὰ πλῆθος ἁμαρτιῶν σου* here, a doublet of v 18.

c 𝔗 elucidates אזהרא "as a warning."

18 18a 𝔐 עוניך would be the only place in the book of Ezekiel with a masculine plural form of עון. The feminine plural form is found in 24:23; 36:31, 33; 43:10 (32:37 a textual error). Thus, with MSS Edd, the singular עונך should be read here.

b 𝔊 𝔙 𝔖 have the copula, but, in view of the clear variation of the prepositions (ב–מן) in the two expressions, this cannot correspond to the original text.

c 𝔊 𝔙 𝔗 𝔖 express vv 18b–19 in the future.

Form

In the present oracle the difficulties of interpretation have emerged already in the mere translation. But even the exact determination of its formal structure comes up against considerable difficulties, since it has obviously undergone a considerable amount of secondary retouching.

In its introduction (v 12a) the oracle is described as a קינה ("lament"). This classes it along with the great קינה ("lament")-poems about the kings of Israel (chapter 19) and the city of Tyre (chapter 27; see also 26:15–18) with their uneven five-stress rhythm.[1] As already in chapter 27 (following chapter 26) and in chapter 19 (following chapter 17),[2] so here too the lament follows directly after a divine judgment oracle. The same pattern will be repeated in chapter 32 (following chapter 29–31) and has also been seen in the secondarily expanded complex of chapter 26 in the linking of vv 15–18 to vv 1–14. In the exposition hitherto it must have struck the reader that in the book of Ezekiel at no other point have such purely metrical structures been so noticeable as in the case of these קינה ("lament")-forms. Obviously the early exilic period—and this is further confirmed by collections of קינה ("lament")-forms in Lamentations—cultivated this form of metrical poetry in particular. This can be understood (even from the internal situation) from the unique lament-situation which arose in Israel with the complete disintegration of her existence as a state.[3]

On the other hand, 28:11–19, in its present form and especially in the first half, gives in the first instance a metrically very obscure impression. It is certainly not to be overlooked that the five-stress rhythm is perfectly clear in a number of places, e.g. right at the beginning of the lament in v 12bβ, in its original form as attested by 𝔊. Vv 18b,19a are also clear. But in between there are verses of a quite irregular form. Thus, for example, C. Budde says of vv 12–17: "It would be pointless to trouble to indicate more than faint echoes of it (*sc.* of the קינה "lament"-meter)," and he believes that only in vv 18f can we see a return to the metrical structure.[4] In view, however, of the otherwise clear metrical stamp of these sections called קינה ("lament") in the book of Ezekiel, the supposition seems not entirely unjustified that this meter was originally also to be found in these intervening verses. This point can be made right at the outset against Widengren's analysis, which in any cast is limited to vv 12–14.[5]

If one tries by means of critical analysis to approach the original form of the oracle, then it ought to be clear first of all (from v 12bβ [note d]) that reference to the wisdom of the king of Tyre, which also in 28:1–10 stood out clearly as an addition, has been added here too only secondarily.[6] On this basis v 17aβ is suspect, a three-stess line which separates the three-stress line v 17aα from the two-stress line which follows at the beginning of v 17b. If it is deleted, the remainder of v 17 forms two five-stress lines.

It may further be noticed that the punishment, which is announced in the judgment oracle by Yahweh in the first person and which is spoken of in vv 17b and 18, is interrupted in v 18a by a clause which is metrically different (2+2+2) and which goes back to the invective. From the content point of view, this derives from the overall theme of the oracle, the beauty and pride of Tyre, to the extent that it speaks in the form of a historical exposition, of sin in commercial practice, the theme which also in the קינה ("lament") of Ezek 27 belonged to the interpretative additions (27:9b, 12–25, 27, 33, 34b). Thus, this exposition too should be removed from the basic text. Then, too, the corresponding statement in v 16a, whose keyword חמס ("violence") appears in secondary expansions in 7:11 (note a), 23; 8:17, will also be part of the secondary interpretation.[7] The word ותחטא ("and sinned"), which closes the half-verse, could, especially if it may be read with a double stress, form the complement to the solitary three-stress line v 15b, which is likewise preceded by a five-stress line in v 15a.

1 See 1,391f.
2 See 1,391.
3 See also the information given about Jeremiah in 2 Chr 35:25 and, on this, also Jer 7:29; 9:9, 16, 19 and, not least, Ezek 2:10.
4 In his fundamental examination of the קינה in C. Budde, "Klagelied," 20.
5 Widengren, *Ascension.*
6 See also Hölscher; Jahnow, *Leichenlied.*
7 See 1,212 (on 7:23); 1,244 (on 8:17), on this basis 12:19b is also suspect; Cooke, 324: "a gloss on v 15."

In the remaining v 16b, the combination of two three-stress lines with a closing two-stress one is difficult. The question arises whether one of the two three-stress lines has not been added secondarily. This is most easily assumed of the first of the two clauses, which anticipates the statement about Yahweh's personal intervention in punishment which is then made explicit in vv 17f, while in v 16 originally only the expulsion by the cherub can have been referred to. Finally, the 2+2 line of v 19b is well known to us from 26:21; 27:36. It forms the editorial refrain-like conclusion.

While in the second half of the unit the קינה ("lament")-structure can still be brought out with a fair degree of certainty, the first half, not least also on account of the obscurity with regard to the contents of a number of expressions, affords much greater difficulties. Here, first of all, the original text of v 12bβ (notes c,d) contains a clear five-stress line. In v 13 the nine names of the precious stones are to be deleted as a secondary illustration (note b). At the end of v 13 the כוננו "they had been fixed" was suspect (note f). The remaining ביום הבראך ("on the day when you were created") forms a good concluding two-stress line which, moreover, recurs with slight variation in the מיום הבראך ("from the day when you were created") of v 15a. The three-stress line corresponding to this can only be achieved if (against BH³) תפיך (see note d) is connected with the following ונקביך (see note e). There then remains in 𝔐 a two-stress line וזהב מלאכת ("and of gold was it woven"), which joins up, across the gap caused by the deletion of the nine names of the precious stones, with כל אבן יקרה מסכתך ("of precious stones of every kind was your garment") to form a five-stress line. This association is wholeheartedly supported from the content point of view by the parallelism of "precious stones of every kind"//"gold." However, מלאכת must then be read with a suffix referring to מסכתך (see v 13 note c). That, finally, the passage at the beginning of the verse, בעדן גן אלהים היית ("You were in Eden, the garden of God"), represents a surprising anticipation of v 14, where the transportation to the proximity of the כרוב ("cherub") on the mountain of God is first mentioned, has already been correctly noted by Hölscher. The clause can be explained as intending to introduce more intelligibly the description of the mysterious being right at the beginning by mentioning his dwelling place which, as distinct from v 14 (15), is described as גן עדן ("the garden of Eden").

V 14 also affords difficulties. The concluding התהלכת ("you walked"), in the case of which it is not entirely clear whether it is attested by 𝔊, 𝔏ᶜ, must on other grounds (see note d) be taken with v 15. If then נתתיך ("I associated you . . .") is taken with v 14a (note a), then the expected five-stress line remains in v 14b. But what are we to make of v 14a? Since the obscure ממשח, in contrast to the second attribute of the כרוב ("cherub"), does not recur in v 16 and is, moreover, not attested by 𝔊, 𝔖 (not at any rate together with הסוכך "guardian," which however is assured as an original element by the 𝔊 of v 16, see v 16 note b), one is inclined to see in it an additional, secondary remark. There then remains in v 14a, including נתתיך ("I associated you . . ."), a simple three-stress line. Has the two-stress line belonging to it been lost? Or must the three-stress line בהר אלהים היית ("on the mountains of God you were"), which otherwise conflicts with the beginning of v 14, be deleted (analogously with the beginning of v 16b) as a secondary interpretation? One hesitates, however, to dispense with every reference to the mountain of God.[8]

The analysis so far has led to a unit of thirteen five-stress lines which lament the fate of the king of Tyre. It may further be asked whether the lament shows a more developed structure in distichs (as in chapter 27) or strophes (see chapter 19). Since at the beginning two groups, each of three five-stress lines, are each rounded off by an almost identical two-stress lines (ביום/מיום הבראך "on the day/from the day when you were created"), one is inclined initially to arrange each of these groups of three five-stress lines into a strophe. The third group of three five-stress lines describes the sin and the fall of the king of Tyre, while the last four five-stress lines, exactly like the closing distichs of chapter 27, have to do with the effect on the surrounding nations who are witnessess of this judgment. The question arises whether in this last group, too, originally a strophe of three five-stress lines was not intended. In fact, in this final section what is said in v 18b is noticeably foreign to the context.

8 On the deletion of אתה in v 15 see note a.

It describes once again the process of judgment, and this strikes one as being a strange repetition after the two five-stress lines of v 17, which had already made the transition to the subject matter of vv 18bβ/19a. In addition, it makes this description in a way which is noticeably different from the earlier one (expulsion from the mountain of the gods, fall to the earth). From the point of view of content, this is a resumption of what had to be described in the expansion (vv 10–14) of the קינה ("lament") in chapter 19 as an addition.[9] Here, too, in v 18bα we must have to do with a secondary expansion. Accordingly, in the basic text here too, in the fourth strophe, three five-stress lines have been grouped together. Thus, the basic text of the קינה ("lament"), on the basis of this analysis, runs as follows:

You were a completed signet of perfect beauty.
Of precious stones of every kind was your garment,
and of gold was it woven.
Your . . . and your . . . were on you on the day when
you were created.

I associated you with the guardian cherub ....(?)
On the mountain of God you were, in the midst of
stones of fire.
You walked blameless on your way from the day when
you were created.

Until wickedness was found in you and you sinned.
Then the guardian cherub drove you into destruction
out of the midst of the stones of fire.
Your heart became proud on account of your beauty,
I have thrown you to the ground.

I have given you into the hands of kings so that they
may look their fill at you,
and I have made you dust on the ground in the eyes of
all who see you.
All who know you among the nations have become
terror-struck at you.

While the outward form of the קינה ("lament") (assuming the above reconstruction to be correct) is of an unusual conciseness with regard to its structure, if one looks at its internal structure, then one must admit with Jahnow that what we have here is a disintegration of the original genre. Admittedly the motif of the contrast between the past and the present can still be recognized in the structure of the whole, but the figurative language has here surpassed that of chapter 19 and 27, reaching the realm of mythical language, and has moved further away still from the straightforward lament over a human death. Above all, however, the קינה ("lament") here is now put entirely in the mouth of Yahweh, who speaks in the first person of the distinction bestowed and of the punishment subsequently inflicted. In this respect the קינה ("lament") comes very close to the prophetic judgment-oracle, from which it is distinguished only in that it turns towards the past and describes in the style of a lament a judgment which had already happened instead of proclaiming a judgment which is still to come.

Setting

One hesitates to determine the point of origin of this oracle. Even if one can scarcely share Morgenstern's assessment in the period between 490 and 480,[10] the question arises, "Does the fall of the city of Tyre and the surrender of her king lie behind the oracle?"[11] Is, in the end, the king of Tyre mentioned in Nebuchadnezzar's Court Calendar Jehoiachin's companion in misfortune?[12] Does Ezekiel already have this event in mind? Or is it, here too, a case of prophetic anticipation of the judgment threatened at the time of the siege of the city? The analogy of the קינה ("lament") in Ezekiel 19 would suggest the first assumption, while a comparison with Ezekiel 27 would suggest the second. Since, however, it becomes clear in 29:17–21 that Ezekiel assessed the end of the siege of Tyre with an essentially more subdued judgment, the second assumption is the more likely. In 28:11–19 Ezekiel is still awaiting the fall of the city of Tyre, which is here included in the figure of her king, in the large dimension of a total deprivation of power.

Interpretation

■ **28:11–12** In a new formula for the receiving of God's word, the prophet is addressed and commanded to raise a lament over the king of Tyre and to address him, under the rubric of the messenger formula, with the word of Yahweh.[13] This corresponds to the introduction to the קינה ("lament") of Ezekiel 27. However, in the fact that the קינה ("lament") itself is then in the form of a speech of Yaweh, 28:12–19 goes a stage further than

9 See 19:14 note b and on that 1, 398.
10 Morgenstern, "Jerusalem" 152.
11 Messel, 101.
12 See above p. 23.
13 See 1, 144f; on "son of man" see 1, 131f; see 1, 133.

chapter 27, and this reveals (as has already been mentioned) the disintegration of the original form of the genre.

It is again remarkable that the ruler of Tyre is here described with the title of king. V 2 had called him נגיד ("prince"). Steinmann, taking up the suggestions of Mackay, has asked whether what we have to do with here is not, in the sense of the later apocalypses, the "angel of Tyre," her heavenly protector, which Steinmann, in a remarkably modern fashion, equates with "what we would today call 'her soul' (*son âme*)."[14] J. Dus would prefer to take as his point of departure the older "theology of the gods of the nations" as this is discernible in Dtn 32:8 (𝔊) and Ps 82. According to this, a judgment oracle over the earthly king who considers himself divine (vv 1–10) is expanded in vv 11–19 by means of a similar oracle over his מלך ("king"), namely Melkart, the "king of the city." Since the latter misuses his divine wisdom, he is, like the gods of Ps 82, called to judgment by Yahweh as an "official responsible to him." At the basis of this concept lies the equation, which is also made by other commentators, of the "king of Tyre" with the cherub (on the basis of 𝔐 of v 14).

In the above analysis of the text this has proved to be untenable, but above all the use of the title "king" elsewhere in the book of Ezekiel disallows this theory. The מלך בבל ("king of Babylon") (17:12; 19:9; and elsewhere), the מלך מצרים ("king of Egypt") (29:2f; and elsewhere), the מלכי ארץ ("king of the earth") (27:33 cf. v 35) are always the earthly rulers of these nations and countries. There is, in addition, the parallel layout of the oracles against Tyre and Egypt. In both, there appears alongside the address to the city or nation the address to the ruler described as מלך ("king"). Can the Tyre oracle in 28:11–19 be so isolated from its context that here, all of a sudden, a different understanding of מלך ("king") is to be accepted? There would have to be much stronger evidence in the text itself in order to justify the application of 28:11–19 to Melkart. The use of mythical material for the description of the ruler is found also in the oracles against Egypt (see, e.g. chap. 31). The juxtaposition of נגיד ("prince") and מלך ("king") in vv 2 and 12 is to be explained, therefore, not on the basis of a differentiation between the human and divine ruler of Tyre within the framework of the consciously constructed composition of the total complex of 28:1–19, but quite simply on the basis of the separate origins of the two oracles, the first of which has been secondarily prefixed to the second with a variation in the title applied to the ruler.[15]

The קינה ("lament") which follows is clear as far as the understanding of the whole is concerned, but it affords, for more detailed exposition, difficulties which have not so far been resolved. In the first instance, with the use of material which is mythical in origin, there is reference to a creature who lived in a magnificent place on the mountain of the gods. As a result of his sin he is expelled from this place. In this a part is played by the figure of a cherub, who has to do with the expulsion from this place of the creature who is being addressed. The identification of the creature addressed with this cherub, which is attempted by 𝔐, cannot be maintained on the basis of the critically emended text. In any case one would have expected this equation right at the beginning of the address in v 12.

It can scarcely be overlooked that from a traditio-historical point of view this account has close connections with Genesis 2f, the Yahwistic paradise narrative, and that it reveals an independent form of the tradition which is at the basis of that narrative. Genesis 3 tells of the expulsion of the first human pair from the divine garden and of the shutting off of this garden by the cherubs posted at its entrance. Instead of a human couple, Ezekiel 28 speaks only of a single figure, and this preserves the older form of the tradition. That Ezekiel 28 is also concerned with primeval man is strengthened by the two-fold emphatic reference to the creation of this figure (vv 13, 15). Only here in an original Ezekiel oracle

14 Steinmann, *Le prophète Ézéchiel,* 147.

15 On such a variation see the similar juxtaposition of מלך ("king") and נשיא ("prince") for the members of the Davidic dynasty (1:2; 17:16; 43:7–9 alongside 12:10, 12; 19:1) and even for the coming David (32:22, 24 alongside 34:24; 37:25; on this see the exposition).

does the verb ברא ("to create") occur, the *terminus technicus* of the creation story in P.[16] Humbert has shown that it is likely that ברא ("to create") was a technical term of specifically cultic language, one which did not find its way into profane every-day speech, and that it belonged to the specific vocabulary of a Yahwistic cosmogonic myth which was part of Israel's pre-exilic liturgy.[17] It is, as a matter of fact, not used in J's primeval history with which the tradition of Ezekiel 28 has its associations. With its element of the "mountain of the gods" and of this "warding off" (סוכך) cherub, this tradition of the expulsion of primeval man from the seat of the god points clearly back to pre-Israelite contexts. Yet, it has not so far been possible to indicate any closer correspondence to it. In its present form too, which clearly distinguishes the creature from the creator, it has clear Yahwistic overtones. The understanding of הבראך ("you were created") in vv 13, 15 as "self-creation" by Morgenstern is, in view of the findings of Böhl and Humbert on ברא ("to create"), a serious misunderstanding.[18]

In Ezekiel 28, however, a second series of statements is connected with this basic material. The king of Tyre is compared to an exquisite signet. The context makes it clear that this comparison has been chosen in order to depict, as in the קינה ("lament") of chapter 27 (though with a quite different image), the extraordinary beauty of Tyre in her royal representative. That the image of the ornament should offer itself particularly for this purpose is immediately understandable in view of the subject matter. In the light of traditio-historical observation, however, the question arises: "Is the comparison with the precious signet already an element of the tradition about primeval man? Or has it, in its application to Tyre, been freely added by Ezekiel himself in order to illustrate Tyre's particular beauty?" The two-fold reference to the place of habitation being "in the midst of stones of fire" and to the expulsion being "out of the midst of stones of fire" makes one suspect that elements have been taken up here which were already woven into the tradition of primeval man, who lives in the place of the creatures of the light.[19]

In this marked use of mythical colors, which has its counterpart in chapter 31, one can again recognize the aim of making non-Israelite local coloring noticeable precisely in the address to the heathen ruler. On the other hand, whether one can actually say that here Ezekiel presents "the fragment of a Tyrian hymn" (van den Born) is questionable in view of the unmistakable Yahwehization of the material.

The first strophe of the קינה ("lament") begins with a direct address to the king of Tyre in the form of a figurative identification. The form recalls the introduction to the great קינה ("lament") about the stately ship Tyre (27:3 and note f) (cf. also the קינה "lament" in 32:2b). The comparison of a ruler with a signet(-ring) is found also in Jer 22:24 and Hag 2:23, where Jehoiachin and Zerubbabel are described by means of this image. There, however, the close connection between the signet ring and its owner is used as an image for the ties between the Davidic king and his God and expounded in Jeremiah in the sense that in the hour of judgment not even these ties will survive. In Ezekiel 28, however, the image is completely detached from the thought of the wearer of the ring and is used as an illustration of the beauty of the king of Tyre, of the glorious past which is now followed by the tragic present. The second half of the introductory five-stress line in v 12bβ corresponds exactly to the addition in 27:3bβ.[20]

Unfortunately, a full understanding of the statement is closed to us, since the traditio-historical background of the reference to the "signet" in the present passage is not elucidated. Is this a description of primeval man which is already to be found in the mythical tradition? Does the connection with the אבני אש ("stones of fire") (vv 14,16) point to an astral background? Is there in the reference to the "signet" also the thought of that which is definitive, as there is in a quite different context in the description of Muhammad as the "seal of the prophets" (*ḫātamu-*

16 In 21:35 it occurred in a secondary addition; the pi'el occurred with a different meaning in 23:47, likewise a secondary section of the text.
17 See 1, 449f on 21:35; Humbert, "bârâ," 419.
18 Morgenstern, "King-God," 154.
19 See the detailed exposition below.
20 On תכנית, which cannot be defined with complete certainty, see note c.

nnabiyyīna, Surah 33:40)? Did the process of sealing, which is emphasized even more strongly in 𝔐 (with its participial vocalization) as the offical function of the person addressed, have its own significance in the present mythical tradition, or was "signet" already a figurative word there too?

■ **28:13** In the continuation, v 13, the specific idea of the "signet" then fades completely into the background (otherwise than in 27:3ff). Here the reference is more to the mythical figure who is addressed in this image and with whom the king of Tyre is compared. Its beauty is described by means of further adornments, the more precise significance of which unfortunately also remains obscure. Reference seems to be made to a splendid "garment" (מסכתך) woven out of gold thread and set with precious stones, and of other splendid adornments (תפיך ונקביך). It is possible that the thought is of specifically royal or priestly ornaments.[21] The use of the verb ברא ("to create") brings the creature described here into the context of a statement about creation. This creature, with which the king of Tyre is compared, has about it the dignity and splendor of the primeval.

The strophe has then been several times enriched and expanded. Thus, to the beauty there has been added a reference to the wisdom of the king of Tyre (see v 12 note d). The reference to the precious stones has been enriched by a borrowing from the list in Ex 28:17–20.[22] Widengren, who finds here a description of the breastplate of the king of Tyre, would expand the list to twelve on the basis of Ex 28. Finally, already in the first strophe the reference has been inserted to the effect that the person addressed as the magnificent signet has been set in close proximity to God. Instead of the mountain of God (vv 14, 16), however, there is mentioned here "Eden, the garden of God." The image of the garden of trees corresponds to Gen 2:8f. Gen 2:15; 3:23f speak of the גן עדן ("garden of Eden") (see also 2:10), while the גן בעדן ("garden in Eden") of 2:8 refers more widely to a country called Eden.[23] The name "Eden" was used in the trade list in 27:23 for a place in Upper Mesopotamia. "The trees of Eden" will recur in 31:9, 16, 18 in the context of a secondary elaboration of the text, in 31:9 with the more precise definition that they stood "in the garden of God." And in 36:35 "the garden of Eden," in a quotation of the words of the astonished nations round about, is an image for this name for paradise with a reference to the "loveliness" (עדן) of the place.[24]

■ **28:14** In the basic text, it is not until the second strophe that there is any reference to the dwelling place of the magnificent creature who is referred to as the "signet." In so far as removal to this place is explicitly ascribed to Yahweh, and this has its correspondence in the וישם שם את האדם ("and there He put the man") of Gen 2:8, this clearly proves that the information given at the beginning of v 13 is a clumsy anticipation. The place is first described with reference to the cherub dwelling there. 10:2 had referred to the cherub in the Jerusalem sanctuary. He appeared there as guardian of the ark and as bearer of the throne of Yahweh.[25] In the present passage only the protective function of the cherub is discernible. The sacred object which he "blocks off" (סכך) is, as opposed to Ex 25:20; 37:9, not the covering of the ark over which Yahweh appears, but the lofty mountain seat of God, far removed from human proximity. In a secondary expansion (note c) this is explicity described as "holy." Even the totally obscure ממשח (missing in v 16) seems to be a secondary expansion (see note b).

In contrast to the addition in v 13a, it is not the garden (of trees) which appears here as the dwelling place of God, but the mountain of God, which in Is 14:13 in clearly polytheistic terminology is called הר מועד "the mountain of assembly" (i.e. certainly of the assembly of the gods), "a kind of Canaanite Olympus."[26] For earlier Israel "mountain of God" meant Sinai (Horeb) (see Ex 3:1; 18:5; 24:13; and elsewhere). This is subsequently replaced by Zion, which in Ps 48:3, in an amalgamation with Canaanite-Phoenician tradition which knows Ṣaphon in north Syria as the mountain of God, can be

21 See notes a, c, and d.
22 For the details see v 13 note b.
23 On this see G. Castellino, "Les origines de la civilisation selon les textes bibliques et les textes cunéiformes" in *Volume du Congrès, Strasbourg 1956,* VT Suppl 4 (Leiden: Brill, 1957), 122f.
24 On the "garden" see also Brock-Utne, *Gottesgarten.*
25 See 1, 250f.
26 John Gray, *The Legacy of Canaan,* VT Suppl 5 (Leiden: Brill, ²1965), 21 note 7.
27 On this see Kraus, *Psalmen,* excursus 5 (on Ps 46).

described as "Mount Zion in the far north" (ירכתי צפון).[27] Paradise as a place on the universal mountain in the north (from a Mesopotamian perspective) is also to be inferred from the geography of paradise in Gen 2:10–14. This concept must also lie behind Ezekiel 28. There is nothing here that compels us to think of Lebanon.[28]

That the splendid creature who is described as a signet is associated with the cherub on the mountain signifies his admission to the place of glory, where he may now dwell among the other creatures who are there. These latter are described as אבני אש ("stones of fire") in vv 14, 16. The authenticity of this description has been questioned, and attempts have been made to replace it with בני אל ("sons of God")[29] or with בני אש ("sons of fire") (Bertholet). The fact that it occurs twice, in v 14 and again in v 16, argues against such an alteration of the text. Pope, as others have done before him, points to the Akkadian *aban išāti* "fire stone." He thinks that he can establish, by cross references, that these stones have gone through a process of smelting, and he would like to connect with this the Ugaritic account of the miraculous founding of Baal's dwelling place on the mountain *ṣpn*.[30] Baal's house was built of silver, gold, lapis lazuli and other precious stones. These various building stones have been fused by means of a fire which burned for seven days inside the house.[31] Thus he assumes that in Ezekiel 28, too, the reference to dwelling "in the midst of stones of fire" is to be interpreted as living in a palace whose precious building stones have been fused by fire. But if such were the meaning, would not the text have spoken explicitly of living in a house or palace made of such stones? E. Rohland imagines a kind of surrounding wall of fire when he speaks of "the location on the mountain of God, surrounded by fiery stones" and associates the passage with Is 54:11f.[32] F. C. Fensham, on the basis of Akkadian *aban išāti,* with which he compares the Ugaritic *abn brq* of text V AB.C 23, thinks of "lightning stones, thunderbolts" hurled in a thunderstorm by the weather-god Baal who lives on *ṣpn*.[33] However, after the magnificent creature himself has been compared with a signet, it is more likely, in the case of the "stones of fire" in whose midst he dwells, that the reference is to his fellow inhabitants—who are thus thought of as creatures of light, either the stars or the originators of the powerful flashes of lightning that fall from heaven. Thus Bertholet favors a connection with a thunderstorm; Ziegler, with stars (so, too, Fohrer) or angels.[34] In any case the polytheistic environment on the "mountain of assembly" is clear. It is only lightly concealed by the image.

■ **28:15** The remark that the magnificent creature walked blamelessly is also, however, part of the description of the beginning of his stay in the residence of God. The closeness to the language of P is once again particularly clear at this point. Thus, according to Gen 6:9 Noah was "blameless" (תמים) and "walked (התהלך) with God" (said also of Enoch in 5:22, 24). But this is also exactly how the narrative of the covenant-making between God and Abraham begins in Gen 17:1, with the summons, "Walk (התהלך) before me and be [or: 'and you will be'] blameless (תמים)." The connection of התהלכת ("you walked") (v 14) with תמים ("blameless") (v 15) is thus confirmed by these parallels.

The third strophe, however, describes the fall of the one who has been so highly exalted. To begin with this is described in very general terms. Unrighteousness is found in the king of Tyre and he has sinned. The full עולה ("wickedness") is not otherwise found in Ezekiel.[35] This does not justify replacing it (BH³), however, by the more frequent (especially in the didactic expositions in 3:20; 18:8, 24, 26; and elsewhere) עול, which then reappears in the addition in v 18. The absolute use of חטא ("to sin") is found in 3:21; 18:4,20; and elsewhere.

■ **28:16** A later hand has then felt obliged to be more specific. Using the formula-like מלא חמס ("full of violence") (7:23; 8:17; 12:19) he refers to the violence which has arisen as a result ot Tyre's trading. The idea of the basic text, which referred not to the commercial city

28 Dussaud, "Phéniciens au Négeb," 40.
29 Dussaud, "Phéniciens au Négeb," 40 note 3; van den Born.
30 On this dwelling place of Baal see also A. S. Kapelrud, *Baal in the Ras Shamra Texts* (Copenhagen: Gad, 1952), 132.
31 II AB VI, 22–35; see also Driver, *Canaanite Myths,* 98f.
32 Rohland, *Erwählungstraditionen,* 201.
33 Fensham, "Thunder-Stones."
34 See also J. de Savignac, "Note sur le sens du terme *ṣâphôn* dans quelques passages de la Bible," *VT* 3 (1953): 96.
35 A poetically archaizing lengthening to עולתה is also found, in Hos 10:13; Ps 92:16; 125:3; see Gesenius-Kautzsch §90g and Beer-Meyer §45, 3c.

but to the "signet"-creature of surpassing beauty, then finds expression in v 17.

■ **28:17** As a consequence of his beauty, the heart of the king of Tyre has become presumptuous. A second hand, which has already been observed in v 12, has expanded this by a reference to the destruction of the wisdom of Tyre which takes up again the יפעה ("splendor") of v 7. Tyre founders on what was given to her as a precious gift from the moment of her origin. Like the foundling Israel in Ezekiel 16, she founders on her beauty of which she has been proud. The later expansion in vv 1–10 starts in its invective section (v 2) at this very point and gives expression to the pride of the king of Tyre in the quotation of his own words.

In v 17 there is no more than a brief mention of the serious offense which leads to judgment. The description of that judgment is made in two parallel expressions, in one of which the cherub is the subject and in the other Yahweh himself. While in Gen 3:24 a plurality of cherubs are placed as guardians at the entrance to Paradise after man's expulsion, here, to begin with, again only one cherub is mentioned, whose title without the article sounds like a proper name (v 14 note b) and who is the instrument of the expulsion which is described in very strong terms as a "destruction" out of the midst of the stones of fire. אבד ("to destroy") piʿel occurs also in 6:3 of the destruction of the high places and in 22:27 of the destruction of life; the qal is used of the loss of hope in 19:5; 37:11 and of the fall of Tyre in 26:17. In case it might appear as if the cherub himself were master and owner of the mountain of God, this is at once corrected by what follows. Yahweh himself judges him who has exalted himself against him. This is the Yahwistic reshaping of the old myth. But Yahweh's judgment brings the true reality to the eyes of the world when he dashes to the ground the one who impudently claimed as a possession that which was only a gift. The motif of the fall to earth or, more intensely, the fall to the underworld of the one who in hubris strives to reach heaven is expounded most forcefully in Is 14:4–21. The descent to the pit has been mentioned in vv 8–10 as well as in 26:20. It is fully developed in 32:17–32. In the present passage the reference is simply to the fall from the top of the mountain of God to the earth. Here again, then, one should refrain from thinking, with Pope, of the Ugaritic tradition of the banishment of the god El to the underworld.

Then, like the concluding section of chapter 27, the fourth strophe develops the following idea. What happens in this divine judgment on the king of Tyre is judgment before the eyes of the whole world.

■ **28:18f** This casting down into the dust of the earth happens before the eyes of all the acquaintances of Tyre. The קינה ("lament") could scarcely be constructed as a proof-saying. In fact, however, here too the concern is with the proof of Yahweh before the tribunal of the public at large, which is horror-struck at this event. The wording of v 19a is closely related to that of 27:35a. But then the redactor has concluded this third group of oracles against Tyre with the refrain-verse of 26:21 and 27:36.

This last strophe, too, has been enriched with secondary expansions. It is surely the same hand as in v 16a that has inserted in v 18a the reference to the guilt and injustice of Tyre's commercial activity. The linguistic difference from the basic text can be seen in the use of the masculine עול ("unrighteousness") (otherwise in v 15). The remark that Tyre has desecrated her sanctuaries through this guilt is unique. Starting from this remark, Bevan tries to explain the whole oracle. Since masons from Tyre also built the Jerusalem temple, the temple in Tyre is identical with Jerusalem temple. The king of Tyre is consciously described as a servant of the sanctuary. Because he commits an offense at the sanctuary, he is also driven from the mountain of God by the cherub who, in Jerusalem as guardian of the ark, guards the holy place. This reconstruction is not very likely. On the basis of the general OT way of thinking, one could suppose that what is meant here is the desecration of the temple by goods which have been forcibly seized from people and have found their way into the temple treasury. But it is completely possible that the person responsible for the expansion was thinking of still more specific events in Tyre which had happened in his own day.

In v 18b*α*, exactly as in 19:14a*α*, there is the additional idea that the fire of judgment bursts forth from the very place of the sin itself and destroys it. It is inadvisable to think of the death of the phoenix which is consumed in the fire.[36] Expressed in fairly general terms, reference to the fire sent by God is already firmly embedded in the stereotyped phraseology of the Amos oracles against foreign nations (Am 1:4, 7, 10; and elsewhere). This new statement, which separates the statements of v 17 and v 18bβ (which belong together), has nothing to do with the falling to the earth which was expressed in v 16 and continued in v 18bβ, even if it does express the valid awareness that sin, in the last resort, is destroyed by its own fire.

Aim

The narrative about the king of Tyre is mysteriously cryptic. It is told as the story of a prince of really princely splendor. Astonishment at the splendid nobility and beauty of a lofty personage permeates the whole description of this favored person who has been so highly exalted.

But then the picture darkens. The prince comes to grief precisely on his exalted state and on his splendor. Instead of ennobling him, his beauty makes him ignoble, highhanded, proud of himself. What is a gift, he seizes to himself with greedy hands as his own property. But why, in actual fact, is there this puzzle of deep falsification, in which the outward fall from the heights has to follow the inward fall?

"The tragedy of princes," one might be inclined to answer, thereby categorizing what is reported here as a puzzle of political history such as can happen again and again. But then, surprisingly, the text leads on to still greater depths. What is narrated here as the fate of princes is narrated in terms of primeval man, of man at the beginning, of man pure and simple. He was the one who was richly endowed, summoned to be beside God, adorned with perfect beauty. But he was then the proud one, the one turned in on himself, who seized for himself and acted highhandedly with what was, as a gift, a great favor.

And so he was dashed from the dwelling place of God to the earth, from the heights to the dust, a puzzle to all who have followed his paths.

The lament over the prince of Tyre laments in prophetic anticipation the fate of an individual who nevertheless represents the political entity Tyre, a single political power in the neighborhood of Israel. To begin with there is proclaimed judgment on the ruler (and his city), who has become presumptuous and violent in his beauty and, as the secondary expansions clearly emphasize, in his commercial capacity. This is the immediate aim of the oracle. But in so far as the proclamation is embedded in the story of primeval man, as this is related quite directly in Genesis 2f with the deletion of all royal characteristics, this prevents the reader, whoever he may be, from an overhasty withdrawal of himself from this event. In the pride and fall of the Prince of Tyre, there is repeated the story of "primeval man." This is "Everyman's story"; in other words, it is more than a mere episodic occurrence.

From this point, however, the text, understood in all its profundity, moves inexorably to the question whether in fact the whole of human history is included here. Is man really represented only by this one primeval man, who was created for God's magnificent presence but who lost it because, as *homo incurvatus in se,* he could relate his nobility only to himself and esteemed what was gifted to him only as "a thing to be grasped"? In Phil 2:5–11 the proclaimer of the gospel is able to relate a remarkable counterstory and to summon people to it as the true story of mankind.

36 As does Morgenstern, "King-God," 153.

3. An Oracle against Sidon and Conclusion of the Oracles against Israel's Palestinian Neighbors

Bibliography

Otto Eissfeldt
"Phoiniker," *PW* NB 1st series 20 (= 40th half-volume) (1950), 350–380.

Ernst Honigmann
"Sidon," *PW* NB 2nd Series 2 (1923), 2216–2229.

28

20 And the word of Yahweh came to me:
21/Son of man, set your face towards
Sidon and prophesy against her 22/ and
say: Thus has [the Lord][a] Yahweh said:
See, I am against you, O Sidon, and I will
glorify myself in the midst of you, and
they[b] shall know that I am Yahweh when
I sit in judgment over her[c] and reveal
myself as holy in her[d]. 23/ And I shall
send a pestilence against her[a] and blood[b]
into her streets, and the slain <shall
fall>[c] in her[d] midst when the sword is
against her[e] on every side, and they shall
know that I am Yahweh.
24 And the house of Israel shall henceforth
feel no malignant brier[a] and no stinging
thorn on the part of all those who live
round about them and who despise them,
and they shall know that I am [the Lord][b]
Yahweh.
25 Thus has [the Lord][a] Yahweh said: When I
gather the house[b] of Israel from among
the nations amongst whom they have
been scattered and reveal myself to them
as holy in the eyes of the nations[c], and
when they dwell in their land which I
gave to my servant Jacob 26/ and dwell
in it in safety and build houses and plant
vineyards and dwell in safety—when I sit
in judgment on all those who despise
them round about, then they shall know
that I am Yahweh, their God[a].

28: 22a אדני is lacking in 𝔊 𝔎 𝔄, see Appendix 1.
22 b 𝔐 וידעו. 𝔊 *καὶ γνώσῃ* is clearly an assimilation to the context.
c 𝔐 בה. MSS (𝔊 𝔗[W] 𝔄) בך, see note b.
d MSS (𝔊 𝔄) בך, see note b.
23 23a 𝔐 ושלחתי בה is not attested by 𝔊 𝔎 𝔄.
b 𝔊 changes the order *αἷμα καὶ θάνατος*. 𝔄 mentions only the blood.
c 𝔐 ונפלל is a scribal error for ונפל.
d 𝔊 again assimilates to the second person singular.
e 𝔐 עליה is not attested by 𝔅 𝔖 and is changed by 𝔊 into the second person.
24 24a סלון occurs also in 2:6. ממאיר occurs in Lev 13:51f; 14:44 of malignant leprosy (צרעת ממארת) as opposed to the non-malignant variety.
b אדני is lacking in 𝔊 𝔎, see Appendix 1.
25 25a אדני is lacking in 𝔊 (𝔊[62], Ir[lat]; on the other hand 𝔊[B] *κύριος κύριος*, 𝔊[A] *κύριος ὁ θεός*, 𝔄 attests *αδωναι κύριος ὁ θεός* in its original).
b בית is missing in 𝔊. 𝔗 בני.
c Doubled in 𝔊 *τῶν λαῶν καὶ τῶν ἐθνῶν*.
26 26a 𝔊 expands: *καὶ ὁ θεὸς τῶν πατέρων αὐτῶν*.

Form

28:20–26 begins with the command to the prophet to deliver a divine message to Sidon (messenger formula v 22). A second messenger formula in v 25 separates off as an independent oracle vv 25f, which also, from the content point of view, contain no reference to Sidon and envisage rather the restoration of Israel in her own land. This second oracle is constructed as a two-part proof-saying.

The remainder, vv 20–24, is remarkable for the occurrence of no fewer than three recognition formulae (vv 22,23,24). An examination of the content reveals that v 24 too is no longer directed at Sidon, but looks back to the whole series of oracles against the nations in Ezekiel 25–28. V 24, then, is to be regarded as an independent proof-saying, even though it is connected by the copula with what precedes it. The material that remains, vv 21–23, is from its content clearly directed at Sidon. From the point of view of form it is characterized as an expanded proof-saying by the infinitive בעשותי,

which follows the recognition formula in v 22b and is introduced by ב. Parallels for such expansion by means of the infinitive with בְּ can be found in 5:13; 15:7; 20:42,44; 25:17; 30:8; 33:29. That such an expansion can then, for its part, also be concluded with a recognition formula is confirmed by 6:13f; 12:15f; 30:25f; 34:27–30; 37:13f. The observation that the expansion, which follows the first recognition formula, transforms the direct address to Sidon to indirect speech about Sidon in the third person might make one suspect that we are dealing here (as possibly also, e.g., in 6:13f) with a later expansion. 𝔊 has put the whole expansion into the second person (see v 22 notes b–d and v 23 notes c, e). Cooke would delete vv 22b,23bβb and retain vv 22a, 23aα transformed into direct address, but this seems merely arbitrary. Against the assumption of a secondary expansion of the basic material which is in the form of a direct address, there is the fact that one is then left with a fragment of such terseness as to be internally improbable. Thus one must simply accept the change in style and conclude, in the end, that the complex of vv 20–26 is made up of an expanded proof-saying (vv 22f) and two simple proof-sayings (vv 24 and 25f), the first two of which units have been joined more closely.

■ **28:20–23** *An Oracle against Sidon.* As is shown by the common designation of the Phoenicians as "Sidonians" both in Homer and in the OT, the city of Sidon was, in the earlier periods of Phoenician history, the most important city and the administrative center of the Phoenician cities. Thus also in Gen 10:15 Sidon is introduced by the Yahwist specifically as the first-born of Canaan. The city, which is to be located at modern *ṣaidā*, forty kilometers north of Tyre, also figures with its king Zimrida in the Amarna letters.[1] Papyrus Anastasi I mentions it in the thirteenth century in its north-south list after Byblos and Berytos (Beirut) and before Sarepta and Tyre as cities which the cultured Egyptian scribe ought to know.[2] The prince of Byblos, with whom Wen-Amon (c. 1100) negotiates according to his travel report, knows that there are fifty ships lying in the harbor at Sidon which handle the trade with a trade delegate living in Egypt, Birkat-El (?).[3] Tiglath-pileser I, about the turn of the eleventh-tenth century, refers to tribute from the cities of Byblos, Sidon and Arvad.[4] About the turn of the millenium, however, Sidon seems to have been outstripped by Tyre. Thus we find not only Solomon, but also the Omrids having connections with the kings of Tyre. In this connection, Ethbaal (Josephus "Ithobaal"), king of Tyre and father of Jezebel, can actually be described as "king of the Sidonians" (1 Kgs 16:31).

In the Assyrian period, Sidon, which on account of its position was much more exposed than Tyre, even if Esarhaddon can call it a city "in the midst of the sea" (*ša qereb tamtim*), had to suffer much at the hands of the Assyrians.[5] On his third campaign Sennacherib conquered greater and lesser Sidon and imposed heavy tribute on king Tubalu (Ethbaal), whom he set up in place of king Luli who fled.[6] After the revolt of king Abdi-milkutti, Esarhaddon went even further and laid waste the city in his fourth year. The king of Sidon, who escaped seawards, is captured and killed, his family and his treasures are led away as booty, and in place of Sidon a successor settlement is founded "in another place" with the name Kar-esarhaddon, "Esarhaddon harbor."[7] But this harsh action on the part of Esarhaddon did not succeed in wiping out Sidon completely. It subsequently reappears under its old name. That Sidon suffered much under the neo-Babylonians too may be inferred from the fact that Nebuchadnezzar's Court Calendar mentions a king of Sidon alongside the king of Tyre at court in Babylon.[8] Herodotus knows of a campaign by the Egyptian Apries against Sidon.[9] In the early Persian period Sidon appears to stand once more at the head of the Phoenician city-states. Once again it suffers severe destruction, at the hands of Artaxerxes III Ochus, who punished it for its rebellion under Tennes.[10]

1 Knudtzon, *Amarna*, nos. 144f; on this see Weber in Knudtzon, *Amarna*, 1162f.

2 Erman, *Literatur*, 288.

3 Erman, *Literatur*, 231; *ANET* 27.

4 *ANET* 275; *AOT* 339.

5 Borger, *Inschriften Asarhaddons*, 8, 48; according to pp. 33, 49 *ša ina qabal tamtim.*

6 *ANET* 287; *AOT* 352.

7 *ANET* 290f, 302f; Borger, *Inschriften Asarhaddons*, 48 and elsewhere.

8 See above p. 23; *ANET* 308.

9 2, 161.

10 See, e.g., A. T. Olmstead, *History of Palestine and Syria to the Macedonian Conquest* (New York: C. Scribner's Sons, 1931), 617–619, and Friedrich Karl Kienitz, *Die politische Geschichte Aegyptens vom 7. bis zum 4.*

Interpretation

■ **28:20f** The prophetic oracle in 28:20–23 presupposes the existence of Sidon as a political power. In a divine message, the prophet, addressed as "son of man," is told to turn his face towards the city of Sidon.[11] He is to prophesy against the city and, under the rubric of the messenger formula, to threaten her with the challenging הנני עליך ("see, I am against you").[12] Instead of speaking of a formula of summons to a duel,[13] K. von Rabenau would prefer to be more cautious and speak of a "formula of encounter."[14] The aim of this "encounter" is the self-glorification of Yahweh. The divine intervention is not justified by the mention of any offense on the part of the city, even though immediately afterwards there is a reference to "sitting in judgment" (עשה שפטים 5:10,15; 11:9; 16:41; 25:11; 28:26; 30:14,19; Ex 12:12; see also Ezek 23:10). On the basis of v 24 (the verse which is, however, no longer directed against Sidon alone), one might ask whether Sidon too has been guilty of contempt for an Israel which has been subject to judgment. In the foreground in any case, however, there stands not Sidon's guilt but the fact of Yahweh's self-glorification. The nip'al of כבד ("to glorify myself") is found otherwise in Ezekiel only in 39:13, where the day of Gog's destruction is referred to by Yahweh as "the day when I glorify myself." In P (Ex 14:4,17f) the event at the Red Sea is the action by which Yahweh reveals his glory to Pharaoh, whom he himself has made obdurate. Exactly as in the present passage, there follows there too (14:4,18) immediately the recognition formula of the proof-saying. The proof of Yahweh's "glory" (כבוד) in his historical activity in the eyes of the world is a process of revelation in which Yahweh manifests himself to the world.[15]

If in נכבד ("to glorify oneself") the reference to Yahweh's weight and dignity is in the foreground, then in the נקדש ("to reveal oneself as holy") which is immediately connected with it there is added the reference to the fire of the holiness which burns up all resistance. It is significant that אֶקָּדֵשׁ ("I will reveal myself as holy") is connected with אֶכָּבֵד ("I will glorify myself") in the quotation of a divine oracle by Moses on the occasion of the destruction of Nadab and Abihu by the divine fire (Lev 10:3). The proof of Yahweh's holiness is a dangerous fire. But here too we have a divine manifestation. Everywhere else where the nip'al of קדש ("to reveal oneself as holy") is attested in Ezekiel, it is connected with the endorsement by witnesses "before the eyes of all nations" (20:41; 28:25; 36:23; 38:16; 39:27; also the hitpa'el in 38:23).[16]

■ **28:23** The description of the judgment on Sidon itself, characterized by another recognition formula as proof of Yahweh before the nations, is presented in the stereotyped formulaic language of the plagues, such as has been found already in earlier contexts. Instead of the three-fold "pestilence, famine and sword" (5:12; 6:12) or the four-fold "famine, wild beasts, sword, pestilence" (14:12ff), we have here the three-fold "pestilence, blood and sword" by means of which Yahweh will act against Sidon.[17]

Setting

The colorlessness of this oracle, which differentiates it from all the previous oracles against foreign nations, also makes it difficult to date. From Jer 27:3 it can be seen that in the time of Zedekiah Sidon was a participant in the plans for rebellion against Babylon.[18] At the time of the siege of Tyre, on the other hand (see on 29:17–20), it must have been firmly in Nebuchadnezzar's control. Must we then think of a judgment oracle against proud Sidon in the period after the surrender of Tyre (Kraetz-

Jahrhundert vor der Zeitwende (Berlin: Akademie, 1953), who (in excursus 8, pp. 181–185) calculates that this took place in the year 343.

11 See 1, 144f; see 1, 131f; on the action thus described see 1, 182f.

12 See 1, 133 on 2:4.

13 Humbert, "'hinnenî êlékâ'"; see 1, 175 on 5:8.

14 von Rabenau, "Zukunftswort," especially 67.

15 See, e.g., Rolf Rendtorff, "Die Offenbarungsvorstellungen im alten Israel" in *Offenbarung als Geschichte,* ed. Wolfhart Pannenberg. Kerygma und Dogma 1 (Göttingen: Vandenhoeck & Ruprecht, 1961), 21–41, especially 28–32; also Walther Zimmerli, "'Offenbarung' im Alten Testament (Ein Gespräch mit R. Rendtorff)," *EvTh* 22 (1962): 15–31; note also the δοξάζεσθαι of John's Gospel.

16 See also Reventlow, "Die Völker." The nip'al of קדש elsewhere in the OT only in Lev 22:32; Nu 20:13; Is 5:16; and in addition the ונקדש בכבדי ("and it shall be sanctified by my glory") of Ex 29:43.

17 On this usage of דם cf. 5:17; 14:19; 35:6; 38:22.

18 See above p. 13.

schmar)? It would be more correct to affirm that in the oracle it is impossible to observe any signs of local coloring or any specific indications of Sidon's contemproary history and that there is no mention of any relationship to the judgment on Tyre, but that the oracle remains entirely stereotyped. The only thing that emerges as clearly defined is the statement about Yahweh's self-glorification in this event. This, however, obviously indicates a final, heightened résumé of all the preceding judgments passed on the nations. The oracle against Sidon is a concluding oracle, added in order to bring out the theological statement with which the oracles against foreign nations are really concerned. Sidon is basically the somewhat fortuitious bearer of these statements. The mention of Sidon specifically might have been caused by its proximity here to Tyre and in view of the frequent association of the two cities (Jer 47:4; Joel 4:4; Zech 9:2).

The oracle, therefore, is from the hand of the man who put Ezekiel 25–28 together (and connected it with the already existing complex of oracles against Egypt in chapters 29–32 to make seven recipients of oracles?). One cannot judge the date of the oracle without taking into account v 24, which is after all part of it.

■ **28:4** *Conclusion of the Oracles against Israel's six Palestinian Neighbors.* From the same hand as vv 20–23 comes v 24, which now leaves Sidon behind and looks back once again over the whole collection of oracles against Israel's Palestinian-Canaanite neighbors. The oracle is connected to the preceding verses by means of the copula and is not to be separated from them. From the content point of view also it is an expansion of the concluding remarks found there.

Interpretation

The divine judgment on Israel's neighbors is illuminated in this oracle exclusively from the point of view of help for Israel. In it the statements of the invectives of chapters 25f are taken up again and summarized (cf. 25:3, 6, 8, 12, 15; 26:2). The statements about the hubris of Tyre, which were to be found especially in 28:1–20, are left out of account. The affliction of Israel by her neighbors is first of all described in an image. סלון ("brier") (see note a), which is not found in the OT outside Ezekiel, seems to be a word peculiar to Ezekiel's language. It is used also in 2:6 as an image for the enmity of men. The parallel קוץ, the "prickly weed," the enemy of the arable land (Gen 3:18; Is 32:13; Hos 10:8), is mentioned in Ju 8:7, 16 (קוצי המדבר "thorns of the wilderness") as a means of extremely painful punishment for men (see also Mt 27:29; Jn 19:2). In ממאיר ("malignant") (see note a) Ezekiel uses a technical term of priestly-medical diagnosis. Then, however, the images are dropped. The pain-causing activity of the neighbors is identified, without an image, as (mocking) contempt such as finds expression, e.g., in the האח ("Aha") of 25:3. Here there is used the root שאט – שוט ("to despise") which occurs only in Ezekiel (cf. 16:57; 28:26; as a noun in 25:6,15; 36:5).

Setting

Since v 24, in language and choice of imagery, is closely connected with earlier (and later) Ezekiel oracles and at the same time reveals Ezekiel's characteristic and original figurative language, one will hesitate to be overhasty in denying the oracle to the prophet. In its origin it must belong with the expansions in 25:6–7, 15–17 (see also 36:5, where the key-word שאט "despise" is used for the behavior of the foreign nations). If it is still to be regarded as part of the prophet's own words—and there are no compelling reasons for excluding this possibility—then the hand of the prophet is to be seen here as participating in the collecting of the foreign oracles into a larger complex.

Aim

26:20–23 and 26:24 must be taken together. By the example of the judgment speech against Sidon, this concluding oracle against foreign nations, the prophetic saying in vv 20–23, aims to present fully what the historical activity of God really means for the surrounding nations. The outlines of the city of Sidon, which is mentioned here, remain quite indistinct. The interest of the oracle does not lie there. And even the description of the judgment in its actual execution remains completely stereotyped. The real point of the statement is not arrived at here either. It is, on the other hand, brought out quite clearly that in this judgment on one of Israel's neighbors the concern is, in the last resort, with the complete emergence, before the eyes of all, of the majesty and holiness of God.

The oracle in v 24, which is directly appended to this and which disregards completely the individual judgment on Sidon and includes this simply in the summary of the divine judgment on the whole world of the nations, makes it clear, however, in which direction God's face is actually turned in this judging activity of his. God's majesty and holiness are revealed in the way in which he removes the thorns and briers which cause pain to the body of his chosen one.

If anyone were to think that this statement was a secret expression of a hidden national egoism, in which the particular human group Israel sought greedily to insure for itself full participation in and the whole future of history and world, he would have basically misunderstood the oracle. Then God would have been made a servant of human greed, and the majesty and holiness of God would have been an empty word. But here the majesty and holiness of God in their definitive revelation wish to be really glorified. This is also what is happening in the history of the nations, that God stands by his work and raises from their humiliation those who have been deeply humiliated, who have tasted the majesty of God the judge right to the dregs, but to whom he has pledged his word and his promise. This he does for the sake of his majestic faithfulness and for his name's sake: "they shall know that *I am Yahweh.*"

The history of the nations in its ebb and flow is a constantly recurring agonizing mystery to the human eye. Here the prophetic oracle undertakes to take a final look at this mystery, which is not however explained away. God remembers those whom he has called. He is in the process of removing the thorns from their flesh and of freeing them, so that, in all this, they may recognize his majesty and, in his judging, also his holiness and may honor him.

■ **28:25-26** *Pardon for Israel and the Recognition of Yahweh.* While v 24 widened the horizon of the oracle in vv 20–23 to include all the neighboring nations and showed how Yahweh's act of judgment is directed at freeing his people from oppression, the additional oracle in vv 25–26 widens the horizon inwards and reveals the fullness of Israel's pardon.

Setting

Vv 25f are not to be considered as an independent oracle. They look back to vv 20–24 and, by taking up and quoting statements from these verses, try once more to expand on what is said in vv 20–24. At the same time, however, this verbal "resumption" and what are at the same time new combinations of statements from the preceding verses make clear that this is an addition, which (unlike v 24 in relation to 20–23) did not originally follow vv 20–24. It is no accident, then, that it has a new introductory formula. Vv 25f belong to a very late phase in the formation of the book, one which certainly is no longer from the hand of the prophet himself. This is supported by linguistic observations (see below). It is however also likely on the basis of the content of the oracle, which includes material and expressions of a proclamatory character from the third part of the book (chaps. 33–39). There is a close analogy with vv 25f, from the point of view of both form and content, in the closing verses of Ezekiel 39.

Interpretation

■ **28:25** V 25 looks forward to the day when Israel will be gathered together again (11:17; 20:34,41; 34:13; 36:24; 37:21; 39:27; see also 38:8). At the same time, however, it is confirmed, taking up the closing words of v 22, that in this very gathering together there occurs the proof of Yahweh's holiness in the eyes of the nations. The reference to dwelling in the land given to Jacob comes from 37:25.

■ **28:26** The double reference to living in safety is fully developed in 34:25,27f (38:8,11,14; 39:26). In the reference to the building of houses and the planting of vineyards (כרם "vineyards" occurs nowhere else in Ezekiel; נטע "to plant" only in 36:36) we find what are clearly Jeremianic expressions.[19] Then, finally, the description again takes up phrases from vv 20–24. The sitting in judgment is from v 22; the mention of those round about who despise from v 24.

This whole picture of coming salvation, painted with traits drawn from the following salvation oracles, is again, however, not an end in itself but a pointer to a recognition. In such activity on Yahweh's part it becomes clear that he, Yahweh, is the God of Israel, "their God." What was described in v 24 in much more figurative language as the removal of pain for the house of Israel is

19 See on this Robert Bach, "Bauen und Pflanzen" in *Studien zur Theologie der alttestamentlichen Überlieferungen,* ed. R. Rendtorff and K. Koch (Neukirchen-Vluyn: Neukirchener, 1961), 7–32.

here described more correctly but less colorfully with the covenant formula "Yahweh, their God" (again in 34:30; 39:22,28 also in recognition formulae; see also the direct address "Yahweh, your God" in 20:5,7,19f).

Aim

This expansion from a later hand, with its full delineation of the picture of salvation, still holds fast to what is the aim of the whole divine history of salvation for the people of God. It is not a "security" which is sufficient in itself as an ultimate possession, a prosperity which delights in itself, but all this as proclamation of the ultimate proof of the covenant loyalty of the God who does not forget what he has promised.

B. Seven Oracles against Pharaoh and against Egypt

Bibliography

H. Bonnet
Reallexikon der ägyptischen Religionsgeschichte (Berlin, 1952).

James Henry Breasted
A History of Egypt from the Earliest Times to the Persian Conquest (New York: C. Scribner's Sons, ²1920).

Adolf Erman and Hermann Ranke
Ägypten und ägyptisches Leben im Altertum (Tübingen: Mohr [Siebeck], 1922–23).

Hermann Kees
"Ägypten," *RGL*.

Hermann Kees
Ägypten (München: Beck, 1933).

Hermann Kees
Das alte Ägypten; eine kleine Landeskunde (Berlin: Akademie, 1955).

Friedrich Karl Keinitz
Die politische Geschichte Aegyptens vom 7. bis zum 4. Jahrhundert vor der Zeitwende (Berlin: Akademie, 1953).

Eduard Meyer
Geschichte des Altertums 3 (Stuttgart und Berlin: J. G. Cotta'sche Buchhandlung Nachfolger, ³1954).

Georges Posener
Dictionary of Egyptian Civilization, tr. Alix McFarlane (New York: Tudor, 1962).

Alexander Scharff and Anton Moortgat
Ägypten und Vorderasien im Altertum (München: Bruckmann, 1950).

Of the seven units directed against Pharaoh and Egypt, each introduced by a messenger formula, six of them have a date at the beginning. The sequence of dates is broken in 29:17.[1] 29:17–20 (21) is characterized as a later addition not only by that fact but also by its content, which links the fate of Tyre with that of Egypt. This is not otherwise the case in any of the oracles against Tyre or Egypt. Thus it must remain open whether in this case too the grouping of precisely seven units was intended by the redactor, as has been assumed for the grouping of seven addressees in the overall collection of the oracles against foreign nations.[2] One will, in any case, have to assume that the sequence 29:1–16; 30:20–26; 31:1–18; 32:1–16; 32:17–32 was already established before 29:17–21 was added. It is impossible to reach any definite conclusions about the insertion of the dateless unit 30:1–19, which also from a thematic point of view interrupts the series of oracles directed against Pharaoh (29:1–16; 30:20–26; 31:1–18; 32:1–16), which (like 32:17–32) addresses Egypt generally and, in addition, has other peculiarities with regard to content which will have to be discussed in the detailed exposition. Nevertheless, these peculiarities of content foster the suspicion that it too has been inserted secondarily into the collection of dated oracles.

The sequence of the oracles against Tyre is recalled by the observation that here too the "lament" (קינה, 32:2–16) over Pharaoh is found at the conclusion of the Pharoah oracles. It is followed by the "lament" (נהה, 32:18) over the journey to the underworld of the pomp

1 See below on the dates at 32:1, 17.

2 See above p. 3.

of Egypt. The coincidence of the systematic sequence of literary forms with the sequence of dates is rather striking. Among the observations with regard to form, it deserves to be noted that the form of the proof-saying is found in the first two chapters (29 and 30), but in chapters 31f, on the other hand, apart from the secondary addition in 32:15, it does not recur.

On the question why precisely Egypt and its ruler within the oracles against foreign nations are credited with by far the fullest threat of judgment comprising the half of the eight chapters 25–32, what was said earlier must first be recalled. In the world surveyed by Ezekiel Egypt is the most stubborn opponent of Babylonian power. For Ezekiel, however, as for Jeremiah, Babylonian power is Yahweh's punishing sword before which the house of Israel must yield. 17:15 (see also 16:26 and chapter 23) had earlier already made clear that by this policy Egypt had also become Israel's tempter, preventing her from unreservedly accepting the divine judgment which humiliated her and made her "a vine, spreading low" (17:6).

The Egypt of Ezekiel's day is, in this respect, simply the heir of earlier Egyptian policy, which has already been correspondingly clearly illustrated in earlier Israelite prophecy. In the first place this country was for Israel the distant, dark background from which Yahweh by his act of liberation had summoned his people (20:5–7). In the time of Solomon, a time which was still unaware of any great threat to Palestine from an eastern power, there even developed at the dynastic level something like friendship between the nations (consolidated by a political marriage [1 Kgs 3:1; 7:8; 9:16; 11:1]), which however was destined to collapse again in the time of Pharaoh Shishak (1 Kgs 14:25f).[3] In the time of the rise of Assyria to the status of a great power, the relationship with Egypt took on a new aspect. The southern power of Egypt now became, more explicitly, the political support for the two Israelite states against the fundamental threat from the great power from the east. Even if it is unlikely that the *muṣru,* which appears, according to the account by Shalmaneser III of the battle of Qarqar (853), among the followers of Hadadezer of Damascus and Ahab of Israel with the small complement of a thousand support-troops, is to be regarded as an Egyptian contingent in support of the anti-Assyrian coalition,[4] nevertheless Egypt certainly makes its appearance at the time of the great eruption of Assyria against the west in the eighth century. It entered this conflict very ill prepared politically. The period of the twenty-second and twenty-third dynasties—inaugurated by Shishak, in which Lybian mercenaries had control of the monarchy, and after apparently strong beginnings, in which the campaign of Shishak to Palestine sought to reassert something of Egypt's old importance as a great power—became a period of increasing weakness and of the disintegration of the unity of the empire. Manetho's twenty-fourth dynasty contains only one name, that of Bochchoris (Bekneranef, c. 720–715), the son of a minor prince Tefnakhte in Sais, who for his part had already attempted to gain control of other parts of the Delta.

A new driving force came from the south from Nubia (Napata), which from time to time had belonged to Egypt and which at this period felt itself to be the champion of pure Egyptian beliefs and, as the twenty-fifth "Ethiopian" Dynasty, also took control of political power in Egypt. As early as c. 750 the Ethiopian Kashta was able, by prevailing upon the "God's wife" who ruled at that time in Thebes to adopt his daughter as her successor, to establish his power in Thebais. In 725 his son Pi'ankhy was successful in battle against Tefnakhte of Sais.[5] But only his successors Shabaka, Shabataka, Taharka and Tanutamun, the first three of whom are mentioned by Manetho as representatives of the twenty-fifth (Ethiopian) Dynasty, had control over the whole of Egypt (from 715-663). It is also they who, in the time of Isaiah and of Assyria's last, terrifying rise to power, tried to encourage any movements in Palestine towards independence from Assyria and to stir them up with promises

3 On this see B. Mazar, "The Campaign of Pharaoh Shishak to Palestine" in *Volume du Congrès, Strasbourg 1956,* VT Suppl 4 (Leiden: Brill, 1957), 57–66.

4 So Scharff-Moortgat, 173; Kienitz, *Geschichte Aegyptens,* 7; against this view is Oppenheim in *ANET* 279 note 9.

5 This is fully recorded in the Pi'ankhy-stele; see *ARE* 4, 406–444.

of help, although they were unable at the decisive moment to provide any serious assistance.[6] Thus they could not prevent Esarhaddon's penetrating as far as Egypt in 671 and making large parts of it into an Assyrian province. The victory stele of Esarhaddon at Zinjirli in north Syria lists the king of Egypt (Taharka?) alongside that of Tyre or Sidon as a prisoner of the Assyrian king.[7] An attempt on the part of Tanutamun to win back the Nile valley was replied to by Ashurbanipal on his second campaign (the first was still directed against Taharka) with a counterthrust which penetrated as far as Thebes and during which the sacred city was plundered.[8]

For her freedom from the Assyrian yoke Egypt had to thank the first ruler of the twenty-sixth dynasty, the so-called Saite dynasty, Psammetichus I (663-609). Like his father Necho he first ruled, as an Assyrian vassal, as a minor prince in the Delta. But when Ashurbanipal, as a result of the serious crises in the eastern part of the empire, was no longer powerful enough to maintain Assyrian rule in Egypt, he was able to free himself from Assyrian domination without a fight and, equally without a fight, to include Thebais within his own sphere of rule. Indeed, when the Assyrian empire began to totter under the advance of the Medes and of the Chaldean neo-Babylonians, Psammetichus I and then his successor Necho (609–596) are surprisingly enough to be found with their army at the Euphrates to help the crumbling Assyrian power.[9] At this point Palestine, as once at the high point of the New Kingdom, seems to become part of an Egyptian empire. In the death of Josiah, the short reign of Jehoahaz and the elevation of Jehoiakim to the throne there can be seen the reverberations of this event on the history of Judah.[10] The battle of Carchemish in 605 brings these dreams of becoming a great power to an abrupt end.[11] After the powerful neo-Babylonian heir of the eastern Empire had once again taken control of Palestine, Egypt sank back into the role of encouraging from the wings all movements in Palestine for independence. Nebuchadnezzar's attack on Egypt in 601/600 must, even though it was unsuccessful, have impressed on the Pharaoh the danger in which he found himself.

Necho was followed by Psammetichus II (593–588) and the latter by Apries (Hophra, 588-569 or 567). To the latter's offensives against Nebuchadnezzar probably belong the attack on Sidon mentioned by Herodotus and the sea-battle against Sidon.[12] It is more clearly confirmed by Jer 37:5 that at the time when Nebuchadnezzar lay before Jersalem with his army, Hophra himself dared to challenge the Babylonians with an army in Palestine. According to the passage cited, this led to a temporary relief of the city, from which the Babylonian troops withdrew in order to counter-challenge Pharaoh. The Lachish letter 3, 13ff, which reports that Kebarjahu the army commander "went down to Egypt," may well belong to the pre-history of this relief action. The Egyptian troops, however, as was foretold by the prophet in Jer 37:7f, withdrew again (without a fight or after a defeat?) without being able to delay the fate of Jerusalem. After the catastrophe a flood of Jewish refugees poured into Egypt. Jeremiah was dragged along as well. In the last oracle of the prophet (transmitted by Baruch), spoken against the refugees who thought that in Egypt they were safe from the Babylonians, we hear: "Thus has Yahweh said: See, I shall give Pharaoh Hophra king of Egypt into the hand of his enemies and into the hand of those who seek his life, as I gave Zedekiah king of Judah into the hand of his enemy Nebuchadnezzar king of Babylon and of him who sought his life" (Jer 44:30).

Unfortunately, the Wiseman Chronicle breaks off in the middle of the account of Nebuchadnezzar's eleventh year (594/93) and says nothing more about Nebuchadnezzar's further policy towards Egypt. Only for the thirty-seventh year of the king (568/67) is there again a fragmentary account of the well-prepared expedition against an Egyptian king, only the last syllable of whose name can be made out but which should be reconstructed as Amasis. Unfortunately it too breaks off

6 See Is 36:6; 2 Kgs 18:21; also see below on Ezek 29:6b-9a.

7 See *ANEP* 447, *AOB* 143f, and the text in Borger, *Inschriften Asarhaddons,* 98f.

8 *ANET* 294f.

9 See the Wiseman Chronicle for the years 616/5 and 610/09–609/08.

10 See above on Ezek 19:2–4.

11 The Wiseman Chronicle for the years 606/05–605/04.

12 2, 161.

before the outcome of the undertaking is reported.[13] It can scarcely be accepted that in the quarter of a century lying between these two dates, at the beginning of which Hophra's advance into Palestine took place, Nebuchadnezzar for his part undertook nothing. Indeed Josephus records a campaign in Nebuchadnezzar's twenty-third year, five years after the destruction of Jerusalem, in which, according to the prophecies of Jeremiah, Nebuchadnezzar conquered Coelesyria, the Ammonites and Moabites and finally also Egypt, killed the Egyptian king, set another in his place and deported all the Jews in Egypt to Babylon.[14] But this account should be linked with the Babylonian account of the campaign in the thirty-seventh year. This in fact takes us into the time of the troubles around the Egyptian throne, in the course of which, after an unsuccessful expedition by Hophra against Cyrene, Amasis supplanted him (569) and Hophra lost his life in the subsequent disorders (567). How great the participation of Nebuchadnezzar in these events actually was remains unclear. At any rate, he must have succeeded in preventing Amasis in the future from ever interfering in Palestine. When Josephus dates these events in Nebuchadnezzar's twenty-third year, he may have been influenced by the date in Jer 52:30 (Smend). The full description of Nebuchadnezzar's victory and its consequences for the Jewish refugees in Egypt is determined by the desire to show the fulfillment of the threats of Jeremiah (and of Ezekiel?). According to Josephus, Megasthenes records campaigns of Nebuchadnezzar against the Libyans and Iberians, and this would presuppose his control of Egypt.[15] It is noteworthy, however, that Herodotus, who gives a detailed account of the end of Hophra and of the reign of Amasis, makes no mention of the Babylonians.[16] This leads one to suppose that the intervention of Nebuchadnezzar was no more than "a gigantic military demonstration" intended to show the Egyptians "his military supremacy and warn them of any renewed aggression."[17] It can no longer be a case of a firm domination of Egypt, as in the time of Esarhaddon and in the early years of Ashurbanipal. For the remainder of the reign of Amasis (569-526) there was peace between Egypt and the neo-Babylonian power. Both then subsequently became the victims of the young Persian state (Babylon in 539, Egypt in 525).

Ezekiel's oracles against Pharaoh and against Egypt are along exactly the same lines as those of Jeremiah. With the exception of the secondary addition in 29:17–21, they are all to be dated in the time of the last siege of Jerusalem and the year immediately following. Since, to a large extent, we lack any precise knowledge of the details of the history of the struggle between Babylon and Egypt in this period, the linking of individual statements in Ezekiel's judgment oracles to specific contemporary events is possible only to a very limited extent. In the judgment on Egypt we can discern the same two-fold aspect as in the oracles against Tyre and its prince. The foreign power is regarded, on the one hand, as having become subject, through temptation, to hubris. On the other, however, it is threatened with the word of judgment within the context of Israelite salvation history on account of its offense against Israel.

From the point of view of form, here too, alongside the simple proclamation of judgment, there is the use figurative language. With regard to the total structure of chapters 29–32, it is noteworthy that, as distinct from chapters 25–28, there is no summarizing element at the end.

13 *ANET* 308.

14 *Antiquities* X 9, 7.

15 *Antiquities* X 11, 1.

16 2, 161ff; see also Diodorus 1, 68.

17 Kienitz, *Geschichte Aegyptens*, 31.

29

1. Three Oracles concerning the Judgment and its Limitations against Pharaoh and the Land of Egypt

1 In the tenth year[a], in the tenth month[b], on
the twelfth[c] (day) of the month the word of Yahweh came to me: 2/ Son of man, set your face towards[a] Pharaoh king of Egypt and prophesy against him and against all Egypt 3/ [speak][a] and say: Thus has [the Lord][b] Yahweh said: See, I am against you, Pharaoh king of Egypt[c], you great <crocodile>[d] which lies in the midst of its Nile branches and says," <My Nile branches>[e] belong to me and I have made <them>[f]," 4/ and I shall put hooks[a]

29:
1 1a The ויהי which usually precedes the dates is missing here and in 40:1. 𝔊^{B} (𝔎 𝔄) δωδεκάτῳ. Is this perhaps a correction in view of the fact that this date precedes that in 26:1? But see then 30:20; 31:1. Or has the number of the day been erroneously transferred to the month? To suggest, as does Fohrer, that 𝔊^{B} contains the original date is hardly likely since 𝔊 presupposes the same sequence in the Egypt oracles as does 𝔐, and this sequence is predetermined by the dates which occur in 𝔐. See also note c.

b 𝔐 בעשרי is missing in MS$^{Ken 151}$, 𝔊^{407}. 𝔊^{AV} (𝔎) reads ενδεκάτῳ μηνί.

c 𝔐 בשנים עשר לחדש. 𝔊 μιᾷ τοῦ μηνός, 𝔙 *undecima die mensis,* 'ΑΘ τῇ δωδεκάτῃ. In the text from which 𝔊 was translated שנים עשר must have been missing or been misplaced (see note 1). In its place there appeared an אחד, which arose out of an erroneous dittography of לחד[ש]. Then in 𝔙, or in the text from which 𝔙 was translated, this became "eleven" by the reinsertion of the number "ten."

2 2a על–אל cf. 1:17 note a.

3 3a 𝔐 דבר is quite unusual in the framework of these formulaic, stereotyped introductory words (see 1,182 on 6:2), and, since it is not attested by 𝔊, it was doubtless not part of the original text.

b אדני is lacking in 𝔊 𝔎^{Bo}, see Appendix 1.

c 𝔐 מלך מצרים is not attested by 𝔊 𝔎 𝔄, but this is not to be regarded as a secondary abbreviation, in view of the fact that the title has already been mentioned in v 2.

d 𝔐 תנים here can on no account be the plural of תן "jackal" (Is 13:22; 34:13; and elsewhere), but is to be equated with the תנין ("sea monster" Gen 1:21; "serpent" Ex 7:9f; "dragon" Jer 51:34). Thus some MSS (Ginsburg) read התנין here too. Since, however, the form תנים occurs with the same meaning also in 32:2 (2 MSS^{Ken} read תנין there too), it must be asked whether one has not to reckon with a parallel form תנים alongside תנין. Here the word must mean the "crocodile," the typical Egyptian Nile animal.

e 𝔐 יְאֹרִי should, on the basis of the immediately preceding יאריו, be vocalized as a plural יְאֹרַי. This is how 𝔊 takes it. On the other hand, 𝔖 𝔙 and v 9 of 𝔐 attest a singular form without suffix.

f 𝔐 עשיתני "I have made myself," according to Bauer-Leander §48c the only occurrence of a reflexive form with suffix, is textually suspect. Would one not expect, in the case of such an unusual expression, some emphatic explanatory addition such as אני . . . אֹתִי? Since only 𝔙 attests 𝔐 (𝔊 καὶ ἐγὼ ἐποίησα αὐτούς presupposes the plural ποταμοί as object; 𝔖 ואנא עבדתה presupposes the singular נהרא as object), is 𝔐 not to be regarded as a very possible scribal error for an original עשית[י]ם (if the preceding יאר is read as a singular [see note e], then of

in your cheeks and shall make the fish of your Nile branches[b] stick fast in your scales. And I shall drag you out of the midst of your Nile branches[b] together with all the fish of your Nile branches which cling to your scales[c] 5/ and I shall throw[a] you into the desert[b], you and all the fish of your Nile branches.[c] You will lie in the open, you will[d] not be gathered up nor be sheltered[e]. I shall give you as food to the beasts of the field and the birds of the air, 6/ and all the inhabitants of Egypt will know that I am Yahweh.

Because <you>[a] have been to the house of Israel a reed prop[b]—7/ when they grasp you [with the <hand>][a] you crumple up and wound them all[b] in the <hand>[c]. And when they lean on you, and you break and make all[b] their hips <totter>[d]—8/ therefore thus has [the

עשיתיה or עשיתיו)? On this see Delitzsch, *Schreibfehler,* 120, 132e. Hölscher would read עשיתי on the basis of 29:9.

4 4a Instead of K^{Occ} חחיים, Q^{Occ} Or חחים should be read.

b 𝔐 יאריך. 𝔊 𝔖 have a singular, 𝔙 a plural.

c 𝔐 בקשקשתיך תדבק is not attested by 𝔊. In 𝔊^{B,239} 𝔎 the preceding ואת כל דגת יאריך has fallen out by haplography. The two clauses just mentioned could be understood syntactically as an independent sentence whose subject, by case attraction and with the help of את, is still connected as object to the verb of the preceding sentence ([והעליתי[ך). See Blau, "Gebrauch," 8.

5 5a On this meaning of נטש se 31:12; 32:4 (parallel אטילך) and Driver, "Ezekiel," 299.

b 𝔐 המדברה. 𝔊, with ἐν τάχει, must have misread this as במהרה.

c 𝔐 יאריך. 𝔊 𝔙 𝔖 have singular.

d 𝔊 adds the copula, see 1:4 note a.

e 𝔐 ולא תקבץ. 𝔊 οὐ μὴ περισταλῇς. περιστέλλω describes the dressing and burial of a corpse, see Tob 12:13 and Sir 38:16 where it corresponds to Hebrew אסף which, on this basis, can also describe the burial of a corpse (גויעתי . . . // אסוף שארו περί-στειλον τὸ σῶμα αὐτοῦ . . . τὴν ταφὴν αὐτοῦ). If, then, 𝔗 adds נבילתך in v 5aβ and in v 5aγ renders לא תתכניש ולא תתקבר, then this does not necessitate assuming, as do Cornill, Hölscher, Toy, Herrmann, Bertholet and Fohrer, in תקבץ a scribal error for an original תקבר.

6 6a 𝔐 היותם owes its origin to the erroneous connection with v 6a, the conclusion of the preceding unit. 𝔊 𝔙 𝔖 still attest the original היותך.

b 𝔗, by way of interpretation, adds an additional רעיעא "broken."

7 7a 𝔐 בכפך should be read, with Q, as בכף, from which come 𝔙 *manu* and 𝔗 ביד. 𝔊, on the other hand, has τῇ χειρὶ αὐτῶν and 𝔖 באידיהון. The parallel in v 7b shows that the word is superfluous. See also note c.

b Literally: Every "hand" . . . every hip.

c 𝔐 כתף "shoulder" (𝔙 *humerum*), which Driver, "Ezekiel," 299, would like to take in the sense of "armpit." 𝔊 (πᾶσα) χείρ and 𝔖 אידיהון have retained the original כף, see also Is 36:6 = 2 Kgs 18:21. The corruption is unmistakably connected with the secondary addition (note a). Either after a glossing with בכפם an attempt was made to avoid the ugly doubling of כף by a change to כתף, or else after a corruption of כף to כתף the introduction of כף, which belonged to the traditional expression, seemed a necessary elucidation.

d 𝔐 והעמדת produces exactly the opposite of what is intended. Since the expression המעיד מתנים is attested in Ps 69:24, the text can be corrected by a transposition of consonants (to המעדת). A different approach is taken by Driver, "Ezekiel" 299f, who endeavors to find for העמיד, on the basis of Akka-

Lord][a] Yahweh said: See, I shall bring the sword against you and wipe out from you man and beast, 9/ and the land of Egypt will become a waste and a ruin, and they will know that I am Yahweh.

Because you say[a], "To me belongs the Nile[b] and I have made[b] (it)," 10/ therefore see, I am against[a] you and against[a] your Nile branches and will make the land of Egypt a <ruin> [<sword>] <and> a waste[b] from Migdol <to Syene>[c] and as far as the frontier of Cush. 11/ No foot of man will pass through it, nor will the foot of beast pass through it[a], and it will remain uninhabited for forty years. 12/ And I shall make the land of Egypt[a] a waste among devastated lands, and its cities will become waste among destroyed[b] cities for forty years, and I shall scatter Egypt among the nations and disperse them among the lands.

13/ [For][a] Thus has [the Lord][b] Yahweh said: At the end of forty years I shall gather Egypt from among the nations where they have been scattered. 14/ And I shall restore the fortunes of Egypt and bring them back[a] into the land of Pathros,

dian and Arabic, the meaning "to cause something to be knocked together, bruised."

8 8a אדני is lacking in 𝔊 𝔎[Bo], see Appendix 1.

9 9a 𝔐 אָמַר again goes back (see v 6 note a) to the erroneous connection of what is here the beginning of a new oracle with v 9a, which is the end of the preceding oracle, which in turn had at the end referred to Egypt in the third person (in fact v 9aα has the third person feminine singular, while v 9aβ has the third person plural). 𝔊 𝔏[S] 𝔙 𝔖 connect, more correctly with what follows. Accordingly, as in 35:10, אמרך (so Cornill, Bertholet, Fohrer) or perhaps even only a simple אֹמֵר should be read.

b In 𝔐 the quotation is slightly different from the form in v 3:1) יְאֹר is in the singular, which is attested elsewhere in Ezekiel only in 𝔐 of 29:3 (but see note e) but which is otherwise frequent. 2) עשיתי is without suffix. 𝔊 𝔖 assimilate to v 3; 𝔙 on each occasion reproduces the verb as in 𝔐; 𝔗 paraphrases in both cases. It seems to be a simplified repetition (from another hand? see below).

10 10a על–אל cf. 1:17 note a.

b 𝔐 לחרבות חרב שממה is broken up by 𝔊 into εἰς ἔρημον καὶ ῥομφαίαν καὶ ἀπώλειαν. 𝔏[S] both times suppresses the copula. 𝔗 לחורב צדו ואישתשממו has it at least in front of the third expression. 𝔙 combines (*daboque terram Aeypti in solitudines, gladio dissipatam*), while 𝔖 לחבלא ולחורבא has the two parts of the double expression of v 9a. This must be along the right lines. The basis here too must surely be in a reading לחרבה ושממה (v 9 לשממה וחרבה). The threat of the sword (חרב) has then transferred to here from v 8. Subsequently the לחרבה חרב has necessarily been taken in the manner of a statement of intensification and been combined as 𝔐 לחרבות חרב "an utter waste." As a result of the dropping of the copula, שממה has been added as a further element of intensification.

c 𝔐 סְוֵנֵה should be read as סְוֵנָה with Michaelis (quoted by Smend). See also Driver, "Ezekiel," 156 note 2. Along with ועד גבול כוש it denotes the most southerly point of the description. Smend points to Strabo 118: μέχρι Συήνης καὶ τῶν Αἰθιοπικῶν ὅρων.

11 11a 𝔖 omits the repetition of לא תעבר בה, doubtless on stylistic grounds.

12 12a 𝔐 את ארץ מצרים. 𝔊 (𝔏[S]) τὴν γῆν αὐτῆς is a stylistic abbreviation.

b 𝔐 מחרבות. In the quite similar passage in 30:7, the nip'al participle is used and in 36:35 a verbal adjective from the same root. Accordingly, Joüon, "Notes," 308, suggests emending to נחרבות or, better still, assuming the dittography of the ם, a simple חרבות.

13 13a The introductory כי of 𝔐 is attested only by 𝔙 𝔊[A] 𝔄 Arm, but not by 𝔊 𝔏[S] 𝔗 𝔖. It may be secondary.

b אדני is lacking in 𝔊 𝔏[S] 𝔎[Bo], see Appendix 1.

14 14a 𝔐 והשבתי seems to have been derived from

into[b] the land of their origin[c], and there[d] they will be a small kingdom[e]. 15/ It will be lower[a] than the kingdoms and will no longer exalt itself over the nations. And I shall reduce them so that they will not rule[b] over the nations, 16/ and they will[a] no more be to the house of Israel a source of (false) trust which brings guilt to men's notice[b] when they provide them with followers[c], and they shall know that I am [the Lord][d] Yahweh.

ישב by 𝔊 *καὶ κατοικιῶ*, 𝔏[S] 𝔅 *et collocabo eos* and 𝔖 ואותב.

b אל–על cf. 1:17 note a.

c On מכורה see 16:3 note b.

d 𝔐 שם is omitted by 𝔊 𝔏[S].

e Literally "a low kingdom."

15 15a 𝔐 תהיה שפלה is omitted by 𝔊 𝔏[S].

b 𝔐 לבלתי רדות. 𝔊 (𝔏[S]) *τοῦ μὴ εἶναι αὐτοὺς πλεί-ονας* seems, by way of contrast to המעיט, to have read רבות.

16 16a 𝔐 יהיה. Since not only in what has gone before but also in what follows "Egypt" (the Egyptians) is spoken of in the third person plural, יהיו should be read here too, with all the versions.

b See 21:28. Driver, "Ezekiel," 300, will be right when he states that the expression is used here in a neuter sense "a reminder of iniquity."

c Literally "when they turn after them"; 𝔅 *ut fugiant et sequantur.*

d אדני is lacking in 𝔊 𝔏 𝔖 𝔎, see Appendix 1.

Form

The complex 29:1–16 is clearly divided up and characterized as to its form by the three recognition formulae in vv 6a, 9a, 16. After the introduction, there is found first of all in vv 1–6a a two-fold proof-saying introduced by the summons (or encounter) formula. The element of indictment (invective) that justifies the pronouncement of judgment is found in v 3 in the quotation of the words of the addressee. In contrast to, e.g., 25:3, 8; 35:10, however, this is not put at the beginning in an explicit יען ("because")-clause from which the proof-saying would then have acquired a three-fold structure. A complete three-part proof-saying of the usual type, as found several times in Ezekiel 25, then occurs in vv 6b–9a. The לכן ("therefore")-clause which introduces the threat has at the beginning, as in 25:13, 16, the messenger formula. The structure of the third unit, vv 9b–16, is more complex. It begins, likewise, as a motivated judgment-oracle in the form לכן ("therefore")-יען ("because"). But the threat of judgment in vv 10–12 is then followed in vv 13–16 by a kind of broken proclamation of salvation introduced by a messenger formula. This, in turn, ends in a recognition formula in v 16b. The latter, in turn, also makes the whole complex into a three-part proof-saying.

The question arises whether the complex is to be broken up into three separate oracles (so, e.g., Fohrer). The difference in subject matter between one section and another might be an argument in favor of this view. But from the point of view of form, the complete separation of the three sections runs up against the difficulty that the person addressed in the second and third sections is not introduced afresh, but is simply presupposed from the preceding unit. In addition, there are associations on the level of content. Thus, the quotation in the first section (v 3) is taken up again at the beginning of the third (v 9b). Again, the reference to the temptation to false trust that Egypt signified for Israel connects the third section in v 16 with the second (vv 6b, 7). Thus it is surely more correct to think of 29:1–16 not as a collection of three independent oracles, but as a series of related oracles.

Although the component parts of 29:1–16 are clearly connected, a glance at the differences in form (and content) between the three raises the question whether the present form of the unit as a whole has not arisen as a result of successive enrichments. At any rate one cannot think here of a "series" of three individual parts in the sense, e.g., of Am 1f or 4:6ff. For details see the exposition.

The question of the time and place of origin is best considered after the detailed examination of the section.

Interpretation

■ **29:1–6a** *a. An Oracle of Judgment on Pharaoh, the Crocodile of the Nile*

■ **29:1** The divine message, leading to the commission to speak against Pharaoh, comes to the prophet on the twelfth day of the tenth month of Jehoiachin's tenth year.[1] According to Parker-Dubberstein, that is January 7, 587. Half a year or so later the besieged city of Jerusalem will fall. 29:1–6a is therefore the oldest in date of the oracles against the foreign nations. Although W. F. Albright supposes that at this time the news of Hophra's campaign against the Babylonians who are encamped before Jerusalem (Jer 37:5) reached the exiles,[2] in the immediately following oracle in vv 3–6 there is not the slightest indication of this.[3] The awareness of Egypt's resistance to the divinely-willed guidance of history does not first come from these latest Egyptian operations.[4]

■ **29:2** As in earlier contexts, the prophet, addressed as "son of man," is summoned to the gesture of "turning his face" against Pharaoh and to prophesy against Pharaoh and Egypt.[5] The fact that the title "king of Egypt" is added here to "Pharaoh" (as in v 3 and in 30:21f; 31:2; 32:2) makes it clear that the original meaning of Egyptian *pr-*ʿꜣ "great house," which is certainly attested from the eighteenth Dynasty onwards as the typical description in Late Egyptian for the king,[6] is here completely submerged. The word is already understood almost as a proper name, which then has to be elucidated by means of a specific title. An actual proper name of the Egyptian king is never found anywhere in Ezekiel, and this clearly shows that we are at a further remove from the actual historical events than we are, e.g., in Jer 44:30; 1 Kgs 14:25; 2 Kgs 23:29, 33–35. Since the continuation, especially from v 10 onwards, turns more and more clearly towards the land of Egypt, the mention of the land of Egypt as the addressee of the prophetic oracle has already been included (editorially?) in the commission.

■ **29:3** The Pharaoh is addressed with the summons formula or encounter formula, which also introduced the first oracle against Tyre (26:3) and the oracle against Sidon (28:22) and which recurs in v 10 in the introduction to the third element of the oracle-complex of 29:1–16 (otherwise in the Egypt oracles only in 30:22).[7] Then, however, it passes immediately into figurative language. Pharaoh is compared with a תנין ("crocodile") (note d) which lies in the midst of its Nile branches. The word יְאֹר ("river Nile"), used in the singular in v 9, is an Egyptian loan-word. The original *itrw* "river, Nile" (the plural is used of rivers in the next world) is pronounced, from the eighteenth Dynasty onwards (and found also without the *t*), as *irw*. So, too, in Coptic.[8] The plural usage, which is the most frequent in Ezekiel (29:3–5, 10; 30:12), is orientated towards the Lower Egyptian Delta region, where at this period the political center also lay, with its many Nile branches. The etymologically obscure תנין (here "crocodile") appears in Dtn 32:33; Ps 91:13, parallel to פתן ("adder"), to denote a serpent-like creature. A serpent is also indicated by P's account of the transformation of the staffs of Moses and the Egyptian magicians (Ex 7:9f, 12). However, this account also suggests that in תנין there lies a hint of the uncanny. This becomes quite explicit in Is 51:9; Job 7:12 where תנין, alongside ים ("sea"), רהב ("Rahab"), תהום רבה ("the great deep"), describes the representative of the chaotic primeval ocean against which the creator God has taken up battle. In Ps 74:13, parallel to ים ("sea"), a plurality of תנינים are mentioned, which as enemies of the creator God are crushed. They presumably correspond to the עזרי רהב ("helpers of Rahab") of Job 9:13. In the continuation in Ps 74:14, the לויתן ("Leviathan") is also mentioned, and this recurs in Is 27:1 alongside the תנין אשר בים.[9] Of the תנין of Jer 51:34 there is little to be made beyond his terrifying, dangerous character, while in Gen 1:21 (and in Ps 148:7 which is dependent on that) there is the completely demythologized use of the term as the

1 See 1, 144f.
2 Albright, "Seal of Eliakim," 94.
3 This observation should not, however, be used in reverse to give a late date to this oracle; so Fohrer (see note a).
4 See, e.g., above on Ezek 17.
5 See 1, 131f; see 1, 182f.
6 Erman-Grapow, 1. 516; according to J. J. Hess, "Beduinisches zum Alten und Neuen Testament," *ZAW* 35 (1915): 129f, it is still found in the south of Egypt to the present day.
7 See 1, 175 on 5:8, where it first occurs; also see above p. 98.
8 Erman-Grapow, 1.146.
9 On Is 27:1 see the close Ugaritic parallels found in Cyrus H. Gordon, *Ugaritic Handbook* (Rome: Pontifical Biblical Institute, 1947 1948), text 67, 1ff (*idem, Ugaritic Literature,* 38); Driver, *Canaanite Myths,* 102f.

name of a great (created) sea monster. At what point in this range of meanings is Ezek 29:3 (32:2) to be included? H. Gunkel thought that he could see in the two Ezekiel passages two versions of the myth of the fight with the dragon, which refers to the hubris and fall of the dragon, and in the reference to the Nile branches a discernible Egyptianization.[10] The reference to "lying in the midst (of the Nile)" רבץ בתוך (also in the introduction to the wild-beast image of the lions in 19:2) would suggest, however, that here the identical demythologizing has taken place as has happened to the לויתן ("Leviathan") of Job 40:25, which is unmistakably mythical in its origin, and to the תנין of Gen 1:21. In Ezek 29:3 (32:2) what should be thought of in the first instance is simply the crocodile, which is particularly typical of the Nile region and is therefore worshipped in many cults.[11] That this comparison is not at all unlikely for the Pharaoh, quite apart from any mythology of the fight with the dragon, is shown by a hymn to Thutmose III in which Amun says of the Pharaoh's enemies: "I have made them see thy majesty as a crocodile, Lord of fear in the water, unapproachable."[12]

The Pharaoh thus presented in an animal image is introduced, by means of a quotation of his own words, in all the arrogance of a representative of a great power.[13] In contrast to the statement by the prince of Tyre, who deduced his divinity from his majestic dwelling place (28:2[9]), what is expressed here about the representative of Egypt is his unrestricted right of ownership of the precious waters of the Nile from which Egypt lives, a right which is justified on the basis of his own creative activity. It may be asked whether in this claim to ownership there does not already lie a concealed polemic against a possible foreign claim to ownership, and thus a reference to the abortive attack on Egypt by Nebuchadnezzar in 601/600. Yahweh himself, according to Jer 43:8–13; 44:30 and again according to Ezek 29:19f; 30:20–26, authorizes his instrument Nebuchadnezzar to make this attack. In the substantiation of this right of ownership on the basis of creative power, an attempt is made to invoke the highest possible category. We need certainly look for no myth of the primeval ocean here. How could the chaos god, who by definition is opposed to the creator god, have legitimatized his claim by means of a statement about creation? But we can scarcely find here either a familiarity on Ezekiel's part with statements made by Egyptian deities seeking to claim for themselves the power of creation or (and this would even seem to justify the reading of 𝔐, see note f) who describe themselves, like Atum-Khepri, as "self-created."[14] Ezekiel can scarcely have been aware of such sacral formulae of priestly theology. It must suffice to think in a general way of the claim of rulers the world over to power and to be the source of well-being, according to which, e.g. the Egyptian king can claim for himself the success of the Nile floods.[15] If this is what is expressed in the terminology of Deutero-Isaiah in Is 47:8, 10 by "I am and there is no one besides me," then in the phrase "I have made them" in Ezek 29:3, we can hear a turn of phrase which is typical of Ezekiel. Against the background of divine self-assertion in "I, Yahweh, have spoken and 'I will do it' (ועשיתי)" (17:24; 22:14; and elsewhere), anyone who has heard Ezekiel's words can hear quite clearly the insufferable hubris of the Egyptian claim.

■ **29:4** A divine threat is made against this hubris. The judgment of which it speaks is expressed in terms of the imagery begun in v 3. Yahweh will hunt the crocodile. In the tomb paintings of the Old Kingdom in Egypt there is never a picture of a crocodile hunt, no doubt in view of the widely practiced worship of the crocodile,[16] although these undoubtedly took place and, as early rock scratchings at El-Hosch show, were carried on with ropes and harpoons, in the same way as the frequently depicted hunting of the hippopotamus.[17] In the later period, districts hostile to the crocodile are differentiated more and more sharply from districts friendly to the crocodile.[18] In the late period Herodotus can give an amusing description of a crocodile hunt with hooks to

10 Gunkel, *Schöpfung*, 71–77; on this basis also, e.g., Fredriksson, *Jahwe als Krieger*, 74f, 78f.

11 See, e.g., Bonnet, *Reallexikon*, s.v. "Krokodil," or Posener, *Dictionary*, s.v. "Crocodile."

12 Breasted, *History*, 319.

13 On this see the analogy of the quotations of the words of Babylon in Is 47:7f, 10.

14 Kees, "Ägypten," *RGL*, 1.

15 Frankfort, *Kingship and the Gods*, 58.

16 Kees, *Ägypten*, 58.

17 Erman-Ranke, 271 note 4.

18 Bonnet, *Reallexikon*, 393.

which bait is fastened.[19] Just so will Yahweh attack the crocodile like a huntsman with "hooks" (חחים 19:4,9; the same expression in 38:4 ונתתי חחים בלחייך "I will put hooks in your jaws"), in order to seize it and snatch it from its familiar watery surroundings.

A peculiar feature here is the statement that Yahweh will let the fish of the Nile branches be draped on the crocodile's scales, so that when the crocodile is pulled out he can at the same time pull out all the fish. In this grotesque extension of what is otherwise quite a graphic image, the intention is to give expression to the participation of the inhabitants of Egypt in the fate of their king. Since the overlong expressions in v 4aβ and v 4bβ are metrically longer than the three-stress lines preceding each of them, the suspicion cannot entirely be suppressed that we might here be dealing with a secondary amplification. The original 3 + 3 structure of vv 4aα, 5aα would then have told simply of the capture of the crocodile and its being snatched from the water.

■ **29:5** When it is stated further that the animal is thrown into the desert (on נטש "to throw" see note a) and left unburied in the open country as prey for the birds of the air and for wild beasts (32:4; see also 31:13), then this involves not only the antithesis "water: dry land," but also that of "inhabited land: desert." For the explicit inclusion of the fish of the Nile shows that this is a reference to the desolation of the inhabited land as a consequence of the exiling of its entire population, something which is then explicitly mentioned in v 12.

■ **29:6a** The Pharaoh has only just proudly boasted of his ownership of the Nile regions and has dared to assert this ownership in highhanded fashion on the strength of his rights as creator. In a judgment such as this, however, which is intended to snatch Pharaoh from this sphere of ownership which he claims for himself, Yahweh makes himself known as the true lord, in the mystery of his person, over the king of Egypt.

■ **29:6b–9a** *b. The brittle staff.* The judgment oracle in vv 1–6a has then been expanded, presumably at a somewhat later point in time, by a second assertion which is differently motivated.

■ **29:8** Here, too, the reference is to a judgment. The place of the Pharaoh, however, is taken by the land of Egypt. Without any imagery, Yahweh threatens, in stereotyped formulaic language, to bring the sword (6:3) and exterminate man and beast (14:13, 17, 19, 21; 25:13) so that Egypt will lie waste.

■ **29:6b, 7** The motivation of the judgment is quite different here. The simile which is used to describe Egypt can be found already in the description of Egypt in the book of Isaiah. In the context of the narrative of Sennacherib's campaign, Is 36:6 (parallel in 2 Kgs 18:21) records the scornful remark of the Assyrian king about the Egyptians: "See, you are relying on 'that broken reed' (משענת הקנה הרצוץ הזה) Egypt which will pierce the hand of any man who leans on it. Such is Pharaoh king of Egypt to all who rely on him." The close verbal relationships and the characteristic image can scarcely leave any doubt that Ezekiel is here transmitting a conventional image which at the same time he amplifies and uses in a more concrete fashion. Such borrowing of an image from the book of Isaiah has already been noted in Ezek 5:1f.[20] What the Assyrian king said in Is 36:6 in quite general terms about Pharaoh is now applied specifically to Egypt's offense against the "house of Israel." Instead of the already broken reed (local Egyptian coloring is the intention of this reference to what is surely the bulrush), on two occasions here reference is made to the breaking of the reed under the hand that leans on it. And correspondingly, the subsequent disaster which befalls the person who is deceived by such a support is developed in two ways. The reed pierces his hand and injures him. His hips totter. The latter is an expression found also in Ps 69:24 for the loss of bodily stability.

It might appear as if Egypt is being blamed here for not having been a stronger support to "the house of Israel" against Babylon and for having neglected the duty of rescuing Israel, a duty for which it was actually destined. But this can in no circumstances be the intention of the prophet, who (as has already been mentioned) has the same attitude to Babylon as had Jeremiah. Rather, he sees Egypt's guilt, and this becomes quite clear in v 16, in a much more graphic way in the manner in which it has actually allowed the suggestion to arise that it could possibly be a support and in this way has led Israel astray to a state of false trust. It leads away from

19 2, 70.
20 See 1, 172.

obedience to Yahweh's dispensation and thereby makes the house of Israel unwilling to be penitent and submissive.[21] This is the quite specific "lie" on Egypt's part. What was to have been expected from Egypt according to the will of Yahweh was not greater military strength, but clarity about the fact that there is no possibility of resisting Yahweh's will and that at this point all preparations, even the most efficient, are in any event a "lie." One cannot ask what this other way of "obedience" would have been like for Egypt in practical, political terms. Its "guilt" is judged from a standpoint other than that of normal international politics.

■ **29:9a** Because Egypt has incurred guilt in this objective way, then according to this oracle the judgment which reveals Yahweh's personal will must be carried out against it.

■ **29:9b–16** *c. The Forty Years of Egypt's Judgment.* The third section of 29:1–16 sums up once again the two preceding oracles, expands their threat of judgment and extends them, astonishingly, along the lines of partial clemency for Egypt.

■ **29:9b** Once again the invective in v 9b begins with Pharaoh's presumptuous statement from v 3. The image of the crocodile, however, is not touched further. The quotation is slightly different in word order from v 3 and is simplified by the omission of the suffixes on the noun יאר ("the Nile") and the verb עשיתי ("I have made"). As in 25:8 and elsewhere, it is here incorporated in a motivatory יען ("because")-clause.

■ **29:10** The judgment speech is as in v 3 (see above). After these slightly rephrased borrowings from the Pharaoh oracles at the beginning of the chapter, the threat passes quickly away from Pharaoh towards the land of Egypt and describes its devastation in much greater detail with borrowings from vv 8f, the second section of 29:1–16. The expression "from Migdol to Syene," as an analogy to which one may cite the phrase for the full extent of Israel "from Dan to Beersheba" (Ju 20:1; 1 Sam 3:20; and elsewhere), makes it clear that the devastation covers the whole of Egypt. The expression recurs in 30:6. "Syene" (סונה) is the traditional southern frontier point a little north of the first cataract, modern Aswan.[22] After the expulsion of the Ethiopian rulers by the Saites, Egypt once again reached as far as this southern frontier. Whether behind the insertion "and as far as the frontier of Cush" there lies the memory of the fact that from time to time the territory as far as the second cataract at Wadi Halfa, the land of *wꜣwꜣ.t* in fact even the territory as far as Semneh, belonged to Egypt, one may very well doubt.[23] As the northern frontier-point a place is mentioned which has as its name the Semitic word "tower" (מגדל). This was the name given by the Egyptians in the later period to the watchtowers of the defensive forts which they erected on their eastern frontier.[24] Thus, e.g., in the context of the Exodus story there occurs in Ex 14:2 (Nu 33:7) just such a Migdol, but there is no proof of its identity with the place referred to in the present passage. One is more inclined to equate the place mentioned here with the Migdol in the Delta, known as the location of a community of Jewish refugees and mentioned in the book of Jeremiah (44:1 cf. 46:14) and thus known of in the time of Ezekiel. It must lie right at the northernmost point of the eastern frontier. An identification with *tell es-samūt* east of *el-kanṭara,* where Magdolo, situated (according to ancient information) twelve miles south of Pelusium, is also to be located, or with *tell el-ḥēr* would satisfy these demands.[25]

■ **29:11** The devastation of the whole of Egyptian territory is described in stereotyped expressions. The foot of neither man nor beast will pass through it.[26] The type of the עָבַר ("passing") is found also in 5:14; 14:15; 33:28; 36:34 as well as in Jer 9:9, 11; and elsewhere.

■ **29:12** The expression about the devastation of land and city among lands and cities recurs almost identically in 30:7. Scattering among nations and dispersal among lands were used in 22:15 with reference to Jerusalem (11:16 and elsewhere) (with reference to Egypt see also 30:23, 26). The fate of Egypt in judgment is in all re-

21 Cf., e.g., the event described in concrete terms in Ezek 17.

22 See Kees, *alte Ägypten,* 175ff.

23 On these frontier questions see, e.g., Erman-Ranke, 593ff.

24 See Kees, *Ägypten,* 228 note 6. Migdol of Rameses III on the Phoenician coast is mentioned by Alt, *Kleine Schriften,* 1. 222.

25 For the former identification see Genesius-Buhl, Koehler-Baumgartner; for the latter, Hermann Guthe, *Bibelatlas* (Leipzig: Wagner & Debes, ²1926); Zorell.

26 On this see the peculiar variation in 32:13.

spects completely assimilated to that of Israel or Jerusalem. There is no awareness of the fact that complete devastation and the deportation of the total population is hardly conceivable, in view of the much larger extent of the territory. If one makes a comparison with Jeremiah's threats against Egypt in Jeremiah 43f, the much more realistic attitude of Jeremiah is immediately striking. In the categories "devastation of the land" and "dispersal among the nations" one can easily recognize the categories of those who have been deported into exile. It is only in these categories that they are able to conceive of judgment on Egypt.

■ **29:13** The most surprising statement, however, is the fixing of a time-limit for the period of Egypt's condemnation to forty years. A series of scholars (Plessis, Rothstein, Herrmann and others) have suggested that the messenger formula in v 13 introduces a secondary addition, which has been secondarily connected with the preceding section by the two-fold insertion of the forty years in vv 11f. Against this, however, there is the consideration (mentioned at the beginning) of the form of the proof-saying, which is concluded only with the recognition formula in v 16. This is also observed by Hölscher, who in addition attributes the whole section to the hand of the redactor. To this may be added the factual consideration that a section comprising only vv 9b–12, deprived of vv 13–16 and of the two references to the forty years in vv 11f, would, from the content point of view, hardly be saying anything more than what has already been said in the two preceding oracles. It would be more correct to realize that the reference to the forty years is the real point of the total complex, a point to which full expression is now given, framed as it is between the references back to the two preceding oracles (vv 9b, 16a).[27]

The exile of the Egyptians is to last for forty years. This statement comes astonishingly close to what was said in an earlier context about the fate of the house of Israel. In 4:4–8, in the context of a later expansion of the original text, a mode of reckoning could be discerned according to which the "house of Judah" would have to reckon with a period of punishment of forty years, similar to the period of punishment of the generation of those who participated in the wilderness wanderings.[28] This same mode of reckoning is here applied to Egypt. While in the case of Judah in 4:4–8 there was no mention of what was to happen after the expiry of the forty years (the restoration of Israel's fortunes is mentioned in other oracles in Ezekiel, but without this element of the calculation of the period of time), here what is to happen at the end of the forty years' judgment on Egypt is fully discussed. Yahweh will gather again the nation that has been scattered among the nations. This is also said of Israel in quite related terms in 11:17; 20:34, 41; 28:25; and elsewhere.

■ **29:14** Yahweh restores Egypt's fortunes.[29] Just as the restoration of Israel, according to 20:32–38, was connected with a decree aimed at separating out the sinners, so here the restoration of Egypt is connected with a setting to rights of what was wrong with this world power. Egypt will be led back to Pathros, the land of her "origin" (on מכורה see 16:3 note b). פתרום ("Pathros") is found again in Ezekiel only in 30:14 and in the rest of the OT only in Is 11:11; Jer 44:1, 15 (see also פתרסים "Pathrusim" in Gen 10:14; 1 Chr 1:12). As the Egyptian *pꜣ-tꜣ-rśj* it describes the "land of the south," i.e. Upper Egypt. See also the combination in the title of Esarhaddon as "King of the kings of Egypt, Pathros and Cush."[30] The Esarhaddon texts suggest the idea that Egypt proper (*muṣur* corresponding to מצרים) is to be found in the Delta and that Upper Egypt and Cush are separate parts of the empire. In Ezek 29:14 it is stated that Upper Egypt is the real homeland of the Egyptians. Is there a reflection here of the correct historical recollection that the Egypt which under the Saites had its political center in Ezekiel's day in the Delta had in earlier periods its political center in the Nile valley, for example in the Thebes of the Middle and New Kingdoms? Or is

27 The suggestion by E. L. Dietrich, שוב שבות, 20f, that vv 12aβ–14a be deleted as an editorial expansion has no justification either.

28 See 1, 166–168.

29 On this expression, which is used in 16:53 of Jerusalem, Sodom and Samaria, see 1, 351 (see also 39:25 of Jacob-house of Israel).

30 *mât muṣur mât paturisi u mât kusi;* Borger, *Inschriften Asarhaddons,* 9, 36, 72, 96, 101, 118, and the conquest account on p. 86.

there here a geological theory of the nature of the statements transmitted by Herodotus?[31] According to this, the Delta had been "as the Egyptians themselves say . . . alluvial land and but lately (so to say) come into being," so that even Herodotus is of the opinion that "as the land grew in extent many of them spread down over it, and many stayed behind." Did Israel explain to herself this tradition of the Egyptians, on the analogy of her own history, as an "exodus" from an original homeland and a "settlement" in an originally foreign territory? In the present context of Ezek 29:14 what is in any case in the foreground is the statement that Egypt's claim to be a great power, which is expressed particularly obtrusively for Palestinian feelings in Egypt's proximity to the frontiers of Palestine, is to be restrained. Egypt is to withdraw modestly into the Nile valley.

■ **29:15** The claim to greatness, deriving from the luxurious abundance of the many branches of the Nile in the Delta, is to be humbled, the high is "to become low" (תהיה שפלה) and be made small (והמעטתים "and I shall reduce them") and "exalt itself no more" (לא תתנשא) and not oppress other nations. Is all this intended to remind us of the empty boasting of vv 3, 9?[32]

■ **29:16** In a free interpretation, v 16 adds to this the recollection of the reproach in vv 6b, 7, which is now made quite clear in its inner orientation. The real offense against Israel was not Egypt's lack of real power which failed at the decisive moment, but the tempting of Israel to false trust, as a result of which Israel's sin now appeared quite publicly and became judicially notorious and open to complaint.[33] Thus Yahweh, in all his judging and pardoning, prosecutes, even with regard to Egypt, the activity which makes him recognizable to men.

One cannot suppress the question why precisely with regard to Egypt there should be recounted this sacred, saving postscript which keeps Egypt's name from extinction, whereas there is no such postscript with regard to all the other groups to which the foreign oracles are addressed. One may point to the fact that in the book of Jeremiah also the oracle against Egypt ends with the prospect of restoration (46:26) (see also Is 19). There is no awareness in Ezekiel of the existence of a group of Jewish exiles living in Egypt on whose account Egypt had to be spared. Nor can one speak of particular sentimental relationships on Ezekiel's part towards Egypt, which after all once sheltered Israel's ancestors (see Dtn 23:8). Rather, elsewhere in Ezekiel a strong anti-Egyptian attitude is striking (see chapters 20, 23). Thus, in this final oracle of 29:1–16, there is perhaps expressed a desire to look to some extent also from the position of the surrounding nations for the great turning point for Israel. Among these nations the great power Egypt cannot be entirely wished away. It will still be there as a great power, but now devoted to humility. There then arises the question, however, whether something of this hereafter ought not to be expressed with regard to other world powers (see also on chapters 38f).

Setting

If, in retrospect, we now ask about the point in time at which to set the total complex of 29:1–16, then the date for the origin of the basic oracle in vv 1–6a is to be found in the date given at the head of it. There were no contemporary references discernible in the oracle itself. But then, here too, there has occurred the process which has already been noted on many occasions, that of a secondary expansion of the oracle. While the date in 29:1 for the basic form of the oracle still indicates a period prior to the fall of Jerusalem, the expansion in vv 6b–9a already gives the impression of being a secondary reflection on Egypt's complicity in the fall of the house of Israel. In Hophra's lamentably disastrous expedition, in which Judah had fastened all her hopes and which had strengthened her in her disobedience to Yahweh's true will (on this see also Ezekiel 17), Egypt's evil character as tempter had again become clear. Thus vv 6b-9a, in which the use of older prophetic oracles is also discernible, should be dated after the fall of Jerusalem. The third oracle, on the other hand, which clearly presupposes the two preceding oracles and consciously refers to them and which, both in its historical reckoning and in its use of the vocabulary of restoration, links up with relatively late elements in Ezekiel 4 and 16, should be removed fairly far in time from the first two oracles. It should be derived, like 4:4–6, from the school of Ezekiel. The

31 2, 15 (also 4).
32 See also 1, 367 on 17:22–24, and 1, 446f on 21:31.
33 On the forensic expression הזכיר עון ("to bring guilt to notice") see 21:28f and 1, 445.

derivation of 29:3–6a (and of 32:2ff) from Jeremiah circles[34] is ruled out on the grounds of linguistic structure (proof-saying).

The discernible remoteness from the actual specific realities of Egypt makes it internally probable that the oracles should be attributed to the sphere of the Babylonian exiles.

Aim

The offense of the great power is presented in a double light in the total complex of 29:1–16. It is first made clear how she complacently boasts of the gift that has been granted to her as of a possession which no one can dispute. From this boasting, however, which first of all basks in its own opulence, there then emerges, when a more profound justification for it is sought, the devilish claim to arbitrary creative power. When a man to whom something has been given clutches onto this possession, then it is but a short way to the public disowning of the creator. The insolent hubris is directed first towards the world's goods, but then, with inner inevitability, against the giver of these goods, who now appears as an intruder over against this absolute possessive will.

In this action, power becomes a temptation for the people of God, who ought to know that God's power makes the weak strong. Power which can be seen appears to them to be the power which is able to help. It attracts the eyes of the weak, so that they are no longer capable of following the less obvious call of him with whom alone is all power, no matter how hidden and puzzling his encounters with his own people may be. It entices the people of God especially at the point where God leads them into the heat of his judgment and wishes them to feel his hand heavy in judgment upon them. It dangles the hope of cheap freedom before their eyes, but in the decisive moment it does not save but only injures the one who thought he had found in it a support.

The prophet, however, proclaims that God is in the process of bringing to judgment this great power in its highhandedness and in its power to lead astray. In addition, his word reveals that God's judgment does not simply seek to destroy, even when men encroach upon his creative power and thereby actually forfeit their life. God does not simply disown the sinful world in order to extinguish it in his wrath. His judgment, here too, seeks to set right. God brings monarchs down from their thrones and leads them through periods of devastation, in which he can keep a nation through a whole generation, back to beginnings which are ordered in accordance with his will. The prophetic word proclaims that even the secular power-world can be restored when God leads men in humiliation to a new awareness of the one who alone is great.

34 Proposed by Kuhl, *Prophets*, 110.

2. Egypt: God's Substitute Reward for Nebuchadnezzar's Trouble over Tyre

Bibliography

See above p. 21 on 26:1–28:19 and p. 102 on 29:1–32:32.

29

17 And in the twenty-seventh year, in the first
month, on the first (day) of the month the
word of Yahweh came to me: 18/ Son of
man, Nebuchadnezzar[a], king of Babylon,
has made his army work hard against[b]
Tyre. Every head has been shaved bald,
and every shoulder has been rubbed bare,
but he and his army have carried off no
reward from Tyre for[c] work which he has
carried out[d] against her. 19/ Therefore[a],
thus has [the Lord][b] Yahweh said: See, I
shall give to Nebuchadnezzar[c], king of
Babylon, the land of Egypt. And he will
[carry off its pomp and][d] pillage it and
plunder it, and this will be the reward of
his army. 20/ As the reward[a] for which[b]
he has worked I have given to him the
land of Egypt, [because they have acted
for me][c] says [the Lord][d] Yahweh.
21 On that day I[a] shall make a horn[b] spring
forth for the house[c] of Israel. But I shall

29:18 18a On the orthography of the name Nebuchadnezzar see 26:7 note c.
b על–אל cf. 1:17 note a.
c 𝔊 (𝔏[S]) have a copula here in addition: ἐπὶ Τύρον καὶ τῆς δουλείας.
d 𝔙 here inserts *mihi* as an instinctive theological elucidation. It is Yahweh himself who has commissioned the work.
19 19a 𝔐 לכן is omitted by 𝔊 𝔏[S] 𝔎.
b אדני is lacking in 𝔊 𝔎[Bo], see Appendix 1.
c On the orthography of the name see 26:7 note c.
d 𝔐 ונשא המנה is missing in 𝔊 𝔏[S] 𝔎 and is to be regarded as an interpretative element in which the catch-word המון (30:10, 15; 31:2, 18; 32:12, 16; and elsewhere), which appears frequently in the other oracles against Egypt, should be emphasized here too. See also 30:4 note a. An emendation to הונה (BH[3]) is not demanded by 𝔖 קנינה.
20 20a Van den Born translates "Voor het werk dat hij eraan besteed heeft" because the gloss (note c) seems to presuppose this meaning. פעלה in Jer 31:16 and 2 Chr 15:7 in fact means the work which yields a reward (שכר). But the following בה, in which a ב-*pretii* is to be found (see also note b), suggests here the much more frequently attested sense of "reward" (parallel to שכר). So, too, Paul Humbert, "L'emploi du verbe *pā'al* et de ses dérivés substantifs en hébreu biblique," *ZAW* 65 (1953): 35–44, especially 42f, who feels obliged to derive the noun פעלה, which is attested in the OT only in the later period, from the "contexte sociologique des marchands phéniciens ou des sédentaires de Canaan."
b 𝔐 בה, which undoubtedly refers back to פעלתו, has been wrongly referred by 𝔙 *adversus eam* to Tyre. Here 𝔙 is following 𝔊 𝔏[S] 𝔖, which in fact incorporate into the text ἐπὶ Τύρον, *super Tyrum*, בצור.
c 𝔐 אשר עשו לי is not attested by 𝔊 𝔏[S] 𝔖 𝔄 and is to be regarded as a secondary theological interpretation along the lines of 𝔙 in v 18 (note d). 𝔗 explains it along other lines: "who were liable before me to receive retribution from them."
d אדני is lacking in 𝔊 𝔎[Bo], see Appendix 1.
21 21a 𝔐 אצמיח has been read by 𝔊 (𝔏[S] 𝔙) as an impersonal third person singular ἀνατελεῖ (*orientur*, *pullulabit*).
b 𝔗 renders פורקן "deliverance."
c 𝔊 𝔏[S] are more emphatic "the whole house of Israel."

open your mouth[d] in their midst, and they will know that I am Yahweh[e].

d Literally "give an opening of the mouth."
e 𝔊 is fuller מרא מרותא.

Form

This dated unit contains first of all in v 18 a word addressed to the prophet himself, in which there is described a specific historical situation (Nebuchadnezzar's battle against Tyre). This is followed in vv 19f, introduced by the messenger formula (without there being any mention of a specific commission to proclaim or of any addressee), a divine oracle, which in its central statement recalls the old prophetic oracles of the holy war: "See I shall give to Nebuchadnezzar the land of Egypt."[1] There is, however, more than the bare statement of the surrender of Egypt in the manner of the old prophetic oracles. Rather, the event is further amplified (plundering) and its inner significance is indicated (reward) before the whole is rounded off in v 20a by the repetition of the basic divine oracle. At the beginning this was expressed participially; when it is repeated it is expressed, as in the old oracles, in the perfect tense.[2]

Further, Hölscher is correct, rather than Kraetzschmar and Plessis, when he asserts that what we have here is "not poetry, but prose."[3] It is, however, the exalted language of the oracle as it is widely found in Ezekiel, stylized by the older conventions of language, yet not dispensing with the loose use of parallel expressions.[4] The formula for a divine saying closes this self-contained unit.

In v 21, tacked on as in 30:9 with ביום ההוא ("on that day"), there is added to the unit a proof-saying in two parts with a proclamation of weal directed at Israel and at the prophet personally. Its content is connected with what precedes, but from the point of view of form it is to be thought of as an independent element.

Setting

The oracle is dated to the beginning of Jehoiachin's twenty-seventh year. According to Parker-Dubberstein that is April 26, 571. The oracle itself suggests that at this time a difficult siege of the city of Tyre must have come to an end with a disappointing outcome for the Babylonian king. In the short sketch of the history of Tyre given above, reference was made to the note by Josephus that Nebuchadnezzar had besieged Tyre for thirteen years under her king Ithobaal.[5] According to W. B. Fleming (with whom E. Unger agrees), the siege is to be dated in the years 585–572.[6] O. Eissfeldt calculates the beginning of the siege to the year 586 and therefore dates the end of the siege to the year 573.[7] However these alternatives are resolved, it is in any event clear that the dating of the oracle of Ezekiel is internally highly probable. A slightly different dating, however, is calculated by W. F. Albright with a siege lasting from 588/87 to 575/74.[8]

The Babylonian outlook of the whole account cannot be overlooked. Thus, there is nothing against attributing the oracle to one of those exiled to Babylon. Neither in the style nor in the content of the oracle and of its secondary observations are there (against Hölscher and others) elements which could seriously call into question the authorship of this section by Ezekiel himself.

Interpretation

■ 29:17 In a word of God, received at the beginning of Jehoiachin's twenty-seventh year, the prophet is authorized to deliver an oracle which unites in a unique way in Ezekiel the fates of Tyre and Egypt.[9] It is the latest dated prophetic oracle in the book of Ezekiel. It follows a long time after the earlier oracles against Tyre and Egypt and is chronologically even later than the great vision of the new temple (40:1–42:20). Its content, too, characterizes the oracle as a late one, which presupposes a long

1 On this see von Rad, *Krieg*.
2 Cf., e.g., Josh 6:16, where (against von Rad's translation) the usual נתן ביד is replaced, as in the present passage in Ezekiel, by a simple נתן ל: "Yahweh has given you the city."
3 Hölscher, *Hesekiel*, 147.
4 See, for example, the two parallel expressions about the booty and those about the reward.
5 *Antiquities* X 11, 1, and *c. Apionem* 1, 21 (= Niese 1, 156).
6 Fleming, *History of Tyre*, 44; Unger, "Nebukadnezar II," 314.
7 Eissfeldt, "Datum."
8 Albright, "Seal of Eliakim," 94f. See further Howie, 42f.
9 See 1, 144f.

period of reflection on earlier oracles and of questioning the validity of these oracles.[10]

■ **29:18** When Yahweh points the prophet (who is addressed as "son of man")[11] to a historical event which had taken place before the eyes of all not too long before and when he himself asks the question which this event can raise, then quite unmistakably he is taking a question out of the mouth of the prophet and his environment, a question which had been raised in their minds by the observations and consideration of this event. The army of the king of Babylon had, strangely, departed from the siege of Tyre without any reward. In this respect this siege had been a bitter effort. With the drastic figure of speech, "Every head has been shaved bald and every shoulder has been rubbed bare," the effort is made visible which had been expended on the siege of the city. While it has already been supposed (Hitzig) that this refers to the labor of building a dyke along which the battering rams could be taken from the mainland to the island city—the method of siege successfully used against Tyre in a later period by Alexander the Great and which demanded of the besiegers the carrying of innumerable baskets of earth on their shoulder and heads, with the result that one could see the worn places on their bodies (מרט [here "to rub bare"] used of the polishing of the sword 21:14–22)—this nevertheless remains pure supposition. Otherwise we know nothing of the construction of such a dyke by Nebuchadnezzar. On the basis of the information of Arrian that the channel was shallow in the time of Alexander, to conclude that this was due to the earlier work of Nebuchadnezzar (Hitzig) is inadmissible.[12] Nor can Ezek 26:8ff bear this assumption at all. The expression is a pure figure of speech that is derived from the burden-bearing laborer who works in bondage (Ex 1:14; 2:23).

If, however, one were then to ask with mild astonishment why the prophet in this case thinks so kindly of the poor Babylonian soldiers who have labored without any reward, as if such unrewarded waging of war and even hard labor without pay were really an isolated case in the world, then one comes upon a deeper level of meaning. It is not enough here to point to the particularly strongly-expressed sense of justice and "the strongly felt consequences of Ezekiel's doctrine of retribution" (Bertholet). Rather, there is, in the background, the question of the validity of the word of proclamation in which Yahweh has bound himself. In the oracles against Tyre, the fall and devastation of Tyre and, quite explicitly in 26:7, her surrender to the great king from the north were expressed. The end of the siege of Tyre appeared quite differently. Whatever the details of the end may have been, Tyre was in any case not destroyed and plundered.[13] Behind Yahweh's word to the prophet lies the question how the historical course of events is to be reconciled with the divine prediction. Although the external wording may suggest that the problem is that of a reward for the Babylonian warriors, the real question in the background is the question of divine faithfulness and of the validity of the divine word.

■ **29:19f** The Yahweh oracle replies in the style of older prophecy (see above under "Form") with the statement about the giving of Egypt to Nebuchadnezzar. What in Israel's holy war was said to the people of God through the mouth of the prophet, "Yahweh has given them into your hand," is here transferred to Yahweh's instrument Nebuchadnezzar (Jer. 25:9; 27:6; 43:10 "my servant Nebuchadnezzar"), who wages Yahweh's wars in the world: "I shall give [in v 20 "have given"] the land of Egypt to Nebuchadnezzar." Here too early proclamations of the prophet are taken up afresh. The imminent collapse of Egypt had already been foretold by him a good fifteen years earlier (29:1–16; 30:20–26; 31f). We have no way of knowing to what extent Nebuchadnezzar's threat to Egypt had increased in the interval. It had certainly not yet come to a collapse of Egypt before Nebuchadnezzar. With the end of the siege of Tyre, however, this older proclamation takes on a completely new fervor and again becomes the proclamation of an imminent event which also has its compelling inner logic. The army of the Babylonians was not properly rewarded at Tyre, now it *will* be rewarded![14] There may also be an echo here of the thought that Yahweh will himself exercise the justice which he expects of his people, when he demands of them that "the wages of the day-laborer" (פעלת שכיר) should not lie overnight in the house of the one who hires him (Lev 19:13). He will shortly bestow a

10 On the dating on the first of the month see also the remark above (pp. 23f) on 26:1.

11 See 1, 131f.

12 Arrian II, 18.

13 See above pp. 23f.

14 On פעלה see v 20 note a.

reward on those who have served him (a secondary addition makes quite explicit this thought of working for Yahweh, v 20 note a). It is uncertain how far one can also presuppose in the prophet a knowledge of specific military preparations against Egypt, which may have been intensified by Nebuchadnezzar after the solution of the problem of Tyre. In the year 571, the Amasis crisis in Hophra's government, which might have provided a direct excuse for Nebuchadnezzar's intervention in Egypt, still lies in the distant future.

The present oracle reveals a process which is significant for the understanding of prophecy far beyond the immediate context in Ezekiel. It shows on the one hand how an element of proclamation, the announcement of judgment on Tyre, which in an earlier period had a quite immediate urgency, can become unimportant in the course of history. To what extent Ezekiel was able to see in the conclusion of the siege of Tyre a fulfillment of the threats against Tyre and her prince or to what extent unfulfilled expectations clearly remained, we are unable to say. It is at any rate clear that in this combined Tyre-Egypt oracle the expectation of judgment on Tyre recedes. The genuine prophet knows (and this can be seen particularly clearly in the case of Isaiah) that Yahweh remains the master of history and also has power freely to take back apparently unambiguous pronouncements or to let them fade into unimportance. Jonah, who sticks to the letter of the law (4:1f), is the opposite of an independent prophet.

At the same time, however, it can be seen how in this oracle the proclamation of judgment on Egypt acquires new relevance following on the end of the siege of Tyre. It is not the withdrawal of an earlier oracle that is the dominating feature of 29:17–20; it is the new expression given to the validity of an old proclamation with reference to a new present, an expression which the prophet is authorized to make, that is the real mark of the prophetic oracle against Egypt. It is not the honesty of the prophet who generously intimates that a divine word has failed to be fulfilled that is to be praised in the light of this oracle (Kraetzschmar: "Ezekiel was great enough frankly to admit the non-fulfillment of his prediction"). What should be noted here, rather, is the fresh illumination given in the context of a new present to a statement which has already to some extent faded into insignificance. In the course of the years, questions may have piled up about the long overdue fulfillment of the Egyptian prophecy; *now* its fulfillment is imminent, and Yahweh has given Egypt into the hand of Nebuchadnezzar. This is explained precisely from the point of view of what has happened in the case of Tyre. The reference to this has taken the place of a justification (such as by an invective against Egypt).

■ **29:21** This actualization is also made clear by the addition (perhaps added secondarily) in v 21. It can, at the same time, reveal the wider horizon against which the prophet's address to the foreign nations is set. "On that day," i.e. on the imminent day of the fulfillment of the threat of judgment on Egypt,[15] Yahweh will make a horn spring forth for the house of Israel.[16] Reference is often made to the lifting or raising up of the horn (Ps 75:5; 148:14; and elsewhere). The expression "make a horn sprout" is found elsewhere only in Ps 132:17 where the reference is to the Davidic dynasty (אצמיח קרן לדוד "I will make a horn to sprout for David") (but cf. also Dan 7:8, 20; 8:3, 8f, 22). The oracle is understood by *b. Sanh.*98a as a reference to the coming son of David (so too Herrmannm, Troelstra, Fohrer). Since, however, there is no obvious reference to royal messianic deliverance, and since this idea is any case fairly unimportant in Ezekiel, it is surely more correct to understand the expression, along with most commentators since Rashi, as a general reference to an approaching deliverance for Israel. This deliverance is connected with the judgment on Egypt. At the time when this judgment takes place, deliverance for Israel will also dawn. The judgment on the great power which resists Yahweh is connected with the expectation of the dawning of the great deliverance for the people of God. Israel longs for the coming of this day, not because she is full of revengeful desire for the day of judgment on Egypt, but because she is on the lookout for the beginning of the restoration of her own fortunes.

To this reference to Israel's destiny there is added another reference to the prophet's own office. The expression פתחון פה ("an opening of the mouth") is found

15 On ביום ההוא ("on that day") see Peter Andreas Munch, *The Expression bajjôm hāhū'; is it an eschatological terminus technicus?* (Oslo: Dybwad, 1936), 2.

16 On the horn as a symbol of strength see Ps 18:3 and elsewhere.

also in 16:63, and both times it indicates a cheerful confidence in speaking, the παρρησία (see e.g. Phil 1:20). It is better not to think here of the prophet's specific inability to speak, which is referred to in 3:26 (24:27; 33:22). The fact that the prophet is given this cheerful confidence in speaking by Yahweh reveals that at this time he is far from feeling this confidence. As Isaiah was reproached, according to 5:19, "Let him make haste, let him speed his work, that we may see it," as Ezekiel himself was reproached, according to 12:22, in connection with the prediction of disaster before 587, "the days grow long, and nothing happens of all the visions" or as they felt obliged to affirm, according to 12:27, "the visions which he sees are for many days hence, and he prophesies of distant times," so here he has clearly been reproached, with regard to his oracles against foreign nations and to the related prediction of the restoration of Israel's fortunes, that the message was not being fulfilled. In the imminent judgment on Egypt and in the restoration of the fortunes of the house of Israel which is related to that context, the authentication of the prophet will happen afresh, and he will be granted the freedom to claim the right to be heard.

In both of these, however, in the deliverance of Israel which is connected with the judgment on Egypt and in the new authorization of the prophet, the concern is in the last resort only with one thing, namely that Yahweh reveals himself to the world.

Aim

The oracle in 29:17–21 proclaims anew that God in his work on earth not only uses his hidden heavenly helpers, but makes men, kings and their peoples, his instruments and accomplishes his work through them. It also proclaims that these men, nations and kings are not just dead implements in God's hand, which he uses and then throws away, but that their service has its reward from God. But here, behind this talk of the helper's reward, it is clear that the real, hidden question is whether in God's helpers his work really succeeds and achieves its purpose, whether God remains faithful to his work or whether what he has begun then suddenly falls away.

The prophetic oracle speaks of the mystery of this divine activity and reveals something of the accusation that the work of the servant of God often seems to remain unrewarded. In the complaint of the servant of Yahweh in Is 49:4, "I have labored in vain, I have spent my strength for nothing and vanity," this accusation has found its most profound expression. But in the same oracle, immediate expression is then given to the same assurance which Ezekiel's oracle also contains, "But—my right is with the Lord (Yahweh) and 'my reward' (פעלתי) with my God." The present oracle also promises that God will not leave his servants' work unrewarded and that he will keep to his word even if the human eye cannot at first see it.

But the oracle also speaks of the judgment which God must dispense in the world. It maintains that even in the mystery of the judgment on the nations, which appears to human eyes as the great disaster, God is in the process of delivering his people, of preparing the restoration of their fortunes. The prophet strengthens the faith of his people not to see in every judgment in the world a finality which they can then maliciously enjoy, but a penultimate event. He encourages the belief that they should always keep their eyes fixed beyond the provisional on the definitive and, with his passion, but also with his fear and with his hope, not to fall a prey to the penultimate but to believe in the ultimate.

In the assurance that he intends to stand by his work and his word, God summons his servants again and again to full confidence. No matter how much remains unfulfilled by God, no matter how much the mystery of events in the world challenges faith and accuses the proclaimer of God's promises of folly, God nevertheless promises him certain proof of his power, a proof in which the joyful opening of the mouth will find its profound correctness and its truth. The following is, however, quite clear from this oracle. Not in any personal, historical or moral wisdom on the part of the proclaimer, but only in the promise of the divine self-revelation lie the reason and justification for cheerful certainty with regard to what he proclaims.

3. The Day of Yahweh against Egypt

Bibliography

Albrecht Alt
"Die Deltaresidenz der Ramessiden" in *Kleine Schriften zur Geschichte des Volkes Israel* 3 (München: Beck, 1959), 176–185.

Albrecht Alt
"Taphnaein und Taphnas," *ZDPV* 66 (1943): 64–68.

Karl Baedeker
Egypt and the Sûdân; Handbook for Travellers (New York: C. Scribner's Sons, [7]1914).

Jürgen von Beckerath
Tanis und Theben; historische Grundlagen der Ramessidenzeit in Ägypten, Ägyptologische Forschungen 16 (Glückstadt, New York: Augustin, 1951).

J. Van Doorslaer
"No Amon," *CBQ* 11 (1949): 280–295.

Hermann Kees
Der Götterglaube im alten Ägypten, MVÄG 45 (Leipzig: Hinrichs, 1941).

Pierre Montet
Géographie de l'Égypte ancienne. Première Partie: To-Mehou, La Basse Égypte (Paris: Imprimerie Nationale, 1957).

30

1 **The word of Yahewh came to me: 2/ Son of man, prophesy and say, Thus has [the Lord][a] Yahweh said:**
[Howl:][b] Alas, the day! 3/ Yes, a day is near, the day of Yahweh is <near>[a], a day of clouds[b], it will be a time (of judg-

30: 2a אדני is lacking in 𝔊 𝔏^{S} 𝔎, see Appendix 1.
2 b 𝔐 הילילו is joined to what follows in 𝔗 𝔖 by ואמרו, but is not attested by 𝔊 𝔏^{S} and must be a secondary expansion. הילילי occurs also in 21:17 as a summons to the prophet. Nevertheless, the double cry of lament ὢ ὤ in 𝔊 (𝔏^{S}, also 𝔙 *vae vae,* is doubtless influenced by 𝔊) raises the question whether a second cry of lament was not developed secondarily to הילילו.
3 3a 𝔐 וקרוב יום is not attested by 𝔊 𝔏^{S} 𝔎 𝔄 𝔄̈ and consequently it is omitted by Cornill and others as a secondary repetition. Nevertheless, it is still surely possible that 𝔊 was already trying to tighten up the style (already known from Ezek 7) of these short exclamations about the day of Yahweh, which are not frightened of repetition, and has suppressed one of these repetitions. At any rate, one would then prefer, with 𝔖 (𝔊^{46}), to delete the copula before the second קרוב. 𝔗 gives a free paraphrase of יום ליהוה with יומא דעתיד למיתי מן קדם יהוה.

b 𝔐 ענן is missing in 𝔊 𝔏^{S}. But the text remaining after its deletion is already on rhythmic grounds much less convincing than 𝔐. An emendation of עת to קץ (Fohrer) is not recommended, even though קץ in 7:2f, 6; 21:30 has been rendered by 𝔊 with πέρας. The translator of 𝔊 changed with chapter 28 (see the Introduction, 26:2 note a and, e.g., the different

ment) for the nations. 4/ And a sword will come upon Egypt, and trembling will come upon Cush when the slain in Egypt fall [and they carry away (from it) its pomp][a] and its foundations are demolished. [5/ Cush and Put and Lud <and the Libyans>[a] and the whole crowd of nations[b] <>[a] and those who belong to the land of the covenant[c] will fall by the sword along with them][d] 6/ [Thus has

renderings of עת עון קץ in 21:30, 34 on the one hand and in 35:5 on the other). The πέρας of 𝔊 in the present passage is to be regarded as a free rendering in accordance with the sense.

4 4a 𝔐 ולקחו המונה is missing in 𝔊 𝔏^S 𝔎. Since from the point of view of form it destroys the parallelism, is syntactically jarring alongside the phraseology of the neighboring clauses and, from the point of view of content, is very similar to the expansion in 29:19 (note d), it must be a secondary addition to the text.

5 5a The list of Egypt's allies mentions in 𝔐 first a group of three names each of one syllable and each with the identical vowel: כוש ופוט ולוד. Between two further groups which are described rather more broadly, there appears in the puzzling כוב of 𝔐 a name of the same type as the first group and which one would prefer to associate with that group. 𝔊 (𝔏^S) provides in the first place, before it mentions the last two rather broader groups, four proper names: Πέρσαι καὶ Κρῆτες καὶ Λυδοὶ καὶ Λίβυες. Here one would first of all want to ask whether כוש is not a scribal error for לוב = Λίβυες, which was then in error placed after כל הערב. But Λίβυες is used in Ezek 27:10; 38:5; Jer 46:9 (= 𝔊 26:9) as a rendering of פוט. In Dan 11:43; Na 3:9; 2 Chr 12:3; 16:8, on the other hand, the word corresponding to Λίβυες is לבים or לובים. At the same time, Na 3:9 makes it clear that פוט and לובים are not identical, but represent two different groups of Egypt's allies. Thus the assumption of a corruption to כוב from לוב, and its removal in error from alongside לוד where 𝔊 still seems to have found it, is not impossible. 𝔙 renders 𝔐's first group of three by *Aethiopia et Libya et Lydi,* finding, that is, the Lybians behind the name פוט and letting the name Cub, which it did not understand (on this see Jerome, mistakenly, *quod Symmachus vertit in Arabiam,* see Ziegler, *Ezechiel*), follow in the same place where it is in 𝔐. 𝔗 and 𝔖 follow 𝔐, with the one deviation that 𝔖, in place of 𝔗's לודאי (𝔐 לוד), has לוביא.

b 𝔐 וכל הערב. 𝔊 καὶ πάντες οἱ ἐπίμεικτοι, 𝔙 *omne reliquum vulgus,* 𝔗 וכל סומכותא "all auxiliary troops," 𝔖 וכלה ערביא. Thus one could hesitate whether one should stick to 𝔐 "mixed race," with which may be compared Ex 12:38; Jer 25:20; 50:37; Neh 13:3, or whether one should revocalize as הָעֲרָב "Arabians" (cf. 27:21). But see the exposition.

c 𝔐 בני ארץ הברית, 𝔊 (𝔏^S) τῶν υἱῶν τῆς διαθήκης μου, 𝔙 *filii terrae foederis,* 𝔖 בני ארעא דקימא. See the exposition.

d The whole of v 5 is pure prose and without any metrical structure and thereby stands apart from the context, in which a certain tendency to parallelism can after all be recognized (see "Form"). It disrupts the context of vv 2–4, 6 (see also v 6 note a) and, from the content point of view, is to be understood as an interpretation of the reference to the סמכי מצרים in v 6.

Yahweh said:][a] And those who supported[b] Egypt will fall, and its proud strength will collapse. From Migdol <to Syene>[c] they will fall in it by the sword, says [the Lord][d] Yahweh.

7 And <it will> be laid waste[a] in the midst of lands that have been laid waste, and <its> cities[b] will be in the midst of cities that have been laid waste, 8/ and they will know that I am Yahweh when I set fire[a] to Egypt and all its helpers collapse.

9 On that day messengers will go out [from me][a] in ships[b] in order to terrify carefree[c] Cush, and trembling will come upon them on Egypt's day[d], for, see, it is coming![e]

6 6a 𝔐 כה אמר יהוה is not attested by 𝔊 (𝔏^{S} is different) and represents a later introductory formula, which was felt to be necessary after the break in connection between vv 4 and 6. Also the lack of אדני (which is omitted only in 21:8) in the messenger formula, which occurs in Ezekiel a total of 126 times, betrays the fact that the expression is unique from the traditio-historical point of view. As opposed to 𝔐, 𝔊, 𝔏^{S}, 𝔗, the expanded formula is found in 𝔊^{OL}, Arm, 𝔅, 𝔖.

b סמך occurs elsewhere in Ezekiel only in 24:2 (in a different meaning).

c 𝔐 סְוֵנֵה should be vocalized סְוֵנָה as in 29:10.

d אדני is lacking in 𝔊 𝔏^{S} 𝔎, see Appendix 1.

7 7a 𝔐 ונשמו and so, too, 𝔅 𝔗 𝔖. 𝔊 (𝔏^{S}) is different with καὶ ἐρημωθήσεται which points to ונשמה. This is probable on the basis of 29:12 and is demanded by the syntactical context. See also note b.

b 𝔐 ועריו does not make sense either as a sequel to 𝔐 נשמו (note a) or in relationship to the otherwise feminine מצרים. It must, on the basis of 𝔊 (𝔏^{S} 𝔖 𝔗) καὶ αἱ πόλεις αὐτῶν, be emended to ועריהם or else, graphically easier, with 𝔊^{L} αἱ πόλεις αὐτῆς and 29:12, to ועריה.

8 8a 𝔗 interprets "strong nations like fire."

9 9a 𝔐 מלפני is not attested in 𝔊 𝔏^{S}. It may therefore be an addition, which emphasizes explicitly that even Cush's terror is personally caused by Yahweh.

b 𝔐 בצים is derived by Q 𝔅 (*in trieribus*) from "ship" (singular occurs in Is 33:21, the plural in Dan 11:30, also in וצים Nu 24:24?). 𝔗 too בליגיונין, with its interpretation as "troops"could also come from this sense. On the other hand, 𝔊 (𝔏^{S}) σπεύδοντες, 𝔖 מסרהבאית seem to point to a reading אצים. The day of Yahweh, suddenly erupting, would then correspond to the "swift messengers." Driver, "Ezekiel," 300, suggests a reading בצים from a root בוץ "to run away" based on Arabaic *bāṣa.* The unmistakable relationship to Is 18:2, however, strongly advises the retention of 𝔐.

c 𝔐 בֶּטַח. This is found as an adverbial adjunct not only with a verb (Dtn 12:10; 33:28), but can also, according to Gen 34:25, be found with a noun (העיר בטח). 𝔗 דשריא לרוחצן and 𝔖 דיתבא בשליא both interpret in line with the sense. Thus, an emendation to בֹּטַחַ (Erlich, *Randglossen,* Bertholet) is not at all necessary. Rather, one might suggest that, in view of its non-attestation by 𝔊 𝔏^{S}, it might be a secondary expansion of the text. Otherwise in the book of Ezekiel only the phrase ישב (היה) לבטח is attested. See 28:26; 34:25, 27f; 38:8, 11, 14; 39:6, 26.

d L C MSS Edd ביום, 𝔅 MSS Edd כיום. Since here no comparison is intended, the first reading is to be preferred.

e The feminine הנה באה is meant consciously to be indefinite neuter, cf., e.g., 24:14. On the באה of 7:6b, 10a see the notes there. 𝔅 elucidates the impression given by the expression in accordance with

10 **Thus has [the Lord][a] Yahweh said: Thus I**
shall put an end to Egypt's pomp by the
hand of Nebuchadnezzar[b], king of Baby-
lon. 11/ He and his people with him[a], the
most brutal people, will be brought[b] to
destroy the land, and they will draw their
swords against Egypt and fill[c] the land
with slain. 12/ And I shall dry up[a] (the)
Nile branches[b] [and shall sell the land
into the hands of wicked (men)][c] and
shall lay waste the land and what it con-
tains by the hands of strangers. I, Yah-
weh, have spoken.
13 **Thus has [the Lord][a] Yahweh said: [And I**
shall destroy (the) idols.][b] And I shall
make an end of the <great ones>[c] in
Memphis and <the prince>[d] in the land of
Egypt [(he) will be no more][e] [and I shall
strike terror in the land of Egypt][f] 14/ and

the sense: *quia absque dubio veniet.*

10 10a אדני is lacking in 𝔊 𝔏^{S} ℜ^{Bo}, see Appendix 1.

b On the orthography of the name see above on 26:7.

11 11a 𝔐 אתו is omitted by 𝔊 𝔏^{S}.

b 𝔐 מובאים. 𝔗 אתן 𝔖 דאתין seem to presuppose באים. The parallel in 28:7 argues in favor of 𝔐.

c 𝔐 ומלאו את. 𝔊 (𝔏^{S}) πλησθήσεται = מלאה?

12 12a Instead of חָרָבָה, attested only here in Ezekiel, but otherwise found in Gen 7:22; Ex 14:21; Josh 3:17, and elsewhere, Var^{G} read, erroneously, חָרְבָּה, which occurs in Ezekiel fourteen times.

b 𝔐 יארים. 𝔊 τοὺς ποταμοὺς αὐτῶν 𝔗 נהריהון. In 29:3ff the plural of יאר was used consistently with a suffix. But see also 29:9.

c V 12aβ is missing in 𝔊 𝔄 and is surely a secondary variant of v 12bα. It is also shown to be such from its unusual use of language (מכר does occur in 7:12f; 48:14, but never in a figurative sense; absolute use of רעים, in comparison with which at most the רעי גוים of 7:24 could be mentioned). According to Herrmann and Cooke, רעים is a scribal error for an original זרים, and this would be the catchword by means of which the accidentally omitted stichos was noted again in the margin. Instead of being put in place of the ביד זרים of v 12b, the clause was wrongly inserted *in toto* before v 12b.

13 13a אדני is lacking in 𝔊, see Appendix 1.

b 𝔐 והאבדתי גלולים is missing in 𝔊. It was inserted when the following אילים was corrupted (note c) and expands the reference to the idols in the usual terminology of the book of Ezekiel.

c 𝔐 אלילים is rendered in 𝔊 by μεγιστᾶνας. Since the word is used parallel to נשיא, a scribal error for אלים = אילים (see 17:13; 31:11; 32:21) is possible. On אלם "magnates" in Phoenician, see Eduard Meyer, "Untersuchungen zur phönikischen Religion," *ZAW* 49 (1931): 3. אליל is quite foreign to Ezekiel's language. Thus it has been glossed secondarily by means of the preceding clause (see note b).

d 𝔐 נשיא (𝔗 מלכא). The plural ἄρχοντας of 𝔊 (𝔏^{S} *principes*) suggests a נשיאים, the ending of which has been lost by haplography (before מארץ). The parallel אילים (note c) also suggests the reading of the plural.

e 𝔐 לא יהיה עוד, which corresponds to the singular נשיא of 𝔐 (note d), is taken by 𝔊 καὶ οὐκ ἔσονται ἔτι as an independent unit and, with the addition of the copula (1:4 note a), has been accommodated to the preceding plural (note d). The originality of the clause, which destroys the parallelism of the verse that originally preceded and does not fit the context of vv 13–16aα, which is in the form of a speech of Yahweh in the first person, is subject to grave doubts.

f V 13b is missing in 𝔊 𝔖. It destroys the sequence of details about individual cities and regions of Egypt and is also linguistically, on the strength of the use of יִרְאָה, which is completely unusual in

I shall lay waste <the land>[a] of Pathros and shall set fire to Zoan and shall sit in judgment on No[b]. 15/ And I shall pour out my wrath upon Sin[a], the stronghold of Egypt, and shall wipe out the pomp from <Noph> (Memphis)[b]. 16/ And I shall set fire to Egypt. <In agony> Sin (= Syene?)[a] shall writhe[b], and in No[c] breaches will be made[d], and in Noph (Memphis) there will be oppressors in broad daylight(?)[e]. 17/ The young men of <On>[a] and Bubastis[b]

Ezekiel, to be assessed as a later addition.

14 14a 𝔊 𝔏ˢ 𝔙 𝔖 speak of the "land of Pathros." 29:14 (Jer 44:1) and the metrical structure make it likely that this reading should be adopted and that in את we have a scribal error for ארץ (Cornill).

b 𝔐 נא. 𝔊 ἐν Διοσπόλει (𝔏ˢ *in Jovis civitate*) 𝔙 (𝔗) *in Alexandria.* The identification with Alexandria, which was founded in 331 by Alexander the Great, is of course an obvious anachronism, which Jerome also clearly finds to be such in his comment on this passage. He writes: "And he has said, 'I shall pass judgment on Alexandria,' and this is its present-day name. It had another, earlier name: No . . . But we, instead of 'No,' have put 'Alexandria,' in anticipation, what is called *πρόληψις* in Greek, like that line of Virgil: 'And he came to Lavinian shores.' They were not called 'Lavinian' at the time when Aeneas came to Latium, but they were later called 'Lavinian,' and the place would thus be more obvious to the reader's understanding." [Trans.]

15 15a 𝔐 סין. 𝔊 Σάιν, 𝔏ˢ *Sain,* 𝔙 *Pelusium.* See the exposition.

b 𝔐 נא is strange, since in the list one does not expect the recurrence of a name just mentioned, but a new name. The Μέμφεως of 𝔊 (𝔏ˢ) suggests a correction to נף, concerning which v 13 has already threatened the destruction of its leaders but not the destruction of the city itself. 𝔙 𝔗 Alexandria as in v 14.

16 16a 𝔐 סין, 𝔊 (𝔏ˢ) Συήνη, 𝔙 *Pelusium.*

b 𝔐 חול תחיל has been correctly understood by the versions as an expression strengthened by the use of the infinitive absolute. 𝔊 *ταραχῇ ταραχθήσεται,* 𝔙 *parturiens dolebit,* 𝔗 מזע תזוע. Only 𝔖 has the simple נתדלח. Thus it should be vocalized חוֹל תָּחִיל.

c 𝔐 נא. 𝔊 Διοσπόλει, 𝔙 (𝔗) *Alexandria.*

d On 𝔐 להבקע, cf. the similar use of the pu'al of בקע in 26:10 (hop'al in Jer 39:2). Jerome takes the expression to refer to the destruction of the dykes and the resultant flooding of the land, which is to be understood as referring to the inundation by the troops of the Chaldeans.

e 𝔐 ונף צרי יומם is attested by 𝔙 𝔗 (paraphrasing: ומפים בעלי דבב יקפונה יום יום), while 𝔊 (𝔏ˢ) *καὶ διαχυθήσεται ὕδατα* (= ונפוצו מים?) tries to get an approximate sense out of a slightly different sequence of consonants, and 𝔖 solves the problem by using a general turn of phrase. Driver, "Linguistic Problems," 177, wants to read ומים יפרצון "and the water shall burst in," while Cornill and others conjecture ונפרצו חומותיה, which would be a parallel repetition of the preceding statement about No. The verb פרץ, however, is not otherwise attested in Ezekiel.

17 17a 𝔐 און is, on the evidence of 𝔊 (𝔏ˢ) Ἡλιουπόλεως, 𝔙 *Heliopolis,* to be vocalized as אוֹן.

b 𝔐 פִּי־בֶסֶת, 𝔊 Βουβάστου, 𝔙 *Bubastis.* 𝔖 has misunderstood the context, in which it also seems to include the יומם of v 16, "And the young men of

will fall by the sword and they them-
selves(?)[c] will go off into captivity.
18 And in Tahpanhes the day will <grow
dark>[a] when I break there the <staff>[b]
(of the rulers) of Egypt and its proud
strength comes to an end in it. The land
itself[c] will be covered by a cloud, and its
daughters[d] will go into captivity. 19/ And
I shall sit in judgment on Egypt, and they
will know that I am Yahweh.

Bubastis (מפי־בסת?) will be like water."

c 𝔐 הנה is unusual. In v 18 the subject of the expression is בנותיה, which would be a meaningful correspondence to the parallel בחורי. 𝔊 *αἱ γυναῖκες*, 𝔏[S] *civitates* each in their own way find the right sense.

18 18a 𝔐 חָשַׂךְ "to hold back" is, on the basis of 𝔊 (𝔏[S]) *συσκοτάσει*, 𝔅 *nigrescet*, 𝔗 אייתי חשוך, 𝔖 נערב, to be emended to חָשַׁךְ. Or even to תֶּחְשַׁךְ? See the exposition.

b The reference in 𝔐 to מֹטוֹת "yoke (poles)," the breaking of which is elsewhere the image of liberation (Jer 28:10), misses the sense intended here. On the basis of 𝔊 (𝔏[S]) *τὰ σκῆπτρα*, 𝔅 *sceptra*, 𝔖 חוטרה מַטּוֹת, should be read (cf. 19:10ff).

c 𝔐 היא literally "it," i.e. Egypt "itself." 𝔊 (𝔏[S]) 𝔖 introduce the clause with the copula. 𝔗 interprets.

d See v 17 note c.

Form

30:1–19 is prefaced by the formula for the receiving of God's word and is the only unit of this type among the oracles against Egypt to remain undated. For this reason, as well as on account of other peculiarities in its content, it is clearly differentiated from the other Egypt oracles.

From the point of view of form the complex is divided up by the two introductory messenger formulae in vv 10 and 13 (on the formula in v 6 see note a) into the three oracles vv 1–9, 10–12 and 13–19. Of these, vv 1–9 in its concluding verse, v 9, which is linked to the preceding unit in the same way as 29:21 by an introductory ביום ההוא ("on that day"), has been subject to an expansion, the contents of which also show it to be a secondary interpretation of the preceding section. V 8 is then, also by its (expanded) recognition formula, clearly seen to be the conclusion of a proof-saying. There is a certain difficulty about the formula for a divine saying at the end of v 6. It might be considered whether vv 7f might not be a secondary expansion of an original unit comprising vv 1–4, 6. Since, however, the late unit in 29:9b–16, which in v 10 seems to presuppose what is said in 30:6, immediately afterwards (v 12) recapitulates 30:7, the author of that section surely had the connected unit 30:1–4, 6–8 in front of him. The formula for a divine saying is therefore to be thought of as a context-formula marking a slight caesura. Vv 1–4,6–8 are to be regarded, however, as a connected unit.

Of the three units, the first (vv 1–4,6–8) and the third (vv 13–19) each have the form of a two-part proof-saying in which Egypt is condemned with no reason given. The central oracle (vv 10–12), a pure declaration of judgment, is concluded by the formulaic אני יהוה דברתי ("I, Yahweh, have spoken") (on which see 5:15,17; [17:24] 21:22; and elsewhere). Further, through all three units elements of *parallelismus membrorum* can be discerned, as well as rhythmically structured individual verses (such as vv 4aα, 11b, 14), without it being possible to discern a consistent metrical structure in the unit as a whole. It should further be mentioned that in vv 3f, e.g. and elsewhere, the terse two-stress lines appear which already in chapter 7 depicted in such characteristic fashion the hammer-blows of the description of the day of Yahweh.[1] But there is no further evidence, here either, of a desire for form for form's sake. Here too there can be seen later, degenerate oracular forms.

Setting

Jahn has passed the following judgment on 30:1–19: "It reveals repetitions and imitations of other passages and is of such little value that it appears unworthy of an Ezekiel. It seems to be the concoction of a later hand, for whom the description of Egypt's fall in chapter 29 was not good enough."[2] Hölscher, Cooke and others have followed this evaluation. It is in fact difficult to provide any convincing arguments against this harsh judgment, especially in the case of vv 10ff. Most probably one can suggest an origin from Ezekiel himself for the introductory section (vv 1–4,6–8), which describes the day of Yahweh which is about to fall upon Egypt. Nevertheless, here too the comparison with Ezek 7, the proclamation of the day of Yahweh over the land of Israel, works to

1 See 1,201f.
2 Jahn, *Buch*, 213.

the disadvantage of Ezekiel 30. The oracle lacks the taut strength of chapter 7, so that in this respect too there is the possibility that the oracle comes from the school of Ezekiel and is a later exposition, utilizing the prophet's language and motifs, of divine judgment on Egypt. The lack of a date in the otherwise consistently dated context of the oracles against Egypt might also argue along these lines.

Nevertheless, the oracle already seems to have been known to the authors of the prose section 29:9b–16 (see above). Certainly 30:10–12 and 30:13–19 come from the school of Ezekiel. The confused sequence in the enumeration of Egyptian cities and districts in vv 13–19 shows how far removed actual conditions in Egypt were from the Babylonian exiles. In the very full list of names one can discern more of a show of learning than actual knowledge. The oracle in vv 10–12 must, however, have originated still in the lifetime of Nebuchadnezzar and probably also before the campaign in his thirty-seventh year.

Interpretation

■ **30:1–4(5), 6–8(9)** *a. The Day of Yahweh against Egypt.*

■ **30:1f** 30:1–19, too, in its opening verse makes the claim to be part of the divine message.[3] The prophet is to proclaim that the day of Yahweh dawns and that this is, in particular, Egypt's fate.[4] The proclamation of this day is expressed first in language familiar from Ezekiel 7. The introductory imperative, which is not attested by 𝔊 (note b), has, however, no parallel in chapter 7. In Is 13:6 it introduces dramatically the proclamation of terror which, as in Joel 1:15, must be shouted out, howled even, by hearer and victim in an inarticulate cry of fear.[5]

■ **30:3** In what follows one cannot fail to notice an internal heightening in terms of an increasing clarification. In the immediately following justificatory proclamation of the approaching day,[6] out of the uncannily indefinite "Alas, the day!," there is extracted first of all a quite indefinite and for that very reason uncanny יום ("day"), which is then (still without the article) characterized as to its ominous origin by means of repetition as יום ליהוה ("day of Yahweh"), only then to be more clearly defined as "a day of clouds" (Joel 2:2; Zeph 1:15) and to be more precise as to its direction from v 4 onwards. In the present passage the parallel description of it as "a day of the nations" (parallelism of יום "day"-עת "time" in 7:7,12) is unique. The day of Yahweh is a "day of the nations," that is undoubtedly a day of battle on an international scale. If the "clouds" recall the elements of the old Yahweh theophany (Ex 19:9,16,18), then the levy of the nations recalls a worldwide international uprising. In all this, however, Yahweh is the real center and threat of the day. Thus, in the rest of the section vv 1–9 nothing is said of the nations as Yahweh's instruments. Only the nations which are on Egypt's side are mentioned, and they in fact on this day are powerless.

■ **30:4** On Yahweh's side, however, the sword, strangely depersonalized, is mentioned as his instrument coming and acting against Egypt.[7] In its train comes the "terror." Here the paralyzing panic of the holy war of the earlier period can be recognized. G. von Rad speaks in fact of "sacral panic."[8] The terror is described as חלחלה "trembling" (on account of the assonance with the immediately following חלל "slain"), a word used in Is 21:3 to refer to the writhing of a woman in childbirth. The noun occurs again in v 9 and in Na 2:11. The phrase is expressed verbally in v 16. Terror on account of the fallen also spreads to Cush, the neighboring territory to the south, beyond the frontier (29:10). What is said here incidentally is then amplified in greater detail in the addition in v 9 (see below). Alongside the terror at the slain there is the terror at the demolishing of the foundations of the country. In 13:14 the reference was to the laying bare of the foundations (Mic 1:6; cf. Hab 3:13; Ps 137:7), an image which is immediately clear. By "demolition" must be meant the complete destruction of the foundations as well, something which is perhaps expressed also in Ps

3 See 1, 144f.

4 On "son of man" see 1, 131f.

5 On the imperative הילילו in connection with the day of Yahweh see also Zeph 1:11; Joel 1:5, 13 (in Ezekiel, in a different context, in 21:17).

6 On קרוב ("near") see 1, 205 on 7:7, 1, 247 on 9:1; 1, 281 on 12:23.

7 On this see Ezek 21 in the context of threat against Israel.

8 von Rad, *OT Theology*, 2. 124.

11:3 by a different expression (השתות יהרסון "the foundations are destroyed").

■ **30:6** The key-word, however, which remains in the continuation in v 6 (which connects directly with v 4), is that of "falling." The helpers of Egypt, i.e. the auxiliary troops at her disposal, will fall. In this way her proud strength will be "brought low" (ירד).[9] From Migdol to Aswan they will fall by the sword.[10]

■ **30:5** The catchphrase "those who supported Egypt" has occasioned a learned expansion in v 5, which explains the phrase in historical terms and also seems to be well informed. Six groups are mentioned here who will "fall by the sword." With this concluding phrase the expansion fits into the general theme of vv 4 and 6. At the beginning there are three names which rhyme with each other, names which otherwise tend to be grouped in pairs (Cush and Put: 38:5; Jer 46:9; Put and Lud: 27:10; Is 66:19 [emended text]). Of these, Cush is Egypt's neighbor to the south and has already been mentioned in 29:10; 30:4 (and will recur in 38:5). In P's table of nations Gen 10:6 (1 Chr 1:8) it is mentioned along with Put as the son of Ham and brother of Egypt. At times it had been closely dependent on Egypt, but in the twenty-fifth dynasty it supplied Egypt's rulers from 715 to 663.[11] Subsequently, however, it again lived its own life under its own rulers. Thus, in the case of the Cush mentioned here, it is not referring to the auxiliary troops of a vassal state, but to recruited contingents of mercenaries.

On Put and Lud see also the discussion above on 27:10.[12] According to that Lud refers to groups of Lydian mercenaries who have enlisted in Egypt. With the information on the Rassam cylinder, according to which Gyges of Lydia in the time of Ashurbanipal sent troops to Egypt in support of Psammetichus I, there should be connected, according to Kienitz, the information supplied by Herodotus that Psammetichus I, in his fight for the throne against his Egyptian rivals, had the help of "men of bronze," i.e. of Ionians and Carians, who had come to Egypt by ship.[13] That relations between Egypt and Lydia were not subsequently broken off is shown by Herodotus's account of the treaty between Croesus and Amasis and of the bodyguard which Amasis created out of the Lydians settled in Egypt by Psammetichus I.[14] According to Rüger this relationship is also referred to in the Lydian inscription found at Silsilis, although textually this is not always clear.[15] According to what was said above, Put refers to the Libyan contingents from the area of Cyrene.[16] It may well be that the fragmentary notice referred to above about the campaign of Nebuchadnezzar against Egypt in his thirty-seventh year actually even explicitly refers to the participation of Put in the battle against Nebuchadnezzar.[17] It refers to a ". . . -*ku ša puṭu-iaman*" as an ally of Amasis. "In the case of this *puṭu-iaman,* the reference can only be, as the name indicates, to a territory whose population is composed equally of *puṭu*-people and Greeks. This presupposition is fulfilled in Cyrenaica" (Rüger).

If the fourth rhyme-word, which goes with this group of three but which is separated from them in 𝔐 and is therefore perhaps a secondary addition, was originally Lub (note a), then here again the reference is to contingents from Libya proper lying east of Cyrene. "Libyans" are mentioned in the OT (only with the gentilic ל[ו]בים) also in Dan 11:43; 2 Chr 12:3; 16:8 alongside (Egyptians and) Cushites and in Na 3:9 alongside Egypt, Put and Cush. It may be recalled in this connection that the Pharaohs of the twenty-second and twenty-third dynasties came from the ranks of Libyan mercenaries.

In Jer 50:37 ערב refers to the "mixture of nations" in Babylon who are to "become women," i.e. lose the warlike bravery which is normally expected of them. The group thus described belongs, like the previously mentioned גבורים ("warriors") (and the "horses and chariots," which are missing in 𝔊 and are perhaps a secondary addition), to the Babylonian army. It must refer to the vassal peoples of the empire gathered in the capital city, Babylon. The same is suggested by the phrase כל הערב

9 On גאון עזה ("its proud strength") see 1, 212 on 7:24 and 1, 507 on 24:21.
10 See above p. 113 on 29:10.
11 See above p. 103.
12 See above pp. 59f.
13 Kienitz, *Geschichte Aegyptens,* 12; Herodotus 2, 152.
14 Herodotus 1, 77; 2, 154.
15 A. H. Sayce, "Silsilis in Upper Egypt" in *Sardis,* Publications of the American Society for the Excavation of Sardis 6: Lydian Inscriptions part 2, ed. W. H. Buckler (Leiden: Brill, 1924), 66–68.
16 See above p. 59.
17 See above pp. 104f.

("all the foreign folk") in Jer 25:20, which is to be connected with v 19 and which describes, alongside Pharaoh's own people (כל עמו "all his people"), his auxiliary, foreign mercenaries. Thus in the present passage the reference is likewise to mercenaries, especially of Greek origin, who also serve the Pharaoh alongside the groups mentioned by name.[18] Now *Epistle of Aristeas* 13 mentions that Psammetichus I had Jewish mercenaries in his army on his campaign against Nubia, a campaign which is also corroborated historically not only by Herodotus, but also by Greek, Carian and Phoenician mercenary inscriptions on the Ramses Colossus of Abu Simbel and by a stele from Karnak.[19] We know definitely of fairly strong Jewish communities in Egypt since the time of Jeremiah and the first deportation of 597 (Jer 24:8 and later chapters 43f). For a still earlier period Dtn 17:16 suggests that there were Jewish (Israelite) mercenaries in Egypt.[20] Among the mercenary groups mentioned so far in Ezek 30:5, the Jewish groups are not included. In any case the Jews would certainly not include themselves in the rather contemptuous collective term ערב (see also Ex 12:38—see also the paraphrase with אספסף "rabble" in Nu 11:4—and Neh 13:3). This forces us in the present passage to find, in the veiled expression "sons of the land of the covenant" these very mercenaries from among their own people. The reading of 𝔊 is then to be regarded not as an indication of a different text, but as a mild, clarificatory interpretation (see note c). Since the land of Cannaan, according to P, was part of the divine covenant promise to Abraham (Gen 17:7f), a description of Palestine as the land of the covenant is easily understandable.[21]

■ **30:7** V 6 had described the havoc of the sword among the population of Egypt and her helpers. V 7, alongside that, refers to the general devastation of the land. This is done, in words which are repeated in 29:12, with what is here a rhythmic structure of 4 + 4 rendered into prose (see above).

■ **30:8** As in Ezekiel 7 the proclamation of the day of Yahweh ends with the recognition formula of the proof-saying. In its expansion in v 8b, with the reference to the "fire" and the "collapse," we have the traditional language of the foreign oracles as we find it already in Amos 1f.[22]

■ **30:9** Then, however, this first oracle has been subject to a secondary addition, in which can be seen a particularly fine example of the "exegesis of scripture by means of scripture." Is 18 in the time of Isaiah points to a situation in which ambassadors from distant Cush, who have traveled over the water in vessels of papyrus, deliver their message in Jerusalem. The expression in Ezek 30:4, to the effect that trembling would befall Cush, has caused a reader who had Isaiah's oracle in mind to explain the process in more detail. Here, too, there are ambassadors, but they come from Yahweh and go in the opposite direction, up the Nile, carrying terror to a Cush that is carefree and secure, "on Egypt's day, for, see, it is coming!" This closing expression imitates once again the uncanny, two-stress neutral language of the reference to the day of Yahweh. At the same time the expression "day of Yahweh" is independently varied to "day of Egypt."[23]

■ **30:10-12** *b. The Historical Exposition. Nebuchadnezzar will wield the Sword.*

■ **30:10** The short oracle in vv 10–12 fulfils with regard to vv 1–9 the same function as did 26:7–14 with regard to the Tyre oracle in 26:1–6. A general declaration of impending judgment on Tyre/Egypt is followed by the historically determined reference to Nebuchadnezzar as the one who will carry out Yahweh's judgment. In its details, the oracle, which seems to follow the layout of

18 See above the Ionians and Carians as well as the second component of the *puṭu-iaman*. This cautions against the emendation to הָעֲרָב which is already opposed by 𝔊 (see note b).

19 Kienitz, *Geschichte Aegyptens,* 26, 128; Herodotus 2,161.

20 See also the discussions in Eduard Meyer, *Der Papyrusfund von Elephantine* (Leipzig: Hinrichs, 1912), 32ff, and Vincent, *religion,* 357ff, on the date of the founding of the Jewish military colony at Elephantine, and the texts discussed there.

21 See too J. Pedersen, *Das Eid bei den Semiten,* Studien zur Geschichte und Kultur des islamischen Orients 3 (Strassburg: Träbner, 1914), 42f. On the broader aspects of this connection see, e.g., Buber, *Israel.* On the groups of nations in v 5 see also Hölscher, *Drei Erdkarten,* 26f.

22 See שלח אש in Am 1:4, 7, 10, 12; 2:2, 5; הצית אש in Am 1:14; in Ezekiel, with the use of נתן which is typical of him, נתן אש ב. See also שבר Am 1:5.

23 On this cf. the "day of Midian" in Is 9:3.

the basic text in vv 1–9, is expressed in everyday terminology and betrays no specific peculiarities. In the introductory statement, according to which Yahweh, through Nebuchadnezzar, will make an end of the pomp of Egypt (והשבתי המון "I shall put an end to the pomp" also in 26:13; [ו]השבתי "I shall put an end . . ." on its own in 7:24; 12:23; 23:27,48; 30:13; 34:25; with suffix 16:41; 34:10), המון ("pomp") contains a mild reference to the reason for the judgment. Egypt is condemned on account of her המון ("pomp"). This word, of whose total of 25 (5:7 is a textual error) occurrences in the book of Ezekiel no fewer than 16 occur in the four chapters 29–32 and 13 of these specifically refer to Egypt, gives expression to the bold arrogance of mankind, here of the great power Egypt (cf. 29:3,9).[24] It is thus noticeable that the secondary supplementers are particularly fond of the use of this word. That it is, however, already a catchword of older prophetic invective is shown by the proof-saying in 1 Kgs 20:13.

■ **30:11** Alongside Nebuchadnezzar his troops are mentioned, as in 26:7.[25] The אתו ("with him") which is added after the second word recalls the language of P (Gen 6:18; 7:7; Ex 29:21; so Cooke, following Driver).[26] As in vv 4–6, more detailed reference is made first to the sword and then to the devastation of the land. The drawing of the sword is described in the words of 28:7 (see also 5:2, 12; 12:14).[27]

■ **30:12** While v 11 spoke of Nebuchadnezzar as the agent, the final verse (12) changes over again to Yahweh as the real subject of the act of judgment. He dries up the branches of the Nile (Is 37:25 as an arrogant statement by the Assyrian).[28] He sells the land to the "wicked" (but see note c) and what it contains (19:7, also 12:19; 32:15) to "strangers."[29] It is particularly stressed that all this that will happen has already been realized in the word which Yahweh has just spoken.

■ **30:13–19** *c. The Execution of the Judgment on Individual Places in Egypt.* Characteristic of vv 13–19, which once again describe the execution of the judgment as entirely an act of Yahweh himself, is the number of individual places which are now listed as places of judgment. In this respect the comprehensive reference to the great day of Yahweh (as is still found in vv 10–12) is found no more. Fohrer is right when he points out that prophecy provides other examples of such a listing of threatened cities (see Am 1:3–5, 6–8; Mic 1:10–15; and elsewhere). What is actually said concerning the judgment is once again quite unspecific; indeed there is an obvious falling away in the variety of verbal expressions used, and this leads to a repetition of identical phrases: ונתתי אש ("and I shall set fire") vv 14–16; ועשיתי שפטים ("and I shall sit in judgment") vv 14,19; בשבי תלכנה ("they will go into captivity") vv 17,18; as well as והשבתי ("and I shall make an end")—ונשבת בה ("and comes to an end in it") vv 13, 18. Generally one can observe that first of all a number of statements are made in the first person by Yahweh himself (vv 13–16aα, 9 verbs). Then, in an effort to achieve a certain variety of expression, the impersonal third person is chosen, where Yahweh no longer appears, but the suffering of the cities and their inhabitants or the actual process of judgment is described (vv 16aβ–18), before the closing lines return once again to the first person (v 19). A difficulty is created, however, by the fact that the series of places cited reveals no discernible order with regard to their sequence. In addition, some places appear several times in different positions (נא "No" vv 14, 16; נף "Memphis" vv 13, 15 emended text, 16). Herrmann endeavored to explain this strange confusion on the basis of the conflation of two parallel texts, the first of which in vv 13–15 remains "corrupt beyond correction," while in vv 16–18, provided that in v 16 סון ("Syene") is read instead of סין ("Sin"), there is an order which is geographically possible. Fohrer, on the other hand, assumes that at the basis of the three strophes vv 13–14; 15–16; 17–18aα there lie three different short lists of names which possibly delimit Egypt as a whole or describe specific areas. Both these explanations raise serious questions, but there are no really satisfactory alternatives.

---

24 See also 1,210 on 7:11–13.

25 On עם "troops" see L. Rost, "Bezeichnungen," 141–147.

26 On the description of the instruments of judgment as עריצי גוים see 28:7 (31:12; 32:12).

27 On the filling (of the land) with slain see 9:7; 35:8.

28 On יארים ("Nile branches") see above p. 110 on 29:3.

29 On רעים ("wicked men") see רעי גוים ("the worst of the nations") in 7:24; on זרים ("strangers") see 7:21; 11:9; 28:7, 10; 31:12; on both see 1,212.

■ **30:13** The text speaks first of all of the liquidation of the authorities in the land.[30] Is 3:1–8 (with reference to Jerusalem) paints an uncannily real picture of the anarchy which can arise from the removal of all authorities. נף ("Noph") is used in the OT, alternately with the form ("Moph") (Hos 9:6), and is an abbreviated rendering of the Egyptian *mn-nfr* = Greek Μέμφις.[31] Memphis, twenty-seven kilometers south of the point of the Delta (Cairo), achieved its significance through (and according to legend was founded by) Menes, the man who united the kingdom. In spite of many fluctuations, it remained an important city throughout the whole history of Egypt. In the sixth century the Saite Amasis made it his capital. Later, according to Herodotus, he also transferred there the Greek mercenaries in order to make them into "his bodyguard against the Egyptians."[32] This new situation which arose under Amasis (569–526) could be presupposed in the present passage. Later the text of the introductory stichos was wrongly copied and was interpreted, by means of a specific addition (note b) in the language of the book of Ezekiel, to refer to the removal of the gods of Memphis, amongst which the creator god Ptah had assumed the most important position.[33] A further addition, missing from 𝔊 (note f), refers in a colorless phrase to the inflicting of fear on the land of Egypt. It has been supposed that this is an echo of the statement in vv 4aβ, 9 about Cush.[34]

■ **30:14** Devastation (והשמתי "and I shall lay waste" v 12), fire (v 8) and judgment are then threatened against the land of Pathros (note a), i.e. Upper Egypt, which has already been encountered under this name in 29:14, and the two cities of Zoan and No. צען ("Zoan"), Greek Τάνις, modern *ṣān-el-hagar,* on the second eastern branch of the Nile Delta, first acquired political significance under the Hyksos, who found a settlement already there called *ḥw.t w'r.t* (= Αὔαρις).[35] The period of Tanis's greatness began when Ramses II (1292–1225) decided to build his capital there.[36] Here the weak twenty-first Tanite Dynasty also had its capital. Subsequently Tanis lost its position of first importance. However, the "Venice of the Delta" (Kees) maintained its importance for maritime trade and for the defense of Egypt's eastern frontier.[37] נא ("No"), described more fully in Na 3:8 as נא אמון ("No-amun"), to be connected with Egyptian *nw.t,* or *n.t*[38] "the city (of Amun)" (hence the rendering of 𝔊 Διόσπολις and 𝔏^S *civitas Jovis*), is, in spite of the attempt by J. van Doorslaer to justify 𝔅's identification of it with Alexandria (see note b), to be equated with the great capital and religious center, Thebes, in Middle Egypt. This city achieved importance as the capital of a world power and as the splendid metropolis of the cult of Amun, first of all in the Middle Kingdom and then especially in the New Kingdom. In the late period Thebes retained its importance as a spiritual principality under the rule of the "God's wife" and then subsequently became completely forgotten by the Mediterranean world. Today the place is famed for the impressive evidence of the past in Luxor and Karnak and for the extensive city of tombs on the west bank of the Nile. In the sixth century, when the center of the empire was in the Delta, Thebes, with its theocracy, had already become provincial from the political point of view. When 𝔅 and 𝔗 render the נא ("No") of 𝔐 here and in vv 15f by "Alexandria," this is to be explained by the desire that the center which was particularly significant in the later period, especially for the Jewish diaspora, with regard to Egypt's politics and trade should also appear with its wealth (𝔐 of v 15 המון נא "pomp of No") in this list. נא ("No"), which can still be designated by 𝔊 as Diospolis, the city of Jupiter, had become a few centuries later for Jerome a small, insignificant place: "For some reason or another, the Septuagint called it Diospolis, though it is a small city in Egypt." Ezek 30:13–19, on the other hand, with its double reference to נא ("No") reveals something still of the old splendor of Thebes.[39]

■ **30:15** With the pouring out of divine wrath (7:8; 9:8; 14:19; and elsewhere), annihilation (הכרית "I shall wipe out" 14:8, 13, 17, 19, 21; 17:17; 21:8–10; and else-

30 On אילים see note c; on נשיא see 1, 209 on 7:27.
31 Erman-Grapow, 2. 63.
32 2, 154.
33 On גלולים ("idols") see 1, 187.
34 On Memphis see also Kees, *alte Ägypten,* 80–101; Montet, *Géographie,* 27–34.
35 On the problem of the equation of Avaris and Tanis see von Beckerath, *Tanis und Theben,* 31–33.
36 On the discussion about the equation of the "city of Ramses" and Tanis see von Beckerath, *Tanis und Theben,* 28–31, but also Alt, "Deltaresidenz."
37 See Kees, *alte Ägypten,* 109–115; Montet, *Géographie,* 192–199.
38 The reading is uncertain; Erman-Grapow, 2. 210.
39 On Thebes see Kees, *alte Ägypten,* 142–163.

where) and fire (see above on v 8) the two places Sin and Memphis (already mentioned in v 13; see v 15 note b), as well as Egypt as a whole, are threatened in vv 15,16aα in a further group of three. While v 13 referred to the removal of the rulers in Memphis, here the reference is to the wiping out of all its pomp, i.e. surely the destruction of the city itself. 𝔐 סין ("Sin") seems to be taken by 𝔊 𝔏S to refer to Sais, the city from which the twenty-sixth dynasty (Psammetichus I) comes, which then under Amasis transferred the capital to Memphis. The little that remains of Sais, which was known as the cult center of the goddess Neith, can be found today half-an-hour north of *ṣān el-hagar* on the Rosetta branch of the Nile, northwest of Tanta.[40] A reference to the city of Sais would certainly in fact be expected in the period of the Saites, from which obviously this list of places comes. In 𝔅, however, 𝔐 סין ("Sin") is rendered by "Pelusium." The remains of this famous eastern port, the "key" to Egypt, where in the year 525 Psammetichus III lost the decisive battle against Cambyses and where Egypt lost her freedom to the Persians, are still to be found in the ruins of *tell el farama* and *tell el-fadda* in the northeast corner of the Delta, a good thirty kilometers northeast of *el-kanṭara.*[41] Montet refers to the Egyptian name *śnw* for this region.[42] According to W. Spiegelberg, it should be called *śjn* or *śwn*, "the fortress."[43] However, according to Erman-Grapow, Egyptian *śwn.w* "fortress" is attested only in the pyramid texts and in the Middle Kingdom.[44] In explanation of the description of this place as "stronghold of Egypt," Jerome points to its safe harbor and its lively trade. As a frontier post at the entry to the Delta it may also have been particularly well known to its Eastern neighbors. Thus 𝔅 will have been on the right track, and perhaps then 𝔊 and 𝔏S should be differentiated from Sais as a transcription of 𝔐 סין ("Sin").

■ **30:16** With v 16aβ there is a change in the way the judgment is described. Yahweh withdraws as the agent, and instead there is a description of how סין ("Sin") writhes in agony (on חלחלה "trembling" see above v 4), how No is broken open (i.e., how breaches are made in its walls [interpreted differently by Jerome, see note d]), while another reference to Memphis, which is admittedly textually very uncertain, seems to indicate invasion by the enemy in broad daylight. 𝔐 סין ("Sin") is here rendered in 𝔊 (𝔏s) by Syene (note a); that is, it has been read, with a very slight graphic alteration, as סון. This would then indicate Aswan, which has already been mentioned in the description of the boundary points in 29:10; 30:6, as the southern frontier-post of Egypt proper.[45] In this case, at least in v 16, for once the geographical direction south-north would have been maintained in these three places.

■ **30:17** The fate of having their young men killed and their wives (? note c) taken captive will overtake און ("On") (note a) and פי בסת ("Bubastis"). On, Egyptian *'iwnw,*[46] was, as the Greek translation "Heliopolis" records, the great center of Egyptian sun-worship. Ancient Heliopolis, whose few remains (traces of an enclosure-wall and, above all, a temple obelisk still stand) are to be found at modern *maṭarīja,* ten kilometers northwest of Cairo, lies thirty-three kilometers due south of the center of ancient Memphis. Their mutual boundary marked the dividing line between Upper and Lower Egypt. The sun theology of Heliopolis, in which the sun god was worshipped as Re-Atum and Re-Horakhty, became widespread especially from the third dynasty onwards in the Old Kingdom and determined the solarization of Egyptian beliefs far into the future.[47] While the royal palace of the Thinites formed the center of what later became Memphis,[48] Heliopolis, lying east of the Nile, was distinguished above all by the "House of Re," in which the god of the rising sun was worshipped as "Horus of the land of light" (Horakhty). On the "high sand" north of Heliopolis, an artificial hill which was described as the primeval hill, stood the main sanctuary of Heliopolis. In it there stood the "benben" stone, the model for the later obelisk, before which, in the sun temple of the Old Kingdom, sacrifices were made on the

40 Baedeker, *Egypt,* 32; on this see Montet, *Géographie,* 80–83.

41 Baedeker, *Egypt,* 186.

42 Montet, *Géographie,* 199.

43 Wilhelm Spiegelberg, "Der ägyptische Name von Pelusium," *Zeitschrift für Ägyptische Sprache und Altertumskunde* 49 (1911), 81–84; "Augustus 'Ρωμαῖοα'," *Zeitschrift für Ägyptische Sprache und Altertumskunde* 49 (1911), 85–87.

44 Erman-Grapow, 69.

45 See above p. 113.

46 Erman-Grapow, 1. 54.

47 Kees, *Götterglaube,* 214ff.

48 Kees, *alte Ägypten,* 80.

altar in the open court. In the later period, admittedly, Heliopolis receded considerably in favor of Memphis, which became once again the capital, and its famous Apis cult. There is no trace in Ezek 30:17 of its particular cultic qualification. It cannot be deduced from the text that the young men mentioned here were neophytes and candidates for the priesthood.[49] Along with Heliopolis reference is made to פי בסת ("Bubastis"), the Egyptian *pr.bꜣst.t*[50] ("house of [the goddess] Bastet"), whose gigantic festival, with seven hundred thousand participants arriving from all directions, is referred to by Herodotus.[51] Bubastis, which under the twenty-second (Libyan) dynasty (the so-called Bubastites) became the capital, lies near *tell basṭa,* half an hour southeast of Zakazik in the eastern Delta on a level with *wādi ṭumīlāt.*[52] The cult of the goddess Bastet in the form of a cat became famous especially in the time of the Bubastites.[53]

■ **30:18** In v 18, finally, the manifestations of judgment are intensified along cosmic lines: the darkening of the sun and the land's being covered in cloud. In the latter we may perhaps hear an echo of the description of the day of Yahweh, which in v 3 was described as a day of clouds. Why the first-mentioned phenomenon should be connected specifically with the place תחפנחס ("Tahpanhes") cannot be determined. (Should one think of an original תחשך "grow dark," which then on account of the similarity in sound stood next to תחפנחס "Tahpanhes"?) This place, which is also mentioned in Jer 43:7–9; 44:1 as the residence of Jewish refugees in the year 587 and where there was (according to Jer 43:9) also a "house of Pharaoh,"[54] has, according to W. Spiegelberg, a name which means "the fortress of the Nubian."[55] W. F. Albright, on the other hand, would rather translate the supposed Egyptian *tꜣ-ḥ(t)-(n)pꜣ-nḥśj* as "the fortress of Penaḥse (=Phinehas)" and see in Phinehas a Theban general of the eleventh century after whom several places have been named.[56] The Tahpanhes mentioned in these passages (also in Jer 2:16 emended text; 46:14) is transcribed in 𝔊 as Ταφνας and is mostly identified with Hellenistic Δάφναι and located at the modern *tell defenneh.*[57] Further, the text states that there the breaking of Egyptian power will take place.[58] It may therefore be asked whether this means that the actual decisive battle between the destroyer of Egypt and the army of the Pharaoh is expected to take place at Tahpanhes in a battle which will also bring (is this to be understood figuratively?) great darkness over Egypt. Are we to think of the influence of the threat-oracle in Jer 43:8–13, which affirms the triumph of Nebuchadnezzar at that very spot? Or are we to assume that the campaign in Nebuchadnezzar's thirty-seventh year led to a clash at that spot, a clash which, in an enlarged form, was also expected at that very spot as a final victory over Egypt? Or must one even think of an echo (admittedly a very imprecise one) of the battle of Pelusium in which Egypt collapsed before Cambyses? At any rate it is clear that the text, in this final statement, envisages the political collapse of the Egyptian power structure (on מטות "yoke(poles)" or "staffs" see note b)—in which her bulwark collapses (v 18aγ takes up the statement of v 6), the cloud of the day of Yahweh covers her (v 3), her daughters are dragged away (see v 17) and judgment is dispensed (v 14)—as taking place at Tahpanhes. There Yahweh will reveal himself to Egypt in the mystery of his person.

If one reviews the names mentioned vv 13–19, then they point for the most part to the Delta (Zoan, Heliopolis, Pelusium [?], Bubastis, Tahpanhes) or its edge (Memphis). Upper Egypt is referred to only in the mention of Thebes, in the regional name Pathros and perhaps in Aswan. This reflects, perfectly correctly, the transfer of the center of the Egyptian state in this late period. It may, however, equally be the case that one can discern the knowledge of places where there were groups of Jewish refugees (or military colonies?), even if these groups are not mentioned at all. Jer 44:1 refers to Migdol, Tahpanhes, Memphis and the land of Pathros.

---

49 So Cooke. See also, Montet, *Géographie,* 156–160.

50 Erman-Grapow, 1. 423.

51 2, 60.

52 Baedeker, *Egypt,* 171f.

53 See Kees, *Götterglaube,* 82f, and Montet, *Géographie,* 173–178.

54 A government building; see Rudolph, *Jeremia.*

55 Wilhelm Spiegelberg, *Ägyptologische Randglossen zum Alten Testament* (1904), 38ff.

56 W. F. Albright, "Baal-Zaphon" in *Festschrift Alfred Bertholet* (Tübingen: Mohr [Siebeck], 1950), 13f.

57 Baedeker, *Egypt,* 185. So, too, Albright and Montet, *Géographie,* 192. Alt, "Taphnaein und Taphnas," on the other hand, thinks of a site further east.

58 On the expression see note b.

The first three names are also mentioned in Jer 46:14.

Aim

In vv 1–19 any internal justification for the judgment on Egypt is almost entirely absent. Only quite incidentally does the catchword המון ("pomp") appear, in which there is concentrated everything that is vain and immoderate, everything boastful from the political or the religious point of view. In v 4 a later hand has appended an expansion which (as in 7:12–14) seems to have added this idea explicitly. A later reinterpretation of v 13 then explicitly added the statement that in Egypt it is not only men but also the power of idols that is opposed to the one lord of history.

The main point of the oracle as a whole, on the other hand, lies in the proclamation that the judgment which falls upon Egypt is the work of the one who alone has power in history. It is the Day of the Lord, and it is therefore inescapable. When the sword begins to be wielded, even though it may be in "the hand of Nebuchadnezzar" (v 10), a man, it is God who is the real opponent. Not any god, but the God of history, the history that God's covenant people have experienced. And therefore even if Egypt summons her helpers (v 8), those who are to support her (v 6), even if she increases these auxiliary troops—the person who added v 5 even makes so bold as to say, "Even if people from the covenant nation, that is the nation of the divine encounter, are among these hired helpers"—God will sit in judgment, the helpers will fall, and the neighboring peoples will be horror-struck and will writhe in terror. And no region will be spared. From Migdol to Aswan there is no corner where one can hide from this judgment. This is in fact underlined by the enumeration of all the places. There is no place, neither the place of the famous sanctuary nor the place of the strongly defended frontier post, where one can be safe from this God (cf. Am 9:1–4). Therefore control is taken also of the forces of nature. The Nile dries up, the sun grows pale, the clouds cover all the light which man thinks he has to help him.

The oracle is the denial of all that trivializes life, but also of any illusion about the possibility of flight. It contains the great proclamation that God is at work even in the history of nations beyond the frontiers of the land of Israel and even beyond the places where the exiles live, carrying out his will and revealing himself in his glory—in such a way that men will recognize him.

While the oracle in its different parts, coming as they do from different hands, is directed quite decisively towards this single proclamation, it does also provide profound consolation and comfort to a people that has experienced in its own life this inevitability of God in his judgment (see the "Day of the Lord" of Ezekiel 7), with the statement that in the whole world there is no other historically decisive encounter than the encounter with this one lord. This lord reveals himself even where, for the time being, it appears as if he has nothing to say.

4. Pharaoh's Broken Arm

Bibliography
Johannes Hempel
Heilung als Symbol und Wirklichkeit im biblischen Schrifttum (Göttingen: Vandenhoeck & Ruprecht, [2]1965).

30

20 In the eleventh year[a], in the first month[b],
on the seventh (day)[c] of the month, the
word of Yahweh came to me:
21 Son of man, I have broken the arm[a] of
Pharaoh king of Egypt and see, it is not
bound up so that it can be healed[b], that a
bandage be put on it [to bind it][c], to
<strengthen>[d] it, so that it might be able
(once again) to wield a sword.
22 Therefore thus has [the Lord][a] Yahweh
said: See, I am against[b] Pharaoh king of
Egypt and will break his arms, the strong
and the broken one[c] and will knock the

30:20 20a 𝔊^{967,62,763} "tenth year."
b 𝔏^{S} "third month."
c 𝔏^{S} "seventeenth day"; ℜ^{Bo} "first day."

21 21a 𝔐 זרוע. 𝔊 (𝔏^{S}) τοὺς βραχίονας. An apparent heightening by the extension of the reference to include both arms, but in reality a weakening, since in the OT "arm" means the fullness of strength. See, however, vv 22ff. 𝔗 again interprets: תקוף מלכות (פרעה).

b 𝔐 רפאות is usually understood in an abstract sense, see Gesenius-Buhl, Koehler-Baumgartner. The other occurrences of the word in Jer 30:13; 46:11 (singular in Sir 3:28) also admit the possibility of the concrete sense; see, e.g., Hempel, *Heilung*, 239: "administer medicines."

c 𝔐 לחבשה repeats inelegantly the verb which has just been used (in the pu'al). It is missing in 𝔊 𝔏^{S} and must have been added secondarily as a gloss on חתול.

d 𝔐 לְחָזְקָה "so that he might become strong." Perhaps better is pi'el לְחַזְּקָה.

22 22a אדני is lacking in 𝔊 𝔏^{S}, see Appendix 1.
b אל–על cf. 1:17 note a.
c As distinct from v 21, Pharaoh's "arms" are now mentioned in the plural in v 22. One may, however, ask whether the odd specification את החזקה ואת הנשברת, which is clearly meant to provide a logical harmonization with v 21, is not a secondary insertion. On no account should one, with Joüon, "Notes," 308f; Bertholet; BH[3], by appeal to 𝔖, delete only את הנשברת and and change זרעתיו to the singular זרעו. 𝔖 removes the absurdity that the broken arm should be broken again quite simply by leaving out the offending element, a radical simplification of the kind 𝔖 loves. The other versions show that they are also struggling with this difficulty in sense. As distinct from 𝔖, however, they try somehow to come to terms with the text. 𝔊 translates: τοὺς βραχίονας αὐτοῦ τοὺς ἰσχυροὺς καὶ τοὺς τεταμένους, thus equalizing the two expressions, so that 𝔏^{S} can then without difficulty omit the copula and translate: *brachia eius fortes et extensos* [*sic!*]. Similarly 'A τὸν κραταιὸν καὶ ὑψηλόν and Θ τὸν ἰσχυρὸν καὶ τὸν μέγαν. 𝔗, in its interpretation ("I shall break his staffs and his strong power with which he has broken kingdoms"), shows that it

sword from his hand. 23/ And I shall
scatter Egypt among the nations and
disperse them among the lands. 24/ And
I shall strengthen the arms of the king of
Babylon and shall place my sword in his
hand and shall break the arms of Phar-
aoh, and he shall groan before him like
one pierced (by the sword).[a]
25 **And I shall strengthen[a] the arms of the king**
of Babylon, but the arms of Pharaoh will
fall, and they shall know that I am Yah-
weh when I place my sword in the hand
of the king of Babylon and when he
stretches it out against[b] the land of
Egypt. 26/ And I shall scatter Egypt
among the nations and disperse them
among the lands, and they[a] will know
that I am Yahweh.

understands נשברת in an active sense (as משברת). 𝔅, on the other hand, comes close to 𝔐: *et comminans brachium eius forte, sed confractum* (i.e. the arm that was broken but is still strong). "Arm" there is wrongly understood as singular. See further the exposition.

24 24a Instead of v 24b, 𝔊 (𝔏[S]) reads: *καὶ ἐπάξει αὐτὴν ἐπ' Αἴγυπτον καὶ προνομεύσει τὴν προνομὴν αὐτῆς καὶ σκυλεύσει τὰ σκῦλα αὐτῆς*, a sentence which, on the basis of 29:8, 19 corresponds to Hebrew והביא אותה על מצרים ושלל שללה ובזז בזה. The sentence is of doubtful authenticity, in that it ascribes to Nebuchadnezzar the הביא חרב, of which Toy correctly affirms that it is otherwise said only of Yahweh (5:17; 6:3; 11:8; 14:17; 29:8; 33:2; associated with these are the references to the coming of the sword 21:24f; 30:4; 32:11; 33:4, 6). Thus it remains (against Cornill, Fohrer) more likely that 𝔊, for some reason or another, has replaced the more original text of 𝔐 by borrowing from Ezek 29. See the exposition.

25 25a 𝔐 והחזקתי is odd alongside the וחזקתי of v 24 (see also v 21 note d). Is it a scribal error or a variation of the kind that the living language shows over and over again?

b על-אל cf. 1:17 note a.

26 26a Strengthened in 𝔊 (𝔏[S]) by *πάντες*.

Form

The dated oracle in 30:20 26 recalls, in its formal structure, the form of 29:17–21. The word of Yahweh which is received is directed first of all to the prophet himself and speaks to him, in the perfect tense, of an event which has clearly already occurred. To this there is joined the actual proclamation, with the messenger formula, introduced as in 29:19 by לכן ("therefore"), but without any specific commission to speak. It begins in 30:22 with the הנה ("see") of the formula of summons or formula of encounter.[1] In 29:19 הנה ("see") was followed by a simple proclamation without this particular introduction. The conclusion of 30:20–26 is then in the form of an expanded proof-saying, in which, at the end of the expansion, the recognition formula is repeated.

If, however, after these statements regarding merely the form, one looks at the content of what is said, then there are not inconsiderable problems of comprehension. While in 29:17–21 the train of thought continued without difficulty from the introductory exposition to the prophet himself (vv 17–18) to the divine oracle (vv 19-20) which contained the prediction of renewed divine action, and where the לכן ("therefore") was logically perfectly in place, the transition from the introductory descriptive words in the perfect tense in 30:21 to the menacing words of proclamation in vv 22–26 is less obvious, and לכן ("therefore") is logically more difficult. Thus, the suggestion of Hölscher carries weight that behind v 21 there may be an originally independent saying. A short, basic oracle has thus, here too, been developed and had its thought carried further by means of a secondary expansion.

The further difficulty, that vv 22–26 in their present form are undoubtedly overloaded, is best discussed in the context of the detailed exposition. The question of the "setting" of the unit as a whole is also best asked in connection with the detailed exposition.

Interpretation

■ **30:20** The divine word which comes to the prophet is dated on the seventh day of the first month of Jehoiachin's eleventh year.[2] According to Parker-Dubberstein, that is April 29, 587, a date approximately three months short of the day on which, according to 2 Kgs 25:3f, the walls of Jerusalem were breached.

■ **30:21** The oracle in the perfect tense, which is

1 See 1, 175; see above p. 98.
2 See 1, 144f.

addressed to the prophet[3] and which forms the kernel of the later expansion of the oracle as a whole, speaks of a blow on Yahweh's part directed against Pharaoh, a blow from which he cannot recover. Rashi thinks of Necho's defeat at Carchemish in 605.[4] More probably, however, the reference is to the event which is reported in Jer 37:5 (cf. 34:21f), when Pharaoh Hophra leapt to the assistance of besieged Jerusalem from which he then had to withdraw having achieved nothing. The present passage may suggest that the withdrawal followed a military defeat. The relief attempt is best dated in the year 588. The news of this will also have reached the exiles; they too will have heard of the failure of the attempt. But at the beginning of 587 many may have seen fresh hope that the relief might be more successful in the new year and Jerusalem be saved. The oracle in v 21 would fit very well into this context and could then be understood, exactly like the threat in 21:23–32, as an oracle directed in the first instance against the false hope of the house of Israel here and yonder. The translation preferred by Hölscher (following Cornill and Jahn) in the present tense (with future meaning), which takes the divine word as the proclamation of a defeat of Pharaoh that is still to come, is not advised either by the date or by the grammatical structure of the sentence (where otherwise it is preferable [as in the divine speeches in Josh 6:2; 8:1; Ju 7:9; but also in Ezek 29:19] to read the verb at the beginning).

The prophetic oracle uses the image of the broken arm. The arm was mentioned as a sign of strength already in the creedal phraseology of the exodus from Egypt: "with strong hand and outstretched arm."[5] In 22:6 it was used as the image of the brutal force of the wicked ruler.[6] In the present passage it refers to the military power of Pharaoh. The expression about the "breaking of the arm" is also found elsewhere as an image for the depriving of the strong of his power (Ps 10:15; Job 38:15; Jer 48:25; with the plural of זרוע "arm" Ps 37:17). It is used with the verb גדע ("to cut off") in 1 Sam 2:31, with דכא ("to crush") in Job 22:9. The breaking of the arm from its socket is referred to in Job 31:22.[7]

The defeat of Pharaoh is expressed in these words of Yahweh in the first person as his deed, and from this it acquires its importance. But the real emphasis of the oracle must lie in the further explanation which is introduced weightily by והנה ("and see"). The blow is followed by no act of healing from which one might have hoped optimistically at the beginning of the new year that Pharaoh could again swiftly seize his sword. It is here graphically depicted what therapeutic actions are normally subsequently taken. The vocabulary has in individual phrases its correspondence in 34:4,16.[8] Normally the broken arm is "bandaged" (חבשׁ, used of the putting on of clothes in 16:10, of the turban in 24:17) in order to effect healing (but see note b) and so that it might lie in a "soft wrapping" (חתול only here; the verb חתל in 16:4 "to wrap in swaddling clothes"; the noun חתלה "swaddling band" in Job 38:9). It is bandaged so that it might find new strength to grasp a sword again. All this, so the prophet proclaims, has been omitted in Pharaoh's case.

■ **30:22** The oracle has then been further expounded in a secondary expansion. Only now does it become a foreign oracle which threatens Pharaoh quite specifically. It is difficult to be certain whether in this expansion an independent threat against Pharaoh, which spoke of the breaking of (both) his arms, has been secondarily connected with v 21 by the insertion of the conciliatory but not exactly skillful statement of v 22aγ (which is therefore deleted by many [Cornill, Jahn, Hölscher and others] as an addition), or whether the expansion was always connected by means of this transitional sentence. In any case the introductory לכן ("therefore") of v 22 seems to presuppose the following line of thought. Because Yahweh, when he smashed Pharaoh's arm, did not bother about the healing of it but had further destruction in mind, therefore he has now broken not only Pharaoh's one arm but both arms. Since in this heightened expression an explicit reference to "*both* arms" is missing, one can scarcely dispense with the phrase which replaces it in the present text, which is continued by לכן ("therefore"), "the strong (whole) one and the broken one." Ps 37:17 shows that the phrase about the "breaking of the arms (plural)" was also quite common. This presupposes that Pharaoh has again taken

3 On "son of man" see 1, 131f.
4 According to Breuer.
5 See 1, 414f on 20:33.
6 See 1, 457.
7 See also Hempel, *Heilung,* 303.
8 On this see Hempel, *Heilung,* 239.

up the sword. One should not ask pedantically whether he now holds it in his left hand. The image simply starts off afresh because it now obviously envisages Pharaoh in the sphere of his own Egyptian sovereignty.

■ **30:24** It can then quickly be seen that the oracle corresponding to v 22 is to be found in v 24, where it is explained that the sword has now been given into the hand of the king of Babylon. In a clear intensification of the statement, instead of the indefinite reference by Yahweh to *a* sword (v 22), we now have the reference to "my sword." And corresponding to that is the fact that it is not simply the strong arm of the Babylonian king that is referred to, but the fact that Yahweh himself makes his arm strong. With a resumption of the statement about Pharaoh's broken arm, v 24b explains how the wounded Pharaoh breaks out in groaning before that other, who now as Yahweh's servant attacks him with the sword.

■ **30:23** V 23, with its reference to the scattering of Egypt (= the Egyptians), now breaks the original connection between vv 22 and 24. This is doubtless to blame for the fact that 𝔊 has subsequently assimilated v 24b to what was said in 29:19 and here too speaks of the plundering of Egypt. Cornill is correct in deleting v 23 as an addition which anticipates what is said in v 26.

The expansion of vv 20f will, therefore, in the first instance have comprised vv 22,24. The basic oracle, which was directed in the first place at the house of Israel and aimed at destroying there all her false hopes, has become in vv 22,24 a foreign oracle which stands against a wider background and speaks of the victory of the king of Babylon over Pharaoh.

■ **30:25** In vv 25–26, however, yet another expansion has been added. This can be seen from the linguistic point of view from the fact that the repetition in v 25 uses the hip'il החזיק ("strengthen"), while v 24 (also v 21? see note d) had used the pi'el. This extension, which first of all with a complete "resumption"[9] repeats what has been said both about the arms of the king of Babylon and about the arms of Pharaoh (with slight variation in the latter instance), broadens the horizon still further by also including the land of Egypt in the threat.

■ **30:26** When the thread is taken up again after the first recognition formula, this whole aim of the sword sent by Yahweh against the land of Egypt and the dispersal of the Egyptians among the nations which this occasions are now fully stated and rounded off by the second recognition formula. This latest expansion in vv 25–26 is along the same lines as the latest expansion within 29:1–16 without, however, mentioning a later gathering in again of Egypt after her dispersal.

Setting

The detailed survey has shown that at the heart of 30:20–26, in vv 20f, there lies an oracle which, as the date in v 20 intends, belongs to the last phase of the siege of Jerusalem. To this there has been joined an expansion which makes the oracle into a foreign oracle against Pharaoh and—analogous to the expansion of the Tyre oracle in 26:1–6 by means of vv 7ff or of the Egypt oracle in 30:1–8(9) by means of vv 10–12—quite openly mentions the Babylonian king as Yahweh's helper in carrying out the judgment. For this part one will have to think of a slightly later period (after 587). Finally, the third part, vv 25–6, extends the threat to include all of Egypt and envisages the dispersal of its population on the model of Israel (see above on 29:10–12). This could point to a time close to Nebuchadnezzar's campaign against Egypt.

Aim

World history appears to the observer again and again as the work of strong arms. And those who cannot reflect on it from the outside as dispassionate observers, but endure it personally in affliction, look fervently for the strong hand which can deliver them and will approach it and reach out to it so that it might help them. Thus Jerusalem, and the exiles who were linked to her, looked to the strong hand of Egypt so that that hand, which once held Palestine firmly in its grip, might become her helper against the oppressors.

The prophet proclaims that, over and above the strong human arms in world history, another is at work, who in his freedom breaks the strong arm on the one side and on the other knows how to make the arm of a foreigner really strong, who on the one side knocks the sword out of one person's hand and on the other hands

9 Kuhl, "'Wiederaufnahme.'"

out his sword to someone else, so that he might thereby complete his work and his judgment.

In all this activity, man should be aware that he is not in the grip of the imponderable course of history, not even in the grip of the all-powerful historical forces of men, however great they might be, but should let himself be brought to the point of recognizing and honoring the only lord, who makes himself known in the mystery of his being through the judgment of history, and of obeying his word which is proclaimed through the mouth of his prophet. This removes man from the role of a mere spectator, but removes him also from all despair of succumbing to the terror of sheer, uncomprehended power. God, who has called in his own name his people to himself and in this has made it possible for them to name him, stands above all power.

5. Splendor and Fall of the World Tree: An Image of Pharaoh

Bibliography

Albrecht Brock-Utne
Der Gottesgarten; eine vergleichende religionsgeschichtliche Studie (Oslo: Dybwad, 1936), especially 120–127.

Hermann Gunkel
Das Märchen im Alten Testament (Tübingen: Mohr, 1917), especially 21–26.

U. Holmberg
Der Baum des Lebens, Annales Academiae Scientiarum Fennicae 16 (Helsinki, 1922/23).

Geo Widengren
The King and the Tree of Life in Ancient Near Eastern Religion: King and Saviour IV, UUÅ (Uppsala: Lundequists, 1951).

August Wünsche
Die Sagen vom Lebensbaum und Lebenswasser; altorientalische Mythen, Ex Oriente lux 1 (Leipzig: Pfeiffer, 1905).

31

1 **In the eleventh year[a], in the third month, on
the first (day) of the month, the word of
Yahweh came to me: 2/ Son of man, say
to Pharaoh king of Egypt and to his pomp:
To whom[a] are you like[b] in your greatness?
3/ See, <a cypress(?)>[a],**

31:1 1a Here too 𝔊^967 and others read δεκάτῳ, see 30:20 note a.

2 2a Driver, "Ezekiel," 300 (where Ezek 30:3 is cited by mistake), wants to take 𝔐, in comparison with 1 Sam 18:18; 1 Chr 29:14, and elsewhere, in a neuter sense.

b 𝔐 דמית is understood by 𝔊 (𝔏^S) *ὡμοίωσας σεαυτόν* with a more strongly active emphasis. The arrogance is positive guilt.

3 3a 𝔐 אשור is unanimously attested by all the versions. 𝔊 Ασσουρ has been incorrectly copied by 𝔏^S as *(ecce) ad sur (est).* 𝔙 *Assur.* 𝔗 paraphrases in a complete sentence: הא אתוראה דמי לארזא בליבנן, 𝔖 אתוריא. Ewald prefers to understand the word אשור here as the description of a type of cedar with the same meaning as the תאשור of 27:6. Since Smend, אשור is emended by most (Cornill, Herrmann, Bertholet, Fohrer, Koehler-Baumgartner) to תאשור. This should be read. The initial ת could have fallen out by haplography after the preceding ה. At the same time, the replacement of the no longer understood תאשור (see also the wrong division into two words in 𝔐 of 27:6) by the more familiar אשור was obvious. On the uncertainty with regard to the precise sense of תאשור see 27:6 note d. In the parallelism here the tree is described as a type of cedar from Lebanon. See the exposition. Cornill then emends ארז to אדיר, while Herrmann, Bertholet, Fohrer unhesitatingly delete the whole expression ארז בלבנון as a gloss. When one realizes, however, that from the metrical point of view v 2b is not (against BH[3]) to be linked with the beginning of

a cedar on Lebanon
with fine branches [and a shady place][b]
and of great height,
and its top reached
the clouds[c].
4/ (The) waters made it great,
(the) torrents in the depths made it grow tall.
Its streams <it (i.e. the torrent) had made to flow>[a]
round about the place where it was planted[b]
and had sent out its channels
to all the trees of the field[c].
5/ Therefore it grew[a] higher
than all the trees of the field,
and its boughs[b] became numerous,
and its branches[c] became long[d]
because of the abundant water [when

v 3, then ארז בלבנון is indispensable as a parallel two-stress line alongside הנה תאשור. Driver, "Ezekiel," 300 (where 30:3 is an error for 31:3), wants to read אשור as אֲשֶׁר and understand it on the basis of *Gen Rab* 15: "Lo! he is strong (as) a cedar." Joseph Plessis, *Les Prophéties d'Ezéchiel contre l'Egypte* (1912), reads אָשׁוּר and understands it on the basis of Hos 13:7. "Voici que je vais (te) considérer (comme) un cèdre sur le Liban." Bewer, "Textual Notes," 164f, leaves אשור in its usual sense and finds in this word, which should be deleted as a gloss which nevertheless may come from Ezekiel himself, a reference to the example of a great power that has fallen. See also Toy. That Asshur is cited as the first world power would also be attested by 32:22. Joüon, "Notes," 309 note 1, retains אשור as original and refers the whole account narrated in the perfect in vv 1–17 to Asshur.

b 𝔐 וחרש מצל is not mentioned in 𝔊 (𝔏^{S}). Since the two phrases יפה ענף and גבה קומה, which have the same structure and are obviously parallels, are separated by this differently structured expression (noun with attributive participle), we must regard the latter as a later expansion. חרש is found also in 2 Chr 27:4 "wooded place" (Koehler-Baumgartner). On the hip'il participle מֵצַל see Gesenius-Kautzsch §67v, and Leo Prijs, "ṣll Hifil," *ThZ* 5 (1949): 152. A radical emendation to bring it into line with the structure of the neighboring expressions (Driver, "Linguistic Problems," 177f: וּמֵצַל חֹרֶשׁ "and overshadowing the forest") is not to be recommended.

c Driver, "Linguistic Problems," 178, sees in עבתים a *forma mixta* of עבות and עבים. A scribe wanted to replace the feminine plural form of עב (attested only twice) by the more common (seven times) masculine plural. Thus עבות will have been the original reading. But the reading of 𝔐 must be very old, since it has also found its way into 19:11.

4 4a 𝔐 הֹלֵךְ should be emended to הֹלִכָה on the basis of 𝔊 ἤγαγε 𝔏^{S} *duxit.*

b 𝔐 מטעה should, on the basis of 𝔊 𝔏^{S} 𝔙 𝔖, be vocalized מַטָּעָה. 𝔗 explains it allegorically as a reference to the nations who help Pharaoh.

c Joüon, "Notes," 309, suggests deleting כל עצי השדה (as a vertical dittograph from v 5) and to read in its place an original מקמו. See the exposition.

5 5a 𝔐 גבהא is an Aramaic spelling.

b 𝔐 סרעפתיו reveals an Aramaic (cf. Syriac סרעיפיתה) expanded form of סעפתיו, which is attested immediately afterwards in vv 6, 8. See also note a.

c פארתיו should be read with Q.

d In 𝔊 𝔏^{S} one of the parallel clauses of v 5b is missing. Thus, Cornill would like to delete ותארכנה פארת[י]ו as a secondary addition, by pointing to the unusual use of ארך to refer to spatial length. Driver, on the other hand, "Linguistic Problems," 178, in view of the Aramaizing סרעפתיו, which he regards as a gloss on בשלחו misunderstood as בשלחיו (note e),

<they> were sent out][e].
6/ In its boughs nested
all the birds of the air,
and under its branches all the beasts of the field
brought forth their young,
and in its shade <there lived>[a]
all great nations of every kind[b].
7/ And it became beautiful[a] in its greatness
through the length[b] of its branches[c];
for its roots
reached[d] abundant water.
8/ (The) cedars could not rival it in the
garden of God, the[a] (boughs of the)
juniper[b] could not rival its boughs, and
the (branches of the) plane trees were
not to be compared with its branches.
No tree in the garden of God was like it
in its beauty[c]. 9/ [I have made it
beautiful.][a] On account of the mass of
its branches [all][b] the Eden trees, that[c]
were in the garden of God, envied it.
10 **Therefore thus has [the Lord][a] Yahweh**
said: Because <it has grown tall>[b] and
has let its top tower up into the clouds[c]
and its heart has become proud of its
height, 11/ therefore <I have given>[a] it

thinks that the original text should read ותרבינה פארתיו.

e 𝔐 בשלחו creates difficulties. It is not attested in 𝔊 𝔏^{S}. It is rendered by 𝔖 as דרביוהי (as in 𝔐 גדלוהו in v 4) and in 𝔙 it is explained as follows: *cumque extendisset umbram suam* and linked with v 6. One should perhaps regard the word (read as בִּשְׁלָחָם?) as an addition in the nature of a gloss, which takes up again the שלח of v 4. Ehrlich, *Randglossen*, reads בִּשְׁלָחוֹ and sees there a noun "watercourse." Toy and Cooke read the word as בשלחיו and link it with v 6, where they then delete בסעפתיו as a secondary description which became necessary as a result of the wrong text division.

6 6a 𝔐 יָשְׁבוּ is strange. It is preferable to read here too a perfect יָשְׁבוּ, parallel to the preceding perfect and presupposed by the versions.

b 𝔐 כל גוים רבים can be understood only if גוים רבים is already a fixed comprehensive expression. It occurs also in 26:3; 38:23; 39:27 (does the article in this last instance point to the same awareness?). See also the expression עמים רבים in 3:6; 27:33; 32:3, 9f; 38:6, 8f, 15.

7 7a L 3MSS^{G} read וַיְּיִף, with retention of the first consonant of the root, instead of the more normal וַיִּף of C, 𝔙.

b 𝔐 בארך. 𝔊 (𝔏^{S}) διὰ τὸ πλῆθος, 𝔖 בסוגאא seem to suggest an original ברב, which could have been wrongly copied as in 𝔐 under the influence of the ארך in v 5.

c On the meaning of דליותיו see 17:6 note d. It must be rendered here by "branch."

d על-אל cf. 1:17 note a.

8 8a 𝔊 𝔏^{S} add the copula, see above 1:4 note a.

b See 27:5 note a.

c 𝔙 *et pulchritudini eius* adds the copula.

9 9a 𝔐 יפה עשיתיו is missing in 𝔊 𝔏^{S}. Since, with this speech of Yahweh in the first person, it at once introduces a theological emphasis which has hitherto been lacking in the description, it should be regarded as a secondary addition which aims at interpreting the יפי of v 8 as a beauty that has been given to the tree.

b 𝔐 כל is missing in 𝔊 𝔏^{S} and is certainly a secondary emphasis.

c 𝔐 אשר, which is not attested by 𝔊 𝔏^{S} 𝔖, is meaningful only if one regards עצי עדן as a pure description of quality, without any geographical reference. See the exposition.

10 10a אדני is lacking in 𝔊 𝔏^{S} 𝔎^{Bo}, see Appendix 1.

b 𝔐 גבהת בקומה begins with a direct address, but then in v 10b passes into the descriptive third person, which is then maintained in what follows. In 𝔊 𝔏^{S} v 10b*α* is also in the address form. With 𝔙 𝔖 the third person (גבה) should be read from the outset. In addition, 𝔖 suggests the reading בקומתו.

c On 𝔐 עבותים see v 3 note c.

11 11a 𝔐 וְאתנהו is determined by the following imperfect יעשה (see note c). Since the continuation

into the hands of a brutal nation[b]. [She
will act against it as thoroughly as its
wickedness deserves. <>][c] 12/ And
strangers, the most brutal nations, have
cut it down and thrown[a] it on to[b] the
mountains, and its branches lay in all the
valleys, and its boughs have been broken
in all the watercourses of the land, and
from its shade all the peoples of the earth
have flown away[c], and it has been
thrown down. 13/ On its fallen trunk
<lived>[a] all the birds of the air, and on[b]
its branches dwelt[c] all the beasts of the
field, 14/ so that no more trees should
grow tall by the water nor let their tops
tower up into the clouds[a], nor should all
(trees) that drink water stand <upon
themselves>[b]; for[c] they are all given over
to death, to the land below, amongst
men, with those who go down to the pit.
15 **Thus has [the Lord][a] Yahweh said: On the**
day when it went down to the under-
world I made the torrent in the depths
mourn for it [I covered (it with it)][b] and

in vv 12ff is in *waw*-consecutive imperfects and perfects, here too with 𝔊 (cf. 𝔅) וָאתנהו should be read.

b On איל see 30:13 note c.

c 𝔐 עשו יעשה לו כרשעו גרשתהו is abbreviated by 𝔊 and translated by καὶ ἐποίησε τὴν ἀπώλειαν αὐτοῦ. This makes it likely that גרשתהו, which is already remarkable by virtue of its defective writing (cf., e.g., נטשתיך 32:4), and כרשעו are variants of the same word, which 𝔊, however, can hardly have found as כרשעו. The imperfect יעשה, impossible in the context and difficult to emend, makes one suspect that the whole sentence is an addition. From the content point of view, too, it stands outside the metaphor of the tree which is continued in v 12. With Toy, Hölscher it should be deleted as an addition. Driver, "Linguistic Problems," 178, retains 𝔐 and takes גרש (as he does also מגרש in 36:5), on the basis of Arabic *jarasa,* to mean "to expose to public contempt."

12 12a On נטש see 29:5 note a. Driver, who in "Linguistic Problems," postulated a root יטש on the basis of Arabic *waṭasa* "crush, smash," withdrew this suggestion in "Ezekiel," 301, and understood נטש on the basis of 𝔊 κατέβαλον as "fling down." In addition, the parallel statements in 29:5; 32:4 make it likely that, against the accents of 𝔐, the verb should be connected with what follows and the athnah placed under ההרים (see van den Born).

b על–אל cf. 1:17 note a.

c 𝔐 וירדו, literally "have gone down." So, too, 𝔊 καὶ κατέβησαν, 𝔅 *recedent,* 𝔗 ונחתו, 𝔖 ונחתון. Hitzig emended to וידדו "and they fled," which is graphically attractive; Cornill, to ויחרדו.

13 13a 𝔐 ישכנו should be emended, on the basis of 𝔊 𝔅 𝔗 and with the context, to שכנו. י is dittography of the preceding ו. 𝔖 reads תשכן, but also assimilates to this the following verb (תהוא). According to Joüon, "Notes," 309f, the imperfect here (as also in 𝔐 of v 11) can be easily understood psychologically from the feeling that after לכן (v 10) a future threat should follow.

b על–על cf. 1:17 note a.

c Literally "were."

14 14a See v 3 note a.

b 𝔐 אֵלֵיהֶם "their gods" or "their strong ones" is surely to be vocalized אֲלֵיהֶם. See 𝔊 𝔗 and Diehl, *Pronomen,* 34. 𝔅 omits the word, but see Ziegler, 40f. On על–אל cf. 1:17 note a. עמד על is found also in 33:26.

c כי is not attested by 𝔊.

15 15a אדני is lacking in 𝔊 𝔎^{Bo} 𝔄̈, see Appendix 1.

b 𝔐 כסתי is not attested by 𝔊, which in addition renders 𝔐 האבלתי and ואקדיר with the third person (the latter thus in 𝔅 as well), ויכלאו, on the other hand (with 𝔅), with a first person (active). According to G. R. Driver and J. C. Miles, *The Babylonian Laws* 2 (Oxford: Clarendon, 1955), 181 note 1, it should be deleted as a gloss on האבלתי, which is to be

stopped up its streams, and the great
waters were held back. And on its ac-
count I dressed Lebanon in mourning,
and on its account all the trees of the
field <have fainted away>[c]. 16/ I have
made (the) nations quake at the crash of
its fall, when I made it go down into the
underworld with those who go down to
the pit. In the land below[a], however, all
the trees of Eden were comforted, the
choice ones [and the good (or best)
ones][b] from Lebanon, all those that were
watered[c]. 17/ They too went down with
it to the underworld, to those who have
been slain by the sword, and <perished
are(?)> those who <dwelt>[a] in its shade
in the midst of the nations.
18 **To whom have you become [so][a] like in**
splendor and height among the trees of
Eden?[b] Thus you will be brought down
with the trees of Eden to the land below.
Amongst the uncircumcised you will lie
along with those who have been slain by
the sword.
That is Pharaoh and all his[c] pomp, says [the
Lord][d] Yahweh.

understood, according to Chajes, as "shut (like a door)." Cornill is more correct when he points, for an understanding of the addition, to 26:19. See also 32:7.

c 𝔐 עֻלְפֶּה seems to be intended to be taken as an adjective "languishing." One must, however, read עֻלְּפָה (Cornill, Toy) or עֻלְּפוּ (Herrmann, Bertholet, Fohrer); cf. the versions.

16 16a 𝔐 תחתית is not attested by 𝔊, but it can scarcely be dispensed with (cf. v 17).

b 𝔐 וְטוֹב is not attested in 𝔊. Alongside מבחר one would rather vocalize it וְטוּב or else read וְטוֹבֵי. But it is undoubtedly a gloss. מבחר is found also in 23:7; 24:4f.

c Literally "drinking water."

17 17a V 17b remains obscure. 𝔐 וזרעו ישבו "and his arm—they sat" is rendered by 𝔅 as *et brachium uniuscuiusque sedebit.* 𝔊 𝔖, on the other hand, find in זרע the word זֶרַע: 𝔖 וזרעה יתב, while 𝔊 in what follows seems to presuppose a quite different text: *καὶ τὸ σπέρμα αὐτοῦ οἱ κατοικοῦντες ὑπὸ τὴν σκέπην αὐτοῦ ἐν μέσῳ ζωῆς αὐτῶν ἀπώλοντο.* On this basis, Cornill, who takes זרע to mean "undergrowth," reads וזרעו ישבי צלו בתוך חייהם אבדו "and its undergrowth, which grew there in its shade, perished in the midst of its (most flourishing) life." Graphically more likely would be a correction of וזרעו to וגועו (Bertholet, Fohrer). Driver, "Linguistic Problems," 179, suggests וְזֹרְעוּ יֹשְׁבֵי בְצִלּוֹ, which, with reference to Syriac זרע (Jas 1:1; 1 Pt 1:1), he renders as "they that dwelt in his shadow were dispersed." But everything here is very uncertain.

18 18a 𝔐 ככה is explicitly attested only by 𝔗 (כדין) among the versions. There is the suspicion that it is an (erroneous) dittography of the following בכבוד.

b Bewer, "Textual Notes," 165, suggests, on the basis of 𝔊 (*κατάβηθι*), the insertion of רדה before והורדת and refers in that connection to 32:18.

c On the spelling הֲמוֹנֹה see Bauer-Leander §29k.

d אדני is lacking in 𝔊, see Appendix 1.

Form

In a dated receiving of God's word the prophet is commissioned to address Pharaoh and his pomp. The introductory messenger formula, which would be expected at this point, first appears in v 10, introduced by לכן ("therefore"), and then appears for a second time in v 15. The complex as a whole, therefore, divides into the sections vv 2b–9, 10–14, 15–18. Since the section vv 10–14, introduced by לכן ("therefore") and the messenger formula, proclaims judgment, one would expect vv 2b–9 to provide the justification for this declaration of judgment.

The initial section vv 2b–9 is surprising in the first instance from the point of view of form, in the fact that the personal address in the second person disappears completely after the introductory question of v 2. In its place, from v 3 onwards, an image is developed with graphic description in the third person. The solitary, brief interruption in v 9*aα*, where unexpectedly Yahweh himself speaks in the first person, is shown by its absence from 𝔊 to be a secondary item (v 9 note a). The image in vv 3–9 has the character of a pure line drawing in which one descriptive sentence follows the other in pictorial fashion. The only place where a statement is developed with detailed logic from what has gone before (v 5 with its introductory על כן "therefore") is shown, both by the two clear Aramaisms (notes a and b), one of which (סרעפתיו "its boughs") contrasts quite clearly with the context (סעפתיו "its boughs"), and by the disturbance of the rhythm, to be a secondary insertion (Jahn). On the other hand, the justificatory clause in v 7b cannot be quarreled with. As secondary elaboration, however, v 8a$\alpha^2\beta$ is also suspect (see the exposition). V 9, too, was probably added only later. V 8b, where the phrase בגן אלהים ("in the garden of God") should be deleted (see the exposition), provides, from the point of view both of form and of content, a good conclusion to the actual description. In v 9, on the other hand, there appears a new range of concepts and an expression of the thought which has not hitherto been applied. Otherwise in vv 3–8 the 2+2 rhythm predominates almost entirely. A reading of it in קינה ("lament")-meter (van den Born) cannot be carried through without doing violence to the text. In any case, the catchword קינה ("lament"), which otherwise characterizes the sections in קינה ("lament")-meter (19; 26:17f; 27; 28:12–19; 32:2 [16]), is missing here. To the lucidity of the form corresponds the clarity of the contents of the description in the basic material of vv 2b–9, which therefore runs as follows:

(To whom are you like in your greatness?)
See, a cypress,/a cedar on Lebanon,
with fine branches/and of great height,
and its top reached/the clouds.
The waters made it great/the torrent in the depths made it tall.
Its streams it (the torrent) had made to flow/round about the place where it was planted
and had sent out its channels/to all the trees of the field.
In its boughs nested/all the birds of the air,
and under its branches all the beasts of the field/brought forth their young,
and in its shade there lived/all great nations of every kind.
And it became beautiful in its greatness/through the length of its branches;
for its roots/reached abundant water.
The cedars could not rival it/in the garden of God
no tree/was like it in its beauty.

Vv 3–8(9) describe a strong stately tree. While at first it seems to be a tree from Lebanon that is being described, the description soon broadens out beyond the normal earthly proportions and sketches the picture of the great world tree, whose roots lie in the depths of the subterranean ocean by whose waters it is nourished, whose top reaches up into the clouds as far as heaven itself and whose shadow shelters all life on earth. The description was already sketched in 17:23 (see also the addition in 19:11). It has its parallels in Dan 4, which is possibly even derived from here. It is paralleled also in Mk 4:32. The motif of the world tree, which has its roots in mythological concepts, is to be differentiated at the outset from that of the tree of life, with which it is often unthinkingly connected (see Wünsche, Holmberg).[1] The world tree, which reaches all three regions of the world, aims as *'imago mundi'* (Eliade) to represent the world as a whole in the totality of its life-force. In Babylonian literature, in the myth of the plague-god Irra, mention is made of a "sacred tree, whose root(?) in the broad ocean of a hundred double hours of water . . . [covers(?)] the bottom of the underworld, whose top reaches into the heavens [Anus]."[2] The more precise significance of the tree is certainly not very clear from this context. Again, Sumerian mythology, in the creation narrative "Gilgamesh, Enkidu and the Underworld" knows of a *ḫuluppu*-tree (willow?) which Inanna finds on the banks of the Euphrates and plants in Erech in her sacred garden, where it then grows strongly. In the end Inanna can no longer fell it because at its base "the snake who knows no charm" (i.e. cannot be affected by any charm?) has built its nest, in its crown the mythical Zu-bird is raising its young and in the middle of it the destructive Lilith has taken up residence.[3] Here the characteristics of the world tree, which offers shelter and living quarters, seem to be used in a particular way. When G. van den Leeuw describes the Germanic world tree Yggdrasill as "an immensely developed form of the *vårträd,* the protective tree of the community," this emphasizes strongly the protective function of the world tree, which emerges clearly in the Biblical passages mentioned.[4] In a unique reversal of the root motif, ancient Indian mythology speaks of the Bodhi-tree (the tree of Buddha's enlightenment) as "a huge fig tree with many roots, which overshadowed the world and sends its roots up towards heaven."[5] Elsewhere there is found the connection between the world tree and the navel of the earth.[6] It is, further, not surprising that subsequently characteristics of the world tree

1 Thus, correctly, Widengren, *King and Tree of Life,* 57; also M. Eliade, "Lebensbaum," *RGG*³ 4, 250f.

2 *AOT* 218.

3 S. N. Kramer, *Sumerian Mythology,* Memoirs of the American Philosophical Society 21 (Philadelphia: The American Philosophical Society, 1944), 33.

have become mixed with this central tree, which represents the life of the world (see on this also 47:12). In spite of the fact that the image of the world tree both in Ezekiel 31 and in Daniel 4 is applied to a ruler, one cannot go so far as to claim it fundamentally for royal ideology.[7]

In Ezek 31:3–8(9) it is surprising how free of specific political references the description is. If one had in front of one only the description of the tree, one could never guess that by this image is meant specifically the Pharaoh of Egypt. The nourishment by the waters of the primeval ocean is nowhere connected exclusively with the Nile, which some have thought was meant here (Hölscher and others). It is also free of any belittling tendency. To what extent it can be considered to be the justification for an invective can be seen only in retrospect, from v 10 onwards. This purely contemplative description explains also from within why an introductory messenger formula has fallen out of the text. One is felt to be reminded of the analogy of the קינה ("lament") of Ezekiel 19 where the references are admittedly much more strongly historical.

However clearly the basic unit vv 3–8(9) can be understood and described in terms of its tradition-material and its form, the sequel is then rather obscure, a sequel which Hölscher, perhaps in somewhat exaggerated terms, has reckoned as belonging "stylistically to the most unpleasant of the whole book."[8] First of all, the concluding section, vv 15–18, stands out fairly clearly with its prose description of the journey of the noble tree to the underworld and the phenomena accompanying it on earth and in the underworld. V 18 sums up the whole with a conclusion which looks back to the superscription of the whole oracle in v 2 and which provides a concluding framework to the complex as a whole.

One would expect to find in the central section, vv 10–14, the actual completion of the story of the splendid tree with its fall from majesty to wretchedness. In fact, this too tells of the fall of the tree and this is accounted for in v 10 by the tree's sin of arrogance (this is how its proud splendor is now retrospectively evaluated). The concluding verse 14 is surprising in its evaluation of the whole event in terms of mankind in general and in its reference to the general mortality of the great, who are only slightly concealed behind the image of the "trees by the water." It is to be regarded as a secondary expansion, which, in its generalization of the application, faintly recalls the addition to the story of Oholah and Oholibah in 23:46–49. What remains, vv 10–13, perhaps with the exception of v 11b (note c), ought then to contain the original text of the announcement of judgment. There is no further trace of metrical form in these verses. Two clear 2+2 lines can possibly be discerned in v 13, which is constructed as a counterpart to v 6a. The rest is in the kind of elevated prose which is often met with in Ezekiel. The different analysis by van den Born, who tries to find in vv 12 (from ובכל גאיות "and in all the valleys")–14a the metrical conclusion of the lament (which is in קינה "lament"-meter), is not really convincing.

Thus, the problem of form in chapter 31 as a whole once again consists in the combination of a metrically constructed presentation of an image with a continuation in prose that is only occasionally replaced by a metrically structured element. The figurative speech of chapter 17, with its interpretation in prose, revealed a similar form.[9]

Hölscher's radical statement that the prose sections are non-genuine is not satisfactory here either. One is led rather to a stylistic usage according to which the full poetic amplification is certainly possible in the description of the image, but where the first person proclamation of the divine action is in the oracular prose which is found again and again in Ezekiel. 31:10–14 is quite clearly such a proclamation.

4 Gerardus van der Leeuw, *Phänomenologie der Religion* (Tübingen: Mohr, ²1956), 39.

5 *Chant.* I, 35.

6 On this see 38:12 and 1, 174f. on 5:5. See also Holmberg, *Baum.*

7 Thus Widengren, *King and Tree of Life,* 56–58, with reference to Lam 4:20. See Mowinckel, *He That Cometh,* note IV (453f) and note VII (456f), on the relationship between Tammuz and the tree of life. Also Gressmann, *Messias,* 266–268. Brock-Utne's (*Gottesgarten*) attempt to interpret Ezek 31 solely on the basis of the motif of the garden of God (a forest in Lebanon) is unsatisfactory.

8 Hölscher, *Hesekiel,* 154.

9 See 1, 359f.

In vv 10–14, to the description of the world tree there has been added the motif of the fall of the lofty one, and this is actualized in vv 15–17 by the tradition-element of the journey to the underworld. It is difficult, on this basis, to interpret the whole account as "an allegory within an allegory"[10] and to find in chapter 31 simply the tradition of 28:11–19 in a new guise, i.e. to find disguised in the tree, which is compared in v 8(9) with the trees of the garden of paradise, the primitive being that was driven out of God's garden.[11] Equally unsatisfactory is Gunkel's understanding of it as "a fable with fairy-tale motifs."[12] Rather, one must consider that the mythical image of the world tree is here connected, in a peculiarly Israelite turn of thought, with the proclamation of the fall of the lofty one (cf. e.g. Is 2:12–17). It can be noticed in vv 10–14 that what is said about the fall has been added secondarily to the already completed image of the world tree, without there having been complete success in the attempt really organically to connect the tradition of the world tree with that of the journey of the lofty one to the underworld.

A final problem for the evaluation of the form of the whole arises out of the question of tenses. The whole unit is in the perfect throughout all its formally varied components.[13] The perfect (imperfect consecutive) in the description of the judgment has been regarded as a prophetic perfect and understood as a future.[14] But the structure with the perfect dominates not just the prophetic proclamation of judgment in vv 10–14, but also the introductory section. Thus the observation made by van den Born and Fohrer is more likely to be along the right lines, that here, in the manner of the dirge (though without the קינה "lament"-meter, see above), a coming event is already mourned for in the image of the felling of the noble tree.

Setting

The date in v 1 determines the time of origin (proclamation?) of the oracle, which subsequently contains no references to contemporary events. Nor do the expansions, which have been added to it secondarily, contain any information which allows their period of origin to be determined more precisely. An interpretation of the איל גוים ("brutal nation") of v 11 in terms of Cambyses (Hölscher) is forbidden by the above analysis of the text.

There is nothing against assuming that the oracle originated among the Babylonian exiles.

Interpretation

■ **31:1** The divine word which gives rise to 31:1–18 is dated on the first day of the third month of Jehoiachin's eleventh year.[15] According to Parker-Dubberstein, that is June 21, 587, a point within the period of the siege of Jerusalem, which almost two months after the date mentioned in 30:20, is now nearing its end. In the content of the oracle, however, by way of contrast with 30:21, there is no trace of the specific historical situation of this particular month.

■ **31:2** The prophet is addressed as son of man and is given the task of speaking about Pharaoh and his proud pomp.[16] The word המון ("pomp") is already a pointer to the content of the oracle which now follows and which has to do with Pharaoh's pride (v 10). The question which then leads over to the description of the magnificent tree and which returns, slightly expanded, in v 18 emphasizes the "greatness" of the person addressed (גדל occurs in vv 7, 18 but nowhere else in Ezekiel; it is used of God in Dtn 3:24; 5:21; 9:26; 11:2; Ps 150:2). From the point of view of content, the question of v 2b is the equivalent of a hymnic glorification (cf. the name מיכאל "Michael," perhaps also the use in 19:2, while 15:2 contains a genuine question). The question in 31:2 should not be connected too closely with the continuation in v 3. The prophet is not looking for a suitable figurative comparison, but is glorifying the greatness of the addressee. The fact that the form of the address is subsequently completely dropped (on the sole apparent exception in 𝔐 see v 10 note b) is a distinct difficulty in

10 Hermann, 206.
11 Thus, following Herrmann, also Humbert, "Démesure," especially 75.
12 Gunkel, *Märchen*, 25.
13 On v 11 𝔐 see notes b and c and v 13 note a.
14 Thus, e.g., Cook on 31:17.
15 See 1, 144f.
16 On "son of man" see 1, 131f.

the transition and would lead us to suppose that v 2b has been secondarily prefaced to the originally independent description of the tree in vv 3–9.

■ **31:3** The presumed original reading in v 3, תאשור ("cypress") (note a), is mentioned in Is 41:19 alongside ברוש ("juniper") (see below on v 8) and תדהר "pine" (see Koehler-Baumgartner) as a species of tree with which Yahweh will adorn the desert transformed into a processional way. The juxtaposition of the same three names then appears, certainly not independently of Is 41:19, in Is 60:13, the enumeration of the types of wood of which the glorious new temple is to be made. The parallel statement there paraphrases the three types of tree in summary fashion as כבוד הלבנון ("the glory of Lebanon"). As far as ברוש ("juniper") is concerned, the connection with the Lebanon is explicit in 2 Kgs 19:23 (Is 37:24) and implicit in Is 14:8; Zech 11:2. Thus the parallel description of the תאשור ("cypress") as ארז בלבנון ("a cedar on Lebanon") is not of itself remarkable. From the rich and varied tree population of the Lebanon, which can be summarily described as ארז ("cedar") a particularly noble and lofty ארז ("cedar")-species is here singled out and described in what follows.[17] In the further description of the tree with its wealth of branches and its lofty height whose top reaches the sky, its particular type is already indicated. In an addition (note b), anticipatory reference is already made to the tree's shade, which is then mentioned in v 6 in the correct place.

■ **31:4** The great height of the tree can reveal the unusual source of nourishment from which it lives. Thus, alongside the "water," i.e. the plentiful water which nourishes it, there is mentioned "the subterranean deep" (תהום) which "makes it grow" to its unusual height. This subterranean river, the existence of which can be deduced from the spring water which bursts from the earth but which conceals within itself quite different powers from those which might be suggested by the tamed channels of normal springs, is the one described, for example, in P's flood narrative. It describes the coming of the flood: "Then all the springs of 'the great deep' (תהום רבה) burst forth, and the windows of heaven opened" (Gen 7:11). And the end of the flood: "Then the springs of the great deep were closed and (also) the windows of heaven" (8:2). Here it can be seen how the hidden, lower deep corresponds to the great deep of the heavenly ocean and how, in the flood, the one above flows with elemental passion towards that other deep and endeavors to join with it so that there might exist only the single deep of the primeval ocean of chaos, the תהום of Gen 1:2, and the created and ordered world would no longer exist.[18] While the flood narrative reveals the uncanny power of chaos lurking in the תהום,[19] Ezek 31:3 seems to speak of a tamed deep, one which has been made into a blessing for the cosmos and which in Gen 49:25; Dtn 33:13 is invoked on Joseph's head in the "blessings of heaven above, blessings of the deep that couches beneath." Always, however, the occurrence of תהום contains a reference to a power which surpasses the normal, everyday, earthly measure and still hints at the mythical power which once dared to enter into battle with the creator himself. Thus Is 51:10. From such primeval springs in the background the tree lives; indeed that power in the deep gave it its help. V 4b gives to that very thought personified expression when it allows the תהום to appear as an active force. The mention of the "streams" (נהרות), too, can sometimes contain something of an echo of mythical speech (cf. e.g., Ps 74:15; Is 44:27). In the present passage they have become beneficial helpers sent by the תהום, to some extent like servant-girls, to the place where the tree is "planted" (מטע 17:7; 34:29). תעלה ("channel"), on the other hand, seems to have a more technical meaning and to recall a country with irrigation canals.[20] In 2 Kgs 18:17 and elsewhere it describes a water channel built by human hands. One cannot logically play off the description of the splendid tree with its

17 On the uncertainty of the precise definition of תאשור see 27:6 note d.

18 See also the historicization of this chaotic destructive process in 26:19 (p. 39 above).

19 See especially Gunkel, *Schöpfung*.

20 According to Bauer-Leander §61 zη, the word originally meant "scar."

roots planted in the well-watered ground against the reference to the "cedar of Lebanon" (v 3). The proper description of the largest tree known to man has had imperceptibly foisted on to it here the improper use of the image for the cosmic world tree, which stands on a watered plain and whose roots reach down to the primeval deeps which wash round it and nourish it. Then one is struck, of course, by the conclusion of v 4, which speaks in general terms of "all the trees of the field." It must have been secondarily influenced by v 5 (note c).

■ **31:5** In both language and style v 5 is clearly a later addition. From the content point of view it anticipates the references to boughs and branches in which, according to v 6, the creatures of the world shelter. It seeks to explain the astonishing growth of these boughs, a growth which exceeds all other trees (cf. also v 8), and the number and length of the branches (סרעפתיו "its boughs" has been borrowed from v 6 in an involuntary Aramaism, likewise פארתו "its branches"). This is due to the abundance of water. The expression מים רבים ("abundant water"), which is attested ten times in Ezekiel, is used also in 26:19 parallel to תהום.[21]

■ **31:6** In what follows, just as in 17:23 (Dan 4:9; Mk 4:32 and parallels), there is the description of the motherly, protective nature of this mighty world tree on which all life depends. In its boughs the birds build the nests in which they know that they are safe. Beneath its branches the animals bring forth their young. In this place of refuge they are able to risk, unthreatened, the mysterious process of the birth of new life. In the sheltering shadow of this tree, however, the whole breadth of mankind, free from care, dares to seek out a home for itself. What is expressed in ישב ("to live") is not the warlike activity of attacking and fleeing, but the peaceful activity of sitting at rest (see e.g., 1 Kgs 5:5; Mic 4:4).

■ **31:7** With the majesty of the tree there is associated its beauty. This characteristic had otherwise been found especially in the Tyre oracles (27f). This beauty, too, is to be attributed to the position of the tree beside plentiful water.

■ **31:8** Lastly, the incomparability of the tree, which had already been stressed in the introduction in v 2b, is now expressed in greatly exaggerated terms. Not even the most magnificent trees of paradise (in terms of such an exaggeration the cedars are mentioned here too) can be compared with this magnificent tree. The "garden of God" (28:13) was always represented as a garden of trees. But while Gen 2f thinks of the splendid trees of the garden, both the tree of knowledge and the tree of life, as trees with edible fruit (also 17:23; Dan 4:9 and Ezek 47:21), this characteristic is completely absent from Ezekiel 31. The tree here is a royal tree that provides exclusively shelter and shade. There is no thought of fruit. This corresponds to the usage in Deutero-Isaiah. There, too, the dominant thought is that of the majestically towering ornament which embellishes Yahweh's processional way through the desert. The statement about the incomparability of the tree is repeated in v 8b parallel to v 8aα^1. In the repetition, the expression בגן אלהים ("in the garden of God") must originally have been lacking. It became necessary as a result of the insertion of the two intervening lines v 8a$\alpha^2\beta$, which are metrically difficult to accommodate into the context, but which also from the content point of view are inferior to the preceding climax of the statement ("cedars of the divine garden"). In dependence on v 6, this addition also speaks of the boughs and branches of the world tree. They are compared with the boughs of the juniper (27:5 note a) and the branches of the "plane trees" (ערמון also in Gen 30:37).

■ **31:9** The original description of the tree's splendor would originally have ended with v 8. In 𝔐 v 9 first of all expands the reference to the beauty of the tree (vv 7f) by saying that this beauty is Yahweh's doing. The theologically correct statement that all beauty comes from Yahweh is to be attached to the misleading mythical statement about the power of the waters of תהום. In the remainder of v 9, which was already known to 𝔊, the thought is then expressed that the Eden trees in the garden of God (עדן "Eden" here seems to be used in a purely qualifying way, see note c) have become jealous of the magnificent tree. This goes beyond what has already been said and introduces a living and judging "environment" for the tree. The addition paves the way for what is said later in vv 16, 18 about the Eden trees. In the original oracle in v 8, the comparison with the other

21 On the obscure שלח see note e.

trees in the garden of God was already made, but there was no mention there of a reaction on the part of these other personified beings. From the point of view of content this statement is thinking of the rivalry between the various world powers. In the original text, as is clear from the continuation, the height of the tree was thought of only with regard to its relationship to God.

■ **31:10** This becomes quite clear in the following statement of Yahweh's reaction, which is characterized by means of the messenger formula as an explicit word of Yahweh. V 10 sums up the whole figure of speech hitherto, in that it interprets from within the image which has been depicted. The great height of the addressee, the reaching of its top into the clouds (v 3), its "growing tall" (רום v 4)—everything that has been developed hitherto quite objectively without any hint of detraction, but rather, one could almost say, with a secret amazement—is now illuminated from within: "Because its heart has become proud of its height." The magnificent external aspect of the height has an internal aspect, a "heart." But when the "heart" is high, then the one who alone is high must exercise judgment. The root רום was used in v 4 in direct association with the expressions cited a moment ago from v 3. The question can be asked whether v 11 thinks that the originator of the רום ("to be proud") is not unexpectedly the תהום, the primeval opponent of the creator God.

■ **31:11** The divine response to the pride of the magnificent tree is to surrender it to a brutal nation.[22] The meaning of v 11b remains uncertain. The use of the imperfect, which has subsequently also influenced the vocalization of v 11a (note a), makes the originality of the sentence questionable (note c).

■ **31:12** The fact that the enemies who carry out the sentence under the command of the brutal nation are described as זרים ("strangers") (see already 7:21; 11:9; 28:7, 10; 30:12; in 28:7 and 30:11f this is also associated with עריצי גוים "the most brutal nations") suggests that in all these passages the same nation is meant, i.e. the Babylonians. Here they are pictured as woodcutters who "fell" (כרת) the giant tree and scatter the "body of the tree" over the whole world. נטש ("to throw down") recurs persistently in the Egypt oracles. According to 29:5 the corpse of the Nile crocodile is thrown into the wilderness. 32:4 uses the same image to refer to the throwing of the captured monster on to the land. In 31:12, where נטש ("to throw down") (not attested in Ezekiel other than in the passages just cited) is repeated quite specifically in an absolute usage at the end of the verse, the throwing to the ground of the felled tree is developed by a figure of speech that is frequent in Ezekiel; it is scattered over mountains, valleys and streams.[23] Is what is meant here that the trunk of the tree is thrown on to the mountains, "its branches" (דליותיו from v 7, see there note c) into the valleys and "its boughs" (פארתיו from v 6) into the watercourses? It is more correct not to look for such detailed elucidation in a statement which is working with formulaic expressions and where the double phraseology of boughs-branches is spread over the three-fold reference to localities.[24]

The fall of this magnificent tree of course also brings to an end its protective shelter for birds, wild beasts and men to which reference was made in v 6. All peoples of the earth (they are mentioned first here, but with a different expression) abandon it since it no longer can provide protective shelter.

■ **31:13** Birds and wild beasts, however, which are also mentioned in 29:5 and 32:4 in connection with the "throwing aside" (נטש) of something that has been cut down, instead of being creatures which trustingly sought shelter beneath the tree, have now become creatures which sit unheedingly on its remains without expecting any further shelter from it.

■ **31:14** The account of the fall of the magnificent tree, which till now (with the exception of the לבב "heart" in the justification in v 10) has remained within the framework of the figure of speech, is followed in v 14 by a unique paranesis, which, both from its content and also

22 On איל "ram," then metaphorically "leader," see 17:13; 32:21, as well as 39:18 and 30:13 (emended text). There is no other occurrence of an association of it with גוים, though one can compare the related expression עריצי גוים (28:7; 30:11; 32:12).

23 On this trio, which is expanded to a quartet in 6:3; 35:8; 36:4, 6 by the addition of the hills, see also 32:6. Only mountains and valleys occur in 34:13.

24 Cf. the analogy (1,191) on 6:12.

from the new range of concepts which can be seen in it, is shown to be an addition by another hand. Mention is made of "water trees" (עצי מים) and "drinkers of water" (שתי מים) who are not to be presumptuous, since they are journeying towards death in the "land below" (ארץ תחתית in 31:14, 16, 18; plural ארץ תחתיות in 26:20; 32:18, 24; elsewhere תחתיות[ה]ארץ Is 44:23; Ps 63:10; 139:15) and belong among the "children of men" with "those who go down to the pit" ([ו]ירדי בור v 16; 26:20; 32:18, 24f, 29f). The plural בני אדם ("men") is not found elsewhere in Ezekiel. Like the simple אדם ("men") of Ps 73:5, it means here mortal created men, subject to sorrow.[25] The "water trees" and the "drinkers of water," on the other hand, are those only lightly disguised by the image who have drunk of the mighty waters described in v 4 and who are thereby tempted to forget that they belong to mortal humanity. Thus the paranesis of v 14 is directed in a quite general way at all those who have been made great by water from below (v 4). This refers to the rulers of the world. The association with Dan 7, where the world empires are compared to beasts which emerge from the great deep, is natural and obvious. By means of the warning example of the magnificent tree which has been felled, they are admonished to remain mindful of their creatureliness. Trees are supposed to grow in this world, not up into heaven.

■ **31:15–18** V 14b also clearly leads to the final section, vv 15–18, which expounds the motif of the journey to the underworld, a motif which subsequently finds its fullest exposition in the book of Ezekiel in 32:17–32, but which was already intimated in the Tyre oracles in 26:19–21 and 28:8.

■ **31:15** The term שאול ("the underworld"), which is found in Ezekiel, apart from 31:15–17, also in 32:21, 27, has not yet been fully explained etymologically. L. Koehler envisages a derivation from שאה "to lie waste" (with an additional ל which is not part of the stem).[26] On the other hand, W. Baumgartner finds a loan-word connected with Babylonian *šu'āra,* the name of Tammuz's dwelling in the underworld.[27] The lack of the article in all the occurrences in the OT would certainly suggest that the word still had something of the ring of a proper name about it. In the present passage it is incorporated into the range of imagery which has been expounded at the beginning of the chapter. In this respect one can observe once more how the תהום, the hidden, opposing power of chaos, lurks in the background of the whole history of human arrogance. On the day when the magnificent tree falls, Yahweh, who is now introduced here as the only real protagonist, allows the waters beneath to mourn—in this speech they are again quietly personified (see also, however, statements such as Is 24:4; Jer 23:10; Am 1:2, and elsewhere). As once, on the day on which (according to Gen 8:2) he halted the flood, he stopped its streams (see above on v 4) and dammed the "many waters," thereby bringing mourning to Lebanon and the trees of the field, since their magnificence will now wither.[28] In a different fashion the "covering" (כסה, see note b) of the stars in the sky is connected with their being "made to mourn" (הקדיר) in Ezek 32:7.

■ **31:16f** As in the case of the fall of Tyre, however (26:15), the earthquake will also affect nations on earth. Only below in the underworld is there a strange "consolation," when the trees of Eden (see above on v 9), the magnificent trees of Lebanon (v 3), "those who drink water" (v 14), who have all likewise gone down to the underworld, recognize the arrival of the Pharaoh, who is meant here. With this scene of contented observation of a similar fate there can be compared the graphic exposition in Is 14:10, 16f.[29]

■ **31:18** In repetition of the statement in v 2b, the concluding verse 18 once again breaks into direct speech. Cooke wishes to regard this, by analogy with the quotation in Is 14:16, as the word of the mighty ones who are already in the underworld, the word with which they greet the new arrival. Nothing in the text leads to this assumption. Thus, it is to be supposed that here (as a

25 On the singular בן אדם see 1, 131f.

26 Ludwig Koehler, "Alttestamentliche Wortforschung: schᵉ'ōl," *ThZ* 2 (1946): 71–74.

27 Walter Baumgartner, "Zur Etymologie von schᵉ'ōl," *ThZ* 2 (1946): 233–235, following W. F. Albright, "Mesopotamian Elements in Canaanite Eschatology" in *Oriental Studies published in Commemoration of the Fortieth Anniversary (1883–1923) of Paul Haupt as director of the Oriental Seminary of the Johns Hopkins University* (Baltimore: Johns Hopkins Press, 1926), 143–154.

28 On the connection between withering and mourning see, e.g., Is 24:7; 33:9; Jer 14:2.

29 On the striking concept of consolation see also the נחם in 5:13; 14:22f; 16:54; 32:31.

kind of framework) the voice which was heard in v 2b speaks once more and, by way of conclusion, poses the opening question again, including this time the process of the journey to the underworld and the description of it in vv 15–17. In contrast to the hymnic quality which the words had to have in the opening section, here the effect is that of the political lament such as is heard in Is 14.

The concluding remark that the song refers to Pharaoh and his pomp (v 2a) is in no sense superfluous. The song itself is, in all its parts, remarkably free of any concrete references to Egypt as a world power. Thus the interpretative reference at the beginning and at the end is indispensable.

Aim

In a remarkably "typical" oracle, Egypt the world power is addressed in Ezekiel 31. In the comparison with the magnificent tree which acquires its size and beauty from the rich waters of the primeval deep, it is shown with the boldness of mythical terminology that mysterious, primeval forces are at work in earthly power complexes. What transpires here is not immediately explicable in terms of everyday rationality. When the NT speaks of the δυνάμεις ("powers") which are active in the world (Rom 8:38f; singular 1 Cor 15:24; Eph 1:20f), it is giving expression to a related perception.

In this bold description of the world power, the prophetic word reveals how greatly and constantly all human power complexes and leaderships are at risk. The misunderstanding of greatness as one's own greatness and arrogance of heart constantly dog him as virtually inescapable temptations.

The prophet, however, does not speak in general terms of possibilities and phenomena, but in historical directness addresses a world power of his own time. To it he proclaims, in the form of an anticipatory lament, that in any event God does not let trees grow up to the sky. In his judgment he will, rather, insure that the ruler who has grown too high and who conceives of himself as a world power will, in due course, be felled. In his journey to the realm of the dead he then experiences his unalterable, indissoluble solidarity with other created beings, with the "children of men." We must, at the same time, observe that this is no fatalistic reference to a general condemnation to death. We are, rather, pointed to one who, as a person known by name, has the power to fell in due course the arrogance of the one who is great among the nations. The prophet knows that for this he does not need a thunderbolt from heaven, but has the power to make a person from the human sphere, a "strong one among the nations," into his instrument and to fell the tree which overshadows the whole world and all nations.

6. Lament and Judgment over Pharaoh the Crocodile of the Seas

Bibliography

Hermann Gunkel
Schöpfung und Chaos in Urzeit und Endzeit (Göttingen, ²1921), especially 71–77.

Hedwig Jahnow
Das hebräische Leichenlied im Rahmen der Völkerdichtung, BZAW 36 (Giessen: Töpelmann, 1923), especially 228–231.

32

1 **In the <eleventh>[a] year, in the twelfth**
month, on the first of the month, the
word of Yahweh came to me: 2/ Son of
man, begin a lament over Pharaoh, king
of Egypt, and say to him:
You have become like a young lion of the nations . . .[a],
and you were like a crocodile[b] in the seas
and have bubbled forth[c] <with your nostrils>[d],
and you have troubled[e] the waters with your feet
and have stirred up their streams[f].
3 **Thus has [the Lord][a] Yahweh said: And I**
shall spread my net over you [by means
of a levy of many nations][b] and <shall

32: 1 1a 𝔐 בשתי עשרה שנה. 13 MSS 𝔊 (attested by $\mathfrak{G}^{A}$ and others) 𝔖 point to the eleventh year (. . . בעשתי). $\mathfrak{G}^{967,B}$ and others = 𝔐. $\mathfrak{G}^{L}$ has the tenth year. Since otherwise (with the exception of the addition in 29:17–21) the oracles against Egypt are arranged in chronological order, the reading בעשתי instead of בשתי is, alongside 32:17, quite probable.

2 2a 𝔐 נדמית is, in 𝔊 *ὡμοιώθης*, 𝔙 *assimilatus es*, 𝔖 אתדמית (cf. also 𝔗), derived from דמה "to be like." The nip'al of דמה is, however, not clearly attested anywhere else in 𝔐. Its reconstruction has, however, been suggested with considerable probability in 19:10 and 27:32. See the notes there. Since this נדמה is otherwise constructed with כ, one might indeed wonder whether in place of כפיר an original ככפיר should be read. It is not absolutely necessary. This renders superfluous all other attempts to improve the text and understand נדמה as "be destroyed" (Smend, Gesenius-Buhl) or even as "be silenced" (Koehler-Baumgartner, Fohrer). Thus, e.g., Cornill inserts after גוים an עליך איך and renders: "A young lion of the nations (comes) upon you; how you have perished!" Bertholet reads אוי לך פרעה מה נ׳, while Fohrer suggests כפי דג ים נ׳. See further, however, the exposition. In addition, the suspicion is aroused that after v 2aγ a corresponding two-foot line has dropped out.

b On 𝔐 תנים see 29:3 note d.

c 𝔐 ותגח is erroneously derived by the versions from נגח. 𝔊 *ἐκεράτιζες*; 𝔙 *et ventilabas cornu;* 𝔖 דקרת.

d 𝔐 בנהרותיך, which clashes with the following נהרותם, should be emended, according to Ewald's attractive suggestion, to בְּנְחִרוֹתֶיךָ (cf. Job 41:12).

e The reading of Eb 22, ותדלחם, is a simple mistake which, for metrical reasons as well, is not to be regarded as the original text.

f 𝔊 *τοὺς ποταμούς σου.*

3 3a אדני is lacking in 𝔊, see Appendix 1.

b 𝔐 בקהל עמים רבים is an interpretative element which destroys what seems to have been intended to be a five-stress line. 𝔊, which still does not attest בקהל and which connects *λαῶν πολλῶν* directly to *δίκτυα* by suppressing the suffix of רשתי, reveals a first stage of the glossing process, whereby עמים רבים is simply set as an interpretative phrase alongside רשתי. The allegorical analysis of Ezek 31 in 𝔗 is

haul you out>[c] in my dragnet. 4/ And I shall throw you[a] to the ground, fling you[b] on to the surface of the ground, and shall let all the birds of the air take up their dwelling on you and let all the beasts[c] of the earth gorge themselves on you. 5/ And I shall spread your flesh on the mountains and fill the valleys with your carcass(?)[a] 6/ and shall water the land with your outflow[a] [from your blood][b] [on the mountains][c], and (the) watercourses will be full of your <blood>[d]. 7/ And when you <expire>[a], I shall cover the sky and darken its stars. The sun I shall cover with clouds, and the light of the moon will shine no more. 8/ All[a] the bright lights in the sky I shall darken on your account, and I shall set darkness over your land[b], says [the Lord][c] Yahweh[d].

an instructive example of such an equation of specific images with political realities. By the later insertion of בקהל, the עמים רבים has then been clearly incorporated, from the syntactical point of view, into the text. See also note c.

c 𝔐 והעלוך reveals the accommodation of the verb to the glossed text of v 3a, from which the עמים רבים have become the subject. 𝔊 *καὶ ἀνάξω* 𝔙 *et extraham* still reveal, here too, the older form of the text in which, as in v 3aβ and then again in vv 4–16, Yahweh himself is the subject. Without doubt והעליתיך should be read.

4 4a On נטש see above 31:12 note a.

b 𝔊 renders v 4aβ by *πεδία πλησθήσεταί σου*; it has read אטילך as מלאך and has then simply ignored על פני in the translation.

c On the basis of 4MSS 𝔊 𝔖, the parallels in v 4bα and related passages (31:6, 13; 34:5, 8; 39:17), one would gladly read 𝔐 חית כל הארץ rearranged as כל חית השדה.

5 5a V 5b has been rendered by the versions in very different ways. 𝔊 *καὶ ἐμπλήσω ἀπὸ τοῦ αἵματός σου πᾶσαν τὴν γῆν* (𝔏^{C} *colles*); 𝔙 *et implebo colles tuos sanie tua;* 𝔖 ונתמלון נחלא מן רמתך. 𝔗 has a freer interpretation. רמותך, according to Gesenius-Buhl "high heap of corpses," Koehler-Baumgartner "rubble," is perhaps (Toy, Herrmann) to be emended to רִמָּתְךָ. Smend suggests רִמּוֹתְךָ [*sic!*] on the basis of Σ *τῶν σκωλήκων σου*.

6 6a 𝔐 צפה is a *hapax legomenon.* 𝔊 *ἀπὸ τῶν προχωρημάτων σου*; 𝔏^{C} *quae de te procedunt;* Σ *τῷ ἰχῶρί σου* (lymph). Hitzig, followed by Gunkel, *Schöpfung,* 73 note 1, and others, emends to צאתך.

b 𝔐 מדמך is missing in 𝔊 𝔏^{C} and is surely to be understood as an interpretation of צפתך or as a corrective gloss on ממך (note d).

c 𝔐 אל ההרים gives a secondary effect and must have been added secondarily as a contrast to אפיקים. On על–אל cf. 1:17 note a.

d 𝔐 ממך, in spite of unanimous attestation, is hardly original. The additional מדמך in v 6a (note b) must contain the correction. המלא מן, instead of the usual construction with the accusative, is found also in Eccl 1:8.

7 7a 𝔐 pi'el בכבותך certainly presupposes Yahweh as the unexpressed subject: "when I wipe you out." Hence the expository interpretation of 𝔗, which nevertheless uses the verb כהא: באכהיותי ית זיו יקר מלכותך מן שמיא. The lack of specific mention of the subject is, however, remarkable. Thus it is advisable to read with 𝔊 (𝔏^{C}) *ἐν τῷ σβεσθῆναί σε*, 𝔙 *cum extinctus fueris,* 𝔖 בדעבך, בִּכְבוֹתְךָ. This image is unique in Ezekiel, and for this reason Ehrlich, *Randglossen,* would prefer to read במותך and Bertholet, בכלותך.

8 8a 𝔖 inserts the copula.

b 𝔐 ארצך, and so 𝔊 𝔏^{C} 𝔗 𝔖 𝔙. 𝔊^{B*} has simply *ἐπὶ τὴν γῆν*, and on this basis Cornill, Fohrer read "over the land."

c אדני is lacking in 𝔊 𝔏^{C}, see Appendix 1.

9 **And I shall trouble[a] the hearts of many**
nations when I lead <your host of
captives>[b] among the nations, to[c] lands[d]
which you (formerly) did not know. 10/
And on your account I shall fill many
nations with horror, and on your account[a]
their kings will stiffen with terror when I
wield[b] my sword against them, and they
will tremble[c] with agitation[d], each for
himself, on the day[e] of your downfall.
11 **For thus has [the Lord][a] Yahweh said: The**
sword of the king of Babylon will come
upon you[b]. 12/ By the swords of heroes[a] I
shall cause your host to fall—the most
powerful nations are they all. And they
will lay waste that of which Egypt is
proud, and all its pomp will be destroyed.
13/ And I shall wipe out all[a] its beasts
from beside (the) many waters, and no
human foot will trouble them any more,
nor will any <animal's hoof>[b] trouble
them any more. 14/ Then I shall allow
their waters to clear[a], and I shall make
their streams flow like oil, says [the
Lord][b] Yahweh.
15 **When[a] I make [the land of][b] Egypt into a**
wilderness and the land <lies waste>[c],
stripped of all that fills it—when[a] I smite[d]

d 𝔙 offers a further addition: *cum ceciderint vulnerati tui in medio terrae, ait dominus deus.*

9 9a והכעסתי is surely to be thus translated here. Gesenius-Buhl, Koehler-Baumgartner "grieve." 𝔗 ואזיע seems to presuppose והרעשתי. On this basis, Joüon, "Notes," 310f, emends the text.

b 𝔐 שברך "your collapse" (𝔙 *contritionem tuam,* 𝔗 תבירי קרבך 𝔖 תברך) should, on the basis of 𝔊 αἰχμαλωσίαν σου, 𝔏[C] *captivitatem tuam,* be emended to שביך. Driver, "Linguistic Problems," 179, wishes to read שביריך, but this is nowhere attested in the OT.

c על–אל cf. 1:17 note a.

d 𝔐 ארצות. 𝔊 (𝔏[C]) reads singular εἰς γῆν. On this basis, Cornill and Herrmann emend. But the frequent parallelism of גוים–ארצות should help us to understand the ארצות here too, especially since it is also defended by the suffix of ידעתם (on the masculine suffix see Bauer-Leander §48j). 𝔊 simplifies.

10 10a 𝔐 עליך is not attested by 𝔊 𝔏[C] 𝔖, no doubt as a result of stylistic simplification.

b 𝔐 בעופפי cannot be doubted in its approximate meaning. Alongside the usual derivation from the po'lel of עוף "to cause to fly" (𝔊 ἐν τῷ πετασθῆναι; 𝔊[B,Q,86] πέτασθαι; 𝔏[C] *cum volare coeperit*), there is the suggestion of Driver, "Studies.6," 375ff (followed by Koehler-Baumgartner, Fohrer), that we have here a stem עפף "to double." For this, however, in 21:19 the verb כפל is used. Joüon, "Notes," 311, reads בעוררי "quand je brandirai" and refers to 2 Sam 23:18; 1 Chr 11:11, 20; Is 10:26.

c V 10bα is misunderstood by 𝔊 προσδεχόμενοι τὴν πτῶσιν αὐτῶν, 𝔖 ונדחלון ונתרהבון אנש בנפשה; see also 𝔗.

d On לרגעים see 26:16 note d.

e 𝔐 ביום. Has 𝔊 ἀφ' ἡμέρας read מיום?

11 11a אדני is lacking in 𝔊 𝔎[Bo] 𝔄, see Appendix 1.

b 𝔐 תבואך. On בוא with its object in the simple accusative see, e.g., Ps 44:18; Prv 2:19; Job 15:21.

12 12a 𝔊 takes בחרבות גבורים as part of v 11 and then inserts the copula (𝔖 similarly before v 12aβ; 𝔖 renders freely with the singular בחרבא).

13 13a 𝔐 כל is omitted by 𝔖.

b 𝔐 ופרסות. The versions and the following תדלחם suggest the reading ופרסת (parallel to רגל).

14 14a 𝔐 אשקיע correctly understood by 𝔙 *purissimas reddam.* 𝔊, which has the impersonal expression ἡσυχάσει, and 𝔗 אשקיט seem to presuppose אשקיט. But שקע is used of water also in Am 9:5 (qal); 8:8 (nip'al); see also משקע in 34:18.

b אדני is lacking in 𝔊 𝔎, see Appendix 1.

15 15a The ב also includes the emphasis "from the fact that," see Zimmerli, *Erkenntnis,* 14–16.

b In 𝔊, 𝔐 ארץ is not attested. The meter too might suggest that the expression ארץ מצרים was originally distributed over the two parallel members of the sentence.

c 𝔐 וּנְשַׁמָּה. The syntactical context here demands the finite form of the verb וְנָשַׁמָּה. Cf. the related expression in 12:19 (19:7).

all who dwell in it, then they will know that I am Yahweh.

16 This is a lament, and as a lament you[a] shall sing it. The[b] daughters[c] of the nations shall sing it as a lament. Over Egypt and over all its pomp they shall sing it as a lament, says [the Lord][d] Yahweh.

d 𝔐 בהכותי 𝔊 ὅταν διασπείρω might have בזרותי before it. Once again 𝔗 avoids the anthropomorphism and points to the human instrument of judgment: באתיותי מחא.

16 16a 𝔐 וקוננוה. 𝔊 καὶ θρηνήσεις might point to an original וקוננתה (Cornill, Bertholet). 𝔗 is concerned to underline clearly the prophetic character of this קינה: אמר נביא איליא היא נבואתא ותהי לאיליא; on this see 19:14b.

b 𝔊 adds the copula, see 1:4 note a.

c I.e. the female members. 𝔗 here too interprets "daughters" in terms of the villages (כפרני); see 26:6 note a.

d אדני is lacking in 𝔊 𝔄̈, see Appendix 1.

Form

At first sight, the dated complex in 32:1–16 seems to be sufficiently characterized by its own data as to its formal characteristics. At the opening (v 2) the prophet receives the commission to utter a קינה ("lament") over Egypt. And the concluding v 16 once again emphatically underlines the fact that what has gone before has been a קינה ("lament") raised among the nations as a lament over Egypt and its pomp.

These details link 32:1–16 with Ezekiel 19 where the identical framework was found. There the metrical structure of the five-stress lines and the contents fully confirmed the data of the introduction and the conclusion.[1]

A closer examination, however, leads to a peculiar embarrassment in the case of 32:1–16. It is true that the assertion in v 2, that it is a קינה ("lament") that follows is supported by the fact that the commission to the prophet leads into the text of the קינה ("lament") without a specific introductory messenger formula.[2] Also, after the introduction in v 2aβ, which has its own problems, the oracle in v 2b is undoubtedly in קינה ("lament")-meter. So far so good.

But now, surprisingly, the messenger formula appears in v 3. It is repeated (with introductory כי "for") in v 11. The units to which these give rise, vv 3–10 and vv 11–15, are each in turn provided with a caesura by means of the formulae for a divine saying at the end of vv 8 and 14. The further formal features of the four units thus created and their contents completely confirm the assertion made in these formulae. It is no longer a question of a (prophetic) lament over an event which has already taken place and which is spoken of in retrospect in the perfect tense, but of a clear divine announcement about the future in which Yahweh himself is the speaker. In the first two units, vv 3–8 and 9–10, the consecutive perfect predominates; this is continued in the final clauses in vv 4a, 7b, 8a, 10a by the imperfect. The unit vv 11–14 begins with the imperfect and varies this in vv 12b and 13a by the consecutive perfect. Finally, the concluding oracle in v 15 is a proof-saying in two parts (constructed with the infinitive), and this, from the point of view of form, is a considerable distance from the קינה ("lament"). It is no longer the lament but the forensic proof (on ב as the introduction to the proof element see v 15 note a) that dominates this oracle. All of these observations in vv 3–15 are strongly opposed to the assertion of the framework in vv 2a and 16 that this is a קינה ("lament"). A glance at the metric structure leads in the same direction. Even if one can still discern the unequal קינה ("lament")-meter without difficulty in vv 3 (see note b) and 8a and, at a pinch, in vv 12b and 13a, on the other hand the majority of the phrases, in so far as they appear to be metrically structured at all, are dominated by balanced lines, especially by the 3+3.[3] All of these individual observations lead to a specific conclusion concerning the assessment of the total complex 32:1–16. The kernel of this unit as a whole is formed by a short קינה ("lament") (or by the fragment of a longer קינה "lament"?). In the final redaction, in vv 2 and 16 this kernel has provided the label for the whole section.

This kernel has then been heavily annotated and

1 See 1, 391–393. There were further examples of the קינה ("lament") in 26:17–18; 27:2–36; 28:12–19. On 32:17ff see below.

2 So too in 19:1ff, whereas in 27:3; 28:12 the formula has incorrectly intruded.

3 See also C. Budd, "Klagelied," 20f; otherwise

expanded by means of the four units 3–8, 9–10, 11–14, 15, whose inner unity will be discussed in the exposition. With regard to formal characteristics, the expansion has freed itself completely from the basic statement. The lament over a past event has been replaced by a divine threat which proclaims this event as God's judgment and as in the future. The real possibility for this formally surprising expansion lies in the suggestion that this is not a primary קינה ("lament"), but one which has been used secondarily to lament not a death which has already taken place, but, in anticipatory prophetic fashion, one which is still to happen and which will be brought about by God's judgment.[4] It will then be a matter for discussion whether the exposition in vv 3ff has suppressed an original continuation of the קינה ("lament") in v 2b, in which the fall of the Pharaoh was described and lamented in the narrative style of the funeral lament, or whether it was in this different form from the outset. The observations concerning 31:1–18 certainly do not rule out this second possibility.

But then the possibility must also be left open that this deviationary continuation might come from the prophet himself. This, too, is best considered in association with the detailed exegesis.

Setting

A date at the head of the unit as a whole records the time of origin of the basic oracle (see below on v 1). V 2, however, was certainly never proclaimed on its own. Thus, to the given date must also be ascribed either possibly a lost continuation of the קינה ("lament") or else part of the continuation of 𝔐, which is expressed in a different form. There is a lack of historical points of reference for the dating of the other components, with the exception of the supposition that vv 11–14, which threaten the arrival of the king of Babylon, can scarcely be earlier than the reign of Nebuchadnezzar and scarcely even earlier than the date of his Egyptian campaign in the thirty-seventh year of his reign (568/67).

Interpretation

■ **32:1** The receipt of God's word in 32:1[5] is dated by 𝔐 on the first day of the twelfth month of the twelfth year, i.e. according to Parker-Dubberstein on March 3, 585. 𝔊 and 𝔖, which are perhaps to be followed (see note a), refer to the eleventh year, i.e. March 13, 586. It is, in any event, a time after the capture of Jerusalem.[6] There is, however, nothing in the oracle against Egypt about the fate of Jerusalem.

■ **32:2** *The funeral lament.* The prophet, addressed as "son of man," receives the commission to utter a lament over Pharaoh, king of Egypt.[7] There is uncertainty about the understanding of the beginning of this lament. If the textual reconstructions in 19:10 and 27:32 are correct, then both of those passages (along with 31:2,18) show that a lament in Ezekiel is often introduced by a דמה ("to be like")-sentence, in which a comparison or the incomparability of the addressee is expressed. Thus the versions also understand the introductory statement as a comparison in which the Pharaoh is compared to a "young lion of the nations." The addition of גוים ("nations") is intended to differentiate him from the simple כפיר ("young lion") which is used almost as a title in 19:3,5f for the king of Judah. One may also ask whether the addition of גוים ("nations") is intended to qualify the preceding expression more strongly in a theological direction (a heathen king as opposed to the lion in God's people) or whether it is underlining the power aspect (a great king as opposed to a petty prince). This understanding of the דמה ("to be like") is made difficult by the harsh transition to v 2b, where, immediately after the emphatic introduction of a first image, a second, quite different one is encountered. Is the latter then in contrast to the first or simply meant as a parallel? The harshness is somewhat lessened if one can see in the כפיר ("young lion") something more like a royal title, in which the element of comparison is much less prominent: You have become like a great king. A translation such as "Young lion of the nations, you have been destroyed"

Mowinckel, "metrische Aufbau," 183; Georg Fohrer, "Über den Kurzvers," ZAW 66 (1954): 205.

4 Jahnow, *Leichenlied,* 162ff.

5 See 1, 144f.

6 On the date of the announcement of this event to the exiles see below on 33:21.

7 On "son of man" see 1, 131f; see above p. 110.

will also have to reckon with a similarly watered down significance for the expression כפיר גוים ("young lion of the nations"), to which the איל גוים of 31:11 affords a good parallel. This understanding has the advantage that the קינה ("lament") then contains not only the description of the Pharaoh's former strength (v 2b), but also that of his destruction; that is, it is a complete, though short, lament. Would one not, in that case, have to expect in v 2b, which leads back into the distant past, a specifically perfective statement right at the beginning (see, e.g., 26:17)? Also in v 2aβ, if it contains the lament for the lion of the nations, one would expect, according to the parallels in 26:17f, Is 14:4,12, the verb in the emphatic first position, as in, e.g., the expression: "How you have been destroyed, O lion of the nations!" So one will nevertheless adhere to the first-mentioned translation. The comprehension of the statement is, however, made more difficult by the fact that after v 2aγ, on the evidence of the meter, we must assume that part of the text has been lost.

The real figure of speech which more fully characterizes the Pharaoh, the prince of the territory of the Nile, is to be found in v 2b.[8] It occurs here for the second time in an extended figure of speech. The local coloring which was given to the image in 29:3 by the mention of the "arms of the Nile" (יארים) as the dwelling place of the תנין ("crocodile") is missing here. According to v 2b the animal lives "in the seas." Reference is also made to the spray from his nostrils, the troubling of the waters with his feet and the stirring up of the streams (34:18). The first-named characteristic might be more appropriate to a hippopotamus than a crocodile.[9] But here too it must be stressed that the prophet does not have a specific Egyptian animal precisely or directly in mind. In addition, the characteristics of the uncanny size of a mythical dragon can be explicitly noted in the parallel reference to "seas" and "streams" (on this see above on 31:4). The echoes of cryptic, mythical allusions to the political "world power" in chapter 31 are also to be heard in the background here too. While the animal is described raging in its own element of waters, its primitive destructive force in that sphere which lies closest to primeval chaos is clearly expressed, even if there is no specific mention of the chaos monster of the mythical primeval battle (so Gunkel). To this extent, vv 3–8, which then deal with it as a creature which exceeds all human dimensions, form, from the point of view of content, the legitimate continuation of the קינה ("lament") in v 2.

■ **32:3–8** *The proclamation of judgment against the dragon.* In vv 3–8, the קינה ("lament") breaks down. The place of the "lament," which envisages a disaster which has already taken place, is taken by the commanding proclamation of the one who, as powerful judge, will himself bring about the disaster. This makes it clear that in reality it has not yet taken place. In the first section, which is rounded off by the formula for a divine saying in v 8, the proclamation of judgment is still wholly directed against the dragon-type figure of v 2. This might be an argument in favor of the idea that here we in fact have the original continuation of v 2. In this respect it cannot be ignored that certain cliché-type expressions reappear which have already occurred in earlier oracles. They are here modified in terms of the judgment on the dragon-like creature.

■ **32:3f** Thus, for example, the stretching out of the "net" (רשת) has already been referred to in 12:13 and 17:20 in connection with the judgment of Zedekiah. Instead of the word מצודה ("snare"), which is suitable for hunting on land, the parallel here uses the word חרם "dragnet" (Koehler-Baumgartner), which is a more suitable image for drawing out of the water.[10] In view of the varying use of the image in Ezekiel, it cannot be said with certainty whether in fact, as is generally assumed, we have here an echo of the Babylonian account of the fight against the monster that tells how Tiamat is caught in Marduk's net.[11] A later hand has felt obliged to add to the concept of Yahweh's personally entering the fray with his hunting weapon, the idea that this happened "by means of a levy of many nations" (see also 23:24). In this way he has broken the image by actually mentioning what it depicted. The image goes on to describe in v 4 how Yahweh throws the corpse of the slain opponent on to dry land and leaves it as food for the birds and wild beasts. This was also expressed with different words in the parallel passage in 29:5, while the second parallel in

8 On the comparison with the תנין (תנים) see above pp. 110f on 29:3.

9 See above p. 111.

10 On this see 26:5, 14; 47:10 and Hab 1:15–17.

11 *Enuma eliš* IV, 95; *AOT* 119; *ANET* 67. Besides Gunkel, *Schöpfung*, see e.g., Fredriksson, *Jahwe als*

31:12f altered it all in terms of the image of the tree and spoke of its being thrown on to the hills and valleys and watercourses (on אטילך see, e.g., Jer 16:13; 22:26[28]).

■ **32:5f** The same three places appear in 32:5f in the context of a gruesome extension of the image. The flesh, the carcass, the (festering?) discharge and the blood of the slain beast fill all these places in the land.[12] But the image lacks clarity just as much as that in 31:12f. We have here the schematic re-use of a figure of speech which was still to some extent meaningful, even although hyperbolic, in its original context in the war inscriptions. There is an unmistakable heightening of the gruesome traits from 29:5 through 31:12f to 32:4–6. In any event this heightening makes it clear that the "monster" is not simply a normal beast of normal size, but, analogous with the world tree of chapter 31, is a "world beast" of cosmic dimensions.

■ **32:7f** Finally, this cosmic background is again fully expressed in vv 7f, which conclude the section vv 3–8. The whole process of judgment is accompanied by the darkening of the sky and of the stars. These are elements of cosmic eschatology, with which Joel 2:10; 4:15 may be compared, features which are otherwise to be found in the description of the day of Yahweh in the latter's later, apocalyptic expression. In contrast to 30:1–19, however, the catchword of the day of Yahweh does not occur here, even although reference is made here also to a darkening by means of clouds (see 30:3,18). The verb כסה ("to cover"), explicitly used twice here, recalls 26:19 and the addition in 31:15, where it was used in connection with תהום; הקדיר ("to darken"), which also occurs twice, recalls 31:15. The mention of the "luminaries" recalls distantly the language of P in Gen 1:14–16, where, however, the feminine plural form is used. It is striking that the day of judgment is described as the day of "your extinction." Here, with its vocalization as pi'el, 𝔐 runs "when I extinguish you," while 𝔊 𝔖 𝔙 suggest a qal reading "when you expire." The reference is hardly, as Smend suggests, to the constellation of the dragon, which Yahweh extinguishes. One thinks, rather, of the concept of the "lamp" (נר) which goes out. This idea has already occurred in the speech of the woman of Tekoa to David in 2 Sam 14:7 and in 2 Sam 21:17. Approximately contemporary with the Ezekiel passage is the phrase in Is 43:17 which describes the defeat of the enemies by means of the image of the wick which is extinguished (see also Is 42:3).

Thus the passage vv 3–8 refers to the defeat of the monster. In its details it cannot be separated from 29:5 and 31:12f, but it presents a fuller development of what is said there.

■ **32:9–10** *The effect on the surrounding nations.* The second person singular who is addressed in vv 9–10 is still the representative of Egypt. There is, however, no other reference to the monster in these two verses. Also, the second person singular referred to in "your host of captives" is, rather, a personified Egypt rather than the individual figure of the Pharaoh. The motif of the reaction of the surrounding nations to the fall of Egypt, which has been added here in a secondary expansion, has been particularly conspicuous in the oracles against Tyre (thus in 26:15–21, where the catchword מפלת "fall" in v 15 provides the link). In 27:28–36 the expression יום מפלתך ("the day of your fall") occurs in the preceding additional verse, v 27. In 28:17, 19 the motif was touched on without being more fully developed. There was a faint echo of it in the Egypt oracles in 30:4,9, and the catchword מפלת ("fall") occurred also in 31:16. The same word rounds off the series in 32:9f. Here too there is reference to the terrifying effect on the hearts of "many nations" (see 31:6 note b) that occurs when they hear of the deportation of the Egyptians to "nations whom you did not know."[13] Also the use of הכעים, especially in the sense of "arouse, trouble," is unusual in Ezekiel (see 8:17 note b). On the concept of the scattering of the Egyptians see 29:12, 13; there is no other reference to the deportation. Hölscher wishes to see here a reference to the deportation of Psammetichus III, whom (according to Ctesias) Cambyses deported to Susa

Krieger, 74f, 79f.

12 Müller, *Ezechiel-studien,* 56–58, has already pointed to parallels in the annals of Tiglath-pileser I (III, 23–27: "The corpses of their warriors I threw on to the tops of the mountains like a downpour, their blood I shed over ravines and the tops of hills" = *ARAB* 1, 78 and elsewhere) and in those of Ashurnasirpal (I, 53 = *ARAB* 1, 142 and elsewhere).

13 This expression recalls passages in Jeremiah (15:14; 16:13; 17:4; 22:28); Miller, *Verhältnis,* 94 note 1. See also Is 55:5.

along with six thousand distinguished Egyptians. Even if the conclusion that this must refer to the fall of a Pharaoh that has already taken place is not necessary, nevertheless vv 9f, after they originated, must be dissociated from either v 1 or vv 3–8.

■ **32:11–14** *The sword of Nebuchadnezzar.* Vv 11–14, which have probably been attracted by the catchword "sword" (חרבי "my sword" v 10) and therefore presuppose the prior existence of vv 9–10, certainly still belong to the Babylonian period.

■ **32:11** Here first of all, in an oracle which presupposes the sword almost as an independent force and in this respect recalls Ezekiel 21 (see also the addition to 21:24 and note a there), the threat of the king of Babylon's sword is held over them.

■ **32:12** Then, however, reference is made to the swords of cruel (עריצי גוים "the most brutal nations" 28:7; 30:11; 31:12) "warriors" (גבור in Ezekiel also in 32:21, 27; 39:18, 20), who lay waste the country's splendor, which is described as גאון "pride" (used alone in 7:20; 16:49,56, but mostly strengthened to גאון עז) and המון ("pomp").[14]

■ **32:13** But once again, in a peculiarly artificial turn of thought, the oracle tries to link up with the קינה ("lament") of v 2 when it says that even the animals will be exterminated from the "many waters" (the Nile?),[15] so that neither foot of man nor hoof of beast will trouble these waters ever again.

■ **32:14** This thought is further intensified into an image of the Nile untroubled by any pollution and flowing peacefully like smooth oil. Clearly the author of this oracle knows something of the slimy brown appearance of the Nile at the time when it floods. He does not, however, attribute this troubling to the mud which is the source of Egypt's fruitfulness, but to the stirring up of the mud of the bank by the cattle that are being led to water. To what extent the reference to the Nile smoothly flowing "like oil" contains an echo of the mythical language discernible in the Ugaritic Baal texts must remain open. In a dream which is a symbol of the resuscitation of Baal, there is a reference to the heavens raining oil and the streams flowing with honey, obviously the expression for a luxuriant, paradisal abundance.[16] Does there lie hidden behind the statement, which in 32:14 is simply introduced as a comparison, a hint of a great picture of paradise? In any event the allusion, if such it be, is quite new in Ezekiel. In an entirely different way, Rabbi Ḥanina finds in this passage, which he combines with 29:21, a sign of the nearness of the Messiah when he says: "The Son of David will not come until a fish is sought for an invalid and cannot be procured, as it is written, 'Then will I make their waters deep, and cause their rivers to run like oil'; whilst it is written, 'In that day will I cause the horn of the house of Israel to bud forth.'"[17]

■ **32:15** *Judgment on Egypt as a proof of Yahweh.* The larger unit of 32:1–16 is rounded off with a proof-saying expressed in stereotyped phraseology. The devastation of the land is expressed in quite similar words in 33:29 in terms of the land of Israel (see further 15:8; 29:10, 12).[18] The whole agony of the devastation of Egypt and the slaughter of the population can be understood, according to what is said in this concluding oracle, only if it is acknowledged as a sign in which Yahweh reveals himself. This statement is put at the conclusion of the whole judgment-oracle of vv 3–14 with the express purpose of insuring that the central point of the proclamation comes over unmistakably clearly. The movements of national history and of nature that were described there serve the one end, the proclamation of Yahweh to the world.

■ **32:16** *Postscript.* The unusually expansive postscript (contrast 19:14) seeks to affirm once again that what has gone before has been a funeral lament. In addition it states that it will be intoned throughout the world by the "daughters of the nations." This makes it clear that the prophetic lament is a secondary use of the literary type. It has its real setting in life among the women of the nation.[19] Beyond all national frontiers the lament of the

14 On גאון עז see 1,212; on המון see above p. 131 on 30:10.

15 But see also above p. 39 on 26:19 and p. 150 on 31:5.

16 *šmm. šmn. tmṭrn / nḫlm. tlk. nbtm* 49.III.6f, 12f; see Gordon, *Ugaritic Literature,* 46; Driver, *Canaanite Myths,* 112f.

17 According to *b. Sanh.* 98a.

18 On the combination נשמה ארץ ממלאה see also 12:19; 19:7; 30:12.

19 Jahnow, *Leichenlied,* 60.

women (otherwise in 26:16f; 27:29–33) now proclaims throughout the world Yahweh's judgment on the great power.

Aim

In this oracle, the powerful ruler is described only quite briefly in the image of the lion and of the dragon-like monster. In the light of the chapter about the shepherds (34:18), it is clear that its inconsiderate snorting and unruly troubling of the waters are signs of unrestrained self-assertion. In the face of such activity on the part of the great ruler, no matter how much it may mythicize itself and act with superhuman powers, the prophet is bidden to intone the lament. For such activity already stands under judgment.

The main point of the oracle is the description of the judgment. God is able to remove from his element the one who is apparently all-powerful in his own waters. And what is he then? A rotting, stinking corpse at whose putrefaction the whole world will be shrouded in darkness because God has extinguished its light. In these apocalyptic features there is expressed the truth that where God raises up the terror of his judgment, even among the great leaders in the created world, even in the case of sun, moon and stars, there are no areas of aristocratic exclusion. The created world is a whole, in every sphere at the service of its creator and called to proclaim his work.

If, in the first place (vv 2–8), the great ruler himself was in the field of vision, in what follows it is the people on whom his greatness shines. In the summons to the earthly instruments of judgment, in the deportation of the people and the devastation of the land, God will inflict judgment on what was "pride" (גאון) and "pomp" (המון). And—here the oracle returns to its point of departure—it will become peaceful in the sphere where the powerful ruler formerly held sway because his wild fury and that of his people will be swept away.

The oracle is addressed by the prophet, and by those who further expounded it, directly against Egypt. It should not, however, be overlooked that in it the purely regional restriction will be surpassed and there will be revealed something of the far-reaching triumph which God will win wherever power vaunts itself against him. This oracle against the world power which thinks it can manage the world with its own powers is also expressed in terms of an ultimate self-revelation of God.

7. The Descent to Hell of Egypt's Pomp

Bibliography

Otto Eissfeldt
"Schwerterschlagene bei Hesekiel" in *Studies in Old Testament Prophecy presented to T. H. Robinson,* ed. H. H. Rowley (Edinburgh: Clark, 1950), 73–81.

Paul Humbert
"Démesure et chute dans l'Ancien Testament" in *maqqél shâqédh. La branche d'amandier. Hommage à Wilhelm Vischer* (Montpellier, 1960), 63–82.

Hedwig Jahnow
Das hebräische Leichenlied im Rahmen der Völkerdichtung, BZAW 36 (Giessen: Töpelmann, 1923), especially 231–239.

Josef Kroll
Gott und Hölle, der Mythus vom Descensuskampfe (Berlin: Teubner, 1932).

A. Lods
"La 'mort des incirconcis'" in *Comptes rendus des séances de l'Académie des inscriptions et belles-lettres* (Paris, 1943), 271–283.

32

17 And in the twelfth year[a], . . .[b], on the fifteenth (day) of the month, the word of Yahweh came to me: 18/ Son of man, utter a lament[a] over Egypt's pomp and bid it go down <> in the midst of mighty

32:17 17a 𝔊[397] 'A Θ name the tenth year, which is unlikely according to the series of dates in 29:1; 30:20; 31:1; 32:1. 𝔖 has the eleventh year.

b The absence of the name of the month is striking. 𝔊 has an additional τοῦ πρώτου μηνός, which might presuppose an original בראשון. Origen has put an obelus against this since it seemed to him ἀλόγως προσκείμενον after the date in 32:1; see the quotation in Ziegler, *Ezechiel,* 33 and 242. If, however, 32:1 is a scribal error (see 32:1 note a), then his argument falls to the ground. But the text of 𝔊 is suspect, not only because it mentions the first most convenient month to offer itself but also on linguistic grounds. A בראשון in the Hebrew original, if it is not as in 29:17 immediately connected with the name of the day (μιᾷ τοῦ μηνὸς τοῦ πρώτου), would, on the evidence of all the other occurrences of information about the month, have to be translated by ἐν τῷ πρώτῳ μηνί. The τοῦ πρώτου μηνός which precedes the note of the day (πεντεκαιδεκάτῃ τοῦ μηνός) does not seem to derive from an original Hebrew בראשון and can also therefore not (cf. the majority of commentaries) be regarded as original. 𝔊 has simply filled in what was missing. Has perhaps an original בחמשי fallen out due to haplography? Hölscher (note 1, p. 155) assumes, on the basis of 32:1, the twelfth month. The question remains open.

18 18a 𝔐 נהה. 𝔗 איתנבי, which is subsequently repeated after גיים אדרם (= 𝔗 עממיא תקיפיא) (איתנבי דיתמסרון לארעא ארעייתא), explicitly underlines the prophetic character of this lament as already in 32:16 (note a).

nations[b] to the land <below>[c], to[d] those who go down to the pit: 19/ Are you then lovelier than others?[a] Go down[b] and lie[c] with (the) uncircumcised 20/ among (those who are) slain by the sword[a] [they lie beside him, [[the sword is destined]]

b 𝔐 והורדהו. 𝔊 *καὶ καταβιβάσουσιν* might suggest a plural reading. On this basis, e.g., Fohrer, who then finds the subject in גוים ("since the nations cast it down"). Quite different is Bewer, "Exegese," 200, who reads הוי רדה אתה בתוך גוים אדרם "Ho! go down amidst mighty nations." He is here partly dependent on Heinisch, who reads "since I make them go down among mighty nations." An emendation of the verb of 𝔐 is not, however, necessary. But surely Heinisch and Bewer are on the right lines in their understanding of the second half. Here an original בתוך was corrupted at an early stage to בנות. This was understood in dependence on v 17 (𝔗 again ולכפרני), and to it, since in the first instance it was the prophet himself who was summoned to lament, there was prefixed an אתה to which the בנות was connected by the copula. This אתה, as Hitzig, Cornill, Toy, Cooke and others already supposed, was then corrupted to אותה, whose feminine suffix is quite unsuited to the context. Bertholet and Cooke (cf. Herrmann) believe that they can recognize in אתה ובנות גוים אדרם a later gloss.

c 𝔐 ארץ תחתיות see 26:20 note c.

d The somewhat surprising את of 𝔐 could have been chosen with the intention of providing a variation on the immediately preceding אל. 24MSS read אל, 𝔊 *πρός*.

19 19a 𝔐 ממי נעמת literally "To whom are you superior in loveliness?" 𝔊 (v 20) *τίνος κρείττων εἶ*; 𝔙 *quo pulchrior es?* 𝔗 somewhat more freely ממן את גיבר. 𝔖 מן מיא בסימא corresponds to Θ (𝔊[A]) *ἐξ ὕδατος εὐπρεποῦς*.

b 𝔐 רדה "climb down." The רדה, strengthened by the cohortative ה, can be heard also, e.g., in the imperious royal command of 2 Kgs 1:9, 11.

c 𝔐 וְהָשְׁכְּבָה is a hop'al in a reflexive sense; see Bauer-Leander §46k′. It occurs again in v 32.

20 20a In the transmission of vv 19–21 𝔊 goes its own way. It first of all omits the summons in v 19, in which, according to 𝔐, the prophet himself is heard speaking, and it connects v 20 (v 20b in a somewhat altered wording, see note b) directly with v 18. Then follows v 21a (with no equivalent for את עזריו), which then forms the introduction to v 19. On this basis 𝔐 v 19 becomes the speech of the *γίγαντες* (גבורים). To begin with, this altered sequence impresses. But on closer examination it can be seen that the words of the *γίγαντες* again end with the *ἐν μέσῳ τραυματιῶν μαχαίρας* which 𝔊 has already reproduced in the translation of 𝔐 v 20. This means that it is not advisable simply to rearrange the order of verses on the basis of 𝔊, as do Cornill, Herrmann, Bertholet, Fohrer. 𝔊 no doubt deserves to be trusted in the first instance in its connection of the בתוך חללי חרב of 𝔐 v 20 with 𝔐 v 19. Uncircumcised and those slain by the sword are always used in parallelism in what follows (see vv 25, 26, 28 and also v 30). See further note b.

and all its pomp is laid low]^b! [21/ There
will speak with him[a] the strong heroes[b]
from the midst of the underworld [[with
his helpers]][c]. There have gone down,
have lain down, the uncircumcised, slain
by the sword.][d]
22 **Assyria is there and all her array <round>**
about <her grave>[a], all of them slain,

b The remainder of v 20 in 𝔐 is undoubtedly corrupt. 𝔊 affords help insofar as its (*ἐν μέσῳ τραυματιῶν μαχαίρας*) *πεσοῦνται μετ' αὐτοῦ καὶ κοιμηθήσεται πᾶσα ἡ ἰσχὺς αὐτοῦ* (placed before 𝔐 v 19 but, as note a showed, including the end of the summons contained in vv 19, 20aα) might possibly suggest an original יפלו אותה (= אִתָּהּ) וישכב כל המונה. On this basis, it would seem that the חרב נתנה of 𝔐 should be deleted as a still later addition. On its translation see Driver, "Linguistic Problems," 179. In 𝔐 משכו (𝔙 *attraxerunt,* cf. 𝔖 וננעגונה) there is to be found a corrupt derivative of שׁכב, one of the key words of the whole section (vv 19, 21, 27–30, 32). The impossible המוניה should be read as המונה. אותה (= אִתָּהּ cf. 2:1 note a) might originally have stood in a different place. The whole, however, is to be regarded as a secondary expansion which already presupposes the false separation in 𝔐 between vv 19 and 20. In 𝔊 the whole of 𝔐 v 20 has found its way secondarily into a quite different position in the text, and this caused the fact to be overlooked that בתוך חללי חרב was translated twice.

21 21a 𝔐 ידברו לו. 𝔊 *καὶ ἐροῦσί σοι*, 𝔖 ונמללון עם גדודיהון make the reading וְדִבְּרוּ of 2 MSS[Ken] appear possible. On the other hand, 𝔐 לו has been harmonized by 𝔊 *σοι* only secondarily to the second person direct address which follows immediately in 𝔊 (= 𝔐 v 19).

b 𝔐 אלי גבורים is attested by 𝔙 *potentissimi robustorum,* 𝔗 תקיפי גיבריא and doubtless also 𝔖 שׁליטנא דעממא. 𝔊 *γίγαντες* is in v 27 the rendering of גבורים alone. One might consider whether 𝔐 אלי does not represent a secondary expansion of the expression (on this see, e.g., the אילי הארץ of 17:13 and the איל גוים of 31:11). It is more likely, however, that 𝔊 is harmonizing the אלי גבורים of v 21 with the גבורים of v 27. See also note c.

c 𝔐 את עזריו with its singular suffix is dependent on what is said in v 21a, but it is not attested by 𝔊 or 𝔖. It is a secondary addition, which, along the lines of and with the wording of 30:8, associates with Egypt her "helpers," who suffer the same fate. עזר occurs in Ezekiel only otherwise in 12:14 (emended text). The whole of v 21a, as is clear from the terminology which is altered vis-à-vis v 17 (אלי גבורים), presents a secondary amplification along the lines of Isaiah 14.

d V 21b is not attested by 𝔊 and is, on the basis of content and choice of vocabulary, one of the accretions typical of this section. Its purpose is to define rather more closely the גבורים who are mentioned here (prematurely). 𝔙 and, even more markedly, 𝔖 try by means of connecting particles to make the text syntactically more acceptable, and they are followed by many commentators.

22 22a 𝔐 סביבותיו קברתיו (to be emended, on the basis of 𝔖 and vv 23f, to סביבות קברתה) is missing in 𝔊 𝔏[C], which must have omitted it in favor of v 23. The parallels in vv 24 and 26 suggest the retention

<fallen>[b] by the sword 23/ [,to whom
<her grave> <was>[a] given in the lowest
depths, and her array lay (buried) about
her grave, all of them slain, fallen by the
sword][b], who (once) had spread terror
<before them>[c] in the land of the living.
24 Elam is there and all her pomp round about
her grave, all of them slain, <fallen>[a] by
the sword, [who went down uncircumcised to the land below,[b]][c] who (once)
had spread terror before them in the land
of the living and who bear their shame
with those who go down to the pit. 25/

of the expression. In vv 22–26 𝔐 derives all the plural forms from קֶבֶר (plural קְבָרוֹת) but the singular in vv 23aβ, 24 from קְבֻרָה. This is surely to be attributed to an artificial secondary arrangement. According to Driver, "Ezekiel," 301, at any rate, a distinction is to be made between קֶבֶר "grave," which is attested only in v 23a, and קְבֻרָה "burial, buried ones," which occurs everywhere else.

b The form with definite article הנפלים, which occurs also in v 24, is surprising. As in v 23 (see also the corresponding indefinite form [מ]חללי חרב of v 26), נפלים should be read. 𝔊 𝔏[C] also omit 𝔐 (ה)נפלים בחרב. Driver, "Linguistic Problems," 179, wishes, on the other hand, to read הנפלים in v 23 as well.

23 23a 𝔐 אשר נתנו קברתיה 𝔊 ἐκεῖ ἐδόθησαν καὶ ἡ ταφή and 𝔏[C] *illuc dati sunt et sepultura eorum* make the אשר נתנו of 𝔐 into the conclusion of v 22, but, at the same time, bear witness to a reading שם in place of 𝔐 אשר. But since in v 23abα, as later in v 24b (note c), we have an explanatory expansion (note b), the loose connection of 𝔐 אשר should be retained. 𝔊 (𝔏[C]) is here trying, as with the insertion of the copula before ἡ ταφή (1:4 note a), to effect a stylistic improvement. To be followed, on the other hand, is the singular reading קברתה, attested also by 𝔖 and 𝔗, which then demands before it either an impersonal qal plural נָתְנוּ or a feminine singular נִתְּנָה.

b It is noteworthy that v 23abα, which in its first part (v 23aα) described the burial place more precisely, goes back in its second part (v 23aβγ) to the statement of v 22a and in its third part (v 23bα) repeats word for word v 22b. The literary phenomenon of "resumption" (Kuhl, "'Wiederaufnahme'"), as a result of which insertions in the text are easily revealed, is found here in its pure form. Thus v 23abα, connected with the loose particle אשר (note a), is to be regarded as an addition.

c 𝔐 חתית. 𝔊 τὸν φόβον αὐτῶν and the parallels in vv 24–26 (see also vv 27, 30, 32; 26:17) suggest the reading חתיתם. 𝔗 (דאיתמסרו לתבר על דשליטו בארעא דישראל) here, as in vv 24–27, 32, points in particular to the violation of Israel, which, in the case of Elam (v 24) and Thubal-Mesech (v 26), then appears historically particularly strange.

24 24a 𝔐 הנפלים should, as suggested in v 22 note b, be read as an indefinite.

b On ארץ תחתיות see 26:20 note c. An emendation to תַּחְתִּית (Driver, "Linguistic Problems," 179) is not recommended.

c The existence of two relative clauses introduced by אשר is surprising. Since the second clause is firmly attached to the pattern, since the immediate sequence of the clauses is extremely harsh and since the first poses problems with regard to its content and is also missing in the doublet in v 25 (v 26), it is the first that is to be regarded as an addition (analogous to v 23abα, which is introduced in the same way).

<They have been placed>[a] in the midst of
the slain. [She was given a resting place
in all her pomp (or: <Mesech-Thubal is
there and all> her pomp?)[b] <round about
her grave>[c]; they are all uncircumcised,
slain by the sword; for <they had>[d]
(once) spread terror before them in the
land of the living and (now) bear their
shame with those who go down to the
pit. <They have been placed>[e] in the
midst of the slain.][a]
26 Mesech-Thubal[a] is there and all her[a] pomp
<round about her grave>[b], all of them
uncircumcised, slain by the sword[c]; for[d]
they had (once) spread terror before
them in the land of the living <and (now)
bear their shame with those who go
down to the pit. They have been placed in
the midst of slain>[e].

25 25a In 𝔊 v 25 is reduced to the introductory words בתוך חללים, which are understood as the conclusion to v 24. A closer examination reveals, however, that in the opening words of v 26 ἐκεῖ ἐδόθησαν Μοσοχ . . . there is incorporated the נתנו which follows בתוך חללים in 𝔐 v 25 and to which 𝔊 again adds the copula (1:4 note a). 𝔐 נָתְנוּ is here understood as נִתְּנוּ. The remainder of v 25 is not attested by 𝔊 and is thus shown to be a somewhat expanded doublet of v 24—or of v 26? On this see note b.

b The beginning of the doublet is, according to 𝔐, interlocked with the conclusion (also attested by 𝔊) of the preceding basic text. The phrase which this produces, נתנו משכב לה, is not found anywhere else in 32:17–32. This suggests that a second possibility of understanding the expansion of v 25, which is missing in 𝔊, should be seriously considered. Is it a doublet of the immediately following Mesech-Thubal strophe? In this case the beginning of the insertion in 𝔐 משכב לה בכל המונה would represent a corrupt doublet of the (שם) משך תבל וכל המונה which follows in v 26. An argument in favor of this view is the fact that the wording of v 25 in detail lies much closer to the wording of the Mesech-Thubal strophe (v 26) than to that of the Elam strophe (v 24). It would then have preserved in its full extent the Mesech-Thubal strophe, the end of which as it now stands seems to have been shortened. P. Rost, "Miscellen," 393, presented the opposite suggestion, that in v 26 we have a correction of v 25.

c Instead of 𝔐 סביבותיו קִבְרֹתֶהָ we should read סביבות קְבֻרָתָהּ; see 𝔖 and v 22 note a.

d נתן, which does not fit syntactically, should with 𝔙 𝔖 (𝔗) and the parallels in vv 23f, 26 be emended to נתנו. In addition, the wording of this part of the sentence, like that of the preceding part, is close to that of v 26.

e The context and 𝔙 𝔖 𝔗 demand here too the reading נתנו. See the beginning of v 25.

26 26a 𝔐 משך תבל. 𝔊 𝔙 𝔖 insert the copula between the two names which, as the suffix in the following המונה and קברתה (note b) shows, were understood by 𝔐 as a combined unit.

b 𝔐 סביבותיו קברותיה should be emended to סביבות קברתה; see v 22 note a. 𝔊 (𝔏^{C}) adds after it an additional πάντες τραυματίαι αὐτοῦ.

c 𝔐 מחללי חרב has perhaps grown out of the usual חללי חרב (vv 20, 21, 25, 28–32) through dittography of the final ם of the preceding ערלים.

d 𝔊 𝔏^{C} do not reproduce the כי.

e It is surprising that the Mesech-Thubal strophe breaks off prematurely in comparison with the Assyria and Elam strophes. If the supposition is correct that the parts missing in 𝔊 v 25 are a doublet of v 26, then the two missing final sections will be found there too. The expansion of these two missing sections may precisely have been the reason for the addition of the expansion, which then found its way

27 **And they do not[a] lie beside (the) heroes who fell <in days of old>[b] who went down to the underworld with all their weapons of war and who laid their swords under their heads and whose <shields>[c] lie on their bones; for terror at the heroes[d] lay on the land of the living.**
28 **You will now in the midst of the uncircumcised [be broken and][a] lie with (those who are) slain by the sword.**
29 **Edom is there[a] [,her kings][b] and all her princes who in (all) their heroic might[c] are laid among those killed by the sword. They lie beside the uncircumcised [and][d] those who go down to the pit.**
30 **The princes of the north are there[a], all of them[b], [and all Phoenicians][c] who went**

as a unit into the text. The addition of these clauses also creates an organic transition to v 27.

27 27a The negation is missing in 𝔊 𝔏^{C} 𝔖, and this considerably alters the meaning. See the exposition.

b 𝔐 מערלים represents an accommodation to the context: the heroes of old lie apart from the uncircumcised. 𝔊 ἀπ᾽ αἰῶνος (𝔏^{C} *a saeculo* 𝔄) has undoubtedly preserved the correct reading מעולם. נפלים מעולם could also be translated: "Those who lie there from of old." Does this contain a word play on the נְפִלִים of Gen 6:4? Cornill, Ehrlich, *Randglossen,* Herrmann in fact read נְפִלִים.

c 𝔐 עונתם "their indebtednesses" is out of place in this concrete description, but is attested by all the versions. Cornill's conjecture צנתם (or צנותם) is convincing and provides a fully satisfactory text.

d Driver, "Ezekiel," 301, wishes to read, instead of the second גבורים, the abstract גְּבֻרָם "their power."

28 28a 𝔐 תשבר, by its absence from 𝔊 𝔏^{C}, is revealed as a (slightly corrupt) dittography of the adjacent תשכב, with which it was subsequently connected by the copula. 𝔖 תשכב ותדמך treats the two expressions as synonyms.

29 29a 𝔐 שמה, which recurs in v 30, is not to be assimilated to the שם of vv 22, 24, 26. From the point of view of content this fuller form does not have a different meaning from the שם of vv 22, 24, 26; see, e.g., 48:35. See further on "Form."

b 𝔅 𝔖 ease the harshness by the insertion of the copula. Oddly, 𝔊 has misunderstood v 29aα. Dependent on v 26, 𝔊 expresses it thus: ἐκεῖ ἐδόθησαν οἱ ἄρχοντες Ασσουρ. 𝔏^{C} *illuc datus est assur et omnes principes eius* is closer to 𝔐, but still omits 𝔐 מלכיה which 𝔅 𝔖 then add with the copula. מלכיה could be a later addition.

c ב here has almost the meaning of "in spite of." Instead of בגבורתם Ehrlich, *Randglossen,* wishes to read the similar sounding בקבורתם. But this is ill-advised in view of the recurrence of the word in v 30. In any case, conscious assonance may have been intended in the use of בגבורתם, which also of course echoes the גבורים of v 27.

d In 𝔐 ואת, the copula should be deleted as an example of dittography. It is not attested in MSS 𝔊 𝔏^{C} 𝔗 𝔄.

30 30a On שמה see v 29 note a.

b 𝔐 כלם is not attested by 𝔊 𝔏^{C} 𝔖, but this can easily be understood as an attempt at stylistic improvement in view of the immediately following וכל. Joüon, "Notes," 310, suggests that the words צפון כלם are a scribal error for an original צר וכל, after which, of course, the following וכל should be deleted.

c 𝔐 וכל צדני אשר is understood by 𝔊 as πάντες στρατηγοὶ (= סרני?) Ασσουρ and 𝔏^{C} as *omnes duces assur,* while 𝔅 derives צדני from the root צוד and renders *venatores.* With MSS 𝔗 𝔖 (𝔅) it is preferable to read the plural צדנים. The whole expression (designation of a nation in place of what occurs

down with[d] (those) slain by the sword, who for (all) the terror spread abroad by them[e] have been put to shame[f] in their might, and they have lain down uncircumcised with those slain by the sword and bear their shame with those who go down to the pit.

31 Pharaoh[a] will see them (all) and will console himself for all his pomp[b], [slain by the sword are Pharaoh and all his army][c] says [the Lord][d] Yahweh. 32/ For I have spread[a] terror[b] before him in the land of the living, and he shall be laid among the uncircumcised along with those slain by the sword—Pharaoh and all his pomp, says [the Lord][c] Yahweh.

otherwise in vv 29f, a reference to the princes) has surely been added secondarily.

d 𝔐 את is missing in 3 MSS, see also 𝔊 𝔏^{C}.

e 𝔐 בחתיתם is best understood along the lines of the earlier use of the expression. Driver, "Linguistic Problems," 179, wishes, on the basis of 𝔙 *paventes* (after which, however, 𝔙, with 𝔊 𝔏^{C}, has the copula), to read בַּחֲתִיתִים and translate "amongst them, that are terror-struck (and) reft of their might, ashamed." Cornill and Ehrlich, *Randglossen*, read חַתִּים "broken," since otherwise the emergence of the gloss בושים would be incomprehensible.

f 𝔐 בושים is not attested in 𝔊 𝔏^{C} but can scarcely be dispensed with after מגבורתם.

31 31a 𝔊 βασιλεὺς Φαραω.

b 𝔐 המונה = המונו. 𝔊 (𝔏^{C}) τὴν ἰσχὺν αὐτῶν.

c V 31bα is unattested in 𝔊 𝔏^{C} and may, on the grounds of content and of stylistic arrangement, be suspected of being an addition.

d אדני is lacking in 𝔊 𝔎^{Sa}, see Appendix 1.

32 32a 𝔐 נתתי is attested by 𝔊 𝔙 𝔖, while 𝔗 (as in v 23 [note c]) paraphrases at great length without making the first person clear. In view of the explicitly secondary character of v 32, the possibility of an expression in the first person, which would, by way of conclusion, throw a certain theological light on the whole complex, can by no means be discounted.

b With K, חתיתו should be read.

c אדני is lacking in 𝔊 𝔎^{Sa}, see Appendix 1.

Form

The question of the structure of the oracle in 32:17–32 must be preceded by a critical analysis which tries to discover its basic form. The textual criticism has already frequently shown that this basic form has been obscured by additions and accretions.

According to v 18 the prophet is commissioned to utter a lament. As in the introduction to the קינה ("lament") in chapter 19 and 32:1f (contrast chapters 27–8) and to the extended simile in 31:2–9, there is no other indication that this is a divine address, by, for example, the introductory messenger formula. Thus, the formulae for a divine saying which conclude vv 31 and 32 present a surprise. They appear not to correspond to the original structure of the oracle. The final verse (v 32) has already shown itself, by its formulation as a divine address in the first person, to be different from what precedes it. It is to be regarded as a secondary expansion. A further caesura, which also reveals itself by a certain change in language, can be recognized at the beginning of v 29. What is surprising here is that after the description of the great powers of the world (Assyria, Elam, Mesech-Thubal) has moved by way of climax to that of the heroes of prehistory, there is again a repetitious enumeration of contemporary nations. They are introduced formally as in vv 22, 24, 26. The different hand is clear already in the use of language, in the use of the fuller form שמה ("there") in place of the שם ("there") found in vv 22, 24, 26. There are, in addition, differences in the content of the description. While in vv 22,24,26 the name of the nation represented the personality of the nation (feminine!), which was of course primarily represented by rulers round whose grave her "array" (קהל) or her "pomp" (המון) were encamped, here, alongside the reference to the name of the nation or region, there is the mention of the "princes" (אדום וכל נשיאיה "Edom and all her princes" or נסיכי צפון "the princes of the north"). Instead of the "grave" (קבורה) it is the "might" (גבורה) that is mentioned. The basic formulaic material that recurred identically and with a certain monotony in the case of the three great nations mentioned at the beginning is certainly echoed once more from v 29 onwards, but has lost the strict order which it had earlier. So vv 29–31 must be set apart as an expansion which is roughly rounded off by the formula for a divine saying in v 31. The original lament ended in v 28 without such a formula.

In the introduction in vv 17f it is remarkable that after the instruction about the lament, there is, unlike 19:2; 31:2; 32:2, no specific command given to the prophet to "speak" (ואמרת or אֱמֹר). The נהה ("utter a lament") in v 18 has obviously itself already the weight of such a direct command to speak. But then it would be best if the direct address of v 19 followed directly on the נהה על המון מצרים ("utter a lament over Egypt's pomp"). Do the remaining words of v 18 then represent a secondary expansion, which is meant to indicate in advance something of the content of the lament? The harshness in 𝔐 of the transition from v 18 to v 19 makes it easy to understand why one is always tempted to follow the reading of 𝔊, which puts the address of v 19 in the mouth of the אלי גבורים ("strong heroes") (on the difficulties of such an assumption see v 20 note a). Over and above what was said there, it can be stated here that while vv 22–26 can certainly be thought of as still part of the speech of the אלי גבורים ("strong heroes"), v 27 certainly cannot since it speaks of the גבורים ("heroes") themselves in the third person. Following v 27, v 28 returns to a direct address to Egypt, thereby linking up formally with the beginning of the oracle in v 19. One cannot regard the oracle as ending before v 27, nor with Hölscher, before v 28.

Thus the following emerges as the text of the original lament:

> Are you then lovelier than others? Go down and lie with (the) uncircumcised among (those who are) slain by the sword.
> Assyria is there and all her array round about her grave, all of them slain, fallen by the sword, who (once) had spread terror before them in the land of the living.
> Elam is there and all her pomp round about her grave, all of them slain, fallen by the sword, who (once) had spread terror before them in the land of the living and who bear their shame with those who go down to the pit. They have been placed in the midst of the slain.
> Mesech-Thubal is there and all her pomp round about her grave, all of them uncircumcised, slain by the sword; for they had (once) spread terror before them in the land of the living and (now) bear their shame with those who go down to the pit. They have been placed in the midst of the slain.
> And they do not lie beside (the) heroes who fell in days of old, who went down to the underworld with all their weapons of war and who laid their swords under their heads and whose shields lie on their bones; for terror at the heroes lay on the land of the living.
> You will now lie in the midst of the uncircumcised with (those who are) slain by the sword.

This lament is not described as a קינה "lament." The noun נהי ("lamentation"), which is derived from the verb נהה ("to utter a lament") used in the introduction (also Mic 2:4; cj. in Ps 102:8; the nip'al in 1 Sam 7:2 surely does not belong here, see Koehler-Baumgartner), is attested also in Am 5:16; Mic 2:4; Jer 9:9, 17–19; 31:15. It always describes an uttering in a lament situation and can be used simply as a parallel to קינה (Jer 9:9, 19). It is difficult, on the basis of these passages, to differentiate between נהי and קינה. Is it possible to recognize such a difference in the metric sphere, since Jer 9:18 describes as נהי a lament with two 2+2 lines while in 9:20 the reference to a קינה in 9:19bβ (the parallel in 9:19bα nevertheless also referred to a נהי) is followed by a lament in the limping five-stress rhythm? In Ezekiel it is possible to see such a metrical differentiation between a קינה and נהי. In the sections cited as קינה, the limping five-stress rhythm has hitherto always been in evidence.[1] Although, on the other hand, C. Budde, referring to Ezek 32:17–32 affirms that "in this passage too the submerged and buried rhythm occasionally comes to the surface," this hesitant statement can be made only with difficulty with reference to the קינה-rhythm.[2] As the observation concerning the נהי of Jer 9:18 might confirm, the occurrence of a two-stress rhythm (a favorite elsewhere in Ezekiel) is much more frequent, although one is still not justified in venturing to speak of a prescribed meter.

But also on the grounds of content-structure and of motif the נהי of 32:17–32 is markedly different from the much more frequent occurrences of the קינה in Ezekiel. While there the contrast-motif "once—now" was developed again and again, it is completely absent from

1 See above p. 157.
2 C. Budde, "Klagelied," 21.

32:17–32. Here all that is described is the journey to the underworld and the shameful state that exists down there. In this H. Jahnow discerns the inversion of the motif which occurs in the genuine lament, that of the "honorable burial." Instead of the consolation that the person buried will be reunited in death with friends and nobles,[3] here in the prophetic-political reapplication of the lament it is the unworthiness of the burial that is fully developed. Only the addition in v 31 contains a "consolation" along the usual lines. Thus, the נהי of Ezek 32:17–32 lacks the brilliance and the inner range of the laments in Ezekiel which are specifically described as קינה. This can best be affirmed in comparison with the great "mocking lament" (משל) of Isaiah 14, with which Ezek 32:17–32 has again and again been compared and indeed as the echo of which it has even been understood (van den Born). The contrast-motif of the hubris of the great ruler, which can be seen in 28:1–10; 31:1–19 as well as in Isaiah 14, finds expression in Ezek 32:17–32 in only a very restrained way in the key-words המון ("pomp") and נתן חתית ("to spread terror").[4] The description here is concentrated above all on the shameful burial place in the underworld. To what extent such a concentration on a single motif might also distinguish the נהי from the קינה cannot be decided.

Otherwise, the basic text of 32:17–32 reveals a clear, formal, consistent shape. The lament is framed by addresses in the second person (vv 19, 28). These framework statements clearly express the theme of the oracle as a whole: "Go down! Lie with the uncircumcised and those slain by the sword." The framework then embraces a consistently descriptive central section, which first (in three parallel strophes) describes the fate of three militant world powers in the underworld and then, by way of contrast, differentiates this in a fourth strophe from that of the heroes of old. What in the address of v 19 at first remains unfulfilled has achieved a certain vividness in the concluding address in v 28 as a result of the description in vv 20–27. There is, of course, no comparison between the colorful image of Isaiah 14 and the strongly stylized description of Ezek 32:17–32. H. Jahnow endeavors to regard the section, in which she inserts vv 29f before v 27, as a litany—scarcely with justification. We have already encountered in Ezekiel the stylized monotony of a series of parallel sections in quite differently placed contexts (see, e.g., 18:5–32; 20:5–26).

Setting

The oracle is dated in the period shortly after the fall of Jerusalem and threatens Egypt with a shameful downfall. The comparison with the downfall of the three powers Assyria, Elam and Mesech-Thubal shows that this is still close to direct experience. There is no reference to a fall of Babylon. Thus, the dating offered by the text itself inspires confidence.

The reference to the three northern and eastern powers seems to reflect directly the experience of the Babylonian plain, which was threatened by these three border and hill nations ranged round her in a semi-circle. Thus it seems certain that this oracle emerged in the place where the prophet lived in exile in Babylon (against Bertholet).[5]

Interpretation

■ **32:17** The divine word comes to the prophet on the fifteenth day of an unnamed month in the twelfth year of the reign of Jehoiachin, that is, according to Parker-Dubberstein, in the year which stretches from April 13, 586 to April 1, 585.[6] It is the period after the fall of Jerusalem, in which the forces of the Babylonian king have now become free for the expected onslaught on Egypt, which was the force behind Judah's uprising (Ezekiel 17). The absence of the number of the month probably, as already in 27:1, indicates later tampering with the date. Here, consideration may have been given in retrospect to the date in 33:21.

■ **32:18** The prophet is addressed as "son of man" and is commissioned to utter lamentations over Egypt's pomp.[7]

3 Examples in Jahnow, *Leichenlied,* 236f.
4 See also W. Staerk, "Zu Habakuk 1:5–11. Geschichte oder Mythos?" *ZAW* 51 (1933): 26f.
5 See further the exposition.
6 See 1, 144f.
7 On "son of man" see 1, 131f; on נהה see above; on המון see 29:19 note d.

The commission is made plain by the command to thrust Egypt into the underworld. ירד ("to go down"), too, is a motif word in the oracles against Tyre and Egypt, where no fewer than 26 out of the total 29 occurrences of the word in the book of Ezekiel occur.[8] In the use of the hip'il in 26:20; 31:16 Yahweh is the subject of the "bringing down" of the mighty (in 34:26 of the sending down of rain). In 28:8 it is the powerful enemy nations who force the prince of Tyre to go down to the pit. That here the prophet himself is to see to the "bringing down" by means of his word is (whether the second half of the sentence, which begins with this word, is original or is only a secondary expansion) obviously stated in anticipation of the רדה ("go down") in v 19. From this point of view too, then, this should not be put, as does 𝔊, in the mouth of the אלי גבורים ("strong heroes"). Behind the command to "bring down" Pharaoh there can be seen an awareness of the power of the prophet's word, which does not only proclaim what is to come but brings reality to pass.[9] Like the sword of brutal enemy nations (28:7), the word of the prophet is to bring down to the underworld Egypt in all her pomp among the "mighty" (אדיר, used in 17:23 of the lofty cedar) nations that preceded her.[10]

■ **32:19** The lament begins with a question, in the phraseology of which the negative form of a hymnic question of boasting can be easily recognized. "'Who' (מי) is (wonderful) like me?," asks Yahweh in Is 44:7.[11] "'Than whom' (ממי) are you then lovelier?" (note a), asks the prophet here and thrusts aside all the prerogatives to which Egypt, addressed as a person (masculine), might lay claim. In this phraseology it is possible to hear implicitly Egypt's claim to be beautiful and, in consequence of this, her right to a "beautiful" destiny. נעים ("lovely") is used of a country in Gen 49:15, of a friend in 2 Sam 1:26, of the beloved in Song 7:7. This beauty has already been represented in the image of the tree in Ezekiel 31. This element emerged still more strongly in the oracles against Tyre in chapters 27f. This claim is harshly interrupted by the רדה, "Go down."[12]

With the uncircumcised, among those slain by the sword is Egypt to lie. Here now are mentioned the actual key-words of the characteristic prophetic "lament." The understanding of what follows depends on the correct understanding of these remarks. They introduce the wider sphere of conceptions of the underworld of the dead. Already the introduction to the lament (v 18) had brought out two principal ideas which are associated in one's mind with this world: 1) the picture which is derived from the contemplation of burial, that of the "pit" (בור, also שחת 28:8) in which man is laid when he is buried deep in the ground; 2) the extended image of a "land below" (ארץ תחתיות), which lies far below the everyday world known to man, the "land of the living" (ארץ חיים vv 23–27, 32; 26:20), and which has its own order. The image of the gloomy pit fuses with the mythical image of the realm of the underworld, which is then described by a word which has not yet been linguistically clarified with any certainty: שאול ("the underworld") (vv 21, 27; 31:15–17).[13] Of the fact that this netherworld of the dead can acquire an uncanny vitality which affects even the world of the living[14] there is no trace in Ezek 32:17–32. Here there is maintained the sharp contrast between the "land of the living" and "the land below," which one enters when one dies.

With this mythical view of a land of the dead, the OT—even if otherwise it banishes all thought of divine powers who rule this realm of the dead, completely demythologizes them and rationalizes them in terms of philosophical conceptions—nevertheless stands in a close relationship to the ideas of the world of the ancient Near East. The twelfth tablet of the Gilgamesh epic expresses through Enkidu how gloomy the order of the netherworld is: "If I were to tell you the order which I have seen, you would have to sit down and weep."[15] The vision of the underworld seen by an Assyrian crown prince shows, in the cry of horror uttered by him as he awakens, how oppressive what he has seen is.[16] Sumerian

8 See above p. 38.
9 See what was said (1, 156) on prophetic sign-actions.
10 On ארץ תחתיות see 26:20 note c; יורדי בור already in 26:20; 31:14, 16; it recurs in 32:24f, 29f.
11 On this see above p. 61 on 27:32.
12 See also 21:31.
13 On this see above p. 152.
14 As has been shown by C. Barth, *Errettung vom Tode.*
15 *AOT* 185; see also *ANET* 98.
16 Wolfram von Soden, "Die Unterweltsvision eines assyrischen Kronprinzen," *Zeitschrfit für Assyriologie* 43 (1936), 1–31; *ANET* 109f.

and Akkadian myths describe the journey to the underworld of specific gods and reveal a varied picture of that netherworld with its demonic helpers, with its seven gates through which the new arrival must pass before he reaches the throne of the goddess of the underworld. Such are the accounts of Inanna's and Ishtar's descent to the underworld, the myth of Nergal and Ereshkigal. Here too everything is painted in tones of deep gloom when the nether kingdom is described as a "dark house," as a "house which none leave who have entered it . . . where dust is their fare and clay their food, (where) they see no light, residing in darkness, (where) they are clothed like birds, with wings for garments, (and where) over door and bolt is spread dust."[17]

By comparison with the varied conceptions from Babylonia, that which lies behind Ezek 32:17–32 appears relatively simple. The component of the conception of the grave here steps decisively into the foreground and thrusts into the background the features of an organized dominion. In this respect, Ezekiel 32 comes close, to a certain extent, to the much more colorfully depicted and more passionately glowing taunt song in Is 14:4–21.[18] In both, in the description the distinction between the "honorable" and the "dishonorable" burial comes decisively into the foreground. While, according to Is 14:18, the rulers of the nations normally rest "all of them in honor" (כלם שכבו בכבוד), the corpse of the powerful ruler, who is cast down from heaven and behind whom one has doubtless to look originally for an Assyrian king,[19] is to be thrown out of the grave, be covered with the corpses of those who have been "pierced with the sword" (מטעני חרב v 19) and thereby be transformed to a state of the greatest impurity.

These concepts have, however, become much more strongly schematized in Ezekiel. What appears in Isaiah 14 as an unprecedented individual measure taken against a particularly evil despot has become in Ezekiel a general, lower category of burial. It will not come as a surprise that with Ezekiel, who as a priest (1:3) is particularly concerned with the separation of clean and unclean and with related cultic practices (22:26; 44:23), the category of the "uncircumcised" is particularly prominent. But Lods has drawn attention to the fact that in the foreign oracles in Ezekiel groups are often put into the category of the uncircumcised, although historically the practice of circumcision must be accepted in their particular case. Thus 28:10 threatened the king of Tyre with the "death of the uncircumcised." According to Sanchuniaton, however, the Phoenicians practiced circumcision.[20] For the Egyptians, whose king (according to 31:18) was to lie "amongst the uncircumcised," a fate with which here in 32:19, 28 all Egypt is threatened, Herodotus appears as counter-witness.[21] These observations lead to the conclusion that in the "death of the uncircumcised" and the "lying with the uncircumcised" we have a category of existence in the underworld which need not in every case agree with the earthly circumstances of the nations who are banished to that place. This category has been formed, according to Lods, primarily from the standpoint of members of Israel's own community. Whoever of that community did not bear the sign of circumcision remained excluded from the family grave. Among the Greeks, it is the ἄωροι, those who died prematurely, who find no rest after death.[22] In the belief in the *limbus infantium* there is the echo of such concepts in the period of the Christian church. In Ezek 32: 17–32, this death has become a category of punishment which stretches far beyond the sphere indicated by its name.

Eissfeldt has completed Lods's investigation in terms of "those slain by the sword" as well. In their case, too, it is basically a question not simply of people killed in war generally, but of the category of those who have been "murdered and put to death," who, like the miscarriages and the uncircumcised, are "thrown on to a place separated from the resting place of those who have received honorable burial or have been buried there and who, correspondingly, have been designated in the under-

17 *ANET* 52–57; *AOT* 206–210, *ANET* 106–109; *AOT* 210–212, *ANET* 103–104; *AOT* 206, *ANET* 107. On Egypt see Hermann Kees, *Totenglauben und Jenseitsvorstellungen der alten Ägypter* (Berlin: Akademie, ²1956). See further Kroll, *Gott und Hölle.*

18 On this see, e.g., Gottfried Quell, "Jesaja 14:1–23" in *Festschrift Friedrich Baumgärtel zum 70. Geburtstag* (Erlangen: Universitätsbund Erlangen, 1959), 131–157.

19 Hempel, *Literatur,* 29; Quell (see preceding fn.).

20 Fragment 36.

21 2, 104; on this see *AOBAT* 158; *ANEP* 629; the text in *ANET* 326; and Josephus *c. Apionem* II, 13 (§137, 142).

22 According to E. Rohde, *Psyche* (Freiburg i. B.: J. C. B. Mohr [Paul Siebeck], 1898), 373f.

world a dishonorable abode separated from the place of those others."[23] In the above-cited passage in Rohde, alongside the ἄωροι, mention is made also of the βιαιοθάνατοι as men who after death find no rest. In this connection reference may be made to the Aeneid VI, 426–441, where "those who have died young" (*infantium animae*), "those who have been falsely condemned to death" (*falso damnati crimine mortis*) and "the innocent suicides who were weary of life" (*qui sibi letem insontes perperere manu lucemque perosi proiecere animas*) have their special place in the underworld. In the OT see, for example, Jer 16:4 with its strange ממותי תחלאים ("of deadly diseases").

These rather general statements pave the way for the correct understanding of the lament in vv 19–32. When the prophet proclaims the רדה ("go down") against Egypt, this is, in the first instance, only a general sentence of death. In the associated command to lie with the uncircumcised and those slain by the sword, the declaration of punishment is made more specific. They are threatened not simply with death, but with a dishonorable death, expulsion to the spheres of uncleanness and unrest even in the underworld below, disgrace among the "people of old" (עם עולם 26:20).

■ **32:20f** To the pronouncement of judgment there have been appended in vv 20b, 21 a group of additions, which individually can no longer be clearly interpreted and which in 𝔊, in so far as they are even attested there (see notes on vv 20f), are arranged differently. Among them v 21a stands out, speaking of Egypt's being addressed by the גבורים ("heroes") of the underworld, who are referred to in v 27. The strange hand is revealed in the divergent description אלי גבורים ("strong heroes"). 𝔊 assimilates the two descriptions to each other. It is unlikely, as suggested by Hölscher (following Hitzig, Cornill, Jahn), that in the אלי גבורים ("strong heroes") there is a reference to the conquerors of Egypt, who are described in גבורים ("heroes") in 32:12, and that, on the basis of the איל גוים of 31:11, this refers to the leaders of these conquerors. Just as unlikely is any reference to the אל גבור ("Mighty God") of Is 9:5 (so Procksch). Rather, a later hand seeks to introduce here the heroes, or their spokesmen, mentioned in v 27, in phraseology that is heightened in the manner typical of Ezekiel. V 21a may in fact be aimed, as a marginal note, at v 19 understood as the word of these spokesmen, as 𝔊 too has understood it and arranged it. The expansion presupposes Is 14:10, 16f. This speaking on the part of the figures of the underworld does not belong to the original text.

■ **32:22f** This, rather, began immediately after the cry in vv 19, 20a[1] with the more detailed description of the underworld and its inhabitants. Three great nations are first presented, who lie in the place of dishonorable burial. They are each introduced by their name, which is here (by contrast with מצרים "Egypt") treated as feminine, the national personality regarded as a kind of collective mother figure who has her great grave, round which lies her great people (קהל "array" or המון "pomp"), just as, for example, at Giza the mastaba tombs of the nobles lie round the pyramid of the king.

In first place Assyria and her "array" (קהל, 17:17 note a) are mentioned. This is the great power which immediately preceded the Babylonian state. Details of its fall, which is here presupposed as an event of the past, are given in the Gadd-Wiseman Chronicle with the cool objectivity of an annalistic chronicle. In the prophecy of Isaiah, on the other hand, we hear the echo of the horror experienced at the cruel hand of this great power, which arbitrarily thrust aside nations' frontiers, plundered their treasures (10:13f) and thus had spread terror in its path on earth above. It is possible to hear clearly the echo of this prophetic indictment in the expression, unique to Ezekiel, נתן חתית ("to spread terror"). While this may also have been used once in 26:17 in a lament over Tyre, yet it is essentially predominant in 32:17ff (seven times in vv 23–27, 30, 32; from v 27 onwards it is partly abbreviated and used differently), the passage which characterizes Assyria in the first instance with this expression. Here speaks a period of time which has experienced something of the terror spread by the great military powers. Thus over the fate of this power, which ends up in the underworld with its hordes of those ignominiously "pierced by the sword," even if the reference to the terror spread abroad by it is not introduced, as in v 26, explicitly by means of the causative particle, there lies nevertheless the accent of well-deserved, divine retribution.

23 Eissfeldt, "Schwerterschlagene," 81.

The statement about Assyria, which no longer mentions explicitly the "lying amongst the uncircumcised," has then had added to it in the relative clause of v 23abα a later, explanatory interpretation, which by the method of "resumption" (note b) has been inserted into the text. Assyria's grave is to lie in the "lowest depths," just as is said in Is 14:15, the only other passage where ירכתי בור occurs in the OT, of the fallen head of state. This is clearly a designation of the dishonorable place apart.

■ **32:24f** Alongside Assyria is Elam. The history of this eastern neighbor of Babylon, whose capital Susa still lies in the plain but whose hinterland stretched far up into the mountains, is in large areas still quite obscure.[24] The Assyrian chronicles reveal, however, that in the forties of the seventh century B.C. there was a great struggle for power between Assyria and Elam. Ashurbanipal reports immeasurable booty which he had snatched from the conquered Susa. In the subsequent period, too, Elamite kings are still mentioned. The oracle of Jeremiah against Elam, dated at the beginning of Zedekiah's reign (49:34–39), could be directed against hopes which expected a rebellion in Elam to lead to the fall of the hated neo-Babylonian power (Rudolph, *Jeremia*). The period of Cyrus is still aware of kings in this area. But the power and significance of Elam seems to have been broken by Ashurbanipal. "At that time Elam received its death blow . . . from then on there is no more Elamite history."[25] Ezekiel speaks from the experience of the contemporary political hegemony in Mesopotamia when he presents Elam as a power in the realm of the dead. Similarly, when Elam—which in P's table of nations (originating in Babylonia?) in Gen 10:22 (the basis for 1 Chr 1:17) precedes, as Shem's firstborn, the second-born Asshur—appears as a power which has spread terror among the nations of the world, this too is a statement made on the basis of this area's political past. At times, Elam, by its attacks and raids into Babylonian territory (the Hammurabi stele was discovered in Susa, a piece of captured booty), was the dreaded tormentor of this region.

Like Assyria it now lies dishonored in its grave deep in the underworld along with its pomp. It is doubtless the expression of historically correct knowledge when a later hand has added the supplementary observation (v 24 note c) that it had gone uncircumcised to its grave. For the present this information cannot be confirmed. The basic text has, then, in the case of Elam gone beyond what was said about Assyria and has explicitly maintained that Elam in its ignominious burial is bearing shame as punishment for the terror which it spread abroad.

■ **32:26** On the power mentioned in third position (v 26, see also v 25 note b), Mesech-Thubal, see above.[26] The unconnected occurrence of the two names is unusual, but there is hardly justification for the deletion of תבל ("Thubal") with Bertholet or for the insertion of the copula (note b, Ehrlich, *Randglossen*, and Fohrer). Against the latter is the treatment of the double name as a singular in what follows; against the former is the observation that the two names are otherwise always found connected (with the exception of the uncertain משך "Mesech" in Ps 120:5). The names point to the area of Asia Minor, from which in the seventh century came the sinister attacks of the Cimmerians and the Scythians, the echo of which can still be heard in chapters 38f.[27] If these powers still played a dangerous role in the final phase of the history of Assyria, if, for example, an Esarhaddon still "lived in perpetual fear particularly of the *Gimirrai* (Cimmerians) in the north east,"[28] then this danger receded after the fall of Assyria, doubtless as a result of the assimilation of the Cimmerians by the Medes, whose successors were then of great historical significance in the Persian empire. If Ezekiel here regards Mesech-Thubal, which historically is viewed as vaguely part of these dangerous northern groups, as a power which is already dead in his period and is buried in the depths of the underworld, then this will correspond to the experience of the inhabitants of the Babylonian plain at the height of Nebuchadnezzar's power, the period when, according to v 17, the oracle was uttered. That then in another context this nightmare could recur will be shown by chapters 38f. 32:26, on the other hand, looks back on Mesech-Thubal as on a historical power in the past and describes its dishonorable burial place with the words which have already been used of Assyria and Elam. Except that the basic text, too, which ought to preserve for us reliable information, speaks of them as uncircumcised and slain by the sword and mentions

24 See, e.g., *RA* 2, 324ff; Hartmut Schmökel, *Geschichte des alten Vorderasien*, HO II, 3 (Leiden: Brill, 1957).

25 Schmökel, *Geschichte*, 281.

26 Pp. 65f on 27:13.

27 On this see Hölscher, *Drei Erdkarten*, 21f.

28 Schmökel, *Geschichte*, 274.

specifically that the terror spread abroad by them is the reason for their rejection to the lowest depths of the realm of the dead. The end of this strophe, which is contained in the addition to v 25 (v 25 note b), maintains, however, that the northern peoples, like Elam, bear their shame and lie among the slain.

■ **32:27** With this dishonorable burial, however, there is contrasted the honorable one of a fourth group, from which the first three groups are spatially separated. Gen 6:1–4 retains in a fragment the memory of that early period of the "heroes." The latter are thought of there, on the basis of some uncanny feeling, as the fruit of the intermarriage of heavenly beings with earthly women. Greek traditions about the heroic age speak with untroubled vividness of the demi-god figures of this period (Heracles, Theseus, and others). But even the Babylonian epic can say of Gilgamesh: "Two-thirds of him is god, one-third is human."[29] These characteristics of the terrible presumption which, according to Humbert, precisely gives to the giants in the OT the description נְפִילִים ("those who have been cast down") have disappeared entirely in 32:27.[30] Even if the נפלים ("who fell") of 𝔐 is a play on the word נְפִילִים or should even be replaced by it (note b), the reference to these figures of "hoar antiquity" (עולם)[31] is unaffected, as if to a distant human memory. Reports have been made of mighty deeds done by these early heroes (see, e.g., what is recorded in Gen 10:8–12 of the גִּבֹּר "hero" Nimrod), and these win for them an honorable grave in the next world. The Gilgamesh Epic attests the great age of such an idea of the possibility of a better life in the grave, if there, in the conversation between Gilgamesh and Enkidu after the preliminary cries of terror, it can be read: "Him who died the death of iron, have you seen?" "I have seen him. He lies upon a couch and drinks pure water." "Him who was killed in battle, have you seen?" "I have seen him. His father and his mother raise up his head, and his wife is bent over him." Alongside this, there stands immediately again the threat of a calamitous fate: "Him whose corpse was cast out upon the steppe, have you seen?" "I have seen him. That which has been left in the pot, morsels of food which have been thrown into the street he eats."[32] If there is here a reflection of the burial of the slain and of the cult of the dead practiced at the grave which determines the difference in people's fate in the world of the dead, then in the description of Ezek 32:17–32 there is mingled something of the nature of a doctrine of world ages, with which Hesiod can be compared as a close parallel.[33] The heroes of the heroic age went to their rest in honor, in possession of their full military armor which they use in the underworld as pillow and blanket. The great ones of the present, on the other hand, those of this wicked harsh age with its terrors, are condemned to the ignominy of a dishonorable grave. The counterpart of the fate of the גבורים ("heroes"), which is not presented by Ezek 32:17–32, can be found in Is 14:11: "Your pomp is brought down to the underworld . . . maggots are the bed beneath you, and worms are your covering."

It is therefore strange that it is said of the heroes of antiquity also, with the explicit use of the particle of causality, that terror of them reigned among the living. The logic of this causal connection is not entirely clear. Thus it is possible that the clause has been added rather unthinkingly by a later hand in dependence on the preceding statement about Mesech-Thubal. If one wishes to assert that it is part of the basic text, then one will have to understand the כי (here "for") in a very neutral sense, analogous to the אשׁר ("who") of vv 23, 24. The "terror at them" is then to be regarded as a simple statement, quite devoid of any judgment about the great power of these figures, in which it is noteworthy that the explicit use of the expression נתנו חתית(ם) ("they spread terror [before them]") of vv 23, 24, 26(25) is avoided, the expression whereby the spreading abroad of terror is attributed to Assyria, Elam and Mesech-Thubal as an active wrong.

■ **32:28** After this description of the two types of burial in the underworld, v 28 by way of conclusion returns to

29 *AOT* 151, *ANET* 73.
30 Humbert, "Démesure," 70.
31 See Jenni, "Das Wort ʿōlām," 28, 29f.
32 *AOT* 185f, *ANET* 99.
33 *Works and Days,* lines 109ff. For the heroic age and the fate of the heroes in the next world see especially lines 156–173.

Egypt, who is the person directly addressed by this whole description: "You [on the basis of the introduction in v 18a we may expand here to: 'Egypt and your pomp'] will share in the dishonorable burial with uncircumcised and those put to death or murdered by the sword." That is the judgment passed by the prophetic word, which now fits Egypt too into the group of powers which have fallen and been buried without honor.

■ **32:29** At a later point in time the oracle has experienced a continuation. This is connected to what has gone before in the same style, but can no longer achieve the severity of these statements. Also the Mesopotamian arena has been abandoned, and we find, in the first instance, the product of a Palestinian situation. Edom, on which comparison may be made with 25:12–14, becomes in what follows, since it abuts on Judaean territory, the real enemy in the land.[34] Thus it is mentioned here in first place (it is otherwise in Ezek 25). And the difference between here and vv 22ff is that the mention of Edom among the inhabitants of the world of the dead is no longer a reference to a fall which has already taken place, but is a threat of one that is still to come (analogous to 25:12–14; 35). In the description, it becomes noticeable, however, that Edom is not comparable with the great powers. As its representatives, נשיאים ("princes") are mentioned. Only a later expansion feels obliged to add the kings (see, e.g., Gen 36:31–39).[35] Also, doubtless out of a proper awareness of Edom's relative size, nothing is said of the terror it spread among the living, but, more restrainedly, simply of its "strength." גבורה, apart from the secondary vv 20f, occurs nowhere else in the book of Ezekiel.[36] Edom, for which Josephus attests circumcision in the Maccabean period, is forced to lie in the underworld in the dishonorable place of the uncircumcised.[37]

■ **32:30** Alongside the princes of Edom there are mentioned the נסיכי צפון ("princes of the north"). According to van der Ploeg, נסיך ("prince") is a foreign loan-word to be connected with the Akkadian *nasīku*.[38] Since Arabic *nasaka* means "to sacrifice," it may originally have designated the tribal chief as priest and sacrificer. It no longer has these overtones in Hebrew but denotes the sheikh, the prince, the ruler. It is found also in Josh 13:21; Mic 5:4; Ps 83:12 (Sir 16:7). But what is meant by the "princes of the north"? Jer 25:26 with "kings of the north" is thinking of the great empires of the far north. Elam and Media have been mentioned immediately previously.[39] Since the north was already mentioned in vv 24, 26, one wonders what the renewed mention of it here should signify. Is the added כֻּלָּם ("all of them") specifically intended to complete the circle of princes of northern nations? Presumably what is envisaged here, as in v 30, is still further destruction of enemies and a forward reference to the event of chapters 38f.

The name of the inhabitants צדני[ם] (here "Phoenicians"), which is then added (note c), is probably intended to include in this "north" also the north that is adjacent to Palestine. By צדני is meant not only the inhabitants of the city of Sidon, but in a wider sense the Phoenicians generally.[40] It can no longer be determined with certainty what actual political polemic is involved in the use of this particular name. Should one think of the extension of Sidonian power to the regions of Dor and Joppa, of which, for example, Eshmunazar speaks?[41] The description in v 30 is somewhat fuller than in the case of Edom. There is an (abbreviated) account of the terror spread by the northern kings. There is also a reference to their valor in which they have been put to "shame" (בושׁ in Ezekiel only otherwise in 16:52, 63; 36:32 of the shame felt by a pardoned Israel). When it is then said that they lie down uncircumcised with those slain by the sword, there is there a recollection which fits the more distant northern nations (see on vv 24, 26).[42] V 30bβ takes up vv 24bβ, 25bα^2.

■ **32:31** With a characteristic turning to consolation, which for the first time corresponds to the genuine lament, the first addition, vv 29–31, closes.[43] In the discovery of the similarity between his ignominious fate and that of the nations mentioned, the Pharaoh will

34 See above pp. 16f. See also chapter 35.
35 On the gradation מלך–נשיא see 1, 209.
36 On the use of this expression see Fredriksson, *Jahwe als Krieger,* 64–66.
37 *Antiquities* XIII 9, 1.
38 van der Ploeg, "chefs du peuple," 51.
39 See also the ממלכות צפונה of Jer 1:15 which belong with the mysterious "foe from the north" whose apocalyptic arrival is spoken of in Ezekiel chapters 38f.
40 See above p. 97.
41 *AOT* 447, *ANET* 662. On this see Kurt Galling, "Die syrisch-palästinische Küste nach der Beschreibung bei Pseudo-Skylax," *ZDPV* 61 (1938): 82.
42 On the Phoenicians see above p. 173 on Tyre.
43 See above pp. 170f.

console himself for what has happened to his pomp. The same thought was expressed in 31:16 from the point of view of those below who experience the coming of the Pharaoh (represented in the image of the tree). The secondary character of vv 29–31 is clear also from the fact that the Pharaoh is explicitly mentioned here, whereas in vv 17–28 it was personified Egypt. The addition in v 31b*a* (note c) is also to be understood as an explicit interpretative note, the aim of which is to regard the whole as referring to Pharaoh.

■ **32:32** The second addition, which like the first points to the Pharaoh, is not entirely unambiguous in what it says, taking as it does the vocabulary of the basic oracle in a new sense. What is clear is that it is referring to an act of Yahweh. But does it refer to it retrospectively: Yahweh had given Pharaoh power to spread terror on earth, but now (consecutive perfect) he will have to lie with the uncircumcised? Or is the clause with the consecutive perfect to be subordinated to the preceding clause: Yahweh now spreads terror at Pharaoh among the living when they see how he must depart in death and shame?[44] חתיתו ("terror before him") would then be being used consciously in a different sense.

Aim

The oracle in 32:17–32 is, in its basic form, extremely restrained in its theological expression. Only the introduction, which states that the prophet has been summoned by God to utter his lament which is basically a proclamation of judgment, reveals that this is an action between God and the great power. Only in the brief reference to the origin of the proclaimed oracle is it clear that this is God's great reckoning with all that on the political stage, "in the land of the living," declares itself to be "pomp" (המון) and powerful "array" (קהל; the appendix adds to these the key-word "might" גבורה).

Thus the prophetic oracle, with great ease, reaches out into the old tradition of its period and of the world around it—at any rate in such a way that it takes from that tradition all that it might contain in the way of mythical power hostile to God. There are memories of gigantic human figures of a vigorous early period in man's history. All that power has now been summoned to death. It now lies in the depths, eliminated, sunk, banished to an eternal silence.

But the prophetic oracle achieves its real passion when it comes closer to its own time. There were powers before whom the world trembled—the memory of this, handed down by fathers and grandfathers, still echoes with full vigor in the present. These powers believed themselves to be lords of their era, empowered to terrify the whole world of the living. And then death summoned them, brought them down in death and shame—"put to shame in their might" says the expander (v 30). With this reference the prophetic oracle opens for its hearers a view into their history. Man must see and hear what has already happened as a result of the cry of "Down!," a cry authorized by God. He must remain alive to the history which he experiences and not forget how powers that yesterday terrified him to the very borders of despair are recalled and banished to shame.

Against this background, then, there comes the actual call that the prophet, at the command of his God, addresses to the pomp of the power which, in its day, thought that it could defy God with its own politics: Down! God will banish you too below.

The basic oracle does not attempt to make any general observation about the transitoriness of all things. Nor does it try to lead only to the weary consolation which the later expander (v 31) allows to the Pharaoh. It tries to proclaim what God has to say to the "pomp" of the great powers in the land of the living.

Only the final expander has slightly disrupted the reticence of the original oracle when he makes God speak explicitly of his own activity—either the activity in which God gives men power for a time to exercise their freedom, an activity over which God certainly does not fall asleep, or the other activity, that God in his judgment bestows saving terror on those who see it, in the hope that they awake to a proper fear of him and return to him.

44 On this see, e.g., the terror felt by the surrounding country at the fall of the king of Tyre, referred to in 26:15ff; 27:28ff; 28:19. On Pharaoh see 31:15ff.

The Watchman and his Consolation: the Freedom to Repent

Bibliography

See 1,369 on chapter 18.

David Heinrich Müller
Ezechiel-studien (Berlin: Reuther & Reichard, 1895), 34–48; reprinted as *idem, Biblische Studien* 1 (Wien: Hölder, 1904).

P. P. Nober
"Sein Blut komme über uns und unsere Kinder!" *Freiburger Rundbrief,* Nummer 41/44 (1958/59): 73–77.

Henning Graf Reventlow
"Sein Blut kommer über sein Haupt," *VT* 10 (1960): 311–327.

H. Staudigel
Die Begriffe Gerechtigkeit und Leben und das Problem der Gerechtigkeit Gottes bei Ezechiel, Unpub. Diss. (Rostock, 1957).

33

1 [a]And the word of Yahweh came to me: 2/ Son of man, speak to the members of your people and say to them:

If I bring the sword[a] over a land and the people of the land take a man from their midst[b] and make him their watchman[a], 3/ and if he[a] sees the sword[b] coming against the land[c] and blows the horn and warns[d] the people, 4/ and (if then) anyone[a] hears the sound of the horn but does not take warning[b] and the sword[c] comes[b] and takes him away[b], then his (the man's) blood[d] will be on his own head. 5/ He has heard the sound of the horn but has not taken warning[a]. His

33: 1a 𝔖 prefixes a superscription זוהרא ולובבא "ad-
1 monition and comfort."

2 2a 𝔗 again has an elucidatory paraphrase דקטלין בחרבא; 𝔊^{A} theologizes *κρίμα αἵματος.*

b 𝔐 מקציהם. קצה denotes, in the first instance, the outermost, the edge and then also the whole surrounded by that edge, cf. מקצהו 25:9. In the watered-down sense of "from the midst of" also, e.g., Gen 47:2. Ehrlich, *Randglossen,* is different, "from their ablest." Fohrer "(the citizens) without exception." 𝔊 *ἐξ αὐτῶν,* Θ *ἐκ μέρους αὐτῶν,* 𝔙 *de novissimis suis.*

c 𝔗, which renders 𝔐 צפה in 3:17; 33:7 by מליף, here harmonizes with the following command to הזהיר and translates למזהרא. Should מזהרנא be read as in v 6?

3 3a 𝔙 elucidates *et ille viderit.*

b 𝔗 as in v 2, see note a.

c 𝔐 על הארץ is abbreviated by 𝔖 to עליהון.

d 𝔐 והזהיר is rendered more colorlessly by 𝔊 *καὶ σημάνῃ,* 𝔙 *et annuntiaverit.* 'Α Σ are more precise with (*καὶ*) *προφυλάξει.*

4 4a The internal subject of ושמע השמע is rendered literally by 𝔊 *και ἀκούσῃ ὁ ἀκούσας,* while 𝔙 *audiens autem, quisquis ille est* is concerned to bring out the indefiniteness of the subject which is intended by the Hebrew expression.

b 𝔐 at this point passes to the narrative perfect (נזהר) with the following consecutive imperfects (ותקחהו . . . ותבוא).

c 𝔐 חרב without the article as already in v 2. 𝔊 *ἡ ῥομφαία* and 𝔖 חרבא scarcely necessitate the emendation to החרב (so Herrmann, Bertholet, Fohrer). On 𝔗 see v 2 note a.

d 𝔗 makes explicit חובת קטוליה.

5 5a V 5a is recapitulatory and is simply omitted by

blood[b] will be upon himself. If he had
taken warning, he would have saved his
life[c].
6 But if the watchman sees the sword coming and does not blow[a] the horn and the
people are not warned[a] and the sword[b]
comes[a] and takes one[c] of them away[a],
then that man is taken away because of
his guilt, but I shall require his[d] blood at
the hand of the watchman.
7 It is you, son of man, that I have made
watchman for the house of Israel. If you
now hear a word from my mouth[a], then
you are to warn them of me[b]. 8/ If I say to
the godless <>[a]: You shall certainly die[b],
and if you have not spoken to warn the
godless[c] of his way[d], then he, the godless[c], will die because of his guilt, but his
blood I shall require at your hand. 9/ But
if you have warned the godless[a] [of his
way, so that he turn aside from it][b], and
he has not turned aside from his way,
then he will die because of his guilt, but
you will have saved your life.
10 But you, son of man, say to the house of
Israel: This is what you say[a]: Our transgressions and our sins are upon us, and in

𝔖, which likes to abbreviate the text.

b 𝔗 see v 4 note d.

c 𝔐 נזהר is, following Wellhausen (in Smend), almost universally emended to הזהיר (Cornill; Ehrlich, *Randglossen;* Herrmann; Toy; Bertholet) and the הוא referred to the watchman. But the versions, with great unanimity, attest the נזהר of 𝔐. Since, in addition, the saving of his life in the case of the watchman is otherwise always expressed by means of the root נצל (3:19, 21; 33:9—the root is also found in Ezekiel at 7:19; 13:21, 23; 14:14, 16, 18, 20; 33:12; 34:10, 12, 27), the statement which differs from that by the use of מלט (also in 17:15, 18) is surely to be read as in 𝔐 and referred to the person warned. Fohrer in any case believes that the whole of v 5, which he reads as in 𝔐, is to be regarded as an explanatory gloss. See also note a.

6 6a Here too the description again passes to the narrative perfect (נזהר . . . תקע) and consecutive imperfect (ותבוא . . . ותקח), see v 4 note b.

b 𝔐 חרב. 𝔊 ἡ ῥομφαία, 𝔖 חרבא do not necessitate the emendation to החרב here either (Herrmann, Bertholet, Fohrer); see v 4 note c. 𝔗 as in v 2, see note a.

c 𝔐 נפש "a living being." 𝔖 repeats נפשא after the immediately following הוא, which then, in 𝔖, is consequently read as הי.

d In 𝔊 the suffix remains untranslated. Otherwise in 𝔊^{26,410,544} 𝔎^{Bo} 𝔄̈ Arm (αὐτοῦ), 𝔊^{AL} 𝔎^{Sa} 𝔄 (αὐτῆς), 𝔏^{CS} *huius sanguine(m).*

7 7a 𝔗 ממימרי softens the anthropomorphism of 𝔐.

b 𝔐 והזהרת אתם ממני remain unattested in 𝔊 𝔏^{CS}, but are factually necessary and in the parallel passage in 3:17 are also attested by 𝔊. In addition, see 3:17 note a.

8 8a The רשע which is still found in 𝔐, which 𝔅 *impie* understands as a vocative and which 𝔗 makes definite (רשיעא—as a vocative?), is not attested by MS$^{Ken\ 251}$ 𝔊 𝔏^{CS} 𝔖 𝔎 𝔄 or the parallel passage in 3:18 (33:14) and should be deleted as dittography.

b See 3:18 note a.

c 3:18 too attests here on both occasions רשע without the article. On this basis (against Herrmann, Bertholet, Fohrer), in spite of 𝔊 𝔗, it should not be emended. See also 33:9, 11.

d In 3:18 there follows הרשעה לחיתו. But see note d there.

9 9a On רשע without the article see v 8 note c.

b 𝔐 מדרכו לשוב ממנה, which is supplementary to 3:19 and which leads to the circumstantial translation of 𝔅, while 𝔖 once again abbreviates, gives the impression of being a secondary interpretative element. See also 3:18 note c.

10 10a The כי which introduces the quotation in 𝔐 is attested only in 𝔊^{L} and in the earliest hexaplaric textual witnesses, which betray the influence of 'A (on 62' see Ziegler, *Ezechiel,* 35). One would also gladly dispense with the לאמר which is missing in 𝔖, but it occurs in the introduction to a quotation also

them we are wasting away[b]; how can we
then live? 11/ Say[a] to them: As I live,
says [the Lord][b] Yahweh, I have no de-
light in the death of the godless, but (in
the fact)[c], that the godless[d] turn from his
way and live. Turn back, turn back from
your evil[e] ways! Why will you then die, O
house of Israel?
12 **But you, son of man[a], say to the members**
of your people: The righteousness of the
righteous man will not save him on the
day when he sins, nor will the godless-
ness of the godless man bring him down
on the day when he turns from his god-
lessness[b] [and the righteous cannot live
by it (i.e. his righteousness) on the day
when he sins][c].
13 **If I say of the righteous: He shall live[a]—but**
he relies on his righteousness and does
unrighteousness, none of his righteous
deeds[b] shall be remembered. <>[c] Be-
cause of the unrighteousness that he has
done—because of it he shall die.
14 **If, however, I say to the godless: You shall**
surely die![a], and he turns from his sin and
does what is just and right, 15/ gives

in v 24; 35:12; 37:18.

b 𝔏^{CS} *(in ipsis) non tabescimus* is doubtless a scribal error for *nos tabescimus.*

11 11a 𝔏^{CS} make the transition to v 11 with *propter hoc.*

b אדני is lacking in 𝔊^{L}, 𝔏^{CS} 𝔎, see Appendix 1.

c On the construction with כי אם see Brockelmann §168.

d On רשע without the article see v 8 note c.

e 𝔐 הרעים remains unattested in 𝔊 𝔏^{S}, which read the singular ὁδοῦ *(via).* It is not attested earlier than 𝔊^{A} 𝔄 Arm. The expression דרכיכם הרעים occurs in Ezekiel also in 20:44; 36:31 (see also 2 Kgs 17:13; Zech 1:4; 2 Chr 7:14). Thus 𝔐 may be original. 𝔊 could have been influenced by v 9.

12 12a The introductory ואתה בן אדם is missing in 𝔊 𝔎, but is attested by 𝔏^{S} 𝔙 𝔗 𝔖. It is clearly justified by the discernible new beginning in v 12.

b A literal translation would be: "The righteousness of the righteous does not serve him on the day of his offense, and the godlessness of the godless—he will not be brought low by it on the day of his turning from his godlessness."

c 𝔊 (𝔎) read in v 12b only καὶ δίκαιος οὐ μὴ δύνηται σωθῆναι. This is as unlikely as the original form of the text as is 𝔐, whose בה has no discernible point of reference in the self-contained v 12b. Toy's reading, which has the וצדקת הצדיק from v 12a in place of the simple וצדיק, would give a more comprehensible text, but has no support in the tradition, in which 𝔙 (see also 𝔊^{L}) expands the בה to *in justitia sua,* while 𝔖 simply omits it. Thus it is more correct to see in v 12b a gloss, which, in an unskillful fashion, repeats the thought of v 12aα and disturbs the parallelism between v 12aα and v 12aβ, a parallelism which is continued in vv 13//14–16.

13 13a 𝔐 חיה יחיה is strongly emphatic: "He shall certainly live," see also 3:21; 18:9(13), 17, 19,21,28; 33:15, 16. The omission of חיה יחיה ו in 𝔊 𝔎 𝔄̈ is certainly to be regarded as an error. The reading ζωῇ ζήσῃ, which is offered by individual hexaplaric witnesses (and 𝔏^{S} 𝔄) and seems to suggest a חיה תחיה (so Cornill, Herrmann, Toy, Bertholet, Fohrer), is impressive, first of all because of its formal uniformity to the word to the godless in v 14. But it is immediately suspect, for the very same reason, as an attempt at harmonization. 𝔐 deserves the preference. See the exposition.

b With Q (𝔊 𝔏^{S} 𝔙 𝔗) the plural צדקתיו should be read against K (𝔖) צדקתו and as already in 3:20. See also 18:24.

c Instead of 𝔐 ובעולו, בעולו should be read with 𝔊 𝔏^{S} 𝔗 𝔄; see also 18:26.

14 14a 𝔐 מות תמות 𝔊 θανάτῳ θανατωθήσῃ, see 3:18 note a. The assimilation made by Ehrlich, *Randglossen,* to the third person of the speech to the righteous (v 13) is a harmonization just as inadmissible as the opposite process in v 13 (note a). See the exposition.

back a pledge <>[a], restores what he has stolen, walks in the statutes (which lead) to life without doing injustice—he shall live[b], not die[c]. 16/ All the sins[a] which hs has committed[b] shall not be remembered against him[c]. He has done what was just and right. He shall live.

17 **The members of your people say: The way of <Yahweh>[a] is not just[b], when it is their own[c] way that is not just. 18/ If the righteous turns from his righteousness and does unrighteousness, then he will die because of them (i.e. the unrighteous deeds)[a]. 19/ But if the godless turns from his godlessness and does what is just and right, then he will live as a result of them (i.e. of the righteous deeds)[a]. 20/ But you say[a]: The way of <Yahweh>[b] is not just[c]. I shall judge each one of you according to his ways, O house of Israel[d].**

15 15a The meaningless רשע of 𝔐, which is not attested by 𝔊 (𝔊^{L} 𝔖^{h} Tht ὀφείλοντος, 𝔏^{S} *debitoris* is a harmonization with 18:7), is either a corrupt doublet of ישיב or a making explicit (Toy). It should at any rate be deleted. Cf. 18:(7) 12 (16) and 3:19 note a.

b See v 13 note a.

c 𝔊 𝔏^{S} 𝔖 insert the copula in three places in v 15, see 1:4 note a.

16 16a The plural verb form necessitates the reading of Q (𝔊 𝔏^{S} 𝔖 𝔅 𝔗) חטאתיו against K חטאתו. Cf. v 13 note b.

b The lack of the ἃς ἥμαρτεν in 𝔊^{L} 𝔄̈ does not permit the deletion of 𝔐 אשר חטא (Cornill). 𝔐 חטא has been replaced in eleven MSS by the weaker עשה, cf. 𝔖 דעבד, also 18:24.

c On 𝔐 לו see 18:22 note a.

17 17a See 18:25 note a.

b 𝔅 *non est aequi ponderis via domini*, 𝔖 לא שפירא אורחה דמריא. 𝔗 clearly softens the rebellious statement לא מפרשן לנא אורחת טובא דיהוה.

c On the prefixed המה see Gesenius-Kautzsch §143a, note 1.

18 18a See 18:26 note a. The בהם here, which corresponds to the עליהם there, is an embarrassment because of the absence of a clear word of reference. 𝔊 𝔏^{S} 𝔅 solve this by translating the preceding עול as a plural (ἀνομίας, *iniquitates*). 𝔖, on the other hand, renders 𝔐 בהם by a singular בה, while 𝔗 faithfully reproduces 𝔐. The reciprocal reference of 18:26 and 33:18 is also very clear at this precise point and is not to be deleted as a simple scribal error on the assumption of vertical dittography (Ehrlich, *Randglossen*). This also militates against Driver's suggestion ("Linguistic Problems," 180) to emend בהם to כמו (the latter unusual in Ezekiel). As in 18:26, it is to be assumed that the author of the text still had in mind from the earlier discussion the number of unrighteous deeds. 𝔐 ומת must not be emended here either (against Bertholet) to ימות.

19 19a עליהם is rendered literally, like בהם in v 18, by 𝔊 ἐν αὐτοῖς, 𝔏^{S} 𝔅 *in eis*, 𝔖 בהון.

20 20a 𝔊 (𝔏^{CS}) more expansively καὶ τοῦτό ἐστιν ὃ εἴπατε.

b See 18:25 note a.

c 𝔅 here has *non est recta* (𝔏^{CS} *directa*) *via domini*. Otherwise see v 17 note b.

d 𝔊^{A} (𝔎 𝔄) adds the concluding formula λέγει κύριος (see 18:30a).

The section 33:1–20 introduces the great third part of the book of Ezekiel. In that third part the proclamation of the coming salvation dominates the stage from chapter 34 onwards. The present section has, in the process of the editing of the book, been deliberately set at the beginning of that section and has pushed 33:21f, the account of the reporting of the fall of the city, which one would have expected immediately after chapter 24, still further away from its original context. The sequence chapter 24/33:21f has thus been severed in the editorial process by the great double insertion chaps 25–32 and 33:1-20.

33:1–20 speaks first of all of the prophet's appointment as watchman and addresses the cry for repentance to Israel and to each individual in her. The appointment as watchman has already been expressed at the beginning of the first part of the book in 3:17–21 in a secondary insertion connected with the call account. In the present form of the book, therefore, 33:1–20 has something of the weight of a second call to the prophet for the phase of proclamation at and after the fall of Jerusalem.

33:1–20 is not a self-contained, seamless complex. True, the only formula for a divine saying (v 11) has no divisive, but simply an emphatic function.[1] But the fourfold specific address to the prophet (simply בן אדם "son of man" in v 2, the fuller form ואתה בן אדם "but you, son of man" in vv 7, 10, 12) certainly divides the whole into four sections vv 2–6, 7–9, 10–11, 12–20. Of these, vv 2–6 and 7–9, which deal with the office of watchman, certainly belong more closely together, just as, on the other hand, do vv 10–11 and 12–20, which have their close correspondence in the complex 18:21–32 (and in 3:20–21). D. H. Müller has understood the three sections 3:17–21, chapter 18 and 33:1–20, under the heading "Plans and Achievement," as an increasingly more fully formed sequence of statements on the same theme, where "the third section seems to be a literary exposition of the first two."[2] It is, however, advisable first of all to examine the two sections vv 1–9 and vv 10–20 individually and only then to ask about their unity.

Form

■ 33:2–9 1. *The Watchman:* vv 2–6, 7–9. The first section, vv 2–6, contains the commission to the prophet to make a proclamation to his fellow countrymen. This is stylized in the form of a casuistic law suit in which the כי ("if") following the subject (vv 2, 6) points more specifically to the language of priestly legal casuistic.[3] In a long-winded subordinate clause, vv 2aβ–4a, the "case" is first of all paraphrased.[4] In contradistinction to the introductions of the individual cases in the Book of the Covenant, the "case" here is not so much defined and delimited as rather described in narrative style by a sequence of events.[5] The principal clause in v 4b, which proclaims the consequential punishment, is on the other hand terse and formulaic. That, however, no strict legal style is present is clear from v 5a with its remarkable recapitulation of the first case (vv 2–4). Here is not only legal order promulgated in unbiased objectivity, but it is explicitly enjoined with a decided parenetic tendency. The other possibility with regard to the person who has been warned by the watchman is then expounded quite tersely in v 5b without strict formulaic language. On the other hand, the style once again becomes austere in the description of the further possibility that the watchman could fail to proclaim the warning. The concluding expression of punishment, however, shows, as already the beginning of the description of the first case in v 2 (אביא "I bring"), the irruption of the personal divine speech into a neutral legal address. The neutral expression of punishment in v 5aβ is, in v 6bβ, changed to a divine address in the first person. The case, in which first of all the concern seems to be with the legal situation between the nation and the watchman appointed by it through its representatives, thereby acquires its full background. In this legal act of appointment of a watchman—this is already clear from the observations of the form—Yahweh himself is involved.

The second section vv 7–9, which is paralleled almost verbatim in 3:17–19, contains no further command to speak. Here Yahweh speaks to the prophet. One could speak of an oracle of appointment, in which Yahweh gives to the prophet his office and the commission included in that office. In the more detailed exposition of that commission, the casuistic style of the description of the office of watchman then becomes quite clear, parallel to the preceding section. The description itself is somewhat shortened, insofar as there is here no consideration of the two possibilities of behavior on the part of the person at whom the watchman's call is directed, but only

1 See 1,176 on 5:11.
2 Müller, *Ezechiel-studien*, 35.
3 See 1,302 on 14:1ff; p. 312 on 14:12ff; and p. 375 on chapter 18.
4 See Albrecht Alt, "Die Ursprünge des israelitischen Rechts" in *Kleine Schriften zur Geschichte des Volkes Israel* 1 (München: Beck, 1953), 286–288.
5 See v 4 note b and v 6 note a.

of the two possibilities on the part of the watchman himself. To the והצפה כי ("but if the watchman") of v 6 there corresponds the ואתה כי ("but if you") of v 9. The element of tradition used in v 8 in the description of the godless is best discussed in the context of the detailed exposition.

The close correspondence in form between vv 2–6 and vv 7–9 advises against a simple separation of the two units. They seem fundamentally to be mutually connected. Vv 2–6 have never, as is clear above all from v 6, been an independent section. The most that could be suggested is the possibility that in the first instance vv 7–9 existed as an independent oracle to which vv 2–6 were then added by way of exposition. In no case is it justified to delete, with Fohrer, vv 7–9 as a spurious later element and to replace it with 3:17–21. As has already been mentioned above, 3:20f is dependent on 18:24.[6]

Interpretation

■ **33:1, 2** In an undated oracular encounter Yahweh addresses the prophet ("son of man") and commissions him to speak to his fellow countrymen.[7] בני עמך ("members of your people") was encountered in 3:11, where the prophet was sent in particular to the exiles (אל הגולה אל בני עמך "to the exiles, to the members of your people"). It recurs in 33:12, 17, 30; 37:18. Elsewhere in the OT is it found in Dan 12:1 (11:14) (see also the בנות עמך "daughters of your people" Ezek 13:17). In comparison with the much more frequent בית ישראל ("house of Israel") (less common בני ישראל "people of Israel"), it expresses more forcefully the idea that in the exilic community it is a question of individuals who are to be addressed as such and not as the representatives of the people as a whole. In view of its content, the law suit developed by the watchman in vv 2–6 can be understood only with difficulty as a proclamation to the community. Thus it is not accidental that the introductory messenger formula is missing at the beginning. Rather, vv 2–6 are clearly (most of all in v 6) intended as a preparation for vv 7–9. The "exposition" in vv 7–9 is, however, directed only at the prophet himself. A corresponding exposition, directed at the people addressed by the watchman-prophet, would have been quite possible but does not occur. In its place there appears in vv 10–20 an address to the people (described as בית ישראל "house of Israel" in v 10 and as בני עמך "members of your people" in v 12), which makes no further reference to the image of the watchman but the content of which unmistakably expresses what was intended in the watchman oracle.

The watchman is introduced as a figure of a time of war. Even the casuistic oracle in 14:12–23, which in v 13 also begins with ארץ כי ("if/when a land"), speaks in its third case (v 17) of the sword which Yahweh summons (חרב אביא על הארץ "I bring a sword upon the land") and means by it the beginning of periods of warfare (see also 21:13–22). Both there and here the אביא ("I bring") right at the beginning expresses the idea that Yahweh himself in the sword approaches a nation as the hidden enemy. In such a case the watchman is the guard appointed by the responsible citizens,[8] who is to discover in time the dangerous attacks of the approaching enemy and to frustrate these by his warning of the defense troops. There is no lack in the OT of graphically described scenes which clearly depict the function of the צפה ("watchman").[9] In 2 Sam 18:24ff the watchman is on the roof of the gate keeping watch in the direction of the field of battle, in order to report as soon as possible the coming of messengers or the approach of the enemy forces. Similar is the watchman who, according to 2 Kgs 9:17ff, stands on the tower in Jezreel and keeps watch down into the Jordan valley.

■ **33:3** While here, as in 2 Sam 13:34 (1 Sam 14:16), the watchman reports by word of mouth, in Am 3:6 ("Is a trumpet blown in a city and the people are not afraid?") we see the raising of the alarm (by night?) by means of a horn (see also Jer 4:5, 19, 21; 6:1, 17 and other passages, as well as Joel 2:1). שופר ("horn"), originally a designation for the wild sheep (Akkadian *šaparu*), describes in the OT the ram's horn, which permits of only certain signal notes and which achieved significance not only for war but also for the cult in Israel and in Judaism (new and full moon Ps 81:4; year of jubilee Lev 25:9).[10]

■ **33:4f** Every watchman has a limited function. He can do nothing whatsoever to prevent the "coming" (בוא) of and the "taking away" (לקח) by the sword. Only the man who heeds the alarm warning and takes the necessary defen-

6 1, 143, 145f.

7 See 1, 144f; on "son of man" see 1, 131f.

8 On עם הארץ see 1, 209 on 7:27.

9 See Bardtke, "Erweckungsgedanke," 19–21.

10 See H. Seidel, "Horn und Trompete im alten Israel unter Berücksichtigung der 'Kriegsrolle' von Qum-

sive measures has the chance to save his life. The man who pays no heed to the signs, however, is himself responsible for forfeiting his life. This responsibility is described in the first instance by the graphic expression דמו בראשו יהיה ("his blood will be on his own head").[11] According to P. Nober this phrase reflects the oriental custom of carrying one's burdens on one's head. Thus a man's burden of guilt can also come on his head. The warning repetition in v 5 uses the weaker blood-guilt formula from 18:13 דמו בו יהיה ("his blood will be upon himself").[12]

■ **33:6** The watchman's responsibility is to give the alarm. If he fails here, then he is to be held responsible for the life of the person who has been taken away. In the closing phrase of v 6, however, it becomes clear what is really meant by the war image which is firmly to the fore. The idea that the person who is not warned is taken away "because of his guilt" reveals that what is meant by the person who is not warned is the unwarned sinner of v 8. And when Yahweh himself actually appears as the avenger of the blood of the person who has lost his life because of the watchman's negligence, then it must not be overlooked that we are not here dealing with an ordinary war among humans. Instead of the expression בקש דם ("to require blood") (3:18, 33:8), the unique expression דרש דם ("to require blood") occurs here.

■ **33:7–9** Thus vv 2–6 spill over into the oracle vv 7–9, in which Yahweh, in a direct address to the prophet, now fully reveals what is meant by the image of the watchman. There Ezekiel himself is now described as the watchman, and this idea has its pre-history in prophetic modes of speech. Already Jer 6:17 mentions that Yahweh has appointed watchmen for his people and is thinking there of the prophets. When in Hab 2:1 the prophet can say that he will take his stand on his "watchtower" (על משמרתי) and will look forth "to see what he will say to me," one might think of a kind of mechanized prophetic activity and think of the prophet waiting for the word. Particularly impressive is the description in Is 21:6ff of how prophetic observation is directed to the goal of a real (visionary) perception. F. Küchler has raised the question whether behind such observation of visionary processes there might not lie at an earlier stage the observation of concrete omens in the sacrificial process, such as comes through in Ps 5:4, "In the morning I prepare a sacrifice and watch."[13] This looking out for someting to appear has then, in prophecy, grown into the expectant listening for the divine word. But the Jeremiah passage already shows how, with the genuine prophet, to this listening there belongs also quite directly the sounding of the alarm, the call to give heed for the people to whom the prophet is sent: "'Give heed' (הקשיבו) when the horn sounds" (*ZB*).

■ **33:7** Ezekiel now hears in the oracle of appointment in v 7 that Yahweh has made him a watchman of this kind to the house of Israel, a watchman who, when he hears a word from Yahweh's mouth, warns his people of God. The complete irrationality of the divine activity is discernible in this announcement: Yahweh, the enemy of his people, who draws the sword against them to annihilate them because of their disobedience—Yahweh at the same time, however, the God who sets up a watchman for his people, who will warn them of the sword in which he himself comes, and thus tries to make that sword ineffectual. For, as v 11 then openly states, he takes no pleasure in the death of the transgressor, but would rather that he live. Such is divine logic!

In obedience to this appointment, Ezekiel, as chapters 1–24 have already shown, has, like Jeremiah, untiringly blown the horn in the ear of the house of Israel and has proclaimed to his people the coming of the sword (see, e.g., 21:13–22).

■ **33:8f** If v 7 is still wholly within the orbit of Jer 6:17, vv 8f contain the turn of phrase characteristic of Ezekiel. We should note, in the first instance, that the reference

---

ran," *WZ* 6 (1956/57): 589–599; Ovid R. Sellers, "Musical Instruments of Israel," *BA* 4 (1941): 42f.

11 On this see 1, 366 on 17:19 and p. 204 on 7:4.

12 On this see also Reventlow, "Blut"; on 18:13 see 1, 384.

13 Friedrich Küchler, "Das priesterliche Orakel in Israel und Juda" in *Abhandlungen zur semitischen Religionskunde und Sprachwissenschaft Wolf Wilhelm Grafen von Baudissin,* BZAW 33 (Giessen: Töpelmann, 1918), 295f.

here is no longer in general terms to the hearing of the word of Yahweh, but that this word is cited directly: "If I say to the godless: You shall certainly die . . ." The question arises whether this is not a ready-made expression which has its specific setting in life.

In the analysis of chapter 18 it became clear that there were situations of specific affirmation of life in the sanctuary.[14] The חיה יחיה ("he shall live"), which then recurs in v 13 in an analogous citation as a word spoken to the righteous, was addressed to the visitor to the temple if he had given the correct answer to the question of obedience to the laws. Were there not analogous situations in which the מות תמות ("you shall surely die") was addressed to the guilty? The observation that the two expressions appear in characteristically different forms (alongside the חיה יחיה "*he* shall live" in the third person in v 13, there is the מות תמות "*you* shall die" in the second person in direct speech in vv 8,14; 3:18) warns us against an immediate schematic equation of the two formulae.[15] Now in fact מות תמות ("you shall die") (not to be confused with מות יומת "he shall be put to death")[16] is attested several times in the OT. It is the formula of the apodictically announced death sentence (1 Sam 14:44; 22:16; 2 Kgs 1:4, 6, 16) or the threatened death sentence (Jer 26:8) or the death sentence that is under certain conditions hypothetically imposed (Gen 2:17 [3:4] 20:7; 1 Kgs 2:37, 42). In contrast to the affirmation of life, there is here no single setting in life. This death sentence can be spoken by God (Gen 2:17; 20:7), the king (1 Sam 14:44; 22:16; 1 Kgs 2:37, 42), the prophet (2 Kgs 1:4, 6, 16) or the temple functionaries (Jer 26:8; delete וכל העם "and all the people"). Always, however, it is the response to disobedience to a quite specific command. Infringement of the law and death sentence belong together. And in every case it is a question of a sentence passed on an individual.

But this now leads straight into the specific character of what is said about the watchman in Ezekiel. While v 7, like Jeremiah 6, envisaged the task of the prophet vis-à-vis the people as a whole, v 8 now turns to the individual. The מות תמות ("you shall surely die") no longer describes the historical onslaught of the "sword" against a whole nation, but the death sentence which (as in Gen 2 or 1 Kgs 2) is associated with the breaking of a particular law. Thus, too, the looking out on the part of the prophet is no longer only the hopeful waiting on the watchtower for specific information from God. It comes to signify the paying heed to the law with the breaking of which the death sentence is connected. The prophet's task, then, is to proclaim the danger which from this point of view is discernible for the individual.

In this expression it becomes clear that the great judgment of the people has meanwhile already begun. The prophets proclaimed it and thereby fulfilled their duty. But prophetic duty does not stop here. Vv 11–16 will make clear all the mercy to found here. They are also still to give warning of the death sentence and, implicit in this, also promise of "life." In the conscription of the prophet as the warner sent to the condemned of Israel, God makes it plain that there is still time between the present and the final death sentence. Insofar as God makes it clear in the watchman that he is still in the process of frustrating his own judgment and in the warner of blocking his own way, he betrays the fact that he wishes to remain with the exilic community, the "members of his people." One does not do full justice to the office of the prophet if one describes him as the "spiritual adviser" of his people. The life to which he summons on instruction from his God, in that he warns of the death sentence which God in his mercy still holds back, although the מות תמות ("you shall die") seems to be formulated in apodictic terms—this life is more than a mere life of the "soul" in the sense of pure inwardness. In the context of 18:9, it has been expounded how much fuller hope for the house of Israel lies in the affirmation of life given by her God.[17]

Vv 8f deal with this hope. On its account not only is the godless man called back to the right path by his God. The prophet, too, who has been appointed to warn and whose "watching" in a new way affects the individual in respect of his God's commands, is summoned to be faithful in his office. Yahweh himself will demand from the watchman an account for the man who meets death without having been warned, as v 6 has already stated. In the event of the warning's having been given, however, the watchman, too, will "save his life" (הציל).

14 See 1,376f, 381f.

15 On the secondary assimilation in v 13 see note a.

16 On this see 1,384 on 18:13.

17 See 1,381f.

Form

■ 33:10–20 *2. The Proclamation of the Freedom to Repent.* The section vv 10–11, directed at the house of Israel, is, like the beginning of chapter 18, in the style of a disputation. A lament of the people, which is cited in the text and which the prophet, at Yahweh's command, is to quote to them, is followed by Yahweh's reply, introduced by the oath formula as in 18:3, ending in a call to repentance. This latter is emphatically underlined by means of an additional question.

Vv 12–20, on the other hand, reveal in their first part, vv 12–16, the character of a didactic debate. It has its close parallel in 18:21–24, although not inconsiderable variations occur in the sequence of statements, and the personal divine address is more prominent in chapter 33 than in chapter 18. The second half in vv 17–20, on the other hand, is an abbreviated reproduction of the discussion in 18:25–30a. It takes its starting point from a quotation of the words of the Israelites and returns to that quotation via the intervening scholarly debates.

Thus, in the case of vv 10–20, one could also speak of a tripartite construction in three speeches, in which conversational discussion and scholarly debate alternate.

Interpretation

■ 33:10 The first part begins with a quotation of words of the "house of Israel." They are words in which the total collapse of the remnant of the people finds expression, and they undoubtedly belong to the period after 587. In the tripartite construction of the sentence, the first two statements in synthetic parallelism are contrasted with a third clause in the form of a question which expresses the people's despair at "life." The first clause with its triple rhyme (in *-ēnū*) has the stamp of a lament.[18] The content describes the man who is crushed under the heaviest burden (עלינו "upon us"). It is the burden of the rebellious deeds of Israel's disobedience[19] and sin. The Deuteronomistic history is the great penitential confession of an Israel crushed beneath the weight of these deeds. Ezekiel 16, 20, 23 may also be read as a commentary on this. The parallel statement describes the punishment that follows that sin with an image of wasting taken from that of a festering wound (Ps 38:6), an image in which can be discerned the language of Ezekiel and of the Holiness Code. נמק בעון ("to waste away in iniquity") occurs also in 4:17; 24:23 as well as in the Holiness Code Lev 26:39 (descriptive of the remnant scattered in exile among the nations and escaped from destructive death). Finally, the איך נחיה ("how can we then live?") of the concluding despairing quesion has its parallel in the ואיך נמלט אנחנו ("and we, how shall we escape?") which also concludes a quotation from the words of disillusioned men in Is 20:6. It is, however, not mere chance that the root חיה ("to live") appears here in Ezekiel. The question about "life" is raised in vv 11f, as well as in the following debate, which is therefore not to be separated from vv 11f.[20]

Thus Israel's despair finds expression in words of lamentation (stylized by the prophet himself). All pride has gone, all clinging to possible hopes has been crushed, all faith in a future and in a continuation of life has been extinguished (see also 37:11). This has in mind not only the disastrous political turn of affairs, but also the acknowledgment that this turn of affairs has its basis deep in their own guilt, which as a burden which could not be shaken off had to bring about this destruction. In this, God does not explicitly appear as judge. But he can be sensed as such behind the confession of sin. פשע ("transgression") implies a personal encounter.

■ 33:11 The divine response to the lament follows, first of all in the words of 18:23 and 18:32.[21] While these were expressed in 18:23 in the form of a question and in 18:32 in the form of a simple statement, here they occur with great vehemence in the form of an oath. Yahweh now emerges with the disclosure of his hidden will and attests that his "pleasure" (חפץ) is in life—even vis-à-vis

18 Cf. the similar rhyme in the lament in Jer 14:7 (alternation of *-ēnū* and *-ānū*), 9b (threefold *-ēnū*), 20 (*-ēnū* and *-ānū*).

19 On פשע see 1,309.

20 On the understanding of this "life" see the discussion 1,381f on 18:9.

21 On 18:23 see 1,385; on 18:32 see 1,386.

the godless, for whom access to it remains open by way of repentance. Thus the sentence ends with the impressive call to repentance.[22]

■ **33:12** The second question, vv 12–16, is specifically directed at the prophet's fellow countrymen.[23] It begins with an impersonally didactic statement which links the fate of the righteous man who commits sin with that of the godless man who repents of his sin. Instead of the expressions "live" and "die" here, the paraphrases "be saved" (הציל, see v 9 and especially 14:14, 16, 18, 20) and "be brought down" (נכשל, emended text of 21:20) are used. The sentence has no parallel in chapter 18 (but see the formally reminiscent expressions in 18:20). But from the content point of view also it does not quite represent the continuation which one expected after 33:11. While that verse dealt with the consolation of the despairing sinner, this verse deals in a more general way with the question of righteousness and life. The fact that this question concentrates on the problem of the turning away from righteousness and the "returning" to righteousness shows once again that this continuation comes from the "returning" oracle in vv 11f.

■ **33:13–16** This juxtaposition also dominates the continuation of the didactic section in vv 13–16, which in its wording has a close parallel in 18:21f, 24.[24] Nevertheless one must draw attention to a number of discernible differences from the parallel in chapter 18. The fact that the sequence of the cases is here reversed (33:13 corresponds to 18:24; 33:14–16 to 18:21f) is connected with the fact that the trend of the discussion is, as already in v 2, downwards in the direction of the sinner who repents. This once again reveals the origin of vv 10f. The same trend is discernible in the fact that in vv 14–16 there is a much fuller discussion of the godless man who repents than there is in v 13 of the righteous man who again becomes a sinner. A further difference lies in the fact that to the more neutral phraseology of 18:24 ("When a righteous man turns away . . .") there corresponds in chapter 33 the more vivid phraseology ("If I say of the righteous: He shall live—but he relies on his righteousness . . ."). There is a corresponding comparison in the case of the godless between 33:14 and 18:21a. The citation of specific judgments on the righteous (godless) gives us here too, as was discussed in connection with 33:8, a glimpse into the specific situations of the assurance of life (sentence of death).

Particular attention should be given to the additional element which can be determined in vv 14–16 in the description of the godless man who repents, in comparison with v 13, the description of the righteous man who has become unrighteous. The turning aside from his righteousness of the righteous man who has received the "life-sentence" is described succinctly: The righteous man "trusts" in his righteousness and does wrong.[25] On the other hand, the repentance of the godless is developed in detail. He repents of his sin, practices justice and righteousness, gives back pledges, restores stolen property, walks in the statutes which lead to life, does not do what is wrong. Particularly noteworthy are the two specific statements about behavior with regard to pledges and stolen property, which have then, in an equalizing tendency, been deleted as additions (Müller, Fohrer). Both clauses occurred in 18:7 as elements in a more detailed series of clauses, which were discernible as a decalogue-type formulary. They have been singled out here rather by chance in order to show how the just life reveals itself in obedience to specific divine ordinances. The clauses of these series are described in the following summary clause in shorthand fashion as חקות החיים "statutes of life." 20:11, 13 and 21 had spoken precisely so of statutes and laws by which a man, if he does them, lives. Obedience to these statutes had formerly in the land given him free access to the sanctuary, that is the way to "life." Thus, here it is also said of the one who has been thus obedient: "He shall live, not die."[26]

By way of summary it can be said of the second section in vv 12–16 that it is certainly different from the immediate attitude of the consolatory address to the de-

22 On the double שובו cf. the שובו והשיבו of 14:6; 18:30; on the concluding question cf. 18:13; on the whole see 1, 308, 386.

23 For an analysis of it see Zimmerli, "'Leben' und 'Tod,'" 496–498.

24 See 1, 385.

25 On בטח in Ezekiel see 1, 342 on 16:15.

26 On details reference should be made to what was said in the context of chapter 18.

spairing that is found in vv 10f and passes over into a more strongly didactic discussive style, which bears in mind not only the immediate consolatory situation but examines various possibilities. In subject matter, however, it expounds in greater detail what was said there. It too speaks of the great freedom which Yahweh opens up in the possibility of repentance for the man who believed that he was dead and lost in his sin. The prophet proclaims to his exilic surroundings: Even you who sigh "Our transgressions . . . weigh upon us . . . how can we then live?" are not finally cut off from life.

■ **33:17-20** Lastly, the third section, vv 17–20, appears as a somewhat abbreviated repetition of 18:25–30aα.[27] The differences are insignificant. Thus 33:17 is in the third person to begin with, while 18:25–30a is in the style of a direct address. The latter asserts itself here only in v 20. While in chapter 18 the response to the people's bold reproach that Yahweh has not acted justly is in the form of a counter-question about the correct behavior of the questioners, in 33:17 it is in the form of an impersonal declaratory statement. In 33:20 it is missing completely. While 18:25 addresses the "house of Israel," 33:17 mentions the prophet's fellow countrymen (בני עמך "members of your people") as those addressed, though admittedly it too mentions in 33:20b, with the verbal repetition of 18:30aα, the "house of Israel." There is nothing in chapter 33 corresponding to the remarkable v 28 in chapter 18.

Pertinently the question arises here how then the rebellious arguments which Yahweh directs at the dock can be reconciled with the shattered sighing of the people in 33:10. One can, in any event, suppose that vv 10–20 are not of a piece. Vv 17–20 presuppose an attitude of rebellious muttering against Yahweh which could already be discerned in 18:2, while vv 10–16 are more strongly addressed to the transgressor who is willing to repent. Since, however, vv 17–20 reveal the strongest dependence on their parallel in chapter 18 and, in contrast to vv 10–16, show no characteristics independent of that parallel, but must rather be described as a careless abbreviation of their original (in which perhaps 18:28 was missing), it can be seriously suggested that vv 17–20 have probably been added only secondarily.

Setting

In 33:1–20 we have a section which was added secondarily to the context at this point. Its thematic purpose is to reveal a new side of the prophet's office, a side which must have acquired particular significance in the period after the fall of Jerusalem, which will be reported immediately after this. The content of the second half of the section is closely connected with chapter 18, a passage which has also only editorially acquired its present position between chapters 17 and 19, which must once have followed each other directly.[28] 3:17–21 is a section worked secondarily on the basis of 33:1–20 and chapter 18.

With the placing of 33:1–20 at the head of the preaching of the prophet's later phase (after 587) the redactors have struck the right note. The components of 33:1–20, which were not formed simultaneously, all belong, from the point of view of content, to the period of the final destruction of the Judaean state. The quotation in 33:10 reveals the despair of a people aware of their sins after the judgment has taken place; the quotation in 33:17, 20 reveals the bitterness at God's judgment. And the combined watchman oracle presupposes the prophet's turning to the individuals in the world around him. In this new way Ezekiel has now to be the watchman and the warner of his people. (The fact that alongside this there continues a great proclamation of total deliverance for the people is shown in chapters 34ff.) It is impossible to fix a more precise time within the period after 587.

When, on the other hand, Herntrich concludes from v 2 that the prophet felt himself responsible particularly for the עם הארץ ("people of the land") and consequently must have been active in Jerusalem prior to 587, he is transferring a characteristic of the earlier figurative presentation of the watchman image to the application in vv 7–9. And when he sees in the proclamation of coming disaster by the watchman the preaching of Ezekiel before 587, then he does not perceive precisely the particular radical change in the understanding of the watchman in vv 8f, which leads on from Jer 6:17 and speaks of a new task of warning the individual under the law.[29] The office of the warner vis-à-vis the individual (בני עמך "members of your people") leads to the situation of the

27 On this see 1, 385f.

28 See 1, 391, 397.

29 Herntrich, *Ezechielprobleme*, 111; on the "individualism" of Jeremiah and Ezekiel see also Miller, *Verhältnis*, 112f, 136–139.

exile, in which the all-important thing is that individuals stand firm in obedience to the divine law and thereby wait for life.

Aim

God appoints his messenger as a watchman, so that the latter can warn the members of his people about him, and quite inexorably urges him to be faithful in that office.

In this activity the whole mystery of God's sacred compassion finds expression. God is on the way to judgment. When insubordination to him obtrudes itself and men believe that they can live without him, war breaks out and the death-bringing sword draws near.

But God does not then allow this war to descend like a lightning flash so that it slays without a word. He makes room for his self-restraint.[30] In this room he places his warner, whose function in an amazing reversal of the fronts consists precisely in hindering God's war and making it ineffectual. In this warner he reveals that behind his will for war and divine destruction there lies a different, much stronger will. His real will, his "delight" (חפץ v 11) is for peace and life—even for the sinner.[31]

The appended proclamation no longer explicitly refers to the watchman, but reveals the watchman sent by God at his activity. Here are men who not only see God's judgment and their death looming as a distant possibility on the horizon, but who are already in the midst of that judgment and death. They are aware not only that they are condemned to death, but, over and above that, that they are justly condemned to death. They have given up their life. But now here below, where there is no more room, God creates anew through the word of his messenger room for the freedom to reach out for life. It is expressed still more precisely. At the point where he himself has pronounced his sentence of death: "You will certainly die" and where, in that explicit word of God, everything ought to be decided, there he creates anew through the call of his messenger room for freedom to repent. And he reveals the will to take back again the word he has already pronounced, in favor of the sentence of life: "He shall live."

The same word, however, applies also to those others who feel they must be bitter against God and blame him for their death. For such is man. He despairs today and tomorrow is full of defiance and the day after is again in despair. To these embittered men too God's freedom is shown, a freedom which desires that even the embittered should live.

The offer of such freeom lies in the call to repentance. The call to repentance does not summon to a merely inner realm of escapism. It refers to the whole of human life, to the carelessly hoarded pledge as well as to the unjustly appropriated stolen property. It rejects all lazy confident trust in the fact that it has now been said once and for all: You shall live. For in the last resort God does not summon to life alone—a life which then, if need be, could be lived without God and even without the other men to whom God has also turned. But it is to himself that God summons and to turning towards him. For "with thee is the fountain of life; in thy light do we see light" (Ps 36:10).

30 Cf. the ἀνοχή Rom 3:26.

31 On this see the remarks of Staudigel, *Begriffe*.

The News of the Fall of Jerusalem

Bibliography

Julius A. Bewer
"Das Datum in Hes 33:21," *ZAW* 54 (1936): 114f.

Moshe Greenberg
"On Ezekiel's Dumbness," *JBL* 77 (1958):101–105.

33

21 In the <eleventh>[a] year, in the tenth[b] month, on the fifth (day) of the month[c] after our deportation, a man who had escaped from Jerusalem came to me with the message: The city[d] has been taken. 22/ And the hand of Yahweh had come over[a] me in the evening, before the fugitive arrived[b]. And he (i.e. Yahweh) opened my mouth by the time he (i.e. the fugitive) came[c] to me in the morning. And my mouth was opened, and I was no longer dumb.

33:21 21a 𝔐 בשתי עשרה שנה. 8 MSS 𝔊^{L} 𝔖 (cf. Tht in Ziegler, *Ezechiel*) read the "eleventh," 𝔊^{88} 𝔖^{h} the "tenth" year. See the exposition.

b 𝔊 reads the "twelfth," 𝔏^{S} (*pace,* Ziegler, *Ezechiel*) the "eleventh." 𝔊^{QV} 𝔏^{C} 𝔖 read, as 𝔐, the "tenth" month. See the exposition.

c Bewer, 114, proposes reversing the figures for month and day, reading בחמשי בעשור לחדש. See the exposition.

d 𝔏^{CS} expand with *hierusalem.*

22 22a על-אל cf. 1:17 note a.

b 𝔊 *πρὶν ἐλθεῖν αὐτόν* is to be regarded as a stylistic device which tries to avoid the ugly repetition of פליט, which has just occurred in v 21.

c The bare בוא has a very harsh effect and is perhaps to be regarded as a scribal error for בֹּאו (Bertholet, Fohrer, Cooke). On the displacement of א and ו see 10:3 note a.

Form

This brief report in 33:21f, which is connected to the context neither at the beginning nor at the end, belongs from the point of view of content as a direct sequel to 24:15–24. The secondary addition in 24:25–27, which proved to be an element composed on the basis of 33:21f, has made this connection quite explicit even in its wording.[1] According to it, what is related in 33:21f appears as the fulfillment of a prediction which was made by Yahweh to the prophet at the time of his wife's death.

From the point of view of form, the report represents a novelty compared with all that has preceded it, insofar as here we have a pure narrative (in the first person) without any indication that it is a divine saying. The nearest approach to this form would be the basic text of the great vision report in chapters 8–11, where, however, the elucidatory and condemnatory divine word broke through the description again and again (see further chapters 40–42). The place of the divine saying has been taken in 33:21f by the report of the פליט ("fugitive"). It is followed immediately by a divine action with regard to the prophet, one which has the power of a sign. So even behind the human word of the פליט ("fugitive") can be heard the speech of Yahweh. Thus the formal uniqueness of the oracle does not, from the content point of view, really lead us outside the structure of the statements of Ezekiel hitherto.

Setting

There should be no doubt as to the originality and genuineness of this brief report (Hölscher, van den Born). Its strong radiation into the remainder of the oracles in the prophetic book (3:26f; 24:25–27; reference must also be made here to the expression specifically characteristic of Ezekiel פתחון פה "opening of the mouth" in 16:63; 29:21) shows that it was of importance for the message of the prophet.[2]

The desperate efforts of Herntrich, *Ezekielprobleme,*

1 See 1,508f.
2 For details of the date see the exposition.

and Bertholet to prove, on the basis of the secondary data of 24:25–27, that Ezekiel was living in Palestine at the time of the fall of the city not only lack a reliable literary-critical basis, but are also quite improbable from the point of view of the content of the statement.[3] 33:21f is an important part of the evidence for the fact that the prophet was living in exile.

Interpretation

■ **33:21** The verses report the coming of a פליט ("fugitive") who brings the news of the fall of Jerusalem. Expression has been given to the amazement occasioned by the fact that a fugitive from the vengeance of the Babylonians should have fled precisely to Babylon. Fohrer supposes that he must first have remained in hiding and then when living conditions became intolerable have fled to Babylon, since judicious men (Jeremiah) had pronounced themselves against flight to Egypt. On the other hand, however, it is surely wiser first of all to examine the linguistic usage of פלט ("to escape") in the book of Ezekiel. פלט ("to escape") undeniably plays a certain role in the book. 7:16, in the description of the day of Yahweh, speaks in general terms of escape to the mountains. In 6:8–10 on the other hand, a passage added after 587, the פליטים ("fugitives") are described as men who have been "carried away" (נשבו) among the nations. And it can be seen still more clearly in 14:22 that the פלטה ("survivors") (יתר "remnant" as in 6:8) left over from Yahweh's judgment come into exile and join those addressed by Ezekiel (הנם יוצאים אליכם "behold, they will come out to you") and there, by what they have to tell, make visible the justice of the divine judgment.[4] It is clear from this that an understanding as "fugitive" in the usual sense (secret, voluntary flight) does not correspond to the sense of פליט. The word describes the man who has remained alive in the battle (פליטי חרב "those who have escaped the sword" 6:8). He can then be a "fugitive" in the more restricted sense of the word. But he can also be a prisoner who is subsequently deported. When Hölscher, in this connection, tries to understand פליט as a collective describing all those deported, this is not in line with the linguistic usage in the rest of the book of Ezekiel, where the plural of פליט is used quite freely.

All of this sheds light on the date in v 21. 𝔐 states that the פליט arrived on 10 (month) / 5 (day) / 12 (year). The dating of the era by לגלותנו ("after our deportation") is also found in 40:1; in 1:2 we find לגלות המלך יויכין ("after the deportation of King Jehoiachin").[5] 𝔐 states that the פליט arrived on 10/5/12. In comparison with the information given in 2 Kgs 25:2f (on the basis of 𝔖) and Jer 30:2; 52:6f, according to which on 4/9/11 breaches were made in the city wall, and in 2 Kgs 25:8f, according to which the city was destroyed by fire on 5/7/11 (MSS, 𝔊ᴸ, 𝔖 on 5/9/11; Jer 52:12 on the tenth of the month), this creates the difficulty that there is a time-gap of about one and a half years between the capture or destruction of the city and the reporting of it to Ezekiel. This is highly unlikely.[6] Steuernagel has made the ingenious attempt, already made before him in the seventeenth century by the Jewish commentator David Altschul in his מצודת דוד (see Aalders, Fisch), to circumvent the difficulty by supposing ancient Israelite autumnal reckoning in the case of the years and Babylonian spring reckoning in the case of the months.[7] In this way there would be a gap of only half a year between the fall of the city and the arrival of the פליט. Thus Hölscher, Cooke, Aalders, Fisch. But this assumption is difficult in the case of such nearly contemporaneous texts as Jeremiah and Ezekiel. Thus it is a more probable assumption that only a later conscious assimilation of the dates in 33:21 was made in the light of the date in 32:17, and that the eleventh year should be read as the original date (see also note a). The emendation is not necessary for Kutsch, since he counts the year 598/7 as the first year of the deportation and thus has the years of the deportation running at one less than the years of Zedekiah.[8] The result, therefore, is a period of just under six months from the capture of the city and one of just under five months from the burning

3 See, e.g., 1, 508f.
4 See 1, 315f.
5 On this see 1, 113–115.
6 See also above pp. 33f on 26:1.
7 Steuernagel, *Lehrbuch,* 576.
8 Ernst Kutsch, "Zur Chronologie der letzten judäischen Könige (Josia bis Zedekia)," *ZAW* 71 (1959): 274.

of it. The deportation order of 587 will not have happened before the return of Nebuzaradan from headquarters in Riblah, from where he brought the order to destroy the city. If one further considers the technical preparations for the train of prisoners and assumes that the newly deported prisoners would probably not simply be taken to those who had previously been deported, but might well have been settled in the first instance in a different place in Babylonia, then the period of just under five months between 5/7 (9 or 10?)/11 and 10/5/11 produces a completely probable period of time between the fall of Jerusalem and the arrival of the first eyewitnesses in Tel-abib. With this compare also the time from 1/12 to 5/1 which Ezra, according to Ezr 7:9; 8:31, needed for the straight journey between Babylonia and Jerusalem. This also disposes of the incisive conjecture of Bewer (note c), which tries to show that the פליט who fled when the city fell, then, according to 24:25f, arrived at the prophet precisely on the day when it was set on fire. Ezekiel will already have heard in an indirect way about the end of the city. 6:8–10 and 14:22 can, however, show how important for the prophet the word of eyewitnesses from his own people was.[9] According to Parker-Dubberstein, the day of the arrival of the פליט is to be fixed on January 19, 586.

■ **33:22** The arrival of the פליט is of great importance. According to *b. Roš Haš* 18b, R. Simon, differing from R. Akiba, derives the fast of the tenth month (Zech 8:19) precisely from this event. For the prophet himself its importance is discernible in a symbolic event which affects his personal life. With the coming of the פליט the prophet is released from his inability to speak and is again able to open his mouth. This process is described as an event occasioned by Yahweh. In this way it acquires its significance within the framework of the prophetic mission. Elsewhere in the book of Ezekiel the "hand of Yahweh" is mentioned only in the framework of the great visionary encounters.[10] 3:14f shows how the heavy weight of Yahweh's hand on the prophet on one occasion puts him for a whole week into a state of speechless rigidity. In the present passage the different phases of the occurrence are, as already in 12:7f and 24:18, divided between the evening and the morning.[11] In the evening the hand of Yahweh comes upon the prophet. In the morning the פליט arrives and Ezekiel's mouth is opened. This statement, which should not be abbreviated by the deletion with Jahn, Herrmann,[12] Hölscher of v 22a (from בערב "in the evening"), is best understood as follows. The state of rigidity and loss of speech "fell" (cf. the נפל of 8:1) on the prophet in the evening, and in the morning, with the exciting event of the arrival of an eyewitness with his message, it left him.[13] At any rate it is not necessary to conclude that the silence lay on the prophet for any longer.

When, subsequently, with emphatic repetition of the פתח ("to open") (now in the nip'al), it is emphasized that Ezekiel is "no longer" (לא עוד) dumb, then it appears as if this expresses not only the cessation of the loss of speech which came upon him specifically in that night, but a change of his condition in a deeper sense. From now on he is quite free to speak, while the preceding period was under speech restraint. Even if one feels obliged to understand 3:27 not as iterative but as a glimpse ahead to the decisive process of release in 33:21f,[14] nevertheless it is a likely assumption that the prophet, until 12/5/11, had had to experience over and over again the divinely decreed speech restraint, which was at the same time (3:25f) also determined by human resistance. This announcement restores to him the "freedom to speak," the *παρρησία*.

This now leads to the full recognition of the significance of what is reported here. In 16:63, in a school-addition which is, however, in the language of Ezekiel, it is stated that the faithless woman will be unable to open her mouth for shame after she has been unexpectedly forgiven. On the other hand, the late oracle in 29:21 states that the definitive arrival of the salvation promised to Israel will give to the prophet complete freedom to

9 On the phraseology of the message see also 40:1.
10 See 1,118.
11 On this see 1,506.
12 J. Herrmann, *Ezechielstudien*, 75f; differently in his commentary.
13 On a similar removal of loss of speech see also Lk 1:64.
14 See 1,160.

open his mouth. Here Ezekiel distinguishes himself from, amongst others, the other writing prophets in that he particularly emphasizes the imminent proof of Yahweh before his people and "before the eyes of the nations."[15] The "proof-saying" is the literary form particularly characteristic of his book. The fall of Jerusalem is now the great historical proof of Yahweh, which reveals that Ezekiel with his message will not be frustrated and will not have to remain speechless with shame. In this event, which is proclaimed to the prophet on a specifically dated day by an eyewitness, Yahweh stands beside his prophet and proves that he has not spoken "in vain."[16]

Aim

So this apparently quite factual report of two events in the life of Israel and in the life of the prophet, even if it contains no explicit word of Yahweh, is a witness to the power to effect events of the divine speech. What is subsequently stated in Deutero-Isaiah in the quite different coloring of his message and is indeed developed there didactically—that Yahweh's word does not return empty (55:10f) and that Yahweh's divinity is revealed in that he declares what is still to come (41:26f; 44:7; 45:21; 48:3), so that man can recognize in the word of Yahweh the reality of what is happening, while the idols lack such power—here sustains the whole account. In this sense Ezekiel, as the later expansion in 24:27 in the light of the event described in 33:21f has stated, becomes a sign for Israel.

In Ezekiel's person it becomes clear what God's word is. It is event which moves the world and itself becomes history.[17] For this very reason it must, even when it leads through periods of contested waiting (12:21–25), hold the field as the essential reality. Over and above all unbelief and all mockery (Is 5:19; Jer 17:15), beyond all periods of apparently ignominious silence it must be heard because in the long run it will stand (יקום לעולם "will stand for ever" Is 40:8) and will not fall.

What in the eyes of the world seems to be the fall and the end of Israel is in reality the proof of the efficacy of the call that is proclaimed over Israel.

15 On this see 1,459 on 22:16.
16 On this see also 6:10; 14:23.
17 On the formula for receiving God's word see 1, 144f.

33

Against Unreadiness for Repentence at Home and Abroad

23 The word of Yahweh came to me: 24/ Son
of man, the inhabitants of the[se][a] ruins
in the land of Israel say[b]: Abraham was
an individual[c], and he gained possession
of the land. But we are many, and the
land is given to us to possess.
25 Therefore say to them: Thus[a] has [the
Lord][b] Yahweh said: Along with the blood
you eat (sacrificial flesh), and you lift up
your eyes[c] to your idols and shed blood—
and you expect to possess the land? 26/
You have resort to your sword[a], you
commit[b] atrocities, and each of you de-
files his neighbor's wife—and you expect
to possess the land?
27 This is what you are to say to them: Thus
has [the Lord][a] Yahweh said: As I live,
those who are among the ruins shall fall
by the sword; whoever is in the open
country, him have I given to the wild
beasts as fodder[b]; and those who are in
the hill fortresses and in caves shall die
by the plague. 28/ And I shall make the
land into a desolate waste[a], and an end
shall be made of her proud might, and the
mountains of Israel shall lie waste with
no one passing through them, 29/ and
they will know that I am Yahweh when I
make the land a desolate waste because
of all the atrocities which they have
committed.
30 But you, son of man—the members of your
people who talk[a] about you by[b] the walls
and in the doors of the houses and who
say[c] to one another[d], each to his brother:

33: 24a 𝔐 האלה is not attested by 𝔊 𝔏^{CS}. It could
24 have been added secondarily in order to make clearer the connection with vv 21f. "These ruins" refers to Jerusalem, the fall of which has just been reported.

b 𝔐 לאמר is not attested by 𝔊 𝔏^{CS} 𝔖. But see v 10 note a.

c 𝔗 underlines the חד, which corresponds to 𝔐 אחד, by means of the important addition יחידאי בעלמא "an isolated individual in the world."

25 25a In 𝔊 𝔏^{CS} the whole reproach of vv 25f is missing. As a result of homoioteleuton, the eye has obviously jumped from לכן אמר אלהים in v 25 to the כה תאמר אלהם of v 27, and the translation of the intervening section has not been completed. From the factual point of view, the motivation in vv 25f cannot be dispensed with before vv 27ff.

b On אדני, which is lacking in the introductory formula of v 27 in 𝔊 𝔏^{CS} ℜ, see Appendix 1.

c 𝔐 ועינכם should be read, with MSS Edd, as ועיניכם.

26 26a 𝔖 על סיפיכון, 𝔙 *in gladiis vestris* seem to go back to a plural חַרְבֹתֵיכֶם, but should rather be understood as an accommodation to the plural subject. An emendation to חָרְבֹתֵיכֶם (BH^3 following Ehrlich, *Randglossen*) "you behave as rulers of these ruins" (עמד על "be in charge of") is not to be recommended. 𝔗 is more probably on the right lines with its interpretative rendering איתעתדתון על תוקפכון "you hold yourself ready in your strength"; עמד על (אל) occurs again in 31:14 (note b).

b 𝔐 עשיתן is either a simple scribal error for עשיתם or else an attempt to ease pronunciation by trying to avoid a ם before a ת. Cooke compares also 44:8; Mic 3:12. See Gesenius-Kautzsch §44k.

27 27a אדני is lacking in 𝔊 𝔏^{CS}, see Appendix 1.

b 𝔐 לאכלו "to eat him" is not incomprehensible. 7 MSS Var^{P} 𝔊 𝔏^{CS} 𝔖 𝔙, however, go back to the usual reading of the phrase נתן לאכלה, which is attested also in 15:4, 6; 29:5; 35:12; 39:4. See also היה לאכלה in 21:37; 34:5, 10.

28 28a 𝔐 שממה ומשמה, see 6:14 note a. It recurs in v 29 and in 35:3. The immediately following resumption of the double expression in v 29, where it is attested by 𝔊, decidedly advises against the deletion, with Fohrer, of ומשמה which is not attested by 𝔊 𝔏^{CS} 𝔄, in v 28. See also Cornill.

30 30a The reciprocal nip'al "speak with each other" is attested elsewhere in the OT only in Mal 3:13, 16; Ps 119:23. The article in הנדברים is strange. Thus Driver, "Linguistic Problems," 180, would prefer to divide the text עמכה נדברים. On his reference to 16:3, however, see note d there.

b Literally "near."

c 𝔐 ודבר is rendered by 𝔊 καὶ λαλοῦσιν, 𝔏^{CS} *loquuntur*, 𝔙 *et dicunt*, 𝔖 וממללין as a plural. Only 𝔗

"Come and hear what the word is[e] that comes from Yahweh"—31/they come[a] to you as (the) people used to come[b] and sit before you [as my people][c] [and listen to your words but do not do them, for a longing for love[d] is in their mouth [[they do]] <and>[e] their heart goes after their gain[f]][g]. 32/ And see, you are to them as

וממליל is singular. If we do not wish to assume an original ודברו, we will have to vocalize ודבר as an infinitive absolute.

d 𝔐 חד את אחד is unattested in 𝔊 𝔏^{CS}. 2 MSS^{Ken} harmonize the Hebrew אחד to the aramaizing חד: חד את חד while one MS^{Ken} reverses the process and reads אחד את אחד. The synonymous expression used immediately following איש–אחיו is found also in 24:23; 38:21 (see also 4:17; 47:14). For the double usage אחד–אחד, 37:16, 17, though not exactly parallel, could nevertheless be cited. Cornill, Herrmann, Toy, Cooke, Bertholet, Fohrer regard חד את אחד as a secondary expansion. Yet the doubling of the expression could also arise from the intention to depict as vividly as possible the excessive whispering in the vicinity of Ezekiel.

e 𝔐 מה הדבר is unattested in 𝔊 𝔏^{S}. Since the neuter *τὰ ἐκπορευόμενα* would correspond to a feminine היוצאת, while 𝔐 היוצא demands the הדבר before it, 𝔊 will once again have abbreviated the expression and 𝔐 will be original.

31 31a After the long introductory description of the people surrounding Ezekiel in v 30, there follows now, appended by means of ו-apodosis (Gesenius-Kautzsch §143d, also Brockelmann §123f), the verbal clause.

b 𝔗 gives added emphasis in a particular direction: כמיתי גברין תלמידין "come running like disciples." Driver, "Ezekiel," 301f, emphasizes correctly that עם here is to be differentiated from עמי.

c 𝔐 עמי is not attested by 𝔊 𝔏^{S} and is surely an interpretative element, which purports to describe from God's point of view the apparent willingness of the people to listen. Cf. 37:12f.

d 𝔐 עגבים is rendered by 𝔊 with ψεῦδος (𝔏^{S} *mendatium*), 𝔖 דגלותא "lie," and this has raised the question whether a corruption of כזבים does not perhaps lie behind this. So Cornill, Herrmann, Toy, Cooke, Bertholet, Fohrer. In that event, however, the rendering of it in 𝔊 by a singular is strange. In addition, elsewhere in Ezekiel כזב is found only in the singular (13:6–9, 19; 21:34; 22:28). 𝔗 renders תולעבא "scorn" while 𝔙 renders v 31b*α* as follows: *quia in canticum oris sui vertunt illos* [*sc. sermones*]. See also notes e and g.

e 𝔐 המה עשים is omitted by 𝔊 𝔏^{S} 𝔖. It will have been inserted when the meaning of v 31b*α* had become no longer clear, but was to be understood along the lines of 𝔙's rendering of it (note d). The copula, which is still attested in front of אחרי by 𝔊 𝔏^{S} 𝔙 𝔖, has been lost in 𝔐.

f 𝔐 בצעם (בצע also in 22:13, 27) has been understood by 𝔊 as *μιάσματα*. 𝔊 *μίασμα* corresponds in Lev 7:18 to פגול, in Jer 32 (𝔊 39):34 to שקוץ. From this it has been assumed that the original was עצבים (BH^{3}). But 𝔐 should be retained.

g It is noteworthy that the section ושמעו את דבריך ואותם לא יעשו recurs in v 32 with a slight rephrasing of the second half, and so does עגבים, which occurs

<one who sings love songs>[a] with beautiful tone and fine playing, and they listen to your words but do not do them. 33/ But when it comes—see, it comes![a]—then they will realize that a prophet has been in their midst[b].

there in a quite clear context. That this is not equally the case in v 31 is shown by the gloss המה עשים (note e), which tries to coordinate the word more correctly. These observations suggest the possibility that v 31aβb arrived in the text only secondarily (Hölscher). It is probably an additional note, which was appended to the catch-word (v 31aβ; quoted in a slightly emended fashion from v 32) and which subsequently found its way from the margin into the text. Once it is removed there remains a perfectly clear, self-contained text. In the phraseology of v 32b (with the prefixed עשים in v 32bβ) the antithesis עשה–שמע is also quite clearly expressed.

32 32a 𝔐 שיר עגבים is rendered in 𝔊 by φωνὴ ψαλτηρίου (𝔏[S] *vox psalterii*), 𝔙 *carmen musicum*, 𝔗 זמר אבובין and in 𝔖 by simple זמירתא. According to this, the prophetic word is compared to a song. The image would be clearer if one could read שָׁר and find there a comparison with the singer of the song. So Herrmann, Bertholet, Fohrer. Spiegel, "Ezekiel," 295 note 22, sees in שיר a *qaṭil*-form analogous to ציר (Jakob Barth, *Die Nominalbildung in den semitischen Sprachen* [Leipzig: Hinrichs, ²1894], 188) with the meaning "singer." Ewald suggested a form שַׁיָּר as did Hölscher.

33 33a 𝔊 (𝔏[S]) has not acknowledged the strongly assertive parenthesis as a word of the prophet, but has, by the addition of an ἐροῦσιν *(dicent)*, put it into the mouth of those who have been overtaken by the fulfillment of the word. 𝔙 and 𝔖 have again felt obliged to expand more fully on what was obscurely indicated in the suffix of בבאה and have added *quod praedictum est*, פתגמיך הידין.

b 𝔏[S] 𝔖 have expressed the statement of recognition to apply directly to the prophet: "and they will realize that you have been a prophet in their midst."

The section 33:23–33, subsumed under a single formula for the receiving of God's word, comprises two oracles, which basically have no connection with each other: vv 24–29 and vv 30–33. Each of the two oracles begins with the address to the prophet (vv 24, 30), but then directs attention to quite different human circles. The units have been linked because both belong to the period after the fall of the city and because both speak for this period of resistance to which the word of the prophet sees itself opposed. Since from the point of view both of form and of content vv 23–29 and vv 30–33 go their own ways, it will be best to treat them separately.

Form

■ 33:23–29 *1. The pious security of those who have not been deported*

Vv 23–29 are, to begin with, in the form of a debate. In this connection the quotation of the opponents in the debate is given to the prophet by Yahweh himself. This is followed by the commission to speak, which is, however, as is shown by its double formulation and by the repetition of the introductory messenger formula (vv 25, 27), artificially divided into two parts. The proclamation proper (judgment oracle) occurs in vv 27–29. It begins with an introductory oath and, by ending in an (expanded) recognition formula, proves to be a proof-saying. It is preceded in vv 25f by a preliminary speech in the form of two parallel questions, which, in the confrontation with specific legal commands, reveal the impossibility of those who have remained in the land laying claim to the possession of it.

If we look at the oracle as a whole, the structure of a tripartite proof-saying shines through. The motivatory section in vv 24–26 provides, in the style of a debate, the rejection of a false claim. The judgment oracle is in the form of an oath, and the recognition formula is expanded by means of a repetition.

Setting

To call the population of the country "inhabitants of these ruins" is scarcely feasible prior to 587. Against Noth, who wants to place it before 587 because of the closeness of 33:24 to 11:15, the oracle is to be dated to the period after the destruction of Jerusalem.[1] It is not entirely clear why this oracle "could not possibly have been written in Babylonia" (Herntrich). Would a prophet who found himself in Palestine state quite so explicitly that the quoted word of opposition was circulating "in the land of Israel"? Here there is revealed the same distance with respect to the land as in 11:15, where the "inhabitants of Jerusalem," who were saying something quite similar, were very clearly differentiated from the exiles who were being addressed. The oracle is spoken from Babylonia. It can be seen elsewhere that Ezekiel had knowledge of remarks which were circulating among those who had been left behind. It must certainly not be assumed that he has just learned of it through the פליט ("fugitive") mentioned in vv 21f (so Hermann). The remark seems rather to betray already a certain distance from the burning of the city, a distance in which "the people had become cocky" (Bertholet) because they have begun to establish themselves in the property of those who had been deported.[2]

Interpretation

■ **32:23f** In a new divine saying Yahweh points the prophet ("son of man") to a remark which is circulating among the people who are trying to find their feet again in a war-ravaged Judah (and in the destroyed city of Jerusalem?).[3] The remark gives a penetrating insight into the mood of those people in the land who had escaped not only the first, limited disaster of 597, but also the much more severe recurrence of 587. It is not only a purely pragmatic re-orientation which is discernible in their words, but also a process of reflection about the fundamentals in which Israel bases her life. Already the Deuteronomic period had newly called to mind that Israel's life was wholly based on the love in which Yahweh had called to himself the ancestors of the nation, had sworn to give the land to Abraham, Isaac and Jacob (Dtn 1:8; 6:10; 9:5; 30:20; 34:4) and had promised them that he would be their God (Dtn 29:12). In the Deuteronomic view, Moses, in the period of threat, had called on God to remember the ancestors (Dtn 9:27). This makes it possible for us to understand why now, in an hour of even stronger attack, the name of Abraham appears in the words of the two prophets of the exile. In Is 41:8, in an oracle of Yahweh in answer to a prayer, Israel is addressed as the "seed of Abraham." In Is 51:2 she is summoned to look to Abraham her father who was "called as an individual" (אחד קראתיו) and then richly blessed and multiplied. When in the present passage, similarly, the possession of the land (ירש "to gain possession of" Dtn 6:18; 12:29; 16:20; and elsewhere; מורשה "possession," which is attested seven times in Ezekiel, occurs elsewhere only in Ex 6:8; Dtn 33:4 in an uncertain text) is connected with the recollection of the insignificance of Abraham, the individual separated from his family (אחד היה "he was an individual"), this reveals how intensively the men of this time of judgment sought refuge, in their hour of attack, in God's promises to the patriarchs.

But in the words of those who are left in the land it is possible to see, in two senses, a fatal breakdown in the appeal to the ancestor of the promise to Israel. In the claim of those who have been spared to the right of "possession" of the land (מורשה), there are heard unmistakably the echoes of what was said in 11:15 by those who remained in the land in 597.[4] It is true that here, as distinct from 11:15, the gloating sideways glance at the exiles has been omitted. Once again, however, a right is

1 Martin Noth, "La Catastrophe de Jérusalem en l'an 587 avant Jésus-Christ et sa signification pour Israël," *RHPhR* 33 (1953): 92 note 10.

2 On this see 2 Kgs 25:12 (=Jer 52:16); Jer 40:10.

3 See 1, 144f; on "son of man" see 1, 131f.

4 See 1, 261.

derived from the fact of their having been spared. What should have been understood only as grace here becomes a claim. And a similar malevolent certainty also characterizes the reference to Abraham. While the divine oracle in Is 51:2 proclaimed the exuberant wonder that Yahweh gave to the individual great riches, here the amazement at that event has disappeared and been replaced by a false sense of self-security. As an individual, Abraham was thrown completely on the blessing of God. Those who are left in the land, on the other hand, assert with satisfaction that they are after all in not such a bad state. They are after all still "many." Yahweh is certainly not to be polemically excluded here. But man has a satisfactorily large share of things: "We are many, we will certainly succeed." One may marvel at the will to rebuild and the strength to overcome catastrophes which find expression here. It should not, however, be overlooked that in this self-security on man's part the real power of the promise is betrayed.

■ **33:25** The prophet is summoned to speak against this security. He points in the first instance to Israel's covenant ordinances. In the failure to keep these the fragile nature of the claim of those addressed becomes clear. Once again there appear in the background specific formulaic ordinances such as we have already found in chapter 18 and in chapter 22.[5] In respect of these the prophet accuses the Palestinians of sin. The ordinance about abstention from blood, which is found in 1 Sam 14:32ff; Lev 19:26, subsequently found its way, in P's legislation alongside the prohibition of shedding blood which follows here in third place (on this see especially 22:1–16), into the basic humanitarian ordinances of the Noachic covenant (Gen 9:4–6). Because "the lifting of eyes to idols" is preceded in 18:6 and in 22:9 by "eating on the mountains,"[6] Cornill, Kraetzschmar and Fohrer wish to read here too ההרים ("the mountains") in place of הדם ("the blood"). There is no support for this in the tradition. It is surely possible that the terms of the pre-Josianic formula, which can still be seen in chapters 18 and 22, seemed outmoded in the specific application to the population of Jerusalem after 587 and were replaced by the present stipulation about shedding blood, the increase in the significance of which can be so clearly seen in what follows.

■ **33:26** The first transgression of the second group of three statements appears, in contradistinction to those which follow ("commission of atrocities" and "defilement of a neighbor's wife"),[7] in none of the lists of commandments. Thus one may ask whether this is not a reference, directly conditioned by the contemporary situation, to the lawlessness of a land that had been laid waste by a long war. Jeremiah 41 and the report in Jer 52:30, to the effect that in the twenty-third year of Nebuchadnezzar (582/81) a further deportation was made by the Babylonians, suggest that the years after 587 remained years of unrest and violence for the land. Can, however, asks the prophet, a people who find themselves in such a state of social and ritual disarray be heirs to the promised land?

■ **33:27** With all the passion of the oath formula, Yahweh replies to this with his negative, in that he pronounces judgment on the remnant who have remained in the land. The three great instruments of judgment, sword, wild beasts and plague, are summoned against these men.[8] Unique here is the juxtaposition of the three spheres affected by the judgment: 1) those among the ruins (corresponds to v 24, in which connection the word-play בחרבות בחרב "among the ruins by the sword" should be noted); 2) those in the open country (7:15; cf. 26:6, 8); 3) those in the refuges and caves (Ju 6:2). This enumeration unmistakably reflects the actual situation of that period immediately after 587, with its struggle of each against all and the more extensively smouldering struggle against the Babylonian forces of occupation.

■ **33:28** If then here the land, in words which recall 6:14 (15:8; 29:10, 12; 32:15); 30:18 (30:6; 7:24) and 14:15, and the "mountains of Israel"[9] are threatened with further devastation and deprivation of population, the

5 On chapter 18 see 1, 375f, 379–381; on chapter 22 see 1, 454f, 457–459.

6 On 18:6 see 1, 380; on 22:9 see 1, 458.

7 On תועבה see 1, 190 on 6:9 and 1, 383 on 18:13; see 1, 380 on 18:6.

8 On a similar deliverance to three or four judgments see, e.g., 5:1–2, 12; 6:11f; 7:15; 14:12ff.

9 See 1, 185 on 6:2.

following period with its renewed Babylonian invasion (Jer 52:30) seems to have fulfilled this threat to some extent.

■ **33:29** Emphatically placed at the end, however, is the statement that in this devastation brought about by the atrocities committed by the people, Yahweh will reveal himself in his self-mystery.

Aim

The oracle in vv 23–29 makes it clear that God remains on the scene even after his great judgment on his people. In every divine judgment it is never a question simply of a judgment which is accomplished in its actual occurrence, but again and again of the fact that God is made known in his revelation.

In the conflagration of Jerusalem God has spoken to his people and in taking from them all their possessions has recalled them to their fundamental ordinances, in which they of themselves are nothing. The present oracle reveals that an element of reflection occurred among the people. With renewed urgency they asked after the origins of the people of God and of the basic order according to which Israel's ancestor Abraham was called.

In the destruction by the divine judgment, however, some were nevertheless spared. There are people who have escaped and have preserved something of the life and of the pledge of the divine mercy. Now, however, the present oracle shows the terrible process of how those who have been spared do not acknowledge, in what has been left to them in mercy, the merciful one who has given this to them, but deduce from it their own special rights. This does not take place in insolent opposition to God and to his dealing with his people from the beginning. Rather, it occurs in the apparently pious way in which the present is understood in the light of these beginnings. In reality, however, both are falsified by the godless self-assertiveness of men. What men should have regarded as a sign of mercy, which God in his forbearance has given to them in the midst of judgment, becomes a right. Instead of allowing themselves to be thrown back to the true poverty of the beginning when God's gift was everything, the relative wealth, with which in their own strength something can be rebuilt, is affirmed. And men remain as of old, with their old idols and their licentious impurity and their violence towards their weaker neighbors.

Where men pass through God's judgment in this way, then God says to them in his unmistakable word that he will remain active in judgment. Where judgment is survived in such a way that from the final outcome the old man begins to rebuild his old way of life, God remains active, no matter how much this rebuilding clothes itself ideologically with pious tradition, and will really make himself known in new judgment.

Form

■ **33:30–33** *2. Misunderstanding on the part of those deported.* The second oracle, vv 30–33, is from the point of view of form entirely in the style of an address to the prophet. Yahweh speaks to the prophet about his experiences in his immediate environment.

The stylization of Ezekiel's oracles becomes particularly clear in an oracle such as the present one. From the point of view of subject matter it is a question here of a state of affairs which should have found its natural expression in the form of a lament by the prophet followed by a divine response. One could point here to passages such as the confessions of Jeremiah, 12:1–6 and 15:15–21, which are in the form of a psalm-lament with a subsequent divine response (so too Is 49:1–6). Ezek 33:30–32 corresponds to the lament and 33:33 to the divine reply which answers this lament. In Ezekiel, however, the whole is in the form of a divine address to the prophet. Insofar as Yahweh here himself describes the attitude of those around the prophet to his proclamation (vv 30–32), he takes from the mouth of the prophet the description of what it is that troubles the prophet. With no clearly marked transition, it then passes in the final part to what Yahweh says by way of consolation to the prophet in these circumstances, which may of course also contain what the prophet has to say by way of proclamation to those around him.

This alienation of the form, which gives expression to many situations only in the indirect phraseology of a divine saying, is one of the principal form-critical problems of Ezekiel's oracles.

Setting

The positioning of this oracle after 33:21f as well as its content make it probable that this oracle comes from after the fall of Jerusalem. In 14:3; 20:3 we saw how the prophet gave a harsh negative response to the elders who asked him for a (consolatory) divine response. Again, the vision of chapters 8–11, which (according to 11:25) the prophet reported to the exiles, was a harsh word of judgment. According to 33:30–33 the situation for the prophet seems to be much more open. The men come, discuss what he says and listen to it as to "a love song." All this would be much more understandable in the period after the fall of Jerusalem. Here the word about the new life which Yahweh plans to establish (e.g. 37:1–14) could be proclaimed much more directly. That the prophet is here speaking to the exiles is clear not only from the reference to the בני עמך ("members of your people" in v 30)[10] but also from the content of the oracle. Herntrich is therefore forced to attribute the "section, vv 30–33, which is in itself unclear" to an "exilic redactor,"[11] while Bertholet assumes that it emerged in the prophet's later exilic period. There is no justification whatsoever for denying such an independent oracle to the prophet (Hölscher).[12]

Interpretation

■ **33:30** The divine saying addressed to Ezekiel ("son of man") gives first of all a graphic description of the commotion aroused in Ezekiel's vicinity among his fellow countrymen in exile after his mouth has been opened (v 22).[13] By the walls of the houses, in the doorways, that is in shady places, they stand and talk with each other about Ezekiel and are unexpectedly ready to come running to hear what the prophet has to say from God. The call to attention with which elsewhere the prophet must summon his people (Am 3:1; 4:1; 5:1; Ezek 6:3; 13:2; and other passages) can now, unexpectedly, be heard in the mouth of the people themselves, somewhat fuller in wording but exactly corresponding in its content.

■ **33:31aα** So they summon one another, come running, as people have come running through the ages whenever something sensational is to be seen, and sit down in front of the prophet (8:1; 14:1; 20:1).[14]

If all this appears from the outside to be a situation of prophetic success, there is nevertheless for the eye which really sees (that of the prophet, whose anguished observation has here been inserted into the divine address) no doubt that the situation is in reality quite different.

■ **33:32** V. 32, which originally followed directly after v 31aα, reveals the real situation. The prophet's word is heard like the love song of the minstrel, whose voice is pleasant and who is skilled in playing the accompanying stringed instrument (Is 5:1–7 shows the daring prophetic secondary use of this type of song).[15] But that is not the way in which the divine word really ought to be heard—binding, so that hearing should be translated into action.[16]

■ **33:31aβb** In a secondary addition (see v 31 note g) there has been added a further motivation: The mouths and hearts of the listeners are sick, for they have been driven by lust and avarice (on בצע "unjust gain" see 22:13, 27).

The description permits a specific conclusion concerning the nature of the prophetic word which is here presupposed. It is a word which invites men to hear it. There is, on the one hand, the fact that we have here an inflammatory proclamation of judgment over a Jerusalem which is still in existence.[17] It is a word which opens up a future. On the other hand, however, it is also a word which summons man to obey God and which demands a decision from him. If we keep in mind, for example, the continuation of Ezekiel 20 which was added after 587 (20:32ff), we will find both aspects united there. Here too there is a reminiscence of the office of watchman.

Quell has described impressively the vexation of the prophet found here, the vexation of being listened to meekly and even eagerly and at the same time not being heard properly. Can one, under these circumstances, still be a prophet?

■ **33:33** It is characteristic that the divine response which confronts the vexation of the prophet produces no other reasons for the endorsement of the prophetic office save

10 On this see above p. 184.
11 Herntrich, *Ezechielprobleme,* 115 note 1; 127 note 3.
12 On the arguments of Torrey see Spiegel, "Ezekiel," 294–296.
13 On "son of man" see 1, 131f.
14 On this see 1, 236.
15 On the stress on lasciviousness to be found in עגב and its derivatives full information is given in Ezek 23 (see 1, 484 on 23:5).
16 See also Quell, *Propheten,* 184f.
17 Quell, *Propheten,* 184 note 2, is different: "It is, precisely, harsh preaching which often pleases most."

the one: When the word arrives—and it *will* arrive—it will be realized that a prophet has been there.[18] God stands by his word, which in any case has a content of reality and event.[19] It is not a question of a predictive mechanism of whose functioning the prophet is convinced, but of a belief in the reliability of Yahweh in his actions.

But what is it that is to arrive? After what has been said it must be a double event. Yahweh will continue his work with Israel along the lines that he has promised. At the same time, however, he will also stand by the word to the individual which he has established through his watchman.

Aim

While 33:21–29 made it clear that even after the collapse of Judah and the destruction by fire of Jerusalem there existed in Israel survivors who had not understood what God had said, one might be inclined to add that among the exiles the guarantee had been given that God's word has its hearers.

Vv 30–33, on the other hand, reveal the great vexation of the prophet, that he certainly finds many to listen but few to obey. Where the human heart refuses to have anything to do with repentance, the word of God is again and again exposed to misinterpretation. It has its beauty. But then men can be caught up in its outward beauty. It has its topicality. But then men can make it into a topical subject of conversation, become excited about it, hold long brilliant discussions about it—and fail to hear the living God in it. Thus helplessly is the divine word exposed to the possibility of being misunderstood. Thus is the prophet unprotected and open to misunderstanding.

Escape into a system of external securities for correct understanding, into the ingenuities of language, into the obscurity of lofty debate which is no longer accessible to all—this would be obvious. The prophet could feel tempted to submit his particular nature to proof by the external accessories of his preaching (Jer 23:25ff). The present divine saying knows nothing of such securities and bulwarks for the transmitter. It knows only the one security. God himself promises to stand by his word to prove its validity. The preacher, however, is called to hazard it with this security alone.

18 On v 33abα see 24:24; on v 33bβγ see 2:5 (1, 133f).

19 See also the criterion for prophecy in Dtn 18:21f; Jer 28:9, but also Is 55:10f.

The Shepherds of Israel and Israel as God's Flock

Bibliography

Karl Begrich
"Das Messiasbild des Ezechiel," *ZWTh* 47 (1904): 433–461.

William Hugh Brownlee
"Ezekiel's Poetic Indictment of the Shepherds," *HTR* 51 (1958): 191–203.

L. Dürr
Ursprung und Ausbau der israelitisch-jüdischen Heilandserwartung; ein Beitrag zur Theologie des Alten Testamentes (Berlin: Schwetschke, 1925), especially 116–124.

Witold Gronkowski
Le messianisme d'Ezéchiel (Strasbourg, 1930).

Erling Hammershaimb
"Ezekiel's View of the Monarchy" in *Studia orientalia Ioanni Pedersen . . . dicata* (Hauniae: Munksgaard, 1953), 130–140; reprinted in *idem, Some Aspects of Old Testament Prophecy from Isaiah to Malachi* (København: Rosenkilde og Bagger, 1966), 51–62.

V. Hamp
"Das Hirtenmotiv im Alten Testament" in *Episcopus; Studien über das Bischofsamt. Festschrift seiner Eminenz Michael Kardinal von Faulhaber, Erzbischof von München-Freising zum 80. Geburtstag dargebracht* (Regensburg: Gregorius, 1949), 7–20.

Joachim Jeremias
"*ποιμήν*," *TDNT* 6, 485–502.

Dieter Müller
"Der gute Hirte; Ein Beitrag zur Geschichte ägyptischer Bildrede," *Zeitschrift für ägyptische Sprache und Altertumskunde* 86 (1961): 126–144.

Jean Gabriel Rembry
"Le Thème du berger dans l'oeuvre d'Ezéchiel," *Studii biblici Franciscani* 11 (1960/61): 113–144.

Albert Schott
Die Vergleiche in den akkadischen Königsinschriften, MVÄG 30 (Leipzig: Hinrichs, 1925) 2, esp. 70–72.

See also on 37:15–28.

34

1 **And the word of Yahweh came to me: 2/**
Son of man, prophesy against the shep-
herds of Israel. Prophesy[a] and say to
them [,the shepherds][b]: Thus has [the

34:2 2a On the doubling of הנבא, see 13:2 note b. 𝔏^{S} reads after the second *prophetiza* another *fili hominis.*

b 𝔐 אלהים הרעים contains a difficult doublet. 𝔊 𝔙 𝔏^{S}, which do not attest the אלהים (𝔏^{S} has here *pastores Israel;* 𝔊^{Ant} [see Ziegler, *Susanna,* 77] omits v 2bα completely, as far as לרעים, as it does also the following הוי רעי ישראל), seem to suggest the required solution. This is accepted by Bertholet, Ehrlich, *Randglossen;* Fohrer. But it is difficult to understand the secondary insertion of an אלהים alongside the לרעים. A different solution seems to be offered by 𝔖, which takes לרעים as a vocative.

Lord][c] Yahweh said: Woe to the shepherds of Israel who feed themselves[d]! Should shepherds not feed the flock? 3/ <The milk>[a] you consume, and with the wool you clothe yourselves. The fatlings[b] you slaughter—the flock[c] you do not feed. 4/ <The sick>[a] you have not made

Following this, Bertholet emends to הרעים, while Driver, "Ezekiel," 302, with reference to the Aramaic texts in W. F. Albright, "An Aramaean Magical Text in Hebrew from the Seventh Century B.C.," *BASOR* 76 (1939): 8–10, simply takes the ל as the vocative particle. But a vocative, followed directly by the introductory messenger formula, would be quite unusual. One would expect the vocative to be followed at least by a summons to pay attention, as, e.g., in vv 7, 9. Thus, the most likely assumption is that the לרעים originally stood at the beginning as a content indicator, such as the יהודה לבית מלך in Jer 21:11 or the לנבאים in Jer 23:9, and found its way secondarily into the context of v 2. It is missing also in 𝔊^{A} and 𝔄. This is followed by Cornill, Toy, Herrmann, Brownlee.

c אדני is lacking in 𝔊 𝔏^{S} 𝔎^{Sa} 𝔄, see Appendix 1.

d אשר היו רעים אותם "who fed themselves" is attested by 𝔖 𝔅 𝔗. 𝔊 (𝔏^{S} 𝔄) *μὴ βόσκουσιν οἱ ποιμένες ἑαυτούς* presupposes an original הירעו רעים אותם, which is accepted by Cornill, Bertholet. But the analogy of 13:3 makes completely possible a descriptive clause which characterizes more precisely the groups of people addressed as רעים. On the expression of the reflexive by means of the verb with את and a suffix, see Ex 5:19; Gesenius-Kautzsch §135k.

3 3a 𝔐 הַחֵלֶב "the fat" (𝔖 שמינא; 𝔗, colorlessly, טובא). 𝔊, which in addition prefixes an *ἰδοὺ* (𝔏^{S} *ecce*), has *γάλα*; 𝔅 𝔏^{S} have a lacuna. Since the slaughtering of the beasts is mentioned only later, the word should be vocalized הֶחָלָב. In any event, one may seriously ask whether, in view of the אכל associated with it, the word is not to be understood, on the basis of 1 Sam 17:18 (Is 7:22), as "curds" or "cheese." Of milk 25:4 says שתה חלב (Ju 4:19 שקה).

b 5 MSS 𝔊 𝔏^{S} 𝔖 𝔅 all add the copula. On 𝔊 see 1:4 note a.

c 𝔐 הצאן 𝔊 *καὶ τὰ πρόβατά μου*; 𝔏^{S} *et oves meas;* 𝔅 *gregem autem meum.* 𝔖 וענא has only the copula, but no suffix, while 𝔗 ועמא interprets the image in terms of the world power which it describes, just as 𝔐 רעה "feed" is rendered here and already in v 2 by פרנס (cf. Greek *πρόνοος*) "care for, be in charge of." See note b. The rough style of 𝔐 should not be altered.

4 4a 𝔐 הנחלות is attested by 𝔊 *τὸ ἠσθενηκός*, 𝔏^{CS} *infirmum,* 𝔖 כריהא (singular) and is no doubt a copyist's error for הנחלה. Driver, "Linguistic Problems," 180, tries to avoid the ugly repetition of חלה in v 4a by assuming a stem נחל (Syriac נחל *macie confectus est,* Arabic *naḥala* "be emaciated") and reading here and in v 21 הַנֹּחֶלֶת. But the association of the two חלה-clauses in v 16 counsels against such a differentiation of חלה and נחל, for the latter of which there is no other OT evidence. A glance at v 16 would also counsel against the deletion of the first part of v 4a (so Cornill, Hölscher). In any case, a certain variation in the statement is achieved through the alternation of qal and nip'al. On this, see e.g., the שובו והשיבו in 14:6.

strong again[b], the ill you have not healed, the broken you have not bound up, the strayed you have not brought back, the lost you have not sought; and <the strong>[c] you have <brutally>[d] downtrodden. 5/ And (the beasts of) <my flock>[a] were scattered because there was no shepherd and became food for all the wild beasts (of prey)[b] [,and they were scattered 6/ <> (the beasts of) my flock][a]. On all the mountains and on

b The description in the imperfect in v 3 passes over in v 4 to the historical description in the perfect (v 5 the consecutive imperfect). Cf. 33:4ff.

c 𝔐 וּבְחָזְקָה. Thus, e.g., Rembry "et par la force." 𝔊 *καὶ τὸ ἰσχυρόν*, 𝔏^{CS} *et forte* suggest the adjective וּבַ,חֲזָקָה, and this is also supported by the repetition in v 16. On רדה ב see 29:15. The wrong vocalization in 𝔐 is a consequence of the dittography in the closing section of v 4. See note d.

d To 𝔐's אתם ובפרך there corresponds in 𝔊 the simple *μόχθῳ* (𝔏^{CS} *labore*). 𝔖 simply omits the concluding ובפרך since it does not know how to deal with it. The אתם—which is consequently lacking in the older tradition and which, after the preceding feminine and before the following ותפוצינה, ought to be read more correctly אתן (16:54), אותהן (23:47) or אותנה (34:21) (cf. however, אתהם in v 12) and which also, as a result of its defective writing, stands apart from the אותם of the context (vv 2, 8, 10; but then differently in vv 14, 23)—is surely to be understood as an erroneous dittography of the preceding [ר]דיתם which was inserted unskillfully be means of a copula before בפרך and necessitated the understanding of בחזקה as a noun (note c). On the possibility of a later positioning of the second of two coordinate nouns, Cooke points to Gen 28:14; Ex 34:27b; Dtn 7:14. Delitzsch, *Schreibfehler*, 160b, on the other hand, thinks that the misunderstanding of ובחזקה has necessitated the insertion of אתם ו. But is בחזקה so easily misunderstood after what has gone before? Driver, "Linguistic Problems," 180, reads ובחזקה רדיתם אַתֶּם בפרך. Hölscher deletes the whole of v 4b and, in addition, sees in ובפרך a gloss on ובחזקה.

5 5a 𝔊 *τὰ πρόβατά μου*, 𝔏^{CS} 𝔙 *oves meae*, 𝔖 עני attest the specification of the subject צאני. The originality of this reading is also supported by the repetition of the ותפוצינה צאני in vv 5/6. See v 6 note a.

b Here too 𝔗 explains the image לכל מלכות ארעא.

6 6a 𝔐 ישגו, not only by its lack of relationship but above all by its lack of agreement with the feminine plural subject, falls completely outside the context and is not attested by 𝔊 𝔏^{CS}. Since it also disrupts two words which belong together (ותפוצינה צאני) and since it is a form of the verb שגה "go astray" which does not otherwise occur in Ezekiel, Driver's emendation to שָׁגוּ ("Linguistic Problems," 181) does not really remove the difficulty. The word has come into the text as a very superficially achieved expansion in consequence of the wrong sentence division. Elsewhere it always describes human behavior. 𝔖 silently passes over ותפוצינה, which has already been expressed in v 5a and which seems superfluous alongside ישגו. But even the phrase ותפוצינה צאני, which remains after the deletion of ישגו, is suspect from the point of view of its originality, since, taken with its continuation, it disrupts the following sentence which has נפצו צאני as its predicate and subject, while it expresses, with the words of the preceding v

every high hill and over the whole land[b]
(the beasts of) my flock were scattered,
and there was no one who looked (for
them) or sought (them)[c].
7 **Therefore, you shepherds[a], hear the word[b]**
of Yahweh: 8/ As I live, says [the Lord][a]
Yahweh, indeed[b], because (the beasts
of) my flock have become the prey and
because (the beasts of) my flock have
become the food for all wild beasts (of
prey), because there was no shepherd
and <the shepherds>[c] did not look for
(the beasts of) my flock and the shep-
herds fed themselves but did not feed
(the beasts of) my flock, 9/ therefore, you
shepherds, hear the word of Yahweh[a]:
10/ Thus has [the Lord][a] Yahweh said:
See, I am against[b] the shepherds, and I
will demand (the beasts of) my flock from
their hand and will make an end of them
so that they no longer guard (the beasts
of) <my flock>[c]; and the shepherds shall
no longer feed themselves[d], and I will
tear (the beasts of) my flock from their
jaws so that they are no longer food for
them.
11 **For thus has [the Lord][a] Yahweh said: See,**
I myself[b] will seek (the beasts of) my
flock and will care for them. 12/ As a
shepherd cares for[a] his flock on the day
<of the storm>, [when he is in the midst
of the <scattered> (beasts of the) flock,][b]

5a, predicate and subject again at the beginning of the sentence. Thus, Herrmann is surely on the right lines when he finds in ותפוצינה צאני a catchword gloss which featured the word צאני (which has fallen out of v 5a) along with the catchword ותפוצינה and which then found its way into the wrong place in the text of vv 5/6.

b Since 𝔐 על כל פני הארץ is rendered in 𝔊 (𝔏^{CS}) by ἐπὶ προσώπου πάσης τῆς γῆς, it may be asked whether 𝔐 did not originally read על פני כל הארץ or whether the כל should not be deleted entirely (with 𝔊^{B}). So Cornill, Fohrer.

c 𝔙, remarkably, has *non erat, inquam, qui requireret.*

7 7a Instead of the vocative without the article רעים, it is preferable to read, on the basis of v 9, הרעים. See Gesenius-Kautzsch §126e.

b 𝔐 את is missing in 20 MSS^{Ken} (cf. v 9). The addition of the article in 𝔊^{O} in contrast to 𝔊 must be connected with the secondary insertion of the את.

8 8a אדני is lacking in 𝔊 𝔏^{CS} 𝔎^{Bo}, see Appendix 1.

b In 𝔐, after the formula for a divine saying, in continuation of the introductory חי אני there follows the introduction to the oath formula אם לא. This beginning, however, is not developed but is left as an anacoluthon. The recapitulation in v 8 of the invective (in the style of a lament) of vv 2–6 is subsequently subordinated as a clause of motivation (יען) to a הנה-clause (vv 9f), which is provided with a new introduction. This is expressed insufficiently clearly both in Gesenius-Kautzsch §149c and in Cooke on v 10.

c 𝔐 רעי is quite unusual alongside the normal usages [ה]רעים (vv 2, 7–10) or רעי ישראל (v 2). 𝔊 𝔏^{CS} 𝔖 doubtless attest the original reading הרעים, which in 𝔐 alongside צאני was also then wrongly changed to the suffixed form.

9 9a In 𝔊 (but not in 𝔏^{CS}) the summons to pay attention, which ought to follow the vocative here, has inadvertently fallen out.

10 10a אדני is lacking in 𝔊 𝔏^{CS} 𝔎^{Bo}, see Appendix 1.

b על–אל cf. 1:17 note a.

c 𝔐 צאן. 𝔊 (𝔏^{CS}) τὰ πρόβατά μου. The suffix has fallen out by haplography before the following ו.

d The אותם, which is taken by 𝔊 αὐτά (*sc.* τὰ πρόβατα), 𝔏^{S} *eas* (there is nothing corresponding to it in 𝔏^{C}) to refer to the sheep of the flock (cf. the secondary אתם in v 4), should no doubt be understood as in v 2 (note d).

11 11a אדני is lacking in 𝔊 𝔏^{CS} 𝔎^{Bo}, see Appendix 1.

b 𝔗 renders 𝔐 הנני אני by האנא מתגלי, thereby emphasizing the revelatory character of this prefixed formula of self-introduction.

12 12a 𝔐 כבקרת רעה. The Aramaizing form of the infinitive is eliminated by many (Herrmann, Bertholet, cf. Fohrer, BH^{3}) by the graphically slight emendation to כבקר הרעה.

b The text of 𝔐 ביום היותו בתוך צאנו נ׳׳ is obviously corrupt. 𝔊 solves the difficulty by characterizing the "day" mentioned here with the data of v

so shall I care for (the beasts of) my flock and rescue them from all the places where they were scattered on the day of cloud and darkness. 13/ And I will lead them out from among the nations and gather them from other lands and bring them into their own land and let them feed on[a] the mountains of Israel, in[b] the watercourses and in all the inhabited places[c] of the country. 14/ I will feed them on good pasture[a], and[b] on Israel's high mountains[c] will be their grazing-land. There they will lie down in good

12bβ as (*ἡμέρα*) *ὅταν ᾖ γνόφος καὶ νεφέλη* and, leaving out the suffix reference of צאנו to the shepherd and presupposing a reading נפרשות, renders the rest literally *ἐν μεσῳ προβάτων διακεχωρισμένων*. Similarly, too, 𝔏^CS. 𝔖 leaves the second-named complex completely unattested and renders the first by the simple ביומא דזיקא "on the day of storm." On this basis, Cornill, e.g., reads ביום סופה and deletes the rest as a gloss. In fact, one would (with 𝔊 𝔏^CS 𝔖) expect a statement along these lines and describe as a gloss-like addition the uninspired and, from the point of view of content, not very satisfying reference to shepherds "in the midst of" the scattered flock (נפרשות should certainly be read [on this see 17:21] and the determining suffix in צאנו is suspect alongside the indeterminate attribute). Those who wish to maintain that the second complex is original will have to regard, as do, e.g., Toy, Cooke, בתוך as an erroneous dittography of היות (which is to be read without a suffix) and thus read "on the day when (the beasts of) his flock were scattered." Driver, "Linguistic Problems," 181, conjectures, on the basis of Syriac תכב pe'al *celeravit, praevenit, advenit, invasit, oppressit, vexavit* and Aramaic תכף "attack suddenly," a word תכוב (in the day of unforeseen disaster), but changes his mind in "Ezekiel," 302, where he translates 𝔐: "on the day when he is in the midst of his sheep, scattered as they are."

13 13a על–אל cf. 1:17 note a.

b 𝔊𝔏^S 𝔖 add the copula, see 1:4 note a.

c 𝔐 מושבי. The (suffixed) plural form of מושב (8:3; 28:2; 48:15) is elsewhere in Ezekiel formed with the feminine plural ending (6:6, 14 and everywhere else in the OT [on 37:23 see note b there]). An emendation to מיטב (Ehrlich, *Randglossen;* Herrmann; Bertholet) is, however, scarcely justified. Driver, "Linguistic Problems," 181, distinguishes two roots ישב: 1) Arabic *waṯaba* "sit down." Hence מושב, plural מושבות "dwelling place." 2) Arabic *wasaba* "have much grass." Hence מושב, plural מושבים "grassy meadow."

14 14a Koehler-Baumgartner (under נוה) distinguishes bewteen נוה "place where one grazes" and מרעה "fact that one grazes." The present verse makes clear, however, that in what follows מרעה too can describe quite concretely the food (found at the grazing place), the "pasture" (so too Koehler-Baumgartner under מרעה) and thus comes close to the meaning of נוה.

b 𝔊 𝔏^S suppress the copula here, but insert one on the other hand before their rendering of 𝔐 תרבצנה. The latter is then expanded, doubtless in order to give more weight to a clause which has consequently become too brief, by means of a *καὶ ἐκεῖ ἀναπαύσονται* (*et illic requiesci[en]t*). 𝔐 should be adhered to. On the double translation in 𝔊 see 16:14 (note a); 17:23 (note b); 20:18 (note b); and elsewhere.

c 𝔐 בהרי מרום ישראל. 𝔊 (𝔏^S) singular as in 17:23; 20:40. 𝔗 בטור קודשא דישראל (cf. 20:40). But in the

pasture-land and have good grazing[d] on[e]
the mountains of Israel. 15/ I (myself)
will feed (the beasts of) my flock, and I
(myself) will make them lie down[a], says
[the Lord][b] Yahweh.
16 I shall seek the lost, bring back the strayed,
bind up the broken, heal the sick and
<watch over>[a] [the fat and][b] the strong. I
shall feed it[c] in righteousness.
17 As for me, you (beasts of) my flock[a], thus
has [the Lord][b] Yahweh said: See, I shall
declare the right of one sheep against
another, against rams and goats.[c] 18/ Is
it too little for you—[a]you feed on the good

passages cited, which speak of the establishment of the messianic and cultic center, the singular is used, in view of the subject matter, in a different way from here, where later the plural is used once again (attested also by 𝔊 𝔏^{S}) to refer to the mountains of Israel as the pasture-land of the flock.

d Literally, with *figura etymologica*, "graze a grazing."

e אל–על cf. 1:17 note a.

15a 𝔊 𝔏^{S} follow this with yet another recognition formula and, with their then following *τάδε λέγει κύριος*, *haec dicit dominus*, which would correspond to כה אמר יהוה, give the impression that a new section begins at v 16 with a new introductory messenger formula. See further below under "Form."

b אדני is lacking in 𝔊 𝔏^{S} 𝔎^{Bo}, see Appendix 1. But see also note a.

16 16a 𝔐 אשמיד "I shall wipe out" presupposes a negative evaluation of the "fat and strong" who have just been mentioned. Such an evaluation can also be discerned in 𝔗, which once again expounds the intention of the image and speaks of "sinners" (חטאייא) and "guilty" (חייביא). The rest of the tradition (𝔊 𝔏^{SW} 𝔙 𝔖) presupposes a reading אשמר, and this is also to be expected in view of v 4. So most of the commentators. Rembry, as already in v 4, adheres to 𝔐.

b 𝔐 ואת השמנה is not attested by 𝔊 𝔏^{SW}. It is highly probable, in view of the heavy dependence of v 16 on v 4, that the expression did not originally occur in the text. שמן was used only in v 14 to describe the succulence of the pasture.

c Not only is 𝔐 ארענה introduced by the copula in 𝔊 𝔏^{SW} 𝔙 𝔖 (see 1:4 note a), but the object of רעה, which is contained in its suffix, is rendered in the plural. This has led Cornill and others to emend to ארען Fohrer deletes ארענה as an explanatory gloss on אשמר. But one hesitates to destroy the expression רעה במשפט. The singular suffix of 𝔐 must continue the singular objects of the preceding verbs, unless (which appears to me to be probable) one refers the just grazing quite specifically to the "strong" who has been mentioned immediately before and on whom Yahweh also bestows his justice. This already leads on to what follows (see "Form"). 𝔗 again expounds ואפרנס עמי בדינא.

17 17a 𝔐 אתנה צאני. 𝔊 𝔏^{SW} do not reproduce the suffix and seem to point to an original אתן הצאן (Cooke, BH^{3}). For this, reference could be made to v 31, the only occurrence of אתן in the OT. See also, however, v 31 note a. אתנה occurs also in 13:11, 20; Gen 31:6.

b אדני is lacking in 𝔊 𝔏^{W}, see Appendix 1.

c 𝔖 translates the last two words of 𝔐 parallel to what has gone before: (הא דאן אנא בית נקיא לנקיא) ובית דכרא לדכרא. 𝔗 again neutralizes the image and refers to "sinners" and "guilty."

18 18a Not only do 𝔊 𝔏^{SW} introduce a copula at the beginning of v 18 (1:4 note a), but make the tran-

pasture and what remains of your pasture you trample down with your feet, and you drink the clear water[b], but what remains over you trouble with your feet? 19/ And (the beasts of) my flock must feed on what your feet have trampled[a] and drink what your feet have troubled[b].

20 Therefore thus has [the Lord][a] Yahweh said [to them][b]: See, I—I myself[c]—declare the right of the lean beast against the fat beast[d], 21/ because you have all pushed aside the weak with side and shoulder and have knocked them down with your horns[a] until you have scattered them abroad. 22/ And I shall rescue (the beasts of) my flock, and they shall no longer become a prey. And I shall declare the right of one beast against the other[a].

23 And I shall set [over them][a] a single[b] shepherd, who will feed them[a], (namely) my servant David. [He will feed them[a]][c] and

sition from the introductory question to what follows by means of a ὅτι (*quoniam, quod*). On this see 𝔐 of Nu 16:9, 13. Is 7:13 has an infinitive following on המעט.

b 𝔐 משקע, a *hapax legomenon.* Literally "water in which the dirt has sunk" (שקע 32:14).

19 19a מרמס, a favorite word with Isaiah (5:5; 7:25; 10:6; 28:18), elsewhere only in Mic 7:10; Dan 8:13.

b מרפש, a *hapax legomenon* formed from רפש (v 18; 32:2) on the analogy of מרמס.

20 20a אדני is lacking in 𝔊 𝔏^{SW} ℜ, see Appendix 1.

b The extension of the introductory messenger formula by אליהם (𝔙 *ad vos*) is unusual. Since it is not attested by 𝔊 𝔏^{SW}, it is scarcely original (Cornill, Toy, Herrmann, Bertholet).

c On 𝔗 see v 11 note b.

d Literally "between the fat beast and the thin beast." 𝔐 בְּרִיָּה should either be vocalized as בָּרִיָּה or be considered a scribal error for בְּרִיאָה (so v 3). See Bauer-Leander §74h'.

21 21a The versions have treated the text with remarkable freedom. Not only do 𝔊 𝔏$^{W(S)}$ 𝔙 𝔗 put the verbs of v 21a in the past and 𝔊 𝔏$^{W(S)}$ smooth the absolute phrase בצד ובכתף by the addition of a suffix (the fact that 𝔗 refers to "strength" instead of "horns" and speaks of expulsion among the nations is in line with its general tendency), but 𝔖 goes still further and puts everything into the third person plural. Everything that follows תנגחו in 𝔐 is summarized by 𝔊 (𝔏^{W}) in the concise sentence καὶ πᾶν τὸ ἐκλεῖπον ἐξεθλίβετε.

22 22a 𝔖 expands the text on the basis of v 17 (note c).

23 23a 𝔐 reveals a remarkable variation in the use of suffixes. Alongside the masculine forms עליהם and אתם, there are the feminine forms אתהן and להן (the להם of MSS Eb 24 must, against BH^{3}, be an assimilation to what follows). This is connected with the fact that the image referred to by the feminine form, that of the beasts of the flock, is abandoned in what follows and from v 24ab on (with the exception of the אתן in v 31, see note a there) exclusively masculine usage is employed. In v 23 now the אתם in v 23bα belongs to a secondary expansion (note c). Consequently the masculine עליהם, which is missing in Eb 24 and which Driver, "Linguistic Problems," 181, wishes to emend to עלהן, is of doubtful originality. The text of v 23 depends originally on the preceding verses (images of shepherd and flock). The following references to prince (נשיא) and people (also Jer 23:4?) have affected it only in secondary additions.

b 𝔐 אחד. Misread by 𝔊 ἕτερον 𝔏^{W} *alium* as אחר. See also 11:19 note a. According to Cooke "an attempt at reconciliation with v 15."

c 𝔐 הוא ירעה אתם is not attested by 𝔊 𝔏^{W}. The passage, which with regard to content simply repeats the ורעה אתהן of v 23a, is revealed as an addition only by its masculine אתם (see note a).

he will be[d] their[a] shepherd. 24/ and I,
Yahweh[a], will be their God. And my
servant[b] David will be prince in their
midst. I, Yahweh, have spoken[c].
25 **And I shall make a covenant of salvation**
with them[a] and shall make an end of the
wild beasts in the land, and they will
dwell in safety[b] in the wilderness and
will (be able to) sleep[c] in the woods. 26/
And I shall send < <> (showers of) dew
in its season> <>[a] and shall cause rain to
fall[b] in its season—they will be showers
of blessing[c]. 27/ And the trees of the
field will bear fruit, and the land will yield
its produce, and they will dwell[a] in
safety[b] in their land and will know that I
am Yahweh when I break the bars of

d In $\mathfrak{L}^{W}$ v 23bβ is also missing. Did 𝔊, *καὶ ἔσται* (*αὐτῶν ποιμήν*) have before it simply והיה? The fuller formulation of 𝔐 (והוא יהיה) might then have been chosen, exactly like the expansion of v 23bα, with an eye to the continuation in v 24.

24 24a 𝔐 יהוה is attested by the versions generally, but is missing in Eb 24. The corresponding *κύριος* is missing in $𝔊^{130,544}$ Hil. Ps 131:1 *ἐγὼ κύριος* in Eus. *ecl.* Does that go back to an older form of the text in which the two four-stress lines of the covenant formula in vv 23bβ, 24aα were metrically precisely balanced, or must we reckon with a secondary assimilation?

b 𝔐 עבדי is not attested by 𝔊 $\mathfrak{L}^{W}$. 𝔐 could represent a secondary assimilation to v 23.

c The concluding formula of v 24b is missing in 𝔖.

25 25a In a secondary re-application of the thought, 𝔊 $\mathfrak{L}^{W}$ make David the recipient of the covenant.

b 𝔐 לבטח remains unattested in 𝔊 $\mathfrak{L}^{W}$. But (against Cornill, Fohrer) it can scarecely be dispensed with from the point of view of subject matter. Did 𝔊, in view of the repetition of the word in v 27, want to abbreviate?

c 𝔐 וישנו. 𝔗 ויתעתקון "they will become old." 𝔙 subordinates the first part of v 25b as a relative clause to the second part, with which לבטח is associated with the omission of the copula before ישנו.

26 26a 𝔐 ונתתי אותם וסביבות גבעתי ברכה "and I shall make them and what is round about my hill a blessing" can scarcely be regarded as the original text. The unusual designation of the temple hill (𝔗 בית מקדשי) as גבעתי (גבעה in Ezekiel, in 6:3, 13; 20:28; 34:6; 35:8; 36:4, 6, is always used in a different way), the varying evidence of the versions, but also the sequence of thought in the transition from v 25 to v 26b lead one to suspect a more far-reaching corruption. This is also against Driver, "Ezekiel," 302, who believes that he can repair the text by transposing וסביבות גבעתי to the end of v 25. 𝔊 (with $\mathfrak{L}^{W}$ 𝔙 𝔗 𝔖) does not attest the copula before סביבות or (with $\mathfrak{L}^{W}$) ברכה at the end of v 26a. 𝔗 expands the end of v 26a to ויהון מברכין. 𝔖 abbreviates v 26a considerably and rearranges the text to read ואתל להון בורכתי חדר רמתי. So, on the basis of 𝔊, ברכה must surely be a secondary expansion. What remains may then tentatively, parallel to v 26b, be read with Bertholet (partly on the basis of Cornill) as את הרביבים בעתם. There can be no possibility of certainty. The thought of the restoration and of the temple hill is certainly not original, however, between v 25 and v 26b.

b Literally "come down." 𝔊 ($\mathfrak{L}^{W}$) has the colorless expression *καὶ δώσω . . . ὑμῖν*. 𝔗 להון.

c 𝔊 *ὑετὸν εὐλογίας* leaves יהיו unattested and puts the remaining expression in the singular (as does also 𝔖).

27 27a Literally "be."

b 𝔐 לבטח 𝔊 translates here more fully *ἐν ἐλπίδι εἰρήνης*. Σ *μή φοβούμενοι*.

their yoke[c] and rescue them from the hand of those who enslaved them[d]. 28/ And they will no longer be a prey to the nations, and the (wild) beasts of the land[a] will no longer devour them, and they will dwell in safety, and no one shall make them afraid. 29/ And I shall set up for them a <prosperous> plantation,[a] and they will no longer be assailed by hunger[b], nor will they (any longer) (have to) suffer the reproach of the nations, 30/ and they[a] will know that I, Yahweh, am their God [with them][b] and that they are my people, the house of Israel, says [the Lord][c] Yahweh.

31 **[But you are][a] (the beasts of) my flock, the [human][b] flock of my pasture are you. But[c] I am your God[d], says [the Lord][e] Yahweh.**

c 𝔐 את מטות עלם. 𝔊 (𝔏^W) *τον ζυγὸν αὐτῶν*, 𝔙 *catenas iugi eorum*. 𝔗 ניר תוקפהון, 𝔖 נירהון. מֹטָה is not otherwise attested in Ezekiel (on 30:18 see note b there), and על, too, occurs only here. 𝔊 𝔖 must have shortened the usual expression (e.g. Lev 26:13; on this see Jer 27:2; 28:13), which 𝔙 and 𝔗 do not correctly understand either.

d Literally "who work with them."

28 28a 𝔗 "the kingdoms of the earth."

29 29a 𝔐 מטע לשם "an honorable (famous) planting"; cf. 𝔙 *germen nominatum*. 𝔗 ניצבא לקיימא. 𝔊 *φυτὸν εἰρήνης*, 𝔏^W *plantationem pacis*, 𝔖 נצבתא לשלמא suggest a reading מטע שלם (or מַטַּע שָׁלֵם), which is more meaningful as a contrast to the following statement about dying of hunger. *ZB* "garden of salvation."

b Expanded by 𝔊^LC Tht by the statement *καὶ οὐκέτι ἔσονται ὀλίγοι ἀριθμῷ ἐν τῇ γῇ*.

30 30a MSS Edd introduce the explanatory "the nations" (הגוים) as the subject of the recognition (on which see, e.g., 37:28).

b 𝔐 אתם, which from the point of view of form disrupts the two-part covenant formula, is not attested by 3 MSS, 𝔊 𝔏^W 𝔖. Its purpose is to develop more fully the content of the covenant formula. See the exposition. 𝔗 interprets אנא יהוה מימרי בסעדהון אלההון.

c אדני is lacking in 𝔊 (in 𝔏^W the whole formula for a divine saying is missing), see Appendix 1.

31 31a 𝔐 אתן, as a feminine form within vv 24ff where the masculine forms have been used consistently (v 23 note a), is surprising. Since it is not attested by 𝔊 𝔏^W 𝔎 and since it gives too great a weight to the first half of the verse in the antithetical structure of v 31a and v 31b, it should be deleted as an addition. Before צאן 𝔊 adds the copula, see 1:4 note a.

b 𝔐 אדם refers the image specifically to the people whom it depicts, see also 36:38. It is missing in 𝔊 𝔏^W and is not expressed in the admittedly very free text of 𝔗. Thus the suspicion is aroused that the word is a secondary insertion. For the possibility of the addition of a qualifying noun in the accusative, Driver, "Ezekiel," 302, refers to 16:27.

c Before the antithesis one would expect a copula: ואני. Such is attested by 𝔊 𝔙 𝔖. In 𝔏^W v 31b*a* is missing.

d At this point 𝔊 𝔙 𝔖 also have the equivalent of יהוה. But this is not the formula of introduction but the two-part covenant formula, so 𝔐 should be preserved.

e אדני is lacking in 𝔊 𝔏^W, see Appendix 1.

Form

Ezekiel 34 deals with the shepherds of Israel and with the condition of the people of God under good and bad shepherding. The relatively self-contained nature of the theme, which is vigorously taken up again at the end in v 31, does not however correspond to an equally self-contained form in the chapter.

To assist in the dividing up of the extensive complex there are, in the first instance, a series of introductory and concluding formulae. Introductory messenger formulae are to be found in vv 2, 10, 11, 17, 20; formulae for a divine saying, in vv 8, 15, 30, 31. In addition, there are the summons to pay attention in vv 7, 9, the emphatic concluding אני יהוה דברתי ("I, Yahweh, have spoken") in v 24 and the two recognition formulae in vv 27, 30. If this formal material is to be used to divide up the chapter, then it must be associated with other observations with regard to form and content.

The first complex vv 2–6, introduced by the introductory formula in v 2, is initially in the style of a woe oracle over the shepherds of Israel. The form of the woe oracle can be found in Ezekiel also in 13:3–16, 18–23 and has been discussed above.[1] As in chapter 13, the woe oracle has been integrated from the formal point of view into a divine speech. From the point of view of content it contains an element of invective, which one expects to be followed by an oracle of judgment. This seems to follow the second address to the shepherds, which is introduced by לכן ("therefore"). The shepherds are here called to hear the word which Yahweh introduces by the oath formula (with the emphatic formula for a divine saying).[2] But this emphatic new beginning is, surprisingly, followed by another invective against the shepherds, introduced by יען ("because"). Only vv 9f, again introduced by לכן ("therefore"), an address and summons to pay attention, contain the expected threat of judgment against the shepherds. Since vv 7f, by the use of the *nota accusativa* in the summons to pay attention (unique in Ezekiel), by the exact repetition of v 5b and further literal dependence on vv 2–6, are suspect as a later expansion, the original continuation of the invective must be found in vv 9f. The statement of judgment which is uttered here is introduced by the formula of summons to a duel or formula of encounter.[3] But also the unit which then follows, vv 11–15, which is again introduced by an introductory messenger formula and concluded by a formula for a divine saying, should not be separated from what precedes. With once more a strong emphasis on the fact that God now acts (הנני אני "see, I myself"), it brings out the positive side of the judgment oracle on the bad shepherds which was pronounced already in v 10: Yahweh himself takes care of his flock. At the same time there is developed the historical significance for Israel of the intervention of the good shepherd. V 15, with its repeated, emphatic אני ("I [myself]") and formula for a divine saying, gives the impression of being the concluding statement of this oracle of salvation. The expansion in 𝔊 by means of the recognition formula (note a) underlines and emphasizes this concluding character.

But how then is v 16 to be adjudged, standing oddly in the no man's land between the concluding formula of v 15 and the new introductory formula of v 17? V 16 is striking, on the one hand, by its literal dependence on what is said in v 4. On the other hand, it contains in its concluding phrase ארענה במשפט ("I shall feed it in righteousness") the key-word which dominates the discussion that follows: the reference to the justice of Yahweh's judgment against his flock (שׁפט "to declare the right" vv 17, 20, 22). Thus this verse, deleted by Hölscher, has the role of a connecting link, joining the discussion that follows in vv 17ff to vv 1–15.

V 17 opens with a renewed summons directed now at the flock. The following complex, which ends at the latest with the formulaic אני יהוה דברתי ("I, Yahweh, have spoken") of v 24, is divided into two sections by the two introductory messenger formulae (vv 17, 20). Vv 17–19 begin by proclaiming the judgment in succinct terms (v 17), but then continue as an invective (vv 18f). In v 20 there follows, introduced as in v 11 by הנני אני ("see, I myself"), a speech of judgment, which then soon turns into a proclamation of salvation. But here too, in v 21, introduced by יען ("because"), there has been incorporated a belated invective. On account of the original content of the latter, one cannot, on purely formal grounds, delete it. In vv 23f the transition from the topic of the flock to that of the nation had become noticeable

1 1, 290.

2 On this see 1, 176, and Baumgärtel, "Formel," 279.

3 See 1, 175; see above p. 98.

(v 23 note a). Whether this grammatical transition must lead to the separation of vv 23f from the original text will have to be discussed in the course of the exposition. From the point of view of form, v 24, with its concluding formula, would no doubt provide a good, resounding conclusion to the preceding section, vv 17–24.

Of what remains, vv 25–31, v 31 itself is set apart by the concluding formula for a divine saying in v 30. Also from the point of view of content v 31 proves to be an addition, in that it pointedly takes us once again to the theme of the beginning and refers what was said in v 30 to the image of the flock, which was not in evidence in vv 25–30. The latter, on the other hand, cannot be further subdivided. The two-fold appearance of the recognition formula in vv 27 and 30 is not to be attributed to two separate oracles (Hölscher), but to the already noted form of the expanded proof-saying, whose expansion (introduced with ב and the infinitive) ends once more in a fuller form of the recognition formula.[4]

Thus Ezekiel 34 can be divided into the two complexes vv 1–6, 9–15 and vv 17–22 (24?), which both reveal the sequence invective—oracle of judgment—oracle of salvation, and the bipartite proof-saying with double conclusion, vv 25–30. In addition, there is the insertion in vv 7f, the transitional verse 16 and the thematic concluding oracle in v 31.

Brownlee elaborates from vv 1–10 a poem consisting of nine or ten tristichs, each consisting of three (or, in v 3, of two) stresses. This he considers to be an independent oracle of disaster from the period before 587. Now it certainly cannot be denied that in vv 3f, e.g. (and even elsewhere), we find exalted language which shows a series of brief sentences with two (v 3) and three (v 4) stresses. But the elaboration of a self-contained metrical structure of consistent regularity is possible only with difficulty. So here too, especially since there is a lack of any more precise special characteristic, it is not possible to go beyond what has already been said about chapter 16.[5]

The time and place of of origin will be discussed after the detailed exposition.

Interpretation

■ **34:1,2** In another divine word the prophet ("son of man") receives the commission to prophesy against "the shepherds of Israel."[6] As in 13:2; 37:9 (cf. 11:4), the הנבא ("prophesy") is repeated before the ואמרת ("and say"). When Ezekiel describes the leaders of Israel as "shepherds," he enters into an old form of speech traditional in the Near East. Already in the Sumerian sphere it can be affirmed of the lofty language which is set apart from normal language: "The stock term for 'king' is 'shepherd' or 'good shepherd.'"[7] Ur-nammu of Ur receives this title from the mouth of Enlil who has summoned him "from among his numerous people": "Let him be shepherd! ran Nunamnir's majestic word."[8] The same image is found in the Akkadian royal inscriptions.[9] Thus Hammurabi can describe himself as "the shepherd who brings salvation and whose staff is righteous."[10] But the shepherd title is found also among the Assyrians and Neo-Babylonians. Of Merodach-baladan II it is said on a boundary stone: "He is truly the shepherd who gathers together again those who have strayed."[11] *re'û* "graze" becomes a technical term for "rule." Even gods such as Enlil, Marduk and especially Tammuz[12] can adopt the title. In ancient Egypt too, in the Pyramid texts, the blind sky-god is described by this name when, e.g., the dead person is addressed: "O Osiris X, may Mekhenti-irty, your shepherd who is behind your calves, protect you"[13] or when it can be said in the Teaching of Merikare: "Well-tended are men, the cattle of God."[14] Here, too, alongside the divine shepherd, there stands the protective king. Müller has described in detail the various aspects under which the shepherdhood of the god and of the earthly ruler is regarded through the millenia (particularly frequent in the eighteenth and twentieth dynasties).

The OT stands in this tradition (Dürr, Hamp). In this

4 See above pp. 96f.
5 Otherwise than in the examples of the קינה (on this see above p. 87). On chapter 16 see 1,334.
6 See 1,144f; on "son of man" see 1,131f.
7 Falkenstein-von Soden, 29.
8 Falkenstein-von Soden, 87.
9 See, e.g., the survey in Schott, *Vergleiche,* 70–72.
10 Dürr, *Ursprung,* 118.
11 Dürr, *Ursprung,* 119.
12 See 1,242.
13 Dieter Müller, "gute Hirte," 128.
14 Adolf Erman, *The Literature of the Ancient Egyptians,* tr. Aylward M. Blackman (London: Methuen, 1927), 83.

connection we must observe that the image of the shepherd here preserves its full vividness to a much greater extent than in the courtly style of Israel's powerful neighbors and does not become fossilized into a conventional formula of courtly language (Jeremias). The vocation of shepherd has preserved its significance in Palestine right to our own time.[15] Both Israel's kings (David) and her prophets (Amos) still had direct contact with it. Thus the conventional language has been filled over and over again with insight. In the OT too, in the first place Yahweh can be addressed as the "shepherd of Israel" (Ps 80:2; Gen 49:24, emended text), and his caring activity towards the people (Ps 77:21; Is 40:11) and towards the individual (Psalm 23) can be fully described in this image. But then here too, the rulers of the people can be described as shepherds, even though there is no evidence of the name "shepherd" being used for the individual ruler in any of the extant royal titles. This is particularly frequent in the book of Jeremiah (2:8; 3:15; 10:21; 22:22; 25:34–36; 50:6; see also 31:10; 50:7f,17,19,44–45, as well as Zech 11:4–17). In the present context, however, reference must be made above all to Jer 23:1ff, a passage which is unmistakably the model for Ezekiel 34. Miller has listed in detail the links between Jer 23:1f and Ezekiel 34.[16] In both we find the form of the woe-oracle directed against the shepherds. The fact that the flock belongs to Yahweh is specifically underlined. The key-words אבד ("destroy"), פוץ ("scatter"), נדח ("to drive away") are to be found. The description צאן מרעיתי ("flock of my pasture") links Jer 23:1 and Ezek 34:31 (with the suffix of the second person also in Ps 74:1; 79:13; with the suffix of the third person Ps 95:7; 100:3). Brownlee's attempt to work out a basic text of Ezek 34:1–10 which would be independent of Jeremiah 23 is not really convincing.

While this may be repeating here the observation already made in connection with chapter 13, chapter 16 and chapter 23 that Ezekiel in many passages is influenced by Jeremiah not only in his choice of themes but also in the way in which he works them out, here too we must at once and once again emphasize what is unique in Ezekiel's treatment.[17] As was the case in chapters 16 and 23, chapter 34 is also characterized by the much broader layout and the fuller amplification of the common theme, which is developed in quite new directions and which receives an exhaustive treatment. Ezekiel's style (e.g. in v 4) is characterized by the series of sentences, parallel in structure, which instantly recall series of commands and lists. A certain inclination for stereotypes and for parallel repetition can also not be overlooked here. Yet even in Ezek 34 the image remains vigorous and lively.

Typical of Ezekiel is the address to those involved right at the ouset as "shepherds of Israel." What has been said above about the "prophets of Israel" can here be repeated with the appropriate variations.[18] In the address to the "shepherds of Israel" God's people are regarded as a whole.[19] Here too the question whether Ezekiel is thinking specifically of the leaders of the people in exile or in Judah-Jerusalem or, even further back, of those of the northern kingdom of Israel should not be posed. Here too, in marked distance from what is merely contemporary, the oracle is directed to the history of Israel as a whole—in judgment in the first instance, but then in promise. Here too, therefore, there is a lack of that passion which comes from direct personal involvement and which could still be felt in, for example, the royal oracles in Jeremiah 22 and even in Ezekiel 17. The prophetic word here is trying to say something total to the history of Israel as a whole. Brownlee's arguments overlook this side of Ezekiel 34.

The nobility and dignity of the office of shepherd reside in the fact that the shepherd works wholeheartedly for the flock. Jn 10:11 expresses it: "The good shepherd lays down his life for the sheep." Is it possible in this context to think that רעה ("shepherd") might suggest an Aramaism for רצה "take pleasure"? The shepherds of Israel have denied this nobility by thinking of themselves while busy with the flock. They thought of what benefit they could derive from the flock, but not of the well-being of the flock itself.

■ **34:3** It is not quite clear whether what is said in v 3 is already intended to describe reprehensible behavior on the part of the shepherds. That the shepherd in an outlying district should feed on the milk of the animals and live on the products which they provide is surely a natural process (1 Cor 9:7). The choice of the verb אכל

15 Dalman, *Arbeit,* 6.

16 Miller, *Verhältnis,* 106.

17 On chapter 13 see 1,291; on chapter 16 see 1,336f; on chapter 23 see 1,482.

18 See 1,292.

19 See also Appendix 2.

("to eat") has led here to the wrong vocalisation חֵלֶב ("fat") and has thus given the impression that what is referred to here in the first place is the consumption of the animals' flesh (their fat, of course, is not eaten in the case of a זבח "sacrifice," but is burnt on the altar Lev 3:17; 7:25; Dtn 32:38). The slaughtering of the beasts is, however, mentioned only in third place.[20] Also the fact that the shepherd takes some of the sheep's wool for his clothing seems at first sight to be irreproachable. Jewish law prohibits the purchase of wool, milk and kids from a shepherd.[21] The Gemara, on the other hand, permits the purchase of milk and cheese from a shepherd out in the desert.[22] This presupposes that the shepherd himself can, of course, live off these things. One could ask whether he has a right to take some of the animals' wool in order to clothe himself. The "harvest festival" of sheep-shearing is held in the presence of the owner of the sheep (1 Sam 25:2). The slaughter of the fat beasts, however, in any case goes beyond what is permitted and is a dereliction of the true office of the shepherd.

■ **34:4** With this active transgressing of the rights of shepherds, there is contrasted in v 4 a "negative mirror for shepherds" (Ziegler), whose statements are then used positively about Yahweh in the secondary linking-verse 16. Here there become clearly visible the dangers to which the flock is exposed in the lonely rugged territories on the edge of the inhabited country, how animals can fall ill, break a leg (Ex 22:9,13), allow themselves to be "separated" from the flock (נדח Dtn 22:1) or "lose" themselves (אבד Jer 50:6; of she-asses 1 Sam 9:3,20). It would be the shepherd's task to set the weak beasts on their feet again (חזק "to make strong"), to heal and bind up (30:21 of men), bring back and look for.[23] At the end 𝔐 summarizes the whole dereliction of duties in a reproach of their brutality (רדה "rule over" also in 29:15). Here there is mentioned again the category of the strong and healthy animals against whom the shepherds have acted brutally (note c). פרך ("brutality") is used more frequently in the Priestly writings: Ex 1:13f of the oppression of the Israelites by the Egyptians and Lev 25:43,46,53 רדה בפרך ("rule over with brutality") of the (forbidden) behavior towards one of one's own people who has become a slave through debt.

■ **34:5** As a consequence of this irresponsible behavior on the part of the shepherd, the flock has been scattered and has become the prey of the wild beasts who always constituted a danger in Palestine, lying in wait on the edge of the desert (cf. the shepherds' law in Ex 22:12 and see also Am 3:12).

■ **34:6** While the reference to the mountains and the high hills over which the flock is scattered still envisages, to begin with, the horizon of Canaan with its high places (גבעה רמה "high hill" 6:13; 20:28)[24] and the straying there of the sheep without a shepherd, the mention of the "whole world" goes far beyond that. This is surely an echo of the reality of Israel's exile. It is surely not permissible to eliminate, as Brownlee does, this conscious ambiguity of the "being scattered." The exile is the bitter fruit of the bad shepherding in which no one really sought or cared for his flock. דרש ("to seek") will return in vv 8, 10, 11 as a key-word. "Seek" is a crucial key-word of the shepherd imagery in the NT also (Mt 18:12; cf. Lk 15:4).

■ **34:7f** Against such dereliction on the part of the shepherds Yahweh threatens his judgment. Following on the résumé in vv 7f, which begins with a sharp oath formula but then proves to be a recapitulation of phrases which have already been used, vv 9f refer first of all to Yahweh's action against the shepherds.

■ **34:9f** In the challenge or summons to approach (see above under "Form") directed at the shepherds, he himself now promises to his flock true "seeking" (דרש), the first effect of which is the removal of the bad shepherds. Just as, according to 13:21,23, he rescues them from the "jaws" (מפיהם) of the bad shepherds, who thus suddenly appear as the ravening wolves who devour the flock.

■ **34:11–15** But then in the final section of the unit vv 1–

20 On חלב see further note a.
21 *b. B. Qam.* 10:9.
22 *b. B. Qam.* 118b.
23 On the treatment of sick animals see Hempel, *Heilung*, 239–241, 254.
24 On this see William L. Holladay, "'On every high hill and under every green tree,'" *VT* 11 (1961): 170–176.

15, once again forcefully introduced by the messenger formula, Yahweh's vengeful punitive action is completely superseded by the great promise of salvation. Yahweh himself will care for his flock. In this motivation (כי "for") it becomes quite clear that the real intention of the shepherd-oracle, by contrast with the originally independent oracle in Jer 23:1f, is no longer an actual polemic against specific shepherds of Israel who are still active. The catastrophe is already in the past, and the prophet wishes to speak now of the new thing that Yahweh will do for his people.

■ **34:11** No human figure now comes as mediator any longer between Yahweh and his flock. Only Yahweh's activity is mentioned. As the true shepherd he will care for his flock. Once again the verb דרש ("to seek") is repeated. The verb בקר ("to care for") also appears and, as the three-fold use of the stem in vv 11f makes clear, it can describe in a particular way the genuine activity of the shepherd. In Lev 13:36, in the diagnosis of leprosy, בקר ("to examine") describes the precise examination of the rash of the disease; in Lev 27:33 it describes the examination of an animal with a view to its suitability for sacrifice; in Prv 20:25 it is used more generally for critical reflection (before taking a vow). With regard to Ps 27:4 (also 2 Kgs 16:15?), Mowinckel has already posed the question whether the reference is not to the cultic examination of the sacrifice.[25] With the Nabataean official title מבקרא, which possibly describes the person who observes the sacrifice,[26] one may also compare the community office of מבקר referred to in the Damascus Document (13:7ff) and the Manual of Discipline (6:12, 20), in which J. Jeremias supposes a prototype of the NT *ἐπίσκοπος*.[27] CD 13:9f describes the fuction of the מבקר as follows: "And he shall have pity on them as a father of his children and shall carry them in all their despondency as a shepherd his flock. He shall unloose all the bonds which bind them that there may no more be any oppressed or broken among his congregation."[28] At any rate the verb בקר implies a careful and painstaking examination of the circumstances given in the respective context. In the present context it is the careful observation and enumeration of the flock and the readiness which these imply to look for the lost and to bring back the strayed. It is precisely in this latter direction that the image is further developed.

■ **34:12** When the occasion of the scattering of the flock is given as "the day of cloud and darkness," we can, on the basis of 30:3, see here a motif of the description of the day of Yahweh. What is meant here by "day of Yahweh," as by the יום יהוה of 13:5, is, retrospectively, the day of the destruction of Jerusalem and the final collapse of the political entity "Israel" (Judah), followed by the definitive dispersion of a people which has lost its shepherds.

■ **34:13** So Yahweh's "shepherding (רעה)" (in all the rich linguistic usage the participle רֹעֶה used as a noun to refer to Yahweh is avoided in vv 13–15) will lead to a renewed deliverance from the places where the people have been scattered, to a new exodus (הוציא "lead out"), to a new gathering (קבץ) and to a new entry (הביא) into the land. 20:34f (41) had already said this in similar terms. Here the flock will graze on the pasture designated for them by God on the mountains of Israel, in the watercourses and in all the inhabited places.[29]

■ **34:14** That will then be the good grazing place in which they can lie down in peace and find "good" (שמן) pasture. On this see Ps 23.

■ **34:15** With the emphatic reference to the one who gives pasture and resting-place (two-fold אני "I") and with the formula for a divine saying the section vv 1–15 comes to an end.

A summary comparison with Jeremiah 23 shows that there in vv 1f we have first of all a pure woe-oracle against the bad shepherds, threatening them with judgment. It has subsequently been expanded by further (salvation) oracles. The tripartite section Ezek 34:1–15, on the other hand, certainly begins, in dependence on Jer 23:1f, from the woe-oracle against the bad shepherds, but the latter here is much fuller in content and

25 See further Kraus, *Psalmen*, 1. 224.

26 Charles F. Jean and Jacob Hoftijzer, *Dictionnaire des inscriptions sémitiques de l'ouest* (Leiden: Brill, 1960–65), 41.

27 Joachim Jeremias, *Jerusalem in the Time of Jesus*, tr. F. H. and C. H. Cave (Philadelphia: Fortress, 1969), 260f.

28 Dupont-Sommer, *Essene*, 157.

29 On the "mountains of Israel" see 1, 185f on 6:2; on אפיקים see 1, 185; on "inhabited places" see v 13 note c.

then clearly goes beyond the judgment oracle directed at the bad shepherds to the proclamation that Yahweh will "shepherd" his people and aims to deliver them from the darkness which has closed in on the "day of cloud." The periods of time of the oracles Jer 23:1f and Ezek 34:1–15 are different. The expansion in Jer 23:3ff, even if there is still genuine Jeremianic material in it (Rudolph), should not obscure that fact.

■ **34:16** The oracle has then been linked with vv 17–23 by the transitional addition in v 16. In the case of v 16 one might in the first instance wonder whether one ought not to consider it (at least the first half of it) still part of v 15 and regard the formula for a divine saying in v 15b as an emphatic contextual formula. This is contradicted, however, by the quite clear final character of v 15 with its double אני ("I")-statement and its climax, from the point of view of content, in the reference to the peacefulness of the "lying down" (רבץ).

First of all v 16 repeats what has been said in v 4 and this, referring to Yahweh, now becomes positive and describes the work of the good shepherd. The sequence of the statements of v 4 is altered to the extent that the first two elements (attitude towards the sick) are telescoped into a single clause, but otherwise the series, apart from the final clause, is repeated, verbally identical but in the reverse order: 1)האבדת ("the lost") 2)הנדחת ("the strayed") 3)לנשברת ("the broken") 4)החולה ("the sick"). Only the final element (החזקה "the strong") remains in its place. Even the strong animal, described in an expansion as the fat one, receives the proper protection from Yahweh. In שמר ("to watch over") (note a) one might see a reference to restraint with regard to the unjust misuse of its strength. The reference to the righteous feeding (במשפט "in righteousness") secures the connection with the following oracle vv 17–24.

■ **34:17–22** If the subject matter of vv 1–15 was the opposition of shepherds and flock, in vv 17–22 the topics are that of brutality within the flock when the strong animal displaces the weak and that of the protection exercised by the shepherd who sees that justice prevails. Thus his protection here is subsumed under the key-word "judge" (שפט). Hölscher's assertion that this is the only passage in chapters 34–39 which speaks of a judgment on the people which is still to come does not prove that the oracle is secondary in the present context. The key-word שפט dominates in v 17, the first section of the oracle, and in v 20, the second section, and returns once again at the end in v 22 as a kind of signature. From the point of view of its thought, this oracle, in spite of its otherwise independent form, comes close to the oracle in 20:32ff, especially 20:35–38. There, in the context of the new exodus, reference was made also to a judgment of separation in which the godless would be weeded out. The animals will have to pass under the raised rod as before a shepherd, who counts them off and separates them.[30] So here also there is reference to a separation-judgment held by Yahweh as the righteous shepherd. It is not clear whether the separation, as in Matthew 25, is thought of as between sheep and goats. In favor of such a view is the fact that the flock (צאני "my flock") which Yahweh supports is referred to in what follows as feminine (vv 19,21f, see also אתנה "you" [fem.] in v 17), while the wicked thoughtless animals are referred to in vv 18,19 (רגליכם "your [masc.] feet"), 21 as masculine. On the other hand, there is again the observation that in v 20 the two feminine forms שה בריה ("fat beast") and שה רזה ("lean beast") stand side by side.

■ **34:17–19** The two-part unit in vv 17ff begins, after Yahweh has first of all generally proclaimed his judgment over "sheep" (שה in v 20 and in 45:15 is treated as feminine), rams and goats (27:21; 39:18), with an invective directed at the thoughtless animals who push forward to the pasture and water and, when they themselves have been satisfied, thoughtlessly trample and make muddy what is still to serve as food and water for others.[31]

■ **34:20** One would expect the second section, after its introductory לכן ("therefore"), to contain the judgment on the thoughtless animals. This is described in v 20, with a certain variation of phraseology by contrast to v 17, as a judgment of separation between the fat (note d) and the "thin" animals (רזה also in Nu 13:20), which are here both treated as feminine.

■ **34:21** Then, however, in v 21, the thoughtlessness of the strong is once again depicted in graphic terms as the thoughtless thrusting aside of the weaker animals.

30 See 1,416.

31 On משקע מים see 32:14 and on רפש 32:2.

Indeed more, the sick are attacked with the horns. In the "scattering abroad" which is seen as the consequence of this thrusting aside, it is possible to hear again an echo of the exile-terminology of vv 5f.

■ **34:22** Over such heedlessness on the part of the strong, however, God will establish his justice. The development of this thought makes it clear that the point of the statement here too is not the punishment of the wicked, but the proclamation of deliverance for those who have hitherto been oppressed. Just as, in the representation of the book of Judges, the sending of the judges means deliverance for Israel, and the "judge" (שׁפט) can therefore also be described as a "deliverer" (מושׁיע Ju 3:9, 15), so here justice is described as deliverance. הושׁיע ("to deliver, rescue"), according to the Arabic *wasiʿa* "to be roomy," originally meant "to make room." "Deliverance" is "living space (*Lebensraum*)." The weak will no longer be a prey to the strong.[32]

■ **34:23f** Yahweh's act of deliverance leads, in vv 23f, to the promise of a good earthly shepherd. If our understanding of vv 17–22 along the lines of 20:32ff is correct, then the first impression of this expansion, which sets alongside the divine judge a man whose uniqueness (אחד "a single") as it were challenges the uniqueness of the divine shepherd and judge, is one of surprise. Ezek 34:1ff has as its probable prototype the oracle in Jer 23:1f. The expansion of that in Jer 23:3f, certainly composed after 587, after an analogous introduction והקמתי עליהם ("and I shall set over them"), refers to a plurality of רעים ("shepherds") whom Yahweh will appoint. Then there is added there, of course, in vv 5f the independent oracle about the "righteous branch" of David, which once again reveals the characteristic introductory word (והקמתי (לדוד ("I shall raise up [for David]").

On the special features of the phraseology in Ezek 34:23f one can in the first place state the following:

The emphatic אחד ("a single") is to be understood in terms of 37:15ff. It is certainly not intended to be directed against the uniqueness of Yahweh, but promises emphatically, in contrast to the historical plight of the division of Israel into two separate political entities, the unity under one ruler which God brings to his people.[33]

Peculiar to Ezekiel is the use of the title נשׂיא ("prince") for the one shepherd. The title מלך ("king") is avoided in this emphatic statement.[34] But this is not so much a sign of polemic against the title מלך ("king") as the desire to describe the dignitary in an archaically solemn fashion by means of a genuine ancient Israelite title, which avoids an outworn everyday word current in the international world (see further, however, on 37:24f).

The most striking element lies in the use of the name David for the future shepherd. David is, in the first instance, a figure of past history. He is the great ancestor of the royal house in Jerusalem and, at the same time, the king whose name most fully recalls the time when Israel was united. In addition, he is the king to whom, according to 2 Samuel 7, there was given by the mouth of a prophet Yahweh's promise of continuing permanence for his royal house. The election of David is for the faith of Judaean Israel indissolubly linked with belief in the election of Israel.[35] The Deuteronomistic History sees in Yahweh's fidelity to the house of David (and to Jerusalem) the particular proof of Yahweh's close relationship to his people.[36] On this soil there has subsequently arisen the expectation of a coming member of the house of David, in whom God's promise concerning the house of David and his associated promise to Israel will be completely fulfilled. Thus Isaiah speaks of the "son" who will be given to the house of David and who, after the "night of liberation," incorporates the kingdom of justice and salvation (Is 9:5f).[37] Jer 23:5f speak of a "righteous branch (צמח צדיק)" which is given to "David," i.e. the house of David. Zech 3:8; 6:12 show how significant this expression was in the early post-exilic period.

On the other hand, Ezek 34:23f (37:24f) is remarkable for its announcement that David himself will be the future good shepherd. Apart from Ezekiel, there are

32 הושׁיע occurs in Ezekiel also in 36:29; 37:23; בז also in vv 8, 28.

33 See further on 37:15ff.

34 On נשׂיא ("prince") see also 1, 209 on 7:27a; 1, 273 on 12:10; 1, 364 on 17:12.

35 See, e.g., Martin Noth, "David and Israel in II Samuel VII" in *The Laws in the Pentateuch and Other Studies*, tr. D. R. Ap-Thomas (Philadelphia: Fortress, 1967), 250–259.

36 On this, Gerhard von Rad, *Studies in Deuteronomy*, Studies in Biblical Theology 9 (London: SCM, 1953), 74–91.

37 See Albrecht Alt, "Befreiungsnacht und Krönungstag" in *Kleine Schriften zur Geschichte des Volkes Israel* 2 (München: Beck, 1953), 206–225; Hans Wildberger, "Die Thronnamen des Messias, Jes 9:5b," *ThZ* 16

only two passages in the OT which speak of a future David. The Judaean who made additions to the book of Hosea has added in 3:5, to Hosea's reference to the return of the Israelites to Yahweh, the note about the return "to David their king."[38] Still closer to Ezekiel's phraseology is the insertion in Jer 30:9f (in the "Booklet of Consolation for Ephraim"), which says of the coming state of liberation (of Ephraim? of all Israel?): "And they shall serve Yahweh their God and David their king whom 'I will raise up for them' (אקים להם)." Here it is quite explicitly stated that in the future Yahweh will raise up a David. While Hitzig is of the opinion, "Thus, Ezekiel expected the latter's resurrection," Begrich on the other hand has correctly noted that fact that הקים ("to raise up") is used also for the raising up of judges (Ju 2:16) "deliverers" (Ju 3:9), prophets (Jer 29:15; cf. also Dtn 18:18) and kings (1 Kgs 14:14).[39] Jer 23:4 uses הקים ("to raise up") for the appointment of a plurality of future shepherds, and here no one can think that the reference is to a resurrection of the dead. So Smend, in his reworking of the commentary, quietly passes over Hitzig's opinion and understands "David" as "a king or rather a series of kings like him." Since the idea of a series of kings is in no way indicated here, in contrast to Jer 23:4, the singular interpretation is to be preferred. Begrich may be correct in speaking of a "David *redivivus*," to the extent that this serves to underline the idea of the similarity between the promised righteous ruler and the David of the earlier period. In addition, however, one can see in this also a reference to the fidelity of Yahweh, who will not go back on his initial promise about the house of David. Further speculation concerning the identity of the historical David with the coming David should be ruled out.

On the other hand, the question arises as to how this future human power is to be connected with Yahweh's power. The concluding summary verse 24 attempts to answer this question. The two non-Ezekiel passages show that here the formulaic double statement "Yahweh their God and David their king" has been developed. This form of the formula might still be operative in 37:23f (see below). As far as the origin of this phrase is concerned, it is not without interest to observe that it appears among the transmitters of Hosea and Jeremiah as well as in Ezekiel.[40] At any rate the normal phraseology discernible in Hos 3:5 and Jer 30:9 finds in Ezek 34:24 its linguistic transformation.[41] Language which is characteristic of Ezekiel in the expression can be seen in the first person, with the formula of self-introduction set arrogantly at the beginning אני יהוה ("I Yahweh") and with the equally authoritarian concluding phrase אני יהוה דברתי ("I, Yahweh, have spoken").[42] It should be noted further that the coming David is not simply designated as נְשִׂיאָם ("their prince") i.e. as *the* נשיא ("prince") of Israel (so in the singular 21:30; in the plural 19:1; 21:17; 22:6). The expression נשיא בתוכם ("prince in their midst"), even if it has, in the הנשיא אשר בתוכם ("the prince, who is in their midst") of 12:12, a certain parallel where the context is of course somewhat different, represents a more detached phraseology which deviates from the usual formula. The נשיא ("prince") holds an office in Israel, but is not Israel's ruler. One can at least raise the question as to whether this does not betray already a step along the road to the conception of the נשיא ("prince") found in chapters 40–48 (see below on 44:1–3). On the other hand, the description of David as Yahweh's servant comes from a widespread tradition. An עבד ("servant") is someone who belongs entirely to his master and is committed to obedience, but who, within that, is nevertheless entrusted with great freedom in the fulfillment of his office.[43]

The question has still been left open whether vv 23f are to be regarded as the conclusion of the section vv 17–24 or as an independent addition to a unit comprising vv 17–22. Considerations of form might, in the first instance, argue for an original connection between the two. The final character of v 24 is considerably more marked than that of v 22. On the other hand, there are

(1960): 314-332; Otto Kaiser, *Isaiah 1–12; a Commentary*, tr. R. A. Wilson. The Old Testament Library (London: SCM, 1972).

38 Wolff, *Hosea*, 57, 63.

39 Hitzig, 265; Begrich, "Messiasbild," 446f. See also Bardtke, "Erweckungsgedanke," 12–15.

40 On this see, e.g., the pedigree of the tradition of Ezek 16 (23) which runs from Hosea to Ezekiel via Jeremiah.

41 On the replacement of מלך by נשיא see above.

42 On this see 1, 176 on 5:15. Cf. also the reminiscence of the first half of the two-fold covenant formula (see 1, 262f on 11:20).

43 See Walther Zimmerli and Joachim Jeremias, "παῖς θεοῦ," *TDNT* 5, 654–717 (Zimmerli, 654–677; Jeremias, 677–717).

also arguments against such an original connection. Vv 17–22 are held together by the catchword שפט ("judge") and speak of the judgment which Yahweh will exercise within his flock. There is no further sign of that in vv 23f. They are basically much closer to the interrogation of vv 1–15. Vv 17–22 envisage the image of animals. Within vv 23f, on the other hand, v 24 clearly leads back to the covenant people (see also v 23 note a). There is also the fact that with the emphasis on the one shepherd ideas from 37:15ff begin to play a part, ideas which have no direct connection with the details of the two preceding units in Ezekiel 34. So v 23f were probably added to vv 17–22 at a somewhat later date.

From the point of view of content there is no compelling reason for denying the origin of the verses to Ezekiel. The point where the prophet came to speak of the new single ruler who is expected in the person of the new David seems in the first instance to have been the question about the unity of Israel, which is taken up in 37:15ff. Thus the full discussion of the meaning of this "messianic" statement will arise most suitably in the context of the exposition of 37:15ff. There, too, the connection with 17:22–24 will be discussed.

■ **34:25–30** In vv 25–30 the shepherd theme fades completely into the background, to reappear only in the independent concluding verse 31. In its place, there occur here more general statements about the promised state of prosperity in the land. These are remarkable for their unusually close dependence on expressions found in the introductory curse section of Leviticus 26.[44]

■ **34:25** Yahweh promises to conclude with his people a covenant of peace. The conclusion of a new covenant in the future has already been promised in 16:60.[45] The word שלום ("peace") which is added here (as also in Is 54:10), indicates in the first instance the reality of which a covenant in any case consists. Covenant means the establishment of a relationship of well-being between the partners of the covenant.[46] Somewhat different is the view of J. Pedersen, who wishes to render ברית שלום ("covenant of peace") in 34:25; 37:26; Is 54:10 by "unbreakable covenant."[47] When Yahweh is the covenant partner, this well-being will extend over the whole sphere of life of the nation and will bring about peace there. It is this emanation of well-being that is thought of particularly here. According to 5:17; 14:15,21; 33:27, the wild beasts assist Yahweh in his judgment. Their removal from the land is the sign of the establishment of peace. This element belonged already to Hosea's proclamation of well-being (2:20). Is 11:1ff shows how in this context old concepts of paradise can be revived. Now H. W. Wolff has asked whether behind Ezek 34:25 one cannot see the divergent view of Yahweh as "covenant mediator."[48] M. Noth has shown in the case of Mari the form of covenant in which a third person mediates the covenant and the peace included in the covenant between two disputing parties.[49] In fact, Hos 2:20 seems to understand the covenant with the beasts as just such a "covenant of reconciliation" established by Yahweh. In so far as Ezek 34:25 speaks of the removal of the animals, however, then this structure in Hosea is destroyed in favor of the usual conception of the two covenant partners Yahweh and Israel. In Ezekiel there further emerges in particular the motif of the removal of anxiety. The people will dwell "in safety" in the uncanny wilderness (Jer 2:6) and in the woods, where usually dangerous wild beasts have their hiding place and attack men (Jer 5:6). לבטח ("in safety") is, in 28:26; 34:25,27f; 38:8,11,14; 39:26, the key-word for the freedom from fear that is bestowed in the great, future God-given peace. What in Lev 26:5bβ,6 is the reward of human obedience appears here as Yahweh's free gift to his people.

■ **34:26f** To this belongs also the blessing of the land with great fruitfulness. Abundant rain, which enables the trees to bear their fruit and the land to bring forth its produce (Lev 26:4), will be the sign whereby Yahweh reveals himself as himself. In the words that follow the recognition formula, however, there appears the motif of

44 On the relationship between Ezekiel and the Holiness Code see the Introduction (1, 46–52). On what follows see also Heinrich Gross, *Die Idee des ewigen und allgemeinen Weltfriedens im Alten Orient und im Alten Testament,* Trierer theologische Studien 7 (Trier: Paulinus, 1956).

45 See 1, 352f.

46 See, e.g., von Rad, *OT Theology,* 1. 130.

47 Pedersen, *Eid,* 33 note 2.

48 Hans Walter Wolff, "Jahwe als Bundesvermittler," *VT* 6 (1956): 318f.

49 Martin Noth, "Old Testament Covenant-Making in the Light of a Text from Mari" in *The Laws in the Pentateuch and Other Studies,* tr. D. R. Ap-Thomas (Philadelphia: Fortress), 108–117.

liberation from the yolk and hard labor imposed by political overlords, who have enslaved the people as the Egyptians once did at the beginning of Israel's history (עבד ב [literally "work with"] as in Lev 25:46; Jer 22:13; 25:14).[50] The expression שבר מטות ("to break the bars") occurs in Ezekiel also in 30:18. על ("yolk") is attested nowhere else in Ezekiel, but see Is 9:3; 10:27; 14:25; Jer 28:2,4,11; 30:8.

■ **34:28** Insofar as the surrender to the nations as prey and to the wild beasts for food is connected with this, one can perceive here a faint echo of expressions from the two shepherd oracles (vv 5, [8], 10, 22), of which otherwise there is no recollection here.

■ **34:29** Once again expression is given to that peace in which no one is afraid any more (39:26; cf. Lev 26:6a), with freedom from hunger (5:12,16f; 6:11f; 7:15; 12:16; 14:13,21; cf. Lev 26:5bα) as in 36:29f and from the scorn of the nations as in 36:6f,15. The phrase about the "prosperous plantation" (note a) is not entirely clear. It might be determined by the Jeremianic attribution of salvation to the idea of "planting."[51] While the word מטע ("plantation") as used elsewhere in Ezekiel (17:7; 31:4) is not in itself formulaic, such a usage can hardly be overlooked in Trito-Isaiah (61:3; cf. 60:21).

■ **34:30** The conclusion with its second recognition formula is once again formed entirely from Ezekiel's linguistic stock. At any rate the expression of the recognition is amplified independently with material from the covenant formula. By this unheard-of blessing of the covenant of well-being in which Israel participates, the world (or Israel?) perceives not only Yahweh in the mystery of his person (so v 27), but at the same time—and herein consists his world-orientated nature—his gracious relationship with Israel. While the covenant formula said: "I am Yahweh, their God," the character of the covenant as gift is explicitly underlined by an addition in 𝔐 (see note b): "I, Yahweh, their God, am with them."[52]

The main theme of Ezekiel 34 has disappeared completely in vv 25–30. There is no longer any reference here to good and bad shepherds, but to the salvation which Yahweh has established in his covenant of salvation. Only in the priority given to and the strong emphasis laid on the elimination of the wild beasts is it possible to hear an echo of the particular enemies of the flock. There is, however, no further interpretation along these lines. The fruitfulness of the land and the elimination of hunger, freedom from foreign domination and the removal of the scorn poured on them by the nations are here the great blessings by which Yahweh reveals himself as his people's God.

■ **34:31** It is not until the concluding verse, v 31, that a return is made to the shepherd motif. At the same time it clearly presupposes the immediately preceding context, insofar as it too contains elements of the covenant formula (cf. vv 24, 30), though the latter (at least in the first half of the verse) is clothed in the imagery of the shepherd chapter; "You are my flock—I am your God," so runs the present variation of the covenant formula: "You are to be my people and I your God" (11:20; 14:11). This takes up the צאן ("flock") which predominates in vv 6,8,10,11,12,15,17,19,22, incorporates it into the covenant formula and thus brackets the two shepherd oracles in vv 1–15, 17–22 on the one hand with the covenant oracle in vv 25–30 on the other. The first half of the covenant formula also echoes v 24a (David oracle) once more. But then the צאן "flock" is expounded in v 31 in two different ways: 1) by the addition of the suffixed form מרעיתי ("my pasture"), which, with the exception of Jer 23:1, is found only in the language of the Psalms (see 74:1; 79:13; 95:7; 100:3); 2) by the addition of אדם ("human"), which then (certainly secondarily, see note b) makes the figure of speech apply to man (see also 36:38). Of course this does not mean that the אדם ("human")-predicate is limited to Israel, as R. Simeon b. Yohai thinks: "You are called *men* (אדם) but the idolaters are not called *men*."[53] In this final sentence all polemic against the evil shepherds has faded away to be replaced by the basic promise of blessing which is fundamentally present in all sections of the chapter: You, Israel, are my flock, my people, and I am your God.

Setting

Ezekiel 34 is a clearly edited chapter, rounded off by its closing verse. Once again one can see here a process of

50 On this see Lev 26:13b.

51 Bach, "Bauen und Pflanzen."

52 On this see A. Feuillet, "La formule d'appartenance mutuelle (II, 16) et les interprétations divergentes du Cantique des Cantiques," *RB* 68 (1961): 24f.

53 *B. Yebam.* 61a; *b. B. Mes.* 114b; *b. Ker.* 6b.

gradual expansion to its final form. Again it cannot always be decided with certainty where the prophet's own words are to be found and where the later work of expansion by the prophetic school begins. In the first instance one could perhaps derive from the prophet himself the two large initial sections, vv 1–15 and 17–22. The fact that they vary the same theme in two different directions is a not uncommon process with Ezekiel (see, e.g., on chapter 16). Both oracles belong in the period after 587, in that both basically proclaim not so much judgment on the wicked shepherds and the inconsiderate strong animals of the flock as rather the beneficent restoration and gathering of the scattered flocks. Brownlee's separation of vv 1–10 as an oracle of doom to be dated before 587 does not commend itself. It is impossible to decide whether Ezekiel himself brought the two sections together by means of the verse 16. The David oracle in vv 23f should not be denied to Ezekiel, even though it did not originally form the conclusion of vv 17–22. If Ezekiel himself added it (secondarily) to vv 17–22, then the whole composition vv 1–23 (including v 16) is to be derived from his hand, since vv 23f link together the two preceding sections. V 12 clearly looks back to the great day of disaster. The origin of the oracles among the exiles is, in view of the discernible distance from the immediate royal history in Jerusalem, internally completely possible.

One should most probably attribute vv 25–30 and the redactional conclusion in v 31 to the circle of Ezekiel's disciples. Linguistically we are in the sphere from which the prophet himself stems (proof-saying, concluding formula v 24). But vv 25–30 give the very strong impression of having been compiled. They contain a more general proclamation of salvation, which is unusually heavily dependent on Lev 26. But here too there is no need to go beyond the end of the period of the exile. There is nothing to indicate a recent resumption of life in Palestine. Contrast, e.g., the language of Haggai and Zechariah.

Aim

Ezekiel knows something of the responsibility of the individual before his God (chapter 18; 33:10ff). But in this connection he never forgets that God has called not individuals, but his people and has allocated individual responsibilities within that people. There are "shepherds" who are entrusted with the duty of guarding the flock. This is a reference to the allocation of political power to men who have to see to the external leadership of the people. Over and above this, however, these shepherds also have the duty of creating in the heart of this people the place for God's law which God wishes it to have.

In thinking of the "shepherds of Israel" the prophet is confronting a shattered history of the people of God, one that has been called in question. The shepherds have abused their office in two respects. They had no concern for the weary and the burdened, for the weak and the sick, the lost sheep who ought to have been the particular concern of the shepherd if he really wanted to have God's law respected. Instead, they have succumbed to the intoxication of power, have carved out their own "positions," opportunities for themselves in life, have regarded power as their domain and the flock as their prey. In their office they see their "prey" (on this see Phil 2:6), the "food" on which they are allowed to fatten themselves and clothe themselves in rich array. In such activity they have wronged both the weak and the strong in their flock. As the result of such disregard of true shepherdhood, however, the flock has been scattered and lost. It has fallen victim to the error of being led astray on the "heights" and of being scattered abroad.

Thus God's anger turns against the shepherds. In the historical judgment on the political leadership of his people (vv 17,19), the prophet in his day has in mind the answer of the holy one. But because God, over and above all the failure of the evil human shepherds, himself remains his people's good shepherd, the word of judgment cannot remain the final word. As the good shepherd, God promises to the people whom he has called that he himself will take care of the lost, will gather them, lead them to good pasture and bring them to the land which he has allotted to them as the land of promise.

God's "justice" will also manifest itself in another direction. It has not already achieved its goal, in that the wicked authorities have been done away with. The crisis of the people of God over whom the rule of the good shepherd is established goes deeper than that. The prophet does not give voice to the pathos of the anarchist and the revolutionary, who expects all salvation to come from the mere removal of the authorities. The flock itself is equally called to the justice of God. The heedlessness which is spread about also "below" among those who are ruled and in which the lust for power of those "above" simply reappears in miniature is no less assailed by God's justice. Here "below," too, God means to see that the strong do not heedlessly thrust aside the weak from their sphere of living with sides and shoulders and horns, that is do not push and fight their way through with fist and elbow and abandon the weak as worthless on the battlefield of life.

But even in the face of such activity in the lower spheres, the prophet promises, above and beyond judgment, deliverance by the good shepherd. In the figure of the returning David he promises God's fidelity to his original history. In what he says he does not satisfy the curiosity of the questioner who would like to know what the relationship is of the new to the old, of the new David to the first David. It is enough for him to proclaim that in the one who will come there will be "in their midst" a shepherd who will gather his flock again into their original unity and who, as the true shepherd, will cause God's justice for his people to be respected. The nature of this "prince," who at the same time will be wholly "God's servant," is not more closely described. Suffice it to know that in him and over him God remains the God of his people and that his divine rule knows no eclipse. In the connection between this promise and the two introductory shepherd and flock oracles, suffice it to know that in this "prince" there exists the shepherd who no longer lives off his sheep and "looks after himself," but the shepherd who lives for his sheep, even for those who labor and are heavy-laden (Mt 11:28), the weak and the lost whom he will seek even as the good shepherd does (Luke 15; John 10). Suffice it to know that in him there exists the shepherd who in his flock brings to victory the true "righteousness of God," whereby the powerful member of the flock gives to the weak his right to life and no longer thrusts the other away with fist and elbow. The prophet looks to the coming of this shepherd and proclaims it as the certain future towards which God's people move.

Then, however, a final expansion makes it quite indubitably clear how much God's desire for salvation really means the complete deliverance of his people, a deliverance in which those who hunger and thirst will be satisfied (Lk 6:21; Mt 5:6), those who are in danger of losing their peace receive "peace on earth" (Lk 2:14; Jn 16:33) and in which every heavy yoke of constraint and enslavement is done away (Jn 8:36). In the removal of all shame, God's people will find their full glory (Jn 17:22). In all this, however, there is no question of the establishment of human dominion, but of the event in which God reveals himself as the God of his people. "Your God—among you." Such a future is proclaimed to God's people by his prophet.

Judgment on Mount Seir and Salvation for the Mountains of Israel

Bibliography
Julian Morgenstern
"The Rest of the Nations," *JSS* 2 (1957): 225–231.

35

1 And the word of Yahweh came to me: 2/
Son of man, turn your face to[a] Mount Seir
and prophesy against it 3/ and say to it[a]:
Thus has [the Lord][b] Yahweh said: See, I
am against[c] you, Mount Seir! and I shall
stretch out my hand against you and
make you into a horrible wasteland[d]. 4/ I
shall make your cities[a] into ruins, and you
will become a wilderness and will know
that I am Yahweh.
5 Because from of old you cherished enmity
and delivered up the Israelites[a] to the
sword in the time of their misfortune[b], in
the time of the final punishment[c], 6/
therefore, as I live, says [the Lord][a] Yahweh, [I shall make you into blood, and
blood shall pursue you][b] <you have made
yourself guilty of blood>[c], so blood shall

35:2 2a על–אל cf. 1:17 note a.

3 3a The *αὐτῷ* corresponding to 𝔐 לו is missing in the original reading of 𝔊[B], but is already attested in 𝔊[967] (𝔏[W]). Thus 𝔊[B] must represent an unintentional assimilation to the mode of expression found in a corresponding context in 13:18; 28:22; 29:3; 38:3.

b אדני is lacking in 𝔊 𝔏[W] ℜ[Sa] 𝔄, see Appendix 1.

c 𝔐 אליך, 3 MSS[Ken] עליך; on על–אל cf 1:17 note a. On the formula הנני אליך see 1,175 and above p. 98.

d On the rhymed expression שממה ומשמה see 6:14 note a.

4 4a 𝔐 עריך. 𝔊 𝔏[W] 𝔖 add the copula. See 1:4 note a. 𝔏[W] abbreviates 4aα and 4aβ to a single clause.

5 5a 𝔐 ותגר את בני ישראל was not understood by 𝔊 *καὶ ἐνεκάθισας* (𝔏[W] *insidiasti;* 𝔏[S] *insedistis,* according to Dold a scribal error for *insidiasti*) *τῷ οἴκῳ* Ισραηλ *δόλῳ*, which must derive תגר (or תגד) from גור or גדד. See already 21:17 note a. 𝔅 *concluseris* envisages a derivation from סגר. The individualistic בני ישראל of 𝔐 is, in a context of "delivering up," better than the collective "house of Israel" of 𝔊.

b 𝔐 בעת אידם certainly seems to have been read by 𝔊 (*pace* BH[3]), but not understood. Cornill is surely right to see behind the strange *ἐν χειρὶ ἐχθρῶν μαχαίρᾳ* of 𝔊 (𝔏[SW] *in manu inimicorum gladio;* 𝔊[A] [𝔄] *ἐν καιρῷ ἐχθρῶν ἐν χειρὶ μαχαίρας*) the more original form of the text and to regard it as the equivalent, with the two parts transposed, of 𝔐 חרב בעת אידם על ידי with אידם misunderstood as איבים. Thus 𝔐 is to be retained with the possibility that אידם contains an intentional word-play on אָדָם (Cooke). See also the word-play in 25:16.

c 𝔐 בעת עון קץ. 𝔗 בעידן תושילמת חוביהון corresponding to 21:30.

6 6a אדני is lacking in 𝔊 𝔏[S], see Appendix 1.

b The passage in 𝔐 כי לדם אעשך ודם ירדפך is not attested by 𝔊 𝔏[S] ℜ 𝔄̈ 𝔄 and is also proved to be a secondary expansion in that it separates the continuation of the oath address in v 6b (אם לא) from its first part (חי אני). From the point of view of content it is a slightly altered dittograph of v 6b. 𝔗 paraphrases 𝔐 דם by דקטלין בחרבא "people who kill by the sword (will pusue you)."

c 𝔐 דם שנאת "blood have you hated" is meaningless in the context. 𝔊 *εἰς αἷμα ἥμαρτες* (𝔏[S] *in sanguinem peccasti*) attests the original reading לדם אשמת, from which the reading of the dittograph (note b) also derives, לדם אעשך. Cf. 22:4; Lev 5:4f. Driver, "Linguistic Problems," 181, wishes to read דם נשאת with the omission of עון in an elliptical

pursue you. 7/ And I shall make Mount Seir into a horrible wasteland[a] and shall wipe out from it (all) who go to and fro[b], 8/ and shall fill its mountains with its slain—[your hills and your valleys and your water-channels][a] those slain by the sword will lie upon them. 9/ I shall make you into a wilderness[a] for ever, and your cities will be uninhabited[b], and you will[c] know that I am Yahweh.

10 Because you say: The[a] two nations and the[a] two lands belong to me and <I take

phrase as in Nu 14:33. 𝔗 tries to make sense of 𝔐 by reading into it a statement about "hate for the blood of circumcision" (דמא דמהולתא). The דם of the last part of the sentence is paraphrased (differently from in v 6a, see note b) by אשדי דמא "those who shed blood."

7 7a 𝔐 לְשִׁמְמָה וּשְׁמָמָה, which tries to differentiate the two שממה artificially through the vocalization, surely results from a scribal error for an original לשממה ומשמה, as is attested in 6:14; 33:28f; 35:3. See also BH^3.

b 𝔐 עבר ושב is rendered in 𝔊 (𝔏^S), in accordance with the usual phraseology in 14:13, 17, 19, 21; 25:13; 29:8; 36:11, by ἀνθρώπους καὶ κτήνη. On 𝔐 see Ex 32:27; Zech 7:14; 9:8.

8 8a 𝔊 (𝔏^S) omits the את הריו of 𝔐 and reads the whole of v 8 as a direct address. τῶν τραυματιῶν σου corresponds to חלליו. But here too the hand of 𝔊, smoothing out the syntax, is at work, since in a text reconstructed on the basis of 𝔊 the anticipation of the further object (חלליו or, according to 𝔊, חלליך) before the nearer one (גבעותיך . . .) would, in spite of Cooke, be strange. In addition, there is the fact that in an enumeration of hills, valleys and water-channels, in comparison with 6:3; 36:4, 6, the omission of the "mountains" is strange. Thus it is more probable that the original reference to mountains in the text has been expanded secondarily in anticipation of 36:4, 6 by the three other elements which have, in line with the style of address found in the oracle as a whole in 35:1ff, been provided with second person masculine singular suffixes. The sequence, which is different from that in 6:3; 36:4, 6, and the plural form גאות, which is unique in the book of Ezekiel and on which 6:3 note c should be compared, might also suggest a second hand. In this way v 8b is relieved of the heavy triple subject which is caught up in בהם (but cf. the difficulty of the allocation in 𝔊).

9 9a 𝔐 שממות עולם. The plural is supported by (36:2, cf. note b there) Jer 25:12; 51:26, 62. 𝔊 𝔖 𝔗 translate as a singular. Apart from the combination found in the passages just mentioned, the plural שממות is not found either in Ezekiel or anywhere else in the OT. On the other hand, there is no example anywhere in the OT of a construct singular either. Is this the usage of a living language or a secondary systematization?

b With K תישבנה, as opposed to Q תשובנה, one should think of a derivation from ישב, cf. Gesenius-Kautzsch §69b, note 1. According to Bauer-Leander §55c', it is an orthographic error for תֵּשַׁבְנָה. On ישב in the sense of "be inhabited" see Koehler-Baumgartner.

c 𝔐 וידעתם. 𝔊 𝔏^S 𝔖 assimilate to the singular of the context. See also v 4.

10 10a According to Blau, "Gebrauch," 14f, the grammatical subject after היה ל is felt as an object, hence the usage of את. It might also be an antici-

them>[b] into possession, though Yahweh was there[c], 11/ therefore, as I live, says [the Lord][a] Yahweh, I shall deal[b] (with you) according to your anger and according to your envy which you have shown[c] because you hated[d] them; and I shall make myself known <to you>[e] when I judge you, 12/ and you will know that I, Yahweh, have heard[a] all[b] your abuse[c] which you uttered against the mountains of Israel when you said: They lie waste[d] and are given to us to devour[e]! 13/ And

patory effect of the following ירש. Brockelmann §31b assumes that the subject can be emphasized by means of את.

b 𝔐 וירשנוה is strange after the preceding speech in the first person. 𝔊 *καὶ κληρονομήσω αὐτάς*, 𝔗 ואירתינון, 𝔖 ואנה ארת אנון, 𝔙 *hereditate possidebo eos* seem to go back to an original וירשתין.

c Ehrlich, *Randglossen*, Bertholet, referring to the two-fold שמעתי in vv 12f, wish to emend 𝔐 ויהוה שם היה to ויהוה שמע. Such an anticipation of the שמע takes away the force of its occurrence in vv 12f. There remains the oddity of the reference to Yahweh in the third person in the context of a Yahweh oracle, which immediately afterwards in v 11 has a quite unmistakable first person. The suspicion that we have here an interpretative sentence added secondarily cannot be entirely suppressed. 𝔗 interprets the words in a sense in which they can scarcely have been intended: וקדם יהוה גליין מחשבת לבא.

11 11a אדני is lacking in 𝔊 𝔏^{S}, see Appendix 1.

b 𝔐 absolute ועשיתי. On this see 8:18 note a; 20:9 note a. 𝔊, in accordance with the meaning, adds (*ποιήσω*) *σοι*. 𝔏^{S} *faciam tibi*. 𝔖 לך (אעבד). 𝔗 confirms 𝔐.

c 𝔊 𝔏^{S} leave 𝔐 כאפך וכקנאתך אשר עשיתה unattested. Yet the suspicion remains that 𝔊 has drastically curtailed the more detailed phraseology of the clause in 𝔐, in which כאפך וכקנאתך seems to be saying the same thing as the following משנאתך (note d), but which ought to be preserved because of the internal correspondence of the absolute usage עשיתה–ועשיתי. 𝔐 should be retained.

d 𝔐 משנאתיך is a scribal error for משנאתך, see 13 MSS^{G}.

e 𝔐 בם inadvertently repeats the preceding בם. On the basis of 𝔊 𝔏^{S}, בך should be read. Driver, "Ezekiel," 302, prefers to retain 𝔐 and understand בם in a neuter sense "by these deeds of mine." 𝔗 interprets the content of the divine revelation: ואיתגלי לאטבא מינהון.

12 12a 𝔗 שמיע קדמי tries to avoid the anthropomorphism of 𝔐.

b 𝔐 כל has been misheard by 𝔊 (𝔏^{S}) as קול, *τῆς φωνῆς*.

c 𝔐 נָאָצוֹתֶיךָ. The noun, formed on the basis of קְטָלָה, is found again in Neh 9:18, 26 with the vocalization נְאָצוֹת. See also נְאָצָה 2 Kgs 19:3; Is 37:3.

d 𝔊 𝔏^{S} clearly translate here rather freely (v 11 note c) and take הרי ישראל as the subject of שממה and omit על and לאמר. According to Q, שממה should be understood as a third person plural שָׁמֵמוּ and be referred to הרי ישראל. So 𝔖 חרבין אנון. K שָׁמֵמָה must be understood, as in v 15a, as a third singular feminine, but this is harsh in the context. 𝔗 supplements the meaning by inserting (צדיאת) ארעהון. It is preferable to read the noun שְׁמָמָה. On this see vv 4, 15.

e 𝔐 לאכלה is attested beyond question. The *εἰς*

you have magnified (yourselves)[a] with
your mouths against me and have made
your words <impudent(?)>[b] against me. I
have heard it[c].
14 Thus has [the Lord][a] Yahweh said: As you
rejoiced . . . the whole land a desolation,
thus shall I do to you[b]: 15/ [As you re-
joiced over the inheritance of the house
of Israel because it[a] was laid waste, so
shall I do (the same) to you.][b] Waste you
will be laid, Mount Seir and all Edom
together[c], and they shall[d] know that I am
Yahweh[e].
36:1 But you, son of man, prophesy to[a] the
mountains of Israel and say: You moun-
tains[b] of Israel, hear the word of Yah-
weh: 2/ Thus has [the Lord][a] Yahweh
said: Because the enemy says of you:
Aha! <Desolation>[b] for ever! To us is it[c]

κατάσχεσιν of 𝔊[AL] (𝔄) can be explained as an echo of 33:24.

13 13a 𝔊 (𝔏[S]) harmonize v 13 with the second person singular of v 12. The plural is, however, quite understandable as a resumption of the "we" of v 12a. In 𝔐 there is no return to the second person singular until v 14 after the messenger formula.

b 𝔐 והעתרתם, translated by 𝔗 with ואסגיתון "you make many," by 𝔙 with *derogastis* "restricted(?)" and omitted by 𝔊 𝔏[S] along with the whole of v 13aβ, cannot be understood on the basis of the usual qal, hip'il "ask, pray." Hitzig's assumption of an Aramaic equivalent of the hebrew עשר with the meaning "be many" (Arabic *kaṯura*) rests on weak foundations. Thus Koehler-Baumgartner conjectures והעתקתם, Krätzschmar הרביתם, Ehrlich, *Randglossen*, and others העתקתם, a denominative from עָתָק "bold." The translation offered here is on the basis of this last suggestion. N. S. Doniach, "Studies in Hebrew Philology: √ עתר," *AJSL* 50 (1934): 178, points to Arabic *'aṯara* "push" and translates: "Ye have caused me to stumble with your words." The omission of v 13aβ in 𝔊 doubtless results from this difficulty in translation, but one ought not to delete the parallel to v 13aα.

c On the rendering in 𝔗 see v 12 note a.

14 14a אדני is lacking in 𝔊 𝔏[S] 𝔄, see Appendix 1.

b V 14b gives the impression of being garbled. In v 15a, which is missing in 𝔊 𝔏[S], there appears alongside v 14b a syntactically complete paraphrase of it in strongly theological, abstract language (נחלת בית ישראל). This is to be understood as a correction of what remains of the corrupt v 14, which has found its way from the margin into the text. 𝔖 has tried to make the text of v 14 readable by the insertion of a לטורא דסעיר after the introductory messenger formula, to which what followed was connected by the free expansion of a דשרא.

15 15a 𝔗 is fuller: ארעהון.

b See v 14 note b.

c 𝔊 ἐξαναλωθήσεται has misunderstood the כָּלֵה 𝔐 as כָּלָה. 𝔊 𝔏 (Sabatier) also insert the copula before it.

d 𝔊 καὶ γνώσῃ.

e 𝔊 expands (κύριος) ὁ θεὸς αὐτῶν.

36: 1a 4 MSS[Ken] על, see 1:17 note a.
1 b The vocative address, which is meaningful before the summons to attention (6:3; 16:35; 34:7, 9; 36:4; 37:4), has been connected in 𝔊 𝔖 in the manner of 21:3; 25:3 as yet another statement of address with ואמרת (τοῖς ὄρεσι, לטורי).

2 2a אדני is lacking in 𝔊. 𝔊[B et al.] κύριος κύριος, see Appendix 1.

b 𝔐 ובמות עולם. The copula is strange. 𝔙 simply suppresses it, while 𝔖 tries to alleviate the harshness by the repetition of the אמר (= ואמר). 𝔊 ἔρημα (𝔊[967] ἐρημία) αἰώνια seems, as the comparison with 35:9 ἐρημίαν (𝔊[147,L] Tht ἔρημον) αἰώνιον shows, to go back to the שממות עולם, of which in fact 𝔐 is said to be a corruption (Toy). The graphically more similar

given for a possession! 3/ therefore prophesy and say: Thus has [the Lord][a] Yahweh said: Therefore, <yes therefore>[b], because you have been laid waste and persecuted[c] on all sides so that you have become the possession of the rest of the nations and have become[d] the subject of gossip[e] and of the (mocking) calumny of people, 4/ therefore, you mountains of Israel, hear the word of [the Lord][a] Yahweh: Thus has [the Lord][a] Yahweh said to the mountains and to the hills, to[b] the water-channels and the valleys, and to the desolate ruins[c] and

שמות assumed by Cornill and others is not found in Ezekiel and occurs only in Ps 46:9. On the plural, which, against Herrmann, Bertholet, Fohrer, should not be changed to the singular, see 35:9 note a.

c The singular היתה could be explained as due to a grammatically loose attraction to the nearby מורשה, unless one wishes quietly to add ארץ as the subject. Cf. 11:15; 33:24; 36:5. The statement bears a strongly aphoristic stamp.

3 3a אדני is lacking in 𝔊. 𝔊[B et al.] *κύριος κύριος*, see Appendix 1.

b 𝔐 יען ביען. On the basis of 13:10; Lev 26:43 one might expect יען וביען. 𝔊 𝔖 𝔙, as already in 13:10, telescope into a single expression. 𝔗 seeks to preserve the asyndetic repetition by means of the insertion of two verbs: חלף דאיתררבו חלף דחשיבו לאחרבא.

c 𝔐 שמות ושאף. 𝔊 translates (*ἀντὶ*) *τοῦ ἀτιμασθῆναι ὑμᾶς καὶ μισηθῆναι ὑμᾶς*, 𝔗 (חלף דחשיבו) לאחרבא ולאצדאה, 𝔙 *pro eo quod desolati estis et conculcati,* while 𝔖 even splits into three expressions (על ד) אצטערתון ואתחרבתון ואתגדפתון. These differing translations already indicate that the sense is not beyond question. It can be said, in the first instance, that we have here clearly a double statement with alliteration which one should not disturb. The first, after יען, must be understood as an infinitive construct, while the second passes to the infinitive absolute. On this see Gesenius-Kautzsch §113e. Since v 3 is unmistakably an interpretative exposition of the quotation of v 2, it is inadvisable to depart from the root שמם, which has been initiated here by the שוממת of v 2 (see there note b). Thus, e.g., Driver, "Linguistic Problems," 181f, who, with Perles, emends to שְׂמוֹת and derives the verb from Arabic *šamita* I *gavisus fuit ob alterius malum,* II *ignominiam affecit.* Rather, שַׁמּוֹת is a rare form of the qal infinitive, attested in Ps 77:10 from חנן and in Ps 77:11 from חלל, see Gesenius-Kautzsch §67r (Bauer-Leander §58p'). שמם is to be understood here in a transitive sense. Thus emendations to שמוה (BH[3], Fohrer), שאות (Cornill), נשם (Hitzig, Kraetzschmar, Herrmann) are all unnecessary. On שאף "lay traps for" see, e.g., Am 8:4; Ps 56:2. Here, too, an emendation to שאט (BH[3], Fohrer) is not to be commended. The sense of v 3 demands information 1) about the devastation of the land, 2) about the falling into foreign possession brought about by that and 3) about the subsequent mockery. 𝔙 𝔗 have achieved the sense more accurately than 𝔊 (𝔖 in the first and third of its expressions).

d On the mixed form וַתַּעֲלוּ see Bauer-Leander §57t''. Literally: you have been brought up.

e 𝔐 על שפת לשון, literally: on the lip of the tongue. Bertholet wants to read על שפת לצון.

4 4a אדני is lacking in 𝔊, see Appendix 1.

b As in 6:3, 𝔊 𝔖 insert the copula, see note b there and also 1:4 note a.

c 𝔊(𝔏[S]) *καὶ τοῖς ἐρημωμένοις καὶ ἠφανισμένοις* splits

the abandoned cities, which have been given up to plundering[d] and mockery for the rest of the nations round about—5/ therefore thus has [the Lord][a] Yahweh said: Indeed, with the fire of my jealousy I speak[b] against the rest of the nations and against all[c] Edom which took possession[d] of my land[e] in all the joy of their heart[f], in utter contempt[g] in order to plunder. . .[h]—6/ Therefore prophesy over

into two expressions linked by the copula, see 1:4 note a.

d 𝔐 לבז. 𝔊 understands the following ללעג in terms of בז: *εἰς προνομὴν καὶ εἰς καταπάτημα*; 𝔗, on the other hand, לבז ,לחיך וללעיב in terms of ללעג. Thus Bertholet, BH[3] propose the reading לבוז. Since the root בוז, as opposed to בזז, is not otherwise attested in Ezekiel, it is preferable, with 𝔖, to keep to 𝔐.

5 5a אדני is lacking in 𝔊 𝔏[S] ℜ[Bo] 𝔄 Arm[p]. 𝔊[B] *κύριος κύριος*, see Appendix 1.

b The perfect (דברתי) is rare after אם לא (Cooke). An analogous דברתי, which in Ezekiel always contains an echo of the formulaic אני יהוה דברתי (5:15, 17 and frequently), is connected with הנני in v 6. According to Brockelmann §40e, this reveals the subjective aspect "under which the speaker simply substantiates an event as having happened."

c 𝔐 כֻּלָּא represents an (Aramaizing?) scribal error for כֻּלָּה, which is found correctly, linked with אדום, in 35:15. On כל with the suffix, in second place, see 11:15 note a.

d 𝔐 (. . . להם) נתנו is here not to be understood in the original meaning of "give (oneself?)," but in the secondary meaning frequent in Ezekiel of "put, take (for oneself)," which then in the present context has the meaning "take (to oneself)."

e 𝔗 elucidates ארע בית שכינתי.

f Literally "in the joy of the whole heart." In view of the clearly recognizable paraphrastic character of v 5, it is inadvisable to delete כל (as, e.g., Cornill, Toy) on the evidence of 𝔖, which elsewhere also often smoothes the text. In 𝔊 𝔏[S] כל לבב is unattested.

g 𝔐 בשאט נפש, in 25:6 בכל שאטך נפש, 25:15 בשאט בנפש. 𝔊 *ἀτιμάσαντες ψυχάς*, 𝔏[S] *iniuriam adficientes animas*, 𝔖 צערו נפשתא. 𝔙 abbreviates to *ex animo.*

h 𝔐 למען מגרשה לבז is presumably to be understood along the lines of what it says. But it has not yet been possible to give a specific meaning to מגרש. 𝔊 (𝔏[S]) *τοῦ ἀφανίσαι ἐν προνομῇ* assumes for גרש, which would then have to be understood as an Aramaic infinitive, a meaning "destroy." The verb *ἀφανίζειν* is used in vv 4, 34–36, and elsewhere in 𝔊, to render derivations of the root שמם. In 34:25 the corresponding Hebrew word is השבית, in 30:11 שחת. 𝔖, which resolves the expression into two verbs דנשבון אנין ונבזון אנין, tends towards an understanding of the Hebrew גרש as "drive away," and this is clearly the case also with 𝔗 לתרכותה למבזה and 𝔙 *et eiecerunt eam ut vastarent.* If 𝔐 is correct (Cornill conjectures למצא בז; Ehrlich, *Randglossen*, למורשה ולבז; Toy למען רשתה ובזה), then one will have to reckon with another, unknown meaning for גרש. Driver, "Linguistic Problems," 182, postulates, on the basis of Arabic *ǧarasa* II "drive out shamefully, expose to view in the streets" (see also 31:11 note c), a reading למען מגרשה לָבֹז. But see v 4 note d.

the land of Israel and say to the mountains and the hills, the[a] water-channels and the valleys: Thus has [the Lord][b] Yahweh said: See, in my jealousy and in my anger do I speak[c] because you have suffered the reproach of the nations. 7/ Therefore, thus has [the Lord][a] Yahweh said[b]: I have raised my hand (in an oath): Indeed[c], the nations[d] round about you shall suffer their reproach. 8/ But you, O mountains of Israel, shall shoot forth your branches and bear your fruit[a] for my people[b] Israel[c], for they[d] are coming soon. 9/ For see, I (come) to you and turn to you[a], and you will be tilled and sown. 10/ And I shall multiply men upon you, the whole house of Israel together[a], and the cities will be inhabited (again), and the ruins will be built up (again). 11/ And I shall multiply upon you men and cattle [and they will multiply and be fruitful][a] and I will make you dwell as in your former times[b] and will do more good (to you)[c] than in your beginnings[d], and you

Cooke, Fohrer prefer to delete the entire phrase as a textually corrupt gloss.

6 6a 𝔊 $\mathfrak{L}^S$ 𝔖 insert the copula, see v 4 note b.

b אדני is lacking in 𝔊 $\mathfrak{L}^S$ Tyc, see Appendix 1.

c See v 5 note b.

7 7a See Appendix 1. On 𝔊 see note b.

b In 𝔊 $\mathfrak{L}^S$ Tyc there is no rendering of כה אמר אדני יהוה. This textual lacuna is undoubtedly the result of a harmonizing of the text in 𝔊, which also eliminates the formula when it occurs in v 6. From the expression διὰ τοῦτο (= לכן), which has survived in 𝔊 ($\mathfrak{L}^S$ Tyc) and which is likewise superfluous after the לכן of v 6, it is clear that 𝔊 has before it the complete text of 𝔐. See further on "Form."

c If 𝔊 ($\mathfrak{L}^S$) seems to presuppose an אל in place of the introductory oath formula אם לא, that could indicate an abbreviation א' ל'. See also 12:23 note c.

d 𝔗 adds דבזו יתכון.

8 8a On the form פֶּרְיְכֶם see Diehl, *Pronomen*, 60.

b 𝔊 ($\mathfrak{L}^S$) link τὴν σταφυλὴν (= ענפכם) καὶ τὸν καρπὸν ὑμῶν καταφάγεται ὁ λαός μου and seems, therefore, to have read יאכל עמי in place of 𝔐 תשאו לעמי and, as a consequence of having misunderstood ענפכם, to have suppressed the תתנו in order to make the text more compact. The related expressions in 17:8, 23 advise adherence to 𝔐.

c 𝔐 ישראל is not attested by 𝔊 $\mathfrak{L}^S$ 𝔎 𝔄, doubtless because 𝔊 wishes to avoid the two-fold occurrence of the word in the same verse. עמי ישראל is found also in v 12; 14:9; (25:14) 38:14, 16; 39:7.

d 𝔗 reinterprets: קריב יום פורקני למיתי.

9 9a 𝔗 educidates the beginning as a statement of revelation: ארי אנא מתגלי, and the turning as a proof of salvation through Yahweh's word: ואיתפני במימרי לאיטבא לכון.

10 10a See v 5 note c. 𝔊 attempts to render the כלה by εἰς τέλος ($\mathfrak{L}^S$ *in finem*), while 𝔖 𝔅 dispense with rendering this repetition of כל. 𝔅 also softens the statement by inserting the copula: *homines omnemque domum Israel.*

11 11a 𝔐 ורבו ופרו. This reversed sequence of the Priestly source's verbs of blessing (Gen 1:22, 28, and elsewhere) remains unattested in 𝔊 $\mathfrak{L}^S$. Since the words also interrupt the style of direct address to the mountains, they probably represent a secondary interpretative element. Karl Marti's reference ("Die Spuren der sogenannten Grundschrift des Hexateuchs in der vorexilischen Propheten des Alten Testaments (Schluss)," *JPTh* 6 [1880]: 326) to Lev 26:9 with its verb sequence . . . והפריתי . . . ופניתי והרביתי is not really conclusive, since in the present passage, 36:9–11, the same three verbs certainly occur more than once, but nowhere in the uniform sequence of the statements in Lev 26.

b 𝔐 קדמותיכם, singular in 16:55.

c On the form הטבתי see Gesenius-Kautzsch §70e, Bauer-Leander §56u″.

d 𝔐 רֵאשִׁתֵיכֶם is from the singular רֵאשָׁה, a *hapax*

will know that I am Yahweh. 12/ And I
shall make men wander[a] over you, my
people Israel [and they will take posses-
sion of you, and you will become their
inheritance and will never again make
them childless][b].
13 **Thus has [the Lord][a] Yahweh said: Because**
<men say to you>[b]: You[c] devour men and
have made your people[d] childless, 14/
therefore (I say): You will not devour men
again, and your people[a] you will never
again <make childless>[b], says [the Lord][c]
Yahweh. 15/ And I shall no longer let the
reproach of the gentiles be heard over[a]
you, and you will no longer suffer the
scorn of the nations [and your people you
will no longer <make childless>][b], says
[the Lord][c] Yahweh.

legomenon.

12 12a 𝔐 והולכתי. 𝔊 καὶ γεννήσω, 𝔏 (Sabatier) *et generabo* seem to presuppose והולדתי. From the point of view of content, a reference to Yahweh's "begetting" would, in view of the context, be extremely odd. Thus 𝔐 is to be preferred. 𝔗, in dependence on v 11, ואסגי.

b The second half of the verse turns unexpectedly into an address in the second person masculine singular. Since this contains phrases from vv 13–15, which have been occasioned initially by the quotation in v 13, it is to be regarded as a secondary addition. 𝔊 𝔖 harmonize it with the second person plural of the preceding verses.

13 13a אדני is lacking in 𝔊. 𝔊^{B} κύριος κύριος, see Appendix 1.

b 𝔐 יען אמרים לכם. The association of יען with a following participle remains unusual, in spite of Driver's attempt ("Ezekiel," 302f) to prove on the basis of Ps 122:1 the possibility of the association of a preposition and an indefinite participle. It is not attested elsewhere in Ezekiel, in spite of the fairly frequent occurrence of a construction with יען. Thus, undoubtedly the infinitive אָמְרָם is to be read. On this see, e.g., 25:3, 6, 8 and elsewhere. On the use of indefinite plural before quotations see 8:12; 13:7; 37:11. 𝔐 לכם links up with the address to the mountains of Israel to be found in vv 1–12. In the sequel it changes to an address in the second feminine singular, which must refer to the land (ארץ). The related saying in Nu 13:32 speaks specifically of the ארץ אכלת יושביה. 𝔊 𝔖 𝔗 attest the second feminine singular address already in v 13aβ. The consequently necessary reading, לך, could then be easily explained on the basis of a wrong word division, if one can read the pi'el participle מאכלת (לך), which is admittedly never found and is not attested in Nu 13:32 either. But this is quite uncertain.

c On the archaic form of K אתי see Bauer-Leander §28f. Q reads את.

d K גויך, singular, is to be preferred to Q גוייך, plural. So 𝔊 𝔙 𝔗. 𝔖 is remarkable with its אנתון for את and עמה for גויך.

14 14a See v 13 note d.

b 𝔐 תכשלי "you cause to stumble" is doubtless a scribal error for תשכלי, see 𝔊 𝔗 𝔖 (𝔙).

c אדני is lacking in 𝔊 Tht. 𝔊^{B} κύριος κύριος, see Appendix 1.

15 15a על–אל cf. 1:17 note a.

b V 15bα has been inadvertently recopied from v 14 (with its scribal error). It is missing in 𝔊. On גויך see v 13 note d. On תכשלי see v 14 note b.

c אדני is lacking in 𝔊. 𝔊^{B} κύριος κύριος, see Appendix 1.

Form

The section 35:1–36:15 has been editorially placed under the single messenger formula (35:1). It is, therefore, against the chapter division of 𝔐, to be regarded as a homogeneous unit. From the point of view of content it is divided by the twofold address to the prophet as "son of man" (35:2; 36:1) into two large main sections, which are also differently addressed. The introductory commission to speak, 35:2f, which at the same time contains the summons to a gesture,[1] is directed against Mount Seir, which in the parallel statement in v 15 is equated with "all Edom." In 36:1, on the other hand, there follows the commission to prophesy to the mountains of Israel. The connection between the two sections is expressed from the content point of view also by the common catchword הר ("mountain") (הרי "mountains (of)"). In addition, the two sections are also contrasted in their content: the judgment on Mount Seir-Edom is followed by the proclamation of salvation to the moutains of Israel. Since, in the justification for the latter, the behavior of Edom is once again expressly mentioned (36:5), one cannot disregard the possibility, at least as far as the final form of 𝔐 is concerned, that the two sections have been intentionally dovetailed. Thus the two sections have been put together in a precise, logical relationship. One could even speak of a kind of "motivated declaration of salvation," a counterpart to the motivated declaration of judgment. But one will have to be clear from the outset that the "motivation" here is to be understood differently from that in the oracle of judgment. This will have to be kept in mind in the exposition.

While in this respect the total complex is relatively clearly laid out, the analysis of its separate parts affords greater difficulties. They prove to be composite structures, which have been in part secondarily expanded. In the first instance, the first half 35:1–15 is still relatively clear. By means of introductory messenger formulae in vv 3 and 14 two sections of the judgment speech against Edom are here introduced. The form of the second of these (vv 14f) can be described as a variant of the tripartite proof-saying. The first two parts of the latter are not bracketed, as is normal in this type of oracle (see, e.g., 25:3–5), causally by means of יען ("because")-לכן ("therefore"), but are introduced, against a background of a kind of retaliation thinking, by means of particles of comparison: כ – כן "so . . . as." Behind this there does, of course, lie a causal element. The section vv 3–13, on the other hand, breaks up into a sequence of three separate oracles which follow each other directly without further introductory formulae: 1) vv 3–4 provide a bipartite proof-saying introduced by the challenge or encounter formula (v 3 note c). 2) In vv 5–9 there follows a tripartite proof-saying, the first two parts of which are introduced in the usual way with יען ("because")-לכן ("therefore"). The beginning of the judgment oracle (the second part) is in the form of an oath, which is amplified by the formula for a divine saying.[2] Exactly the same form is to be found in 3) vv 10–13, though now enriched by a number of special elements. Thus the introductory motivatory section (יען "because"-clause) is enlivened by a quotation of the words of Edom (cf. 25:8; 26:2). The third element of the proof-saying, the recognition formula, is, on the other hand, strengthened in an unusual manner by means of an anticipatory ונודעתי בך ("and I shall make myself known to you") (see v 11 note e). After the recognition formula, however, there follows in vv 12f an expansion, which looks back once more to the motivation element (v 10) and lets us hear for the second time the words of the Edomites in the form of a quotation with the specific framework of an introductory and a concluding שמעתי ("I have heard").

Thus 35:1–15, the judgment oracle against Edom, appears as a series of no fewer than four self-contained proof-sayings in which Yahweh, consistently in the first person, directly addresses Mount Seir (second person masculine). Since the addressee is explicitly mentioned by name only at the beginning (v 2), the sequence of oracles is to be understood in its uniform address as a "series," without, however, the presupposition of a strict uniformity having been imposed on its individual parts. Thus it would also be possible that here a number of originally independent separate oracles have been secondarily linked.

From the point of view of form, on the other hand, the complex 36:1–15, the declaration of salvation to the mountains of Israel, is much more obscure. To be sure,

1 See 1, 182f on 6:2.

2 See 1, 176.

here too the section vv 13–15 can, in the first instance and without difficulty, be separated off as an independent element on the basis of its own introductory messenger formula. Its form is that of a "motivated salvation oracle," in which Yahweh directly addresses the land in the second person feminine singular. In its motivation (יען "because") clause it again provides a quotation. The declaration of salvation, on the other hand, is expounded in two sentences, each of which is concluded by the formula for a divine saying.

But how is the remainder, vv 1–12, to be regarded? Since v 11 closes with the recognition formula and the following verse (12) already contains the key-word of v 13 and also, in its course, abandons the address in the second person plural and passes to the address in the second person (masculine) singular, v 12 will have to be regarded as an editorial transitional verse similar to 34:16. But how are we to judge the confusing plethora of commissions to the prophet to speak (vv 1, 3, 6), summonses to attention (vv 1, 4) and introductory messenger formulae (vv 2, 3, 4, 5, 6, 7), which cannot be clearly assessed on the basis of the logically classificatory יען ("because") (vv 2, 3b [6])-לכן ("therefore") (vv 3, 4, 5, 6, 7) statements? The impression of a text greatly overfilled with additions, in which the logical layout has been broken, suggests itself (see, by way of analogy, a passage such as 5:5ff). Thus, if one is looking for the basic text, one will not be able to avoid deletions. In this respect Hölscher is along the right lines when he finds in v 2, with its quotation of the enemy's words, the original motivatory element of the oracle of salvation. V 3b, in contrast to what the introduction in v 3a (לכן "therefore") would lead us to expect, provides a fuller paraphrase of v 2. In v 4 there follows an unusually expansively phrased new introduction and address for the expected oracle of salvation (לכן "therefore"), which finally seems to follow in v 5 with yet another introductory formula (לכן "therefore"). Closer examination shows that in it are bound up elements of what is said in v 6 (בקנאתי "in my jealously") along with a clear reference back to the threat against Edom in chapter 35. The language also echoes sections of chapter 25. V 6, however, marks a fresh beginning with a commission to the prophet to speak, and the oracle once again contains an address and an introductory messenger formula. For the whole section vv 3–6 (as far as יהוה "Yahweh"), Hölscher would regard only the address introduced by לכן ("therefore"), v 4abα (as far as and including ולגאיות "and to the hills"), as original. This separation of the bulk of vv 3–6 as later exegesis has, in fact, much in its favor. But there still remains the difficulty that v 7 immediately begins again with the introductory messenger formula, introduced by לכן ("therefore"). Thus one might consider whether the remainder of v 6 does not also belong with the secondary additions and v 7 is to be connected directly with v 2. The text would then be, from the point of view of form, concluded. On the other hand, however, v 7 corresponds so clearly with the divine address v 6b (and continues it and intensifies it) that one must simply accept the harshness of the renewed beginning with לכן ("therefore") in v 7. In addition, v 10—with its "resumption" of the beginning of vv 11,[3] its explanatory addition כל בית ישראל ("the whole house of Israel") and its change of person in v 10b—is much more remarkable. It is to be regarded as a secondary amplification (Jahn, Hölscher).

Thus 36:1–11 contains in the first instance a "motivated salvation oracle," in which Yahweh addresses the mountains of Israel in the second person plural and makes his promise to them in response to the scorn of the enemies which is cited in the oracle. In vv 13–15, to which v 12 is the transition, this oracle has acquired an addition which addresses the land in the second person feminine singular. Above all, however, vv 1–11 have been expanded internally by all kinds of additions and explanations. Its theme presents a counterpart to the oracle of doom against the mountains of Israel (chapter 6).

Now Jahn, Herrmann and Hölscher have put forward the theory that Ezekiel 36 did not originally presuppose Ezekiel 35 before it, but, on its own, presented the counterpart to chapter 6.[4] Behind this assertion there lies the correct observation that the basic form of 36:1ff speaks quite generally of the "enemy" (v 2) and the "nations round about you" (v 7). The specific reference to Edom has been added only secondarily in v 5. On the other

3 Kuhl, "'Wiederaufnahme,'" 4.
4 J. Herrmann, *Ezechielstudien*, 36f.

hand, it is not to be assumed that in the book as a whole Ezek 36:1–15 ever formed the counterpart to chapter 6 without chapter 35. Here too the character of the book as a collection must be taken into account. In this collection the word of consolation to the mountains of Israel, which were threatened by the possessive claims of her neighbors, has been linked with words of judgment on the hill country of the Edomites, who in particular laid claim to Israelite (Judaean) territory. Above the judgment on Edom there rises salvation for Israel. An analogous surpassing of the threat of judgment by a promise of salvation was seen also in chapter 34. From this point of view it also becomes clear why these Edom-oracles have not been put alongside 25:12–14. Structurally they have acquired in chapter 35f another meaning and have become pre-oracle motivation for the proclamation of salvation.

Setting

35:1–36:15 certainly emerged only in the period after 587. Besides, in comparison with chapter 25 it can be said that they reflect a later state of affairs. While there Ammon was the neighbor of Jerusalem that was mainly threatened by Yahweh, here it is Edom. While there it was a question of mockery at the fall of Jerusalem and, in a more general way, of the enmity and vindictiveness of the neighboring peoples towards Jerusalem, here it is claims to possession of the land that are rejected. While 33:24 disclosed claims to ownership on the part of the nationals who had remained behind in the land, here it is the world of the neighboring peoples, among whom Edom in particular stands out, that is involved. This leads away from immediate proximity to the fall of Jerusalem to somewhat later years. This is also indicated by the very specific proclamation of 36:8 that the time of return for the exiles is near. Does this assertion arise from the calculation that part of the forty years of exile envisaged in 4:6 has elapsed? Or does it originate in specific political observations which already point to the period of Deutero-Isaiah, so that we can discern here the voice of the school of Ezekiel in the late exilic period? In any event, this observation prevents a dating later than the period of the return of the exiles under Zerubbabel.

Bertholet reckons with the origin of the section in Babylon, while Herntrich reckons in the case of chapter 35, on account of the strong interest in Edom, with an origin in Palestine. Since, however, the polemic concerning rights of ownership in the land runs through Ezekiel's preaching in all its phases equally (11:15; 33:24; 35:10 (12); 36:2), without a change of location being anywhere perceptible, there is nothing to prevent chapters 35f too from being derived from an exilic context.

Interpretation

■ **35:1–4** The reference to the reception of God's word introduces the divine address to the prophet ("son of man") and the summons to a gesture in which the prophet is to turn his face towards Mount Seir.[5] The name "Seir" (שׂעיר vv 2, 3, 7, 15) has already occurred in a gloss in 25:8 (see note b) alongside Ammon and means, according to Koehler-Baumgartner, in the first instance a "small forest" or, according to P. Haupt, "rough" i.e. "rugged, rocky, uncultivated land."[6] As a proper name the word is usually used throughout the OT in the combination הר שׂעיר ("Mount Seir") (Gen 36:8f; Dtn 1:2; 2:1; and elsewhere) as a designation for the hill country to the east of the *'araba* in which Edom settled and found its home.[7] To the Edomite nation there was addressed in 25:12–14, in the context of the peoples neighboring on Palestine, Yahweh's judgment. The reason given for this was Edom's implacable thirst for revenge. In the present passage judgment is proclaimed on this land, in the first instance without any further justification, in formulaic language such as is found elsewhere in Ezekiel.[8] It is impossible to isolate in more detail the formulaic stock, so that it is best to think here of formulae from the Ezekiel school.

---

5 See 1, 144f; on "son of man" see 1, 131f; see 1, 182f.

6 Paul Haupt, "Die Schlacht von Taanach" in *Studien zur semitischen Philologie und Religionsgeschichte Julius Wellhausen zum Siebzigsten Geburtstag*, BZAW 27 (Giessen: Töpelmann, 1914), 211.

7 On this see above p. 17.

8 On the introductory call of the summons to a duel or to an encounter see 1, 175 and above p. 98. On the remainder of v 3 see 6:14. On v 4a see 12:20.

■ **35:5** The second proof-saying, vv 5–9, motivates the proclamation of judgment. In doing so it goes back to the circumstances mentioned in the two Edomite-Philistine oracles in 25:12–17. There (v 15) איבת עולם ("long-standing enmity") described the longstanding Philistine hatred.[9] The expression על ידי חרב ("to the sword") is found also in Jer 18:21; Ps 63:11.[10] The hatred vented itself in a particularly cruel fashion at the time of the disaster (עת אידם "time of their misfortune"), a time to which it is looked back here from a certain distance. יום איד is a technical term for the "day of disaster." Ob v 13 uses it in the context of his graphic retrospective description of the events of the summer of 587 (Ob vv 1–14) no fewer than three times. Elsewhere it occurs without suffix in Job 21:30, with suffix 2 Sam 22:19 (= Ps 18:19, first person); Prv 27:10 (second person); Dtn 32:35; Jer 18:17; 46:21 (third person plural). Alongside it there appears the expression, typical of Ezekiel, the "time of the final punishment" (עת עון קץ).[11]

■ **35:6** In this way Yahweh's judgment will come about. That this is described as vengeance for blood-guilt (דם אשמת "you have made yourself guilty of blood," note c) is in keeping with Ezekiel's categories of thought and judgment.[12] Unique is the expression about the "pursuit" (רדף in Ezekiel only here) by blood, an expression which is also taken up in the gloss (note b). In the context of language about a deed entailing its own consequence, the shed blood becomes precisely the active pursuer of the guilty person.[13] On this see, e.g., Gen 4:10.

■ **35:7** V 7 gives expression to the desolation in stereotyped formulae. שממה ומשמה ("horrible wasteland") (note a) has already occurred in v 3; it occurs also in 6:14; 33:28 (see also 23:33 note b). הכרית מן ("to wipe out from") occurs in 14:13,17; 21:8; 25:13; 29:8. The wiping out of the עבר ושב ("[all] who go to and fro") has been mentioned already in 33:28 (see 14:15), as well as in Is 34:10; 60:15; Jer 9:9,11; Zeph 3:6. They are referred to as witnesses in 5:14; 36:34. The combination עבר ושב occurs also in Ex 32:27; Zech 7:14; 9:8.

■ **35:8f** The filling of a place with slain has already been referred to in 9:7; 11:6; 30:11 (see also 32:5f). On the whole of v 9 see the related formulation in 29:12; 30:7.[14] The eruption of the concluding recognition formula in the midst of plural phraseology is unusual. But such a protuberance of the concluding formula from the context is not without analogy in Ezekiel (see 6:13; 7:4,9; and elsewhere). In this way the oracle against Edom in vv 5–9 also remains strongly enmeshed in the stereotyped language of the Ezekiel school.

■ **35:10** The third proof-saying is, from the point of view of form.[15] and of content, much more individualistic. In the motivation for the judgment proclaimed here two quotations of words of the Edomites are cited. In the first, Edom bluntly announces its right of ownership of the whole land. The description of the territory of Israel as "the two nations and the two lands" corresponds to the "two nations and two kingdoms" in 37:22. It is not to be referred to the two nations Edom and Judah, but means, like the "two houses of Israel" in Is 8:14, Judah and North Israel as the two parts of Israel as a whole. In the light of actual historical circumstances the claim seems very strange. Edom never penetrated beyond Jerusalem. In the wording of this statement, the formulation of which does not come from the Edomites but from Ezekiel (or his school), one can hear very clearly the voice of the exiles who are far removed from the actual circumstances in the land. In exile news has been received of the penetration of Judaean territory by the Edomites. This is regarded as a threat to Yahweh's land, and this is then formulated comprehensively as a threat to the land as a whole. That, once again, this is not really a geographical statement, but a theological one is clear also from the observation that "Yahweh is there" (see 48:35), whether this is from the original author of the oracle or as is, for reasons both of form (note c) and of content (according to chapter 11 Yahweh has departed from Jerusalem), more probable, from an expander. The attempt to seize the land is an attempt to seize Yahweh's

9 On the hatred of Edom, already mentioned in the (secondary?) Amos oracle 1:11f, implacable, venting itself to the full in the use of the sword, see above p. 17.

10 On this see Miller, *Verhältnis,* 104.

11 On this see 1, 446 on 21:30, 34.

12 On this see 1, 456f on 22:1ff, as well as the אשם of 25:12.

13 Koch (see 1, 204).

14 On שממות עולם see v 9 note a.

15 See above p. 232.

property. Hos 5:10 had already denounced it as the crime of removing boundary marks that Judah should have annexed Israelite territory. In another way Ezek 11:15; 33:24 had spoken against false territorial claims within Israel. That here a nation from outside lays claim to the land which was given by Yahweh to his servant Jacob (28:25; 37:25) must summon Yahweh to the scene.[16]

■ **35:12f** In the second quotation, however, the claim to take possession of the land or, as it is now stated quite blatantly in terms of the image of a beast of prey, to take it "to devour" (note e; see also 29:5; 34:5, 8, 10; used figuratively of fire in 15:4, 6; 21:37), is motivated by the political fiasco of the holy land: "They (the mountains of Israel) lie waste." And thereby, as the (certainly secondary, note the second person plural) exposition in v 13 shows, to the unlawful claim there is added the crime of blasphemous arrogance and boasting against Yahweh which arises from the misunderstanding of his divine desire for justice.

■ **35:11** So Yahweh announces with an oath that in his judgment on this anger and jealousy and hatred on Edom's part he will make himself known. The land of Israel may lie waste and the house of Israel itself be struck dumb, but the God of Israel will not fail to hear what is said in self-confident arrogance against his people, to whom he has pledged his name.[17] In vv 12f, framing the second quotation, it is twice emphatically underlined שמעתי (יהוה) אני ("I [Yahweh] have heard").

■ **35:14f** The final oracle, set somewhat apart by its own introductory formula (added at a second stage?), in vv 14–15, expresses clearly in the expository correction (v 15) to the mutilated v 14b (v 14 note b) the theological intention which was concealed in the preceding oracle. It is a question of the "inheritance" of the house of Israel. נחלה ("inheritance"), apart from the thirteen occurrences in chapters 44–48, occurs again in Ezekiel only in the redactional verse 36:12.[18] To Edom's gloating over the devastation of the land (v 2) Yahweh will reply by the infliction of devastation on Edom. Thus the final oracle of chapter 35 goes back, even in its language, to the first and concludes the circle of threats against Edom, all of which are emphatically described as proclamation of the divine self-revelation.

■ **36:1** But this brings us to the transition to the second part of the oracle, 36:1–15, the oracle of salvation for the mountains of Israel, which is introduced with a new, full commission to the son of man to prophesy. The keyword of the address, "mountains of Israel," by means of which the whole unit 35:1–36:15 is clearly made, in the composition of the book as a whole, to correspond to chapter 6 in the first half of the book, was heard already in 35:12. In it there is now addressed openly the nation whose deliverance has already been the subject, in veiled terms, of the judgment oracles against Edom.

■ **36:2** This happens anew in the form of a motivated divine saying (יען "because"-לכן "therefore"). As motivation, once again the words of the opponents are cited. The opponent is described in a remarkably general term, which recalls the language of the Psalms, as "the enemy." אויב ("enemy") occurs in Ezekiel otherwise only in 39:27 (איביהם "their enemies") and איבה ("enmity") in 25:15; 35:5. Only v 6 explains: "the nations" and v 7 still more fully: "the nations round about you." The insertion which is v 5, however, specifies: "The rest of the nations and all Edom." The oracle in 36:1ff is, as is clear from its quite different terminology, undoubtedly in the first instance quite independent of the Edom oracles. In the content of what the enemy is quoted here as saying, however, the oracle comes very close to what was put into the mouth of Edom in chapter 35. The scornful האח ("Aha!") with which the speech of the enemies begins has its correspondence in the words of the Ammonites in 25:3 and of the inhabitants of Tyre in 26:2. There then follows, here too, the reference to the desolation of the land. In the שממות עולם ("desolation forever") which is to be accepted as the original reading (note b), as in 35:9, the definitive nature of the state of destruction of Israel's

16 See Albrecht Alt, "Hosea 4:8–6:6. Ein Krieg und seine Folgen in prophetischer Beleuchtung" in *Kleine Schriften zur Geschichte des Volkes Israel* 2 (München: Beck, 1953), 177 note 1.

17 See 1, 407f on 20:5.

18 On the theological meaning of the term, which is of great significance in the Deuteronomic writings, see von Rad, "Promised Land."

habitations, a state which will last "from now on until the most distant future,"[19] is expressed, and any hope of a reversal of fortune for Israel is dashed. H. Haag, who wishes to retain 𝔐 and then find in the expression the everlasting nature of Yahweh's promise of land to Abraham, surely pays too little attention to this embedding of the text in its context.[20] As in 35:12, the enemies derive from this their claim now to be able to remove the land definitively from the hands of Israel and take it into their own "possession" (מורשה, as in 11:15; 33:24).

■ **36:3** The attitude of the enemies which found expression in the quotation has been further expounded in the secondary addition v 3. In a direct address to the mountains of Israel, it is there declared that they have been devastated in order to fall into the possession of the "rest of the nations." The sentence is very forcefully introduced with a double alliteration.[21] שאף (note c), chosen alongside שמות for the sake of the alliteration, describes primarily the gasping or panting for air (Jer 2:24; 14:6), for shade (Job 7:2), for the repose of the night (Job 36:20), but can also already in Am 8:4 describe the hostile attack on the poor. The reference to the "rest of the nations" certainly does not mean only "the other nations," but is intended to indicate that a first judgment has already been pronounced over the nations.[22] Nothing necessitates thinking with Morgenstern here of the "rest of the nations" decimated in the course of Xerxes' Persian campaign against the Greeks. Then with particular emphasis, reference is made, in terminology not otherwise attested in Ezekiel, to the mockery to which the mountains of Israel have been subject in their devastation. דבה ("[mocking] calumny"), which here, as in Jer 20:10=Ps 31:14, describes the "whispering of hostile people,"[23] is not attested elsewhere in Ezekiel, but occurs four times in P (Gen 37:2; Nu 13:32; 14:36f). It occurs also in Prv 10:18; 25:10.

■ **36:4** In 𝔐 v 4 now begins Yahweh's reply. This verse, which reveals itself by the reference to the "rest of the nations" to be, like v 5, part of the insertion which begins with v 3, may still contain a part of the original introduction to the proclamation of salvation (Hölscher). But the introduction, which begins with the vocative address to the mountains of Israel, with a summons to attention and a renewed, addressed introductory messenger formula, has then certainly been expanded. Alongside the references to four types of terrain which correspond to the addressees of 6:3,[24] there is also the mention of the desolate ruins and abandoned cities (vv 10, 33, 38), of which it is said that they have become for the "rest of the nations" objects of plunder and "mockery" (לעג otherwise only in the gloss on 23:32, see note b). Once again there appear side by side the objective element of desolation and the subjective one of mockery.

■ **36:5** The immediately following speech of Yahweh within the insertion formed by vv 3–5 is clearly seen from its beginning to be a slightly varied (באש קנאתי "with the fire of my jealousy" instead of בקנאתי ובחמתי "in my jealousy and in my anger") borrowing from the beginning of the Yahweh speech of the basic text (v 6b). In the form of an oath Yahweh confirms his word of judgment on the rest of the nations and on all Edom, and then needlessly recapitulates once again the crimes of the nations: the unjustified claim to ownership (in an unusual formulation נתנו את ארצי להם למורשה "they took possession of my land"),[25] the gloating (vv 14f; 25:6), the disdain (25:6,15). V 5bβ remains unclear (note h).

■ **36:6f** The transition from the insertion formed by vv 3–5 back to the basic text is then made by means of a new introduction. This introduction corresponds partly to the beginning of v 4, but by reference to the "land of Israel" proves to be not original.[26] Does it already envisage the continuation in vv 13–15 which is then in fact directed towards the land (second person feminine singular)? The basic text which then begins immediately is, with its declaration of salvation, addressed to the mountains of Israel (second person plural). Here too, to begin with, attention still focuses on the nations round about. Insofar as the mountains of Israel have hitherto

19 Jenni, "Das Wort 'ōlām."
20 Haag, *Untersuchung*, 19f.
21 On יען ביען see note b.
22 On this see 25:16, but already Am 1:8; 9:12.
23 Haag, *Untersuchung*, 20.
24 See 1, 185f.
25 On מרשה see otherwise vv 2f; 11:15; 25:4,10; 33:24, and the ירש of 35:10 (corresponding to the לאכלה of 35:12).
26 On this see 1, 203 on 7:2.

had to bear the reproach of the nations (נשא כלמה "to suffer reproach" 16:52, 54; 32:24f, 30; 34:29; 36:6f; 39:26; 44:13), Yahweh now swears with uplifted hand (20:5f, 15, 23, 28, 42; 44:12) that the latter will now suffer their reproach, i.e. on their part will have to come under the judgment which they intended for Israel.

■ **36:8** Against this background, however, Yahweh's word now turns towards his land and discloses what will happen on the mountains of Israel when the reproach is removed from them. It is characteristic how their new "honor" is described: "But you, O mountains of Israel, shall shoot forth your branches and bear your fruit for my people Israel, for they are coming soon." The mountains are, in accordance with their real, God-given function, "mountains of Israel." It is not simply in a new blossoming which would restore life and fruitfulness that their honor lies, but in the mountains' becoming once again Israel's mountains and in their blossoming and flourishing becoming again a blossoming and flourishing for Israel. Thus Israel's return, which is proclaimed in an impressive statement of proximity, is at hand. Such statements of proximity have been heard earlier in the proclamation of the day of Yahweh (7:7;[27] 30:3), of the days of judgment (12:23) and of the executioners of the divine judgment (9:1 and note a). Here it is an element in the promise of salvation. For Israel, before long, once again branch and fruit will grow on the mountains of Israel. One can scarcely conclude, with Haag, from the fact that Lev 23:40 also mentions branch and fruit together that Ezekiel here had in mind the legislation for the feast of booths in Leviticus 23 and meant: "Once again the feast of booths will be celebrated in remembrance of the second return from a foreign land."[28] Branch and fruit are also mentioned in Ezek 17:23 in the description of the new tree on the mountains of Israel in connection with that tree. The flourishing of a tree is described there by means of a fairly general expression.

■ **36:9** This interpretation is borne out by an allusion in the following verse to the blessing formulae of Leviticus 26. The challenge or approach formula הנני אליכם (here "see, I [come] to you") (note c on 35:3), which is not to be deleted, with Humbert,[29] simply because it is used here for the only time in the OT in a beneficent sense, is followed by the promise of Yahweh's "turning to" them (פנה אל Lev 26:9) and of the cultivation and sowing of the mountains.

■ **36:10** The multiplication of people, which is also promised in v 11 in the same words, is referred in the expansion in v 10 specifically to "the whole house of Israel" (37:11). To this is added the reconstruction of the cities and the ruined places.

■ **36:11** The basic text speaks in v 11 in more general terms of the multiplication of "people and cattle" (אדם ובהמה 14:13, 17, 19, 21; 25:13; 29:8), to which a later hand has added the blessing formula of P (note a), of the re-inhabiting as before and of an increase of good beyond what it once was. In such activity Yahweh will reveal himself in the mystery of his person.

■ **36:12** The transitional v 12, however, which turns to an address in the second person (masculine), once again takes up the proclamation that the men of the people of God (v 10) are to be carried off. In antithesis to 35:10, it speaks of the Israelites "taking possession" (ירש) of the land so that (here 35:15 is taken up again) it is once more their inheritance, a place which Israel will never again make childless.

■ **36:13–15** Here, however, the key-word of vv 13–15 has already appeared. This oracle of salvation makes clear in a broader perspective how the reproach is removed from the land. It can be seen in the OT to what extent childlessness was regarded by a woman as a reproach. "Yahweh has taken away 'my reproach' (חרפתי)," says Rachel after the birth of her first son (Gen 30:23; see also 1 Samuel 2).

■ **36:13** Thus now an evil rumor is circulating about the land of Israel to the effect that the shame of its childlessness is its own fault. The image is indeed heightened in the quotation in a strange fashion. The land which ought to be the mother and bearer of children (on this see, e.g., the תוצא "let . . . bring forth" of Gen 1:24) seems to resemble the wild ravening beast seeking and devouring its victims. Thus, not only did it once "spew out" its Canaanite population (Lev 18:25,28), but it also devoured Israel in the catastrophes of 732, 722, 597 and 587. This expression of the dangerousness of the land in which one can perish has a remarkable parallel in the

27 See 1,205.

28 Haag, *Untersuchung,* 21.

29 Humbert, "'hinnenî êlékâ,'" 104.

Priestly narrative in Nu 13:32, which speaks of the "hostile slander against the land" (דבת הארץ, see above v 3) in the mouth of the spies: ארץ אכלת יושביה הוא (it is "a land that devours its inhabitants"). See also 2 Kgs 2:19, where the blame for childlessness in the land is attributed to a spring: המים רעים והארץ משכלת ("the water is bad and the land is unfruitful").

■ **36:14f** These evil words against the land, which according to v 15 circulate in the mouth of "the nations," i.e., however, here no longer the neighboring Palestinian nations, but (as in v 20) the host nations of the exiles and the refugees, Yahweh will counter with a new future in which all this slander will no longer be true. The oracle obviously speaks to a hidden despondency on the part of the exiles who are concerned with the question: "Will in fact a newly bestowed history in the land work out any differently from the first history?" Yahweh's word points to a future in which the threat from the land will be definitively removed.

Looking back on 35:1–36:15, the question must now be finally asked in what way the "motivations" which proliferate here are to be understood. With regard to the יען ("because")-לכן ("therefore") formulations within chapter 35 the question presents no difficulty. Edom will experience divine judgment as a punishment for its malevolence, its gloating and its blasphemous claims to ownership of Yahweh's land. But how is the יען ("because")-לכן ("therefore") in 36:1–5 to be understood? Here too, to begin with, where punishment of enemies is mentioned (vv 5,6f), the same holds true as in chapter 35. But to what extent is salvation for the mountains of Israel the "consequence" of misdemeanor on the part of the enemies? Here it must be a question of a different kind of "therefore." Yahweh's blessing is not to be derived as a necessary consequence of the malice of the enemies or even from Yahweh's judgment understandable in such a situation. Rather, here we have the "consequence" of the free divine mercy which refuses to leave in the lurch those who have been derided by the enemy, who have been condemned to death, who have been displaced, but which will turn to them as it once already did at Israel's beginnings. For the sake of his inner faithfulness, Yahweh keeps his word to the mountains of Israel and to the land of Israel, above all, however, decisively to the people of Israel, to "my people Israel" (34:30; 36:12).

This immediately answers the question which was left open at the beginning, the question of the logical connection between chapter 35 and 36:1–15. The oracle against Mount Seir is not a "motivation" for the oracle directed towards the mountains of Israel in the way that the reference to the sins of the Edomites is "motivation" for the judgment on Edom. Rather, here too it is a question of the free decision based on Yahweh's inner faithfulness. In the face of the mockery of the victors of the moment, whose claim to the land of defeated Israel seems to be supported by all the logic of normal human reasoning, he promises to this defeated Israel and to his land covered in disgrace the future of a new life. In this deeper sense of a divine logic in which God remains true to himself, chapter 35, the oracle against the Edomites, forms the "motivation" for the oracle directed towards the mountains of Israel.

Aim

The oracle starts from the realities of Israel's history. Israel had been thrown into a judgment which had taken everything from her: her two nations, her hill country, without which she could not properly be Israel since her God had there established the place of his proximity (35:10), just as the mountains could no longer properly be the "mountains of Israel" without the nation Israel. In this complete collapse of all her earthly securities and also of the guarantees of her spiritual life, Israel was forced to recognize the reality that stood over her and could not take refuge in a different spiritual world. God himself had led her, through this disaster which he had brought about, into the reality of the most naked deprivation.

It now seemed, according to all the rules of logic, to be part of this reality that the neighboring nations, as well as the related nation of the Edomites, should have penetrated this empty space and have felt themselves to be the rightful owners and have said so. Whatever of human unpleasantness, malicious joy, pent-up hatred and sheer striving for power may have accompanied all this, they seemed simply to be taking seriously in their own way the reality which God had created in his judgment on his people.

Into this reality the prophetic word has to bring, in God's name, a quite different message. It turns, first of all, against the enemies of God's people, who realistically think they can act in accordance with the new situation, and it says to them that God's judgment is in no sense handing out to the instruments of that judgment a charter enabling them to regard those judged and their possessions simply as objects to be liquidated. Here too God is against hatred. Here too he is against the malicious joy of the victors of the day. He is against the greedy dividing up of the victim's clothes and will in his time call all this to account.

At the heart of the prophetic word, however, there stands something else. It proclaims the mysteriously strange logic of God. At the point where, in his judgment, nothing more than the reality of death seems to hold sway and where in the normal logic of human understanding the thought arises that one can pass over the victim as someone who is done with, there God proclaims the logic of His faithfulness. In order to show to all who, in reality, he is, he will, precisely at this point, grant new life. And this not from a spirit of stubborn contradiction which always insists on being right in the end and in doing so shows itself to be merely fickle, but for the sake of his own inner faithfulness. Because, even when he has pronounced sentence of death, he does not abandon his work and will not allow his name, which he has entrusted to men, to be dishonored, he will for that reason have mercy on the condemned, allow the dead to flourish again, will rebuild what was destroyed and will again bring back the displaced so that they will "come soon." This is what God does for his people. In this activity he shows himself to the world to be acknowledged.

But the following oracle, 36:16–38, will speak of the inner logic of this activity quite unmistakably.

Israel's New Life: The Free Gift of the God who is true to himself

Bibliography

Floyd V. Filson
"The Omission of Ezek. 12:26–28 and 36:23b–38 in Codex 967," *JBL* 62 (1943): 27–32.

Herbert Haag
Was lehrt die literarische Untersuchung des Ezechiel-Textes? (Freiburg in der Schweiz: Paulusdruckerei, 1953), especially 19–51.

H. St. J. Thackeray
"The Greek Translators of Ezekiel," *JTS* 4 (1903): 407f.

36

16 **And the word of Yahweh came to me: 17/**
Son of man, when the house of Israel
lived[a] in their land, they made it unclean
by their behavior and their deeds[b]. Like
the uncleanness at menstruation was
their behavior (unclean) before me. 18/
Then I poured out my anger upon them
[because of the blood which they shed in
the land and because they have defiled it
with their idols][a] 19/ and scattered them
among the nations so that they were
dispersed[a] throughout the countries.
According to their behavior and their
deeds I judged them. 20/ But wherever
<they came>[a] to the nations, there they
profaned my holy name while it was said
of them: These are the people of Yah-
weh, and they have had to leave his land.
21/ They I grieved[a] for my holy name
which the house of Israel had profaned
among the nations to whom they came.

36: 17a ישבים without the article is to be understood
17 grammatically as a complement and not as in apposition to בית ישראל. Smend, following Ewald: relative clause.

b 𝔊 translates 𝔐 בעלילותם by *ἐν τοῖς εἰδώλοις αὐτῶν* and adds (as a double translation of בעלילותם?) *καὶ ἐν τοῖς ἀκαθαρσίαις αὐτῶν*, thus preparing the way for v 17b. דרך parallel to עלילה also in v 19; 14:22f; 20:43f. Against Cornill, ובטמאתם should not be added in 𝔐.

18 18a V 18aβb is missing in 𝔊 and presents a second (superfluous in the context alongside v 17), more detailed description of Israel's sin. V 18aβ is thus linked to v 18aα by means of the catchword שפך. Bloodshed (chapter 22) and idol worship (chapter 8) are Israel's typical sins.

19 19a 𝔐 ויזרו. 𝔊 *καὶ ἐλίκμησα αὐτούς*, 𝔖 ודרית אנון are assimilated, as far as form is concerned, to the preceding ואפיץ אתם (on this see 22:15; 29:12; 30:23, 26). 𝔐, however, is not to be deleted as a gloss (Cornill) nor emended on the basis of 𝔊 𝔖 (Fohrer). 𝔗 has, more fully, "evil ways" (אורחתהון בישתא) and "depraved deeds" (עובדיהון מקלקליא).

20 20a Literally: "And 'they came' (read ויבאו; see 10:3 note a) to the nations to whom they came, and they profaned. . . ." 𝔐 אשר באו שם does not seem to be attested by 𝔖 (BH^3). In reality, however, the reference to this phrase in 𝔖, which again and again freely rearranges the text in the interests of readable language, is in the addendum which it provides later in the phrase: ואמרין הוו להון עממא הלין. The passage, which is not literally attested in 𝔖, identifies the nations more precisely as hosts of the exiles for the time being. Vriezen, "*'Ehje*," 504, speaks with regard to the present passage, of the "intensive sense" in which the indefinite construction is used here: "Everywhere, wherever they came."

21 21a 𝔊 (𝔏 Sabatier) *καὶ ἐφεισάμην αὐτῶν* finds the divine mercy for the people promised here already and thereby alleviates the sharpness of the statement that Yahweh is first concerned for his name. On no

22 Therefore say to the house of Israel: Thus
has [the Lord][a] Yahweh said: Not for your
sake do I act[b], O house of Israel, but for
the sake of my holy name[c] which you
have profaned among the nations to
whom you have come, 23/ and I will
sanctify my great name which has been
profaned among the nations, which you
have profaned in their midst. And the
nations will know that I am Yahweh,
says [the Lord] Yahweh[a], when I show

account should 𝔐 be emended, with Fohrer, on the basis of 𝔊.

22 22a אדני is lacking in 𝔊 𝔎^{Bo} Tyc. 𝔏^{Ver} *dominus omnipotens*, see Appendix 1.

b On the absolute use of עשה see 20:9 note a.

c The parallel use of למען and ל occurs also in Is 55:5 (Ehrlich, *Randglossen*). 𝔊 in the first occurrence uses a simple dative *οὐχ ὑμῖν*, and then the preposition *διὰ* (*τὸ ὄνομά μου*).

23 23a 𝔐 נאם אדני יהוה (on the אדני see Appendix 1) is not attested by 𝔊 𝔏^{Ver} 𝔎^{Bo} Tyc. In the oldest 𝔊 MS, 𝔊^{967}, the whole passage vv 23bβ–38 is missing. Already H. St. J. Thackeray, in his *A Grammar of the Old Testament in Greek according to the Septuagint* 1 (Cambridge: University Press, 1909), 11f, had established for this passage in the 𝔊 of Ezekiel a different style of Greek and had asked whether this were not an independent translation which might have come, e.g., from a Jewish or Christian lectionary. On this see further H. St. J. Thackeray, *The Septuagint and Jewish Worship; a Study in Origins,* The Schweich Lectures 1920 (London: Oxford University Press, 1921), 124–129. Now, in fact, this assertion about 𝔊^{967} contains a certain element of uncertainty which has not found sufficiently clear expression in the discussion about 𝔊^{967} hitherto. In the surviving parts of the Scheide Papyrus, 36:23bα is followed directly by 38:1–39:29, then by 37:1ff. In 37:4 the surviving text breaks off. In view of these readjustments, which have a distant correspondence in 𝔏^{W}, where chapters 38f follow chapter 42 and chapter 36 is missing, and in view of the absence of the continuation, it is not absolutely necessary to conclude that 36:23ff, a section which is so significant from the content point of view, could still not have followed after chapter 37. It is not probable, but not absolutely impossible. Perhaps the discovery of the missing sheets of 𝔊^{967} will one day give us more certain information. But how is the probable absence of vv 23bβ–38, a section which is already linguistically suspect, from the present form of 𝔊^{967} to be interpreted? Irwin (*Problem,* 62f) assumes a correspondingly shorter Hebrew original and leaves open, for the emergence of the section vv 23bβ-38, the period from the end of the third century B.C. to the third century A.D. Even if, for many reasons, one cannot concur with this radical suggestion, on the other hand the attempt of Filson, "Omission," to understand the omission of vv 23bβ-38, like that of 12:26–28 in 𝔊^{967} (see 1,283, Preliminary note), as a simple copyist's error due to homoioteleuton is not convincing either. See also Ziegler, *Ezechiel,* 10, note 1; A. E. Brooke, "Review of F. G. Kenyon, *The Chester Beatty Biblical Papyri. Descriptions and texts of twelve manuscripts on papyrus of the Greek Bible.* Fasciculi V–VII," *JTS* 39 (1938): 167–169. The question will be considered further in the context of "Form" and "Interpretation."

myself holy through you[b] in their midst.
24/ And I will take you from among the
nations and gather you from all[a] coun-
tries and bring you to your land. 25/ And I
will sprinkle clean water over you[a] so
that you may become clean[b]. From all
your uncleannesses and from all your
idols I will make you clean[c], 26/ and I will
give you a new heart[a], and a new spirit[a] I
will put within you. And I will put away
the heart of stone[b] out of your body and
will give you a heart of flesh[b], 27/ and I
will put my spirit within you and cause[a]
you to walk in my statutes and observe
and do my ordinances. 28/ And you shall
dwell in the land which I gave to your
fathers and shall be my people[a], and I[b]
will be your God.
29 **And I will deliver you from all your unclean-**
nesses. And I will summon[a] the grain and
make it abundant and will lay no (more)
famine upon you. 30/ And I will make the
fruit[a] of the trees and the produce of the
field abundant so that you no longer[b]
have to suffer abuse[c] among the nations
on account of famine. 31/ And you shall
think[a] of your wicked ways and your evil
deeds[b] and shall loathe yourselves[c] on
account of your guilty deeds and your
atrocities. 32/ Not for your sake do I act,
says [the Lord][a] Yahweh; that you must
know[b]. Be ashamed and humiliated[c] on
account of your ways[d], O house of Israel.
33 **Thus has [the Lord][a] Yahweh said: On the**
day when I cleanse you of all your guilty
deeds, then I will make the cities to be
inhabited, and the ruins will be rebuilt.
34/ And the waste land will be cultivated
instead of[a] its lying waste in the eyes of
everyone who passes by, 35/ so that it
will be said: This[a] waste land[b] has be-

b 𝔐 בכם. MSS בהם lays the emphasis on God's punishment of the nations, while 𝔐, which is certainly original, envisages Yahweh's merciful activity in the eyes of the astonished nations. Thus בעיניכם, MSS and 𝔅, is not to be read either.

24 24a MSS Eb24 𝔖 make a smoother parallel by suppressing the כל.

25 25a 𝔗 illustrates on the basis of the ritual of purification in Nu 19: "And I will remit your sins like those that are cleansed with the water of sprinkling and with the ashes of the heifer of the guilt offering (תורתא דחטאתא)."

b 𝔖 abbreviates by omitting וטהרתם. In its place, אידכי יתכון, corresponding to 𝔐 אטהר אתכם, is put at the beginning of v 25b.

c 𝔊 καὶ καθαριῶ ὑμᾶς makes the final verb independent by inserting a copula (see 1:4 note a) and links the preceding nouns to וטהרתם.

26 26a 𝔗 interprets the obedience in terms of the fear of God: לב דחול ורוח דחלא.

b Here too 𝔗 interprets: "a godless heart which is hard as stone" and "a heart, fearful (דחול) of me, to do my will (רעותי)."

27 27a On the construction ועשיתי את אשר see Cooke and Gesenius-Kautzsch §157c; Brockelmann §161bβ.

28 28a 𝔗 adds a fine nuance, undoubtedly on conscious theological reflection: ותהון קדמי לעם ואנא אהוי לכון לאלה. On היה ל see Brockelmann §107g.

b Only here in the whole book of Ezekiel does the form אנכי occur. On the distribution of אני and אנכי in the OT see Zimmerli, "Jahwe," 193 note 2. MSS[Ken] Eb 24 assimilate secondarily (against BH[3]) to the normal usage.

29 29a 𝔗 renders 𝔐 וקראתי, which is unusual in this expression, by the more common ואיבריך.

30 30a 𝔐 singular פרי, see Brockelmann §17.

b 𝔐 עוד is not attested by 𝔊 𝔎[Bo].

c See Ehrlich, *Randglossen,* and Wolff, *Hosea,* 171 note o on Hos 10:6.

31 31a 𝔖 adds תמן.

b The Jeremianic מעלל is attested only here in the book of Ezekiel. See 1,316 on 14:22f.

c On ונקטתם בפניכם על see also 6:9; 20:43. 𝔗 has the lovely paraphrase: "You will sigh when you see (ותידנקון ותהון חזן)."

32 32a אדני is lacking in 𝔊 𝔎[Bo] Tyc; 𝔊[B] κύριος κύριος, see Appendix 1.

b *ZB.* Literally: Let it be (made) known to you. See also, e.g., the ואודע להם of 20:5.

c On בושו והכלמו see 16:52 בושי ושאי כלמתך.

d 𝔖 expands בישתא ולא תמותון (מן אורחתכון).

33 33a אדני is lacking in 𝔊 𝔎[Bo]; 𝔊[B] 𝔖[h] αδωναι (κύριος); 𝔊[A] 𝔄 (κύριος) ὁ θεός; 𝔊[Q] κύριος (κύριος). See Appendix 1.

34 34a תחת אשר only here in the book of Ezekiel.

35 35a On הלזו, attested only here in the OT, see Gesenius-Katuzsch §34f; Bauer-Leander §30f.

b 𝔗 adds "Israel."

come like the garden of Eden[c], and the
ruined[d], devastated and demolished
cities are fortified and inhabited[e], 36/
and the nations which are left round
about you shall know that I, Yahweh[a],
rebuild what was demolished, replant
what was laid waste[b]. I, Yahweh, have
spoken and will do (it).
37 **Thus has [the Lord][a] Yahweh said: This**
too[b] I will allow the house of Israel to ask
me[c] to do for them. I will multiply their
men[d] like a flock of sheep[e]. 38/ Like
sheep for sacrifice, like sheep in Jeru-
salem[a] at the time of its feasts[b], so shall
the ruined cities[c] be filled with flocks of
men[d]. And they will know that I am
Yahweh[e].

c 𝔐 כגן עדן. 𝔊 *ὡς κῆπος τρυφῆς*. In 28:13 *ἐν τῇ τρυφῇ τοῦ παραδείσου τοῦ θεοῦ* corresponds to בעדן גן אלהים; in 31:9 *τὰ ξύλα τοῦ παραδείσου τῆς τρυφῆς τοῦ θεοῦ* corresponds to עצי עדן אשר בגן אלהים, and in 31:16, 18 *τὰ ξύλα τῆς τρυφῆς* to עצי עדן. The גן אלהים of 31:8 is rendered (twice) by *παράδεισος τοῦ θεοῦ*. Κ*ῆπος* is not attested elsewhere in 𝔊 of Ezekiel.

d The plural חֳרָבוֹת for the singular חָרֵב only here and v 38.

e Literally: They are inhabited as fortified.

36 36a 𝔊[A] (𝔎[Bo] 𝔄̈ Arm Tyc) inserts an *εἰμί*. In this way it makes the self-contained recognition formula independent and makes a new sentence begin with the following verbs. That is certainly grammatically possible without any difficulty.

b 2 MSS[Ken] 𝔊 𝔖 𝔙 add the copula in order to soften the harshness of the statement. To correct 𝔐 by inserting a ו before נטעתי does not, however (against Cornill, Bertholet, Fohrer), come into question since ונטעתי would then have to be translated as a future. See the immediately following ועשיתי. The harshness of the asyndetic parallelism of the two clauses in 𝔐 is intentional.

37 37a אדני is lacking in 𝔊 𝔎[Bo]; 𝔊[A] 𝔄 (*κύριος*) *κύριος ὁ θεός*; 𝔊[B] *αδωναι* (*κύριος*), see Appendix 1.

b עוד זאת occurs also in 20:27 as an introduction to the secondary passage 20:27–29. See 1,412 and 20:27 note b.

c אדרש also occurs in 14:3; 20:3, 31. 𝔗 again guards against the direct statement of the approach to God by the insertion of במימרי.

d On this double accusative see Gesenius-Kautzsch §117ff.

e 𝔗: I will multiply them in regard to men and make them rich (ואצלחינון) in flocks.

38 38a 𝔗 paraphrases: Like the holy nation that lives [*sc.* in Jerusalem] and comes to Jerusalem at the festival time of Passover.

b מועד, in Ezekiel only otherwise in 44:24; 45:17; 46:9, 11, is "the agreed time." Thus 𝔗 and 𝔖 also correctly emphasize the "time" (בזמן, בזבנא).

c 𝔗 adds: "of the land of Israel."

d There is no reason to delete צאן (Bertholet, BH[3]). 𝔗 again interprets צאן אדם as עמא בית ישראל.

e 𝔊 *ὅτι ἐγὼ κύριος* is different from the usual way of translating in 28:22–48:35. See 1,193f, Preliminary Remarks.

Form

As a result of the formulaic stock used, the construction of the section 36:16–38 can be easily discovered. A direct address to the prophet himself, in which Yahweh presents him with the past history of his people and his (Yahweh's) own experience in the present situation (vv 17–21), is followed by the command to the prophet to speak. The introductory messenger formula, with which the proclamation begins (v 22), is repeated in vv 33 and 37, so that the two further, smaller units, vv 33–36 and vv 37–38, stand apart from the main body in vv 22–32. It is clear from their introductions that both units are secondary additions. Already in 20:27 עוד זאת ("this too") had introduced an addition which clearly stood apart from the original framework of the text. Vv 37f are in the form of a bipartite proof-saying. A personal promise by Yahweh (v 37), which is amplified by means of a figurative comparison (כְּ "like"-כֵּן "so") in v 38a, is followed by the recognition formula. The unit is couched in the impersonal third person. The immediately preceding unit, vv 33–36, on the other hand, is characterized, by the introductory ביום טהרי "on the day when I cleanse," as a further exposition of the preceding promise of purification (טהר "to cleanse"). Here too we have a bipartite proof-saying. The recognition formula at the end has acquired a two-fold expansion. The subject of the recognition is paraphrased in full and the content of the recognition has been developed to a verbal statement, which, for its part, is also underlined by means of the final assurance אני יהוה דברתי ועשיתי ("I, Yahweh, have spoken and will do [it]"). The unit begins with a personal address (second person plural), but goes over to factual description (third person).

In contrast to this, the main section of the prophetic oracle in vv 22–32 reveals a more complex structure. A first part, vv 22–23bα, begins first of all with a passionately and antithetically worded assertion and then ends, as a bipartite proof-saying, with a recognition formula emphasized by a formula for a divine saying. There then follows, introduced by an infinitive with בְּ ("when"), an expansion of the proof-saying. In verbal clauses this unfolds, mostly with consecutive perfects, the activity of God. Like a framework, v 32 then finally turns back again to the initial thesis of vv 22f. It is heavily underlined by means of a formula for a divine saying and the immediately following יִוָּדַע לָכֶם ("that you must know"), which emphasizes that the aim of all divine activity is recognition by man, and finally ends with a double imperative. These draw the conclusion for the behavior of those who are addressed.

Now the text-critical examination (v 23 note a) led to the conclusion that the whole passage vv 23bβ–38 seems to be missing in the old textual witness 𝔊⁹⁶⁷. Thus the question arises whether v 23bβ is not the beginning of a section which was still absent from the Hebrew original of 𝔊⁹⁶⁷ and which therefore represents a later component of the book of Ezekiel. Now in 𝔐 vv 23bβ–38 there is in fact also a series of linguistically unusual elements, such as the unique אנכי ("I") of v 28 (note b), the only occurrence in Ezekiel of מעלל ("deed") in v 31 (note b), the תחת אשר ("instead") of v 34 (note a), the הלזו ("this") of v 35 (note a), as well as the antithesis "build-plant," characteristic of the language of Jeremiah but attested in Ezekiel only in the later addition in 28:26.[1] All this might argue for allowing an original unit to end with the formula for a divine saying in v 23bα and regarding what follows as a later addition. On the other hand, there is still the fact that the section which ends with v 23bα gives, on its own, a fragmentary impression. The real material exposition of Yahweh's proving that his name is holy is missing from it. There is the additional fact that the end of the section vv 22–32 comes back to the beginning (v 32aα'=v 22aβ¹). A similar framework was found already in 20:1–31, so it is not unique. This might advise against breaking up vv 22–32 and instead regarding it as an original (later) unit. The possible absence of the passage from 𝔊⁹⁶⁷ and the peculiar character of the translation of it would then be a problem for the history only of 𝔊, but not of 𝔐.

Setting

The oracle in vv 16–31 presupposes the exiled people in specific spiritual distress. As "Yahweh's people," who, if they want to justify themselves in their belief, must speak of Yahweh who led them out of Egypt and into the promised land,[2] they will be asked without fail about the efficacy of this activity on the part of their God. Is the story of the loss of their homeland not a counter-proof against Yahweh? Vv 16ff answer this question, which represents real spiritual distress. Thus, in fixing a period for the oracle we cannot go beyond the time of the first return or perhaps of the rebuilding of the temple (Haggai, Zechariah). The same holds good also for the two additions.

On the other hand, it is remarkable how near these oracles come in many respects to the problems and the questions which are discernible in the preaching of Deutero-Isaiah. In Deutero-Isaiah, too, the question of

1 See above p. 100.
2 20:5ff; see 1,405f on Israel's "Credo."

the justification for Yahweh's new act of mercy towards Israel is asked, and is answered in 43:25 basically no differently from here in vv 22, 32. Deutero-Isaiah, too, is concerned with the question of the rebuilding of what has been destroyed, especially the destroyed city of Jerusalem (44:26, 28; 49:17 emended text; 54:11f), which has here occasioned the addition in vv 33–36. And in Deutero-Isaiah, too, there is a discussion (54:1–3) of the question of the repopulation of the country or the city, a subject which is discussed here in the second addition. That the promise of new fruitfulness for the land was a lively hope for the returning exiles and that their disappointment in this respect was a challenge to them is clear from Haggai and Zechariah. In the latter there is also encountered in a new way the problem of the purification of the unclean people and the removal of sin from the land (3:1–7; 5:5–11). The observation of these links, especially with Deutero-Isaiah, makes it possible to date vv 16–32 further into the period of the exile than those oracles which still reflect directly the shock of the fall of Jerusalem. Also linguistically vv 16–32 are particularly closely associated with the late components in the book of Ezekiel. Thus it is possible that here (and certainly in vv 23bβ–38, the passage which is missing from 𝔊⁹⁶⁷) it is no longer Ezekiel himself who is speaking, but the school which continues his line of thinking and is dependent on his forms of speech.

But all the oracles, even the second addition, will have to be derived from the prophet's exilic environment. The reference to the many sacrificial animals in Jerusalem does not presuppose the idea of the Jerusalem of the period after 587, but the radiant memory of the great festivals in the still intact temple.

Interpretation

■ **36:16,17** In the receiving of God's word the prophet himself ("son of man") is addressed by Yahweh.[3] In a succinct résumé he is presented with the period when Israel lived in her land and its outcome. How exactly אדמתם ("their land") (see v 24; 34:13, 27; 37:14, 21; 39:26, 28), the suffixed equivalent of the more frequent construct אדמת ישראל ("land of Israel") (7:2; 11:17; and elsewhere), is to be understood is stated in Ezek 28:25 with its "their land which I gave to my servant Jacob" (see 37:25). It is a possession which has been gifted to them and for which they are therefore responsible. But Israel has made the land unclean (also Lev 18:28; Dtn 21:23). With the offensive reference to the uncleanness of menstruation, a category of uncleanness (Lev 15:19ff) mentioned in Ezekiel also in 7:19f; 18:6; 22:10, the uncleanness of their way of life before Yahweh is illustrated.

■ **36:18f** So Yahweh poured out his wrath upon them (as 7:8; 9:8; 14:19; 20:8, 13, 21; 22:22; 30:15). A later hand, taking up שפך ("to pour out"), has here added bloodshed and idolatry (linked in 22:4 also) as the typical grievous sins (note a). Thus Yahweh scattered the people (the same expression also in 12:15; 20:23; and elsewhere) and judged them according to their deeds (24:14).

■ **36:20** Although everything to this point has been expressed in stereotyped language, the specific point to which the present oracle has been leading becomes discernible in vv 20f. Those who have been thus scattered rob, precisely through their dispersion, Yahweh's holy name of its holiness and make it profane.[4] The name appears in vv 21–24 like a personal being capable of suffering.[5] With this personification of the name one might feel oneself reminded in the first instance of the Deuteronomic theological material on the name of Yahweh. But the difference must not be overlooked. While the author of Dtn 12:5, when he speaks of the place which Yahweh has chosen to put his name there, is thinking of Israel's cultic center where Yahweh has made it possible for men to call on his name, the present passage is thinking of other spheres which Yahweh has chosen as the "dwelling place" of his name. When the nations say of exiled Israel, "These are the people of Yahweh and they have had to leave his land," then the name of Yahweh as a proprietor's name[6] applies to two entities: 1) "the people Israel" (עם יהוה; 20:5 had spoken of the election [בחר ("to choose")] of Israel in which Yahweh had moved defenselessly into the sphere of availability to men);[7] 2) the land (ארצו "his land"), which as a result of Yahweh's gift to the patriarchs had become the "land of Israel" (28:25; 37:25).[8] The fact of the exile had now revealed to the nations the fact that Yahweh can

3 See 1, 144f; on "son of man" see 1, 131f.

4 On the antithesis חל – קדש see 22:26; 44:23.

5 On the significance of the name in the OT see Grether, *Name*.

6 Kurt Galling, "Die Ausrufung des Namens als Rechtsakt in Israel," *ThLZ* 81 (1956): 65–70.

no longer hold together the two entities, Israel and the land, on both of which his name lay. What Moses, according to Nu 14:16, held up to Yahweh in prayer as a thing to be feared now became reality. The nations are speaking of a powerless Yahweh (מבלתי יכלת יהוה להביא . . . "because the Lord was not able to bring . . .") or, what is far worse, as Moses feared according to Ex 32:12, of a malicious and destructive Yahweh. Thus the name of Yahweh—the one who is holy in his irresistible power and in the majesty of his justice (Is 6), that is the one who is set apart from all that is commonplace—where it is mentioned among the nations with respect to Israel, becomes "commonplace, profane," the name of one who is powerless, malicious. But this profanation is not Yahweh's fault. It is, rather, the people in exile who make Yahweh's name profane, insofar as on account of their wicked past they have had to be banished by the holy one from his land because he is, on account of his majesty, jealous for his right.

■ **36:21** Therefore, so the story which Yahweh tells to his prophet continues, Yahweh was grieved for his name (חמל "to grieve" + negative 5:11; 7:4, 9; 8:18; 9:5, 10; cf. 16:5). It is remarkable that ואחמל ("then I grieved") is in the consecutive imperfect, and here too therefore it is something that has already happened that is looked back upon. We would actually expect here a statement about the future. The consecutive imperfect could mean that the decision has already been made by Yahweh and that he is telling the prophet about the event which has already taken place for him even if the people know nothing about it. More probably, however, it shows that the prophetic proclamation of salvation has already been clearly made to the people and that the real foretelling in this oracle consists in making clear how such a declaration of salvation is at all possible. Already the oracle 35:1–36:15 had raised the question of the "motivation" of Yahweh's promise of salvation. The question obviously posed itself to the exilic community: "How can the holy one possibly forgive again his sinful people whom he has had to drive away on account of his holiness?" The present oracle tries to answer this question.

■ **36:22** This becomes clear in the commission to proclaim with which the prophet is now to go to the people. This begins not with the proclamation of salvation itself, but with a sharply polemical rejection of a wrong motivation for Israel's future of salvation. The oracle has a remarkably close factual parallel in Is 43:22–28. Admittedly Deutero-Isaiah's oracle is in the form of judgment oracle (Begrich: appeal speech of the accused). Israel is confronted with the wicked past history of her failures (לא "not" with perfect, vv 22–24a) and her active sins (v 24b) in a direct address (second singular). Then, however, with a sharp turn to Yahweh's activity (אנכי אנכי "I, I"), forgiveness is promised on Yahweh's free decision (למעני "for my own sake"). A comparison of the two passages makes quite clear the uniqueness of Ezekiel's (or his school's?) language. According to Deutero-Isaiah Yahweh promises the deletion of the guilt; the present passage formulates what it says remarkably formally with the absolute use of עשׂה ("to do") of which Ezekiel is so fond (see 8:18 note a). In Deutero-Isaiah Yahweh's lively turning to his people in love can be discerned; here, in language which is much more strongly detached, the concept of the "name" intervenes. It is out of compassion (חמל "to grieve") for his "name" that, according to v 21, Yahweh turned to his people. 39:25 will later speak of "zeal" (קנא) for the holy name. Both features link closely the present passage with 20:9, 14, 22 (44) and the absolute usage there ואעשׂ למען שמי ("but I acted [mercifully] for my name's sake"). Apart from 36:20–22 the qualified expression שם קדשי ("my holy name") is found also in 20:39; 39:7, 25; 43:7f. In v 23 there is also the expression שמי הגדול ("my great name"). What was said above on 20:9 can be repeated here with appropriate variations.[9] Not only in the past, on the different occasions in Israel's early history, was Yahweh, in consideration of his honor, which at the same time signifies the acknowledgement of his inner faithfulness, driven to spare the sinful nation. Now too after the judgment in which everything seems to be at an end, this consideration is once again revealed, this time in a new depth of activity on Yahweh's part. Here too Ezekiel is devoid of all soft-hearted features and warmer tones. There is no mention of mercy, love, covenant faithfulness, the justice that brings salvation. This whole vocabulary is missing from the book of Ezekiel. חסד, רחמים, אמונה, ישועה, ישע,

7 See 1,408.
8 See von Rad, "Promised Land"; Wildberger, "Israel."
9 See 1,409.

אהבה are sought in vain in the book of Ezekiel. צדקה and אמת are attested only in a strictly forensic use, while אהב occurs only in chapters 16 and 23 of human lovers. Only the verb הושיע ("to deliver") occurs three times (34:22; 36:29; 37:23). In place of these in Ezekiel the dominant concept is that of the majesty of Yahweh and the revelation of his honor and glory. For the sake of this revelation he will not abandon his people, but will again validate his honor in the eyes of the world. To a period and a nation who believed that they could willfully manipulate Yahweh, he is presented in all his majesty. From this majesty there comes also his work of deliverance for his people.

■ **36:23** Yahweh will once again reveal as holy his great name, which his people have brought into disrepute among the nations, so that the nations will acknowledge it. This too is said with formulaic stringency. Once again it is Deutero-Isaiah who first undertook the graphic description of the movement which takes place among the nations as a consequence of Yahweh's new saving activity (45:14ff). In Ezekiel all the details are still locked away in the formulaic phraseology.

The additional clause in v 23bβ, which at the same time provides a syntactical bridge to the actual development of the individual actions in the divine activity towards Israel, in which probably we have a later expansion (see above), first of all recapitulates the important statements of vv 22f. Is this "resumption" also a sign of a later addition?[10] In the בהקדשי בכם לעיניהם ("when I show myself holy through you in their midst") the three partners in the great event are again mentioned together, most succinctly, in three words: Yahweh, who shows himself to be holy (as opposed to vv 20–23bα there is no further reference to the name here!): Israel, the sinful nation, on whom the proof of God's holy faithfulness to himself will operate; and the nations, before whose eyes this assertion of Yahweh's holiness happens so that they too may acknowledge it.[11] Ps 115:1f gives expression to a faith which has understood this proclamation.

■ **36:24** But then there follows the unfolding of the individual acts in which Yahweh will act for Israel. The first consists in the bringing of them back from among the nations. This is described with the terminology of 34:13a. In place of הוציא ("to lead out") there appears, as in 37:21, לקח ("to take"). The mocking statement of the nations in v 20 is rendered void as a result of this repatriation. Yahweh's people and land will once again be united. But does this not again endanger all Yahweh's work in the way described in 20:1–31?

■ **36:25-27** Vv 25–27 attempt to make clear that Yahweh will now act "for his name's sake" in a way which far surpasses his activity as described 20:9, 14, 22 and which creates something fundamentally new.

Pre-exilic Israel foundered on her disobedience. In this disobedience she had broken away from the ordinance of the covenant in which she belonged to her God and had neglected Yahweh's will as laid down in the covenant law (44:7). As a result there had grown in the two prophets of the late pre-exilic period the grim realization that Israel was incapable, by her very nature, of obedience (Jer 13:23; Ezek 2:3f; 15). Thus it is not surprising that in the three great prophets of the beginning and end of the exilic period the question of "covenant" found full expression.[12] All three speak of the covenant which Yahweh makes with the people (Jer 31:31f; cf. 32:40; Ezek 16:60, 62; 37:26; cf. 34:25; Is 54:10; 55:3). Jeremiah openly uses the expression "new covenant" and thereby affirms the end of the old covenant. Jeremiah and Ezekiel also see in full acuteness that this covenant, if it is to be a "lasting covenant" (ברית עולם Ezek 16:60; 37:26; Is 55:3), must come to grips in a new way with the problem of the obedience of God's people to Yahweh's commands. Jer 31:31–34 comes up with the expression that in this new covenant Yahweh will write the law in his people's heart. In this way Yahweh will himself instill in the human heart proper hearing (שמע is also "obey"). Jer 32:40(39) means the same when Yahweh says there, "I will put fear of me into your heart." In Ezekiel 36 this promise acquires its own characteristic wording.

The renewal of the nation, which alone can offer a guarantee of continued existence in the land, takes place here in three stages.

■ **36:25** The first is purification from what in their past still clings to them. When reference is made here to

10 Kuhl, "'Wiederaufnahme.'"

11 Reventlow, "Die Völker."

12 von Rad, *OT Theology*, 2. 266–272.

"sprinkling with clean water," then, even though the verb זרק ("to sprinkle") is mostly used otherwise in connection with the sprinkling of blood (Ex 24:6; Lev 1:5,11; and elsewhere), we should see behind this the image of a ritual act of sprinkling with water for the purpose of cultic purification. Nu 19:9–22 refers to such an act of sprinkling with water (v 17 מים חיים "running water"), but uses the verb הזה ("to sprinkle"). O. Betz believes that he can deduce from 1 QS III, 4–9 that at Qumran there was proselyte baptism which modifies Ezekiel 36 and became the prototype of Christian baptism.[13] The promise in 1 QS IV, 21, "And he will sprinkle upon him the spirit of truth like waters of purification,"[14] shows to what extent the phraseology of the Ezekiel passage must have stimulated cryptic interpretation. Thus even the critical Apollinarius finds in this passage a pointer to Christian baptism.[15] In Ezekiel 36 itself the act is understood as a ritual introductory act which is intended to remove the old uncleanness, even that of the גלולים ("idols").[16] That the water of purification in Ezek 36:25 was water from the temple spring remains sheer speculation.[17] Haag believes that he can deduce a connection with the great Day of Atonement from the fact that the plural טמאות ("uncleannesses") occurs, apart from here (vv 25,29), only in Lev 16:16,19.[18]

■ **36:26** This is followed immediately by the second stage: the gift of a new heart and a new spirit. In connection with the ritual purification of the body there follows the renewal of the heart. The same expression of this renewal has already occurred in 11:19.[19] It corresponds to the assurance of Jer 31:31–34. The heart which has till now been hard as stone and has remained deaf to the call to obedience will become alive. The key-word "new," which Jer 31:31 associated with the covenant, is here associated with the heart, which changes as a result of Yahweh's new activity. According to *b. Sukk.* 52a "stone" is one of the seven names of the "evil inclination." The removal of stone from man strikes at the evil inclination.[20]

■ **36:27** In the third stage, however, the putting of Yahweh's spirit in the human heart, the new being finds its full strength. For "spirit" in the OT is never simply an "insight, understanding," but a power which gives a man strength to do new things (1 Sam 10:6f). The new thing here is the obedience which is now possible with regard to Yahweh's commands and the new way of life. This was mentioned already in 11:20, where, however, there was no specific reference to the spirit of God. See also the formulation of Lev 26:3, where obedience within the framework of the demands of the law is described in similar words. Jer 31:31ff had referred to the putting of the law in the human heart. Ezek 36:27 speaks of putting the spirit there and in this way goes beyond Jer 31 and allows Yahweh to participate directly in man's new obedience.

■ **36:28** This obedience is the precondition for remaining in the land, the explicit subject matter of v 28. The covenant formula is used to describe the new situation achieved by the people.[21] This is the definitive realization of what Yahweh intended from the very beginning for his people in the covenant. In the present formulation from a later hand there appears here for the only time in the book of Ezekiel (cf. e.g., the covenant formulae in 11:20; 14:11; 34:31; 37:23) the form of the pronoun אנכי ("I"). This could also be due to the influence of Jeremianic phraseology (see Jer 24:7; 30:22, as well as 11:4). In the covenant formula, which in 11:20 originally marked the end of the divine speech, a certain pause is reached.[22]

■ **36:29** But then a new beginning is made describing the changes in the external life of the country, changes which go hand in hand with the inner renewal. To what extent, in the immediately post-exilic period, inner obedience to the divine command and the external condition of the country are considered together is very clear from Haggai. Thus here "deliverance" from uncleanness (הושעתי also in 34:22; 37:23) is linked with abundant growth of corn and removal of famine (on this

13 Otto Betz, "Die Proselytentaufe der Qumransekte und die Taufe im Neuen Testament," *RQ* 1 (1958/59): 213–234.
14 According to Dupont-Sommer, *Essene*, 81.
15 Neuss, *Buch*, 50.
16 On these see 1, 187.
17 So Widengren, *King and Tree of Life*, 36 note 2.
18 Haag, *Untersuchung*, 38. Cf. also the removal of the old clothes from the high priest Joshua (Zech 3:4).
19 See 1, 262f.
20 Cf. in this connection the imperative formulation in 18:31 and see 1, 386.
21 See 1, 262f on 11:20.
22 See 1, 262f.

cf. Hos 2:23f). With the remarkable turn of phrase "summon the grain" a phrase such as 2 Kgs 8:1 "summon" a famine (קרא ל) may be compared. On the increase of fruit trees see Ezek 34:27. That verse uses a different expression to describe the produce of the field. On תנובת השדה "produce of the field" see also Dtn 32:13; Lam 4:9. תנובה "produce" (from נוב "grow") occurs also in Is 27:6; Ju 9:11 (olive tree); Sir 11:3 (bee). It is noteworthy that the famine in the land, explicitly mentioned twice, is linked with the abuse of the nation. Here it seems to be being stressed, in response to a quite sharp attack, that the "land of Israel," which has obviously, in this connection too, been reproached with devouring its inhabitants instead of giving them food (v 13), is not a "land of famine."

■ **36:31** Then, however, the exposition turns back rather sharply to the point of departure, once again recalling Israel's early sinful history and at the same time warning that this should not be suppressed in the memory, but should be "thought" of, with real revulsion at the guilt and horror of the past.[23]

■ **36:32** Finally, with caustic pungency, by means of a formula for a divine saying and explicitly underlined by a following יודע לכם ("that you must know"), once again the main concern is stressed, which was put at the beginning of the whole oracle of proclamation in v 22aβ, "Not for your sake do I act." The passionate rejection of all self-glorification and of "possession" in terms of election dominates this whole oracle, which therefore even in its closing imperative (at this point vastly different from Deutero-Isaiah) does not summon its hearers to jubilation and rejoicing in response to God's activity, but to shameful repentance.[24] We must not here play off Deutero-Isaiah against Ezekiel on intuitive grounds. However little an isolated proclamation of a call to repentance which is unable to break through to rejoicing over that activity of God which makes repentance possible[25] will be able to come fully alive, so on the other hand a message of mercy to the elect which does not rest upon the solid foundation of repentance and of knowledge of the "justificatory" לא למענכם ("not for your sake") can become a diabolical temptation. Ezekiel and Deutero-Isaiah each have their function in their proper place. But together they proclaim the same activity of the same God.

■ **36:33-36** Vv 24–32 have developed the בהקדשי בכם ("when I have showed myself holy through you") of v 23bβ and have shown how Yahweh's holiness will create for himself his obedient people and round about the repatriated people will give to his land also the honor of new fruitfulness. The addition in vv 33–36 tries to add two more features to this image. To the renewal of nature it adds the rebuilding of the human settlements and the cultivation of the fields accomplished by human hands.

■ **36:33** On that day, which is described not on the basis of its outward prosperity, but, in relation to v 25, as the day of the divine cleansing from guilty deeds, the rebuilding of the settlements will also take place. This was stated in the same words also in the supplement in v 10 (see above). See also the words of judgment in 6:6; 12:20 and those against Egypt in 29:12; 30:7. The close association with Deutero-Isaiah in this rebuilding theme has already been established.[26]

■ **36:34f** The devastated fields will again be cultivated (עבד [here "to cultivate"] as in v 9). On the other hand, this addition is also concerned with developing more fully the לעיניהם ("in their eyes") of v 23bβ. Thus then the figure of the non-Israelite observers is at once introduced with the quotation of their observations. As unsuspicious witnesses they affirm the miracle of the rebuilding: the land that previously lay waste—now a paradise garden of the most luxuriant fertility. Is the mention of the גן עדן ("garden of Eden") intended to bring a somewhat pagan local coloring into the language of the foreigners?[27] The cities that once were devastated (this is expressed by means of no fewer than three participles) will once again be inhabited and fortified.[28] The contrast with the description of the resettled land in 38:11, where it is said of the inhabitants that they live without wall or bars or gates, has been pointed out. One might ask whether בצורה ("fortified") here does not refer figuratively to the protection which, according to Zech 2:9, Yahweh offers to Jerusalem like a wall of fire. More probable, however, is still the assumption that the particular theological statements of 38:11 were not yet

23 On this see 1, 188–190 on 6:8–10 and 1, 417 on 20:43f. On the description of the evil deeds as לא טובים ("not good") see 1, 385 on 18:18.

24 On בושו והכלמו see 16:52 (16:63; 32:30).

25 Wolff, "'Umkehr.'"

26 See above p. 247.

available to the author of 36:35.[29]

■ **36:36** But the real aim of the oracle is not the observation of a specific situation in the country, but the confession of the surrounding nations which encounter the process of reconstruction in the country and acknowledge Yahweh in that process. As subjects of this recognition there are named "the nations which have been left in the land." The שארית הגוים ("the rest of the nations"), which was encountered three times in the expansion in vv 3–5, is here paraphrased more fully. From this paraphrase it emerges that judgment has been pronounced over Israel's neighbors. The fact that they have not completely perished in that judgment receives here a deeper significance in the task of remaining as witnesses to Yahweh's faithfulness in fulfilling his promise to Israel.[30]

■ **36:37–38** A second addition recalls Ezek 20:1–31 (and 14:1ff) not only by the use of the secondary addition formula עוד זאת ("this too") (which occurred in 20:27), but also by the further development of its address. There the men who came to question Yahweh were promptly told in all abruptness that Yahweh would not allow himself to be questioned (20:3, 31; correspondingly 14:3, 7, 10). Here, by contrast, in an oracle of salvation it is promised that Yahweh will allow himself to be entreated to act on behalf of the house of Israel. And then follows the reference to the increase in the population which has occurred already in the preceding oracle in 36:11 (and in the additions in vv 10,12). Covenant and population increase also belong closely together in Gen 17:2 and Lev 26:9.

■ **36:38** The abundance of people is described with the image of the flock and, further, with the image of the abundance of sacrificial animals at the feasts in Jerusalem. The promise of abundant population is also strongly developed in Deutro-Isaiah (49:19; 54:1ff). The problem of the repopulation of the depopulated countryside was obviously of great concern to the exiles. In Zech 2:8, in the early post-exilic period, the expectation of a large population in Jerusalem is linked with the prophetic disowning of human preparations (rebuilding of the walls). In the reference to the abundance of sacrificial animals at the festival in Jerusalem we are to find not an indication of the (meagre) reality of the Jerusalem cult of the post-exilic period, but the idealized memory of the lost pre-exilic period.[31] When the priestly writer here compares the new population with the flock of "sacrificial" animals (קדשים) this might also conceal the thought of the new sanctification of the people. Thus Yahweh reveals himself as the holy one (v 23bβ) in the abundance of his holy "flock of men" (צאן אדם). Can we perhaps recognize in this addition the hand of the person who added 34:31 (note b) and who describes an Israel which has become Yahweh's flock as אדם (צאן מרעיתי) ("the human [flock of my pasture]")?

Aim

In the darkness and distress of his people, over whom no light ever seems to shine now, the prophet is summoned by God. He is to speak to them of a future, of rebuilding and of future blessing. The blessing is not to be an event that remains hidden. It is to happen before the eyes of the world. It is to arouse the amazement of the "nations" so that the latter begin to discuss the particular distinction which lies over God's people. Without having wished it, since they were more likely to indulge in mockery of the nation that had suffered disaster, the nations are to become witnesses of the unique event that has taken place here. God has raised his own people on high.

The one who has been chosen is, however, unexpectedly also the one who is most especially exposed to danger. Is he not the one who has been elevated, distinguished? Does he not have a possession of which he can boast before others and a privilege which distinguishes him from others? Besides, his distinction comes not from men but from God.

It is at this point that the proclamation of the present oracle begins. It is at once protection against the falsifica-

27 On this see 28:13 (31:9, 16, 18); on the comparison of a landscape with the garden of God see Gen 13:10, but especially the related, contemporary statement in Is 51:3.

28 בצורה occurs also in 21:25, of Jerusalem; see 1, 442.

29 See also below on chapters 38f.

30 On "building" and "planting" as an echo of Jeremianic phraseology see above p. 245. On the concluding formula, which maintains that Yahweh's word will also be followed by his action, see 1, 176.

31 On this see, e.g., the idealized calculations of 1 Kgs 8:63 or the chronistic data of 1 Chr 29:21; 2 Chr 7:4f; 29:32f; 35:7–9.

tion of and confirmation of the truth of this proclamation.

Protection against falsification. God confronts his people with their history insofar as it is history controlled by themselves. In this history there is nothing praiseworthy, but much offense to God, life lived in impurity and destruction of the good ordinances. Thus then has God's judgment taken place, has God's people found itself in a state of wretched loss to which the world has pointed and in respect of which the world has reviled the name of God. What a miserable crowd God's people are and what poor advocates of the holiness of their God. In what a dubious light God appears as a result of his community. There is nothing of which to boast there, but much of which to be deeply ashamed.

And then, however, the other aspect remains unshaken. God has arisen over this dubious crowd. Not because somewhere in it something praiseworthy is to be found. But also not for any sentimental emotion, but because he keeps his word and does not go back on what he has promised in the freedom of his condescension—for his name's sake. Thus he establishes his history upon this crowd—not the boastful crowd but the crushed and deeply unworthy one—leads them along his ways, establishes new life while he washes away the old uncleanness by his sprinkling, removes stony hearts and, through his spirit, effects obedience in the hearts of those who can know in their deep shame that they have been accepted anew by him.

The prophet proclaims all this as the certain future of his lost people. The New Testament community too, who have through Christ become participants in this promise, know that this is also their future. At the same time, however, they confess that in the fullness of time (Gal 4:4) this future has already begun, that sins have been forgiven, guilt washed away, the obedience of faith awakened by God's spirit. God is already in process of rebuilding what has been destroyed and of increasing the number of his people. They know at the same time, however, that all the glory and all the worth of this new history of God is attributable alone to God's free action which he accomplishes for his name's sake. All true understanding of God, which happens as a result of God's activity towards the shattered, will perceive and acknowledge not human piety, but only God himself in the wonder of his sacred majesty.

The Resurrection of Dead Israel

Bibliography

W. Emery Barnes
"Ezekiel's Vision of a Resurrection (Ezekiel 37:1–14)," *The Expositor* 8th series 14 (1917): 290–297.

Harris Birkeland
"The Belief in the Resurrection of the Dead in the Old Testament," *Studia Theologica* 3 (1949): 60–78.

A. Díez-Macho
"Un segundo fragmento del Targum Palestinense a los Profetas," *Bibl* 39 (1958): 198–205.

Herbert Haag
Was lehrt die literarische Untersuchung des Ezechiel-Textes? (Freiburg in der Schweiz: Paulusdruckerei, 1943), especially 51–60.

J. Henniger
"Zum Verbot des Knochenzerbrechens bei den Semiten" in *Studi orientalistici in onore di Giorgio Levi Della Vida* 1 (Rome: Istituto per l'Oriente, 1956), 448–458.

Aubrey R. Johnson
The Vitality of the Individual in the Thought of Ancient Israel (Cardiff: University of Wales Press, 1949).

Emil G. Kraeling
"The Meaning of the Ezekiel Panel in the Synagogue at Dura," *BASOR* 78 (1940): 12–18.

Robert Martin-Achard
De la mort à la résurrection d'après l'Ancien Testament (Neuchâtel: Delachaux & Niestlé, 1956), especially 78–85.

Harald Riesenfeld
The Resurrection in Ezekiel XXXVII and in the Dura-Europos Paintings, UUÅ (Uppsala: Lundequists, 1948).

Leonhard Rost
"Alttestamentliche Wurzeln der ersten Auferstehung" in *In memoriam Ernst Lohmeyer* (Stuttgart: Evangelisches Verlagswerk, 1951), 67–72.

Rachel Wischnitzer-Bernstein
"The Conception of the Resurrection in the Ezekiel Panel of the Dura Synagogue," *JBL* 60 (1941): 43–55.

Walther Zimmerli
"'Leben' und 'Tod' im Buche des Propheten Ezechiel," *ThZ* 13 (1957): 494–508; reprinted in *idem, Gottes Offenbarung,* ThB 19 (München: Kaiser, 1963), 178–191.

37

1 **[a]The hand of Yahweh came[b] upon me, and**

37:1 1a Here too 𝔖 adds a superscription על חית מיתא, see above 25:1 note a.

b The abrupt beginning with היתה עלי is striking. 𝔊 *καὶ ἐγένετο ἐπ᾽ ἐμέ*, 𝔖 והות עלי assimilate to the usual expression with its introductory ויהי. A comparison with 40:1 raises the question whether a date might have fallen out (Herrmann, Kraetzschmar). Bertholet wishes to link vv 1ff with 3:24a. See the

he[c] led me out <in the spirit of Yahweh>[d] <and set me>[e] down in the midst of the plain[f]. But it was full of bones[g]. 2/ And when he led[a] me through them[b] all around, see there they lay in very great number (scattered) over the plain, and

exposition.

c An analogous masculine continuation occurs also in 3:15; 40:1. It is Yahweh himself who acts in his "hand."

d 𝔐 ברוח יהוה is surprising in a sentence in which Yahweh himself is the subject. So 𝔊 *καὶ ἐξήγαγέ με ἐν πνεύματι κύριος* 𝔖 ואפקני ברוחה מריא take the divine name יהוה as the subject of the clause. We would then expect this to come immediately after ויוצאני. Cornill deletes the second יהוה as explicative. But in view of its good attestation it should be retained and understood as a fixed technical term with the same sense as ברוח אלהים in 11:24. רוח יהוה occurs otherwise only in 11:5.

e Instead of 𝔐 וַיְנִיחֵנִי, which nevertheless recurs in 𝔐 40:2, one should perhaps vocalize וַיַּנִּיחֵנִי.

f 𝔐 הבקעה presupposes that the plain, as in 3:22f, is something already known.

g 𝔊 (𝔏 Sabatier 𝔗) (*ὀστῶν*) *ἀνθρωπίνων* is an unnecessary elucidation.

2 2a 𝔐 והעבירני. The use of the perfect with ו instead of the more usual consecutive imperfect is a feature which has already occasionally been observed in Ezekiel (13:6 [note b], 8; 17:18 [note a]; 19:12 [note c]; see further 40:24, 35; 41:3 [?], 8[?], 13, 15; 42:15). It occurs frequently in the present section in vv 2, 7, 8, 10. Twice (vv 2, 8) it is the case of the direct introduction to a הנה-clause; twice (vv 7, 10) it is followed by a consecutive imperfect. One might ask here too whether a slight trace of hypotaxis is not to be observed: a statement in the perfect with ו, describing the precondition, leads by way of preparation to the really accentuated main statement which is introduced by הנה "in most cases an interrupting call for attention" (Koehler-Baumgartner) or by narrative consecutive imperfect (which is also followed immediately in v 7 by a הנה-clause). The resumption of ונבאתי in v 7 by כהנבאי is clear evidence for this logical arrangement. One cannot then on any account consider that we have here already a complete amalgamation of the perfect with ו into the general usage of the perfect such as is then to be found, e.g., in the late language of Qoheleth. For all that, one cannot fail to notice a displacement of the expression, e.g., in the וראיתי והנה of v 8 in contrast to the וארא[ה] והנה of 1:4, 15; 2:9; 8:2, 7, 10; 10:1, 9, but also in the והעבירני והנה of v 2 in contrast to the ואקום ואצא . . . והנה of 3:23 or the ויבא א[ו]תי of 8:14, 16; (11:1) 40:3; (43:5; 44:4).

b In the treatment of the gender of עצמות a remarkable variation pervades the whole section. רבות and יבשות in v 2, התחיינה in v 3, היבשות in v 4 point to the feminine. Alongside these, however, עליהם v 2, שמעו עליהם v 4, בכם, וחייתם v 5, עליכם, בכם, וחייתם, וידעתם v 6, עצמו v 7, עליהם, בהם v 8 point to the masculine; see also v 7 note f. The personal conception which then clearly comes through in the בהרוגים of v 9 already lies behind what has been said about the עצמות.

see[c], they were very dry.
3 And he said to me: Son of man, can these
bones come to life again? Then I said:
[Lord][a] Yahweh, you know. 4/ But he said
to me:[a] Prophesy over[b] these bones and
say to them: You dry bones, hear the
word of Yahweh. 5/ Thus has [the Lord][a]
Yahweh said to these bones: See, I will
put the spirit of life in you so that you
come to life[b]. 6/ And I will make sinews
for you and will put flesh upon you and
cover you with skin and put the spirit of
life[a] in you so that you come to life, and
you will know that I am Yahweh.
7 When I prophesied[a] as I had been bidden[b],
there arose, when I prophesied[c], a
noise[d], and see (there arose) a rustling,
and the bones moved closer together[e],
one to the other[f]. 8/ And as I looked[a], see
there (appeared) sinews on them, and
flesh grew and skin <stretched>[b] over
them, but there was (as yet) no spirit of
life in them.
9 Then he said to me: Prophesy over[a] the
spirit of life, prophesy, son of man, and
say to the spirit of life: Thus has [the
Lord][b] Yahweh said: Come from the four
winds, spirit of life[c], and breathe on
these slain so that they come to life
(again).
10 And when I prophesied[a], as he had bidden
me, the spirit of life entered into them,
and they came to life and rose to their
feet, a mighty host.

c The second וְהִנֵּה does not need to be vocalized as וְהִנָּה. In the doubling of the והנה, expression is given to the unprecedented nature of what is seen. Its omission from 𝔊 𝔖 is to be regarded as a stylistic improvement.

3 3a אדני is lacking in 𝔊. 𝔊[967] (κύριε) ὁ θεός. See Appendix 1.

4 4a MSS (𝔊[Q] 𝔏 Sabatier) insert בן אדם.

b 𝔐 על. V 9 has אל (הנבא). On אל–על cf. 1:17 note a.

5 5a אדני is lacking in 𝔊, see Appendix 1.

b 𝔊 telescopes 𝔐 רוח וחייתם to πνεῦμα ζωῆς.

6 6a 𝔊 (𝔏 Sabatier) πνεῦμά μου, see Appendix 3.

7 7a See v 2 note a.

b 𝔐 כאשר צויתי. 3 MSS כאשר צוני, to which 𝔊 𝔏 (Sabatier) 𝔖 𝔙 correspond. That could be assimilation to v 10. 𝔗 = 𝔐.

c On the construction ויהי . . . כהנבאי cf. 9:8; 11:13. Thus there should be no emendation to בהנבאי with 32 MSS (𝔊 𝔗 ?).

d 𝔐 קול is omitted by 𝔊 doubtless because from the point of view of content it recurs in רעש.

e 𝔐 ותקרבו may be retained, with Driver, "Ezekiel," 303, as an erroneous dialect form of the third person feminine plural of the imperfect, which has a parallel in Jer 49:11. According to Gesenius-Kautzsch §60a, note 1, on the other hand, the form is "to be regarded as a clumsy correction of the original 'וַיִּק intended to suggest the reading וַתִּקְרַבְנָה, to agree with the usual gender of עֲצָמוֹת." Or does the ו ending conceal a mutilated article belonging to the following עצמות? On the construction of a verb in the feminine singular before a plural subject see Gesenius-Kautzsch §145k. The deletion of עצמות (2 MSS[Ken], BH[3], Fohrer) is not to be recommended.

f Literally: A bone to its (other) bone. Since עצם is of common gender (Albrecht, "Geschlecht," 73; in the Mishna it is only masculine, H. Rosenberg, "Zum Geschlecht der hebräischen Hauptwörter," *ZAW* 25 [1905]; 336), there is no objection to the reading of 𝔐 עצמו.

8 8a on 𝔐 וראיתי see v 2 note a.

b Since v 6, the only place in which קרם otherwise occurs in OT, showed that the qal was transitive, nip'al וַיִּקָּרֵם should be read with most commentators.

9 9a See v 4 note b.

b אדני is lacking in 𝔊, see Appendix 1.

c 𝔐 הרוח is unattested in 𝔊 𝔎[Bo] 𝔄 Arm 𝔄̈, but (against Cornill) can scarcely be dispensed with.

10 10a 𝔐 והנבאתי. On the perfect with ו see v 2 note a. The form הִנַּבֵּאתִי, which can be understood only as a hitpa'el with assimilated ת (Bauer-Leander §59c; on this see above 5:13 note a והנחמתי), for which some MSS[Ken] read והתנבאתי, is strange alongside the nip'al form in v 7. The only other occurrence of the hitpa'el of נבא in Ezekiel (13:17) is the emphatic statement "behave as a prophet(ess)." One might consider whether in 𝔐 in the present passage

11 **Then he[a] said to me: Son of man, these bones are the whole house of Israel. See, they[b] say: Our bones are dried up, our hope <is blighted>[c], we are cut down[d]. 12/ Therefore prophesy and say to them[a]: Thus has [the Lord][b] Yahweh said: See, I will open your graves and bring you out of your graves [as my people][c] and lead you into the land of Israel. 13/ And you will know that I am Yahweh when I open your graves and when I bring you out of your graves [as my people][a]. 14/ And I will put my spirit in you so that you come to life and will establish you in your land and you shall know that I, Yahweh, have said it and will do it, says Yahweh.[a]**

an (outward) reminiscence of the emphatically repeated הנבא of v 9 is intended. Cornill, Herrmann suppose a scribal error for an original ונבאתי.

11 11a 𝔊 expands the subject with *κύριος*.

b 𝔐 המה הנה. Driver, "Linguistic Problems," 182, proposed reading הִנֵּה as הֵנָּה and placing המה after it. In "Ezekiel," 303, he prefers to adhere to 𝔐, and for הִנֵּה without a suffix he points to v 2; Is 28:2; before a participle, to Is 65:6; Am 7:4. Bertholet, Fohrer on the basis of 𝔗 (אינון הא אינון) emend to הֵנָּה וְהִנָּם. 𝔊 adds the copula, but see 1:4 note a. הנה is unattested in 𝔊 𝔙, and with their *καὶ αὐτοί* (*ipsi*) these seem to presuppose a personal pronoun.

c With 37 MSS[Ken] (𝔊 𝔗 𝔏 Sabatier) אבדה should be read. The copula has found its way into the text through dittography of the preceding ו.

d For 𝔐 נגזרנו לנו Felix Perles, "'Gewebe' im Alten Testament," *OLZ* 12 (1909): 251f (followed by Koehler-Baumgartner on גזר), proposes reading נגזר נוֹלֵנוּ "our thread of life has been cut off." The language and imagery of this reading, however, are attested nowhere else in the OT, so this ingenious conjecture should be declined. On לנו see Gesenius-Kautzsch §119s.

12 12a 𝔐 אליהם is unattested in 𝔊.

b אדני is lacking in 𝔊, see Appendix 1.

c 𝔐 עמי is not translated by 𝔊 𝔖 (see also v 13 note a). Since it introduces into the text the fully theological interpretation of covenant renewal and acceptance as the people of Yahweh, i.e. the removal of the curse pronounced in Hos 1:9, and since it cannot be seen why 𝔊 and 𝔖 would have suppressed this important statement for the sake of making the text more compact, one will have to reckon with the secondary addition of the עמי in 𝔐.

13 13a Here too 𝔖 has preserved the original reading without the theologically interpretative עמי, see v 12 note c. 𝔊 copes with the already expanded text of 𝔐 only by suppressing אתכם and the suffix in מקברותיכם (which, however, are made absolutely necessary by the preceding parallel and by the analogy of v 12) and by subordinating the last part of the verse: *τοῦ ἀναγαγεῖν με ἐκ τῶν τάφων τὸν λαόν μου*.

14 14a 𝔙 *ait dominus deus*, 𝔖 אמר מרא מרותא show here too, against 𝔐 𝔗 𝔊, the doubling of the divine name which usually occurs in the formula for a divine saying in 𝔐.

Form

37:1–14 begins in vv 1–10 with a dramatically fashioned report of a vision which has its parallels in 1:1–3:15 (3:22ff); 8:1–11:25 and chapters 40ff. In the grip of Yahweh's hand the prophet is led out to "the plain," which he finds strewn with bones. Here, after a preliminary question by Yahweh who does not actually himself appear, he is commanded to prophesy. Under the influence of his word the bones begin to come to life again. But then the prophet, once again addressed as "son of man," is, in a shorter second part (vv 11–14), commanded to preach. After what he saw in the vision has been interpreted for him by an explicit indentification with the house of Israel (v 11), the command comes to him to speak to Israel and make her a prophetic promise. The image of the bone-strewn field is replaced in this proclamation by the image of the graves from which Israel is to be awakened in the repatriation to her own land.

The two main sections, vv 1–10 and vv 11–14, thus stand in a relationship of image and interpretation, where the interpretation contains at the same time the real proclamation to the people. From the point of view of form this recalls Ezekiel 17 and 21:1ff. The transition from the first part to the second is achieved by means v 11. The fact that in the proclamation to the people the image of the dead bones is replaced by that of the graves should on no account lead to the separation of the two parts, not even in the form of allowing v 11 to stand as an original interpretative explanation of vv 1–10 (Herntrich). For vv 11–14, which are introduced by a new address, are for their part quite clearly in the form which is frequently attested in Ezekiel, that of the disputation.[1] V 11 begins with a quotation of the words of the people, which is followed by the divine response in vv 12–14, which quite unconcernedly introduces a new image. No exception need be taken to this fluctuation in the language (against Hölscher). Thus v 11 fulfills a double function: 1) It interprets the imagery of the vision and in this respect has a backward reference. At the same time it introduces 2) the form of the disputation in vv 11–14, in which God, as, e.g., in 33:10ff, counters the people's resignation with his word of promise. It is, however, also not necessary to delete with Jahn and Herrmann[2] vv 13b,14 or with Bertholet and Fohrer vv 12b,13 as variants to vv 12,13a or vv 12a,14 respectively. (Kraetzschmar regards vv 12,13a as a parallel to vv 13b,14). Rather vv 12–14 are in the form which has already been noted several times, that of the expanded proof-saying.[3] The bipartite proof-saying in vv 12–13a is followed in v 13b, introduced twice by an infinitive with ב ("when"), by a repetition of the promise of v 12, and this is developed in v 14a by further promises in the consecutive perfect. With yet another recognition formula which has been expanded by verbs, contains the emphatic דברתי ועשׂיתי ("I have said it and will do it") (17:24; 22:14; 24:14; 36:36) and ends with the formula for a divine saying, the section reaches its resounding conclusion. The range of possibilities of different forms in Ezekiel is here handled with a certain panache.

The same may also be said, from the point of view of form, of the vision in vv 1–10. This is in the form of a first person narrative. But it does not only provide the development of what is in itself a static vision, but shows, as already 1:1–3:15; chapters 8–11; chapters 40ff, that the prophet participates in the divine activity. And this not only in the role of the one who is guided by Yahweh to be receptive of vision and word, as in the three great visions mentioned above, nor only as one who is asked for his response (v 3), but in such a way that, with the full activity of prophetic proclamation in the midst of the visionary event, he participates in the latter. So, too, in the secondary expansion in 11:1–13. He is to address the dead bones in an instructive proclamatory oracle (messenger formula; vv 5f). This is in the form of a bipartite proof-saying. Then, now precisely in the imperative, he is to proclaim once again the divine command to "the spirit of life" (הריח) with all his prophetic power (v 9). Under the influence of this activity on the part of the preacher there begins to emerge, within the visionary experience, life from death. None of Ezekiel's other visions reaches such dramatic heights as does this vision of the dead bones. The closest comparison is with 11:1–13.

In this passage, when one examines the formal structure one is particularly reminded of the call vision. In the examination of the account of the ordination in 2:8–3:3 we noted that the process of incorporation of the scroll was expanded into an event characteristically in two stages. The same observation can be made with regard to 37:1–14.[4] The introductory word of the prophet concerning the dead bones would lead us to expect a single process of revival. But then this is expanded into the two stages of the reconstitution of the body and the revival of this still dead body by the רוח. Certainly this expansion does not appear in any way unnatural, for it takes as its hidden model the process of the primeval creation of man as this is reported in Gen 2:7. The creation of the

1 See 1,280 on 12:21–25.
2 J. Herrmann, *Ezechielstudien*, 36.
3 On this see above p. 96f.
4 See 1,135f.

body is followed by endowment with the breath of life, which alone makes man into a living being. But the formal stylistic element of expansion into several stages must not thereby be overlooked. It is in line with the stylistic observations made hitherto in the book of Ezekiel.

These last questions have already led us into the realm of questions about the subject matter of the vision reported here. Is there anything more to be said, let it be asked finally here in the context of these introductory general remarks, about the traditio-historical origin of this bizarre vision of the field of dry dead bones? Herntrich would understand it against a background of contemporary experience and use it to locate the prophet in Palestine: "In the time of the terrible siege many battles will have taken place here (i.e. near Jerusalem); for it is to be assumed that Ezekiel, exactly like Jeremiah in his visions, first sees something real and that the prophetic vision links on to that."[5] On the other hand, however, another observation emerges much more forcefully from the text. The real point of origin of the whole picture which the prophet sees quite obviously lies in the words which, according to v 11, the prophet cites from the mouth of the people. This sentence contains, in the first of its three verbal clauses, the impressive image of the dry bones. In the context of the detailed exegesis we will have to examine its sphere of origin. From this image, which is at first not properly understood and which the prophet encounters in the people's lament, the vision comes to him in a process of dramatic realization of its content. In the case of Ezekiel we have already noted in the call narrative that figures of speech could unexpectedly acquire a dramatic reality in the prophet's experience before his God.[6] The same was true of the symbolic action of the cutting of the hair.[7] It is only too natural that this image, which comes from the people's figurative language, should be interpreted to refer to the "slain" (הרוגים v 9), and this might give the impression that we are here dealing with the type of the "battlefield saga."[8] But this element does not bear the main emphasis. The latter lies, rather, on the image of the dry bones, which has its roots in the quotation of the people's words. Thus, in inquiring about the origin of the pictorial material of the vision one must not go back either to images from the contemporary memory or to older Israelite traditions, nor even take as a starting point the motif of the battlefield saga. The oracle as a whole itself reveals the immediate origin of the image of the dry bones, which is then dramatically confronted with the promise of the God who, as creator of man, also has the power to refashion dead bones into living men. At the same time, however, with this understanding of the development of the image one encounters afresh a characteristic of Ezekiel's language which confirms anew what has been asserted elsewhere.

Setting

With all these considerations, however, the question of the origin of the oracle has been largely prejudged. Already the analysis of its form suggests extreme proximity to the genuine words of Ezekiel. "To deny him this vision (Hölscher) is an error" is Bertholet's judgment. This is undoubtedly correct.

The quotation in v 11 which determines the whole section suggests, exactly like the quotation in 33:10, a period of resigned despair on the part of the men around the prophet. There is nothing against assuming that these are the exiles for whom "Israel's resurrection" would in fact have to consist in the return of those who had been deported. This is what is stated explicitly in vv 12 and 14. One does not have the impression from this oracle that the prophetic proclamation of salvation had become well established. The polemic formulation of the proclamation of a new restoration also suggests that in the case of the prophet himself we are not dealing with a well polished message that has already been proclaimed over a long period. Thus, with the dating of the section, in spite of the confirmation of certain elements of Ezekiel's later language (v 2 note a), it is better not to go too far into the exilic period and to date it in any event earlier than 36:16ff. There is some evidence to suggest that the oracle once had at its head a date (see below on v 1). This would then have been set aside by an editor, although it is not easy to see the reasons for this. It is probable that this would have been a date between that of 33:21 and that of 40:1.

5 Herntrich, *Ezechielprobleme*, 117.

6 See 1, 136f.

7 See 1, 172.

8 Walter Baumgartner, *Zum Alten Testament und seiner Umwelt; ausgewählte Aufsätze* (Leiden: Brill, 1959), 361.

Interpretation

■ **37:1** In a way which is unusual for Ezekiel the section 37:1–14 begins with a simple perfect. Closer examination reveals that v 1a is fairly closely related to the beginning of the great vision of the new temple in 40:1ff. There, after a complex double date, the text continues with the same words as are found in 37:1 היתה עלי יד יהוה ("the hand of Yahweh came upon me"). Instead of the words which follow here, ויוצאני ברוח יהוה ויניחני ("and he led me out in the spirit of Yahweh and set me down"), there follows there an analogous expression . . . ויבא אתי . . . במראות אלהים . . . ויניחני ("and he brought me . . . in the visions of God . . . and set me"). Since the other descriptions of visions which are formulated, partly at least, in similar terms (1:1ff; 8:1ff [also 3:16a, 22f]) are also dated at the beginning, the suspicion arises that in 37:1 a date (corresponding to 40:1) must have fallen out. The following portion of text will then have survived in its fragmentary form (with introductory perfect). Now Bertholet has suggested that by means of 37:1b, 37:1ff was originally connected directly with 3:16a, 22–24, where the prophet was also sent out into the בקעה ("plain"). In this way, 3:16a would then provide, for this vision too, the missing date.[9] Against this association, however, there arise not inconsiderable objections. First of all, from a purely textual point of view, the connection cannot be made quite so smoothly as it appears in Bertholet. At the point of connection further emendations would have to be made. Also, from the point of view of content, there is the question whether the scene in 37:1ff, as is asserted in 3:22, is really to be thought of as in the presence of the כבוד יהוה ("glory of Yahweh"). Above all, however, the date suggested by 3:16a, namely a period seven days after the prophet's call, is internally quite improbable. 37:11 clearly attests the complete collapse of all the exiles' hopes. To this is addressed the message of salvation, of the revival of the whole nation. This message is certainly not to be expected in the period before the fall of Jerusalem, which is suggested by the date of 3:16. Thus any connection between 3:16a, 22–24 and 37:1ff is to be denied. The original date of 37:1 remains impossible to discover.

The hand of Yahweh has come upon the prophet and has snatched him from the normal sphere of everyday life.[10] In this state Yahweh leads him out "in the spirit of Yahweh." In ברוח יהוה ("in the spirit of Yahweh"), יהוה ("Yahweh") (against Smend) is not to be understood as the subject of ויוצאני ("led me out"). Rather, this expression is to be understood as a technical term of the language of prophetic schools, so rigid that it cannot, as would really be expected here, be changed into the suffixed form ברוחו ("in his spirit"). In Ezekiel it is used also in 11:5 for the spirit that instantly comes. A closer parallel to the present passage is the ברוח אלהים ("in the spirit of God") of 11:24.[11] The fact that in the passage corresponding to this in 40:2 במראות אלהים ("in the visions of God") appears (מראה "vision" is combined with רוח אלהים "spirit of God" in 11:24) reveals how interchangeable are all these terms which describe the prophet's state of possession. In all this it cannot be decided with certainty whether the prophet is led bodily out into the בקעה ("plain") or whether this is an imaginary transportation like the transportations to Jerusalem in chapters 8ff and chapters 40ff. The parallel in 3:22f would, nevertheless, suggest the former.[12] L. E. Browne assumes that here, on the basis of Gen 11:2, the thought is of the plain in which the tower of Babel was built "as typical of a place where evil was rampant."[13] J. Morgenstern, on the other hand, with reference to Zech 14:4f, believes we have to think of the valley at the foot of the Mount of Olives in which the resurrection of the dead takes place.[14] In this connection he points to the representation of the event of Ezekiel 37 in the synagogue at Dura (see below).

Outside in the plain there opens before the prophet's eyes the terrifying picture of a field of corpses. The bones have been lying about unburied for a long time, naked, already picked clean by the birds of the sky, stripped of their skin and flesh and sinews, bleached and dried out by the heat of the day. Miller tries to see in this

9 See note a 1, 142.
10 On this see 1, 117f.
11 On the אלהים see 1, 116f.
12 On בקעה see 1, 157 on 3:22f.
13 Browne, *Ezekiel and Alexander,* 18f.
14 Morgenstern, "King-God," 181.

picture the influence of Jer 8:1–3.[15] It is not only with his eyes that Ezekiel registers this death. He is led all over the field (does the העביר על explicitly refer to the climbing over of individual piles of bones?). In the fatigue caused by this action, there is to be impressed upon him the idea that this is not simply a symbol of death but death in all its fulness—the great death.

It is surprising that no reaction is indicated on the prophet's part to the uncleanness of this terrain and to the danger of contamination to which he is exposed by his traversing of this field. The reaction expressed in 4:14 and then again the careful purification of the land from all remains of bones in 39:12–16 might have led us to expect something of this nature here. It is omitted doubtless because the whole section is orientated specifically along the line of thought "death-life" and is not to be diverted from that by any subsidiary considerations of "clean-unclean."

■ **37:3** But then a voice comes to him, "the son of man,"[16] and asks him a monstrous, one is almost tempted to say ludicrous, question: "will (and that means 'can' here) these bones come to life again?" In this way a penetrating question is asked about the evidence of triumphant death.

The prophet's answer is very restrained. In it we hear not the man of God who is gifted with special insight and transported into proximity to God, but simply the man who knows about God: "You know" (cf. Rev 7:14). This has two sides to it: the admission of the powerlessness of man, who, faced with such an irrefutable victory on death's part, is incapable of saying anything about he possibility of life for these dead bones; at the same time, however, the knowledge that he is replying to the God whose abilities are not curtailed by man's lack of abilities. Haag affirms, correctly, that this response reveals that the period of Ezekiel, exactly like Job 14:14, knows nothing of a general eschatological resurrection of the dead, but does not wish, either, to deny to Yahweh the possibility of awakening, thanks to his power as creator, some time the dead to life again. Thus 1 Kgs 17:17–24 and 2 Kgs 4:31–37 recount how Yahweh, through the prophets, once effected such a thing.[17] And the description of Yahweh as אל אלהי הרוחת לכל בשר ("God, the God of the spirits of all flesh") in Nu 16:22 (27:16) (P) is obviously affirming precisely this sovereign power of Yahweh. Nor must it be limited, for example, by the belief, which Henninger attests by a rich array of religio-historical material, that unbroken bones still possess their soul and therefore the possibility of revivification. Henninger himself rightly states that such thoughts have quite lost their power in Ezekiel 37, insofar as here the bones no longer appear as bearers of the life force, but, rather, it is their lifelessness that is strongly emphasized. Thus with the prophet's reply everything is transferred back from man's impotence to God's powerful decision.

■ **37:4f** This decision is described in what follows, where the prophet is suddenly transformed from being the spokesman of human impotence into the spokesman of divine omnipotence. He receives the commission to proclaim over the dry bones the prophetic word, which, with the summons to attention, calls the dead to pay attention, and, as authorized messenger,[18] delivers the divine message in which the "God of the spirits of life for all flesh" himself proclaims that he will bring his spirit of life and will make the dead bones come to life.

■ **37:6** This general statement is developed further in v 6, insofar as the reconstruction of the living beings from the bones upwards is described on the basis of a certain anatomical knowledge. Such knowledge may be located in a particular way in the priestly circles from which Ezekiel comes and which are entrusted with the dissection of the sacrificial animals. With this we may compare the medical knowledge of the Egyptians, who are "particularly skillful as a result of the practice of embalming."[19] The bones are first of all fastened to each other again by means of sinews. גיד occurs in the OT also in Gen 32:33 (twice); Jer 48:4; Job 10:11; 40:17. On this, see, e.g., the phraseology of the Pyramid Texts, which do not yet

15 Miller, *Verhältnis*, 92.

16 On "son of man" see 1, 131f.

17 See also the statement, in somewhat different circumstances, of 2 Kgs 13:20f.

18 Introductory messenger formula; Rolf Rendtorff, "Botenformel und Botenspruch," *ZAW* 74 (1962): 165–177.

19 Hermann Grapow, "Medizinische Literatur," *HO* 1/2 (Leiden: E. J. Brill, 1952): 181-187; idem, *Über die anatomischen Kenntnisse der altägyptischen Ärzte* (Leipzig: Hinrichs, 1935).

seem to presuppose the mummification of corpses[20] and which summon the dead to life: "Now then, NN, your head is fastened to your bones, your bones are fastened to your head. The doorposts of heaven will be opened for you, the great bolts will be broken for you . . . ." Or: "Protect the head of NN, so that it does not come loose. Gather together the bones of NN so that they do not come loose."[21] Over this there grows flesh, which for its part is protected by the skin. And to this reconstruction of the body there is added true animation through the breath in which the spirit of life is discernible. The whole proclamation, however, is in the form of a proof-saying. What Yahweh proclaims is orientated towards the acknowledgement of the mystery of his person.

■ **37:7** Thus speaks the prophet. And then his ears hear a noise beginning in the background of the prophetic speech. קול ("noise"), as in 1:24f; 3:12f; 10:5; 43:2, in 3:12f is in a construct relationship with רעש ("rustling"), which is here used as a parallel and in which the impressions of shock (12:18 note a) and of rustling are linked. The bones rustle as they come together.

■ **37:8** Then growth begins to take place on the dry bones exactly as the word of Yahweh had proclaimed: sinews, flesh, skin. When a pause is then made in the process, insofar as the spirit of life is at first missing, only to reappear under a new powerfully spoken word, this is not the expression of a weakness in the initial divine word. Rather there breaks through here, alongside the stylistic desire to expand the process (see above on "Form"), also the compulsion of a specific tradition. A dichotomistic concept of man led already in the old Yahwistic creation narrative to a shaping of the account of the creation of man in two stages (Gen 2:7). This dichotomistic picture remained in force until the time of Qoheleth (3:20f; 12:7). It is not to be confused with Idealism's dualistic concept of man, insofar as it does not contrast with a creaturely body which is from below an immortal soul which is from above. Rather it distinguishes between the body, which can be seen with the eyes and felt with hands, and the life force, which animates the body, is intangible, but is no less effective and can be discerned in the breath.[22] As a mysterious intangible power in man this has the advantage of special origin. Gen 2:7 has the "breath" (נשמה) directly breathed into man by the creator from his fullness of life. When, on the other hand, in the creation of the animals (Gen 2:19) there is no mention of this particular breathing in of life, this is meant to indicate the greater proximity to God of the human lifeforce (P, in Gen 1:26f, speaks much more fully of man's being made in the image of God). In the statement of Eccl 3:20f the puzzling questioning after the peculiar nature of human life can be clearly heard.

In the context of the common ground with Genesis 2, Ezekiel 37 however now shows once again a particular variation in the concept of the place of origin of the spirit of human life. By contrast with the נשמת חיים ("breath of life") of Gen 2:7, reference here, as in Ecclesiates, is to the רוח ("spirit").

■ **37:9** But by contrast with Eccl 12:7, it is not a רוח ("spirit") which comes from God. Rather, this possibility of life seems to be regarded as something which pervades the whole world, which now blows upon the human corpses like a wind in order to transform them into living creatures (cf. the נפש חיה "living being" of Gen 2:7). But while the wind, for all its capricious veering from south to north (Eccl 1:6) and for all the unpredictability of its origin at any given moment (Eccl 11:5; Jn 3:8), can blow from only one place at a time, the irruption of the breath of life into the dead bodies is represented as an event which happens from all four points of the compass simultaneously—a רוח of a mysteriously peculiar kind. Can the "fourfold wind" of the *Enuma eliš* 4, 46 be compared with it?[23] On the "four winds" as a description of the four points of the compass see also 42:20; Zech 2:10; 6:5; 1 Chr 9:24; Dan 8:8; 11:4.[24] Thus the prophet then receives the commission to address the רוח ("spirit") with a command (imperative) and to summon it to come and breathe upon the "slain." The fact that the reference to

20 Hermann Kees, "Pyramidentext," *HO* 1/2 (Leiden: E. J. Brill, 1952): 32.
21 Pyramid Texts 572, 730.
22 But also in the power of the blood (see 1,500 on 24:7).
23 *AOT* 117, *ANET* 66.
24 On this see J. M. Powis Smith, "The Syntax and Significance of Genesis i.1–3" in *Old Testament Essays* (London: Charles Griffin and Co., Ltd., 1927), 166–169. K. Tallqvist, *Himmelsgegenden und Winde,* StOr II, 1928, 105ff. See also 1,203 on 7:2. On רוח see also Appendix 3.

the bones has been replaced by a reference to the "slain" is in the first instance connected with the fact that meanwhile the bones have become bodies again, which are now lying there like corpses. It is only at this point that the image of the vision first connects up with the reference to the slain. Here too the thought of those who once fell in the battles with the Babylonians may also have been an influence. The oracle as a whole is not, however, referring to the resurrection of those who fell at that time. The allusion is only quite incidental and is not a central element of the image.

■ **37:10** At this divine command, which again is to happen specifically following the messenger formula, the dead move because the breath of life has entered into them and stand up. When it is explicitly stated that this was "a mighty host," there is of course here in no way the thought of renewed warfare on the part of a rearmed Israel (see then chapters 38ff!), but simply the idea of a large number. With this "standing up" (ויעמדו על רגליהם "and they rose to their feet") on the part of the crowd, however, the description breaks off. On this see also the prophet's "standing on his feet" after he had collapsed at the visionary experience in 2:1f; 3:24. There too standing up means the regaining of wakeful vitality.

■ **37:11–14** The spectacle had arisen before the prophet, to begin with without any element of interpretation—at the most in the הרוגים ("the slain") of v 9 might, from afar and quite incidentally, something of contemporary experience have been touched upon. Nowhere at all is it now said that the prophet is to communicate this spectacle to the people. Rather, according to v 11 Yahweh informs the prophet alone of the meaning of what he has seen. The commission to speak which follows in vv 12–14 does not go back in what it says to the imagery of vv 1–10. It clothes what it has to say (and from the content point of view this is exactly what vv 1–10 said) in a new image. Thus, according to the wording of the text itself, the vision to begin with remains a kind of symbolic assurance for the prophet himself. What is to be proclaimed to the people in vv 12–14 has already taken place before his very eyes in the visionary spectacle.

■ **37:11** By means of the renewed address to the prophet ("son of man," as in v 3) the interpretation of the vision becomes the prelude to a new section. The bones which the prophet saw are interpreted as referring to "the whole house of Israel." The interpretation is not applied from without to the house of Israel. Rather, the latter has equated the dry bones with itself in words which the prophet quotes. The exposition in v 11 sees in them the appropriate description of the "whole house of Israel" (so also in the secondary addition in 36:10).[25]

The citation of the words of lamentation on the part of the house of Israel is, formally, in three parts like that of 33:10 and contains, like it too, the darkly plaintive rhyme syllables *-ēnū* and *-ānū*.[26] Also in terms of its form of language it is, in its stock of both words and images, in the language of the Psalms (and Proverbs). Here a man's bones can be mentioned as representative of the whole man. This happens in the language of praise: "All my bones say: Yahweh who is like you" (Ps 35:10). But equally so in the language of the lament: "Yea, my life goes past in sorrow and my years run on in sighing. My strength fails 'in misery,' my bones grow weak" (Ps 31:11).[27] Prv 17:22 comes closest to the imagery of Ezek 37:11: "A cheerful heart enlivens 'the body' [Koehler-Baumgartner גויה], but a downcast spirit 'dries up the bones' (תיבש גרם)."[28] The loss of hope was described in the same words in Ezek 19:5 (אבדה תקותה "her hope was lost"), but see also Ps 9:19; Prv 10:28; Job 8:13; 14:19. The verb גזר has the meaning "cut off." In metaphorical terms one can think of the "cutting down" of grass or flowers. 2 Kgs 6:4 uses the verb of cutting wood. But it is also used in an absolute sense when, e.g., Lam 3:54 says: "Water streamed over my head. I said: 'I am cut off' (נגזרתי)." Or when Is 53:8 says of the servant of Yahweh: "For 'he was cut off' (נגזר) out of the land of the living"; see also Ps 88:6. In all three clauses of the quotation, full expression is given to lamenting the hopeless fading, dying, being cut down. Israel, who in the events of the years 733/32, 722 and 597 was pushed further and further into disaster and defeat, sees herself finally sentenced to death in the event of 587. The concentration of the vision on the single image of the dried bones has fully grasped the basic element of this hopeless self-assertion on the part of the people.

■ **37:12** To this hopelessness, however, the prophet has to

25 On this see also Appendix 2.

26 See above p. 187.

27 See Kraus, *Psalmen.*

28 Ps 102:5 uses the expression ויבש לבי ("and my heart withered"); see further Johnson, *Vitality,* 69f.

deliver the divine proclamation. Yahweh promises in the proof-saying in vv 12–13a, in the first instance, that he himself will open the graves, lead his people out of the graves and bring them into the land of Israel, and that in all this he will let himself be recognized. Here it is no longer the image of the unburied bones lying on the field, but that of correct burial, in which the corpse is shut in a cave or in a pit in the ground and sealed off securely from being seized by the living,[29] but is thereby also definitively excluded from the sphere of the living. Yahweh will burst this prison of the grave and will lead out his people—here the oracle turns ambiguously to the exodus terminology (leading out of the grave—leading up to the land, cf. the העלה "to bring up" of 1 Sam 12:6; Hos 12:14; and elsewhere), and in the third statement of the new settlement (הביא "to lead" in this sense also in v 21; 36:24) the grave terminology is completely left behind. In the עמי ("my people") (v 12 note c and v 3 note a) perhaps a later hand wished to give expression to the covenant reality in which the people are to stand once again. On this see the two-part covenant formulae in 14:11 and elsewhere.

■ **37:13f** The expansion of the proof-saying recapitulates once again the first two clauses of the divine saying in v 12, which spoke of the historical act of Yahweh's liberating his people, and then goes beyond them in v 14a with a statement of a final goal. The transfer to the land (the reference to a new settlement is recapitulated with the change of the והבאתי "and I will lead" of v 12 to והנחתי "and I will establish") will be connected with the bestowal of Yahweh's spirit by which the people will live. The statement is in deliberately ambiguous terms. On the basis of the vision one thinks in the first instance of the newly bestowed spirit of life in v 9. But it is remarkable that the reference here is explicitly to "my spirit" (רוחי), i.e. the spirit of Yahweh, which in the language of the רוח-statement in the vision was studiously avoided. Thus one must think beyond the mere revivification to the promise of the spirit in 36:27 (39:29), by which also the inner transformation of the people comes about. This alone makes it possible for the first time that the old history of disaster in the land will not again be repeated.[30] In this respect the oracle comes close to what was said in 36:16ff.

The double recognition formula, which in v 14 ends in the divine assertion דברתי ועשיתי ("I have said it and will do it") (36:36), again affirms that this miracle of the revivification of the people will not create earthly prerogatives, but reveals the Lord of this history as the Lord who is able to keep his word. The revival of Israel will be God's great revelation of himself to the world.

Ezek 37:1–14 depicts an unusually stirring visionary event. It is no wonder that in art it later played a significant role. In early Christian art it was, among the representation of scenes from the book of Ezekiel, the episode which was "presented earliest and most frequently."[31] In Western art, in sharp contrast to oriental art, the scene surprisingly disappears completely. Thus, e.g., it is no longer represented in the great Ezekiel cycle of Schwarzrheindorf.[32] Particularly impressive is the Jewish representation on the lower frieze of the north wall of the synagogue at Dura-Europos.[33] To what extent the prophetic narrative in this representation moves into the light of the surrounding non-Israelite tradition can be seen, according to R. Meyer, from the fact that in the revivification scene there appear winged creatures, which must be regarded as figures representing the soul.[34] Behind this can be discerned the Hellenistic dualism of body and soul, which (as has been observed above) lies far from the biblical text.

29 See, e.g., *BRL*, "Grab."

30 See above p. 248.

31 Neuss, *Buch*, 141. On early Christian art see further pp. 141–154; on post-classical oriental art, 180–188; on the Rosas Bible, 211; on the Farfar Bible, 224; on Western art, 261–263.

32 Neuss, *Buch*, 265–296, and Albert Verbeek, *Schwarzrheindorf. Die Doppelkirche und ihre Wandgemälde*, 1953.

33 See Carl H. Kraeling, *The Synagogue*, The Yale University Excavations at Dura-Europos final report 8, part 1 (New Haven: Yale University Press, 1956); also Riesenfeld, *Resurrection;* Wischnitzer-Bernstein, "Conception"; Martin Noth, "Dura-Europos und seine Synagoge," *ZDPV* 75 (1959): 164–181; Werner Georg Kümmel, "Die älteste religiöse Kunst der Juden," *Judaica* 2 (1946): 29–56.

34 Rudolf Meyer, "Betrachtungen zu drei Fresken der Synagoge von Dura-Europos," *ThLZ* 74 (1949): 29–38.

The picture in the synagogue at Dura understands the resurrection of the dead not as an image for the liberation of the exiles of Israel, but as a real resurrection of the dead. Insofar as it represents this resurrection against the background of a mountain which is split in two and on which there is a house collapsing in the earthquake, it reveals that it has understood the רעש ("rustling") of 37:7, on the pattern of the earthquake in 38:19f, as an eschatological event and finds expressed in Ezekiel 37 the promise of a future resurrection of the dead. This understanding of Ezek 37:1–14 has also given to the episode its significance in Christian representations. Thus, many Church Fathers found the final resurrection of the dead proclaimed here.[35] At the same time, there is found in Jewish tradition also the conception that this resurrection refers to a historical event at the time of Ezekiel.[36] According to *b. Sanh.* 92b R. Eliezer said, "The dead whom Ezekiel resurrected stood up, uttered song, and immediately died." To the question of the song which they sang R. Joshua replied, "They sang thus, 'The Lord killeth and maketh alive: he bringeth down to the grave, and bringeth up' (1 Sam 2:6)." To the supposition that Ezek 37:1–14 could be only a parable, R. Eliezer the son of R. Jose the Galilean opposes a different version, "The dead whom Ezekiel revived went up to Palestine, married wives and begat sons and daughters." And R. Judah b. Bathyra adds, "I am one of their descendants, and these are the *tefillīm* which my grandfather left me as an heirloom from them." Further thought is given to the question of who in particular could have been meant by those who were revived by Ezekiel. Rab is in a position to say, "They were the Ephraimites who counted the years to the end of the Egyptian bondage, but erred therein." The fragment of the Palestinian Targum published by Diez-Macho also moves in this realm of thought. It prefaces the whole narrative with the observation that Ezekiel thought to himself "what would happen to the dead who die in exile." It is then able to say that those who are brought to life are the 30,000 Ephraimites who left Egypt thirty years "before the end" (קדם קצא; is this a reference to the contemporary exiles in Egypt and to the period of exile from the homeland which has been allotted to them?) and were killed by the Philistines. Here, on the evidence of *b. Sanh.* 92b, there is also the influence of 1 Chr 7:20f. The later Haggada which is attested in the Mahzor Vitry can even speak of 200,000 Ephraimites.[37] Here the house of Israel is interpreted specifically in terms of the northern kingdom.

In contrast to all these later interpretations of Ezek 37 it must now once more be finally and unambiguously stated that Ezek 37:1–14, with the two different images of the revival of unburied dead bones and of the opening of graves and the leading out of those buried there to new life, expresses the event of the restoration and the regathering of the politically defeated all-Israel. There is no thought of a resurrection of individuals from the dead nor of an event exclusively the concern of the exiles of the northern kingdom. This was already recognized by the Antiochenes as well as by Jerome.[38] Nevertheless, exegetes who reckon with the figurative character of the two statements in the present context have raised the further question whether, in the use of these metaphors, it is nevertheless not to be recognized indirectly "that the idea of the resurrection of the dead was not wholly unknown to the prophet and his contemporaries."[39] In the metaphorical traits in the vision Riesenfeld believes that he can recognize a series of echoes of the royal New Year festival, from which the belief in the resurrection of the dead is supposed to have taken its origin (role of the spirit, situation of the battlefield which echoes the ritual mock battle, repatriation tradition, etc.). The material cited is not, however, convincing (see also Birkeland's criticism). What is described in Ezek 37 has all the marks in it of something surprising and unusual. It is thought of as historically unique. Here, as Rost has pointed out, there is no link with, e.g., the concept of Sheol, in which one is most likely still to find in early Israel the thought

35 See Neuss, *Buch:* Justin, p. 25; Irenaeus, 26; Tertullian, 32; Cyprian, 32; Cyril of Jerusalem, 43; Epiphanius of Constantine, 47; Severus and John of Damascus, 85; Ambrose, 89; not, on the other hand, Augustine, 89.

36 But also in Epiphanius of Salamis (Neuss, *Buch,* 85f).

37 Díez-Macho, "Targum Palestinense," 201.

38 Neuss, *Buch,* 50, 56f; 71.

39 Riesenfeld, *Resurrection,* 3.

of the continued existence or, more correctly, of the continued shadowiness of the individual after death. Rather, the concept of the disintegration of man in death (along the lines of Eccl 12:7) is taken completely seriously. Only in the sending out anew of the breath of life, that is through an event which connects up with the point where, according to Gen 2:7, the creation of the first man took place, can new life arise.[40] In the visionary description in vv 1–10 the creator is proclaimed, who has the power to make a new beginning at the point where everything seems to have come to an end. And the second image of the opening of the graves (vv 12–14) speaks exactly the same language.

Aim

The prophet's word in 37:1–14 is directed towards the community which sighs in deepest need in exile after 587 and which feels that it is at the end of all its hope. Only the image of death, of bleached bones, of flowers cut down is really appropriate to their situation (v 11). This awareness is all the bitterer since it arises in a people who once had known something of hope and of a great future. Their God had drawn them close to himself. But like the prodigal son they squandered and wasted the father's goods. Thus their misery is not only fate but sin. The prophet himself had said that quite unmistakably to his people in his harsh discourses (chapters 15, 16, 20, 23).

Now, however, this same prophet is sent to this very same people with a quite new message of life. Life is here proclaimed quite unconditionally, with no preconditions nor in such a way that God's activity here and there left aside a godless person and in this way, at least in this negative counterpart, made it clear that man should to some extent cooperate in his life. The fragment of the Palestinian Targum (Díez Macho), which in the resurrection event leaves at least one dead body lying on the ground and has God's angel reply to a question about that body, "For interest and surcharge he has lent (his money), therefore he is not honest (enough) to receive life along with his brothers," has undoubtedly quite rightly been aware of the unprecedented nature of such a proclamation, but has wrongly tried to soften it. Thus unprecedented is in fact the will of God which is proclaimed over the people who realize definitively that they are subject to death, thus unconditional is the will of God for his people's life. However clearly it is said in another passage to a people who are going around in defiance or despair with the thought of assimilation to the heathen world around them (20:32) that entry into life will not take place without judgment on everything that is opposed to God, however clearly it is also said elsewhere (18:23) that God's promise of life to man demands a return to God, so here there is clearly revealed the great profundity of the divine promise of life (see already the חיי "live" of 16:6) which also stands behind those apparently conditional statements promising life.[41] The man who is in the depths of despair is confronted by the unconditional nature of the divine promise of life. There is no sign of a connection with any merit which might seem to exist somewhere on the part of the people of God. From his free will God gives life to his own who are condemned to death. Even the prophet himself knows of no way whereby the people could somehow or other lay claim to such life. The question whether life is still possible for this people he must, in view of the evidence of the dry bones, pass back to God: "Lord, you know."

This vision granted to the prophet and the word with which he is charged speak, however, not simply of possibilities which God might have intended. They proclaim as firmly as possible an imminent action on God's part, "I the Lord, have said it and will do it." In the resurrection of the man whose cross inscription designated him as the king of his people, the New Testament community encountered this reality which is more than a mere divine plan and experienced the validity of God's promise of life to his people—certainly of a new, remarkably altered kind. But yet at the same time in such a way that they have seen expression given to what was promised by the prophet to his people and, in its deepest intention, made universally valid. The prophet has been able to promise to his people return from being dispersed and lost. He proclaims life where it has become clear that the life of the one called by God is now definitively at an end. He looks to the day of the new settlement when that which was separated far apart finds itself

40 On this cf. the καινὴ κτίσις of 2 Cor 5:17.

41 On 20:32 see 1,414; on 18:23 see 1,385; on 16:6 see 1,339.

together again. As the real goal of this divine activity, however, he acknowledges the new life in which God's spirit will dwell in the midst of his people. The person who added עמי ("my people") in vv 12 and 13 hits exactly what is meant, that God's people should be wholly the people of God—that is the aim of this new gift of life. Where the return of God in a new freedom and in a new linking of what was previously separated becomes a reality, there God will have achieved his aim.

The other side must certainly also be heard. Only when, as a result of this event, the great awareness dawns and men no longer appear with their own achievements, no matter how magnificently righteous these might be, but when they realize that God reveals himself in the miracle of his free promise of life—only there does God's action achieve its goal. There all ecclesiastical prerogatives collapse, and there remains only the praise given to the God who in the majestic freedom of his faithfulness (לשם קדשי "for the sake of my holy name" 36:22) has revealed himself to his community.

It is, finally, important for the understanding of this promise that the way it is expressed is not debased into a divine programme of history and that the two stages of the revival of the dead bones are not reckoned as a prediction of two phases of human history and interpreted literally in terms of specific events. The unit 37:1–14 has only one word to say, no matter how God may then manipulate history and its various phases. It speaks of the free gift of life coming from God's fidelity to his early promises, through which and in which God, the merciful creator of his "new creature" (2 Cor 5:17), acquires his perfect glory.

The Two Sticks

Bibliography

W. Emery Barnes
"Two Trees become One: Ezek 37:16–17," *JTS* 39 (1938): 391–393.

Julius Boehmer
"מלך und נשיא bei Ezechiel," *ThStKr* 73 (1900): 112–117.

Hugo Gressmann
Der Messias, FRLANT 26 (Göttingen, 1929), especially 256–258.

Herbert Haag
Was lehrt die literarische Untersuchung des Ezechiel-Textes? (Freiburg in der Schweiz: Paulusdruckerei, 1943), 64–78.

E. Power
"The shepherd's two rods in modern Palestine and in some passages of the Old Testament," *Bibl* 9 (1928): 434–442.

Edzard Rohland
Die Bedeutung der Erwählungstraditionen Israels für die Eschatologie der alttestamentlichen Propheten, Unpub. Diss. (Heidelberg, 1956).

See also on 34:1–31.

37

15 **[a]The word of Yahweh[a] came to me: 16/**
You[a], son of man, take a stick[b] and write
on it: For Judah[c] and the Israelites asso-
ciated[d] with him. And <take>[e] another[f]

37: 15a 𝔖 inserts a superscription: על דסלקין והוין
15 חד עמא וחדא מלכותא.
16 16a 𝔐 ואתה is not attested by MS$^{Ken\ 181}$ 𝔊. See 7:2 note a.

b 𝔐 אחד is not translated by 𝔊, but as a contrast to the following אחד (עץ) (see note f) should not be omitted. While 𝔊 understands עץ as ῥάβδον, 𝔗 translates לוחא.

c The ל in ליהודה and ליוסף is understood mostly, on the basis of Gesenius-Kautzsch §119u, as a *lamed inscriptionis* and reference made to Is 8:1f. It is, however, surprising that in 21:25, where one would positively expect it, such a ל does not occur. Serious consideration should therefore be given to the different conception of Hölscher; Kurt Galling, "Ein Stück judäischen Bodenrechts in Jesaia 8," *ZDPV* 56 (1933): 211, 213 note 3, according to which the ל is part of the inscription and denotes possession. See the exposition.

d 𝔐 K חברו. With Q, חבריו should be read on both occasions. 𝔊 renders προσκειμένους ἐπ᾽ αὐτόν or προστεθέντας πρὸς αὐτόν. 𝔗 אחיהון.

e 𝔐 וּלְקַח is unusual alongside the introductory קח לך. While 𝔗 𝔖 סב assimilate the expression in both places, 𝔊 differentiates them λάβε σεαυτῷ . . . λῆμψη σεαυτῷ. 𝔙 differentiates them still more strongly *sume tibi . . . tolle.* If one does not wish to read here

stick and write on it: For Joseph[c]
[Ephraim's stick][g] and <the whole>[h]
house of Israel[i] associated[k] with him. 17/
And join them together into one stick,
that they may become one[a] in your hand.
18 **But when[a] the members of your people say**
to you:[b] Will you not tell us what you
mean by these things?[c] 19/ then say[a] to
them: Thus has [the Lord][b] Yahweh said:
See, I will take the stick[c] of Joseph that
is in Ephraim's hand[d] and the tribes of

an infinitive absolute וְלָקֹחַ, then one will have to conjecture another קח (or, on the basis of 𝔊, the fuller קח לך, so BH[3], Herrmann, Fohrer) or ולקחת (Cornill).

f 𝔐 אחד. Since 𝔊 renders it as *δευτέραν*, 𝔅 as *alterum*, 𝔖 as אחרנא, this is mostly emended to אחר. In the juxtaposition of 19:3, 5, however, . . . אחד אחד is clearly attested in the sense "the one . . . the other." But see also v 17 and Jer 24:2. Thus an emendation is inadvisable, especially since אחד is clearly the key-word of the whole section.

g עץ אפרים, which, in comparison with the parallel of the first inscription, is additional, is to be judged an explanatory interpretative element.

h 𝔐 וכל. The parallel in the first inscription, MS[Rossi 892] 𝔅 suggest a reading ולכל. Yet the deficient insertion of the element, which would then have been inserted more smoothly by the witnesses mentioned, could also point to the secondary expansion of the text. See the exposition.

i 𝔐 בית ישראל, 𝔊 *υἱοὺς* Ισραηλ, 𝔖 בני איסראיל.

k 𝔅 *sociorumque* fails to recognize the attributive character of the plural חבריו (see note d) alongside the singular בית ישראל and sees here a reference to Israel's covenant partners.

17 17a 𝔐 לאחדים has been misunderstood by 𝔊 *τοῦ δῆσαι αὐτάς* as a verbal form, and this has consequently brought about the independence of the conclusion in the form *καὶ ἔσονται ἐν τῇ χειρί σου*. 𝔖 alters the sentence much more. On this basis Driver, "Linguistic Problems," 182–3, supposes an אחד "unite," related to the verb יחד, and reads, with transposition of the words, לך לאחדם יהיו לעץ אחד בידך. But 𝔐 must not be emended. See Brockelmann §83a. With the plural אחדים cf. the דברים אחדים of Gen 11:1. 𝔅 *et erunt in unionem in manu tua.* V 19bβ uses, for the same expression, the singular אחד.

18 18a 𝔊 has the fuller Hebraizing introduction *καὶ ἔσται ὅταν λεγωσι.* והיה should be inserted; see Cooke.

b Since in analogous counter-questions on the part of the people (12:9; 21:5, 12) the difficult לאמר is missing and since there is no indication of such a word in 𝔊 𝔖, it perhaps represents a later addition.

c Literally: What these things are to you.

19 19a 𝔊 *καὶ ἐρεῖς* has here had before it the grammatically more correct ודבר (or ודברת?).

b אדני is lacking in MS[Ken] 𝔊, see Appendix 1.

c 𝔐 עץ is rendered twice in 𝔊 by *τὴν φυλήν* and then the following לעץ again by *εἰς ῥάβδον*. 𝔗 twice has ית שיבטא and לעץ is interpreted as לעמא.

d The עץ אפרים of v 16 (note g) is here interpreted more fully. In this case ביד cannot be understood, with Robert Gordis, "A Note on YAD," *JBL* 62 (1943): 341f (with reference to Amarna letter 245, 35), as the equivalent of בעד ("the stick of Joseph, which stands for Ephraim"), but means surely the staff which is in a man's hand. The inter-

Israel associated[e] with him and will lay
upon[f] [them] the stick[c] of Judah and will
make them into one stick[g], and they will
become one in my hand[h].
20 **And the sticks on which you write should**
lie before their eyes in your hand[a]. 21/
And say to them: Thus has [the Lord][a]
Yahweh said: See, I shall take the Israel-
ites[b] out of the midst of the nations
amongst whom they have gone and will
gather them from all sides[c] and will bring
them into their land[d] 22/ and will make
them into one nation in the land, on the
mountains of Israel[a], and one king[b] will
be king[c] over them all, and they will[d] no

pretation already presupposes the gloss in v 16 (note g).

e See v 16 note d.

f The text here is clearly corrupt. 𝔊 καὶ δώσω αὐτοὺς ἐπὶ τὴν φυλὴν Ιουδα already seems to have 𝔐 in front of it. But עליו should be reduced to על and the following את deleted. The אותם of 𝔐 refers back to the "tribes of Israel" in which the image of the stick finds its exposition. On the other hand, the following עליו still has the stick in mind, and this occurs again in what follows. Thus it should be preferred to אותם, which represents a secondary glossing.

g 𝔗 again interprets לעמא חד.

h 𝔐 בידי. Its suffix seems to have been understood by 𝔊 ($\mathfrak{L}^{W}$) ἐν τῇ χειρὶ Ιουδα as an abbreviation of יהודה. While 𝔐 speaks of the unity of the nation of Yahweh, 𝔊 ($\mathfrak{L}^{W}$) accentuates Judaean messianism.

20 20a 𝔖 "take them into your hand."

21 21a אדני is lacking in 𝔊 $\mathfrak{L}^{W}$, see Appendix 1.

b 𝔐 בני ישראל. 𝔊 ($\mathfrak{L}^{W}$) πάντα οἶκον Ισραηλ.

c 𝔐 מסביב. 𝔊 ($\mathfrak{L}^{W}$) more fully ἀπὸ πάντων τῶν περικύκλῳ αὐτῶν.

d 𝔐 אל אדמתם. 𝔊 ($\mathfrak{L}^{W}$) interprets more fully εἰς τὴν γῆν τοῦ Ισραηλ, while 𝔖 omits the whole expression.

22 22a 𝔐 בארץ בהרי ישראל. 𝔊 ($\mathfrak{L}^{W}$) ἐν τῇ γῇ μου καὶ ἐν τοῖς ὄρεσιν Ισραηλ eases the expression by inserting the copula, see 1:4 note a. Also its τῇ γῇ μου following the immediately preceding אדמתם is suspect and (against Cornill, Bertholet, BH^3) is no reason for emending 𝔐 to ארצי. Rather בארץ is the completely unemphatic resumption of באדמתם which is then more closely defined by the additional בהרי ישראל along the lines of the באדמתם of v 21. Nevertheless it might be wondered whether the whole complex, which is decidedly superfluous in the parallel structure of v 22a/b, is not a secondary theological interpretation.

b 𝔐 ומלך אחד. 𝔊 ($\mathfrak{L}^{W}$) καὶ ἄρχων, which, on the basis of 34:24, seems to point to a נשיא in the original. To this it is mostly emended (Herrmann, Bertholet, Fohrer, as well as O. Procksch, "Fürst und Priester bei Hesekiel," *ZAW* 58 [1940/41]: 116, and Karl Heinz Bernhardt, *Das Problem der altorientalischen Königsideologie im Alten Testament* VTSuppl 8 [Leiden: Brill, 1961], 116 note 5). But the clear correspondence with the following ממלכות, which is also attested without any doubt by 𝔊 βασιλείας, is a much stronger argument for the retention of 𝔐 and for believing that 𝔊 has assimilated to 34:24. See further the exposition.

c 𝔐 למלך, which is not attested by 𝔊 $\mathfrak{L}^{W}$ 𝔖 and is introduced in 𝔗 by an added (מלכא) למיהוי, at first sight seems superfluous and is therefore mostly deleted (Cornill, Toy, and others). But when it is noticed that the two closely related clauses v 22aβ/bα, positive and negative, are both built on the basic verbal expression היה ל, the justification for

longer be two nations and no longer be divided into two kingdoms <>[e]. 23/ And they will no longer defile themselves with their idols [and with their detestable things and with all their transgressions][a], and I will deliver them from all their (manifold) backsliding[b] in which they have sinned and will purify them, and they will be my people, and I[c] will be their God, 24/ and my servant David will be king[a] over them, and they will all have one shepherd.

24b **And they will walk in my ordinances and observe my statutes and do them[b]. 25/ And they will dwell in the land[a] which I gave to my servant Jacob, in which <their>[b] fathers dwelt, and they and their children and their children's children will dwell there for ever[c], and David my servant will be their prince[d] for ever. 26/ And I will make with them a covenant of salvation. It will be an everlasting covenant[a] <>[b], and I will multiply them**

this deletion becomes questionable.

d K יהיה is, incorrectly, still referring to the king: "He will no longer be for two nations," which would suggest a king for each nation. The parallel structure of v 22, however, strongly demands a reading יהיו. See also the versions and 𝔗 יהיו.

e 𝔐 עוד is missing in 𝔊 𝔏[W] 𝔙 and, alongside the preceding עוד and the one that follows in v 23, represents a superfluous overinterpretation. 𝔖 seems to have read עוד, but transfers it to the beginning of v 23 (after the copula) and therefore omits the following עוד.

23 23a 𝔐 ובשקוציהם ובכל פשעיהם is unattested in 𝔊 𝔏[W] and gives the impression of being a secondary overloading.

b 𝔐 מכל מושבתיהם, 𝔙 *de universis sedibus,* 𝔖 מן כלה בית מעמרהון, 𝔗 מכל מותבניהון. On the plural of מושב in Ezekiel see 34:13 note c. The word cannot originally have stood in the present passage. 𝔊 *ἀνομιῶν* (𝔊[L] Tht *ἀσεβειῶν*) and still more clearly Σ *ἀποστροφῶν* (𝔖[h]) point to an original משובותיהם, which admittedly does not occur elsewhere in Ezekiel but belongs clearly to the language of Jeremiah (2:19; 3:22; 5:6; 14:7; singular in Hos 11:7; 14:5; Jer 3:6, 8, 11f; 8:5; otherwise only in Prv 1:32; see Miller, *Verhältnis,* 114f).

c 𝔊 (𝔏[W]) adds *κύριος* after *ἐγώ*. Did the following אהיה and the thought of Ex 3:14 already lead in a Hebrew *Vorlage* to an additional יהוה? But see also, e.g., 34:30.

24 24a 𝔊 (𝔏[W]) *ἄρχων ἐν μέσῳ αὐτῶν*, see v 22 note b. 𝔖 has a verbal expression נמלך עליהון.

b 𝔏[W] omits ועשו אותם.

25 25a 𝔐 על הארץ. 𝔊 (𝔏[W]) *ἐπὶ τῆς γῆς αὐτῶν.*

b 𝔐 אבותיכם, so too 𝔙 𝔗. 𝔊 𝔏[W] 𝔖 suggest אבותיהם, which alone is possible in the context, but they are suspected of secondary assimilation. Probably in this second relative clause, which clashes with the immediately preceding one, we can recognize a secondary addition.

c In 𝔊 𝔏[W], 𝔐 ובניהם ובני בניהם עד עולם remains unattested. But since the המה which introduces this series and which on its own is superfluous is attested, the remainder must have fallen out accidentally in 𝔊 𝔏[W].

d 𝔐 נשיא. Here 𝔗 has מלכא. This, in comparison with 𝔊 (vv 22, 24; see v 22 note b), is the reverse tendency of adjustment.

26 26a 𝔏[W] omits the second ברית: *testamentum pacis aeternum.* The remainder of v 26 is missing. 𝔗 𝔖 link the two ברית-statements by means of the copula.

b 𝔐 אותם ונתתים והרביתי אותם ונתתי cannot be correct, as is clear from the perplexity of the versions. 𝔊 (on 𝔏[W] see note a) translates אותם by *μετ' αὐτῶν* and omits אותם . . . ונתתים. 𝔙 guesses in the translation of ונתתים *et fundabo eos* "and I will establish them" and omits the second אותם. 𝔗 guesses ואיברכינון, 𝔖 omits ונתתים. The most helpful suggestion is that of Herrmann, that אותם ונתתים is a slight

and will put my sanctuary[c] for all time in their midst, 27/ and my dwelling place shall be with them, and I will be their God, and they will be my people, 28/ and the nations will know that I am Yahweh who sanctifies Israel[a]—when my sanctuary[b] will be in their midst for ever.

textual corruption of a marginal catchword, which has then found its way back into the text, and that it is a doublet of אותם ונתתי.

c 𝔐 מקדשי. 𝔙 here and in v 28 has *sanctificationem meam* (as also in 11:16; 28:18). Jerome, who as a rule correctly renders מקדש as *sanctuarium* (see, e.g., 8:6; 9:6, and elsewhere) remarks on this: "And I shall set, he says, my sanctification or sanctuary in their midst for ever. This the Jews interpret with regard to the temple which was built under Zerubbabel. But how can it be said to stand 'for ever' since that temple which was built by Zerubbabel and afterwards restored by many was destroyed by fire by the Romans? All these things are to be applied to the church and to the time of the Savior [i.e. the Christian era] when his tabernacle was set up in the Church" [Trans.].

28 28a 𝔐 מקדש את ישראל. 𝔊 ($\mathfrak{L}^W$) ὁ ἁγιάζων αὐτούς.
b See v 26 note c.

Form

37:15–28 recount how Yahweh summons the prophet to a sign-action. This has as its theme, briefly summarized, "Repurification of the two parts of Israel." Subsequently the section ends in a much more broadly conceived promise of salvation to Israel in which the various themes of the proclamation of salvation in chapters 34, 36f (shepherd, new covenant, purification of Israel etc.) are taken up afresh. Thus, in assessing the form of the present section the first question to be asked is whether it is to be regarded as an original unit.

The divine address begins twice in vv 15–28 with the introductory messenger formula (vv 19,21). In both places it is preceded by a specific command to speak (דבר אל[י]הם "say to them"). This is motivated in v 19 by the preceding speech of Yahweh to the prophet (vv 16–18). Correspondingly, the command in v 21 is not to be separated from the immediately preceding divine address to the prophet. It will not do simply to delete the latter with Hölscher, Cooke, Herntrich, nor should it be placed with van den Born (considered by Hölscher as a possibility) after v 17b in the context of the first address to the prophet (vv 16–18). Rather does the content too suggest that v 20 introduces a new section. While the divine oracle in v 19 was still couched in the metaphorical language of the two sticks, this image is completely abandoned in the divine oracle of vv 21ff, and only the subject matter described in the image is spoken of.

Are then vv 20–28 to be regarded as a self-contained section? From the point of view of form here, there stand out distinctly and consistently the proclamations in the consecutive perfect. In v 28 they are rounded off by an expanded recognition formula (v 28b, ב "when" with infinitive). But the observation with regard to content that in v 22 a king is proclaimed and in v 24 David is explicitly designated as this "king" (מלך), while v 25 then speaks of David as a נשיא ("prince"), is an argument against the whole of vv 20–28 having originally belonged together. This gives weight to the observation that there is a covenant formula not only in v 23 but also in v 27. In 11:20; 14:11; 34:30(31) the covenant formula had stood at the end of a section. In 34:24 it had been slightly expanded. In 36:28 it revealed at least a break in the speech. In chapter 37, too, the covenant formula in v 27 rounds off the divine proclamations before the expanded recognition formula follows in v 28. Thus it is likely that in the covenant formula in v 23b we find a hint that a section once ended here. The statement about David, which with its מלך ("king") is clearly dependent on v 22, would then be a secondary addition to vv 20–23, which, in dependence on 34:24, here too, in the combination of vv 23bβ, 24a, is meant to call to mind the expression "Yahweh their God and David their king."[1] A connection with 34:23f, which for its part seems to presuppose

1 On 34:24 see above pp. 218f.

37:20–23, is also suggested by רועה אחד ("one shepherd").[2] The new beginning of the next section would therefore be found in v 24b. Also from the point of view of content the taking of vv 24b–28 together as a single unit with a common theme is recommended. No fewer than five times in these verses does the key-word עולם recur, which is otherwise wholly absent from chap. 37 (עד עולם "for ever" v 25; לעולם vv 25,26,28 "forever"; ברית עולם "everlasting covenant" v 26). This shows that the underlining of the duration of the promise is the object which unites vv 24b–28.

Thus in 37:15–28 we have to reckon with three units: vv 15–19; 20–23(24a) and 24b–28.

In vv 15–19 there is first of all a sign-action. As we have already found in Ezekiel, here too the whole action is included in Yahweh's words. The completion of it is not reported.[3] Vv 16f contain the divine instruction to the prophet. In its introductory קח לך ("take") it corresponds to the three sign-actions of the basic text of chapters 4f (4:1–2,9–11; 5:1f) (see also the עשה לך "prepare for yourself" of 12:3). To this there is added, as a second element, the puzzled question of the people about the meaning of the prophetic activity. As in 12:9; 21:12, it is also included in the divine proclamation (21:5 is slightly different). In v 19 there then follows the interpretation which the prophet is to pass on to the questioners as a divine proclamation. With regard to this it is remarkable that basically it does not contain an interpretation of the metaphorical elements of the sign-action, but simply says, with regard to the prophet's action, that Yahweh himself will act in the way that the prophet was told to act in the sign action.

Thus one will regard the continuation in vv 20–23 (24a) as an essentially necessary further interpretation. The section vv 20–23(24a) is somewhat awkwardly introduced by v 20, which, with slight modification, repeats the content of v 17. With its הנה אני לקח (" see, I shall take"), the divine speech begins exactly like the one in v 19, but then from the content point of view turns in a quite different direction and contains an expansive proclamation of salvation. This goes far beyond the mere exposition of the sign-action and at the end concludes with the (secondarily expanded) covenant formula.

Finally, vv 24b–28 are in the style of a bipartite proof-saying. The first element, the announcement of salvation in vv 24b–27, ends, like that of vv 21–23 (24a), with the covenant formula. The beginning in v 24b is scarcely accentuated. From the point of view of content there is no reference to the introductory sign-action.

Setting

Against the derivation of the account of the sign-action in vv 15–19 from Ezekiel, from the aspect of form (in view of the relationship with chapters 4f; 12 [21:23ff]) no decisive objections arise. Since the question of the reunification of the divided Israelite states had acquired a new topicality from the time of Josiah[4] and has also found clear expression in the book of Jer (3:6ff and chapters 30f), it is also from the point of view of content completely probable that Ezekiel came to speak of it in his proclamation of salvation. "The idea that the prophetic action is 'incredible' is itself incredible."[5] It shares its minimal action-content with the sign-actions of chapters 4 and 24. Like the former it is more representational than dramatic. But the same is also true of, e.g., Jeremiah 27.

Herntrich's thesis that the sign-action must have taken place in Palestine soon after the destruction of Jerusalem is not probable. Anyone who is clear in his own mind, in the light of the information in the book of Jeremiah, about the turbulent state of affairs in Judah after the collapse, will rather have the impression that the action, which looks back reflectively on a state of affairs which was no longer thus topical in Palestine after 587, has its point of origin at a certain temporal and physical distance from the destruction of Jerusalem.

The further exposition in vv 20–23(24a), on account of the unself-conscious use of the title of king for the future ruler of the reunited country, comes from a period earlier than vv 24b–28, where the title of king, along the lines of the later establishing of terminology, has been replaced by the title of נשיא ("prince").[6] The fact that vv 20–24a were not deleted at the later change in terminology could be an argument that they were still protected by the authority of the prophet himself. But certainty here is of course not to be reached. See the

2 See above pp. 218f.

3 See 1, 156f.

4 On a possible earlier stage in Hos 2:1–3 see Wolff, *Hosea*, 25ff.

5 Bertholet, 129, citing the view of Hölscher, *Hesekiel*, 176.

exposition.

The expansion in vv 24b–28, on the other hand, in view of the close contact of, e.g., v 25 with 28:25, is best attributed to the later hand who was at work in 28:25f.[7] This might also be supported by the particularly close linguistic relationship with Leviticus 26 which is observable in vv 24b and 27a.

Interpretation

■ **37:15,16** The formula for the receiving of God's word and address to the prophet ("son of man") introduce the unit in which Yahweh commands the prophet to take two sticks, to inscribe each of them and then to join the two of them into a single "stick."[8] In this instruction the עץ ("stick") remains remarkably undefined. As a rule it designates the tree (6:13; 17:24; and elsewhere) from which one harvests fruit (34:27), but it can also designate an individual piece of wood which is used as raw material for the craftman's work (15:3) or as material for lighting a fire (24:10; 39:10). In the present passage 𝔊 translates עץ by *ῥάβδος* (𝔏ʷ in v 20 has *virga*), thereby envisaging a wooden staff. This recalls Nu 17:16–26, the story of the staffs of the tribal princes of Israel and of the staff of Aaron, where 𝔊 renders the מטה ("staff, rod") of 𝔐 by *ῥάβδος*. In this priestly text the command given to Moses is קח מאתם מטה ("get from them rods"). Then, here too, there follows the commission to inscribe: איש את שמו תכתב על מטהו ואת שם אהרן תכתב על מטה לוי ("write each man's name upon his rod, and write Aaron's name upon the Rod of Levi"). 𝔗, on the other hand, points in a different direction by rendering עץ by לוחא along the lines of Is 8:1, where it renders the גליון ("tablet") of 𝔐 also by לוח, thus thinking of a wooden tablet on which writing can be inscribed. With this Hab 2:2 may be compared. In the interpretation in v 19, on the other hand, 𝔗 interprets עץ יוסף ("the stick of Joseph") and עץ יהודה ("the stick of Judah"), under the influence of 𝔐 שבטי ישראל ("the tribes of Israel"), as שיבטא דיוסף ("the tribe of Joseph") and שיבטא דיהודה ("the tribe of Judah"). The commentators of chapter 37 (vv 15ff) usually follow the exegetical tradition of 𝔊. In this case, however, one must not think of the two shepherd's staffs (club and crook) which the Palestinian shepherd still has with him to this day[9] and on the basis of which Power throws new light on the passages Ps 23:4; Zech 11:7ff; 1 Sam 17:23. An interpretation in terms of a shepherd's staff already seems to be present in the allegory in Zech 11:4–17, which speaks of the staff "Grace" and the staff "Union" as a shepherd's "two staffs" (שני מקלות).[10] More probably, however, one should think of the ruler's staff. Ezek 37:17ff seems to have been understood in this way already by Sir 47:21, where the division of the kingdoms is described as a separation "into two scepters" (לשני שבטים).[11] That the kingdom can be represented by the shoot of a tree (vine?) could be seen already in 19:11f, where in any case reference was openly made to שבטי משלים ("royal scepters"). At any rate one cannot think of a scepter in the form of a club,[12] since then the fitting together of the two pieces into a single piece is not conceivable. A different direction is taken by Barnes, who believes that the real intention of the image is along the lines of an "ingrafting" of one tribe into the other, but that this was not carried through by Ezekiel. Thus there remains an uncertainty about the understanding of the text by 𝔊. In view of the indefiniteness of עץ, which is strictly consistent in 𝔐, the interpretation of 𝔗 cannot definitely be excluded, especially since the fitting together of two wooden tablets to form a new entity can be more easily envisaged.

According to Yahweh's command, the "wood" is to be written upon. If עץ is a ruler's staff, then (as was the case with the staffs of the tribal princes in Nu 17:16–26) one would have to think of a carved mark of ownership. In the case of a wooden tablet, the recording of a dedicatory inscription can be easily envisaged. K. Galling thinks, in this instance, on the basis of his understanding of the גליון of Is 8:1f as a property title-deed, of the allocation of a portion of land to Joseph and Judah and

6 See below pp. 276–279.

7 See above p. 100.

8 See 1, 144f; on "son of man" see 1, 131f.

9 Dalman, *Arbeit*, 6. 222, 238.

10 On the relationship between Zech 11 and Ezek 37 see Friedrich Horst in Horst-Robinson, *kleinen Propheten*, and William Walter Cannon, "Some Notes on Zechariah c. 11," *AfO* 4 (1927): 146.

11 See also Rudolf Smend, *Die Weisheit des Jesus Sirach* (Berlin: Reimer, 1906), 456.

12 *BRL:* "Keule."

of the subsequent union of the portions into a larger unit, Israel.[13] In that case the sign-action would already contain not only the statement about the reunification of both parts of Israel, but also the promise of renewed allocation of land. But the whole further exposition, even in vv 20–24a, where v 21 certainly speaks of a repatriation but not of the allocation of a new portion of land, provides no further evidence for this understanding. The possibility must, however, be kept open that Ezekiel's sign-action could be determined by that of Isaiah (8:1f).[14] If we do not wish to explain the ל of the inscriptions by the uncertain assumption of a ל-*inscriptionis,* but find in it the expression of an allocation (note c), we will be unable to evade the question of what it is that is allocated. In the interpretation of the staff as a ruler's staff we can find here the confirmation of a kingdom of Judah and of Joseph and then of Israel (on this cf. the ממלכה "kingdom" of v 22). On the understanding of the "wood" as an inscribed wooden tablet the definition of what precisely is allocated remains in the balance.

The allocatory inscriptions each mention first of all a name: Joseph and Judah. Joseph was the leading tribe in the northern kingdom, which for that reason can be called (e.g., in Am 5:6,15; 6:6) simply (house of) Joseph. It is significant for Ezekiel that he does not refer to the northern kingdom by its usual name Israel. In Ezekiel the name "Israel" is confined to the covenant nation as a whole.[15] Here it first appears in the addition which mentions alongside Judah "the Israelites associated with him" (בני ישראל חבריו) and alongside Joseph "the whole house of Israel associated with him" (כל בית ישראל חבריו). These expansions of the dedicatory notes are of suspect originality to many (Hölscher, Cooke, Bertholet). If עץ is the ruler's staff then this broad designation of the ruler is in fact surprising. In the expansions "Israel" is to be understood in its original extent. Israel is the whole nation, including all twelve tribes (on this see also the allocation of land in 47:13–48:29). In both parts of divided Israel other groups are associated with the leading tribes Joseph and Judah: with Judah, Simeon and parts of Benjamin, not to speak of the Calebites, Kenizzites and Jerahmeelites who are not included in the twelve-tribe reckoning.[16] The remainder of the twelve tribes were associated with Joseph. The term חָבֵר ("associate") is not found elsewhere in Ezekiel. In Song 1:7; 8:13 it describes the companions, fellow shepherds; in Is 1:23 comrades, accomplices. In Ju 20:11 one can still hear echoes of the technical political sense "confederate." It is on this basis that the present passage is to be understood. In a secondary gloss (note g) the remark "Ephraim's stick" has been added to Joseph. The hill country of Ephraim forms the heartland of the former northern kingdom and in 733, as all that remained of the state, it received a final reprieve.[17] Thus, e.g., in Isaiah (7:2,5,8f, and elsewhere) and Hosea (4:17 and elsewhere) the name Ephraim is used for the state itself.[18] The gloss is intended to explain the less usual "Joseph."

■ **37:17** The prophet is given the further order to "bring together" (קרב) the two pieces of wood (staves?) in order to fit them together in his hand as one piece. Thus, as in v 7 the bones which were separated in death "grew together" (קרב), so that which was separated is reunited in his hand. The process, it is true, remains much less graphic than the one in v 7. The placing together of two tablets lying neatly one against the other is much more easy to visualize than the fitting together of two sticks which continue to appear as two. But the argument of clearness of presentation is much less forceful in Ezekiel than with one of the other prophets.

■ **37:18f** The interpretation of this strange action is provoked by the counter-question of the people who look on, puzzled.[19] Its wording recalls 24:19, while 12:9; 21:5,12 express the same thing more succinctly. With great emphasis the reply is then given to the prophet in v 19 as the real message which is to be proclaimed to the outside world. The content of this first "interpretation" is strange. What it contributes to the action which has just been described is simply the word of Yahweh emphasized

13 Kurt Galling, "Ein Stück judäischen Bodenrechts in Jesaia 8," *ZDPV* 56 (1933): 213 note 3.

14 See 1, 172 on the sign-action in 5:1f.

15 See Walther Zimmerli, "Israel im Buche Ezechiel," *VT* 8 (1958): 75–90, and Appendix 2.

16 On this see Noth, *History of Israel,* 55ff, 76f.

17 See Albrecht Alt, "Israels Gaue unter Salomo" in *Kleine Schriften zur Geschichte des Volkes Israel* 2 (München: Beck, 1953), 76–89.

18 See Albrecht Alt, "Die Rolle Samarias bei der Entstehung des Judentums" in *Kleine Schriften zur Geschichte des Volkes Israel* 2 (München: Beck, 1953), 319 note 1.

19 On בני עמך "members of your people" see above, p. 184.

as strongly as possible: It is I who do all this. The קח לך ... ולקח ("take ... and take") of the beginning is taken over and rephrased as הנה אני לקח ("see, I will take") in the mouth of Yahweh. Everything else, the reference to the "stick of Joseph" (to which the glossator of v 16 here adds the remark "that is in Ephraim's hand" which already seems to be thinking of a scepter), the reference to the stick of Judah, to the joining of the two into one stick and to the holding of it fast in the hand (here the hand of Yahweh) returns. A slight variation on v 16 is admittedly to be seen in the fact that as "confederates" of Joseph "the tribes of Israel" are mentioned, while there is no reference to Judah's confederates. This could lend support to the idea that this association of the חברים ("confederates") is a secondary addition which was not consistently carried through.

V 19, on this basis, contains a divine promise rather than a real interpretation of the sign-action. The latter, in its comparative lucidity, is not developed further. Quite decisively, on the other hand, the promise is made by Yahweh himself that he personally will fasten together into one unit in his hand that which was separated.

■ **37:20-24a** Thus it is understandable that, presumably somewhat later, a new attempt was made by the prophet himself or by the "school" which handed on his oracles, and the interpretation was carried out more fully.

■ **37:20** Vv 20–24a are introduced in v 20 by a free recapitulation of the sign-action with the "sticks" (עצים here in the plural). To this there is added simply the fact that the action took place "before their eyes."[20]

■ **37:21** The interpretation, which (analogous to v 19) is in the style of a proclamation to the prophet's environment, begins with the "resumption" of the הנה אני לקח ("see, I shall take").[21] In contrast to v 19, however, this has nothing more to do here with the "taking" of the sticks, but is applied to the "leading out" of the Israelites from among the nations. This has already been mentioned in 36:24, a verse which recurs here almost literally but transposed into the third person plural. The gathering together of those who have been scattered has here become the really urgent problem. The historical object of the "reunification" of the two kingdoms takes on a new shape from this futuristic aspect. Yahweh leads out his people, gathers them and brings them into their land.

■ **37:22** Here he will make them into one nation under one king. The unfortunate split into two nations and two kingdoms which burdened the past will then no longer obtain (לא יחצו עוד "they will no longer be divided"). The clearly parallel correspondence of the גוי אחד ("one nation") and מלך אחד ("one king") in v 22a to the שני גוים ("two nations") and שתי ממלכות ("two kingdoms") in v 22b strongly advises the retention of the מלך ("king") in 𝔐 (note b).[22]

■ **37:23** Then in v 23 the inner renewal of the people, which was the great theme of 36:25ff, is promised. There will be an end to their defilement by their "idols" (on גלולים see above), their "detestable things" (שקוצים 5:11; 7:20; 11:18,21; 20:7f,30) and their "rebellious deeds" (on פשע see above).[23] Yahweh will "deliver" them (הושיע also 34:22; 36:29) and purify them (36:25) so that they become his covenant people.[24] The expansion in v 24a returns once again to the theme of v 22 in that, doubtless in dependence on 34:23f (see above), David is designated as king and as the one shepherd in whom the schism is healed.[25]

By contrast with vv 15–19, vv 21–24a reveal a not inconsiderable shift of point of view. Vv 15–19, exactly like the pre-exilic statements of Jer 3:6ff; chapters 30f, spoke of a reunification of that which had been separated. Judah contrasts with "Joseph" just as, in the days of Josiah, the politically intact Judah contrasted with the house of Joseph—which was violated under the scourge of the Assyrian and was politically shattered—and sought to bring the latter home again. The basic element, vv 15–19, which doubtless stems from Ezekiel himself, is still entirely in the mold of Jeremiah's "reunification statement." Vv 21–24a, on the other hand, reveal a more realistic and serious appraisal of the situation

20 On לעיניהם ("before their eyes") in the sign-actions see 1, 170.
21 See Kuhl, "'Wiederaufnahme.'"
22 On the "mountains of Israel" see 1, 185 on 6:2f.
23 On גלולים see 1, 187; on פשע see 1, 309 on 14:11.
24 See above p. 218. On the covenant formula see 1, 262f, and Rudolf Smend, *Die Bundesformel,* ThSt 68 (Zürich: EVZ, 1963).
25 עבדי דוד ("my servant David") as in 34:23f; see above pp. 218–220, and below pp. 278f.

which had altered since 587. Here there is no longer expected the "reunification" of the two kingdoms, both of which have now disappeared, but rather the gracious divine protecting of the newly gathered people from a new schism. It is in this sense that emphasis is laid on the "one nation, one king." New in contrast with vv 15–19 is also emphasis on the concern for the inner renewal of the nation. There is no reference to any specific function which the future king might have in this context, as, e.g., a righteous judge along the lines of Is 11:9.

■ **37:24b–28** Another shift of emphasis can then be discerned in vv 24b–28, which was added somewhat later still as a further explanation. The initial theme of the sign-action in vv 15–19 has now completely disappeared. In words which recall 11:20; 20:19 but also Lev 26:3, reference is made (in relation to v 23a?) to the people's new obedience as well as to their new dwelling in the land (see v 21).

■ **37:25** The latter is expressed here in words which, partly literally, correspond to 28:25a. But then from v 25b onwards, we can discern the statement which was really intended, the key-word of which, עולם, predominates in all that follows.[26] Here is the confirmation of the sustained duration of that which has been promised anew by God. עולם serves as the "designation of the definitive nature of the coming salvation."[27] This promise is expressed in four different ways: 1) The people will acquire a lasting dwelling place in the land. They will live there till their children's children, "for ever."[28] That is God's definitive rejection of a renewed threat of exile. 2) David's rule will last "for ever."[29] Here the key-word given in v 24a is taken up and at the same time altered. Even if one were to regard the change of word order from the עבדי דוד ("my servant David") of v 24 (=34:23, 24) to דוד עבדי ("David my servant") as no more than an essentially unimportant stylistic variation, which, for all that, could reveal the hand of a different author, nevertheless the replacement of the מלך ("king") of v 24 (v 22) by נשיא ("prince") (v 25) is due to conscious reflection. This will require specific consideration.

■ **37:26** 3) The covenant of salvation is to be an "everlasting covenant." The ברית עולם ("everlasting covenant") has been mentioned already in 16:60. It was also promised during the exile by Deutero-Isaiah (55:3, see also 61:8). According to Jenni the oldest instance of this expression (2 Sam 23:5) reveals, by its following predicates ערוכה בכל ושמרה ("ordered in all things and secure"), its origin in legal language.[30] P describes God's two unconditional covenants of mercy with Noah (Gen 9:16) and Abraham (Gen 17:7, 13, 19; see also Ps 105:10; 1 Chr 16:17) as ברית עולם ("everlasting covenant"). "The predicate עולם does not here describe any transcendentalizing of these entities."[31] ברית עולם ("everlasting covenant") in the present passage describes the ברית שלום ("covenant of salvation"), which was already promised in 34:25 and to which is thereby attributed inviolability.[32] The increase in population, which is briefly mentioned as the only specification of the salvation (missing in 𝔊, see note b), was more fully treated in 36:10f, 37. This echoes the old promise to the patriarchs. 4) Finally, "for ever" (לעולם)—and here obviously the highest climax of the promise is reached—Yahweh's sanctuary is to stand in the midst of his people. There is to be no further destruction of the temple by fire. The reference to the new sanctuary touches on the great theme of chapters 40–48, which was already indicated in 20:40f. What is revealed in chapters 40–48 of the reality of the new sanctuary (the בתוכם "in their midst" is made geographically visible in the allocation of land in 48:1–29) is here described as an irrevocable gift. The sanctuary is described first of all by the term usual in Ezekiel מקדשי (5:11; 8:6; 9:6; and elsewhere).

■ **37:27** Alongside this, however, there appears a term which is quite unique in the book of Ezekiel, משכני ("my dwelling place"). משכן ("dwelling place") also occurs in 25:4 in a secular context. In that 2 Sam 7:6 speaks of Yahweh's moving about in Israel's pre-Jerusalem period באהל ובמשכן ("in a tent for my dwelling"), then this

26 On this see Jenni, "Das Wort 'ōlām."
27 Jenni, "Das Wort 'ōlām," 70.
28 On עד עולם ("for ever") see Jenni, "Das Wort 'ōlām," 34–38.
29 On לעולם ("for ever") see Jenni, "Das Wort 'ōlām," 39–43.
30 Jenni, "Das Wort 'ōlām," 74.
31 Jenni, "Das Wort 'ōlām," 73.
32 See above p. 220.

passage might suggest that the expression משכן ("dwelling place"), which is frequently used by P in connection with the אהל מועד ("tent of meeting," has a long prehistory.[33] The expression, which was originally connected with the old tent of revelation, would then have been used in a later period in isolated passages to refer in an archaizing way also to the Jerusalem temple. So 1 Chr 6:33; 2 Chr 29:6; Ps 26:8; 74:7.[34] According to von Rad, משכן ("dwelling place") belongs in the sphere of presence theology associated with the ark.[35] A different view, however, is presented by L. Rost, who feels that 2 Sam 7:6 is, at the earliest, Deuteronomic.[36] And W. Schmidt points to the Ugaritic parallels which suggest that the word is to be attributed originally to the Canaanite-Jerusalem sphere.[37] In the present passage the משכן ("dwelling place"), on account of the verbal element which stands out more strongly in it, may have been added: Yahweh dwells "with" (על) his people.[38] Thereby this people, as is finally stated by means of the covenant formula (see above on v 23), really become the people of the covenant. V 27 is remarkably closely related to Lev 26:11f.

■ **37:28** The recognition formula in v 28 concludes the proof-saying of vv 24b–28, and thus Yahweh is recognized in the international world as the one who has sanctified Israel, i.e. reserved her for himself. The proximity of this קדש ("sanctify"), which is surrounded by the verbal range of the election concept, to the idea of election is pointed out by K. Koch.[39] 20:12 had mentioned the Sabbath as the sign of recognition of this sanctifying separation of Israel.[40] Here it is the fact that Yahweh's sanctuary stands in Israel's midst "for all time" (לעולם). By this final accentuation it is once more underlined that this is the greatest of the four עולם-gifts mentioned in vv 25–27. In the citing of the nations, however, it is made clear that the realization of the מקדשי בתוכם ("my sanctuary in their midst"), which is described in chapters 40–48 without any reference to the nations, is to be understood as the central event in which Yahweh is acknowledged throughout the world.

At this point a brief pause must now be made and, looking back on what has been said hitherto in the book of Ezekiel about Israel's ruler, a summary drawn up.

First of all, as far as the terminology is concerned, it can be stated at the outset that both מלך ("king") and נשיא ("prince") are used to describe non-Israelite rulers. The great king of Babylon and the Pharaoh of Egypt (30:13 probably does not refer to the Pharaoh, see note d there) are always called מלך ("king"). The king of Tyre is also called מלך ("king") in 28:12 (28:2 נגיד "prince"). נשיאים ("princes") is the name given to princes of the coastlands (26:16; alongside that in 27:35 also מלכי איים "kings of the coastlands"), of Kedar (27:21), of Edom (32:29; on the מלכיה which occurs here see note b *ad loc.*). See also the נשיא ראש ("chief prince") Gog (38:2f; 39:1). In the designation of the earlier and contemporary rulers of Israel (Judah) the title נשיא ("prince") predominates (7:27; 12:10, 12; 19:1; 21:17, 30; 22:6).[41] מלך ("king") occurs in the (secondary) superscription 1:2, in the gloss 7:27 (see note a), in the prose narrative in 17:12 (it is also implied in the ממליך אתו "made him king" of 17:16).[42] See also 43:7, 9. On this basis one can conclude that נשיא ("prince") is the title for the king of Jerusalem which is preferred by Ezekiel, especially in elevated language, but that (against Böhmer and others) the title מלך ("king") is by no means excluded in basic polemic. This picture is confirmed even where Ezekiel (and his school) is speaking of the future king. Where the juxtaposition of "nation" (גוי) and "kingdom" (ממלכה)

33 So Cross, "Tabernacle," 65–68; Fritz Dumermuth, "Zur deuteronomischen Kulttheologie und ihren Voraussetzungen," *ZAW* 70 (1958): 59–98.

34 See Dumermuth (see preceding fn.), 65.

35 von Rad, *OT Theology*, 1. 235ff.

36 Leonhard Rost, "Die Wohnstätte des Zeugnisses" in *Festschrift Friedrich Baumgärtel zum 70. Geburtstag* (Erlangen: Universitätsbund Erlangen, 1959), 158–165.

37 Werner Schmidt, "מִשְׁכָּן als Ausdruck Jerusalemer Kultsprache," *ZAW* 75 (1963): 91f.

38 On this see the שכן בתוך in 43:7, 9.

39 Koch, "Geschichte," 219.

40 See 1,410.

41 On this see 1,209, and E. A. Speiser, "Background and Function of the Biblical *nāśī'*," *CBQ* 25 (1963): 111–117.

42 See 1,364 on 17:12.

suggests the parallels גוי ("nation") and מלך ("king"), the future ruler can also actually be described as מלך ("king") (37:22 and the related v 24). Only in the latest sections does נשיא ("prince") seem to be more firmly established. Thus the expansion in 37:24b–28 no longer takes up the מלך ("king") proffered by 37:22 (24a), but goes back to the נשיא ("prince") of 34:24. Above all, it will be seen in chapters 40–48 that the title נשיא ("prince") for the future ruler of Israel has clearly won the day, even in the prosaic legal texts. Even here, however, 43:7, 9 are retrospective and are different.

But this leads directly on to the factual question about Ezekiel's "messianic" statements. What does the prophet say about the role of Israel's future ruler?

One cannot answer this question at all without a brief consideration of Ezekiel's position with regard to Israel's older traditions. Ezekiel belongs to later prophecy. In his oracles (and in the expansions by those who passed on his oracles) different streams of tradition begin to mix. Thus we believed it possible to find in him elements of the prophecy of Amos, Hosea, and especially of Jeremiah.[43] In awareness of and with the acceptance of older traditions, some of which are themselves very heterogeneous, the prophet formulates his own message which has doubtless been determined by very personal factors.

This is true where the prophet's statements about Israel's future ruler find expression. Israel is aware of voices which are sharply and critically opposed to earthly kingship among the people of Yahweh because they see in it a threat to Yahweh's kingship, which is alone admissible. Among the prophets, the prophet of the northern kingdom, Hosea, in the context of his theology of the exodus tradition, is the champion of these voices, which in the narrative sphere can be heard particularly in 1 Samuel 8; 10:17–27; 12.[44] It is scarcely entirely by chance that the only passage which in the book of Ezekiel gives emphatic expression to the kingship of Yahweh (verbal מלך "to be king") is to be found in 20:33 in the introduction to the description of the new exodus.[45] In the description of the new settlement which then follows there is no mention at all of a future ruler of Israel. Instead, the description ends with the promise of a new cult on "the high mountain of Israel" (20:40). Of a specific polemic against kingship because that institution was the equivalent of a "breach of covenant," there is certainly no trace.[46]

Rather, a majority of other passages show that the prophet, for all his harsh polemic against Israel's sinful princes (22:6, 25), especially the last, covenant-breaking king Zedekiah (17:12ff; described as נשיא "prince" in 21:30; see also 12:10ff), is also aware of the divine promise to the house of David and, in this the successor of Isaiah, cannot see the consummation of Israel's salvation without a divine affirmation of the royal house of David. Thus 17:22–24 spoke of the restoration to new glory of the one who had for the time being been brought low. Nevertheless, it may appear strange that no further individual characteristics of the description of the future royal figure are to be found and, above all, that the future glory is specifically connected, as in 20:40, with "the high mountain of Israel." In what happens up there the majesty of Yahweh is revealed in the eyes of the nations and demands their acknowledgment. From quite a different aspect 34:23f expresses its point of view of the future ruler. In association with the Jeremianic tradition the latter is here presented as the counterpart of the wicked shepherds. It is also strange here that the active function of this shepherd is not in any way more closely defined. In this respect the רעה אחד ("single shepherd") in 34:23 seemed already to presuppose what was said in 37:20–23, where, once again in new perspective, reference was made to the future ruler. It was a question of the re-establishment of Israel's unity. The one future ruler is here the representative of the newly-won unity. In 34:23f the statement about the future shepherd, as discussed above, has then been linked with the oracle of expectation which was

43 For Amos see 1, 203 on 7:2; for Hosea, 1, 335 on chapter 16; for Isaiah, 1, 172 on 5:1f; for Jeremiah, 1, 136f on 3:1–3, 1, 482 on chapter 23, and elsewhere.

44 See Wolff, *Hosea*, 167, on Hos 9:15; 227, on Hos 13:10.

45 See 1, 414f.

46 Haag, *Untersuchung*, 75.

probably coined in the period of Josiah, "Yahweh their God and David their king" (Hos 3:5; Jer 30:9).[47]

At the same time, the term נשיא ("prince"), which is more frequent in Ezekiel, found its way into the formula. That the representative of Israel's unity was described precisely as "David" is easily understandable. Was not David not only the recipient of the Nathan promise in 2 Samuel 7, but, alongside his son Solomon, also the only ruler under whom Israel was a united nation? On the basis of the formulation in 34:24 there has been added, at a somewhat later time, to the bipartite covenant formula in 37:23 the reference to David in v 24a, whereby in dependence on v 22 the title מלך ("king") has been happily retained. Only the final addition in 37:24b–28 has replaced it by the title נשיא ("prince"). In this last formulation, however, there emerges unmistakably a tendency which had already appeared clearly in 17:22–24. The expectation of the prophet (and of his school) envisages something new which Yahweh will do on "the high mountain of Israel." On this mountain, which Yahweh describes at the same time in 20:40 as הר קדשי ("my holy mountain"), it is not in the long run the prince of Israel who is the decisive factor, but the sanctuary newly founded there by God—and God's own dwelling in it (on this see also Is 2:2–4; Mic 4:1–4). This has already been stated in 20:40. In 37:24b–28 it is further underlined by placing the David promise before the clearly emphasized promise of God's holy dwelling place. And thus, finally, in the eschatological plan in chapters 40–48 and in the assignment of the נשיא ("prince") there, even details are regulated. H. Meulenbelt correctly evaluates the "messianic statements" of the book of Ezekiel: "Zij hebben meer betrekking op het heil, dan op eenen 'Heiland.'"[48]

From this it is understandable that the figure of the future king never at any point acquires fuller life as a person and in this respect remains far behind Is 9:5f; 11:1–9 and even Mic 5:1–3 and Zech 9:9. The prince is shepherd, representative of Israel's unity, is object of a glory whereby the nations recognize how Yahweh can bring low and raise up. In no passage, however, is there any specific activity ascribed to him as there is, e.g., even to the anointed one of Haggai and Zechariah with regard to the rebuilding of the temple. The name David, to which Yahweh adds the usual apposition עבדי ("my servant"), is the only concrete element.[49] But this name carries with it here something of the timelessness of a cipher, to which the לעולם ("for ever") can then also be added and which demands no further graphic development. The more concrete delineation of the "messianic salvation" which is found throughout Ezekiel takes a different path in spite of its adherence to the David-Messiah promise. In the great description in chapters 40–48 all the glory of the time of fulfillment rests on Yahweh's presence in the midst of his people and on the place where this presence becomes reality. The "prince" stands as a servant figure on the fringe of this event. It is remarkable that in the case of the other prophet of the exile, with regard to the David promise, in spite of all the differences in the details in Is 55:3–5, one can make basically very similar observations.

Aim

Judah had experienced under her king Josiah a liberating reformation. From the multiplicity of cultic centers and forms of belief there has been a turning towards Yahweh, the unique one (Dtn 6:4) who wished to have his worship practised in the one place chosen by him. In these days a wound in Israel's history has begun to throb anew. There was once *one* people of God, one Israel of twelve tribes. After an elevated initial period it was shattered. Two different standards were raised and supporters rallied round. Two scepters were raised and claimed superiority and tore the unity of the people of the twelve tribes of the community of God into two separate "confederacies" (חברים): Judah here! Joseph here!

The wound continued to throb in the decades after Josiah and in the terrible events of that period. The prophet Ezekiel, who was called in the days of deep darkness to proclaim the salvation of his God who wishes to save his people from death, is sent to proclaim healing for this wound also. His hand, which "brings together" (קרב) the two "sticks" on which he had previously scratched the two party slogans "Judah" and "Joseph," may be the symbol for the mighty hand of God, who will

47 See above pp. 218f.

48 Hendrik Huibrecht Meulenbelt, *De prediking van den profeet Ezechiël* (Utrecht: Breijer, 1888), 185, quoted by Haag, *Untersuchung*, 69: "They are more concerned with salvation than with a 'savior'" [Trans.].

49 See above pp. 218–220.

seize those who have been separated and will bring them together into the unity of his community. God does not wish the separation of his community but its unity. But because he is the God who promises a future for his community, he does not simply stand lamenting before the breach in his community, but promises that he will bring together with his own hand what has gone astray along separate roads and in reciprocally hardening attitudes. This is proclaimed to God's people.

The promise had subsequently acquired a heightened exposition. Men were still staring at the one "historical" schism in God's community which had occurred at a given point in time. And meanwhile God's judgment had struck them much more severely and more threateningly and had torn them apart and scattered them in all directions, so that the "historical" schism might now appear, in the face of that, almost only like a slight knock. So the prophet is summoned to proclaim, concerning this more serious distress, that God's hand will reach out here too and will bring together that which had been torn a thousandfold. Here too God stands by the promise made to his own, one, holy people, the promise which their belief in God can acknowledge in their confession of faith down through the ages. At the same time, however, the promise in its exposition extends in two directions: this unity will not be created by a human organization which would then be able to drive the people of God into a forced unity more successfully than in an earlier period or in the long run with more powerful means and more powerful threats than in an earlier period (1 Kgs 12:10f), but the one king set by God over his own people will be the symbol of the unity. And the other direction is connected directly with this: God will heal and rescue (והושעתי "I will rescue") his people, so that they put away their idols and detestable things round which they had previously gathered and as a result of which they had split in two. God will make his people clean (וטהרתי "I will make clean"). Without the turning away from the things of old, unity cannot become a reality. Only the "new heart" of which 36:26 had spoken as the result of purification (v 25) can, in God-given innocence, become free to renounce all the obduracies in which new standards are raised, new "confessionalities" and "confederacies" to false standards could emerge. Only the new heart will be able to leave as simply one what God in his mercy has called to oneness.

When in v 24a the name "David" is again set over this unit, this is undoubtedly not intended as the call of a reactionary reversion to some kind of "conservative" programme around which, as round a new symbol of schism, a new sect could gather. The "anointed one" is not set in the community by God so that the new party of "Christ people" (1 Cor 1:12) could in a new way be aware that their special righteousness was confirmed in him.

The last expansion in vv 24b–28 has then gone beyond what was said and on the basis of that has declared that what God promises to his community will become definitive. The community of the people of God are to know that they are moving towards a goal in which they can remain at home "in the land" and need no longer wander homeless abroad. "There remains still a rest for the people of God" (Heb 4:9). They are to know that the saving covenant made by God is unbreakable, that the name of his servant "David" which he has set over them is irremovable and that in all this God will, once for all, take up his dwelling among his people.

It is towards such hope that the prophetic word directs the people of God, so that, on such a basis, they can also bear the affliction of the present with upturned face. It assures them that in this fourfold final act by which God sanctifies the people amongst whom he himself dwells the mystery of the divine truth will be discernible to all nations.

Assault on and the End of Chief Prince Gog of Meshech and Tubal

Bibliography

J. G. Aalders
Gog en Magog in Ezechiël (Kampen: Kok, 1951).

W. F. Albright
"Contributions to Biblical Archaeology and Philology," *JBL* 43 (1924): 363–393 (3. 'Gog und Magog,' 378–385).

George Ricker Berry
"The Date of Ezekiel 38:1–39:20," *JBL* 41 (1922): 224–232.

Julius A. Bewer
"Das Tal der Wanderer in Hesekiel 39:11," *ZAW* 56 (1938): 123–125.

Julius Boehmer
"Wer ist Gog von Magog? Ein Beitrag zur Auslegung des Buches Ezechiel," *ZWTh* 40 (1897): 321–355.

A. van den Born
"Études sur quelques toponymes bibliques," *OTS* 10 (1954): 197–214 (1. 'Le pays du Magog,' 197–201).

George Wesley Buchanan
"Eschatology and the 'End of Days,'" *JNES* 20 (1961): 188–193.

Wilhelm Caspari
"*ṭabur* (Nabel)," *ZDMG* 86 (1933): 49–65.

Brevard S. Childs
"The Enemy From the North and the Chaos Tradition," *JBL* 78 (1959): 187–198.

E. Dhorme
"Les peuples issus de Japhet d'après le chapitre X de la Genèse" in *Recueil Édouard Dhorme; Études bibliques et orientales* (Paris: Imprimerie nationale, 1951), 167–189 (= *Syria* 13 [1932], 28–49).

L. Dürr
Die Stellung des Propheten Ezechiel in der israelitisch-jüdischen Apokalyptik, AA IX 1 (Münster: Aschendorff, 1923), especially 63–108.

Gillis Gerleman
"Hesekielsbokens Gog," *Svensk exegetisk årsbok* 12 (1947): 132–146.

Hugo Gressmann
Der Messias, FRLANT 26 (Göttingen, 1929).

Hugo Gressmann
Der Ursprung der iraelitisch-jüdischen Eschatologie, FRLANT 6 (Göttingen, 1905).

Severin Grill
"Der Schlachttag Jahwes," *BZ* 2 (1958): 278–283.

Hermann Gunkel
"Gog und Magog," *RGG*² 2, 1303.

J. Halévy
"Gog et Magog," *Revue sémitique* 12 (1904): 370–375.

Johannes Herrmann
Ezechielstudien, BWAT 2 (Leipzig, 1908), especially 37–48.

H. Holma
"Zum 'Nabel der Erde,'" *OLZ* 18 (1915): 41–43.
Gustav Hölscher
Drei Erdkarten; ein Beitrag zur Erdkenntnis des hebräischen Altertums (Heidelberg: Winter, 1949).
G. Hüsing
"Gūgu (678–643)," *OLZ* 18 (1915): 299–303.
Paul Joüon
"יַד = *jet* (Nombres 35:17–18; Ez 39:9)," *Mélanges de la faculté orientale de l'université Saint Joseph. Beyrouth* 6 (1913): 166f.
Carl A. Keller
"Gog und Magog," *RGG*³ 2, 1683f.
A. Knobel
Die Völkertafel der Genesis. Ethnographische Untersuchungen (Giessen: Ricker, 1850).
E. König
"Zur Vorgeschichte des Namens Russen," *ZDMG* 70 (1916): 92–96.
Aarre Lauha
ZAPHON, Der Norden und die Nordvölker im Alten Testament (Helsinki: Der Finnischen Literaturgesellschaft, 1943), especially 68–72.
John L. Myres
"Gog and the Danger from the North in Ezekiel," *Palestine Exploration Fund, Quarterly Statement* (1932): 213–219.
Conrad von Orelli
"Gog und Magog," *Realencyklopädie für protestantische Theologie und Kirche*³ 6, 761–763.
Louis Piotrowicz
"L'invasion des Scythes en Asie Antérieure au VIIᵉ siècle av. J.-C.," *Eos* 32 (1929): 473–508.
Edzard Rohland
Die Bedeutung der Erwählungstraditionen Israels für die Eschatologie der alttestamentlichen Propheten, Unpub. Diss. (Heidelberg, 1956).
W. H. Roscher
Der Omphalosgedanke bei verschiedenen Völkern, besonders den semitischen. Ein Beitrag zur vergleichenden Religionswissenschaft, Volkskunde und Archäologie (1918).
H. Schmidt
Der heilige Fels in Jerusalem (Tübingen: J. C. B. Mohr [Paul Siebeck], 1933).
K. F. Smith
"The Tale of Gyges and the King of Lydia," *American Journal of Philology* 23 (1902): 261–282, 361–387.
W. Staerk
"Der Gebrauch der Wendung באחרית הימים im at. Kanon," *ZAW* 11 (1891): 247–253.
Max Uhlemann
"Ueber Gog und Magog," *ZWTh* 5 (1862): 265–286.
Roland de Vaux
"Magog-Hiérapolis (Histoire d'une fausse exégèse)," *RB* 43 (1934): 568–571.

Arent Jan Wensinck
The Ideas of the Western Semites concerning the Navel of the Earth (Amsterdam: Müller, 1916).

H. Winckler
"Gog" in *Altorientalische Forschungen* 2 (Leipzig: Pfeiffer, 1898), 160–171.

On later history

Andrew Runni Anderson
Alexander's Gate, Gog and Magog, and the inclosed Nations (Cambridge, Mass.: The Mediaeval Academy of America, 1932).

Hugo Bieling
Zu den Sagen von Gog und Magog, Wissenschaftliche Beilage zum Programm der Sophien-Realschule. Ostern 1882 (Berlin: Weidmannsch Buchhandlung, 1882).

Hans Bietenhard
Das tausendjährige Reich; eine biblisch-theologische Studie (Bern: Graf-Lehmann, 1944), especially 51f.

Wilhelm Bousset and Hugo Gressmann
Die Religion des Judentums im späthellenistischen Zeitalter, HBNT 21 (Tübingen: Mohr [Siebeck], ^{3}1926), especially 219–222.

Theo. Brown
"A Note on Gog," *Folk-lore* (London) 61 (1950): 98–103.

M. J. de Goeje
De muur van Gog en Magog, 1888.

Bernhard Heller
"Gog und Magog im jüdischen Schrifttum" in *Jewish Studies in Memory of George A. Kohut,* ed. Salo W. Baron and Alexander Marx (New York: The Alexander Kohut Memorial Foundation, 1935), 350–358.

S. H. Hooke
"Gog and Magog," *ET* 26 (1914/15): 317–319.

K. G. Kuhn
"Γὼγ καὶ Μαγώγ," *TDNT* 1, 789–791.

Hermann L. Strack and Paul Billerbeck
Kommentar zum Neuen Testament aus Talmud und Midrasch 3 (München: Beck, ^{2}1956–1961), 831–840.

38

1 **[a]And the word of Yahweh came to me: 2/**
Son of man, turn your face towards Gog
[<to the land of Magog>][a], the chief

38: 38a 𝔖 prefixes the superscription: Against those of
1 the house of Gog and Magog who came up against
those who had returned from Babylon (סלקו "have
come up"). 𝔊$^{Qmg\ sup}$ 𝔖^{h} (Arm) ἐπὶ Γωφ καὶ μαγωγ.
2 2a 𝔐 ארץ המגוג is linked in 𝔊 καὶ τὴν γῆν τοῦ
Μαγωγ, 𝔖 ועל ארעא דמגוג by means of the copula
with גוג (see 1:4 note a), is completely omitted by
𝔊^{62}, while 𝔅 𝔗 attest 𝔐. The occurrence of the
article with מגוג, which is otherwise attested only
without the article (39:6; Gen 10:2; 1 Chr 1:5), is
strange but is already presupposed by 𝔊 (𝔖), which
in addition seem to understand the word as a per-

prince[b] of Meshech and Tubal, and prophesy against him 3/ and say[a]: Thus has [the Lord][b] Yahweh said: See, I am against you[c], Gog[d], you chief prince[e] of Meshech and Tubal, 4/ [and I will turn you round[a] and will put hooks in your jaws] and will lead you out[b] (- you) and all your army, horses and riders, all of them[c]

sonal name. So too the superscription (v 1 note a); Rev 20:8; *Sib. Or.* III 319f, 512. An easier reading would be gained by dividing the words ארצה מגוג (Cooke and others). On the ה of direction in the gesture recommended see דרך תימנה in 21:2, which is admittedly not exactly similar in form. But since the expression does not subsequently recur, but in a strange way separates the name of Gog from his title, it is most probably to be regarded as a secondary addition. See further the exposition.

b In 𝔐 נשיא ראש משך ותבל 𝔊 ἄρχοντα Ρως Μοσοχ καὶ Θοβελ takes the ראש as the name of a country, while 𝔖, which coordinates נשיא ראש by the insertion of the copula (מדברנא ורישא), finds in the expression a title. So too 𝔅 (Jerome dependent on 'A) *principem capitis* and 𝔗 רב ריש, which in close relationship to 𝔐 connect the words and correctly see in them an intensification of the title of נשיא. On the basis of the grammatical consideration that the construct formation נשיא ראש with the following designation משך ותבל should then, more correctly, have been connected by means of ל, Cooke regards נשיא as a secondary interpretation of ראש. See the exposition.

3 3a 𝔊 amplifies (καὶ εἶπον) αὐτῷ.

b אדני is lacking in 𝔊, see Appendix 1.

c 𝔗 again paraphrases הא אנא שלח רוגזי עלך. Humbert, "'hinnenî êlékâ,'" 108, correctly perceives in the present passage a use of the summons formula which deviates from the normal. It is not, however, to be emended. See the exposition of 39:1.

d 𝔐 גוג. 𝔊[87] Μαγωγ. Tht Γωγ καὶ Μαγωγ. The address is missing in 𝔊[B,967] Arm.

e See v 2 note b.

4 4a 𝔐 ושובבתיך occurs also in 39:2 and the po'lel of שוב also in 39:27; Is 47:10; 49:5; 58:12; Jer 8:5; 50:19; Ps 23:3; 60:3 and the po'lal in 38:8. 𝔅 renders *et circumagam te*, 𝔖 less precisely ואכנשך, 𝔗 ואשדלינך "I persuade you." On 𝔊 see note b.

b To the whole passage in 𝔐 ושובבתיך ונתתי חחים בלחייך והוצאתי אותך there corresponds in 𝔊 simply καὶ συνάξω σε. Only the later tradition in 𝔊[OL] 𝔎[Bo] 𝔄 Arm Tht follows 𝔐 and reads καὶ περιστρέψω (𝔊[26,239] 𝔄 συνάξω) σε (κυκλόθεν) καὶ δώσω χαλινὸν εἰς τὰς σιαγόνας σου καὶ συνάξω (𝔊[149,26,239] 𝔄 πλανήσω) σε. Thus 𝔊 does not seem to attest 𝔐 ושובבתיך ונתתי חחים בלחייך. But a certain difficulty remains in the fact that 𝔐 ושובבתיך in 39:2 is translated in 𝔊 by συνάξω, and this raises the question whether 𝔊 in 38:4 did not also have ושובבתיך before it, while in the original then the words ונתתי . . . והוצאתי אותך might have been missing. שובב in 39:27 (38:8) is rendered by ἀποστρέψαι. At any rate the image which is known from 29:4 (Is 37:29) of subjugation with hooks will originally have been foreign to the text, since one certainly does not expect it here in the exposition of the whole event. 𝔖 explicates the "leading out" by the addition of מן אתרך.

c 𝔐 מכלול see 23:12. 𝔊 makes the reference to armor more precise (ἐνδεδυμένους) θώρακας and is

armed, a great company [buckler and shield, all of them armed with swords][d] 5/ [Persia, Cush and Put are with them, all of them: shield and helmet][a], 6/ Gomer and all his hordes[a], Beth Togarma, the furthest north [and all his hordes[a]][b], many nations are with you. 7/

followed by 𝔙 *loricis,* 𝔖 זינא "weapon."

d The unconnected addition of 𝔐 צנה ומגן . . . תפשׂי is strange but is attested by 𝔊, which does admittedly deviate slightly *πέλται καὶ περικεφαλαῖαι* (וכובע ?, v 5 note a) *καὶ μάχαιραι.* 𝔖 tries to create a smooth syntactical connection, links בניזכא ובסכנא ("with lances and shields") to what goes before with the addition of a ב and connects what follows by means of the copula ואחידי סיפא. The final כלהון is connected with v 5 (see v 5 note a). 𝔙 connects צנה ומגן as an accusative with the following (חרב) תפשׂי, necessitating the insertion of the copula, and also omits the כלם: *hastam et clipeum arripientium et gladium.* 𝔗, finally, inserts a transitional participle דמזיינין ("who are armed") and a preposition בעגילין ותריסין; v 4bβ=𝔐. The whole addition in 𝔐 is to be regarded (with Herrmann, Cooke, Fohrer) as a secondary enrichment. On מגן וצנה see 39:9, as well as 23:24. The concluding תפשׂי חרבות כלם, on the other hand, copies in its formation the preceding לבשׁי מכלול כלם.

5 5a As in v 4, here too there an be observed the effort on the part of the versions to correct syntactically a text which has been pieced together out of two later additions. 𝔊 *Πέρσαι καὶ Αἰθίοπες καὶ Λίβυες* (Θ Αιλαμ *καὶ* Χους *καὶ* Φουδ; 𝔊[A] 𝔄 Arm *καὶ* Λυδοί cf. 27:10) *παντες περικεφαλαίαις καὶ πέλταις* not only inserts (as does 𝔖) the copula before פוט (see 1:4 note a) and omits אתם, but takes מגן וכובע in an instrumental sense. So too 𝔙 *scutati et galeati,* 𝔖 with the insertion of the preposition בסכרא ובסנורתא. 𝔗, as in v 4, with a participle מזיינין בעגילין וקולסין. In addition, 𝔖 also takes the כלם of the end of v 4 with v 5a and suppresses the כלם of v 5b. In fact, v 5a is to be regarded as the addition of typical mercenary troops, who now stand in a clumsy way before the reference in v 6 to the real allies, who are geographically connected with Gog. In this connection see the descriptive אתם alongside the אתך of v 6 which fits the address form of the text. In v 5b, however, one can recognize the variant (added by means of the catchword כלם) of the צנה ומגן of v 4b (cf. 𝔊, note d).

6 6a 𝔐 אגפיה (אגפיו). 𝔊 *οἱ περὶ αὐτόν*; 𝔖 (חילהון) חילה; 𝔙 *agmina eius* (*robur eius,* corresponding to 𝔊[L] Tht *τὰ ὑποστηρίγματα αὐτοῦ*); 𝔗 משירייתהא (משיריתהון).

b 𝔐 ואת כל אגפיו with introductory את, which should not be lightly deleted, does not fit the context. The expression is a secondary expansion which is formed in dependence on v 6a*a* and which fails to notice that the original text introduced the two proper names each with an addition of its own. Here one cannot avoid noticing a slight rhythmic element in uniform three-stress lines. The conjecturing (Bertholet, Fohrer) of a מירכתי in 𝔐 on the basis of 𝔊 *ἀπ' ἐσχάτου βορρᾶ* and of v 15, where the expression occurs in a different context, is not recommended either. Also, the insertion of the copula at

Stand and prepare yourself[a], you and your whole company which have been mobilized for[b] you, and be at <my>[c] service. 8/ After a long time[a] you[b] will be summoned[c], at the end of the years you[b] will come to a land which has been recovered from the sword,[d] has been gathered together again from among the many nations on the mountains of Israel[e] which for long[f] lay waste—which has been led out[g] from among the nations, and they all dwell securely—9/ and you will arise like the thunderstorm, will come[a] like the cloud, to cover the land <>[b] [you and all your hordes and many

the beginning of v 6b in 𝔊 𝔖 𝔙 represents a secondary smoothing. See 1:4 note a.

7 7a 𝔐 הכן והכן לך. 𝔊 makes it more concise here by omitting the copula *ἑτοιμάσθητι ἑτοίμασον*, 𝔖 by telescoping into a single verb אתטיב ("make ready"). Ezekiel is elsewhere fond of such double expressions, cf. שובו והשיבו 14:6; 18:30; without variation of the verbal form התשפט (אתם) התשפט 20:4; 22:2; but also יען [ו]ביען 13:10; 36:3.

b אל–על cf. 1:17 note a.

c 𝔐 והיית להם למשמר is attested by 𝔖 והוי להון מטרתא, 𝔗 ותהי להון למטרא and in another way also by 𝔙 *eis in praeceptum.* 𝔊 is different *καὶ ἔσῃ μοι εἰς προφυλακήν*. In 𝔐 one will think rather of the function of care and protection which the commander exercises towards his troops (Koehler-Baumgartner היה למשמר "give cover") than with 𝔙 of the command which they have to obey for him. Driver, "Ezekiel," 303f, takes משמר as "place of assembly," i.e. as something which is under observation (שמר). This could be compared with Ewald's earlier suggestion "and for those for whom you serve as a banner." This line of thought, which has to do with the relationship between Gog and his followers, is somewhat surprising after the sharp imperative which seems to be a command to Gog from Yahweh. Thus 𝔊, which refers the משמר to submission to Yahweh (לי), has probably preserved the original reading. On this basis then Cornill has "Be my reserves," following Hitzig "Be at my command."

8 8a 𝔐 מימים רבים. 𝔖 מן יומתא קדמיא "from earlier days." 𝔊 *ἀφ' ἡμερῶν πλειόνων*.

b 𝔊 misunderstands 𝔐 תפקד and תבוא as third person feminines and also translates תבוא twice *ἑτοιμασθήσεται . . . ἐλεύσεται καὶ ἥξει*. 𝔗 inserts before תפקד: "Your camp (משיריתך) (is counted)."

c 𝔊 𝔖 add the copula, see 1:4 note a.

d 𝔙 𝔖 add the copula.

e 𝔊 *ἐπὶ γῆν Ισραηλ*.

f 𝔐 תמיד literally "constantly."

g 𝔖 reveals a text which is freely transposed and greatly curtailed. V 8aβ is inserted into v 8aα על טורא דאיסראיל ועל ארעא דאשתינת מן חרבא; v 8aγ and v 8bβ are omitted entirely. In 𝔏^{W}, on the other hand, the translation jumps, as a consequence of homoioteleuton, from the first מעמים to the second מעמים and omits the intervening text.

9 9a 𝔊 (𝔏^{W}) connects the verb, by means of the copula, to what precedes; see 1:4 note a. 𝔖 adds the copula but omits any rendering of תבוא. 𝔙 (*ascendens,* cf. 𝔏^{W} *ascendentes*) subordinates the first verb to the second, thus rendering the copula unnecessary (it is retained, inconsistently, in 𝔏^{W} in dependence on 𝔊), but in its place it adds one before the second comparison (*et quasi nubes*). All these are free, secondary, stylistic variations. So too 𝔗 כענא דסליק וחפי ית ארעא.

b 𝔐 תהיה, which 𝔊 introduces with the copula

nations with you][c].

10 Thus has [the Lord][a] Yahweh said: And it
will be[b] on that day that thoughts[c] will
arise in your mind and you will think of an
evil plan 11/ and say: I will go up against
an undefended country[a], will come upon
peaceful people[b] who dwell securely—
they all dwell securely, without walls
and[c] bars, and (even) gates they do not
have—12/ to seize spoil and carry off
booty, to turn your hand[a] against (re-)
inhabited ruins and against[b] a nation
which has been gathered from among
the nations[c], (<people) who have>[d]
acquired (for themselves) cattle and
goods[e], who live at the navel[f] of the
earth. 13/ Sheba and Dedan and the
merchants of Tarshish[a] and all <their
traders>[b] say to you: Do you come to

(1:4 note a) and which 𝔖 𝔙 correctly omit, is an inelegant secondary insertion which disrupts the syntactical context. But see also v 16 note b.

c 𝔐 אוֹתָךְ = אִתָּךְ, see 2:1 note a. V 9b arouses the suspicion that it is an addition, supplied from the vocabulary of v 6, which has the duty of summarizing once again vv 3–9 (which have been heavily expanded by additions).

10 10a אדני is lacking in 𝔊 𝔏^{W}. 𝔊^{B} *κύριος κύριος*, 𝔊^{A} *κύριος ὁ θεός*, see Appendix 1.

b 𝔐 והיה is omitted by 𝔏^{W} 𝔙 𝔖—for stylistic reasons? See also v 18; 39:11.

c 𝔐 דברים "words," 𝔗 הרהורין cf. Dan 4:2.

11 11a 𝔐 על ארץ פרזות. 𝔊 *ἐπὶ γῆν ἀπερριμμένην* (𝔏^{W} *super terram projectam*) "a rejected land." 𝔖 על ארעא כהינתא "a rich (prosperous) land." On the meaning of פרזות see Zech 2:8, hence 𝔙 *ad terram absque muro*, 𝔗 על ארעא דיתבא קירוי פצחיא "which is inhabited in open village settlements."

b 𝔐 אבוא השקטים should be divided more correctly as אבואה שקטים. Cornill, Fohrer insert על. 𝔊 emphasizes more fully *ἡσυχάζοντας ἐν ἡσυχίᾳ*, while 𝔖 adds the copula but as a result omits השקטים as well as the following כלם ישבים. 𝔗 links the two consecutive participles with the copula. As an object to ישבים 𝔊 adds *γῆν*, 𝔏^{W} *civitatem*.

c 𝔙 suppresses the copula and connects up *vectes et portae non sunt eis*.

12 12a 𝔐 ידך. 𝔊 *χεῖρά μου* finds here the continuation of the quotation in v 11. 𝔏^{W} 𝔖 𝔙 𝔗 (which gives an exposition of the content משירייתך [לכנשא]) attest 𝔐.

b אל–על cf. 1:17 note a.

c 𝔊 (𝔏^{W}) *ἀπὸ ἐθνῶν πολλῶν*.

d 𝔐 עשה. The following parallel ישבי makes an original עשי probable here too (Herrmann, Bertholet, Fohrer). The two words מקנה וקנין (the verb קנה ony in 7:12), which are not attested elsewhere in Ezekiel apart from here in vv 12f, are telescoped in 𝔊 (𝔏^{W}) to simple *κτήσεις*. 𝔙 *qui possidere coepit*, 𝔖 דקנו בעירא וקנינא, 𝔗 אצלחו בניכסין וקניינין.

e 𝔖 𝔙 add the copula.

f 𝔐 טבור. 𝔊 (𝔏^{W} 𝔙) *τὸν ὄμφαλον*, 𝔖 (דארעא) שופרה "best part," 𝔗 תוקפא "stronghold."

13 13a 𝔐 וסחרי תרשיש. 𝔊 (𝔏^{W}) *καὶ ἔμποροι Καρχηδόνιοι*, 𝔗 תגרי ימא (without copula).

b 𝔐 וְכָל־כְּפִרֶיהָ (𝔙 *et omnes leones eius*), misunderstood by 𝔊 *καὶ πᾶσαι αἱ κῶμαι αὐτῶν*, 𝔏^{W} *et omnes regiones eorum*, 𝔖 וכלהון קוריא as כְּפָרֶיהָ (cf. 1 Chr 27:25; 1 Sam 6:18). 𝔗 interprets along the lines of 𝔐 וכל מלכהא. On כְּפִיר in the sense of "ruler" see above pp. 158f on 32:2. According to *LidzEph*, 1.235, we have to reckon also with "warrior" as a meaning for כפיר. The context makes it more likely, however, that parallel to סחר we should think of a description of a trader. Cornill proposes reading כנעניה. It is more likely that we should regard it, with Toy, BH[3], Koehler-Baumgartner, Fohrer, as a textual corruption of רכליה. רכל[ת] occurs alongside

seize spoil[c], have you summoned your
hosts in order to carry off booty, to carry
away silver and gold, to take away cattle
and goods[d], to seize much[e] spoil?
14 Therefore prophesy, son of man, and say to
Gog[a]: Thus has [the Lord][b] Yahweh said:
On that day when my people Israel dwell
securely will you not <arise>[c] 15/ and
come from your home in the furthest
north, you[a] and many nations with you,
all riding on horses, a great company and
a great army[b], 16/ and come up against
my people Israel, like a cloud, to cover
the land[a]? At the end of days it will be[b]
that I will allow you to come against my
land[c] so that the nations[d] acknowledge
me[e] when I show myself holy in their
eyes[f], Gog[g].
17 Thus has [the Lord][a] Yahweh said[b]: It <is
you>[c] of whom I spoke in earlier times
through my servants the prophets of
Israel, who prophesied[d] in those days
[years][e], that I would bring you against
them.
18 And it will be[a] on that day, the day[b] when
Gog comes against the land of Israel,

[ת]סחר also in 27:12/13, 15/16, 17/18, 20/21a, 21b/22.

c 𝔊 adds the copula (1:4 note a), as do 𝔗 𝔖, the latter inserting it additionally three times in what follows. 𝔙 here has *ecce* and then a two-fold insertion of the copula.

d See v 12 note d. 𝔙 here has *supellectilem.*

e 𝔐 גדול is missing in 𝔊 𝔏^{W}. The triple accentuation of the three parallel infinitive clauses suggests the originality of 𝔐.

14 14a 𝔖 ואמר לגוג ומגוג see v 2 note a.

b אדני is lacking in 𝔊 𝔏^{W}, see Appendix 1.

c 𝔐 תדע is attested by 𝔖 𝔙 𝔗, with 𝔗 adding the explanatory תידע פורענות גבורתי "you will acknowledge my powerful retribution." 𝔊 ἐγερθήσῃ. 𝔏^{W} *exsurges* (𝔏^{S} *exsurgens*) points to an original תֵּעֹר which since Ewald ("you will bestir yourself") has been regarded, correctly, by the majority as the original text. Aalders defends 𝔐.

15 15a 𝔐 אתה is omitted by 𝔊 𝔏^{WS} 𝔖, but can scarcely (against Cornill, Gressmann) be dispensed with.

b 𝔙 *exercitus vehemens,* 𝔏^{W} *virtus multa* (𝔏^{S} *copiosa*).

16 16a 𝔗 as v 9, see note a.

b 𝔐 תהיה is taken by 𝔙 *eris* as a second person. 𝔖 freely תאתא. Driver, "Linguistic Problems," 183, wishes to put the *athnah* at תהיה and understand תהיה as in 𝔐 of v 9. But see v 9 note b.

c 𝔗 על ארע בית שכינתי.

d 𝔊 (𝔏^{WS}) παντα (τὰ ἔθνη).

e 𝔐 אתי (דעת) is strange since only here in Ezekiel does the accusative formulation of the recognition formula occur; see Zimmerli, *Erkenntnis,* 34 note 49, and see further under "Form." 𝔗 again paraphrases פורענות גבורתי (. . .דידעון). See v 14 note c.

f 𝔗 paraphrases לעיניהם by ויהון חזן בפורענותך.

g 𝔐 גוג is included by 𝔊 in the introductory formula of v 17 (note b) and is completely unattested in 𝔖. Thus its originality is suspect.

17 17a אדני is lacking in 𝔊 𝔏^{SW}; 𝔊^{B} κύριος κύριος, see Appendix 1.

b 𝔊 adds τῷ Γωγ, see v 16 note g.

c 𝔐 האתה is in the form of a question. Since 𝔊 𝔖 𝔙 𝔏^{SW} have no indication of this and since a question at this point is in fact surprising, one may suppose that the initial ה is a dittograph.

d 𝔊 𝔏^{SW} omit 𝔐 הנבאים.

e 𝔐 שנים is already an embarrassment to the versions and is linked in 𝔊 𝔏^{SW} 𝔖 to the preceding ימים by the copula. 𝔙 *in diebus illorum temporum* is grammatically impossible as a translation of 𝔐. 𝔗 inserts a linking text ביומא דאינון מלקדמת דנא שנין סגיאן. Cf. the analogous difficulty in 𝔐 of Dan 11:13. On the whole question see Shemaryahu Talmon, "Double Readings in the Massoretic Text," *Textus* (Annual of the Hebrew University Bible Project) 1 (1960): 144–184, especially 171.

18 18a As already in v 10, 𝔖 omits the introductory והיה of 𝔐.

b 𝔖 𝔏^{W} omit the resumption of the ביום.

**says [the Lord][c] Yahweh, that my fury
will infuse[d] my anger[e] 19/ and my
jealousy[a]. In the fire of my fury I have
spoken: Indeed[b], on that day I will cause
a great earthquake to happen in the land
of Israel. 20/ And the fish of the sea and
the birds of the sky and the wild beasts of
the field and all insects that creep on the
earth and all men who are on the face of
the earth will quake before me[a], and the
mountains will be thrown down, and the
terraces (on the slope)[b] will collapse, and
every wall[c] will fall to the ground, 21/
and I will summon against him <terrors>[a]
of every kind, says [the Lord][b] Yahweh.
The sword of the one will be against the
other[c]. 22/ And I will enter into
judgment[a] with him, with plague and
with bloodshed. And I will pour streaming rain and hailstones,[b] fire and
brimstone over him and his hordes[c] and
(the) many nations who are with him 23/
and will show myself great and holy[a] and
will proclaim myself[b] in the eyes of many
nations, and they will acknowledge that I
am Yahweh.**

**39:1 But you, son of man, prophesy against Gog
and say: Thus has [the Lord][a] Yahweh
said: See, I am against you[b], Gog, chief
prince[c] of Meshech and Tubal, 2/ and I
will turn you round[a] and will lead you by**

c אדני is lacking in 𝔊 𝔏^{SW}; 𝔊^{B} *κύριος κύριος*, see Appendix 1.

d 𝔐 תעלה חמתי. 𝔖 נאקד רוגזי. 𝔗 ידלק רוגזי וחימתי. Driver, "Ezekiel," 304, prefers to take עלה here, on the basis of Arabic *ġly* ("cook," see Zorell, 601) as "snort."

e 𝔐 באפי, which is omitted by 𝔊 𝔏^{SW}, is to be connected with ובקנאתי in v 19.

19 19a See v 18 note e. 𝔊, in the rendering *καὶ ὁ ζῆλός μου*, connects ובקנאתי with v 18 and understands it as a second subject of תעלה.

b 𝔗 again paraphrases: באיתגלאה פורענותי במדלק אשת רוגזי (גזרית במימרי). 𝔖 tones it down by breaking down the oath formula, while 𝔏^{S}, on the other hand, strongly emphasizes it by prefixing the formula for a divine saying (*dicit dominus*).

20 20a 𝔐 מפני, so too 𝔙 𝔗. On the other hand, 𝔊 *ἀπὸ προσώπου κυρίου*, 𝔏^{SW} *a facie domini*, 𝔖 מן קדמוהי turn the whole into a narrative third person. Since vv 21–23 continue in the first person, 𝔐 is to be retained.

b 𝔐 מדרגות occurs also in Song 2:14, where, parallel to בחגוי הסלע, reference is to סתר המדרגה. Hence Cornill "steep cliffs," Herrmann "steep cliff peaks," Koehler-Baumgartner "mountain path." See also Hans Zirker, "דרך (derekh) = potentia?" *BZ* 2 (1958): 292. According to *b. Šeb.* III, 8a, the sense is "terraces" which are supported on the slope by wall structures, see D. Correns, *Schebiit* (Berlin: Töpelmann, 1961), 69f. So too Dalman, *Arbeit,* 4. 320, and Plate 34. 𝔊 *αἱ φάραγγες*, 𝔏^{S} *valles*, 𝔏^{W} *colles*, Σ *αἱ νάπαι*, Θ (𝔖^{h}) *οἱ φραγμοι* corresponding to 𝔙 *saepes*. Different are 𝔖 מגדלא, 𝔗 מגדליא "towers" on the basis of Is 2:15, where too מגדל and חומה are juxtaposed.

c 𝔗 וכל שור רם לארעא יתחמר "and every high wall will become a heap of rubble on the ground."

21 21a Attempts are made to render 𝔐 לכל הרי חרב by 𝔖 חרבא בכלהון טורי and 𝔙 *in cunctis montibus meis gladium*, while 𝔗 "and I appoint him to fall by the sword on the mountains of my people" interprets freely. 𝔊 *καὶ καλέσω ἐπ' αὐτὸν πᾶν φόβον* (partly assimilated to 𝔐 in 𝔏^{S} *omnem timorem gladii*) has preserved the original reading וקראתי עליו לכל חרדה.

b אדני is lacking in 𝔊 𝔏^{S}, see Appendix 1.

c 𝔙 amplifies with *dirigetur*.

22 22a Literally nip'al "commit myself for trial."

b 𝔊 𝔖 𝔏^{S} insert the copula, see 1:4 note a.

c 𝔊 (𝔏^{S}) *ἐπὶ πάντας τοὺς μετ' αὐτοῦ*. 𝔖 על רברבנוהי.

23 23a 𝔊 *καὶ ἐνδοξασθήσομαι*, 𝔏^{S} *et glorificabor* add a further element of glorification.

b 𝔐 ונודעתי is again dogmatically confirmed by 𝔗 ואיגלי גבורתי. 𝔖 omits the statement since it appears superfluous before the following recognition formula.

39:1 1a אדני is lacking in 𝔊 𝔏^{S}, see Appendix 1.

b על–אל cf. 1:17 note a and 13:8 note c.

c See 38:2 note b.

2 2a On 𝔐 ושבבתיך see 38:4 note a. Here 𝔖 has

the nose[b] and will let you come[c] from the
furthest north and will bring you to the
mountains of Israel. 3/ And I will smite
your bow out of your hand and will let
your arrows fall[a] from your right hand. 4/
On the mountains of Israel you will fall[a],
you and all your hordes and <many>
nations[b] who are with you. To the birds
of prey[c], to everything that has wings,
and to the[d] wild beasts of the field I will
give you as fodder. 5/ In the open field
you will fall[a], for I have spoken (it), says
[the Lord][b] Yahweh.
6 And I will send fire against Magog[a] and
against those who dwell[b] securely on the
islands, and they shall know that I am
Yahweh. 7/ And I shall proclaim[a] my holy
name in the midst of my people Israel and
will no longer profane[a] my holy name,
and the[b] nations will know that I am
Yahweh, holy in Israel[c]. 8/ See, it is coming and will happen[a], says [the Lord][b]
Yahweh. That is the day of which I
spoke.
9 And the inhabitants of the cities of Israel
will go out and will [burn and][a] set fire to

ואכנשך, which is chosen as the rendering of ושבבתיך in 38:4, in second place. See note b.

b 𝔐 וששאתיך is a *hapax legomenon.* 𝔊 *καὶ καθοδηγήσω σε,* 𝔙 𝔏[S] *et educam te,* 𝔗 ואטעינך "I will carry you." Is the ואשינך "I will calm you," which appears in first place in 𝔖 (note a), intended as a rendering of וששאתיך? The root is surely to be understood on the basis of Ethiopic *sosawa* "walk along."

c 𝔐 והעליתיך is omitted by 𝔏[S].

3 3a 𝔐 אפיל is introduced in 𝔊 (*καὶ καταβαλῶ σε*) with the copula (1:4 note a) as a new clause and is linked with v 4. It is completely omitted by 𝔖, which also twice leaves the preceding יד untranslated.

4 4a 𝔊 (𝔏[S]), which has linked the beginning of v 4 with the final verb of v 3 (note a), links תפול, again by the insertion of the copula (1:4 note a), with what follows. 𝔊[967] also inserts before that the clause which is taken from v 7 "and my name will not be profaned." 𝔗 interprets תיתרמי נבילתך.

b 𝔐 ועמים. 𝔊[967] (𝔏[S]) *ἔθνη πολλά,* 𝔖 𝔗 strongly suggest the addition of רבים. 𝔙 *et populi tui.*

c 𝔐 לעיט צפור. On עיט "bird of prey" see also Gen 15:11; Is 18:6; 46:11; Jer 12:9; Job 28:7. The following צפור כל כנף is a closer description of it. On the addition of an apposition by means of the construct relationship see Gesenius-Kautzsch §130e. The versions no longer understood this. 𝔊 (𝔏[S]), which inserts an extra verb (*δοθήσονται*), translates *εἰς πλῆθος ὀρνέων παντὶ πετεινῷ,* 𝔖, still less clearly, simply לפרחתא דשמיא, while 𝔙 *feris avibus omnique volatili* and 𝔗 לעופא צפור וכל דפרח make the כל כנף, which is dependent on the צפור, independent by the insertion of the copula.

d 𝔊 (𝔏[S]) *καὶ πᾶσι τοῖς θηρίοις.*

5 5a 𝔗 תתרמי נבילתך.

b אדני is lacking in 𝔊 𝔏[S] 𝔄̈, see Appendix 1.

6 6a 𝔊 (𝔏[S]) *ἐπὶ Γωγ.* See the exposition.

b 𝔐 ובישבי has been misread by 𝔊 (𝔏[S]) *καὶ κατοικηθήσονται* as וישבו, which produced a declaration of salvation for the (hitherto unmentioned) islands. In what follows 𝔗 has an explanatory expansion וביתבי נגוותא דשרן ברוחצן.

7 7a 𝔊 *γνωσθήσεται* (𝔏[S] *innotescent*) . . .
σεται (𝔏[S] *contaminabitur*) transforms Ya
sonal speech into an impersonal passiv

b 𝔊 (but not 𝔊[B] 𝔏[S] 𝔎[Bo] 𝔄̈) *πάντα.*

c 𝔐 קדוש בישראל is transformed, doubtless under the influence of the linguistic usage of the book of Isaiah, by 𝔊 (not 𝔊[B]) 𝔖 𝔙 𝔏[S] into the simple genitive relationship. 𝔗, on the other hand, tries to safeguard the understanding of 𝔐 by a fuller paraphrase in the framework of its particular theology ארי אנא יהוה קדישא אשריתי שכינתי בישראל.

8 8a 𝔊 (𝔏[S]) more fully *ἰδοὺ ἥκει καὶ γνώσῃ ὅτι ἔσται* (*γνώσῃ ὅτι* is missing in 𝔊[967]). In 21:12 𝔊 ran as follows: *ἰδοὺ ἔρχεται καὶ ἔσται.*

b אדני is lacking in 𝔊 𝔏[S]; 𝔊[B] *κύριος κύριος,* see Appendix 1.

9 9a 𝔐 ובערו והשיקו. 𝔊 *καὶ καύσουσιν,* 𝔏[S] *et succendent*

**the armor [and shield and buckler][b] bow
and arrows, javelin[c] and spear and will
make a fire with them for seven years.
10/ And they will not gather any wood
from the fields nor cut down[a] (wood) in
the forests, but will fuel fires with the
armor and will rob those who robbed
them and plunder those who plundered
them, says [the Lord][b] Yahweh.**
11 **But on that day it will be[a] that I will give to
Gog a place where[b] there is a grave (for
him) in Israel: the Oberim(?) Valley[c], east**

attest only one verb, but the fuller ונשבקון נורא of 𝔖 may suggest that they had the double expression in front of them and telescoped it. Athough 𝔊 again translates the ובערו which follows in v 9b by *καὶ καύσουσιν* (𝔏^S is slightly different, *et comburens*), the unusual והשיקו, which has doubtlessly been consciously placed alongside בנשק because of the assonance, is probably more original. Has it subsequently been interpreted by ובערו, which now inelegantly appears in the same verse? השיק also occurs in Is 44:15 (Sir 43:4, 21). The nip'al is found in Ps 78:21. According to Bauer-Leander §52u, this is derived from שלק, but it is more probably to be derived, with Gesenius-Buhl and Koehler-Baumgartner, from נשק. The solution of Driver, "Linguistic Problems," 183f, who postulates on the basis of Syriac בער *perlustravit, quaesivit* a meaning "gather together," is not to be recommended in view of the בער "burn" which is attested twice immediately after. In "Ezekiel," 304, Driver then proposes deleting והשיקו as a gloss on ובערו.

b 𝔐 ומגן וצנה stands out from the context in that unlike the preceding, summarizing בנשק and the following individual enumeration of weapons it is not introduced by ב. 𝔖 assimilates in respect of both expressions, 𝔗 in respect of the first (בעגילין). A further stylistic harmonization is to be seen in that 𝔊 deletes the copula before מגן (*πέλταις*), which in the (expanded) 𝔐 begins the individual enumeration of weapons, but adds it, on the other hand, accordingly before בקשת (*καὶ τόξοις*). 𝔖 𝔏^S add it in the latter place without deleting it in the former. 𝔙 𝔗 delete it before מגן (*clipeum*) and for the rest follow 𝔐. The original text had referred only to a burning of the weapons of attack. This is obscured, however, in 𝔊 𝔏^S 𝔖 𝔙, who translate צנה by "lance" (*κοντοῖς, contis,* בניזכא, *hastas*). In addition, 𝔏^S translates מגן by *ballistis* "sling."

c See the exposition.

10 10a 𝔖 makes for stylistic conciseness by the omission of the second verb.

b אדני is lacking in 𝔊 𝔏^S 𝔄, see Appendix 1.

11 11a As already in 38:10, 18 𝔖 suppresses the introductory והיה.

b 𝔐 מְקוֹם־שָׁם. 𝔊 *τόπον ὀνομαστόν*, 𝔏^S 𝔙 *locum nominatum* seem to point to a reading מְקוֹם שֵׁם. 𝔖 presupposes 𝔐, while once again (by altering the position of שם) making for stylistic smoothness (אתל תמן דוכתא לגוג (לקברא. 𝔗 comes closest to 𝔐, although it understands שם freely in the sense of "fitted for" (אתין לגוג אתר כשר (לבית קבורא. On the relative clause presupposed by 𝔐 and dependent on the construct state see Gesenius-Kautzsch §130c, d; Brockelmann §144. In contrast to 21:35 it is here constructed asyndetically.

c 𝔐 גֵּי הָעֹבְרִים (גי is a defective form of גיא, Bauer-Leander §72v'). 𝔊 *τὸ πολυανδρεῖον* (common grave, 𝔏^S *multorum virorum congestum*) *τῶν ἐπελθόντων*. As a translation of גיא (= valley of Hinnom?) *πολυανδρεῖον*

of the sea[d], and it will block (the way) for those who pass through[e]. And there they will bury Gog and all his proud host and will call it <Valley of Gog's Hordes>[f]. 12/ And the house of Israel will bury them in order to cleanse the land—for seven months. 13/ And the whole people of the land will bury (them)[a], and it will be to their honor[b] on the day when I glorify myself, says [the Lord][c] Yahweh. 14/ And they will set apart people with a continuing commission[a] who pass through the land, who bury[b] those [who pass through][c] who are left lying on the open field in order to cleanse it. At the end of seven months they are to stop

is also attested in Jer 2:23; 19:2, 6. 𝔙 *vallem viatorum;* otherwise 𝔖 נחלא רבא and 𝔗 חילת מגזתא "valley of the ford, of the defile" and Σ *ἡ φάραγξ τῶν διαβάσεων*. The further precision "east of the sea" raises the question whether one should not read here the name עֲבָרִים which occurs in Jer 22:20 and as הַר הָעֲבָרִים Nu 27:12; Dtn 32:49 or as הָרֵי הָעֲבָרִים Nu 33:47f to describe the northwestern part of the Moabite uplands (Mount Nebo). According to P. Wernberg-Møller, "Observations on the Hebrew Participle," *ZAW* 71 (1959): 59, participle and segholate form can appear as variant forms of one and the same word, so that an equation without emendation of 𝔐 would be possible. See the exposition.

d 𝔗, strangely and certainly not in accordance with the meaning of 𝔐, מדנח ים גניסר; see further the exposition.

e חסם in Dtn 25:4 of muzzling. On Sir 48:17 Smend, *Weisheit,* 465, observes: "חסם certainly also had a technical building sense." גי here is feminine (cf. Zech 14:4). 𝔊 *καὶ περιοικοδομήσουσι τὸ περιστόμιον τῆς φάραγγος*, similarly 𝔖 ונסכרונה לנחלא which omits 𝔐 את העברים. Σ *ἡ ἐμφράσσουσα τὰς διαβάσεις*. 𝔙 takes a different direction *quae obstupescere facit praetereuntes.* 𝔗 has a quite free exposition וסמכא היא לתרין טורייא "and it is supported by the two cliffs" (i.e. forms a defile bounded by two cliffs?). Bewer, "Textual Notes," 165, suggests, on the basis of 𝔊 𝔖, as the original reading וחסמו את הגי and the deletion of את העברים as a gloss: "and they shall dam up the valley."

f 𝔊 *τὸ γαι τὸ πολυανδρεῖον τοῦ Γωγ*. According to this, *πολυανδρεῖον* appears, otherwise than in v 11a, as a translation of המון. See also v 15. 𝔖 נחלא דסופנה דגוג "Gog's death's valley."

13 13a 𝔊 adds *αὐτούς*, 𝔖 אנון, while 𝔙 *eum* thinks of Gog personally.

b 𝔐 לשם. 𝔊 *εἰς ὀνομαστόν*, 𝔙 *nominata* (*dies*), 𝔏^{S} *in nominatissimum* (*diem*).

c אדני is lacking in 𝔊 𝔏^{S} 𝔄 𝔖, see Appendix 1.

14 14a 𝔐 תמיד is referred adverbially to the verb by the versions (𝔊 *διὰ παντός*, 𝔖 אמינאית [מהלכין], 𝔙 *jugiter*, 𝔏^{S} *semper*, 𝔗 תדירא), while in 𝔐 it is dependent on the construct אנשי and describes as perpetual the office of those who are set apart for it.

b Driver, "Linguistic Problems," 184, and Bewer, "Textual Notes," 66, propose emending 𝔐 מקברים to מבקרים "searching for" (cf. 34:11f). Bewer, in addition, would also like to emend the העברים of v 15 to המבקרים. Since, however, in v 15b המקברים appears again in an unimpeachable passage and since the versions attest 𝔐, the latter should be retained.

c 𝔐 את העברים does not fit the context and, since it is not attested by 𝔊 𝔏^{S} 𝔖 (is the expansion in 𝔙 *qui sepeliant et requirant* a reference to the obscure element found here?), is to be regarded as an addition. So too Driver and Bewer (see note b). 𝔗 tries

searching[d]. 15/ And when the searchers[a]
pass through the land and one of them
sees a human bone, then he is to erect
beside it a marker[b] until the buriers have
buried it in the <Valley of Gog's
Hordes>[c]. 16/ [But also the name of a
town is Hamonah.][a] And they will
cleanse the land.
17 **But you, son of man[a], thus has [the Lord][b]**
Yahweh said: Say to the birds, to every-
thing that has wings[c], and to all the wild
beasts of the field: Assemble and come,
gather together[d] from round about to my
sacrifice which I will slaughter for you[e],
on the mountains of Israel. And you shall
eat flesh and drink blood. 18/ [a]The flesh
of heroes you shall eat, and the blood of
the princes of the earth you shall drink:
rams, lambs and goats—bulls, fatlings
from Bashan are they all[b]. 19/ And you

to make sense of the text by taking the את as equivalent of עם "together with."

d 𝔊 (𝔏^{S}) separates 𝔐 יחקרו from what goes before by the insertion of the copula (1:4 note a).

15 15a Literally "those who pass through." 𝔊 𝔏^{S} 𝔖 make the text more concise by omitting ועברו. 𝔗 expands ועדי אורחא דעדן. See the exposition.

b 𝔐 ציון, correspondingly 𝔖 צויא, 𝔗 צוואה. 𝔊 *σημεῖον*, 𝔏^{S} *signum*, 𝔙 *titulum*,

c 𝔐 גיא המון גוג. 𝔊 as in v 11b (note c). 𝔖 abbreviates נחלא דגוג.

16 16a 𝔐 המונה. 𝔊 *πολυανδρεῖον*, see v 11 note c. Σ *πλῆθος*. 𝔖 עשינתא. 𝔗, on the other hand, surprisingly inserts here a reference to the wars with Rome (Gog = Rome): ואף לתמן יתרמון קטילי רומי קרתא דסגיאין איתרגושתהא. The fallen Romans are also to be buried there. The whole first clause of v 16 is an obvious addition, which separates the second clause from v 15. Driver, "Linguistic Problems," 184, reads וְגָמַר שֵׁמַע הֲמוֹנֹה "and the fame of his multitude (or 'mob') shall come to an end." See the exposition.

17 17a 𝔊 (𝔏^{S}) inserts here an *εἶπον*, which is then repeated after the introductory messenger formula (corresponding to 𝔐). 𝔖 has put this introductory formula in the correct place after the commission to the prophet and immediately before the plural summonses.

b אדני is lacking in 𝔊 𝔏^{S} 𝔄, see Appendix 1.

c 𝔐 לצפור כל כנף. 𝔖 לכלה פרחתא דשמיא. 𝔗 expands לעופא ציפר כל דפרח; 𝔙 here too has two expressions linked by the copula *omni volucri et universis avibus* (see v 4 note c).

d 𝔖 omits the third, 𝔏^{S} the second and third imperatives.

e 𝔗 replaces the sacrifice by the object intended על קטילי דאנא קטיל and קטול סגי.

18 18a 𝔏^{S} adds the copula.

b The enumeration in v 18b, which Fohrer would like to delete as an explanatory gloss, apcars in the versions in somewhat different form. To be sure, with the exception of 𝔏^{S}, which telescopes the half verse into the concise double statement *arietes et vituli pingues,* they attest the full range of the vocabulary of 𝔐. 𝔗, again in its characteristic manner, changes the images into the objects intended, but for the rest, in the syntactic structure and the placing of the copula, reproduces 𝔐 exactly מלכין שילטונין וטורנין גיברין עתירי נכסיא כולהון. 𝔙 adds the copula before כרים (*agnorum*) and understands the second half (from פרים on), inserting the copula before every noun and translating בשן freely (in association with 𝔊), as an independent statement, as a simple apposition to the first half of v 18b: *taurorumque et altilium et pinguium omnium.* 𝔖, to be sure, does not break the construct relationship מריאי בשן, but for the rest understands the whole passage as an unclassified enumeration and inserts a copula three times, so that the text in it runs: (בסרא. . .) דדכרא ודמפטמא ודתישא ודתורא ודארונא

shall eat the fat[a] of my sacrifice[b] which I
have slaughtered for you until you are
filled and drink the blood until you are
drunk, 20/ and you shall be filled at my
table[a] with horses[b] and chariot horses[c],
with heroes[d] and all warriors, says [the
Lord][e] Yahweh.
21 **And I shall reveal my glory among the**
nations[a], and all nations will see my[b]
judgment which I have executed and my
hand[c] which I have laid upon them, 22/
and the house of Israel will know that I,
Yahweh, am their God,[a] from that day on
and for ever.
23 **And the nations[a] will know that the house[b]**
of Israel has gone into exile because of
its guilt, because they were faithless
towards me and I hid my face from them[c]
and gave them into the hands of their
oppressors so that they all fell by the
sword. 24/ I have done to them[a] accord-
ing to their uncleanness and according to
their crimes and have hidden my face
from them[b].
25 **Therefore thus has [the Lord][a] Yahweh**
said: Now I will restore the fortunes[b] of
Jacob and have mercy on the whole[c]
house of Israel and will be jealous for my
holy name[d]. 26/ And their shame[a] and

דבישן כלהון. 𝔊, on the other hand, again comes close to 𝔐, dividing v 18b into two parts, thereby setting the caesura, against the accents of 𝔐 but surely more correctly, before פרים, but inserting, against 𝔐, a copula before פרים and before the now independent second half in which פרים is determined and understood as subject (see 1:4 note a): κριοὺς καὶ μόσχους καὶ τράγους καὶ οἱ μόσχοι ἐστεατωμένοι πάντες. Undoubtedly 𝔐 should be retained; it provides, in the first place, a threefold enumeration of animals, only the last element of which is joined by means of the copula. To this there is joined a second statement in which (against 𝔊) the גבורים from v 18a, to whom reference was also made in the animal images at the beginning of v 18b, remains the subject. Alongside the comparison with the sacrificial small cattle there appears now the comparison with the large fatted beasts.

19 19a 𝔐 חלב. 𝔖 בסרא, 𝔏[S] *carne.*

b 𝔐 מזבחי is confirmed by 𝔊 𝔏[S]. 𝔙 *de victima* for stylistic reasons suppresses the suffix, which is actually superfluous alongside the following relative clause. 𝔖 adds to this an adjective מן דבחתא רבתא, while 𝔗 again discards the image מבסר קטילין.

20 20a 𝔗 again interprets על טורי עמי. 𝔏[S] has an addition in dependence on v 19 *quam parui* (*paravi*) *vobis.*

b 𝔖 𝔗 add "in the flesh."

c 𝔐 וָרֶכֶב (23:24; 26:7, 10) is understood by 𝔊 καὶ ἀναβάτην, 𝔖 ודרכביהון, 𝔙 *et equite forti,* 𝔏[S] *et sessorem* as וְרֹכֵב. Since this pair of words סוס ורכב occurs also in 26:7, 𝔐 should be retained (with 𝔗), but רֶכֶב understood along the line of 2 Sam 8:4.

d 𝔊 𝔖 𝔏[S] destroy the structure of the text by inserting the copula (1:4 note a), 𝔙 by connecting ורכב גבור *et equite forti.*

e אדני is lacking in 𝔊 𝔏[S], see Appendix 1.

21 21a 𝔐 בגוים. 𝔊 (𝔏[S]) ἐν ὑμῖν. The emendation to בגוג, proposed by Cornill but with no support in the tradition, overlooks the fact that v 21 sees the beginning of an appendix in a more general style.

b 𝔐 משפטי. 𝔖, for the same stylistic considerations as in v 19 (note b), suppresses the suffix.

c 𝔐 ידי. 𝔗 גבורתי.

22 22a 𝔏[S] *et ex hac die.*

23 23a 𝔊 (𝔏[S]) πάντα τὰ ἔθνη.

b 𝔖 בני.

c 𝔗, in the context of its theological terminology, formulates as follows: על דשקרו במימרי וסילקית שכנתי מינהון.

24 24a 𝔐 אֹתָם–אוֹתָם, see 2:1 note a.

b 𝔗 as in v 23, see note c.

25 25a אדני is lacking in 𝔊 𝔏[S]; 𝔊[B] κύριος κύριος; see Appendix 1.

b K שבית, Q שבות. See 16:53 note a.

c 𝔐 כל is not attested by 𝔊 𝔏[S]. In its place 𝔏[S] adds *adhuc.*

d The jealousy for the name is turned by 𝔊 𝔏[S] into "on account of the jealousy" (διά, *propter*) of the

all[a] their faithlessness with which they were unfaithful to me[b], they will take upon themselves[c] when they dwell securely in their land and no one terrifies (them), 27/ when I bring them back from amongst the nations[a] and gather them from the countries of their[b] enemies and show myself holy in the eyes of [many][c] nations. 28/ And (by this) they will know that I, Yahweh, am their God, that I, after I had led them away[a] among the nations, will gather them into their land and no longer[b] leave any of them behind. 29/ And I will no longer[a] hide[b] my face from them, after[c] I have poured out my spirit[d] on the house[e] of Israel, says [the Lord][f] Yahweh.

name. 𝔗 develops v 25b in terms of punishment of the nations for their sins: ואתפרע פרענות גבורתי מן עממיא על דאחילו ית שמא דקודשי.

26 26a 𝔐 את כלמתם ואת כל מעלם. 𝔖 כלה בהתתהון ועולהון makes a stylistic improvement by placing the כל before the double expression, while 𝔊 𝔏^{S} omit the כל.

b 𝔐 בי is omitted by 𝔊 𝔏^{S}. 𝔗 במימרי.

c 𝔐 ונשו, according to Bauer-Leander §59c = ונשאו. So Q, MSS, subsequently 𝔊 καὶ λήμψονται, 𝔏^{S} *et accipient*, 𝔖 ונקבלון, 𝔙 *et portabunt*, 𝔗 ויקבלון. Since a statement of salvation for Israel is expected at this point, the text has, since Hitzig, been emended to וְנָשׁוּ "they shall forget" by most commentators (Cornill; Ehrlich, *Randglossen;* Toy; Rothstein; Herrmann; Bertholet; Fohrer; Ziegler). The qal of נשה is attested with certainty only in Lam 3:17, possibly also Dtn 32:18; Hab 3:10. Nip'al, pi'el, hip'il also occur. The root is never found in Ezekiel. But since the phrase נשא כלמה occurs very frequently in Ezekiel (16:52, 54; 32:24f, 30; 34:29; 36:6f; cf. 36:15; 44:13) and since the phrase both here and in 16:54 follows immediately on שוב שבות, all the comparative material argues against the emendation of 𝔐, which is so unanimously attested by the versions. See further the exposition.

27 27a 𝔙 makes a new beginning: *et reduxero eos.*

b 𝔐 איביהם. 𝔊 τῶν ἐχθρῶν, 𝔏^{S} *gentium.*

c 𝔐 הגוים רבים is unusual. Can one justify the article on the grounds mentioned in 31:6 note b? Ehrlich, *Randglossen;* Bertholet; Fohrer emend to גוים רבים. Since, however, רבים is not attested by 𝔊 𝔏^{S}, it is more probable that הגוים is original and that רבים is a secondary gloss which has not been fully assimilated into the syntax (Cornill, Cooke, and others).

28 28a 𝔐 בהגלותי אתם. 𝔊 ἐν τῷ ἐπιφανῆναί με αὐτοῖς (𝔏^{S} *dum apparebo illis*) takes the form as a nip'al בְּהִגָּלוֹתִי, certainly incorrectly. This correcting of the understanding is connected with the fact that 𝔊 (𝔏^{S}) did not have v 28aγb in its original. But these words can scarcely be dispensed with from the point of view of subject matter. 𝔗 adds two justificatory clauses, the aim of which is to guarantee Yahweh's righteousness. The deportation occurred "because they sinned before me" (דעל דחבו קדמי), the return "when they repented" (וכד דתבו).

b 𝔐 עוד is missing in 𝔖 𝔙.

29 29a 𝔐 עוד is omitted by 𝔖 as well as by 𝔊^{967} 𝔎^{Bo}.

b 𝔗 as in v 23, note c.

c 𝔐 אשר. 𝔊 ἀνθ' ὧν, 𝔏^{S} *pro eo quod*, 𝔙 *eo quod*, 𝔖 אלא.

d 𝔐 רוחי. 𝔊 τὸν θυμόν μου, 𝔏^{S} *iram meam* take it to refer to Yahweh's anger; 𝔗 ית רוח קדשי (𝔙 *spiritum meum*, 𝔖 רוחי), to the spirit that brings salvation.

e 𝔖 amplifies על כלה בית איסראיל, so too 𝔙 *super omnem domum Israel.* Is this a reminiscence of 37:15ff?

f אדני is lacking in 𝔊 𝔏^{S}. 𝔊^{B} κύριος κύριος, see Appendix 1.

Form

The great Gog pericope in chapters 38f, which is introduced in 38:1 by an undated messenger formula, must first be examined with regard to its unity. At the same time, attention must be paid to the formal structure of the individual components.

An initial survey indicates that chapters 38f, as a result of the commission directed four times to the prophet to speak (38:2f, 14; 39:1, 17), is divided into the four units 38:2–13, 14–23; 39:1–16, 17–29. In the first three sections Gog himself is addressed (38:3, 14; 39:1), while the fourth speech is, according to its introduction, directed at the birds and the wild animals (39:17).

If, first of all, one looks more closely at this last, particularly characteristic unit in 39:17–29, then it quickly becomes clear that the address to birds and beasts is maintained only as far as v 20 which is concluded by means of a formula for a divine saying. There then follows a more general divine speech. Within it, vv 21f could possibly still be connected with the Gog episode. Vv 23ff, from the content point of view also, have no further connection with that episode. Vv 21f are in the form of a promissory, bipartite proof-saying. The acknowledgment statement in it is strongly emphasized. Vv 23–29, for their part, are divided into two parts in v 25 by means of the introductory messenger formula introduced by לכן ("therefore"). The second of these two parts is characterized, as a result of its expanded recognition formula in vv 28f, as a proof-saying. Here too the whole is concluded by a formula for a divine saying. Thus, as the original component of that section, which is introduced in v 17 by the command to speak, one can designate simply vv 17–20.

The first of the three sections directed against Gog (38:2–13) is, in the first place, divided into the two parts vv 3–9 and vv 10–13 by the two introductory messenger formulae in vv 3 and 10. The first of these, as the text-critical discussion has shown, has acquired all kinds of amplificatory additions in vv 3–5, 9. After their deletion there remains an oracle which is entirely in the style of an address to Gog. It begins with the challenge or encounter formula.[1] The promise which follows, of Gog's being led out, is enlivened again in v 7 by a direct imperative summons to Gog. Vv 10–13, which are also in the form of a direct address to Gog and which describe the flourishing of Gog's evil intentions towards Israel, twice (vv 11, 13) use the form of the quotation in order to give dramatic life to the narrative. One can hear in them the thoughts of Gog and the encouraging words of the merchants to him. Since vv 10–13 appear somewhat surprisingly secondary to Gog's inner motive for his campaign against the mountains of Israel and since they are formally introduced by the colorless (והיה) ביום ההוא ("[and it will be] on that day") which served in 29:21 and 30:9 to introduce additions, it may be supposed that they were first added at a second stage for the subjective justification of Gog's campaign.

The second section, 38:14–23, gives rise to more difficult considerations. The fact that here too in vv 14 and 17 the introductory messenger formula appears and that therefore the whole is to be divided into two parts, vv 14–16 and 17–23, that then in the second part two emphatic formulae for a divine saying are to be found in vv 18 and 22, does not initially give rise to any doubts. More difficult is the fact that with v 18 the direct address to Gog disappears and in vv 18–23, a section which signifies a most vivid threat against Gog and his army, Yahweh simply speaks more descriptively of the great blow which is to fall upon the land of Israel. In addition to these observations of form there is also the difficulty concerning the content, a difficulty which has been observed again and again by commentators, namely that the judgment on Gog's power is described quite differently in 38:18–23 from the way in which it is described later in 39:1–5, a section which in its formal structure is quite irreproachable. The answer to this is scarcely the two-source theory for the whole Gog pericope as suggested by Kraetzschmar, Bertholet. Nevertheless, one is forced by the convergence of considerations of form and of content to regard vv 18–23 as a secondary expansion. In the image of Gog's fall it contains cosmic characteristics which were not originally part of the image. The addition, which is characterized as a proof-saying by a double recognition formula at the end (וידעו . . . ונודעתי "and I will proclaim myself . . . and they will acknowledge"), is joined at the beginning to

1 See 1, 175 and above p. 98.

what precedes it by the clumsy double expression והיה ביום ההוא ביום בוא גוג על אדמת ישראל ("and it will be on that day, the day when Gog comes against the land of Israel"). On the first half of this expression see what has already been said in connection with v 10. The second half gives the impression of being a recapitulatory connecting remark. Thus, as the original components of the section vv 14–23, there remain only the two elements vv 14–16 and 17, which, from the point of view of their style as a direct address to Gog, correspond to what the introduction in v 14a would lead us to expect.

It cannot, however, be denied that not inconsiderable doubts arise as to the originality of even these two components. In the case of vv 14–16 these are doubts of a formal kind. The verses are in the form of a proof-saying with concluding recognition statement. But the latter reveals an unusual formulation. Admittedly its infinitive form has a certain correspondence (although in fact in a different context) in 20:12, 20. The use of למען ("so that") in order to emphasize the final element of the recognition statement is found, however, in the book of Ezekiel only in the secondary phrase למען אשר יֵדְעוּ ("that they might know") of 20:26b (see note b).[2] Finally, quite unique in the book of Ezekiel is the accusative formulation of the recognition statement, which corresponds to the ידע ("recognition")-statements which, formally, are found especially in Hosea and Jeremiah. This does not fit the style which is otherwise consistently maintained in Ezekiel. In addition, there is further the remarkable stylization of vv 14–16 in the form of a question. This is connected with the peculiar nature of the content of the present passage. In vv 1–9 an event was proclaimed in its successive stages. Vv 14–16 contribute no new element of this event. Rather, they recapitulate it in single words and partly in whole phrases which had already occurred in vv 1–9 (ישב לבטח "to dwell securely" v 8, ירכתי צפון "the furthest north" v 6, עמים רבים אתך "many nations with you" v 6 [v9], סוסים "horses" v 4, קהל "company" v 7, חיל "army" v 4, כענן לכסות הארץ "like the cloud, to cover the land" v 9, באחרית [הימים] "at the end (of days)" v 8). The new thing which vv 14–16 try to say lies simply in the summons to reflect on the inner meaning of the event which has previously been reported. Gog comes so that the nations see how Yahweh will glorify himself against him before their eyes. The "proof-saying" is used in this question of reflection in a modified, secondary way. The question which summons to reflection has grown out of the divine proclamation to which the type of the proof-saying basically belongs and which one also expects here after the full introduction in v 14a (לכן "therefore," command to speak, introductory messenger formula). Finally, a further difference in the nature of the oracle strikes one. While vv 1–9 referred, in a very distanced manner, to the people gathered on the mountains of Israel (v 8, subsequently also 39:2, 4, see below), vv 14, 16 (see below on 39:7) speak much more personally of עמי ישראל ("my people Israel"). Thus one can scarcely regard vv 14–16 as the original continuation of the basic text.

But v 17 too, which in 𝔐 (under the influence of the preceding vv 14–16?) has been wrongly written as a question (note c), gives rise to similar considerations. Here too there is no continuation of the event, but a kind of interpretation of Gog who appears initially in puzzling terms. He is described as the one who has long been designated by the prophets of Israel of "earlier days" (the phrase עבדי נביאי ישראל "my servants the prophets of Israel" is a combination of the language of the Deuteronomist and of Ezekiel). This undoubtedly catches the original intention of the Gog proclamation (see below on the tradition-history of chapters 38f). The theological interpretation is, however, significantly different from the unrestrainedly descriptive and dramatic nature of the basic text.

The Gog proclamation resumes again only in 39:1ff, where the destruction of Gog by Yahweh on the mountains of Israel is promised. The beginning of 39:1–16 is, in style, parallel to the beginning of 38:2–9 with the challenge or encounter formula. This is followed, first of all, by the expected direct address to Gog. The graphically restrained description of the event on the "mountains of Israel" (vv 2, 4) corresponds to 38:8. With v 5 the address to Gog breaks off. V 5b, with its formula for a divine saying and the preceding formulaic כי אני דברתי ("for I have spoken [it]"), bears a clearly final stamp.

Vv 6–16, in which the direct address to Gog is not

2 Zimmerli, *Erkenntnis*, 13.

again resumed, are not, from the formal point of view, a unit. First of all vv 6–7 with the conclusion in v 8 (formula for a divine saying with additional emphatic assurance) stand out by reason of their strongly emphatic recognition formulae. They recall 39:21f. From the point of view of thought and language (עמי ישראל "my people Israel") they belong, moreover, closely with the expansion in 38:14–16. The next section, vv 9–10, which describes the destruction of the weapons of Gog's army, is concluded in v 10 with a formula for a divine saying. Finally, the remaining verses, 11–16, which deal with Gog's burial and the cleansing of the land from the dead bones, is separated into two sections by the formula for a divine saying. Concerning these two sections one can ask the question, but cannot answer it with certainty, whether the second is a secondary, more meticulous elaboration of the great purificatory action in the land. Content-wise, vv 14–16 are a continuation of vv 11-13.

But the question now arises whether the description of the destruction of Gog's weapons (vv 9–10) and of his burial (vv 11–16) is not in fact the genuine continuation of the announcement of his destruction (vv 1–5), even if they are no longer in the form of a direct address to Gog. As a justification for the difference in form one might adduce the fact that the two themes treated in vv 9–16 are not, in their nature, suited to being in the form of a direct address to Gog. But in the way of this hypothesis there stands the major difficulty from the content point of view that 39:17ff, the original element of which was reckoned to exist in 39:17–20, could by no means any longer be understood as the continuation of vv 9–16. In this passage (vv 17–20) the birds and wild beasts are summoned to a meal on the battlefield which represents Yahweh's place of sacrifice. After the great clearing up operation of vv 9–16, which is spread over seven years (v 9) or seven months (v 12), there is no further place for this meal. Thus then many judge 39:17–20 to be an addition spun out of 39:4 and consider that it is to be removed as secondary from the original text (Hölscher, van den Born). But this is to overlook how closely the call in 39:17–20 stands from the point of view of form to the calls in direct speech which are directed at Gog. Is an expander, after in the preceding sections the possibility of purely descriptive exposition had emerged, supposed to have gone back once again in a late addition to that most direct and most vital form of the basic elements? But also from the content point of view everything is in favor of vv 11–16, a passage painstakingly concerned with the cultic purity of the land, being later that the marvelously carefree summons of vv 17–20, which in addition links up quite naturally with vv 1–5 as a highly colored exposition of the motif touched upon in v 4. Thus, on considerations of both form and subject matter, it is probable that 39:17–20 represents the concluding section of the original Gog oracles. But because over the field of the slain Gog himself can scarcely be personally addressed any more, the divine summons turns to the birds of the sky and the beasts of the field and bids them complete the final judgment on the field of the dead. Stylistically this lies entirely along the lines of the preceding oracles.

Thus the oldest element of the Gog pericope is to be found in 38:1–9 (without the additions which were excluded in the discussion of the text); 39:1–5, 17–20. It runs as follows:

> And the word of Yahweh came to me:
>
> Son of man, turn your face towards Gog, the chief prince of Meshech and Tubal, and prophesy against him and say: Thus has Yahweh said:
>
> See, I am against you, Gog, chief prince of Meshech and Tubal, and I will lead you out, (you) and all your army, horses and riders, all of them fully armed, a great company. Gomer and all his hordes, Beth Togarma, the furthest north, many nations are with you. Stand and prepare yourself, you and your whole company which have been mobilized for you, and be at my service. After a long time you will be summoned, at the end of the years you will come to a land which has been recovered from the sword, has been gathered together again from among many nations on the mountains of Israel which for long lay waste—which has been led out from among the nations, and they all dwell securely—and you will arise like the thunderstorm, will come like the cloud to cover the land.
>
> But you, son of man, prophesy against Gog and say: Thus has Yahweh said: See, I am against you, Gog, chief prince of Meshech and Tubal, and I will turn you round and will lead you by the nose and will let you come from the furthest north and will bring you to the mountains of Israel. And I will smite your bow out of your left hand and will let your arrows fall from your right hand. On the mountains of Israel you will fall, you and all your hordes and many nations who are with you. To the birds of prey, to everything that has wings, and to the wild beasts of the field I will give you as fodder. In the

> open field you will fall, for I have spoken (it), says Yahweh.
>
> But you, son of man, thus has Yahweh said: Say to the birds, to everything that has wings, and to all the wild beasts of the field:
>
> Assemble and come, gather together from round about to my sacrifice which I will slaughter for you, a great sacrifice on the mountains of Israel. And you shall eat flesh and drink blood. The flesh of heroes you shall eat, and the blood of the princes of the earth you shall drink: rams, lambs and goats—bulls, fatlings from Bashan are they all. And you shall eat the fat of my sacrifice which I have slaughtered for you until you are filled and drink the blood until you are drunk, and you shall be filled at my table with horses and chariot horses, with heroes and all warriors, says Yahweh.

This self-contained composition is characterized as to form by the consistent presence of the direct address, first of all to Gog and then to the wild beasts and birds who hold judgment feast over him. This gives it its liveliness. More specifically, its language, as has been observed again and again in Ezekiel, can be described neither as prose nor as tightly controlled speech.[3] Rather, it reveals the character of a rhythmical elevated prose, in which there appear two-stress and three-stress lines which are occasionally connected in clear parallelism (see, e.g., 38:9; 39:17f) without being linked by fixed laws into a metrically self-contained whole.

The three-fold commission to speak divides the whole into three strophes. The fact that the first two begin in stylistically similar ways may distantly recall the similar beginnings of the description of the two young lions in the קינה ("lament") of chapter 19 (v 3 // vv 5b, 6). It appears, further, to be an intentional artistic element that in each of these three strophes, by a twice recurring element which acts as a kind of refrain, there is given at the same time the key-word for the content of the strophe in question. In strophe one it is עמים רבים אתך ("many nations with you") which recurs at the end of each half-section (38:6, 9). It underlines the large numbers of people in Gog's army which are described in strophe one. In strophe two, על הרי ישראל תפול ("on the mountains of Israel you will fall") (39:4a) recurs in variation to על פני השדה תפול ("in the open field you will fall") (v 5)—and this describes the content of this strophe too, which narrates Gog's fall. And the third strophe, על זבחי אשר אני זבח לכם ("to my sacrifice which I will slaughter for you") (39:17), which recurs, again slightly varied, in the מזבחי אשר זבחתי לכם of v 19 ("my sacrifice which I have slaughtered for you"), brings out the main content of vv 17–20, which speak of Yahweh's great sacrificial meal. But even this concealed element of form is handled quite freely and does not become firmly fixed as a refrain.

The basic text of chapters 38f then experienced expansions which emphasize individual features more clearly or else add completely new elements. Alongside expansions which are still in the form of an address (38:10–13, 14–16, 17) there appear others which abandon this address form. A prosaic character emerges more strongly from some of these additions (e.g. 39:9–16).

On the tradition-history of the Gog pericope. With the question about the "bricks" of the Gog prophecy one comes anew upon the observation that in Ezekiel traditions from various spheres are brought together into a new creation.

Let us first ask about the origin of the name Gog. It is clear in any event that Gog is understood to be an unusually powerful prince (נשיא ראש "chief prince") "from the far north" (מירכתי צפון 39:2) who also has around him followers from the far north (38:6). A mysterious foe from the north who will suddenly erupt into the land and spread terror in Judah and Jerusalem is found above all in the early prophecies of Jeremiah (especially Jer chapters 4–6). "See, a people is coming 'from the north country' (מארץ צפון), a great nation is 'stirring' (יעור, with this cf. the תער 'arise' in the expansion in Ezek 38:14) 'from the farthest parts of the earth' (מירכתי ארץ)" (Jer 6:22). At a later stage the place of this foe in the preaching of Jeremiah is taken by the Babylonian king. It is in this way that even King Jehoiakim interprets the words which are read out to him from Jeremiah's scroll: "Why have you written in it [i.e. the scroll]: The King of Babylon will certainly come and destroy the land, and will cut off from it man and beast?" (Jer 36:29). On the basis of an account by Herodotus of

3 See, e.g., 1, 334.

a Scythian invasion as far down as the Egyptian frontier many have tried to see the Scythians in this "foe from the north."[4] Gunkel and Gressmann thought of the Medes. Or else, with a stronger disregard of the historical situation, the idea has been explained on the basis of the mythical sphere of the ominous north.[5] However one may resolve this question with regard to Jeremiah and however much one may reckon for Jeremiah already with a given prophetic tradition,[6] for Ezekiel 38f it is in any event clear that his references to the foe from the north are based on the Jeremianic preaching available to him (see also the image of clouds and storm wind in Jer 4:13 and Ezek 38:9 [16]). The secondary explication in 38:17 and 39:8 then openly states that Gog's invasion is the fulfillment of earlier prophetic preaching. One feels able still clearly to discern in 38:1–9, filling a self-contained first strophe, the original traditio-historical independence of the description of the uprising of this foe from the north along the lines of the Jeremianic "Scythian oracles."

But then there follows the announcement of the destruction of the foe on the "mountains of Israel"—this key-word runs emphatically through all three strophes (38:8; 39:2, 4, 17). There was nothing of such an end in Jeremiah's oracles about the foe from the north. But this expectation is expressed as clearly as one would wish in the framework of Isaiah's preaching about the Assyrians: "As I have planned, so shall it be, and as I have purposed so shall it stand. I will shatter Assyria in my land, will trample him under foot 'on my mountains' (על הרי)" (Is 14:24f). The two prophets express things differently. Isaiah regards the mountains of Palestine in terms of Yahweh's dwelling on Zion ("my mountains"), while Ezekiel defines them in terms of the people who live on them ("the mountains of Israel").[7] In fact, however, they coincide. Both speak of the end of the assailant in the heart of the mountains where Yahweh's temple stands and where Yahweh's people dwell. In the case of Isaiah too there arises the question of the origin of this expectation. We have recently become more strongly aware how decisively Isaiah's thought moves in the framework of a Zion theology, which is supported by the certainty that Yahweh's enemies must be shattered on his chosen holy city. Psalms 46; 48; 76 attest the existence of this Zion tradition, which in the case of Isaiah has penetrated deep into the substance of his preaching.[8] The fact that then in the expansion in 39:9f reference is also to the great destruction of the weapons—a feature which is found in Ps 46:10; 76:4 and, with different associations, in Is 9:4—is additional confirmation of these observations. Again at this point, however, one may suppose that Ezekiel 38f are not determined in their proclamation in a general way by "Zion traditions," but quite definitely have the preaching of the prophet Isaiah in mind and are concerned with the question of the fulfillment of that preaching. The end which Yahweh, in Isaiah's words, had promised to the Assyrians on the mountains of the chosen land will be fulfilled in the end of the foe from the north, the mention of which echoed Jeremiah's preaching. Thus in Ezekiel 38f there are intertwined elements of the preaching of Isaiah and Jeremiah. In the rather inelegant recapitulation of the details of the first strophe at the beginning of the second (39:1f) one can almost feel the effort which it requires to join together two elements of prophetic tradition which had previously been separate and to bring the Jeremiah tradition, which was still treated very independently in the first strophe, into line with statements of promise from Isaiah.

The third strophe adds nothing essential to the course of the great action, but simply illustrates further the end of Gog. In developing Yahweh's victory with the image of the sacrificial meal prepared by Yahweh himself there is certainly taken up again a motif which can be traced already in pre-exilic prophecy. Zeph 1:7 (Jer 46:10) uses it in his description of the day of Yahweh. The summoning of the wild beasts to the day of judgment has its prototype in Jer 12:9.[9]

But where do the name and figure of Gog originate?

4 Herodotus 1, 103–106. See Duhm; Piotrowicz, "L'invasion," and others.

5 Lauha, *ZAPHON*, 62–68. On the whole question see Rudolph, *Jeremia*.

6 Lauha, *ZAPHON*, 55–62.

7 On this see 1, 185f; correspondingly, 1, 203, "the land of Israel," 1, 292, "the prophets of Israel," 1, 445f, "the prince of Israel," above p. 214, "the shepherds of Israel"; see also Appendix 2.

8 See Rohland, *Erwählungstraditionen*, 119–208; von Rad, *OT Theology*, 2. 155–169; Aubrey R. Johnson, *Sacral Kingship in Ancient Israel* (Cardiff: University of Wales Press, 1955), 77–93.

9 On the whole range of imagery connected with Yahweh's sacrificial meal see Gressmann, *Ursprung*, 136–141; Grill "Schlachttag Jahwes."

The mention of a Reubenite Gog in 1 Chr 5:4 can contribute nothing to the illumination of the question. The translators of 𝔊 not only found the name Gog in Nu 24:7 (see also ﮃ, 𝔏, 'A, Σ, Θ), where 𝔐 reads the name of the Amalekite king Agag, but also understood the גזי of Am 7:1 𝔐 as Gog, and this has raised the question of a possible mythical interpretation of the figure of Gog. Gressmann considers Gog as a "locust giant" after the manner of the scorpion man in the Gilgamesh epic.[10] Heinisch believes that we can understand Gog, on the basis of Sumerian *gūg* "darkness," as the personification of darkness. But these are scarcely satisfactory explanations.

The question is further complicated by the observation that the land of Gog (although only in the secondary addition in 38:2 and its expansion in 39:6) is called Magog. This name recurs in Gen 10:2 (1 Chr 1:5) in the enumeration of the sons of Japheth. The eldest of these, Gomer, who is mentioned in 38:6 among Gog's allies and who is mentioned in Gen 10:3 as the father of Togarma who is also mentioned in 38:6 as an ally of Gog, is followed by Magog and then by Madai, the representative of Media. After Javan, the representative of the Greek world, there follow Tubal and Meshech, which are mentioned in 38:2; 39:1 as the actual area of Gog's dominion. One is reluctant to separate Magog from Gog. Albright believes he can find in the linking of the two names a conscious desire for rhyme such as exists also in the juxtaposition of כרתי and פלתי in 2 Sam 8:18 and elsewhere, of אלדד and מידד in Nu 11:27 and of Jabal, Jubal and Tubal(-Cain) in Gen 4:20–22. Is then Gog or Magog the original name? Aalders thinks it is Magog, alongside which Gog would be Magog's representative.[11] Boehmer tries to understand the word, in an artificial variation of an "athbash" type of formation, as a cryptogram of בבל ("Babylon") and to regard גוג ("Gog") as a derivation of that. More probable is the reverse derivation, which regards Magog as Gog's domain. Admittedly the explanation of it as a contraction of an original Akkadian *^{māt}Gôg* involves linguistic difficulties.[12] Still more far-fetched is Albright's supposition that Magog is a mixture of Manda and Gog, where Manda is a reference to the Umman manda, the northern barbarians. One would then rather, from a linguistic point of view, think of a bold analogy with the formation of nouns of place by means of prefixed מ, with which there has been formed an original designation for the "land of Gog" over and above the traditional names "chief prince of Meshech and Tubal." Genesis 10 (P) stands close, traditio-historically, to Ezekiel 38f.

For the name Gog, which will thus have been the primary element,[13] certain names of peoples have further been pointed out. On the basis of Amarna letter I, 38 Albright thinks of a country *gaga,* which should really be *gasga* and which is to be located in Cappadocia near the border with Armenia. Since in Hittite this name is used to describe swineherds, it is a derogatory term ("barbarian"). Dürr prefers to think of a princely tribe *gâgi* in the region to the north of Assyria, a tribe which is mentioned in the Annals of Ashurbanipal.[14]

But the present text speaks very definitely of a ruler who bears this name. Thus a search has been made in the old tradition for persons with a similar names. F. Delitzsch drew attention to a city prince *gâgu,* mentioned in the Annals of Ashurbanipal, "the powerful ruler of a warlike mountain people not too far to the north of Assyria."[15] Messel[16] unhesitatingly postulated an officer of this name under Cyrus the Younger, while Gerlemann, according to whom Ezekiel took the name Gog from the Balaam oracle in Nu 24:7, foregoes any more precise historical designation. In the present state of our knowledge, the greatest probability is surely still to be accorded to the connection with Gyges (Γύγης), who appears as a powerful Lydian king in the Annals of Ashurbanipal under the name *gûgu.*[17] That he subsequently was a great preoccupation of later ages can be deduced from the legendary tradition in Herodotus.[18]

10 Gressmann, *Messias,* 128 note 1.
11 Aalders, *Gog en Magog.*
12 M. Streck, "Das Gebiet der heutigen Landschaften Armenien, Kurdistân und Westpersien nach den babylonisch-assyrischen Keilinschriften," *Zeitschrift für Assyriologie* 15 (1900), 321, fn. 1; see also Driver, "Linguistic Problems," 183.
13 So too Koehler-Baumgartner; Hölscher, *Drei Erdkarten.*
14 Dürr, *Apokalyptik,* 98f.
15 Friedrich Delitzsch, *Wo lag das Paradies? Eine biblisch-assyriologische Studie* (Leipzig: Hinrichs, 1881), 246f.
16 Messel, 125f.
17 See above pp. 59f and 129, and *ARAB* 2, 779–785, 847f, 876.
18 1, 8ff.

The domain of Magog in Gen 10:2 would then be Lydia.[19] However, it is immediately clear how poorly defined is the precise geographical and historical knowledge behind the statements of Ezekiel 38f. There is admittedly some knowledge of the legendary mountain peoples on the northern edge of the known world, of Tubal and Meshech, of Gomer and Togarma, but no distinction is made between the area of the Lydian kingdom with its king Gyges and the areas encompassed by these four names. But perhaps we are already going too far in assuming any knowledge at all of the connection between Gog and Lydia. It is also possible that the name Gog had already become a cipher for a legendary great ruler who rules over the multiplicity of threatening northern powers on the edge of the then-known world and as such is the exemplary representative of the "foe from the north."[20] But all this remains very uncertain.

Thus, in the proclamation about Gog, if one can describe these hazy details about nations as a common stream of tradition, traditions run together from three principal tributaries and produce the material for what is said in Ezekiel 38f, which vis-à-vis all these individual traditions also has something new to say.

Setting

When and where did this Gog proclamation arise in its original concise form?

While commentators up to the turn of the century saw no problem in deriving Ezekiel 38f from the exilic prophet Ezekiel,[21] distrust arose subsequently. Chapters 38f have been attributed to a later redactor of the book.[22] Messel wished to refer the oracle to the campaign of Cyrus the Younger against Babylon (described by Xenophon), during which an officer called Gog wanted to push on to Egypt, and thus justify, here too, his dating of Ezekiel to the period around 400 B.C. Torrey, who sees in the ראש ("chief") of 38:2; 39:1 the circumlocution for Javan-Greece which has broken away from the triad Javan-Tubal-Meshech of 27:13 (Gen 10:2; 1 Chr 1:5) and which is then designated here as "head" ("chief" of the kingdoms), finds in Gog the "Greek" Alexander the Great.[23] On the basis of other considerations Browne comes to the same conclusion. A further step still is taken by van den Born.[24] In the ארץ המגוג ("the land of Magog") of 38:2 𝔐, he assumes a scribal error for an older abbreviation ארץ המג׳, behind which there lies an original ארץ המגדן "the territory of the Macedonian" in which the Macedonian Alexander is clearly discernible. And Berry even believes that he can recognize in the events described in 1 Macc 6:18f the background of the Gog pericope and that he ought to identify Gog with Antiochus Eupator (163–162).

But if, after all this, we examine the text itself, then it can first of all be affirmed that the basic text is in no way stylistically different from what is usual elsewhere in Ezekiel, but rather in many respects corresponds to that: in the introductory gesture to which the prophet is summoned, which was directed towards persons also in 13:17 and 29:2; in the challenge or encounter formula; in the reference to the הרי ישראל ("mountains of Israel"); in the word that is exclusive to Ezekiel, אגפים ("hordes") (12:14; 17:21) in the description of the army.[25] Ezekiel's language is recalled by the elevated prose style, the emphasis by means of the concluding formula כי אני דברתי ("for I have spoken [it]") in 39:5 (see 23:34; 26:5; 28:10). But also the broad development of the image of Yahweh's sacrificial meal in the third stophe in comparison with the briefer mention of it in Zeph 1:7 is in line with the unique character of the prophet most recently confirmed in chapter 34.[26]

But alongside these stylistic considerations there are also those of a factual nature involving the content which suggest that the basic text of chapters 38f should not be removed too far from Ezekiel, even that a derivation from the prophet himself is not impossible. Thus the unmistakable traditio-historical dependence of the Gog pericope on Isaiah and especially on Jeremiah is completely bound up with the observations which one is able

19 Hölscher, *Drei Erdkarten*, 54.

20 See what has been said above (p. 279) on the name David.

21 Ewald, Hitzig, Smend, Haevernick, Bertholet, Kraetzschmar.

22 J. Herrmann, *Ezechielstudien;* Hölscher; Cooke.

23 Torrey, *Pseudo-Ezekiel*, 96 note 37.

24 van den Born, 'pays du Magog.'

25 On the "introductory gesture" see 1, 182f; on the "challenge or encounter formula" see 1, 175 and above p. 98; on the "mountains of Israel" see 1, 185.

26 See above p. 214.

to make about completely genuine Ezekiel texts.[27] The nature of the dependence is, admittedly, not the same in the case of chapters 38f as that of Ezekiel 23 on Jer 3:6ff. Here, as the explanation in 38:17 clearly explains secondarily, it is a question of the central problem of the historical resolution of those old prophetic pronouncements which still lay unresolved in the presence of the prophet. But this question certainly does not lead to a later period. That precisely the period of the exile was quite urgently preoccupied with the question of the fulfillment of divine promise is clear not only from Ezek 29:17ff,[28] but above all from the preaching of Deutero-Isaiah. That of which the prophet Jeremiah was already assured by Yahweh in the vision in 1:11f—namely that Yahweh is watching over his word—becomes in the exilic period one of the great themes of Israel's reflection on the mystery of her God in this period of disaster. Israel clings to the divine word which has been given to her—the only thing which has remained for her in this time of total collapse—and questions it, in passionate involvement, as to what it contains of truth and validity.[29] In the Gog pronouncement we see the prophet of the exile, in the completely new exposition of older prophetic word, busy at this very task. Into the announcement of the foe from the north (Jeremiah) and of Yahweh's victory over his enemy in the holy land itself (Isaiah) which has come to him from older prophecy, he introduces the concrete details about the northern king Gog and his hordes which were completely absent from the older Jeremiah preaching and actualizes them by means of these references.

In view of these concrete actualizations, however, it is worthwhile to look back once again on 32:17ff and on what was said there.[30] In the enumeration of the three great dead ones, Assyria, Elam and Meshech-Tubal, we believed that we could observe the historical and temporal experiences of the Mesopotamian plain. The three great disrupters of the Mesopotamaian world in the preceding centuries were there presented as inhabitants of the underworld. From these three there is selected here the geographically most remote as the one who is least known, the most strange with regard to his political structure (see below on נשׂיא ראשׁ "chief prince") and the one who is, consequently, the most sinister. Even if he is, at the moment, historically remote (32:17ff, more boldly, said "dead"), he is nevertheless pronounced here to be the one who could unexpectedly again be dangerously near. This too was probably spoken from the experiences of life and history of those living in Mesopotamia, who had witnessed, in the fall of Nineveh for example, the sinister irruption of the mountain peoples into the plain. The question will then arise here of the earliest possible period in the Mesopotamian plain for such an experience of danger brewing in the region of (Lydia?) Meshech-Tubal, Gomer and Beth Togarma (a danger which is then directed, in the context of the Israelite Gog prediction, predetermined by Jeremiah's preaching, not against Mesopotamia but against the holy land to which Israel is to return). This would be more probable in the period in which the northern mountain country is not yet joined with the plain in the unity of the Persian empire than in the period after 539. One would prefer to locate the Gog pericope before the conquest of Babylon by Cyrus also because the situation of an Israel gathered from among the nations and dwelling securely in her land is painted in 38:8 in colors to which the reality of the situation after the dispensation of the edict of Cyrus and the incipient return corresponds but little (cf. Haggai and Zechariah 1–8). Gathering and return are here depicted quite unconcernedly on the basis of pure prophetic promise. The geographical location of the actual center of the danger in Meshech-Tubal, i.e. in Asia Minor, also suggests location in a period in which the formation of the new political center of gravity in Persia, which becomes manifest in the period of Deutero-Isaiah, is not yet discernible.

27 On Jeremiah see, e.g., 1, 482 on Ezek 23; on Isaiah, 1, 172 on 5:1f.

28 See above pp. 118–120, as well as pp. 192f on 33:21f.

29 On this see Walther Zimmerli, "Der Wahrheitserweis Jahwes nach der Botschaft der beiden Exilspropheten" in *Tradition und Situation. Studien zur alttestamentlichen Prophetie Artur Weiser zum 70. Geburtstag dargebracht* (1963), 133–151.

30 See above pp. 171f and 175f.

In this context, two questions have yet to be considered. Again and again it has been observed with justified astonishment that nowhere in the book of Ezekiel is Babylon specifically threatened with Yahweh's judgment. The concealed threat admittedly to be found in the addition in 21:33–37 is much too obscure to be able to alter the total impression.[31] The conclusion has then been drawn from this (most forcefully by Boehmer) that Babylon must be concealed behind the Gog pericope. Against this assumption, however, there is the association of Gog with Meshech-Tubal, Gomer and Togarma, which, if it is taken seriously, clearly points in a different direction. Although in Jeremiah the Babylonian power may subsequently have taken the place of the "foe from the north" of the early preaching, this substitution is forbidden sufficiently clearly in the case of Ezekiel 38f.

But this leads directly to the second question: Is it feasible in the context of Ezekiel's preaching, which in the rest of the oracles always very clearly points to a following stage, that the prophet for once on this occasion is also pointing to a stage after the following one, i.e. to a second stage of divine activity over and above the one that is expected first (the gathering of the exiles)? There is no doubt that something new is happening here. A first step is taken on the way to apocalyptic, the aim of which is to set up a sequential order of future events. In the biblical sphere this step cannot be taken in the realm of free speculation about the future. The future is God's and therefore cannot be reached by any human acumen. But God had spoken. Thus the step will be taken where men hear and in heedful questioning submit to the word previously spoken by God and allow their thoughts of hope to be led by him in the direction of the future.

Is it then feasible that precisely Ezekiel could have taken this step of heedful reflection into the stage beyond next? This is often very swiftly denied, mostly by appealing to statements in the later additions to Ezekiel 38f.[32] The examination of Ezekiel's preaching has, however, made it clear that this prophet, much more than the prophets before him, formulated his word of judgment and salvation again and again out of words which had previously been heard. From Jeremiah he had learned to see in the Babylonian power and in Nebuchadnezzar the instrument of divine judgment. The limit of this vision is never overstepped in the genuine words of Ezekiel. He never speaks (in this he is very different from a Deutero-Isaiah and also from the author of Jeremiah 50f who refers the announcement of the "foe from the north" to the Medes and applies it polemically against Babylon) of judgment on Babylon. Against the background of this peculiarity it seems not unthinkable that the reckoning with the world power of the heathen nations, the reality of which must have been completely obvious even to an Ezekiel, is concentrated in a separate event alongside the judgment pronounced over individual neighboring powers in the oracles against foreign nations. In Jeremiah's announcement of the foe from the north, in Isaiah's promise of deliverance for the holy land he hears the previously issued divine proclamation of this event. But in this he refrains from any further "apocalyptic" development of this event. Just as the judgment on individual nations (with the single exception of the prouncement against Edom-Seir which has laid claim to Israel's land 35:1–36:15)[33] remains quite separate from the proclamation of salvation to Israel, so too the announcement of the final judgment on the enemy peoples from the north, as something which happens "at the end of years" (38:8), is not incorporated into the description of ultimate salvation in chapters 34–37 and chapters 40–48, far less combined with that in a total apocalyptic picture (thousand-year empire). The sequence of chapters 34–37, 38–39, 40–48 is not to be systematized, as the later apocalyptic development of the Gog prophecy does, in terms of a temporal sequence.[34]

Really compelling reasons for denying the oracle about Gog in its original form to the prophet Ezekiel who lived in the Mesopotamian region before the appearance of Cyrus cannot be adduced. The derivation of the Gog prophecy from Ezekiel's late preaching remains in the sphere of possibility.[35]

Interpretation

■ **38:1f** *The basic text.* The Gog prophecy too is confirmed by its introductory formula as a word event which contains teaching linked to a specific time.[36] The prophet is

31 See 1, 448.

32 See, e.g., Bertholet-Galling; Rohland, *Erwählungstraditionen,* 189f; Kuhl, *Prophets,* 135.

33 On 25:14 see above pp. 20f.

34 Kuhn, "Γὼγ καὶ Μαγώγ."

35 So, correctly, J. Herrmann in his commentary;

addressed as "son of man" and is summoned by Yahweh to turn against Gog with the gesture mentioned in 6:2 and elsewhere.[37] In contrast to all other passages it is here directed not against an already publicly known person (false prophetesses, Pharaoh) or locality (Jerusalem, Ammon, Sidon, Mount Seir), but against a figure who is still hidden from universal knowledge and who will irrupt into history "after many days, at the end of the years." If the name Gog is intended to be the name of a ruler already known in the past (Gyges), then this "hiddenness" could be compared with what was said above about the future David, who is equally still "hidden" as far as the present of the exile is concerned.[38]

The one who is to come is located geographically more precisely. Certainly ראש ("chief") is to be connected with נשיא ("prince") and is not to be interpreted as a geographical indication (note b). This renders superfluous the various attempts to find an equivalent for ראש in "the ἔθνος Σκυθικόν which lives in the northern Taurus and which the Byzantines call οἱ ʿΡῶς"[39] or in the tribe of the ʿΡωξολανοί or Roxalani and then in the Russians.[40] Gog's actual sphere of rule is Meshech and Tubal. These groups from Asia Minor were enumerated in the trade list in 27:13 as trading partners of Tyre (in the reverse order), cited in 32:26 as brutal nations of the past.[41] Here they are political powers which will once again, in the future, unfold all their menace. Jeremiah's "foe from the north" remained nameless. Above the supposition was expressed that the present geographical location of this foe arises from the horizon of the population of the Mesopotamian plain, which (as was already clear from 32:22–26), alongside the oppressors Assyria and Elam, was also aware of the danger of the northern peoples (Scythians, Cimmerians) invading uncannily from the mountains.[42] Jeremiah 50f indentified the "foe from the north" with the Medes.

Gog, to whom secondarily a land Magog has been attributed,[43] is described as "chief prince" of Meshech and Tubal. The title נשיא ראש ("chief prince") is unusual. In spite of the somewhat deviant grammatical structure vis-à-vis the כהן הראש ("the chief priest") of 2 Kgs 25:18; 2 Chr 19:11 (also Ezr 7:5 הכהן הראש; 1 Chr 27:5 הכהן ראש), it is to be understood as a description of the one who stands out from a plurality of princes. The title מלך ("king") which in Ezekiel is characteristic in the first instance of the high king and which in Jer 25:26 is also used naturally for the 'kings of the north' (cf. also in Ezek 26:7 Nebuchadnezzar in the role of the high king who is to come from the north), is avoided.[44] At the same time, however, by means of the added ראש ("chief"), Gog is also to be set apart from the circle of second rank נשיאים ("princes").[45] Over and above this, there seems also to be implied a correct knowledge of the strange governmental structure of the northern princes, which, in the relationship of a number of national groups and their leaders over which there stands the unifying authority of a נשיא ראש ("chief prince"), differs from the political structure of those settled in the cultivated land.[46] Thus already in his title Gog is introduced not as the ruler of a great united empire, but as the leader of a number of national groups.

■ **38:3** With the challenge or encounter formula the prophet is to address this ruler in the divine word (introductory messenger formula) and to announce to him Yahweh's action.[47] In contrast to all the other passages in which Yahweh announces his activity in such a summons, it is not here a question of an act of Yahweh which punishes (5:8; 13:8f, 20; and elsewhere) or which brings salvation (36:9) and in which he has responded with his action to the addressee's "previous history." Rather he initiates such a history here for the first time.

■ **38:4** He leads Gog out of his land so that he can begin his terrible work. The thought that, like the Assyrians in Isaiah and the "foe from the north" and then Nebuchadnezzar in Jeremiah, he might be coming as Yahweh's

Eissfeldt, *OT Introduction;* Fohrer.

36 See 1, 144f.

37 On "son of man" see 1, 131f; see 1, 142f.

38 See above p. 279.

39 Orelli, "Gog und Magog."

40 Knobel, *Völkertafel,* countered by König, "Vorgeschichte," and Uhlemann, "Gog und Magog."

41 See above pp. 65f; see above pp. 175f.

42 See above p. 303.

43 Note a, see above pp. 283f.

44 See above p. 277; see above pp. 35f.

45 See above p. 277.

46 On this "*nāśî*'-in-chief" see also Speiser, "*nāśî*'," 113.

47 See 1, 175 and above p. 98. See also 1, 133.

instrument against Israel is here quite non-existent. A later hand has subsequently (note b) vigorously shown, with the image of the beast that is dragged in, subdued by means of hooks, how restricted Gog is in all his wild activity and how, in the last resort, he is led by Yahweh. The image comes from 19:4 (29:4).[48] It is certainly to overload ושובבתיך ("and I will turn you round") to find hidden in it the reference to a previous first campaign of punishment by Gog against Babylon.[49] Rather one might wonder whether it does not contain an element of bringing back, so that this would contain a reminiscence of a Gog of the past.

Gog comes with a great army (otherwise in the case of Pharaoh 17:17), with horses and riders (23:6, 12), in full armor (23:12) and with a great company. קהל רב ("a great company") occurs also in 17:17 (see also 26:7; 32:3). The description has been expanded secondarily by the enumeration of protective and offensive weapons (note d).

■ **38:5** In a further addition from a later hand three groups of mercenary soldiers, from Persia, Cush and Put, have been added, but they basically have no business in the army of these wild, warrior tribes who are capable of waging their own wars.[50] The secondary character of v 5 naturally prevents the use of the reference to the Persians for the dating of the basic text of chapters 38f.

■ **38:6** The continuation of the original text in v 6 mentions as Gog's allies two further tribes from the Asia Minor-Armenia mountains in the north. בית תוגרמה ("Beth Togarma") appeared in 27:14 as a trading partner of Tyre immediately after Javan, Tubal and Meshech. סוסים ופרשים ("horses and riders"; at 27:14 "draught-horses and saddle-horses"), which, according to v 4, characterize Gog's army, were there mentioned as exports. The priestly table of nations in Gen 10:3 (1 Chr 1:6) mentions Togarma among the Japhethites as a son of Gomer. גמר ("Gomer"), which is not otherwise mentioned in Ezekiel, is to equated with the *gimirrai* of the Akkadian annals and with the Κιμμέριοι of the Greeks. According to the Odyssey the Cimmerians live where no ray of sunlight ever reaches, ἠέρι καὶ νεφέλῃ κεκαλυμμένοι, at the entrance to Hades.[51] According to the Akkadian annals, at the end of the eighth century they attacked the Armenian kingdom of Urartu from the north, were themselves attacked in the seventh century by the Scythians from the north and became a source of anxiety to Esarhaddon.[52] To their onslaught Gyges of Lydia, who, in the event that Gyges is to be found behind the figure of Gog, here will have become their leader, later fell victim.[53] Subsequently, however, their force was subsumed under the power of the Medes.[54]

■ **38:7** With a summons to be ready, which recalls Am 4:12, but which in its doubling of the verb reveals a favorite stylistic feature of Ezekiel (note a), the speech begins a second fulfillment. If v 7b is correctly reconstructed on the basis of 𝔊 (note c), it refers the command to be ready specifically to readiness for "obedience" (משמר) to Yahweh. Gog is put on the alert by Yahweh for his (i.e. Yahweh's) service.

■ **38:8** The details concerning the time of Gog's envisaged active attack (מימים רבים "after a long time" and the parallel באחרית השנים "at the end of the years") have received much attention. According to Staerk באחרית הימים ("at the end of days"), which is found thirteen times in the OT and with which he suddenly associates "the analogous באחרית השנים ("at the end of years")," is first attested in 38:16 and is to be regarded as a coinage of the exilic period.[55] It "served to describe the time in which, after complete repentance and perfect realization on the part of the people, the expected messianic kingdom would appear as the just reward for the faithful."[56] Dürr, on the other hand, who would prefer to accept a pre-exilic time of origin for ten out of the fourteen (including Dan 2:28) occurrences, finds in it an older eschatological term which indicates the turning point which begins with the day of Yahweh. What is new in Ezekiel is that the older, national eschatology extends, in the prophetic Gog oracle, to a universal expectation of

48 See 1,395 (pp. 111f).
49 Herrmann, 252f.
50 See note a. On the three mercenary groups, where פרס appears in place of an earlier לוד, see what has been said above pp. 59f. And on the repeated addition of parts of armor which leads to the inelegant double occurrence of מגן, see note a also.
51 Odyssey XI, 12ff.
52 Schmökel, *Geschichte,* 166, 267; 274, 276.
53 Schmökel, *Geschichte,* 280.
54 Schmökel, *Geschichte,* 282, 311.
55 Staerk, "Gebrauch," 248.
56 Staerk, "Gebrauch," 253.

judgment on the nations, thereby paving the way to the apocalyptic understanding of the day of Yahweh as the "absolute eschatological final act."[57] Now it is clear that we cannot reckon in the OT with an abstract concept of time nor with an "absolute end."[58] Time is time filled with event. Thus here we are not to think on the basis of a given eschatological scheme in which time is given in advance as the housing for the event which is to fill it and into which, at the end of a stretch of time which is previously thought of generally as "empty," the events presented here are to be set. The expression מימים רבים ("after a long time") used at the beginning of v 8, understood at its most straightforward, says quite simply that the events will take place at a not inconsiderable time in the future. This at the same time predetermines the understanding of the parallel expression באחרית השנים ("at the end of the years"). This formulation, which is found only here in the OT, expresses the conclusion of the period consisting of years (not of all theoretically imaginable years in the world) after which Gog will erupt.

This period, however, is filled by the immediately following details which speak of what will happen beforehand. In mysterious secrecy the "mountains of Israel" are not instantly named as the goal of Gog's campaign, but these mountains are spoken of as a land whose population (to be understood as an intermediate element) has been brought back from having been slaughtered by the sword (37:1–14) and has been gathered together again from among the many nations (20:32ff). Only then does there follow the reference to the mountains of Israel, which have "long" (תמיד, note f) been under the shame of devastation, but which are now re-inhabited in undisturbed peace by those who have been brought back from among the nations. In all this, the process which chapters 34–37 had described in full is presupposed to have been completed (on the re-inhabiting of the devastated land see 36:34f, on the living "in security" and peace [לבטח] 28:26; 34:25, 27f). The "many days" and the "years" which first must come to an end refer to the fulfillment of the salvation which has been promised in the prophet's earlier preaching. At the end of the time which is filled with this event, at history's furthest horizon, which has only just been glimpsed and from which the statements of chapters 40ff (in so far as these originate with Ezekiel) are not to be excluded as an account of what is only an event at one remove (there is no speculation here on the problem of the discontinuation of time), there will follow the uprising of Gog, who is summoned like one who has been conscripted for military service. The person of the one who summons remains unexpressed in allusive language in a passive expression. פקד ("to summon") is frequent in Jeremiah; in Ezekiel only otherwise in 23:21.[59]

■ **38:9** Gog will draw near like a mighty thunderstorm to cover the land with his great hordes. Jer 4:13 had described the foe coming down from the north with the same imagery: "See, he 'comes up like clouds' (כעננים יעלה), his chariots like the whirlwind. . . ." The key-word שאה ("thunderstorm") might come from Is 10:3: "What will you do on the day of 'punishment' (פקדה), in the 'storm' (שואה) which will come from afar?"[60] With the repetition of the thematic key phrase which has already occurred at the end of the first part (v 6b), ועמים רבים א[ו]תך ("and many nations with you"), the first strophe ends. It has concentrated completely on the description of God's mighty mobilization and therefore has been still very close to the oracles about the "foe from the north" in Jeremiah (see also Is 5:26–29). There is no mention at all of any subjective guilt on Gog's part. Everything has been objectively arranged by God, the fulfillment of what has been proclaimed earlier, as the addition in v 17 will then later, quite correctly, affirm.

■ **39:1-5** Divine activity, however, then also dominates the second strophe, 39:1–5, the beginning of which is stylistically identical with the beginning of the first. But then it changes from the statement about the approach of the enemy, which is in line with the Jeremiah oracles, to the statement about the destruction of the foe on the mountains of Israel, the old proclamation of Isaiah. Here the challenge (encounter) formula which hangs threateningly over the first strophe finds its development in the

57 Dürr, *Apokalyptik,* 104.

58 See, e.g., von Rad, *OT Theology,* 2. 99ff.

59 See Josef Scharbert, "Das Verbum PQD in der Theologie des Alten Testaments," *BZ* 4 (1960): 209–226.

60 On שאה and ענן see Scott, "Phenomena," 24.

full proclamation of judgment on Gog.[61]

■ **39:2** V 2 succinctly recapitulates the content of the first strophe in four verbal statements.[62] The immediately following עלה ("to arise") was used in 38:9 and בוא ("to come") in 38:8, 9 in the qal, in the active, of Gog, but here these two verbs are used to refer strictly to Yahweh's activity and are put into the hipʿil. The whole journey with its point of departure in the "furthest north" and its goal on the "mountains of Israel" is under Yahweh's guidance. Here too there is no mention whatsoever of any subjective guilt on Gog's part.

■ **39:3** The judgmental event which now follows takes the form in vv 3–4a of a duel between Yahweh and Gog. The latter is represented as an archer. This might be a reference to the particular weapons of the northern peoples, of whom the basic text of the first strophe had simply said that they came with horses and riders (on this see Is 5:28; Jer 4:29; 6:23). In the book of Ezekiel bows and arrows are referred to, other than in 39:9 only in quite different contexts (קשת "bow" in 1:28; חצים "arrows" in 5:16; 21:26).[63] The details of the duel are described just as little as those of the battle in 30:22 with the Pharaoh, whose arm is broken and whose sword is struck out of his hand. The archer's left hand is in the habit of holding the bow, while the right hand takes the arrow from the quiver (so-called Gorytus, worn on a belt over the left hip)[64] which is worn on the left side, lays it on the string and stretches the latter. Yahweh strikes Gog's bow out of his left hand and the arrows out of his right.

■ **39:4** Once again the field of battle on which, around the chief prince, his armies also fall is specifically said to be the mountains of Israel. And just as on a battlefield after a battle between men wild beasts and birds of prey gather ("Wherever a body is there the vultures gather" Mt 24:28; see also 2 Sam 21:10), so over this field of divine battle the animals gather for the gruesome meal which Yahweh has here prepared.

■ **39:5** So Gog will fall—no more closely descriptive stroke illustrates the details of God's battle with the army of the nations. The concluding remark establishes concerning it simply that it is promised in Yahweh's word. Yahweh's victory will reveal itself as Yahweh's fulfilled word.

One can again observe, in this second strophe too, the complete lack of any internal motivation. For the prophet it is sufficient to say that in this event divine proclamation is fulfilled. The motivation of the Jeremiah oracles of the foe from the north, which, according to Jeremiah 3–6, irrupts over a sinful nation as Yahweh's instrument of judgment, is here totally abandoned. In Ezekiel's emphasis, on the other hand, that this whole event takes place on the mountains of Israel and obviously also *for* the mountains of Israel and for the nation which has returned there, one cannot fail to hear the reference to God's fidelity to his relationship with Israel.

■ **39:17–20** The third strophe, 39:17–20, grows quite organically out of the second. It takes up the graphic stroke, delineated in v 5, of the wild beasts and birds of prey which hold feast on the field of battle, develops it more graphically and at the same time animates it along the lines of the dramatic structure of the first two strophes and puts the whole in the style of a direct address as Yahweh's mobilization of the wild beasts and the birds of prey (see also Jer 12:9; Is 56:9).

■ **39:17** Again it begins with the commission to the son of man, who must now command the wild beasts and birds (cf. 37:4ff the command to the dead bones and 37:9 to the spirit of life). In addition, however, the image changes as a result of the introduction of a new element, which can show that in this gruesome section too we are dealing with something that has been arranged by Yahweh in all his majesty. The feast of the animals becomes the sacrificial feast to which Yahweh himself invites. This motif, which is older than Ezekiel, is used in Zeph 1:7 in the context of the description of the day of Yahweh, on which the people in Jerusalem are "sanctified" like sacrificial animals for slaughter. In a later

61 This connection is overlooked by Humbert, "'hinnenî êlékâ,'" 108 (see 38:3 note c).

62 On the introductory ושבבתיך ("and I will turn you round") see what was said on 38:4; on the *hapax legomenon* ששא ("to lead by the nose") see note b.

63 On bows and arrows as the most important weapons of, e.g., the Scythian horsemen see Tamara Talbot Rice, *The Scythians* (New York: Praeger, 1957), 73.

64 Rice (see preceding fn.).

passage, Is 34:5–8, it is used in the context of an oracle of judgment on the nations, in particular on Edom, in whose land Yahweh brings about the great slaughter. Gressmann thought he could find there the prophetic obverse of the eschatological picture of Yahweh's salvation feast.[65] Grill points, in addition, to Jer 46:10; 50:26f (Rev 19:17–21) as passages in which undoubted expression is given to the motif of Yahweh's day of battle. He finds references to it in Is 30:33; Ps 22:20; 37:20; 49:15; Lam 2:21f (Jas 5:5). The point of the use of precisely this motif in Ezekiel 39, where Gog and his hordes, the sacrificial animals, the wild beasts and the birds are guests at the feast, is supposed to lie in lending to Gog's fall the character of world-wide publicity. Just as, according to 17:24, all the trees of the earth are to observe how Yahweh deals with his royal house, so here the whole non-human animal creation (see the emphatic כל "all" in the address to beasts and birds) participates in the event of divine victory on behalf of his people on the mountains of Israel. Gog himself, however, is completely effaced from this final description.

■ **39:18** Here revealed stands his mighty army, which is now clearly seen to be the army of representatives of the earthly powers: heroes, princes of the earth are named before the discourse returns once more to the figurative language of animal sacrifice: rams, lambs, goats, cows, fat beasts from Bashan.

■ **39:19** When v 19 speaks of satiation and drunkenness with the fat and the blood of the sacrificial animals, then the recollection of the fact that in the normal sacrificial meal the fat and the blood are reserved for Yahweh (44:7, 15; see, e.g., Lev 3:16f) can show how boldly exaggerated is what is said here.

■ **39:20** In the concluding verse, however, which first of all insures once again that the guests will not have to rise hungry from Yahweh's table, the phraseology returns without figure of speech to the mention of horses and chariot horses, heroes and warriors.

On the detailed terminology there are the following references. גבור ("hero") occurs also in 32:12, 21, 27. With נשיאי הארץ ("princes of the earth") may be compared the נשיאי הים ("princes of the sea") of 26:16.[66] אילים (here "rams") is an ambiguous word which mediates between the two spheres of the animal and the human worlds. It occurred in 27:21 in the trade list between כרים ("lambs") (in Ezekiel otherwise only as a siege instrument 4:2; 21:27) and עתודים ("goats") as an import from Arabia. Thus איל figures also in the enumeration of the offerings in chapters 40–48 (43:23, 25; 45:23f; 46:4–7, 11) as an important sacrificial animal. Already the shepherd chapter could show, in 34:17, how the two strong animals איל and עתוד (which is not attested elsewhere in Ezekiel) could also designate the "strong" in a human context.[67] איש מלחמה ("warrior") occurs again in the plural in the (secondary) passages 27:10, 27. פר ("bull") occurs elsewhere only as a sacrificial animal in chapters 43, 45f (*passim*). On מריאי בשן ("fatlings from Bashan"), which is attested only here in the OT, see what was said above on Bashan.[68] That the "fat beast" (מריא) is the preferred sacrificial offering is clear from 2 Sam 6:13; Is 1:11; Am 5:22. Whether the "fat beasts" here intentionally also "smack of those hostile to God" remains questionable.[69] Insofar as Yahweh, the sole recipient of all sacrifices, is here depicted as the one who arranges a great sacrificial meal on the (cultic) heights (הרי ישראל "mountains of Israel," cf. 6:2 and 18:6, 11, 15), this is a particularly bold anthropomorphism for the priest/prophet Ezekiel. In the general picture it is undoubtedly not the elements of cruelty that should be brought out, but the elements of the great feast at which no one must leave Yahweh's table unsatisfied (on this see the שלחני "my table," which is only attested otherwise in the OT in Ezek 44:16, and the שלחן יהוה "table of Yahweh" in Mal 1:7, 12), just as no one left David's feast unsatisfied in 2 Sam 6:19. It may seem strange that this last strophe of the basic text of the Gog pericope does not end with a specific statement of glorification (recognition formula). In the content of this third strophe its place has been

65 Gressmann, *Ursprung*, 141. So too Mowinckel, *Psalmenstudien, II*, 296f.

66 On נשיא see 1,209; 1,273; 1,364; and above pp. 277f.

67 From this result then the references to the אילי הארץ in 17:13, to the איל גוים (Nebuchadnezzar) in 31:11, to the אלי גבורים in 32:21 and to the אילים in Memphis in 30:13 (corrected text, see note c there). It occurs also in 31:14, but is there a textual error.

68 See above p. 300.

69 Grill, "Schlachttag Jahwes," 281.

taken by the matter of the unprecedented sacrificial meal itself. The concluding formula of the second strophe remains valid for this too: "I have spoken it."

The expansions. The basic text of the Gog pericope has subsequently been subject to expansions. The additions are not all from the same hand nor from the same period. They reveal a process of continuing reflection and exposition in the "school" of Ezekiel from different points of view.

■ **38:10–13** The concern of the expansion in 38:10–13 can, in the first place, be very clearly recognized. It is appended by means of a new introductory messenger formula and of the loose connecting formula והיה ביום ההוא ("and it will be on that day"), which is the sign of a secondary expansion. The marked objectivity of the basic text, according to which Gog alone, on Yahweh's mysterious, free resolve, is on the alert and is then summoned to the mountains of Israel, has subsequently been felt to be intolerable. It has been expanded here by means of a subjective motivation in the behavior of Gog and his followers which has revealed the judgment on Gog as an act of divine justice.

■ **38:10** Thus, coming strangely after vv 8f, reference is made to the wicked thoughts (חשב "to think" occurs also in 11:2) which "arise in Gog's heart" (on עלה על לב see 14:3f, 7; also 11:5; 20:32) and set him on his way.

■ **38:11** The quotation of these thoughts in the first person gives to the whole a great liveliness. There is in Gog's heart, in the first instance, the evil desire to commit an atrocity against the defenseless, who are to be attacked where they least expect it—a desire which is rooted deep in the mysterious depths of the human heart. The secure dwelling in the land of those who have returned there, which was spoken of in v 8 (connected with 34:25, 27f), is here interpreted more graphically in different words. They live in open, undefended settlements. The word פרזות ("undefended") occurs, apart from Est 9:19, otherwise only in Zech 2:8. This passage shows how soon after the exile minds in Jerusalem were concerned with the question: Rebuild the walls or have an unfortified Jerusalem protected only by Yahweh? Nehemiah's rebuilding of the walls then finally satisfied them. Thus it is felt that the expansion in vv 10–13 points to the period about or after 520. The person who added vv 10–13 is on the side of Zechariah, who was told in his third night vision (2:5–9) that Yahweh would be a protective wall of fire roundabout his city. In the Gog prophecy he hears, in respect of the question which vexes his period, the promise that Yahweh will, in the hour of greatest danger, reveal himself as the true protector of his people who live in open settlements. שקט ("peaceful") occurs in 16:42, 49 in a different usage. It may be supposed that the question of the refortification of Jerusalem also greatly concerned the exiles. The answer given here (and in Zechariah) is different from that given by the politician Nehemiah sent from the exilic community about the middle of the fifth century. But even Ezek 48:30–35 speaks quite naturally of gates for the future city of Jerusalem (see also Is 54:12).

A specific problem is also raised in vv 10f by the particularly close relationship to Jer 49:30f. There reference is made to Nebuchadnezzar's plans (חשב . . . מחשבה "he made . . . a plan") against Arabian Kedar (see above on 27:21)[70] where there follows also the direct quotation of the words of Nebuchadnezzar who summons to war against a carefree nation (גוי שלוי יושב לבטח "a nation at ease that dwells securely") who live apart without fortified settlements (לא דלתים ולא בריח לו בדד ישכנו "that has no gates or bars, that dwells alone"). Has the person who added vv 10–13 this Jeremiah oracle in mind?[71] At any rate the dwelling in open settlements, which was "natural" for those desert groups, is here given new, deeper significance.

■ **38:12** With this evil intention of attacking the weak there is instantly associated in Gog also the greedy desire for enrichment by the possessions of the defenseless. Once again, in the description of these defenseless people, reference is made back to v 8 with the idea of the ruins being now reinhabited (36:10, 33 referred to reconstruction, ni'pal of בנה "to build"), and the people being gathered from among the nations (עם מאסף מגוים "a nation which has gathered from among the nations" instead of [ארץ] מקבצת מעמים "(a land) which has been gathered together again from the nations" in v 8). But here too the description with its interpretation goes beyond what was said in v 8, when reference is made to

70 See above p. 68.

71 See Hans Bardtke, "Jeremia der Fremdvölkerprophet. II," *ZAW* 54 (1936): 256 note 2 (IX. 'Das Orakel wider Kedar und Hazor 49:28–33,' 255–256); Rudolph, *Jeremia*.

the rich possessions of cattle and goods. The thought takes up again what was said in 34:25ff and in 36:7ff about the new blessing in the land. The vocabulary used here, however, is not found anywhere else in the book of Ezekiel (see note d).

The name given to the dwelling place of the repatriated people is quite unusual. There is no further reference to the "mountains of Israel," but it is the "navel of the earth" which is mentioned as the place of residence of this people. A connection between טבור ("navel") and תבור ("Tabor") as suggested by D. W. Thomas,[72] and a subsequent translation as "raised ground, height, hill," is scarcely probable on linguistic grounds. Whether behind this figure of speech there lies in the long run the idea of the world as a mythical primeval being in human shape can no longer be decided. The name "navel," in any event, claims for the place so designated a location in the center of the world. This claim was expressed in non-mythical terms for Jerusalem in 5:5: "This is Jerusalem! I have set it in the midst of the nations with the lands round about it."[73] While what was expressed, theologically correctly, in 5:5 was the divine positioning, 38:12 speaks in a much more exposed way of a simple discovery of a position in the geographical world sphere. The passage in Ju 9:37 which records incidentally, without any secondary theological purpose, that Abimelich's armies advancing against Shechem come from טבור הארץ (according to Caspari to be translated as "from the navel of the land") would suggest that Gerizim near Shechem, the old sacred mountain and later site of the rival Samaritan sanctuary, also made the claim to be the central locality.[74] The wealth of material gethered by Wensinck and Roscher (see also Holma) makes it additionally clear that not only the assertion of living in the center of the world,[75] but also the specific reference to the "navel" (ὄμφαλος) is attested in a wide surrounding area. In Greece, alongside the dominating claim of Delphi, there stands the conception (apparent only in monuments rather than in literature) of the Eleusinian mystery cults that Athens, the *μητρόπολις τῶν καρπῶν*, was the place of the *ὄμφαλος*.[76] In the wider Greek world the same claim is made by Paphos, Branchidai, Delos, Epidauros. In post-biblical tradition it gained significance through its connection with the Adam legend in its relationship to Golgotha,[77] Zion and Moriah and perhaps also with Hebron. Islam, for its part, has transferred the tradition to Mecca. In the present passage it is surprising that Jerusalem is not explicitly mentioned, but only the "land" (v 11) and the people gathered on it—corresponding to the הרי ישראל ("mountains of Israel") of the basic text. Is the claim to be the "navel of the earth" here extended to the land as a whole or does Jerusalem nevertheless lie hidden in the background? In chapters 40–48, where the claim of the temple mount is most vigorously asserted, the expression does not recur. In any event, in this quite different language of 38:12, it is stated that Gog's campaign is not an undertaking similar to many other wars, but is a war at the center point of the world in which there is therefore also involved a decisive event of world history (see also "Aim").

■ **38:13** But then in v 13, by the addition of a quotation of words of others who are interested in this war, there is added to the whole a dramatic note. There is turmoil in the world of the merchants. The question of booty arouses their interest so that they ply Gog with wordy, verbose questions (see. e.g., the piling up of word plays in שלל שלל "to seize spoil," בזז בז "to carry off booty" [see also 29:19], הקהיל קהל "to summon hosts" as well as מקנה וקנין "cattle and goods"). Insofar as these questions in part imitate literally the phraseology of v 12, which described the intention of Gog himself, they reveal once more, as in a mirror, the evil greed of the brigand Gog. In addition, one can hear in this quotation of the trading nations Sheba (27:22), Dedan (25:13; 27:21), Tarshish (27:12) and their "traders" (סחרים and רכלים) an echo of the trade list of chapter 27.[78]

■ **38:14–23** There follow in vv 14–23 three additions with a completely new introduction, which, like 38:2;

72 D. Winton Thomas, "Mount Tabor: The Meaning of the Name," *VT* 1 (1951): 230.

73 On this see 1, 174f, and Schmidt, *heilige Fels*, 37f.

74 See Bernhard W. Anderson, "The Place of Shechem in the Bible," *BA* 20 (1957): 10f.

75 For Babylon see, e.g., Unger, *Babylon*, 20–24.

76 Aristides, cited by Roscher, *Omphalosgedanke*, 76.

77 Joachim Jeremias, *Golgotha*, ΑΓΓΕΛΟΣ Archiv für neutestamentliche Zeitgeschichte und Kulturkunde 1 (Leipzig: Pfeiffer, 1926), 43–45, 67.

78 On Sheba see above p. 68; on Dedan, p. 19; on Tarshish, p. 65; on "traders," note b and pp. 63f.

39:17, addresses the prophet as son of man, like 38:2 and 39:1(17) contains the command to prophesy and the commission to speak and like 38:3; 39:1, 17 marks a new beginning with the introductory messenger formula. They scarcely belong originally together. The second (v 17) is again introduced by its own messenger formula. The fact that they are secondary insertions is revealed from the point of view of form by the introductory לכן ("therefore") which is not found in the second and third strophes of the basic text and which here too fulfils no genuine logical function.

■ **38:14–16** The first, in the form of an interrogative reflection, whose introductory formula has therefore changed from the normal form והיה ביום ההוא ("and it will be on that day") (so vv 10, 18; 39:11) to the question הלוא ביום ההוא ("will it not be on that day"), contains (as note d above) largely simply a recapitulation of what was said in the first strophe of the basic text.[79] Admittedly עמי ישראל ("my people Israel") (vv 14, 16) and the ארצי ("my land") (v 16) reveal a terminology which differs from that of the basic text.

■ **38:14f** Also new is the reference to Gog's "coming" (note c), in which can be heard an echo of the "Scythian oracle" of Jer 6:22.[80] V 15 adds nothing new to vv 1–9. The statement to which vv 14–16 are actually leading up is to be found in v 16b.

■ **38:16** Here, in the first instance, the unique formula of v 8, באחרית השנים ("at the end of the years"), is changed to the common formula באחרית הימים ("at the end of days") (see Staerk). The recognition formula, linguistically altered and, from the point of view of its formal arrangement, strange as to its word order, states that the bringing of Gog to Yahweh's land is aimed at achieving recognition in the world of nations.[81] In the fact that Yahweh reveals himself to Gog as holy in the eyes of the nations he will be acknowledged. The formulation has its parallels in 20:41; 28:25; 36:23 and 39:27, where the proof of Yahweh's holiness consists in the repatriation of his people to his land, and in 28:22, where this proof occurs in the judgment on Sidon.[82] The present passage is along the lines of 28:22. In the judgment on Gog, which has already been indicated, Yahweh reveals to all the world his consuming holiness, which, however, as these earlier statements already show, is always linked with the proof of his loyalty to his people. The same thought will also be emphasized in the expansion in 39:6–8 in association with the second strophe of the basic text (see also 39:21f at the end of the third strophe).

■ **38:17** The second addition (v 17) expresses openly what could already be discerned in the basic text, namely that in Gog's arrival older prophetic declamation is fulfilled. To this extent, from the point of view of content, there can be no objections to attributing the oracle to the author of the basic text, and that could well mean to Ezekiel himself. Objections to such an assumption arise, however, from the details of the phraseology. The reference to "my servants the prophets of Israel" is unique in the book of Ezekiel. It links Ezekiel's turn of phrase "the prophets of Israel"[83] with the phrase עבדי הנביאים ("my servants the prophets"), which is found in Deuteronomistic texts (2 Kgs 9:7; 17:13) and Deuteronomistically colored Jeremiah texts (7:25; 26:5; 29:19; 35:15; 44:4) and Zech 1:6. What is also surprising is the backward look to "earlier times" and to the prophetic word spoken in them. This already recalls the phraseology of Zech 1:4 with its reference to the נביאים ראשנים ("former prophets") and seems to represent a stage of distanced reflection on past prophecy which one does not expect in Ezekiel, who himself, even when he clearly goes back to older prophetic oracles (chapters 16, 23, 34), still stands directly in the prophetic experience of the word. Also this additional observation, which, even if it is in the form of an address to Gog, nevertheless refers to the listener in Israel who is waiting for elucidation, does not quite fit into the style of the impetuous summons to Gog and the animals who wish to hold a feast on the field of battle. It is, rather, to be understood as a didactic, interpretative observation.

■ **38:18–23** Of a quite different kind and much more markedly distinct from the original Gog pericope is the third addition, vv 18–23. In what it says it leads straight into Yahweh's judgment on Gog and thus anticipates what will only be recounted in the second strophe of the basic text in 39:1–5 in the form of a duel between Yahweh and Gog. But it shapes it quite differently. The personal element fades into the background. Here Gog

79 See above p. 297.

80 On this see also Bardtke, "Erweckungsgedanke."

81 See above pp. 296f.

82 See above p. 98.

83 See 1,292.

falls in the framework of a cosmic world-shattering event.

■ **38:18** The section begins with the customary, loose connecting formula והיה ביום ההוא ("and it will be on that day") and elucidates "that day" as the day on which Gog comes against "the land of Israel."[84] The basic text of the Gog pericope referred consistently to the הרי ישׂראל ("mountains of Israel"). Contrary to the factual account of Yahweh's victory in a duel over Gog in the second strophe of the basic text, here the whole event erupts from the passion of Yahweh's mounting wrath.

■ **38:19** The linking of אף ("anger") and קנאה ("jealousy") occurs also in 35:11 of Edom's wrath; אשׁ עברתי ("fire of my fury") of Yahweh's anger also in 21:36; 22:21, 31 (see also 7:19). In all these pasages we are dealing with an annihilating reality. In such wrath Yahweh now swears that "on that day" he will bring on the land of Israel a mighty earthquake. רעשׁ ("earthquake") occurs several time in Ezekiel, but never in the sense of an earthquake caused by Yahweh. In 12:18 it described the prophet's trembling, in 37:7 the rattling of the dead bones coming together and in 3:12f the roaring at the termination of the theophany. Even where the verb רעשׁ ("to quake") is used it describes roaring or trembling as a consequence of a noisy event and is always linked with preceding מקול or לקול ("at the noise") which points to the noise of the invading destroyers of Tyre (26:10, 15), of the fall of the city of Tyre (27:28) or of the great cosmic tree (31:16). Only in 38:19f are the noun and verb used of the earthquake directly brought about by Yahweh, which is not the result of a previously described event but the cause of all that follows. Cosmic changes in association with divine intervention are referred to in the book of Ezekiel only in secondary expansions. 30:12 referred to the drying up of the arms of the Nile, 32:7f to the darkening of the stars. While 13:11, 13 speak of the downpour which causes the wall to collapse or 26:3, 19 of the surging of the sea against the island fortress of Tyre and 27:26 of the storm from the east which causes the ship Tyre to founder, these statements are on a different plane. Ezekiel himself has not used these characteristics of cosmic earthquake, which then become significant in later apocalyptic (Joel 2:10; 3:3f; 4:15),[85] even in his great description of the day of Yahweh in chapter 7. This also sets him apart from the early post-exilic expectation of a Haggai, according to whom the eschatological salvation-event begins with the great shaking of the world (2:6, 21), but also from certain statements in Deutero-Isaiah.[86] Jer 4:23–26 and the specific announcement of an impending earthquake in Amos (see Am 1:1) are certainly to be judged somewhat differently.[87] Thus in comparison with the original Ezekiel oracle, the later apocalyptic style of vv 18–23 is unmistakable.

■ **38:20** A certain lack of balance is to be found in the fact that v 19 first of all speaks only of an earthquake "in the land of Israel," while v 20 then clearly goes beyond this and, in the context of universal judgment, speaks of the quaking of the fish in the sea, the birds in the sky, the wild beasts and creeping things of the earth,[88] of the collapse of the mountains, of the terraces carefully constructed by human hands on the hillsides (note b) and of the walls. In these last one may hear the echo of the great proclamation of the day of Yahweh in Isaiah (2:12–17). In addition, in the מפני ("before me") there is a reference to the fact that in this cosmic upheaval we are dealing with an event in the presence of the judge who will come. To the sphere of the holy war, the background against which, according to von Rad, the reference to the "day of Yahweh" must in the last resort be understood,[89] there then belongs the reference to the "panic terror" which Yahweh will summon against Gog's army (קרא "to summon").[90] 26:16 referred to the "putting on of terror" (חרדות). Under its influence the sword of the one in Gog's army will turn against the other, as long ago in Gideon's war against the Midianites in Ju 7:22.[91] But then, in order to describe the divine judgment (nip'al of שׁפט "to enter into judgment" 17:20; 20:35f) the most varied elements are listed in an indis-

84 On this designation, which recurs in v 19, see 1,203 on 7:2.

85 See Hans Walter Wolff, *Joel and Amos,* tr. Waldemar Janzen, S. Dean McBride, Jr., and Charles A. Muenchow, ed. S. Dean McBride, Jr. Hermeneia (Philadelphia: Fortress, 1977).

86 Begrich, *Studien,* 79.

87 But see also Ps 46:7 and, on all this, Childs, "Enemy."

88 On this terminology see Gen 1 (P) and Siegfried Herrmann, "Die Naturlehre des Schöpfungsberichtes; Erwägungen zur Vorgeschichte von Genesis 1," *ThLZ* 86 (1961): 413–424.

89 von Rad, *OT Theology,* 2. 119–125.

90 Fredriksson, *Jahwe als Krieger,* 95 note 5. On the reading חרדה see note a.

91 On this see von Rad, *Krieg,* 10f.

criminate collection. Plague and bloodshed, the specific troubles of time or war, were also found in 5:17 and 28:23 in expansions. As an objective illustration of the destruction of a great army in this way we may compare a passage such as Is 37:36 (= 2 Kgs 19:35).[92] גשם שׁ[ו]טף ("streaming rain") occurred in 13:11, 13 in the context of the image of the collapsing wall. Only there in the OT are the אבני אלגביש ("hailstones") also mentioned. The OT otherwise uses the word ברד for "hail" (Is 28:2, 17; Hag 2:17; and elsewhere).[93] According to Gen 19:24 Yahweh caused "sulphur" (גפרית) and fire to rain on Sodom and Gomorrah (see also Is 30:33). All these blows, which cannot be fitted into a unified picture, fall on Gog and his army, which is again described with the vocabulary of the first strophe of the basic text.

■ **38:23** In all this Yahweh reveals himself as great and holy and makes himself recognizable to the world of the nations. The concluding formulation, on which reference may be made to what has been said above about v 16, is particularly fully developed. The hitpaʿel of גדל ("to show oneself great") is not otherwise attested in Ezekiel. On התקדש ("to show oneself holy") see what was said on v 16. On the nipʿal of ידע ("to proclaim oneself") in the context of the expanded recognition formula see 35:11 (also 20:5, 9).

On the expansion in vv 18–23 as a whole, it can therefore be affirmed that it is clearly distinguishable from the original Gog proclamation. Anticipating what is first proclaimed in the second strophe of the basic text in 39:1–5, it places Yahweh's victory over Gog in the context of a cosmic event in the style and with the pictorial features of later descriptions of eschatological events. This elevation into the realm of world history and eschatology is admittedly not entirely successful. The location of it in the "land of Israel" and the citation as witnesses of the surrounding nations, who themselves are obviously not affected by the event, still bear the contours of Ezekiel's preaching. The tension between the features of the cosmic judgment and the judgment on the enemy who has irrupted into the land of Israel and from whom Israel is to be rescued can be further seen in that, when mountains and walls collapse in the land of Israel where the judgment takes place, it is still actually Israel who suffers from that event. The tension which also exists between the two additions which come from different hands, vv 10–13 and vv 18–23, may be pointed out only incidentally. According to v 11 the settlements are without walls. V 20, on the other hand, must refer, along the lines of Is 2:15 (חומה "wall" here parallel to מגדל "tower"), to walls erected for defense. One cannot say that the description of Gog's end has gained in clarity by its extension into the cosmological sphere. The image of the duel in 39:3 remains, in spite of the greater terseness of what it says, clearer than the picture described in the accumulation of possibilities of judgment in 38:20–22.

■ **39:6-16** The second strophe of the basic text in 39:1–5, which, with the כי אני דברתי ("for I have spoken it") and the formula for a divine saying in v 5, has reached an unmistakable conclusion, has been expanded in vv 6–16 by several expository additions.

■ **39:6-8** The first element among them, vv 6–8, recalls so strongly the expansion of the first strophe in 38:14–16 that one wonders whether it does not come from the same hand. It is true that it is formally different from the latter, is not in the form of a question, but develops the proclamations of the basic text in 39:1–5 with the proclamatory consecutive perfect and gives expression, exactly like 38:14–16, to Yahweh's self-glorification in which the latter wishes to be acknowledged by the nations. As in 38:14, 16, in 39:7 reference is to "my people Israel." Also in the key-word for the revelation of holiness, which is forcefully expressed in 39:7 in the threefold recurrence of the root קדש ("holy"), it recalls 38:16 where this key-word occurred, in more restrained fashion, only once.

■ **39:6** According to 39:1–5, Yahweh's intervention had brought about the fall of Gog and his army. The expansion widens the framework. Insofar as it describes the judgment as a "sending of fire against" (שלח אש ב"), it takes up the formula of threat of judgment against foreign nations which can be found in profusion in the foreign oracles in Am 1f (1:4, 7, 10, 12; 2:5; in 1:14 it is והצתי אש ב" "and I will kindle fire in"). In Ezekiel it is completely lacking in all his many foreign oracles. While the formula of setting fire to something in Amos 1f

92 See also Gressmann, *Ursprung*, 85–98.

93 On Yahweh's fighting with this weapon see Fredriksson, *Jahwe als Krieger*, 49.

naturally refers in the first instance to human constructions (חומה "wall" parallel to ארמנות "strongholds" in 1:7, 10, 14), 1:12; 2:2, 5 show that it can be abbreviated simply to a place name or the name of a people (Teman, Moab, Judah) with ארמנות ("strongholds") retained in parallelism. Similarly in Ezek 39:6 the expression is applied to the name Magog, which is therefore not to be replaced, as in 𝔊, by the easier reading Gog (note a). The reading Gog is also not likely, since here there is obviously being described a judgment on the judgment which has already been described in vv 1–5 and in which Gog himself falls. But to attempt to interpret v 6 in terms of a later burning of Gog's corpse is ruled out in view of v 11, where Gog's burial is explicitly described. Therefore the aim of v 6 is to extend the proclamation of judgment to Gog's hinterland. Thus the person who formulated the expansion is already aware of the attribution, expressed in the gloss on 38:2 (note a), of Gog to the land (or people?) of Magog. This is connected with the area of the "isles" or "coast" (איים) which appears again and again in the oracles against Tyre, the trading power in the Mediterranean world (26:15, 18; 27:3, 6f, 15, 35). The connection between Gog (Magog) and the Greek world, for which reference can be made to the proximity of Magog to Javan in Gen 10:2, certainly does not give us the right to find another reference to Alexander the Great in this addition.[94] Rather one thinks back to 38:13, where among Gog's followers the merchants of Tarshish were also to be found. Tarshish figures in Gen 10:4 among the sons of Javan. In the trade list in 27:12f Tarshish (v 12) is immediately followed by Javan, Tubal, Meshech (v 13) and Beth-togarmah (v 14). That is, the Greek Mediterranean world is followed by groups from Asia Minor, which, according to the basic text, represent the most limited area of Gog's rule. When it is said of this commercial world which is connected with Gog that its inhabitants dwell in security, this is what the basic text said in 38:8 (followed by vv 11, 14) about Israel, transferred to the world of their opponents who attack Israel with thoughtless levity.

■ **39:7** But Yahweh intends to make himself known in his true nature in his judgment on this world of warriors and merchants. This is expounded here in the context of a theology of God's holy name. When it says that Yahweh will reveal his holy name in the midst of his people and will no longer profane it and that the nations will acknowledge Yahweh as "holy in Israel" (Isaiah said "the holy one of Israel"), there stands behind that, as its dark counterpart, the earlier disastrous history of the profanation of his holy name. 36:20–23 was the fullest account of that. שם קדשי ("my holy name") occurs in Ezekiel also in 20:39; 39:25; 43:7f. In this expansion the Gog pericope is brought into the light of Israel's total history and is understood as the proof of the continuing holiness of Yahweh among his people. The time of the dishonoring of Yahweh's name, the great tribulation of the exiles, will definitely lie in the past. This will be clear precisely from the great Gog crisis and will achieve universal recognition.

■ **39:8** The confirmatory statement הנה באה ונהיתה ("see it is coming and will happen") occurred already in 21:12.[95] By contrast with that passage, however, it here asserts the inevitability of the coming salvation. In addition, taking up the thought of the expansion in 38:17, it is finally asserted that the day of the judgment of Gog is the day of which Yahweh had previously spoken. Isaiah's proclamation of the end of the enemy in the midst of the land of Israel is now fulfilled. At the same time, the key-word היום ("the day") may also evoke the association of the "day of Yahweh."[96]

■ **39:9–16** This theological interpretation of the event is followed, as was the case with the first strophe, by further additions which aim to depict graphically the consequences of the day of judgment on Gog. They may recall 38:18–23, in that with their description they are still further removed from the basic account, which then follows with its third strophe in vv 17–20, and indeed make what will be said in that third strophe not only superfluous but even impossible.

■ **39:9–10** This is not yet so true of the first illustration of the event in vv 9–10. This speaks of the destruction of Gog's weapons. It takes up a motif which was already in the older tradition connected with the destruction of God's enemies. Thus Is 9:4, after having spoken earlier of the breaking of the yoke and of the oppressor's rod, speaks of the sequel to this victory: "For every boot

94 See above p. 302.

95 See 1, 425.

96 See 1, 201f and Wolff, *Joel and Amos,* 33 on Joel 1:15.

which tramples in battle tumult and (every) cloak which is trailed in blood will be burned, become fuel for the fire." Here it is the combustible armor which is burned. Ps 46:10 is supposed to show that these statements represent an old Zion tradition when it is said there, subsequent to the victory over the enemies of Yahweh's holy city: "He curbs wars to the end of the earth, breaks bows, shatters spears, burns chariots (or better: shields) with fire."[97] In Psalms 48 and 76, which also belong here, explicit mention of the burning of armor—here weapons—is missing.

But if this statement remains, in the passages mentioned, entirely within the realm of the mystery in which God himself acts, then in Ezek 39:9f it has acquired a modest development. Now it is the inhabitants of the cities of Israel who "emerge" (יצא) to do this work. It is not clear whether the thought here is still of the reference to the undefended living in open areas (as in 38:11) or whether here there are not, rather, presupposed defended cities from behind whose walls the people have observed the fall of Gog's army, which (on the analogy of 2 Kgs 19) is effected by the mysterious power of angels or plague (cf. 38:22 בדבר ובדם "with plague and with bloodshed"), and from which they now emerge just as, according to 2 Kgs 7:16, the people of Samaria, miraculously delivered from the siege, "go out." The plundering of the camp, which follows there, is admittedly pushed entirely to the side here by the motif of the destruction of the weapons (v 10b). With detailed enumeration, all the "armor" (נשק occurs only here in Ezekiel, but see, e.g., Is 22:8; 2 Kgs 10:2) is spread out before the listener. In conformity with the basic text in 39:3, bow and arrow come first. A later hand has failed to observe this relationship and, as in 38:4 (note d), though there in reverse order, has added the two kinds of shields (see also 39:5b [note a] and Ps 46:10 [emended text]). To these are added other combustible weapons מקל יד ("javelin") and רמח ("spear"). On רמח ("spear") see, e.g., Nu 25:7; Ju 5:8; Joel 4:10. Alongside it the "hand stick" appears somewhat strangely, and one is not very sure what kind of weapon it was. Thus one might prefer to follow Joüon, who would connect יד here and in Nu 35:17f with the root ידה "throw," and regard יד מקל as a pointed stick, possibly provided with an iron point (*bâton de jet, javelot*), which might possibly be compared with the מטה ("staff") of 1 Sam 14:43. Then in this second pair also two similar weapons would be joined, the long and the short lance.

So great is the mass of weapons that fires can be kept burning with them for a whole week of years.[98] The thought (implied in Is 9:3f and Ps 46:10) of the final elimination of war, which can be clearly heard in Is 2:4 in a "remarkably bold transformation of the old motif of the destruction of the weapons,"[99] is not here expressed.

■ **39:10** In its stead, there follows in v 10 a very rational, second element when the practical usefulness of these supplies of wood is pointed out. See also 47:11. If, on the basis of v 9, one thinks that throughout the seven years the fires outside in the fields burn high when, in the process of clearing the fields, the rubbish is thrown on to the fire (Mt 6:30; 13:30, 40), here it is explained that the weapons of Gog's army supply the domestic needs of the people in place of the wood that would otherwise be cut down in the forest. When, in addition, in transformation of the phraseology of 38:12f (29:19), reference is made to the plundering of the plunderers, this abandons completely the motif of Is 9:3f and Ps 46:10 and describes the normal course of a human victory with its division of the booty (see Ju 5:30; 8:24ff; 2 Kgs 7:16; Is 9:2). The strongly God-oriented character of the original Gog pericope is here completely abandoned. Quite unconcernedly what is mentioned is what pleases the people (who did not participate in the actual battle). The formula for a divine saying concludes this first addition, which is quite distinct in its carefree "worldliness" both from the basic text of the second strophe and from the theological, interpretative addition in vv 6–8.

■ **39:11-16** The second addition, vv 11-16, which is again

97 Rohland, *Erwählungstraditionen*, 142.

98 In contrast to Ernst Kutsch, "Erwägungen zur Geschichte der Passafeier und des Massotfestes," *ZThK* 55 (1958): 27, one must not understand the seven years, with Fohrer, simply as "many years," but, in an Israel which knows the sabbatical year, with Gordon, *Ugaritic Literature*, 5, think of a clearly defined cycle of time. See also the seven months in vv 12, 14.

99 Rohland, *Erwählungstraditionen*, 176 note 1.

appended by means of the addition formula והיה ביום ההוא ("and it will be on that day"), then stands in open contradiction to the third strophe of the basic text. While there it was a question of the great sacrificial feast prepared by Yahweh for the birds and beasts of prey, here it is of the burial, carried out by men, of the corpses of Gog and his army. One may raise the question whether vv 11–16 are not divided by means of the formula for a divine saying in v 13 into two halves, the second of which would have been added only secondarily. Since, however, v 12 clearly paves the way for vv 14–16, one had better regard the whole as belonging together and understand the formula in v 13 as an emphatic context formula which creates an emphatic pause after the ביום הכבדי ("on the day when I glorify myself"). At any rate vv 11–13, with their threefold וקברו[ם] ("and they will bury [them]"), are stylistically ponderous.

■ **39:11** V 11 recounts, in the first instance, how Yahweh himself is concerned about a burial for Gog "in Israel" (the basic text here would undoubtedly phrase that as "on the mountains of Israel"). The location of this burial place is defined more precisely as the Oberim Valley, east of the "sea." This valley is not simply to be equated with Gog's battlefield.[100] The site of the battle and the site of the grave are clearly differentiated. If the name Oberim were simply a secondary form of Abarim (note c), the הים ("the sea") could here be understood as referring to the Dead Sea and one could think of a valley running from the Jordan towards Mount Nebo. One would then be not far from the region of שטים ("Shittim") and בעל פעור ("Baal-peor"), which, according to Nu 25:1ff and Hos 9:10, was forbidden territory for Israel. This Transjordanian location is accepted by many commentators, but is burdened with a triple uncertainty: 1) the meaning of על קדמת is not necessarily "in the east." The few other occurrences, Gen 2:14; 4:16; 1 Sam 13:5, clearly admit the possibility of "opposite."[101] 2) It is uncertain whether by הים is meant the Dead Sea, which is called "the eastern sea" (הים הקדמוני) in 47:18, or, as is otherwise the case, the Mediterranean. Admittedly the latter is referred to in 47:10, 15, 19 as הים הגדול ("the great sea"). Or whether the thought is not perhaps of the Sea of Galilee, the Lake of Gennesaret. So 𝔊, see note d. 3) Finally, it remains questionable whether the Abarim region can still be thought of as lying "in Israel." According to Nu 33:47f Israel finds herself, after her descent from the uplands of Moab and from the Abarim region, when she is encamped in the plain opposite Jericho, in the "plains of Moab." And the land distribution programme of the school of Ezekiel in chapters 47f regards the Jordan as Israel's eastern frontier.

So, then, other solutions have been sought. Bewer, who refers הים to the Lake of Gennesaret, finds the "Valley of the Wanderers" in the *wādi fejjās* through which the caravan route, the *darb el hawarneh,* the 'Way of the Hawanians,' passes. Similarly van Deursen.[102] The Plain of Jezreel, which lies "opposite" the Mediterranean, is favored by Hengstenberg, Troelstra and Noordtzij, while Aalders thinks he ought to find the שְׁפֵלָה ("lowland") here as a caravan transit region.[103] But against the last two identifications, however, the definitive argument should be the use of the term גיא ("valley"). No serious consideration should be given to Gressmann's reference to Herodotus, according to which what we have here is really an Egyptian tradition.[104] Thus any definite location of the burial place of Gog and his hordes remains uncertain. The statement that the valley (filled with corpses and therefore also now unclean) should block the way for those who "pass through" (עברים) is derived, in a somewhat forced way, as a further comment based on the name of the valley, Oberim. The valley is now to receive the new name, "Valley of Gog's hordes." Is the גיא המון ("valley of the hordes") supposed to refer, with its loose assonance, to the גֵיא הִנֹּם ("valley of Hinnom"), the valley of abomination κατ᾽ ἐξοχήν, so that the latter name would now be associated with Gog? That an etymological aetiology is intended here is in any case probable.

100 As it is by Leo Krinetzki, "'Tal' und 'Ebene' im Alten Testament," *BZ* 5 (1961): 217, who finds in the expression גיא המון גוג ("Valley of Gog's Hordes") the motif of the "valley" of the eschatological battlefield.

101 See Gesenius-Buhl; Koehler-Baumgartner; Theodor Nöldeke, "Review of Friedrich Baethgen, *Sindban oder die sieben weisen Meister. Syrisch und deutsch,*" *ZDMG* 33 (1879): 532 note 3.

102 Aalders, *Gog en Magog,* 103.

103 Aalders, *Gog en Magog,* 105.

104 2, 75.

■ **39:12** In this context v 12 introduces the further thought of the cultic purification of the land. Alongside the week of years during which the burning of the weapons of Gog and his hosts takes place, there appears here the week of months during which burials take place and the land is cleansed from the contaminating corpses (on contamination by corpses see Nu 19:11ff). The motif of the destruction of weapons after God's great victory over his enemies, a motif which dominated vv 9f, has disappeared and been replaced by the field of thought of the "holy land," which will then dominate chapters 40–48. One can recognize in the background here priestly traditionists of the book of Ezekiel.

■ **39:13–16** While v 12 expresses the task of burial first of all in general terms with reference to the whole "house of Israel," vv 13–16 develop the instructions for the more precise accomplishment of this which is now to follow in two stages.

■ **39:13** First of all the whole עם הארץ ("people of the land") sets to the task. E. Würthwein is of the opinion that here we no longer have the upper class, but, because in the future everyone will have his own property (47:14), the people as a whole.[105] For seven months the corpses will be buried. If such a long period of clearing away of the whole army is necessary, how immeasurable must the number of the fallen have been. The 185,000 dead of 2 Kgs 19:35 can give some idea of the proportions which must be thought of here. In this context once again mention is made of the glory of all these occurrences, a ray of which now falls on Israel's men whose honor is thereby enhanced. In this connection it must not be overlooked how neatly, from the terminological point of view, the differentiation is made. The day of Gog's fall, which is here openly regarded as the same as the day of the burial, is the day on which Yahweh glorifies himself.[106] The כבוד ("glory") is Yahweh's prerogative. Only 31:18 uses the substantive, which is attested nineteen times in Ezekiel (mostly in the combinations כבוד יהוה "the glory of Yahweh" or כבוד אלהי ישראל "the glory of the God of Israel"), in relation to a man (see also the verb in 27:25). The honor which falls to a man is expressed by means of the term שֵׁם. "Name" here is continuing reputation, posthumous name. It is significant that Israel and the "name" which she acquires as a result of this whole event first find expression here in connection with the burial of Gog. Israel is not an active participant in the victory over Gog and in his destruction. This remains entirely Yahweh's deed. Rather Israel's share consists exclusively in the clearing up of the battlefield.

■ **39:14** But this activity on the part of Israel's manpower is insufficient. One can see particularly the way of priestly carefulness and precision when vv 14f, over and above what has already been said, refers explicitly to the work of a control commission scrutinizing what has been done. אנשי תמיד, "men with a continuing commission," "professionals,"[107] are sent out to "pass through" (עבר) the land and bury those who were not buried in the first, main wave of burials. For a second time there is a wordplay with the name of the burial place mentioned in v 11. If the את העברים ("who pass through"), which was deleted as a gloss (note c), really refers, as Aalders thinks, to the enemies who had "passed through" the land, then the glossator would be punning with עבר ("to pass through") in a third direction. However, it is just as possible that 𝔗 with its rendering of את by עם ("together with") is in the right. Then there occurs in the gloss the correct insight that in the commission which appears in vv 14f the two groups of the עברים ("searchers") and the מקברים ("buriers") must be differentiated.

■ **39:15** The procedure of the commission, which sets to work after the expiry of the seven months' work of the עם הארץ ("people of the land"), is described so exactly that one could see behind it a usage which is actually practiced. The unclean spot where remains of bones are found is, in the first instance, marked by the control men (עברים "searchers") in the narrower sense (by setting up a stone?). צִיּוֹן (here "marker") is attested in Jer 31:21 in the sense of a "signpost" and in 2 Kgs 23:17 in the sense of

105 Würthwein, *'amm*, 48f. See 1, 209 on 7:27.

106 On the הכבד said of Yahweh, which is found in P in Ex 14:4, 17f, in the context of Yahweh's triumph over the Egyptians, but in Lev 10:3 also in the context of the mysterious self-glorification of Yahweh through the destruction of those who infringed the purity of the sacrificial order, see above p. 98 on 28:22.

107 Aalders, *Gog en Magog*, 109.

"gravestone." Only then do the second group, the actual מקברים ("buriers"), come behind them and bring the bones that have been found to the burial place in the "Valley of Gog's hordes." In this way the land is cleansed.

■ **39:16** In v 16 a brief remark, inserted only secondarily before the final sentence (note a), adds once more an aetiological reference, the meaning of which can unfortunately no longer be understood. A town which must surely be located in the vicinity of the גיא המון גוג ("Valley of Gog's Hordes") recalls by its very name, המונה ("Hamonah"), the burial place of Gog's hordes. The identifications which have been suggested: Bethshan-Skythopolis (Smend), Megiddo-Legio (Troelstra), Emmaus which in 𝔊^A in 1 Macc 3:40 is called Αμμαουν,[108] remain in the realm of free speculation.

■ **39:21–29** A last expansion is to be found, finally, in vv 21–29, connected with the third strophe of the basic text. As has already been established, vv 21–22 still look back to the Gog pericope, while vv 23–29 leave that behind and once again reflect, comprehensively, on the prophet's total message.

■ **39:21–22** From the point of view of content, vv 21f are along the same lines as the expansions to the first two strophes in 38:14–16 and 39:6–8, which one would therefore be happy to regard together as components of a first stage of revision of the Gog pericope. Again it is maintained that Yahweh's battle against Gog was aimed at universal recognition.

■ **39:21** While in the two previous passages, especially in 39:6–8, the revelation of Yahweh's holiness was emphasized, here the reference is to the revelation of Yahweh's glory (כבודי "my glory") among the nations, and this recalls the phraseology of v 13. The phrase נתן כבוד ב ("to reveal glory among") is unusual in Ezekiel. The replacement of the verb ידע ("to know") by ראה ("to see") in the recognition formula was found also in 21:4 (parallel in v 10). With the משפטי אשר עשותי ("my judgment which I have executed") we may compare the ועשיתי בתוכך משפטים ("and I will execute judgment in your midst") of 5:8. The ידי אשר שמתי בהם ("my hand which I have laid upon them") is without parallel in Ezekiel. In the powerful (ידי "my hand") act of judgment (משפטי "my judgment") "upon them," the thought is of the judgment of the nations on Gog in which Yahweh's glory becomes manifest.

■ **39:22** But Israel too, who is named here for the only time in the book of Ezekiel as the subject of recognition in a recognition formula, is to be aware from this that Yahweh is her God. Insofar as it is expressly affirmed at the same time that the awareness is to be effective "from that day on and forever," it becomes clear once more that the Gog affair "at the end of the years" (38:8; "at the end of days" 38:16), even in this late stage of the work, is not understood as an event at the absolute end of time as much as it brings to a definitive end that period of judgment in which Yahweh's relationship with Israel seemed to become questionable.

■ **39:23–29** *A final oracle looking back on Ezekiel's total message.* The second addition in vv 23–29 connects directly with vv 21f. It looks back on Yahweh's dealings with Israel with no further specific reflection on the Gog episode. We must have, here again, an element of concluding editorial activity such as was found at the end of chapter 28. From the point of view of content it also links with other elements of the final stages of work on earlier units.

■ **39:23f** Yahweh's dealings with Israel are regarded, following on vv 21f, from the point of view of their evidential character in the eyes of the world. There is, admittedly, nothing here of a visible hastening on the part of the nations to the salvation of Israel, of an explicit acknowledgment of Yahweh or even of a journeying with the returning exiles such as is expected by Deutero-Isaiah and Zechariah.[109] The international world is here simply the forum before which the revelation takes place. In its presence, and therefore demanding its acknowledgment, the judgment of deportation on Israel has taken place (גלה "to go into exile" in this sense occurs in Ezekiel, apart from v 28, only otherwise in 12:3). The deportation was the divine punishment for "guilt" and "faithlessness" (on מעל see above; it occurs again here in v 26).[110] Three time in vv 23–29 is the divine reaction of punishment described by the expression, which does not occur elsewhere in Ezekiel, of "hiding the face" (vv 23, 24, 29). Behind this expression, which is common in the language of the psalms (13:2; 22:25; 27:9; and

108 Aalders, *Gog en Magog.*

109 On this see Zimmerli, "Wahrheitserweis Jahwes" (see above p. 303).

110 See 1,313f.

elsewhere) but is also favored by Deutero- and Trito-Isaiah (54:8; 57:17; 59:2; 64:6; see also 50:6; 53:3), lies the knowledge that man lives only by the grace of Yahweh's face turned towards him, which is prayed for in the Aaronic blessing (Nu 6:25f), but comes to grief if God's face is turned away (Ps 104:29). Thus Yahweh has handed Israel over to the oppressors and to the sword (cf. chapter 21) and has dealt with them in accordance with their deeds of impurity and "rebellion" (on פשע see above).[111] צר ("oppressor") is found frequently in the Psalms, in Ezekiel only in the secondary passage 30:16.

■ **39:25** But then Yahweh's word changes. The promise of change begins in the style of a proclamation, introduced by the introductory messenger formula. Change of fortune has already been mentioned in the addition in 16:53–58 and in 29:14 with reference to Egypt.[112] The expression can now also be compared with the חשבו אלהן [שיבת בי]ת אבי of Stele III from *Sefire* which A. Dupont-Sommer translates: "The Gods have brought about the restoration of the ho[use of my father]."[113] שוב שבות ("to restore the fortunes") in the present passage can be exegeted from the point of view of content, exactly as in Jer 33:26, as "mercy" on Israel.[114] The verb רחם ("to have mercy"), which plays a significant role in the language of the Psalms, in Hosea and Deutero-Isaiah and which cannot be separated from the noun רֶחֶם ("womb") (attested in Ezekiel only in the technical term פֶּטֶר רֶחֶם "firstborn" in 20:26) or רַחַם ("womb") (does not occur in Ezekiel), and its plural רחמים "mercy," is never attested in a genuine Ezekiel oracle. He uses in its place the verb חמל ("to have compassion"). Here too the redactor betrays his proximity to the language of the Psalms. The parallelism Jacob-Israel occurs also in 20:5. Jacob alone as the bearer of the promise occurs in 28:25; 37:25. The expression "be jealous for my holy name," which one might definitely expect in 36:16ff, where the intervention of Yahweh on behalf of his name is recounted most fully, is, surprisingly enough, lacking elsewhere in Ezekiel. The verb קנא/ה ("to be jealous") occurs in 8:3; 31:9 in other contexts. Close to Ezek 39:25 lies Joel 2:18.[115] The noun קנאה ("jealousy") occurs ten times and often refers to Yahweh's zeal. On שם קדשי ("my holy name") see above on v 7.

■ **39:26** In what follows it is surprising that there is reference to the bearing of shame and faithlessness on the part of those who are now living peacefully in the land. The direct logic of the thought seems to argue forcefully for an emendation of 𝔐 ונשו ("and they will take upon themselves") to ונשו ("and they will forget"). Many exegetes make that emendation (note c). The following considerations, however, argue for the retention of 𝔐: The unanimous witness of the versions, even of 𝔊 and 𝔖 which otherwise happily smooth out awkward parts of the text, confirms 𝔐. The thought of earlier sins being "forgotten" is quite unheard of in the book of Ezekiel. Rather 16:53, where the restoration of fortune is also referred to, shows that the text continues directly to precisely the thought attested here by 𝔐, even the verbally similar phraseology of "bearing disgrace" (נשא כלמה). Thus in the present passage the same thought is expressed as in 16:54, that Israel, in the midst of her having been pardoned, takes her shame and guilt upon herself and, in the midst of her experience of salvation and of peaceful dwelling in the land, remains aware of her previous history. Mercy is not a summons to blind forgetfulness. The newly bestowed peace is spoken of in the words of 34:28.

■ **39:27** On the phraseology of v 27 see 28:25. The renewed gathering together of the people (the disturbance by Gog is left out of consideration) is, as is now said in this addition, the way in which God reveals his holiness in the eyes of the nations (so 38:16; 39:7 of the Gog incident).

■ **39:28ff** V 28 beings once again with a recapitulation: That Yahweh is Israel's God is seen in the way in which he led Israel away among the nations, but has now brought every single one of them back to their land. The definitive nature of this "turning of the face" (vv 23f) is

---

111 See 1,309.

112 See 1,351 on 16:53.

113 A. Dupont-Sommer, *Les inscriptions araméennes de Sfiré,* Mémoires présentés par divers savants à l'Académie des Inscriptions et Belles-Lettres 15 (Paris, 1958), 132.

114 See Baumann, "שוב שבות," 28f.

115 See Wolff, *Joel and Amos,* 61.

sealed by the outpouring of the divine spirit upon the house of Israel. Here the statements of 36:27 and 37:14 are taken up with different terminology (שׁפך רוח על "to pour spirit on" instead of נתן רוח ב[קרב] "to put spirit within"). The communication of the spirit is here described as the final irrevocable union of Yahweh with his people. Here too Joel, which is related in its terminology to 39:29, will carry further the proclamation of salvation found in the book of Ezekiel (3:1ff).[116]

In the final section, vv 23–29, it has been noticeable again and again that it has no connection whatever with the Gog pericope. This has led Herrmann, e.g., to the assumption that in vv 25–29 we have the concluding oracle of chapters 34–37 which as yet is quite unaware of the Gog pericope. 38:1–39:24 would then have been inserted secondarily after chapter 37. Against this hypothesis it can, however, be said that vv 25–29 can scarcely be separated from vv 23–24 (see the connecting phrase הסתיר פנים "to hide the face" which is not otherwise found in the book of Ezekiel). On the other hand, 39:23–29 can, from its introductory words, very easily be understood as an expansion of vv 21f. While v 21 looked back to the Gog pericope and spoke of what the nations "learn" (ראה) from this activity on Yahweh's part and adds in v 22 what Israel can "perceive" (ידע) from this event, v 23 goes back again to v 21 and describes what the nations too can "perceive" (ידע). From the point of view of content, v 23 does not carry the full weight of the genuine recognition formula in which the recognition of Yahweh is usually described. Rather, v 23 with its repetition of the recognition formula is intended as a "resumption" of the combined beginnings of vv 21f.[117] At the latest in v 25 it becomes clear that vv 23–29 are, in the first instance, proclamation to Israel which then achieves its goal in the recognition formula of v 28 which once again takes up v 22. Israel is to know that Yahweh is her God.

If, however, vv 23–29 were intended from the beginning as the conclusion of chapters 38f, then the question arises as to how it is possible that the redactor who added this conclusion could disregard so completely the content of the Gog pericope and refer solely to the earlier proclamation of judgment and salvation. One cannot avoid the conclusion that for him the Gog incidents signified no new emphasis in the history of Yahweh's dealings with his people, but simply bore the weight of a final enactment of the salvation already proclaimed for Israel. This can still warn against attributing to the Gog pericope in the book of Ezekiel the weight of an apocalyptic final episode having an independent value in the plan of calculation of the end time. For the redactor of the book whose hand is to be found here, it is completely integrated into the great proclamation of salvation for Israel. Thus in the formulation of the sum total of this proclamation it can take a sufficiently back place that it need no longer be mentioned as of any special significance.

On the history of later interpretation. Later exegesis no longer kept to this line. Theodoret of Antioch, who believed that the propheies against Gog were fulfilled immediately after the return of the Jews under Cyrus, remains a solitary figure.[118] For an understanding along these lines see also, for example, the views of Ephraim the Syrian, who is aware also of an identification of Gog with the Holofernes of the book of Judith.[119] The main stream of later commentators has made what is proclaimed here as the fulfillment of earlier prophetic oracles into a universal event of unique importance in apocalyptic imagery. The inspiration for this can be detected already in the secondary expansions within chapters 38f, especially in a passage such as 38:18–23. Mention must also be made here of the book of Joel, which, alongside the Ezekiel oracles of the Day of Yahweh (Ezekiel 7; 30) and of the description of the temple stream (Ezekiel 47), clearly makes quite specific use of Ezekiel 38f. A locust and drought catastrophe becomes for this prophet an omen of the nearness of the Day of Yahweh, which, with cosmic traits (2:10), is described as the invasion of an enemy which in the retrospective 2:20 is called the "northern" (הצפוני). "Day of Yahweh" and "northerner" are here completely linked. Admittedly the names Gog and Magog do not

116 See Wolff, *Joel and Amos,* 65ff. See also Appendix 3.

117 Kuhl, "'Wiederaufnahme.'"

118 Neuss, *Buch,* 57.

119 A. M. Dubarle, "La mention de Judith dans la littérature ancienne, juive et chrétienne," *RB* 66 (1959): 541.

appear in this connection.[120]

On the other hand the double description Γὼγ καὶ Μαγώγ ("Gog and Magog") is used in the great picture of the Johannine Apocalypse (Rev 20:8f) as the name of the mythical army of the nations whose attack ends the thousand-year period of peace. Here it is no longer God but Satan who sends Gog and Magog as the world of the nations deceived by him. In countless numbers Gog and Magog, the hordes from the four corners of the earth (the northerly direction has disappeared here completely), pour forth against the camp of the saints, against "the beloved city," only to be consumed by the fire of heaven (cf. Ezek 38:22; 39:6 and 2 Kgs 1:9ff). Then the deceptive devil is also thrown into the pool of fire and sulphur. Gog and Magog have here become entities in a dualistic concept of the end of history. While the names Gog and Magog occur elsewhere in the Apocrypha and Pseudepigrapha only incidentally (*Sib. Or.* 3:319, 512), Rabbinic tradition speaks fully of the "war of Gog and Magog," the details of which are arranged very differently with regard to the sequence of the apocalyptic events of the Messianic period.[121]

Subsequently the Gog-Magog tradition entered into a unique relationship with the Alexander tradition. Already Josephus knows of a Scythian tribe of Alani who lived in the north, on the other side of a pass which Alexander the Great had closed with iron gates.[122] Muhammad connects this tradition in Sura 18:86ff with *D̲hu'lqarnain,* behind which is to be found Alexander the Great, and calls the nations shut off behind the iron gates, *Yajūj* and *Majūj.* Behind these probably lie the names Gog and Magog.[123] The episode of the building of this wall is reported also in the Greek *Historia Alexandri* (Pseudo-Callisthenes). The localization of the wall, about which later Arabic tradition also has much to say, has subsequently shifted a great deal as a result of the widening of the geographical horizon. It has moved from the region of the Caucasus and of the Caucasian Gates as far as the Great Wall of China. Correspondingly the identification of Gog and Magog has also shifted.[124]

An unexpected twist to the tradition is found in the fact that behind the wall some have sought to find the ten lost tribes of Israel.[125] To what extent the Gog and Magog tradition could take root in quite unexpected places, doubtless as a result of quite extraneous associations, is shown by the identifications of two figures in London's Guildhall with Gog and Magog and the subsequent explanatory story.[126] The location of Magog in Heliopolis, on the other hand, owes its origin, according to de Vaux, to a misreading of a text of Pliny.

Aim

The original prophetic oracle of Ezekiel 38f attempts to answer the question of the aim of God's ways with his people. The prophet speaks on the subject as one who knows about the great promises make by his God to the exiled people awaiting their return. He knows of the promise of restoration and of God's protection for his people snatched from judgment. At the same time, however, he is aware of national powers which are still threatening and hostile. Implicit in this awareness may be the experience, conditioned by contemporary events, of those who live in the Babylonian plain and who are conscious of disaster brewing against them in the northern mountains. Over and above this, however, it is noticeable that the prophet is conscious of an older prophetic message according to which a massed northern enemy will once again pour down upon God's people. It is possible that in all this there lies hidden for the prophet, quite basically, the question of the "powers." Belief in

120 For the details see Wolff, *Joel and Amos,* 12ff, and at various points throughout his commentary. See also Georg Fohrer, "Die Struktur der alttestamentlichen Eschatologie," *ThLZ* 85 (1960): 407.

121 Bietenhard, *tausendjährige Reich;* Kuhn, "Γὼγ καὶ Μαγώγ"; Bousset-Gressmann. On the Rabbinic material see Strack-Billerbeck, 3. 831–840 (name, time of appearance, Gog's motives, Gog's armies, length of campaign, scene of the defeat, Gog's destroyer, means used against Gog, judgment on Gog, Gog's grave). For Hasidic Judaism see, e.g., Martin Buber, *For the Sake of Heaven,* tr. Ludwig Lewisohn (Philadelphia: Jewish Publication Society, 1945).

122 *Jewish War* VII 7 (4).

123 In spite of Denise Masson, *Le Coran et la révélation judéo-chrétienne; études comparées* (Paris: Adrien-Maisonneuve, 1958), 443.

124 For more precise details see Anderson, *Alexander's Gate;* de Goeje, *muur;* Heller, "Gog und Magog."

125 Anderson, *Alexander's Gate,* 58ff.

126 Bieling, *Sagen;* Brown, "Note"; Anderson, *Alexander's Gate,* 81f.

God's promise is beset (not only in Ezekiel's time) by the question why the powers of international history still conflict so indomitably with all that God has promised to do for his people. Must it then not, over and above all that can be expected more immediately in the way of divine help and liberation, eventually come to a final, decisive confrontation which will directly reveal God's victory over the "powers"?

The prophet is empowered to address to these questions a declaration from God. Even in its form this reveals the challenge with which God finally meets the "powers." The challenge to the wild chief prince, irrupting from the edge of the known world, could not be shaped in a more majestic style than it is here. With superior certainty the prophetic oracle makes it known that it is none other than God himself who brings about the coming of the threatening foe. If Gog in his insolence believes that he can accomplish his own act of violence, the truth is that it is God himself who has brought him from afar and has "led him by the nose" (39:2) like a child. An interpreter has added to this the harsher picture of the wild beast kept in check by means of hooks (38:4). The chief prince, who, according to the picture of him added analogously in 38:10–13, believes that he can collect his booty without encountering any resistance and for whom the good prospects of his undertaking are fully attested by the unscrupulously jostling commercial world of the traders, is in reality the one who is led, the one who is brought to the place of his destruction by God himself. In such a free and unconcerned manner are the dangers spoken of which seem so powerfully to threaten the people of God on the part of their enemies.

To this confidence expressed at the beginning of the prophetic speech there corresponds then also the narrative of the continuation of Gog's campaign. The basic text avoids all colorful picturing of the event in which the enemy power is brought to nothing. It is enough that it is God himself who, like an individual combatant in a duel, strikes the weapons out of the hands of the one who is the strong one in human eyes, disposes of all his army—in a land in which Gog thought he would find a defenseless people an easy prey. In this respect there is no singing the praises of an armed people of God, no extolling the cleverness of the pious which itself might have resisted the wiles of the enemy. In clear objectivity there stands here alone the proclamation of the self-glorification of God which alone is to be extolled.

"Helpers" are needed by God only after the victory has been won. Insofar as the summons of the wild beasts is described as an invitation to a sacrificial meal, this simply emphasizes once again that God remains the only host for his creatures. There the clearing up is done with that arrogant conceit which believes, either in pious self-righteousness or in timid faint-heartedness, that God's affairs must be brought to a victorious end by his saints. God alone is the master of his great, joyful feast. The community is summoned to fearlessness, to waiting in joyous anticipation for the great victory feast of their God.

Later interpreters have added to the Gog proclamation stronger emphases in two directions. There are first of all statements which explicitly emphasize the divine self-revelation in his action. God's holiness (38:16, 23; 39:7), his mighty judgment (39:21) and his majesty (39:13, 21), which reveal him, in his intervention on behalf of his people, judged and in themselves powerless, as the "holy one in Israel" (39:7), are visible throughout the world in the eyes of the nations (38:16, 23; 39:6f, 21, 23). At the same time, however, the victory over Gog, in which old prophetic preaching is fulfilled (38:17), makes it clear that even the most uncanny crises in the history of the people of God are encompassed by God's word.

The second line is taken up by the expansions concerned with the fuller illustration of the one who is coming. Thus the great number of Gog's followers is described more fully. The business and commercial interests of the world traders who wish to change the faith of the helpless people of God into resignation by means of their apparent power (what can faith do against the interests of high finance!) make themselves heard (38:10–13). On the other hand, the divine intervention is heightened by means of the summons of the forces of earthquake, of the holy war and of all kinds of apocalyptic phenomena into a cosmic event and developed as an act of the lord of all the forces of nature. The enormity of Gog's defeat is graphically illustrated by means of the fires which are fueled by Gog's weapons and of the arrangements for the burial of Gog's army. At the same time there comes the assurance that the enormous catastrophe which befalls God's enemies in the midst of God's land can inflict no lasting harm on the purity of the latter. The pure land is the final goal of God's dealings. Chapters 40–48 will go on to speak of that in their own particular way.

In his final word, however, the final redactor allows the whole thrilling unique act of God towards the world powers to fade into the background in favor of the really decisive history which lies beind that act, the history of the relationship between God and his people. That God, after a period of anger against the people's offenses, once again turns his face to them in grace (v 29; cf. vv 23f), has mercy on them (v 25), brings them back again to his land, i.e. close to God (v 27), and pours out his spirit on them (v 29)—that is real history. It is on this that God's people may meditate in the peace newly granted to them, without forgetting the darkness of their own arrogant history, and be conscious from this of who God is—the God who does not abandon Israel to her own devices because he is jealous for the holiness of his name, who remains true to his people because he remains true to his name.

The Great Vision of the New Temple and the New Land

Bibliography

Gerhard Charles Aalders
"Ezechiël's Herstellingsvisioen (Capp. 40–48)," *Gereformeerd theologisch tijdschrift* 13 (1912/13): 453–474, 509–532.

J. J. Balmer-Rinck
Des Propheten Ezechiel Gesicht vom Tempel. Für Verehrer und Forscher des Wortes Gottes und für Freunde religiöser Kunst übersichtlich dargestellt und architektonisch erläutert, 1858.

George Ricker Berry
"The Authorship of Ezekiel, 40–48," *JBL* 34 (1915): 17–40.

Alfred Bertholet
Der Verfassungsentwurf des Hesekiel in seiner religionsgeschichtlichen Bedeutung (Freiburg i. B.: Mohr, 1896).

Julius Boehmer
"Die prophetische Heilspredigt Ezechiels," *ThStKr* 74 (1901): 173–228, especially 217–222.

Julius Friedrich Boettcher
Neue exegetisch-kritische Aehrenlese zum Alten Testamente, 2. Abtheilung ed. F. Mühlau (1864), 183–191.

Julius Friedrich Boettcher
Proben alttestamentlicher Schrifterklärung nach wissenschaftlicher Sprachforschung mit kritischen Versuchen über bisherige Exegese und Beiträgen zu Grammatik und Lexicon (1833), 218–365 (XII. "Exegetisch-kritischer Versuch über die ideale Beschreibung der Tempelgebäude Ezech. C. 40–42; 46:19–24").

James Oscar Boyd
"Ezekiel and the Modern Dating of the Pentateuch," *PrincTR* 6 (1908): 29–51.

C. Chipiez and G. Perrot
"Restitution du temple de Jérusalem d'après Ézéchiel," *RGATP* 4 Ser. 12 (1885): 151–167, 193–233.

G. A. Cooke
"Some Considerations on the Text and Teaching of Ezekiel 40–48," *ZAW* 42 (1924): 105–115.

J. E. Dean
"The Date of Ezekiel 40–43," *AJSL* 43 (1927): 231–233.

George C. M. Douglas
"Ezekiel's Temple," *ET* 9 (1897/98): 365–367, 420–422, 468–470, 515–518.

George C. M. Douglas
"Ezekiel's Vision of the Temple," *ET* 14 (1902/03): 365–368, 424–427.

Walther Eichrodt
"Land und Volk der Heilszeit nach Hes. 40–48," *Der Freund Israels* 71 (1944): 57–60, 82–88; 72 (1945): 17–22.

F. W. Farrar
"The Last Nine Chapters of Ezekiel," *The Expositor* 3rd series 9 (1889): 1–15.

Hartmut Gese
Der Verfassungsentwurf des Ezechiel (Kap. 40–48) traditionsgeschichtlich untersucht, BHTh 25 (Tübingen: Mohr, 1957).

Joachim Jeremias
"Hesekieltempel und Serubbabeltempel," *ZAW* 52 (1934): 109–112.

Ed. König
"Die letzte Pentateuchschicht und Hesekiel," *ZAW* 28 (1908): 174–179.

Ernst Kühn
"Ezechiels Gesicht vom Tempel der Vollendungszeit. Kap. 40–42; 43:13–17; 46:19–24. In redivierter Übersetzung und mit kurzer Erläuterung," *ThStKr* 55 (1882): 601–688.

W. F. Lofthouse
"The City and the Sanctuary," *ET* 34 (1922/23): 198–202.

Cameron M. Mackay
"The City and the Sanctuary," *ET* 34 (1922/23): 475f.

Cameron M. Mackay
"The City and the Sanctuary. Ezekiel 48," *PrincTR* 20 (1922): 399–417.

Cameron M. Mackay
"Ezekiel's Sanctuary and Wellhausen's Theory," *PrincTR* 20 (1922): 661–665.

Cameron M. Mackay
"The Key to the Old Testament (Ezek 40–48)," *CQR* 199 (1935): 173–196.

Cameron M. Mackay
"Prolegomena to Ezekiel 40–48," *ET* 55 (1943/44): 292–295.

O. Procksch
"Fürst und Priester bei Hesekiel," *ZAW* 58 (1940/41): 99–133.

Willy Rautenberg
"Zur Zukunftsthora des Hesekiel," *ZAW* 33 (1913): 92–115.

Georg Richter
Die ezechielische Tempel; eine exegetische Studie über Ezechiel 40ff, BFChrTh 16,2 (Gütersloh, 1912).

Martin Anton Schmidt
Prophet und Tempel; eine Studie zum Problem der Gottesnähe im Alten Testament (Zollikon-Zürich: Evangelischer, 1948), especially 163–171.

Theo. G. Soares
"Ezekiel's Temple," *The Biblical World* 14 (1899): 93–103.

Chapters 40–48 of the book of Ezekiel describe, like chapters 8–11, a great ecstatic vision on the part of the prophet. He is transported to the temple mount in the land of Israel. There a man leads him through the sanctuary area. In a series of silently accomplished measurements and with a few concise explanatory remarks, the construction of this area is set out for him after he had been told right at the beginning that everything that he saw was to be the object of a proclamation for the house of Israel (40–42). Next, the prophet sees how the glory of Yahweh returns to the temple and listens as he is told the statutes of the temple, the measurement of the altar and the ordinances for the dedication of the altar (43). After he has also been informed of the ordinances for the outer East Gate through which Yahweh's glory had entered and which was subsequently closed (44:1–3), he is told, after he has once again observed the presence of that glory in the temple, the ordinances for the life and service of Levites and priests (44:4–27). The priests' emoluments (44:28–31), the regulations for the possession of property by the sanctuary servants, the city dwellers and the prince (45:1–8) and, after an invective directed at the unrighteous princes of Israel (45:9), the system of measurements, the size and purpose of the various offerings by the people are regulated in his hearing (45:10–17). After the exposition of the sacrificial ordinances for the great feasts, reference is made to the conduct of the cult (46:1–12) and to the prince's property rights (46:16–18), while in between these there occur the regulations for the תמיד-offering (46:13–15), before there follows in 46:19–24, in a surprising repetition, a section descriptive of the temple area (kitchens for the sacrifices). But then the perspective widens in the last two chapters. The description of the temple spring, again in the form of a visionary guidance experience, a spring which swells to a river on its way to the valley (47:1–12), directs the gaze towards the country. After a description of the boundaries of the country (47:13–20), its division among the sanctuary, the sanctuary servants, the prince and the twelve tribes is described (47:21–48:29) with a resumption of the regulations of 45:1–8 before, finally, "the city" is described in its full extent with its gates and their names.

This enormous final vision in the book presents, as already remarked, a counterpart to chapters 8–11. In both the prophet is transported from his place of exile to Jerusalem and is there led from the outside into the inside of the Temple and is confronted, at various points along his way, here with the ordinances for the new sanctuary, there with the disorder of the old. In both, the whole section circles round the question, more or less clearly explicit, of the presence of the glory of Yahweh in the Jerusalem Temple. While, however, chapters 8–11 show how Yahweh's glory departs from the unclean, sinful former sanctuary, chapters 40–48 show how it once again takes possession of the now cleansed temple area, which, in its ideal layout, provides a protective citadel for the sanctuary.

These areas of correspondence are countered on the other hand by marked differences. This begins already in the case of the formal design. While chapters 8–11, notwithstanding the later expansions which were identified, afforded the rounded description of an ecstatic vision at the end of which the prophet was restored once more to his place among the exiles (see also 1:1–3:15), there is lacking in chapters 40–48 (as in 37:1–14) a concluding report of the return of the prophet and of the end of his vision. The differences, however, also concern the character of the content. While chapters 8–11, especially in their original form, are filled with continuous movement and are in narrative style, the effect of chapters 40–48 for long stretches is that of the description of a static situation in which only what is at hand is observed and revealed as to its order. There appear on a large scale legal regulations which recall the legal style of many sections of the Pentateuch. This could be the reason why chapters 40–48 have been called, for short, "draft constitution."

This description, however, does not fully grasp the actual state of affairs. Chapters 40–48 are not simply concerned with a situation legally imposed on men, the proper "constitution" of which is here regulated, but just as much with the proclamation of a new reality miraculously brought about by Yahweh. This can be seen most clearly in 47:1–12, but also in 43:1ff. The statements of chapters 40–48, in the orientation of their content, are connected quite unmistakably with the words of promise in chapters 34–37. There 37:26–28 had also quite explicitly spoken of the erection of the new, everlasting sanctuary in the midst of the people by Yahweh and had added to that the covenant formula.[1] In the sanctuary newly founded by God the lasting covenant relationship between Yahweh and his people was to be made quite clear in the sight of the nations. Above all, however, reference must be made here to 20:32ff, where the promise of the new exodus in vv 40f leads to the promise of the new worship, well pleasing to God, on "my holy mountain, the high mountain of Israel."[2] When reference is also made there to the "gifts" (תרומות) which Yahweh will receive with favor, there occurs there precisely the key-word which holds together the various sections of 44:30–45:17. All this stands in 20:32ff, however, in the context of the great promise of Yahweh's future action. The whole vision of the new temple and its ordinances appears from this point of view as the complete fulfillment of the future which Yahweh had promised for Israel.

All this makes clear the inner tension which dominates the whole of chapters 40–48. The many regulations which are laid down here and are also in fact formulated in the jussive (see e.g., 45:10) weave themselves into a total plan, which, exactly like the vision in 37:1–14, is under the sign of the free divine promise. Only when both basic aspects, the promise of a future seen in a vision and proclaimed as a divine gift and (on the basis of this gift) the commitment to new ordinances born of thoughts of reform and imposed on the men of Israel as law, are given their due weight will the pericope chapters 40–48 be correctly understood.

Ezekiel 40–48 are not all the product of the same mold. The penetrating analysis of Gese, who has carried powerfully forward the analyses of his predecessors, shows that behind the present text there lies a lively process of growth and redaction. Thus it will be best to consider one by one the individual components with regard to form and content and then, in conclusion, to evaluate the whole complex by way of a survey and to determine its "location" in the total context.[3]

As the first great complex, chapters 40–42 in the first place stand apart from what comes after them. Here the layout of the temple in its outer form is measured and described. 42:15–20, which, after the description of the individual structures in the temple area, returns to the measurements of the complex as a whole, marks the conclusion of this first part of the great vision.

1 See above pp. 276f.
2 See 1,416f.
3 See below the conclusion of the exegesis of chapters 40–48 (pp. 547–553).

A. The New Temple

Bibliography

Gustaf Dalman
"Der zweite Tempel zu Jerusalem," *PJ* 5 (1909): 29–57.

Kurt Galling
"Serubbabel und der Hohepriester beim Wiederaufbau des Tempels in Jerusalem" in *Studien zur Geschichte Israels im persischen Zeitalter* (Tübingen: Mohr, 1964), 127–148.

Kurt Galling
"Serubbabel und der Wiederaufbau des Tempels in Jerusalem" in *Verbannung und Heimkehr. Beiträge zur Geschichte und Theologie Israels im 6. und 5. Jahrhundert v. Chr., Wilhelm Rudolph zum 70. Geburtstage dargebracht* (Tübingen: Mohr [Siebeck], 1961), 67–96.

Rudolf Kittel
Studien zur hebräischen Archäologie und Religionsgeschichte, BWAT 1 (Leipzig, 1908), 1–96 (1. "Der heilige Fels auf dem Moria. Seine Geschichte und seine Altäre").

Kurt Möhlenbrink
Der Tempel Salomos; eine Untersuchung seiner Stellung in der Sakralarchitektur des Alten Orients, BWANT 4 (Stuttgart: Kohlhammer, 1932)

Martin Noth
Könige, BK 9 (Neukirchen-Vluyn: Neukirchener, 1964–1968).

This analysis of the first part of the great final vision, which is limited to chapters 40–42, shows that these chapters too are in no way formed as a unit. Its formally self-contained basic element, to which further parts have been added and on which, partly, these are formally more or less clearly dependent, can be discerned in 40:1–37, 47–49; 41:1–4. It has now been split into two parts by the insertion of 40:38–46. To this are connected the sections 41:5–15a; 41:15b–26; 42:1–14 and 42:15–20, but these are each best considered individually.

1. The Visionary Guidance of the Prophet from the East Gate to the Threshold of the Holy of Holies

Bibliography

Carl Gordon Howie
"The East Gate of Ezekiel's Temple Enclosure and the Solomonic Gateway of Megiddo," *BASOR* 117 (1950): 13–19.

Hermann Schult
"Der Debir im salomonischen Tempel," *ZDPV* 80 (1964): 46–54.

Wolfram von Soden
"Akkadisch *ta'û* und hebräisch *tā'* als Raumbezeichnungen," *WO* 1, 5 (1950): 356–361.

G. Ernest Wright
"A Solomonic City Gate at Gezer," *BA* 21 (1958): 103f.

Yigael Yadin
"Solomon's City Wall and Gate at Gezer," *IEJ* 8 (1958): 80–86.

Walter Zimmerli
"Ezechieltempel und Salomostadt" in *Hebräische Wortforschung; Festschrift zum 80. Geburtstag von Walter Baumgartner,* VT Suppl 16 (Leiden: Brill, 1967), 389–414.

See also Bibliography above pp. 325f.

40

1 **In[a] the twenty-fifth year of our exile, at the**
beginning of the year[b] on the tenth[c] (day)
of the month, in the fourteenth year
after[d] the city had fallen, on this very day

40:1 1a On the model of the majority of the other dated oracles (see 1:1 note a) 𝔊 begins, here too, with an introductory καὶ ἐγένετο (in 𝔊[88] with an obelus, 𝔏[S] *factum est*). But since 29:1 attests even in 𝔊 the possibility of beginning with the date, 40:1 𝔊 is doubtless a case of secondary assimilation to normal usage. 𝔖 adds here too a superscription: בנינא דביתא.

b 𝔐 בראש השנה. 𝔊 ἐν τῷ πρώτῳ μηνί (𝔏[S] *in primo mense*) shows that 𝔊 is no longer aware of the old New Year's date of Lev 25:9, but, in dependence on the usual dating by year, month and day, puts the month which it assumes in place of the ראש השנה which it understands as only an approximate indication of date. An emendation to בראשון (Toy, Richter, *ezechielische Tempel*) is therefore not advisable. See the exposition.

c 𝔐 בעשור. While the tenth month in the date is designated by the ordinal numeral (בעשרי 29:1; 33:21; cf. Gen 8:5), in the corresponding note of the day the noun form עשור occurs throughout. So 20:1; 24:1; see further Ex 12:3; Lev 16:29; 23:27; 25:9; Nu 29:7; Josh 4:19; 2 Kgs 25:1; Jer 52:4, 12.

d אחר אשר occurs again only in Ruth 2:2; otherwise אחרי אשר or אחר alone. See also Brockelmann §163b.

the hand of Yahweh came upon me[e] and
he[f] brought me [there][g] 2/ in the visions
of God[a] [he brought me][b] to the land of
Israel[c] and set me[d] on[e] a very high moun-
tain. And on it was a building[f] like a city
[in the south][g].
3 **And when he had brought[a] me there, see,**

e 𝔗 paraphrases שרת עלי רוח נבואה מן קדם יהוה, so too 8:1; 37:1.

f see 37:1 note c.

g The שמה of 𝔐 is puzzling and is premature at this point. 𝔊 ($\mathfrak{L}^{W}$ 𝔖) *καὶ ἤγαγέ με* (2) *ἐν ὁράσει θεοῦ εἰς τὴν γῆν τοῦ* Ισραηλ does not attest either the שמה of v 1 or the הביאני of v 2, which takes up inelegantly the ויבא אתי of v 1. Gese sees in this a smoothing out of 𝔐 by 𝔊 and supposes that ויבא אתי שמה had already at an early stage found its way into v 1 from v 3a*α*. But since all the other passages which speak of the coming of Yahweh's hand on the prophet in a verbal clause (1:3; 3:22; 8:1; 37:1; cf. 33:22) are continued by a verbal statement in the consecutive imperfect, the phrase which would result from the deletion of v 1b*β*, viz. היתה עלי יד יהוה במראות אלהים הביאני, is perceptibly out of step with the usual phraseology. In particular, the comparison with 37:1, where ברוח יהוה occurs in place of the במראות אלהים of 40:1f and where, further, the identical sequence of verbs occurs היתה עלי יד יהוה ויוצאני . . . ויניחני, suggests a reconstruction of the text on the basis of 𝔊 (deletion of שמה in v 1 and of הביאני in v 2). Thus, the indication of place in v 1 has, like the שם in 1:3; 3:22; 8:1, been added secondarily. The addition made it necessary for v 2a to become an independent clause by means of the insertion of הביאני.

2 2a 𝔐 במראות is rendered by a singular in 𝔊 *ἐν ὁράσει* ($\mathfrak{L}^{W}$ *in visione*) as in 8:3. It is plural in 1:1. Here too 𝔗 levels out theologically ברוח נבואה דשרת עלי מן קדם יהוה, see v 1 note e.

b See v 1 note g.

c ארץ ישראל "land of Israel" occurs also in 27:17; 47:18; see above pp. 66f.

d On ויניחני see 37:1 note e.

e על–אל cf. 1:17 note a.

f מבנה *hapax legomenon,* but cf. Phoenician מבנת, H. Donner and W. Röllig, *Kanaanäische und aramäische Inschriften* (Wiesbaden: Harrassowitz, 1962–64), 60,2.

g 𝔐 מנגב. 𝔗 מדרומה, 𝔙 (*civitatis*) *vergentis ad austrum,* Σ *ἀπὸ νότου,* Θ *ἀπὸ μεσημβρίας.* 𝔊 *ἀπέναντι* ('Α *ἐξέναντι,* $\mathfrak{L}^{W}$ *contra*) seems to presuppose a מנגד which is accepted by Hitzig, Cornill, BH^{3}. Toy מנגדי, Fohrer-Galling נגדי. But Gese correctly draws attention to the fact that elsewhere מנגד always presupposes a distance between the observer and that which is observed, which, according to what follows, is not the case here. On the other hand, מנגב cannot be original in the context of chapters 40–42 which otherwise refer to the south always as דרום and never as נגב, which is used frequently only from chapter 46 onwards. It must be a secondary addition which inadvertently refers the כמבנה עיר to the city which, according to chapter 48, is to be located to the south of the temple (see below on 48:15–19).

there was (there) a man whose appearance[b] was like bronze[c], and he had a
linen cord[d] in his hand and a measuring
rod. And he stood at the gate. 4/ And the
man spoke to me[a]: Son of man, look with
your eyes and listen with your ears and
pay attention to all that I show you. for in
order that I should show it to you have
you been brought here[b]. Proclaim[c] all
that you see to the house of Israel.
5 And see, a wall ran round the temple
(area)[a] on the outside. But the measuring
rod which the man had in his hand measured six cubits, (the cubit measured) at a
(normal) cubit and a hand-breadth. And
he measured the thickness[b] of the structure[c]: one measuring rod, and the
height[d]: one measuring rod.
6 And he entered the gate[a] which faced east

3 3a According to Bauer-Leander §59p, ויביא is a late *plene* form of ויבא.

b 𝔐 מראהו. 𝔊 (𝔏^{W} 𝔖) καὶ ἡ ὅρασις αὐτοῦ may have found a ומראהו in its original (Ehrlich, *Randglossen;* Cooke).

c 𝔊 (𝔏^{SW}) elucidates χαλκοῦ στίλβοντος, which in Dan 10:6 (Θ) corresponds to an original Hebrew נחשת קלל.

d 𝔊 σπαρτίον οἰκοδόμων, 𝔏^{S} *resticula turtorum,* 𝔏^{W} *resticula structorum.*

4 4a The ἑόρακας which is read additionally by 𝔊 (𝔏^{SW}) (cf. הראית 8:12, 15, 17) is unusual before the beginning of the actual vision and directly preceding the following imperative רְאֵה and is certainly not original.

b After the הראותכה, for which, after the preceding אשר אני מראה אותך the איש who is speaking is the most obvious subject, even if the impersonal translation "that one should show it to you" (e.g. *ZB*) is also grammatically possible, 𝔐 הֻבָאתָה (on the form see Bauer-Leander §54a), with its transition to the second person, is surprisingly clumsy. The alteration to the first person εἰσελήλυθα in 𝔊$^{L',36,764,\text{ and others}}$ (𝔏^{S} 𝔄̈ Arm), which is also made by Ehrlich, *Randglossen,* Herrmann, Fohrer-Galling, Eichrodt (see also Dan 9:22), represents, however, an obvious harmonization and has against it not only 𝔗, which, with its איתיוכא (one has brought you), clearly paraphrases 𝔐, but also already 𝔊 (𝔏^{W}) εἰσελήλυθας (𝔖 אתית can also be understood as a first person, so Herrmann, Fohrer-Galling). One might then still ask whether an original באתה should not be read and the ה deleted as dittography. But it is surely more correct to retain 𝔐. It should be emphasized that it is not the man who "has come" (there has been no previous reference to such a "coming"), but it is the prophet who has come or, more precisely, been brought. The hopʻal thereby unmistakably harks back to the double (𝔐 triple) hipʻil of vv 1, (2) 3. Thus the harsh transition in 𝔐 from הראותכה, oriented towards אני מראה, to הבאתה, oriented towards ויבא אתי of v 1 (3), must be borne.

c 𝔊 𝔏^{SW} 𝔖 alleviate the harshness of the transition by the insertion of the copula, see 1:4 note a.

5 5a בית "house" here means the total temple complex.

b 𝔐 רחב "breadth."

c 𝔐 בנין. According to Driver, "Ezekiel," 304f, better rendered by "structure" than by "building." 𝔊 προτείχισμα "outer work, outer wall"; misunderstood by 𝔏^{SW}: *quod ante murum.*

d 𝔊 (𝔖) smooth out the text καὶ τὸ ὕψος αὐτοῦ.

6 6a 𝔐 שער is doubtless to be understood as definite, cf. 𝔊 𝔖 𝔗. The parallel passages 40:20 (but see there), 22; 42:15; 43:1 might suggest reading השער with MS$^{\text{Ken 96}}$. But since the form without the article occurs again in 43:4, the originality of 𝔐 cannot be contested with certainty. See also 9:2 note b.

and climbed[b] its steps and measured the threshold of the gate: one measuring rod deep [and the threshold <of the gate>: one measuring rod deep][c], 7/ and the recess: one measuring rod long and one measuring rod deep, and the space between[a] the recesses: five cubits[b], and

b 𝔊 does not render ויעל but in its place reads ἐν ἑπτὰ ἀναβαθμοῖς. With Gese, this is to be regarded (against Cornill, Bertholet-Galling, Eichrodt, Howie) as a secondary accommodation to the description of the other outer gates (vv 22, 26), where 𝔊 admittedly then speaks of κλιμακτῆρες. Instead of K במעלתו, which suggsts a singular form (thus according to the note in BH^3, cf. Ginsburg; in the text BH^3 points בְּמַעֲלוֹתָו), the vocalization should, of course, be plural. The defective writing of the third person masculine plural suffix is encountered so often in what follows that one should speak here not of a scribal error, but more correctly of a scribal peculiarity characteristic of Ezek 40ff.

c ואת סף אחד קנה אחד רחב is to be regarded as a slightly corrupt (אחד in place of שער) dittograph of the preceding words, which is accommodated by 𝔖 (אחר in place of אחד "another threshold") and 𝔙 (*id est limen* . . .) each in their own way. In 𝔊 not only is the dittography missing, but also the preceding contextually indispensable רחב which here refers to the depth of the threshold. In its place there occurs in 𝔊 (except in 𝔊^B) after διεμέτρησε (וימד) the addition τὸ θεε ἔξ ἔνθεν καὶ ἔξ ἔνθεν καὶ . . . which is marked with an obelus in 𝔊^Q (Jerome) and which anticipates (inaccurately) the data of v 7. When 𝔊 renders סף by αιλαμ (᾽Α Θ πρόθυρον, Σ οὐδόν), it is possibly thinking not of the threshold, but of a vestibule similar to the one behind the gate structure. The latter is also referred to in 𝔐 v 8. It is, of course, also possible that 𝔊 does not associate any specific concept with αιλαμ. Thus Gese: "The technical term עלם = αιλαμ, which was not understood by 𝔊, is vague enough to serve as the description of any architectural intervening section" (131). On no account is 𝔊 to be followed here and translated (as, e.g., by Howie) by "vestibule."

7 7a בין in 𝔐 here still has substantival force. 𝔗 interprets more fully ובין תוייא כותלא "and between the recesses was a wall." 𝔊, on the other hand, in its καὶ τὸ αιλαμ ἀνὰ μέσον τοῦ θαιηλαθα, might already be introducing here, in an appropriate interpretation, the technical term which appears from v 10 onwards (איל) for the sections between the recesses. The fact, however, that this appears in the plural form אילם (= αιλαμ), which is correct in v 10 but inappropriate here, suggests rather (against Bewer, BH^3) not adducing 𝔊 here as evidence for an original reading האיל, but accepting that it is providing a free interpretation. In view of the varying use of αιλαμ (v 6 it renders סף; v 9 אֻלָם; v 10 אֵילָם), the evidence of 𝔊 here remains in any case very uncertain. See also v 6 note c.

b 𝔊 six cubits. In an addition, in which 𝔊 (𝔏^W), anticipating the data of v 10, introduces in vv 7f three recesses and the intervening pillars, there emerges also the figure of five cubits for the breadth of the second pillar. 𝔐 v 7b is to be found in 𝔊 in the opening words of v 9. As a result of homoiote-

the threshold of the gate to the vestibule[c] of the gate inwards: one measuring rod. 8/ And he measured the vestibule of the gate [inwards: one measuring rod. 9/ And he measured the vestibule of the gate][a]: eight cubits, and its pillars[b]: two cubits. And the vestibule of the gate lay on the inside. 10/ And the recesses of the east gate[a] lay three on the one side and three on the other. The three had one and the same measurement, and the pillars on either side (also) had one and the same measurement. 11/ And he measured the inside width[a] of the gate opening: ten cubits, the [b] (full) width[a] of the gate: thirteen cubits. 12/ And in front of the <recesses>[a] there was a barrier[b]: one cubit (deep), and one cubit (deep) was the barrier on the other side[c]. And the recess measured six cubits on the one side and six cubits on the other. 13/ And he measured the gate from the (beginning of the) roof of one recess to (the beginning of) its (opposite) roof[a]: twenty-five cubits, with doorway facing

leuton the 𝔊 text then jumps from the second השער in v 7b directly to the שמנה אמות after the השער of vv 8/9, whereby the dittography of 𝔐 in vv 8/9 is not yet presupposed; see v 9 note a.

c On אולם see 8:16 note a; on the change in the spelling אולם and אילם in chapters 40–48 see Cooke, 441. On the construct form אֻלָם see Bauer-Leander §71x.

9 9a The repetition in 𝔐 vv 8/9 of the words מהבית קנה אחד 9 וימד את אלם השער from vv 7/8 is missing in a majority of MSS Edd as well as in 𝔖 𝔙 𝔏[W]. It was also not found by 𝔊, which has the πηχῶν ὀκτώ (שמנה אמות v 9) follow directly on the second השער of v 7, to which πύλης corresponds. On the form of 𝔊 see also v 7 note b.

b 𝔐 ואילו is to be understood with Q as ואיליו. This reading also seems to be presupposed by 𝔊 καὶ τὰ αιλευ. 𝔙 singular *et frontem eius.* The plural form of איל is clearly recognizable in vv 10, 16, 49 (v 14 text uncertain). The K ואילו, however, is also found in vv 21, 24, 26, 29, 31, 33, 34, 36, 37 so that we have here, without doubt, a consciously preserved defective spelling. See also v 6 note b and v 7 note a.

10 10a 𝔊 καὶ τὰ θεε τῆς πύλης θεε κατέναντι does not point, since 𝔊 in 47:3 renders קדים by ἐξ ἐναντίας (see also 1 Sam 13:5; Hab 1:9), to a different original, but is a rendering of a misunderstood, rearranged 𝔐. So, correctly, Cooke, Gese against Hitzig, Cornill, Herrmann.

11 11a On this understanding of רחב and ארך see v 49 note a and below pp. 349f.

b 𝔊 𝔙 make the text easier by the insertion of the copula, see 1:4 note a.

12 12a 𝔐 תאות. Since 𝔊 transliterates θειμ, instead of the completely unique feminine plural form, here too the usual masculine form תאים should be read.

b 𝔐 גבול, 𝔙 *marginem,* 𝔗 𝔖 תחומא "border" must designate a barrier in front of the recesses facing the passage. 𝔊 καὶ πῆχυς ἐπισυναγόμενος ἐπὶ πρόσωπον τῶν θειμ ἔνθεν καὶ ἔνθεν (𝔏[W] *et cubitum concollectum contra faciem thein hinc et inde*) obviously had no idea what the expression meant.

c 𝔊 𝔖 abbreviate the somewhat circumstantial but textually irreproachable phraseology of v 12a. With Gese (against Toy, Herrmann, Fohrer-Galling) 𝔐 is to be preferred.

13 13a 𝔊 ἀπὸ τοῦ τοίχου τοῦ θεε ἐπὶ τὸν τοῖχον τοῦ θεε has repeatedly tempted scholars to emend 𝔐, which is clearly attested by 𝔖 𝔗 𝔙 (אגר, *tectum*). Cornill, since τοῖχος in about twenty instances (see, e.g., 41:5f) corresponds to קיר in 𝔐, reconstructs האתיון לקירו מקיר; Kraetzschmar and Richter, *ezechielische Temple,* מגו התא לנגדו; Bertholet-Galling and Fohrer-Galling, מגו התא לגו התא. None of these is supported by any versional tradition. Also, nowhere else is גו ever an architectural term (Gese). Since this measuring is inside the gate, גג here will mean the point at which the roof sits on the walls.

doorway[b]. [14/ . . .][a]. 15/ And <from the front>[a] of the gate where one enters (?)[b] to[c] the front of the vestibule of the gate <inwards>[d]: fifty cubits. 16/ And there

b By פתח here is meant the opening of the fenced-off recess facing the corridor of the gateway. According to Gese (see also Bertholet-Galling and Fohrer-Galling), v 13b will have been added in order to elucidate the obscure adverbial definition of v 13aβ.

14 14a 𝔐 ויעש את אילים ששים אמה ואל איל החצר השער סביב סביב "he made the pillars sixty cubits—and by the pillar of the vestibule the gate round about" does not make any sense and is clearly corrupt. On the basis of careful consideration of the rendering in 𝔊 and 𝔖 there can be recognized in v 14 textually corrupt elements from vv 15 and 16 which have found their way by mistake to the beginning of v 15 between vv 13 and 15. For the detailed proof see Gese, 140–148. Since, also, v 15 is the direct continuation of the complete measurement of the gate begun in v 13, v 14 can be seen, also from the point of view of content, to be a secondary addition.

15 15a V 15, as is clear also from 𝔊, contains details of measurements which do not refer to an object which can be designated by a single word, but mentions the beginning and the end point of the measurement. The comparison with v 19, which contains a similar measurement, is obvious; we are to read instead of על פני (at the front) an original מלפני on the assumption of the corruption of a מ to an ע. לפני—which 𝔊, with a correct feeling that this must be a specific part of the gate structure, translates, technically inaccurately, by *αἴθριον* (open place) in the four places in vv 15 and 19 (see also v 14)—means the area fronting the building.

b היאתון K, האיתון Q has not so far been identified with certainty. The context, however, leaves scarcely any doubt that what is meant here is the outer side of the east gate as the starting point of the measurement. The *ἔξωθεν* of 𝔊, which contrasts with the following *ἔσωθεν* (𝔐 פנימי), might suggest an original חיצון in 𝔐. See, e.g., 41:17. So Cooke. Yet the possibility cannot be excluded that איתון (or originally אתיון?) conceals a no longer extant noun or adjective which describes the outer facade of the gate "the side at which one enters" (Gese).

c על–אל 1:17 note a. The corruption of מלפני into על פני (note a) could here have brought quite particularly in its train the form על פני instead of the expected אל פני. But a corruption of עד לפני is not impossible. So 2 MSS, Toy, Cooke, Bertholet-Galling and Fohrer-Galling. 𝔊 *εἰς τὸ αἴθριον*.

d The innter gate, i.e. the one leading to the inner court, can certainly not be meant here. After the sketch of the parallel gate measurements in vv 20–23, 24–27, the measurement of the distance to the corresponding inner gate follows only at the end when all the detailed measurements of the gates have been given. Thus it is added for the east gate, quite correctly, by way of conclusion in v 19. The measurement of fifty cubits, as is clear from the

were framed windows[a] in the recesses [and in their pillars][b] round about inside the gate, and similarly[c] there were windows <in its vestibule>[d] inside round about, and on <its pillars>[e] there were palms[f].

17 **Then he led me into the outer court and see, there were rooms, and there was a pavement[a] laid[b] round about the court.**

parallels (vv 21, 25), refers to the total length of the gate structure. Thus either הפנימי will have to be deleted (Gese) as an addition which has erroneously found its was into v 15 on the basis of the textual corruption in v 19 (see below) or else, in the event that the specific emendation to לפנימה (so Fohrer-Galling) is felt to be undesirable, the expression השער הפנימי will have to be understood as a counterpart to השער האיתון (? see note b), in a quite unique usage, as the description of the inside of the (outer) gate.

16 16a 𝔐 חלנות אטמות literally "closed windows." אטם in Is 33:15; Ps 58:5; Prv 21:13 of the closing of the ears; Prv 17:28 of the closing of the lips. Hence 𝔗 כוין סתימן. Somewhat differently 𝔊 *θυρίδες κρυπταί*, 𝔏[W] *fenestrae occultae*, 𝔙 *fenestras obliquas*. 𝔖 paraphrases more fully כוא דשטיפן מן לגו וקטינן לבר "windows open on the inside, narrow on the outside." Here 𝔖 seems to be thinking of windows which are not completely closed but which grow narrower towards the outer wall. Galling "framed windows." Already in the Solomonic temple חלוני שקפים אטמים were mentioned (1 Kgs 6:4). According to Noth, *Könige*, 95 (note f), "framed windows with bars." Driver, "Ezekiel," 305: "narrowed windows, loopholes."

b On 𝔐 אליהמה Gese points to the spelling of the suffix as found at Qumran. Cf. Millar Burrows, "Orthography, Morphology, and Syntax of the St. Mark's Isaiah Manuscript," *JBL* 68 (1949): 209, and Bauer-Leander §29z and §72v'. This word with its strange spelling, although it is attested in the versions (𝔊 imprecisely has *ἐπὶ τὰ αιλαμ*), is, however, difficult to fit into the context and is surely to be regarded as an addition.

c וכן introduces the second half of the sentence. The *atnaḥ* which divides the verse should, therefore, be transferred to the second סביב.

d 𝔐 לאלמות וחלונות. 𝔊 *τοῖς αιλαμ θυρίδες* (𝔏[W] *fenestrae aelam*) does not seem to have had the copula in its original. In 𝔐 this, along with the preceding ת, will have found its way into the text as a corrupt dittograph of the preceding מו. With Gese לאלמו חלונות should be read. In vv 16–30 in 𝔐 א[י]לם is consistently found, while earlier and later it is אֻלָם or אולם. The consistent transcription in 𝔊 *αιλαμ* shows that subsequently the form אילם has prevailed. Why it is used in 𝔐 only in 40:16–30 is not discernible.

e 𝔐 איל (𝔊 *αιλαμ*, 𝔗 אלא) has arisen from a transposition of the consonants of אלו (= אילו, cf., e.g., v 9).

f 𝔊 adds *ἔνθεν καὶ ἔνθεν*. On the form תִּמֹּרָה "artificial palm tree" see Bauer-Leander §61wβ, note.

17 17a On the aspirated pronunciation of the פ in רצפה see Bauer-Leander §75f.

b 𝔐 עשוי stands out as a result of its lack of grammatical agreement with רצפה. Therefore, and especially since it is not attested by 𝔊 (𝔖 is much further

Thirty rooms gave on to[c] the pavement. 18/ And the pavement ran along the side of the gates, the same depth as the gates. (That is) the lower pavement. 19/ And he measured the distance[a] from the front of the <lower> gate <to the front of the inner gate>[b], (which faces) outwards: one hundred cubits [in the east and in the north][c].

from the text), it is deleted by many (Cornill; Ehrlich, *Randglossen;* Herrmann), while others such as Bertholet-Galling and Fohrer-Galling emend it to עשויה. But since another עשוי, similarly lacking in grammatical agreement, occurs in 41:18f (46:23?; it is otherwise in 41:20, 25), it may be considered whether 𝔐 should not be retained and עשוי, similar to מחקה in 8:10; 23:14, considered to be a fixed technical term used as a noun or, with S. R. Driver, *A Treatise on the Use of the Tenses in Hebrew* (Oxford, 1892) §135,6, Obs.3, as an impersonal passive participle. Gesenius-Kautzsch §121d prefers to understand רצפה as a preceding accusative of result. 𝔖 here finds a reference to the ascending steps (דרגין): וחזית דרגא כד חדרא תלתין דרגין חד לעל מן חד.

c על–אל cf. 1:17 note a.

19 19a Literally "the breadth," see the exposition. 𝔊 ($\mathfrak{L}^W$) adds the explanatory *τῆς αὐλῆς*.

b 𝔐 מלפני השער התחתונה לפני החצר הפנימי "from the front of the lower gate in front of (opposite?) the inner court" not only stands out as a result of the feminine adjective התחתונה, concerning which, according to Bauer-Leander §62y, those who pointed the text already recommended by their accentuation the masculine form as the correct one, but can also not be correctly fitted in from the point of view of content. 𝔊 *ἀπὸ τοῦ αἰθρίου τῆς πύλης τῆς ἐξωτέρας ἔσωθεν ἐπὶ τὸ αἴθριον* (also 𝔙 *usque ad frontem*) *τῆς πύλης τῆς βλεπούσης ἔξω*, which admittedly describes the "lower gate" in free translation as the "outer," adds an interpretative *ἔσωθεν* "inwards" and understands הפנימי as הפנה, has surely preserved the correct reading. Thus, comparing v 15, the following should be read: מלפני השער התחתון אל לפני השער הפנימי מחוץ.

c 𝔐 הקדים והצפון looks back, in its first word, to vv 6–16(19), the description of the east gate, and forward, in its second word, to vv 20–23, the description of the north gate. These orienting keywords do not fit the text and are best regarded as additional observations appended secondarily. They have been woven into the context by 𝔊 ($\mathfrak{L}^W$) but not by 𝔖. הקדים has been linked to the reference to the gate in v 19a, in a way quite impossible in the Hebrew text, going back beyond the numeral and repeating the *βλεπούσης*: *τῆς βλεπούσης κατὰ ἀνατολάς*. The הצפון in 𝔊, however, has become a component of a new guidance formula: *καὶ ἤγαγέ με ἐπὶ βορρᾶν*. On this basis the original text has been conjectured by the marjority to be ויולכני דרך הצפון (Cornill, Herrmann, Bertholet-Galling and Fohrer-Galling, Eichrodt; see also Gese). The *καὶ ἰδοὺ πύλη* which follows in 𝔊 in v 20 seems to justify the reference to v 24, where this guidance formula occurs. Now it is difficult not to be aware that 𝔊 already had before it the text of 𝔐 and is harmonizing it with what might have been expected on the basis of v 24. Thus 𝔊 should not become the basis for a reconstruction of the text. Gese judges correctly: "Thus 𝔊

20 (Also) at the gate in the outer court which faces north he measured length and breadth[a]. 21/ And its recesses[a]—three on the one side and three on the other—and its pillars[b] and its vestibule[c] corresponded[d] (exactly) to the measurements of the first[e] gate: fifty cubits was its length[f], and the breadth: twenty-five

is already reconstructing the text" (153). But are we justified in going on to state with Gese: "So, with 𝔊, we must assume that ויולכני דרך הצפון (והנה) once stood in the text or was at least envisaged"? Such a decision cannot be taken without regard to v 20.

20 20a On the basis of 𝔊 (v 19 note c) two emendations are mostly made in v 20: 1) והשער is, with reference to v 24, emended to והנה שער; 2) the resultant syntactical transformation of v 20a into an independent noun clause makes v 20b also into an independent clause and necessitates the emendation (again on the basis of 𝔊 and of v 24) of 𝔐 מדד to ומדד. But if v 20 is considered quite independently of 𝔊 or of v 24 it requires no emendation. It is a completely self-contained compound noun clause with a backward pronominal reference in the verbal clause of the predicate (מדד ארכו ורחבו), where an introductory ו is certainly possible but in no sense obligatory (Beer-Meyer §92,4). While 𝔐 thus affords a completely satisfactory text, the same can scarcely be said of the form emended on the basis of 𝔊. The beginning, introduced by the "call for attention" הנה (Koehler-Baumgartner), leads one to expect a brief reference to the entity which is now appearing for the first time and which is only then precisely examined and described. Thus in v 24 והנה שער דרך הדרום. This is contradicted by the fuller description of the north gate in v 20a והשער אשר פניו דרך הצפון לחצר החיצונה which cannot easily be combined with an introductory הנה. Thus we can scarcely avoid the conclusion that in v 20 we have a good, original text according to which the north gate of the outer court, into which the prophet has already been led in v 17, is described without a specific guidance formula. The tendency of 𝔊 to insert different formulae for a guidance situation can be seen again particularly clearly in v 44a.

21 21a The suffixed plural form תאו is always written defectively by K in what follows (vv 29, 33, 36). 𝔊 transliterates it as a singular תא in v 7 and as a construct plural in v 10 by (τὰ) θεε.

b On K אילו see v 9 note b. By contrast with θεε (note a), 𝔊 in its transliteration here (τὰ) αιλευ gives expression to the suffix.

c 𝔐 ואלמו is here and in vv 24 (אילמו), 29, 31, 33, 36, against Q, to be read as a singular ואלמו. This is indicated also by 𝔊 αιλαμμω and by 𝔙 *et vestibulum eius* (singular). See also v 16 note d. 𝔊 ($\mathfrak{L}^{W}$) also adds here, erroneously, καὶ τοὺς φοίνικας αὐτῆς which then recurs in its original place in v 22.

d If one is unwilling to read 𝔐 היה as הָיָה (= היו), one must assume that the singular verb refers to the immediately preceding singular אלמו (emended text).

e 𝔊 equalizes here too in form of expression in that it describes the first-named (𝔐 ראשון) gate in accordance with v 6 and the one immediately following in v 22 as πύλη βλέπουσα κατὰ ἀνατολάς.

f In ארכו, which (against BH³) should not be

cubits. 22/ And <the windows of its vestibule>[a] and its palms (were) like [the measurement of][b] the gate which faces east. And by seven steps one climbed up to it, and <its vestibule>[c] faced <inwards>[d]. 23/ And a gate to the inner[a] court lay opposite the gate, on the north as on the east[b]. And he measured (the distance)[c] from gate to gate: one hundred cubits.

24 **And he led me towards the south and see, there lay a gate facing south. And he measured it pillars[a] and <its vesti-**

emended to ארך, the connection is back beyond v 21a with the phraseology of v 20b. The parallel רחב then remains without suffix and should not (against Herrmann) be provided with a suffix on the basis, e.g., of 𝔊. In the recurrences in vv 25, 29, 33, 36 (in vv 33, 36 the chiastic structure is replaced by the precise parallelism of the word order) both dimensional terms remain without suffix. Throughout (in vv 29, 33, 36 only with *μῆκος*) 𝔊 inserts the possessive *αὐτῆς*.

22 22a In 𝔐 וחלונו ואלמו the further reference to אלם in the enumeration is strange in view of the fact that this was already mentioned in v 21. A glance at the description of the other gates shows that in every case reference is made to the windows of the אלם. So here too this juxtaposition should be restored and, with Kraetzschmar, Herrmann, Bertholet-Galling and Fohrer-Galling, חלוני אלמו or, graphically closer, חלונות אלמו should be read. The complete harmonization with vv 25, 29, 33 (see also v 36) by means of a reading וחלינים/חלונות לו ולאלמו (Gese, 18 note 3) is not advisable, since the description of the north gate, as the continuation of v 22 immediately shows (note b), also goes its own way. On the juxtaposition of feminine and masculine plural forms of חלון see on v 25; on the singular reading of אלמו see v 21 note c.

b 𝔐 מדת is not attested by 𝔊 (𝔏^{W}) *καθὼς ἡ πύλη* and is also meaningless from the point of view of content, since there is no reference to the measuring of the windows and ornamental palm trees with regard to the east gate. Read כַּשַּׁעַר.

c Here too, against 𝔐, the vocalization should be אֵלָמּו; see v 21 note c.

d 𝔐 לפניהם, for which, in relationship to מעלות, one would strictly speaking expect לפניהן, is surprising after the description of the east gate, since the vestibule does not lie on the outer side of this, where (according to v 6) the steps are to be found, but faces inwards (מהבית, vv 7, 9). Thus the *ἔσωθεν* of 𝔊 (𝔏^{W} *interius*) points to the correct reading לפנימה. The wrong reading has found its way also into v 26.

23 23a 𝔐 הפנימי treats as masculine חצר, which in 8:16; 10:3–5; 40:17, 20, and elsewhere is treated as feminine. Since the same happens in 40:27f, 44; 42:3; 43:5 (Jer 36:10), one must assume (against Albrecht, "Geschlecht," 49) that חצר (exactly like חלון, see v 25 note b) can be both masculine and feminine.

b 𝔐 ולקדים will have been correctly interpreted by 𝔊 (𝔏^{W}) *ὃν τρόπον τῆς πύλης τῆς βλεπούσης κατὰ ἀνατολάς*. Gese wishes to see in ולקדים the hand of the glossator of v 19.

c 𝔊 here too (see v 19 note a) adds the interpretive *τὴν αὐλήν*.

24 24a On 𝔐 אילו see v 9 note b. 𝔊 (𝔏^{W}) here too prefixes the *καὶ τὰ θεε* which is to be expected on the basis of the scheme of the enumeration in the case

bule>[b]—corresponding to the previous measurements. 25/ And it (i.e. the gate) and its vestibule[a] had windows[b] round about, corresponding to the windows previously mentioned. Fifty cubits was the length and twenty-five cubits the breadth. 26/ And <it had seven steps>[a], and its vestibule[b] faced <inwards>[c]. And it had palms[d], one on the one side and one on the other, on[e] its pillars[f]. 27/ And the inner[a] court had a gate facing south. And he measured (the distance)[b] from gate <to gate> [southwards][c]: one hundred cubits[d].

28 **And he led me through the south gate into <the>[a] inner[b] court and measured the [south][c] gate—corresponding to the previous measurements—29/ and its recesses[a] and its pillars[b] and its vestibule[c]—corresponding to the previous measurements. And it (i.e. the gate) and its vestibule had windows round about. Fifty cubits was the length and twenty-five cubits the breadth. [30/ And vestibules round about. Twenty-five cubits was the length and five cubits the breadth][a]. 31/ And its vestibule[a] faced**

of the other gates. Has an original וימד תאו ואילו here become corrupted and been abbreviated as the result of haplography? In view of the freedom with which variety occurs in the details of the descriptions of the gates and the repeated repetition of ומדד in the text that follows (40:35; 41:13, 15) this cannot be maintained with certainty.

b See v 21 note c.

25 25a See v 21 note c.

b 𝔐 חלונים is very strange alongside the חלנות which follows in the same verse, but in view of the many occurrences of both forms (masculine also in v 22; 41:16, 26 as well as 1 Kgs 6:4; Jer 9:20; Joel 2:9; see also Jer 22:14; feminine in vv 16, 25, 29, 33, 36; 41:16; Song 2:9) it should not be assimilated. See the identical phenomenon in the case of חצר, v 23 note a.

26 26a In שבעה עלותו, first of all, the feminine form of the numeral is odd. The numeral, in the case of those between 3 and 10, is normally of the opposite gender to that of the noun to which it belongs (Beer-Meyer §59,1) and is treated thus in vv 22, 31, 34, 37. Next, the form עלותו is surprising, where K and Q read an infinitive or a participle respectively; see P. Wernberg-Møller, "Observations on the Hebrew Participle," *ZAW* 71 (1959): 57. The simple assumption of a scribal error of ה for מ leads to the reading שבע מעלותיו which also seems to lie behind 𝔊 ($\mathfrak{L}^{W}$) καὶ ἑπτὰ κλιμακτῆρες αὐτῇ. This dispenses with the complete assimilation to the parallel vv 31, 34, 37 (Bertholet-Galling and Fohrer, Gese) or to v 22 (so 𝔅).

b See v 21 note c.

c See v 22 note d.

d 𝔅 *caelatae palmae.*

e על-אל cf. 1:17 note a.

f On אילו see v 9 note b.

27 27a 𝔐 הפנימי, see v 23 note a.

b 𝔊 adds τὴν αὐλήν, see v 23 note c.

c 𝔐 השער. About 30 MSS 𝔊 𝔗 attest here too the שער which would be expected on the basis of v 23. The article of 𝔐 is due to the addition דרך הדרום, which is missing completely in 𝔖 but appears in 𝔊 at the end of the verse in the free rendering τὸ εὖρος πρὸς νότον.

d With the numeral "100" usually the singular אמה occurs (vv 19, 23, 47). See Brockelmann §84c.

28 28a 𝔐 חצר is read by MSS^{Ken} (cf. 𝔊 𝔗 𝔖) as החצר before הפנימי. According to Brockelmann §60a, however, 𝔐 could be original.

b 𝔐 הפנימי, see v 23 note a.

c 𝔐 השער הדרום is impossible (see the first half of the verse). But since 𝔊 ($\mathfrak{L}^{W}$) does not render הדרים, the latter should be regarded as an interpretative element which is also factually superfluous.

29 29a See v 21 note a.

b See v 9 note b.

c See v 21 note c.

30 30a The verse is not attested by 𝔊 $\mathfrak{L}^{W}$ and is to be

the outer <court>[b], and it had palms on
its pillars[c], and <its stairway>[d] had eight
steps.
32 And he led me into the inner court[a] in an
easterly direction and measured the
gate—corresponding to the previous
measurements—33/ and it recesses[a] and
its pillars[b] and its vestibule[c]—corresponding to the previous measurements.
And it (i.e. the gate) and its vestibule[c]
had windows round about. Fifty cubits
was the length and twenty-five cubits
the breadth. 34/ And <its vestibule>[a]
faced <toward the>[b] outer court, and it
had palms[c] on its pillars[d] on either side,
and <its stairway>[e] had eight steps.
35 And he led me into the north gate and
measured—corresponding to the previous measurements—36/ its recesses[a],
its pillars[b] and <its vestibule>[c]. And it[d]
had windows round about. Fifty cubits
was the length and twenty-five cubits
the breadth. 37/ And <its vestibule>[a]
faced the outer court[b], and it had palms
on its pillars[c] on either side, and <its
stairway>[d] had eight steps.
47 And he measured the court, the length: one
hundred cubits, the breadth: one hundred
cubits, square. But the altar stood in
front of the temple building. 48/ And he
led me into the vestibule of the temple
building and measured the pillars[a] of the
vestibule: five cubits on the one side and
five cubits on the other. And the breadth
of the entrance to the gate <was fourteen cubits and the sides of the entrance
to the vestibule>[b]: three cubits on the
one side and three cubits on the other,
49/ the breadth[a] of the vestibule: twenty

regarded as a slightly corrupt doublet of v 29, one which alters the figures.

31 31a See v 21 note c.

b As in v 28, here too the article of חצר has fallen out of 𝔐 as a result of haplography.

c See v 9 note b.

d 𝔐 מַעֲלָו should be read מַעֲלוֹ with K. On this suffixed form of the noun מעלה see Bauer-Leander §73 l.

32 32a 𝔐 החצר הפנימי (see v 23 note a) is rendered in 𝔊 (𝔏^{W}) by *εἰς τὴν πύλην τὴν βλέπουσαν* (*κατὰ ἀνατολάς*). This causes Cornill, *ZB*, BH^{3} to emend to השער הפנה, while Bertholet-Galling and Fohrer-Galling, Eichrodt emend the דרך of 𝔐 to שער with no support in the tradition. The fact, however, that 𝔊 must then translate השער in v 32b by *αὐτήν*, and thus makes a double emendation of 𝔐, gives greater weight to the *lectio difficilior* of 𝔐. See the exposition.

33 33a See v 21 note a.

b See v 9 note b.

c See v 21 note c.

34 34a See v 21 note c.

b 𝔐 לחצר, which also occurs in the parallel passage in v 37 and should therefore not be emended, is doubtless to be understood on the basis of v 31 (emended text) as אל החצר. So also 𝔊 here as in v 31 (and in v 37) *εἰς τὴν αὐλήν*.

c 𝔙 *palmae caelatae*, see v 26.

d See v 9 note b.

e See v 31 note d.

36 36a See v 21 note a. 𝔊 𝔏^{W} 𝔖 prefix here too the copula as in vv 21, 29, 33. Its omission, however, is in line with the otherwise more concise wording of this verse.

b See v 9 note b. 𝔊 𝔏^{W} 𝔖 𝔙 prefix the copula, but see note a.

c See v 21 note c.

d 𝔊 *τῷ αιλαμμω αὐτῆς* seems to suggest the insertion of ואלמו, so Cornill, Toy, Herrmann, Galling, Eichrodt, BH^{3}. But the more concise wording of the verse, in which the כמדות האלה of vv 29, 33 is also missing (Toy, Herrmann, Galling, Eichrodt add it without any support in the tradition), advises against this addition which would mean that two אלמו would then stand inelegantly close together.

37 37a 𝔐 ואילו, as 𝔊 𝔏^{W} 𝔙 attest and the sense demands, is a scribal error for ואלמו.

b On the meaning of לחצר see v 34 note b.

c See v 9 note b.

d See v 31 note d.

48 48a 𝔐 אל is omitted by 𝔙 and transliterated by 𝔊 as *αιλ*, which would suggest that in the Hebrew *Vorlage* of 𝔊 there was the form איל.

b 𝔐 has lost through haplography a passage which has been preserved in 𝔊 (𝔏^{W}) *πηχῶν δέκα τεσσάρων καὶ ἐπωμίδες τῆς θύρας τοῦ αιλαμ*. On this basis, to 𝔐 should be added ארבע עשרה אמות וכתפות פתח האילם.

49 49a Here it becomes particularly clear that, without reference to the position of the observer, the

cubits, and the depth[a]: <twelve>[b] cubits. And one climbs up to it by <ten>[c] steps. But there were columns by[d] the pillars, one on the one side and one on the other.

41:1 And he led me into the temple and measured the pillars: six cubits was the depth on one side and six cubits the depth on the other [the depth of the <pillars>][a]. 2/ And the breadth of the doorway was ten cubits, and the side walls of the doorway (measured) five cubits on the one side and five cubits on the other. And he measured its (i.e. the temple's) depth: forty cubits, and the breadth: twenty cubits.

3/ And <he went>[a] inside and measured the pillar of the doorway: two cubits, and the doorway: six cubits, and the <side walls>[b] of the doorway: seven cubits <on the one side and seven cubits on the other>[c]. 4/ And he measured its (i.e. the inner room's) depth[a]: twenty cubits, and the breadth[a]: twenty cubits beyond the temple[b]. And he said to me: This is the holy of holies.

longer measurement is described as ארך and the shorter as רחב. From the standpoint of the observer here ארך is the width, רחב the depth. See Gese, 124–126.

b 𝔐 עשתי עשרה, which gives an impossible figure in view of the total measurement, should be corrected on the basis of 𝔊 δώδεκα to שתי עשרה.

c 𝔐 אשר is, according to 𝔊 (𝔏[W]) δέκα, a scribal error for עשר. 𝔙 *octo*.

d אל–על cf. 1:17 note a.

41:1 1a 𝔐 רחב האהל is a remarkably lame appendage. From the point of view of content, too, it does not fit the context as a result of the אהל, which never recurs in chapters 40–48 and which is rendered by 𝔗 𝔖 with משכנא (𝔙 *tabernaculum*) and is understood on the basis of P's אהל מועד. 𝔊 καὶ πηχῶν ἓξ τὸ εὖρος τοῦ αιλαμ ἔνθεν fits the expression, which it appears to have found in its *Vorlage* in the form רחב האיל (Gese), into the preceding text by combining the last two occurrences of רחב. It has rendered the first רחב by πλάτος. 𝔊[O] then adds at the end, corresponding to 𝔐, yet another πλάτος τῆς σκηνῆς; so too does 'A (on the basis of 𝔊[Q]). The two words in 𝔊 are to be regarded as explanatory glosses.

3 3a One is tempted in the first instance to regard 𝔐 ובא, with many, as a corruption of ויבא (so MS[Ken]). But the analogy with the ומדד of 40:24, 35 (41:13, 15; 42:15) makes a ובא not wholly impossible. The consecutive perfect occasionally seems to languish in Ezekiel; see, e.g., 13:8; 17:18 (note a) and 37:2 note a.

b 𝔐 ורחב. 𝔊 καὶ τὰς ἐπωμίδας still attests the כתפות which has fallen out of 𝔐 but is expected on the analogy of v 2 (see also 40:48, emended text) and is, factually, the only word which makes sense.

c Corresponding to v 2, 𝔊 reads more fully πηχῶν ἑπτὰ ἔνθεν καὶ πηχῶν ἑπτὰ ἔνθεν. The omission of the מפה ושבעה אמות מפה which one must therefore assume to have been there originally could be connected with the corruption of the כתפות to רחב (note b), as a result of which these concluding words became meaningless.

4 4a On the understanding of ארך–רחב see 40:49 note a.

b אל–על cf. 1:17 note a. על פני literally "at the front, in front of." רחב thus refers to the measurement of the square area which corresponds to the narrow side of the היכל.

Form

After a double date the visionary transportation of the prophet to the temple mount is reported (40:1–2) in brief words which recall the terminology of the ecstatic scene of chapters 8–11. There he sees the man who will lead him in what follows, sees the measuring instrument with which the latter will undertake the measurement of the sanctuary area and hears from his mouth the commission to proclaim to the house of Israel what he is about to see (40:3–4).

After a brief mention of the surrounding wall and its measurements, where surprisingly the measuring instrument in the man's hand is once again described (v 5), there occurs first of all the detailed measurement of the outer east gate (vv 6–16). After brief remarks about the outer court which is now entered (vv 17–18) and after the measurement of the distance from the outer east gate to the inner one (v 19), there follows the more summarily conceived description of the outer north (vv 20–23) and south (vv 24–27) gates; after the entry to the inner court, comes the measurement of the inner south (vv 28–31), east (vv 32–34) and north (vv 35–37) gates; and after a brief measurement for the inner court and the reference to the altar which stood there (v 47), comes the description of the temple building towards which the whole has clearly been moving. In three measurement processes its vestibule (vv 48f), main hall (41:1f) and inner sanctuary (41:3f) are described. In the case of this last structure, for the first time on the whole progress through the temple a brief word of interpretation is heard from the man who (after the introductory instruction 40:4) has hitherto completed the whole process of guidance and measurement in silence. From the point of view of form, too, this is the goal of the whole leading of the prophet from the periphery of the temple buildings to the threshold of the innermost, central part.

It is also easy to discover the remaining formal structure of this process which has a clear goal in view. The activity of the man who alone appears alongside the prophet in the vision and whose measuring rod is described twice (but see the remarks on 40:5) dominates the whole process. In this respect his activity is divided into two different types of action.

He is, in the first instance, the prophet's guide through the various parts of the building. This finds expression in the formulae of movement and guidance. These are in stereotyped form, but not with any absolutely standardizing strictness: ויב[י]אני ("and he led me") (40:17, 28, 32, 35, 48; 41:1); ויולכני ("and he led me") (40:24); ויבוא (ויעל) ("and he entered [and climbed]") (40:6); the ובא ("and he went") of 41:3 has been preserved as an exception undoubtedly on theological considerations (see below). The prophet is brought by the man who guides him to the different parts of the temple area, and what he sees there can be introduced occasionally by the favorite expression of the vision-style, הנה ("see") (40:5, 17, 24; cf. also v 3). Here too, however, in contrast with the guidance statements of chap. 8, there is no fixed rule. See v 20 note a.

The main stress in the man's activity, however, lies on his measuring with the measuring rod which is so emphatically introduced (40:3, 5). No fewer than nineteen times is mention made of the completion of this process of measurement with, here too, scope for slight variation of expression: וימד ("and he measured") 40:5, 6, 8 (9 is dittography), 11, 13, 19, 23, 27, 28, 32, 47, 48; 41: 1, 2, 3, 4; ומדד ("and he measured") 40:24, 35; מדד ("he measured") 40:20. All the emphasis of this description lies on the measurements, as is shown also by the ten occurrences (as well as 40:3, 5) of the noun מדה ("measurement") (40:10a, 10b, 21, 22, 24, 28, 29, 32, 33, 35). Alongside this everything else fades into the background on the way to the goal formed by the declaration of 41:4b. Even for the pavement of the court the measurement is also given in 40:18. Only the steps which lead up to the gates and to the temple building (40:6, 22, 26, 31, 34, 37, 49) and the pillars in front of the vestibule of the temple building (40:49) are simply counted. The windows and the wall decoration of the gate structures are neither counted nor measured. More precisely, the situation is that the measurements of the individual parts of the structure of the east gate are carefully and individually recorded, while in the case of the five other gates there is simply a summary reference back to the measurement of the first gate.

With regard to these measurements, it is further significant that they give only the measurement of the ground plan. Only in the case of the surrounding wall is a height given in 40:5 (v 5bγ is missing in $\mathfrak{G}^{967}$); otherwise all measurements are confined to breadth and length, i.e. the ground measurements of the sections of the building. What dominates the picture as a whole is not the sight of a building rising before one's eyes, as one would expect in a spontaneous vision, but a ground plan (cf. e.g., by way of contrast, the totally different "vision" of the pilgrims to Zion in Ps 48:13f). The question has been asked, with justification, whether the description in Ezekiel 40f does not envisage just such a ground plan already drawn. But not only are the heights missing, but also, and this emerges clearly from a comparison with 1 Kings 6f, all the details about the building material to be used, about the interior furnishings (that is found later with respect to the temple building in 41:15b–26) as well as all the details concerning the purpose for which the buildings are to be used. With almost ascetic severity the text concentrates on the exact description of a ground plan. Only the mention of the steps leading up to the gates and to the temple building reveals any sign of movement in the temple area. But here only the number of the steps is given with no mention of a measurement of elevation.

The scene, with its guidance statements, recalls, as has already been mentioned, the ecstatic vision of chapters 8–11. There too the prophet was led (though not by the leadership of a "man") from the outside into the innermost part of the temple area.

The comparsion with the visionary guidance experience of chapter 8 leads to another peculiarity of the guidance vision of 40f. In chapter 8 the four abominations which were shown to the prophet on his way to the sacred central part of the temple building were supposed to reveal the totality of Jerusalem's sins.[1] In the vision of chapters 40f the figure four disappears completely, in spite of the square layout of the whole which might suggest the observance of this number (see e.g., 42:15–20). On the other hand, one might wonder whether, in the two times three gates and the triple ascent to the temple building, which in turn is divided into three rooms, the figure three is not a conscious element of the stylization. If the two times three gates are followed, as a seventh structure, by the temple building, can the figure seven also be regarded as an element of the construction, with the seventh, particularly sacred element being set apart from the six elements of the way of approach just as, in the Priestly creation narrative in Gen 1:1–2:4a, the seventh day, the particularly sacred one (2:3 ויקדש אתו "and he hallowed it"), is set apart from the six working days? More clearly, however, in the construction there appears the figure twenty-five and its multiples: the gate (inside measurement) is twenty-five cubits wide; its length (outside measurement) is fifty cubits; a hundred cubits is the distance from gate to gate; the inner court is a hundred cubits square; so that the total measurement of the temple area, as the measurement in 42:15–20 makes quite explicit, is five hundred square cubits. This system of measurement is still effective in the undoubtedly later description of the allocation of land in chapter 48 in the measurement of the תרומה in the narrower sense (48:20) at twenty-five thousand cubits by twenty-five thousand. But that is not all. The measurement of the steps of the ascent to the level of the sanctuary begins with the figure seven, which is again of significance here (40:22, 26). The inner court is reached by eight steps (40:31, 34, 37), while the level of the temple building is reached by a further ten steps (40:49, emended text). Thus the measurement of the steps forming the ascent as a whole again comes to the figure twenty-five. From this point of view one cannot suppress the question whether the figure in the date in 40:1, the twenty-fifth year, is not also to be evaluated in this context of numerical stylization.

In the question of the origin of the high estimation of precisely the number twenty-five and its multiples, which does not emerge particularly strongly anywhere else in the OT, one might refer in the first instance to 1 Kgs 7:2 with its measurement of the House of the Forest of Lebanon as one hundred cubits long and fifty cubits broad (and thirty cubits high), where the corresponding numerical system can be seen in one part of the Solomonic (palace!) buildings. In connection with the date in 40:1, however, the further question is worthy of serious consideration whether the calculations concerning the year of jubilee, which are discernible in Leviticus 25, are not the decisive factor here. Since the figure fifty for the calculation of the year of jubilee is to be understood not in terms of a decimal system but as a sacred pentecost, i.e. the number following seven squared (7x7 = 49), then the system of calculation which seems to be orientated quite soberly along decimal lines really has its starting point somewhere quite different. We shall return later to the significance of this supposition from the point of view of content. In the framework of the considerations of form which can be made in the present context, one thing is at any rate clear. The guidance vision of chapters 40f, which begins in the "full vision style of the description of a building" (Gese), ends with a system of harmoniously regulated measurement constructed on the basis of significant figures. It presents a whole, structured in the strictest stylization, which speaks through its mysterious symmetry and proportion.

1 See 1, 235.

Setting

From this point of view also the question of the "setting" of this vision will be answered. One can certainly not regard this structure as the fortuitous result of a dream vision in which recollection and programmatic mingle unchecked. No more, however, does it afford straightforward recollection of the Solomonic temple burned to the ground by the Babylonians in 587. Caution in the use of Ezekiel's temple vision for the reconstruction of the Solomonic temple, which Noth urges, is fully justified.[2] Nevertheless, the question to what extent traditions concerning the Solomonic temple have been introduced into the new plan will have to be discussed in the context of the detailed exegesis.

Whatever may be said in detail concerning the genuineness of the visionary experience, which cannot basically be disputed, the vision reveals in any case a variety of new reflections on the place of worship which was established in Israel at the end of the period of judgment. These reflections can in no sense disregard, in spiritualizing fashion, the actual reality of a temple. However much, according to Ezek 36:26 (11:19), Israel's future is determined by the new heart promised by Yahweh to his people, it certainly cannot neglect the correct design of the temple, even down to the measurements for its construction. The disorder of the temple which was revealed in the vision of chapter 8 must not recur. The outline in chapters 40f in the first place completely disregards those who will serve in this temple and who, according to chapter 8, were actually responsible for the disorder. It concentrates decisively on the structural aspect and speaks of the new symmetry of the temple which is promised to the restored nation. The spiritual background of the vision in chapters 40f is, as a result of a penitent change of heart, characteristic also of the structural foundation of Israel's place of worship. Concerning the content of the statements which give expression to this "change of heart," something will have to be said under the heading "Aim."

In the earlier oracles of Ezekiel it was possible to recognize throughout a strong leaning towards stylization. Thus, with respect to the question of the "setting" where the form of the vision in chapters 40f arose, one cannot conclusively exclude the possibility that this vision of the new, symmetrically arranged temple area, however strongly conscious stylization determines the individual features, could come from the priestly prophet Ezekiel, who (according to 29:17) was still delivering his oracles two years after the twenty-fifth year of his exile. On the other hand, it can also certainly not be excluded as a possibility that the visionary experience of the prophet in the twenty-fifth year of his exile also occasioned reflections in the wider circle of priestly exiles who surrounded the prophet, in the "school" which then handed on and expanded the prophet's words. That this "school" had a substantial share in the further enrichment of the vision cannot be doubted. The question of the "origin" of the present section will have to be considered again once we have gained an overall picture of chapters 40–48.

Interpretation

■ **40:1** The visionary experience is fixed in time by a double date. The first date is reckoned, as are the great majority of the dates in the book, in terms of the reign of Jehoiachin, which coincides with the years after the deportation of 597. The latter is explicitly mentioned here, as in 1:2 and 33:21, as the starting point of the reckoning. The beginning of this year, according to Parker-Dubberstein, falls on 4/19/573. What is strange, however, is the more precise information "at the beginning of the year on the tenth of the month." Already 𝔊 no longer understood this and, as in the case of the date in 32:17 (note b) which in 𝔐 has also been transmitted with no information about the month, has read the first month. So, too, $\mathfrak{G}^{A,410}$ in 26:1 (see note b there). But 𝔐, as *lectio difficilior,* deserves the preference.[3] Already Wellhausen drew attention to the connection with Lev 25:9, according to which the Year of Jubilee was proclaimed by trumpet blasts on the tenth day of the seventh

2 Noth, *Könige,* 106f.

3 Otherwise Ernst Kutsch, *Das Herbstfest in Israel,* Unpub. Diss. (Mainz, 1955), and *idem,* "Chronologie," 273. Kraus, *Worship,* 67, understands ראש השנה as the name of a month, but this is difficult to maintain.

month.[4] Thus in 40:1 we encounter an older date for the New Year in terms of the ancient Israelite year beginning in the autumn.[5] It remains obscure why the beginning of the year should be on the tenth of the month and not on the first. While Barrois sees here the influence of Egyptian decimal reckoning,[6] Begrich asks whether it is not caused "by the methods of intercalation in the Israelite calendar, methods of which we do not know the precise details" in comparison with the beginning of the Babylonian month. Snaith thinks of the difference between a sun year and a lunar year. In the later strata of P the great Day of Atonement then falls on the date in Lev 25:9. Thus, if the date in 40:1 "at the beginning of the year on the tenth of the month" is to be fixed in terms of Lev 25:9 on the tenth day of the seventh month, then the great temple vision falls, according to Parker-Dubberstein, on 10/22/573, i.e. approximately eighteen months before Ezekiel's last dated oracle in 29:17–21.

The connection with the "ecclesiastical calendar" discernible in Lev 25:9 ought, however, to go a step further. In the discussion of the "form" of chapters 40f the remarkable dominance of the number twenty-five and its multiples was noted, along with its influence even on the dating. Now twenty-five is the half of fifty, the number of the Year of Jubilee, the real content of which, according to Lev 25:10, is the summons to the great "liberation" (דרור).[7] This year of liberation will be mentioned explicitly in 46:17. See also Jer 34:8, 15, 17, where דרור is used in connection with the "liberation" of the slaves in the seventh year. Now Is 61:1, the last remaining occurrence of דרור in the OT, shows that reference to the year of "liberation" was obviously also used to refer to liberation from the captivity of exile. Admittedly the expression is not attested in Deutero-Isaiah, where one would first expect it. But the language of the Trito-Isaiah passage in the narrower sense appears so clearly as a spiritualizing re-interpretation of Deutero-Isaiah's terminology that the supposition does not appear wrong that the expression "Year of Liberation" was already not foreign to the terminology of the exilic period.[8] In this context reference might also be made to Lev 26:34, where the period of exile is itself understood as a making up for the land's lost sabbaths. The problem of the sabbatical year and the year of liberation has unmistakably been of considerable interest for the deported in the period of exile.

Is it then, from that point of view, sheer chance that the great vision of the new temple comes to the prophet precisely in the middle of a fifty-year period, i.e. half way through the period which must elapse before the proclamation of the great year of release (Is 61:1)? Just as the year begins to turn on midsummer's or midwinter's day, so New Year's day of the twenty-fifth year of the exile can also be understood as the halfway point with regard to the coming great liberation by Yahweh. One must simply accept the slight imprecision in view of the fact that, on a strict calculation, the second half of a fifty-year period would begin with the beginning of the twenty-sixth year, especially since the calculation of fifty years is already burdened with the imprecision that in this reckoning the first and the fiftieth years are years of Jubilee

4 Julius Wellhausen, *Prolegomena to the History of Ancient Israel* (Edinburgh: Black, 1885), 110.

5 On the calendar year in the monarchical period see Begrich, *Chronologie,* 66–90. On Ezek 40:1 see Begrich, *Chronologie,* 87f. On the equation "beginning of the year" = New Year see Sigmund Mowinckel, *Zum israelitischen Neujahr und zur Deutung der Thronbesteigungspsalmen* (Oslo: Dybwad; 1952), 27f, and N. H. Snaith, *The Jewish New Year Festival; its origin and development* (London: S.P.C.K., 1947), 131–133.

6 Barrois, *Manuel,* 2. 172.

7 On דרור as an Akkadian loan-word and on the practice of the summons to such "freeing from burdens" see Martin Noth, *Leviticus; a Commentary,* tr. J. E. Anderson. The Old Testament Library (Philadelphia: Westminster, 1966), 187; Elliger, *Leviticus,* 351ff, where also what is necessary has been said about the calculation of the "year of fifty years" (שנת החמשים שנה), Lev 25:10, which strictly speaking belongs in the context of a cycle of seven weeks of years (= forty-nine years).

8 Walther Zimmerli, "Zur Sprache Tritojesajas" in *Gottes Offenbarung,* ThB 19 (München: Kaiser, 1963), 217–233.

and that the intervening period is strictly speaking one of only forty-nine years. But if the date in 40:1 is understood as the day in the middle of the period of captivity leading up to the great liberation, then the whole system of the temple measurements, whose inner structure is built on the numerals twenty-five, fifty and their multiples, acquires a hidden depth of significance with regard to the occurrence of the great liberation in the "year of fifty years."

In a different direction Morgenstern believes he can establish a particular connection between New Year's Day and the building of the temple.[9]

The second date, which mentions only the year, is calculated with regard to the fall of "the city," i.e. Jerusalem. This is expressed by means of the vocabulary that is already familiar from the messenger's report in 33:21. Gese tries to see here the establishment of the connection with chapters 8–11, where the departure of the כבוד יהוה ("glory of Yahweh") and the destruction of the temple were depicted. But one might also wish to see here an anticipatory indication already of 43:1ff, the account of Yahweh's return to the new temple. The question may also be asked whether the mention of this second date, which lies a good ten years after the first one with its reference to Jehoiachin's exile, does not imply an adjustment to the expectation of the end of Judah's exile after forty years, as is presupposed in 4:6 (see also the statement about Egypt in 29:13). In the fiftieth year of the "liberation" of those who were deported with Jehoiachin, the halfway point of which is reached with the occurrence of the vision of the new temple, approximately forty years will have passed since the destruction of the city and the end of Jerusalem and of the monarchy in Judah. But this consideration should be entertained only peripherally. In contrast to the fairly strong pointers towards a fifty-year reckoning, the text here makes no firm statement.

The vocabulary with which the prophet's visionary experience and transportation are described corresponds to the descriptions in earlier parts of the book.[10] That the phraseology as a whole is particularly close to 37:1 has already been noted above.[11]

■ **40:2** In his transportation (the verb לקח "to take" and all the harsh scenery of 8:3 are missing here), in which by contrast with 8:1ff no other figure participates and the "spirit" too is not mentioned, the prophet is brought to a high mountain in the land of Israel. On ארץ ישראל ("land of Israel"), attested elsewhere in Ezekiel, apart from 40:2; 47:18, only in the trade list in 27:17, see above.[12] The expression אדמת ישראל ("land of Israel"), which is characteristic of Ezekiel, is not used in this context which is simply giving a piece of geographical information.[13] The place name Jerusalem is not actually mentioned. But it is not to be understood, with Richter, that "its location is a purely ideal one." Also the thesis of Mackay, that it is the area of Shechem that is meant here, certainly does not catch the sense of the passage. The הר גבה ("high mountain") of 17:22 is there caught up in the immediately following verse 23 by הר מרום ישראל ("the high mountain of Israel"), the expression which here and in 20:40 (plural in 34:14) describes the city and temple mount of Jerusalem. The idea that in the eschaton an elevation above all other mountains is expected for this particular mountain finds its clearest expression in Is 2:2. This elevation of the temple mount in Jerusalem to the form of the mythical divine mountain is doubtless also presupposed here. 43:12 then speaks simply of "the mountain." For the present passage it is further characteristic that, just as the natural description of the temple buildings which the prophet is subsequently shown appears as a "building like a city" (כמבנה עיר), the city of Jerusalem does not appear at all alongside the temple area. The later land-distribution list in 48:1ff, which is not presupposed here, then shows clearly enough the detached way in which only the city is brought into a spatial relationship with this exclusive vision of the temple. The lack of a reference to the city was also noticed at a very early stage and led to the glossing of the

9 Julian Morgenstern, "The Three Calendars of Ancient Israel," *HUCA* 1 (1924): 36ff.

10 With היתה עלי יד יהוה cf. 1:3; 3:14; 37:1, as well as 8:1 (see 1, 117f). On מראות אלהים, 1:1; 8:3, as well as 11:24 (see 1, 116f). On ויניחני, 37:1.

11 See above p. 259.

12 See above pp. 66f and 27:17 note a.

13 See 1, 203.

text (note g). The extremely lively announcement of the city's rights then finds expression in the addition in 48:30–35.

■ **40:3** On the mountain the prophet, in his divine vision, sees first of all a man (הנה "see" is vision style). His form shining like bronze recalls the creatures which carried the throne in the expanded text of 1:7 and characterizes him as a supernatural being.[14] On the other hand, the idea that Yahweh himself was present in the man (so Herrmann, Jahn) has been refuted, on good grounds, by Rautenberg.[15] The man's function is limited to leading the prophet and measuring the temple area. In 8:2f the man saw to the prophet's transportation, while the leading of him into the temple building and the commentating of what he saw emanated, in that earlier passage, from Yahweh himself.

Two measuring instruments can be seen in the man's hand. The linen cord does not explicitly appear anywhere again in the measuring that follows. It may be compared with the חבל מדה ("measuring line") of Zech 2:5 which is there used to measure the city. It is a measure with which longer distances can be measured. פתיל ("cord") is never encountered elsewhere with this function. In the other passages it designates the cord, possibly of purple or even of gold, but even in one passage (Ju 16:9), of tow, with which something is tied fast. By way of contrast, the קנה המדה ("measuring rod") is the measuring rod for short measurements. A. Parrot[16] finds measuring cord and measuring rod linked on several occasions in Mesopotamian representations, e.g., on the stele of Ur-nammu of Ur.[17] But this interpretation of the symbols is not uncontested.[18] The length of the measuring rod is described more precisely in v 5. The position of the man with the measuring instruments "at the gate" indicates already the place where, in v 6, the principal measurements will begin.

■ **40:4** Before beginning the measuring, however, the man addresses the prophet and tells him the significance of what is to follow. He urges him to pay close attention. Seeing is put before hearing since in what follows there will be much measuring but almost no speaking. In the description of what the man intends to do it is the "showing" that is more often referred to. The closest attention is to be paid to what is seen, since, so runs the third expression, the prophet has been brought here in order that he might be shown something, be given something to see. To this is added the explicit command to proclaim what is seen. The visionary perception, which above all characterized the old seers of pre-classical prophecy, is here fully linked with the commission to proclaim, which, as a rule, has to do with the heard word. See also 44:5f.

■ **40:5** From the position of the man at the entrance to the gate one might expect that his measurements would begin at that very spot. It is mildly surprising that v 5 in the first instance speaks of the wall which surrounds the whole temple area (בית "house") and contains the report of its measurement. It is equally surprising that the measuring instrument in the man's hand is once again explicitly mentioned. And finally, the third peculiarity of v 5 resides in the fact that, departing from the rule which is otherwise strictly adhered to in 40:1–37, 47–49; 41:1–4, it gives a height measurement. Now, with regard to the first of these, one can observe, correctly, that the outer wall will at once catch the eye of the observer coming from outside and that the mention of it is in that respect understandable. But why then the explicit reference to the man's position בשער ("at the gate") (v 3), which is so clearly continued in the ויבוא אל שער ("and he entered the gate") of v 6? With regard to the second, it can be observed that the renewed mention of the measuring rod here serves to append the precise definition of the unit of measurement, which in fact finds its place better before the first measurement than in the general description of v 3. The third observation remains peculiar. If one adds to it also the remarkable resumption of the חומה ("wall") by בנין ("structure") and the element of obscurity concerning the measurement of the thickness of the wall (see below), then one can scarcely avoid the suspicion expressed by Galling that v 5 has been added only secondarily and then doubtless in connection with the conclusion in 42:15–20, where the mention of the surrounding wall (in v 20) recurs. Admittedly one can scarcely in this respect retain the argument which was adduced mainly by Galling, that with the consistent principle of internal measurements one would then arrive at a measurement of only four

14 See 1, 126.

15 Rautenberg, "Zukunftsthora," 92f, 98.

16 Parrot, *Babylon*, 145f.

17 *ANEP* 306, *AOB* 661.

18 See also E. D. van Buren, "The Rod and the Ring," *Archiv Orientální* 17, 2 (1949): 434–450.

hundred and eighty-eight cubits for the length of the side of the court (against 42:20).[19]

It is the principal concern of v 5 to make clear that what is used in the measurements in the sanctuary is the "long cubit" which consists of "a (normal) cubit and a hand-breadth." When in 2 Chr 3:3, in connection with Solomon's building of the temple, the use of "cubits of the old standard" (במדה הראשונה) is established, this is surely a reference to the same double standard for the cubit. Since the "hand-breadth," which, measured at the wrist, comprises the breadth of four fingers (hence 𝔙's translation of טפח in Ex 25:25 [37:12] by *quattuor digitis*), stands to the cubit in the relationship of 1:6, then the relationship of short cubit and long cubit to each other is one of 6:7. According to Galling, long cubit and normal cubit were also differentiated in Babylon and Egypt.[20] Here the relationship of the Egyptian "royal cubit" (long cubit) to the normal cubit of 458:525 mm. corresponds more closely to the relationship expected in Ezek 40:5 than does the Babylonian cubit with 495 (the cubit of Gudea) or 518 (cubit of Nippur): 556 mm. Barrois gives for Egypt the figures 525:450 mm.[21] From the information in the Siloam inscription he reckons a normal cubit as 444 mm. and a 'hand-breadth' as 74mm. and therefore for Ezekiel's cubit arrives at a length of 518 mm. Similarly, R. B. Y. Scott calculates the normal cubit to have been 444.5 mm.[22] The "measuring rod" of six long cubits is therefore to be calculated at a little over three meters long. The reference to the long, or, according to 2 Chr 3:3, "old" cubit clearly involves the desire to link up with the old tradition, a desire which can also be seen, e.g., in an account by Esarhaddon of the erection of a new temple "with the long cubit . . . in accordance with its old plan."[23] 𝔊[967] ἐν πήχει ἀνδρὸς καὶ παλαιστῆς seems to describe the normal cubit as a "man's (=people's?) cubit." Where the limit of the link-up with the past lies in the case of Ezekiel 40f is a question for later. In what follows, measuring by the measuring rod is encountered only at the beginning in vv 6–8 and then gives way completely to measurement by the cubit. It recurs in 41:8 and 42:16–19.[24]

In the measurement of the wall it is noteworthy that thickness and height have the same measurement (a good three meters). The idea (or tradition?) that lies behind that is no longer discernible. One might also ask how the man measured the thickness of the wall. Was it done on the inside of the gate where it would then be identical with the width of the threshold (v 6)? Or is the divine being thought of, as in Gudea's dream of the building of the temple ("In the dream there was a man, huge as the sky and huge as the earth"), as a giant who is able to survey and measure the wall from above?[25] Nothing else in the context points to such a concept. Thus the process of measurement here, as opposed to that in what follows, remains unclear.

■ **40:6–16** In vv 6–16 we are told what was to be expected in view of the man's position at the gate, namely the measurement of the gate structure through which access is gained to the temple area. In contrast to what follows, nothing is yet said here of the leading of the prophet into that area, but simply of the man's entry. It is, of course, tacitly assumed that the prophet follows him and notes the results of his measurements. It is otherwise in 41:3f.

The measuring takes place in a clearly ordered sequence. After the report of the ascent by steps (v 6aβ) there follows first the measurement of the depth of the individual parts of the gateway (vv 6b–9a). The details of the sequence of these parts which have already been named (details which are indispensable for the reconstruction of the structure and alignment, vv 9b–10) are followed by the measurement of the width. Finally come the details of the total measurement of the gateway (vv 13, 15; on v 14 see note a) and of the windows and their ornamentation (v 16).

In order to understand the measurements, it should be mentioned in advance that the "length" (ארך) and the "breadth" (רחב) of a measured element are not in terms of the perspective of someone who is passing through,

19 Against this see the arguments of Gese, 13 note 3.
20 *BRL*, 367.
21 Barrois, *Manuel*, 2. 244–247.
22 R. B. Y. Scott, "The Hebrew Cubit," *JBL* 77 (1958): 205–214. See also *idem*, "Weights and Measures of the Bible," *BA* 22 (1959): 22–40.
23 Borger, *Inschriften Asarhaddons*, 22.
24 On vv 5–16 see below figure 1 (p. 353).
25 Falkenstein-von Soden, 141.

but, as is already clear from 1 Kgs 6:2f[26] and particularly so in the present context from the juxtaposition of 40:49aα and 41:2b, describe quite objectively the longer and shorter dimensions of an object to be measured.[27] In the present translation, for the sake of clearer understanding, the terms have been accommodated to English linguistic usage.

■ **40:6** While v 3 mentioned, still quite imprecisely, that the man was standing at the gate, it is now clearly stated that the measurement of the temple begins at the east gate—the gate through which, according to 43:1ff, Yahweh's glory will make its entry, just as, according to 10:19, it had left the temple through this same gate. According to chapter 8 the prophet was led into the city and the temple from the north. The references to the gates in the section 40:1–37, 47–49; 41:1–4 and in other places too are not uniform. In the most concise formulation the direction can be simply added to the gate: in a construct relationship 40:28 (שער הדרום "the south gate"), also v 35 and in 44:4; without the article 46:9 (with ה *locale* of the direction in 40:40; 47:2aα); with ל 40:23; with the adjective הקדמוני ("the east") only 10:19; 11:1. Alongside this occurs the insertion of דרך: so השער דרך הקדים ("the east gate") 40:10; see v 24; and more frequently still the fuller indication of the direction by a noun clause appended with אשר ("which") with the noun פנים ("face") as subject (40:6, 20, 22; further 42:15; 43:4). Formations with the participle of פנה ("to face") do not occur in the present section, but are found (with or without אשר "which") in 8:3; 9:2 (note c); 11:1; 44:1; 46:1, 12; 47:2.

By means of steps (the fact that there are seven may be deduced from vv 22, 26; see also note b), which are to be thought of as outside the gate structure, the man first sets foot on its six-cubit deep outer threshold. It must be bordered on each side by the equally thick walls of the gateway, which are then continued, as envisaged by v 5, in the walls round the temple area which have the same measurement.

■ **40:7a** The next part of the building is described as תא. With regard to this word, von Soden has shown that it is an Akkadian loan-word and that it has no fully corresponding English equivalent: "Dependent on the design, the תָּאִים are recess-like rooms or room-like recesses."[28] The floor surface is given as one measuring rod, i.e. six cubits, square. The immediately following reference to the intervening section "between" the recesses (בין, v 7 note a) already shows that in the corridor of the gateway we are not dealing with only one such recess.

■ **40:10** V 10 makes it clear that there are three recesses on each side. The addition to v 6 in 𝔊 (note c) made that six per side. From v 10 on, the intervening section, five cubits broad, is described as איל ("pillar"). This architectural expression is attested outside Ezekiel 40f only in 1 Kgs 6:31, where Noth translates as "gate walls." Here איל ("pillar") is defined by the בין ("[spaces] between"), which is used first in 𝔐, as the partition wall between the recesses. Boettcher understands it to be the wall-faces on both sides.[29] The corridor of the gateway, which thus measures from beyond the threshold three times six and two times five, i.e. *in toto* twenty-eight cubits, is also cut off from the inner side by a six-cubit deep threshold, which then opens not immediately into the open courtyard but into yet another room of the gate structure, the אולם ("vestibule").[30]

■ **40:8f** The derivation of the word referred to in 8:16 note a, from Akkadian *ellamu* "before" (used of space and of time), faces certain phonetic difficulties, so that, with Noth, just as serious consideration should be given to the derivation from a root אול "to be in front" (cf. Arabic *'awwalu* "first").[31] Here and in vv 48f it denotes a vestibule extending in front of a building complex, which may be thought of in the first place as open but which subsequently can develop into an enclosed room forming a more or less broad entrance door. It is this further development that is obviously presupposed here (and in vv 48f). The measurement of the room at eight cubits deep and of a thickness of two cubits for its outer wall,

26 See Noth, *Könige,* 111.
27 See Gese, Appendix I (pp. 124f).
28 von Soden, "Raumbezeichnungen," 361.
29 Boettcher, *Proben,* 302ff; idem, *Neue Aehrenlese,* 183f.
30 On the varying spelling of this word in 𝔐 see v 7 note c.
31 Noth, *Könige,* 97, note d on 1 Kgs 6:3.

איל ("pillar"), which encloses it at the front, forming a doorway, completes the measurement of the length (depth) of the gate, for which, in v 15 too, the total of fifty cubits is calculated. It is explicitly stated in v 9b of the אלם ("vestibule") what could already be deduced from the way in which the measuring was done, namely that it lies "on the inside."[32]

■ **40:11** The details of the measurements of the width help further in the elucidation of the whole. Admittedly a difficulty is provided by the very first piece of information which speaks of ten cubits רחב ("width") for the door aperture and thirteen cubits ארך ("width") for the gate. One cannot solve it by suggesting that these refer to the two sides of a right angle. The figure of twenty-five cubits width for the gateway in v 13 (inner measurement), from which six cubits for each of the side recesses (vv 7, 12) must be deducted, means that thirteen cubits remain as the width of the actual gateway, and this should correspond to the thirteen cubits ארך ("width") in v 11. Thus here פתח השער ("the gate opening") must be differentiated from the simple שער ("gate"). The supposition of Gese (following Galling) that the ten cubits refer to the width of the passageway after the deduction of the space occupied by the opened leaves of the door, while the thirteen cubits refer to the complete door opening in the wall, has therefore much to commend it. Therefore, if one takes into account the use of dimensional data which deviates from modern concepts, it is not at all necessary to emend with Galling (following Ewald, Bertholet, Richter and others) ארך ("width") to דרך.

■ **40:12** The form of the architectural element of the גבול ("barrier") in front of the recesses cannot be more precisely defined. It must be a barrier which shields the recesses on the corridor side. Von Soden, following others (such as Richter), sees in it "a railing projecting from each pillar one cubit into the recess or a wooden partition" which gives a certain protection in the recesses to the guards on the gate. Galling (in Bertholet-Galling) thought, in 1936, in terms of the "prohibited area," of a "raised pavement," but this would again imply a measurement of height which is not to be expected here. In 1955 (in Fohrer-Galling), he thought in terms of the "demarcation" by a railing one cubit thick and one cubit high. Since in v 13 the width of the gate is measured not at ground level but at the point where the roof begins, the obvious question is whether what is meant is not a barrier wall of half height, which gives protection to the guards but also allows an uninterrupted view of the gateway. Thus גבול appears to mean in 43:13 also a low ledge, which prevents the blood and water from the altar from flowing out on to the court. Such a conception allows the retention of the measurement of six by six cubits for the area of the recesses.

■ **40:13** The measurement of the width of the gate from side to side at the point where the roof begins keeps the process of measurement in the sphere of what can be clearly envisaged, but at the same time leaves unanswered the question of the external width of the gate and therefore also of the thickness of the side walls. The attempts which were made to include the outer walls within the given width show in the narrowness of what remains for the thickness of the outer walls the impossibility of this assumption.[33] Howie's statement that we are here dealing with a visionary spectacle and that it should therefore not be surprising to find incorrect information for once is a statement of despair and is, in view of the great precision of the information which is discernible elsewhere, unsatisfactory.[34]

■ **40:14** On v 14, for which it is completely impossible to reach meaningful sense and which has confused quite beyond recovery the understanding of the description of the gate, see note a.

■ **40:15–16** After the total measuring of the length of the gate (v 15), v 16 without giving measurements, provides two further details concerning the lighting and the decoration of the interior of the gate. חלוני שקפים אטמים ("framed windows with bars" [Noth]) have already been mentioned in connection with the temple itself in the account of the construction of the Solomonic temple (note a).[35] Through these windows, about the number of which and their more precise location nothing more is said, light enters the inner gate structure and its vestibule. The palm-tree decoration, which, according to Galling, appears on stone reliefs such as are known from

32 On the definition of "inside" and "outside" in chapters 40–48 see Gese, 125f.

33 Galling in Bertholet-Galling, but otherwise in Fohrer-Galling; Howie.

34 Howie, "East Gate," 18.

35 As illustrations for the חלנות אטמות (lit. "closed

tell ḥalaf, is also found in Solomon's temple.[36] There it is mentioned as decoration of the temple itself on the outer wall, doors and moveable stands (1 Kgs 6:29, 32, 35; 7:36) along with other forms of ornamentation.[37] The emphasis in Ezek 40:16 surely lies on the sole mention of palm-tree decoration and must be aimed polemically at the figurative representations mentioned at several points in Ezekiel 8.

■ **40:6–16** The construction of the temple gate has become extremely clear, at least as regards its interior measurements, as a result of the precise details in vv 6–16. In the search for archaeologically comparable temple-gate structures, there is nothing analogous in Palestinian temple buildings. On the other hand, surprisingly great similarities have been most recently encountered with city-gate structures of the Solomonic period. In 1950, Howie, taking up a suggestion of Albright, drew attention to the north gate of Megiddo, which, in a somewhat smaller format, reveals in the passageway of the gate immediately behind two gate-towers in a line with the city wall the identical three gate recesses which have been described in Ezekiel 40. In his excavation at Hazor Yadin, in 1957, came across a quite similar gate structure of the time of Solomon. Here a tower projects from the wall in front of each of the three recesses on both sides of the passageway. Yadin has subsequently reexamined a structure in Gezer in a publication of Macalister. What was described as part of a "Maccabean castle" turned out, on closer examination, to be the western half of a quite identical gate-structure with three recesses and projecting defensive towers on a level with the casemate wall.[38] Wright and de Vaux have also adopted this third example as typical of the structure of Solomonic city-gates.[39] The question to be considered after the completion of the detailed examination of the present section is: How does it come about, this undeniably close relationship between the temple-gates in the vision in Ezekiel 40f and Solomon's city-gates in Megiddo, Hazor and possibly also in Gezer?[40]

■ **40:17–18** The description of the outer east gate is followed in vv 17–19a, before the prophet is led to the outer north gate, by a succinct description of the area between the outer and inner gates, which, as v 19a shows, is still entirely dependent on the description of the gate in vv 6–16. The man has led the prophet through the gate and into the court where new elements come into view (והנה "and see"): rooms (porticos), a stone pavement (so Koehler-Baumgartner) running round the whole court. Both are described in more detail and in the same order in vv 17b, 18. With regard to the rooms only their number (thirty) is given. Nothing more detailed is said about their layout beyond the fact that they give on to the pavement and that they therefore also, according to v 18, lie along the outside wall of the court. In what follows there are many references to לשכות ("rooms") in the expansions in 40:38–46; 42:1–14 (41:10; 44:19; 46:19; textual error in 45:5). None of these passages, however, is dealing with the rooms of the outer court mentioned here. Jeremiah 35 and 36 show how in the pre-exilic temple distinguished people, by no means exclusively temple officials, occupied such rooms in the temple precincts. The fact that Baruch, according to Jer 36:10, reads the words of Jeremiah's scroll "in the hearing of all the people" in Gemariah's room makes it probable that that room was like a portico open to a court. Neh 13:4ff records how Nehemiah tries to impose stricter rules with regard to rights of possession of these rooms in the post-exilic temple (see also Ezr 8:29; 10:6). The text of Ezekiel 40 says nothing about whether, in its opinion, only temple servants or also "laymen" could occupy such rooms, which served as storerooms, cloakrooms, council rooms and rooms for sacrificial meals.

In the case of the pavement, too, no process of measurement is reported. But the information that the pavement extended as far into the court as the front of the gate shows that it extended into the court a distance of fifty cubits from the surrounding wall (outer façade). The thirty cells are doubtless of smaller dimensions than

windows") of v 16, there can, e.g., be cited, according to Galling, the ivory carvings in *AOB* 191; *ANEP* 131; Watzinger, *Denkmäler,* 1. figure 84.

36 *ANEP* 654.

37 On the technique of these decorations, which are undoubtedly carved in wood, see Noth, *Könige,* 125f.

38 See the ground plans of these three buildings, figures 2–4 (p. 357).

39 Roland de Vaux, *Ancient Israel, its Life and Institutions,* tr. John McHugh (New York: McGraw-Hill, 1961), 234.

40 See below pp. 359f.

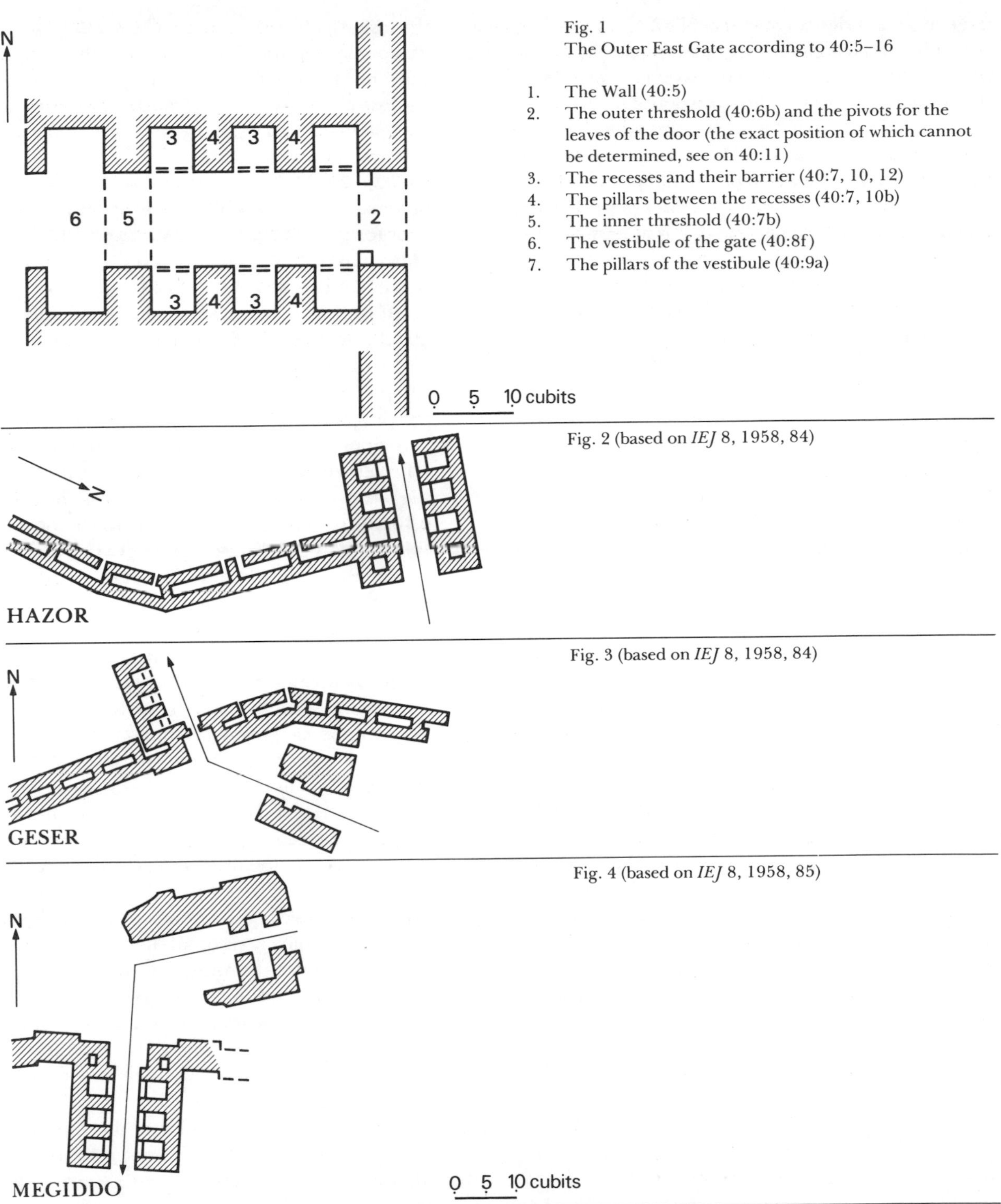

Fig. 1
The Outer East Gate according to 40:5–16

1. The Wall (40:5)
2. The outer threshold (40:6b) and the pivots for the leaves of the door (the exact position of which cannot be determined, see on 40:11)
3. The recesses and their barrier (40:7, 10, 12)
4. The pillars between the recesses (40:7, 10b)
5. The inner threshold (40:7b)
6. The vestibule of the gate (40:8f)
7. The pillars of the vestibule (40:9a)

Fig. 2 (based on *IEJ* 8, 1958, 84)

Fig. 3 (based on *IEJ* 8, 1958, 84)

Fig. 4 (based on *IEJ* 8, 1958, 85)

the two great priestly chambers of 42:1–14 which stretch from the sacred area for fifty cubits along the pavement of the outer courts (42:3). The pavement is described as the "lower pavement." This is no doubt to differentiate it from the pavement of the inner court which lay somewhat higher. Nothing is said later, however, of such a pavement in the inner court. The full paving of the inner court appears to be attested for a later period in *Arist* 88. As far as 2 Chr 7:3 is concerned, it is impossible to know for certain what this proves with regard to the inner court of the post-exilic temple, since the post-exilic author of Chronicles could have been envisaging the outer court reserved for the worship of the people.

■ **40:19** V 19 returns once again to the more detailed description of the east gate when it once more, this time with a specific measurement, gives the distance from the outer to the inner gate as one hundred cubits. This information is repeated in vv 23 and 27 in the further descriptions of the outer gates. Once again we encounter here, in the reference to the "lower gate," an indication of the difference in height between the two courts. This is made quite clear in vv 31, 34, 37 in the eight steps which in each case lead up to the three inner gates.

■ **40:20–23** Without an introductory guidance formula (the leading in to the inner court was already expressed in v 17), vv 20–23 describe the outer north gate, the reference to which corresponds to that of the east gate in v 6. The description itself, however, can now be made much more summarily. Of the architectural elements enumerated in vv 6b–12, only the three recesses, the pillars and the vestibule are mentioned here. סף ("threshold") and גבול ("barrier") are not mentioned. For the dimensions, reference back is made to the measurements of the "first gate." On the other hand, the total measurement of length and width is repeated. Immediately afterwards the elements of v 16 (vestibule windows and palm trees), are repeated and these are subsequently connected more and more closely with the introductory specification (see vv 25f, 29f, 33f and then vv 36f). It is significant that here, over and above the general information of v 6aβ, it is explicitly stated that one ascends to the outer gate by means of seven steps. In view of the otherwise strictly maintained identical schematism of the gates, this information should be transferred to the outer east gate as well. The information about the inward orientation of the vestibule, in which the מהבית (here "on the inside") of v 9b is replaced by לפנימה ("inwards") (v 22 note d), and the measurement of the distance from the outer to the inner gate (corresponding to v 19) conclude the more succinctly shaped description of the gate. Factual deviations from the structure of the gate on the east are not discernible.

■ **40:24–27** The same is true also of the description of the outer south gate, to which the prophet is now led (guidance formula ויולכני "and he led me" with directional indication דרך הדרים "towards the south"). The description of the gate שער דרך הדרום ("a gate facing south") is more succinct than the analogous designation in vv 6, 20 (22), as is also the following enumeration of the structural components where the recesses are missing completely. The elements which follow correspond to the recapitulation in the case of the north gate with variations in expression and in the order of the list. The only new element is the information that of the palms on the pillars of the vestibule there is one on each side.

■ **40:28–31** The transition to the inner court, from which subsequently the three inner gates are measured even though they all project into the outer court, is expressed with the stereotyped guidance formula ויביאני ("and he led me"),which is then also used in the case of the other inner court gates and the two front chambers of the temple building (vv 32, 35, 48; 41:1). The prophet is led into the inner court through the inner south gate, which lies opposite the previously measured outer south gate and is designated quite succinctly as שער הדרום ("the south gate"). The description of this, as of the other inner gates, is even more succinct in its expression, even though the recesses appear in the list once again. The measurement of the distance to the opposite gate, which was never missing in the case of the outer gates, is no longer necessary here. The ascent to the higher platform of the inner court is accomplished by eight steps, which, on the analogy of the outer east gate, are to be thought of as extending in front of the gate structure which projects far into the outer court, admittedly in the opposite direction. One might therefore imagine that the three inner gates, the level of which rises above the outer court, are built on terraces.

■ **40:32–34** In the description of the inner east gate, which, except for small variations in expression, is identical with the description of the south gate, the only strange feature is that it is again introduced with the prophet's being led into the inner court. Is this due to an inattentive, literal repetition of v 28? In the information about the measurements, the gate itself is referred to, still more baldly than in all the previous descriptions, simply as השער ("the gate"), since the guidance formula has already mentioned the easterly direction of the move.

■ **40:35-37** In the description of the inner "north gate" (שער הצפון), to which the prophet is finally led, even the mention of the gate no longer features in the measurement formula. מדד ("to measure") is here used absolutely. In what follows, too, minor abbreviations vis-à-vis vv 32–34 are also discernible.

■ **40:47** Just as in vv 17f brief details of the outer court were appended to the measurements of the outer east gate (vv 6–16), so in v 47, following on the compressed description of the inner gates, there is appended a terse piece of information about the inner court. It measures one hundred cubits by one hundred. Nothing is said about its being shut off by walls which one must assume to have flanked the enormous gates, which, in turn, only make sense as openings in a wall. Even a reference to the pavement, which one would expect on the basis of v 18b, is missing. Instead, reference is made, without any more precise measurement being given, to the altar, undoubtedly the great altar of the burnt offerings referred to in 43:13ff. Concerning its position it is said only that it stands "in front of the temple building." Insofar as that is usually tacitly assumed to mean that it stood in the middle of the court (see the plans in Cooke, Bertholet-Galling, Eichrodt), then such a location reveals the unconscious influence of the square shape not only of the inner court, but also of the temple area as a whole. Must not this square layout have a center? And will this center not be the altar? Closer consideration, however, makes this assumption questionable. In contrast to the great Temple of Heavenly Peace in Peking, the layout of the temple in Ezekiel 40f is not conceived symmetrically around the center. Already the absence of gates on the west side of the temple area can draw attention to this. It becomes quite clear, however, in the continuation of the leading of the prophet, which has its goal not at the altar, but in the temple building to the west of the altar and there in the most westerly room of that building, the holy of holies. Everything is orientated towards that spot, as will also be emphasized in the later complex in 43:1ff and as is also expressed indirectly in the rules of procedure in the temple. Even the altar is orientated towards that spot, for of it is precisely said not that it stands "in the center of the court," but "in front of the temple." It does not signify a new center of gravity, but stands submissively in front of the sanctuary whose core is in the holy of holies. How close the altar was to the temple cannot be determined. In all this, however, Ezekiel's temple will once again simply reflect the circumstances of the Solomonic temple. When 1 Kgs 8:64, in the account of Solomon's dedication of the temple, states that in addition Solomon dedicated "'the middle of the court' (תוך החצר) that was before the house of the Lord" because the bronze altar before Yahweh could not contain all the offerings, it becomes clear from that that this center was usually an open space and that therefore the altar is to be located closer to the temple building.[41] The situation in Ezek 40:47 is no different.

The bald note about the altar, which, exactly like the account of the building of the temple in 1 Kings 6f, says nothing about the erection of the bronze altar, was subsequently found to be unsatisfactory. In 43:13–17 precise details about the altar have been added, which admittedly do not answer the question about its more precise location in the court either.[42]

■ **40:48-41:4** The guidance of the prophet does not stop at the altar, but reaches its proper goal with the tripartite temple building. Here too the description confines itself in a quite strict and restrained manner to the sphere of enumeration and measurement. Its precise arrangement shows, nevertheless, very clearly that here the final goal of a journey with a direction has been reached. For the third time mention is made of an ascent, this time by ten steps. With this there is reached, as the total number of steps from the temple entrance to here, twenty-five, that number which mysteriously dominates the whole description. This figure may not, on any account, be surpassed by a further ascent to the holy of holies.[43] There is, in addition, the increasing narrowing of the gateways. While one enters the vestibule through an entrance

41 See also 2 Kgs 16:14; *b. Mid.* V 1.

42 On this see also de Groot, *Altäre,* and the contrary opinion of William McKane, "A Note on 2 Kings 12:10 (Evv 12;9)," *ZAW* 71 (1959): 260–265.

43 Galling in Fohrer-Galling, 230.

fourteen cubits wide, the entrance to the second chamber narrows to ten cubits and the entrance into the innermost room, which the prophet himself is not allowed to enter but which he must allow the man to enter on his own (in that 𝔊[967] already translates the ויביאני "and he led me" in v 1 with καὶ εἰσῆλθεν, its intention is to forbid the prophet to enter the front chamber too), even to six cubits. Correspondingly, the side walls of the doors grow wider. While in the vestibule, which is therefore not to be thought of, as is the vestibule of the Solomonic temple,[44] as a completely open vestibule, the sides are each three cubits wide, in the middle chamber they are each five cubits and in the inner chamber they are each seven. This increase towards the third chamber is not, however, continued in the thickness of these side walls or in the "pillars" which flank the doors. Admittedly this increases from five cubits thick in the vestibule to six cubits in the middle chamber—that corresponds to the thickness of the temple wall according to 41:5. But then it falls to two cubits in the case of the back chamber with its broad side walls flanking the doors. The same changes can be seen in the surface measurements of the chambers. While it increases from the vestibule, twenty cubits broad but only twelve cubits deep, to the middle chamber, forty cubits deep and also twenty cubits broad, it falls again in the case of the back chamber to twenty cubits broad by twenty cubits deep.[45]

It should not be disregarded that here the elements of increase are influenced by a contrary factor which one can best grasp from the point of view of a specific combination of traditions. The same can also be supposed in the case of the reference to the two columns which stand "beside" (על/אל) the pillars of the vestibule. It is impossible, on the basis of the wording, to regard, with Richter, these columns as the pillars themselves. They are an additional element which can be understood only from the point of view of the tradition.

But before posing the question about the tradition which is given for the temple building, the element with which this whole guidance scene closes must be once again strongly emphasized and its significance evaluated. The whole guidance through the temple area has taken place, from 40:6 on, in complete silence. Thus the prophet had been told to direct his closest attention to the "observance" of the process of measurement—the fourfold use of ראה ("to see") in 40:4 is clear enough. Now at the conclusion of this great guidance the man's mouth opens and the "hearing," which is mentioned once in 40:4, can now also come into its own: "And he said to me: This is the holy of holies." The tenor of the whole account has been directed towards the showing of the location of the realm of the sacred at its highest. The succinct naming formula which concludes the account gives expression to this goal.

In the case of the temple building it is now for the first time possible to make a precise comparison between the details in the visionary guidance narrative and the account of the building of Solomon's temple. 1 Kings 6f describe, with detailed measurements, the construction of the temple and the manufacture of a series of furnishings for it. Against this background, then, the first "structural elements" to be seen at the entrance to the temple, the two columns beside the pillars of the entrance to the vestibule, at once achieve their full elucidation. 1 Kgs 7:15–22, 41f describe in detail the preparation and erection of two cast, hollow bronze columns in front of the temple. The account there makes it probable that these were not bearer elements in the construction of the temple but were free-standing works of art. Concerning the names of the columns, Jachin and Boaz, and the symbolism implied in them, many theories have been advanced, but these have not, so far, led to any secure understanding.[46] The columns are mentioned again in 2 Chr 3:15–17; 4:12f. Their removal as booty at the destruction of Jerusalem is reported in 2 Kgs 25:13, 16f; Jer 52:20–23. It is characteristic of Ezekiel's temple vision that the columns are certainly mentioned but that not a word is said about their appearance, their names or even their significance. They belong to the picture of the temple of pre-exilic memory, which is faithfully preserved but which is obviously given no new significance.

This cautiously conservative connection at the very heart of the temple building with the temple of Solomon destroyed in 587 goes still further, however. According to 1 Kgs 6:2f, Solomon built the temple, according to its internal measurements, sixty cubits long, twenty cubits

44 Noth, *Könige*, 111.

45 See figure 5 (p. 357).

46 See, e.g., Walter Kornfeld, "Der Symbolismus der Tempelsäulen," *ZAW* 74 (1962): 50–57. There is a fundamental discussion of 1 Kgs 7:15–22 in Noth, *Könige*, 148–155, 162f.

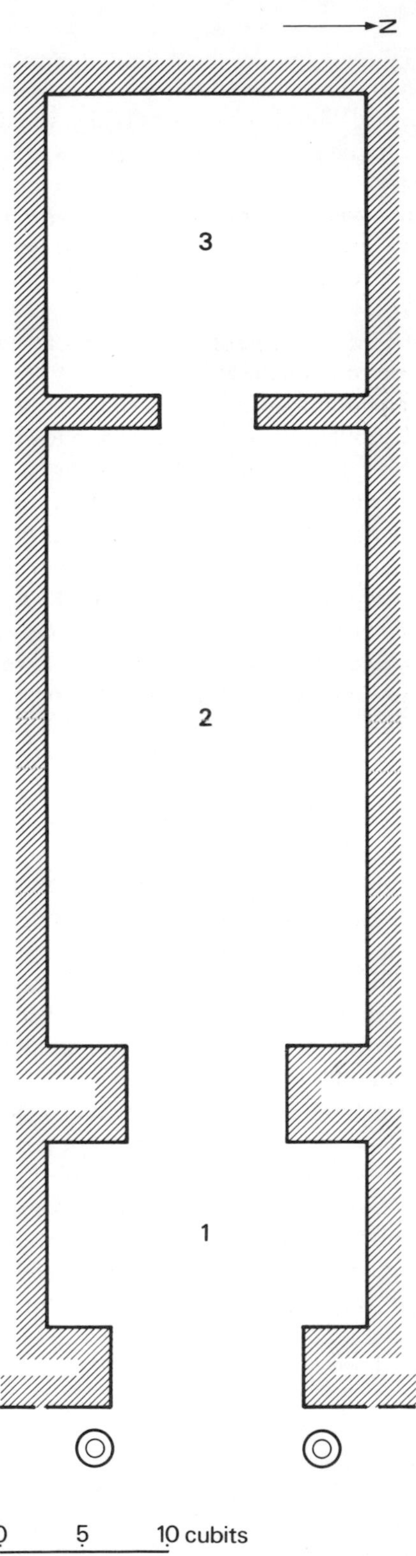

Fig. 5
The interior of the temple building according to 40:48–41:4

1. The vestibule (40:48f)
2. The temple hall (41:1f)
3. The holy of holies (41:3f)

broad and thirty cubits high. To this was added the vestibule, which, according to v 3, did not belong to the actual "house" but lay in front of it (על פני היכל הבית), twenty cubits broad and ten cubits deep. Vv 16f supply the additional information that the דביר in the innermost chamber was twenty cubits deep, so that for the outer chamber (היכל) there remained forty cubits. This corresponds, with the exception of one slight variation in one single measurement, to the description in Ezekiel 40f. While Noth, by the comparison with the temple of *tell taʿjīnāt,*[47] is led to assume for the Solomonic structure an open porch protected only at the sides by the temple walls projected forward, here the mention in 40:48 (emended text) of the "side walls" (כתפות) each three cubits broad indicates the beginning of a closing off at the front, which admittedly in its "front opening" (השער), with a width of fourteen cubits, stands wide open for any who emerge. While the width of twenty cubits agrees with the measurement of the Solomonic אולם ("vestibule"), the increase in its depth from ten to twelve cubits must be considered more closely later on.

The measurement and the name of the principal chamber (היכל), on the other hand, coincide completely with the data in 1 Kgs 6:17.[48] In Ezek 8:16 היכל was the term for the whole temple building. That is entirely correct if Schult is right with his theory that the דביר is a self-contained unit incorporated into the היכל of the Solomonic temple. But it is also understandable on the basis of Schult's theory why in the description in Ezek 41:3, which, in contrast to 1 Kings 6, regards the innermost area as an independent chamber, the wall which separates it from the היכל is so remarkably thin and why the increase which was discernible in the thickness of the walls from the אלם to the היכל is not continued but falls far behind. According to this there was no stone wall in Solomon's temple between היכל and דביר, but the דביר was entirely constructed of wood and separated from the rest of the היכל by a wooden wall which was not taken into account in the measurements.[49] In the Herodian temple a curtain separated the holy of holies from the sacred area.[50] Thus here too is revealed the desire to assimilate to the pre-exilic temple and its proportions. The technical term דביר is not taken up again, however, but the innermost part of the temple where holiness is most fully concentrated is described by a phrase expressing just this very quality, קדשׁ קדשׁים ("the holy of holies").

But now we must also briefly turn our attention to the differences from Solomon's temple. 1 Kgs 6:2 mentioned a measurement for the temple of sixty cubits by twenty. If one adds to that the vestibule mentioned there in v 3, the result is a measurement of seventy by twenty. If, on the other hand, one makes an exact calculation of the measurements in Ezekiel 40f, then to that figure there must be added not only the two cubits by which the depth of the vestibule exceeds that of 1 Kgs 6, but, by the inclusion of the thickness of the various walls, an additional five (40:48) plus six (41:1) plus two (41:3) cubits. The depth of the inner chamber from the entrance to the אלם ("vestibule") to the back wall of the holy of holies is increased to eighty-five cubits. What is the reason for these differences? The question cannot be answered from the context of 40:48–41:4. But it does become clear from the measurements given in 41:5ff. As a result of the "side structure" (צלע), which, like the אלם ("vestibule"), is built on to the main building, the extent of the latter is increased on both sides and at the rear by a further fifteen cubits, so that here too, surprisingly, once again there emerges a main structure determined by the number fifty and its multiple, a building measuring one hundred cubits by fifty.

Thus two things are revealed in these figures. It becomes clear, on the one hand, that the details of the guidance vision with regard to the temple building very cautiously endeavor to preserve the measurements known from Solomon's temple. On the other hand, however, they try to accommodate these to the total plan of chapters 40f, which is determined by the figures

47 Noth, *Könige,* 148–155, 162f; Noth draws on C. W. McEwan, "The Syrian Expedition of the Oriental Institute of the University of Chicago," *American Journal of Archaeology* 41 (1937): 9 (fig. 4).

48 On the loan-word היכל, which Noth translates by "room" (*Saal*), see 1,243 and Noth, *Könige,* 100 (note z on 1 Kgs 6:17).

49 Noth, *Könige,* 119, 121.

50 Josephus, *Jewish War* V 5, 5; Mt 27:51 (and parallels); Heb 6:19; 9:3; 10:20.

twenty-five, fifty and their multiples. Equally, it has also become clear that the section 40:1–37, 47–49; 41:1–4, which nevertheless clearly reveals the way to a goal which can no longer be surpassed, is not fully comprehensible on its own, but represents an extract from a far-reaching architectonic blueprint, to which further elements, which are also necessary for the understanding of 40:48–41:4, are added only in later sections, which, as we shall see, are from a form-critical point of view, very differently shaped.

■ **40:1–37, 47–49, 41:1–4** After these observations on 40:48–41:4, we have now reached the point of asking, with regard to the *overall plan of the present unit as a whole,* which parts of it derive from *tradition* and which, on the other hand, are a *programmatic new plan.* Only after the clarification of this question will it be possible to ask, under the heading "Aim," what exactly this visionary temple plan is "saying."

If one compares 1 Kings 6f with the layout in Ezekiel 40f, one is quickly confronted with a first difference. Ezekiel 40f involves a temple precinct which contains, on the wide area of five hundred meters square (this should be extended on the basis of 42:15–20), as its true center a temple building doubly protected by courts each with three gates. On the other hand, 1 Kgs 6f involves a temple building surrounded by a court which, in turn, is part of an extensive palace complex of Solomon enclosed within a "great court" (7:9, 12). There is no trace whatsoever of this surrounding palace complex in Ezekiel 40f. Now it was observed in connection with 8:3 that other statements in the books of Kings already reveal a development in the pre-exilic period in accordance with which elements of the palace area were attached to the temple as a second forecourt.[51] Ezekiel 40f shows how this development was radically carried to its conclusion. The land round the temple is claimed in its entirety, in a way that is not beset by any other territorial claims, for the temple and its large-scale gate structures, which are not mentioned at all in 1 Kings 6f. These enormous gate structures known to us from elsewhere in ancient Palestine but which are given great and emphatic prominence in Ezekiel 40, might thus appear as something new and revolutionary. The gates of the first temple which are mentioned incidentally, such as the "upper gate" (2 Kgs 15:35) and the "new gate" (Jer 26:10; 36:10), were undoubtedly much more modest structures.

Thus one might be inclined to think of Babylonian influences on the fuller design of the temple gates. One cannot simply reject the contribution of such influences (see below on 44:1–2). But over and above this, precisely for the gate structures described in Ezekiel 40, there has emerged the astonishing observation that with regard to an element which is particularly characteristic of them, namely the three recesses on each side of the passageway of the gate, clear parallels are to be found in the older city-gates of Megiddo, Hazor and perhaps also Gezer.[52] The building of these, however, should be connected with the note in 1 Kgs 9:15, according to which Solomon "built" Hazor, Megiddo and Gezer. This "building" was doubtless the development of them into fortified cities (see also 1 Kgs 9:19). Since 1 Kgs 9:15 speaks in the same context also of Solomon's building work on the temple and palace, the Millo and the wall of Jerusalem, it is very probable that the type of city-gate which archaeologists have found at Megiddo, Hazor (and Gezer?) as structures from the Solomonic period was also used in the development of Jerusalem.[53] But then we would have discovered at this point too a commemorative element handed down from Jerusalem's pre-exilic tradition. The revolutionary process in the temple vision consists in the fact that this type of city-gate, which is conceived as military protection for the city and can provide for the city-guards a place in the gate recesses (can one, in this connection, compare תא הרצים "guardroom" in 1 Kgs 14:28?) from which eventually to fight against enemy attackers, has, in Ezekiel 40, been made into a temple-gate, which thus acquires a defensive characteristic. Thus in this particularly unusual element of Ezekiel 40 preservation of tradition and revolutionary innovation in the service of new intellectual orientation lie side by side. Yadin has calculated the following measurements for Megiddo, Hazor and Gezer respectively: the depth of the gate: 20.3, 20.3, 19.0 m; the inside width: 17.5, 18.0, 16.2 m; the space between the two entrance towers: 6.5, 6.1, 5.5 m; the width of the gate opening: 4.2, 4.2, 3.1 m. Thus the depth is a little less than the measurement in Ezekiel

51 See 1,237.

52 See above p. 352.

53 On this see Zimmerli, "Ezechieltempel."

40, while the width is greater than in the case of the gates in Ezekiel 40. The width of the gate opening, again, remains in the three places less than in Ezekiel 40.

Yet another difference is characteristic within the context of the similarity. Ezekiel 40 lacks completely any indication of gate towers flanking the entrance and contributing to the defense possibilities at the city-gate. In its place here there is the additional, characteristic element of the אולם, the "vestibule." It will become clear from 44:3 and 46:2 that this portico in the inner and outer east gate has particular significance for the temple service of the נשיא ("prince"). The question has been posed by Galling on the basis of purely architectural considerations whether one should not see in this אולם ("vestibule"), structurally, a new element which has been added in Ezekiel 40 over and above the traditional form of the gate. The inner threshold between recess passageway and אולם ("vestibule") (40:7b), which, like the outer one (40:6b), corresponds to the thickness of the wall, would suggest that Howie's proof that the structural element of the אולם ("vestibule") is present in the city gates is not, on the other hand, convincing. Over and above Galling, however, it must then be asked whether in the omission of the towers and the addition of the אולם ("vestibule") the specific transformation of the military defense gate to the cultically significant sanctuary gate has not also found its architectural expression.

The fact that the court of Solomon's temple already had a pavement is rendered likely by 2 Chr 7:3, but not definitely proved. The skillful accommodation of the traditional measurements of the temple into the quite different system of measurements in Ezekiel 40f has already been discussed. Thus there emerge, at more than one point, impressive examples of the adoption of what is already given into a bold, new total concept. To what has been taken over from earlier times there belonged also the two columns in front of the temple building.

Nothing more precise is said about the spot on which the temple is to stand. But after what has been said it may be fairly safely assumed that the location given in the tradition is thought of as the site of the temple building.[54] To the picture of the locality there belongs for Ezekiel 40f also the correct recollection of an inner "upper" court lying up on a terrace. To assume over and above this that the author of chapters 40f had in front of him the temple ruins[55] does not seem to me to be necessary. The measurements of the ascent are then not given in cubits but simply in the number of steps, which regarded as a whole are counted in an unmistakably schematized way. Thus the supposition that Ezekiel 40f envisages the erection of the temple on the highest point of the temple mount, i.e. doubtless on the rock of the modern *qubbet eṣ-ṣaḫra,* is still the most probable one.[56] Also the orientation of the temple towards the east, which perforce emerges from its location on the west side of the inner court, the only side still available, corresponds to the easterly orientation of Solomon's temple which can be deduced from 8:16.

According to Jeremias and Möhlenbrink, the temple of Zerubbabel can be discerned in the plan in Ezekiel 40f.[57] Now admittedly we know very little about the second temple. Nevertheless, this suggestion is contradicted by (amongst other things) the measurements of Cyrus's edict in Ezr 6:3, which were originally sixty cubits long, twenty cubits wide and thirty cubits high and according to which the Zerubbabel temple was to be built.[58] These figures show not the slightest influence of the ideal picture of Ezekiel 40f, about the message and import of which we must now inquire.

Aim

The fact that the "vision" of 40:1–37, 47–49; 41:1–4 has the weight of a "proclamation" can be seen from the commission in 40:4 to "proclaim" (הַגֵּד) what is seen to the house of Israel. The "proclamation" does not simply mean the making known of a new picture of things to come which Israel should add to other pictures which she already has. It undoubtedly means direction and sum-

54 On this see Galling, "Serubbabel und der Wiederaufbau," and *idem,* "Serubbabel und der Hohepriester."

55 Galling in Fohrer-Galling.

56 See Schmidt, *heilige Fels.* A site between the modern *eṣ-ṣaḫra* and the *el-'aqṣā* is envisaged (for the Herodian temple, which, however, can scarcely have abandoned the old site) by B. Bagatti, "La posizione del tempio erodiano di Gerusalemme," *Bibl* 46 (1965): 428–444.

57 Möhlenbrink, *Tempel,* 31f.

58 According to Galling, "Serubbabel und der Wiederaufbau," 71.

mons at the same time for an Israel that is uncertain of her way and is not yet fully determined on going. The fact that in the vision which is proclaimed here much human thinking and much reflection on the part of the prophet himself, condensed as far as possible into sketch plans, has been precipitated does not detract in the slightest from the weight of the "proclamation" which is aware of having acquired a new authority.

The "vision," in which the prophet's reflection and careful planning takes shape as the experience of the divine commission, comes to him at the cultic New Year of the twenty-fifth year of his exile, the middle year of a fifty (or forty-nine) year period culminating in the year of release. In the transportation to the land of Israel, which no longer bears the dramatic experiential emphasis of the transportation of 8:1ff, there is shown to him what has already been newly prepared there. The detailed examination of the vision has already made it clear how new elements mingle with recollections of the old, of the form of the Solomonic temple and of the Solomonic (post-Solomonic) city. In the old elements, which are ratified for the prophet in the vision, there is confirmed the word of faithfulness on the part of Israel's God who does not allow what he has once begun to be torn down. In the new, to which everything is transformed, can be heard the call to depart from what was once sinful and evil and displeasing to God.

The "proclamation," therefore, has a twofold, inner aspect. It is, on the one hand, an indicative announcement of what is shown to the prophet in the vision as already existent. On the "high mountain"—behind this lies an echo not only of 17:23; 20:40 but also of Is 2:2; it is not only a natural geographical phenomenon but the height granted by God by way of distinction to his own mountain—stands God's new sanctuary, already visible to the eye which God has already opened. No human laborer's hand is shown, no human king's pomp (by contrast with 1 Kings and Chronicles) was involved. Only the figure of the man sent by God, who, with his measurements, participates in the whole procedure seen by the prophet. As if a heavenly being who has about him the bright gleam of heavenly light (40:3) should have to measure human work. The prophet's vision is the promise of the goal of the homeland which is prepared by God and which, according to 20:34ff, awaits them in the year of release after the new exodus and the day of future liberation.

At the same time, however, it should not be overlooked that this proclamation also has an imperative aspect. Against the background of that earlier temple vision of chapter 8 what is revealed as new is a judgment on what has happened and a summons to turn their whole mind and all their own resolve towards the new.

The language in which this new factor is enshrined is, moreover, unusual enough. It is the language of objective architectural forms and measurements. Its decipherment and its translation into the word which addresses man as one who is lost in the imprisonment of the exile, and at the same time as one who is called to responsibility for himself, is not easy. It is perhaps possible to find a similar "language" in Psalm 48, where a Song of Zion presents this command: "Walk about Zion, go round about her, number her towers, 'consider well' her ramparts (שִׁיתוּ לִבְּכֶם לְ; cf. Ezek 40:4), go through her palaces; so that you may tell the next generation: This is God, our God for ever and ever. He will guide us."

The prophet's way leads through six gates to the building in which he reaches his goal, to the threshold of the holy of holies which alone is given a name by the figure of the guide. The orientation towards the holy is unmistakably expressed as guidance for man.

Along the whole road it is further made clear to the prophet that in the ascent to this holy place nothing else can be important. By contrast with the powerful tradition of the Solomonic period, no splendor of a royal palace is discernible, but nor does any side chapel of a protector or suppliant, in the manner of Ezek 8, interrupt the prophet's way. This single-mindedness extends even to the restrained decoration in the vestibule of the gates, where, by contrast with the unbridled disorder of the old temple (8:3, 10), only the rather ornamental palm trees are to be seen. The whole space on the temple mount belongs here, undoubtedly in a vast extension of the area which was at that time available for the temple precinct, to God alone.

The greatly enlarged gates, which have adopted the form of the old defensive gates of the royal city, in which in the three recesses on either side of the passageway the guards keep watch and ward off any enemy, proclaim God's exclusive and defensive holiness, which does not demean itself with human affairs, even with the governmental affairs of a human king. The transformation of the gates by the omission of the combat towers and the building of the projecting vestibule, which, as will appear later, is destined to become a place of worship (44:3; 46:1–3), could also at the same time give expression to the other statement that the gates are not only places of defense but places which summon people to a correct turning towards that which is holy.

It may, in this connection, be of significance that this will be stated only with respect to the two east gates. They lie opposite the real center of the temple precinct, which is not to be equated with the geometrical center of the square sanctuary area. The temple building with the holy of holies lies on the west side of the square inner court. The worshippers do not stand round about a sacred center. Their worship has a clear direction, a direction which turns away from the false direction discernible in 8:16. It is not the easterly direction offered by nature, the direction of the rising sun, but the westerly direction—not derivable from nature, but, in the experience of Ezekiel 40f, quite simply determined by the will of Yahweh—that is revealed to Israel. Thus then the west side, on which God's sanctuary lies, remains without a gate. One cannot approach God from behind. One must come before his face and bow there.

If thus the simple, geometrically harmonious alignment falls on the center of the square and if there is something arbitrary in the orientation of the temple as a whole, yet at the same time something of the harmony of the undisturbed divine order in the sanctuary is expressed by the numbers included in the plan. In two times three gates there is opened the access to the similarly tripartite seventh structure at the goal of this whole guidance. In this there seemed to be discernible something of the rhythm of the Priestly creation narrative with its culmination in the seventh, sanctified day. But then it is the twenty-five (and its multiples) which becomes significant. While this may have a distant footing in the Solomonic tradition in the measurements of the House of the Forest of Lebanon (1 Kgs 7:2), the introductory date of the middle year of the period culminating in the great release seems to give to this figure in its present context a new, immediately significant emphasis. Already in the measurements of the gates and then of the temple building, which, in a bold increase on the sacred measurements of Solomon's temple, is oriented on the number fifty, there is reflected at the same time the number of the year of the great release. Under the symbol of these measurements, the one who comes to worship in the temple, in the event that access to the sacred house is granted to him as a priest, climbs by means of twenty-five steps to the site of what is holy. While the vision of chapters 40f fails to give any other details of heights, nevertheless the prophet's route is upwards by means of that ascent. One is tempted to think of God's Jerusalem name, which is admittedly not found in Ezekiel, עליון ("Most High"), and how it rings through a Psalm like Psalm 47: מאד נעלה ("he is highly exalted") (v 10).

The objective language which is spoken in Ezekiel 40f is particularly difficult for a modern to understand with his orientation towards personal address. Even if the details of the interpretation cannot be determined with certainty on every point, the common denominator by which the whole is to be understood cannot be missed. The prophet is charged by his vision with proclaiming to his downcast people that their God is already in the process of erecting his sanctuary in their midst in faithfulness to his earlier promise. God's people move towards the day on which once again the cry goes out to a life which has become perplexed, the cry which gives to life a direction and a way: "Enter his gates with thanksgiving" (Ps 100:4) and on which men encourage each other: "Come, let us worship and bow down and let us kneel before the Lord . . ." (Ps 95:6).

2. Two Additions about the Chambers in the Inner North and South Gates

Bibliography

Friedrich Blome
Die Opfermaterie in Babylonien und Israel 1 (Rome: Pontifical Biblical Institute, 1934).

William McKane
"A Note on 2 Kings 12:10 (Evv 12:9)," *ZAW* 71 (1959): 260–265.

40

38 And there was a chamber whose door
opened <into the vestibule of the gate>[a].
There the burnt offering is washed[b]. 39/
In the vestibule of the gate, however,
there stood two tables on one side and
two on the other[a], on[b] which the burnt
offering[c] and the sin offering and the guilt
offering were to be slaughtered. 40/ And
on the side wall, outside the <vestibule>[a]
beside the doorway[b] of the gate which
faces north[c] there stood two tables, and
on the other side wall of the vestibule of
the gate there stood (likewise) two
tables. 41/ Four tables (stood) on the one
side and four tables on the other, on the
side wall of the gate, (all together) eight
tables, on[a] which the sacrifices were to
be slaughtered[b]. 42a/ And (the) four
tables for the burnt offering were (made)
of hewn stone. Their length was one and
a half cubits and their width one and a
half cubits[a] and the height one cubit.

40: 38a 𝔐 באילים השערים. 𝔊 (𝔏W), which was
38 obviously not able to make anything of v 38 at all, shows however in its *αιλαμμω* that it read not the plural of איל but the word אילם. Similarly, the following *ἐπὶ τῆς πύλης* points to a singular שער. The continuation in 𝔐 v 39 confirms that באילם השער should be read.

b 𝔊 *ἐπὶ τῆς πύλης τῆς δευτέρας ἔκρυσις* seems to have read השער השני instead of 𝔐 השערים שם. Is in what follows the root "wash" connected with *ῥέομαι*?

39 39a V 39a is missing in 𝔊 (𝔏W).

b אל–על cf 1:17 note a.

c 𝔐 העולה is not attested by 𝔊 (𝔏W). See the exposition of v 42.

40 40a 𝔐 לעולה "for him who comes up" is read by 𝔊 (𝔏W) 𝔖 as עֹלָה "burnt offering." Fohrer-Galling proposes the emendation to למעלה and the deletion of לפתח, in order to avoid the difficulty of the neglect of the differences in level. The corresponding statement in v 40b makes it clear, however, that 𝔐 לעולה is a scribal error for an original לאולם (לאילם).

b לפתח gives the impression of being superfluous, but is not to be deleted, with Fohrer-Galling, since it affirms that the tables do not stand to the side of the gate structure, but in front against the side walls which flank the gate entrance.

c הצפונה does not refer (as suggested by many commentators) to the side wall (כתף), which would then indicate a gate situated to the east, but is a more precise direction indicator referring to the gate (השער) or perhaps to the whole phrase (פתח השער). See the careful considerations of Gese, 156. As is to be expected from the direct connection with vv 35–37, the whole is located in the area of the north gate. It is not clear how 𝔊 (𝔏W) intended the twice added statement that the tables are aligned *κατὰ ἀνατολάς* to be understood.

41 41a אל–על cf 1:17 note a.

b 𝔊, which transposes the two halves of v 41b, inserts a second *θύματα* (=זבח): *ἐπ᾽ αὐτὰς σφάξουσι τὰ θύματα κατέναντι τῶν ὀκτὼ τραπεζῶν τῶν θυμάτων*; 𝔏W suppresses the word, which is incorrectly rendered by it with *holocautoma,* in the second passage. See the exposition.

42a 42a a 𝔊 two and a half cubits.

43a/ [a]And the storage trays(?)[b], a hand's breadth wide, were fixed round about on the inside (of the building). 42b/ On[a] them <were laid>[b] the implements with which the burnt offering was slaughtered—and the sacrificial offering[c]. 43b/ On[a] the tables, however, (is laid)[b] the flesh of the offering[c].

44 And outside at the inner gate[a] there were
<two>[b] chambers in the inner court[c],
<one>[d] on the side wall of the north gate

43a 43a The sense demands the placing of v 43a before v 42b since the broad tables cannot have been the place, as it now appears in 𝔐, where the sacrificial knives were laid, while the sacred flesh of the sacrifice must find its place on the storage trays which are only a hand's breadth wide (note b).

b 𝔐 השפתים. The word is attested also in Ps 68:14, where Ju 5:16 is cited, in which משפתים seems to be used in the sense of "sheepfolds." But already 𝔊 *γεῖσος* (𝔊[967] *κυμάτιον*) and quite clearly 𝔙 *labia* as well as 𝔖 ספותהון understand the word as שפה "lip, edge." Quite different here is 𝔗 which is clearly interpretive ועונקלין נפקין פשך חד קביעין בעמודי בית מטבחיא מגיו לאולמיא סחור סחור, which is thinking of hooks in the wall. On the plural significance of the dual see Bauer-Leander §63s. For the rest, see the exposition.

42b 42b a על–אל cf. 1:17 note a.

b 𝔐 ויניחו is, according to 𝔊 (𝔏[W]) 𝔙 𝔖 𝔗, a scribal error for יניחו (dittography).

c 𝔐 והזבח seems to be secondary in the text, so BH[3], following Cornill; Ehrlich, *Randglossen;* Herrmann; Bertholet-Galling; Fohrer-Galling, suggests deleting it as an addition. But see the exposition.

43b 43b a על–אל cf. 1:17 note a.

b The text would be made easier if one could, with 𝔖 סימין, here too insert a יניחו. But 𝔐 can be completely original.

c On the orthography of קֻרְבָּן (otherwise always קָרְבָּן), see Bauer-Leander §20k. In the place of v 43b 𝔊 (𝔏[W]) reads the following passage which begins with the identical words: *ἐπὶ τὰς τραπέζας ἐπάνωθεν στέγας τοῦ καλύπτεσθαι ἀπὸ τοῦ ὑετοῦ καὶ ἀπὸ τῆς ξηρασίας* "above the tables, however, were roofs to give protection from the rain and the heat." See the exposition.

44 44a 𝔊 (𝔏[W]) begins the verse with a new guidance statement: *καὶ εἰσήγαγέ με εἰς τὴν αὐλὴν τὴν ἐσωτέραν, καὶ ἰδοὺ δύο ἐξέδραι.* This reading, even by reference to the end of v 43 (so Galling ויקרבני אל החצר הפנימית), cannot be graphically connected with 𝔐. Thus, as already in the case of vv 19/20 and its related formulation in 𝔊 (v 19 note c, v 20 note a), it must be assumed that 𝔊 has here too independently accommodated its text to the situation of the guidance vision. It is still strange, however, that 𝔊, where 𝔐 speaks of לשער הפנימי, mentions *αὐλὴν τὴν ἐσωτέραν*, which seems to point to לחצר הפנימי. Hence Cornill, Herrmann, Bertholet-Galling, Fohrer-Galling. Since, however, השער הפנימי already occurs in 40:19 (note b; on v 15 see note d) and 𝔐, from the point of view of sense, is unobjectionable, 𝔐 should be retained.

b 𝔐 שרים "(chambers of the) singers." 𝔙 (*gazophylacia*) *cantorum,* interpreted by 𝔗 as referring to the Levites (לישכת ליואי), while 𝔖 דרברבנא presupposes a שרים. 𝔊 (𝔏[W]) has, on the other hand, with its *δύο*, preserved the original reading שתים which is confirmed also by the continuation of the statement.

<facing>[e] south, <the other>[f] on the side wall of the <south gate>[g] <facing>[h] north. 45/ And he said to me: This chamber[a] which faces south is for the priests who see to the service in the temple 46/ But the chamber which faces north is for the priests who see to the service at the altar—they are the Zadokites, those of the Levites who (may) come near to Yahweh to minister to him.

c On בחצר הפנימי see v 23 note a.

d Instead of 𝔐 אשר, according to 𝔊 (𝔏^W) *μία*, 𝔙 *una*, an אחת should be read which is immediately taken up by a corresponding אחת (note f) and is also demanded by the continuation in vv 45f.

e 𝔐 ופניהם originated by adjustment to לשכות after the antecedent אחת was corrupted to אשר. ופניה should be read.

f 𝔐 אחר. The connection with לשכה demands the feminine אחת.

g 𝔐 הקדים should, on the basis of 𝔊 (𝔏^W) *νότου*, be emended to הדרום, as is demanded also by the recapitulation in v 46.

h 𝔐 פני must, by analogy with what precedes, be emended to פניה.

45 45a According to Gesenius-Kautzsch §136d note 1, הלשכה is to be regarded as in apposition to זה. On the unusual construction, which avoids what one would actually expect, הלשכה הזאת, see the exposition.

Form

The complex 40:1–37, 47–49, 41:1–4 had come seamlessly together with no gap discernible in the progress of the guidance vision. We must now look at the omitted intervening section, 40:38–46, and examine it with regard to its form and its connection with the context. The content of these verses makes it clear at once that we have here two sections, vv 38–43 and 44–46, quite independent as to content. From the point of view of form, too, they prove to be two completely independent structures.

Vv 38–43 speak of a "chamber" (לשכה) opening into the vestibule of the inner north gate which had just been described in vv 35–37 and of the furnishing of vestibule and chamber with a view to the preparation of the various types of offerings. This section lacks all the elements which characterized the unit 40:1–37, 47–49; 41:1–4. There is no mention of the prophet's being led. The textual emendation of Cornill to ויוליכני פתח האילם ("and he led me to the opening of the vestibule") is unconvincing.[1] Nor is there any talk of measurement undertaken by the guide. This is all the more surprising since in v 42 measurements are given for the tables in the vestibule and these could, without any difficulty, have been presented to the prophet's eye in a process of measurement. In comparison with the unit referred to, it is also surprising that here for the first time, quite one-sidedly, a structure on the north side is singled out and described in considerable detail. The great harmonious plan, which in the guidance vision unmistakably intentionally tries to say something essential about the ordering of the future temple, is disturbed by the inclusion of vv 38–43. It is also unprecedented that a chamber is here described down to the smallest details of its furnishing. One may compare the summary mention of the thirty chambers of the outer court in v 17. Here too, in the אבני גזית ("hewn stone") of v 42, there is the first mention of a material for an element of the temple furnishing. Quite new also is the reference to an intended purpose for the various parts of the room and of the furnishings which are mentioned. This can occur in the imperfect (with jussive emphasis, Gese); so vv 38, 41, 42. It can be expressed in the form of an infinitive (v 39) or of a simple nominal sentence (v 43).

The absence of the element of guidance and measurement is also characteristic of the second section, vv 44–46, which describes two cells at the inner north and south gates. Here too there would have been nothing to prevent a reference to the prophet's being led to the south gate. In what follows there are no further details in the description of the chambers in v 44. Only the direction of the gates is given. Instead, there follows in vv 45f an element which at first might recall the visionary guidance scene. The man opens his mouth and says some-

1 Though followed by *ZB;* see also Bewer, "Textual Notes," 166f.

thing about the owners of the two cells. But from the point of view precisely of the formal structure of the guidance vision it must be said that this premature statement by the man about the chambers destroys the effect of the statement about the holy of holies in 41:4, which clearly formed the conclusion and real object of the visionary guidance scene. The tense stillness which leads up to that final statement is prematurely destroyed if vv 44–46 were original in the context. One may certainly affirm that the structure of vv 44–46 clearly has before it the model of the structure of the visionary guidance account ending in a declamatory statement. Linguistically the different hand is admittedly revealed by the וידבר אלי ("and he said to me") in contrast to the ויאמר אלי ("and he said to me") of 41:4. The model of 41:4 can even be seen in the fact that what the man says begins here too with the demonstrative pronoun זה ("this") (here feminine). But closer examination then reveals at once that זה ("this"), in contrast to 41:4, does not form with the following word a nominal sentence with demonstrative character: "That is . . . ." Rather it is a demonstrative which has been prefixed in a grammatically unusual way for the sake of the (apparent) similarity to 41:4. See note a.

From the content point of view vv 44–46 are differentiated from the guidance vision also by the fact that here we have the first explicit mention by name of a group of people who serve in the temple. Vv 44–46, too, certainly did not originally stand in their present context (against Galling). Both form and content of the verses advise against this. Here too we are dealing with the secondary insertion of two structural elements, which, in the framework of the vision narrative, could appropriately have been inserted at two different points—the chamber on the south side after vv 28–31 and that on the north after vv 35–37.

Setting

The dislocation of the plan of the guidance vision by vv 38–46 suggests that in the two inserted sections there is at work a later hand who could no longer fully reproduce the severe style of 40:1–37, 47–49, 41:1–4. Even the spurious imitation of one element of this style in the man's speech in vv 45f suggests a later hand who is concerned to complete the plan of the new temple. The same type of imitation of form will be encountered again in 41:22 and 42:13f. Since vv 38–43 entirely and vv 44–46 at least partly have to do with additions concerning the inner north gate, both expansions have been added after vv 35–37 where the prophet finds himself at that very gate.

Whether both expansions were added simultaneously can no longer be discerned with certainty. It is, however, clear in any case that vv 44–46 with their introduction look back to the already preceding section vv 38–43. After vv 38–43 have dealt with furnishings in the vestibule of the north gate, v 44 begins with the assertion: "Outside the inner gate structure however . . . ."

On the still later addition in v 46b see the exposition.

Interpretation

■ **40:38–43** *1. The furnishings at the inner north gate for the preparation of the sacrifices.* Vv 38–43 describe the furnishings in and at the inner north gate which serve for the preparation of the sacrifices. The various operations of the sacrificial process—the slaughtering, the washing of the parts, the laying down of the sacrificial meat and of the implements necessary for the slaughtering—are envisaged here as well as the varied quality of the types of sacrifice.

■ **40:38** The description begins by mentioning a room built onto the gate structure and opening into the vestibule, i.e. into that part of this structure which protrudes furthest into the outer court. According to v 37 one ascends to the gate structure by means of eight steps. Is the built-on chamber also constructed on this higher level? Must one, then, in this case reckon with substructures or with a terrace? Since one must assume such for the inner gates which extend into the outer court, this assumption will not enounter any insuperable difficulty. The question cannot, however, be completely suppressed whether, in the case of this annex constructed in accordance with the ground plan, full reckoning is really taken of the differences in height. We are dealing, in this whole temple plan (and clearly so also in the case of the land distribution in chapter 48), with planning from afar. A clear regard for the differences in level will be affirmed in 42:1–14.

In this room the burnt offering is to be washed. 2 Chr 4:6, according to Gese a statement "dependent on this passage," remarks in an additional note to the original in 1 Kgs 7:38 with quite related vocabulary that the bronze basins of the Solomonic temple were to be used for the washing of "what was used for the burnt offering":[2] את מעשׂה העולה ידיחו בם.[3] One may associate this information with the instructions in Lev 1:9, 13, according to which in the burnt offering the "entrails" (קרבו) and the "lower legs" (כרעיו) are to be washed. According to Blome, this washing is not intended to be of a ritual nature but the purely physical cleaning of the two most soiled parts.[4] It is clear that this process of washing will take place only after the slaughtering which is mentioned in what follows. The sequence which is preserved in vv 38ff is determined not by the sequence of the sacrificial process, but by the description of the buildings which moves from outside to inside.[5]

■ **40:39** Thus there follows next the description of the interior of the vestibule of the gate structure itself. To the left and right as one passes through the door (so we must expand) there stand in this entrance room of the gateway, which, according to vv 8f (the measurement of the outer east gate holds for all the gates), is eight cubits deep and surely (by analogy with v 13) twenty-five cubits broad, two tables on each side. On them burnt offering, sin offering and guilt offering are to be slaughtered. The individual types of offering will have to be discussed more closely in connection with 45:10–17.[6]

■ **40:40–41** Before v 42 continues in more detail the description of these tables, vv 40f mention two further pairs of tables which are found outside the vestibule, i.e. already in the area of the outer court. Once again there is no further mention of the difference in level between the gateway, which is reached by means of steps, and the court. The "side" (כתף) of the vestibule, in contrast to that of the vestibule of the temple (v 48, note b), is not measured. Its width, since both outside and inside two tables of one and half cubits stand before it, undoubtedly at a certain distance from each other, will have to measure more than the three cubits of those "sides" (shoulder walls).

What is more important is that here explicitly the north gate is given as the site of these sacrificial tables. The placing of this addition after vv 35–37 of the basic text suggested from the outset that it must be the north gate that was in question here. The transfer to the east gate (from Hitzig, Ewald, Cornill on to Fohrer-Galling) is from the first completely lacking in probability and is clearly excluded by v 40 (note c). Even Lev 1:11 speaks of the killing of the animal for the burnt offering "on the north side of the altar." In the case of Herod's temple *b. Mid.* III 5 speaks of "rings" (טבעות) on the north side of the altar on which one killed the sacred offering and mentions the house of those who do the killing as being to the north of the altar. McKane, in his discussion of 2 Kgs 12:10, comes to similar conclusions.

■ **40:42a** Thus, then, on both sides of the entrance to the vestibule stand two tables on each side, on both the outer and the inner side of the wall, eight tables all together, all intended for the killing of the animals. The interest is concentrated, however, as the sequel shows, in particular on the tables standing inside the vestibule for the killing of the burnt offering. They alone are described by their measurements (1½: 1½: 1 cubits) and by their material (hewn stone blocks). It is strange that here only tables for the burnt offering are mentioned, while v 39 mentioned three types of offering in all. Has 𝔊, as a result of this observation, suppressed the burnt offering in order to make a clear distinction? It will be more correct to decide with Gese that עולה ("burnt offering") here is the comprehensive term for the sacred offering in which the people have no share.

■ **40:43a** The information about purpose which follows in v 42b can in any case no longer refer to the tables. It should be preceded by v 43a which mentions yet another element of the furnishing of this area. Unfortunately the meaning of שׁפתים (here "storage trays") can no longer be determined with certainty. The dual might lead one to think of a double element. Hence Galling: "fork hooks" fastened to "pegs" (ביתדות instead of בבית). 𝔗 thinks along these lines. The translation given here, "storage

2 Wilhelm Rudolph, *Chronikbücher*, HAT 21 (Tübingen: Mohr, 1955), 206: "the prepared portions of the burnt offering."

3 On this see also Noth, *Könige*, 161f.

4 Blome, *Opfermaterie*, 1. 136f.

5 See also the "chamber of the washers" (לשכת המדיחים), *b. Mid.* V 3.

6 See below pp. 478f.

trays," follows 𝔊 𝔙 𝔖. The giving of their measurement as טפח "a hand's breadth," i.e. about six centimeters (see above on v 5), suggests rather a ledge running along the wall.

■ **40:42b** Such a ledge would provide enough space for laying down the knives and hooks. When the text here speaks of implements (knives) for the burnt offering and the "cereal offering" (זבח), this statement envisages both the sacrifice killed inside the אלם ("vestibule"), in the sacred precinct, as well as the one killed on the tables outside, i.e. surely even in the outer court. The distinction in sanctity will be brought out particularly strongly in the regulations in 46:19–24 for the sacrificial kitchens of the two areas. עולה here too refers to the sacred offering, while זבח includes the cereal offering enjoyed also by the people in the outer court and all its possible subgroups. The implements for the sacrificial slaughterings in both areas are, logically, stored inside the vestibule.

■ **40:43b** The final observation in v 43b surprisingly introduces yet another sacrificial term. קרבן "offering" occurs otherwise in the book of Ezekiel only in 20:28. It therefore need not be called in question here,[7] since it is clearly summarizing by means of a general term all the sacrifices which are prepared on the tables inside and outside. What is said about the tables is concluded with this comprehensive indication of purpose. The reading of 𝔊, which speaks of protective roofs against the rain (note c), could refer only to the tables against the outside walls, tables which are not more closely described, but which surely ought to be explicitly noted in connection with the precise description of the tables inside the vestibule. We have to reckon with a free interpretation on the part of 𝔊.

■ **40:44–46** *2. The two priestly vestries at the inner north and south gates.* Vv 44–46 in their description of the two rooms at the north and south gates of the inner court are much more meager. Their location is given. In spite of Gese, the "outside the gate" should not be emended, on the basis of 𝔊, to "outside the inner court." Only in a very forced way could this be linked with the immediately following "in the inner court" by means of the suggestion that the rooms were still counted as part of the inner court because their entrances led directly into the inner court although they actually lay outside it. By contrast with other passages (40:7, 9, 19[8]), it is not the temple as a whole which is evisaged here, but the north-gate complex which has just been discussed. The two rooms are thought of as inside the inner court, immediately beside the two gates, directly opposite each other. On which side of the gate they lie is not stated. The whole emphasis lies on the ownership designation which follows in vv 45f. The room to the north is allocated to the priests who "see to the service in the 'house'" (שמרי משמרת הבית), the southern one to those who "perform the service at the altar" (שמרי משמרת המזבח). This clearly refers to two categories of priests, both of whom have their room in the area of the inner court and who therefore, with regard to their sanctity, are not subject to any discernible gradation. One can speak of an order of precedence only at the most insofar as here משמרת הבית ("service in the temple") doubtless designates the varied services in the broad sphere of the temple as a whole, whereas משמרת המזבח ("service at the altar") means the sacrificial service in the narrower sense. The problem of this terminology as well as of the relationship to the related chapter, Numbers 18, will have to be discussed when the priesthood is discussed in context, i.e. in 44:6–31.[9]

■ **40:46b** The same is true of the observation in v 46b, which, as an explanatory secondary interpretation, equates the second-named group of priests with the Zadokites, who among the Levites are particularly chosen to approach Yahweh in service.

Aim

Both additions to the visionary guidance narrative aim, each in their own way, to bring elucidation to the picture of the temple seen by the prophet. Vv 38–43 are emphatically interested in the slaughtering of the sacrificial animals and in the place where this happens. In addition, there is discernible the fairly sharp distinction between what happens in the holy of holies and what happens in the outer court. While the great guidance vision still betrayed no awareness of such distinctions but was wholly orientated towards the location of the holy of

7 Roland de Vaux, *Studies in Old Testament Sacrifice* (Cardiff: University of Wales Press, 1964), 30; Herrmann; Bertholet-Galling and Fohrer-Galling.

8 On this see Gese, 125f.

9 See below pp. 453–463.

holies, here inner differentiations are discernible which there were at the most foreseen in the gradation of the ascent to the holy of holies.

On the other hand the addition in vv 44–46, which, for the first time, introduces the men who will perform the service in the temple, indicates differences in the service but no difference in the evaluation of those who perform the service. Both priestly groups have their vestries, symmetrically arranged with regard to each other, in the inner court. In their person it at once becomes clear that God establishes his sanctuary so that men can, within it, become ready to care for and obediently to attend to (משמרת "service") the realm of the sacred.

3. The Annexes of the Temple and Its Surroundings: The Area to the West Behind the Temple

Bibliography

Leroy Waterman
"The Damaged 'Blueprints' of the Temple of Solomon," *JNES* 2 (1943): 284–294.

41

5 **And he measured the wall of the temple: six cubits, and the breadth of the side chamber[a]: four[b] cubits round[c] about the temple. 6/ And the side chambers, side chamber above[a] side chamber, [thirty-] three times[b]. And terraces(?)[c] against**

41:
5 5a צלע, first of all "rib, side," is here a technical building term referring to the annexes at the side (and the back) of the temple. So already 1 Kgs 6:8. In the plural the word will refer to the individual rooms of the side annexes.

b 𝔖 has misread 𝔐 ארבע as שבע.

c The overloaded סביב סביב לבית סביב of 𝔐 is rendered in 𝔊 by the terse *κυκλόθεν* (𝔏^{W} *in gyro*). 𝔖 says more fully כד הדר ביתא, 𝔙 *undique per circuitum domus,* while 𝔗 סחור סחור מקף לביתא סחור סחור even surpasses the verbosity of 𝔐. The analogous, even if somewhat differently arranged expression in v 10 prevents an overhasty abbreviation of the text, which one would rather, however, (with Herrmann) read in the arrangement of v 10.

6 6a על-אל cf. 1:17 note a.

b 𝔐 שלוש ושלשים is also attested by the versions, of which also 𝔊 𝔙 take the following פעמים of 𝔐 as a dual and render it by *δίς* and *bis* respectively. This explains the at first puzzling figure of thirty-six in 𝔏^{W} as the sum of thirty and "twice" three. The addition חדא עיסרי בסידרא (eleven per row) of 𝔗 distributes the thirty-three structural units explicitly among three stories. In spite of its impeccable attestation, however, the "thirty-three times" of 𝔐 is incomprehensible. Since it is impossible to envisage a thirty-three story building in view of the three-storied nature of the annex attested by v 7 as well as by 𝔗, one would have to translate the אל of 𝔐 quite generally with "by" and (with 𝔗) calculate a total of thirty-three rooms. Herod's temple, according to *b. Mid.* IV 3, had thirty-eight such rooms. But what then is the meaning of פעמים? Thus the suggestion accepted by Herrmann, Bertholet-Galling, Fohrer-Galling, Gese that ושלשים is a secondary addition (intended to indicate that thirty was the total number of rooms?) is highly probable.

c 𝔐 באות must contain a building term corresponding in content to the מגרעות of 1 Kgs 6:6 without one therefore having to emend the text to מגרעות (so Toy, Bertholet-Galling, Fohrer-Galling). That no further conclusions can be drawn from *διάστημα*, with which 𝔊 translates both terms, as to the Hebrew original because in 𝔊 we have a colorless expression of difficulty which is used to translate the most varied unknown words (v 8; 42:5, 12f;

the inner wall of the temple for the side chambers round about. so that there might be supports[d], but no supports[d] in the wall of the temple (itself). 7/ And <the widening by the "gallery">[a] which led higher and higher up the side chambers, for the temple was enclosed[b] right to the top and round about the temple—thus the temple grew broader towards the top. <From the lowest>[c] story one climbs through the middle one to the topmost[d] one. 8/ And <the . . . of the temple>[a]—a <raised pavement>[b] round

45:2; 48:15, 17) has been shown by Gese, 164. According to Driver, "Ezekiel," 305, באות is to be understood on the basis of בוא "insets, intakes in the wall," while מגרעות from the opposite perspective speaks of "withdrawals." The combination of perspectives is shown by 𝔙 *eminentia quae ingrederentur* (*per parietem*).

d אחוזים will also contain a technical building term, since the connection of the masculine participle of אחז with the feminine צלעות is scarcely possible. 𝔙 *ut continerent et non attingerent parietem.* 𝔗 paraphrases very broadly but with correct understanding למיהוי רישי שריתא נייחין על זיזיא ולא יהוין שרייתא מעברן בכותלי ביתא "so that the ends of the beams rested on ledges but do not penetrate the walls of the temple." So too the phraseology of 1 Kgs 6:6 with the verb לבלתי אחז בקירות הבית.

7 7a The form-critical structure of the present enumeration would lead us to expect a noun at the beginning such as is afforded by 𝔊 *καὶ τὸ εὖρος* (𝔏[W] *et latitudo*), 𝔙 *et platea,* 𝔗 ופותיא. The ורחב which should be read on the basis of these (Gese) then finds its more precise explanation in v 7aβ על כן רחב לבית. As a consequence of this reading ורחב, however, the verbal form ונסבה (for an explanation of it see Bauer-Leander §58t) of 𝔐 becomes suspect. 𝔗 מסיבתא suggests a noun here too. The מְסִבָּה which can be reconstructed on the assumption of a graphically easily understandable scribal error, and to which the ה which has been wrongly linked in 𝔐 with the preceding word should be added as the article, occurs in *B. Mid.* IV 5a as the name of the ramp which leads round three sides of the temple building to the upper story. This element, too, is then more precisely explained in the כי-clause of v 7aα by the participle מוסב.

b Literally: the house was surrounded. An emendation to במוסף הבאות (Driver, "Ezekiel," 305—בסוסף here is surely a printer's error) is unnecessary.

c 𝔐 (התחתונה) וכן is meaningless. 𝔊 *ἐκ* (*τῶν κάτωθεν*) 𝔏[W] 𝔙 *de* (*inferioribus*) 𝔖 (לתחת) מן point to the original reading (התחתונה) מן.

d 𝔐 על העליונה לתיכונה is attested by 𝔙 𝔗, while 𝔊 *ἐπὶ τὰ ὑπερῷα καὶ ἐκ τῶν μέσων ἐπὶ τὰ τριώροφα* (𝔏[W] *in superiora et de mediis in tertia lacunaria*) and, still more forcefully, 𝔖 למצליתא ומן מצליתא לעליתא give a fuller interpretation. The more succinct form of 𝔐, however, can certainly contain the original text, in which case concerning על consideration should be given to the possibility of confusion with אל as established in 1:17 note a. In place of the somewhat difficult לתיכונה, which must certainly be understood along the lines of 𝔗 באורח מציעיתא, Gese suggests the reading בתיכונה.

8 8a In view of the form-critical structure of the section vv 5–12 (see below), 𝔐 וראיתי, even though it is attested by 𝔖 𝔗 𝔙, can scarcely be correct. When 𝔊 translates as *καὶ τὸ θραελ* it can scarcely have had before it the straightforward וראיתי. Rather it tran-

about, the foundation site[c] of the side chambers: a full[d] measuring rod, six cubits, was <its top terrace> (?)[e]. 9/ <And> the thickness[a] of the outer wall of the side chamber: five cubits. And the open space[b] <between the>[c] side cham-

scribes by it, analogously to the *αιλαμ* and *θεε* of chapter 40, a word which it did not understand but considered to be a noun (𝔏[W] *thraniel,* 𝔊[L] *θροελ*, 𝔊[V] *θροαια*, 𝔊[449] *θροαιλ*, 𝔊[407] *θραιλ*, 𝔊[130] *θρααιλ*). A comparison with 𝔐, which will therefore have arisen as a result of the transposition of consonants and the loss by haplography of the final consonant, suggests תראל or תראיל (graphically more likely than the תרעל reconstructed by Cornill "with absolute certainty" and also accepted by Gese). This word is probably a building term (a foreign loanword? cf. אראל). It has not so far been explained. The meaning of the structural element designated by it can be assumed, however, from what follows.

b 𝔐 גבה "height" is also presupposed by the versions. One might, however, wonder whether the word here, analogous to the רחב "widening" of v 7, is to be understood as "heightening." Yet the suggestion made by Siegfried and then adopted by Herrmann, Bertholet-Galling, Fohrer-Galling, Gese may be right, that what is meant here is גַּבָּה (cf. the *Γαββαθά* of Jn 19:13), to be derived from גב "back, boss" attested in various expressions in Ezekiel (1:18; 10:12; 6:24, 31, 39; see also 43:13). If in what follows אַצִּילָה (note e) were to be read and this were to be related to גַּבָּה and not to *θραελ* whose gender we do not know, then this feminine form would be also grammatically necessary and be preferable to the masculine גֹּבַהּ.

c Q מוסדות is to be preferred to K מיסדות since we are here dealing with the description of the foundations and not with a measurement "from the foundation" which would demand a corresponding term for an end point.

d 𝔐 מלו is with MSS, Eb 22, Edd to be understood as מלא ("phonetic writing," Bauer-Leander §67f). Elsewhere this is always connected with measurement terms (cf. מלא קומתו 1 Sam 28:20; מלא החבל 2 Sam 8:2; מלא רחב Is 8:8).

e 𝔐 אַצִּילָה masculine plural in 13:18, feminine plural in Jer 38:12 in the sense of "joint, shoulder." In the present passage it will be a technical building term and the reading אַצִּילָה is to be preferred. So Bertholet-Galling "side measurement"; Fohrer-Galling, on the basis of K. Elliger, "Die grossen Tempelsakristeien im Verfassungsentwurf des Ezechiel (42:1ff)" in *Festschrift für A. Alt* (Tübingen: Mohr, 1953), 92, "top terrace." Here too 𝔊 offers the colorless *διάστημα* (𝔏[W] *intervallorum*), see v 6 note c. 𝔙 *spatio,* 𝔗 רוח. Driver, "Linguistic Problems," 184, wishes to read אֶצְלָהּ "beside it."

9 9a 𝔐 רחב. 𝔊 𝔏[W] 𝔙 𝔖 (but not 𝔗) begin with the copula, in line with the style of the enumeration hitherto. Thus ורחב should be read.

b 𝔐 ואשר מנח. The אשר still reveals the feeling for the original verbal character of מנח "that which is left free." 𝔊 *τὰ ἀπόλοιπα*. 𝔏[W] *residua.* 𝔗 אתר שביק still seems to be aware of the original nominal significance of אשר: "the space left free." So too Driver,

bers of the temple. 10/ and the cham-
bers: twenty cubits broad right round the
temple. 11/ And <the doors>[a] of the side
chamber on to the open space (were
arranged as follows): a door to the north
and a door to the south. And the breadth
of <the walls>[b] of the open space: five
cubits round about.
12 **And "the building"[a] which lay to the west**
opposite[b] the "restricted area"[c]: the
depth (was) seventy cubits. And the wall
of the building[a]: five cubits thick round
about. And its length: ninety cubits.
13 **And he measured[a] the[b] temple: one hun-**
dred cubits long, and the restricted area
and the "building"[c] and its walls: one
hundred cubits deep, 14/ and the breadth
of the front of the temple and the re-
stricted area to the east: one hundred
cubits. 15a/ And he measured[a] the
breadth of the "building" alongside[b] the
"restricted area" at the <back>[c] [and its

"Linguistic Problems," 184, referring to Akkadian *ašru.* Furthermore מנח then appears twice on its own in v 11. The אשר in v 9, however, is not to be rejected. 𝔙 scarcely knows what to do with מנח, translating it in v 9 by *interior,* in v 11, on the other hand, twice by *ad orationem* (so too Σ εἰς προσευχήν and τῆς προσευχῆς).

c In 𝔊 ἀνὰ μέσον (𝔏[W] *inter media*) corresponds to 𝔐 בית. Since the ובין of v 10 demands something corresponding to it in v 9, we should assume that בית is a corruption of בין. In the second downstroke of the ת in 𝔐, however, there is concealed a part of the article of צלעות now lost in 𝔐 (attested in 𝔊). Read הצלעות. In view of the lack of clarity in 𝔐 of v 9b, 𝔊 has expressed this part of the verse abruptly as a counterpart to v 9a. Outer wall (אסתא . . . דלבר) and inner wall (ודמן לגו) are, according to this (in contrast to v 5), five cubits thick.

11 11a 𝔐 ופתח. 𝔊 Καὶ αἱ θύραι (𝔏[W] *et ianuae*) makes the text easier, since in what follows it refers to a door on each side of the temple. Against the view of most commentators, however, 𝔊 is not to be followed, since, in the first instance, 𝔐 is envisaging only one side of the temple and extends the point of view to the two sides only in v 11aβγ.

b 𝔐 מקום is incomprehensible. Driver, "Linguistic Problems," 184, understands it as the equivalent of אשר "place" in v 9. The equally puzzling rendering of 𝔊 τοῦ φωτός (𝔏[W] *lumen*) is, however, on the track of the original text. Since φῶς in 𝔊 42:7, 10, 12 is used to render גדר or גדרת, here too 𝔊 must have had גדר in its original Hebrew text (Gese). This illuminates the text completely even if the way in which the text became corrupted to the מקום of 𝔐 remains obscure.

12 12a 𝔐 בנין. The masculine form is protected by the masculine suffix in ארכו. See further v 15; 42:1, 5, 10. It should not (against Cornill, Cooke) be emended to the feminine בניה which occurs in v 13. 𝔊 τὸ διορίζον (𝔏[W] *quod* or *qui separat*), corrupted to αἰθρίζον in 𝔊[B], derives the word from the root בין.

b אל–על cf. 1:17 note a.

c 𝔐 גזרה, equated with מנח by 𝔊 and, like it, rendered here and in vv 13–15; 42:1, 10 by τὸ ἀπόλοιπον or τὰ ἀπόλοιπα, in 42:13, like באות (v 6) and אציל (v 8), by διάστημα.

13 13a 𝔐 ומדד see 40:24, 35; 41:15; 42:15.

b 𝔊, with a false assimilation to v 14, κατέναντι (τοῦ οἴκου), 𝔏[W] *contra* (*edem, sic!*).

c 𝔐 here והבניה, see v 12 note a. It is protected by the suffix in קירותיה. 𝔊 here has the equivalents of גזרה and בניה in the plural καὶ τὰ ἀπόλοιπα καὶ τὰ διορίζοντα.

15 15a See v 13 note a.

b 𝔐 אל פני (אל–על, 1:17 note a) "opposite."

c 𝔐 אֲחֲרֶיהָ is better read as אַחֲרֶיהָ with Eb 22. Referring to persons, אָחֹר is found in the plural in 8:16.

embankments on both sides][d]: one hundred cubits.

d 𝔐 אתוקיהא is not to be separated from the אתיק in 42:3, 5 but refers, also from the point of view of content, to the אתיקים mentioned there, see below and also v 16 note c. The remarkable *plene* writing of the suffix, however, which recalls the forms in 1QIsa[a] (Beer-Meyer [[3]1966] §9,3; see, e.g., עליהא Is 34:11; 37:33; 42:5; 45:12; 66:10; against Bauer-Leander §29w and §67f which speak of a "scribal error"), as well as the fact that here one and the same measurement (one hundred cubits) is given for the measurement in a second dimension, make it likely that in ואתוקיהא מפו ומפו we have an addition by a second hand.

Form

In the conclusion to the great guidance vision in 40:48–41:4, the temple had been described with its vestibule with their internal measurements. Nothing was yet disclosed about its external measurements and how these fitted into the temple area as a whole. 41:5–15a here provide the necessary supplementation. At the same time they answer the question how the square which, on the basis of the symmetry of the square layout of the total area, was to be expected immediately behind the temple building itself was formed. In this way vv 13–15a, with their total measurement of the two areas, form the obvious conclusion of the unit vv 5–15a with its individual descriptions in vv 5–12.

Stylistically vv 5--15a are very different from the introductory guidance vision. There is no further mention of the prophet being led by the man, although it remains impossible to visualize how the prophet from the last position reached by him in 41:1, the inner room of the היכל, could have followed the measurements of the outer and back sides of the temple. Thus, in vv 5–15a we are dealing with an independent section of text, stylistically different from 40:1–41:4.

On the other hand, however, the desire to connect the section with what precedes cannot be mistaken. The very first word reports an act of measurement (וימד "and he measured"). The subject of this measuring action is not introduced anew but is presupposed as known. The measuring process is mentioned again in the summary conclusion (vv 13, 15a) where the consecutive perfect used there, ומדד ("and he measured"), has its parallel in 40:24, 35.

In the complex bracketed by the וימד ("and he measured") in v 5 and the ומדד ("and he measured") in v 13, however, there can be seen yet another stylistic deviation from the guidance vision. Although in vv 5–12 a considerable profusion of very varied measured objects are listed, the verb מדד ("to measure") is not used again in this middle section.. The individual structural elements and their measurements are, rather, described in a consistent nominal sentence style which in 𝔐 is broken only in vv 6b and 7 (on 𝔐 v 8 see note a) by subordinate verbal clauses. Thus vv 5–12 give the impression of being a "catalogue of individual structural elements with their construction and their measurements" (Gese). In complete contrast to the great guidance vision, there is discernible in this presentation no movement towards a climax. The whole is dominated by sheer statistical factuality.

Setting

If one inquires about the origin of the section vv 5–15a, one is forced by considerations of content to the conclusion that in spite of its stylistically different structure, it cannot be separated from 40:1–37, 47–49; 41:1–4. The guidance vision had revealed the temple area as a great, harmonically shaped whole in which specific measurements played a dominant role. At decisive points, however, such as the giving of the total measurement of the temple or the question of the structure of the western part of the temple layout, it left open points which precisely cried out for supplementary information. What is specified in 41:5–15a fits, from the point of view of content, precisely into what one expects from the guidance vision and supplies what is lacking exactly as one would expect on the basis of the vision.[1] So, in spite of the great stylistic differences, one can assume behind the present section the same hand as that from which the guidance vision also comes.

One would then, of course, wish to ask why the measurements of 41:5–15a have not also been included in the great guidance vision. To this it may be answered that the guidance vision aims at the rhythm of the two times three gates and the goal of the seventh structure reached in the tripartite temple building and moves in a consciously structured trend towards the center formed by the holy of holies—a trend which would be disturbed if, for example, there followed even the move to the בנין ("building") (41:12) which lay behind the temple. Thus the description of the structural elements which lay outside the temple remained outside the guidance vision. The latter reached its objective at the entry to the holy of holies. It is in its factual statements certainly very consciously expanded by this section, which has no further significant emphasis and reports quite technically in the manner of a catalogue and whose only sign of slight disruption is from the measurement statements which frame it.

Interpretation

■ **41:5** While the description of the gates failed to give the measurements of the thickness of the side walls, these are now measured in the case of the temple building without its being clear at what point the measuring process takes place. The thickness of six cubits, which is to be assumed also for the rear west wall, corresponds to the thickness given in 41:1 for the wall between vestibule and היכל. This indicates that the אלם ("vestibule"), whose "pillars," i.e. front walls on each side, have a thickness of only five cubits (40:48), was not originally reckoned to be part of the temple structure. Thus, as already mentioned, Noth reckons for Solomon's temple with a hall open at the front.[2]

The next structural element is "the rib" (צלע "side chamber"). This word designates side annexes to the inner temple described in 40:48–41:4. צלעות are also mentioned in connection with Solomon's temple in 1 Kgs 6:5f, 8(15f).[3] The view of Möhlenbrink that the structures round the temple designated in 6:5f, 8 by this name belonged only to Zerubbabel's temple and are to be understood on the basis of Persian palace building (*apadana*) is rejected by Noth.[4] With Möhlenbrink, however, he believes he ought to follow the view of Friedrich that these "ribs" (the term could, according to Friedrich, have been taken over from ship-building) in Solmon's temple were of wooden construction. The singular צלע there refers to each of the three wooden stories built into the temple. 1 Kgs 6:8 may suggest that the lowest of these was an open gallery. The conception of Ezekiel 41 is different from that. When v 9 gives the thickness of the outer wall of the צלע as five cubits, then, even though there is no specific mention of the material, it is a massive stone structure that is envisaged. Similarly in the Ezekiel plan the light wooden wall which in Solomon's temple separated the דביר from the main hall of the temple has become "petrified" into a wall two cubits thick (see above on 41:3).

In addition in Ezekiel 41 one is struck by a lack of terminological clarity. V 5b speaks of צלע in the singular. This singular recurs in vv 9 and 11. In between, however, vv 6f, 8b change to a plural mode of expression. In this connection, v 6 shows that here the singualr צלע, exactly as in 1 Kings 6, describes each of the three superimposed stories. The return from the plural to the singular is given no further motivation. The reference to צלע in the singular fits completely the observation which we made in relation to the guidance vision, namely that everywhere we have only ground-plan measurements. In the passages which use the plural צלעות, on the other hand, what are envisaged are the stories which are built upwards. The first passage which uses the plural צלעות, vv 6f, is noteworthy in another respect. In both parts of v 5 we find measurement details. This type of description continues from v 8 to the end of the section. In vv 6f, on the other hand, no measurements are given. Instead there is a more detailed description of the position of, construction of and ways of access to the צלעות. May one also draw attention to the more remarkable phenomenon that in the case of the measurements, which proceed from inside to outside, in v 5 in a clear sequence first the wall of the temple is measured, then the inside measurement of the צלע, but that the outer wall of the צלע

1 On this see figure 6 (p. 376).
2 Noth, *Könige*, 111.
3 On this see the detailed discussion by Noth, *Könige*, 113ff, 135f.
4 Möhlenbrink, *Tempel*, 141–153.

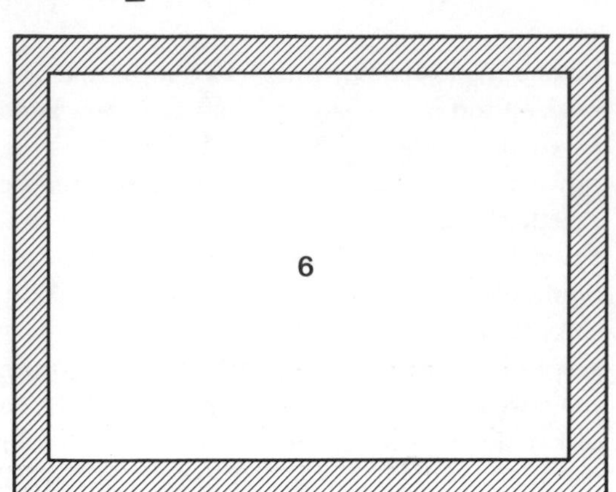

Fig. 6
The additional details about the temple building and the area to the side of and behind it (41:5–15a)

1. The temple wall (41:5a)
2. The side structure (41:5b)
3. The outer wall of the side structure (41:9a)
4. The open space at the side (41:9b)
5. The wall of the open space (41:11b)
6. 'The building' (41:12)
7. The restricted area of 41:12f
8 The restricted area to the east of 41:14

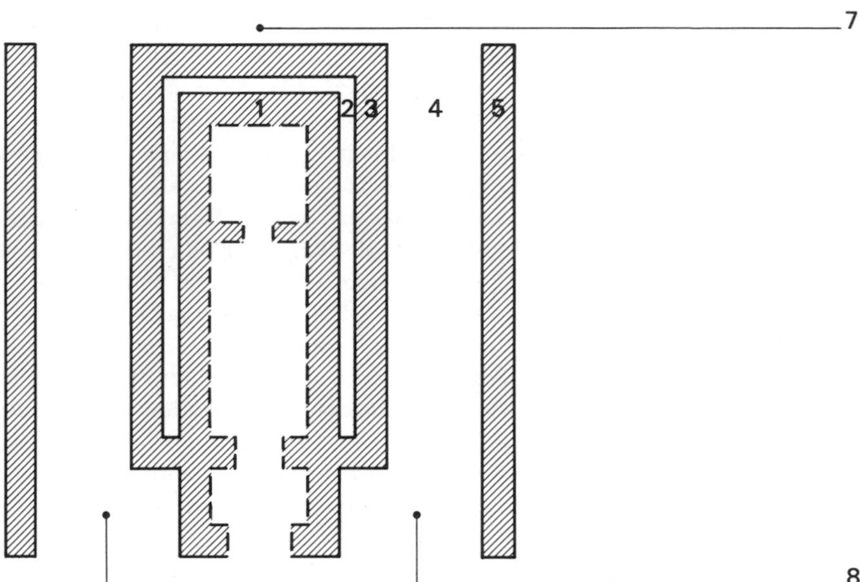

follows only in v 9 after, meantime, in vv 6–8, quite different elements are mentioned, the relationship of which to the sequence of description from inside to outside is difficult to see? Thus one cannot entirely suppress the suspicion that the description, which is otherwise quite clear in its sequence of measurements of the temple area (vv 5–11) and of the adjoining western area behind the temple building (v 12), a description which confines itself to giving the ground measurements, has been the object of secondary amplification which adds other elements. A trace of such secondary editing might also still be found in v 9 where the plural צלעות occurs.

■ **41:6** V 6 introduces the fact that there are three צלעות, just as in 1 Kgs 6:6, even if the way this is expressed is different. By the insertion of the numeral thirty (note b) a later hand may have given expression to his reckoning of the number of the individual rooms in the three stories of the annex. *b. Mid.* IV 3a speaks quite explicitly of "chambers" (תאים)[5] as the individual units of the annex and is able also to indicate the division of these amongst the three sides of the temple concerned. Of the thirty-eight rooms enumerated by *b. Mid.*, fifteen (i.e. three rows of five) are superimposed along the north and south walls, while the eight rooms of the west (rear) wall are divided three in each of the two lower stories and two in the top story. In this connection, the term צלע is no longer used by *b. Mid.* As in 1 Kgs 6:6, *b. Mid.* IV 4 is further aware that the upper rooms are broader than the lower ones. Ezek 41:6 does not mention this, but does mention what is also according to 1 Kgs 6:6 the reason for this broadening. The roof beams of the צלעות are not let in to the temple wall, which for reasons of sanctity was not to be damaged, but were built on the ledges of the temple wall which thus three times recedes by a cubit and is only three cubits thick at the top.[6]

■ **41:7** The sense of v 7 is confirmed by *b. Mid.* IV 5, where מְסִבָּה (here "gallery"), as in I 9d, describes a passage which "turns" (סבב) its direction as it goes. The noun associated with it, רחב "broadening," is used here in a sense different from its usual meaning. This necessitates the addition in v 7aα of the involved explanation of what is meant. Deviating from Galling, who wishes to locate the rising passageway in the interior of the צלעות, it should be assumed with Gese that it is a staircase or ramp running round the outside of the temple and "broadening" it.[7] Once again, *b. Mid.* IV 5a knows (in addition to Ezekiel) that the מסבה which leads upwards begins in the northeast corner of the temple, that is on the right as one stands in front of the temple building, leads along the north side, turns south along the rear of the temple and on the south side comes eastwards to reach the "top story" (עליה). The plan in Ezekiel says nothing of all this. Here this passageway serves only to reach the upper צלעות. Solomon's temple does not have this outer ramp or stairway. There the upper צלעות are reached, according to 1 Kgs 6:8 by לולים (Noth "trap doors"). The fact that the outer ramp or stair is mentioned in Ezekiel 41 before the outer wall of the צלע in v 9 is strange and, as already mentioned, leads one to suspect the originality of this information in the text.

■ **41:8** The same misgivings could, to begin with, arise against the information in v 8, where the building term תראל (note a), which has not so far been explained, must be understood, on the basis of what follows, as a designation for a raised foundation. The plural צלעות is suspect here too, while the mention of a measurement might arouse confidence. Admittedly one is surprised by the double measurement in which, moreover, an identical measurement is denoted in two ways (measuring rod alongside cubit measure [on this see above on 40:5]). One would actually expect such doubling of expression least of all in the "catalogue" of 41:5ff, which is characterized by its extreme functionalism. Thus the question arises whether the words מוסדות הצלעות מלו הקנה ("the foundation site of the side chambers: a full measuring rod") do not represent a secondary expansion. What then follows immediately after the statement about the גבה ("raised pavement") (note b), namely שש אמות אצילה ("six cubits was its top terrace"), would then, including its feminine suffix, acquire an obvious relationship. The thought, both in the basic text and in its possible secondary expansion, is of the elevated foundation on which the "house" (cf. the ten steps in 40:49) and, according to the supposed expansion, also the צלעות stand. In the addition then surely a height measurement for the foundation is given. It is identical with the measurement of the founda-

5 On this see above on 40:7.

6 On the technical term כאות ("terraces") (corresponding to מגרעות in 1 Kgs 6:6) see note c; on אחוזים ("supports"), note d.

7 See also Driver, "Ezekiel," 305.

tion which occurs also in *b. Mid.* IV 6, which is described there by the word אטם.[8] In the case of the אצילה ("top terrace") of the unexpanded text one could also envisage a measurement taken on the surface: six cubits till the falling away of the base of the foundation. The whole of v 8, however, because of its position before v 9 is not entirely above suspicion with regard to its originality (in this place?).

■ **41:9a** Now at last v 9a produces the information which has long been awaited as the continuation of v 5. With a thickness of five cubits for the outside wall of the צלע, the measurement of fifteen cubits is arrived at for the exterior of the temple building (including the צלע), and this, added on both sides to the width of the inner hall of the temple, gives a total breadth for the building of fifty cubits. The length of the structure, which, according to 40:48–41:4, as far as the inner hall was concerned was eighty-five cubits, is increased by the rear wall with צלע to one hundred cubits, thus giving for the temple building the total of one hundred by fifty cubits.

■ **41:9b–10** However the measuring still continues at the sides in an outward direction. The area left free on both sides of the building (on אשר מנח "open space" see note b), the "freedom" (Galling), a kind of fire gap (Elliger), reveals a width of twenty cubits. The closer definition of this width as being "between the צלעות of the temple and the chambers" raises doubts not only because of the plural צלעות but equally because of the mention of the "chambers" (לשכות). Neither in this section nor in the following is anything said about chambers, which are supposed to lie parallel to the long side of the temple building. In addition, this information clashes seriously with the reference to the "wall" which shuts off the מנח ("open space") and which is mentioned correctly in v 11b as the next structural element in the continuing outward movement. Is such a wall supposed to rise directly in front of the chambers mentioned here, which then would have to be located at distance not of twenty but of twenty-five cubits? Thus both observations make it likely that here we have a secondary expansion, which, from a knowledge of later circumstances, knows of chambers on the sides of the square temple area. The priestly vestries described in 42:1ff lie further to the west.[9]

■ **41:11a** But before the last measurement in the progression from the wall of the sanctuary outwards, v 11a mentions in addition the exits which lead from the צלע, here once again in the singular, into the מנח ("open space"). Galling notes, correctly, that nothing is said here of a stair down from the higher level to the lower one of the area round the temple, and this seems to suggest once more that what is envisaged here is a ground plan which does not yet take account of the present text of v 8. On each of the long sides of the temple a door leads to the outside. In the case of Solomon's temple 1 Kgs 6:8 mentions only a single "entrance" (פתח) to the middle story on the right side of the building. It is reached by means of the לולים (Noth "trap doors") mentioned there. Waterman's idea that the entrances of the annex did not lead outside but into the inner room of the temple, and the conclusion drawn from this, that in the case of Solomon's temple it was a question primarily of a treasure chamber, have rightly found no echo. It is clearly contradicted not least by the careful treatment of the temple's outer walls in which not even holes for beams could be made.

■ **41:11b** The reference to the five cubit thick boundary wall (note b) concludes the description of the side areas of the temple and its annexes. The addition of the side area, twice twenty-five cubits, to the width of the temple, fifty cubits, produces here too, the figure of one hundred cubits which is then explicitly cited later in the total measurement.

■ **41:12** First of all, however, in v 12 the necessary information is given about the building of the same width and length which lies to the west. As the principal structure here, there is mentioned a building of unusually large dimensions and described by the quite colorless descriptive expression בנין ("building"). Since its larger measure-

8 Holtzmann: "The part of the structure which blocks up the excavations; the foundation wall, the foundation cf. Par III 6."

9 See further the discussion by K. Elliger, "Die grossen Tempelsakristeien im Verfassungsentwurf des Ezechiel (42:1ff)" in *Festschrift für A. Alt* (Tübingen: Mohr, 1953), 83.

ment is given as ninety cubits and its smaller one as seventy cubits and since the wall is of five cubits, one arrives at an outside measurement of eighty cubits by one hundred. Since it is more particularly stated that it lay on the western side opposite the גזרה ("restricted area"), there emerges the picture of a building lying broadside on opposite the temple with a depth of eighty cubits, thus almost filling one hundred cubits square. In front of it lies the area known as גזרה ("the restricted area"). Apart from Ezek 41:12–15; 42:1, 10, 13 where it refers to this area lying beside the temple building, גזרה occurs only in Lam 4:7, a sentence which can no longer be interpreted with certainty. גזר means "cut off, cut up." Thus גזרה is usually understood as "blocked off area" (Gesenius-Buhl), "detached area" (Koehler-Baumgartner), *spatium separatum* (Zorell). In later Hebrew it can describe a building level or a balcony-like annex to a building[10] (see also Arabic *jazīra* "island," i.e. detached land). Does it, then, like *τέμενος* in Greek, describe an area inaccessible to the ordinary man without consecration? Once again the text provides no further information. The analogy of the terms בנין "building" (used in 40:5 for the walls) and מנח "open space" would make it probable that here, too, we have not a specifically defined term like a proper name but a descriptive word. The fact that the term is used in v 14 also for an area in front of the temple supports this understanding of it.

■ **41:13–15a** Finally, in vv 13–15a the total measurement of the area described in vv 5–12 is undertaken and defined, a process which could still be rather indeterminate with regard to the measurements. First of all in v 13 are given the measurements of the depth of the two squares to the west of the inner court: 1) The measurement of the depth of the temple which could already be reckoned on the basis of the information in 40:48–41:4 and 41:5, 9a as one hundred cubits; 2) the measurement of the depth of the area behind the temple building for whose גזרה lying in front of the "building" (here described in free variation as בניה) a depth of twenty cubits could thus be calculated. This corresponds to the "open space" (מנח) at the side of the temple. In vv 14, 15a there follows 1) the measurement of the breadth of the hundred cubit square of the temple building. These hundred cubits, too, could be calculated from the information in 40:48–41:4 and 41:5, 9f, 11b. It will be noticed that in the description of the front of the temple building it is not בית, צלע, מנח and גדר which are listed as elements of this front, but only בית and גזרה. This suggests that the side annex (צלה) of the temple (בית) does not come forward as far as the אלם, but flanks only the היכל and the קדש קדשים, so that at the front on either side of the אלם there is still an open space to which is added also the forward extension of the מנח. Like the space behind the temple, this too is described as a "restricted area (גזרה)." Once more, in the fact that the צלע does not come forward as far as the אלם, the original restriction of the temple building to היכל and קדש קדשים perhaps is revealed. 2) The measurement of the breadth of the square lying to the west of and behind the temple building. Its width of one hundred cubits was also deducible from the earlier information about the בנין ("building") which occupies its whole width (v 12aβb). By way of closer definition it is simply stated that it lay behind the restricted area.

■ **41:5–15a** After this survey of details, it must be asked here too to what extent what has been described in vv 5–15a differs from the Solomonic temple which had been destroyed in 587. In this connection, observations which have been made in connection with the great guidance vision can be reaffirmed. The connection with *what has been asserted by the tradition* is closest here too in the case of the innermost part of the temple building. This has been discussed in the context of 40:48–41:4. The connection, however, becomes weaker the further away one moves from this sacred center. Thus in 41:5–15a, the annex (צלע), which in Solomon's temple was undoubtedly a wooden structure, is firmly incorporated into the structure which is to be accommodated to the ideal measurement of fifty by one hundred cubits. This is clear not only from the fact that it is extended by strong stone walls (as can be concluded from the measurement of the thickness), but also from the fact that its measurement figures become a fixed element in the total measurement of the building which is orientated towards the figures fifty and a hundred. Admittedly the time-honored measurements for the inner room are carefully pre-

10 Levy, *Wörterbuch*.

served. They are, however, no longer the relevant figures for the layout of the new plan. The harmonization with the new, harmonious symmetry of the figures is achieved by means of a powerful arrangement of the annexes which are now supplied with imposing outside walls.

A strongly stylized arrangement must also have been imposed on the hundred cubit square area behind the temple building, four fifths of which is covered by the בנין ("building"). If one follows the most probable assumption that the location of the holy of holies is on the sacred rock of the temple area (Schmidt), then if one keeps in mind the natural slope of the temple hill towards the Tyropoeon valley and does not presuppose the great terrace of Herod's temple preserved in the present-day *ḥaram,* there is no room for an area of one hundred cubits behind the temple building. This is not given sufficient expression in the discussion by Galling.[11] If 42:1–14 correctly takes up the conceptions of chapters 40f, then it is presupposed there that the hundred cubit square area lying behind the temple is on the same level as the inner court. The enormous בנין ("building"), whose dimensions exceed quite considerably the great House of the Forest of Lebanon in Solomon's palace precinct (according to 1 Kgs 7:2, one hundred cubits by fifty) and whose roof would have to have been supported by a still greater number of rows of pillars than was the case there, is clearly the product of an embarrassing situation. Its intention is to forbid all access to the area behind the temple, that is behind the back of the Lord of the holy of holies who is facing forward i.e. eastwards. Hence there is never, even in the latest expansions, the slightest indication of the use of this, the most enormous structure in the whole temple area.

This does not, however, prevent one from asking what—certainly in much smaller dimensions—could have stood in the pre-exilic temple on the west side of the temple building. Since, in the account of the building of temple and palace in 1 Kings 6f, no information is given about this, the assumption has at most a claim to a certain probability that it is there that the element described as פרבר in 1 Chr 26:18 is to be located. Admittedly in the interpretation of the פרבר opinions diverge hopelessly. While some associate it with the פרורים of 2 Kgs 23:11, a building "at the entrance to the temple by the chamber of the chamberlain Nathan-melech" in which the sun horses were kept which Josiah then removed, Rudolph, for example, following Yahuda, keeps the two expressions severely apart.[12] With Rothstein and van Selms he finds in פרבר, on the basis of late Hebrew and Aramaic,[13] the description of a square. Alongside the four Levitical gate-keepers who were placed on the west side of the temple area on the "road" (מסלה), two more were delegated for the פרבר. The consideration of what is said in Ezek 41:12 might rather suggest that west of the Solomonic temple building we should reckon with a structure which might then here, under the influence of the schematizing measurements, have been expanded to quite improbably large proportions. Also the unmistakable function of this building as a barrier makes it appear as not impossible that precisely at this spot an earlier misuse of the place, such as is discernible in 2 Kgs 23:11, had to be warded off as forcefully as possible. But all the discussions are here moving in the realm of supposition.

If we also take into consideration the information about Herod's temple,[14] then there is no trace whatsoever of this large western structure. It seems, therefore, not to have become important for the practical needs of the second temple. This could confirm from hindsight that the בנין ("building") of 41:12 fulfills no genuine useful function but has been constructed, on theological grounds, as an element for blocking off the western side. Something of this function as a barrier may also have been reflected in the naming of the open intervening strip in front of it as גזרה ("restricted area").

Aim

41:5–15a is fully integrated into the plan which has become discernible behind the guidance vision. Thus for the "language" of the measurement calculations and the way in which they are expressed reference should be made back to what was said there.

In this connection it is particularly clear that the structure of the temple building too, with all the conservative preservation of the measurements of its inner rooms and,

11 Bertholet-Galling, XXI.
12 Rudolph, *Chronikbücher,* 172, note a on 1 Chr 26:18.
13 Levy, *Wörterbuch.*
14 See, e.g., the attempted reconstruction of Holtzmann, *Middoth,* Giessener Mischna VIII, and Dalman, "zweite Tempel," 55.

in a certain sense, also of the annexes, has been integrated into the harmonious total structure of the whole temple area. The measurements of its annexes as well as the surrounding side chambers are orientated towards these total measurements.

A new emphasis, not hitherto discernible, is to be detected, on the other hand, in the arrangement of the area to the rear of the temple building. The symmetry discernible with regard to the gates of the three directions other than the west is clearly broken on the western side. What already had to be stated in the context of the guidance vision, namely that the whole arrangement is not orientated towards the middle of the square, where one would then expect to find the altar, is once again explicitly confirmed. The three gates are not orientated towards the geometrical center of the square, but towards the temple which lies on the west side of the inner court. Its rear thus (in contrast to 1 Chr 26:18) has no entrance of its own, no "road" (מסלה) nor a gate in alignment with it. It in fact leaves no place for a building such as the פרורים of 2 Kgs 23:11 in which symbols of a foreign cult could be housed. This western side is blocked off by the restricted area immediately behind the temple building and by the shapeless "structure" which is nowhere explained by means of a particular indication as to its purpose. Here there is presented once again, in a manner impossible to overlook, the idea that one can approach God only face to face but not from behind. The apparently opposite statement of Ex 33:23, according to which Yahweh allows Moses to look back on his majesty (וראית את אחרי "and you shall see my back"), is not speaking about the possibility of approaching God on one's own initiative from behind. It is speaking rather of the particular grace of God which preserves the one who has been called by God at the point where God's burning majesty, which cannot be borne by men, approaches them.

41

4. Wall Decoration and Interior Furnishings of the Temple

15b **And the inner[a] temple (room) and <its outer vestibule>[b] 16/ were <paneled>[a]. And the framed windows[b] and the ledges[c] round about had in their three parts [opposite the ledge][d] round about a wood**

41: 15b a 𝔐 הפנימי has been read by 𝔊 *καὶ αἱ γωνίαι*
15b (𝔏[W] *et anguli*) as הַפִּנּוֹת and been inserted with the copula (1:4 note a).

b 𝔐 ואלמי החצר is attested by 𝔙 𝔗, obviously found difficult by 𝔖 and understood to refer to the vestibules of the gate structure lying against the outer court ופרוסתדא דתרעא דדרתא. The original wording is suggested by 𝔊 *καὶ τὸ αιλαμ τὸ ἐξώτερον* (𝔏[W] *et aela exterius*) which corresponds to והאלם החיצון and, graphically close to 𝔐, should be read as ואלמו החיצון.

16 16a 𝔐 הספים "the thresholds," so 𝔙 *limina* 𝔗 𝔖) is,
on the evidence of 𝔊 *πεφατνωμένα* (𝔏[W] *praetiata* must be a corruption of the *retiata* that follows later), a scribal error for ספונים. In the article of 𝔐 we can see a vestige of the preceding scribal error for החיצון (v 15b note b).

b On חלונים אטמות see 40:16 note a and 40:25 note a. 𝔊 renders here with *θυρίδες δικτυωταί* (𝔏[W] *retiatae* "closed off with netting?").

c אתיק (אתוק), attested only in Ezek 41:15, 16; 42:3, 5, is compared by Driver, "Studies.3," 363f, and "Linguistic Problems," 185, as an Akkadian loan-word, with *mūtaqu* "passageway" (from *etēqu*). Yet, according to Elliger, "grossen Tempelsakristeien," 85, an internal Hebrew derivation from נתק "tear off, cut off" with prosthetic א is perfectly possible, and this would then lead to the meaning "something torn off, cut off" and further to "ledge, step, sharp edge." In the present passage the word can then designate the ledge by which the framework of a window recedes in steps, such as is to be seen on the ivory carving "Woman's Head in a Window" from Nimrud (*AOB* 191, *ANEP* 131) and from Samaria (Watzinger, *Denkmäler,* 1 figure 84 bottom right). 𝔊 *ὑποφαύσεις* (𝔏[W] *subluminaria*) "dormer windows" scarcely assists in the explanation. 𝔗 עתיקיא is obscure and is perhaps, like 𝔙 *ethecas,* a phonetically approximate adaptation of the word which was not understood.

d The antecedent of 𝔐 לשלשתם cannot be discovered with certainty. Most obviously, in view of the grammatical incongruence of the numeral three, one would think of a connection with אתיקים, and this would suggest a depth to the framework of three steps, and for this again the ivories cited in note c could be adduced. The נגד הסף, which is not attested in 𝔊 (𝔏[W]) and therefore doubtless added secondarily, seems on the other hand to represent the interpretation that by שלשתם the three sides of the framework which are opposite the "threshold," i.e. the lowest side, the "ledge" of the window, which surely does not reveal the threefold gradation, are meant. Thus then the illustration cited shows the triple framework only on three sides, with only a simple finish at the bottom.

veneer(?)[e], <from the>[f] floor, however, up to the windows [and the windows] there stretched a . . . veneer (?)[g] 17/ <to>[a] above the (door-) opening[b]. And <in the>[c] inner room and outside and on[d] the whole wall round about, the inner and

e 𝔐 שחיף will once again contain a technical craft term. 𝔙 *stratumque (ligno)*, 𝔗 דחפי ניסרין דארזא "which [referring to the 'threshold'] was covered with planks of cedar," 𝔖 קרם קיסא "paneling of wood" (referring here to a freely added תרעא) all point to wood paneling. Thus Driver, "Ezekiel," 305f, adduces Syriac סחפא "row, layer (of wood, stone)," סחפתא "covering" and Talmudic Aramaic סחף "lay a cover over." He is thus able to make probable a meaning "covered, paneled." The word is then used here as a noun (in contrast to ספונים, not made plural). But עץ is not (against Cooke) to be deleted as a gloss. 𝔊 is strange with ὥστε διακύπτειν, which is taken up again at the end of v 16 in an addition: εἰς τὸ διακύπτειν. That could suggest השקיף and result in an astonishing link with 1 Kgs 6:4. On this see Noth, *Könige*, note f. In addition, 𝔊 (𝔏^{W}), with no support in the tradition, makes a completely new beginning here for the rendering of the עץ: καὶ ὁ οἶκος καὶ τὰ πλησίον (ἐξυλωμένα).

f In place of 𝔐 והארץ, on the basis of 𝔊 καὶ ἐκ τοῦ ἐδάφους (𝔏^{W} *et pavimento*), ומהארץ should be read, thus preparing for the following עד החלונות. 𝔖 ואורכה seems (wrongly) to presuppose in its original a וארכה.

g In 𝔐 והחלנות מכסות one expects now the description of the wall decoration below the windows, corresponding to ספונים and שחיף עץ in what has gone before. But the repeated והחלנות, once again introduced by a copula, intrudes between. Although it is attested by all the versions it is to be regarded as a dittograph (Bertholet-Galling, Fohrer-Galling, Gese). The expected information is concealed in מכסות, in which Galling sees a "paneling" of plaster or wood relief. 𝔊 interprets the two final words of v 16, which are made independent by the inserted והחלנות, on the basis of its understanding of what has gone before, in a free expansion: καὶ αἱ θυρίδες ἀναπτυσσόμεναι τρισσῶς εἰς τὸ διακύπτειν, 𝔏^{W} *et fenestrae replictiles tripliciter ad prospiciendum.* The exact opposite sense is found here by 𝔙 *et fenestrae clausae.* 𝔗 וכוין סתימן. 𝔖 וכוא מכסין.

17 17a The analogy of v 20a suggests that instead of 𝔐 על we should, with 𝔗, read עד.

b The whole passage is not attested by 𝔊 (𝔏^{W}), which admittedly has expanded the end of v 16 in very arbitrary fashion. If it is original (Gese deletes it) it should be regarded as the conclusion of v 16. The space "from the ground to above the door-opening," which has been described from v 16b to here, also appears in v 20, in an identical description, as the area decorated with palms and cherubs.

c 𝔐 ועד, which is attested by 𝔊 𝔙, replaced in 𝔗 by ומן, while 𝔖 simply omits it and links הבית directly to what precedes, is out of place here, where there is no question of indicating a terminal point, and is surely a scribal error for ועל. For the reverse scribal error see note a.

d על-אל cf. 1:17 note a.

the outer, there were fields(?)[e] 18/ and (artistic) work[a] of cherubs and palms. And there was a palm between each cherub. And the cherub had two faces. 19/ On one side a human face was turned towards the palm, and on the other side it was the face of a lion that was turned to the palm. In the whole room round about it was done[a] (thus). 20/ From the floor to above the door-opening the cherubs and the palms were carved[a].

20b And in the wall [of the main hall][b] 21/ of the main hall (was) <a fourfold graded door-frame>[a]. In[b] front of the holy place, however, there was <something to be seen which looked like>[c] 22/ <an>[a] altar of wood[b]. Three cubits was <its>[c] height, its length two cubits <and two

e 𝔐 מדות is missing in 𝔊 (𝔏W). The difficulty of its insertion is reflected in 𝔙 *ad mensuram* and 𝔖, which without hesitation convert it into a verbal form governing the two preceding words: "And he measured inside and outside." Driver, "Linguistic Problems," 184f, proposes to read the transition from v 17 to v 18 as נעשו (עָשׂוּ) דמות כרובים; in "Ezekiel," 306, as עשויה דמות כרובים. See also Ehrlich, *Randglossen.* Yet דמות, which is suitable for the style of a vision (1:5, 10 and elsewhere), is out of place in this technical description. Thus, if one does not simply delete מדות as a gloss (so Cornill "completely meaningless," Herrmann, Gese), it should be asked whether מדות here is not to be understood as "measured off area, strip, field." On this see, e.g., the מדה בחבל in *b. B. Bat.* VII 2,3.

18 18a On the awkward עשוי "something made, concoction" see 40:17 note b. 𝔗 has a noun גלף (כרובין).

19 19a See v 18 note a. But see also v 20.

20 20a The postponed עשוים agrees here with the preceding subjects. 40:17 showed that even in this position lack of agreement is not excluded.

b The *puncta extraordinaria* over the ההיכל (Bauer-Leander §6s) show that this word, which represents a doublet of the following one, was already suspect in the eyes of the Masoretes. The simple וקיר (instead of the ובקיר which might have been expected and apparently read by 𝔊 καὶ τὸ ἅγιον as והקדש) is explained by the enumeratory style of this and the following information (Gese, 178f). On this, however, see also the remarks on the "form" of the section vv 15b–26 as a whole.

21 21a 𝔐 מזוזת רבעה, the form of which at a pinch could be understood if it were to be thought of as a comprehensive term telescoped for emphasis, is surely rather to be read as מזוזת רבועת; on this see also Noth, *Könige,* notes on 1 Kgs 6:31, 33. Driver, "Ezekiel," 306, proposes the inversion מזוזת ההיכל רְבֻעֹת. 𝔊 𝔖 did not understand מזוזת; 𝔖 simply omits it, while 𝔊 ἀναπτυσσόμενος (𝔏W *replictilis*) uses the word by which מכסות was rendered in v 16.

b On the style of 𝔐 see v 20 note b.

c מַרְאֶה כְּמַרְאֵה should be read. 𝔐 with its disruption of the construct relationship by the verse ending is trying to make it clear that the independent כמראה refers to the proximity of the numinous. On this see the accumulation of מראה in chapter 1. This becomes even clearer in 𝔗 ואפי בית כפורי חיזוויה כחיזו יקרא.

22 22a 𝔐 המזבח. The addition of the article, which is missing, surely correctly, in 𝔊, is, like the addition of the article in the preceding word (v 21 note c), a consequence of the inappropriate verse division.

b On the giving of the material of a thing by means of a predicate in a nominal clause see Brockelmann §14b*α*.

c 𝔐 גבה is, on the evidence of 𝔊 (𝔏W) 𝔖 𝔗, to be read with a suffix גבהו.

cubits the breadth>[d]. And it had <corners>[e] and <its pedestal>[f] and its sides were of wood[b]. And he said to me: That is the table which stands before the face of Yahweh.

23 But the main hall had two doors and the holy place[a] 24/ had <two>[a] doors. But the doors had two leaves which could be swung back (to the wall): the one door had two leaves[b] and the other[c] had two leaves. 25/ And on them [on the doors of the main hall][a] cherubs and palms were carved[b] on the walls. And a . . .[c] of wood was on[d] the facade of the hall on the outside. 26/ And the framed windows[a] and palms[b] on both sides on[c] the side walls[d] of the vestibule. And the side chambers of the temple and the . . .[e]

d 𝔊 (𝔏^{W}) reads in addition *καὶ τὸ εὖρος πηχῶν δύο*, the equivalent of which in 𝔐 must have fallen out through haplography. But see the exposition.

e Since the suffix of 𝔐 ומקצעותיו is not attested by 𝔗 either (nor by 𝔊 𝔏^{W} 𝔖; 𝔙 is different), the reading ומקצעות is advisable.

f 𝔐 וארכו makes no sense. 𝔊 *καὶ ἡ βάσις αὐτοῦ* (𝔏^{W} *et basis eius*) has the original reading ואדנו, which, on the basis of the other occurrences, of which about fifty alone occur in Ex 26–40, must be understood as plural וַאֲדָנָו. In the passage about the table of the showbread, Ex 25:23–30 (to which 37:10–15 corresponds), there is admittedly no mention of אדנים.

23 23a The separation of the sense units of the complex vv 23–24, which is textually almost completely intact, has not yet been understood by the accentuation of 𝔐. Thus ולקדש belongs with what follows. On the whole see Gese, 180–183. Contrast Driver, "Ezekiel," 306.

24 24a With 𝔊 (𝔏^{W}) the copula of 𝔐 ושתים should be deleted. The following *atnaḥ* should be moved from לדלתות to דלתות.

b The sense division is against the accents of 𝔐 between מוסבות and דלתות.

c 𝔊 transfers its *τῇ θύρᾳ*, in free restyling, from "the one" to "the other" (door).

25 25a An old gloss, already attested by 𝔊, factually correct, but syntactically not fitting into the context.

b The word עשוי is inflected here on both occurrences, on the first occurrence even at the opening of the verse. See also v 20 note a. An emendation of עשויה to עשוים is not necessary; see the analogous lack of agreement in Ps 37:31b.

c 𝔐 עב is unexplained. 𝔊 *σπουδαῖα* (*ξύλα*) is already not understood by 𝔏^{W} and is simply omitted. 𝔙 *grossiora* (*ligna*), 𝔗 סקופתא "post," 𝔖 קרימן (קיסא) "covered (with wood)" are not of much help either. The word seems to recur in v 26 in the plural. See the exposition.

d על-אל cf. 1:17 note a.

26 26a See 40:16 note a.

b 𝔐 ותמרים has surely been found by 𝔊 *καὶ διεμέτρησεν* corrupted to ותמר.

c על-אל cf. 1:17 note a.

d 𝔐 כתפות. 𝔊 (*εἰς τὰ*) *ὀροφώματα* (𝔏^{W} [*in*] *lacunaria*), which in 2 Chr 3:7 corresponds to Hebrew קירות.

e 𝔐 וְהָעֻבִּים is certainly not to be separated from the עָב in v 25. The versions show the same puzzlement with regard to the word. 𝔊 *ἐζυγωμένα* (𝔏^{W} *coniuncta*) connects it with צלעות (𝔙 *latitudinemque parietum*), 𝔗 𝔖 translate as in v 25. Bauer-Leander §67f wishes to derive it from a singular עָב "threshold (?)."

Form

It is with a certain amount of surprise that one reads, in the continuation of chapter 41 from v 15b on, a precise description of the interior furnishings of the temple. The inside of the temple had already been described in terms of its measurements in 40:48–41:4. In 41:5–11 there was added to that the description of its annexes and the area around it. After the description of the square at the back in v 12, vv 13–15a had summarized everything in a total measurement clearly intended as a conclusion. The return to the temple interior once again is unexpected.

While this description begins, although the later verse division has very unskillfully included the end of the previous section with the start of the new description in the one verse (15), in v 15b with a clear beginning, it ends in v 26 in a very fragmentary fashion. There can be no doubt of the fact that a new section begins in 42:1, in view of the guidance formula at the beginning. The conclusion of 41:26, on the other hand, is undoubtedly corrupt. After the description of the interior of the temple (including its vestibule), in v 26b we have reference to the "ribs = side chambers" (plural!) and to the עבים, which can no longer be determined with certainty. Nothing, however, is said about them. One has the impression that at this point a text which originally continued has been abruptly broken off by the even more corrupt quotation of the beginning of the next section.

From the point of view of form and style, too, the section 41:15b–26 does not fit its context. There is no guidance formula recounting the leading of the prophet back into the temple. And, although there is actually a measurement in v 22, there is no measurement formula of the kind found in vv 5–15a at least at the beginning of the catalogue-like enumeration and which recurred twice in the summary-like conclusion in vv 13–15a. In vv 15b–26, on the other hand, one cannot even speak of a purely catalogue-like style in spite of the occasional enumeratory style (v 20 note b and v 21 note b). Rather, here individual parts are from time to time described more fully: paneling, relief decoration on the walls, altar table, doors. Only vv 21b–22 show any desire to link up with the wider context, insofar as here the figure of the guide unexpectedly appears and (is it by chance that only in these verses do some measurements appear?) even opens his mouth and in the style of the conclusion of the great guidance vision (41:4) explains the significance of the altar table (זה השלחן אשר לפני יהוה "that is the table which stands before the face of Yahweh"). But if 41:4 is the final goal of the guiding through the temple, after which there was no further area to be visited, the statement here is made quite casually and incidentally. It goes on at once to the description of the doors. But one cannot see in vv 21b–22, for example, a misplaced fragment of the great guidance vision. That is advised against not only by the introductory וידבר אלי ("and he said to me"), which reveals the altered linguistic usage of the addition in 40:44–46 (cf. v 45) in contrast to the ויאמר אלי ("and he said to me") of 41:4, but also by the content. The guidance vision had not said anything about the presence of Yahweh in the temple. That can happen only after 43:1–9. To that extent the לפני יהוה ("before the face of Yahweh") of v 22 is premature. Rather one must suppose that vv 21b–22, which speak of the altar table and which are in a style dependent on the guidance vision, have been added by the hand which took over vv 15b–26 from another, fuller context in which process v 26b was broken off in fragmentary fashion. See further the exposition.

Setting

In what has been said the question of the origin of the section has already been touched upon. That it cannot come from the hand which composed 40:1–37, 47–49; 41:1–4 and 41:5–15a[1] is made clear also by the altered linguistic usage. See the contrasting usage of ההיכל הפנימי ("the inner temple room") and אלמו החיצון ("its outer vestibule") (v 15b), which recur in varied form in the הפנימי הבית ("the inner room") and the לחוץ ("outside") as well as the בפנימי ובחיצון ("the inner and the outer") of v 17, while in the case of the מהחוץ ("on the outside") of v 25b it is not certain but it is also not impossible that it describes the location of the אלם ("vestibule") in the structure as a whole. Also the description of the holy of holies קדש ("the holy place") (vv 21, 23) is terminologically different from 41:4. In

1 So Gese, 32.

contrast to the hitherto strict reluctance to give information about materials, here עץ ("wood") is mentioned as a material several times (vv 16, 22 twice, 25).

Whether one can go beyond this negative assertion and, in view of the sequence of the description of the wall paneling, the wall decoration and the doors, a sequence which is found similarly in 1 Kings 6, even if with different terminology in the details, can conclude that the author had before him an older description of Solomon's temple is uncertain. Nevertheless it is noteworthy that the antithesis of inside-outside is also to be found in 1 Kgs 6:29f. The interpretation hazarded by Noth "behind-in front" (i.e. of the figurative representations) is admittedly not to be recommended on the basis of Ezekiel 41.[2] In addition, however, the variations between the description in Ezekiel 41 and that in 1 Kings 6 with regard to ornamentation and materials show that the intention here is to describe something unique, something new. Thus this late section, inserted secondarily into its present context (at an awkward point), may also have arisen in the priestly circle that was planning in exile the rebuilding. Admittedly the possibility cannot be definitely excluded that the influence of the reality of the second temple is not already being felt here.

Interpretation

■ **41:15b–16** The description begins with a summarizing, comprehensive statement for the inside of the temple and the vestibule outside. The whole interior of the temple is paneled. ספן ("to panel") occurs in this technical sense also in the account of the building of Solomon's temple in 1 Kgs 6:9; 7:3, 7, where cedar wood is consistently mentioned as the building material. The same wood is also mentioned in connection with Jehoiakim's palace in Jer 22:14. Hag 1:4 does not mention any material. By "inner temple" are meant the two rooms of the inner temple building. Unfortunately, however, in the subsequent particularization of the general description, the technical details which are important for the actual conception are obscure. Thus it is clearly a question of a particular technical treatment of the wood-covering of the framed windows and their ledges (note c). But in this connection it is not clear whether there is envisaged a recessing in three ledges or else the particular treatment of the three upper parts of the frame in contrast to the lowest part, the "sill" (note d). Above all, however, שחיף (here "veneer"), which must describe a particular technique of dealing with wood, remains completely obscure (see note e). As a second special area there is singled out the area from the floor to the windows and to the point above the door opening. Since one must surely reckon with a height for this area which remains the same all the way round, there follows what is also probable on the grounds of general consideration, namely that the windows must be situated very high. And from this the conclusion can again be drawn that the temple "annex" (צלע) does not reach right to the top of the building, but that above it there is still room for window openings. Nothing further is said about the covering of floor or ceiling or of the part above the area mentioned. 1 Kgs 6:15 has a fuller report to the effect that in Solomon's temple the floor was covered with cypress wood and the walls right up to the ceiling with cedar wood. Once again, however, the details of the treatment of this second area of wall in Ezek 41 remain unclear, since the precise meaning of מכסות cannot be determined (see note g). In view of the generalizing introductory statement of the first sentence, however, one must surely think of a particular form of wood paneling.

■ **41:17–20a** The information becomes clearer only when in vv 17–20 the ornamentation of the walls is described in more detail. In this connection v 20a again asserts explicitly that it is a question of the ornamentation of that second area between floor and windows and of strips above the doorways. The ornamentation, which is found, as is confirmed once again in assimilation to v 15b, both inside and outside the temple building round about (but clearly not in the—only whitewashed?—upper part of the wall), corresponds in part to the ornamentation of Solomon's temple as reported in 1 Kgs 6:29. If the מדות of v 17 (note e) is correctly understood as "fields," then that refers to the geometrical division of the ornamented area into precise fields into which the figures are then set. All that is necessary concerning the technique used in such figurative representations and the probability

2 Noth, *Könige*, 126.

that wood reliefs were fixed as fillings in the broad walls has been said by Noth,[3] as it has also about the "very old motif of the tree of life flanked by two animals facing each other" which lies behind the representation of the cherubs and palm trees.[4] In comparison with the ornamentation of the walls of Solomon's temple the lack of "open flowers" (פטורי צצים) is to observed. Whether this is a conscious elimination or simply a somewhat greater unpretentiousness in the decoration of the temple, such as can also be observed elsewhere, cannot be said with certainty. In comparison with the ornamental decoration of the gates (40:16 and elsewhere) the enrichment of the adornment by the motif of the cherubs can be observed. These are described further than in 1 Kgs 6:29 as two-headed creatures. This indicates that, if the wall is divided into fields, on one field at any rate there is a continuous presentation, comprising several groups, of the sequence of cherubs and palm trees, so that what are envisaged by the מדות are fairly broad "strips."[5] The form of the cherubs of the wall relief mentioned here is to be distinguished from the throne-bearing cherubs of chapter 10, as are the cherubs in the דביר of Solomon's temple described in 1 Kgs 6:23–28 from the cherubs of the wall representations in 1 Kgs 6:29.[6] In both cases, however, they doubtless basically fulfill a protectively apotropaic function.[7]

■ **41:20b–25a** As in 1 Kings 6, the details about the ornamentation of the walls (the lack of any information about the floor, corresponding to 1 Kgs 6:30, has already been mentioned; Noth considers v 30 to be a catchword gloss) are followed immediately by the description of the doors of the two inner rooms and their doorposts. This is reported in 1 Kgs 6:31–35 in proper order: 1) vv 31f door and doorposts of the דביר, 2) vv 33–35 door and doorposts of the היכל. By contrast, Ezek 41:20b–25a reveal a disrupted sequence: 1) vv 20b, 21a speak of the doorposts of the היכל, 2) vv 21b–22 of the altar table standing in front of the קדש, 3) vv 23–24a[1] (see v 23 note a) mention in parallel clauses the doors of the היכל and the קדש, which are then discussed with regard to their construction and their ornamentation in summary fashion in vv 24a[2]–25a. The most marked difference compared with 1 Kgs 6:31–35 is in the insertion of vv 21b–22, the passage about the altar table, which has its factual correspondence in 1 Kgs 6:20b, 21b, 22b. It separates the description of the doorpost of the היכל in v 21a from the description of the doors to the היכל and קדש. Since vv 21b–22 do not fit the context of vv 15b–26 from the stylistic point of view either and are dependent on 41:4, the passage is, as already mentioned, to be regarded as an addition. A comparison with 1 Kgs 6:31ff makes it probable that it has taken the place of the description of the doorposts at the entrance to the innermost room.

The original text of vv 20bff seems, in comparison with 1 Kings 6, to have followed the order 1) היכל 2) קדש. This order occurs also in vv 23–24a.

■ **41:20b–21a** Thus vv 20b–21a mention, first of all, the doorposts of the היכל. The מזוזת רבועה ("fourfold graded door-frame") of v 21 (see note a) corresponds to the expression which in 𝔐 of 1 Kgs 6:33 has been corrupted to מאת רבעית, which Noth emends, surely correctly, to מְזֻזֹת רְבָעוֹת and understands to be a fourfold gradation, becoming narrower towards the rear, of the door casing.[8] The temple of *tell taʿjīnāt* can be cited as archaeological evidence for such a gradation (there it is triple).[9] The parallel in 1 Kgs 6:31 makes it likely that once at this point there followed information about the corresponding "fivefold" doorposts at the entrance to the innermost room.[10]

■ **41:21b–22** In its place there follows, in Ezekiel 41, the mention of the altar of 1 Kgs 6:20ff, which there too was described as standing לפני הדביר. The change in style in the transition to v 21b is very marked. In the midst of a description which is quite technical and factual in style there appears here quite unexpectedly the mysterious vision style: "something which looked like an altar."[11] There is, in addition, the unmistakable dependence on

3 Noth, *Könige*, 125f.
4 See the text and illustrations in Moortgat, *Tammuz*, 4–9.
5 On the association of lions' faces and human faces see 1:10 (1, 126).
6 On this see Noth, *Könige*, 122–124.
7 See also the כרוב . . . הסוכך of 28:14, 16.
8 Noth, *Könige*, note tt to 1 Kgs 6:33, without reference to Ezek 41:21.
9 On this see the upper (*hilani-*) ground plan in C. W. McEwan, *American Journal of Archaeology* 41 (1937), 9 (fig. 4).
10 On the text of 1 Kgs 6:31 see Noth, *Könige*, note pp to 1 Kgs 6:31.
11 On מראה which is used here cf. the frequent usages of this word in, e.g., chapter 1 (vv 1, 13, 16, 26–28).

41:4. Surprisingly, in the course of a vision which has till now proceeded in silence, the man begins to speak with a remark expressed quite succinctly, suggestive but in content extremely important. That the description of the altar as a "table before the face of Yahweh" seems premature at this point, before the arrival of Yahweh in the sanctuary is described, has already been mentioned—as has the fact that the introductory וידבר ("and he said"), compared with the ויאמר ("and he said") of 41:4, recalls the secondary expansion 40:45. In addition, the secondary addition in 40:38–43 is recalled by the measurements, with no explicit introductory measurement formula, of the altar which is described as a "table." The measurements, both there and here, follow the reference to the materials—there אבני גזית ("hewn stone"), here עץ (מזבח) ("[altar] of wood"). Then follow the individual measurements: 41:22 height three cubits (in 40:42 one cubit), length two cubits (in 40:42 one and a half cubits) and width two cubits (in 40:42 one and a half cubits). When, in addition, the "corners" are explicitly mentioned, these must be equated, even if the term מקצעות is never used elsewhere of the altar (see 46:21f, also Ex 26:24; 36:29; Neh 3:19f, 24f; 2 Chr 26:9), with the "horns" of the altar which 43:15 mentions in connection with the great altar of the burnt offerings. This is all the more remarkable since this "altar," which is described as a structure of wood and can scarcely then be used for the burning of offerings by fire, is described by the man as a "table" (שלחן). Since wooden sides and a wooden pedestal (note f) are mentioned, it must be a "table" the structure of which resembles an altar.[12]

From 1 Kgs 6:20–22, a passage heavily overlaid with additions,[13] it can be deduced concerning the table "in front of the דביר" of Solomon's temple that it was made of cedar wood and overlaid with gold. In greater detail P in Ex 25:23–30 describes the table, which measures two by one by one and a half cubits, as made of accacia wood with gold overlay, moldings round the edges and fixtures for carrying it, an item of furniture in the tent of meeting. It specifies in conclusion: "You shall at all times lay on the table 'showbread' (לחם פנים) before 'my face' (לפני)." The explicit emphasis in what the man says on the fact that the table stands before Yahweh's "face" (פנים) makes it probable that for Ezekiel 41 what is really meant is this table on which, in a more primitive sacrificial scheme, offerings were "laid" before Yahweh. From this it is highly probable that the golden table which is explicitly mentioned in the case of Solomon's temple and on which the "bread of the presence" has to lie is to be equated with the "altar" of 1 Kgs 6:20. The fluctuation in designation, which can equally well be seen in Ezek 41:21f, reflects the insoluble fusion of presentation and sacrifice in the case of the showbread, which are shown by 1 Sam 21:5 to be an old form of offering. See also Lev 24:6. An interpretation in terms of the altar of incense is not recommended.[14]

■ **41:23–25a** Disregarding the intervening section, vv 21b–22, the description of the doors is continued in vv 23ff. Once the correct division of a wrongly divided 𝔐 has been made (v 23 note a) the description becomes quite clear. It corresponds exactly to the doors described in *b. Mid.* IV 1ab. Thus we are not dealing, as seems to be suggested by 𝔐 in its present form and as has already been proposed by Rabbi Juda in *b. Mid.* IV 1c, with two door leaves which can fold in on each other. Galling has correctly shown that the hinge technique necessary for such a construction is attested no earlier than the Roman period. Rather, as is clear from vv 23, 24a with the sequence 1) היכל 2)קדש, what is envisaged are two doors, i.e. a double door at each entrance. According to *b. Yoma* V 1b, the sanctuary and the holy of holies were separated even in Herod's temple by two curtains which were separated by the space of a cubit and which were pulled up one on the north side and the other on the south side (V 1d). The מוסבות ("leaves") which are mentioned in v 24b are then the door leaves, of which two opened into the room and two opened out of the room on to the side wall.[15] The same meaning should be attributed (against Noth) to the גלילים of 1 Kgs 6:34. The door leaf, which is set in the pivot hole at the front and rear corner respectively of the partition wall which divides the rooms, "turns" (סבב or גלל) on its own door hinge. As in 1 Kgs 6:31ff these doors too have the same figurative decoration as the temple walls. Here too the doors of the temple in Ezekiel 41 lack the flower ornamentation of

On the present double expression מראה כמראה cf. 40:3; 43:3.

12 On the usual form of the table see Galling, *BRL.*

13 Noth, *Könige.*

14 E. Power, *Verbum Dei* II, 603f.

15 See the sketch in Gese, 187.

Solomon's structure. Similarly there is no mention here of a gold overlay.

■ **41:25b–26a** The description, which has depicted in vv 23–25a the doors at the ends of the two inner rooms of the temple building, turns in vv 25b–26a to the vestibule. The latter has framed windows like the two inner rooms. Since the "side annex" (צלע) does not run along the side of the vestibule (see the reference to the eastern גזרה "restricted area" v 14), the windows in the vestibule could be lower than those in the inner rooms. The ornamental decoration of the walls is here restricted to the palm trees. What is meant by the עב "in front of the vestibule outside" has not so far been successfully clarified from the etymological point of view. The term occurs also in 1 Kgs 7:6 in the context of the description of the vestibule of Solomon's House of the Forest of Lebanon. The analogy of the preceding elements in the description in 41:23ff suggests the sense proposed by Galling and Noth of a railing closing off at the front, rather than that of "canopy" (proposed by Koehler-Baumgartner) or "projecting roof" (Zorell), "protective roof" (Herrmann), "cornice" (Montgomery on 1 Kgs 7:6). A. Cohen concludes from the equation of the עבים of v 26 with מרישות in *b.B.Qam.* 67a (העבים אלו המרישות) that עב has the meaning "supporting beam, joist."[16] Levy, *Wörterbuch:* "thresholds." עב is a means of closing off the wide open entrance "gate" (שער 40:48) of the אלם ("vestibule") at the front

■ **41:26b** When then in v 26b mention is again made of the צלעות ("side chambers") of the temple building and of the עבים, which must once again be the עב of v 25, with no further details being given concerning these two structural elements, one can only suppose that the larger context from which vv 15b–26 have been taken contained more precise information about the temple annexes and about the "railings" which were possibly used there too to close off the front. But here we have nothing but suppositions.

Aim

The description of the interior of the temple presented in 41:15b–26 is not from the hand of the author of the great guidance vision. The possibility cannot be excluded that it already has before it the second temple and describes its interior with a certain parallelism to the description of Solomon's temple in 1 Kings 6. But precisely this comparison makes it clear that here everything has become much more modest. This is also true if one regards 41:15b–26 still as a programmatic description preceding the rebuilding of the temple and sketching in anticipation the planned new structure. Here (as also in all of Ezekiel 40–48) there is nothing about decoration with gold. The ornamented paneling of the temple building no longer reaches to the ceiling. Nothing is said either about the use of cedar wood. Only "wood" is mentioned. The ornamentation of the inner room of the temple is more restrained, insofar as the flower ornaments are no longer mentioned. It is restricted to cherubs and palm trees. It is impossible to discern any specific theological preoccupation in the basic text.

Such a preoccupation cannot, however, fail to be heard in vv 21b, 22, even if there is a connection with what is said in 1 Kgs 6:20a. The man who inserted into the description the statement about the altar table in front of the sanctuary of the temple clearly wished to revive the situation of the great guidance vision by means of the stylistic transformation occasioned by the reference to the altar table. He introduces the latter as a mysteriously visionary prospect (מראה כמראה "something to be seen which looked like") and lets us hear the man's words describing the table, in the form of the designation statement of 41:4, as a table before the divine presence. Already the rabbis have reflected on this statement: "It begins with 'altar' and ends with 'table'." R. Yoḥanan and R. Eleazar both said: "As long as the sanctuary existed the altar used to atone for Israel, but now man's table (i.e. his feeding of the poor) atones for him."[17] This interpretation of the table in terms of man's charity, behind which, as Spiegel shows,[18] one can discern the halakhic difficulty of the juxtaposition of altar and table, is doubtless not the opinion of the author of 41:21b, 22. The latter is here thinking of the table on which men lay their gift in honor of God (the showbread) before the holy of holies. The presupposition of this, however, is the still greater concept that it pleases God to

16 Cohen, "Studies," 178.

17 *b. Ber.* 55a, identically *b. Menaḥ* 97a and *b. Ḥag* 27a.

18 Spiegel, "Ezekiel," 259.

be close to his people in the inmost part of the temple and to look upon this table. In this respect one may compare the phraseology of Solomon's prayer at the dedication of the temple in 1 Kgs 8:29. In this statement, however, the present passage, even though it occurs too early within the total context of chapters 40–48, before the event described in 43:1ff, nevertheless hits the nub of what is before all else being expressed in this total context: The God of Israel will once again take up his dwelling among his people and will be present here for his people's adoration and sacrifice. That is the great future salvation towards which God's people are moving.

5. The Great Priestly Vestries

Bibliography

K. Elliger
"Die grossen Tempelsakristeien im Verfassungsentwurf des Ezechiel (42:1ff)" in *Festschrift für A. Alt* (Tübingen: Mohr, 1953), 79–103.

42

1 **And he led me out into the outer[a] court <>[b] northwards and led me into the building with chambers[c] which lies (diagonally)[d] opposite the restricted area and the "building" to the north. 2/ <>[a] Its length (was) <a hundred cubits>[b] on the <north side>[c] and the width fifty cubits. 3/ Diagonal to the twenty[a] (cubits) of the inner**

42:1 1a 𝔊^{B} (𝔏^{W}) here has ἐσωτέραν, see also 46:1. All that follows shows that 𝔐 is correct.

b 𝔐 הדרך can scarcely be tolerated before the following דרך and should be deleted as a dittograph. This דרך is read as שער by 𝔊, which offers an expanded text here: κατὰ ἀνατολὰς κατέναντι τῆς πύλης τῆς (πρὸς βορρᾶν). 𝔗 seeks to do justice to 𝔐 by means of an insertion, which, however, can scarcely be harmonized with 𝔊 and is conclusive for a more authentic form of the text: באורח תרעא דפתיח לאורח ציפונא.

c 𝔊 (𝔏^{W}) introduces here (as already in 40:20, 44) the fuller vision style: καὶ εἰσήγαγέ με, καὶ ἰδοὺ ἐξέδραι πέντε. Over against the plurality of buildings with chambers, which in 𝔊^{A} 𝔄 even reaches the number ten, 𝔐 is correct, as the continuation shows.

d On נגד "diagonally opposite," see Elliger, "grossen Tempelsakristeien," 83.

2 2a 𝔐 אל פני was perhaps already read by 𝔊 (𝔏^{W}), the word-order of which in the rest of the verse deviates from 𝔐 (ἐπὶ πήχεις ἑκατὸν μῆκος). According to Elliger, this could conceal the fragment of a further description of location. The words could, however, also be a corrective addition to (or replacement of?) פתח which has strayed from its original position. Bewer, "Textual Notes," 167f, wishes to read אל פניה "on its front."

b Here too 𝔐 has become disarranged as a result of the displacement of words. The placing of המאה in front of אמות, with the introductory ה being also attached to ארך as a suffix, clarifies the text. מאה אמות occurs also in 40:27. The rule is מאה אמה. Here too 𝔗 seeks to do full justice to 𝔐 by the insertion of an element: לקביל אורכא דאמין מאה תרעא חד פתיח לציפונא.

c 𝔐 פתח makes no sense. 𝔊 πρὸς βορρᾶν points to an original reading פאת צפון, with which may be compared 41:12, where פאת דרך הים is similarly translated by πρὸς θάλασσαν. Further 47:17–20; 48:1.

3 3a 𝔐 העשרים has been misunderstood by 𝔊 (𝔏^{W}) 𝔖 as השערים. But it is not clear why 𝔊 (𝔏^{W}) prefaces it by διαγεγραμμέναι (ὃν τρόπον αἱ πύλαι). There is a (scarcely satisfactory) attempt at an explanation in John P. Peters, "Critical Notes," *JBL* 12 (1893): 47f.

court[b] and diagonal to the (stone) pavement of the outer court (it rose) ledge by ledge[c] <in three steps>[d]. 4/ And in front of the chambers was a passage, ten cubits broad, leading inwards[a]; <the length was a hundred cubits>[b]. And its entrances[c] lay on the north side. 5/ But the upper chambers were foreshortened[a], for the ledges <took away (a part) from them>[b]. From the lower and

b On לחצר הפנימי see 40:23 note a.

c On אתיק see 41:16 note c.

d 𝔐 בשלשים. V 6 and the renderings of 𝔗 𝔖 (על תלתא סדרין) make the reading מְשֻׁלָּשִׁים probable.

4 4a At first glance 𝔐 אל הפנימית does not appear to be attested by 𝔊 (𝔏^W). Yet the remarkable ἐπὶ (πήχεις ἑκατόν) recalls the identical beginning of v 2, where a suggestion of the introductory אל פני of 𝔐 was supposed. Thus, here too 𝔊 may well have had אל פני[מית] in front of it.

b To the difficult expression of 𝔐 דרך אמה אחת, in which Galling, Elliger, Eichrodt and Bewer, "Textual Notes," 168, emend, in pure conjecture, דרך to וגדר, there corresponds in 𝔊 (𝔏^W) (ἐπὶ) πήχεις ἑκατὸν τὸ μῆκος, correspondingly in 𝔖 ואורכא מאא אמין, which suggests a (or אמה ?) וארך מאה אמות in the original. This text is supported both by the juxtaposition of רחב and ארך and by its content, which suggests a passage running along the whole side of the building.

c Instead of 𝔐 פתחיהם, 13 MSS Edd read פתחיהן, which is grammatically more precise. Yet this precision is by no means always maintained in the case of the third person feminine plural suffix.

5 5a 𝔐 קצרות has not been understood by 𝔊 ὡσαύτως (𝔏^W *similiter*). 𝔙 with *humiliora* is different, but thinks of a lowering of the height rather than of the width of the rooms. 𝔗 has דחיקן "pressed," which is then used in v 6 also as the rendering of נאצל. In both places 𝔖 uses זעורין "small."

b 𝔐 יוכלו אתיקים מהנה. 𝔊 ἐξείχετο τὸ περίστυλον ἐξ αὐτοῦ (𝔏^W *eminebat columnatio eius*), as well as the readings of 𝔖 דעאלין הוו בהין דרגא "projected into the steps" and the paraphrastic, expansive 𝔙 (*quia*) *supportabant porticus quae ex illis eminebant* (neither of which can be understood apart from the influence of 𝔊), suggest the concept of the "projection" of structural elements. It is, of course, quite remarkable that the "shortening" of a structural element should go back to projecting elements. So Elliger, with his translation "rocky ledges projected into them," comes to think of elements of the natural landscape which are covered by the visible buildings. It would, however, in the total description of the building, be a quite unique phenomenon if here details were given about the characteristics of the terrain which were covered by the visible structure. This then also suggests the possibility of not suddenly having to understand אתיק in v 5 in a different sense from that in v 3. Thus 𝔗 נסיבן זיזיא מינהן, "זיזיא (balconies, extensions—does it have here precisely the sense 'ledges'?) were removed from them" seems to come closest to what was meant by the text, which states that in the topmost story of the building the total structure, which was described in v 2 by the measurement one hundred by fifty, seems to be reduced. Elliger will be correct when he supposes behind יוכלו, with reference to נאצל v 6, an original perfect. Must one then read יכלו מן and consider the

middle (stories) upwards <the> building was constructed[c]. 6/ For it was (arranged) in three stories and had no pillars like the pillars of the <outer> (chambers)[a]. So (the building) was terraced[b] from below from the lower and middle (chambers). 7/ And there was a wall[a] there, which ran outside, parallel to the chambers, towards the outer court in front of[b] the chambers. Its length (was) fifty cubits, 8/ for the length of the chambers of the outer court (was) fifty cubits. <The latter>[a], however , lay <opposite them. In total>[b] there were a hundred

meaning "assert oneself (in contrast to)" to be modified in the direction of "remove (from)"? If the יאכלו read by MSS Q pointed to an original אכלו, then the "removal" would be expressed very pictorially. The rendering of נאצל in v 6 with the same verb which corresponds to the יוכלו in v 5 by 𝔊 (𝔏^{W}) 𝔙 can also raise the question whether the original was not אצלו, which is admittedly graphically a bit further removed, in the sense of "put to the side, remove" (Nu 11:17; Eccl 2:10).

c 𝔐 מהתחתנות ומהתכנות can in no case be in apposition to מהנה, by which the topmost row of rooms is meant. Thus these words will begin a new sentence unit whose predicate בנין one should then read with 𝔗 בניינא as definite. 𝔊 renders the two words with *ἐκ τοῦ ὑποκάτωθεν περιστύλου καὶ τὸ διάστημα*, in which the word *διάστημα* (41:6 note c) here too probably reveals that 𝔊 has not understood the word ומהתכנות. The concluding בנין is paraphrased by a summary reference to the third story which was mentioned in the preceding: *οὕτως περίστυλον καὶ διάστημα καὶ οὕτως στοαί*. 𝔖 quite simply omits the last words, while 𝔙 connects them wrongly *de inferioribus et de mediis aedificii.* There is no reason to assume with Elliger, Eichrodt that there is something missing from the text of v 5b.

6 6a 𝔐 החצרות. 𝔊 *τῶν ἐξωτέρων* (𝔏^{W} *exteriores*) presupposes a reading הַחִיצֹנוֹת, which is preferable to 𝔐 since here, and immediately following in v 8, there is a reference back to 40:17, in the basic text of which in the first instance only rooms were mentioned.

b On נאצל "terraced" see Elliger, "grossen Tempelsakristeien," 91f, and Driver, "Linguistic Problems," 185, who sees in אצל a form parallel to נצל "remove, take away" and points to Arabic *'ṣl* (as distinct from *wṣl* with which Hebrew אֵצֶל is to be connected).

7 7a 𝔐 וגדר 𝔊 (𝔏^{W}) *καὶ φῶς* (*et lumen*). On this scribal error, which goes back to an original ואור, see also 41:11 note b. 𝔖 abbreviates the information as to position (omits v 7aβ).

b על–אל cf. 1:17 note a.

8 8a 𝔐 והנה is strange. It is certainly, as Elliger observes, an element of the vision style. It is otherwise, however, completely absent from 42:1–14. Moreover, it is found in chapters 40–48 only where new visionary content comes into view. The introduction of a measurement by means of הנה would be quite unique. That explains why not only 𝔖 and 𝔙 but even 𝔗 silently omit it. Thus Gese (27) would prefer to see הנה here being used in another function. But in the framework of the description of a vision that is still quite unusual. So it is more correct to read with 𝔊 *καὶ αὗται* וְהֵנָּה and to refer that back to the לשכות of v 7.

b 𝔐 על פני ההיכל, which in spite of its attestation by 𝔙 𝔗 𝔖 affords really enormous difficulties, should be emended on the basis of 𝔊 (𝔏^{W}) *ἀντιπρόσωποι*

cubits. 9/ And <the doors of these chambers>[a] <one entered>[b] from the east side if one wanted to enter them[c] from the outer court, 10/ <at the top>[a] of the walls of the forecourt.

10b **To the <south>[b] there were at the restricted area and along[c] the side of the <building> rooms 11/ with a passage in front of them. (They looked)[a] like the rooms which lay on the north, as long and <as broad>[b] as they and with <exits>[c] and layout and doors like them. 12/ And**

ταύταις τὸ πᾶν (πηχῶν ἑκατόν) to על פניהן הכל. Driver, "Ezekiel," 306f, reads על פניה הכל which is graphically closer to 𝔐. That a feminine singular suffix can be linked with a feminine plural is shown by 2 Kgs 3:3; 10:26; 13:2, 6, 11; Jer 36:23; Mic 2:9.

9 9a 𝔐 ומתחתה לשכות, in which in any case the final ה of the first word should be attached to the second as the article, is unusual. How is one to envisage "underneath the rooms" whose proximity to the courtyard has just been mentioned? It is remarkable that the commentators have never given serious consideration to the reading of 𝔊 𝔖, which, moreover, is confirmed by 𝔐 in the parallel description of the southern structure in v 12. Cornill mentions 𝔊 *καὶ αἱ θύραι τῶν ἐξεδρῶν*, 𝔖 תרעא דאכסדרא, but puts them aside with the remark "a plural פתחות is unheard of." Jahn finds here a textual corruption of ובכתף הלשכות. In comparison with 𝔐 v 12, ופתחי הלשכות should be read. 𝔐 has arisen from the miswriting of two letters and wrong word division. V 9a*α* represents a compound nominal sentence: "And with regard to the doors of these rooms—the entrance, if one wanted to enter them, was from the east, from the outer court."

b With K הַמָּבוֹא should be read.

c להנה only otherwise in 1:5, 23; Zech 5:9. See Bauer-Leander §81f′.

10 10a 𝔐 ברחב is factually difficult to incorporate. 𝔊 (𝔏^{W}) *κατὰ τὸ φῶς τοῦ ἐν ἀρχῇ περιπάτου* attests, in a strangely misplaced word order, the three substantives גדר (see v 7 note a), ראש and חצר. That רחב must be a scribal error for ראש is clear from the recapitulation for the southern structure in v 12.

b 𝔐 הקדים should, on the basis of 𝔊, which in an erroneous doubling of the expression has the reading *τὰ πρὸς νότον κατὰ πρόσωπον τοῦ νότου* (similarly 𝔏^{W}), be emended to הדרום. The content of what follows makes it clear that we are dealing here with the southern counterparts of the northern rooms described in vv 2–10a*α*.

c על–אל cf. 1:17 note a.

11 11a 𝔊 *κατὰ τὰ μέτρα* wrongly presupposes a כמדות in place of the כמראה of 𝔐.

b 𝔐 כן רחבן. 𝔊 (𝔏^{W}) *καὶ κατὰ τὸ εὖρος αὐτῶν* makes it likely that here, by analogy with the other expressions, וכרחבן should be read.

c 𝔐 וכל מוצאיהן is certainly attested by the versions but should surely be reduced to וכמוצאיהן, since its כל, without a preceding particle of comparison, which is quietly added by 𝔊 (𝔏^{S}), does not fit the context. 𝔅 𝔖, which reproduce כל precisely without the particle of comparison, then quietly omit these in the following expressions where they actually occur in 𝔐. In addition 𝔖 expands to מפקניהין ומעלניהין. 𝔊 after *κατὰ πάσας τὰς ἐπιστροφὰς αὐτῶν*, which must correspond to 𝔐 ובמשפטיהן, adds *καὶ κατὰ τὰ φῶτα αὐτῶν* behind which, on the basis of v 7 note a, must lie a כגדריהם.

to <the doors>[a] of the chambers on the south side there led an entrance at the top of the path along the protective wall[b] <>[c], (open)[d] on the east when <one went in>[e].

13 And he said to me: The chambers to the north <and>[a] the chambers to the south, which lie beside[b] the restricted area, are the sacred chambers where the priests who approach[c] Yahweh eat the sacred gifts. There they are to deposit the sacred gifts and the cereal offering[d] and the sin offering and the guilt offering, for the place is holy. 14/ When the priests have gone in[a], they must not (without

12 12a The beginning should certainly not be emended with Galling, Elliger, Eichrodt on the basis of the corrupt ומתחת of v 9. Rather the original text of v 9 attested by 𝔊 (note a) is here presupposed and what it says transferred to the southern structure. Admittedly here in 𝔐 and in the versions a slight textual corruption can be ascertained. 𝔊 ($\mathfrak{L}^{W}$) fuses the וכפתחיהן of v 11 with the וכפתחי of v 12 and allows the comparative style with כ (*καὶ κατά*) to continue to be operative as far as the פתח בראש of v 12a*β*. In 𝔐 this style predominates still in v 12a*α*. In reality, however, it ceases with the end of v 11. After, in the closing words of v 11, reference has been made in general terms to the similarity of the פתחים in the northern and southern buildings, v 12 goes back again to a quite particularly important פתח and describes it by way of contrast to vv 9–10a*α*. Thus, at the beginning, instead of 𝔐 וכפתחי a simple ופתחי should be read with Bertholet-Galling, and in what follows the same construction of a compound nominal sentence is to be found as in v 9ab*α*.

b On 𝔐 הגדרת הגינה see Elliger, "grossen Tempelsakristeien," 99–101. The technical term has not been understood by 𝔊 ($\mathfrak{L}^{W}$), which again here employs the helping word *διάστημα* (41:6 note c): *ὡς ἐπὶ φῶς* (see 41:11 note b) *διαστήματος καλάμου*. But even 𝔙 *vestibulum separatum* is only guess work. 𝔗 even finds here דוכן ליואי "the platform of the Levites." 𝔖 באורחא דנחלא seems to find a גיא behind הגינה.

c The twofold דרך of 𝔐 is not attested by 𝔊 (though it is by 𝔖 𝔙 𝔗) and could be a dittograph. If not, we have to do with the beginning of a new sentence: "The path ran along the protective wall."

d The parallel description in v 9, המבוא מהקדים בבאו להנה, necessitates this understanding.

e On the basis of the parallel in v 9, 𝔐 בבואן should be read as בבואו. On this same basis מבואו would also be possible: "(open) to the east was their (i.e. the rooms') entrance."

13 13a With 𝔊 𝔖 𝔙 the copula should be inserted.

b על–אל cf. 1:17 note a.

c 𝔐 אשר קרובים. In 40:46 the expression was הקרבים. In adaptation to the word-order of that formulation 𝔊 ($\mathfrak{L}^{W}$) adds *οἱ υἱοὶ Σαδδουκ*, while 𝔗 adds לשמשא.

d 𝔙 omits והמנחה.

14 14a 𝔐 בבאם הכהנים is paraphrased very freely by 𝔊 ($\mathfrak{L}^{W}$) *οὐκ εἰσελεύσονται ἐκεῖ πάρεξ τῶν ἱερέων* (*οὐκ ἐξελεύσονται* . . .). Even the beginning of v 14a*β* is expanded *διὰ παντὸς ἅγιοι ὦσιν οἱ προσάγοντες καὶ μὴ ἅπτωνται τοῦ στολισμοῦ αὐτῶν*. Bewer, "Textual Notes," 168, proposes deleting הכהנים as a gloss, transferring בבאם to v 13 and then reading יציאום instead of יצאו (cf. 44:19). But it is not impossible to retain 𝔐. Gese wishes to emend 𝔐 and in the light of the ושם in v 14a*β* read שמ(ה) יבאו also at the beginning of v 14a*α*. On the proleptic suffix of 𝔐 see Bauer-Leander §65i, Brockelmann §68b. Since

further ceremony) emerge from the sanctuary into the outer court. They should, however, remove there the clothes in which[b] they perform their duties, for they[b] are holy <and should>[c] put on other clothes; (then) they may approach the place where the people are[d].

10:3 may contain a scribal error (note a), reference may best be made for the usage to Job 29:3, but see the commentaries on that passage.

b 𝔐 בהן (only otherwise in 1 Sam 31:7; Is 38:16; Bauer-Leander §81f') and הנה are unusual, since בגדים is otherwise masculine and is such, in fact, in the close parallel 44:19, and are corruptions of בהם and המה. See also Albrecht, "Geschlecht," 97.

c In 𝔐 ילבשו the copula should be added on the basis of 𝔊 (𝔏^{W}) 𝔖 𝔗 𝔅. Read וילבשו.

d 𝔊 (𝔏^{W}) modifies as follows: *ὅταν ἅπτωνται τοῦ λαοῦ*, 𝔗 ויתערבון עם עמא, 𝔖 ומקרבין קורבנא חלף עמא.

Form

With 42:1 there begins a new section, which, as is clear both from the content and from the formal shape, ends in v 14. It tells of the two large room structures which delimit on its two sides, north and south, the square area lying to the west behind the temple building, the area which was described in 41:12 and measured in 41:13, 15a.

In its formation this section is dependent on the great guidance vision of 40:1–37, 47–49; 41:1–4. In introductory guidance formulae (ויבאני "and he led me", ויצאני "and he led me out") there is described how the prophet is led out of the outer court to the northern building. After the measurements of the two complementary room structures have been given, the section ends, analogously to 41:4, with a speech by the man. In what he says, which is introduced as in 41:4—but in contrast to 40:45 and 41:22—by ויאמר אלי ("and he said to me"), he explains to the prophet what he has seen. This brings the section to its final goal.

In contrast to this relationship of form, however, there are also unmistakable differences. On no single occasion here does the measurement formula occur, according to which the man would have completed the measurement in the prophet's sight—the formula which in the great guidance vision dominates the whole description with a particularly montonous repetition. And in contrast to the great guidance vision there is no mention here either of the prophet's being led from one place to the other, i.e. from the northern building to the southern one. In the detailed description there is no further mention of any movement on the part of the prophet through the temple area, just as the man is mentioned again only in the concluding words. By contrast with 41:4, however, these words themselves are no longer simply the brief statement mentioning the location (41:22, in this respect, was from the point of view of form much closer to 41:4). Rather the man's words contain a general instruction as to what should be done with these annexes. The introductory nominal sentence, which still reflects something of the character of the designation of 41:4: "The chambers . . . are the sacred chambers," is followed by a series of statements in the imperfect regulating the behavior of the priests in these chambers. And this makes it already clear that now, as in the appendix in 40:44–46, but in clear distinction from the great guidance vision, the officials who will populate the temple make their full appearance.

Setting

This leads to the question of the origin of this section. One certainly cannot regard it as the original continuation of the guidance vision which has grown around the description of the temple building in 41:5–15a. This is also confirmed by the continuation in 42:15–20. This latter can be connected without any difficulty with 41:5–15a and, from the point of view of form, again comes much closer to the style of the guidance vision. 42:1–14 does not originally belong in this context. On the other hand, it is now equally clear that 42:1–14 presupposes that 41:5–15a immediately precedes it and that it seeks to explain questions which were left open by that description section. 41:15b–26 interrupts the connection between 42:1–14 and 41:5–15a. Thus the conclusion must be that first of all into the expanded guidance vision, which continues as far as 42:20, 42:1–14 has been inserted—a section which from the point of view of content stands close to the expansion in 40:44–46. Only somewhat later has the description of the interior of the temple (41:15b–26) been added.

The section originated in the circle of priestly groups in the exile who reflected further on the plan of the sanctuary for the coming time of restoration, of which the prophet has had a vision, and expanded it at those points which seemed to require expansion. To what extent, here too, they did so on the basis of conditions in

Solomon's temple will have to be examined in connection with the detailed exegesis. Here the more general observation may suffice that the priestly circles who find their voice here are particularly concerned with the distinct separation of priests and "people" (v 14) and with insuring that in the temple itself the sacred realm of the priest should not come into forbidden contact with that which is of the people. There has not so far in what has been said in the guidance vision been any trace of this particular concern. Even in the related addition in 40:44–46 it does not emerge with this degree of emphasis.

Interpretation

■ **42:1** The immediately preceding guidance statement had recounted in 41:1 that the man led the prophet inside the temple building. The attached measurements in 41:5–15a, which say nothing about his being led anywhere else, presuppose that the prophet is still inside the temple. 42:1, which tells of him being led out into the outer courtyard to the building opposite the restricted area and בנין ("building"), links up with that report. There follows a description of this building (at first described in the singular as לשכה "chamber" but from v 4 onwards consistently in the plural לשכות "chambers"), for which Elliger appropriately used the term "temple sacristy." The situation of the building "opposite" the "restricted area" (גזרה) and "building" (בנין) presupposes that it borders the side of the square which lies to the west behind the temple building and which is formed for eighty cubits by the בנין ("building") and for the remaining twenty cubits by the northern, narrow side of the גזרה ("restricted area"), that it lies diagonally, therefore, to the בנין ("building") which is orientated towards the east. The explicit observation "to the north" makes it certain that what is envisaged is the northern side of the hundred cubit square area lying behind the temple building.

■ **42:2f** After the familiar hundred by fifty cubits are mentioned as the measurements of the building, the exact length is mentioned once again in v 3—on this occasion, unfortunately, less precisely than in v 1 so that again and again different ways of understanding this specification have arisen. We must surely, however, understand the statement in the light of v 1. By the "twenty (cubits) of the inner court," opposite which the building lies, must be meant once again the narrow side of the restricted area. But why is it only this that is mentioned here and not the בנין ("building") as well? On the other side of the building (so it must be understood) there lies, diagonally opposite, the pavement of the outer court. It and the rooms built on it were mentioned in 40:17f, where it was ascertained that the pavement projected fifty cubits into the outer court along the perimeter wall. This depth is then presupposed in 42:8 also as the "depth" (ארך) of the rooms of the outer court. When it is said further of the building described here that it is constructed אתיק אל אתיק ("ledge by ledge"), then by אתיק is meant, as in 41:15f, a "ledge," a backward-sloping part of the structure. The building, which lies at the point where the upper terrace (of the inner court, of the square of the temple building and of the square which lies behind the temple to the west) falls to the outer court, loses height in three ledges. Its roof, seen from below, reaches its full height in three stages.

■ **42:5–6** The same phenomenon is described again in vv 5f, from the other side. There is, admittedly, no complete unanimity as to the understanding of these details. Elliger, followed by Fohrer-Galling and Gese, believes that in the information which explains the "curtailment" of the upper chambers they ought to find an element of the terrain lying beneath and covered by the building: "Rocky ledges projected into them."[1] There are, however, difficulties in accepting that the אתיקים already mentioned in v 3 are to be referred there to three regular gradations in the terrain.[2] More correctly, one thinks there, as is also considered by Elliger, of the ledges in the visible form of the building which the prophet can see from the place where he is standing. Can, however, אתיק in v 5 be understood in a completely different way? Is it at all likely that into the description of the outwardly visible shape of the sacristy there have also been inserted secondarily details about the nature of the terrain which is concealed beneath the building? Thus more probably here too what we find described is the external shape of the building, the topmost story of which is described as

1 Elliger, "grossen Tempelsakristeien," 88.

2 This also finds expression with Elliger, "grossen Tempelsakristeien," 86.

"shortened" because its roof does not extend the whole fifty cubits to the northern edge, but after a third of the fifty cubits (one must surely supplement thus) falls step-like to a lower level. And the same is correspondingly true of the middle level, which, from the point of view of the lowest, is "higher." Thus the end of v 5, which once again begins from the opposite side, says that the structure is built up from below via the middle level. And the end of v 6 reiterates, using the root אצל "squared off," which is known from 41:8, and adding a מהארץ: "From below" the building is constructed terrace-like from the lowest level via the middle level. The roof-surface which falls in terraces "eats away" (if אכלו is correct, see v 5 note b) more and more of the total area of the building. The transition from the singular לשכה ("chamber") to the plural לשכות ("chambers") makes it clear that a plurality of chambers is presupposed in the interior of the total building. When, in addition, it is explicitly stated that this structure has no pillars, as had the "outer (chambers)," there are presupposed in this reference structural elements which were not mentioned in the great guidance vision, but which are clearly visible to the author of this section. Is the thought that of substructures, which one might happily accept in the case of the chambers mentioned secondarily in 40:38–46, or of open pillared halls, in the case of the rooms mentioned in 40:17f?[3]

There is still lacking in the picture of the spatial layout of the sacristies the passage which is symmetrically adjacent on both sides and by which one enters the sacristy building from the outer court and leaves it on the inner side after one has, in the building itself, doubtless by steps, reached the height of the inner court.

■ **42:4** V 4 describes the "passage" (מהלך) which runs inwards along the sacristy building with a width of ten cubits. It follows in the first instance (this is not explicitly stated) for a length of eighty cubits the north wall of the בנין ("building"). The first twenty (of its total of one hundred) cubits of length are open on one side to the restricted area. This may also explain why the description of the site of the sacristies in v 3 is, contrary to that in v 1 (and v 10), limited to the mention of the restricted area (= העשרים "twenty").

■ **42:7** For the passage (the word מהלך is no longer used here) which runs along the north side and for which the same measurement of one hundred cubits is given, there is specific mention of a (protective) wall. It measures there fifty cubits, since the remaining fifty cubits are formed by the wall of the adjacent chamber of the outer court. This measurement is identical with the figure given in 40:18 only for the pavement of the court.

■ **42:8** The area of the building, measuring a hundred by fifty cubits, is extended by these lateral strips to a hundred by seventy cubits, a figure which is not in accord with the basic figures twenty-five, fifty, one hundred mentioned in the guidance vision. This might also suggest that this building was not envisaged in the original temple plan, which was strictly in accord with these figures and endeavored to accommodate to them older, traditional measurements (such as those of the temple building). The dependence on the basic plan of the measurement of the building itself as a hundred by fifty cubits should not deceive us on this.

■ **42:9** The description then lays particular emphasis on the precise layout of the "exits" (פתחים) from the building. Already v 4b, in the context of the description of the passage lying to the south of the building, established that its "entrances" (פתחיהם) lay on the north side. In v 9 this piece of information is made precise. From the east one enters from the outer court the passage which lies, shielded by the wall, on the north side of the building and on to which the (north facing) doors open. One cannot enter the building directly from the court. The whole is clearly intended to insure against an unprepared entrance into this building from the court, since the building, as vv 13f will show, already belongs to the sphere of the highly sacred.

■ **42:10–12** The description of the sacristy building on the south side of the western square behind the temple building is presented in an abbreviated fashion—if it is indeed the description of an exactly similar building. The same was the case with the description of the gates in the great guidance vision. So v 10 describes the position of the southern sacristy building precisely as v 1 does—with the slight difference that the building is described here right at the beginning as plural לשכות ("chambers"). The "passage" (דרך) mentioned in v 11a*a*

3 On 40:38ff see above pp. 366f. See also Galling, *BRL:* "Säule."

corresponds to the "passage" (מהלך) on the inner side which v 4a described for the northern sacristy. For the measurements of the whole structure reference is made to the first description (see v 2), just as in quite summary fashion to its exits (see vv 4b, 9f), its layout—here the thought must be of the type of construction described in vv 3b, 5, 8—and doors. This last, however, since it is clearly considered to be particularly important, is taken up once again in v 12 (corresponding to vv 9f). With the use of a new technical term the "protective wall" (see note b), which provides security for access from the outer court to the southern sacristy too, is explicitly mentioned and the easterly orientation of the passage thus created is emphasized.

■ **42:13–14** In the words addressed to the prophet by the man who accompanies him the descriptions reaches its goal in vv 13f. The location of the sacristies is described, as in v 1, only as being "opposite" (here על פני) the restricted area (on this see above v 4). It recalls 41:4 (and 41:22) when first of all, in a nominal sentence, there follows the cultic designation of the buildings as לשכות הקדש ("the sacred chambers"). This nomenclature is taken up later by 46:19. From this qualification of the sacristies as a sacred place there arise the subsequent regulations about behavior in this area, which at the end of v 13 is once again specifically described as מקום קדש ("a holy place"). Already the expansion in 40:38–43 had brought out the distinction between the sacred whole burnt offering and the "cereal offering" (זבח) which is also consumed by the "people." This distinction becomes discernible with particular clarity in the description of the sacrificial kitchens in 46:19–24. Of these particularly sacred offerings—the designation קדשי הקדשים ("sacred gifts") appears twice in v 13—the עולה is burnt in its entirety on the altar as a sacrifice for Yahweh. In the case of חטאת ("sin offering") and אשם ("guilt offering") it is laid down in the priests' law in 44:29 that the portions not consumed on the altar should fall to the priest as his income. In the regulation of P in Leviticus 4f there is no further mention of this. To this in 44:29 the מנחה is also added as a vegetable offering, the unburnt parts of which according to P, too, in the regulation in Lev 2:3 fall to the priest.[4] The priestly portions are not to be taken out of the sacred inner area. The priests are to eat them in the sacristies and are to leave there what is not directly used as food.

A second regulation, which finds it counterpart among the priestly laws in 44:19, concerns the clothes in which the priests serve. After his service, the priest may not simply pass through one of the doors of the inner court directly into the outer court. Rather, he must first change his clothes in the sacristies before he emerges into the realm of the people, i.e. here clearly of the "laity." For even the clothes are impregnated with the holiness which fills the inside of the temple area. They are "holy," says the text quite directly.[5] It should also be noted that there is no reference here, in contrast to 40:44–46, of an allocation of the two sacristy buildings to two different groups. They are both equally intended for "the priests who approach Yahweh."

■ **42:1–14** Finally, with regard to 42:1–14 the question must be asked to what extent in the description of the great sacristies *tradition* from Solomon's temple is here adopted. What has been said in 41:5–15a about the stylized arrangement of the rear of the temple building is scarcely favorable to the assumption of such a tradition of large structures serving as "holiness sluices" of the innermost temple precinct. In Herod's temple too, if the sketch drawn by Holtzmann on the basis of what is said in *b. Mid.* is reasonably accurate, there is no sign of them.[6] There is, in addition, the double observation that the great sacristies, with their measurement of a hundred by fifty cubits, are clearly harmonized with the dimensions of the temple plus annexes which are fitted into the schema of the guidance vision. Also, the observation that the sacristies fulfill an eminently important function in the context of the refined holiness theology of the temple, which is undoubtedly first fully developed in the secondary expansions, can only strengthen the doubt that what we have here is older, traditional material. On this basis, one must precisely ask whether the older tradition of the priestly sacristies is not to be found in 40:44–46, which speak of two chambers for the sanctuary servants beside the two inner gates to the north and the south, while 42:1–14 represent a replanning which goes far beyond that and which has been formed

4 On the sacrifices see further on 45:10–17.

5 On this concept of holiness, on the basis of which taboo zones of the holy are constituted, see, e.g., van der Leeuw, *Phänomenologie* §57, "Heiliger Raum."

6 Giessener Mischna.

in the wake of the more refined ideas of holiness. In this connection the possibility must not be entirely excluded that in these structures the recollection of smaller buildings at the sides of the פרבר has been much expanded in the context of the great blueprint.[7] There could also be connected with this the recollection of a sloping away of the terrain at the sides of the terrace of the old inner temple court, which is here, of course, considerably lengthened towards the rear (the west), and of structures whose purpose was to counteract this terraced drop. In Herod's temple, as far as such structural elements are concerned, one would think first of the area of the "warm house" (בית המוקד) to the north of the temple building, described in *b. Mid.* I 6–9, whose two northern chambers lie in the domain of the profane and two southern ones in that of the sacred and which are divided by "stone projections" (ראשי פסיפסין). Such stone projections separating the sacred from the profane are also mentioned in II 7b as separating the priestly court from the court of Israel, as well, of course, as in the division of the holy from the holy of holies in the upper room of the temple (IV 5b).

Aim

The description of the two priestly sacristies which match the temple building plus annexes in size is unmistakably at the service of very distinct concepts of holiness. This is not just true of the concluding words of the guiding figure which mark the climax of the whole description. It is already clear from the layout of the buildings which reveal their bridging function in their terrace-like ascent from the lay sphere to the priestly sphere. A wall built on the side of the building which faces the lay sphere prevents direct access to the buildings which already belong to the realm of greater holiness. The only entrance on the east side of the passage guarded by the wall makes possible an exact control of those who enter.

At the same time, there is proclaimed in the design of the building, and then quite clearly in the man's explanatory words, that any admittance of the profane, far less of the unsanctified, into the sphere of the sacred is strongly forbidden. And vice versa—this emerges explicitly in vv 13f—any direct exposure of the sacred to the profane outside must be prevented.

Behind this can be seen a passionate desire not to betray the sacred to the unclean, not to throw it to the dogs (Mt 7:6). This whole layout carries the turning away from the debasement of the sacred which has already been discernible in chapter 8. At the same time, however, the danger which threatens to arise in this intensified guarding and delimiting of the sacred is not overlooked. The thought that the sacred, precisely in the assertion of its character as "wholly other," finds its greatest realization at the point where it is holy not in detachment from, but in turning to, the sick world round about (on this see 47:1–12) could easily come off badly in such perfection of the expectation of holiness. In the middle of the Bible there can be heard the proclamation of the holy God who, precisely as the "wholly other," was there in his wholeness on the side of the world of the sinners and the lost.

7 See above p. 380.

42

6. The Conclusion of the Measuring of the Temple Area

15 And when he had completed the measure-
ment of the interior of the temple pre-
cinct he led me through the door that
faces east and measured it[a] round about.
16/ He measured[a] the east side[b] with the
measuring rod[c]: five hundred (cubits)
[measuring rods][d] (measured) with the
measuring rod. He turned[e], 17/ meas-
ured[a] the north side: five hundred (cubits)
[measuring rods][b] with the measuring

42:15 15a 𝔐 ומדדו must, if it is retained, refer to the total complex of the בית. 𝔊 interprets it in this way *καὶ διεμέτρησε τὸ ὑπόδειγμα τοῦ οἴκου κυκλόθεν (ἐν διατάξει)*; on this see Ex 25:9–40. 𝔏^{W} *et mensus est templum aedis.*

16 16a 𝔊 (𝔏^{W}) here too expands the text by a fuller introduction *καὶ ἔστη κατὰ νώτου τῆς πύλης τῆς βλεπούσης κατὰ ἀνατολὰς καὶ (διεμέτρησε).*

b 𝔐 רוח הקדים literally "(side of the) east wind." On this see Appendix 3.

c 𝔊 (𝔏^{W}) makes the verse more concise by omitting the first בקנה המדה.

d 𝔐 חמש אמות קנים, which in K would be rendered: "five cubits, measuring rods," has already been corrected by Q to "five hundred (חמש מאות) measuring rods," corresponding to the reading of vv 17–19. Now 40:5 has given the length of the measuring rod as six large cubits, so that vv 16–19 lead to a total measurement for the temple precinct of three thousand by three thousand cubits. This cannot be made to coincide with the five hundred by five hundred cubit which results from the information given hitherto. Thus the suggestion that the קנים in the measurement figures in vv 16–19 is of secondary origin is highly probable. It has been inserted because the information to be found in all these verses, that the measurement was made בקנה המדה, was understood as an indication of the measurement and not simply as an indication of the measuring instrument. This informaion is missing in v 20, where then also the insertion of the קנים did not take place. Here the original form of the text can be seen, according to which the measurement figures appeared originally without the addition of the unit of measurement. This unit of measurement is undoubtedly to be found in the אמות which was then read into K in the wrong place.

e סביב "round about" is also attested by 𝔙 𝔗. In 𝔖 it is entirely missing, while 𝔊 (𝔏^{W}) *καὶ ἐπέστρεψε* has understood it verbally as סבב and, with the insertion of the copula, has connected it with the following statement. That corresponds to the transition in vv 18/19 of 𝔐 too and must, even to the addition of the copula (see 1:4 note a), represent the original text. Thus, here and in v 17, סבב should be read and be connected with what follows. 𝔖 simply omits סביב.

17 17a 𝔊 𝔖 𝔏 always add the copula before מדד too, in order to alleviate the harsh beginning with מדד which is strictly maintained in 𝔐 in vv 16–19. 𝔙 in v 16 *autem,* in vv 17–19 *et.* In 𝔏^{W} vv 17, 19 are missing. 𝔊 expands the direction indication right at the beginning: (*καὶ ἐπέστρεψε*) *πρὸς βορρᾶν,* but then follows 𝔐.

b See v 16 note d.

rod. <He turned>[c] 18/ <to the>[a] south side, measured: five hundred (cubits) [measuring rods][b] with the measuring rod. 19/ [a]He turned to the west side, measured: five hundred (cubits) [measuring rods][b] with the measuring rod. 20/ On the four sides he measured it (i.e. the temple precinct)[a]. It had a wall round about, (in) length: five hundred (cubits), (in) breadth: five hundred (cubits). (It had the task) of dividing the sacred from the profane[b].

c See v 16 note e.

18 18a 𝔐 את is the result of the wrong verse division (see v 16 note e) and should be emended on the basis of 𝔐 v 19 to אל, dependent on סבב. 𝔊 reverses vv 18 and 19 in the interests of the clear sequence of the points of the compass. See, on the other hand, also Rev 21:13.

b See v 16 note d.

19 19a 𝔐 v 19 correspnds to 𝔊 v 18 and is missing in 𝔏^W.

b See v 16 note d.

20 20a 𝔊 again reads more fully *τὰ τέσσαρα μέρη τοῦ αὐτοῦ καλάμου. καὶ διέταξεν αὐτὸν καὶ (περίβολον . . .)* and then after the numeral a *πρὸς ἀνατολάς*.

b 𝔊 *ἀνὰ μέσον τῶν ἁγίων καὶ ἀνὰ μέσον τοῦ προτειχίσματος τοῦ ἐν διατάξει τοῦ οἴκου*, with which 𝔊 48:15 may be compared. 𝔙 *inter sanctuarium et vulgi locum.*

Form

The section 42:15–20 can be recognized immediately by its introductory words, which have the character of a superscription, as the concluding section of the great measuring process.

Stylistically the proximity to the concluding measurements of the temple building and the square behind it to the west with בנין ("building") and גזרה ("restricted area") in 41:13–15a cannot be mistaken. Except that here at the end the two elements which characterized the great guidance vision at the beginning of chapters 40–42 are once more connected. The closing measurement formulae are preceded by a guidance statement. The measurement statements then follow, strongly stylized, in a fourfold repetition of identically formulated sentences. Here too of course it is the case that in details the freedom of slightly varying the formula is not entirely abandoned (omission of the בקנה המדה "with the measuring rod" immediately after the stating of the direction from the second measurement on, transposition of the מדד "he measured" after the stating of the direction from the third measurement on).

In addition, however, in this section it is noteworthy that the consecutive imperfect in the verbal forms has completely vanished, and both the guidance statements and the measurement statements, including the prefixed סבב ("he turned") in the measurements of sides two to four, are to begin with in the perfect with ו and then from v 16 on in asyndetically arranged perfects. The formulation with the syndetic perfect is by no means new. It has occurred already in the guidance formula at the end of the great guidance vision in 41:3. In the measurement formulae there it occurred occasionally in 40:24, 35 and then dominated the conclusion of the section 41:5–15a (in vv 13, 15). The asyndetic formulation in the perfect from 42:16 on is presumably to be regarded as a particularly emphatic, conscious stylization of the conclusion. At any rate one cannot separate 42:15–20 from 41:13–15a.

Setting

Thus, with regard to the question of the origin of the concluding section one may assume that it is from the same hand as 41:5–15a. But since 41:5–15a appears as a continuation of what has been described in the great guidance vision, 42:15–20 will also come from the hand of the author of the guidance vision. Thus 40:1–37, 47–49; 41:1–15a; 42:15–20 form the basic text (possibly written down in two stages) of the great temple vision which has been secondarily expanded with other components. If the reference to the perimeter wall in 40:5 belongs to the original text, then one can recognize a clear return of the conclusion (42:20a) to the beginning, thus rounding off the whole.

Interpretation

■ **42:15** By means of the introductory sentence of the conclusion of the measurements, it is underlined that the real content of the guidance experience lies in the communication of the size of the temple area. As in 40:5, the latter is described as בית ("house").

Now the prophet is led out of this area through the east gate, through which he was led in, to take note of its size from outside.

■ **42:16–19** In the sequence E, N, S, W (so, too, Rev 21:13), which is altered by 𝔊 to the sequential order E, N, W, S, the man measures the four external sides of the exactly square temple precinct. The measurements in *B. Mid.* II 1 must have been harmonized, in biblicistic fashion, to those in Ezek 42:15ff. There they have been expanded by information about the inequalities which exist in reality between the two temple terraces. The description of a side by means of the "wind" direction as רוח is possibly also attested in the inscription *CIS* 2, 213.[1] On the concluding ארבע רוחות ("four sides [winds]") of v 20 see 37:9 and Appendix 3. Also in this detail about the measuring instrument the conclusion goes back to the beginning of the guidance vision, where the measuring rod was said to be in the man's hand (40:3) and where the first measurements were made with this measure (40:6f). The mention of this measuring instrument has then led secondarily to the misunderstanding that, here too, the "measuring rod" refers to a unit of measurement (see note d). The measurement in cubits, which is certainly intended by the text, corresponds to the measurements which are to be expected on the basis of the internal measurements of the individual parts. A slight, certainly unnoticed lack of clarity unfortunately arises from the fact that one arrives at the measurement of five hundred cubits only if in the east-west direction one can equate the rear wall of the בנין ("building") with the perimeter wall of the temple. Then one achieves the following sum: depth of the gate: fifty cubits; distance to the inner east gate: one hundred cubits; inner east gate: fifty cubits; inner temple court: one hundred cubits; temple building with annexes: one hundred cubits; גזרה ("restricted area") and בנין ("building") including the (five cubits thick) rear wall: one hundred cubits. This gives the total of five hundred cubits which corresponds to the lateral measurement from north to south. From this it becomes questionable whether the information that reckons the thickness of the perimeter wall at six cubits (40:5) is really part of the original dimensions. In the course of a secondary expansion of the text by that passage, this lack of balance could simply have been overlooked.

■ **42:20** The concluding information about the wall, which dispenses with a measurement of breadth and mentions only a measurement of length, adds a quite distinctive statement on the basis of which the whole original temple plan is laid out. The wall has the task of marking the division between the sacred and the profane. This expression was used in 22:26 in the enumeration of the priest's duties.[2] It recurs in 44:23 in the same context. It states here explicitly what has already emerged in the consideration of the structure of the great guidance vision: In its new, pure dimension the layout of the temple precinct is understood as a clear isolation of the sacred domain from the profane, by means of which for the future every new "profanation" is repulsed by means of "abomination." There is no trace in all of the basic stratum of chapters 40–42 of any other differentiation between degrees of holiness such as is found in 42:1-14. Only the innermost chamber in the temple building is described in it as "holy of holies." It seems that the more pronounced differentiation of degrees of holiness is to be attributed to the further, reflective work of the later expander.

Aim

The concluding formulation of the great description, undoubtedly composed from the literary point of view in two stages, of the measuring of the sanctuary reveals what lies behind this entirely objective activity, which apparently belongs to the professional realm of the architect. As the verbal link with 22:26 shows, the office of priest is visible in it. The measurements of the building are meant to speak. 40:4 had already shown that the prophet, when he informs the house of Israel of the temple's dimensions, becomes a preacher. The divine ordinance, according to which the sacred should not be polluted, nor inadvertently mixed or confused with the profane because it belongs to God and because God does not wish to be confused with the world, becomes visible in the architectural layout.

But the holy cannot be thought of or understood in

1 J. T. Milik, "Notes d'épigraphie et de topographie palésteniennes," *RB* 66 (1959): 557.

2 See 1, 468f.

the biblical sphere apart from the holy one. Till now, in the context of the measuring (in the basic text) there has not been any mention of him. Thus what follows in 43:1ff represents with internal logical consistency the fulfillment of what has till now been made visible: The holy is found where God himself is present.

B. The Entry of Yahweh into his Sanctuary and the New Ordinances for the Prince, the Priests and the People

While the first three chapters of the great final vision stood out as a more or less self-contained unit and while, for the two final chapters 47–48 too, with their vista of the land outside the sacred precinct, a certain common denominator can be found, this will be less successful in the central section, chapters 43–46. The introductory account of Yahweh's entry into his sanctuary, which subsequently clearly influences certain regulations, is followed by a mass of heterogeneous ordinances, the structure of which is not very obvious and which have to do with the construction of the altar, the temple service and those who participate in it and which, in 45:1–8 for example, already clearly move on to the subject matter of chapter 48. Thus the collection in chapters 43–46 represents a certain, not entirely satisfactory expedient for a main central section of chapters 40–48. The examination of the individual sections, which here too will be undertaken one by one, reveals in this central section a particularly lively process of tradition, about which something will be said in summary fashion after the examination of chapters 40–48 as a whole.

1. Yahweh's Entry into his Sanctuary

Bibliography

W. F. Albright
"The High Place in Ancient Palestine" in *Volume du Congrès, Strasbourg 1956,* VT Suppl 4 (Leiden, 1957), 242–258.

George Ricker Berry
"The Glory of Yahweh and the Temple," *JBL* 56 (1937): 115–117.

Kurt Galling
"Erwägungen zum Stelenheiligtum von Hazor," *ZDPV* 75 (1959): 1–13.

David Neiman
"*PGR:* A Canaanite Cult-Object in the Old Testament," *JBL* 67 (1948): 55-60.

43

1 **And he led me to the gate <>[a] which**
<faces>[b] east. 2/ And see, the glory of
the God of Israel came[a] from the east[b],
and its rushing was like the rushing of
many waters[c], and the land shone with
its brightness[d]. 3/ And <> <his appearance <> was exactly like the appear-
ance>[a] which I had seen when <he>[b]

43: 1 1a In 𝔐 השער is followed by another שער without the article, which is, however, unattested in 𝔊 𝔖 𝔙 (otherwise in 𝔗) and which should, with most commentators, be deleted as a dittograph (see also 42:12).

b 𝔐 אֲשֶׁר פָּנָה is unusual, since otherwise the direction of the gates is expressed either by אשר פניו (40:6, 20 and elsewhere) or by the simple participle (8:3; 11:1; 44:1; 46:1, 12; 47:2). See also 9:2 note c. Thus פנה here will be a scribal error for an original פניו. At the end 𝔊 adds *καὶ ἐξήγαγέ με* no doubt in view of the renewed "bringing in" in v 5. The "leading out" of 42:15 is thus understood by 𝔊 as referring only to the inner east gate.

2 2a 𝔗 tones down the over-anthropomorphic בא of 𝔐 and reads איתגלי.

b 𝔊, on the basis of v 1, makes the sense more precise *κατὰ τὴν ὁδὸν τῆς πύλης τῆς βλεπούσης πρὸς ἀνατολάς*.

c 𝔊 *καὶ φωνὴ τῆς παρεμβολῆς ὡς φωνὴ διπλασιαζόντων πολλῶν* takes the וקולו of 𝔐 to refer to the sound in the camp of the heavenly armies. 𝔗 קל מברכי שמיה emphasizes their praise; on this see also 3:12 note a. It is on this basis that the comparison added in 𝔐 1:24 with the "camp" (1:24 note b) is here really understood. In the second half of the passage (Schleusner translates: *vox multorum qui se duplicant in acie*) Cornill and Jahn presuppose in the place of the מים of 𝔐 a שנים in the text translated by 𝔊.

d 𝔗 more fully מזיו יקריה.

3 3a The beginning of 𝔐 וכמראה המראה אשר ראיתי כמראה אשר ראיתי is overloaded. The versions, except 𝔗, give a somewhat different picture. In place of the first two words 𝔊 gives a simple *καὶ ἡ ὅρασις*. 𝔙 renders the first four words of 𝔐 freely by *et vidi*

came to destroy[c] the city, and <the appearance>[d] was exactly like the appearance which I had seen by[e] the river Chebar. And I fell on[e] my face. 4/ And the glory of Yahweh entered[a] the (temple-) house by the way through the gate[b] which faces east. 5/ And (the) spirit raised me up and brought me into the inner[a] court, and see, the (temple-)house was filled with the glory of Yahweh.

6 And I heard[a] someone from within[b] speaking[c] to me—but the man[d] stood beside me—7/ and he spoke to me: Son of man, (see) the place[a] of my throne and the

visionem, while 𝔖 omits them entirely. Consideration of the word order in 𝔐 raises the question whether the beginning of v 3 might be a scribal error arising out of the dittography of the phrase כמראה אשר ראיתי (on this cf. the dittograph in 40:6, 8f) and a slight, secondary adaptation to the present text. The formula of backward reference is then, on its first occurrence in the present corrupt 𝔐, taken to refer to the vision which, according to v 2, is just beginning (והנה) and in this connection the beginning has been altered to וכמראה המראה. The original text may have read המראה כמראה; with this cf. 8:4; 41:21 and the immediately following v 3b (note d).

b 𝔐 בבאי is, in spite of its attestation by 𝔊 𝔖, scarcely original. 𝔗 interprets באיתנביותי לחבלא ית קרתא. Jahn supposes a dogmatic alteration to avoid a statement about a destruction of Jerusalem by Yahweh himself. On the basis of 𝔙 Θ 𝔖^{h} בבאו should be read with MS$^{\text{Ken 145,250}}$.

c 𝔊 τοῦ χρῖσαι seems to go back to a textual corruption למשחת which has then been derived from משח.

d 𝔐 ומראות, omitted by 𝔖, rendered by 𝔊 καὶ ἡ ὅρασις and even by 𝔗 וחזוו (otherwise 𝔙 *et species*) as a singular, would originally have been singular parallel to v 3a ו(ה)מראה. 𝔊 ἡ ὅρασις τοῦ ἅρματος speaks explicitly here of throne carriages, on which see 1,127–129.

e על–אל cf. 1:17 note a.

4 4a 𝔐 בא is rendered by 𝔗 as in v 2 (note a) with איתגלי.

b שער without the article in 𝔐 is strange. 6 MSS^{Ken} (𝔊 𝔗?) read השער, hence Bertholet, Fohrer, Gese. But see also 9:2 note b and 40:6 note a.

5 5a On הפנימי alongside החצר see 40:23 note a.

6 6a 𝔊 καὶ ἔστην καὶ ἰδοὺ φωνή.

b On the form מהבית see Bauer-Leander §81p′.

c On the form מִדַּבֵּר see 2:2 note c and Rashi: "מדבר with *šwa* [i.e. pi'el] is used of a man who speaks to his fellow face to face, but מדבר with *ḥireq* [i.e. hithpa'el] of the *škina* who speaks to himself in glory and whose messengers hear it only: translated בורפאליץ [cf. French 'pour-parlers']," quoted from Gese, 34 note.

d Since in the איש it is undoubtedly the figure known from 40:3ff who is to be found, 𝔐 ואיש must be emended to והאיש with Cornill, Ehrlich, *Randglossen,* Gese and others. 𝔙, wrongly, finds in the man the speaker of the following words: *et vir qui stabat iuxta me dixit ad me.*

7 7a 𝔐 את מקום כסאי ואת מקום כפות רגלי is attested by 𝔖 𝔙. 𝔊 ἑόρακας seems at first sight to presuppose a הראית, which might then have fallen out by homoioteleuton alongside את (so Cornill, Herrmann, Bertholet). Somewhat differently Driver, "Ezekiel," 307, wishes to regard את as an abbreviation of אתה תראה. 𝔗 . . . דין אתר בית כורסי . . . ודין אתר makes Ehrlich, *Randglossen;* Toy; Fohrer suppose an original זה instead of את. In this connection one might think of

place[a] of the soles of my feet, where[b] I
will dwell for all time in the midst of the
Israelites. But the house of Israel must
no longer make my holy name unclean—
neither they nor their kings—by their
harlotry and by the memorials[c] of their
kings <at their death>[d] 8/—by setting
their threshold beside my threshold[a] and
their doorposts beside by doorposts[b] so
that (only) a wall lay between me[c] and
them, and they again and again[d] made
my holy name unclean by their abomina-
tion which they committed so that I (had
to) destroy them in my anger[e]. 9/ Now[a]
let them keep their harlotry and the
memorials[b] of their kings far from me[c]
and I[c] will dwell for all time in their midst.
10 You[a], son of man, describe to the house of
Israel the (temple-)house so that they

the ואת persistently corrupted from וזאת in 47:17–19, as well as in 16:22. More probably, however, 𝔐 should be retained here and את should be regarded, according to Gesenius-Kautzsch §117i, with Gese, who also refers to Moses Hirsch Segal, *A Grammar of Mishnaic Hebrew* (Oxford: Clarendon, 1958) §416f, as a strong particle of reference which implicitly presupposes a verbal statement along the lines of the expansion in 𝔊. Thus 𝔊 and 𝔗 faithfully reproduce 𝔐 each in its own way. To find, with Blau, "Gebrauch," 15f, the anticipation of the later שם קדשי in the two statements is not to be recommended.

b 𝔊 takes 𝔐 שָׁם as שֵׁם and translates the passage, with slight distortion of the text along the lines of Deuteronomic theology (see, e.g., Dtn 12:11): *ἐν οἷς κατασκηνώσει τὸ ὄνομά μου ἐν μέσῳ οἴκου* (did its text read בית?) Ισραηλ. In 𝔗, where already the powerful מקום כפות רגלי was rendered by בית אשריות שכינתי, here too the expression is דאשרי שכינתי תמן.

c 𝔐 ובפגרי מלכיהם. 𝔊 *ἐν τοῖς φόνοις τῶν ἡγουμένων*. 𝔙 *in ruinis regum suorum*. 𝔖 בשלדא (corpses) דמלכיהון. 𝔊 has misunderstood 𝔐 and certainly does not give the right unhesitatingly to emend the text here and in v 9 (note b) to בהרגם or את הרגיהם (Fohrer).

d 𝔐 במותם is to be derived from במה (see above on 6:3) which then appears, however, in a syntactically strange way, not to be fitted in to the context. Thus 𝔙 *et in excelsis* inserts a copula, as does 𝔖 ובפתכריהון "and with their idols." 𝔗 במותהון Θ (𝔖[h]) *τῶν τεθνηκότων* points, with about 20 MSS Edd, to a reading בְּמוֹתָם which commends itself also from the point of view of content. Thus Gese as well as Ehrlich, *Randglossen;* Toy; Bertholet, which last, however, propose a deletion of the word as a gloss. 𝔊 *ἐν μέσῳ αὐτῶν* points to a reading בתוכם (so Fohrer). Graphically it might also be wondered whether במותם might not be a corrupt dittograph of the following בתתם. See further the exposition.

8 8a 𝔗 elucidates by the addition of "in my sanctuary."

b 𝔗 more graphically: "its structures beside the court of my sanctuary (עזרתי)." On both occasions 𝔊 transposes: *τὸ πρόθυρόν μου ἐν τοῖς προθύροις αὐτῶν καὶ τὰς φλιάς μου ἐχομένας τῶν φλιῶν αὐτῶν*.

c 𝔗 tones down the anthropomorphism בין מימרי, while 𝔊 again expounds more broadly *καὶ ἔδωκαν τὸν τοῖχόν μου ὡς συνεχόμενον ἐμοῦ καὶ αὐτῶν*.

d On the frequentative sense of the *waw*-consecutive perfect see Gesenius-Kautzsch §112i.

e 𝔊 more fully: *ἐν θυμῷ μου καὶ ἐν φόνῳ*.

9 9a 𝔐 עתה. 6 MSS[Ken] 𝔊 *καὶ νῦν*, 𝔙 *nunc ergo* might suggest the reading ועתה. So Cornill, Herrmann, Bertholet. On the insertion of the copula in 𝔊 see 1:4 note a.

b See v 7 note c.

c 𝔗 again tones down the direct address in the "I" of Yahweh and reads מלמחטי קדמי and ואשרי שכינתי.

10 10a 𝔐 אתה. 29 MSS ואתה, 𝔊 *καὶ σύ*, 𝔙 *tu autem*, 𝔖

may be ashamed of their transgressions[b]. And if they measure <its layout>[c] 11/ then <they will>[a] be ashamed of all that they have done. Tell them about the shape[b] of the temple and its design[c] and its exits and its entrances[d] and all the relevant instructions[e] and statutes <>[e]

ואנת suggest an original ואתה. So most commentators. Here too, however, one would have to see a secondary easing of the text.

b According to Driver, "Linguistic Problems," 185f, v 10aβ should be deleted as an erroneous anticipation of v 11.

c 𝔐 ומדדו את תכנית is attested literally only by 𝔅 *et metiantur fabricam.* 𝔊 𝔗 (טיקוסיה) as well as 𝔖 (לדמותה דביתא) suggest the correction of תכנית to תכנתו. 𝔐 תכנית (elsewhere only in 28:12) has arisen either through haplography of the ו before the following ואם (v 11 note a) or through transposition of תו to ות (= ית). On a similar transposition of ו see, e.g., 14:1 note a. תכנתו will then have to be understood, on the basis of v 11, as תכונתו. 𝔊 *καὶ τὴν ὅρασιν αὐτοῦ καὶ τὴν διάταξιν αὐτοῦ* has found in the text a מראהו but does not deserve (against Cornill, cf. Toy) to be followed. An emendation to ומדותיו (Herrmann, Galling) is superfluous. Nor is the reading ואת מְדָדֵי תכניתו "the measurements of its proportions" (Driver, "Linguistic Problems," 185f) convincing.

11 11a The conditional ואם נכלמו of 𝔐 is remarkable. The immediately preceding unconditionally proffered proclamation of the temple vision, which is supposed to induce shame, can scarcely be connected immediately with the precondition of such shame. Even an oath formula introduced by אם is unlikely in this context. Thus 𝔊 *καὶ αὐτοὶ λήμψονται τὴν κόλασιν αὐτῶν* doubtless leads along the right track to an original reading והם יכלמו. This is to be understood as a final clause of v 10 (Wellhausen, Cornill, Cooke, Gese).

b 𝔐 צורת הבית has been read by 𝔊 *καὶ διαγράψεις*, with the transposition of the first two consonants, as וצרת and understood as a synonym of the later וכתב, which is rendered by the same word. Hence Koehler-Baumgartner צור III "design, make a plan." One must, however, adhere to 𝔐 and understand צורה as a parallel to the תכונה which is connected with it in a double statement (corresponding to the following ומוצאיו ומובאיו).

c 𝔐 ותכונתו is omitted by 𝔊, which has not grasped the layout of the whole passage in parallel statements (see already note b on 𝔐 צורה, also note d). On תכונה Driver, "Ezekiel," 307, points to Na 2:10. Cowley, *Papyri,* 15,6f: "arrangement, outfit, furniture." So too Job 23:3 of God's heavenly furniture.

d 𝔐 ומובאיו, instead of the phonetically correct derivation from מבוא (26:10; 27:3; 33:31; 42:9K; 44:5; 46:19), is due to assonance with the neighboring ומוצאיו; see also 2 Sam 3:25Q. 𝔊 omits this word too, see note c.

e In the next four expressions in 𝔐 וכל צורתו ואת כל חקתיו וכל צורתו וכל תורתו what is surprising is not only the twofold recurrence of צורה, which has appeared already at the beginning of the enumeration, but also the abandonment of the pairing of terms which had formerly been observed. The

and draw them for them to see so that they may observe all the relevant <instructions>[f] and statutes and do them.
12 **This is the instruction for the (temple-) precinct[a]: On the top of the mount its whole area all around is sacred. [See, that is the instruction for the (temple-) precinct][b].**

pair תורת–חקות attested in 44:5 (alongside מוצא–מבוא) is here severed by the placing of a וכל צורתו in front of each of the expressions. Thus the suggestion becomes highly probable that the two וכל צורתו, which both factually after the preceding צורת הבות and in addition by their plural form do not fit the context, do not represent the original reading. Then surely the וכל צורתו וכל תורתו immediately preceding the הודע is to be understood as a catchword gloss which has come secondarily into the text as a correction of the preceding wrong reading וכל צורתו and which proposes reading וכל תורתו instead of וכל צורתו. So Herrmann, Cooke, Gese. This then leads, of course, in contrast to 44:5, to the sequence 1) תורתו 2) חקתיו. This seems to appear here also in v 11b, see note f.

f 𝔐 וכל צורתו is, on the evidence of 𝔊 *τὰ δικαιώματά* (*μου*), equally a scribal error for an original תורתו.

12
12a 𝔐 ואת תורת הבות. 𝔊 *καὶ τὴν διαγραφὴν τοῦ οἴκου* and 𝔖 הנו חזוא דביתא presuppose here too in the text before them a corruption of the תורת to צורת, see v 11 notes e and f. On the corruption of זאת to ואת, which is also presupposed by 𝔊, see 16:22 note a.

b V 12bβ, which is missing in 𝔊 𝔖, is remarkable also for its introductory הנה and should be deleted as a superfluous repetition of v 12a.

Form

About the fact that there is a new beginning in 43:1 there is, on the basis of criteria of form and content, no doubt. Opinions about the conclusion of the present section, however, are certainly extremely diverse. Bertholet makes a break after v 9 and finds in vv 10–12 an addition by another hand. Hölscher calls vv 10f "a clumsy join which attempts to make the connection with 43:12ff." Fohrer sees in 43:1–9; 44:1–2(3); 47:1–12 a continuous narrative and in 43:10–12 the addition of a later hand. Gese, however, has drawn attention to the fact that between 43:1–9 and 43:10–11 there exists, from the point of view both of style and of content, a strong connection and that a break after v 9 is, therefore, scarcely permissible. V 12, on the other hand, he would wish to regard as a "leftover fragment" or as a "transition piece" leading to the description of the altar in vv 13ff. Neither explanation, however, is particularly obvious. From what has this fragment in v 12 been "left over"? And in what does its "transition" to vv 13ff consist? V 12 certainly connects with vv 10f, but reveals no element of particular connection with the altar which is the subject of vv 13ff. Doubt as to the originality of v 12 in its present context can arise at the most from certain considerations as to the content of this verse. On this see the exposition. Thus, in any event, one will have to reckon with the unity of vv 1–11.

From the point of view of form vv 1–11(12) begin, once again, in the style of the guidance vision. Now, admittedly, all the elements of measurement are missing. Also the guiding figure of the man passes quickly and completely into the background in the face of the appearance of Yahweh. As in earlier theophanies (3:12–14; 8:3; 11:24; cf. 37:1) the prophet is transported by the רוח ("spirit") to a new place. Twice the visionary observation is introduced by הנה ("see") (vv 2, 5). The great call vision, which is specifically referred to in the (undoubtedly secondary) v 3aβ, is further recalled not only by the prophet's reaction (on v 3b cf. 1:28) but also by the introduction of the words of Yahweh (on v 6a cf. 1:28; 2:2). Yahweh's word then dominates the second part of the section from v 7 on. A characteristic style of the pairing of words and of the repetition of clauses[1] links the two parts of Yahweh's speech, each of which begins with the address to the son of man. This reveals, in the first instance, the promise inherent in the theophany. Over and above the invective against the earlier sins in the temple precinct it leads to the demand for new conduct and to the commission to the prophet to proclaim. In v 12 there follows, introduced by its own superscription, the enactment of the תורה ("instructions") for the temple, which is seen in the vision and is now requisitioned by Yahweh and is promised to Israel.

Setting

By contrast with the basic text of chapters 40–42, 43:1–6 reveal a distinct change in style. The process of measurement, the architectural description of the total plan of the temple area are concluded. 43:10f make it clear, however, that what was seen in that earlier vision has not simply been left behind, nor is it unknown to the author of 43:1ff. Rather it enters specifically into the commission to the prophet to proclaim, a commission which is expressed once again here (vv 10f). On the other hand, however, 43:1–11(12) cannot be understood without looking back at chapters 8–11 and at 1:1–3:15. The link between chapters 40–48 and the beginning of the book of Ezekiel is nowhere to be grasped so fully as at this very point.

Now for those who have in mind chapters 8–11 alongside 20:40ff and 37:26ff, it is difficult to conceive that the vision of the new temple has already reached its climax with the perception of the new architectonic relationships on the sacred mountain. The final, decisive element is still missing, the presence of Yahweh at this place. Since now, in spite of the stylistic dissimilarity of chapters 40–42, no observations strongly prohibit the origin of 43:1–11(12) from the hand of the author of the great guidance vision 40:1–37, 47–49; 41:1–4 and its continuations in 41:5–15a; 42:15–20, and since, on the other hand, much of the content of 43:1-11(12), as will be shown, is best understood as inner reflection of this very plan, one can describe the unity of authorship as an entirely possible assumption. The vision of the return of the divine glory into the reconstructed sanctuary represents the climax of the vision of the temple of the future.

For the process of the writing down of this vision it must, of course, be stated once again what already emerged from the juxtaposition of 40:1–37, 47–49; 41:1–4 and 41:5–15a; 42:15–20. The individual elements of the vision have been written down in consecutive sections in which the separate parts each acquired their particular, formal shape. One must explain this process, which is not there in the basic text of 1:1–3:15 and chapters 8–11, by the fact that great significance was attached to the architectonic correctness of the plan. Thus the great guidance vision, the aim of which is towards the holy of holies, pressed forward in the first instance to an independent form in which the measurements of substantial features remained unmentioned. The necessary further details were added in 41:5–15a in a rather artless, list-like fashion. The whole measurement process was finally rounded off by a concluding section in 42:15–20. Now 43:1–11(12), in a renewed narrative beginning, makes Yahweh himself pass along in the way described in 40:1–37, 47–49; 41:1–4, from the east gate to the holy of holies (admittedly without the diversions via the side gates). This process, parallel to chapters 40f, ends in 43:7–11(12) in direct speech of Yahweh in which also what was intended by chapters 40f is given full expression. To this extent 43:1–11(12), alongside chapters 40–42, cannot be dispensed with against the background of the book of Ezekiel as a whole. One will simply have to accept the strange, repeated additions to the arrangement of the section as a whole. There is reflected in this the infiltration of strong elements of reflection, even of graphic meditation on the visionary spectacle.

Let a final consideration which suggests itself to reflection on the juxtaposition of chapters 40–42 and 43:1–11(12) not go unmentioned. If one examines the components of the great, dated final vision in terms of their possible experiential authenticity, then 43:1–11(12) speaks of the occurrence of a direct encounter with God. Behind this one can hear again the echo of the call experience and even, distantly, of Isaiah 6,[2] but also of the experience of chapters 8–11. 43:1ff speak of a genuine vision in the encounter with God. In chapters

1 Gese, 41.

2 See 1,98–100.

40–42, on the other hand, one had the impression of the prophet bent over a sketch plan of the new temple. The complete lack of any impression of height in the buildings presented the "vision" of the new temple in a strangely unreal light. Thus the question arises whether chapter 43 does not stand closer to the real core of prophetic experience, while chapter 40–42, which now precede it, belong much more strongly to the process of reflective, later stylization. What was a datable experience has thus possibly developed reflectively into its individual elements in a "scholarly" process.

Interpretation

■ **43:1** With the guidance verb which was used also in 40:24 (ויולכני "and he led me") the prophet reports of being led to the (outer) east gate. When Hölscher, Gese and others observe here a tension with 42:15, since this gate has already been mentioned as the last place where the prophet stood, and conclude from that the incompatibility of connecting 43:1 to 42:15–20, then that is inexact. 42:15 had stated that the prophet had been led through the east gate out of the interior of the temple. The east gate is not the goal at which this leading came to rest. Rather, in 42:15–20 there followed the measuring by the man of the outer walls on their four sides. Every impartial reader will understand that the prophet follows the man's measurings. On the other hand, in contrast to 42:15, the leading to the east gate in 43:1 is the end point of that leading.

■ **43:2, 4** Here the prophet experiences what is described in vv 2ff. What he now sees surpasses all that has hitherto been seen according to chapters 40–42. Yahweh himself appears in his majesty. As in 1:1ff; 3:22f and chapters 10f, it is not (as it is in Isaiah 6) a question of the unveiling of a presence of Yahweh which was already there but was till then hidden from human gaze. Yahweh comes from the east. It is through the east gate that he enters the temple itself. One certainly cannot conclude from the fact that only the east gate is mentioned, here as already in v 1 in the case of the prophet's own entry, that what is envisaged here is not the plan as drawn in chapter 40 with the two east gates and that one has to do here with the simple conception of a temple with only one east gate. As the consequences which are drawn in 44:1–2 and in 46:1 show, naturally the passage through both gates is reckoned with (on this see also Ps 24:7–10 with its plural address to the gates). Here, however, one cannot overlook the statements of 10:18a, 19b; 11:23.[3] Yahweh's arrival follows in the reverse direction the way along which the prophet, almost twenty years before, had seen the departure of Yahweh's majesty from the temple precinct. Against the background of these statements the immediate question that arises is this: Is this coming of Yahweh to his sanctuary once again a coming which will one day end in a new departure from the temple? In vv 7 and 9 Yahweh himself will answer this question.

First, however, it is worth examining the detailed description of the divine appearance, in which, according to H. Schmid, elements of the Sinai tradition may be observed.[4] The theophany is spoken of first of all with the full expression "glory of the God of Israel," and this is continued in vv 4f with the simpler "glory of Yahweh."[5]

In contrast to 10:18f and 11:22f, where the basic text can be differentiated from secondary expansion, etc., by this very difference in appellation, no such differentiation between two different hands can be undertaken here.[6] Rather, one has the impression that for this first reference to the presence of Yahweh within chapters 40–43 the fuller expression, with its suggestion of Israel's covenant reality, has been consciously chosen. The fuller expression, like the shorter one, surely belongs to already extant tradition.[7] After the solemn introduction the account returns to terser phraseology. For the description of the accompanying acoustic phenomena the image of the "rushing of many waters" is used, an image which is used in the expansion to the call vision in particular for the rustling of the wings of the creatures which

3 See 1,251f.
4 Herbert Schmid, "Jahwe und die Kulttraditionen von Jerusalem," *ZAW* 67 (1955): 191.
5 On this see 1,123f.
6 See 1,232.
7 On the "God of Israel" see Steuernagel, "Jahwe," 334f.

carry the throne.[8] In addition there is the reference to the optic phenomenon of brightly shining light, in which no "solar symbolism" is to be seen.[9] What is envisaged, rather, is an illumination, as if by lightning, of the whole country round about. With different words 1:4 had also spoken of fire and light as characterizing the theophany, while 1:13 then linked the light phenomena, among which the flickering flashes of lightning are specifically mentioned, more closely with the four creatures.[10] The ambiguous use of the term כבוד ("glory") in this connection is worth noting. In v 2a it describes the form in which Yahweh actually appears, but then in v 2b it describes the brightness which emanates from this very figure. Nevertheless, there is no justification for critical interference with the text. In comparison with chapter 1 the concise description of the theophany is striking.

■ **43:3** This perception is doubtless the reason for the double reference back in v 3a, which recalls first of all the theophany in chapters 8–11 and then, secondly, the theophany by the river Chebar which was the subject of chapter 1. In quite similar words there were also references in 3:23 and 8:4 to earlier descriptions. As in these passages, here too we are dealing with secondary, bracketed elements which have been added editorially when the book was being put together as a whole.[11] In the first reference, to chapters 8–11, this can be seen also in the fact that what is mentioned is a "coming" of Yahweh to destroy the city. This represents a view which is derived from the additions in 8:4 and 9:3a. The basic text of chapters 8–11 made no reference to a coming of Yahweh, but to the destruction of the city which would begin from the place of the divine presence in the temple. Connected with this was the departure of Yahweh's glory from the temple. In the reference to chapter 1 𝔊 mentions specifically the "chariot" and thus betrays the speculation with regard to Ezekiel 1 which was already under way in its time.[12] The original text of 43:1ff had, exactly like the basic text of chapters 8–11, dispensed with a closer description of the כבוד ("glory"). It reports solely, with the words of 1:28, the prophet's terrified collapse.[13]

■ **43:5** While, according to 2:2, the "spirit"[14] had then raised the prophet and had rendered him capable of hearing the divine address, here, as in 3:12, 14; 8:3; 11:1, 24,[15] the "spirit" is spoken of as the power which can transport man to different localities. The prophet is transported to the place in the inner court where he hears the voice of Yahweh, the light of whose glory fills the temple. An analogous statement is to be found in the account of the transfer of the ark to the newly built temple of Solomon. Yet surely Noth is correct in seeing in 1 Kgs 8:10f a later, priestly addition to which Ex 40:34f closely corresponds.[16] It will not do, however, for this reason to regard Ezek 43:5, too, for example, as also dependent on P statements. The conception of the presence of Yahweh in the temple, a presence which fills the latter with suffocating smoke, which is more fully developed in Ex 40:34f and 1 Kgs 8:10f, is already too clearly discernible in Isaiah 6, even if there the explicit reference to the כבוד יהוה ("glory of Yahweh") is employed differently. Ezekiel 43 refers to the presence of Yahweh in the temple in a much more restrained fashion. Everything leads up to Yahweh's address to the prophet.

■ **43:6** This is introduced in v 6a with words which recall 2:2 (1:28b).

First of all, however, a brief remark is made about the "man," about whose whereabouts one instinctively wants to ask. While in 43:1 he was still presupposed to be in his role as the prophet's guide, now it is simply observed that he is standing beside the prophet. Why is it not recounted of him that he has led the prophet from the outer east gate into the inner court? Hölscher postulates that the original text must have stated this, deletes the reference to the רוח ("spirit") and the ותשאני ("and . . . raised me up") which goes with it in v 5 and makes the "man" the subject of the guidance statement which is found there. The text of 𝔐 will then have been altered in

8 See 1, 130f on 1:24.
9 Contrary to Herbert Gordon May, "Some Aspects of Solar Worship at Jerusalem," *ZAW* 55 (1937): 278–281, who finds in 43:1ff the reflection of a spring equinoctial ritual. See also Morgenstern, "King-God," 160f.
10 On 1:4 see 1, 118–120; on 1:13, 1, 121f.
11 See 1, 157f and Sprank, *Studien*, 3.
12 See v 3 note d and 1, 127f.
13 On this see 1, 123.
14 See 1, 132 and below Appendix 3.
15 See 1, 139.
16 Noth, *Könige*.

view of the statement in 44:1–3 (46:1) that the east gate is closed. Jahn and J. Herrmann remove the reference to רוח ("spirit") in a different way, by presupposing that it is Yahweh himself who is meant by איש ("man").[17] But 𝔐 should be adhered to. The withdrawal of the man is doubtless to be explained on the basis that in view of the presence of Yahweh in his כבוד ("glory") there is no further place for any further guiding activity. When the sun rises the stars grow pale. When the king enters and begins to speak the courtiers fall back. The concise observation about the man who, as a heavenly being, traverses the way into the inner court with just as much ease as the prophet transported by the spirit simply aims to make one more brief reference to the figure about whom the reader may ask and, in the manner of the observation, to indicate at the same time that his actual service is at an end.

■ **43:7** It is Yahweh alone who now speaks. In the weighty introductory clause in v 7aα, which, in spite of different phraseology, recalls the climactic sentence of the great guidance pericope in 41:4bβ, he points the son of man[18] in an indicative statement to the place of which he has now taken possession and explains it as the place of his presence. What was described objectively in 41:4 as "holy of holies" is now characterized from within, by the Lord who is here present, in all its majesty: "The place of my throne and the place of the soles of my feet"—and to this there is added immediately the promise which God as the faithful one adds in such a characterization of the place: "(the place) where I will dwell for all time in the midst of the Israelites." In this respect the naming of this place expresses old concepts, loaded with tradition. Terminology which was previously connected with the ark here receives new life.

When, according to Jer 3:16f, the people who mourn the loss of the ark of the covenant are antithetically pointed to a time when they will remember the ark no more but will call Jerusalem "the throne of Yahweh," then behind this can be discerned the description of the ark as Yahweh's throne. The description, which is connected with the ark, of Yahweh as "enthroned on the cherubim" (ישב הכרבים 1 Sam 4:4; 2 Sam 6:2) belongs to this realm of thought. The cry which is heard in the people's lament in Jer 14:21, "Do not dishonor the 'throne of thy glory' (כסא כבודך)" extends the expression used of the ark to Zion and Jerusalem as the place of Yahweh's throne. In the phrase "place of the soles of my feet," on the other hand, we can discern only a slight variation of the "stool" on which the feet of the enthroned one rest. By means of this description (הדם רגליו "footstool"), however, in Ps 132:7, after the news of the discovery of the ark in "Kiriath-jearim" (שדי יער) has been announced in a dramatic dialogue, the congregation is summoned to worship: "Let us go to his dwelling, let us throw ourselves (in worship) at his footstool." 1 Chr 28:2, in a speech of David, has the full parallelism of the "ark of the covenant of Yahweh" and the "footstool of our God." In Ps 99:5, where the cry as in Ps 132:7 can be heard, the expression, on the evidence of the parallel v 9, is similarly to be expanded to refer to Yahweh's holy mountain (הר קדשו "his holy mountain").[19] Similarly Lam 2:1. Also the formulation in Is 60:13, which is quite close to that in Ezek 43:7, reveals the parallelism of מקום מקדשי ("place of my sanctuary") and מקום רגלי ("place of my feet"). In a magnificent synthesis Isaiah 6 has already connected the two conceptions. When Isaiah here sees Yahweh seated on a high and lofty throne in the temple, this is a description of the Lord of the ark enthroned high above the cherubim. But when the prophet then speaks of the hem of the divine garment which (flowing down over the feet) fills the temple, then it is not difficult to discern behind this the ark as the footstool for the divine feet. Only Yahweh's feet rest on the ark in the temple. The "high and lofty" divine throne above the cherubim towers high above it into the heavenly heights. The complete disruption of these concepts associated with temple and ark can be seen in the early post-exilic period where Yahweh, according to Is 66:1, in a critical questioning of the rebuilding of the temple, states: "Heaven is my throne and the earth my footstool—what kind of house would you build for me and what kind of resting place would there be for me there?" On the use of the concept מנוחה ("resting place") in the context of the site of the ark see also Ps 132:8: "Arise, Yahweh, to thy resting place—thou and thy mighty ark." H. Schmidt points out "that the sacred rock [the spot on

17 J. Herrmann, *Ezechielstudien.*
18 See 1, 131f.
19 See Schmid, "Jahwe," 194f.

which the holy of holies must have stood][20] is still today 'the site of the footprints,' that the crusaders looked for the footprints of their ascended Lord on this rock just as did and still do today the Muslims the footprint of the Prophet and of other holy men."[21] One can scarcely, however, conclude from this that the period of Ezekiel already knew of a footprint of Yahweh's on the sacred rock. The old ark-footstool tradition is quite sufficient to explain the terminology of Ezek 43:7.

The passage in Ezekiel, from what it says, stands in sharp contrast to Is 66:1 when it makes Yahweh say of the temple building of the promised temple or, as can be made more precise on the basis of 41:4, of the holy of holies in this temple: "The place of my throne—the place of the soles of my feet." Here, in the innermost part of his temple Yahweh is enthroned. He commandeers it as his dwelling place. It will be observed that by not a single word is any mention made of the ark here or in any of the expansions from the school of the prophet. In the negation implied here Ezekiel 43 obviously stands completely in the line of the oracle in Jer 3:16f. On the positive side of what it says, however, it adheres strictly to the association of divine throne and footstool with the temple. This differentiates him not only from Trito-Isaiah but equally from Jeremiah, in whose train he seemed just now to be following. In the P plan of the sacred tent (Exodus 25ff) the ark is then fully restored to its old right. Ezekiel 43, in contrast to this fairly late priestly theology, is still fairly strongly prophetically revolutionary.[22]

Admittedly Ezekiel 43 sets great store by the presence of Yahweh in the sanctuary. Thus the promise of the everlasting dwelling in the midst of his people then becomes the thematic word which, like a framework, introduces (v 7aβ) and concludes (v 9b) the following complex of statements. It should be observed here that in this expression there is nothing about Yahweh's dwelling in his temple, but of his dwelling in the midst of his people Israel. That corresponds to the statement, expressed in different terminology, of 37:26–28, where it was said that Yahweh would set his sanctuary in the midst of his people for all time. The mention there in v 26 of the covenant with the people and the specific quotation of the two-sided covenant formula in v 27 allowed this fact to emerge clearly. Here too it is not a question of the sacred place which might have holiness in itself, but of the relationship of Yahweh to his people, for which his presence in the sacred place is a sign and a seal.[23] Behind the statement of Yahweh's dwelling "in the midst of Israel" G. von Rad believes that he can hear echoes of "the good old Israelite view of Yahweh's presence in the camp."[24]

From this point alone it then becomes fully understandable that in the words which frame the promise there can be embedded an address to this very covenant nation which harshly reprimands them and offers them a new way. Yahweh's dwelling in his sanctuary is no natural phenomenon. It is summons and obligation. In the formulation of these statements the framework technique may be observed for a second time. The summons in the jussive to leave off the previously practiced atrocities frames in vv 7b and 9a the description of these atrocities and the punishment inflicted for them by Yahweh (v 8). This clear literary technique, which also uses the identical words in the framework, advises against following Procksch in his critical reduction of the complex vv 7b–9 to vv 7bα, 8a.[25]

■ **43:8** The fact with which the Israelites and, first of all, their kings in the pre-exilic period are reproached is stated in v 8. In a characteristic tripartite sentence it is stated that in the old temple the palace bordered on the temple, threshold to threshold, doorpost to doorpost so that only a wall separated temple and palace.[26] This corresponds to the description of 1 Kings 6f. The temple was built as one element of the total Solomonic palace complex.[27] The close juxtaposition of temple and palace can be made very clear by means of a narrative such as 2 Kings 11.

20 See above p. 360.
21 Schmidt, *heilige Fels,* 91.
22 On the significance of the loss of the ark see also Noth, "Jerusalem Catastrophe," 262.
23 On משכן ("dwelling place"), used in 37:27 as a description of the divine dwelling (see p. 276), comparison may also be made with Kuschke, "Lagervorstellung," 84–86.
24 von Rad, *Priesterschrift,* 183. On the meaning of "perpetual" (לעולם) see above p. 276 on 37:25f.
25 Procksch, "Fürst," 101f.
26 Gese, 41.
27 This is to be maintained in spite of the disagreement of Hugues Vincent, "Le caractère du temple salomonien" in *Mélanges bibliques rédigés en l'honneur de André Robert,* Travaux de l'Institut Catholique de

■ **43:7bβ, 9** Over and above the general proximity of temple and palace, however, vv 7 and 9 emphasize an effect which is particularly aggravating. In the old temple the Israelites violated the holiness of the divine name by the פגרי מלכיהם ("memorials of their kings"). In this designation, most commentators (including Eichrodt), as a consequence of the secondarily added statement of 6:5 (on this see note a there), have found the "corpses" of the kings in Jerusalem and have heard here the reproach that the graves of the kings had been located immediately next to the temple precinct. Now so far, archaeology has provided no certain information about the royal graves in ancient Jerusalem.[28] The data collected by Simons from Kings and Chronicles reveal as the burial place for the first thirteen kings down to Ahaz the "city of David," i.e. a location somewhat apart from the temple area.[29] The burial places of Manasseh and Amon might suggest somewhere closer to the temple. When, in the case of Manasseh (2 Kgs 21:18; on this cf. 2 Chr 33:20), the "garden of Uzza," which is also mentioned for Amon (2 Kgs 21:26), is described also by the further observation as being "in the garden of 'his palace' (ביתו)," then here one could be brought into very close proximity to the temple terrain.[30] Unfortunately there is lacking in the case not only of Hezekiah, but also of all the kings after Amon, in 2 Kings[31] any more specific information as to burial place, so that the assumption, which is mainly derived from Ezek 43:7, 9, that the graves of some kings must have lain directly alongside the temple court is not in accord with the conclusive confirmation of the royal annals.

Thus the supposition that פגר in this passage should be understood somewhat differently acquires a certain weight. Neiman, by his comparison of two commemorative inscriptions from Ugarit[32] with analogous inscriptions from Phoenicia, has established the meaning "stele" for the פגר which occurs there.[33] On this basis Neiman interprets 43:7 as referring to royal stelae which have been set "on their high places." The same sense of פגר he finds also in Lev 26:30, which would then in the addition in Ezek 6:5 not be cited in the sense of the Leviticus passage. In connection with these considerations Galling, in his discussion of the stele sanctuary at Hazor, has modified the thesis to suggest that what is envisaged is not stelae in the context of an idolatrous cult but stelae in memory of a deceased person: "Precisely if in the case of the royal stelae it is a question of stelae *pro memoria,* the atmosphere of death which is here under judgment may still adhere to them."[34]

If this view, which in fact precisely for this context has much in its favor, is correct, then the revocalization of 𝔐 בָּמוֹתָם ("their high places") as בְּמוֹתָם ("at their death") commends itself. Admittedly, Albright has suggested retaining 𝔐 and understanding it as an abbreviated בְּבָמוֹתָם ("in their high places").[35] By במות he understands elevated spots on which memorial stelae were raised (funeral shrines). The kings are thus reproved because they set up their memorial stelae "in their *bâmôt.*" But since the context compellingly demands that what is in question here is a desecration of the temple area, over which the name of Yahweh stands in a particular way, and since the erection of a במה immediately next to or within the temple area is extremely unlikely after Josiah's reformation, the simple revocalization of 𝔐 has more in its favor. A complete deletion of the במותם (Ehrlich, *Randglossen,* Toy, Herrmann) can certainly not be justified with the reference to the fact that it does not recur in v 9. V 9a otherwise reveals itself as an abbreviated repetition of v 7b.

Alongside the specific reproach for the erection of memorial stelae by the kings there stand the comprehensive reproaches against kings and "house of Israel" in which there recurs the vocabulary which is familiar from earlier contexts of the book of Ezekiel. The "profaning" (חלל) of Yahweh's holy name (שם קדשי "my holy name") has already been mentioned in 20:39; 36:20, 23 (39:7). On the basis of the total context the reproach is to be referred to the wiping out of the clear order of sanctity

Paris 4 (Paris, 1957), 137–148.

28 On this see the discussion in Simons, *Jerusalem,* 194–225, "The Royal Necropolis"; and Kurt Galling, "Die Nekropole von Jerusalem," *PJ* 32 (1936): 73–101.

29 Simons, *Jerusalem,* 201–204.

30 See also Jeremias, *Heiligengräber,* 53–56.

31 On 2 Chr 32:33 see Simons, *Jerusalem,* 207.

32 First translated by R. Dussaud, "Deux stèles de Ras Shamra portant une dédicace au dieu Dagon," *Syria* 16 (1935): 177–180.

33 See also Gordon, *Ugaritic Handbook,* Glossary 1605, "monument, stela"; and texts 69, 70. But see also Joseph Aistleitner, *Wörterbuch der ugaritischen Sprache* (Berlin: Akademie, 1963) 2189.

34 See also Mowinckel, *He That Cometh,* 79 note 3.

35 Albright, "High Place," 247.

of the temple, which will then be enjoined anew in vv 10f (12). The people's infidelity was, as in vv 7, 9, also described as זנות ("harlotry") in 23:27 (but see note a there). The word, which is used in the figurative sense of idolatrous worship also in Hos 6:10; Jer 3:2, 9; 13:27, is here, perhaps because of this figurative general significance, preferred to the תזנות ("harlotry") which is frequently used in Ezekiel 16 and 23 because in the latter, as these allegories show, the real sense of זנה ("to play the harlot") still echoes clearly.[36]

■ **43:8b** The description of the people's offenses has been involuntarily transformed in v 8b into a historical report, which then recounts also the bad end of the sinful period, the destruction of the people by Yahweh in his anger.[37] In this backward looking formulation it is firmly maintained in the midst of this promise for the future which is made to the prophet that what has happened signifies an end (chapter 7), a death (see 37:1ff). The future into which Israel may enter is the miracle of a new awakening. In view of the miracle of this new event, according to which Yahweh will take up his dwelling for ever in the new sanctuary in the midst of his people (v 9b), there issues once again in v 9a the demand to keep far from Yahweh and his temple the "harlotry" which manifested itself in the setting up of the memorial stelae. The intertwining of jussive and indicative is particularly close in v 9, which concludes the first part of the address. What is demanded is not, however, the precondition for Yahweh's return to his people. That is announced quite unconditionally. But v 9 certainly proclaims the quite inevitable consequence of that event. In this connection it is not initially envisaged that traces of buildings or even graves from the distant past should be put aside. Rather will it be the task for the future to keep such for all time far from Yahweh's dwelling place. The fact that in this context the title "king" is freely used, whereas elsewhere in the expectations for the future the title נשׂיא ("prince") comes to the fore, only shows to what extent the demand grows out of the total rejection of the past.[38]

The expression that the horrors referred to are to be kept "far" from Yahweh (רחק) makes it clear, however, to what extent here what is formulated in the jussive is orientated towards the concrete image of the new temple. The most revolutionary element of the temple description in the great guidance vision consisted precisely in the clear separation of the temple from the palace complex. What was expressed there in the cryptic language of a building plan is here translated into a concrete demand: Separate cleanly the sacred from the profane, separate clearly God's sphere of ownership from the sphere of human, even royal claims.

■ **43:10–11** What follows in vv 10f (12) as the second part of the speech of Yahweh then develops the divine demand once again in quite direct reference to the architectural language of the great guidance vision. At the same time the introductory commission to the prophet which was given him prior to the beginning of the visionary guidance (40:4b) is taken up once more. This framework-like return to the beginning of the whole composition, to which 43:1–11(12), on the basis of its content, must be reckoned, surely speaks for a connection between the sections as having been intended by their authors.

In their introduction vv 10f (12) also, of course, reveal the connection with the immediately preceding unit. The commission to the prophet to describe the "house," i.e. the whole temple complex seen by him in the vision, to the house of Israel is followed by the surprising expression, ". . . so that they may be ashamed of their transgressions." For whoever approaches this from the earlier words of the book of Ezekiel this expression is not new. It is a characteristic of the preaching of this book that such shame is spoken of not in the context of the judgment sermon but in that of the proclamation of salvation. In 16:54 it is the salvation which Israel experiences along with Sodom and Samaria, in 16:61 the establishment of the everlasting covenant with Israel and in 36:32 the free act of grace effected by Yahweh for his own sake which

36 On תועבה ("abomination") used in v 8 see 1, 190 and, in addition, Paul Humbert, "L'étymologie du substantif *toʿēbā*" in *Verbannung und Heimkehr. Beiträge zur Geschichte und Theologie Israels im 6. und 5. Jahrhundert v. Chr., Wilhelm Rudolph zum 70. Geburtstage dargebracht* (Tübingen: Mohr [Siebeck], 1961), 157–160.

37 On this use of the piʿel of כלה cf. 20:13; 22:31. אפי occurs in 20:8, 21 as the direct object of the piʿel of כלה.

38 See above pp. 218–220 on 34:23f and below on 47:13–48:29.

drive the people to a sense of shame.[39] The present passage thus fits perfectly into the rest of the preaching insofar as here, too, the shame results from the salvation to be proclaimed by the prophet. Its uniqueness consists, then, in the fact that the shame is to follow from the "proclamation of the (temple-) house," i.e. from the proclamation of salvation encoded in the architectural plan. At the sight of the temple painted for them by the prophet, the temple which is promised to his people by Yahweh, their eyes will be opened to the extent to which they had gone astray in their earlier dealings with the sacred which had also found expression not least in the ground plan of the old temple.

While the emphatic repetition of this statement in vv 10–11a*α* could already recall from the stylistic point of view the repetitions in vv 7–9, the relationship of style is still clearer in the threefold division of the development of the preaching commission which follows in v 11a*β*. In three complementary pairs of concepts there is now developed here what the prophet is to pass on to his people: 1) The shape of the temple and its furnishings. This involves the ground plan of the whole temple area as seen in the guidance vision. 2) Its exits and its entrances. One wonders whether this is concerned quite generally with the knowledge of the gates which played so great a role in the guidance vision or whether, in addition, there are already envisaged particular access and egress ordinances for the temple such as are then developed particularly in chapter 46. 3) All the relevant instructions and statutes for the temple as a whole. Here what are in mind, over and above the mere knowledge of the building structure and the order of the gates, are the rules which are to regulate life in the visionary temple. There was already a hint of this in vv 7–9.

In view of these three areas of proclamation, the prophet is shown a double way of transmission. He is to teach his people.[40] But he is at the same time to picture it for them. כתב (here "draw") here means not only the written record of prophetic words.[41] The explicit remark "for them to see" means, since the normal, written prophetic scroll was to be read and was thus meant for the ears (Jer 36:6 באזני העם "in the hearing of the people", also vv 10, 15, 20, 21), above all that the prophet is to draw what he has seen in a ground plan which he is to let his hearers see (on this cf., e.g., Ex 25:9, 40). The latter, however, are to be willing to "observe" (שׁמר) and "do" (עשׂה) the instructions connected with this. The same linking of the two verbs is found also in 11:20; 18:21; and elsewhere.

■ **43:12** The whole instruction to the prophet to proclaim to his people is concluded by means of the communication of a תורה ("instruction") which is emphatically introduced with its own superscription.[42] It gives expression to the sentence which results from all that has been seen: "This is the instruction for the temple precinct: On the top of the mount its whole area all around is sacred." The giving of Tora is one of the specific duties of the priest.[43] Correct "differentiation" (הבדיל) belongs particularly to the giving of Tora.[44] The process in Hag 2:10ff, in which the priest gives instructions as to behavior with regard to sacred and unclean, has as its point of departure knowledge about the differentiation between these mutually exclusive spheres. In 43:12 the Tora comes directly from the mouth of Yahweh himself.

At this point, of course, the question may well arise as to whether the Tora of v 12 can be connected from the point of view of content with the earlier data in the basic text of chapters 40–42. In 41:4 the figure of the guide had described the innermost room of the temple to the prophet as קדשׁ הקדשׁים ("the holy of holies"). The outer wall of the temple precinct, on the other hand, separated, according to 42:20, the "profane" (חל) from the "sacred" (simple קדשׁ). Thus the question arises whether the Tora of 43:12, which one would like to take seriously as a precise formulation, does not attest a heightened concept of holiness, according to which the whole temple mount is not only "holy" but "very holy." It would then surely come from a different hand. Against this idea it

39 The הכלם of 16:27 is in a different context. See also the occurrence of בושׁ in 16:52, 63; 36:32 (32:30 in a different context).

40 On הודיע as a particular method of priestly instruction see 1, 468 on 22:26 and 1, 336 on 16:2. See also 44:23.

41 Antonius H. J. Gunneweg, *Mündliche und schriftliche Tradition der vorexilischen Prophetenbücher als Problem der neueren Prophetenforschung,* FRLANT 55 (Göttingen: Vandenhoeck & Ruprecht, 1959), 40, among others, wishes to deduce from this passage that at that time there existed written prophetic oracles.

42 See Begrich, "Tora"; Östborn, *Tora.*

43 Cf. 22:26; 44:23 and see 1, 468.

44 See 1, 336 on 16:2.

should be considered from the other side that קדש הקדשים ("the holy of holies") with the definite article in 41:4 is primarily a spatial designation, however much it certainly also contains an expression of quality. In the Tora of v 12, on the other hand, which seeks to differentiate the profane area and the sacred, the קדש קדשים ("sacred") (here indefinite) is a designation of fitness which intentionally implies magnification. It does not reckon with a weaker stage, the simple "holy," which would then come somewhere between the very holy and the profane. In no sense is it seeking to lessen the particular value of the word that is used in 41:4 for the innermost room of the sacred area. It is to be understood on the basis of the emphasis of the declaration of principle which is intended to be from the mouth of Yahweh—an emphasis which is not peculiar to 42:20 which is in a purely factual style.[45]

To this two more general observations may be added. The Tora of 43:12 obviously tries to formulate what had already been said at the conclusion of the external measuring of the building in 42:20 (basically already going beyond the actual measurement itself) about the significance of the perimeter wall of the temple precinct. The wall was to separate the sacred and the profane. Here, admittedly, there is no hint of the heightened holiness statement of 43:12. But the verb הבדיל ("to divide") is used here, undoubtedly intentionally. The parallel endings of the description of the measuring of the temple (42:20) and of the scene of appropriation by the personal appearance of the God of Israel in 43:12 is perhaps more than mere chance. What in the final statement of the measurement report was a factual statement by the narrator here becomes an "instruction" in the mouth of Yahweh himself. The second observation is this. With the transportation of the prophet to a very high mountain the guidance vision began in 40:2. Here the prophet was shown the promised temple. With the Tora about this mountain the report of Yahweh's taking possession of the temple comes to an end. In the total context of chapters 40–48 there is no further reference to this "mountain" (הר). The question whether here too there is not to be seen, perhaps, a consciously formed framework-element in the bringing together of the basic stratum of chapters 40–42 with 43:1–12 may certainly be considered. 43:12 would then be the end of a road which began in 40:1.

These considerations do not remove completely the difficulties already mentioned with regard to the terminology of 43:12. Thus there remains an element of uncertainty regarding the question of whether the Tora of 43:12 originally belonged to 43:1–11.

Aim

The section 43:1–11(12) clearly wishes to give expression to what was already intimated in the cryptic language of the description of the buildings in 40:1–37, 47–49; 41:1–4 + 41:5–15a; 42:15–20. This is not achieved by means of a purely intellectual interpretation of what was originally depicted graphically. Rather it is achieved by means of a majestic act of God who personally enters what had previously been shown to the prophet by a divine guiding figure.

This entry has a double significance. It is, in the first instance, the royal occupation of the new temple, constructed with pure measurements, on the high mountain of Israel (40:2 alongside 20:40). It is, however—and this aspect is especially brought out in the text itself—at the same time the entry of this Lord into the midst of his people and the manifestation of his gracious intention to take up residence "in the midst of his people" (vv 7, 9) for all time. What is shown to the prophet in the vision which is granted to him alone and what he must now say to and depict for his whole people is the great promise with which God encounters his people. These people are not the pious congregation which might have coaxed God's mercy down from heaven by the abundance of their good works. They are the people whom God should have "annihilated" (כלה) because of their "faithlessness" (זנות). It is over this people that there goes, in what the prophet sees and is to proclaim, the announcement of the imminent coming of God who announces himself not just for a limited visit, but for a partnership of dwelling with his people which will never be broken. The vision of the new temple—this is what the scene with which the measuring process ends is saying retrospectively about what has been shown—is not the vision of a new sacred object or

45 See also the observation of Klaus Koch, "Die Eigenart der priesterschriftlichen Sinaigesetzgebung," *ZThK* 55 (1958): 42 note 5.

even of a religious treasure which is to be handed over to the people at this period. It is the preparation of the way along which God himself in his majesty will come, of the house in which he himself will take up residence so that his people may come to him at any time, honor him and find shelter in the shadow of his wings.

Over and above this, however, 43:1–12 tries to make it equally clear that such a coming of God to his people cannot simply be entered by them as assets on the credit side, where it would also remain what it is and was from time immemorial. The account of God's coming to his people shows at the same time how at this coming there occurs first of all a terrifying self-awareness which leads to a deep sense of shame. The people's whole previous history is illumined critically and revealed in its dubiousness.

But that is still too little. At God's appearing there is heard at the same time the summons to something new which must not only be heard but also be done (v 11). This new thing is described in terms of the awareness of the Old Testament priest. The basis of correct obedience is correct differentiation and separation. Profane humanity must not penetrate God's holy domain, but must respect the holy things of God as that which is circumscribed by God's commands. But the priestly/prophetic witness of Ezekiel 43 still knows nothing of that terrifying act of God in which he gives himself in his servant, in order to crown his love, to the unclean world as a pure sin offering (Is 53:10). The priestly-prophetic duty consists in urging that he who is unaware of and does not respect the otherness of the holy one cannot serve him. It is at this frontier that he is aware of being stationed as guardian.

2. A Double Addition. The Altar and its Consecration

43:13–27 does not stand in a recognizable literary context, linked either with what precedes or with what follows. It has been correctly noted that the description of the altar would have its place, from the point of view of content, after 40:47, where the altar in front of the temple building is mentioned. Thus Procksch, e.g., thinks 43:13–17 probably once followed 40:47.[1] But that is certainly not correct. The formally self-contained nature of the guidance vision affords no place for this section, which is formulated stylistically without any reference to guidance or measurement.

The description of the altar is followed by the ritual of its consecration. From the point of view of content there can be no doubt that vv 18–27 belong after vv 13–17. At the same time, however, it becomes quite clear—not only from the expansive, fresh introduction in v 18 but also from the uniqueness of the style—that vv 18–27 form an independent section, which, from the point of view of form, is shaped quite differently. In its detailed treatment of the general topic of "altar" it reveals only in v 20 any indication of a connection with vv 13–17. The messenger formula which introduces the section, as well as the subsequent formulae for a divine saying, differentiate it noticeably from vv 13–17 and come, from the point of view of form, close to later sections. Vv 18–27 were probably added to vv 13–17 only at a somewhat later period.

Thus it is advisable to deal separately with vv 13–17 and vv 18–27.

1 Procksch, "Fürst," 102.

a. Form and Measurements of the Altar of Burnt Offering

Bibliography

W. F. Albright
"The Babylonian Temple-Tower and the Altar of Burnt-Offering," *JBL* 39 (1920): 137–142.

Kurt Galling
Der Altar in den Kulturen des alten Orients (Berlin: Curtius, 1925).

J. de Groot
Die Altäre des Salomonischen Tempelhofes, BWAT NF 6 (Stuttgart: Kohlhammer, 1924), especially 44–52.

Rudolf Kittel
Studien zur hebräischen Archäologie und Religionsgeschichte, BWAT 1 (Leipzig, 1908), 1–96 (1. "Der heilige Fels auf dem Moria. Seine Geschichte und seine Altäre").

Robert deLanghe
"L'autel d'or du temple de Jérusalem" in *Studia biblica et orientalia,* Analecta biblica 10 (Rome: Pontifical Biblical Institute, 1959), 342–360.

Heinrich J. Lenzen
Die Entwicklung der Zikkurat von ihren Anfängen bis zur Zeit der III. Dynastie von Ur, Ausgrabungen der Deutschen Forschungsgemeinschaft in Uruk-Warka 4 (Leipzig: Harrassowitz, 1942).

W. Rosenau
"Harel und Ha-Ariel; Ezechiel 43:15–16," *MGWJ* 65 (1921): 350–356.

Paul Rost
"Der Altar Ezechiels, Kap. 43:13–17" in *Altorientalische Studien Bruno Meissner zum 60. Geburtstag,* Mitteilungen der altorientalischen Gesellschaft 4 (Leipzig: Harrassowitz, 1928/29), 170–174.

Hugues Vincent
"L'autel des holocaustes et le caractère du temple d'Ézéchiel," *Analecta Bollandiana* 67 (1949): 7–20.

43

13 **And these are the measurements of the altar in cubits, the cubit (reckoned) at one (normal) cubit[a] and a hand-breadth: <The projection (surrounding) it was one cubit (deep)>[b] and one cubit wide, and the enclosure[c] round its edge[c] was <one>[d]**

43:13 13a The double אמה אמה of 𝔐 is attested only singly by 2 MSS^{Ken} 𝔊 𝔖. 𝔗 and 𝔙 (*in cubito verissimo qui habetat cubitum et palmum*) have 𝔐 before them.

b 𝔐 וחיק האמה is wrongly divided and must be read as וְחֵיקָה אמה. 𝔊 κόλπωμα βάθος ἐπὶ πῆχυν interprets the measurement correctly as the depth of the depression (חיק) which is filled by the altar so that at the edge all around a channel is left for the blood. The tradition gives no excuse for an emendation of 𝔐 האמה to הארץ (Vincent).

c The suffixes of 𝔐 וגבולה and שפתה do not refer (as Galling suggests) to מזבח but to חיק, which, according to Albrecht, "Geschlecht," 80, is construed as a feminine. Thus a revocalization to the masculine (BH^3, Galling, Gese) is unnecessary.

d 𝔐 האחד, unattested by 𝔊 𝔖, has mistakenly acquired the article. Since זרת, as in later Hebrew

span round about. And that is the base[e] of the altar: 14/ <From the projection>[a] on the ground to the lower ledge[b]: two cubits, and one cubit the width. And from the small ledge to the large ledge: four cubits, and the width <one cubit>[c]. 15/ But the <sacrificial hearth>[a]: four cubits (high) and from the hearth upwards (rose) the horns[b]: four (of them). 16/ And the hearth (measured) twelve cubits long by twelve cubits wide, a square with its four sides[a]. 17/ And the (large) ledge (measured) fourteen (cubits) long by fourteen (cubits) wide on[a] its four sides[b]. And the enclosure <ran round about it>[c] half a cubit (broad) and its protrusion all around (measured) a cubit. And its steps[d] faced[e] east.

(Levy, *Wörterbuch*), must be feminine, אחת should be read.

e 𝔐 גַּב has been read by 𝔊 καὶ τοῦτο τὸ ὕψος τοῦ θυσιαστηρίου as גֹּבַהּ. On this basis Cornill; Toy; Herrmann; Fohrer-Galling (Bertholet-Galling reads גֹּב); Procksch, "Fürst," 103, emend. As a result, the text undoubtedly becomes more easily comprehensible. But then subsequently one misses a corresponding expression to introduce the measurement of the width. Thus 𝔐 should be retained. On גב see also 1,342 on 16:24. 𝔗 טיקום. By contrast with 𝔐, however, which links v 13bβ with what precedes, the clause is understood as an introduction to v 14.

14 14a 𝔐 ומחיק הארץ is rendered very freely by 𝔊 ἐκ βάθους τῆς ἀρχῆς τοῦ κοιλώματος. At any rate it attests the absence of the copula.

b On עזרה Driver, "Ezekiel," 307f, compares Arabic *'dr* "protect, guard." Thus עזרה "surrounding ledge."

c 𝔐 ורחב האמה. According to MS[Ken] 𝔊 𝔖 ורחב אמה should be read.

15 15a 𝔐 וההראל. 5 MSS והאריאל. In vv 15b, 16 the spelling האראיל is found. 𝔊 αριηλ. 𝔙 *ariel.* 𝔖 consistently הראיל. 𝔗 מדבחא; see the exposition.

b 𝔐 הקרנות is clearly attested by 𝔊 𝔖 𝔗 and should not be emended (as is done by Bertholet, Fohrer-Galling, Procksch, Gese) to קרנות. Here too we have the recording style of measurement and enumeration. On the other hand, 𝔊 καὶ ὑπεράνω τῶν κεράτων πῆχυς (G[967] + εἷς) reads the numeral, which surprisingly stands out against the scheme of the measurements, as אמה, but this should not be followed.

16 16a על–אל see 1:17 note a. 𝔙 freely *aequis lateribus.* Bertholet, Fohrer-Galling, Eichrodt want to take the words with the end of v 15, but in the case of the horns one would expect the information "at its four corners." The continuation in v 17 also advises against the transposition. On the formation of רָבַע as an original fraction see Bauer-Leander §79a′.

17 17a על–אל cf. 1:17 note a.

b One misses here another statement about the small ledge, which might have run something like: "And the small ledge measured sixteen (cubits) long by sixteen (cubits) broad on its four sides." It could have become lost as the result of homoioteleuton.

c 𝔐 סביב אותה represents a combination of two possible expressions. Either סובב אותה (on the lack of the article Driver, "Ezekiel," 308, points to Jer 33:2) or סביבותיה should be read.

d On 𝔐 ומעלתהו, which 𝔊 𝔖 𝔙 take as a plural and 𝔗 אתר דסלקין as a singular "its ramp," see Bauer-Leander §29v, and Driver, "Ezekiel," 308. In 40:6 there occurred the noun form מעלותו, and this is demanded by many here.

e Instead of 𝔐 פְּנוֹת, פֹּנוֹת should be read.

Form

A brief superscription introduces the description of the altar and states from the outset that what follows will be dealing with measurements. It is all the more surprising that nowhere in what follows is the measuring process made graphic as in the great guidance vision. The attempt is not even made to connect the whole, which in the manner of the enumeration of the individual parts and their measurements most closely recalls 41:5–15a, with the context of the guidance vision even by means of an introductory statement of measurement in terms of the figure of the guide such as was done in 41:5. At no point does the "I" of the prophet emerge. No reference is made to the unprecedented event of the coming of Yahweh which is reported in vv 1–11(12) and which then in 44:1–3 and in later sections clearly determines the temple rules. As if the "large cubit" had never been mentioned, it is introduced once again with no notice taken of 40:5. But the measurement details here differ from the measurements of the great guidance vision also in that they refer not only to the ground plan but also to the height of the altar. All this shows that in 43:13–17 we have a section which, from the stylistic point of view too, is largely independent of what precedes it.

Setting

The description of the altar gives few clues as to its origin. If the suggestion which has recently been strongly advocated that the altar reflects something of the architectural type of the ziggurat is correct, then this would suggest the exile as the place of origin of the description. And yet, as will be shown, not inconsiderable objections can be made to this interpretation so that no particular weight can be given to this derivation. Nor is the thesis advanced by de Groot that this form of the altar had already been introduced as an innovation by Ahaz and his priest Uriah (2 Kgs 16:10ff) capable of cogent proof.

As far as the period of origin is concerned one can set the composition of the piece, which attempts to supply the information lacking in 40:47, later than the emergence of chapters 40f. On the other hand it surely does not presuppose the conception of the altar in the temple of Zerubbabel.

Interpretation

■ **43:13** By contrast with the speech of Yahweh in vv 7, 10 and with the section following in vv 18ff, in the description of the altar the prophet is not addressed (as "son of man"). The description is introduced by a completely neutral superscription. The unit of measurement is once again defined at the outset as in 40:5. In what follows, the description in vv 13b–15 moves from bottom to top with the height of the individual parts of the altar being given along with the measurement of the recession to the relevant part of the structure. The rest of the description in vv 16, 17, which gives the widths, moves in the opposite direction from top to bottom. The whole ends with an observation about the altar steps.

The formal structure of the description is thus quite clear. Unfortunately the same can not be said of the individual terms used for the description. This begins right away with the first structural element, the חיק ("projection"), which is taken up again more fully in v 14 as חיק הארץ ("the projection on the ground"). According to Albright, it is the exact translation of the Akkadian architectural term *irat erṣeti* or *irat ḳigalli* "edge (originally 'bosom') of the earth."[1] Albright thinks that it describes a base slab let in to the pavement at ground level. The expression is used in inscriptions of Nebuchadnezzar for the ground floor of the divine palace and of the temple tower of Etemenanki. Now חיק elsewhere in Hebrew, however, describes the lap, the fold of a garment above the belt or once, in 1 Kgs 22:35, even the projection, i.e., the hollowed out interior of a war chariot. In any event that signifies a hollow, an indentation which in no way coincides with the Akkadian *irtum* "breast, edge."[2] Thus, then, here too חיק הארץ is best understood as a hollow in the ground, and the equation with Akkadian *irat erṣeti* is best abandoned. The association made by Fohrer-Galling, who, following Albright, wishes to retain the expression as the rendering of the Akkadian architectural term but regards it as describing here a "sunken foundation level," presents a compromise which is surely not possible in its present form. Insofar as "a cubit" is given here as the measurement of the חיק, to begin with without any further dimensional indication, and since all the following measurements which are given

1 Albright, "Babylonian Temple-Tower," and *idem*, *Archaeology*, 150ff.

2 von Soden, *Akkadisches Handwörterbuch*.

without more precise specification refer initially to the dimension of height, here too the idea must be that of the depth of the hollow or excavation in the ground (חיק הארץ). Thus 𝔊 interprets correctly κόλπωμα βάθος ἐπὶ πῆχυν. To this is added the further information "one cubit wide," which gives (as it even seems to do in Galling in the long run) the width of the drain created beside the altar by the excavation into which blood and water flow. The term גבול (here "enclosure") which follows described in 40:12 the barrier of the individual gate niches. Here too must be meant a low barrier a span (= half a cubit) high, which protects the outer "rim" (על שפתה) of the drain at the edge of the חיק into which the blood from the altar flows. If the drain is full it prevents blood from spilling out on to the court and prevents, at the same time, any who approach from falling into the drain, which is, after all, half a meter (= one cubit) deep and broad (Galling).

The statement of v 13bβ must then, against the accentuation of 𝔐, be understood as a superscription for what immediately follows (note e). The גב ("base") mentioned here, made easier by 𝔊 which reinterprets it as גבה ("height"), is to be understood on the basis of 16:24 (cf. the plates mentioned there) as a term for the lower part of the altar, a term best described as the base of the altar. It is contrasted with the upper part, the "sacrificial hearth" mentioned in v 15.

■ **43:14** The lower part is built up in steps. The lowest of them, measured from the bottom of the hollow in which the altar stands, is two cubits high. Then the edge of the altar recedes by one cubit. עזרה ("ledge") is the term for this recession. Apart from vv 17, 20, עזרה ("ledge") appears again in 45:19 in the context of sprinkling of blood. In Sir 50:11 one might wonder whether the עזרת מקדש ("court of the sanctuary") is not to be connected, like עזרה in 2 Chr 6:13; 4:9, in accordance with later linguistic usage, with the temple forecourt. Smend translates "ambulatory of the sanctuary." In Ezekiel 43 it must be an architectural term. The following measurement suggests, almost of necessity, a ledge at the first point where the altar begins to taper.

The next ledge comes four cubits higher. It too recedes by one cubit. It is strange that when this measurement is given, the "lower ledge" (העזרה התחתונה) is called, secondarily, the "small ledge" (העזרה הקטנה) and the upper one is called the "large ledge" (העזרה הגדולה). This description cannot refer to the depth of the recession which is a cubit in the case of both ledges, but only to the smaller distance in height which leads to the recession. In this way the upper ledge, which, from the point of view of width, is narrower, becomes the "large" one while the lower one which is effectively broader becomes the "smaller."

■ **43:15** The name of the topmost part of the structure, which now clearly represents the actual altar hearth, is written in two different ways in its three occurrences in vv 15f (v 15 note a). הראל or אראיל can surely not be separated from the אריאל ("Ariel") which occurs five times in Is 29:1f, 7 and which there described "the city where David encamped," i.e. Jerusalem. In 29:2b this is compared with the sacrificial hearth (on which sacrifices lie and flames burn). Attempts have been made to understand the word on the basis of Arabic *'iratun* "fireplace" (root *'rj*) and to see the אל element either as a divine name ("God's hearth") or as a mere formative element.[3] Even the element ארי "lion" has been thought by some to be found there.[4] More recently, on the other hand, reference has been made to Akkadian *arallû,* for which, alongside the meaning "underworld," the meaning "mountain of God" is also assumed. Thus, e.g., Albright sees in the הראל of Ezek 43:15a "a slight popular etymology of the Akkadian loan-word."[5] In this connection he cites the fact that the summit of the Babylonian temple tower was described by means of a word of similar meaning, *ziqqurratu* "mountain peak." Since representations are found on which the ziggurat is decorated at the top with horns, which are mentioned here as the topmost element of the altar in Ezek 43:15,[6] the picture seems to round itself out according to which the altar in Ezekiel 43 is related to the ziggurat, even down to the nomenclature of its parts, and, as הראל "mountain of God," seems to copy this. Now against this conception of *arallû* there arises, above all, the linguistic difficulty that, according to von Soden, for the Sumerian loan-word *arallûm* the meaning "underworld" is certainly attested, but not the meaning "moutain of god"—whereby the heart of

3 Gesenius-Buhl.
4 Rosenau, "Harel," and others.
5 Albright, *Archaeology,* 151.
6 Cf., e.g., André Parrot, *The Tower of Babel,* tr. Edwin Hudson (New York: Philosophical LIbrary, 1955), 29 (figure II).

Albright's argument is destroyed.[7] One would also have to ask the purely linguistic question of the origin of the "i" sound in the Hebrew אריאל—an intermediate sound which is, admittedly, not indicated in the consonantal form of Ezekiel 43:15f. Thus the linguistic question and then also the specific reference to the Babylonian ziggurat, which is assumed also by de Vaux, Galling, Vincent, must still remain a completely open question. For even for *ziqqurratu, CAD* Z 131, alongside a mass of references with the sense "temple tower," cites only one which suggests the sense "mountain summit," and it assumes for this one passage that the word is used here in this way only in a figurative sense.

After the height measurements, the enumeration of which is terminated by the mention of the four horns, there follow now the width measurements in the reverse order from top to bottom.

■ **43:16** Thus the area of the topmost part of the structure is twelve cubits by twelve. In strict accordance with what is said in the superscription to be the theme of this section, nothing is said about the form of the altar hearth, in connection with which we must assume there to have been a grating and an ash-bin for the ashes to fall into and through which came the influx of air to keep the fire on top burning. All that is given are the measurements and the four directions in which they were measured.

■ **43:17** The same is also true of the עזרה ("ledge"), whose side measurements are fourteen cubits. Since the next lowest part of the structure according to v 14bβ was one cubit broader on each side, then this is in complete agreement with the measurements already given. This is, of course, the "large," i.e. the upper, עזרה ("ledge"). One may wonder why this is not immediately followed by the information about the lower "small" עזרה ("ledge") which would therefore measure sixteen cubits by sixteen (v 17 note b). Has this been omitted because it can easily be calculated? Or has something fallen out as a result of homoioteleuton (Galling, Procksch following Krätzschmar, Jahn)? There is no trace of anything in the versions.

The description in descending order ends with the גבול ("enclosure") and the חיק ("protrusion")—the fact that these elements are in the reverse order from that in v 13 can once again confirm the correctness of the earlier assumption. The "barrier" (גבול) rises above ground level. Since its width (thickness) is measured as half a cubit, it cannot be easily understood why זרת ("span"), the term which is used to indicate its height in v 13 and which must be identical with this measurement, is not used here also. Is there a difference in the calculation of the two? As the lowest element, there follows the measurement of the width of the חיק, which, as in the case of the גבול, is identical with its depth, one cubit. In the reference to the steps, by contrast with the information about steps in the great guidance vision, the number of them is not given, only the orientation of the stairway as a whole. In that it ascends from the east this makes explicit the fact that the altar is oriented towards the west, i.e. towards the temple building. According to 8:16 men with their backs to the temple had prostrated themselves towards the east, in the direction of the rising sun. The present description of the altar makes it clear from this one passage, in which, contrary to what one would expect from the superscription, no measurements are given, that this section, so inexpressive in its sensual considerations, is aware of the concern for the correct direction of prayer in the temple.

■ **43:13–17** From all this, the form of the altar is clearly discernible. It is a structure which from a lowest ledge of sixteen by sixteen cubits tapers slightly towards the top, in two stages of unequal height, to a width of twelve by twelve cubits. It stands in a depression eighteen cubits by eighteen and one cubit deep and rises to a height (excluding the horns) of ten cubits from its own base (nine cubits above the level of the pavement). Behind its tapering stepped shape there may stand, in the distance, the model of the ziggurat. It is better, however, not to argue with Albright on the basis of the architectural terms and seek to deduce from that something of what it signified for the author of vv 13–17. Isaiah of Jerusalem had already spoken of the אריאל. "Horns" on the altar were already known to ancient Israel, as was the possibility of finding refuge there (1 Kgs 1:50f; 2:28—Solomonic period; cf. Am 3:14—period of JeroboamII; also Jer 17:1). They were to be found on the altar table of 41:22 (מקצעות "corners") and play a prominent role in

7 von Soden, *Akkadisches Handwörterbuch.* See also J. Van Dijk, "Le motif cosmique dans la pensée sumérienne," *Archiv Orientální* 28 (1964): 27.

the descriptions of P (Ex 27:2; 29:12; and elsewhere). In view of this abundance of attestations from within the Bible and the no less abundant comparative material from the domain of Syro-Phoenician archaeology[8] the ziggurat, which is occasionally represented with horns, does not need to be involved.

To what extent in this description of the altar the remembrance of the form of the pre-exilic altar survives and to what extent what is programmatically new is to be found in it can no longer be decided, since detailed information concerning the pre-exilic altar of whole burnt offerings has not been preserved, either that of Solomon or the altar of Ahaz. 2 Chr 4:1 describes Solomon's altar as a structure twenty cubits by twenty cubits by ten cubits, but only the height measurement of that coincides with the description in Ezekiel 43. *b. Mid.* III 1a tells (for the second temple?) of a square structure which strongly recalls Ezek 43:13–17, even if the length of the sides is twice what it is in Ezekiel 43: "The altar was thirty-two cubits by thirty-two. It rose a cubit and went in a cubit, and this formed the 'foundation' (היסוד) . . . It then rose five cubits and went in one cubit, and this formed the 'surround' (הסובב), leaving twenty-eight cubits by twenty-eight. The horns extended a cubit in each direction, thus leaving twenty-six by twenty-six. A cubit on every side was allowed for the priests to go round, thus leaving twenty-four by twenty-four as the place of the wood pile."[9] Over and above this R. Jose believed that the return from the Babylonian exile occasioned the extension of the measurements of the sides, and he achieved harmony between Ezekiel 43 and the measurements just given by suggesting that the measurements of Ezekiel 43, of which he cites v 16, were each measured from the middle of a side in either direction "twelve cubits in every direction."[10] On the other hand, the further mention of a "ramp" (כֶּבֶשׁ) which led up to the altar from the south[11] shows that people had become conscious of the contradiction which existed between Ezek 43:17bβ and the altar law in the book of the Covenant (Ex 20:25f). There it is forbidden to build steps at the altar such as even an earth altar or, if it were already a stone altar, one of unhewn stones would have required. *B. Mid.* III 4a and Josephus, who in addition gives the dimensions of the altar as fifty cubits by fifty by fifteen, also speak of adherence to this prescription.[12] Is this law not known to the author of Ezekiel 43? Or does he, because he has a quite different viewpoint (or pre-exilic tradition?) in mind, simply disregard it?

Aim

Owing to a lack of pre-exilic comparative material, Ezek 43:13–17 reveals nothing of possible new architectural ideas which might lie behind its plan. Only one thing can be discerned through its meagre description, namely that it has been at pains, in contrast to the sacrileges of earlier times (8:16), to let the adoration of God, which takes place in the sacrifice, really happen "before God." For this reason its altar turns from the "forward" (i.e. easterly) direction apparently preferred by nature and faces in a westerly direction towards the place in which God has taken up residence in his holy house. Through the orientation of the sacrificial cult and the obedient turning to the place in which it has pleased God to come near to his people, this altar description too gives expression to the idea that true worship of God does not choose arbitrarily for itself the way of its accomplishment.

8 Galling, *Altar,* 65–67 (figures 17–36), and *BRL,* 17ff; also *AOB* 444, 458–465.

9 Translated by Maurice Simon in *The Babylonian Talmud,* ed. I. Epstein (London: Soncino, 1948).

10 *b. Mid.* III 1b.

11 *b. Mid.* III 3b, confirmed by Josephus, *Jewish War* V 5, 6.

12 For Josephus see preceding fn.

b. The Dedication of the Altar of Whole Burnt Offering

Bibliography

Klaus Koch
Die Priesterschrift von Exodus 25 bis Leviticus 16; eine überlieferungsgeschichtliche und literarkritische Untersuchung, FRLANT 53 (Göttingen: Vandenhoeck & Ruprecht, 1959), especially VIII. Anhang, 104–108.

Klaus Koch
"Sühne und Sündenvergebung um die Wende von der exilischen zur nachexilischen Zeit," *EvTh* 26 (1966): 217–239.

Rolf Rendtorff
Die Gesetze in der Priesterschrift, FRLANT 44 (Göttingen: Vandenhoeck & Ruprecht, 1954).

On sacrifice see the bibliography on 45:10–17 below.

43

18 And he spoke to me: Son of man, thus has
[the Lord][a] Yahweh said: These are the
ordinances for the altar: On the day on
which it is erected to offer burnt offerings
on it and to sprinkle blood[b] on it 19/ you
must give to the levitical priests[a], who
are from the descendants of Zadok, who
come near me[b], says [the Lord][c] Yahweh,
to serve me, a bull as a sin offering, 20/
and you must take[a] of its blood and put[a]
(it) on[b] its four horns[c] and on[b] the four
corners of the ledge and on[b] the rim
round about, and you must cleanse[a] it
and make atonement[a] for it[d], 21/ and you
must take[a] <the bull>[b] of the sin offering,
and it is to be burned[c] at the place of
review[d] in the temple outside the
sanctuary.
22 On the second day you must offer[a] a he-
goat[b] without blemish as a sin offering,
and they must cleanse[c] the altar as they
cleansed (it) with the bull. 23/ When you
have completed the cleansing you must
offer[a] a bull without blemish and a ram

43: 18 18a אדני is lacking in 𝔊[967]. 𝔊[B] *κύριος ὁ θεὸς Ισραηλ,* 𝔊[O] (Arm) *κύριος κύριος*, see Appendix 1.

b 𝔗 דם ניכסת קודשיא.

19 19a 𝔙 𝔖 make a separation in the way that later becomes usual: Priests and Levites.

b 𝔐 הַקְּרֹבִים אלי; 40:46 הַקְּרֵבִים.

c אדני is lacking in 𝔊[967,613]. 𝔊[BA] *κύριος ὁ θεός*, see Appendix 1.

20 20a 𝔊 has all the verbs in the third person plural. See the exposition.

b על-אל cf. 1:17 note a.

c 𝔐 על ארבע קרנתיו. 𝔊 *τὰ τέσσαρα κέρατα τοῦ θυσιαστηρίου*. The antecedent, מזבח (v 18), once stood closer to קרנתיו before the substantial expansion of v 19 (see the exposition).

d 𝔐 וכפרתהו is omitted by 𝔊. On the suffix form see Bauer-Leander §48h′.

21 21a 𝔊 third person plural.

b הפר החטאת should surely be emended to פר החטאת. On this see also the שעיר חטאת of v 25.

c 𝔐 ושרפו. 𝔊 *καὶ κατακαυθήσεται*. 𝔙 adjusts to the context: *et combures*. 𝔗 𝔖 as 𝔐.

d 𝔐 מפקד. 𝔊 *ἐν τῷ ἀποκεχωρισμένῳ*. 𝔙 *in separato loco*. 𝔗 באתר דחזי לביתא. 𝔖 גבה (דביתא). The word מפקד is also attested in Phoenician (see *CIS* 1,88,4f), but unfortunately the passage does not help us to reach a more certain understanding. Jean-Hoftijzer, "poss. part d'un temple."

22 22a 𝔊[967] *λήμψῃ*. The remaining witnesses of 𝔊 *λήμψονται*.

b 𝔊[967] renders 𝔐. The remaining witnesses of 𝔊 *ἐρίφους δύο*.

c 𝔗 ותדכי, second person singular.

23 23a 𝔊[967] *προσοίσεις* (𝔏[C] *offeres*), the remaining witnesses of 𝔊 plural *προσοίσουσι* (alongside *συντελέσαι σε*).

from the flock without blemish. 24/ and
you must offer[a] them before Yahweh,
and the priests must sprinkle salt on
them and offer them as a whole burnt
offering to Yahweh.
25 **Seven days long you must prepare daily a**
goat for a sin offering, and they must
prepare a bull and a ram from the flock,
(beasts) without blemish. 26/ Seven
days long[a] they must make atonement
for the altar and purify it and consecrate[b]
it. 27/ So they must complete these
days[a]. But from the eighth day onwards
the priests must offer your whole burnt
offerings and your final offerings[b] on the
altar. And I shall accept[c] you with pleas-
ure, says [the Lord][d] Yahweh.

24 24a 𝔐 וְהִקְרַבְתָּם has been misunderstood by 𝔊 (𝔏[C]) as a second person plural.

26 26a 𝔊 (𝔏[C]) still connects the words with v 25 and makes a new introduction to what follows by means of the copula.

b The expression מלא יד, which in the first instance has undoubtedly been coined with reference to the installation of men to an office, is here used also for the commissioning of the altar. 𝔊 (𝔏[C]) 𝔖 felt that they had to refer it to men (priests) here too and altered the suffix to the third person plural καὶ πλήσουσι χεῖρας αὐτῶν.

27 27a The first sentence is missing in 𝔊 𝔏[C].

b On the translation "final offerings" see below on 45:15, 17.

c 𝔐 ורצאתי, a spelling mistake for ורציתי, Bauer-Leander §57t″.

d אדני is lacking in 𝔊 (𝔏[C]), see Appendix 1.

Form

An introduction which would lead one to expect a prophetic divine word (v 18a*α*) introduces, in v 18a*β*, a sacrificial regulation which is again provided with an explicit superscription. The character of prophetic oracle is underlined also by means of the two formulae for a divine saying which occur in context in v 19 and at the end in v 27. F. Baumgärtel, however, has drawn attention to the fact that this wording contradicts the rule, which is discernible elsewhere in the prophetic sayings, never to connect regulations and commands with נאם יהוה ("says Yahweh").[1] The same will be noticed in the case of other sections within chapters 44–48. His observation that "the prophetic formulaic language has slipped over these legal regulations" draws the correct conclusion from this observation. The prophetic formulaic material can be removed without any damage to the content. There then remains a cultic ordinance formed in the style of many of the regulations of P.

Since this, as has been mentioned, is introduced in 43:18a*β* by its own superscription, one can in fact speak of the "two introductions" to the section vv 18–27. This form of the double introduction is to be found in the same way in P. Only that there, in, e.g., Nu 19:1ff, which one might cite as a close analogy, the superscription זאת חקת התורה ("this is the ordinance of the law") (v 2) is preceded by the introductory formulae of Yahweh's speech to Moses (v 1). The ritual ordinance is thus inserted into the context of Yahweh's revelation to the leaders of the Israel of the wilderness period. Completely analogously here, the ordinance of Ezek 43:18bff with its superscription in v 18a*β* is to be inserted, by means of v 18a*α* and of the formulae for a divine saying in vv 19 and 27, into the context of the divine revelation to the prophet. This formally analogous process of the insertion of an independent cultic ordinance into a specific revelatory situation brings Ezek 43:18ff close to the developmental processes of P.

The cultic regulation which is enclosed within a prophetic framework is to be described from a form-critical point of view as "ritual." Rendtorff, in connection with his analysis of Leviticus 1 and 3, has described the form of rituals in the following terms: "They contain concisely-phrased prescriptions for the course of the sacrifice, in which the individual acts of the process are each expressed in a brief, stereotyped verbal sentence. The sentences are in the impersonal third person singular and—with the exception of the first—in the consecutive perfect. The conclusion is usually formed by a formulaic expression."[2] This style is present from v 19 onwards. It is slightly modified insofar as the ritual here (v 19) begins at once with the consecutive perfect and in place of the neutral third person there is direct address in the second person. If Koch should be right with his

1 Baumgärtel, "Formel," 286.
2 Rendtorff, *Gesetze*, 12.

assumption that behind the passages in Exodus 25–29, which are in "formulaic address" and which reveal precisely this characteristic consecutive perfect, there are hidden rituals, then we would have before us here the identical phenomenon of the transformation of ritual to the form of the direct address.[3]

The particular difficulty of the text, however, is formed by the circumstance that the address in the second person is not maintained but changes in v 21b, without specific mention of a new subject, to the third person singular and in vv 22b, 24b, 25b–27bα to the third person plural with, in the case of vv 24b and 27bα, the priests being named as the new subject, those who had already been mentioned in v 19 as the recipients of the sacrificial animal. The situation is further complicated by the fact that 𝔊 in addition, in vv 20 (note a), 21a (note a), 22a (but not 𝔊[967], see note a), 23b (not 𝔊[967], see note a), has the subject in the third person plural. Now the simple harmonization of 𝔐 to 𝔊 is prohibited not only by the occasional deviation of the important 𝔊[967], but even more by the fact, correctly underlined by Gese, that 𝔊 itself in vv 23a and 25a (𝔊[967] also in vv 22a, 23b) attests the second person singular of 𝔐. That makes the other passages where it deviates from 𝔐 suspect as attempts at harmonization. When, however, Gese, without reference to 𝔊, feels that he has to come to the conclusion on other considerations that in the basic form of the ritual everywhere in place of the second person singular, in which the prophet is made the bearer of the action, the third person plural should be read with the priests as the real agents, then he is not to be followed in this. Koch must surely be more correct here when he decides, on the basis of the comparison with P, that in a differentiated way we have to reckon with a plurality of agents. Only thus is it comprehensible that in vv 24 and 27 the priests are then explicitly mentioned. Thus the exposition must attempt in the first place to take 𝔐 as its starting point.

Procksch attempts to avoid the difficulties of 𝔐 by deleting vv 22 and 25 as secondary additions.[4] But how is one to understand the secondary insertion of these awkward statements? By contrast Rautenberg is surely on the more correct road when he sees in vv 25–27 a secondary expansion of the more concise ritual of vv 18–24.[5] The problems of the changes in subject will be discussed individually in the context of the exposition.

Setting

The ritual pericope vv 18–27, which is in itself composite and not free of tensions and which only in its first part reveals a clear relationship with the preceding description of the altar (cf. v 20), must be later than this latter and is certainly not from the hand of the author of the great guidance vision. On the other hand, it must, from the content point of view, be dependent on older ritual traditions which it reshapes in accordance with its own ideas or to which it even gives new emphases. The present ritual, in its basic form in vv 18–24, will belong to the period in which the altar of the second temple was not yet consecrated. It gives a glimpse of how the exilic congregation, to which the author belongs, begins to reflect in detail on the subject of the approaching restoration of the cult in Jerusalem. The prerequisites for the resumption of regular sacrificial worship are the subject of intense reflection. The imminent proximity of the immediate resumption of the cult can be clearly felt in contrast to the model of the great guidance vision.

On the origin of the expansions in vv 19 and 25–27 see the exposition.

Interpretation

■ **43:18** Although Yahweh had spoken from v 7 onwards, vv 18–27 are introduced afresh with the ויאמר אלי ("and he spoke to me") repeated from v 7. The fact that it is Yahweh who is speaking, and not the man of 40:3, is not already made certain by the address "son of man," since that expression was also used by the man in 40:4 (subsequently 44:4, emended text).[6] But it is admittedly suggested by the prophetic terminology, which is also used from the beginning in what follows, as well as by the absence of the man from 43:6b onwards. This was the understanding also of the author of the expansion in v 19 and of the concluding section vv 25–27 in which the address changes to the first person in the mouth of Yahweh. The phrases לפני יהוה ("before Yahweh") and עלה ליהוה ("whole burnt offering to Yahweh") in v 24 are

3 Koch, *Priesterschrift,* 7–32.
4 Procksch, "Fürst," 105.
5 Rautenberg, "Zukunftsthora," 102.
6 On "son of man" see 1,131f.

used in a quite formulaic way and cannot be cited as arguments against this. Prophetic formulaic language admittedly occurs only in abbreviated form. The commission to the prophet to speak, which in correct style ought to precede the introductory messenger formula since this formula has its setting in the word of the prophet himself, has disappeared.[7] Thus the impression arises that Yahweh himself addresses the prophet with the messenger formula. Such abbreviation was also to be found, however, in 6:11.

The proclamation with which the prophet is charged consists in transmission of a ritual, which, with its independent superscription, is introduced in a fashion characteristic of the priestly style (see also v 12). What follows is then described (with a backward glance at v 11?) as חקות ("ordinances"). This has a (singular) correspondence in the superscription זאת חקת הפסח ("this is the ordinance of the Passover") in Ex 12:43. In Numbers 19 one can observe a fluctuation between the terms חקה and תורה which can appear linked in the superscription (זאת חקת התורה). "This reveals a struggle for priority between these two terms."[8] As in the Tora of v 12 this expresses an ordinance stemming from Yahweh and regulating cultic life.

The present passage is concerned with the measures whereby the altar, when it is completed, can be rendered fit for its proper task. It is on the latter that the real emphasis lies, not on the "day" of completion.[9] The two most significant purposes for which the altar serves are thus specified: it is the place where the whole offering is sacrificed (see above on 40:38f) and where the blood is sprinkled. זרק ("to sprinkle") occurs in Ezekiel otherwise only in 10:2 and 36:25 in a different usage. It describes the blood rite which in the rituals of P is particularly significant in connection with the עולה (Lev 1:5, 11; 8:19; 9:12), the זבח שלמים (3:2, 8, 13; 7:14; 9:18) and the אשם (7:2).

In the detailed examination of the ritual of altar dedication which follows it will be advantageous to take note of the P texts which in another context also speak of the dedication of the altar. In the context of the divine instructions to Moses for the founding of the Israelite cult there is the ritual in Ex 29:36f, which, according to Noth, is one of the additions to the ordinances for the consecration of the priests in 29:1–25.[10] This demands a sin offering and the anointing of the altar in order to cleanse it. In addition, there is the expansive account of Aaron's installation in Leviticus 8. Here, first of all, in what is certainly a later insertion in vv 10f which refers back to Ex 40:9–11, there is an account of the anointing of the whole sanctuary and, in connection with that, also of the altar. Then in v 15 the application of the blood to the horns of the altar is interpreted as a measure of the "cleansing" of it and as an act of atonement (כפר "to make atonement"). An act of cleansing for the altar has also found its way into the ritual of the great day of atonement (especially Lev 16:18f). The close correspondence with Ezekiel 43 enables Koch to suppose behind both "a verbally identical earlier form, which, however, already had behind it a varied tradition-history route when it was taken up by the two writers."[11] Since also the presentation of a sin offering and of a whole burnt offering was a component of the altar dedication of Ezekiel 43, note must in addition be taken of the ritual ordinances for the whole burnt offering (Leviticus 1 and 6:1–6) and for the sin offering (Leviticus 4 and 6:17–23).

■ **43:19** The actual ritual for the dedication of the altar begins in v 19. Here at once there appears the phenomenon which has already been mentioned, namely that the prophet, exactly like Moses in P Exodus 25ff, is summoned in direct address by God to the carrying out of decisive actions of cultic procedure. But what makes sense in the case of Moses, since he was in fact charged with carrying out the first cultic measures, is strange in the case of the prophet, who in the vision was shown events of the future and in whose case, therefore, it is of the carrying out of future activity in the temple that is spoken. Till now the prophet was nowhere presupposed

---

7 See 1, 133 on 2:4.

8 Rendtorff, *Gesetze*, 65 note 52. On חק ("ordinance") see 1, 175 and Richard Hentschke, *Satzung und Setzender, ein Beitrag zur israelitischen Rechtsterminologie*, BWANT 5. F. 3 (Stuttgart: Kohlhammer, 1963), especially 85–89.

9 On the almost conjunction-like character of ביום ("then, when") see, e.g., 16:5; 20:5.

10 Martin Noth, *Exodus; a Commentary*, tr. J. S. Bowden. The Old Testament Library (Philadelphia: Westminster, 1962).

11 Koch, *Priesterschrift*, 105.

as a participant in future activity, but only as the proclaimer of the future seen by him. The original situation of chapters 40ff has been left behind. Obviously quite different structural laws, corresponding to P, are at work here. The prophet is elevated to the role of cult founder. At the same time, however, as in P, other figures can be observed who participate in the cult. First of all the priests are mentioned. The explicit restriction to the Zadokites betrays the same amplifier's hand as was already at work in 40:46b and which tries to harmonize with 44:10–16 (see there). The original text undoubtedly spoke, as in v 24 (v 27), simply of הכהנים ("the priests"). To them the prophet is to give a bull as a sin offering so that they can complete the consecration of the altar.

■ **43:20** Nothing further is said, however, of the slaughtering and preparation of the sacrificial animal which one would expect the priest to do. All that is reported is the blood rite which is especially important here and which is to be carried out by the prophet himself. By means of this rite the cleansing of the altar is correctly effected. Here the verbal contact with Lev 16:18 is particularly clearly discernible (ולקח מדם הפר . . . ונתן על קרנות המזבח סביב "and he shall take some of the blood of the bull . . . and put it on the horns of the altar round about"). At the same time, however, the statement here is developed in dependence on the description of the altar. The smearing with blood, which, as in Leviticus 16, is expressed by the simple נתן (דם) על ("put [blood] on"), here takes place on the four horns (v 15b), the four corners of the ledge (vv 14, 17) and on the "rim" round about (vv 13, 17). It will strike one that as in v 17 only one עזרה ("ledge") is mentioned. The reference is no doubt to the "large" upper ledge. In this context it is once again quietly confirmed that it is in the גבול ("enclosure, rim") but not in the חיק ("protrusion") of the altar that one has to look for a projecting part of the altar's structure. In this application of blood to the top, the middle and the foot of the altar one can easily recognize a certain analogy with the application of the blood of the "ram of ordination" (איל המלאים) to the lobe of the right ear, the thumb of the right hand and the big toe of the right foot at the consecration of the Aaronites (Lev 8:22f). The effect of this application of blood is described by the two verbs "purify" (חִטֵּא) and "expiate" (כִּפֶּר), which occur also in connection with the consecration of the altar in Ex 29:36f; Lev 8:15 and Lev 16:18f. חטא ("purify, cleanse") occurs in Ezekiel outside this passage (vv 20, 22f) also in 45:18 in connection with the purification of the sanctuary. In P it is used in this sense, apart from the two passages mentioned, also in Lev 14:49, 52, of the cleansing of a house from leprosy. Thus, in the context of the consecration of the altar in Ezekiel 43 it is a question not only of a sanctifying of what was previously profane, but of a removal of the sinful substance which is contrary to God and which clings to the altar which has been man-made of earthly material. May one go one step further and think, in the context of the historical situation, of the sin which lies upon the people and on the site of their temple (Ezekiel 8) and which is now to be set aside? On this see, e.g., Zechariah 3. כפר ("to expiate, make atonement") occurs in Ezekiel, apart from here (vv 20, 26), also in 16:63; 45:15, 17 as well as in the texts concerning the consecration of the altar in Ex 29:37; Lev 8:15; 16:18. It is to be connected (as a loan-word?) with the Akkadian word which occurs also in the D-stem *kapāru* "wipe off, purify cultically" and represents in P an extremely central technical term which also in its derivatives כַּפֹּרֶת ("cover" on the ark of the covenant) Ex 25:17 and elsewhere and יוֹם (הַ)כִּפֻּרִים ("day of atonement") (Lev 23:27f; 25:9) has acquired significance in the sphere of objects and periods of expiation.[12]

In comparison with the other details about the consecration of the altar it is remarkable that in what follows nothing is said about either the sevenfold "sprinkling" of blood (הִזָּה) on the altar with the finger (so Lev 16:19; see also Ex 29:12) or the pouring out of the blood on the base of the altar (Lev 8:15) or of its being anointed (Ex 29:36; Lev 8:11). The anointing then corresponds to post-exilic usage.[13] In the sprinkling and pouring of the blood Koch believes he can discern a specific P addition.[14] Similarly the "sanctifying" of the altar (Lev 16:19 "from the uncleannesses of the Israelites"), which is heavily underlined in Ex 29:36f; Lev 8:15; 16:19, is missing in Ezekiel 43.

■ **43:21** It is then part of the general sin-offering ritual

12 See also Koch, "Sühne."
13 Noth, *Exodus,* 238.
14 Koch, *Priesterschrift,* 105.

that the animal for the sin offering is burned "outside the camp" (Lev 4:12, 21; 8:17; 9:11; 16:27). In addition to the expression used in the present context "outside the sanctuary," there occurs also the more precise location במפקד הבית ("at the place of review in the temple"). This could refer to a specific locality in Jerusalem which might be sought in the vicinity of the שער המפקד ("Muster[?] Gate") (Neh 3:31—east of the temple court?). It could also simply mean "the place prescribed for it." מפקד in 2 Sam 24:9 means "mustering," 2 Chr 31:13 "command." Procksch suggests "control." See also note d. The fact that the regulation for the burning "outside" is not directly addressed to the prophet but is expressed in indefinite neutral terms need not, in view of Lev 16:27f, surprise us. There too it is a third person who is sent out to do it. That person has to cleanse himself in a special way after having done his work.

■ **43:22** A distinct deviation from the other ordinances for the dedication of the altar is afforded by v 22 with its fixing of a second sin offering in the form of a he-goat for the second day. That this is not, as Procksch thinks, a secondary addition is shown by the comparison with Leviticus 16, where the sacrifice of the bull for the sin offering which Aaron, according to v 11, makes for himself is followed, according to v 15, by the sacrifice of the goat as a sin offering for the people and where, according to vv 18f, the altar is purified with the blood of both animals. It will strike the reader that v 22a addresses the demand to the prophet, while v 22b expresses the consequent act of purification with a plural subject and, in addition, refers to the act of purification on the first day also in plural terms. It should nevertheless be noted that, in contrast to v 24, where in connection with a further act the priest is specifically mentioned as subject, this subject is missing here. Thus it remains questionable whether one is to refer the plural here solely to the priests or whether it is not to be understood neutrally as a comprehensive statement. There could be included within it both the activity of the prophet and that of the priests, who are no longer named here but who were mentioned in the introduction to the first sacrifice. The fact that the indeterminate statement in v 21b was expressed in the singular can be connected with the fact that there it was a question of the activity of an individual, where here everyone who is involved in the sacrifice is included. In the demand addressed to the prophet to הקריב ("offer"), it may be referring to the initial act of the sacrifice—the "bringing near" which is described in v 19 with the simple נתן ("put") and which was likewise referred to the prophet.

■ **43:23-24** This could be indicated also by the continuation in vv 23f, where the "purification" is first of all made a charge on the prophet as well as the subsequent offering of two sacrificial animals, a bull and a ram, which are now to be offered as whole burnt offerings. There the further acts of the sprinkling of salt and the actual sacrifice (העלה "to offer") are expressly attributed to the priests. Nothing is said about salt as an addition to the sacrifice in the ordinance for the עולה ("whole burnt offering") in Lev 1, but there is in the case of the vegetable cereal offering in Lev 2:13. The reference to the "covenant of salt" (ברית מלח), which is presupposed there and which is made explicit in Nu 18:19 and 2 Chr 13:5, makes it very likely that the use of salt at sacrificial meals was by no means confined to the cereal offering. Salt too has a purifying power, but in the case of a meal, at the same time a binding power.[15] V 24 must fairly certainly represent, vis-à-vis the ritual of Leviticus 1, an older form of the whole burnt offering in which the priests had to carry out a particular salt rite.

More significant, however, is the assessment of the whole activity on the second day. According to v 23 the "purification" reaches its conclusion on this day after the presentation of the second animal for a sin offering. Basically that corresponds to the ordinance in Lev 16:18f. In that passage too the expiation (כפר "to expiate") of the altar is achieved through the blood of two sacrificial animals, which are there, admittedly, offered on the same day. Thus, to use the terminology of Lev 16:19, the altar is purified of the uncleannesses of Israel and thus the way is prepared for the normal regular burnt offerings. The introductory double sacrifice of the two most important sacrifical animals is here entrusted to the prophet as the cult initiator, and it inaugurates the normal use of the altar, whose most important functions were mentioned in v 18b.

15 See also, e.g., Jirku, *Materialen*, especially 13–20.

The fact that with v 24 a certain conclusion is reached could be deduced from the twofold formulaic reference to Yahweh in the "offering before Yahweh" and in the "whole burnt offering for Yahweh." This produces an emphatic concluding effect.

■ **43:25-27** The secondary character of vv 25–27 can be seen, contentwise, above all from the fact that there is given here a comprehensive scheme which cannot be made to agree at all with what has been stated hitherto, but which is surely to be understood as a harmonization with later regulations in P. Ex 29:37 lays down a seven-day consecration of the altar, and this is repeated in Lev 8:33, 35. This same seven-day form of purification is laid down in vv 25–27. In the process, the terminology of vv 18–24 is used without its managing to obscure the fact that it is a different scheme that is envisaged. The only reference to a "sin offering" is connected with the sacrifice of the he-goat. What has become of the sacrifice of the bull of the sin offering which was described particularly in vv 19–21?

■ **43:25** Certainly reference is made in v 25b to the sacrifice of a bull, but is this the bull of the sin offering of vv 19–21? Is it not rather the bull of the burnt offering prescribed in v 23 after the end of the purification? The association with the ram and the fact that it comes after the goat of the sin offering might suggest the latter.

■ **43:26** This burnt offering, however, then becomes, according to what is said in v 26, part of the purification ceremony, which is now described, in contrast to what has gone before but in agreement with Lev 16:19, as a "cleansing" (טהר "to cleanse"). There occurs also the additional technical term מלא יד "to fill the hand." This has its counterpart in Akkadian *mullû ana ḳati* "to hand over (something)" and means, according to Noth, first of all when applied to persons, the "payment of certain fees for the performance of certain offices," and from there it becomes a term for installation to an office.[16] Thus P, at the consecration of Aaron and his sons, speaks of an איל מלאים, a "ram of ordination." Only in Ezek 43:26 is the expression used in the OT also for the consecration of a sacred object.

■ **43:27** After this seven-day consecration is ended the normal sacrificial cult can begin from the eighth day onwards. This is described here by the reference to whole burnt offerings and "final offerings" (on the individual types of offerings see below on 45:10–17). What began, according to v 24, immediately after the presentation of the second sin offering is here postponed to the eighth day. It is possible to see in this the harmonization with the sacrifice ordinance of P. Vv 25–27 have thus been composed later than vv 19–24. They appear already to envisage the usage of the post-exilic community.

A word must still be said about the form of this addition. It is dependent on what precedes to the extent that first of all in v 25 it begins with a phrase in the second person singular. But then this mode of address is immediately abandoned and it switches to a plural mode of expression, which, in the light of the כהנים ("priests") of v 24, is surely to be referred to the priests. These are mentioned explicitly in v 27, where the beginning of the normal sacrificial cult is mentioned. The change of style, however, can be recognized especially in the closing verse, in which the congregation is addressed in the second person plural and Yahweh, in the first person, promises it that its sacrifices on the altar thus purified will find his pleasure.[17] It should be noted, finally, that the linguistic usage for the offering of the sacrificial animals is different from that of vv 19–24. נתן ("put") (v 19) and הקריב ("offer") (vv 22, 23) are replaced here by עשׂה ("prepare") (vv 25 twice, 27).

Aim

The ritual for the consecration of the altar, which in its component parts is dependent on older usage, reveals the reflections of the priestly exiles on the question of how, at the new beginning, sacrifices pleasing to God could be offered on the great altar in the temple court. The person who added vv 25–27, with their culmination in God's promise that he will graciously accept sacrifice, moves in the same realm of thought as permeates the whole ritual. To be able to offer gifts which will be pleasing to God is what the congregation desires. In this connection, the congregation is in no doubt that such pleasure cannot be forced by men but can be bestowed only as a gift.

16 Noth, *Exodus*, 321.

17 On רצה as a specific term of sacrificial vocabulary see 1,417 on 20:40f, the only other occurrence of the verb in Ezekiel.

Thus the whole ritual with its detailed regulations is not understood if it is interpreted as a way discovered by or even made by man.[18] It is presented as the power bestowed on the prophet by God enabling him to follow a specific way. The prophet himself, the charismatic addressed by God, becomes the new Moses who is permitted to inaugurate the new sacrificial cult.

In this way sin is shown to be the real hindrance, which must be removed by the preparation of the altar which is to carried out according to God's instructions. However one is to evaluate the depth of the concept of sin which is presupposed here, it cannot, at any rate, be ignored that God in this ritual shows the way in which sin, which renders impossible God's pleasure in the gift on the altar, may be abolished. He accepts a sacrifice with the blood of which the sin may be removed from the altar. If God's people are willing and ready to walk humbly along this way which cannot be a way of human glory and self pride, then they will encounter the pleasure of their God in what they bring to the altar.

Even when in the letter to the Hebrews OT sacrifice is explained in terms of a greater one who is to come, nothing different is said about the approach to God.

18 Cf., e.g., the heading "Man's Expedient for his own Redemption" under which Ludwig Koehler (in his *Old Testament Theology*) deals with the "Cult."

3. The Closed Outer East Gate

Bibliography

Karl Harmuth
Die verschlossene Pforte; eine Untersuchung zu Ez 44:1–3, partially published Diss. (Breslau, 1933).

A. Kassing
"Das verschlossene Tor Ez 44:1–3. Heilsgeschichtliches Sinnverständnis als ekklesiologisch-mariologische Anregung," *Wort und Wahrheit* 16 (1953): 171–190.

A. Pohl
"Das verschlossene Tor Ez 44:1–3," *Bibl* 13 (1932): 90–92.

Eckhard Unger
Babylon: die heilige Stadt nach der Beschreibung der Babylonier (Berlin and Leipzig: de Gruyter, 1931), especially chapter 19, "Die heilige Pforte," 201–206.

Franz Heinrich Weissbach
Das Hauptheiligtum des Marduk in Babylon, Esagila und Etemenanki, Wissenschaftliche Veröffentlichungen der Deutschen Orientgesellschaft 59 (Leipzig: Hinrichs, 1938).

44

1 **And he brought me back[a] to the outer gate of the sanctuary which faces east, but[b] this was closed. 2/ Then he [Yahweh][a] spoke to me: This gate shall[b] remain closed. It shall[b] not be opened, and no one shall[b] pass through it, for Yahweh, the God of Israel, has gone in[c] through it, so it shall[b] remain closed.**

44: 1 1a 𝔐 וישב אתי. Within the guiding through the temple the verbs of guidance are otherwise consistently in the suffixed form (see 40:17, 24, 28, 32 and elsewhere), even the וישבני of 47:1, 6. In the introductory description of the transportation in 40:1, 3 there can be found also ויבא אתי (ויביא אותי) (see also 8:3). Thus in the fuller form there may lie something of the emphasis of a new beginning.

b 𝔐 והוא has been understood by 𝔖 וחזיתה as והנה.

2 2a The expression ויאמר אלי יהוה is found in Ezekiel otherwise only in v 5. In 9:4; 23:36 יהוה, according to the normal word order (Beer-Meyer §92,3), immediately follows the verb, while as a rule there occurs the simple ויאמר אלי which one would expect here too. The word order is, however, assured by the rendering in $𝔊^{B}$, $𝔏^{C}$, 𝔄̈ 𝔄 Arm. The words in vv 2f, 5ff are thus intended to be words of Yahweh, while the statement of v 5 nevertheless in the related passage 40:4f is clearly a statement of the guiding figure, which is likely also in vv 2f, 5 in view of the reference to Yahweh in the third person. Thus considerations both of form and of content lead to the suspicion that יהוה has been inserted secondarily in v 2 and then surely also in v 5, where the versions no longer reveal the unusual wording of 𝔐.

b 𝔐 יהיה. The instructions are given in vv 2f in the simple imperfect (not jussive) or consecutive perfect and are negated with לא.

c 𝔊 εἰσελεύσεται ($𝔏^{C}$ *transibit*) understands the בא of 𝔐 in a future sense. Does there stand behind this the expectation of an eschatological appearance of

3 **The prince <>[a]—he shall[b] sit in it to eat food before Yahweh. From the vestibule of the gate (-structure) he shall[b] enter, and by the same way[c] he shall[b] go out (again).**

Yahweh from the direction of the Mount of Olives, with which a passage like Zech 14:4f could be compared as a distant parallel? Here too 𝔗 avoids the harshly anthropomorphic בא and replaces it by איתגלי.

3 3a 𝔐 את־הנשיא נשיא הוא affords difficulties. 𝔙 (*eritque clausa*) *principi. Princeps ipse* (*sedebit in ea*) and 𝔗 (ויהי אחיד) לרבא רבא הוא (יתיב ביה) both had 𝔐 in front of them, but connect the introductory את הנשיא of v 3 as a dative to the end of v 2. Or have they understood it as a superscription-like observation in the manner of the superscriptions of Jer 21:11 and 23:9? Driver, "Ezekiel," 308f, finds here the את which emphasizes the subject and sees in the following נשיא הוא the modification: "qua prince." On the other hand, Blau, "Gebrauch," 7–19, disputes, as Karl Albrecht had already done in "את vor dem Nominativ und beim Passiv," *ZAW* 47 (1929): 274–283 (also C. Brockelmann, "Die Objektkonstruktion der Passiv im Hebräischen," *ZAW* 49 [1931]: 147–149), the existence of an את which emphasizes the subject, but admits nevertheless in "Gebrauch," 7 note 3, and in "Gibt es ein emphatisches *'ēṯ* im Bibelhebräisch?" *VT* 6 (1956): 211 note 3, that the present passage is the only one which does not fit into his attempt to understand את as the sign of the accusative. On the basis of the comparison of 𝔗, on which 𝔙 is dependent, and 𝔊, G Joh. Botterweck, "Textkritische Bemerkungen zu Ezechiel 44:3a," *VT* 1 (1951): 145f, believes that את הנשיא is a scribal error for אל הנשיא (so too Harmuth) and that the latter is to be regarded as a marginal note. Since, however, 𝔊 𝔏[C] 𝔖 attest only one (ה)נשיא, the suspicion is more likely that the נשיא without the article (cf. the שער without the article in 43:1) has found its way into the text either as a dittograph or as a marginal note incorporated by mistake. If, then, with Harmuth, Botterweck, an original אל הנשיא is to be assumed, then the whole sentence would be introduced by a prefatory note by way of superscription: "Direction for the prince: he is to stay in it . . ." (Harmuth). If one sticks to 𝔐 את הנשיא, then it must be seriously asked whether one may not understand this הנשיא, which is accentuated by את, dissociated from what follows and taken up again by הוא, as analogous to the repeated . . . את מקום of 43:7. There is no support in the tradition for the emendation made by Toy, Herrmann, Bertholet, Ziegler and others of the את to אך "only."

b Cf. v 2 note b.

c Literally: "and from the direction of its (i.e. of the vestibule) way."

Form

The delimitation of the section 44:1–3 offers no difficulty. It begins anew in v 1 with a guidance formula. At the other end 44:4ff is introduced by another guidance formula. From the thematic point of view it is orientated quite differently and clearly marks a new beginning. Similarly, the inner formal structure of vv 1–3 is quite obvious. The act of guidance which reveals to the prophet a new state of affairs in the temple precinct is followed by an explanatory word from the man explaining this state of affairs and proclaiming at the same time specific regulations for the sanctuary.

In this connection there is controversy over the question of whether the proclamation of this regulation included from the outset v 3, the instructions of the נשׂיא ("prince"), or whether it was confined originally to the proclamation of the closed gate. While Gese, with reference to the analogy of 46:1ff, where the instruction about the closed inner east gate is indissolubly linked with instructions for the cultic conduct of the נשׂיא, also connects 44:3 as an original component along with vv 1–2, Fohrer sees in v 3 a "gloss which alters the subject matter." Rautenberg considers v 3 to be an addition "on account of its completely unprepared appearance."[1] He adheres to the observation, which is in any case correct, that there is mentioned here for the first time in chapters 40–48, and without any preceding introduction, the figure of the נשׂיא ("prince") which is then of significance in chapters 45f, 48.

Now it is remarkable that this topic is at once abandoned again in 44:4ff and there follow extensive discussions about priests and Levites. A return to the נשׂיא ("prince") is made only in the discussion of 45:7. Particularly close to the complex 44:1–3, which links closed temple gate and נשׂיא ("prince"), there lies, as has been mentioned, 46:1ff. While 46:1, with its reference to the closing of the gate for a specific period, is connected so closely with the prerogative of the נשׂיא ("prince") that the literary separation of the statements about the closed gate and the privilege of the נשׂיא ("prince") is impossible, the two statements in 44:2 and 44:3 stand unintegrated side by side. Whether the unusual beginning of v 3 (note a) is to be evaluated as an indication that v 3 was added secondarily to vv 1f is something which, in view of the uncertain text of this beginning, may be asked but cannot be firmly maintained.

Nevertheless one must take seriously the possibility that vv 1–2 were originally independent and that the ordinance about the closed gate was formulated initially without regard to any of the cultic personnel in the temple. Vv 1f are thus close to the basic text of chapters 40–42 and 43:1–11(12), where also a temple ordinance was promulgated quite apart from any human cultic activity. In the rest of chapters 44–48 this kind of description of temple phenomena without reference to persons is found only in 47:1–12, a section which might therefore be regarded as a continuation of 44:1–2. Whether that is possible is something which will have to be examined later.

The statement about the נשׂיא ("prince"), if this assumption is correct, represents a secondary expansion which, factually, forms a curve towards the נשׂיא ("prince")-statements in chapter 45 and above all chapter 46. In this case, too, it will have to be seen whether the intervening passage, 44:4ff, is the interruption of an intervening section which breaks an older connection or whether one can see in it the original continuation of 44:1f. Only this would give us the right to regard 44:3 with Fohrer as a "gloss" or with Rautenberg as an "addition" which rather unskillfully would, in anticipation, broach the subject of the נשׂיא ("prince") already in connection with 44:1–2.

Setting

44:1–2(3) have to be read as a sequel to what has gone before. The closing of the outer east gate is incomprehensible apart from what has happened in 43:1ff. On the other hand, the grammatical observation made concerning v 1 (note a) argues for a new beginning. The use of the term מקדשׁ ("sanctuary") for the whole temple area, appearing here for the first time within chapters 40–48, should not be used, however, to assume a different author for 44:1–2(3) vis-à-vis 43:1ff. מקדשׁ ("sanctuary") has been used frequently within the context of chapters 1–39 (see 5:11; 8:6; 9:6; 11:16; 21:7; 23:38f; 24:21;

1 Rautenberg, "Zukunftsthora," 102 note a.

25:3; 37:26, 28 [28:18 of Tyre]). Further, it will occur eleven times in 44:5–45:4 and later still in 45:18; 47:12; 48:8, 10, 21. One should not be too quick to build a contrast between the use of בית ("house") in chapters 40–43 and מקדש ("sanctuary") in 44:1. In the architectural style of the description of the buildings the use of בית ("house") would readily suggest itself, while in 44:1 the use of מקדש ("sanctuary"), with its more strongly theological emphasis, for the area which is now filled with Yahweh's presence would commend itself. Also, the transition to the designation of the temple area as a whole as מקדש ("sanctuary") immediately after the remarks about what happens in the בית ("house") in the narrower sense, i.e. the temple building (43:4f), is surely understandable.

Thus it is surely possible, the more so in view of the strong connection with regard to content, to link 44:1–2(3) directly to 43:1–11(12). The addition of v 3 will be illuminated by the judgment on 44:4ff. See also the general discussion about the literary pre-history of chapters 40–48 at the end of the exposition of chapters 40–48.

On v 3, the statement about the נשיא ("prince"), see the detailed discussion of the later נשיא ("prince")-ordinances.

Interpretation

■ **44:1** The prophet, according to v 1, is led back by the איש ("man") (who is no longer explicitly mentioned) to the outer east gate from where in 40:6ff and 43:1ff his route began. He finds this gate, through which, according to 43:4, the majesty of Yahweh entered the interior of the temple precinct, closed. Nothing more is said of the way in which it is closed, whether the entrance is walled up or whether simply the leaves of the door are barred.

■ **44:2** The man explains to the prophet that the gate has been closed because of this divine entry. Yahweh is described here for the first and only time in the book of Ezekiel with the full title, "Yahweh, the God of Israel," which (according to Steuernagel) had its original home in the sanctuary of Shechem.[2]

With regard to men a clear ruling has been given: No human foot shall in the future cross the threshold over which Yahweh passed to his sanctuary. The closed gate proclaims the majesty of the one who came. One may ask, over and above however, whether it does not testify to a second aspect, namely the finality of Yahweh's entry into his sanctuary, an entry which has been referred to in 43:7, 9 as לעולם ("for all time"). Yahweh closes behind him the doors which he no longer intends to open for a new departure of the nature of that in 11:23. Thus, in addition, the closed gate could proclaim also Yahweh's fidelity.

Here, one cannot suppress the question as to whether the phenomenon of the closed sanctuary gate emerges here for the very first time in the framework of the vision on the part of this prophet of the exile which has just been sketched (or on the part of the school of his disciples who continue to reflect on this vision).

Now Unger has pointed out a related phenomenon in the city of Babylon. Pohl has followed him in the assumption that the "Sacred (lit. 'pure') Gate" *bābu ellu,* through which Marduk's procession from Esagila passed and returned again and which was possibly also the entrance gate of the god Nabū in the "procession route of the deities Nabū and Nanā,"[3] was a closed gate which was opened only for the gods to pass through. In line 440 of the New Year Festival ritual Unger finds the mention of a "feast of the opening of the gate" which would thus determine the date of the procession.[4] Now, in connection with this interpretation of "gate opening" (*pit bābi*) we should note the observation of B. Landsberger: "'Opening of the gate' is certainly to be understood in cultic terms (of the temple gate), but in general the term denotes access of the people to the temple on the occasion of a festival, but not a specific or generally widespread festival" (see also 4. 112).[5] Also the specific expression "closed gate," which Unger believes he has found, cannot, on closer examination of his reading, be maintained. The fact, however, that there were periods when gates were closed is assured by the opposite expression *pit bābi* which expresses the end of the period of closure. One may perhaps in this context recall the end of Psalm 24 with its summons to the gates to open themselves for the מלך הכבוד ("King of glory"). Furthermore, the assumption of a reservation of the "Sacred

2 See 1, 254 on 8:4. אלהי ישראל on its own is found in 8:4; 9:3; 10:19f; 11:22; 43:2.

3 Weissbach, *Hauptheiligtum,* 71f.

4 See also *AOT* 302, *ANET* 334.

5 Benno Landsberger, *Der kultische Kalender der Babylonier und Assyrer* (Leipzig: Hinrichs, 1915), 87.

Gate" for the passing of the deity is extremely probable.

With reference to the Russian late Byzantine "Sacred Gate," which was built in 1176 A.D. in Susdal east of Moscow, Unger poses the question whether the Sacred Gate in Babylon is not to be conceived analogously to that as an entrance point to the temple which consisted of two gates side by side, one of which stood open for normal traffic while the other was usually walled up and was opened only for specific occasions. In another way one can think of the *porta sancta* which opened only once in twenty-five years in the year of the Jubilee for a whole year. And as more distant analogies there can be mentioned also the "golden gates" through which, in Vladimir, Kiev, Constantinople, for example, rulers passed in triumph.

If what Ezek 44:1–2 recounts is compared with all these different varieties of the closed gate, what strikes one is the complete uniqueness of the justification given here for the closing of the east gate. There is no trace here any longer of the periodic opening of the gate and the sacred procession of the festive crowd or even of a victorious ruler. With complete uniqueness here the gate is to be closed "once for all" because Yahweh has "once for all" taken possession of his sanctuary, and no procession, however sacred, may repeat this event regularly after him. In harsh offensiveness there is to be proclaimed through the medium of this closed gate the divine action which remains strictly over against man and which he is not to penetrate, not even in pious cultic imitation.

■ **44:3** That this is in fact what is meant is emphasized once more by the cultic ruling which follows immediately in v 3, even if this may have been added only later. If here the prince is allowed to sit in the vestibule of the gate structure, which is orientated inwards in the direction of the westwards-facing temple building, in order to eat there his sacrificial meal (this must be what is meant by אכל לחם "to eat food" here), then this renders the eastern gate structure ineffective as a gate. It acquires the function of a cultic room. The prince, as the most distinguished member of the lay congregation, is accorded the privilege of eating his meal in the gate structure which has been sanctified by Yahweh's entry.[6] The sequence in v 3b recurs almost identically in 46:8b.

Aim

With the "closed gate," the author of 44:1–2, obediently reflecting in the Babylonian exile on the layout of the new temple, takes over an architectural feature which may have confronted him particularly impressively in temple structures of Mesopotamia. In its biblical context the feature becomes the bearer of a novel type of statement. Certainly, the element of the divine prerogative can be discerned everywhere. But when the alternation of the gate's being closed and cultically opened must give place to a closing of it once for all, the closed gate in the temple blueprint of Ezekiel 40–48 acquires the character of "sign" in the strictly biblical sense. It has to be the sign established for ever for the new, definitive turning of God to his people, the constant remembrance of the fact that God has taken up his dwelling in the midst of his people.

When the congregation bows, there where the miracle of this new coming of God will take place, in obedient awe before the order established by God, they acknowledge the majesty of God, whose way man can revere with adoration but into which he cannot arbitrarily intrude not even in a worshipful cultic manner. At the same time they thank their Lord, through their obedience, for the fact that it has pleased him to grant his salvation to his people in such a definitive fashion.

Above and beyond this, since the fourth century A.D., the early church believed that it could find, in a way which is no longer possible for the exegesis of our own day, in the vision of the closed temple gate the typological prefiguration of the birth of Christ from the Virgin Mary (Harmuth, Kassing). Thus Theodoret, for example, says: "It is probable that through this there is faintly indicated to us the virgin mother, too, through whom no one has entered or come out except the Lord himself."[7] Or Jerome: "Some have the beautiful under-

6 On the function of the אלם as a cultic room see above p. 441; on the position of the נשׂיא in the blueprint in chapters 40–48 see below on 47:13–48:29.

7 Neuss, *Buch*, 59.

standing of the closed gate through which only the Lord, the God of Israel, enters and the Prince, for whom it remains closed, as the Virgin Mary who remained a virgin before and after the birth."[8] A quite different, spiritualizing interpretation is represented by Origen in his Fourteenth Homily.[9]

8 Neuss, *Buch,* 74f; see also Severus of Antioch, 86; Rufinus, 90; John Cassian, 91; Rupert of Deutz, 130f.

9 Neuss, *Buch,* 41f.

4. Renewed Encounter with God and a Commission

In 44:4f there is found the beginning of a new complex. In a second encounter with the appearance of Yahweh's glory the prophet is ordered to pay heed to all that he is told. There then follows, from the commission to speak in 44:6aα down to 46:18, a series of sections which are introduced by the introductory messenger formula (44:6, 9; 45:9, 18; 46:1, 16), mixed with the formula for a divine saying (44:12, 15, 27; 45:9, 15), with no interruption by any further guidance statement or any other element reporting an event involving the prophet. Such formulae of prophetic speech were to be found hitherto in chapters 40–48 only in the inserted secondary passage 43:18–27. On the basis of these observations the complex 44:4–46:18, for all the variety of its contents, acquires a certain self-contained character as to form.

In addition, one may ask whether in the reprimanding call רב לכם ("enough . . ."), which introduces the section 44:6b–31 dealing with the temple servants and which recurs in 45:9 in the sentence against the "princes of Israel," one should not recognize a further structural element intentionally supplied by the editors of the complex 44:4–46:18. Alongside the temple servants the "princes of Israel" would also thus be set apart as figures about whose correct relationship to the temple cult 44:4–46:18 intends to say something.

Closer examination then shows very quickly, however, that 44:4–46:18, from the point of view both of content and of form, contains very heterogeneous material and is by no means all of a piece.

It is advisable, then, and the above mentioned similarity in the formal elements in 44:4–46:18 suggests this too, to take this complex together, to examine one by one its individual components and to ask the question about the editorial process which lies behind it all only after this total review (see after chapter 48). In such an examination of the individual parts, 44:4–31 stands out first of all as a particular section which deals exclusively with Levites and priests. At the same time, however, particular attention must be paid to its introduction in 44:4f.

44

4 **And he led me through the north gate to the front[a] of the temple(-house), and I looked, and see, the glory of Yahweh filled the house of Yahweh[b]. And I fell on[c] my face. 5/ Then he [Yahweh][a] said to me: Son of man, pay good heed and see with your eyes and hear with your ears all that I say to[b] you about all the ordinances of the house[c] of Yahweh and about the regulations concerning it and apply your mind to <the entrances>[d] of the house <and>[e] all the exits of the sanctuary.**

44:4 4a 𝔐 אל פני here designates the goal of the route and is not to be understood like על פני in the sense of a mere geographical location ("opposite") of the north gate. Cf., e.g., the אל פני (= על פני) of 48:21.

b The juxtaposition of כבוד יהוה and בית יהוה has a stylistically harsh effect. Thus Cornill, Toy, referring to 𝔖 and 43:5, wish to read simply הבית. In the case of 𝔊 one might wonder whether the lack of the *κυρίου* after *δόξης*, in view of the fact that 𝔊[967] has it and also 𝔏[C] renders it, is a conscious smoothing or goes back to a simple scribal error.

c על-אל cf. 1:17 note a.

5 5a Cf. v 2 note a.

b 𝔐 אתך cf. 2:1 note a.

c Here too 𝔖 omits the divine name, cf. v 4 note b.

d A glance at 43:11, on which pasage 44:5 is unmistakably dependent (see the exposition), makes it likely that we should reckon in 𝔐 למבוא with the frequently attested confusion in Ezekiel of א and ו (י) (10:3 note a) and accept the reading למבאי which is also presupposed by 𝔗 למעלני.

e 𝔐 בכל is certainly presupposed by 𝔊 𝔗 𝔅, but is not really intelligible. Thus a scribal error for וכל or ולכל (Ehrlich, *Randglossen;* Bertholet; Fohrer; Gese) is not unlikely. 𝔖 attests the simple copula but might have smoothed over the difficulty secondarily in its usual way.

Form

As became clear from what has so far been said, 44:4–5 have a double character. They are on the one hand the introduction to the immediately following oracle about Levites and Priests. The ואמרת ("and you are to say") of the commission to speak in v 6 connects directly with vv 4f. On the other hand, however, they look forward beyond 44:6–31 and in their present context also claim to be an introduction to the chain of divine ordinances that runs to 46:18.

In the two verses the relationship with the divine manifestation described in 43:1–6 is soon apparent. Thus Steuernagel tried to regard 44:1–8 as a parallel account to 43:1ff. On the other hand, however, the proximity of v 5 to 40:4 cannot be ignored, and this led J. Herrmann to let a second part of the prophet's total presentation begin in 44:4ff.[1] Hölscher, on the other hand, has taken a further radical step and has regarded as secondary the whole of 43:1–11, which because of the parallelism of 43:10f and 44:4f was a disturbing interruption, and has connected 44:4ff directly to chapters 40–42. By contrast, Gese, by a careful comparison of the individual statements, has shown that 44:4f are to be regarded as a secondary formation which picks up elements from all the parallel passages mentioned and fits them into a new combination.

In their formal layout, vv 4f appear as an abbreviated copy of 43:1–6. The account of another divine manifestation, introduced by a guidance formula, is followed by the address to the prophet summoning him to pay attention. The specific commission to speak will then follow in v 6.

Interpretation

■ **44:4** With a new beginning the prophet reports that he is led to the spot in front of the temple building, i.e. the spot in the inner temple court where he had already found himself according to 43:5. While, according to 43:5, he had been transported by the spirit from the outer east gate into the inner court, here the man (who is no longer explicitly named) leads the prophet from outside to inside by the roundabout way via the north gate. The reason for this detour lies in the closing of the east gate for any human person which was reported in vv 1f. Thus it can be stated with certainty that 44:4f presuppose what is recounted in vv 1f.

With slight variation of expression (את בית יהוה "the house of Yahweh" instead of הבית "the house") the observation of 43:5b that the glory of Yahweh filled the temple is then repeated, and we are told, with a verbatim repetition of 43:3b, that the prophet fell on his face. Thus the clear picture of 43:1ff is slightly dimmed. According to chapter 43 the prophet was shattered at the appearance of Yahweh's majesty at the outer gate, was then raised up by the spirit and brought into the inner court. There he hears from the secluded depths of the temple (מהבית "from within") the voice of Yahweh who has withdrawn himself from his gaze. In chapter 44 it remains uncertain what the prophet actually sees, since Yahweh, in the present context, has already after what has happened in chapter 43 entered the seclusion of the sanctuary. What the prophet is enabled to see by his being led a second time into the inner court has, in reality, no longer the character of surprise at the self-manifesting presence of God, by which he was brought to his knees in 1:28 and 43:3. The phenomenon of the coming is here replaced by the circumstance of Yahweh's (hidden) presence. Nor is the raising up of the prophet mentioned, in contrast with 2:1f and 43:5 (implied in the ותשאני "and . . . raised me up"). Thus here already there emerges the impression of secondary reworking of an account already in existence and clear in itself.

■ **44:5** Then the prophet is addressed.[2] Since, in addition, v 5a is closely dependent on 40:4, it is probable that we should assume here too the presence of the guiding figure and that in the יהוה ("Yahweh") added in 𝔐 we have a secondary assimilation to 43:6f (see v 2 note a). In the comparison with 40:4 the impression once again forcefully emerges that the adoption is associated with a transposition of the word order, which blurs what was clear in 40:4. 40:4 occurred in the introduction to the great visionary experience of the new temple, in which the man interpreted for the prophet what had just been seen only right at the end. Thus in 40:4 the admonition to see preceded that to hear. Both were rounded off by the summary statement to "pay attention" to it (שים לבך),

1 J. Herrmann, *Ezechielstudien,* 54.

2 On the address "son of man" see 1, 131f.

i.e. to reflect upon its significance. The שׂים לב ("pay attention") is not simply an introductory call to attention which summons to the opening of the senses, but a following admonition to reflect inwardly upon what has been observed with the senses. Since in what follows in 44:6–46:18 more information is transmitted in the divine word and nothing more is to be seen, 44:5 transforms the introductory exhortation in such a way that the summons to "pay attention" (שׂים לב) is placed at the beginning and then seeing and hearing are arranged in the same order as in 40:4. But what purpose does the visual aspect still serve here? Why is the "reflection" put in a logically inept fashion before the summons to plain observation with the senses which ought to precede reflection? שׂים לבך ("pay attention") is thus devalued to a purely formal call to attention. Thus, too, 44:5a is intelligible only as a secondary readaptation, and not even a skillful one, of 40:4.

In addition, however, the author of 44:5 expands his basic text of 40:4 also by borrowing from 43:11. Alongside the real object of the reflection and observation, which by analogy with 40:4 is added in an object clause in which only the "showing" (מראה אותך "show to you") needs to be changed to "saying" (מדבר אתך "say to you"), there appear, added on by ל as a second object, the ordinances and regulations of the temple from 43:11 (in reverse order). And the ושמת לבך ("and pay attention") repeated from v 5a (= 40:4) is followed in addition by the mention of the entrances (note d) and exits of the sanctuary from 43:11 (again in reverse order).

All these minute observations permit a very specific conclusion. The author of 44:4f had before him a literary complex to which there belonged not only 40:4; 43:1–6, 11 but also already 44:1f. In dependence on these passages he formulates 44:4f as an introduction to the following series of Yahweh ordinances. The remarkably clumsy dependence on some of the passages mentioned, passages which were undoubtedly fixed in literary form, makes it certain that the author of 44:4f is not identical with the author (authors?) of these earlier passages, but follows them at some distance in time. On the other hand, the adoption of the phraseology of 43:11 makes it appear as not entirely impossible that "ordinances" which already followed 43:11(12) in an earlier text form have been incorporated in the complex to which 44:4f is the introduction.

Setting

44:4f thus prove, on precise detailed examination, to be a later editorial heading for a collection of "Statutes and Instructions, Entrance and Exit Rules" for the temple, which has been added secondarily to the already fixed complex 40:1–44:3 (possibly still minus some of its expansions). Through this very introduction in 44:4f, however, it becomes quite clear that the collection of ordinances is entirely along the same lines as the earlier temple description and is to be understood as an exposition of that description. We must look for the transmitters of these ordinances—added at a certain remove in time—among the followers of the Ezekiel school tradition. Whether its continuation is completely in line with the prophet's preaching will have to be examined with regard to the separate units.

Aim

The literary-critical insights on 44:4f can already lead us to guess that what follows makes the claim, with considerable polemical force, to be direct revelation from the center of the divine presence. The gathering together of the contents of 40:4; 43:1–6, 11 shows that the author of 44:4f is not content to let the ordinances which follow be authenticated as divine ordinances by 43:1–6, but that he repeats in concentrated fashion the statements about the divine presence made till now, the commission to speak and the proclamation of sacred ordinances in order to give full authority to what follows. The polemical note will be further confirmed by the content of what now follows.

5. Levites and Priests

Bibliography

E. Auerbach
"Die Herkunft der Ṣadoḳiden," *ZAW* 49 (1931): 327f.

Wolf Wilhelm Graf Baudissin
Die Geschichte des alttestamentlichen Priesterthums (Leipzig: Hirzel, 1889).

Aage Bentzen
"Zur Geschichte der Ṣadoḳiden," *ZAW* 51 (1933): 173–176.

Aage Bentzen
"Priesterschaft und Laien in der jüdischen Gemeinde des fünften Jahrhunderts," *AfO* 6 (1930/31): 280–286.

Aage Bentzen
Studier over det zadokidiske praesteskabs historie (København: Lunos, 1931).

George Ricker Berry
"Priests and Levites," *JBL* 42 (1923):227–238.

John Bowman
"Ezekiel and the Zadokite Priesthood," *Transactions of the Glasgow University Oriental Society* 16 (1955/56): 1–14.

Karl Budde
"Die Herkunft Ṣadoḳ's," *ZAW* 52 (1934): 42–50.

H. Donner
Studien zur Verfassungs- und Verwaltungsgeschichte der Reiche Israel und Juda, Unpub. Diss. (Leipzig, 1956).

Otto Eissfeldt
Erstlinge und Zehnten im Alten Testament; Ein Beitrag zur Geschichte des israelitisch-jüdischen Kultus, BWAT 22 (Leipzig: Hinrichs, 1917), especially 59–71.

Antonius H. J. Gunneweg
Leviten und Priester, FRLANT 89 (Göttingen: Vandenhoeck & Ruprecht, 1965).

Hans Jürgen Hermisson
Sprache und Ritus im altisraelitischen Kult; zur "Spiritualisierung" der Kultbegriffe im Alten Testament, WMANT 19 (Neukirchen-Vluyn: Neukirchener, 1965).

Gustav Hölscher
"Levi," *PW* NB 1st series 12 (1925), 2155–2208.

A. van Hoonacker
"Ezekiel's Priests and Levites," *ET* 12 (1901): 383, 494–498.

A. van Hoonacker
"Les prêtres et les Lévites dans le livre d'Ézéchiël," *RB* 8 (1899): 177–205.

Friedrich Horst
"Zwei Begriffe für Eigentum (Besitz): נַחֲלָה und אֲחֻזָּה" in *Verbannung und Heimkehr. Beiträge zur Geschichte und Theologie Israels im 6. und 5. Jahrhundert v. Chr., Wilhelm Rudolph zum 70. Geburtstage dargebracht* (Tübingen: Mohr [Siebeck], 1961), 135–156.

G. H. Judge
"Aaron, Zakok, and Abiathar," *JTS* 7 (1956): 70–74.

Ed. König
"The Priests and the Levites in Ezekiel 44:7–15," *ET* 12 (1901): 300–303.

J. C. H. Lebram
Das hebräische Priestertum nach J und E, Unpub. Diss. (Heidelberg, 1943).

John A. Maynard
"The Rights and Revenues of the Tribe of Levi," *Journal of the Society of Oriental Research* 14 (1930): 11–17.

Theophile James Meek
"Aaronites and Zadokites," *AJSL* 45 (1929): 149–166.

Rudolf Meyer
"Levitische Emanzipationsbestrebungen in nachexilischer Zeit," *OLZ* 41 (1938): 721–728.

Kurt Möhlenbrink
"Die levitischen Überlieferungen des Alten Testaments," *ZAW* 52 (1934): 184–231.

Julian Morgenstern
"A Chapter in the History of the High-Priesthood," *AJSL* 55 (1938): 1–24, 183–197, 360–377.

Francis Sparling North
"Aaron's Rise in Prestige," *ZAW* 66 (1954): 191–199.

H. H. Rowley
"Zadok and Nehustan," *JBL* 58 (1939): 113–141.

Hans Strauss
Untersuchungen zu den Überlieferungen der vorexilischen Leviten (Bonn: Rheinische-Friedrich-Willhelms-Universität, 1960).

Albert Vincent
"Les rites du balancement (tenoûphâh) et du prélèvement (teroûmâh) dans le sacrifice de communion de l'Ancien Testament" in *Mélanges syriens offerts à M. René Dussaud* 1 (Paris: Geuthner, 1939), 267–272.

Julius Wellhausen
Prolegomena to the History of Ancient Israel (Edinburgh: Black, 1885), especially 121–152, "The Priests and the Levites."

44

6 **And you are to say to the <house of> rebelliousness[a], the house of Israel: Thus has**

44:6 6a מרי on its own in the address to Israel has a parallel in the book of Ezekiel only in 2:7, but there, on the evidence of a large body of tradition, it rests on a textual corrupton (see 2:7 note c). Here too, on the evidence of 𝔊 *τὸν οἶκον τὸν παραπικραίνοντα* (𝔊^{967} = 𝔐), it is shown to be a textual error. It is to be supplemented by בית, which has fallen out due to the proximity of the neighboring בית ישראל. 𝔅

[the Lord][b] Yahweh said: Enough (now) of
all your abomination[c], house of Israel—7/
that you have brought in foreigners, un-
circumcised in heart[a] and in flesh, to be
in my sanctuary, to profane it [my
house][b] when you offer my food[c], the fat
and the blood. Thus <you have>[d] broken
my covenant with[e] all your abomination
8/ and have not kept charge of my sacred
things[a], but have <set them>[b] (i.e. the
foreigners) (as men) who have charge of
the service due to me in my sanctuary.
9 **<Therefore>[c] 9/ [the Lord][a] Yahweh has**
said: No foreigner, uncircumcised in
heart[b] and in flesh, shall enter my sanc-
tuary, (no one) of all the foreigners[c] who

exasperantem me seems to interpret 𝔐 as a participle with suffix, while 𝔖 לביתא דאיסראיל ממרמרנא has recourse to transposition and attributive subordination of the מרי to the בית ישראל. 𝔗 לעמא סרבנא seems already to presuppose 𝔐 and to expand the latter in its own way.

b אדני is lacking in 𝔊. 𝔊^{L,V,46} *αδωναι κύριος ὁ θεός*; 𝔊^{O} Arm *κύριος κύριος*; 𝔊^{B} *κύριος ὁ θεός*; 𝔊^{A} *κύριος ὁ θεὸς τοῦ Ισραηλ*. See Appendix 1.

c With the expression רב לכם מן may be compared the הנקל לבית יהודה מן of 8:17 (cf. Is 49:6). The absolute usage of רב לכם is found also in 45:9; Nu 16:3, 7.

7 7a 𝔗 destroys the figure of speech ערלי לב, has רשיעי ליבא (בני עממיא) and leaves only ערלי ביסרא. This is not attested in 𝔊^{967}, undoubtedly by mistake.

b את ביתי is not attested by 𝔊,which in addition renders 𝔐 לחללו, as does 𝔙 (see also 𝔖), by a coordinated verbal clause appended by means of the copula. It represents an interpretation of the suffix of לחללו, which is then, conversely, not rendered in 𝔙 𝔗 𝔖. It should, with most commentators, be deleted. 𝔗 renders ית עזרתי (ולאפסא).

c 𝔐 לחמי, which is qualified by the following חלב ודם (on this see Driver, "Ezekiel," 309, and the exposition below), has been misunderstood by 𝔊 *ἄρτους*, 𝔙 *panes meos,* but correctly grasped by 𝔗 ית קורבני which then further expounds fat and blood as ניכסת קודשין.

d 𝔐 ויפרו is already suspect by reason of the following תועבותיכם. 𝔊 *καὶ παρεβαίνετε*, 𝔙 *et dissolvitis,* 𝔖 ומבטלין אנתון suggest an original reading ותפרו. Driver, "Ezekiel," 309, believes he can retain 𝔐 by understanding ויפרו as: "They (the foreigners who do not themselves stand in a covenant relationship with Yahweh) cause my covenant to be broken."

e אל-על cf. 1:17 note a.

8 8a V 8a has been omitted by 𝔊, undoubtedly in error. It appears first in the post-hexaplaric recension with asterisk.

b 𝔐 ותשימון must refer to the foreign cult personnel already mentioned. Thus one might expect the reading ותשימום, which is then also assumed by Toy, Herrmann, Bertholet, Fohrer, Gese. Yet it cannot be definitely excluded that 𝔐 arose from dissimilation (avoidance of a double ם) on grounds of euphony and is to be retained as original (Cooke).

c 𝔐 לכם remains unattested in 𝔊. In its place there occurs a *διὰ τοῦτο* which introduces the messenger formula which follows in v 9 and suggests an original לכן.

9 9a אדני is lacking in 𝔊 (Clement, Jerome). 𝔊^{B} *κύριος ὁ θεός*; 𝔊^{O} *κύριος κύριος*; see Appendix 1.

b Cf. v 7 note a.

c On the ל in לכל בן נכר, which occurs also in 6:9 (6:9 note d has, therefore, to be expanded on this basis), see Gesenius-Kautzsch §143e. According to Paul Haupt, "A New Hebrew Particle," *Johns Hopkins University Circulars* 13 no. 114 (July, 1894):

**live in the midst of the Israelites[d], 10/ but
the Levites who went far from me when
(the) Israel(ites) went astray [who went
astray][a] away from me after their idols,
they shall bear their guilt. 11/ They shall
provide in my sanctuary the service of
watching[a] over[b] the gates of the temple
and the service in the temple. They shall
slaughter the burnt offering and the sacrifice for the people and shall serve
them[c]. 12/ Because they <served>[a]
them before their idols and <became>[b] a
stumbling block of iniquity to <the house
of>[c] Israel, therefore I have raised my
hand against them[d], says [the Lord][e]
Yahweh, and they shall bear their iniquity
13/ and shall draw near to me no more to
serve me as priests nor to[a] all my sacred
things[b], the holy of holies[c]. And they
shall bear their shame and their abomination which they have committed[d]. 14/
And I shall appoint them[a] as those who
have to see to the service in the temple in
everything which has to be done and be
seen to in it[b].**

**15 But the Levitical priests, the descendants
of Zadok, who kept what was to be kept
in my sanctuary when the Israelites[a]
went far astray from me, they shall
approach me to serve me and they shall
stand (in service) before me to offer me
fat[b] and blood, says [the Lord][c] Yahweh.
16/ They shall enter my sanctuary, and
they shall approach my table[a] to serve
me, and they shall keep my charge.**

**17 But when they go in through the doors of
the inner court, then they shall put on
linen clothes, and no wool shall be on
them (i.e. their bodies) when they serve
in the gates of the inner court and
within[a]. 18/ Linen headbands they shall
wear on their heads and linen breeches[a]
on their loins, and they shall not gird
themselves with sweat(-inducing garments)[b]. 19/ But when they go out to the**

107f, it is not the preposition ל which we have here but an emphatic particle corresponding to Arabic *la* "indeed." Similarly Driver, "Ezekiel," 309, who finds here an affirmative particle resuming the preceding כל בן נכר and points to, amongst other passages, 1 Chr 29:18.

d 𝔊 ἐν μέσῳ οἴκου Ισραηλ.

10 10a In 𝔊 𝔖, 𝔐 אשר תעו, which once again very emphatically refers the sin to the Levites, remains unattested. Since in the parallel statement in v 15, which speaks of the priests, the expression בתעות בני ישראל occurs again with מעלי referring to the statement about Israel, one should regard the same expression also as the original text of v 10 and consider אשר תעו as a secondary intrusion. Fohrer describes it as a gloss "which defines more closely"; Gese, surely more accurately, as a "rectifying" one.

11 11a 𝔙 expands: *erunt . . . aeditui et janitores* (*portarum domus*). V 11aβ is then omitted by 𝔖.

b על-אל cf 1:17 note a.

c 𝔐 לפניהם has been read by 𝔊 ἐναντίον τοῦ λαοῦ (𝔊[967] + μου) as לפני העם. Since העם has just been mentioned, 𝔐 (against Cornill; Ehrlich, *Randglossen*) is to be preferred.

12 12a 𝔐 ישרתו is rendered by the versions as an account of what is in the past. It is a scribal error for שרתו.

b 𝔐 והיו is emended by Bernhard Stade, "Anmerkungen zu 2 Kö. 10–14," *ZAW* 5 (1885): 293, to ויהיו. On this see also Arie Rubinstein, "The Anomalous Perfect with *Waw*-Conjunctive in Biblical Hebrew," *Bibl* 44 (1963): 62–69.

c 𝔗 𝔖 לבני.

d 𝔗 again speaks the language of its word theology קיימית במימרי עליהון.

e אדני is lacking in 𝔊[967]. 𝔊[B] κύριος ὁ θεός; see Appendix 1.

13 13a על-אל cf. 1:17 note a. The interchange of אל and על in this verse is particular striking.

b 𝔊 οὐδὲ τοῦ προσάγειν πρὸς (𝔊[967] has in place of this πάντα) τὰ ἅγια υἱῶν τοῦ Ισραηλ.

c 𝔊 τὰ ἅγια τῶν ἁγίων μου (μου is missing in 𝔊[967]).

d 𝔊 is rather different ἐν τῇ πλανήσει ᾗ ἐπλανήθησαν, echoing v 10.

14 14a 𝔊 has the plural καὶ κατατάξουσιν αὐτοὺς (φυλάσσειν). Is the plural to be translated by the impersonal "one" or are the priests intended to be the subject of the installation? So Cooke.

b 𝔐 בו is missing in 𝔊.

15 15a 𝔊 οἴκου Ισηαηλ.

b 𝔊 prefixes θυσίαν (not in 𝔊[967]).

c אדני is lacking in 𝔊[967]. 𝔊[B] and others κύριος ὁ θεός.

16 16a Expanded by 𝔗 in terms of the table for the showbread: לפתור לחים אפיא.

17 17a 𝔐 וביתה remains unattested in 𝔊.

18 18a 𝔐 מכנסי, 𝔊 περισκελῆ, 𝔙 *feminalia*.

b 𝔐 ביזע has been transcribed in 𝔊 βιζα (βια in 𝔊[967], a scribal error) as an expression which has not

people into the outer court <>[a] they shall take off the clothes in which they served and leave them in the sacred rooms and put on other clothes so that they do not make the people holy with their garments.

20 They shall not shave their head nor let their hair flow loosely[a]. They shall trim their hair[b].

21 And no priest shall[a] drink wine when he[a] enters the inner court.

22 And they shall not take as wives a widow or a divorcee, but only virgins, descendants of the house[a] of Israel. And the widow who is the widow of a priest they may take.

23 And they shall give my people instructions about the difference between sacred and profane, and about the difference between unclean and clean[a] they shall teach them.

24 And in a controversy[a] they shall <sit in judgment>[b]. In accordance with my laws <they shall conduct it>[c]. And my instructions and my statutes they shall observe at all my appointed feasts and keep my sabbaths.

25 But a dead man[a] <they> shall not go near[b], making themselves unclean. Only in the case of father and mother and son and daughter <and>[c] brother and unmarried

been understood (cf. *αιλαμ*, *θεε* in chapter 40). 𝔗 paraphrases the sentence which it did not understand: ולא ייסרון על חרציהון אלהן על ליבביהון ייסרון. Cooke wonders whether this does not preserve a tradition of ceremonial girding. On this see also his quotation from Kimḥi. 𝔖 simply omits the passage. Only 𝔙, which like the other versions introduces the sentence with the copula, has understood it: *et non accingentur in sudore.* According to Driver, "Ezekiel," 310, we have here an elliptical statement in which the real object of חגר, namely the garment, has fallen out and where ביזע is to be understood as "at the cost/risk of sweating."

19 19a 𝔐 has, accidentally through dittography, repeated the words אל החצר החיצונה. The versions do not attest the addition. Instead 𝔗 inserts מדרתא דקודשא and explains the אל העם of 𝔐 by the addition of לאיתערבא. With the same verb 𝔗 also renders the ולא יקדשו of 𝔐: ולא יתערבון עים עמא. Is 𝔗 trying to avoid the explicit "make holy" referring to the people?

20 20a 𝔗 ופירוע לא ירבון; 𝔖 וקוצתהון לא נרבון; 𝔙 *neque comam nutrient.* 𝔊 *καὶ τὰς κόμας αὐτῶν οὐ ψιλώσουσι* (𝔏^{C} *non tondent*) has misunderstood 𝔐.

b Here too 𝔊 *καλύπτοντες καλύψουσι τὰς κεφαλὰς αὐτῶν* has not understood 𝔐.

21 21a 𝔐 ישתו and בבואם are construed in accordance with the sense.

22 22a 𝔊 (𝔏^{C}) 𝔖 omit 𝔐 בית. 𝔊^{967} replaces *τοῦ σπέρματος* by *τοῦ οἴκου*. 𝔐 is supported by זרע בית יעקב in 20:5.

23 23a 𝔏^{C}, which renders only the second pair of terms by *inter medium sancti et polluti,* then adds, obviously by way of correction: *et inter medium mundi.*

24 24a 𝔐 ריב is interpreted more narrowly in 𝔊 *ἐπὶ κρίσιν αἵματος* (𝔏^{C} *iudicium sanguinis*). Yet 𝔐 (against Cornill, Fohrer, Eichrodt) is not to be supplemented on this basis.

b 𝔐 literally: "stand in order to judge." According to Driver, "Ezekiel," 310, what is reflected here is Babylonian practice according to which the judge stands. In Israel, according to Ex 18:13; Nu 35:12, the parties stand while the judge sits (see also *b. Sanh.* II 4). Q wishes to expand 𝔐 לשפט to למשפט. 𝔊 (𝔏^{C}) *τὸ διακρίνειν* and 𝔗 𝔖 למדן, however, support K.

c 𝔐 ושפטהו is a scribal error for ישפטהו. On this see 𝔊 (𝔏^{C}) as well as 𝔗. Admittedly the suffix is not attested by the versions. 𝔊 (𝔏^{C}) adds, by means of the copula, a second translation of the passage.

25 25a On מת אדם see, e.g., the פרא אדם of Gen 16:12, which Gesenius-Kautzsch §128l understands as a non-genuine genitive (explicative or epexegetic). Otherwise Driver, "Ezekiel," 310, who translates here not "dead person" but "a man's dead."

b 𝔐 יבוא is a scribal error for יבאו, cf. 10:3 note a.

c With 𝔊 (𝔏^{C}) 𝔙 𝔖 (𝔗 = 𝔐) here too the copula should be added.

sister[d] may they make themselves
unclean. 26/ But after he has become
clean (again)[a], <he>[b] shall count off for
himself seven days[c] 27/ and on the day
when he [in the sanctuary][a] enters[b] the
inner court to serve in the sanctuary, he
shall offer[b] a sin offering for himself, says
[the Lord][c] Yahweh.
28 **And <they shall have no>[a] (landed)**
property[b]. I am their property. And you
shall give[c] them no possessions[b] in
Israel[d]. I am their possessions. 29/ They
shall eat[a] the cereal offering and the sin
offering and the guilt offering, and every
devoted thing in Israel shall belong to
them. 30/ And the best of all the first-
fruits of everything[a] and every offering of
everything[b] from all your offerings shall
belong[c] to the priests. And the best of
your coarse meal[d] you shall give to the

d 𝔖 (under the influence of Lev 21:3?) adds בתולתא.

26 26a 𝔐 אחרי טהרתו. 𝔖, differently, מן בתר דמסתיב "after his pollution."

b 𝔐 יספרו, which is attested by 𝔙 𝔗, has surely arisen under the influence of the plural subject in v 25 and should, on the basis of 𝔊 (𝔏^{C}) 𝔖 and Lev 15:13, 28, be emended to יספר. See also 𝔊 in v 24.

c 𝔖 expands, in complete accordance with the sense but certainly without any support in the text in front of it, והידין נתדכא.

27 27a 𝔐 אל הקדש, alongside אל החצר הפנימית before the following בקדש and in comparison with vv 16, 21, has the effect of a superfluous doubling. Since it is missing in 𝔊 (𝔏^{C}), it is to be regarded as a gloss.

b In 𝔊 here, doubtless under the influence of v 25, the plural has intruded in the case of both verbs. 𝔊^{967} singular.

c אדני is lacking in 𝔊^{967}. 𝔊^{AQ} (𝔏^{C}) κύριος ὁ θεός.

28 28a 𝔐 והיתה להם לנחלה "and it shall be to them for a possession." So, too, 𝔊^{AQ} 𝔏^{C} 𝔗 𝔖. This wording, however, in view of the antithetic continuation in v 28aβ as well as that of the parallel in v 28b and of the other statements in the OT (see the exposition), cannot be original. The והיתה of 𝔐 is obviously intended to connect with the חטאתו of v 27 and say that the sacrificial gifts are the "possession" of the priests. Hence the paraphrastic rendering of v 28a in 𝔗 ותהי להון לאחסנא לחולק מותר קורבני חולקהון, which is continued also in the expanded rendering of v 28bβ: מתנן דיהבית להון אנון אחסנתהון. 𝔙 *non erit autem eis hereditas* presupposes a different text. If Gese wants to suggest that this has been corrected by 𝔙, then the reading of 𝔊^{967} καὶ οὐκ ἔσται αὐτοῖς κληρονομία ought now to confirm the age of this reading. Thus the text will originally have read ולא תהיה להם נחלה.

b On the more precise meaning of the terms נחלה and אחזה, which have no exact correspondence in English, see the exposition.

c 𝔊 (𝔏^{C}) οὐ δοθήσεται. So Driver, "Linguistic Problems," 186, תִּתֵּן.

d 𝔊 ἐν τοῖς υἱοῖς Ισραηλ. Cf. 12:23 note c.

29 29a 𝔐 יאכלום. The suffix takes up again the subject in the compound noun clause, see Beer-Meyer §92,4a.

30 30a 𝔊 (𝔏^{C}) divides differently in that it inserts the copula before בכורי כל.

b Otherwise Driver, "Ezekiel," 310, "every offering of every kind" with reference to Dtn 4:25; Ps 145:15, and G. A. Cooke, *A Text-Book of North-Semitic Inscriptions* (Oxford: Clarendon, 1903), 73, B 1–2.

c 𝔐 יהיה does not agree with the subject. Blau, "Gebrauch," 14 note 9, wonders whether this reflects the influence of כל. See also 45:10 note a.

d 𝔐 וראשית ערסותיכם. 𝔊 only τὰ πρωτογενήματα ὑμῶν, but cf. Levy, *Wörterbuch*, 3.702. On the discussion about the meaning of ערסות see Eissfeldt, *Erst-*

priest—to bring blessing to rest on your[e] house.
31 Any[a] beast that has fallen or has been torn, be it bird or animal, the priests shall not eat.

linge, 61–63, who decides for the meaning "dough."

e 𝔐 ביתך, also 𝔅 𝔗, while 𝔊 (𝔏C) 𝔖 have the plural suffix which one would expect. In v 30bβ, however, we can only be dealing with a later gloss which has been fully incorporated into only some of the versions (see the exposition).

31 31a 𝔊 (𝔏C) 𝔖 add the copula, cf. 1:4 note a.

Form

44:6–31 is shown by its continuous theme to be a homogeneous section. It is concerned with the persons who have to serve in the temple in accordance with their two classes: Levites and priests. 45:1ff, even if the connecting catchword תרומה seems to form a certain transition from chapter 44 to chapter 45, turn to a new topic.

From the point of view of form, vv 6–31 present a rather complex structure. The introductory divine commission to speak in v 6aα leads one to expect a prophetic oracle. The introduction of the oracle with the messenger formula heightens this expectation,[1] just as do the recurrent formulae for a divine saying in vv 12, 15, 27. On the connection of these two elements, however, see also the observation of Baumgärtel quoted above on 43:18.[2] Even the oracle itself which then begins in v 6b does not at first disappoint the expectation aroused by the surrounding formulaic material, insofar as it begins with a clear invective which appears to be followed in v 9, introduced by לכן ("therefore") (see v 8 note c), by the word of judgment. This suggests the customary form of the two-part prophetic saying.[3] The invective element, which is prefixed as motivation, has found in that saying its peculiar structure. Instead of the initial יען ("because")-clause of 5:7, 11; 13:8 and elsewhere, the variability of which has already been discernible,[4] there appears here the emphatic exclamation רב לכם "Enough now!" which might recall the woe-cry. The continuation with the following לכן ("therefore") follows the normal style. Yahweh addresses his people directly (second person plural) through the whole invective statement of motivation.

But then in the consequence clause, which is once again emphatically underlined by means of the introductory messenger formula, there comes the surprise. Instead of the expected statement of judgment or punishment in direct address, there follows in v 9 a legal regulation which gives no hint of any punishment which must befall the house of Israel who were addressed in the invective. For this sacral, legal direction, which expresses the non-admission of specific categories of persons to the sacred precinct, a close parallel can be found in the assembly laws of Dtn 23:2–4, in which, of course, לא יבא ("shall not enter") occurs five times at the beginning of each sentence and the sphere to which admission is refused is introduced by ב. Examples where the sacral, legal instructions begin with a generalizing כל ("all") may be found, e.g., in Lev 6:11, 20; 11:9, 12, 20, 42.

The style of the personal address in the second person plural is, however, also abandoned in the bipartite continuation in vv 10–16, which describes the two groups who in the future will be admitted to the sanctuary in place of the excluded "foreigners" (v 9). Here now, unexpectedly, there suddenly appears, in a new association, the punishment element which was missed in v 9. Vv 10–14, first of all, deal with the Levites and are, for their part, still in the form of a word of judgment with a double motivation. In its first version (vv 10–11), v 10a describes in a relative clause the sin of the Levites and introduces the announcement of punishment in vv 10b, 11 with the expression נשא עון ("to bear guilt"), well-known from 14:10 and characteristic of punishment formulae in sacral law.[5] The second version in vv 12–14 reveals the usual יען ("because") in the motivatory description of sin. The fact that this יען ("because")-clause is concluded by an emphatic formula for a divine saying is, of course, unique in the book of Ezekiel and confirms the "uncontrolled" use of this formula which Baumgärtel was forced to observe from another point of view. Here too the declaration of punishment in vv 12bβ-14 is then introduced by the formulaic נשא עון ("to bear guilt, shame"). The difference from a genuine, prophetic declaration of punishment can be recognized in the fact that no irruption of a historical act of punishment on Yahweh's part is announced, but that, rather, the threat of punishment is in the form of a cultic prescription which is to be observed in the future.

The difference from a genuinely prophetic mode of

1 See 1, 133 on 2:4.
2 See above p. 430.
3 See 1, 235.
4 הראית-clause, 1, 235; woe-cry, 1, 290; strengthening to יען וביען 13:10; 36:3.
5 On this see 1, 305.

speech can be further recognized in the fact that the "declaration of punishment" against the Levites is followed in vv 15–16 by a motivated "declaration of reward" for the Zadokite priests. It has been observed in earlier contexts that the genuine, prophetic declarations of salvation were characterized by their lack of worldly motivation.[6] Yahweh's faithfulness is the sole reason for his intervention to save. The oracle concerning the priests differs from that. It justifies the "beneficent" preeminence of the priests in the service of the temple (vv 15aβ–16) by their good behavior in the period of aberration (v 15aα).

Vv 6–16, a section which was composed as a unit, is followed in vv 17–31 by a complex which is of a substantially different structure. It contains isolated instructions to the priests of different types, lengths and forms. The direct address of the people by Yahweh in the second person plural, which was discernible at the beginning of vv 6–16, can be observed with certainty only in v 28, to which, however, vv 29–30a must also belong. Thus one may with Gese recognize in this section, which regulates the access of the priests, the conclusion of the regulations for the priests. The verses which remain, vv 17–27, 31b, represent on the other hand expansions, which, from the point of view of substance, also partly point in a quite different direction. From the point of view of form they are best discussed in the framework of the detailed exegesis, since for the assessment of the total unit, vv 6–31, they contribute nothing more.

The discussion of the "Setting" of the complex vv 6–31 will follow the detailed exegesis.

Interpretation

■ **44:6** In Yahweh's commission to the prophet to speak there appears for the first and only time in chapters 40–48 the description of Israel as "house of rebelliousness," which occurred in the collection of judgment oracles in the first half of the book, frequently in chapters 2f and 12 and then again in 17:12 and 24:3.[7] The desire to formulate a judgment oracle in the prophetic style can be clearly discerned even if subsequently the power to carry it through is lacking. The invective רב לכם ("enough [now]") which introduces the indictment is found in the Priestly Korah narrative as well as in the invective of the Korahites (Nu 16:3) and in Moses' reply (Nu 16:7). Otherwise the expression occurs in Dtn 3:26 and 1 Kgs 12:28.

■ **4:7** The house of Israel is charged with the particular abomination of having admitted "foreigners" to the sanctuary and thus having broken the covenant.[8] "Foreigners" are not otherwise referred to in the book of Ezekiel with the root נכר. When it speaks of them as the זרים this always refers to the political foreign nations who act as instruments of Yahweh's judgment on Israel (7:21; 11:9) and on the neighboring peoples addressed in the foreign oracles (28:7, 10; 30:12; 31:12). Thus 44:6ff stands at an appreciable distance from the genuine oracles of Ezekiel. One may not, with A. Bertholet, charge this passage with being the first example of the equation "the foreigner is the heathen."[9] Rather, Ezek 44:6ff is closely akin to priestly formulations; in Lev 22:25 an expansion prohibits the acceptance and offering of food for the deity (לחם אלהיכם "food of your God") from the hand of a foreigner.[10] The expression בן נכר ("foreigner") occurs only here in Leviticus, but it is found in P regulations also in Gen 17:12, 27; Ex 12:43. Under the designation זר, which according to Gunneweg means there in a somewhat broader sense not only the non-Israelite but what is ritually unfit, the illegitimate,[11] there occurs in Nu 1:51; 3:10, 38; 18:7, in an oracle directed against the priests, the strong expression הזר הקרב יומת ("הזר who comes near shall be put to death"), and 18:4 makes a demand similar to Ezek 44:9 וזר לא יקרב אליכם ("and זר shall not come near you"). In all this there is the background for the rejection of all that is foreign which is clearly discernible in Ezra. On the evidence of the word of consolation to the בן נכר ("foreigner") of Is 56:3–8, this attitude did not go uncontra-

6 See above p. 239, 247, 250.

7 On this see 1, 134.

8 On תועבת see 1, 190 and above p. 418 (fn. 36) on 43:8.

9 Bertholet, *Stellung*, 107.

10 From the priestly source, according to Elliger, *Leviticus*, 269f, 300.

11 Gunneweg, *Leviten*, 201.

dicted. The proximity of the present passage, which judges the participation of foreigners in the service of the sanctuary as a desecration of the same, to the language of P is discernible also in the description of the offering as "food of Yahweh." This can be found also in Lev 3:11, 16; 21:6, 8, 17, 21f; 22:25; 24:7; Nu 28:2.[12] When "fat and blood" are then mentioned as the particular content of this food of Yahweh, what is envisaged is the burning of the fat pieces and the sprinkling of the blood on the altar. Both are connected, for example, in the rituals for animal sacrifices in Leviticus 1–5.[13]

Unusual is the description of the foreigner as "uncircumcised in flesh and spirit." Uncircumcision is spoken of in the book of Ezekiel only in connection with the representations of death in the oracles against foreign nations (28:10; 31:18; 32:19–32).[14] It argues for the origin of the original Ezekiel oracles in the early exilic period that in them there is no mention of the demand for circumcision which then, obviously in consequence of the exilic situation, is in P the great confessional sign of genuine descent from Abraham and is required on pain of death (Genesis 17). In 44:7, 9 the uncircumcision of the heart is connected with the reference to ritual bodily circumcision. This transfer, which doubtless originates in the concept of circumcision as a sign of purification, is found also in Jer 4:4; 9:25; Dtn 10:16; 30:6; Lev 26:41. In addition there is a reference in Jer 6:10 to uncircumcised ears and in Ex 6:12, 30 to uncircumcised lips. Hermisson has discussed this process of "spiritualization" of circumcision.[15] It does not lead to the suppression of the ritual regulations. The combination of the ritual aspect and of the inner purity of the heart is nowhere expressed so clearly as here. Of course, in the overall description of the "foreigner" as "uncircumcised in body and in heart" there is again reflected the beginnings of the exclusive attitude towards all foreigners. In 3:6 Ezekiel himself had spoken very differently of the people of his heathen surroundings.[16]

Israel's sin in allowing "foreigners" to do service in the temple is finally described, by a term which is otherwise unusual with Ezekiel himself, as "breach of covenant."[17]

■ **44:8** In sharp contrast it is observed that Israel has "not kept the observances concerning my holy (i.e. consecrated to me) things,"[18] but has instead allowed the foreigners to do the service in the sanctuary. In this connection, there is a word play in the two halves of the verse on the two senses of the word משמרת ("service"), which is often used in P for the cultic activities of the Levites.

Looking at 44:7f one must ask what concrete facts are envisaged in this reproach of pre-exilic Israel. Josh 9:27 mentions that the people of Canaanite Gibeon had been designated by Joshua as "hewers of wood and drawers of water for the congregation and for the altar of Yahweh to this day" (see also Dtn 29:10). According to Noth, what is thought of is enslaved cultic personnel at the sanctuary of Gilgal.[19] In Ezra 2:43ff in the list of the (returning?) community, נתינים, i.e. "temple servants," are mentioned and in vv 55–57(58) descendants of Solomon's slaves. Must one seek in these circles groups of non-Israelite origin who were recruited for cultic functions? Or must one think, over and above, in this recruitment of foreigners to the temple service of the period, of the great exposure to foreign Assyrian cults under Manasseh and Amon about which, of course, nothing is known? In this connection Cooke points to neo-Babylonian and Phoenician records which seem to attest the installation of "foreigners" (גרים) in the temple service. As far as Israel is concerned, the question cannot be answered with certainty. In the description of the temple abominations in chapter 8 Ezekiel himself has given no indication of this offense.

■ **44:9** As already mentioned, this harsh invective against the house of Israel is not followed in v 9, in spite of its renewed emphatic introduction as a prophetic divine saying, by the expected speech of judgment, but by a sacral legal prohibition, phrased in general terms, to the proximity of which to the prescriptions of exclusiveness

12 On this see Elliger, *Leviticus*, 53.
13 On the "food of God" see F. Nötscher, "Sakrale Mahlzeiten vor Qumran" in *Lex tua veritas* (Festschrift H. Junker) (1961), 145–174, especially 163.
14 On this see above p. 173.
15 Hermisson, *Sprache*, 64–76.
16 See 1, 137f.
17 On this see the observations on the secondary passage 16:59 (1, 352f).
18 Gunneweg, *Leviten*, 191.
19 Martin Noth, *Das Buch Josua*, HAT 7 (Tübingen: Mohr, ²1953), 54.

for the קהל יהוה ("assembly of Yahweh") in Dtn 23:2–4 and its particular proximity to priestly prescriptions reference has already been made in the discussion of the "Form." The fact that we are not dealing simply with the citation of traditional material is shown by its dependence on the characterization of the "foreigners" found in v 7. At the same time it is clear that the formulation comes from a time in which foreigners lived "in the midst of Israel." This already appears clearly to presuppose the post-exilic situation with which Is 56:3ff is also concerned.

The prohibition is followed by the positive regulation of temple duties, which now for its part divides into the double directive for Levites and priests. In this connection the duties are differentiated from the point of view of punishment and reward. On the side of those being punished a completely new, second element of guilt, over and above that in vv 6b–8, is brought into play.

■ **44:10–14** Vv 10–14, in a double parallel structure, speak of the punishment of the Levites by their obligation to menial temple service. In the description of the guilt in vv 10a and 12a, as well as in the separate statements about the punishment, it is remarkable how strongly the phraseology, given the different overall point of view, is dependent on statements in the judgment speeches of Ezekiel in chapters 1–24. The Levites are reproached with having gone far from Yahweh.[20] In this connection there is already very clearly in mind a fixed view of history which is aware of a particular period of sin and temptation, the "time when Israel went astray." The fixed turn of phrase, of which תעה ("to go astray") has already occurred in 14:11 in Ezekiel's preaching, will recur in v 15 and in 48:11.[21] Such a way of speaking easily establishes itself where a generation makes a sharp break with previous history and stands out against a "period dominated by formal principles." This period is characterized for Ezek 44:10 by Israel's following after the "idols." These are designated by the word גלולים, which is well-known from chapters 1–39.[22] According to v 12a the Levites did cultic duty for their people before these "idols" and thus became the cause of sin for their people. Once again there is caught up here a technical term which plays a considerable role in the prophet's preaching of judgment.[23] Because of this sin on the part of the Levites, they will have to bear their guilt or, more precisely, the responsibility for their guilt (vv 10b, 12b), and this is further varied in v 13 to the statement that they will have to bear their shame and their abomination. In these two expressions also the language of Ezekiel's preaching of judgment, which for its part adopts older sacral legal formulae, is taken up.[24] Over and above this general affirmation of guilt and punishment, however, there is now developed more precisely in what the punishment for the Levites will consist. Specific duties are assigned to them:

1) The duty of guarding the gates of the "house," by which must be meant here not the temple building in the narrower sense but the whole temple area. The term פְּקֻדּוֹת ("watching") is used in 2 Kgs 11:18 for the guards whom the priest Jehoiada posts in the temple area in order to secure the proclamation of Joash as king. One thinks involuntarily here of the niches in the strong fortified temple gates of Ezekiel 40, in which surely some of the Levites must have been stationed when performing this duty. But there is no explicit reference to that. Since in Ezra and Nehemiah the "door keepers" (שֹׁעֲרִים) are still differentiated from the Levites, Ezekiel 44 with its allocation of this duty to the Levites does not seem to have prevailed. P does not mention the door keepers. In Chronicles they are reckoned among the Levites.[25]

2) The duty in the "house," where they are to slaughter the burnt offering and the sacrifice of the people and thus serve the people. Here too Ezekiel 44 has obviously not prevailed. The old custom that the donors themselves slaughtered the sacrificial animal (e.g., 1 Sam 14:32–35) has not allowed itself to be suppressed. Not only the rituals for the burnt offering and sacrifice in Leviticus 1 and 3 but also the accounts of the practices in

20 On this see 8:6, cf. 1, 240, as well as the self-righteous ambiguous utterance in 11:15 (see 1, 261).

21 See 1, 309.

22 See 1, 187.

23 See 1, 146 and 211.

24 On נשא עון see 1, 164 and 305; on נשא כלמה, 1, 351.

25 Cf. Baudissin, *Geschichte*, 142f.

the Herodian temple show that the donors of the sacrifice did not allow themselves to be deprived of this right.[26]

In the second version in vv 12–14 the declaration of punishment is introduced with the threatening gesture of the raised divine hand. The benevolent oath gesture of Ezek 20:5f, 28, 42 (47:14) is thus transformed into something hostile (but see also 20:15, 23; 36:7). It is now clearly brought out that the allocation of these menial tasks to the Levites includes correspondingly the prohibition of performing full priestly service (כהן "to serve as priests") and approaching the holy of holies. Numbers 18 can illustrate this even more fully. Thus what is meant is the "service of the temple" (משמרת הבית) in all its varied aspects (on the expression see Nu 3:25f; 4:25f).

The close connection with the linguistic stock of Ezekiel 1–39 might raise the question whether the language here does not after all reveal the speaker to be the prophet himself. On the other hand, however, it must be strongly emphasized how greatly what is said in this language deviates in content from the preaching of the prophet as this became known from the earlier oracles. That preaching astonished by its radicalism in which again and again the people as a whole were accused of rebelliousness and original sin. Where individual figures were made to stand out, they always were instantly characteristic of this totality and were never isolated from it.

■ **44:15–16** Above all, however—and this leads directly to vv 15f—it is, on the basis of that preaching, unthinkable that a whole class, united in one family, should be designated as having held true in a time of error and be adjudged worthy of subsequent reward.

It is precisely this that happens when reference is now made to the "Levitical priests, the descendants of Zadok." Of them it is attested in the introductory statement of motivation that in the time of Israel's going astray (the term of historical classification recurs) they had faithfully maintained the service of the sanctuary (משמרת מקדשי "the service of my sanctuary"). For this reason they are now to acquire the right for the future to approach Yahweh in his service and to stand before Yahweh to offer him the precious gifts of fat and blood at the altar (on this cf. v 7). The antithesis is also expressed in clear language: While the Levites "serve the people" (v 11 יעמדו לפניהם לשרתם "they shall serve them") because they had served them before their idols, the Zadokites are to serve Yahweh (ועמדו לפני "they shall stand (in service) before me"). They are to have the right to enter the "sanctuary." מקדש here must, in contrast to v 1, mean the temple itself in the narrower sense. They are to be permitted to approach "Yahweh's table." The reference to Yahweh's table is connected with the reference to food (v 7). Also in Mal 1:7, 12 it seems that what is meant by the reference to the table is the altar to which fat and blood are brought as Yahweh's food. Thus here too one must think not, e.g., only of the table of showbread (41:22). The last regulation too is clearly directed antithetically against the Levites. While they, according to v 14, have to "see to the service of the house" (שמרי משמרת הבית), which here clearly refers to the larger temple area, so the Zadokites have to see to the service of Yahweh (ושמרו את משמרתי).

■ **44:10–16** It is worth pausing here to consider what is meant by these regulations and how they fit into the *history of the priesthood in the Old Testament.* Only when this context has been clarified can it be judged what the particular characteristic of the present regulation is and in what direction the tendency of what it is actually saying lies.

Now the present passage has again and again played a quite special role for the understanding of the history of Old Testament priesthood. Wellhausen, in his *Prolegomena,* begins the chapter which, within the "History of the Cult," deals in particular with "The Priests and Levites" with an analysis of this very pericope. As a result of its brilliant presentation, a definite view of the history of the priesthood has subsequently been able to achieve wide acceptance. According to this, ancient Israel still knows no difference between priests and Levites. The tribe of Levi is the real priestly tribe. A separation begins to appear only in the wake of Josiah's reform. In this reform all local sanctuaries are abolished. Jerusalem acquires the privilege of being sole sanctuary. Admittedly Dtn 18:6f legislates that "if a Levite comes from any of your towns," i.e. if a priest of a local sanctuary

26 Josephus, *Antiquities* III 9, 1; *b. Zebah* III 1; and other references.

comes to the place of the sanctuary chosen by Yahweh, he can serve there before Yahweh if he so desires "like all his fellow-Levites who stand to minister there before Yahweh." 2 Kgs 23:9 shows, however, how the Jerusalem priests, whose privileges were threatened by this far-reaching regulation, were able to make it inoperative, so that the country priests (here כהני הבמות "priests of the high places") certainly shared in the emoluments of the Jerusalem priests but received no full priestly rights. In this state of affairs, Ezekiel, "a thorough Jerusalemite,"[27] with his programmatic schema for the post-exilic period "drapes the logic of facts with a mantle of morality" and decrees that the "Levites," i.e. the descendants of the country priests who became unemployed in 622, have to perform menial tasks because of their (or more exactly their fathers') sin, while the Jerusalem Zadokites, who were unsullied by the sin of the pre-reform period, could perform the full service. This is then also the state of affairs which P finds and develops in its own way.

This view of Wellhausen's has not remained without opposition. But when, e.g., Baudissin asserted, in opposition, the greater age of P over against Deuteromony, he did not challenge the view that Ezekiel 44 "deals with the Levitical priests of the high cult and seeks to demote them by way of punishment for this very cult which culminated in idolatry."[28] He sought simply to maintain that the gradation of priests and Levites already existed (namely in P, which was adjudged older) and that the polemic of Ezekiel 44 was directed above all against the Aaronite Ithamarites who also participated in the high cult.

But most recently (Strauss, Gunneweg) the question has been posed more and more strongly whether the tacit identification Levites = priests is really reliable for the older period. In a careful analysis of the oldest references to Levites, Gunneweg suggests that in the early period, e.g. Ju 17:7 which mentions a Levite from Bethlehem from the tribe of Judah, both terms are to be clearly separated. The "Levites are persons who have a particular legal and social status. They belong to none of the other tribes of Israel and are therefore everywhere strangers. As such they are reckoned among the *personae miserae.* But although strangers they nevertheless belong to the Israelite amphictyony."[29] Later Levi distinguishes itself by its zeal for the ordering of the life of the Yahweh amphictyony and against the new, formerly Canaanite, Yahwehized sanctuaries. The exemplary priestly figure who becomes increasingly significant in the tradition of those sanctuaries is Aaron.

It is into this state of affairs that the Deuteronomistic programme comes. In Deuteronomy we can see in the "Levite who is within your gates" the landless Levite living in the place as a "stranger," who on no account can be equated with the high priesthood. On the other hand, however, it is possible to see in the references, which are to be clearly separated from this, to the "Levitical priests" the specifically Deuteronomistic programme which demands that priests should be Levites, and, similarly, that the Levites should be permitted priestly duties. According to this all of Levi ought to be a tribe of priests.

This, then, is an outline of the presuppositions on the basis of which what is said in Ezekiel 44 must be understood. In this connection, two things must be made clear at the outset. The one is the emergence of the name Zadok. The information from the time of David makes it completely clear that this Zadok was a historical figure who was priest under David alongside Abiathar, who in turn was introduced as a descendant of Eli, at the ark sanctuary in Jerusalem. There is much to be said for the supposition that David, in the framework of his policy of conciliation between Canaan and Israel, took over in him a member of the old Jebusite royal house whose Melchizedek tradition thus also penetrates the Israelite-Jerusalemite priestly tradition. After the banishment of Abiathar in the wake of the troubles about the throne in 1 Kings 1f, Zadok is the sole representative of the Jerusalem priesthood. In the "sons of Zadok," who subsequently, by taking over the Elide family tree, integrated themselves with the ark-priesthood of Shiloh and, by tracing that genealogy back to Aaron, integrated themselves completely with the Israelite tradition and in the wake of the Deuteronomic reform programme designated themselves Levitical priests, we undoubtedly have before us in Ezekiel 44 the Jerusalem priesthood.[30]

27 Wellhausen, *Prolegomena,* 124.

28 Baudissin, *Geschichte,* 106.

29 Gunneweg, *Leviten,* 220.

30 On this, cf., e.g., Rowley, "Zadok"; Bentzen. The latter's assumption that in Zadok David had precisely made the last Jebusite king his priest is admittedly

The second observation consists in recalling the fact that chapters 40–48 must in no sense be superficially simplified as a unified programme, but reveal clear stages of growth. Thus it could be discerned already in 40:46b and 43:19a that secondary additions endeavored to bring about the harmonization of older formulations with 44:6ff. An observation of a similar kind will have to be made in 48:11aβb. In this connection it is preferable to speak, not with Gese of a "Zadokite layer," but rather with Gunneweg of a Zadokite section in 44:6ff and of its "metastases" in the corrective additions just mentioned.

Above all, 40:45–46a, which have been assimilated to 44:6ff by means of the addition in 40:46b, give us an unrestricted view into an older form of the regulations for priestly duties. The two rooms in the inner north and south gates, which are described in an addition to the original guidance vision, are here divided between two groups of temple priests. Since such a division of the two buildings of 42:1–14 is not mentioned in 42:13f and since, from the point of view of content, such a division is also not likely, it is preferable (against Gunneweg) not to cite that description here. The two priestly groups are differentiated in 40:45–46a according to their functions as כהנים שמרי משמרת הבית ("the priests who see to service in the temple") and כהנים שמרי משמרת המזבח ("the priests who see to service at the altar"). One cannot fail to recognize that in these descriptions the terminology of 44:6ff is anticipated. Here, with slight variation of terminology, the שמרי משמרת הבית ("those who have to see to the service of the temple") (44:14) are contrasted with the group of whom it is said, with a backward glance at the past, שמרו את משמרת מקדשי ("they kept the service of my sanctuary") (44:15) and of whom it is said for the future: ושמרו את משמרתי ("they shall keep my charge"). This was previously explained in detail as entering Yahweh's sanctuary and approaching his table, i.e. the altar (44:16). The "metastasis" of 40:46b then equates this latter group, completely in accord with 44:15f, with "the sons of Zadok, those of the Levites who come near to Yahweh to minister to him." The great surprise, on the other hand, consists in the fact that the שמרי משמרת הבית ("those who see to service in the temple"), who are called כהנים ("priests") in 40:45, in 44:14 are Levites to whom, in v 13, the title כהן ("priest") is explicitly refused.

The conclusion cannot be avoided that 40:45–46a reveal an older situation than the one envisaged in 44:6ff. According to it priestly service is divided into two levels, of which undoubtedly "service at the altar" possesses the greatest honor, the holders of which offices, however, are both described quite simply as "priests." This is still not far from the Deuteronomic situation in which all priests are designated as "Levitical priests" without there being any difference in duties being discernible.

40:46b, on the other hand, leads to 44:6ff. When it is stated here only of the second group of the sons of Levi (such is the designation of both groups), the one equated with the Zadokites, that they may come near to Yahweh in service, this is tacitly stating that the first group does not have this privilege, and this corresponds to the negative statements of 44:13. When in 44:10–14 service in the temple is limited to guarding the gates, slaughtering the sacrificial animals for the people (what is described as "service for the people") and when this group is explicitly forbidden to approach all of Yahweh's holy things (קדשי "my sacred things"), especially of course the holy of holies, then one has the impression that here, by contrast with 40:45, a diminution of the rights of the first group has taken place. This is contrasted with an extension of rights on the side of the Zadokites. What in 40:46a was still restricted to "service at the altar" has, in the retrospective statement of 44:15, become "service in my sanctuary" and is, in the future perspective of v 16, described as service of Yahweh himself (משמרתי "my service"), in which the approach to Yahweh's table is rather only a single element in the entry to Yahweh's sanctuary which is reserved for them.

Gunneweg correctly draws attention to the fact that an analogous reduction in Levitical duties can be discerned also in the later expansions in P. While Nu 1:48ff; 3:5ff; 4:21ff speak simply of Levites carrying and guarding the sacred things, in 4:5–20 and chapter 18 it is possible to observe stricter rules for keeping the Levites from direct contact with the holy (cf. Nu 4:15, 19; 18:3 with Ezek 44:13, and for the extension of the priestly duties of the Zadokites-Aaronites Ezek 44:16; Nu 18:5 and the

not very probable.

statements about the priests in 4:5ff). Here, admittedly, there is lacking in the expressions in P the sharpness of the polemic of Ezekiel 44. נשא עון refers, in the quite neutral sense of "bear responsibility," in Nu 18:1 to the Aaronites exactly as it does to the Levites in 18:23. The "guilt" incurred by the people as the result of a possible contact with the holy is, on the other hand, described as נשא חטא (18:22; see also v 32). Thus the movement of vigorous repression of the Levites is reflected in the later strata of P in a somewhat mitigated form.

The repression of the Levites into menial duties is justified in Ezek 44:6ff in all severity by their particular transgression in the "sinful period." The formation of rigid clichés in looking back on past historical periods, according to which "standing" and "falling" are attributed in black and white terms to specific groups, can be seen to some extent already in the treatment of the history of the northern kingdom in the books of Kings and then intensified in the books of Chronicles. It would also, however, not be difficult to find similar examples of the establishing of resistance heroes and fallen in times of temptation even in the more recent past. The sin of the "Levites" (44:10ff), which admittedly does not lead to an embargo on referring to the Levitical priests (44:15), is expressed, characteristically, in completely stereotyped phrases: going far from Yahweh, following after idols (v 10), serving the people before their idols. All serve as the impetus for their guilt. Nothing is said about cultic service, which has often been silently read into the situation here especially if one thought one ought to find behind the Levites simply lumped together the priestly families of the country sanctuaries. Wellhausen's judgment that here "the logic of facts" had been draped "with a mantle of morality" cannot entirely be rejected. Use is made, after all, of a piece of genuine recollection of an evil time of apostasy in the past, which in the words of Ezekiel had found particularly trenchant expression. The reservation of the harsh judgment for an individual social class and the corresponding exoneration of another class do not, on the other hand, correspond in any way to Ezekiel's preaching about sin, which is directed in 22:23ff equally against all classes and found in chapter 8 its most trenchant expression with regard to the temple and those who served in it. Those who sigh and mourn at the destruction of the temple will be found, according to 9:4, outside in the city. Nothing justifies us in regarding them as the Zadokites who remained righteous.

■ **44:17-31** Polemic and praise then disappear completely in vv 17–31, a collection of instructions of the most varied kind for the duties of the priests mentioned in vv 15–16. Nothing further is said here about the Levites. The survey from the point of view of form showed that in vv 28–30a at most we might still have a section which is to regarded as the original conclusion of 6–16.

■ **44:17-19** Vv 17–19 deal in the first instance with clothing regulations which are to be observed by the priests who enter the sacred precinct. V 18, which has a belated effect after v 17bβ, disrupts the clear sequence of the double rule about entry to the sanctuary and departure from it and has probably been inserted here only secondarily. Stylistically, too, v 18 has a somewhat different character. The rule about leaving is clearly connected with what is said in 42:1–14 about the great temple sacristies which have the function of holiness sluices, although it formulates it with new and independent vocabulary. Similarly Lev 6:4 (16:23). The key words "sacred rooms" come from 42:13. With the conception of holiness represented in v 19 may be compared what was said on 42:13.[31] The "linen" (פשתים) clothing of the priests was described in 9:2, 11; 10:2, 7 by בדים ("linen"), which corresponds to the way P usually speaks of the priestly clothing (see Ex 28:42; 39:28; Lev 6:3; 16:4; and elsewhere).[32] In addition there is found also שש for the finer linen which is used, according to Ex 28:6, for the making of the ephod and, according to 28:39, for Aaron's coat and turban (on this see Ezek 16:10, 13; 27:7).[33] Linen is also attested in Herodotus as the material for priestly dress in Egypt.[34] The expansion in v 18 introduces another two items of priestly clothing made of linen: 1) the headband, which was mentioned in 24:17, 23 among the items of clothing of the prophet himself and which figures also in Ex 39:28 with the same term (פאר) among the items of priestly clothing—alongside the term usually used in P מצנפת (Ex 28:4, 37, 39 and elsewhere); 2) the breeches. That the priest should wear these is directed by P in Ex 28:42 (39:28;

31 See above p. 400.
32 See 1,246.
33 See 1,341 and above p. 57f.
34 2, 37. See also Lucian, *De Dea Syria,* 42.

Lev 6:3; 16:4) with explicit justification. The anxiety that men's nakedness could be uncovered before the holy is expressed already in the Book of the Covenant (Ex 20:26) in the prohibition of building steps up to the altar.

The command to wear linen clothes is contrasted with the prohibition of woolen clothing for the inner precinct of the temple area "in (cultic) service inside the gates of the inner court and within." This inner precinct is understood, as in 42:1–14, as a place of heightened sanctity. Whether the original reason for the prohibition of woolen clothing is really, as v 18b clearly implies, because woolen clothes cause one to sweat and sweat could be regarded, like other human excrementa, as unclean (cf., e.g., Dtn 23:12–14) cannot be said with certainty. It is not impossible that already older taboo regulations sought to keep wool, which comes from animals, away from the cultic sphere.

■ **44:20** V 20 deals with the hair style. Shaving it bald is surely forbidden because of the connection with customs associated with death. Pre-Islamic Arabia testifies to the sacrifice of hair on the graves of the dead (Cooke). The fact that alongside shaving bald at a death (Job 1:20; cf. Jer 7:29; Mic 1:16 גזז "to shave"; on קרחה "baldness" as a sign of mourning see above on 7:18 and on 27:31)[35] the reverse practice of letting the hair fall loose could also be indulged in (both are primarily a ritual of disfigurement in the face of the returning dead person) can be seen already in 24:17, 23 where, as the normal form of mourning, the loosening of the headband can be recognized. פרע ("locks"), which is used here, occurs also (as a verb) in Lev 10:6 in connection with mourning customs (so, too, 21:10?) and with the leper in 13:45. It will be forbidden here too because of the connection with the uncleanness of these conditions and not because of the recollection of the Nazirite (Nu 6:5; also Ju 5:2?), who, because he is under a vow, is not eligible for priestly duty (so Cooke). By means of the trimming of the hair which is enjoined here the two other possible extremes are avoided (see in addition the prescriptions in Lev 19:27 for the people, Lev 21:5 for the priest and Lev 21:10 for the high priest).

■ **44:21** The prohibition of a priest's drinking wine when he enters the inner precinct is perhaps to be understood as arising from old, anti-Canaanite feelings. See the polemic of Hosea (4:11), but also the attitude of the Rechabites in Jeremiah 35. It has its parallel in Lev 10:9.

■ **44:22** The prohibition of a priest's marrying a widow or someone rejected by her husband is connected with the conception of the priest's sphere of holiness, which must not be brought into contact with the alien sphere of the non-priest. The explicit exception made in the case of a priest's widow, who has precisely already been connected with the priestly sphere, makes that sufficiently clear (see also Lev 22:13). The first prohibition occurs also in Lev 21:7 referring to the priest; and the double prohibition, in Lev 21:14 referring to the high priest without any mention of the exception of Ezek 44:22bβ. Also in Nu 30:10 אלמנה ("widow") and גרושה ("divorcee") occur together in a legal prescription (concerning the vow).

■ **44:23-24** Vv 23f, which deal with the duties of the priest, do not fit, from the point of view of form, the context of the surrounding statements insofar as here Yahweh himself speaks in the first person. From the point of view of content the statements largely correspond to what is said about the priests in the class-sermon of 22:23–31 in v 26.[36] The lack of order in the behavior of the priests before the great time of judgment will find no further place in the new temple of the future. Thus, as in 22:26, the reference is to correct instruction in the differentiation of sacred and profane and to teaching about clean and unclean. Behind יורו ("they shall give instructions") there is an echo of the substantive תורה ("instruction") (cf. 43:12) and behind יודעם ("they shall teach them") the noun דעת ("knowledge") (see above on 16:2).[37] As in 22:26 reference is made to the keeping of the sabbaths, the "holy" time, i.e. the time special to Yahweh, for which the priest is to be particularly responsible (see in P the closely related statements of Lev 10:10f).

Over and above 22:26, however, there is reference here not only in a general expression to the responsibility for the "instructions and statutes" (43:11; 44:5) for the "appointed feasts" generally (מועדים also in 36:38; 45:17; 46:9, 11), but also to a responsibility of the priests in the judicial system. The trial system, in which a decision was made on the basis of the "rules of legal decisions"

35 On 7:18 see 1,208; on 27:31, see above p. 61.

36 See 1,468f.

37 See 1,336.

(משפטים) as these are gathered together in, for example, the first part of the Book of the Covenant (Ex 21:1ff), lay, in the early period, in the hands of the local judges in the gate. Subsequently the king, perhaps because of his city kingdom in Jerusalem, acquired influence and responsibility in the court, as can be seen, e.g., in Jeremiah's oracle against Jehoiakim with its description of Josiah (22:15f). In the early period the priests were called upon when a divine decision had to be obtained at the sanctuary (Ex 22:8). Whether instruction in the laws of Yahweh (משפטיך "your laws"), which Dtn 33:10 mentions as a duty of Levi, already belongs in the early period is questionable. In any case, however, the participation of the priests in the responsibility for legal decisions in the later period is then unmistakable. Thus in Dtn 17:9 the Levitical priests are associated with the judge at the central cultic place for the decision on capital questions (see also 19:17). In the ritual in 21:1ff "the priests, the sons of Levi" have been secondarily inserted as those responsible for every trial: על פיהם יהיה כל ריב וכל נגע ("by their word every dispute and every assault shall be settled") (v 5). In the post-exilic period, when the monarchy has been abolished, this development had increased.[38] This is surely reflected in 44:24, where the priests participate fully in legal jurisdiction.

■ **44:25–27** Vv 25-27, which are rounded off by a formula for a divine saying and in which the "I" of Yahweh is no longer to be observed, lead back to the holiness prescriptions for the priest. They might once have followed directly after v 22.

■ **44:25** They deal with the defilement of the priest by a death in the immediate family. The sphere of death is in any case a sphere which defiles particularly severely (cf. Nu 19:1ff). Such defilement is permitted to the priest in the case of the nearest blood relations, among whom are reckoned father, mother, son, daughter, brother and sister, the latter two, however, only if they have not been excluded by marriage from this narrow circle of relationship. This uncovers once again the areas of holiness which were already of significance in v 22b. The rule of v 25 has its exact equivalent in Lev 21:1–3 for the priest. For the high priest, who has not yet been mentioned in Ezekiel 40–48,[39] the valid rule is the stricter one of Lev 21:11, according to which the latter may not defile himself even with father and mother. What is surprising is the failure to mention the priest's wife. According to *b. Yebam.* 90b she is included in the שארו הקרב אליו ("his nearest of kin") which is prefixed in Lev 21:2 to the detailed list.

■ **44:26–27** This prescription, which was clearly found already in its present form by Ezekiel 44, is then linked by means of vv 26f to the general theme of chapter 44, which is concerned with the purity of those who enter the sanctuary. The change to the singular reveals in an ugly way the secondary character of vv 26f compared with v 25. According to Numbers 19 (31:19) the one who has become defiled by a corpse must cleanse himself with the water of purification, the making of which has been described in vv 1–10, on the third and the seventh day after the defilement. It is not clear whether Ezekiel 44 presupposes this or an analogous ritual for the layman. The prescription that the priest should count seven days "after he has become clean" and then should offer a sin offering when he takes up his duties again seems to suppose a prescription of this kind. The general demand for purification, which applies also to the layman, seems, in the case of the priest, who, within the temple, enters the area of intensified holiness, to be increased (cf., however, also v 27 note a and Lev 15:28).

■ **44:28–30a** There follows in vv 28–30a a statement about the income of the priests, in which not only is Yahweh the speaker but also Israel can be seen in the second person plurals of vv 28b, 30a to be the entity that is addressed. This leads back to the phraseology of the beginning in vv 6–8 and reveals the passage to be the original conclusion of vv 6-16. The beginning is obscured in 𝔐 because in its original wording a contradiction will have been seen to the later (45:3f; 48:10–12) division of priestly land (cf. v 28 note a).

■ **44:28** The original text of this passage stated that the priests should have no landed property. In this there is preserved the old Levitical arrangement according to which Levi is a landless גר ("sojourner"). But in the context it is restricted to the "Levitical priests" in the narrower sense (v 15). In two parallel sentences, to which is given consciously a solemn weightiness, this is ex-

38 Cf., e.g., Bentzen, "Priesterschaft."

39 On this see Morgenstern, "Chapter."

pressed, while in a corresponding positive sentence Yahweh each time explains personally that he himself is the priest's real possession. The proximity in form of the statement אני נחלתם ("I am their property") and אני אחזתם ("I am their possessions") to the momentous sentence of self-presentation אני יהוה ("I am Yahweh") can certainly not be ignored.[40] These sentences recapitulate what Dtn 18:2 in the speech of Moses in the third person had already expressed; see further Dtn 10:9; Josh 13:33 and, in P, Nu 18:20.

In these passages the reference is consistently to נחלה ("property") or נחל, to which also חלק "portion" can be added. Similarly then in 47:13f, 21–23 (cf. 48:29). In the present passage there appears as a parallel expression alongside נחלה ("property"), אחזה ("possession") derived from אחז "seize, grasp." In his careful examination of the two terms Horst has shown that נחלה ("property") is the older expression, rooted in the clan structure, for the portion of land allocated in the first instance to the clan. Similarly Donner: "inalienable, heritable land tenure" (*scil.* from the part of Yahweh). The term subsequently acquired a broad range of application in that it can be applied to Israel as a whole as well as to the individual. On the other hand the reference to the נחלה ("property") of God seems to have a Canaanite pre-history.[41] In Mari, too, *naḫālum* is found as an expression for "the gift of ground and land which was in state hands or in the possession of a clan or an individual and which was basically inalienable."[42] On the other hand, אחזה, "the legitimate possession," represents the later term, attested from the sixth century, by which property (possession) can be described. As the stronger, more abstract legal term it achieves significance in P and Chronicles. In Ezekiel it is attested only in the late sections from 44:28 onwards (see especially also on 45:1ff). The English translations "inheritance, property, possession" are quite incapable of covering the full content of the words.

The notion diverting attention away from all worldly possessions, namely that Yahweh is Levi's (heritable) property, is modified in Josh 18:7 in terms of the "priesthood" (כהנה) of Yahweh being the priest's heritage. Josh 13:14 speaks in more concrete terms of the "offerings by fire to Yahweh the god of Israel" as Levi's נחלה. And still more precisely in Nu 18:24 "the tithe of the Israelites which 'they present as an offering to Yahweh' (ירימו ליהוה תרומה)" is given to the Levites as נחלה.

■ **44:29** Along the same lines, too, Ezek 44:29–30a develops the basic tenet of v 28. First of all here there is cited the indirect income, as part of which in first place there is their share in three kinds of offering. Of the cereal offering there falls to the priest, according also to Lev 2:3, 10; 6:9, all that is not burnt on the altar as an אזכרה to Yahweh (Lev 2:2, 9; 6:8). Of these the only exceptions are the offerings which the high priest and the priests themselves present (6:16). The analogous regulations about the sin offering are found in Lev 6:19, 22 (the exception 6:23), about the guilt offering Lev 7:6. All three types of offering are combined in Nu 18:9f completely analogously to Ezek 44:29a, with the addition of the stipulation known from Ezek 42:13 that what is holy is to be eaten in the holy place. There is no reference at all here to the portions of the Israelites' "sacrifice" (זבח) which are set apart in Dtn 18:3 as the due of the priests alone. Do these fall to the Levites (משרתי הבית "temple servants" 46:24b) who prepare the זבח of the "laity" (העם) in the outer court? The stipulation which then follows, to the effect that "every 'devoted thing' (חרם) in Israel" should fall to the priest, has its correspondence in Nu 18:14. What is meant here is no longer what was dedicated to Yahweh in the holy war, which then had to be destroyed.[43] Rather here it is a question of what is, in a wider sense, irrevocably dedicated to Yahweh. So, too, Lev 27:28f.[44]

■ **44:30a** The more precise definition of the two spheres of direct income which are then mentioned is again to be achieved by comparison with the terminologically closely related chapter about priestly emoluments, Numbers 18. There, in vv 25–30, it is laid down that the Levites for

40 See 1, 407f on 20:5.

41 On the exclusion of the Levites from the allocation of a נחלה see Horst, "Zwei Begriffe," 143–145.

42 Horst, "Zwei Begriffe," 152.

43 See von Rad, *Krieg*, 13f.

44 On this see Elliger, *Leviticus*, 391, and C. H. W. Brekelmans, *De ḥerem in het Oude Testament* (Nijmegen: Centrale drukkerij, 1959), especially 66f.

their part should earmark from the tithe which they receive from the Israelites the tithe which is their donation to the priests: "So shall you also 'present' (תרימו) an 'offering for Yahweh' (תרומת יהוה) from all your tithes which you receive" (18:28). It is these "tithes of tithes" which the Levites give to the Zadokites that are envisaged here. But then the question may be asked whether the adjacent, completely parallel expression "the best of all the firstfruits of everything" is not also to be regarded as a deduction from the people's gift of firstfruits. The tribute of the ראשית בכורי אדמתך ("the first of the firstfruits of your ground") is already demanded in the Book of the Covenant, Ex 23:19, which describes the later feast of weeks in 23:16 as חג הקציר בכורי מעשיך ("the festival of the harvest of the firstfruits of your labor") (see further Ex 34:22; Lev 23:20; Nu 18:13).[45] While the stipulations in vv 17–27 could give rise to the question whether they might not be valid also for the Levites who do duty in the temple, then it can be observed with certainty in the case of vv 28–30a that the rules about income detailed here are strictly limited to the Zadokites alone. So, too, Gese. This observation, too, might strengthen the case for regarding vv 28–30a as the original conclusion of vv 6–16.[46]

■ **44:30b** In v 30b there is then added yet another stipulation about gifts, but with the mention of the priest in the singular it differs from vv 28–30a (otherwise, v 21) and is therefore to be regarded as an addition. Here, with the use of the word ערסות ("coarse meal"), which is attested also in Nu 15:20f and Neh 10:38, the priest is also given the best of the coarse meal. Cakes of coarse meal (see note d) are, according to Nu 15:20f, to be dedicated as an "offering" (תרומה) for Yahweh. Neh 10:38 mentions the obligation of the people to give the ראשית עריסת(ינו) ("best of [our] course meal") to the priests. When then in the present passage a further addition in the singular mentions the goal which is thus to be attained, namely the bringing of blessing to rest on Israel, then one might find behind this the recollection of the fact that the priests in particular have the privilege of imposing blessing on the congregation (see Nu 6:22–27).

■ **44:31** Very unskillfully there is added at the end an observation which in no sense refers to the priests alone. Already Ex 22:30 ordains quite generally that no flesh of a fallen or torn animal may be eaten. So too Lev 17:15 (7:24). Then, however, the prohibition emerges also in Lev 22:8 among the specifically priestly rules. One may suppose that it was from there that it was taken over also into Ezekiel 44.[47]

Looking back on vv 6–31, it strikes one how detailed is what is said about the Zadokites and how little can be discerned of the income and rights of the Levites. Now it has certainly been proved that these statements about the priests have been enriched by the secondary addition of vv 17–27 and 30b–31. But this enrichment corresponds entirely to the emphasis imposed by the original unit vv 6–16, 28–30a. The interest and concern of this section are centered on the Zadokites, whose designation as "Levitical priests" occurs solely on account of the incorporation, which is in progress in the wake of Deuteronomy, of all temple servants into the genealogy of Levi. Quite differently from in Deuteronomy, however, here we can discern no longer a movement towards Levi, but (maintaining the genealogical exigencies) a movement away from Levi.

Setting

The slogan which can be heard here, "Zadokites versus Levites," and its historico-theological underpinning have no basis in the preaching of the prophet Ezekiel as this is heard in chapters 1–39 or in the basic stratum of chapters 40ff. In it can be heard the voice of a later period even if one is not prepared to go, with Berry, precisely as far as the Maccabean period. Even within P the deflection of the Levites from central duties at the sanctuary does not belong to the basic stratum. Thus in 44:6–31 we find an expression of the post-exilic period. The reserve of the Levites in the movement for return from exile, which can be seen most clearly in Ezr 8:15ff (but also already in Ezra 2), is undoubtedly to be understood as a reaction to this. In 44:6–31, as could be supposed already from the introduction in v 4f,[48] the older blueprint of Ezekiel's vision of the future is expanded, with discernible polemic, by a completely novel element.

45 See Eissfeldt, *Erstlinge*.

46 On the transfer of the תרומה from a profane linguistic usage to a cultic one see also Vincent, "rites."

47 In addition, see 1, 170f on 4:14f.

48 See above p. 445.

Aim

Ezek 44:6ff comes from the hand of a man who knows that God's people is emerging from a time of grievous error. In this respect he is a disciple of the prophet Ezekiel, in that he knows of the abomination of impurity and of the service of foreign gods through which God has been dishonored by his people.

Admittedly he is not a disciple of Ezekiel in that he experiences the horror in the first instance in the fact that foreigners who do not bear the sign of circumcision have been brought in to serve in the sanctuary. And he is particularly not a disciple of Ezekiel in that in the description of the punishment meted out by God he forgets the solidarity of all in the confession of guilt before God and places the group of the faithful alongside the group of the unfaithful, announces to the former that they are set apart by God for a particularly sanctified ministry while he thrusts aside the latter, as a punishment, to humble, menial functions. The picture of the righteous who deserve to be close to God and of particular sinners who deserve to remain far from God does not fit into the radicalism with which Ezekiel himself had declared the guilt of the whole people (chapters 16, 20, 23) at all levels (chapter 22), and quite particularly in the case of those who served in the Jerusalem temple, and had declared also the end which subsequently comes to all, even to the priests (7:26), and which had its beginning in the sanctuary itself (chapter 9).

Against this background, the hands of later writers have, undoubtedly with the help of already existing regulations, developed the rules of a pure priesthood. Not only in their dress, their hair style, in abstention from wine, the rules for marriage and the avoidance of contact with impurity but also in the active fulfilling of their duty to the people they are to be aware that they are obliged to seek holiness and righteousness. In renouncing landed property of their own and in living off the gifts of the congregation—so, in vv 28–30a, we undoubtedly hear once more from the author of vv 6–16—they are to be conscious of the privilege of having in God their real possession. Thus there is mingled with the questionable justification of the priestly privileges of the Zadokites once again genuine awareness of the grace of divine calling to holy service—a grace which can cause men to forget their other, apparently so "secure" possession and can make them happy in the joy which Psalm 84 extols in such an impressive way.[49]

49 See further below pp. 469f on 45:1–8.

6. A Supplement to the Property Rights of the Levites and Priests within the Consecrated Area

Bibliography

Friedrich Horst
"Zwei Begriffe für Eigentum (Besitz): נַחֲלָה und אֲחֻזָּה" in *Verbannung und Heimkehr. Beiträge zur Geschichte und Theologie Israels im 6. und 5. Jahrhundert v. Chr., Wilhelm Rudolph zum 70. Geburtstage dargebracht* (Tübingen: Mohr [Siebeck], 1961), 135–156.

See further on 47:13–48:29.

45

1 **But when you allocate the land as a pos-**
session, then you shall set apart a conse-
crated area for Yahweh, a holy (portion)
of the land, twenty-five thousand (cubits)
long[a] and <twenty thousand>[b] (cubits)
broad. <It>[c] shall be holy in its whole
extent round about. [2/ Of this[a] (a plot of)
five hundred by five hundred (cubits)
square <belongs>[b] to the sanctuary[c], and
it has all round it fifty cubits of pasture
land[d]][e]. 3/ From this measured area,

45: 1a 𝔐 has ארך both before and after the numeral,
1 but this is attested in the versions only by 𝔗. 𝔊 (𝔏[C]), the oldest witness, appears therefore to argue for the originality of the word in the second position. In 𝔊[967], doubtless due to homoioarchton, the whole passage from the first קדש to immediately before the second קדש has dropped out.

b 𝔐 עשרה is, on the evidence of 𝔊 (𝔏[CW]) 𝔄, a scribal error for עשר[י]ם. The continuation in v 3, as well as the observation that the figure ten thousand is עשרת אלפים in vv 3, 5; 48:(9) 10, 13, 18 demand the emendation on the basis of 𝔊. Besides this see also 2 Sam 18:3; 2 Kgs 24:14 and on this Bauer-Leander §79s. According to S. Krauss, "Textkritik auf Grund des Wechsels von ה und ם," *ZAW* 48 (1930): 324, what we have here is the scribal confusion, attestable elsewhere too, between ם and ה. More probably this (as in 48:9) is a tendentious alteration; see the exposition.

c 𝔐 הוא, in view of the adjacent גבולה, should be read as היא.

2 2a 𝔐 מזה reveals a very loose connection with what precedes. A reference to תרומה would demand מזאת.

b 𝔐 יהיה is, on the basis of 𝔊 𝔗 4 MSS[Ken], to be read as וְהָיָה. This would render inapplicable what is established for the passage by K. Schlesinger, "Zum Wortfolge im Hebräischen Verbalsatz," *VT* 3 (1953): 388, namely the "special effect (suddenness, surprise)" of asyndeton.

c It is quite unique in Ezek 40–48 that the whole sanctuary complex should be described as הקדש.

d 𝔐 מגרש, rendered by 𝔊 again with the vague word διάστημα (𝔏[W] *intervallum*), describes in Nu 35:2ff and elsewhere the pasture grounds around the Levitical cities. In Ezek 48:17 there is mentioned just such an area round the city which is free of buildings. That the temple precinct, for which according to 42:20 the wall was the clear divide between sacred and profane, has another such protective strip round it has no other corresponding

however, <you shall>[a] measure off (a piece with the dimensions) twenty-five thousand[b] (cubits) long and ten thousand[c] (cubits) broad, and on it stands the sanctuary[d]. A most holy (part) 4/ [holy][a] of the land it is. It shall be for the priests who serve in the sanctuary, who come near to serve Yahweh. And to them shall be (given) room (there) for houses and <grazing space for the herds>[b]. 5/ And (an area of) twenty-five thousand (cubits) long and ten thousand (cubits)[a] broad shall be allocated as a possession[b] to the Levites who see to the service in the temple—<cities to live in>[c]. 6/ And as the possession of the city you[a] shall allocate (an area of) five thousand (cubits) broad and twenty-five thousand (cubits) long alongside the consecrated area. It shall belong to the whole house of Israel. 7/ And to the prince (you shall give space) on both sides of the consecrated area and of the possession of the city, alongside[a] the consecrated area and the possession of the city, on the west side westwards and on the <east side>[b]

reference anywhere in chapters 40–48. 𝔙 *suburbana eius*, 𝔗 רווחא, 𝔖 שׁטחה.

e The observations with regard to form and content made in notes a, c and d, along with the fact that v 2 clearly breaks the continuity between vv 1 and 3 (Cornill, Toy, Bertholet wish therefore to place v 2 after v 4, Procksch before v 1a*β*), make it probable that v 2 is a later addition.

3 3a 𝔐 תמור. In spite of the consistent attestation by the versions, it is likely, in view of the plural context, that the form with its unusual *plene* writing (Bauer-Leander §58p′) has arisen by transposition of the consonants from an original תמדו. See also 10:3 note a.

b With Q, חמשׁה should be read.

c 𝔊 (𝔏^W) reads, wrongly, "twenty thousand." The width measurement is missing in 𝔊^967.

d 𝔐 המקדשׁ is not attested by 𝔊^967,B (𝔏^W) 𝔖, but cannot be dispensed with after ובו יהיה which is attested also by the text witnesses just mentioned. The undetermined קדשׁ קדשׁים, which these witnesses connect in its place with ובו יהיה and to which they silently add the article, does not yield the statement expected here.

4 4a 𝔐 קדשׁ is not attested by 𝔊 (𝔏^W). It became necessary when v 3 was separated in the present way. Not only מן הארץ (so Toy, Gese) but also the following הוא belong as conclusion to v 3. So too Herrmann, Eichrodt.

b 𝔐 ומקדשׁ. The (οἴκους) ἀφωρισμένους (𝔏^W [*locus*] *segregatus*) of 𝔊 is to be compared with 𝔊 of Josh 21:13–18, 21, 32, where ἀφωρισμένα consistently corresponds to Hebrew מגרשׁים; see v 2 note d. So it is not incorrect in the למקדשׁ which follows in 𝔐 to find a statement which describes more precisely the designation of the מגרשׁ of the Levitical cities. Nu 35:3 states that they are for pasturing cattle (לבהמתם). Nu 31:9 shows in another context how בהמה alongside מקנה can indicate possession of cattle, and the latter is graphically quite close to מקדשׁ. Thus, with Bewer, Cooke and others, it should be emended to ומגרשׁ למקנה. The fact that the details about the Levitical territory end in a similar indication of purpose supports the proposed emendation.

5 5a In 𝔊 (𝔏^W) here, wrongly, εἴκοσι. Differently in v 1, cf. note b.

b 𝔐 takes up the reference to the Levites with epexegetic ל: להם לאחוה.

c 𝔐 עשׂרים לשׁכת "twenty rooms," even if it is taken up by 𝔙 𝔗 𝔖, is meaningless. 𝔊 πόλεις τοῦ κατοικεῖν has preserved the original reading ערים לשׁבת.

6 6a 𝔐 תתנו 𝔊 (𝔏^W) δώσεις (*dabis*), 𝔊^967 δώσετε—a consequence of the scribal error in v 3 (note a).

7 7a על-אל cf. 1:17 note a.

b 𝔐 קדמה should be read, corresponding to the ים, as קדים.

eastwards and in length corresponding[c] to one of the (tribal) areas[d] from the frontier <westwards>[e] to the frontier eastwards 8/ as landed property[a]. And <it shall be>[b] his possession in Israel. And <the princes of Israel>[c] will no longer oppress my people but will let the house of Israel have[d] the land according to its tribes.

c The plural form לפמות of 𝔐 is not otherwise attested and should be emended to לפמת.

d This already presupposes the allocation of tribal territories in chapter 48.

e Corresponding to קדימה, one would expect ימה here.

8 8a 𝔐 לארץ, which is omitted by 𝔖, should be taken as in 𝔊 with v 7.

b According to 𝔊 ($\mathfrak{L}^{W}$) וְהָיָה should be read. The reading of 𝔙 𝔗 is a consequence of the wrong verse division. 𝔖 has a quite different understanding נהוא יורתנא לבני איסראיל.

c 𝔐 נְשִׂיאַי "my princes" is surprising in this context. 𝔊 (𝔏) ἀφηγούμενοι τοῦ Ισραηλ suggests the correct reading נשיאי ישראל. Does 𝔐 go back to an abbreviation נשיאי י''?

d For this sense Bertholet points to the usage of נתן in 1 Kgs 18:26.

Form

45:1–8, which with its conclusion in v 8b clearly leads on to the invective in 45:9, is surprising in its present context. The allocation of land described in it has its detailed counterpart in 48:8–22. It will not do, however, to see in 45:1–8 simply a briefer, partial first draft of what is then developed more fully in chapter 48 and is there incorporated into the description of a complete allocation of land, which takes account not only of sacred area in the center of the land but also of the surrounding territory of the twelve tribes. Rather, the reference to the חלקים ("[tribal] areas") in v 7b shows that the present passage already presupposes the complete allocation of land of chapter 48. On the other hand, however, it will not do either to speak, with Bertholet, of a doublet of chapter 48. Closer examination shows that 45:1–8 has very characteristic different emphases over against chapter 48, which makes it certain that we have here an excerpt from chapter 48 or, more precisely still, from 47:13–48:29, which has different emphases from a quite specific point of view.

First of all in this connection reference is correctly made to the catchword תרומה (in 45:1 "consecrated area") which unmistakably connects 45:1–8 with 44:30a. Astonishment at the superficiality of this connection is expressed quite openly by Gese, for example: "The catchword principle here is in itself completely superficial, the more so since תרומה is understood in different ways within 44:30a–45:17."[1] A close examination of the situation, however, shows that for 45:1–8a just as important as the catchword תרומה is the catchword אחזה ("possession"). This reveals at the same time a lively interest which makes the addition of 45:1–8 at this point completely understandable from the point of view of content too. The manipulation of the text of 44:28 (note a) had shown that a later age found a certain difficulty with the fact that in chapter 48 the priests are also allocated a portion of land, while 44:28 had stated beyond all ambiguity that the priests in Israel were to receive no possessions. It is this very question that 45:1–8 tries to answer in its gentle re-emphasis of the allocation plan for the "consecrated area."

On the form of vv 1–8a it can be stated that in the total structure we are dealing with an excerpt from 47:13–48:29. This is clear not only from a wealth of individual phrases which, beginning with the introduction in 45:1a, take up expressions from that section, but equally so from the sequence of the land portions dealt with. The sequence: sanctuary, priests, Levites, city, prince corresponds exactly to the sequence of chapter 48. The dependence ends with v 8a. V 8b then leads, somewhat surprisingly to the reader, to the admonition to the princes of Israel in v 9.

1 Gese, 68.

Setting

The sharp differentiation between priests and Levites, which results precisely from the important catchword אחזה ("possession") used in 45:1–8a, shows, equally with the more precise characterization of the tasks of priests and Levites which differs from chapter 48, that 45:1–8 is entirely along the same lines as 44:6ff. While in 44:30a it was established that income regulations referred strictly and exclusively to the priests and that under the term תרומה ("offering") the tithe was also mentioned which the Levites had to hand on to the priests from the tithe which they received but which was not explicitly described, in 45:1–8 it can be seen that in the designation of the land allocation as אחזה ("possession") a clear distinction is made between priests and Levites.

Verbal dependence for long stretches on 47:13–48:29, for which there is no corresponding observation with regard to 44:6–16, 28–30a, makes it likely that 45:1–8a is one of the additions to the priests-Levites complex. It differs from the expansions in 44:17–27, 30b–31 by its noticeably anti-Levitical attitude, which gives the Levites fewer rights to the domain of the holy than is the case in 47:13–48:29. Thus 45:1–8 is from the same circles as 44:6–16, 28–30a, but was composed later than that section and as an expansion of it on the basis of 47:13–48:29.

Interpretation

For the full exposition of the statements in 45:1–8 insofar as they recur in 47:13–48:29 reference must be made to the exegesis of that section. In the present context we are concerned to highlight the particular emphasis which 45:1–8 tries to express through its use of its source.

■ **45:1** First of all, in dependence on the phraseology of 47:14b, 22; 48:29, reference is made to the time when the new allocation of land is to take place. The separation of the "gift of land" (תרומה) and the measuring of it is described with the words of 48:9. The affirmation is made here right at the beginning (and this goes beyond the passages on which it is dependent) that the concern is with the sacred area which is marked off from the land as a whole. Likewise, in v 1bβ, it is emphasized once more in a secondary addition in the style of the declaratory judgment[2] that the whole area round about is holy. When, in the measurement of the area in both places in 𝔐, reference is made, instead of to twenty-five thousand cubits by twenty thousand, to only twenty-five thousand by ten thousand of sacred territory (v 1 note b and 48:9 note b), then this textual alteration is to be understood as a further tendentious distortion in the interests of the anti-Levitical standpoint: only the priestly land is to be described as holy. What follows, however, both in 45:1–8 and in chapter 48, shows that priestly land and Levitical land in both passages are spoken of as the "consecrated area." In both passages 𝔊 has preserved the original reading.

The scribal error has been facilitated in 45:1 by the fact that the continuation in v 3, which speaks of the separation of the priestly share from the total area (המדה הזאת "this measured area") measured out in v 1, has been cut off from v 1 by v 2.

■ **45:2** This verse, which contains information about the sanctuary which one would expect more appropriately only after v 4, is not to be rescued and transposed to that position as originally belonging there (so Cornill, Cooke and others). It represents an accretion in which there is added to the sanctuary area described in the dimensions of 42:20, by analogy with what is said in 48:17 about the city territory even if with smaller dimensions, a pasture zone which is then obviously immediately understood as an additional protective ring for the sanctuary. Thus it is only vv 3f which speak of the measuring off from the total consecrated area of the priestly land in which the sanctuary stands and, in v 5, from the Levitical land. What is said about the priestly land has its correspondence in 48:10; what is said about the Levitical land has *its* correspondence in 48:13f. In these two sections there occur now the most remarkable re-emphases in contrast to chapter 48.

■ **45:3f** The extent of the priestly share (v 3) corresponds in the first instance completely to what is measured in 48:10a, as does the statement that the sanctuary (48:10 מקדש יהוה "the sanctuary of Yahweh") is situated within it. But then vv 3/4 goes beyond its model in 48:10, which had referred to this territory as a part of the תרומה

2 See 1,376 on chapter 18.

קדש ("sacred area"), by stating that this area is to be separated off from the land as particularly holy. This is not to be referred simply to the sanctuary, concerning which this quality was expressed in 43:12 (in 41:4 first of all for the innermost room of its temple building), but refers to the whole priestly share. The priests are thus designated, along the lines of 44:15f, as משרתי המקדש ("those who serve in the sanctuary") and as those who may approach Yahweh to serve him (40:46b, also 43:19). It will be seen later how this elevation of the priestly territory to the sphere of the ultra-holy in the clearly secondary expansion in 48:12 found its way also into that description in which it was originally foreign. As an accretion to what is said in chapter 48 there should be noted, finally, also the observation in 45:4b which states that the land is to serve the priests as "room for houses and grazing space for the cattle."

■ **45:5** This last observation is only fully comprehensible against the background of what is said about the Levites. Here too, to begin with, the measurement of the strip of land corresponds entirely to the measurements in 48:13. In the case of the duties of the Levites, on the other hand, which here too surpass what is described in chapter 48, once again the terminology of 44:11(14) recurs. The Levites serve in the "house" (בית), which here, in contrast to מקדש ("sanctuary") as the sphere of the priests, once again means the whole temple precinct. But then it is said of the land which is allocated to them that it is given to them "as a possession" (לאחזה, according to Horst, "as a lawful holding") so that they might have here cities to live in. While P allocates to the Levites forty-eight cities for their dwellings scattered throughout the land, here the Levitical cities are obviously located in the Levitical territory which as a whole—and this is precisely what clearly differentiates them from the priests—is regarded as their "possession." This abolishes for them the "Levitical rule" (Gunneweg) which was expressed in 44:28 with the use of this very word. Nevertheless the regarding of their share of land as specifically arable land is avoided, though this would be a natural deduction from what is said. It cannot, however, be overlooked that only the priests are now subject to the old, sacred Levitical regulation of non-ownership of land. And this separates them in a new way from the Levites as the group to whom Yahweh in 44:28 has made himself known and whose choicest possession he will himself be.

■ **45:6ff** The word אחזה ("possession") then recurs in connection with the two following recipients of an allocation of land. The "possession" of the city is spoken of in v 6 in dependence on 48:15–20. The original in this case, however, is very much abbreviated. After the measurements which originate in 48:15a there follows immediately the לעמת תרומת הקדש ("alongside the consecrated area") from v 18 and the free reproduction of 48:19—people from all Israel are to have a share of this land. What is said about the prince, finally, recapitulates, with word for word adoption of individual passages, the gist of 48:21a. Here too, however, in v 8a the term אחזה ("possession") is added to the text of the original. To these details about the prince's property there is then added in v 8b, by way of transition to v 9, the admonition to the princes of Israel not to use force on Yahweh's people in matters of landed property. Here Yahweh himself speaks, as he does also in the following invective and exhortation, and makes himself the champion of his people's land rights. The allocation of land to the tribes of Israel, which in chapter 48 is framed by the details about the תרומה ("consecrated area"), can thus be discerned in the distance in the somewhat surprising expression that the princes "give" the people the land according to their tribes, an expression which may in the present context be correctly rendered by the less forceful sense of "let have" (note d). The ideas of this conclusion recur in 46:16–18, a section in which the problem of the אחזה ("possession") of the prince is once again emphatically dealt with and is reflected upon in its effects for the princely practice of giving.

Aim

In the section which speaks of the allocation of the consecrated area (vv 1–8a) two things are to be expressed. There is first of all the securing of the "old Levitical" principle that the person who belongs to the tribe of Levi—and that, after the Deuteronomic reform movement, means the true priest—is to have no personal landed property. This principle seemed to have run into danger as a consequence of the land allocation laid down in chapter 48. Was a piece of land not allocated here to the priest in the same way as land had been allocated to the prince and the inhabitants of Jerusalem? This threat is warded off in 45:1–8 in such a way that in this passage, which in the case of all the other groups speaks of a "possession" (אחזה) of land, a right of usufruct is established for the priests: Their houses are to stand here and their herds can graze here. But "possession" it is not to be. By the declaring of this territory as "most holy" it is associated completely with the most holy sacrificial offerings on which the priest, by ancient right, may live. This right was also specifically promised in 44:29.

This, however, links up with the other factor which links 45:1–8a in particular with 44:6–16, 28–30a—the clear separation from the new-style Levites. It is precisely they who forfeit the old sign of the nobility of the "Levites," i.e. the lack of landed property, insofar as the portion of land which is allocated to them is described as אחזה ("possession"). In the description of the Levites it is again affirmed that they are involved in service in the wider temple area while for the priests, who are here no longer described as "Levitical priests," there remains reserved the service of the "sanctuary," i.e., of the inner area which leads to true proximity to Yahweh. Thus the Levites' land, too, is still part of the "consecrated area," but it is not most holy, not to be compared with the sacrifice which belongs to God alone. Even in their "possession" the Levites are no longer as close to God as the priests in their right to the sole use of what is most holy. While the Levites appear to be given more tangible property, they become poorer in their actual sacred "possession."

Thus in these verses two things are mingled in a strange way. On the one side there is revealed here the awareness of the fact that permission to come close to God is not a matter of course, but the gift of divine permission—and, related to this, the awareness, which was for long prized among the Levites of the old style, that, where God has given himself in this way as a possession and feeds his own with his bread at his table (44:16), tangible, normal proprietary rights are no longer important and fade into the background. The lack of landed property on the part of the "Levites" is their nobility which proclaims their proximity to God. Alongside this, however, 45:1–8a also reveal the other aspect, the struggle of groups of people for the right to this proximity. This struggle can, as is attested by the story of Cain, sometimes even lead to the position where in the fight for God's favor a brother becomes his brother's enemy and murderer.[3] When God's full grace is then encountered by man in the Son, it has then become obvious at once that in the priesthood of all believers all barriers and prerogatives concerning the proximity of God are torn down. There remains no boasting about special election.

3 See Walther Zimmerli, *1. [i.e. Erstes Buch] Mose 1–11. Die Urgeschichte,* Zürcher Bibelkommentare (Zürich: Zwingli, [3]1967), 231f.

7. An Admonition to the Princes of Israel

Bibliography

Joachim Begrich

"Die priestliche Tora" in BZAW 66 (Berlin, 1936), 63–88; reprinted in *idem, Gesammelte Studien zum AT,* ThB 21 (München: Kaiser, 1964), 232–260.

While in the first part of the divine speech which comprises 44:6–46:18, namely from 44:6 to 45:8a, priests and Levites were the center of interest, from 45:9 onwards, introduced by an imperious invective against the princes of Israel, the figure of the נשיא ("prince"), to which 45:7f had already alluded, is in the foreground. The position of this figure within chapters 40–48 will have to be considered in context in connection with the complex 47:13–48:29. The suspicion that the sharp schematization which allows the invective in 45:9 to appear in the present total text of 44:6–46:18 as a correspondence to the invective in 44:6, which begins in a similar way, has materialized in the course of the complicated redaction history of this section of text cannot be completey rejected. This redaction history will be discussed at the end of chapter 48.

45

9 **Thus has [the Lord][a] Yahweh said: (It is) enough (now)[b], you princes of Israel. Put away violence and oppression and practice justice and righteousness. Cease to drive away my people[c] (from their land), says [the Lord][a] Yahweh.**

45:9 9a אדני is lacking in 𝔊 (= 𝔊⁹⁶⁷). $\mathfrak{G}^{B}$ κύριος θεός [sic!]. See Appendix 1.

b Literally: Enough (it is) for you!

c Literally: Cease your driving of my people away! The noun גרשה is attested only here. 𝔊 καταδυναστείαν ($\mathfrak{G}^{967}$ καταδυναστείας) 𝔗 תקלתכון, 𝔖 שועבדכון, while 𝔙 paraphrases: *separate confinia vestra* (*a populo meo*).

Form

After an introductory invective, the princes of Israel are summoned in an address in the imperative to put away injustice. From the point of view of form this admonition recalls the prophetic imitation of priestly Torah as this can be observed in Am 5:14f or Is 1:16f.[1] In the third of the exhortatory clauses there is once again an echo in the verb of the catchword תרומה ("consecrated area"). The whole oracle is introduced, with the greatest significance, by means of the introductory messenger formula, and the intention of this is emphatically to set it off from its context as a particularly significant prophetic saying. In addition, the rhythmic structure of the statement is in lines of three stresses.

Setting

The word עמי ("my people") connects v 9 with 45:8b and the closely related 46:18. In addition v 9 and 45:8b are connected by the plural reference to the princes. Since עמי ("my people") occurs within chapters 40–48 only otherwise in 44:23, which is slightly differently slanted with regard to content and which does not fit in its present context, the question arises whether at any rate 45:8b, 9; 46:18 are from the same hand. This is a question which may tentatively be posed with regard also to 44:23f. The derivation of the Torah from a quite foreign context is not to be recommended in view of the obviously intentional wordplay between הרימו ("cease") and the catchword תרומה ("consecrated area") which is dominant from 44:30 onwards.

1 On this see Begrich, "Tora."

Interpretation

■ **45:9** 45:9 opens the section 45:9–46:18, which subsequently will describe in detail the cultic duties of the נשיא ("prince") (singular), with a summons to the (plural) princes of Israel who were already cited in the plural in v 8b. This shows that here what is envisaged is not, as in 44:3; 45:16f; 46:1–18; 48:21f, "the prince" as the leading figure of the future, but, analogously to 43:7–9, the history of the sins of the earlier kings of Israel who have already been referred to as "princes of Israel" in the superscription of Ezekiel 19. On the invective nature of רב לכם ("enough [now]") see on 44:6. There too it is associtated with a review of Israel's sinful history. The הסירו ("put away") in the exhortation to the removal of evil has its parallel in the prophetic admonitions of Is 1:16 (v 16aβ is a secondary expansion) and Jer 4:4; see also Am 5:23. שד ("oppression") is attested only here in Ezekiel. שד וחמס ("oppression and violence") occurs in Hab 1:3; חמס ושד ("violence and oppression") in Jer 6:7; 20:8; Am 3:10.[2] Thus use is made here of a common combination in (non-Ezekiel) prophetic language. On the other hand, the משפט וצדקה עשו ("practice justice and righteousness") has its correspondence in the description of the righteous in 18:5, 21 and elsewhere. The third clause of the exhortation leads back from these general demands to Israel's royal history with its examples of the forcible removal of people from their lawful territorial possessions (1 Kgs 21:1–16; Is 5:8). The forced expression הרימו גרשתיכם ("cease to drive away"), which links up with the thought of v 8b, is chosen in order to allow the whole admonition (laboriously enough!) to appear as the continuation of the (תרומה) תרימו ("you shall set apart [a consecrated area]") of v 1. In this way the catchword, which then recurs in v 13, is meant to be kept active.

In 44:6ff the correct cultic behavior for Israel was contrasted with their previous wrong behavior as described in the invective. Similarly, in this second half of 44:6–46:18 too, the correct behavior of the princes of Israel is to be described against the background of the wrong behavior of the earlier "princes of Israel." Where this correct behavior is concretized to some extent in v 9bα, the admonition clearly refers back to the question of property ownership already discussed in vv 1–8. However clearly, then, v 9 is meant to be the prelude to the coming discussion, it can nevertheless not be separated from what precedes it.

Aim

Against the background of earlier experience with men in positions of power (cf. 22:25), the author of 45:9, leaving aside the specifically cultic duties which will become increasingly important in what follows, exhorts the princes in quite general terms to keep to the rule of righteousness and to avoid violence. Where God has given talent and power, let the one who has been thus endowed keep himself from allowing his talent to become "robbery" (on this see Phil 2:6) and from becoming, in his greed, a robber.

2 On חמס see also 1,210 on 7:11aα.

8. Right Measures and Right Offerings

Bibliography

Friedrich Blome
Die Opfermaterie in Babylonien und Israel 1 (Rome: Pontifical Biblical Institute, 1934).

George Buchanan Gray
Sacrifice in the Old Testament, its Theory and Practice (Oxford: Clarendon, 1925).

Rolf Rendtorff
Studien zur Geschichte des Opfers im alten Israel, WMANT 24 (Neukirchen-Vluyn: Neukirchener, 1967).

Leonhard Rost
"Erwägungen zum israelitischen Brandopfer" in *Von Ugarit nach Qumran*, BZAW 77 (Berlin, 1958), 177–183; reprinted in *idem, Das kleine Credo und andere Studien zum Alten Testament* (Heidelberg: Quelle & Meyer, 1965), 112–119.

H. H. Rowley
"The Meaning of Sacrifice in the Old Testament," *Bulletin of the John Rylands University Library of Manchester* 33 (1950): 74–110.

Rudolf Schmid
Das Bundesopfer in Israel; Wesen, Ursprung und Bedeutung der alttestamentlichen Schelamim (München: Kosel, 1964).

Dionys Schötz
Schuld- und Sündopfer im Alten Testament, Breslauer Studien zur historischen Theologie 18 (Breslau: Müller & Sieffert, 1930).

N. H. Snaith
"Sacrifices in the Old Testament," *VT* 7 (1957): 308–317.

W. B. Stevenson
"Hebrew 'Olah and Zebach Sacrifices" in *Festschrift Alfred Bertholet* (Tübingen: Mohr [Siebeck], 1950), 488–497.

Roland de Vaux
Studies in Old Testament Sacrifice (Cardiff: University of Wales Press, 1964).

Adolf Wendel
Das Opfer in der altisraelitischen Religion (Leipzig: Pfeiffer, 1927).

45

10 Use[a] just balances[b] and a just ephah[c] and a
just bath.[d] 11/ Ephah and bath[a] are to be
measured[b] the same so that a bath[a]
holds one tenth[b] of a homer[a] and an
ephah[a] amounts to one tenth[b] of a
homer[a]. Its measurement[b] is to be on the

45: 10 10a On the lack of agreement of יהי see Blau, "Gebrauch," 14. By contrast with 44:30, which see, there is no sign here (against Blau, note 9) of any influence of a כל.

b 𝔏^W 𝔅 *statera iusta.*

c 𝔊 *μέτρον δίκαιον*, 𝔗 ומכילן דקשוט, 𝔖 מתקלא דקושתא. 𝔅 transliterates *ephi iustum.*

d 𝔊 *χοῖνιξ δικαία*, 𝔖 כילתא דקושתא, 𝔅 *batus iustus.*

11 11a On the definition of the measurements see Brockelmann §21cδ.

b It is noteworthy that in two juxtaposed expressions the terminology changes. Alongside תכן there

basis of the homer[a]. 12/ And a shekel[a] amounts to twenty gerahs. <Five>[b] shekels are to be five (shekels), and <ten>[b] shekels are to be ten (shekels), and <fifty>[b] shekels are to amount to a mina[a] with you.

13 This[a] is the offering which you are to make: one sixth of an ephah from a homer of wheat and <one sixth>[b] of an ephah from a homer of barley. 14/ And what is due of the oil [the oil is measured by the bath][a]: one tenth of a bath from the cor[b] [ten baths are a homer][c], for the ten baths are a <cor>[d]. 15/ And one item of small cattle from the herd up to two hundred[a]

is מתכנת in the sense of "measurement," and "tenth" is first of all מעשר then עשירת. In 𝔙 and 𝔗 חמר is rendered by *cor(um)* and כורא respectively. For the rest, 𝔗 paraphrases while 𝔖 severely curtails the second half of the verse.

12 12a Cf. v 11 note a.

b The figures in 𝔐 have been corrupted. Since the division of the stichoi was no longer clear, they have been manipulated in such a way that in v 12b there resulted an addition of 20 + 25 + 15 = 60 shekels for the mina, as is specifically stated in 𝔗 in its paraphrastic text כלהון שיתין מניא רבא "a total of sixty makes up a larger mina"—the additional קודשא מני it sanctions at the same time as a "sacred mina." Here too 𝔖 offers a shortened text. Once again it is 𝔊 that leads to the original reading. Its middle clause οἱ πέντε σίκλοι πέντε, καὶ οἱ δέκα σίκλοι δέκα again tries to impress on the reader the fixed equality of the unit of measurement. On this basis the second עשרים should be emended to חמשה and ועשרים to ועשרה. In the calculation of the mina וחמשים should be read, with 𝔊, instead of וחמשה. Thus the quite unique form of the numeral "fifteen" disappears; see Bauer-Leander §79m and q.

13 13a 𝔊 ($𝔏^W$) inserts the copula, cf. 1:4 note a.

b In 𝔐 וששיתם the ם must be an erroneous dittograph of the following article. On the basis of the versions וששית should be read. Here too 𝔙 𝔗 𝔖 render "homer" by "cor." Oddly enough, in v 13bα 𝔊 reads γομορ and in v 13bβ κόρου, and אפה, which it renders with μέτρον in v 13bα, it transcribes in v 13bβ as οιφι.

14 14a 𝔐 הבת השמן is usually deleted by the commentators as a gloss, but it is attested by the versions. Even if Gese points to 𝔗 𝔖 as evidence for the absence of the words, they are nevertheless attested in a paraphrase in 𝔗 במכילתא רטיבא "with the measure for the liquid." And 𝔖, since it simply abbreviates what it does not understand, may not be cited as evidence, since it simply passes over even the introductory וחק and incorporates a much abbreviated v 14b into the first half of the verse. The succinct הבת השמן will need to be understood, on the basis of 𝔗, something along the lines attempted in the above translation.

b 𝔐 מן הכר is not attested in 𝔊. On account of the false association it has become superfluous for 𝔊. From the point of view of content, however, it cannot be dispensed with.

c V 14aβ is a dittograph of v 14b and is thus, correctly, missing in 𝔊 ($𝔏^W$) 𝔖.

d 𝔐 חמר is attested by 𝔊 ($𝔏^W$) (and by the dittograph in v 14aβ). The sense demands הכר, which has already been used in 𝔗 𝔙 in vv 11 and 13 as a rendering of חמר. In 𝔐 חמר is a dry measure and כר is a liquid one.

15 15a 𝔐 המאתים. 𝔊 ($𝔏^W$) δέκα, on the other hand, aims to increase the demand of the tithe (cf., e.g., Dtn 14:22ff).

(beasts) from the <families>[b] of Israel for the cereal offering and the burnt offering and the final offerings in order to make atonement for them[c], says [the Lord][d] Yahweh.

16 **The whole people [of the land][a] is obliged[b] to give this offering to the prince in Israel. 17/ The prince, however, is obliged to provide <the burnt offering>[a] and the cereal offering and the drink offering on the feasts and new moons and sabbaths <and>[b] on all the festivals of the house of Israel. He is to provide the sin offering and the cereal offering and the burnt offering and the final offering to make atonement for the house of Israel.**

b 𝔐 ממשקה. 𝔙 *de his quae* is indeterminate. 𝔗 מפטימא "of the fatling." Again, 𝔖 omits the word which it did not understand. 𝔊 ($\mathfrak{L}^W$) ἐκ πασῶν τῶν πατριῶν seems to point to an original מ(כל) משפחות. Yet one must ask whether 𝔊 is not correcting in its own way a word which it did not undestand. Ehrlich, *Randglossen;* Gese emend to ממקנה. If one cannot accept that 𝔙 and 𝔗, in their understanding of a word משקה which is no longer attested in this sense, are along the right lines, then this conjecture is the most likely.

c 𝔐 עליהם. 𝔊 ($\mathfrak{L}^W$) περὶ ὑμῶν. The preceding "Israel" already reveals that the direct address has been abandoned (see also v 17). A different view is adopted by Gese who assumes that later readers referred the text to the "princes of Israel," whom he tried also to find behind the offerings of vv 13–15, and have correspondingly "improved" the text (70f).

d אדני is lacking in 𝔊 (= $\mathfrak{G}^{967}$) $\mathfrak{L}^W$. $\mathfrak{G}^B$ κύριος θεός [sic!].

16 16a 𝔐 הארץ, which, if it were original, according to the normal rule (but cf. Brockelmann §73c) would demand עם without the article before it, is not attested by 𝔊 ($\mathfrak{L}^W$) and represents an expansion which imposes the duty of giving an offering in particular on the עם הארץ.

b על-אל cf. 1:17 note a. היה אל "to be duty bound to something," see Gesenius-Buhl, under היה k. 5g. Ehrlich, *Randglossen;* Cooke wish to emend 𝔐 יהיו אל, on the basis of 𝔊 δώσει, to יתנו את. BH^3, Bertholet, Fohrer assimilate to the expression in v 17: יהיה עליו.

17 17a 𝔐 העולות should be emended to the singular העולה with 11 MSS and in accordance with the phraseology in v 17b. 𝔊 ($\mathfrak{L}^W$) puts the whole list in v 17a (see also v 17b) in the plural.

b 𝔐 בכל should be read ובכל with 41 MSS, Edd, versions in association with the preceding enumeration.

Form

If one asks about the structure of vv 10–17 then v 13a emerges first from the context as the superscription of a תרומה ("offering")-ordinance. This leaves vv 10–12, the description of the measurements to be used for the תרומה ("offering"), with the appearance of a kind of "Foreword." The details of this ordinance itself follow in vv 13b–15, a section which for its part is rounded off by the formula for a divine saying. The remaining section, vv 16–17, is similar to vv 13–15 in that it too closes with a list of types of sacrifice and a concluding formula which expresses the expiatory significance of these sacrifices. To the לכפר עליהם ("to make atonement for them") of v 15b there corresponds the fuller expression לכפר בעד בית ישראל ("to make atonement for the house of Israel") in v 17b.

While there can thus be no doubt about the threefold division of this section, things are less clear if one asks about who is being addressed here. The superscription of the sacrifice ordinance addresses a plurality of people in the second person plural. If one reads vv 13–15 in isolation, one would think of the people who are addressed also in the ordinance about the priests in 44:6–8 and again in 44:28–30a. Even the prefixed section in 45:10–12 which expounds the measurements reveals a second person plural address. In the context, however, immediately after 45:9, this can be referred only to the princes, and this would then have to hold also for the sacrifice ordinance which follows in vv 13–15. This understanding is suggested also by the observation that the concluding לכפר עליהם ("to make atonement for them"), on the evidence of the parallel statement in v 17b, refers in its third person plural suffix to the "house of Israel," which can surely then not also be addressed in the second person plural. Thus one can scarcely escape the conclusion that in the present context the direct address in vv 10ff is still intended to refer to the princes of Israel referred to in v 9.

With this, however, there emerges the unexpected fact that in an ordinance directed towards the people's future there appears here, uniquely, the plural reference to the נשיאים ("princes"), whose location in what has gone before (45:9) was recognized to have been a retrospective view of Israel's past history. Is that really the original meaning of the text? The suggestion, which is justified in detail by Gese, that this state of affairs only arose at a secondary, redactional stage here becomes highly probable. An instruction which was originally directed at the people (second person plural) has become secondarily a word addressed to the princes as a result of the prior insertion of vv 1–8(9). The expiatory formulae in vv 15 and 17, which speak of the people in the third person plural, have been added in consequence of this redactional transformation.

In addition, however, there is a yet fuller observation. The details which follow in vv 16f after the formula for a divine saying have, on closer examination and from the point of view of content, precisely this significance, to elucidate the juxtaposition of prince and people in the sacrifice ordinance. Here it is said, along the lines of a compromise between the tense statements, in a secondary justification, that the people are to give the תרומה ("offering") to the prince and that the prince has then to complete the performance of the sacrifice. The entire preceding exhortation to the prince thus appears in the light of a figurative mode of expression, in that the direct demand for offering concerns the people and the offering becomes sacrifice only through the mediation of the prince.

The following can be said in detail concerning the form of the three sections. In vv 10–12 the instructions about the right measures are uniformly expressed as jussive clauses concluding with the universally used היה ("to be") (v 10 יהי לכם, v 11a*α*, b*β* יהיה, v 12 יהיה לכם), with the expansion in v 11a being in the form of a final infinitive clause. Vv 13–15a (minus the redactional expansion in v 15b) is in pure noun clauses. The interpretative conclusion in vv 16f, finally, again reveals compound verbal noun clauses (twice with היה "to be").

Setting

Thus vv 10–17 in their present form come from the hand of the late author of v 9 (and of vv 1–8). In vv 13–15 (also in vv 10–12?), however, he has subordinated an already extant תרומה ("offering")-ordinance, about which one might wonder whether it did not once represent the original continuation of 44:28–30a, to v 9 with the addition of v 15b*α* and then endeavored to ease the subsequent tensions by means of the interpretative expansion in vv 16–17.

Interpretation

■ **45:10–11** For a period which was still unaware of any national norms for weights and measures, it was very tempting to use a measure which could be easily manipulated on occasion to one's own advantage. Thus there occurs, not only on the part of the prophet, the attack on the merchants who make the ephah (measure of sale) small and the shekel (measure of purchase) great and falsify balances (Am 8:5; see also Hos 12:8; Mic 6:10f). Wisdom, too, which exhorts to a life of order, regards the falsification of measures as an abomination to Yahweh (Prv 11:1; 20:10; see also 16:11). And in the sphere of the legal texts, both Deuteronomy (25:13–16) and the Holiness Code (Lev 19:35f) enjoin correct measures as Yahweh's command. Thus, in the present context, it does not seem out of place that the general admonition to the princes to practice righteousness is followed by the admonition to use correct measures.

The phraseology here is particularly close to that of H, where, parallel to the demand for "correct balances" (מאזני צדק) there is the demand for correct weights, and to that for the "correct ephah" (איפת צדק) there is that for the correct hin (cf. Ezek 45:24). In the present passage, first of all the correct units of measurement are regulated, and these are then of significance for the sacrifice ordinance in vv 13–15, although there admittedly is no reference to the כר ("cor"). This shows that vv 10–12 are envisaged not primarily from the side of the command to the princes, but from the side of the sacrifice ordinance. The demand for correct balances is prefixed, as in H, in a general sense, without the weights being mentioned alongside them (unlike H). מאזנים ("balances") already in 5:1. The dry measure which is mentioned next, the ephah (= Egyptian *ipt,* de Vaux *'pt*), is a dry measure for grain. Like the liquid measure the bath, it hold 39.3 liters.[1] De Vaux, however, believes that the evidence available from texts and archaeological judgments are insufficient for an exact measurement.[2] He describes the calculations which have just been given as much too high. This is clear especially with respect to the unit of the homer, to which the bath and the ephah are here linked. The homer is to be equated with Akkadian *imēru* (donkey, donkey's burden). The capacity calculated by *BRL* and Barrois, 393.8 liters, is in de Vaux's view much too high for it. With regard to the present passage one may suppose that it was formulated at a time when little order prevailed in the measurement system and when a definite order needed to be established especially in regard to the sacred offerings. Whether in vv 10f existing measurement relationships have been adopted or whether, going beyond what already exists, the aim is to create new order cannot be decided with any certainty.

■ **45:12** With the dry measures v 12 links information about weights and the measurement of the value of money that is associated with these. Since the three measurements mentioned in this connection play no part in the following sacrifice ordinance, the supposition cannot be dismissed that v 12 represents a secondary expansion which goes beyond what the context would lead us to expect. On the measurement of the shekel, which to begin with simply means "weight," see on 4:10.[3] Gerah, perhaps the "grain," the smallest unit of weight, is mentioned also in Ex 30:13; Lev 27:25; Nu 3:47; 18:16. It is one twentieth of a shekel. The mina is found in the OT also in 1 Kgs 10:17; Ezr 2:69; Neh 7:70f and doubtless also in the wordplay in Dan 5:25 on the basis of its original sense.[4] On the basis of the rest of the information in the OT it seems to have been worth fifty shekels.[5] That corresponds also with the original reading of 45:12 (note b). The corrupt 𝔐, on the other hand, ends up with the mina of sixty shekels which is the usual reckoning of it in the sexagesimal system of Mesopotamia. When in the emended text of v 12 it is enjoined, in addition, that five shekels and ten shekels are to have their exact value, then this can mean that these units were used for counting particularly frequently in commercial transactions. In this context, however, we are not dealing with minted coinage which then became widespread in the Persian Empire (cf. e.g., the daric of Ezr 8:27 and the drachma of Ezr 2:69).

■ **45:13–15** This preparation is followed in vv 13–15 by the ordinance for the תרומה ("offering"), which in three sections regulates the offering of grain (wheat and barley)[6] in the amount of one sixtieth part, of oil one hundredth part, and of small cattle, of which one animal for every two hundred is to be offered. Among the measures the cor appears here as a new unit, and this occasions an addition in v 14b to the definitions of the measures. Here the cor[7] is equated with the homer. In two secondary additions to the text it is emphasized that liquids are measured by the bath (note a) and that the bath stands in a relationship of one to ten with the homer. It is not quite clear what is meant by מקשה, which is in any case a scribal error for מקנה (note b). That צאן can be subordinated to the more comprehensive term מקנה is shown by Gen 26:14.

The תרומה ("offering") demanded here is, in contrast to 44:30a (and Numbers 18), not to be understood from the point of view of the tithe. The term is clearly not yet strictly delimited from a technical point of view, but in its usage here stand closer to the loose usage in Dtn 12:6, 11, 17. In the present passage it refers to the gifts which are donated for the regular sacrifice. Thus its meaning here is along the same lines as the תרומה ("offering") ordained in Ex 30:11–16 of half a shekel for the sacrificial service in the tent of meeting. The original ordi-

1 According to *BRL,* 367. So too Barrois, *Manuel,* 2. 250.

2 de Vaux, *Ancient Israel,* 199–203.

3 On 4:10 see 1, 169; also de Vaux, *Ancient Israel,* 203–206.

4 Cf. Otto Eissfeldt, "Die Menetekel-Inschrift und ihre Deutung," *ZAW* 63 (1951): 105–114.

5 See de Vaux, *Ancient Israel,* 204f; *BRL.*

6 See 1, 168f on 4:9.

7 Incorrectly, according to de Vaux, *Ancient Israel,* 200f, who connects it with Akkadian *gur* (von Soden, *Akkadisches Handwörterbuch: kurru*).

nance must have represented the opinion that the gifts from the people were to be given directly to the sanctuary. In the present context the demand is made that at the handing over of these gifts the prince should be included to see that מנחה ("cereal offering"), עולה ("burnt offering") and שלמים ("final offerings") are offered, which then effect expiation for the people.

■ **45:16-17** This is expressed with all the clarity that might be desired in the commentary that is appended in vv 16f. The people as a whole are obliged to give the תרומה ("offering") to the prince and the prince, for his part, is obliged to supply the burnt offerings on the feasts, new moons, sabbaths and all the festivals in Israel. As sacrificial leader he is to "arrange for" (עשה) the sacrifices in order thereby to effect the expiation for the people that was already mentioned in v 15. In vv 15, 17a and 17b, in this connection, there appears three different series of sacrificial lists. The list in v 15 מנחה ("cereal offering")—עולה ("burnt offering")—שלמים ("final offerings") has been expanded in v 17b by the prefixed חטאת ("sin offering"), which is obviously intended (in an addition?) to correct the earlier list. In v 17a עולה ("burnt offering") and מנחה ("cereal offering") (in that order) have been expanded by the addition of נסך ("drink offering").

With regard to the sequence in the sacrificial list, Rendtorff has shown in his studies on the history of sacrifice that the עולה ("burnt offering") was originally the principal sacrifice, which therefore usually came first in the lists. According to de Vaux and Rost, however, the עולה ("burnt offering") cannot be traced back to the Israel of the wilderness period, but is a type of sacrifice adopted in Canaan.[8] The close form-critical relationship of Lev 1 and Lev 3 makes it clear that the עולה ("burnt offering") was often connected with the זבח שלמים ("final offering"). Thus in the enumeration of the Levites' duties in 44:11 עולה ("burnt offering") and זבח ("sacrifice") were cited as the sacrifices which were to be slaughtered by the Levites on the people's behalf.

On the other hand, the listing of the מנחה ("cereal offering") before the עולה ("burnt offering") is unusual. Normally it follows it, as is shown by the priestly ordinance codified in Leviticus 1–3. There, as a result of its close connection with the עולה ("burnt offering") in later ritual, it has forced its way in between עולה ("burnt offering") and זבח שלמים ("final offering"). It represents the cereal offering which, according to the later ordinance, regularly accompanied the עולה ("burnt offering") and which, after the removal of the אזכרה ("memorial portion") for Yahweh, fell to the priest's share.[9] V 17a mentions, in addition, after עולה ("burnt offering") and מנחה ("cereal offering") the second extra offering, the נסך "drink offering." According to Nu 15:1ff every עולה ("burnt offering") and every זבח ("sacrifice") is to be accompanied by these additional offerings. As additions to the עולה ("burnt offering") the two offerings appear also in Lev 23:13, 18, 37; Nu 6:15, 17; 15:24; Ex 29:40f; 30:9. 2 Kgs 16:10ff may also be compared. מנחה ("cereal offering") and נסך ("drink offering") appear alone in Joel 1:9, 13; 2:14 and Is 57:6. As distinguished from the מנחה ("cereal offering") in Leviticus 1–7 the נסך ("drink offering") has not acquired any ruling in an independent ritual section or דעת ("knowledge")-section.[10] The latest phase in the development discernible in the priestly texts is then characterized by the fact that the חטאת ("sin offering") surpasses the עולה ("burnt offering") in significance and often appears at the head of the lists, just as it occurs here in v 17b, in what, for that very reason, is proved to be a later addition.[11]

From the point of view of content, it may be observed with regard to the עולה ("burnt offering") that it is exclusively an animal sacrifice in which various types of domestic animals (bull, ox, ram, lamb, goat) and occasionally also birds are used. In the early period it is found principally as the true royal and festal sacrifice. It then becomes, even as early as the pre-exilic period, also the daily sacrifice. The increased importance of the חטאת ("sin offering"), which initially seems to have been a special dedicatory and purificatory sacrifice for sanctuary

8 On עולה ("burnt offering") see Gray, *Sacrifice,* 7; de Vaux, *Ancient Israel,* 27–51; Stevenson, "'Olah," 489–492; Rendtorff, *Studien,* 74–118.

9 See further Rendtorff, *Studien,* 169–198; Gray, *Sacrifice,* 13–17; Snaith, "Sacrifices," 314–316.

10 On the נסך ("drink offering") see further Gray, *Sacrifice,* 400f; Rendtorff, *Studien,* 169–172.

11 On חטאת ("sin offering") see Schötz, *Sündopfer;* Gray, *Sacrifice,* 57–62; de Vaux, *Ancient Israel,* 91–95; Rendtorff, *Studien,* 199–234; Snaith, "Sacrifices," 316f.

and temple, is to be understood against the increased experience of the need for redemption from sin in the period after the great catastrophe. Yet the עולה ("burnt offering"), in spite of its displacement to second place, still retains great significance even in the later period.

The שלמים ("final offerings") which here appear in all three sacrificial lists seem to have had a particularly eventful history. Leviticus 3 contains the ritual of the זבח שלמים ("final offering") and shows, as do other passages in P, that in the later period זבח ("sacrifice") and שלמים ("final offerings") have entered into close association. In זבח ("sacrifice") there is surely to be found the old communion sacrifice, which doubtless comes from the remote wilderness period and in which the sacrificing community sat down to a meal and only a part was offered to Yahweh.

שלמים (here "final offerings"), on the other hand, is controversial. De Vaux finds in it, since the term is attested also in Ugarit, as in the עולה ("burnt offering"), a Canaanite legacy and translates שלמים by "sacrifice de communion," while Gray understands שלמים as "payments" and finds expressed in it the thought of the gift (restitution).[12] While Schmid finds in the word precisely an allusion to Israel's covenant reality and hence translates it by "covenant sacrifice," others translate it along the same lines, but in a somewhat more restrained fashion, by "peace offerings" (Cooke, following the Revised Version), "salvation meal offering" (Elliger), "salvation offering" (*ZB*). Wendel, similarly, renders "peace offering" or "fraternization offering." The translation "meal offering" (Herrmann, Bertholet, Fohrer, Eichrodt) does not take account of the שלם-element in the word. According to Rendtorff, שלמים is to be understood primarily, quite independently of its association with זבח, as the description of a "final offering" (also suggested by Fohrer, note on 45:15). It subsequently lost its independent meaning and entered fully into association with other types of sacrifice. Thus especially the blood rite in the זבח שלמים sacrifice is to be understood from the point of view of the שלמים.[13]

In vv 15 and 17 the expiatory significance of the sacrifice is emphatically expressed. In 43:20 and 45:19f it can be seen that expiatory power is especially attributed to the blood. Other passages in the Priestly writing admittedly caution against attributing expiatory efficacy exclusively to the blood. Thus the עולה ("burnt offering") seems to have had particular expiatory power with regard to offenses in general.[14] In the present passage it is no longer possible to recognize any very close connection between the expiatory statements and a particular sacrifice.

In v 17a reference was made to specific festival occasions on which the prince (here, again, singular) was to make the offering. 45:18–25 and 46:1ff are directly connected with this and give the impression of being the detailed implementation of the programme intimated in 45:17.

Aim

The ordinance for the gifts from which the sacrifice in the sanctuary is to be provided could be understood in the first place as a purely technical ordinance of dues which has about it, particularly markedly, a transitory character. By its association with the passionate challenge to the princes of Israel in v 9, however, it has acquired an emphasis which raises it from the level of a purely technical regulation. The emphasis of the prophetic summons to the renunciation of all-too-human commercial practices settles on it. Such a summons, however, addresses not only the holders of political power who are here initially directly addressed.

The manipulation of the measures by which is measured the offering which is due to God again and again lies as a temptation in men's path (Acts 5:1ff). But where measures are manipulated with regard to God, it is not long before the same behavior is indulged with regard to human neighbors. The present ordinance urges an integrity in these external matters of calculation—an integrity which corresponds to the integrity of life before God.

12 Gray, *Sacrifice*, 7.

13 On זבח שלמים see de Vaux, *Ancient Israel*, 27–51; Stevenson, "'Olah," 492–497; Rendtorff, *Studien*, 149–168; Schmid, *Bundesopfer*.

14 Rendtorff, *Studien*, 81–83.

9. The Great Festivals and the Prince's Offering

Bibliography

Hans-Joachim Kraus
Worship in Israel; a Cultic History of the Old Testament, tr. Geoffrey Buswell (Richmond, Va.: John Knox, 1966).

Julian Morgenstern
"The Three Calendars of Ancient Israel," *HUCA* 1 (1924): 13–78.

Leonhard Rost
"Weidewechsel und alttestamentlicher Festkalender," *ZDPV* 66 (1943): 205–215; reprinted in *idem, Das kleine Credo und andere Studien zum Alten Testament* (Heidelberg: Quelle & Meyer, 1965), 101–112.

Ernst Würthwein
Der 'amm ha'arez im Alten Testament, BWANT 4, 17 (Stuttgart: Kohlhammer, 1936), especially 47–50.

See also the bibliography to 45:10–17.

45

18 Thus has [the Lord][a] Yahweh said: In the
first (month), on the first of the month,
you[b] shall take a bull without blemish
from the herd and cleanse the sanctuary.
19/ And the priest shall take of the blood
of the sin offering and smear (it) on[a] <the
doorposts>[b] of the temple and on the
four corners of the ledge of the altar and
on[a] <the doorposts>[b] of the gate[c] of the
inner court. 20/ And so also you shall do
on the seventh <of the month>[a] [for the
sake of anyone who has (sinned) through
error or ignorance][b] [and you shall make
atonement for the temple][c].
21 In the first (month) on the fourteenth day of
the month you shall keep the Passover [a
feast][a]; for <seven>[b] days unleavened

45: 𝔐 אדני is missing in 𝔊 (= $𝔊^{967}$). $𝔊^{B}$ κύριος θεός, $𝔊^{AQ}$
18 κύριος ὁ θεός, see Appendix 1.

b 𝔐 תקח. 𝔊 ($𝔏^{W}$) λήμψεσθε tries, as in the ritual in 43:18–27, to smooth out the text; see "Form."

19 19a על-אל cf. 1:17 note a.

b 𝔐 מְזוּזַת. According to 𝔊 𝔙 𝔖, מְזוּזֹת should be read.

c 𝔐 שער is attested by the versions; see the exposition.

20 20a 𝔐 בשבעה בחדש. 𝔊 ($𝔏^{W}$) ἐν τῷ ἑβδόμῳ μηνὶ μιᾷ τοῦ μηνός expands the text and suggests a second expiatory performance at the beginning of the second half of the year. On the other hand, Gese points to the inclination of 𝔊 in Ezekiel, discernible also in 26:1; 32:17; 40:1, to fill out dates. So one ought to keep to 𝔐 and simply emend בחדש to לחדש. For another view see Hölscher, 202 note 2. See the exposition.

b 𝔐 מאיש שגה ומפתי has been completely misunderstood by 𝔊 ($𝔏^{W}$) λήμψῃ παρ' ἑκάστου ἀπόμοιραν and has been read, according to Cornill, as something like מאיש נשא פה. This addition, which is scarcely original, tries to provide an explanation for the duty of regular atonement for the sanctuary along the lines of what is said in Lev 4:13; Nu 15:22.

c 𝔐 וכפרתם with its second person plural form, which is also attested by 𝔊 ($𝔏^{W}$) 𝔗, cannot be the original continuation of v 20a. 𝔖 eases the difficulty by formulating the statement in the third person and seeking to refer it to the priest. 𝔙 assimilates to the second person singular. It must be a secondary expansion.

21 21a The surprising word order in 𝔐 הפסח חג is preserved, astonishingly, by 𝔊 πασχα ἑορτή ($𝔏^{W}$ *pascha dies sollemnis*), 𝔙 *pascha solemnitas,* 𝔗 פיסחא חגא (otherwise 𝔖, פצחא ועדעאדא). Usually the

bread shall be eaten[c]. 22/ And on that
day the prince shall present, for himself
and for all the people of the land, an ani-
mal as a sin offering. 23/ And (through-
out) the seven days of the feast he shall
offer to Yahweh a burnt offering—seven
bulls and seven rams, (animals) without
blemish, every day for the seven days[a],
and as a sin offering every day a goat.
24/ And as a cereal offering <he shall>[a]
give an ephah for the bull and an ephah
for the ram and a hin of oil for an ephah.
25 **In[a] the seventh (month), on the fifteenth**
day[b] of the month, on the feast, he shall
do the same for seven days with sin
offerings <and>[c] burnt offerings and
cereal offerings and oil.

commentators simply reverse the order and explain the unusual word order in 𝔐 as due to intentional inversion by a later hand who wantd to arrive at the 𝔐 reading חג שבעות. It then admittedly is strange that this idea can be discerned in none of the versions (not even 𝔗) which all already have the inversion in front of them. There is the additional factor that the expression חג הפסח occurs only once, in Ex 34:25, and never in the many references in the P tradition, to which the Ezekiel tradition is close. Thus, here the original text will have been simply יהיה לכם הפסח. The חג could then represent an additional remark occasioned by the החג which follows in v 23 and intended to prepare for that reference. A different view is expressed by Friedrich Horst, *Das Privilegrecht Jahves*, FRLANT 28 (Göttingen: Vandenhoeck & Ruprecht, 1930), 83 note 1 (= *Gottes Recht*, 109 note 250), who wishes to read וחג, referring the word to the seven-day feast of unleavened bread, and to delete the remainder of v 21 as a secondary expansion.

b 𝔐 שְׁבֻעוֹת is a very secondary reading which is discernible in none of the versions and whose aim is to take account of the feast of weeks too in this festival calendar, without producing, however, a syntactically possible text. In the spelling of 𝔐 both the absolute form of חג and the construct form of שבעות are strange. In any event שִׁבְעַת should be read.

c 𝔐 יאכל. 𝔊 ἔδεσθε, 𝔖 תאכלון. But the passive formulation of 𝔐 is found also in Ex 13:7 (Lev 6:9).

23 23a 𝔐 ליום שבעת הימים is omitted by 𝔖.

24 24a 𝔐 יעשה. 𝔊 (𝔏[W]) ποιήσεις.

25 25a At the beginning, 𝔊 (𝔏[W]) 𝔖 insert the copula, cf. 1:4 note a.

b 𝔐 יום is unattested in 𝔊 (𝔏[W]) 𝔖. Since it has already occurred in v 21, it may be original, even though it is normally missing in dates (cf. v 18, but also 1:1, 2; 8:1; 20:1 and elsewhere).

c 𝔐 כעולה is introduced with the copula in 𝔊 (𝔏[W]) 𝔖. Since this occurs also in the other items in the list, it should be added here too. 𝔗 has it only with the last item, while 𝔅 corresponds to 𝔐 (at any rate it introduces the first two items in the list with *tam—quam*).

Form

In 45:17 there was sketched the outline of the subsequent detailed statements which now deal separately with the prince's offerings on specific occasions. With a new messenger formula the first section of these elaborations dealing with the sacrifices on the "festivals" (חגים, also vv 21, 23, 25) is introduced in v 18. 46:1ff, with a new introductory formula, will then deal with the sacrifices on the sabbath (vv 1, 3f, 12), new moon (46:1, 3, 6) and other "appointed occasions" (מועדים 46:9).[1]

Within vv 18–25, which appear from the sequence of dates on the first of the first (v 18), the seventh of the first (v 20), the fourteenth of the first (v 21) and the fifteenth of the seventh (v 25) to be structured so clearly,

1 On 46:11, which again mentions חגים ומועדים, see below.

on closer form-critical examination, the beginning, vv 18–20, is different from what follows. We have here the form of the ritual which is already familiar from 43:18–27. Here too this reveals what was observed there, namely the remarkable change of subject. After the introductory address in the second person singular, it passes in v 19 with the description of the blood rite to a statement about the action of the priest (third person singular) only to revert in v 20a to the address in the second person singular. V 20b with its second person plural then clearly leads to the particulars about the great annual festivals, which begin with the address to the people in the second person plural but then recount the activity of the prince in the third person singular. V 20b is to be regarded as a link section which has been added secondarily. Its aim is to connect the self-contained ritual in vv 18–20a with the details, which are expected after the outline of v 17a, about the princely offering on the feasts in vv 21–25. Thus the catchword חג ("festival"), which is also expected after v 17, still does not occur in vv 18–20, but does immediately afterwards on three occasions in vv 21–25. The date in vv 18(20), which fits well into the context, should not therefore obscure the independence of the ritual in vv 18–20a.

While the join in v 20b at the conclusion of the ritual is, like the various verbs which described the individual acts of the sacrificial process in vv 19f, in the form of a consecutive perfect, a new style begins with the festival ordinance of vv 21–25. After an introductory observation about the date of Passover, rules are simply given in a monotonous exposition for the presentation of the various offerings by the prince. An introductory ועשׂה ("and he shall do, make") (v 22) is followed as the only verbal statement by a threefold imperfect יעשׂה ("he shall do, make") (vv 23, 24, 25). The whole emphasis here, apart from the dates, is on the detailed listing of the gifts to be offered. See also 46:4–7.

Setting

Not only in the form of the ritual but also in its content, which refers to the altar which was described in 43:13–17, does 45:18–20a stand so close to 43:18–27 that one would wish to ascribe the two sections to the same hand. So Hölscher, Gese and others. However, the detailed exegesis will also point out differences which make it appear probable that 45:18–20a is of later origin than 43:18–27.

Vv 21–25, on the other hand, bring the prince fully into the picture and are not to be separated from the additional details about the prince's offerings in 46:1ff. The dating of these sections cannot be attempted without a comprehensive consideration of the figure of the נשׂיא ("prince") in chapters 40–48. Such a consideration will be undertaken in connection with the exposition of 47:13–48:29. The assessment of chapters 40–48 as a whole comes after chapter 48.

Interpretation

■ **45:18-20a** Vv 18–20a, composed in the style of a ritual, say nothing about the prince. Rather, this section is concerned exclusively with the cleansing of the sanctuary. מקדשׁ ("sanctuary") refers, in v 18, to the temple area. Then in v 19 the places to be cleansed are listed in detail: "temple building" (בית), altar and gate. While the related passage in 43:18ff dealt with the first cleansing, i.e. with the consecration of the altar, here the reference is to the annually recurring process of a cleansing of temple, altar and gate.

■ **45:18-19** This is located time-wise on the first day of the first month, that is, undoubtedly, the beginning of the year. This is a discrepancy with the new year date in 40:1 (Lev 25:9). But Morgenstern, in his discussion of the various calendar systems, has pointed to the fact that also in the account of the erection of the tent of meeting in Ex 40:2 account is taken of a New Year's Day on the first of the first month which is important for a new cultic beginning. While the great Day of Atonement in Leviticus 16, which subsequently won the day as the great day of cleansing not only of the sanctuary but of the whole community, adheres, in its dating to the tenth of the seventh month, to the old date for New Year, the present dating appears novel. One might ask whether this is not the influence of the Babylonian calendar with its expiatory rites for the sanctuary effected in the context of the great New Year festival As Leviticus 16 shows, this was not successful in its fixing of the atonement ceremony. The cleansing at the beginning of the year has as its goal, as the extensive ritual for the great Day of Atonement is able to show much more fully, the cleansing of the sanctuary (and of the community) from the sin which has accumulated throughout the year.

45:18–20a isolate from the undoubtedly fuller ritual

of this day only the one element of cleansing by means of a blood rite. Quite tersely it is stated that a bull without blemish is needed for this. There is no designation of this as חטאת ("sin offering"). Nothing is said about slaughtering or the further stages of the offering, but all that is laid down is that the cleansing is to be done with its blood. In this connection it is noteworthy that the taking of the animal and the completion of the "cleansing" (חטא) is certainly, as in 43:20, to be the task of the prophet addressed in the second person singular; the completion of the actual blood rite, however, is in the hands of the priest who is introduced (by contrast with 43:18ff) in the singular. This recalls the later rituals of Leviticus 1 and 3, where precisely the sprinkling of the blood is reserved for the priests. Does this argue for the idea that the regulation in vv 18–20a is closer to P than is 43:18ff? The blood rite here admittedly has its particular shape in that the blood is smeared on the doorposts of the temple (this recalls the Passover custom of Ex 12:7), on the four corners of the altar ledge (in 43:20 it was the horns, ledge and rim) and the posts of the gate to the inner court, most probably of the east gate. Here the blood clearly has the power to remove sins. There is no mention of atonement (כפר "to make atonement") in the ritual itself (cf. on 43:20).

■ **45:20a** V 20a prescribes the repetition of the same action on the seventh day of the first month. Most commentators believe they ought to follow 𝔊 here and read the date as the first day of the seventh month (note a), thereby achieving the parallelism of two days of atonement at the beginning of each half of the year.[2] Yet, apart from the graphically not entirely unobjectionable textual emendation which this reading demands (see also note a), the resultant, almost compulsorily essential assignment of an additional New Year's Day on the first of the seventh month argues against this alteration. With Gese, we should retain 𝔐 and see here a septenary pattern for the repetition of the cleansing. For a similar septenary pattern see Passover-Unleavened Bread according to Lev 23:8; Nu 28:25. On the secondary glossing in v 20aβ, which should be referred not only to the action of the seventh day but to the whole act of cleansing, see note b.

■ **45:20b** The transitional sentence in v 20b introduces secondarily the theological concept of expiation (with this cf. the expansions in vv 15bα and 17bβ). It differs from the preceding ritual also by the different usage of בית ("temple"), which in v 19 was used in the narrower sense, but which here must correspond as to content to the מקדש ("sanctuary") of v 18.

■ **45:21–25** In vv 21–25 there then follows the sequel which v 17 led us to expect. Here the reference is now to the "feasts" which were first mentioned there, the feast on the fourteenth of the first month, which lasts for seven days (vv 21–24), and the feast on the fifteenth of the seventh month, which also lasts for seven days (v 25). Only the first feast is introduced with a name of its own.

■ **45:21** The explicit designation as חג ("feast") must, on the other hand, have been added only secondarily (see note a). פסח ("Passover"), whose etymology is still obscure, originally designated the custom of slaughtering a lamb at night and of the meal eaten in traveling garb, as well as the associated blood rite which Rost believes is to be understood as an apotropaic pastoral custom at the beginning of transhumance.[3] With the Passover celebration there was then associated in the settled land (only because of the coincidence in time?) the "week of unleavened bread," which can be understood only against the background of the usages of the cultivated land.

■ **45:22–24** The prince's offerings laid down for the period of the seven days show that the amalgamation of Passover, which provides the name here, and the week of unleavened bread, which determines the duration of the feast, is already quite complete. On the other hand, the clause in v 21b which prescribes the eating of unleavened bread for seven days raises critical objections. The beginning of v 22, which enjoins on the prince a specific offering "on that day," presupposes the naming of a specific day, but not the mention of a seven-day festival ordinance. So this final part, which has its verbal correspondence in the final part of Nu 28:17 (but see also Dtn 16:3aβ: Ex 23:15, 34:18; Lev 23:6), will then have been added secondarily because it was thought to be indispensable in an ordinance for Passover-Unleavened Bread.

■ **45:21b** The influence of the analogy of the other festival calendars is also discernible in the shape of 𝔐 in v

2 Gese, 77 note 2.

3 See also the careful discussion in de Vaux, *Studies*, 1–26.

21b, where by the insertion of חג ("feast") and the revocalization of שִׁבְעַת ("seven") as שָׁבֻעוֹת ("weeks") (note b), an interpretation in terms of the "Feast of Weeks" has been forced on to the text. The absence of a mention of it in the original context, in view of the explicit old regulations of Ex 23:14; 34:23f; Dtn 16:16 according to which all males have to appear before Yahweh three times in the year, seemed unthinkable in an ordinance for the prince of Israel. On the other hand, it must be stated that for the author of 45:21ff the old pilgrimage festival at the beginning of the wheat harvest, which is referred to in Ex 23:16 by the term חג הקציר ("the feast of harvest") and then in Ex 34:22; Dtn 16:10 (cf. Nu 28:26) by the name חג שבעת ("the feast of weeks"), has faded in its significance and is not made the opportunity for a particularly full sacrifice on the part of the prince. That this should be due[4] to "its lunar insignificance" is scarcely probable.

■ **45:25** On the other hand, the old autumn festival in Israel, which is described, as already in 1 Kgs 8:2; 12:32, simply as "the feast" (החג) and in Lev 23:39; Ju 21:19; Hos 9:5 as "the feast of Yahweh," maintains its significance. Ex 23:16; 34:22 refer to it by the name חג האס[י]ף ("the feast of ingathering"). Dtn 16:13, 16; Lev 23:34 call it "feast of booths" (חג הסכות). This shows that to its character as an old Canaanite vintage festival other components have been added.[5] In the present passage, it becomes, like Passover, a festival which is characterized by particular princely offerings. At the same time, however, in the analogous treatment of the two festivals, there is revealed the process which is strongly at work in the course of history, that of leveling out festivals which to begin with in their rituals are clearly distinct. The nocturnal festival, whose domestic character could not subsequently be suppressed either, is here treated in precisely the same way as the festival which, according to Judges 21, is still celebrated out of doors in the vineyards. Admittedly the festivals are here described only from the point of view of the presentation of offerings by the princely representative of the people. There may still have been room alongside this for other elements. It is nevertheless clear how for the priestly author of Ezekiel 45 the effects of the Deuteronomic reform are tacitly assumed, insofar as Israel's representative can, of course, present his offerings only in the one sanctuary in Jerusalem. And here too the leveling process has continued, in that the activity of Israel's true representative which is relevant for the festivals is concentrated on the offerings which are presented in a particularly substantial fashion. Here we are on the way to Numbers 28f, as is clear from the copious sacrificial ordinance for the eight-day autumn festival, an ordinance in which the נשיא ("prince") in no longer mentioned (29:12–38). There is no longer there any special name for the festival, no longer even the general החג ("the feast"). The individuality of this festival now consists rather in the detailed quantification of what is to be sacrificed.

■ **45:21–25** This sacrifice and the prince who presents it on his own behalf and on behalf of the whole community of Israel (v 22) are the really important central elements for Ezekiel 45. This community is no longer described, as in the redactional introduction in v 17b, as בית ישראל ("the house of Israel"). Instead, here and in 46:1ff, there appears the term עם הארץ ("the people of the land"). This appeared in Ezekiel's judicial speeches in 7:27;[6] 12:19; 22:29; 33:2 as a description of the land-owning aristocracy. Würthwein has already shown with regard to 39:13 that in the future expectations in the book of Ezekiel the term acquires an altered significance.[7] This is quite clear in chapters 45f. עם הארץ ("the people of the land") means here (and in Lev 4:27) the whole cultic community, certainly not merely the wealthy upper class. "*'amm ha'arez* refers to this people newly constituted on Palestinian soil. For ארץ here means nothing other than Palestine."[8] The fact that later, after the return, there appeared a foreign local population which was certainly not integrated into the community, to which subsequently the designation עם הארץ ("the people of the

4 As is maintained by Gray, *Sacrifice,* 287.

5 See Kraus, *Worship,* and Albrecht Alt, "Zelte und Hütten" in *Alttestamentliche Studien; Friedrich Nötscher zum sechzigsten Geburtstag,* eds. Hubert Junker and Johannes Botterweck, BBB 1 (Bonn: Hanstein, 1950), 16–25; reprinted in *idem, Kleine Schriften zur Geschichte des Volkes Israel* 3 (München: Beck, 1959), 233–242.

6 See 1, 209.

7 See above p. 318.

8 Würthwein, *'amm,* 49.

land") was transferred and in which is described the hostile opponents in the land (see, e.g., Ezr 4:4f), is here not yet in view. This is an observation which is by no means insignificant for the dating of 45:20–46:12.

On behalf of himself and the community the offerings are to be presented by the prince as sacrificial leader: on the first day of the "Feast of Passover" a bull as a sin offering, throughout the seven days of the festival in addition daily a burnt offering of seven bulls and seven rams, animals "without blemish" (תמים as in 43:22f, 25), and also daily a goat as a sin offering. Hölscher regards the latter as an addition on the basis of Numbers 28.[9] There are, further, the additional offerings: an ephah of flour (that is for each bull and each ram) and a hin of oil as an additional offering with each ephah of flour.[10] In this connection there is an obscurity in the reckoning of the days. The Passover festival begins on the evening of the fourteenth day of the first month. According to the sacrifice regulation in Nu 28:16–25, the week when unleavened bread is eaten begins on the fifteenth of the month; on the first day of this week, i.e., on the fifteenth of the first month, there begins also the seven-day long copious presentation of offerings. In Ezek 45:22, on the other hand, the ביום ההוא ("on that day"), which designated the first day of sacrificial obligation, can refer back only to the fourteenth day of the first month, the day on which Passover was kept. Can one be content with Cooke's assertion that the phraseology is "somewhat loose" and identify the first day of the copious offerings with the day following Passover night? Or should one argue that the day is reckoned from nightfall, so that the first full day is identical with the first day of the week of unleavened bread? But why then is Passover explicitly fixed on the fourteenth day of the first month? And why does Nu 28:16f explicitly separate the dates? Or must one really acknowledge that here, intentionally, a different reckoning is intended which advances the festival complex by a day, something which has no analogy elsewhere? In all this, questions seem to me to remain open.

With regard to the offerings, it should be observed that the most incisive difference in comparison with the older Passover lies in the marked inclusion of the sin offering, the intrusion of which in post-exilic sacrificial practice has already been discussed in the context of vv 16f. A comparison with Numbers 28 shows that subsequently not only was the fourteenth day of the first month relieved of the copious offerings, which do not begin until the fifteenth, but that, although the presentation of a bull as a sin offering disappeared on the first day, the daily presentation of a goat as a sin offering remained. In addition, there the demand is for two bulls as a burnt offering instead of the seven here, for one ram and seven lambs instead of the seven rams here. There the מנחה ("cereal offering") is strongly depreciated, with the oil element reckoned inclusively; three tenths (of an ephah) for every bull as a burnt offering, two tenths for the ram and one tenth for each lamb.

The schematic leveling out of the feast days in Ezekiel 45 again becomes very clear when one also compares the regulation for the feast of the seventh month. Ezek 45:25 prescribes for this feast, in quite general terms, the same sacrificial gifts for the prince as for the feast in the first month. In the sequence of the offerings under consideration, here too the sin offering comes first, followed by the עולה ("burnt offering"), then the מנחה ("cereal offering") and the oil offering, which is here, in contrast to Numbers 29, not linked with the מנחה ("cereal offering") but stands simply as one element among the sacrificial material. Numbers 29, on the other hand, reveals the much greater significance of the autumn festival in that the number of the sacrificial lambs and rams for the seven days of the feast is simply doubled. In the case of the bull- עולה ("burnt offering"), it begins on the first day with thirteen animals and decreases by one animal each day to the seventh day, which has only seven bulls. The eighth day of the feast, added only secondarily, has an עולה ("burnt offering") of only one bull, one ram and seven lambs, which, in the case of the last two types of animals, corresponds to the information for the feast of unleavened bread. מנחה ("cereal offering") and חטאת ("sin offering") remain unchanged compared with the feast of unleavened bread.

The summary comparison with the later sacrifice ordinance in Numbers 28f leads to the following conclusions, that Ezekiel 45 1) changes the calendar of the

9 Hölscher, 201 note 3.

10 On the הין ("hin") see 1, 169 on 4:11 and de Vaux, *Ancient Israel,* 200ff.

major feasts by a reduction to the two great annual festivals, 2) levels out these two festivals from the point of view of the offerings demanded in the requirements and 3) by prefacing the sin offering of a bull gives to both feasts a strong character of atonement. Precisely in this last element it has been felt particularly that one can discern a proximity to the period of judgment experienced in the exile. In all three aspects mentioned later development did not follow Ezekiel 45. In all three points the older tradition made itself felt once again. In the considerable increase, which can be presumed in Ezekiel 45 (in comparison, e.g., with Leviticus 23), in sacrificial activity at the sanctuary in Jerusalem, the later period has admittedly strongly continued the tendency discernible here, at least with regard to the autumn festival.

Aim

To the ordinances for the prince's offerings at the great festivals a second hand has prefaced in vv 18–20 a ritual which has a strong emphasis which is then also found in the ordinance for the prince's festival offerings. In this ritual there is prescribed by divine decree the cleansing of the sanctuary which is to be carried out regularly at the beginning of the year.

In the preaching of Ezekiel it had become clear how the fire of God's wrath had to consume his people because of their sin. The great vision of chapters 8–11 had shown in particular that this judgment could not bypass Israel's sanctuary either. Indeed, in 9:6 the command was given from the mouth of God himself to the men with the instruments of judgment: "At my sanctuary you shall make a beginning." It is against this background that the ordinance given in Ezekiel 45 for the service in the new sanctuary must be heard. Here God ordains in mercy that at the beginning of each new year, by a specific ritual to be carried out at the sanctuary, the threatening stain of sin may be removed. In this ordinance, however, there is revealed the will of the God who would like to protect himself from having to punish sin with his fire, a will which was also discernible already in the commissioning of the watchman in time of danger (3:17–21; 33:1–9).

The prophets, an Amos (5:21ff), an Isaiah (1:10ff), had once with great severity also attacked Israel's cults. Music making, feasting in the temple were abhorrent to the Holy One. When the present ordinance for the offerings at the feasts in the future sanctuary ordains that a great sin offering should precede all burnt offerings, then the intention is to proclaim, over these feasts with their danger of religious whitewashing with false, festal joy, the intention of God that he means to remove sin. Before the burnt offerings in which man could easily see his pious activity and alongside these burnt offerings of every single feast day the sin offering is set. It reminds the community in the midst of their high feasts of their real condition before God—but recalls, as an offering ordained by God, also the fact that God is ready to remove sin.

The truth proclaimed in this ordinance of the sin offering, which is, for its part, never of course secure from being falsified into a new human possibility, has become unmistakably clear at the point where God himself has taken into his own hands the removal of sins in his son. Here he has allowed it to become the crisis point of all independent activity on man's part. At the same time, however, he has made himself known to his world in his offering once for all.

10. Gate Ordinances for Prince and People and the Prince's Minor Offerings with an Appendix on the Tamid

Bibliography

G. Förster
"Die Neumondfeier im Alten Testamente," *ZWTh* 49 (1906): 1–17.

F. Wilke
"Das Neumondfest im israelitischen-jüdischen Altertum," *Jahrbuch der Gesellschaft für die Geschichte des Protestantismus in Österreich* 67 (Festschrift für Josef Bohatec) (1951): 171–185.

See also the bibliography to 45:10–17 and 45:18–25.

46

1 **Thus has [the Lord][a] Yahweh said: The**
gate of the inner court which faces east
shall be closed during the six working
days[b] but be opened on the sabbath day,
and (also) on the day of the new moon it
shall be opened[c]. 2/ Then the prince shall
enter (it) through the vestibule of the
gate structure from outside[a] and (remain)
stand(ing) by the posts[b] of the gate, and
the priests shall present his burnt offer-
ings and his final offerings, and on the
threshold[b] of the gate he shall pay hom-
age (by falling down) and go out (again).
But the gate shall not be closed till
evening. 3/ And the people of the land[a]
shall pay homage before Yahweh (by
falling down) at the doorway of that gate
on sabbaths and new moons.
4 **But the burnt offering which the prince**
shall present to Yahweh[a] (consists) on
the sabbath day (of) six lambs without
blemish and a ram without blemish. 5/
And the cereal offering (consists of) an
ephah for the ram, but for the lambs the
cereal offering (consists of) as much as
his hand is able to give, and oil—one hin
for the ephah[a]. 6/ And on the day of the
new moon (the offering consists of) a bull
<without blemish>[a] from the herd[b] and
six lambs and a ram—they shall[c] be (ani-
mals) without blemish. 7/ And he shall
bring an ephah for the bull and an ephah
for the ram as a cereal offering—but for
the lambs as much as his hand can give,
and oil: a hin for an ephah.
8 **When then the prince enters, he shall enter**
through the vestibule of the gate struc-
ture and come out (again) by the same
way. 9/ But when the people of the land
enter (to appear) at the feasts before
Yahweh, then he who comes in by the
north gate to pay homage (by falling
down) shall go out by the south gate. And
he who comes in by the south gate shall
go out by the north gate[a]. He shall not go

46: 1a אדני is lacking in 𝔊 (= 𝔊[967]). 𝔊[B] *κύριος θεος*
1 [sic!], see Appendix 1.
b 𝔐 ימי המעשה. 𝔗 יומי חולא "profane days."
c V 1bβ is mssing in 𝔊[967], but this is easily explained as due to homoioteleuton. Since in v 3 too, in the regulation for the עם הארץ, the new moon is mentioned alongside the sabbath and is attested also by 𝔊[967] there, its occurrence in v 1 is not to be dispensed with.
2 2a 𝔐 מחוץ is erroneously referred by 𝔊 (except 𝔊[967,26,106]) to "gate": *τῆς πύλης τῆς ἔξωθεν*. This then forces 𝔊[B] (𝔏[W]) to adjust to v 1 with the reading as in 42:1 *ἔσωθεν (interioris)*.
b 𝔐 מזוזה and מפתן are not differentiated in the versions, but are both identically rendered by 𝔊 with *πρόθυρα* (𝔏[W] *vestibulum*) 𝔅 *limen* 𝔖 אסכופתא 𝔗 (א)סקופת "posts." See the exposition. Gese wishes to read plural מזוזות instead of singular as in 45:19.
3 3a הארץ is omitted by 𝔊[967] (𝔏[W]).
4 4a 𝔊 (𝔏[W]) and 𝔅 suppress in their construction, each in its own way, the relative clause.
5 5a 𝔖 anticipates here with the mention of a cereal offering also for the offering of a bull (which is not mentioned until v 6), but compensates by omitting v 5b, the reference to the oil.
6 6a 𝔐 תמימים is a scribal error, due to dittography, for תמים; according to Hölscher, 202 note 1, it is a correction on the basis of Nu 28:11.
b 𝔐 בן־בקר is unattested in 𝔊 (𝔏[W]).
c In 𝔊 (𝔏[W]) 𝔖 it is singular, referring only to איל.
9 9a 𝔐 צפונה is surely not (*pace* Herrmann) to be schematically harmonized with the צפון in v 9aα. See also 47:2.

back through the (same) gate by which
he came in, but <he shall go straight
out>[b]. 10/ But the prince, when they
come, shall come in in their midst, and
when they go out, shall go out[a] (in their
midst).
11 **And on the feasts and festivals the cereal**
offering shall consist of an ephah for the
bull and an ephah for the ram, but for the
lambs as much as his hand can give. And
oil: a hin for the ephah..
12 **And when the prince brings a free-will**
offering, a burnt offering or final offering
as a free-will offering for Yahweh, then
the gate which faces east shall be
opened for him, and he shall bring his
burnt offering and his final offering as he
brings (them) on the sabbath day. Then
he shall go out, and the gate shall be
closed after he has gone out.
13 **And you[a] shall bring daily to Yahweh as a**
burnt offering a yearling lamb without
blemish. Every morning[b] you[a] shall pre-
sent it. 14/ And every morning[a] you[b]
shall present in addition a cereal offering:
one sixth of an ephah and one third of a
hin of oil in order to sprinkle[c] the wheat
groats—a cereal offering for Yahweh as a
perpetual ordinance [Tamid][d]. 15/ And
<they shall>[a] present the lamb and the
cereal offering and the oil every morning
as a Tamid-burnt offering.

b More than 100 MSS, Eb 22, Q, confirmed by the versions, here read singular יצא instead of 𝔐 יצאו. The latter has arisen as a result of dittography.

10 10a Here too the plural יצאו of 𝔐 is, with 37 MSS, Eb 22 and according to 𝔊 (𝔏^{C}) 𝔙 𝔗, a scribal error, due to dittography, for יצא. 𝔖 is much more deviant and repeats the instruction of v 8bβ.

13 13a 𝔐 תעשה is rendered by 𝔊 (𝔏^{C}) 𝔙 𝔖 (which omits the second occurrence) as a third person and referred still to the prince who was the subject of the preceding section. But in vv 13f we have a new, formally independent unit; see the exposition.

b The single occurrence of *πρωί* in 𝔊^{BA} (𝔏^{C}), which is doubled in 𝔊^{967}, does not prove that בבקר occurs only once in the original; cf. Cooke.

14 14a 𝔊^{967} attests here, as do 𝔊^{BA} 𝔏^{C} 𝔄, only a single בבקר, but cf. v 13 note b. 𝔙 *cata mane mane* here and in v 15 is strange. In v 13 it had translated *semper mane*.

b Cf. v 13 note a.

c The verb רסס is attested only here in the OT, but cf. Song 5:2 רסיסים "drops" (of dew). 𝔊 *ἀναμεῖξαι*, 𝔏^{C} *miscere*, 𝔗 ערב. Only 𝔖 למפלה (from פלל "sprinkle").

d 𝔐 חקות עולם should, on the basis of 𝔊 *πρόσταγμα διὰ παντός* (𝔏^{C} *praeceptum semper*), 𝔙 *legitimum iuge atque perpetuum*, 𝔗 קיים עלם, 𝔖 נמוסא לעלם אמינאית and with MSS, be read as singular חקת עולם. The combination חקת עולם is attested more than twenty times in the priestly writing, but חקות עולם never occurs. The firm anchoring of this form in priestly language then also suggests that the expression in 𝔊 (𝔏^{C}), which seems to point to an original חקת תמיד, which again is not attested elsewhere, should be interpreted as an abbreviated rendering of 𝔐. Thus 𝔐 is the original not only of 𝔙 𝔗 𝔖 but also already of 𝔊. The association of עולם and תמיד is, on the other hand, thus unique, while the עולת תמיד of the immediately following v 15 is attested in priestly languge also in Ex 29:42; Nu 28:3 (emended text), 6; Ezr 3:5 (see also 1 Chr 16:40 and, with the definite article, in Nu 28f fifteen times). Thus a secondary intrusion of the תמיד from v 15 (Gese) is very likely. See the exposition.

15 15a 𝔐 וַעֲשׂוּ should be read with K 𝔖 𝔗 as וְעָשׂוּ against Q 𝔗^{W} יעשו. 𝔊 reads *ποιήσετε* (𝔏^{C} *facietis*), while 𝔙 *faciet* wishes to regard v 15 also as still referring to the prince (cf. v 13 note a).

Form

The complex which is introduced by a messenger formula is delimited at the farther end by the section which begins with the same formula, vv 16ff. From the question about its unity, it emerges that down to v 12 it deals in narrative style (third person singular) with regulations for prince and people of the land. In vv 13f, on the other hand, surprisingly there appears again an address in the second person such as last occurred in the ritual in 45:18–20a. The fact that 𝔊 (𝔏^{c}) 𝔖 𝔙 (but not 𝔗) refer the statements here too to the prince and read the third person singular is to be regarded as a secondary harmonization (cf. v 13 note a). In v 15 the language once again changes, this time to the third person plural (where the versions go different ways, cf. note a). Since in vv 13ff there is no further mention of the prince, vv 13f are proved to be, from the content point of view, also a separate section to which, in v 15, a further expansion has been added.

In vv 1–12, from the point of view of content, gate regulations (vv 1–3, 8–10, 12) can be separated from sacrifice regulations (vv 4–7, 11), where the regulations for the sacrifices continue what was begun in 45:20–25 along the lines of the proclamation of 45:17. After the "feasts" (חגים) reference is now to sabbath and new moon (in the reverse order from 45:17) and "festal occasions" (מועדים). It has been considered whether one should not separate the two components from each other and, so Procksch, regard the sacrifice regulations, for example, as coming from the original נשׂיא ("prince")-layer. Yet closer examination shows that the two components are nevertheless very closely connected. New moon and sabbath are referred to both in the gate regulations in v 1 and in the sacrifice instructions in vv 4 and 6. The מועדים are mentioned in v 9 in the context of a route regulation; v 11, on the other hand, from its content proves to be a later addition. A strong link between the two elements can be seen in v 12, where the new sacrificial element of the נדבה ("free-will offering") can scarcely be detached from the context of the gate regulations. Thus, since the two elements in addition are closely linked above all by their common reference to the נשׂיא ("prince"), one will have to abandon any attempt to separate what is connected in vv 1–12, even if one cannot fail to recognize the difference in style in the linguistic formation of the two elements. The gate regulations, after the introductory instruction about closing and opening the inner east gate (v 1), are, in vv 2f and 12, in a lively narrative style, which, in the sequence of its consecutive perfects, is to be characterized as ritual style.[1] In vv 8–10 the perfects are, surprisingly, consistently replaced by imperfects (jussives?), but here too the lively movement of the action, in which the verbal element is dominant, cannot be mistaken. V 12 begins in casuistic style with כי ("when"), but in its continuation it is in the ritual style of v 2 with the typical consecutive perfect (four times). In the sacrifice regulations, on the other hand, as in 45:21–25, it is the noun which dominates, the enumeration, and there is little variation discernible in the verb. But this can be understood unmistakably from the content of the two components, for the content is reflected in the style. Nevetheless, there appears in vv 1–12 a process of growth which has preceded the unity. See the detailed exposition.

In the addition in vv 13f and its appendix in v 15, in the context of further sacrifice instructions, as in 45:22–25 only the verb עשׂה ("to do, make") is used in the verbal arrangement.

Setting

Concerning the origin in time of vv 1–12, what was said about 45:21–25 is valid here too. The two sections doubtless stem from the same hand. Concerning their integration into the total process of the emergence of chapters 40–48, something will require to be said, after the comprehensive consideration of the figure of the נשׂיא ("prince") in chapters 40–48 has also been undertaken, in connection with the total review of chapters 40–48.

Interpretation

■ **46:1** 44:1f had spoken of the unconditional closing of the outer east gate; 44:3 had linked with that an instruction for the cultic behavior of the נשׂיא ("prince"). 46:1ff place alongside that the regulation concerning the intermittent closing of the inner east gate too. Here too there is connected with it a cultic instruction for the נשׂיא ("prince"), who is allowed to enter the gate structure on sabbath and new moon. The closure of the gate on "working days" (ימי המעשׂה, only here in the OT) is unmistakably influenced by the regulation of 44:1f. In v 12, secondarily, there is a further opening for a shorter period. The significance of sabbath and new moon will require to be considered further in connection with the sacrifice regulations in vv 4f and 6f. For the understanding of what follows it is at once important to realize that entry to the inner court is permitted only to the priests. Then it becomes clear, here too, that the defensive

1 Koch, *Priesterschrift,* 107.

function of the gate, which was unmistakable in its original construction, is quite unimportant, as already in 44:3, and that the gate structure acquires a particular function in the cultic celebration. For this process the gate is opened on sabbath and new moon. Nothing is said here about an absolute prohibition on the priests from passing through the whole gate, even though the expansion in 40:38–46 made it clear that the priests were allocated in particular the inner north and south gates beside which their cells were located.

■ **46:2** In a ritual-like description, v 2 makes clear in what way the inner east gate (40:32–34) becomes, on the stated feast days, the prince's cult place. From outside, i.e. from the outer court, he enters the gate structure, which, with its vestibule, opens into this court, goes to the posts of the gate and standing there assists at a distance at the presentation by the priests of the offering donated by him. The priests here are not further subdivided into priests and Levites, but, obviously in the manner of 40:45–46a and in spite of their different tasks in the sacrifice, simply designated as "priests." The prince's offerings consist of עולה ("burnt offerings") and שלמים ("final offerings").[2]

The designation of the places in the gate structure where the different actions are carried out is terminologically not in accord with the description of the gate in chapter 40, so that much remains unclear in our understanding of them. Thus, in the first place, it is not indicated more precisely in what place the מזוזה ("post") is to be located. In chapter 40 the side of the passages is always called איל ("pillar"). "Door posts" in the gate structure are to be assumed first of all at the entrance to the vestibule, then at the entrance to the actual gateway with its niches and finally at the exit into the inner court. Here it is most likely that one should envisage the doorposts at the exit from the gate into the inner court. These are what are surely meant in 45:19b, according to which they are sprinkled with blood by the high priest, who approaches them from the court. Here, at the entrance to the inner court where the eye can take in all that happens in the inner court, the sacrificial leader is present at the offering up of Israel's sacrifice. And here, in connection with that, he completes his act of worship. מפתן ("threshold") too, the place where he falls down, is sought in vain in the description of the gate in chapter 40. In the context of 10:4 (9:3; 10:18),[3] a translation "podium (of the temple building)" was presupposed. In the present passage, if the location of the doorposts is correct, one will have to think, with the older interpretation of מפתן, of the (outer) "threshold" of the gate facing the inner court. It had been designated in 40:6 (with the reverse orientation of the outer gate) as סף ("threshold"). Unfortunately it can no longer be decided whether סף (40:6f; 41:16; 43:8) and מפתן (also in 47:1) are really synonymous or whether the two words each have a slightly different emphasis—whether, for example, מפתן as the word of the literary language differs from the more technical, architectural term סף. After this act of adoration, which seems in the liturgy to follow the presentation of the offering, the prince leaves the gate structure. V 8 will add a clarification concerning the route he has to follow in doing so.

■ **46:3** Once again, alongside the prince, the cultic community is introduced as עם הארץ ("the people of the land").[4] Nothing is said about their offering since, as in 45:22, the prince presents the offering "for himself and for all the people of the land." Thus there is no question, either, of the full participation of the people at the offering. They simply perform an act of adoration at the entrance to the gateway. This must refer to the entrance which faces outwards towards the outer court, which leads first into the אולם ("vestibule") and only then over a threshold into the passageway with its niches. Does this envisage the people being able to see from a distance, through the passageway, which is admittedly fifty cubits long, something of the sacrificial action in the inner court? If so, then it is not entirely clear how that can be, in view of the steps which lead up to the gateway. Are the people permitted to climb these steps and must they then perform their act of adoration on the threshold to the אולם ("vestibule")? Or must one assume that 46:1–3 does not visualize the gateway of chapter 40 in all its details, a fact which would suggest a certain distance between chapter 40 and what is envisaged in chapter 46? At any rate, it is explicitly said of this act of adoration on the part of the people that is happens "before Yahweh." In

2 See above pp. 478f on 45:17.
3 1, 251, following Koehler-Baumgartner.
4 See above pp. 483–486 on 45:21–25.

this connection it is noteworthy that this לפני יהוה ("before Yahweh") also recurs in v 9, in connection with what is said there about the people of the land, while it is not used here of the prince (but cf. 44:3).

■ **46:4–7** In vv 4–7 the exact prescriptions for the offerings for sabbath and new moon begin, and these revert to the style of 45:21–25. In contrast to Passover and autumn festival in 45:21–25, here, as in 45:17a, there is no reference to a sin offering but only to a burnt offering. The fact that here too the שלמים ("final offerings"), which are explicitly mentioned in v 2, are missing suggests perhaps that in vv 4–7 a sacrificial regulation, already independently established, has been joined to the gate regulation of vv 1–3 without being completely adjusted to it. In this connection the thought may have helped that שלמים ("final offerings") is the offering which the prince consumes (according to 44:3) in the vestibule of the outer east gate, undoubtedly in the sacrificial community of his own household (there it is referred to quite generally as לחם "food"), and not the gift offered in fire on behalf of all Israel. Yet it must be stated that the addition in 45:15b and 17b reckons with the fact that the שלמים ("final offerings") too is also one of the offerings that bring about atonement for Israel. On the other hand שלמים ("final offerings") was also missing in the closely related passage 45:21–25.

■ **46:4–5** The sabbath, whose offering is described first of all in vv 4f, has already been mentioned in 20:12f, 16, 20f, 24; 22:8, 26; 23:38; 44:24.[5] Here the sabbath is again mentioned explicitly from the point of view of the offering (see what was said above on the feasts of 45:21ff). This, with six lambs and one ram, is not so copiously provided for as the offerings of the great feasts, but considerably more so than in Nu 28:9 where for the sabbath offering two yearling lambs are required. Admittedly there, in v 10, it is explicitly observed that besides that, the Tamid, the regular daily offering, is also to be offered. According to 28:3, the latter consists of two yearling lambs. Here too the עולה ("burnt offering") is supplemented by the מנחה ("cereal offering"), which, as in 45:24, consists of an ephah for a ram, while the contribution for the lambs is left to the giver's discretion. The instruction for the contribution of oil is a literal repetition of 45:24b. Nu 28:9 requires two tenths of an ephah of fine flour mixed with oil.

■ **46:6–7** The requirements for the day of the new moon are increased vis-à-vis the sabbath by the offering of a bull, to which is added a מנחה ("cereal offering") of one ephah. Nu 28:11ff, on the other hand, requires the increased gift of two bulls, one ram, seven lambs and one goat as a sin offering. The מנחה ("cereal offering") for the bulls there comprises three tenths of an ephah each, for the ram two tenths and for each lamb one tenth of fine flour mixed with oil. The feast of the new moon is occasionally mentioned in older narrative texts (1 Sam 20:5; 2 Kgs 4:23). It even appears in prophetic polemic (Is 1:13; Hos 2:13; Am 8:5). It did not find its way into the older legal texts up to H. Was the connection between this day, which was celebrated by a joyful greeting of the new light (Job 31:26f), and the course of the stars still too strong for Israelite susceptibility? The fact that in Ezekiel 46 and Numbers 28 (cf. in P, also Nu 10:10 as well as Ps 81:4) it reappears with a not inconsiderable emphasis in the offering requirements shows that it had not been suppressed in the people's experience. In the ritualization, strongly focused on the thought of obedience, of the older custom the threat posed by it was no longer so grave. The addition of a goat as a sin offering to the sacrificial requirement in Nu 28:15 can also show how differently the experiences of this day were now orientated.

■ **46:8–10** To the offering regulation there is joined in vv 8–10 a further exposition of the route to be taken in the sanctuary by prince and people of the land. V 8, whose introductory בבוא הנשיא ("when then the prince enters") shows it to be a more precise interpretation of the ובא הנשיא ("then the prince shall enter") of v 2, obviously aims to prevent the misunderstanding that the emergence from the gate structure (ויצא "and he shall go out [again]") of v 2 should be intended as permission to enter the inner court into which he "goes out" from the gateway. At the threshold at which he has been present at the offering in the inner court and on which he has paid homage to God he is to turn round and go back to the outer court by the same way as the one by which he came in. Such, too, was the regulation in 44:3b for the outer

5 See 1,410 on 20:12. But see also Walther Eichrodt, "Der Sabbat bei Hesekiel. Ein Beitrag zur Nachgeschichte des Prophetentextes" in *Lex tua veritas; Festschrift H. Junker* (1961), 65–74.

east gate.

■ **46:9** But the people, on their festive occasions, are commanded not to return, similarly, by the same route, but to go out again through the gate opposite the one by which they entered. The fact that in this connection only the north and south gates are mentioned as entrance and exit gates shows that the regulation of 44:1f about the closed outer east gate here too stands in the background. One may ask whether in this transit regulation there predominates simply the sober intention of preventing congestion on occasions of great crowds in the temple and of insuring an orderly flow of the crowd through the temple from north to south and from south to north. One may ask whether old taboos prohibiting turning round in the sacred precinct are not here ritually consolidated. The southerly direction here (and in 47:1, 19; 48:10, 16 and elsewhere) is נגב. In chapters 40–42 it was always דרום.

■ **46:10** The instruction for the prince, which is added in v 10, is to be closely linked with v 9. Here too we are dealing with the great festival occasions on which the community as a whole comes together. The prince is not to separate himself from the community. As he enters with them (in procession?), so too must he go out with them (see, e.g., the picture in Ps 68:28). Here one must most probably presume a secret attempt to prevent royal veneration, which in the ritual would set the king apart from the community. The prince here is quite strictly regarded as the chief representative of the community.

■ **46:12** This community celebration is contrasted in v 12 with a specific offering on the part of the prince himself. For the נדבה, "the voluntary gift," there is, among the sacrificial laws, no specific regualtion. One may ask whether this special case of the נדבה ("free-will offering"), whose presentation goes back to the austere style of v 2, has not been added to the complex vv 1–3, 8–10 only somewhat later. נדבה ("free-will offering") is frequently linked with נדר, the "voluntary gift" which is promised in a vow and then carries within it as a duty, circumstances permitting, specific temporal obligations. Numbers 30 deals with the redemption of the vow. נדבה ("free-will offering"), on the other hand, seems to signify the gift given spontaneously, with no legal obligation or any preceding obligation in a vow. Thus, according to Ex 35:29; 36:3, the community donates material for the construction of the tent of meeting. So too, however, offerings were spontaneously offered at the sanctuary in the context of the feasts (Am 4:5). Such a spontaneous offering is also presupposed as possible in the case of the prince. It can be עולה ("burnt offering") or שלמים ("final offerings"). In a ritual-type expression, the right to be present in the inner east gate, which he has in the case of the regulated sabbath offering, is granted him on this occasion too. At any rate the gate is not to be kept open for the whole day, but need only be opened for this act on the part of the prince.

■ **46:11** In v 11, then, a disruptive addition has intruded, which repeats the regulation about the מנחה ("cereal offering") at the feast in 45:24 and expands it by the sentence about the מנחה ("cereal offering") for the lamb in 46:5aβ.

■ **46:13–15** *An Appendix on the Tamid: vv 13–15.*

■ **46:13–14** In the form analysis it was shown that vv 13f with their second person singular differ from vv 1–12. From the content point of view we are dealing here with the addition of the presentation of an offering the lack of which has been felt in the sacrifice regulations of 45:18–46:12, but which was not foreseen either in the introductory survey in 45:17. It is a question of the offering which was to be made every day. This is described in vv 13 and 14 in two independent sentences. Initially it is the עולה ("burnt offering") of a yearling lamb without blemish which is to be offered to Yahweh daily in the morning. In addition there is a מנחה ("cereal offering") which is also to be offered to Yahweh every morning. The fact that this cannot be a continuation of the description of the prince's offerings in vv 4–7 can be seen, content-wise, in that here, by contrast with the מנחה ("cereal offering") for the lamb in vv 5–7, the measurement is not left to the person performing the sacrifice, but is precisely regulated: it consists of one sixth of an ephah (of flour) and one third of a hin of oil with which to sprinkle the wheat flour.[6] This recalls the favorite phrase used in P in the description of the מנחה ("cereal offering")—סלת בלולה בשמן ("wheat groats mixed with oil") (Nu 28:12 and elsewhere). But yet, here too, the information is again

6 On סלת see 1,341 on 16:13.

clearly distinguished from the phrases in P by 1) use of language (רסס "to sprinkle") and 2) the measurement of the portion of oil which is omitted in P. The phraseology of v 14 is a halfway stage between the sacrificial regulation in vv 5 and 7, from which it differs by the reduced מנחה ("cereal offering")-requirements, and P. The regulation for this daily מנחה ("cereal offering") is finally designated, as frequently in P (Ex 12:14 and elsewhere), as חקת עולם ("a perpetual ordinance"). The most remarkable thing, however, is the emphasis with which this מנחה ("cereal offering") is also described as מנחה ליהוה ("a cereal offering for Yaweh"). In this connection Gese has correctly observed that one does not have the impression that the מנחה ("cereal offering") is simply an addition to the עולה ("burnt offering"), but that "the two parts are of equal value, standing side by side."[7] But then his further question also acquires significance, whether we do not come across here the pre-exilic situation according to which alongside the daily morning עולה ("burnt offering") there stood an evening מנחה ("cereal offering"). The evening as the time when the מנחה ("cereal offering") was offered is indicated by 1 Kgs 18:29, 36, a text which concerns the northern kingdom. Morning עולה ("burnt offering") and evening מנחה ("cereal offering") are mentioned together in 2 Kgs 16:15 in connection with the Jerusalem cult in the time of Ahaz. By the transfer of the מנחה ("cereal offering") to the morning in Ezek 46:14 the appearance is intended to be given that here too it is a question of an accessory offering as in vv 5 and 7.

■ **46:15** But perhaps the confusion caused by the insertion of the בבקר בבקר ("every morning") of v 13 also in v 14 is to be attributed to the hand which added v 15, in which now any differentiation of the two daily offerings has vanished, and lamb offering and מנחה ("cereal offering") and oil offering are all included in the עולת תמיד ("*tamid*-burnt offering") which is to be offered every morning. Here now we have the explicit mention of the term by which not only the sacrifice ordinance of Numbers 28 calls the daily offering, the absence of which was felt by the person who made the present addition, but also the regulation in Ex 29:38ff. Here too we again find both terms. But now in the morning and in the evening a full עולה ("burnt offering") (each a lamb) and a full מנחה ("cereal offering") (one tenth of an ephah of wheat flour mixed with a quarter of a hin of oil—Ex 29:40 adds further a נסך "drink offering" of a quarter of a hin of wine) are offered. Since the pre-exilic period was already familiar with both morning and evening sacrifice, it is unlikely that Ezek 46:15 intends to reduce the total quantity. Probably its author, by the reworking of vv 13f and the conflation of the two types of offering into a single total offering, was forced to concentrate everything in the morning-*tamid* and to describe only the morning-*tamid*.

Aim

Alongside the offerings for the great festivals, there are placed here the offerings for sabbath and new moon and something is revealed of the order with which prince and people are to observe these days in the sanctuary. Sabbath and new moons are the accents which follow each other in the short periods of the seven-day week and the monthly sequence and which subdivide the normal course of time. With the gift which the prince offers on behalf of his whole people and with their presence, he acknowledges the Lord to whom all time belongs.

In a twofold way the text speaks of the prerogative of the prince among the people and at the same time of his solidarity with them. More closely than all the rest of the community he may approach the sacrifice in the inner court and observe its completion. But this prerogative reaches its highest point where, in this special proximity to which he is called, he throws himself down before his God. To be the first of those who bow before God is the fulfillment of his prerogative. But there is linked with this at the same time the exhortation to solidarity. When the people approach their God on the great festivals, the prince should not set himself apart and seek his own special great festival. In the midst of his people, as leading member of the community he shall be there—there where the community enters the sanctuary as well as there where they leave it.

While all cultic activity on the prince's part on these special days, and even when he wishes to bring his offering out of turn, takes place in the gate to the inner

7 Gese, 84f.

court which is normally closed and which is opened only for these special occasions, there occurs again and again the reminder that access to the presence of God is never simply open, available every day equally to men on their own initiative, but is a gracious possibility ordained always afresh by the will of God.

The person who added vv 13–15 has added to the regulations of vv 1–12 the reference to the offering expected every day by God and has thus made it clear that also the working day which is neither sabbath nor new moon nor great feast expects a gift to God, the God who wishes to be "continuously" (תמיד) honored—just as he has promised "at all times" (לעולם) to be his people's God and to dwell in their midst (43:7, 9).

11. An Appendix on the Inalienable Nature of the Prince's Property

Bibliography

H. Donner
Studien zur Verfassungs- und Verwaltungsgeschichte der Reiche Israel und Juda, Unpub. Diss. (Leipzig, 1956).

Martin Noth
"Das Krongut der israelitischen Könige und seine Verwaltung," *ZDPV* 50 (1927): 211–244.

See also the bibliography to 45:1–8.

46

16 **Thus has [the Lord][a] Yahweh said: If the**
prince gives to one of his sons a present
<out of his inheritance>[b] then it belongs
to his sons. It becomes their property as
an inheritance[c]. 17/ But if he gives a
present out of his inheritance to one of
his servants, then it belongs to him (i.e.
to the servant) until the year of release[a].
Then it returns[b] to the prince. Only with
his sons shall it remain their <inher-
itance>[c]. 18/ And the prince shall not
take any of the inheritance of the people,
displacing them with force from their
property. He shall allocate an inheritance
to his sons from his own property so that
none of my people shall be scattered[a]
each from his property.

46: 16a אדני is lacking in 𝔊 (= 𝔊[967]); 𝔊[B] *κύριος θεός*
16 [sic!]; see Appendix 1.
b 𝔐 נחלתו should, on the basis of 𝔊 *ἐκ τῆς κληρονομίας αὐτοῦ* (𝔏[C] *ex hereditate sua*) and on the basis of the analogous form in v 17, be emended to מנחלתו.
c 𝔖 again abbreviates greatly, omitting the first היא and the whole of v 16b.
17 17a 𝔗 שתא דיובילא mentions here specifically the
year of Jubilee, the regulations for which are to be found in Lev 25. See the exposition.
b On the form ושבת (alongside ושבה Lev 22:13; Is 23:17) see Bauer-Leander §56u".
c 𝔐 נחלתו is, on the evidence of 𝔊 (𝔏[C]), a scribal error for נחלת. Literally: "Only the inheritance of his sons shall belong to them."
18 18a According to Kopf, "Etymologien," 191,
behind Hebrew פוץ stands "the image of the overflowing stream . . . whose waters spread in different directions."

Form

Vv 16–18, in spite of the catchword נשיא ("prince"), are contrasted with what immediately precedes not only by the introductory messenger formula but also by the new subject matter. The section is clearly delimited at the other end by the reintroduction of the guidance scene in vv 19f and thus represents the conclusion of the great complex 44:4–46:18 with its consistent use of messenger formulae.[1] Thematically it is connected with the details about the נשיא ("prince") in the first half of chapter 46. It deals with the prince's right of disposal of his property and with the limits of this right.

Formally, the section at the beginning in v 16 (and v 17) is clearly modeled on the last regulation of the gate ordinances in 46:12 which begins in casuistic style. This rasies the question whether it already presupposes the intervening section, vv 13–15, or whether it once followed directly on v 12. In what follows in vv 16–18 there is admittedly no further sign of the ritual style of vv 2 and 12. As in vv 2–12, here too the נשיא ("prince") is consistently referred to in the third person. In v 18, however, there suddenly appears a first person reference

1 See above p. 443.

to Yahweh which did not occur in vv 1–12. Yahweh speaks of his people as עמי ("my people") which, within chapters 40–48, apart from 44:23, only occurred otherwise in 45:8f.

Setting

There are also other observations in 46:18 which lead to 45:8f. Here too the נשיא ("prince")-section, which clearly presupposes the land allocation to the prince, turns to a gentle polemic against the prince and mentions the temptation to which he is particularly vulnerable, that of oppressing the people. In this connection the verb הונה (here "to displace with force") is used, which occurs also in 45:8 but nowhere else within chapters 40–48. Linguistic form and content as well as the subject matter of the whole complex, which, like 45:1–8, hovers around the question of אחזה ("property"), thus make it very likely that in 46:16–18 the same hand can be seen as was also at work in 45:1–9. The fact that here, in contrast with that passage, the נשיא ("prince") is referred to in the singular, can be easily understood as harmonization with the preceding statements. The person who added 45:1–9 has here too appended an addition to the regulations for the נשיא ("prince").

Interpretation

■ **46:16–18** Pre-exilic accounts reveal that the kings had at their disposal a certain amount of crown property.[2] The basis of this must have been the private landed property of the one who was chosen king. This could have been increased through purchase (2 Sam 24:24; 1 Kgs 16:24; see also 1 Kgs 21:1f). At a change of dynasty the property passed completely to the successor as can be seen, for example, from David's handling of Saul's property (2 Sam 9:7ff; 16:4; 19:30). The continuation of the Naboth story in 1 Kings 21 shows that the king can further increase his crown property by the incorporation of the property of someone on whom a legal sentence has been passed. In addition, 2 Kgs 8:1–6 seems to attest the right to incorporate the property of those who have fled the country. On the "royal right" of incorporation of property 1 Sam 8:14 may also be compared. The same passage makes it clear, in addition, that the king can give away this property as a fief to his "servants," those who are personally bound to him.[3] A similar gift of property as a fief to royal servants is presupposed by 1 Sam 22:7. The spread of crown property throughout the whole of the northern kingdom is clearly attested, according to Noth, by the Samaria ostraca.[4]

By contrast, however, Ezek 45:1–8a, in which the land allocation of 48:1–29 is reflected, shows a very different picture. It is the object of the blueprint of chapter 48 to show the correct and just apportionment of the land, one that is properly regulated with regard to its sacred central point. There is no longer any place here for crown property scattered in this way haphazardly through the land and constantly subject to change. The monarchy, that latecomer in Israel's history, had at one time to establish itself in a land long since divided up among the various groups of people and had to procure its own landed property. In Ezekiel 48 the allocation of royal land, for which, further, the deatils in 48:21–22 should be checked, is removed from such hazards. It is fully assimilated to the allocation of land to the tribes as described in the book of Joshua and incorporated into Yahweh's regulations for allocation.

But then the further conclusion is quite unavoidable. Even in the case of the king's royal property care must be taken that subsequently this good, divine allocation does not fall into disarray. A law like that for daughters' inheritance in Nu 27:1–11 with its appendix in Numbers 36 tries, in the sphere of tribal property, to counter the danger that, in the case of female succession and of the marriage of the woman outside her tribe, landed property from the share of one tribe might pass to that of another. But above all, the law of the year of jubilee in Leviticus 25, in which is incorporated material which goes back to the pre-exilic period,[5] tries to insure that the old, divinely ordained scheme of property does not fall into confusion. In every fiftieth year, according to Lev 25:13b, a clause from the oldest material in the law, "everyone shall return to 'his property' (אחזתו)."[6] That the year of jubilee was known already in the exilic period was also made probable by the discussion about the date in 40:1.[7]

Ezek 46:16–18 now shows the application of these

2 As Noth, "Krongut," has shown.

3 On עבד ("servant") as the royal officer see Zimmerli-Jeremias, 657f.

4 See the map in Noth, "Krongut," 235.

5 According to Elliger, *Leviticus*, 347f.

6 Elliger, *Leviticus*, 336. On Lev 25 see also B. D.

property laws to the crown property allocated to the prince. The legal problem is treated casuistically in two specific cases.

■ **46:16** V 16 deals with the case when the prince shares something of his property with his own sons. מתנה, which can also mean quite generally "gift" (also used in 20:26, 31, 39 of the sacrificial gift), must here too refer to the heritable gift of land. Such a gift of land to a son of the prince is quite harmless since in this case the princely land remains in the prince's family.

■ **46:17** The situation is different in the case of the handing over of princely land as a fief to one of the king's men (עבדיו "his servants"). Here it can be a question only of a temporary grant of the land in question. The year of release will then, here too, restore the original situation and allow the land to revert to the prince.

"Year of release" here certainly does not refer to the sabbatical year (so, e.g., Fohrer). "We know nothing of a seventh year in which property was restored to its original owner."[8] The fact, however, that Jer 34:8, 15, 17 can use the term דרור ("release") in a loose sense even in the context of the liberation of slaves should not allow us to overlook the fact that the present text is dealing only with the return of landed property. In this context the word is used also in Lev 25:10. While Lev 25:13b spoke of the "return" (שוב) of the individual to his property, here it is expressed from the other side, that the property "returns" to the prince. In this way, then, the "inheritance" (נחלה) of the sons is also secured.

■ **46:18** But then v 18 turns aside to warn the prince not to touch the people's property. The term עם הארץ ("people of the land"), which characterized the נשיא ("prince")-sections 45:21–46:12, has vanished here and been replaced by a simple עם ("people"). As in 45:8, but also in Lev 25:14, the verb הונה (here "to displace with force") is used to describe the displacement of individual people from their property, which is warned against, and to make more precise once again the fact that sons are to be given an inheritance from the prince's own property. In the final sentence, which warns against the "scattering" (פוץ) of the people far from their own property, it is possible to hear from afar an echo of the invective against the evil shepherds who had been accused in 34:5f (12) 21 of the wicked scattering of the flocks. The recollection of this passage also shows how here the consideration of the princes (= kings, plural) directed towards the past intrudes from long ago into the sober regulations for the prince of tomorrow.

Aim

46:16–18 selects from the property regulations of the various groups of people the regulation for the prince's property in order to develop it along new lines. In this it becomes clear that even for the most powerful man among the people, who, according to the preceding regulations, had the right to represent the whole people in the sacrifice and to approach the sacred sacrificial act more closely than hitherto anyone from the non-priestly class, property was not something to be treated arbitrarily. Even when dealing with his own property, the powerful ruler must remain aware of the fact that this has been given to him as a gift from God. It is in the last resort to be accounted for as a gift.

This is true in both directions. The prince, when he gives and bestows, may never accomplish this giving in ultimate, personal sovereignty as he alone wishes. His princely giving must take place within restraints; it stands under reservations which no royal power can set aside. Even when the powerful ruler appears to be dealing with his most personal property, his control is a control over property which he has been given.

But it is equally true with regard to what the prince takes. What God has ordained for another is forbidden the prince, even if that other were the least among the people. The image of the flocks which are not to be scattered even by the one who has power over them is in the background of v 18b. Quite explicitly the hand of the real owner stretched out over this flock appears when God describes this people as "my people."

The light in which the prince's property and his freedom vis-à-vis this property are set is equally valid for every property which is given anywhere to someone in power.

Eerdmans, *Alttestamentliche Studien* 4 (Giessen: Töpelmann, 1912), 121–133.

7 See above pp. 346f.

8 Eerdmans (see fn. 6), 125.

12. An Appendix to the Description of the Temple. The Sacrificial Kitchens

Bibliography

A. Lods
"Les cuisines du temple de Jérusalem," *Revue de l'histoire des religions* 127 (1944): 30–54.

46

19 And he brought me through the entrance at
the side of the gate to the sacred <priest-
ly chambers>[a] which face north, and
there was a room at the back[b] towards
the west. 20/ And he said to me: That is
the room in which the priests cook the
guilt offering and the sin offering, <and
here>[a] they bake the cereal offering so
that they do not have to bring it out into
the outer court and (thus) make the
people holy[b].
21 And he led me out into the outer court and
led me to the four corners[a] of the outer
court, and there was a court[b] in (each)
corner of the main court[c]. 22/ In the four

46:
19 19a 𝔐 אל הלשכות הקדש is grammatically impossible and, on the basis of 42:13, to which passage allusion is made here, אל לשכות הקדש should be read. Equally, suspicion is aroused by the following אל הכהנים, according to which the prophet would have been led to the priests in the sacred cells, which, in the context of the whole temple vision of chapters 40–48, would be a completely unique occurrence. Since none of the versions, apart from 𝔙, states this, but the priests are mentioned there (along the lines of 42:13f) as users of the cells, and since, in addition, the immediately following הפנות connects with לשכות as the still grammatically effective substantive, either לכהנים or אשר לכהנים should be read (is 𝔐 אל intended to be an abbreviation of אשר ל'?).

b 𝔐 מקום בירכתם ימה was not understood by 𝔊 *τόπος . . . κεχωρισμένος* (𝔏[C] *locus secretus*), and ימה does not even seem to have existed as a separate word in the text translated by 𝔊 (haplography?). 𝔗 understands, with K, the ending as a suffix, as does 𝔖 אתרא בשפוליה. Thus, Cooke, e.g., believes, with reference to Gen 49:13, that בירכתָם should be read. Since, however, P too, in Ex 26:23; 36:28, knows the absolute usage of בירכתים and indeed even attests in 26:27; 36:32 with its לירכתים ימה the analogous combination with the compass direction, the reading of Q לירכתַיִם is to be preferred. 𝔙 *locus vergens (ad occidentem).*

20 20a The second אשר in 𝔐 can be understood as the resumption of the first אשר, but its asyndetical addition produces a very harsh effect. Thus the reading suggested by 𝔊 *καὶ ἐκεῖ* (𝔏[C] *et ibi,* see also 𝔖 ואפין בה), ושם, is to be preferred.

b 𝔐 לקדש. Hebrew loves to express a consequence in a final position.

21 21a Masculine מקצועי is strange alongside the feminine plural מקצעות in v 22 (41:22; also Ex 26:24; 36:29). Yet the observations made, e.g., in connection with חלון (40:25 note b) prohibit any necessity to make them uniform.

b 𝔙 *atriolum* interprets the חצר, which is used here too in 𝔐, in accordance with the sense and thereby anticipates v 22.

c The distributive repetition of חצר במקצע החצר, which recurs in 𝔊 𝔗 𝔖 (in 𝔖 this time interpreted in

corners of the main court were <small>[a] courts, forty (cubits) the length and thirty (cubits) the breadth. Of one size were all four [at the corners][b]. 23/ And there was a stone wall[a] round about in them[b], in all four, and there were cooking places round about, set[c] at the foot of the walls. 24/ And he said to me: These are the kitchens[a] where the temple servants shall cook the (meal) offerings of the people.

comfortable breadth ודרתא אחרתא בסטרא אחרנא דדרתא), is hinted at in 𝔙 *atriola singula,* is missing in Eb 22 (result of homoioteleuton?).

22 22a 𝔐 קטרות is presupposed by 𝔗 מקטרן "joined" (*DalmanWB,* 359) and doubtless also by 𝔙 *disposita. B. Mid.* II 5b cites the passage and refers it to the smoke which mounts from these unroofed (ולא היו מקורות) places. Kopf, "Etymologien," 199, wishes, on the basis of Arabic *qṭr* "couple together, arrange in a row one behind the other," to understand 𝔐 as "lying in a row one behind the other." Driver, "Ezekiel," 311f, points to Akkadian *qaṭāru* "tie" and suggests a meaning "attached, flanking." But 𝔊 *αὐλὴ μικρά* (𝔊[967] *αὐλαὶ μικραί*), 𝔏[C] *atrium pusillum* and 𝔖 דקדקתא make it probable that we have here a scribal error for קטנות.

b 𝔐 מהקצעות was, as the *puncta extraordinaria* show (Bauer-Leander §6s), already suspect in the eyes of the Masoretes. The word is vocalised by 𝔐 as a hop'al participle: "corner rooms" (? Bauer-Leander §25h'; 51a'). More probably what we have here is the definite noun מקצעות which has again wrongly found its way as a gloss into the text.

23 23a 𝔐 טור is later taken up again by טירה. On this cf. 25:4. 𝔊 translates both, inaccurately, by *ἐξέδραι.* 𝔖, which reproduces only v 23a (abbreviated), similarly by אכסדרא; 𝔗 correctly in both passages נדבכין, while 𝔙 oscillates between *paries* and *porticus.*

b 𝔐 is already attested by 𝔊 and is therefore surely not to be emended (*pace* BH[3]) to the smoother להם attested by 2 MSS.

c The uninflected עשוי of 𝔐 עשוי מתחת has occurred already in 40:17 (cf. note b). Thus the emendation to עשוים תחת suggested by Ehrlich, *Randglossen,* Driver ("Ezekiel," 312) or to עשויות תחת according to Bertholet, Gese and others is not absolutely necessary. Driver takes תחת in the sense of "close up against."

24 24a 𝔐 בית המבשלים, which is rendered by 𝔊 *οἱ οἶκοι τῶν μαγείρων* (𝔏[C]) as a plural, by 𝔙 𝔗 𝔖, disregarding 𝔐 אלה, as a singular, is to be understood with Cooke, following Gesenius-Kautzsch §124r, as a compound expression, which, as a grammatical unit, is inflected only in the second word. Yet a scribal error for בתי המבשלים can also not be excluded (Lods).

Form

From the purely formal point of view one might ask whether the section which begins in 46:19 with a renewed guidance formula and is continued by another in v 21 does not also reach over into chapter 47, which again contains a large number of guidance verbs. In this case it is the observation of content, that 46:19–24 deals with the temple kitchens while 47:1ff then leads the perspective out into the land around the temple, which necessitates the assumption of a caesura after v 24. To what extent there are then other, additional differences between 46:19–24, which, e.g., contain nothing about measurements by the "man," and 47:1ff will require to be shown.

The examination of content also warns against dividing vv 19–24, in spite of the two reported guidances, into two independent sections, vv 19–20 and vv 21–24. The common subject matter of "sacrificial kitchens" links the two sections together. In addition, however, it will emerge that with the separation of the two sections, which in their association link together the statements about priests and Levites, precisely an essential element would be destroyed.

Nor will it do, in view of the quite remarkably late appearance of this section descriptive of the temple structure, to try to find, as Cooke at least endeavors, separate positions in the description of the temple structure in chapters 40–42 for each of the sections vv 19–20 and 21–24, positions in which the two elements might once have stood (vv 19f after 42:14; vv 21–24 after 40:17). The two elements ought to be left together and be understood in their connection with each other.

Formally the two halves of the double unit are constructed quite similarly on the pattern of the guidance narrative, which occurred in 40:1–37, 47–49; 41:1–4 in its most elaborate form, intensified with great restraint towards a specific goal, and was then rudely imitated in the later sections 40:44–46; 41:21b–22; 42:1–14. A guidance which leads to immediately in front of a specific object (in 40:44–46 the verb of leading is entirely omitted) is followed by an interpretative word from the man, which usually begins with a demonstrative pronoun and mentions the object in view in a concise nominal sentence. This form of the declaratory oracle, which is found in its purest form in 41:4 (also 41:22), is internally no longer completely observed in 40:45f and is most extensively transformed in 42:13f, recurs in 46:20 and 46:24 in a relatively pure form. Admittedly there is mingled with the interpretation, which in 41:4 and 41:22 is confined to the naming, here as in 40:45f and 42:13f an element of instruction. There occurs not only a naming in a nominal sentence, but in the imperfect a specific instruction is given. Differences of proportion, whereby the guidance in 46:21–24 is much fuller in its structure than are vv 19f, while exactly the reverse is true of the interpretative words, are of no further significance for an assessment of the form.

Setting

The first guidance scene has the prophet enter once again one of the priestly sacristies which were introduced in 42:1–14. A part of these is described in more detail. In this respect, vv 19f, and therefore then surely the whole complex of vv 19–24, represent a supplement to 42:1–14, a section which itself has already been inserted secondarily in its context. The fact that this supplement was no longer inserted where it really belongs but has found its place at the end of 44:4–46:18, a complex which has arisen as the result of a lively development, shows that it emerged only at a not inconsiderable lapse of time after 42:1–14.

There is, in addition, a second observation. The juxtaposition of vv 19f and vv 21–24 corresponds to the juxtaposition of the priests and the Levites, whose eating places and work places are described in the two sections of the double guidance. In this connection it can be seen that certainly there is a specific reference to "priests" (v 20), but not, on the other hand, to "Levites." For them there is used simply the designation "those who provide the service of the temple" (v 24). That corresponds to the description of the Levites' duties in 44:11 (see also v 14) and occurs in 45:5, also in this participial form, as a description of the Levites. In contrast to 40:46, however, those who see to the service of the temple are not called priests here and not even, as in 44:10ff and 45:5, Levites. The polemical devaluation of the Levites here even seems to surpass what can be ascertained in chapters 44f. Thus one can certainly not consider 46:19–24 as older than 45:1–8, but at most contemporary with it. Since 46:19–24 seems to presuppose the latest sections of the complex 44:4–46:18, it is to be considered, in spite of its skillful imitation of the older forms, as a very late element which can at best have arisen contemporaneous with that appendix which is along the same lines as 45:1–8 and with which it is indeed immediately connected, 46:16–18. There is, here, however, no reference to the נשיא ("prince"). These verses are interested solely in the hierarchy of the priesthood and in the strict observance of the limits of holiness in the temple.

Interpretation

■ **46:19–20** The last guidance route (44:4) had led the prophet to the front of the temple building, where, according to the present text, all the instructions in

44:6–46:18 were addressed to him. Now, with no details being given of the route, he is brought to the entrance at the side of the (inner north) gate which leads to the holy, north-facing priestly sacristies. This is surely the "entrance" (מבוא) mentioned in 42:9 which opens eastwards into the outer court and leads to the northern sacristy, which in 42:1ff is located with reference to the structures of the inner court. The location here "at the side of the gate" is somewhat surprising, since, if the above reconstruction is correct, the entrance after all lies more than a hundred cubits from the gate. Nothing is said here about the layout of the building which rises in steps, but only of that part of it which lies over on the west side. There the prophet observes unexpectedly (והנה) a מקום ("room, place"). The peculiar character of this "place" is not described in any detail. Of its purpose it is simply stated: There the flesh of אשם ("the guilt offering") and חטאת ("the sin offering") is to be cooked and the מנחה ("cereal offering") baked. In everything that is mentioned here what are referred to are those parts of the offerings which, according to 44:29, are the priests' share. The parts of the אשם ("guilt offering") and the חטאת ("sin offering") which are burned on the altar for Yahweh and the additional מנחה ("cereal offering"), the kneaded dough of wheat flour and oil, are not cooked or baked beforehand. On the other hand, the dough which is set aside for the priests' food requires further preparation. In contrast to 1 Sam 2:15, where Eli's greedy sons take the priests' share uncooked because they want to roast it for themselves, only the cooking of the priests' food is referred to here. The showbread, which lies on the table before Yahweh (41:22) and subsequently is no doubt at the priest's disposal (1 Sam 21:5), is not specifically mentioned in this connection. The explicit aim of the passage is the insuring of the highly sacred part of the offering which is the priest's due and which must not be removed from the inner sanctum of the temple. The information in 42:13, according to which the three parts of the offering mentioned there are to be eaten by the priests in the holy sacristies, clearly was insufficient for the author of 46:19f. It must, in addition, be insured that even the preparation of this sacred food must not take place outside that sacred precinct. Similarly, in 44:19, reference was made to the dangerous infection of the people by the "holy." In this prohibition the concern is with the carrying out of the holy to the "people," undoubtedly not only because of genuine concern at the danger to those outside of unprepared contact with the holy. On such a threat see 2 Sam 6:6f and Lev 10:1f.

■ **46:21–24** The parallel guidance narrative in vv 21–24 leads us out into the outer court. The prophet is led into its four corners. In all of them he sees smaller sections marked off, measuring forty cubits by thirty. Nothing more precise is said about the disposition of length and breadth in relation to the temple as a whole. G. Sauer supposes behind the figures forty and thirty the figure seventy as the size actually intended.[1] At any rate it is noticeable that these figures do not accord with the systematic reckoning of the temple measurements in chapters 40–42.

The small courts are marked off by layers of stones. On טור ("wall") see 1 Kgs 6:36; 7:4, 12, where what is envisaged is an artistic wall structure of hewn stones overlaid with wooden beams.[2] In the present passage, what is envisaged is a simpler construction of "stones laid side by side forming a fence,"[3] beside which lie the fireplaces on which the Levites who see to the service in the "temple" cook the portions of the זבח ("sacrifice")-offering for the congregation. Here too we are dealing not with the preparation for the offering which, according to 40:38–43, is prepared in the inner north gate, but with the cooking of the portion used as a meal by the people of the land, who, it is true, must be clean in order to enter the sanctuary but who are not sanctified in a heightened sense. It is, however, significant that no further word is wasted here on the quality of this lay congregation. The real concern of 46:19–24 is with the delimitation of the outer from the inner, sacred precinct. Admittedly in the much more ample layout of cooking facilities in the outer court, one can discern the concern for the large number of participants from the lay congregation for whom the sacrificial meal is to be provided. In addition the possibility cannot be excluded that the present regulation is intended to prevent the abuse of preparing the meal component of the זבח ("sacrifice") outside the temple, perhaps in the houses of the city. But

1 Georg Sauer, *Die Sprüche Agurs,* BWANT 5,4 (Stuttgart: Kohlhammer, 1963), 86.

2 Noth, *Könige,* 128.

3 According to Gesenius-Buhl.

that, too, is not explicitly stated.

Lods has gathered together the scanty references from the pre-exilic period which might refer to the preparation of the meal portion in the sanctuary. They occur in 1 Sam 2:12–17; 9:22–24; possibly in Dtn 16:7. They do not provide a clear picture. P says nothing about sacrificial kitchens. When then 2 Chr 35:11–13, in its description of Josiah's passover, states that the Levites not only prepare the passover animals but also cook the portions to be eaten and bring them to the people for their meal, then one can certainly conclude that sacrificial kitchens had been set up in the temple. *B. Mid.* I 4 refers to two cells at the Nicanor gate. One is said to have been the "cell of the house of the baker of the sacrificial cakes." I 6 mentions in the "warm house" (בית המוקד) *inter alia* the chamber of the bakers of the showbread. In the wider world around Israel excavations have revealed particularly clearly in third dynasty Ur kitchen-structures in the temple of Gig-Par-Ku.[4] H. Frankfort found similar evidence in *tell asmar.* In Egypt, too, reports from Karnak indicate the existence of temple kitchens.

Aim

46:19–24 show the extent to which planning and thinking about the sacrificial cult in the rebuilt temple in Jerusalem entered into the details of how it was to be carried out. The verses show once again the concern already noted in 42:1–14 to protect strictly the ultra holy from the outer sphere. Thus one would have to repeat here what has been said above about 42:1–14.[5]

4 C. Leonard Woolley, "The Excavations at Ur, 1925–6," *The Antiquaries Journal* 6 (1926): 365–401.

5 See above p. 401.

C. The Land Around the new Sanctuary

What is described in the two final chapters of the great temple vision does not represent a formally self-contained unit. It is, however, held together thematically by the intention of saying something about the land, which is determined from the perspective of the center of the sanctuary. While the mysterious visionary spectacle of 47:1–12 makes visible the blessing which flows from the sanctuary into the easterly region, 47:13–48:29 develops, in the style of a list, the regulations for the new allocation of land. The same style is also characteristic of the appendix 48:30–35, which speaks of the gates and of the new name of the city and, in its content, quite surprisingly breaks free from what has been expounded hitherto in chapters 40–48. Here too the various sections, which, both in form and in content, are characteristically different from each other, will be examined separately.

1. The Temple Stream

Bibliography
Felix Marie Abel
Une croisière autour de la mer Morte, 1911.
Felix Marie Abel
"Notes complémentaires sur la mer Morte," *RB* 38 (1929): 237–260.
Max Blanckenhorn
"Entstehung und Geschichte des Todten Meeres. Ein Beitrag zur Geologie Palästinas," *ZDPV* 19 (1896): 1–59.
Gustaf Dalman
"Die Wasserversorgung des ältesten Jerusalem," *PJ* 14 (1918): 47–72.
William R. Farmer
"The Geography of Ezekiel's River of Life," *BA* 19 (1956): 17–22.
B. Mazar, Trude Dothan, and I. Dunayevsky
En-Gedi. The First and Second Seasons of Excavations, 1961–62, *'Atiqot* English Series 5 (Jerusalem, 1966).

47

1 And he led me back[a] to the doorway of the
temple, and there was water coming out
from under the threshold[a] of the temple
flowing eastwards, for the front of the
temple (faced) east[b]. And the water
flowed down [underneath][c] on the right
side of the temple, south of the altar.
2 And he led me out through the north gate[a],
round the outside <to the gate which
faces east>[b] and <the>[c] water trickled[d]

47: 1a 𝔐 וישבני. 𝔊 *καὶ εἰσήγαγέ με* as, e.g., 46:19.
1 Then 𝔐 מפתן is again rendered, as in 9:3; 10:4, by *αἴθριον* (𝔏^C^ *subtus de eo quod erat sub aere*). 46:2 (= 𝔊 v 3) *πρόθυρον*, which is used here (in the plural) as the rendering of פתח.

b The clause is missing in 𝔊, but does not have to be deleted from 𝔐 as a gloss (Cooke and others, following Cornill).

c 𝔐 מתחת is not attested by 𝔊 (𝔏^C^) 𝔅 𝔖 and is a not entirely correct repetition of the preceding מתחת. Here in fact we are no longer concerned with the place where the water wells up but with the first stretch along the south side of the front wall. The altar stands in the way of a direct easterly flow. מכתף does not need to be emended to לכתף, since מן can also express a "locality, direction, side" (Gesenius-Buhl, *s. v.,* 1 c).

2 2a On 𝔐 שער צפונה see 46:9 note a.

b In 𝔐, שער החוץ דרך הפונה should be deleted as a double scribal error. Since there is never any reference to a שער החוץ and since, in addition, החוץ is not attested by 𝔊 (𝔏^C^) 𝔖, the repetition of the immediately preceding חוץ must be regarded as an explanatory gloss. Its insertion will be due to the subsequent corruption of the words to דרך הפונה. The original הפונה דרך קדים naturally belongs to שער; see on this, e.g., 44:1; 46:1, 12. The corruption has caused great confusion. 𝔊 𝔏^C^ 𝔖, since דרך obviously did not seem quite right to them, speak of a court facing east, while 𝔗, with a correct instinct, abruptly inserts after דרך (= אורח) an additional תרעא.

out on the south side.
3 [But when the man came out to the east
with the measuring cord[a] in his hand,][b]
He measured a thousand cubits[c] and let
me pass through[d] the water—water up
to the ankles[e]. 4/ And he measured a
thousand (cubits more) and let me pass
through[a] the water—<water> up to the
knees[b]. And he measured a thousand
(cubits more) and let me pass through[a]—
water up to the loins. 5/ And he meas-
ured a thousand (cubits more)—a
stream[a] which I could no longer walk
through[b], for the water was deep[c], water

c On the basis of 𝔊, since we are dealing with the water already mentioned in v 1, 𝔐 מים should be provided with the article which has fallen out through haplography.

d פכה, an onomatopoetic formation, is attested only here in the OT. But see also פך "bottle, jug" and the same phonetic image also in בקבק "bottle."

3 3a קו only here in Ezekiel. 40:3 mentioned פתיל פשתים and קנה המדה.

b 𝔐 בצאת האיש קדים seems already to have been available to 𝔊 in approximately the same wording *καθὼς ἔξοδος ἀνδρὸς ἐξ ἐναντίας*. But it cannot be the original text. Since statements about changes of place are otherwise usually in the form of guidance statements about the prophet, the reading ויוצאני (cf. v 2) might suggest itself. According to Gese, 90 note 1, 𝔐 בצאת would then be a conscious secondary alteration which endeavored to avoid the false impression that the man leads the prophet out through the closed east gate. Yet, the alteration of the text is not entirely unobjectionable, either graphically or factually, since, besides the unusual בצאת referring to the man, also the explicit mention of האיש at this particular point might seem strange, and since the measuring instrument is designated by an expression not hitherto used (note a), the observation about the man, which at this point gives an impression of being secondary, is probably to be regarded as an addition, the point of which is to mention explicitly once again, just before the measurements which now follow, the measuring instrument in the man's hand. See also what has been said above pp. 348f on 40:5.

c Literally: "a thousand with the cubit." 𝔊 (𝔏[C]) *ἐν τῷ μέτρῳ*.

d 𝔐 ויעברני is understood, here and in what follows, by 𝔊 as a qal *καὶ διῆλθεν*.

e 𝔐 אפסים, *hapax legomenon,* perhaps related to פסים. 𝔊 (*ὕδωρ*) *αφέσεως* is surely a transcription which has subsequently been made to look elegant. 𝔏[C] *usque ad femora* comes nearer the meaning. 𝔙 *ad talos* gets it exactly, as does 𝔖 עדמא לקורצלא. 𝔗 מי קרצולין and 𝔊[Qmg] 𝔖[hmg] 'ΑΣΘ *ἕως ἀστραγάλων*. Boettcher, *Neue Aehrenlese,* 191: "points of the foot."

4 4a Cf. v 3 note d.

b 𝔐 מים ברכים. The parallelism of the other statements and 𝔗 מי דכובין demand מי ברכים. The assumption of a construct form מֵים (L. Kopf, "Arabische Etymologien und Parallelen zum Bibelwörterbuch," *VT* 9 [1959]: 261) is hardly to be recommended. 𝔊[967], in a spiritualizing reference to ברכה "blessing," *ὕδωρ εὐλογίας*. 𝔊[BAQ] *ὕδωρ ἕως τῶν μηρῶν*.

5 5a 𝔐 נחל is missing in 𝔊 (𝔏[C]).

b 𝔊 *καὶ ὀυκ ἠδύνατο διελθεῖν* refers the expression, as it has already done with the earlier expressions about passing through the water, to the man. In the light of the foregoing, 𝔐 provides the original text. The test of the passability of the stream is here too the prophet's affair.

c 𝔐 גאו, really "high." 𝔊 humanizes it *ἐξύβριζε τὸ*

to swim in[d], a stream which can no
longer be walked through[e].
6 And he said to me: Have you seen, son of
man?[a] [And he led me back to the bank of
the stream[b]. 7/ When <I came back>[a],
there were on[b] the bank of the stream
very many trees[c], on both sides. 8/ And
he said to me:][a] This water goes out to
the eastern region[b] and flows down into[c]

ὕδωρ, and 𝔏^{C} is even stronger *contumeliam faciebant.* 𝔙 *intumuerant.* 𝔗 תקיפו, 𝔖 סגיו.

d 𝔐 מי שחו was not understood by the versions. 𝔊 ὡς ῥοῖζος χειμάρρου "like the raging of the winter stream," 𝔙 *profundi,* 𝔗 מי סחוא, 𝔖 עשנת.

e Rautenberg, "Zukunftsthora," wishes to delete completely this clause, which is abbreviated in 𝔊. Cooke, on the other hand, sees in the preceding אשר לא אוכל לעבר a doublet of v 5bβ.

6 6a The question connected with the address הראית בן אדם is elsewhere in Ezekiel (8:12, 15, 17, but see also 1 Kgs 20:13; 21:29; Jer 3:6) the prelude to a further communication from Yahweh. The present passage is unusual in that the speech of Yahweh breaks off immediately after this prelude and continues only after a new guidance statement in v 8, with repeated ויאמר אלי but without a further prelude, and provides precisely the explanation which was expected on the basis of vv 1–5. The guidance statement, which in vv 6b, 7 interrupts the speech, introduces (surprisingly, in a reference back to the route that has already begun) into the vision an element which is then interpreted in v 12 with the same vocabulary only sightly varied (עץ על שפת הנחל מזה ומזה). One can scarcely avoid the conclusion that vv 6b, 7 have been inserted secondarily, in a very unskillful fashion, interrupting the speech that has already begun, and have, by the repetition of the ויאמר אלי in v 8, been accommodated to the text.

b The guidance formula ויולכי has its prototype in 40:24; 43:1. On the וישבני, which has been added to it specifically in the present passage and which is taken up again in v 7 (cf. note a) and is therefore not to be emended on the basis of 𝔖 ואותבני to וַיְשִׁבֵנִי (so BH^3; 𝔊 𝔏^{C} omit it completely), see v 1 as well as 44:1. Thus it seems to be the idea of the addition that the prophet, who has climbed down into the stream (Cornill: "doubtless unable to swim"), is brought back to the bank and thus becomes aware of the trees there. The clause introduces an unexpected element into the basic account which is composed in solemn four-stress lines. שפת הנחל is an accusative of direction, see Brockelmann §89. The insertion of a preposition such as then appears in the versions is unnecessary (*pace* BH^3, Bertholet, Fohrer).

7 7a 𝔐 בשובני. Bauer-Leander §29h: "Scribal error brought about by וַיְשִׁבֵנִי, v 6 (or a formation analogous to that?)." According to Driver, "Ezekiel," 312, transitive שוב occurs only in the expression שוב שבות and in Ps 85:5; Na 2:3. Thus, Driver too proposes the emendation to בְּשׁוּבֵנוּ or בשובי.

b על–אל cf. 1:17 note a.

c 𝔖 already anticipates אילנא דטב.

8 8a Cf. v 6 note a.

b The place references are understood by 𝔊 (𝔏^{C}) as regional names: εἰς τὴν Γαλιλαίαν (τὴν πρὸς ἀνατολάς) and ἐπὶ τὴν Ἀραβίαν. 𝔙 connects גלילה with גל "heap of stones" and translates *ad tumulos sabuli*

the Arabah[b] and into the sea, into the <bitter, salty waters>[d] and the waters will become fresh[e]. 9/ [And it will be that all living creatures which swarm in that place which <the stream>[a] reaches will live. And the fish will be very numerous because that water reaches there—and they (i.e. the waters) will become fresh.][b] And where the stream reaches, everything will live. 10/ [And it will be[a]—fishermen will stand beside it[a]. From En-

orientalis and *ad plana deserti.* 𝔊 לגרביא has misunderstood על הערבה. On גלילה, which has not yet been certainly interpreted, see Noth, *Josua,* 70, 13:2 note a.

c אל–על cf. 1:17 note a.

d 𝔐 הימה המוצאים. The plural ending of the second word, which seems to be in apposition to the first, makes הימה suspect and commends as the original text the המים presupposed by 𝔊 (𝔏[C]) 𝔖. 𝔅 apparently regards אל הימה as a mere repetition and omits it. המים is taken up again in the continuing final clause. But המוצאים too, even if it appears to have been presupposed by 𝔊 (τὸ ὕδωρ) τῆς διεκβολῆς "(the water) of the break-through (or of the outburst)," 𝔏[C] *(aquam) emissionis,* 𝔅 *et exibunt,* 𝔗 מתפקין (לימא רבא), can scarcely be original. Driver, "Linguistic Problems," 186f, wishes to derive it from צוא (cf. צֹאָה): "made dirty." 𝔖 סריא (במיא) "(in the) stinking (water)," even if it shows in what follows ובסמין מיא "and sweet smelling does the water become" how freely 𝔖 translates, at least points in the right direction. The solution which is graphically simplest is afforded by a reading החמוצים, with which may be compared the חמיץ "salted" of Is 30:24. חמוץ contains, not the objective substance designation "salt" (on this cf. v 11), but, as was correctly felt in 𝔖 even in an inexact rendering, the subjective taste experience.

e On the form וְנִרְפּאוּ cf. Bauer-Leander §54r.

9 9a The dual נחלים in 𝔐 is incomprehensible and not attested by any version. At the most in the מי נחלא of 𝔗 could be seen a feeble attempt to come to terms, admittedly in a very free way, with the consonantal text of 𝔐. הנחל should be read. It is perhaps also advisable to read with Eb 22 a preceding שמה.

b The surprising return of וירפאו to the concluding statement of v 8, which is not expected here again, together with the diffuseness of the earlier text of v 9, which appears to be summarized again more concisely in the final part, arouses the suspicion of secondary supplementation. This has the aim (as in vv 6b, 7) of preparing the way for what is to follow. Here it is a question of abundance of fish. Thus the supplementer must already have had in front of him v 10, which does not, however, require this preparation; but cf. v 10 note a. The idea of its being a secondary addition is supported also by the loose connection by means of the formulaic והיה. 𝔖, with its inclination to abbreviate, has omitted the conclusion from וחי on.

10 10a 𝔐 והיה has been read by 𝔊 (𝔏[C]) ζήσεται (𝔊[967] καὶ ζήσεται) as (ו)חיה and connected with the end of v 9. In 𝔅 𝔖 it is missing entirely, while 𝔗 ויהי אתר למקם connects it with 𝔐 ועמדו. On the form of 𝔐, in which והיה represents "a mere introductory formula" for the immediately following verb, see S. R. Driver, *Hebrew Tenses* §121, Obs. 1. Since, then, the עליו which follows ועמדו refers unmistakably not to the הנחל which precedes in v 9bβ but to the ימה of v 8,

gedi as far as En-eglaim nets will be[b] spread out to dry. <Of very many kinds>[c] will <its>[d] fish be, like the fish of the great sea, very numerous.] [11/ Its swamps[a] (however) and its pools[b], they will not become fresh—they will be used for salt[c].][d] 12/ By the stream, however—on both its banks—grow fruit trees[a] of every kind. Their leaves[b] do not wither, nor does their fruit come to an end. Every month[c] they produce fresh fruit, for its (i.e. the stream's) water flows out of the sanctuary, and their fruit is used[d] for food and their leaves[b] for healing[e].

there arises also in the case of v 10 the suspicion that it is a secondary elaboration. This is supported here too by the formulaic והיה, cf. v 9 note b. The statements about the נחל are continued in v 12.

b 𝔐 יהיו regards as the subject of the sentence the two places which have just been mentioned. The versions, however, are unanimous in suggesting a reading יהיה, which also fits the text from the content point of view.

c 𝔐 למינה, on the spelling see Bauer-Leander §67f and 29 1m′. Literally: "According to its kind will its fish supply (=according to their kind will its fish) be."

d 𝔐 דגתם is still determined by והיו, cf. note b. On the basis of 𝔊 𝔙, דגתו should be read.

11 11a 𝔐 בצאתו is, on the basis of the parallel statement, certainly to be regarded as the plural of בצה (occurs also in Job 8:11; 40:21; see also בץ "mud" Jer 38:22) and to be corrected to בצותיו. Bauer-Leander §74h′: "Scribal error." 𝔊 καὶ ἐν τῇ διεκβολῇ ($\mathfrak{L}^{C}$ *emissio*) sees in it, as already in מוצאים (v 8), the root יצא. Is it thinking here of an outlet? The phrase καὶ ἐν τῇ ἐπιστροφῇ αὐτοῦ, which it adds (with no support in 𝔐) by way of correspondence, will then designate the "allocation," i.e. the inflow. The same idea is also suggested by the double expression in 𝔖 ומפקנוהי ומעלנוהי, by the second word of which 𝔖 tries to render the וגבאיו of 𝔐 (note b). 𝔙 correctly *in littoribus*.

b 𝔐 וגבאיו from גבא (also in Is 30:14). 𝔊 καὶ ἐν τῇ ὑπεράρσει αὐτοῦ ($\mathfrak{L}^{C}$ *et in elatione*) connects the word, which it did not understand, with the root גבה. In this connection it may be thinking of flood points. 𝔗 פצידוהי "watercourses." 𝔖 cf. note a.

c 𝔐 למלח. 𝔗 clarifies למחפוריין דמלח "for salt pits."

d This parenthetical observation, which interrupts in somewhat schoolmasterly fashion the description of the marvelous effects of the stream, surely belongs to a later hand.

12 12a Literally: food trees. 𝔊 ξύλον βρώσιμον. 𝔙 *lignum pomiferum*.

b 𝔐 עלהו has, on both occasions, not been understood by 𝔊: ἐπ᾽ αὐτοῦ ($\mathfrak{L}^{C}$ *in eo*), ἀνάβασις αὐτῶν ($\mathfrak{L}^{C}$ *ascensio eius*).

c 𝔐 לחדשיו, misunderstood by 𝔊 ($\mathfrak{L}^{C}$) τῆς καινότητος αὐτοῦ *(novitatis eius)*, too narrowly defined by 𝔖 ובכל ריש ירחא.

d 𝔐 והיו. With Q Eb 22 and on the basis of 𝔊 (καὶ ἔσται), the reading והיה is to be preferred.

e תרופה occurs again in Sir 38:4.

Form

Since 47:13 begins abruptly, without any explicit proclamatory commission, with an introductory messenger formula and since the following description of the frontiers of the future land of Israel leads stylistically, and as to content, into a quite different sphere, there can be no doubt as to the delimitation of the end of 47:1–12.

The unit is again in the form of a guidance scene. From the place in front of the temple, to which the prophet is first of all led back (וישבני "and he led me back"), he is led round (ויסבני "and he led me round") by a detour via the north gate out of the temple precinct

(ויוצאני "and he led me out") and via its northern corner to the outer east gate and then follows the course of the temple stream, through which the man makes him pass three times (ויעברני "and he let me pass" vv 3b, 4a, 4b). By contrast, the information about the prophet's being brought back in v 6b (ויולכני וישבני "and he led me back"), and in v 7 which depends on it, must be part of a secondary addition (v 6 note a).

With these details about transportation there are connected once again, as in the basic unit of chapters 40–42, details of measurements. Four times the man measures off a distance of a thousand cubits (וימד "and he measured" vv 3, 4a, 4b, 5). The exposition will show that the measuring process here fulfills a quite different function from that in chapters 40–42 and could actually be dispensed with without loss. It is to be understood only from the perspective of the model of chapters 40–42. Even in the fourfold nature of the measurement an element of stylization can be observed. The number four has already been noted as the number of comprehensive totality which has a part to play again and again in the book of Ezekiel.[1] In the present passage the declaratory value of the number four is much more in the background. What is expressed, rather, in the various stages is simply a total process which reaches its culmination in the fourth measurement. This fourfold measuring has no deeper significance for what the section is saying.

The earlier guidance scenes are recalled also by the further observation that the guidance and measuring, which have presented the prophet in a visionary way (והנה "and see" vv 1, 2b) with an unexpected state of affairs, are followed by an explanatory statement by the guiding figure. This is no longer, as in 41:4, 22, in the form of declaratory naming. It is, however, also not, as was observed in 40:45f; 42:13f; 46:20, 24, in the form of a veiled legal regulation, but describes the wonderful way in which the stream which flows from the temple spring effects healing in its further course in all the area round about it. We are dealing here with a pure proclamation of healing for the sick places in the land, with which Cooke correctly compares the proclamations of salvation for the delivered land in 34:26–30; 36:8–12, 30–36; 37:25–28. However different the details of content may be, these passages have in common the proclamation of divine deliverance for the land which has hitherto been afflicted with disaster. Within chapters 40–48, 47:1–12 are most closely connected with the proclamation of Yahweh's eternal presence in the temple in 43:7–9. Except that there, in the proclamation of salvation, there was entwined an element of demand, of which there is no trace in 47:1–12.

Setting

When one passes from the double guidance scene of 46:19–24 into the context of 47:1–12 one is at once aware of the different world which one has entered. Reference has already been made to the freedom with which, without any secondary aim of regimentation, future salvation is here promised for the territory outside the sanctuary. Certainly, here too, when the prophet is led out of the sanctuary, the rule about the closed east gate is observed. Thus, in any event, 44:1–2 and 43:1–11 (12) are both among the passages presupposed by 47:1–12. There is no reference to the existence of double doors, so that the knowledge also of 46:1, where a closing (limited as to time and aimed especially at the laity) of the inner east gate is mentioned, cannot be claimed. But in addition in 47:1–12 there is no indication of the narrow concern for the correct gradation of the degrees of sanctity, for the differentiation of the laity from the priests and, within the priesthood, again between the Zadokites and the Levites. Nor is there any hint anywhere of reflections about the prince. Instead there is reported, with great lack of concern, that the water, which is empowered in the innermost sanctum by the abundance of holiness on the part of the most holy one, flows out from the sanctuary into the dried up, salty region of mysterious curses without there being given the least hint of ritual protection from the stream which emerges from the realm of the holy. Out there it heals what is sick. The full beneficent effect of God's taking up residence in his people's midst, which was spoken of in 43:1ff, is here unfolded.

Thus one cannot avoid associating 47:1–12 closely with 43:1ff. In that case, we are dealing with a remarkably non-cultic continuation of what was begun there.

1 See 1,120.

The account of the closed east gate, which in its turn is connected with 43:1ff, forms the transition from chapter 43 to chapter 47. The details of the process of growth of chapters 43–48 will be discussed following 48:30–35.

Interpretation

■ **47:1-12** We will be unable to understand what 47:1–12 is saying if beforehand we have not endeavored to clarify certain *elements of tradition presupposed by the passage.*

The section 47:1–12 first of all refers to the natural phenomena of the land of Israel when it speaks of a spring which sends its water into the Dead Sea and cures its puzzling maladies. In the description of the Dead Sea there is revealed sound knowledge of what can in fact be determined there even up to the present. This inland sea, described in 47:18 as "eastern sea," with which may be compared also the observation made above on the הים ("the sea") of 39:11,[2] lies in the bottom of a tectonic depression which came about in remote antiquity. Its water surface lies c. 390 meters (in 1915, 387 meters; September 1960, 397.36 meters) below sea level. Its high salt content (as much as 26%) prevents any fish life in its waters. Even the Madeba map shows how the fish, which in the Jordan has come near the sea, turns tail in horror and swims upstream again. Even if the story of the destruction of Sodom in Genesis 19 does not refer to the origin of the Dead Sea, it nevertheless clearly reflects the experience which those who live in the land have, at least with regard to the area around the southern edge of the Dead Sea. It is an uncanny place, afflicted with the curse of God, a place of catastrophic judgment.

But how about the spring which arises on the temple mount? The modern visitor to the *ḥaram* in Jerusalem will look for it in vain, however unlikely, in any case, is the eruption of a spring precisely at the highest point of the temple mount. Now, it is true, the *Letter of Aristeas,* in its glorificatory description of Jerusalem, speaks of a natural spring which leads water to the temple, and even Tacitus mentions a *fons perennis acquae.*[3] Yet Aristeas' description is, according to Simons, "wholly imaginary" and must go back to passages like, precisely, Ezekiel 47.[4] The spring from which Jerusalem (and its temple) lives lies, as is shown by the various structures for carrying water, especially the Siloam tunnel built by Hezekiah,[5] at the foot of the city and temple hill in the Kedron valley It is the spring Gihon.

Now the song of Zion, Psalm 46, shows, however, that (certainly already in an early period) there had been references to "waters" in the city of Yahweh: "A 'stream' (נהר)—'its canals' (פלגיו) make glad the city of God, the holy dwellings of 'the Most High' (עליון)."[6] In this phraseology there is reflected ancient mythological language about the mountain of the gods. The continuation in Psalm 46 (as in Psalms 48; 76) speaks of the onslaught of the nations against the city of God and of their defeat. This theological statement was very clearly discernible in the Gog pericope.[7] In Psalm 46, however, the related reference to the abundant waters of the impregnable mountain of God reveals another line of tradition. This can be seen particularly clearly in Gen 2:10–14, where the location of paradise is described as a place of great abundance of water. All the great rivers of the world come down from this place, which must therefore be thought to be on a high mountain.[8] The inhabited world lives on the surplus of the riches of paradise. But paradise, as is shown also by many features in Genesis 2f, is the dwelling place of God—or, to transfer it back to the polytheistic past, of the gods. This motif of the river of paradise, which flows down from the dwelling place of the gods, has been clearly at work in the formation of Ezek 47:1–12 alongside the bare natural phenomena of Palestine (wilderness of Judah, Dead Sea). This is also regarded by J. Gray as a pre-Israelite local Jerusalem tradition.[9] Connections with the cosmic ocean which nourishes the holy city, such as are supposed by A. R. Johnson, have, if they ever existed, completely faded.[10]

In addition, however, a third factor must be mentioned. In a motivated judgment oracle against the

2 See above p. 317.
3 *Letter of Aristeas* 89; Tacitus, *Histories* 5, 12.
4 Simons, *Jerusalem,* 48 note 3.
5 Dalman, "Wasserversorgung"; Simons, *Jerusalem,* 157–194.
6 On this see also Ps 65:10; Is 33:21, and Gunkel, *Märchen,* 42–50; Gressmann, *Messias,* 179–181.
7 See above p. 300.
8 See above p. 347 on 40:2.
9 John Gray, "The kingship of God in the Prophets and Psalms," *VT* 11 (1961): 19f. See also Schmid, "Jahwe," 191f; Kraus, *Psalmen,* 343f.
10 Johnson, *Sacral Kingship,* 9.

faithless people and their king Ahaz, Is 8:6f, in the period of the Syro-Ephraimitic war of 733, expresses the threat: "Because this people have despised the waters of שלח ("Shiloah") that flow gently and melt in fear before Rezin and the son of Ramaliah, therefore, behold, the Lord will bring up against them (i.e. will inundate them with) the waters of the river, mighty and many . . . it will flood all its river valleys and go over all its banks." By the gently flowing waters of שלח ("Shiloah") is meant the system of canals which, before the Siloam tunnel cutting through the hill was built under Hezekiah, led the water of Gihon with a minimal drop along the eastern slope of the hill.[11] By this quite unrepresentative small amount of water there is meant, in Isaiah 8, Yahweh who is enthroned on the height of the temple mount above these waters of Gihon. With this insignificant stream there is contrasted the strongly flowing water of the Euphrates, by which is meant, as the gloss in 8:7aβ correctly interprets, "the king of Assyria and all his glory." The one who is represented by the insignificant water of שלח ("Shiloah"), who is nevertheless the lord of the whole world and also of the great nations, will allow the great king, whom the people hold in awe and whom their king Ahaz has summoned to his aid, to overwhelm the land, to carry out the judgment which he, the hidden, real king, has passed on his people. Thus the insignificant one, the one despised by the people, proves to be the one who has even the great waters under his control. From Ezek 5:1f as well as from the Gog pericope it was observed that the proclamation of Isaiah, specifically that from the Syro-Ephraimitic war, was not unknown to the prophet of the exile. In 47:1–12, too, it seems that we can affirm the same knowledge on the part of the prophet or of the later representative of his school.

What has become of these elements of geographical recollection and of pious tradition in Ezek 47:1–12?

■ **47:1** The prophet is once again led by the guidance figure to the front of the temple. In the section which once immediately preceded this, 44:1f, he had been standing at the outer east gate. In the sequence of the present form of 𝔐 he was last found, in 46:21–24, in the outer court beside the sacrificial kitchens for the people. There is no further mention here of the glory which, according to 43:5, filled the temple, but of a tiny stream which the prophet sees trickling out under the מפתן הבית ("threshold of the temple")—in an easterly direction because the temple, as was clear from chapters 40–42, is oriented towards the east. Since the prophet is standing in front of the temple, the מפתן ("threshold") must be an architectural element visible from the outside. The word is to be understood here, as in 46:2, as an (elevated) threshold. Under it the water flows out, but the point where it wells up is not defined any more closely. *P. Šeqal.* 6,50a,3 cites in this connection the teaching of a Baraitha: "From the holy of holies to the curtain (the waters are as minute) as the feelers of the crab(?) or of the tortoise(?); from the curtain to the golden altar as the feelers of the grasshopper; from the golden altar to the threshold of the temple . . . like the warp thread; from the threshold of the temple to the outer courts (temple vestibules) like the woof thread; from there on like the outflow from the mouth of a bottle . . . ."[12] This detailed working back from the threshold to the innermost part of the holy of holies certainly goes far beyond the threshold of the temple building. But here—and this is entirely in keeping with the text itself—it is strongly asserted that the water emerges from the place of Yahweh's presence.

The course of the water is followed further. Since, according to 40:47, the altar stands "in front of the temple," the water cannot simply run from the threshold straight across the inner court eastwards to the east gate. First of all it follows the front wall of the building.

■ **47:2** Led round via the north gate (more precisely, reference should have been to the two north gates) to the outside of the east gate, here too the prophet sees the water running out under the south side, doubtless of the gate structure. To indicate the south side, the noun נגב (v 1) and the adjective ימני are used, but not, on the other hand, דרום which occurs several times in the architectural description in chapters 40-42. A glance at 21:1, where in a single verse three different terms for the south appear (תימן, דרום, נגב), warns against constructing overelaborate literary-critical conclusions on this observation. When the passage referred to from *p. Šeqal.* measures the emergence of the water at this point with the emergence of water from the mouth of a bottle, then

11 Simons, *Jerusalem*, 177.

12 Strack-Billerbeck, 3. 855.

it has quite correctly grasped the etymological connection of פכה ("to trickle") to פך ("bottle, jug") (cf. v 2 note d), even if it once again, with its measurement, goes beyond what is stated in the text.

■ **47:3–5** It is only vv 3–5 that contemplate measuring the quantity of water. Here, with the measuring instrument known from chapters 40–42, four identical stretches are measured by the guiding figure, and then, in addition, with a second method of measurement, the increasing depth of the water is established. The emergence of the man to carry out the measuring is explicitly stated in v 3aα, in an addition which has not been very skillfully inserted, and the measuring instrument is also explicitly mentioned but with a nomenclature different from that in 40:3. A קו ("cord") of thirty cubits is mentioned in 1 Kgs 7:23; קו המדה ("measuring line") Jer 31:39; נטה קו ("to stretch a line") Is 44:13; Zech 1:16; Job 38:5 (see also note a).

The process of measurement is different from that in chapters 40–42 in that the really considerable and striking measurements of the water's depth are established not by the man himself with his measuring rod but by a different method. The man's measurements have the function only of calling a halt at equal intervals. In that he then on each occasion leads the prophet through the water, he makes him aware of its increasing depth. This may recall the process in 37:2, where the extent of the field of bones is likewise made clear to the prophet by means of an extended tour (והעבירני "and he led me through . . .").

In a mysterious fashion which is not further clarified, the water quickly increases in depth as it proceeds—from the ankles to the knees to the thighs. After the fourth measurement (the number four, here too, as the number of wholeness, concludes the measuring process) it can no longer be crossed on foot but only by swimming. Here too later exegesis has spun more out of the text: "Scripture says: For the waters were high . . . , i.e., they were too high so that one could not swim (מי סחו read as one word = מִסָּחוֹ). Perhaps he could not cross in a small boat but in a large one? Scripture says: No galley with oars can go on it (Is 33:21). Perhaps he could not cross it in a large boat but in a large clipper? Scriptures says: No stately ship can cross it (Is 33:21)."[13] The text of Ezek 47 breaks off after the four measurements and leaves to the reader to imagine for himself the corresponding further increase of the stream to a river and to a large river. What the passage is trying to say has become sufficiently clear in what has been said: small and slight, almost despicable it was to begin with (one thinks of the gently flowing waters of שלח "Shiloah"). But it becomes increasingly powerful until it becomes a mighty river. Such is the mysterious power of what at first sight is so insignificant.

■ **47:6–7** But what this power is aimed at becomes quite clear in the words of the man, who begins in v 6 his explanation to the son of man.[14] The inelegant delay which this explanation suffers in vv 6b, 7, which allow the prophet on his return to see the many trees on both sides of the water, has already emerged in the course of the textual discussion as a secondary addition which is intended to prepare the way for v 12.[15]

■ **47:8** The man's explanatory words first of all describe the water's further course, which the prophet himself no longer follows. Nothing more is said about any further increase in the water. The water flows first of all into the "eastern region." Since this designation is found nowhere else in the OT, it is surely not a specific territorial designation, but is simply a general description of the area between Jerusalem and the Jordan valley.[16] On the other hand, the second term ערבה ("Arabah") elsewhere occasionally designates the Jordan valley east (Dtn 4:49) and west (Josh 12:8) of the Jordan. Thus the Dead Sea (ים המלח "the salt sea") can even be called, in Dtn 3:17; 4:49, ים הערבה ("the sea of the Arabah"). Nowadays the name *'araba* has become attached to the prolongation of the depression south of the Dead Sea.[17] As third stage there is then mentioned "the sea," which is described by

13 Strack-Billerbeck, 3. 854.

14 See 1, 131f.

15 See v 6 note a.

16 On this cf. Josh 13:2 (Joel 4:4) גלילות הפלשתים, which Noth provisionally renders as "regions of the Philistines." But see also Nelson Glueck, "Three Israelite Towns in the Jordan Valley: Zarethan, Succoth, Zaphon," *BASOR* 90 (1943): 21 note 79a.

17 See also Noth, *OT World*, 54.

means of its bitter, salty water (v 8 note d). In connection with this description of the three stages of the course of the river, one wonders to what extent the author of 47:8 still envisaged precisely the actual geographical relationships in the vicinity of Jerusalem and adheres to them. The Kedron valley *(wādi sitti marjam),* into which the water flowing down from the temple mount in an easterly direction would pour, runs first of all in a southerly direction. The *wādi en-nār,* in which the Hinnom and Kedron valleys join south of the city, first turns fairly decidedly in a southeasterly direction, but, only at a certain distance from Jerusalem, definitively turns east towards the Dead Sea into which it flows directly from the mountain region. Why, in 47:8, is the ערבה ("Arabah") described as the area between the eastern region and the Dead Sea? Does the author of the passage not actually have in his mind's eye the direction taken by someone traveling east from Jerusalem to Jericho, from where, via the Jordan valley southwards, the Dead Sea can also be reached? Or must one assume that, along the lines of Zech 14:4, he is envisaging a miraculous cleavage of the Mount of Olives with the subsequent free outlet eastwards to the Jordan valley, where the temple river then first reaches the plain of the Jordan and from there flows south into the Dead Sea?

More important for the author, however, than this question of the precise course of the water is the description of the miraculous effect of this river which emerges from the sanctuary and grows into a mighty force. This river will heal the cursed place in the land of Palestine. The waters of the bitter, salt sea will become fresh. The thought here is after all surely not of the natural process of a gradual change in the relationship between fresh water and salt water in the Dead Sea, but of the act of miraculous healing which comes about through this water of salvation. Just as the sick who climb into the water of the pool of Bethesda when the angel touches it are healed according to Jn 5:7, so the sick, accursed water of the Dead Sea is healed by the good water which comes from the temple mount.[18]

■ **47:9** In the language of P someone has added in v 9 the idea that all creatures that swarm (Gen 1:20f) wherever the healing waters reach will have life and that the fish there will multiply (note b). The original text had stated succinctly that everything in the places which the stream reaches would have life.

■ **47:10** To this then there was added at an early stage the vivid picture of the fishermen who will practice their trade from En-gedi to En-eglaim—a completely unthinkable idea in view of conditions in the Dead Sea at that time. Of the two places named, En-gedi has kept its name to the present day *(ʿain jiddi).* Thanks to the water pouring down in a powerful waterfall into a gorge, it is a flourishing oasis. Excavations on *tell el-jurn,* where more precisely the old location is to be sought, have most recently shed greater light on the history of the locality in its settlement since the late Israelite period.[19] More contentious is the location of En-eglaim ("spring of the calves"?), which seems to bear a name formed in a remarkably analogous way to that of En-gedi ("spring of the kid"). Attempts have been made to link the name on phonetic grounds with *ʿain ḥajle,* which does not, however, lie on the Dead Sea coast but more than five kilometers inland, on the plain a good three kilometers from the Jordan. After the excavations at *ʿain feška* in the neighborhood of Qumran had clearly shown the existence of older settlements at that spring, the equation En-eglaim = *ʿain feška* has been asserted by Farmer in the wake of earlier scholars. He felt that he could point to the fact that the settlement of the Qumran community at this very spot where there was the promise of the advent of salvation for the time of redemption could be readily understood. A. S. van der Woude has associated himself with this thesis of Farmer's.[20] Now, however, Y. Yadin, on the basis of newly discovered documents, has made it probable that for the Bar Kochba period in the southeastern sector, i.e. on the eastern side of the Dead Sea, we have to reckon with a district called עגלתין.[21] Since in

18 Cf., e.g., the "water sweetening" of Ex 15:25.

19 See Mazar-Dothan-Dunayevsky, *En-Gedi.*

20 A. S. van der Woude, *Die messianischen Vorstellungen der Gemeinde von Qumrân,* Studia semitica neerlandica 3 (Assen: Van Gorcum, 1957), 237.

21 See Yigael Yadin, "Expedition D—The Cave of the Letters," *IEJ* 12 (1962): 250f, and Mazar-Dothan-Dunayevsky, *En-Gedi,* 3.

the document published by Yadin the place name הלוחית is also mentioned for that district,[22] it is probable that we should connect with it the "third Eglath" (עגלת שלשיה) mentioned in the Moab oracles in Isaiah 15 (v 5) and in Jeremiah 48 (v 34). הלוחית ("Luhith") in Is 15:5 (cf. Jer 48:5). So then, in En-gedi and En-eglaim places on opposite sides of the Dead Sea are mentioned, which thus in its totality will be as rich in its wealth of fish as the "great sea," i.e. the Mediterranean. What was said in 26:5, 14 to Tyre by way of threat, that the now inhabited rocky island would become a place where fishermen would dry their nets, is asserted here to the glory of the coastal settlements of the Dead Sea. The connection in figurative usage with Ezekiel 26 may thus be recorded here.

■ **47:11** The thoroughness of this transformation frightened a later writer who was aware of the possibility of the extraction of salt from the Dead Sea. So he has added the observation that the swamps and pools of the sea, doubtless little side arms and parts of the edge standing half under water are what are envisaged, keep their salt water and could be used for the extraction of salt. For salt was necessary not only for the seasoning of man's food but equally so for the sacrificial cult (43:24). The observation attests that the extraction of domestic salt from the Dead Sea, which is intensively carried out today especially at the southern end near *jebel usdum*, has its ancient predecessors. Since, according to v 11, the salt is not cut out of the rock but is gathered from evaporation pans, it is the northern end that is envisaged as the location of such "industry" rather than the southern end, where in *jebel usdum*, to which the pillar of salt of Lot's paralyzed wife in Gen 19:26 must refer, crystalline salt can be mined in opencast workings.

■ **47:12** The definitive conclusion of the unit 47:1–12, and doubtless also of the basic text of chapters 43–48, is formed by v 12, which recounts yet another miracle in connection with this healing water. Even the flora on the bank of the river will be of undreamt-of abundance. Fruit trees, whose leaves do not wither, whose fruit is never exhausted and which produce fresh fruit month after month, will grow on both sides of the river. Here one feels reminded in a particular way of the promises of the earlier proclamation of salvation in the book of Ezekiel (cf. e.g., 34:26f, where the new fruitfulness is caused by abundant rain, and 36:30). Here too later Rabbinic exegesis has attempted a more detailed development. While Rabbi Judah (c. 150 A. D.) says: "In this world grain requires six months and tree fruit twelve months . . . , but in the future grain will require one month and tree fruit two months," Rabbi Jose (c. 150) goes still further and discovers, by a comparison with Joel 2:23, that in the future the time for grain will be shortened to fifteen days and that for tree fruit to one month.[23] One may wonder whether the last clause of v 12b does not already belong to the secondary expansive exposition when it affirms particularly, and somewhat belatedly, that the fruit is to be for food and the leaves of the trees for healing. The thought of healing, which was emphasized already in the רפא ("to heal") of v 8(9), is thus once again underlined in a particular way. The original conclusion of the text is probably best found in v 12aβ, where the decisive sentence of the whole complex is expressed once again: Strength and healing are characteristic of the river by reason of the fact that its waters come from the sanctuary. מקדש ("sanctuary") is here used in the wider sense for the sanctuary as a whole and not only for the temple building, which was designated in v 1 by בית ("temple"). Whatever one's judgment of the originality of v 12b, it is at any rate clear that with this reference back in v 12aβ to the sanctuary, the place of the continuing presence of god (43:7f), the whole is pointed towards it proper place.

■ **47:1–12** We can now consider in context the question of the way in which 47:1–12 has treated the traditional material which it has incorporated within it. The paradise tradition discernible behind Gen 2:10ff had exalted the place of the garden of God with its abundant water. This water, which then divides into four arms, is so powerful that with the water which is not needed in the garden of God it is able also to supply the earth with its four great rivers. In a different way, Psalm 46 had exalted the city of God with its strong defense against every enemy as the place which is made glad by God's streams of water. Ezekiel 47 takes up the reference to the place of the divine presence as the source of abundant

22 Yadin (see preceding fn.), 250.

23 Strack-Billerbeck, 3. 856.

water. But not in the way in which we can hear in *Mujir ed-dīn* with direct transference of Gen 2:10–14 to Jerusalem: "Of rivers there are four . . . all the water which the sons of men drink comes from these four and emerges under the rock of Jerusalem."[24] Ezekiel 47 differs both from this phraseology and from Psalm 46 in that at the place of the divine presence it lets only a small trickle arise. It is not the abundance of water at the place of the divine presence that is extolled, but the miracle of the emergence of blessing in the temple stream from small beginnings to an abundance by which the land outside, even down to the place of accursed death, is blessed and restored. Admittedly there is no reference to men, apart from the fishermen who are cited by way of illustration of the abundance of fish in the Dead Sea. But the decisive statement that blessing goes out from the place of the divine presence into the surrounding land cannot fail to be heard. This is particularly surprising after the intensive concentration on the sanctuary which guards its holiness carefully within itself. The existing traditions are here broken up and opened outwards. In connection with that element of Isaiah's preaching, namely that Yahweh shows his power precisely as the one who is at first insignificant, the proclamation here has become that of the willingness to bless the world round about the most holy one. This naturally includes the other idea, namely that fullness of blessing for Israel can be expected from no other place than the one in which Yahweh has taken up his abode for all time in the midst of his people.

The picturesque proclamation of Ezekiel 47 has already had a discernible subsequent history within the OT. In the supplement in Joel 4:18–21, which, according to H. W. Wolff, could still be from Joel himself,[25] in v 18b, in the context of the description of the great future fruitfulness, reference is also made to the spring which erupts in Yahweh's house and waters the valley of accacias. In the name of this valley there could be intended an "apocalyptic cipher" (Wolff). Zech 14:8 no longer refers to the temple. The "living waters" (מים חיים) flow from Jerusalem, when Yahweh will be king over the whole earth (v 9), and divide into two streams which flow into the eastern sea (Ezek 47:18) and the western sea and, by contrast with the usual wadis of Palestine, contain water all the year through. Of the effects of this occurrence nothing more is said. The whole has clearly already become a fixed element of eschatological expectation. We have already mentioned the significance which, according to Farmer, van der Woude, Ezek 47:1–12 might have had for the Qumran community in its choice of a dwelling place.

In the NT the most obvious use of Ezekiel 47 is to be found in Rev 22:1ff. There too the temple, which according to 21:22 will no longer be in the new Jerusalem because God and the Lamb will be the temple of the community, has disappeared in the reference to the temple river. The "water of life" which is as clear as crystal flows from the throne of God and of the Lamb. The leaves of the trees growing at the edge of the river, described as the "wood of life" (*ξύλον ζωῆς*) and thus fully connected with the motif of the "tree of life," serve here in the ultimate extension of the divine will for salvation "for the healing of the nations." A more heavily veiled echo of Ezekiel 47 (and of Zech 14:8) might also be found in Jn 7:38, where there is a reference to the streams of living waters which flow from the body of the believer.[26] On the exegesis in the early church, in which the increase of the river represents the increase in the number of believers, the fourfold measuring the four gospels, the depth of the last measurement the depth of the fourth gospel (Theodoret), the river baptism (Polychronius) or then at the same time the Jewish people gaining new strength after the return from exile represents the church increasing in its number of believers—on all this see Neuss.[27] For Jerome the river is an image of the teaching of the church and of the grace of baptism: "It flows along between two rows of trees, the books of the Old and New Testaments, fructifies everything and even renews the Dead Sea of the souls which died in sin."[28] By way of conclusion there may be cited the final

24 Cited in Schmidt, *heilige Fels,* 63 note.
25 Wolff, *Joel and Amos,* 75.
26 On this see Pierre Grelot, "Jean VII, 38: Eau du rocher ou source du Temple?" *RB* 70 (1963): 43–51.
27 Neuss, *Buch,* 59f, 63.
28 Neuss, *Buch,* 75.

passage of the "Tractate of the Vessels,"[29] which expects from the eschatological temple stream the discovery of the hidden treasures: "At that time a great river whose name is Gihon will flow from the 'place' (בית) of the Most Holy and will flow into the great and fruitful wilderness and mingle with the River Euphrates and 'thereby' (מיד, Milik: *à son passage*) there will emerge all (sacred) vessels."

Aim

In the veiled imagery of the references to the temple spring and to the waters which flow from it 47:1–12 tries to state that the appearance of God in his sanctuary in the midst of his people does not create a self-contained "holy place." All the preparation of the sacred place with its protection against unthinking access on the part of what is ungodly, as this is reflected in the architectural layout of the sanctuary, is meant in the last resort to serve God's intention to allow life and healing to flow out from here into the land. This life and this healing are to be effective precisely where unnatural disease and hostility to life are most obviously operative. The Dead Sea, that enigma of the geography of Palestine, with its magnified hostility to life, must serve as the expression of this proclamation.

In the representation of the water, which from the smallest beginnings swells in its course into a mighty river, there is expressed, however, in addition, what Jesus in another context intended to say in the double parable of the mustard seed and the leaven (Mt 13:31–33): The work that begins in the place of God's presence on earth—the NT here speaks of the kingdom of God—begins in insignificant modesty so that men might well fail to notice it. But then it grows, not through natural tributaries which might come to strengthen it but through its own inner power, into the mighty river which in Is 8:7f can symbolize the great powers. The mystery of divine hiddenness is thus discernible in God's efficacy on earth.

But finally it must be clearly recorded that the prophetic author of Ezek 47:1–12 did not, in all this, intend to compose a fairy tale or blow a soap bubble. He is speaking of the harsh realities of his land and of the riddles contained in it. But, in addition, he is speaking of the place in Israel over which God's ancient promise lies. When he points to that place of God's promise, he is speaking of the miracle which is happening in the midst of his people who have still to return home from exile, the miracle of the healing and the revival of the sick and the dying. What he is proclaiming is not far removed from that message of new life which was expressed in 37:1–14.

29 Partially presented by Milik in "Notes," 567–575, with reference to the Beirut tablets.

2. The New Allocation of Land

Bibliography

Y. Aharoni
"Tamar and the Roads to Elath," *IEJ* 13 (1963): 30–42.

George Ricker Berry
"The Date of Ezekiel 45:1–8a and 47:13–48:35," *JBL* 40 (1921): 70–75.

Alfred Bertholet
Die Stellung der Israeliten und der Juden zu den Fremden (Freiburg, 1896), especially 110–113.

K. Elliger
"Die Nordgrenze des Reiches Davids," *PJ* 32 (1936): 34–73.

Menaḥem Haran
"The Levitical Cities," *Tarbiz* 27 (1958): 421–439 (Hebrew, with English summary).

Menaḥem Haran
"Studies in the Account of the Levitical Cities," *JBL* 80 (1961): 45–54, 156–165.

Yeḥezkel Kaufmann
The Biblical Account of the Conquest of Palestine, tr. M. Dagut (Jerusalem: Magnes, 1953), especially 48–51, "The Land of Canaan."

Cameron M. Mackay
"The City and the Sanctuary. Ezekiel 48," *PrincTR* 20 (1922): 399–417.

Cameron M. Mackay
"The City of Ezekiel's Oblation," *PrincTR* 21 (1923): 372–388.

Cameron M. Mackay
"Ezekiel's Sanctuary and Wellhausen's Theory," *PrincTR* 20 (1922): 661–665.

Cameron M. Mackay
"The Land of the Lost Boundary," *CQR* 116 (1933): 1–23.

Cameron M. Mackay
"The North Boundary of Palestine," *JTS* 35 (1934): 22–40.

B. Maisler
"Lebo-Hamath and the Northern Boundary of Canaan," *Bulletin of the Jewish Palestine Exploration Society* 12 (1946): 91–102 (Hebrew, with English summary).

Martin Noth
"Studien zu den historisch-geographischen Dokumenten des Josuabuches," *ZDPV* 58 (1935): 185-255, especially 239–248.

47

13 **Thus has [the Lord][a] Yahweh said: <This is the boundary>[b] in which you shall take the land as an inheritance for the twelve**

47:13 13a אדני is lacking in 𝔊 (= $𝔊^{967}$). $𝔊^{B}$ *κύριος θεός* [sic!], see Appendix 1.

b 𝔐 גה גבול. 𝔊 *ταῦτα τὰ ὅρια,* 𝔙 *hic est terminus,* 𝔗

tribes of Israel[c] [Joseph <two> parts][d].
14/ And you shall keep it as an inheri-
tance—each (with the same share) as the
other; I have raised my hand[a] (in an oath)
to give it to your fathers, and (thus) this
land shall fall to you as an inheritance[b].
15 **And this is the boundary of the land: On the**
north side[a]: From the Great Sea
<towards>[b] Hethlon to where you go in
<towards Hamath>[c], to Zedad, 16/ <—>[a]
Beroth(ah?)[b], Sibraim[c] which lies be-
tween the territory of Damascus and the
territory of Hamath, as far as Hazar-
<enon>[d] which lies on the border of
Hauran. 17/ So <the boundary>[a] runs
from the sea <as far as>[b] Hazar-enon

דין תחומא suggest the reading which the context also suggests, זה הגבול (cf. v 15). On the use of the definite article after זה and זאת Cooke points also to Nu 34:13; Ps 118:20, 24. Only 𝔖 נחלא דתחומא "valley of the boundary" feels obliged to understand the scribal error גה as גיא.

c On the mode of expression see Nu 33:54; 34:13.

d 𝔐 יוסף חבלים is surely correctly understood by 𝔙 *Joseph duplicem funiculum habet,* 𝔗 יוסף יתקבל תרין חולקין. 𝔖 דיוסף לחבלא. 𝔊 misunderstands, *πρόσθεσις σχοινίσματος* (𝔏[C] *augmentum funiculi*). The use of חבל, which is used otherwise in Ezekiel only in 27:24 in its real meaning of "rope," for the portion of land measured (by the measuring cord), which in Ezek 45:7; 48:8, 21 is called חלק, is already a linguistic indication of a strange hand. See the exposition.

14 14a 𝔗 קיימית במימרי.

b The expression נפל בנחלה ל occurs otherwise in Nu 34:2; Ju 18:1. It occurs subsequently in the hip'il in v 22; 48:29; on this cf. v 22 note b.

15 15a לפאת צפונה. As a close examination of vv 17ff and of 48:2ff shows, the compass directions which end in ה-*locale* can be replaced, without any discernible rule, by forms without the ה. The latter has thus lost here the power to modify the meaning.

b 𝔐 הדרך should, for grammatical reasons and on the evidence of the parallel in 48:1, be read without the article. 𝔊 *τῆς καταβαινούσης καὶ περισχιζούσης* has not understood דרך חתלן. See also 48:1 *καταβάσεως τοῦ περισχίζοντος.*

c In 𝔐 צדדה has forced its way between the two parts of the phrase which, on the basis of 48:1, is to be understood as a unit לבא חמת. Nu 34:8 shows, as does 𝔊, that is should come after לבוא חמת. On the way in which 𝔐 could have arisen see Herrmann, Cooke.

16 16a Cf. v 15 note c.

b Since ברותה is not attested elsewhere, it cannot be determined with certainty whether the ending belongs to the name or, as is the case with the preceding צדדה, represents the ה of direction.

c In 𝔊 there follows here also a Ηλιαμ (Ελιαμ) which could correspond to Hebrew חילם. Cf. 2 Sam 10:16 (v 17 חלאם).

d 𝔐 חצר התיכון. 𝔙 *domus Tichon,* 𝔖 חצר מצעיתא, Σ (according to Jerome) *atrium medium.* The parallel passages in 48:1 and Nu 34:9f have at this point חצר עֵינָן, and the immediately following v 17 has חצר עינון. This reading seems to be presupposed by 𝔊 *αὐλὴ τοῦ Σαυναν* (𝔊[A] *Ευναν*) also in 47:16. 𝔐 is thus a scribal error for חצרה עינון (or עינן). At this point 𝔗 has בריכת עגיבאי "pond of the Agibites (?)."

17 17a Since 𝔊 𝔗 𝔖 attest הגבול with the article, 𝔐 גבול is to be regarded as a scribal error for הגבול caused by haplography.

b 𝔐 חצר עינון is the place at the eastern end of the northern boundary. One expects something corresponding to the מן of the starting point מן הים. 𝔙

where the territory of Damascus [and north][c] lies to the north and (likewise) the territory of Hamath[d]. <That>[e] is the north side. 18/ And the east side: <From Hazar-enon>[a] (the place) between[b] Hauran and Damsacus, the Jordan <forms the frontier>[c] <between>[d] Gilead and <the>[d] land of Israel as far as[e] the Eastern Sea, <as far as Tamar>[f].

usque ad, 𝔖 לחצר עינן indeed give expression to such. Thus 𝔐 should be corrected either to (חצר) עד or (as in v 16 note d) to חצרה. 𝔊, surprisingly, ἀπὸ (τῆς αὐλῆς).

c 𝔐 וצפון is rather awkward alongside the following צפונה and is simply understood by 𝔖 וצפיון דבגרביא as the proper name of a place or of a district. Although it is unanimously attested by the versions (the end of the verse, which is lost in 𝔊, is preserved in $𝔊^{967}$), it should be deleted as a corrupt dittograph of the following word or as a gloss which has erroneously found its way into the text.

d 𝔐 וגבול חמת appears rather belated and is also remarkable in that, although it ought, in an enumeration from west to east, to precede Damascus, it is in fact only mentioned after it. Since, however, the analogous order appears in 48:1, one cannot with certainty delete it. At any rate 𝔊 (*pace* BH^3) should not be cited as evidence for such a deletion, since here the whole of the end of v 17 is missing. $𝔊^{967}$ attests it, cf. note c.

e 𝔐 ואת here and in vv 18f is a scribal error for זאת, cf. $𝔊^{967}$ 𝔖.

18 18a The analogy of the description of the north side (v 15) and of the south side (v 19) makes it likely that in the case of the east side, too, we should look for a clear point of departure in the description of the boundary. On the analogy of the following southern boundary (v 19) (in the case of the western boundary the situation allows a simpler description), this must be identical with the final point of the preceding description of the northern boundary. That is חצר עינון. In 𝔐 there occurs now the location of Hazar-enon in terms which are to be expected in view of v 16, without the place itself actually being named. It is not impossible that it should be added. So most commentators. But 𝔐 is clear without the specific addition. See also note b.

b The starting point for the eastern boundary is already expressed clearly in 𝔐 through the double מבין which should, therefore, not be emended. A completely analogous expression is found in 2 Kgs 16:14.

c 𝔐 מגבול is, on the evidence of 𝔊 διορίζει, 𝔖 מתחם, a scribal error for מגביל.

d In 𝔐 the מן, which was entirely in place earlier for the designation of the starting point of the boundary, has been added even with the following בין . . . ובין, which describes the territory along both sides of the eastern boundary, and this has brought about the obscurity of the continuation in 𝔐. Both occurrences should be deleted.

e על-אל cf. 1:17 note a. This indication of the terminal point should not, on the basis of 𝔊 ἐπὶ τὴν θάλασσαν, 𝔙 *ad mare,* be emended to עד; see also the אל in v 19.

f 𝔐 תמדו, which is attested by 𝔙 𝔗, has been understood by 𝔐 doubtless as an echo of the measurement formulae of chapters 40ff, but it is quite

<That>[g] is the east side. 19/ And the south side facing noon[a]: From Tamar[b] as far as the waters of <Meribath>-kadesh[c], to the brook (of Egypt)[d] to the Great Sea. <That>[e] is the south side facing noon[a]. 20/ And the west side: The Great Sea <forms the frontier>[a] as far as opposite (the spot) where you turn towards Hamath. That is the west side. 21/ And you shall divide up this land for yourselves[a], for the tribes of Israel.
22 And is shall be (so)[a]: You shall allot[b] it as an inheritance for yourselves and for the

impossible in the present context, the style of which is formally concise. The continuation in v 19 points decisively to a reading תמר(ה), which can be discerned hidden behind the Φοινικῶνος of 𝔊 (φοῖνιξ = date palm = תמר) and clearly in the על ימא מדנחיא דתמר of 𝔖. Cf. also v 19 note b.

g Cf. v 17 note e.

19 19a 𝔐 נגב תימנה. The doubling of the indication of direction should not give rise to any critical operations, since it occurs also in 48:28 (Ex 26:18; 27:9; 36:23; 38:9) and in Ex 27:13; 38:13 also in connection with the easterly direction קדמה מזרחה. On תימן cf. 21:2 (note a), where in parallel clauses the three designations for the south all occur תימן, דרום, נגב. 𝔊 links the two designations here and at the end of the verse (in 𝔊 = v 20) by means of the copula, cf. 1:4 note a. 𝔖 has only one designation and omits v 19b.

b 𝔊 here proffers the double information ἀπὸ Θαιμαν καὶ Φοινικῶνος; 𝔊[967] deletes the second, cf. also v 18 note f. 𝔗 מיריחו identifies תמר with Jericho, see the exposition.

c 𝔐 מריבות קדש is written מריבת (קדש) in 48:28, and this also corresponds to Dtn 32:51. 𝔖 also reads thus, while 𝔊 transliterates Μαριμωθ. 𝔙 translates *aquas contradictionis Cades* in reference to the מי מריבה (singular) of Nu 20:13, 24 (Dtn 33:8; Ps 81:8; 106:32; see also the simple מריבה of Ex 17:7; Ps 95:8). 𝔗 עד מי מצות רקם is different again. The place name Kadesh is also rendered in 𝔗[O] in Gen 16:14; 20:1; and elsewhere by רקם, קדש ברנע by רקם גיאה (Nu 32:8; 34:4; Dtn 1:2, 19; and elsewhere). Are there specific local traditions behind this?

d 𝔐 נחלה, rendered by 𝔙 as *torrens,* means the נחל מצרים, which appears in this full form in, e.g., Nu 34:5; Josh 15:4, 47; and elsewhere in descriptions of the southern boundary of Canaan and is to be found in the *wādi-el-ʿariš.* The נחלה has been misunderstood by 𝔗 אחסנא, 𝔖 יורתנא as נחלה "inheritance." 𝔊 παρεκτεῖνον is, according to Cornill, "an explanatory addition which has suppressed the original. παρεκτεῖνον is obviously saying that the boundary runs along the נחל to the sea." Jahn wants to reconstruct a נֹטָה as the original.

e Cf. v 17 note e.

20 20a 𝔐 מגבול is, as in v 18 (note c), a scribal error for מגביל. Cf. 𝔊 διορίζει, 𝔖 מתחם. In 𝔖, in addition, the whole section vv 19b–20aα has dropped out as a result of homoioleuton (הים הגדול).

21 21a 𝔐 לכם. For this usage of ל with a retrospective suffix see Brockelmann §107f.

22 22a On the absolute use of prefixed והיה cf. v 10 (note a). It is omitted by 𝔊 𝔙. 𝔖 has ומא דפלגתונה by way of introduction, but this does not justify reading a כי in its place (BH[3]), since the following clause immediately gives the instruction and is not simply a protasis.

b Initially תַּפִּלוּ should be supplemented by גורל. So 𝔊 throughout, in accordance with the sense,

resident aliens[c] who live amongst you
and who beget sons amongst you. They
shall be to you as native Israelites. Along
with you they shall <acquire (it) by lot>[b]
as an inheritance amongst the tribes of
Israel. 23/ Thus it shall be (so): In the
tribe in which the resident alien[a] lives,
there shall his inheritance be given him,
says [the Lord][b] Yahweh.
48:1 **And these are the names of the tribes: In**
the furthest north, (i.e.) by[a] the side (of
the boundary which is designated by the
places:) way to Hethlon "where you go in
towards Hamath," Hazar-enon[b]—the
territory of Damascus lies to the north,
beside[c] Hamath—<there emerges>[d]
<from>[e] the east side <to the west>[f]:
(for) Dan one (portion)[g]. 2/ And beside
the territory of Dan from the east side to[a]
the west side: Asher one (portion). 3/
And beside the territory of Asher from
the east side to the west side: Naphtali
one (portion). 4/ And beside the territory
of Naphtali from the east side to the west
side: Manasseh one (portion). 5/ And
beside the territory of Manasseh from the
east side to the west side: Ephraim[a] one
(portion). 6/ And beside the territory of
Ephraim from the east side to the west
side: Reuben one (portion). 7/ And beside
the territory of Reuben from the east side
to the west side: Judah one (portion).
8 **And beside the territory of Judah from the**
east side to the west side lies the conse-
crated area which you shall consecrate,
twenty-five thousand (cubits) the width
and the length corresponding to one of
the portions from the east side to the
west side, and the sanctuary[a] shall lie in

βαλεῖτε . . . ἐν κλήρῳ. 𝔙 *mittetis . . . in hereditatem* has lost this insight. Its place can be taken by the actual gift allocated by lot. The hip'il should be read also in the יַפִּלוּ in v 22bβ (not 𝔐 יִפְּלוּ). 𝔊 φάγονται has י[א]כלו before it.

c 𝔐 ולהגרים. On the form with retention of the ה see Bauer-Leander §25x. 𝔊 καὶ τοῖς προσηλύτοις already fully envisages the religious proselytes whom 𝔖 דמתפנין לותי then also explicitly characterizes by their turning to Yahweh. See the exposition.

23 23a 𝔊 καὶ ἔσονται ἐν φυλῇ προσηλύτων ἐν τοῖς προσηλύτοις τοῖς μετ' αὐτῶν speaks, in a period in which the old tribal groupings have disappeared, of a "tribe of proselytes." 𝔊 scarcely has a different text in front of it, but is simply introducing insights of its own period.

b אדני is lacking in 𝔊 ($𝔊^{967}$). $𝔊^{B}$ κύριος θεός [sic!], see Appendix 1.

48:1 1a על-אל cf 1:17 note a. On the basis of 47:15 one might wish to read here מן הים (so Bertholet, Fohrer, Cooke, Gese), but this is attested nowhere in the tradition, and even the continuation cites the list of places from 47:15f only in selection. Thus the loose אל יד, which is also encountered later, should be retained. 𝔖 too על יד.

b 𝔐 חצר עינן cf. 47:16 note d. 𝔗 here also reads חצר עינן.

c על-אל cf. 1:17 note a.

d 𝔐 והיו לו should not simply be deleted (Herrmann, Fohrer). הנחלו, in spite of the reference to Job 7:3 (Bertholet), sounds forced. 𝔊 καὶ ἔσται αὐτοῖς, 𝔙 *et erit ei*, 𝔗 והוה לה, omitted by 𝔖. In the older form of the text at any rate there seems to have been a והיה here which is to be understood in a neuter sense without any specific subject. On this cf. 47:10, 22. לו is to be understood along the lines of Brockelmann §107f.

e 𝔐 פאת קדים. The parallel statements about the other tribes in vv 2–7 (8), 23–27 make the reading מפאת קדים a certainty. The form קדים is found in this formula also in vv 2, 6–8a, while in vv 3–5, 8b, 23–27 the fuller קדימה occurs. There is no justification at all for making the statements identical (*pace* Bertholet).

f In 𝔐 הים one expects the terminal point. Mostly this is expanded, on the basis of vv 2–7, 23–27, by analogy, to [ו]עד פאת ימה. But on purely graphic grounds and on the basis of 𝔊 ἕως πρὸς θάλασσαν, the simple ימה commends itself. The fuller ועד פאת ימה in vv 2ff is rendered by 𝔊 as ἕως τῶν πρὸς θάλασσαν.

g 𝔖 דדן abbreviates here and in all the other references to the tribes.

2 2a 𝔐 עד, and so also in vv 4, 7f, 23–27. In vv 3, 6 ועד. Here too there is scarcely justification for consistent uniformity (Herrmann, Bertholet).

5 5a 𝔖 reverses the order of Ephraim and Reuben.

8 8a 𝔐 המקדש. 𝔗 interprets more fully with the double expression כיבש מקדשא "leveled place

the midst of it[b]. 9/ The consecrated area
which you shall consecrate[a] to Yahweh—
the length shall be twenty-five thousand
(cubits) and the width <twenty
thousand>[b] (cubits).
10 And to the following (persons) the sacred
area shall fall[a]: The priests: To the north
(a portion of) twenty-five thousand
(cubits) and to the west [width][b] ten
thousand (cubits) and to the east
[width][b] ten thousand (cubits) and to the
south [length][b] twenty-five thousand
(cubits), and Yahweh's sanctuary shall
be in the middle of it[c]. 11/ (It shall fall) to
the sanctified priests[a], the descendants
of Zadok who have kept what of mine
was to be kept[b], who did not go astray
when the Israelites went astray, as the
Levites went astray. 12/ And they shall
receive a particular consecrated part[a] of
the consecrated area of the land as a

(*DalmanWB*) for the sanctuary," with which it has translated in 45:4 the supposed original מגרש למקדש (note b).

b 𝔐 בתוכו refers the suffix to חלק. The reading attested in some MSS, on the other hand, בתוכה, doubtless represents the correction to the grammatically more accurate reference to תרומה. So Cornill; Ehrlich, *Randglossen;* Herrmann.

9 9a 𝔐 אשר תרימו. 𝔊 ἣν ἀφοριοῦσι.

b 𝔐 עשרת אלפים as in 45:1 (see there). 𝔊^{967} εἴκοσι χιλιάδες has, by contrast with the other textual witnesses of 𝔊 (πέντε καὶ εἴκοσι χιλιάδες, 𝔊^{AB} εἴκοσι καὶ πέντε χιλιάδες), preserved the original reading demanded by the context.

10 10a 𝔙 *hae autem erunt primitiae* fails to understand the construction. 𝔖 ולכהנא נהוא פורשנא includes the clause, which is of the nature of a superscription and also already envisages the Levitical portion (וללויים, corrected text of v 13), in the statement about the priests.

b רחב and ארך, as the very varied tradition of the versions shows, have been inserted in the text only secondarily. 𝔐 gives the details in the case of the directions west, east and south. In 𝔊 (𝔏^{S}) the information about the east side has accidentally fallen out. In the text attested by 𝔊^{967} the details are missing for this side. In 𝔊^{B} they are missing completely, while 𝔊^{AQ,967} have them for the west and south sides, 𝔊^{Q} also for the east side which it has added. 𝔙 adds them also for the north side where they are missing in 𝔐. 𝔖 gives, after the information for the north, by mistake another (fifth) measurement, admittedly without a compass direction, but by way of compensation, with the dimensions ופתיא עסרא אלפין. On the other hand, it omits the dimensions everywhere else. Thus the haphazard secondary insertion of these details in the text can be clearly recognized.

c 𝔐 והיה מקדש יהוה בתוכו, 𝔗 here again has ויהי כיבש מקדשא דיהוה בגויה cf. v 8 note a, while 𝔊 καὶ τὸ ὄρος τῶν ἁγίων ἔσται ἐν μέσῳ αὐτοῦ seems to envisage as the original text והר המקדש יהיה בתוכם. On 𝔐 cf. v 8 note b.

11 11a 𝔐 לכהנים המקדש מבני צדוק "to the priests belongs that which has been sanctified by the sons of Zadok," so too 𝔙, while 𝔊 τοῖς ἱερεῦσι τοῖς ἡγιασμένοις υἱοῖς Σαδδουκ, see also 𝔖, has preserved the original reading לכהנים המקדש[י]ם בני צדוק. 𝔐 has arisen through false word division.

b 𝔐 משמרתי. 𝔊 (𝔏^{C}) τὰς φυλακὰς τοῦ οἴκου, cf. 𝔐 44:15. 𝔗 מטרת מימרי.

12 12a 𝔐 תרומיה only here. The noun formed from the word of belonging (*nisba;* Bauer-Leander §61wθ-cι) is designated in the versions by the same words as the basic word תרומה. Yet this is no reason to see in this form, which is completely transparent, a scribal error for an original תרומה (so the majority of recent commentators). In 𝔊 ἡ ἀπαρχὴ δεδομένη ἐκ τῶν ἀπαρχῶν (𝔏^{S} *delibationis* [sic!] *data separata deliba-*

most holy place alongside[b] the territory of the Levites.

13 And <to the Levites>[a] corresponding to the territory of the priests: twenty-five thousand (cubits) the length, and the width ten thousand (cubits). <The whole>[b]: The length twenty-five thousand (cubits) and the width <twenty thousand>[c] (cubits). 14/ <>[a] None of it shall be sold[b] or exchanged[c], nor shall the best of the land <be allowed to pass>[d] (into other hands), for it is holy to Yahweh.

15 And the remainder: Five thousand (cubits) in width[a] by twenty-five thousand (cubits in length)—it is profane[b]. It shall belong to the city as living areas and pasture

tionis) could, in addition, positively be a reference to the unusual form which it had before it.

b על-אל cf. 1:17 note a.

13 13a 𝔐 והלוים. Since the new beginning corresponds to the לכהנים (v 10), 𝔊 (𝔏^{S}) τοῖς δὲ Λευίταις, 𝔙 *sed et levitis* suggest the correct reading וללוים, which has been corrupted due to haplography.

b 𝔐 כל. Since v 13b gives the sum of the two parts of the תרומה, הכל should be read. See also 𝔊 πᾶν τὸ μῆκος. 𝔐 has arisen through haplography. On scribal errors with ם and ה see Delitzsch, *Schreibfehler,* 122a. Driver, "Linguistic Problems," 187, suggests reading כֻּלּוֹ אֹרֶךְ.

c 𝔐 עשרת is, as in v 9, a scribal error for עשר[י]ם. The addition of the priestly and Levitical territory gives this total measurement, which has been preserved in 𝔊 εἴκοσι.

14 14a In 𝔊 (𝔏^{S}) 𝔖 the copula is missing, and this suits the new beginning better.

b 𝔐 ימכרו runs in 𝔊 οὐ πραθήσεται, 𝔏^{S} *non dabitur venum datum* (𝔊^{967} οὐ πραθήσετε is, by contrast, secondary), and this could correspond to a יִמָּכֵר. In view of the fact that 𝔊 also renders the two following verbs in the singular, this reading should be considered seriously. Yet 𝔊 might also be envisaging a ימכרו understood impersonally. 𝔙 𝔗 𝔖 support 𝔐. Cf. also note c.

c 𝔐 ימר has been read by 𝔊 καταμετρηθήσεται as יִמַּד, clearly a scribal error for 𝔐. 𝔗 יחלף also confirms 𝔐. On the other hand, 𝔙 *mutabunt,* 𝔖 נחלפון suggest here, too, the plural form ימ[י]רו. This may have been abbreviated to 𝔐 through haplography. Since a passive use of מור is scarcely attested, since the closely related passage in Lev 27:10, 33 is, rather, in the active form, since the third singular in an impersonal usage would be somewhat surprising in the present context and since the preceding ימכרו is fairly well attested, here too ימירו should be read.

d 𝔐 יעבור. 𝔊 ἀφαιρεθήσεται (𝔏^{S} *auferentur*) τὰ πρωτογενήματα, 𝔙 *transferentur primitiae,* 𝔖 active נעברון רישיתא. Only 𝔗 confirms the singular form of 𝔐, which is also unusual in its *plene* form. Thus the erroneous interchange of the two final consonants is possible, and the form should be taken, on the basis of 𝔖, as a transitive hip'il יַעֲבִרוּ. On this technical use of עבר for a commercial transaction, see Nu 27:7f, where the recipient of the goods is introduced by ל, as well as the use of the qal in Is 45:14; Lam 4:21 (על for the introduction of the recipient). The present passage is unusual in that there is no mention of the recipient.

15 15a 𝔐 ברחב here with the article, cf. 42:2. 𝔖 omits it.

b 𝔐 חל הוא is in the form of a declaratory judgment, on this see 1,376. 𝔊 προτείχισμα has understood it as חַל (= חיל) "outer fortification"; cf. 𝔊 2 Reigns (= 𝔐 2 Sam) 20:15; 3 Reigns 20:23 (= 1 Kgs 21:23); Lam 2:8. 𝔖 דוכתאהי "it is its place." Cooke: "belonging to it."

grounds[c]. And the city[d] shall be in the
middle of it[e]. 16/ And these are its (the
city's) measurements: The north side
four thousand five hundred (cubits) and
the south side[a] four thousand five
hundred[b] (cubits) and <the>[c] east side[a]
four thousand five hundred (cubits) and
the west side four thousand five hundred
(cubits). 17/ And the pasture grounds of
the city measure northwards two hun-
dred and fifty (cubits), southwards[a] two
hundred and fifty (cubits), eastwards[a]
two hundred and fifty (cubits) and west-
wards two hundred and fifty (cubits). 18/
And the remainder consists in length[a],
(running) along the side of the sacred
consecrated area, ten thousand (cubits)
to the east and ten thousand (cubits) to
the west, [and it runs along the side of
the sacred consecrated area,][b] and its[c]
produce serves as food for the workers in
the city[d].
19 **And the workers in the city[a] shall work it[b],**
(they alone) from all the tribes of Israel.
20/ The whole consecrated area (meas-
ures) twenty-five thousand by twenty-
five thousand (cubits). You shall set apart
(= consecrate)[a] the sacred consecrated
area as a square[b] together with[c] the

c 𝔐 מגרשׁ. 𝔊 again διάστημα (𝔏[S] *intervallum*), see above 41:6 note c. 𝔙 *suburbana,* 𝔗 רוח "open place," 𝔖 שׁטחא.

d 𝔗 כיבשׁ קרתא, cf. v 8 note a.

e 𝔐 בתוכה. The masculine suffix, which should be read with Q, refers to נותר.

16 16a 𝔖, with the aim of letting the points of the compass follow each other in the way in which they are adjacent to each other, reverses the order of the south and east sides.

b The חמשׁ, which in 𝔐 has erroneously been written twice, has already been noted by the Masoretes as foreign to the text by the omission of all diacritical and accentual signs (כתיבן ולא קרין), see Bauer-Leander §6m.

c 𝔐 ומפאת is a scribal error for ופאת.

17 17a 𝔖 here has the order north-west-south-east, cf. v 16 note a.

18 18a Here too 𝔖 omits 𝔐 בארך, cf. v 15 note a.

b The passage has been accidentally repeated in 𝔐 from what has gone before, but is also attested by the versions.

c The suffix of 𝔐 תבואתה refers to הנותר and should be read as masculine. On this see also the יעבדוהו of v 19. 𝔊 τὰ γενήματα αὐτῆς seems to be thinking of ἀπαρχή as the antecedent.

d In עבדי העיר, as the immediately following form העבד העיר shows, the absolute noun is to be regarded as the object of the construct noun which still has a verbal effect. What is envisaged is certainly not "city workers" or public services in the city. One must, rather, hear in it the phrase which lies behind it, עֹבֵד אדמה (see Walther Zimmerli and Joachim Jeremias, *The Servant of God,* Studies in Biblical Theology 20 [Naperville, Ill.: Allenson, 1965], 11), which here at the same time should be left open for additional workers' services which are found among the city population and which make their life possible. The עבדי המלך, who certainly are also resident in the city, are supported from royal property; see above on 46:17.

19 19a Cf. v 18 note d. This element in the population is designated here collectively. In the continuation, in a *constructio ad sensum,* they are referred to in the plural.

b 𝔐 יעבדוהו refers to נותר. Thus the emendation to יַעַבְדֻהָ (Driver, "Linguistic Problems," 187) is unnecessary, against 𝔊 ἐργῶνται αὐτήν which here too still envisages ἀπαρχή as the antecedent.

20 20a 𝔙 freely: *separabuntur,* referring to the tasks of v 20a (as subject).

b 𝔐 רביעית. The ordinal numeral otherwise usually designates fractions. "Squared" is described in earlier chapters (40:47; 45:2) by מרבע or (41:21; 43:16) by רבוע. But here there can be no doubt as to the meaning "squared," especially in view of the unanimous testimony of the versions (𝔊 τετράγωνον, 𝔏[S] *quadratum,* 𝔙 *in quadrum,* 𝔗 מרבע, 𝔖 omits it). If anyone feels unable to accept this meaning for

property of the city.
21 And the remainder for the prince: On both
sides of the sacred consecrated area and
of the property of the city, opposite[a] the
twenty-five thousand (cubits) <east-
wards>[b] as far as the eastern boundary
and westwards opposite[a] the twenty-
five thousand (cubits) <as far as>[c] the
western boundary, along the side of the
(other) portions[d], (it belongs)[e] to the
prince. And there lies the sacred conse-
crated area and the sanctuary of the
temple in its midst[f], 22/ and <the prop-
erty>[a] of the Levites and <the property>[a]
of the city, in the middle of what belongs
to the prince, lie between the territory of
Judah and the territory of Benjamin. [To
the prince does it belong.][b]
23 And the rest of the tribes: From the east
side to the west side: Benjamin[a] one
(portion). 24/ And beside the territory of
Benjamin from the east side to the west
side: Simeon one (portion). 25/ And be-
side the territory of Simeon from the east
side to the west side: Issachar one (por-
tion). 26/ And beside the territory of
Issachar from the east side to the west
side: Zebulun one (portion). 27/ And
beside the territory of Zebulun from the
east side to the west side: Gad one (por-
tion). 28/ And beside the territory of Gad
towards the south side facing noon[a] runs
<the>[b] boundary from Tamar[c] <as far
as> the waters of Meribath-kadesh[d], to
the brook (of Egypt)[e] and to[f] the Great
Sea.
29 That is the land which you shall allot to the
tribes of Israel <as an inheritance>[a], and
these are their portions, says [the Lord][b]
Yahweh.

רביעית in 𝔐, one is forced to assume a scribal error for מרבעת or רבועה. The latter would present no great graphic difficulty.

c על-אל cf. 1:17 note a. 𝔊, wrongly, ἀπό. 𝔖 מן.

21 21a על-אל cf. 1:17 note a.

b 𝔐 תרומה, even though it is attested by 𝔙 𝔗, cannot be correct. Thus it is silently omitted by 𝔖, while 𝔊 renders it by μῆκος, thus possibly having before it a scribal error for ארך. Since, otherwise, the statements about the western and eastern halves of the prince's property are completely parallel in form, the idea is strongly suggested that תרומה should be regarded as a scribal error, easily explicable, for קדימה (Cornill, following Smend and others).

c Consideration of the parallel structure of the descriptions of the two parts of the prince's territory forces us to regard על as a scribal error for an original עד. So 𝔊 ἕως (𝔏^{S} *usquae*—sic!—*ad*), 𝔙 *ad*.

d 𝔐 לעמת חלקים. 𝔊 *ἐχόμενα τῶν μερίδων*. The reference is to the portions of the tribes, already described in the northern half. Thus, החלקים, with the article, is necessary.

e The insertion of a יהיה (Cooke) is not necessary.

f The suffix here refers to תרומה. Thus בְּתוֹכָהּ should be read.

22 22a The double ומאחזת of 𝔐 is attested by the versions, but is surely to be regarded as a scribal error for an original ואחזת which arose on the second occurrence as a result of dittography and was then transferred to the first occurrence. The wrong verse division of vv 21/22, which overlooks the fact that a summarizing description of the territory that has been described from v 8 onwards began in v 21b and which then ought to facilitate the return to the tribal enumeration in vv 23ff, has also been partly responsible for this.

b The repetition of the לנשיא יהיה from v 22a, which is simply omitted by 𝔖 in its tendency to abbreviate but which is rendered in the other versions, fails to realize that from v 21b onwards we are no longer dealing with the description of the territory of the prince; cf. note a.

23 23a 𝔊^{967} here by mistake passes directly to Simeon and omits v 24.

28 28a Cf. 47:19 note a.

b 𝔐 גבול. 𝔊 *τὰ ὅρια αὐτοῦ*, 𝔖 תחומה. 𝔗 תחומא suggests the reading הגבול. The article has fallen out through haplography.

c 𝔐 מתמר. 𝔊 *ἀπὸ Θαιμαν* (𝔊^{967} Θαιμαρ) 𝔏^{C} *a Theman*, 𝔙 *de Thamar*, 𝔗 מיריחו, 𝔖 מן תמר.

d Cf. 47:19 note c. On the basis of the earlier example, here too עד should be inserted, cf. 𝔙 𝔖.

e Cf. 47:19 note d. 𝔙 *hereditas* misunderstands here the word which it interpreted correctly in 47:19.

f על-אל cf. 1:17 note a.

29 29a 𝔐 מנחלה is, on the basis of 45:1; 47:14, 22 and the versions, a scribal error for בנחלה.

b אדני is lacking in 𝔊 (= 𝔊^{967}). 𝔊^{B} *κύριος θεός* [sic!].

Form

The transition from 47:1–12 to vv 13ff leads into another world. While, according to 47:1–12, the prophet observed the natural phenomena of a new land transformed by God's life-giving river, vv 13ff, introduced by an introductory messenger formula, return to practical regulations. The people, who had remained unseen in 47:1–12, are now again addressed and are instructed about a specific action. The land, in which no miraculous changes are any longer discernible, is to be divided up among the tribes. A description of its borders in terms of the four points of the compass is prefixed in vv 15–20. A renewed summons to divide up the land (vv 21–23), in which specific instructions are given about the attitude to resident aliens, is followed in 48:1–28 by the exact description of the portions of land, in which particular attention is given to the division of the territory inside the "consecrated area" (תרומה) in vv 8–22. V 29 concludes the whole with a tailpiece in which the allocation of land to the tribes is again explicitly mentioned. A formula for a divine saying interrupts the whole complex in 47:23, and one closes it in 48:29.

The unmistakable framing of 47:13–48:29 by the command to allocate land in 47:13f and by 48:29 advises against dividing the great complex into a multiplicity of independent units. The stylistically independent boundary description in 47:15–20, with its principal heading (47:15a) and the headings and endings to its separate parts, is for its part so clearly enclosed by v 21, which immediately follows it and which again summons to the allocation of land, that, even though it is traditio-historically an independent element with a pre-history of its own, one cannot separate it from the context created by the redaction of the complex as a whole without disturbing that context. On the other hand, the statements about the גר ("resident alien") in 47:22f appear to be a secondary expansion. This is possibly indicated from the point of view of form by the loose linking with והיה ("and it shall be [so]") (on this see, e.g., 38:10, 18; 39:11; 47:9, 10). But it is also very probable from the point of view of content. The excision of vv 22f leaves no lacuna in the text. From 47:21, the order to allocate the land to the tribes, it flows on without a break to 48:1ff, the enumeration of the portions of land. Then the formula for a divine saying at the end of 47:23, which seems to suggest a delimitation after v 23, together with the insertion of vv 22f which it concludes, must have found its way into the text (see also, e.g., 45:9). The secondary amplifications which the text has also acquired in 48:11, 12, 21b–22 will be discussed in the context of the detailed exposition.

The formal structure of 47:13–48:29 can thus be clearly discerned. In this section, which is in the form of a personal address (second person plural), there has been incorporated in 47:15–20 a boundary description in an impersonal form. In the same impersonal style of an enumeration is also the description of the twelve tribal portions in 48:1–7, 23–28. The section about the תרומה ("consecrated area") in the strict sense, which is framed by this, passes briefly in its outer parts (vv 9 and 20) into the style of an address, only to revert also in the remainder of it, exactly like the details about the prince's portion of land in vv 21–22a (vv 21b–22 are secondary), once again into the factual descriptive style. The personal "I" of Yahweh emerges only in v 11, a sentence which from the point of view of content also is clearly marked out as an expansion. Otherwise Yahweh is always spoken of in the third person (48:9, 10, 14). This shows how, externally, only the introductory prophetic messenger formula as well as the concluding formula for a divine saying have been added. The text itself does not claim to be a divine speech.

The "Setting" of the section will best be discussed after the detailed exposition.

Interpretation

■ **47:13–48:29** The messenger formula, by which the section is introduced, appears here without any preparation.[1] It has not been preceded by a divine speech let alone a commission to the prophet. The last speaker has been the man in 47:8–12. Thus the section marks a completely new beginning without any connection with what has gone before—a clear secondary section.

But even in its subject matter it reveals something completely new. The domain of the sanctuary with its

1 See 1, 133.

ordinances is left behind. We emerge into the land outside the sanctuary. Therein lies the comparative justification for the connection of this section with 47:1–12, where this emergence from the sanctuary into the surrounding world of the land of Israel also occurred, even if in a quite different manner. 47:1–12 had made clear how, from the starting point of God's sanctuary, the land which has been marked by disease and death will be made miraculously whole. 47:13–48:29 shows the process of reformation in a quite different manner, namely that the house of Israel will somehow or other be taken back to the beginning again and will be given the task of doing better what it had already done at the beginning when it first settled in the land.

According to the point of view which had already become standard in the pre-exilic period (cf., e.g., Deuteronomy), the people as a whole were brought out of Egypt and then, via the intermediate stage of the wilderness wanderings, reached the land of Canaan, occupied it and divided it up among their tribes. This is reported in the book of Joshua. The preparations for the settlement and the allocation of land are already discernible in the book of Numbers. In the book of Ezekiel Israel's new beginning has been described in 20:33ff as a new exodus from among the "nations." Through the "wilderness of the nations" (20:35), after God's refining judgment, it was to reach again its land in whose midst stands "the mountain height of Israel" (20:40). In that section which spoke of the new exodus, the only factors mentioned were this mountain and the correct cult which is practiced here. The other elements of the settlement were not touched upon.

This is what is new in 47:13–48:29. The new settlement is now described in terms of what will happen to the whole land in view of the new arrival of the twelve tribes of Israel. Just as the new exodus will be more glorious than the first exodus (this theme will then be developed in hymnic language by Deutero-Isaiah) and just as the new sanctuary, to which Israel goes after her second exodus, will be erected in a new, exemplary fashion (this has been described in chapters 40ff), so too the allocation of land which concludes the settlement process will take place in a new and exemplary fashion. In this connection, in view of what has gone before in chapters 40–46, it is to be expected from the outset that this new arrangement, by contrast with the arrangement of the period of Joshua, will be structured around the new sanctuary as its central point.

Just as in chapters 40–46 for the erection of the new, model sanctuary no new Moses was summoned—what was new was an order directly effected by God and then enjoined, in its detailed instructions, on the people and their representatives—so, too, in the case of the new settlement and allocation of land no new Joshua is summoned. Here too the land will be re-allocated by God himself. Problems of a renewed conquest of land do not enter into the question. The new arrangement, however, is clothed in the form of a command to the people. The gift given anew by Yahweh is to be allocated in accordance with Yahweh's instructions. It is, however, small wonder that in the formulation of these instructions there is discernible an involuntary dependence on the phraseology with which the first allocation of land is described.

■ **47:13** The first thing to be noted here is that the house of Israel in the context of this new allocation of land appears once more as a tribal people. In 47:13, 21 (22f); 48:29 the שבטי ישראל ("tribes of Israel") are explicitly mentioned as recipients of the allocation of land. 48:1–7, 23–28 then enumerate the twelve tribes individually by name. The way in which the list of twelve is enumerated will need to be discussed in detail in connection with 48:1ff. There, too, the intention of the gloss in 47:13a (note d) will have to be discussed. The tribal structure of Israel is by no means self-evident to those who come to it from the earlier oracles of the book of Ezekiel. Even in Deutero-Isaiah the "tribes of Israel" appear only once and in purely formulaic terms in an עבד ("servant")-song (49:6). "Tribes" of Israel have been mentioned in the book of Ezekiel, apart from 45:1–8 which is dependent on chapter 48, only incidentally in 37:19. In the foreground in 37:15ff there stood, as in chapter 23 (and in 4:4–8), what was much more immediately visible to the contemporary nation, the double entity of the two kingdoms of Israel. To what extent the experience of this schism and its burden, but at the same time the possibility of its elimination, had become fresh again in the time of Josiah has already been emphasized.[2] The full emergence of Israel's tribal structure in Ezek 47f is doubtless connected with the fact that in the case of the new order for the land thoughts turn involuntarily to the processes of the first settlement, with the intervening history of "disorder" being passed over.

■ **47:14** The description of the land as being sworn to the fathers uses the phraseology of 20:(28)42. On the other hand, the terminology of the allocation of land reveals a quite special relationship with Nu 33:50–34:15, an addition to P in which Yahweh speaks with Moses about the imminent settlement. The hitpaʿel of נחל ("to take as an inheritance") is attested, apart from Is 14:2; Lev 25:46, only otherwise in Nu 32:18; 33:54 (twice); 34:13 in the context of settlement statements. The two last-mentioned passages refer explicitly in this connection to the "lot" (גורל) as the means of allocation. The unusual expression נפל or הפיל (vv 14, 22 [twice] and 45:1) בנחלה ("to fall as an inheritance") is found also in Nu 34:2; Josh 13:6; 23:4; Ju 18:1 in an analogous context. The expression איש כאחיו occurs also in Lev 7:10.

■ **47:15–20** *The boundary description.* Particularly noteworthy is, now, the connection of the boundary description of the land which begins in v 15 with Nu 34:3–12. The book of Joshua contains a series of lists of boundary points for individual tribal territories.[3] On the other hand, a description of the total boundary of the land is found only in Nu 34:1–12. In contrast to the sequence of the compass points north-east-south-west in Ezekiel 47, the sequence maintained there is south-west-north-east. The number of names mentioned is usually greater in Numbers 34 than in Ezekiel 47. The connection between the two texts is particularly close in the description of the northern boundary.

■ **47:15–17** The description begins in Ezek 47:15, after the composite superscription, with the "northern side" (פאת צפונה; in Nu 34:7 גבול צפון "northern boundary"). A lively discussion has ensued about this boundary. One might first of all regard לבוא חמת ("where you go in towards Hamath") as the key name for an understanding of the whole. Apart form Ezekiel 47f and Nu 34:8 it occurs fairly frequently in the OT as the most northerly point of Israelite territory (see Nu 13:21 [P]; Josh 13:5; Ju 3:3; 1 Kgs 8:65; 2 Kgs 14:25; Am 6:14; 1 Chr 13:5; 2 Chr 7:8). Unfortunately the identification of the place referred to is extremely uncertain in spite of its frequent occurrence in the OT. The uncertainty begins already with regard to its grammatical understanding. Does the name, as it is usually understood, describe a place from which there opens the approach to the oft-named Syrian Hamath on the Orontes (*ḥama*)? Where then is this place to be located? Does this description have in view the "entrance" from the sea so that one must think of the valley of the Eleutherus (*nahr el-kebīr*) in the north of Lebanon?[4] Or, what ought to be more likely, are we dealing with an expression from the geographical perspective of Israel, and are we therefore to think of the transition from the *beqāʿ* to the basin of Riblah[5] into which the Orontes valley widens as it leaves the Anti-lebanon and flows towards Kadesh, Homs and Hamath? It is inadvisable to think of a place any further south immediately on the northern boundary of the territory actually settled by Israel, e.g. in *merj ʿejjūn,* since Hamath is about two hundred kilometers away from there and since, in addition, the territory north of the bend of the Litani (*nahr el-qāsimīje*) is a termination rather than an "approach."[6] The other grammatical possibility consists in regarding לבוא (here "entrance") as a place name and Hamath simply as a more precise, geographical designation. Thus Noth, where the displacement of חמת ("Hamath") in 𝔐 (v 15 note c) seems to him to make it possible that חמת ("Hamath") is in fact a secondary addition, finds in לבוא a place in the north of the Israelite territory east of the Jordan.[7] On a "quite vague possibility" of identification he points to a *labʾu* mentioned in the inscriptions of Tiglath-pileser III.[8] In addition he believes that he can find in Numbers 34 and Ezekiel 47 an old series of boundary points of northern

2 See above p. 279.
3 See Albrecht Alt, "Das System der Stammesgrenzen im Buche Josua" in *Sellin-Festschrift. Beiträge zur Religionsgeschichte und Archäologie Palästinas* (Leipzig: A. Deichert, 1927), 13–24, and Noth, "Studien."
4 So Guthe, *Bibelatlas,* 3 I.
5 See 1, 191f on 6:14.
6 Elliger, "Nordgrenze," 40.
7 Noth, "Studien."
8 Noth, "Studien," 246 note 2.

Transjordan. In connection with Josh 19:32–39, he speaks more precisely of a "boundary description for Dan" omitted from the book of Joshua.[9] The very general piece of information about the starting of the boundary from the "Great Sea" (= Mediterranean) is judged by him to be a beginning which has been appended secondarily and, as a consequence of the assumption that it is dealing with the northern boundary of the whole Israelite territory, been prefixed to the whole. On the other hand, the חתלן (דרך) ("[towards] Hethlon"), which is missing in Numbers 34, as well as צדד ("Zedad"), ברות ("Beroth"), סברים ("Sibraim"), cannot, in his view, be more precisely determined. Yet the situation of חצר עינון ("Hazar-enon"), which is also to be read in v 16 on the basis of v 17 (48:1), is explained more precisely in v 18 by the information that it lies "between Hauran and Damascus" and "Gilead." This points, against the background of the Assyrian division into provinces which has been closely studied by Forrer,[10] to the spot where the three provinces of Hauran (*ḫaurina*), Samaria and Damascus meet. This, according to Noth, refers to a place west of *leja*, somewhere near *eṣ-ṣanamēn* or *šeḫ meskīn* or even further west near *el-ḥarra.* According to Numbers 34 the boundary then ends by the Sea of Genessareth. Thus Noth sees in Ezekiel 47 and Numbers 34 the description of a line "which began in the vicinity of the sources of the Jordan and then ran in a curve through the territory east of the Jordan until it ended finally on the eastern shore of the Sea of Tiberias."[11] The details have then been misunderstood in both passages and been transformed into the description Israel's northern boundary.

This point of view has been energetically contradicted by Elliger.[12] He finds in Ezekiel 47 the quite correct recollection of the northern boundary of the empire of David at the time of its greatest extent. Most clear, in his view, is the localization of צדד ("Zedad"), which is not to be emended with the Samaritan tradition and 𝔊^MSS to צרד ("Zerad") and then associated with *ḫirbet serada* (*s*, not *ṣ*!). It is to be equated with *ṣadad*[13] just east of the road from Damascus to Aleppo via Homs.[14] לבוא חמת is to be understood as "entrance to Hamath" and located in the vicinity of Riblah. Then Sibraim, which Elliger (as does Noth also) equates with the זפרן ("Ziphron") of Nu 34:9, and Beroth also belong to this central Syrian region. Hazar-enon Elliger finds in *qarjetēn.*[15] Beroth, which is mentioned in 2 Sam 8:8, written as ברתי ("Berothai"), as a town in the territory of Hadadezer of Zobah, he locates in the region of the state of Zobah between Hamath and Damascus somewhere near modern *el-junṭur* or *ḥafar* or *mehīn.* Yet this last place, since it is missing in the parallel in Numbers 34, can have been added only secondarily. Sibraim may have lain on the site of ancient Euaroia of the Roman period.[16] In the present-day name *ḥawwārīn* there could also be preserved the Hauran of vv 16 (18). Finally, in the דרך חתלן ("towards Hethlon") Elliger, in comparison with the הֹר הָהָר ("mount Lebanon") which occurs at this point in the parallel in Nu 34:7, believes that he can find a scribal error for an original הר לבנון which had been written in an abbreviated form הר ל״ן.

But behind this mention of the Lebanon mountains Elliger believes that he can discern the original description of the western boundary of the province of Damascus in the Davidic empire. Like Noth, he is also of the opinion that "the continuation of the northern boundary across Lebanon to the sea represents a secondary addition which falsifies the sense of the original document."[17] While, according to Noth, this was a case of the misunderstanding of the tribal boundary of Dan, here it is a misunderstanding of the northern boundary of the Davidic empire as the general northern boundary of Israelite territory.

From the completely opposite side Kaufmann tackles the question of Israel's northern boundary according to Ezekiel 47 without going into the more precise location of the individual places. He finds in the OT five different conceptions of the "Land of Israel." Alongside 1) the conception of the "land of Canaan," the land of the

9 Noth, *Josua,* 120, and *OT World,* 75.
10 Forrer, *Provinzeinteilung,* especially 61ff.
11 Noth, "Studien," 247.
12 Elliger, "Nordgrenze."
13 As already suggested by Edward Robinson, *Biblical Researches in Palestine, Mount Sinai and Arabia Petraea* 3 (Boston: Crocker & Brewster, 1841), 461, App. 171.
14 Cf. Guthe, *Bibelatlas,* 5 D 3.
15 See also Ernst Honigmann, "Historische Topographie von Nordsyrien im Altertum, II," *ZDPV* 47 (1924): 19, no. 318.
16 Ernst Honigmann, "Historische Topographie von Nordsyrien im Altertum, I," *ZDPV* 46 (1923): 184f, no. 174.
17 Elliger, "Nordgrenze," 71.

patriarchs, there are 2) Moses' land of Israel, 3) Joshua's land of Israel, 4) the land which was actually Israel's area of settlement and 5) the kingdom of Israel. In the case of the first four we have ethnographic conceptions, in the case of the fifth an imperialistic one. Ezek 47 and Nu 34 belong to the first conception, in which the "promised land" of Canaan reaches from the Brook of Egypt to the Euphrates or to לבוא חמת "the gateway to Hamath" (Gen 15:18; Ex 23:31; Nu 13:21; and elsewhere). Thus it includes Lebanon, the territory of Tyre, Sidon, Byblos and the land of the Philistines, but not, on the other hand, the land east of the Jordan.

One certainly cannot simply ignore the point of view expounded by Kaufmann. The assumption of purely accidental misuse of boundary lists is rather unsatisfactory. One will have to take serious note of the possibility that even behind Ezekiel 47 (Numbers 34) there lie consciously affirmed ideal conceptions of the extent of the land promised to Israel. This does not exclude the possibility that such concepts envisage realities of later historical periods in Israel, above all, of course, those of the Davidic period. That must be the case here in the description of the northern boundary. When 6:14 announces the raging of divine judgment "from the wilderness to Riblah,"[18] that seems to be dominated by a similar concept of the northern frontier of the land as that in 47:15–17, where the key word לבוא חמת surely, as Elliger sees it, points to the vicinity of Riblah.[19]

■ **47:18** The description of the eastern boundary is shorter than the corresponding description in Nu 34:10–12. The beginning, at the place "between Hauran and Damascus," which is used here in a way otherwise unusual in the OT as the name of a region and as an abbreviation of the גבול דמשק ("territory of Damascus") of vv 16f, is undoubtedly connected with חצר עינון ("Hazarenon") of vv (16)17, but in what follows, omitting additional information from Numbers 34, simply the Jordan is given as the boundary between Gilead and "the land of Israel."[20] In this expression Gilead is quite unmistakably excluded from the land of Israel. As the southern terminal point of the eastern boundary there is given, beside the "Eastern Sea" (so too Josh 2:20; Zech 14:8; cf. on 47:8), the place Tamar. This is lacking in Nu 34:12, where only the "Dead Sea" (ים המלח) is given as the terminal point (there this was also given in v 3 as the starting point for the southern boundary). The place is mentioned also in 1 Kgs 9:18 (K) as תמר "(place of) palms," in Gen 14:17 and possibly also in 2 Chr 20:2 (wrongly identified as En-gedi) as חצצון תמר ("Hazazon-tamar").[21] Citing the Madeba map, the *notitia dignitatum* and the tax edicts of Beersheba, Aharoni comes to the conclusion that is must be a place in the *ʿaraba* and locates it near *ʿain ḥuṣb.* There is no discernible reason for the omission of this boundary point from Numbers 34.

■ **47:19** The fixed points of the southern boundary are easily identifiable. Of the total of eight items in Numbers 34, which for their part are a mild reduction of the series of fixed points in Josh 15:2–4 (southern boundary of the tribe of Judah), only half are mentioned in Ezekiel 47, with Tamar again in place of the reference to the Dead Sea in Nu 34. Instead of the Kadesh-barnea of Nu 34:4 (also Nu 32:8; Dtn 1:2, 19; 2:14; 9:23; Josh 10:41; 14:6f; 15:3) what is mentioned here is מי מריבת קדש ("Meribath-Kadesh") (note c). This is a reference to the place in the wilderness mentioned in the stories of the wilderness wanderings under the name מריבה ("Meribah") (Ex 17:7; cf. Ps 95:8) or מי מריבה ("waters of Meribah") (Nu 20:13, 24; cf. Dtn 33:8; Ps 81:8; 106:32; the tripartite description occurs, besides 48:28, also in Dtn 32:51). At it, as

18 See 1, 191f.

19 See further the summary considerations on the boundary description (below pp. 531f). On לבוא חמת see also Maisler, "Lebo-Hamath"; on ברותה, Arnulf Kuschke, "Beiträge zur Siedlungsgeschichte der Biḳāʿ," *ZDPV* 74 (1958): 112f; on סברים, A. Sarsowsky, "Notizen zu einigen biblischen geographischen und ethnographischen Namen," *ZAW* 32 (1912): 149f. Albright (*Archaeology,* 220) equates the name with the Sepharvaim mentioned in 2 Kgs 17:31.

20 See above pp. 66f.

21 On this see Mazar-Dothan-Dunayevsky, *En-Gedi,* 3 and note 8. Robinson, *Biblical Researches,* 616, 622f, and Peter Thomsen, "Untersuchungen zur älteren Palästinaliteratur," *ZDPV* 29 (1906): 124, wished to locate it in Kurnub. Albrecht Alt, "Das Institut im Jahre 1933," *PJ* 30 (1934): 20–24, and "Aus der 'Araba II—IV," *ZDPV* 58 (1935): 34f, proposed *qaṣr ej-jehēnīje.*

the name suggests, the nomadic shepherds of the wilderness settled their "lawsuits" (ריב). Thus the place can also be called in a poetic archaizing way עין משפט (Gen 14:7). As is shown by the third element, which also designates the place as a holy place, it belongs to the larger region of Kadesh, in which several wells are to be found, of which one, by no means the most abundant, today bears the name *ʿain qedēs.*[22]

By the נחל ("brook") which is mentioned next is meant, on the evidence of the fuller text of Nu 34:5, the נחל מצרים ("Brook of Egypt"). This "Brook of Egypt" is mentioned also in Josh 15:4, 47; 1 Kgs 8:65; and elsewhere as the boundary wadi with Egypt and is to be equated with the *wādi el-ʿarīš.*

■ **47:20** The description of the western boundary is given, as in Nu 34:6, in the single reference to "the Great Sea." This lays claim, as Israel's territory, not only to Philistine territory but also to the Phoenician coast up to a point "level with" (נכח) "where you turn towards Hamath" (לבוא חמת)—does this mean as far north as Tripolis or the *nahr el-kebīr*?

■ **47:15–20** Looking back on the boundary description as a whole the question arises as to the extent to which simply old tradition is recapitulated here and to which a new regulation is intended in view of a new beginning. The close relationship with Numbers 34 and, in the case of the southern boundary, also with Josh 15:2–4, prevents the assumption that in Ezek 47:15–20 there exists a radical new scheme which is to be found only here. Kaufmann is surely correct with his supposition that already in the older tradition there were various conceptions of the "land of Israel." The tradition circles of the school of Ezekiel, in their desire for clear order, go back to one of these conceptions, one which in many places is in marked disagreement with the actual circumstances of territorial possessions in the Israel of the monarchical period. They see in it the original promise of land made by Yahweh (47:14).

Project and earlier historical reality seem to come closest in the case of the southern boundary. The Judah of the monarchical period before the catastrophe of 701[23] must have extended its sphere of influence into the wilderness to the south of Beersheba. Nevertheless Alt feels obliged to establish for the period of Josiah, the period to which he ascribes the lists of places in the book of Joshua: "The fact that the boundary description of Josh 15:2ff, like Ezek 47:19, still lays claim for Judah to the semi-desert as far as Kadesh has perhaps only theoretical significance."[24]

By contrast, it is remarkable that on the eastern boundary the whole of the territory east of the Jordan, in which, after all, two and a half Israelite tribes settled and to which a judge like Jephthah belonged, is dispensed with. It is, however, scarcely possible—and this must again be emphasized—to speak of a completely novel, post-exilic "policy of renunciation." The conception of the eastern boundary has a quite different lesson. That the experience of the foreignness of the Transjordanian settlement area, as opposed to the actual promised land, was felt much earlier is doubtless revealed by the story, which in its present form is certainly late, of the altar of the tribes east of the Jordan in Joshua 22. Even the system of tribal boundaries in the book of Joshua does not take account of the land east of the Jordan.[25] In accordance with the intention of Ezek 47:15–20, Israel, by its renunciation of the eastern territory beyond the Jordan, finds itself back in the circumstances assigned to it by Yahweh from of old.

On the northern boundary, if Kaufmann and Elliger are correct with their location of לבוא חמת, the plan seems to envisage the ideal extent of the Davidic empire.

It becomes quite clear in the description of the western boundary that Israel also regards Philistine territory as territory basically assigned to itself. Here the old blessing-curse story of the sons of Noah (Gen 9:18–27) can make it clear that already the early period was of the opinion that "Japheth (the Philistines) should dwell in the tents of Shem (Israel)," i.e. simply lead the life of a

22 On this see Y. Aharoni, "Kadesh-Barnea and Mount Sinai" in *God's Wilderness; discoveries in Sinai,* tr. Joseph Witriol (London: Thames and Hudson, 1961), 115–182.

23 On its consequences see Alt, "Sanheribs Eingriff."

24 Alt, "Judas Gaue," 280 note 3.

25 Alt, "Staatbildung," 54 note 1.

stranger in the land of the real owners. In Ezekiel 47 this point of view once again finds its full expression. And as far as the Phoenicians are concerned, whose territory in this blueprint is claimed quite far northwards as the land of divine promise, then the sober enumeration in the "negative list of possessions" in Ju 1:31, which cites, among the cities not conquered by the tribe of Asher, not only Acco but also Achzib and Sidon, shows that Israel has already in an earlier period regarded at least southern Phoenicia as part of the promised land already assigned to her. With the inclusion of the coast as far north as level with לבוא חמת the claim of Ezekiel 47 admittedly goes far beyond these earlier statements.

The recognition that these older traditions were alive in Israel itself removes the necessity of finding here, with Gaster, a particular Samaritan tradition, because the Samaritan book of Joshua also seems to dispense with the territory east of the Jordan.[26]

■ **47:21** After the description of the boundary of the land as a whole, which forms the presupposition of the allocation of land, v 21 returns to the instruction to divide up the land into its tribal portions. In this connection the verb חלק ("to divide up") is used (v 13 נחל "to take as an inheritance")—and one expects immediately the instructions for the חלק ("portion") which is to be allotted to each tribe.

■ **47:22-23** *Allocation of land to the resident aliens.* The fulfillment of this expectation is subject, however, to a further slight delay. The additional observation, which has been inserted secondarily, vv 22f, refers to the attitude towards resident aliens in the allocation of land. In this preliminary remark a ruling is given for a problem which did not arise in such a way for the Israel of the monarchical period. The resident alien in that period was not allowed to own land and was commended to the legal protection of the full citizen. Hence the unremitting admonitions in earlier laws not to oppress the גר ("resident alien") and the admonition in Deuteronomy to allow the גר ("resident alien") along with the widow and the orphan and the Levites, whose legal status was the same as that of the גר ("resident alien"),[27] to participate in the sacrificial meals in the sanctuary (Dtn 12:12 and elsewhere). During the exile something new comes about, the association of non-Israelites with the community of Yahweh worshippers.[28] When now the new entry into the land is being planned, what is to happen when the גרים ("resident aliens") who had joined the Yahweh community in Babylon also came into Yahweh's land? Vv 22f try to answer this question. They answer it fully prepared to assimilate the גר ("resident alien"). He is to receive a share in the land allocation in the tribal area where he wishes to settle, and this surely means also that he is to be incorporated into that tribe. It should be noted that the much stricter practice of Dtn 23:2–9, which will admit only גרים ("resident aliens") from Edom and Egypt, and these only in the third generation, is here clearly relaxed.[29] When Galling refers this regulation only to the second generation of גרים ("resident aliens"), this is not exactly what the text says.[30] It says that גרים ("resident aliens") who beget sons in Israel, i.e. surely have migrated with their whole family or build up their family in the land, are to be given a portion where they live—they themselves, not just their sons. It is unlikely that this whole development would have been started off only through the solidarity of the experience in exile even of a series of גרים ("resident aliens") who might have returned with the others, as Bertholet assumes.[31] The regulation belongs, rather, to the context of the reconsideration of good order in the land, the return to which is being prepared on the basis of new realities. That the practice in the community immediately after the exile must have appeared differently can be supposed from Is 56:1–8.

■ **48:1-29** *The allocation of land* begins in 48:1. In this connection we should recall the presentation in the book of Joshua, the counterpart of the allocation of land at the time of the first settlement in the land. In Josh 13:1ff it is introduced by a command of Yahweh to Joshua ordering

26 Moses Gaster, *The Samaritans: their History, Doctrines and Literature* (London: Oxford University Press, 1925), 138f, following Spiegel, "Ezekiel," 272.
27 See above p. 457.
28 See Zimmerli, "Wahrheitserweis Jahwes."
29 See also Sigmund Mowinckel, "Zu Deuteronomium 23:2–9," *Acta orientalia* 1 (1923): 90.
30 Kurt Galling, "Das Gemeindegesetz in Deuteronomium 23" in *Festschrift Alfred Bertholet* (Tübingen: Mohr [Siebeck], 1950), 190.
31 Bertholet, *Stellung,* 110–112.

him to "divide up" the land "as an inheritance" among the tribes (חלק בנחלה 13:7). After a reference to the allocation of land by Moses on the other side of the Jordan to Reuben, Gad and the half-tribe of Manasseh (13:8–32), the mention of the fact that Levi is to receive no portion but Joseph on the other hand is to receive two (13:33–14:5) and the allocation of a portion of land to Caleb (14:6–15), chapters 15–19 then describe how the remaining tribes have allocated to them by Joshua their share by "lot" (גורל 15:1; 16:1 and elsewhere).

In Ezekiel 48 there is no reference to any actual use of the lot. Everything here is determined in advance by command of Yahweh. After a superscription which would simply lead one to expect a list of tribes in a specific sequence, the allocation to the same twelve tribes as are mentioned in Joshua 13 and 15–19 is commanded. Admittedly a great difference between this and Joshua 13 and 15–19 springs immediately into view. The sequence of the twelve tribes and their portions in vv 1–7, 23–28 is split in two by vv 8–22, the disproportionately expansive description of a thirteenth portion of land. In the context of this latter allocation of land, which appears in eighth position in the series, there are cited also the Levites, who are not mentioned in the tribal enumeration and who are indemnified in Joshua 21 by the allocation of Levitical cities (with "pasture ground" מגרש but without "arable land" אחזה).[32] The conception in Ezekiel 48 is quite different. The thirteenth portion of land, which is not allocated to any tribe as such (not even Levi), is consistently described as תרומה ("consecrated area"). This term has been used, apart from 45:1–8a which is dependent on chapter 48, for the sacrificial gifts (20:40), the tithes for the sanctuary and its servants (44:30) and what was given to the prince for the maintenance of the regular sacrificial cult (45:13, 16). The (התרומה) אשר תרימו ליהוה ("[the consecrated area] which you shall consecrate to Yahweh") by which in v 9 (45:1) the most important part of this תרומה ("consecrated area") is characterized, shows quite clearly that the thirteenth portion of land is primarily a tribute to Yahweh. This is what is new in this view, that not only from the fruit of the field is a portion to be earmarked and handed over to Yahweh, but equally so from the land. This is the new and good order for the land in accordance with which Israel is to live after the second settlement graciously accorded to her. The following period, of course, then shows very clearly that this bold project of a new relationship even precisely with regard to landed property could not prevail.

■ **48:1–7** The layout of the allocation begins at the northern boundary, which is recapitulated, with the omission of some names, from 47:15f. The eastern boundary, from which each tribal portion here and in what follows stretches to the sea, i.e. to the western boundary, is not defined in any more detail. By contrast, at the end (v 28), the southern boundary is described precisely once again with the details of 47:19. The interlocking with 47:13ff, which makes it impossible to separate the two sections 47:13ff and 48:1ff, is thus once again here clearly visible. In addition, the northern tribal portions are listed in a quite stereotyped fashion, one after the other, stretching identically right across the land. The fact that there is an identical measurement for the north-south extent of each of the tribal portions may perhaps be concluded from the איש כאחיו ("each . . . as the other").[33] The northern tribes are listed from north to south in the order Dan, Asher, Naphtali, Manasseh, Ephraim, Reuben, Judah.[34]

■ **48:8–22** There follows, in vv 8–22, the expansive exposition about the תרומה ("consecrated area"), which in its east-west extension reaches, like the tribal portions, from the Jordan to the Mediterranean. Here too, for the one and only time, there is also information about the north-south extent of one of the thirteen portions (twenty-five thousand cubits). The information which is immediately added and which is repeated in v 10 for the priestly zone, namely that the sanctuary lies in the center of it, reveals already something of the most important characteristic of the תרומה ("consecrated area"). Quite clearly the dedication to Yahweh is expressed in v 9 for the zone of twenty-five thousand cubits (east-west) by twenty thousand cubits (north-south) which is to be marked off from the תרומה ("consecrated area") as a whole. In 𝔐 here too the figure twenty thousand has been tendentiously reduced to ten thousand, since the intention has been to regard only the priestly portion as Yahweh-תרומה, i.e. as

32 See Haran, "Studies."

33 On the (unrealistic) enumeration of the tribal portions each with its concluding אחד ("one") cf. vv 31–34; Josh 12:9–24.

34 On this sequence see below pp. 540–542.

sacred תרומה (v 10) (cf. v 9 note b). V 15 will make it clear that his special territory does not lie symmetrically in the center of the תרומה ("consecrated area"), marked off from the tribal portions to the north and to the south by strips two thousand five hundred cubits broad. Rather, we have an asymmetrical division of the central portion which is twenty-five thousand cubits square into two strips each of ten thousand cubits and one of five thousand broad (north-south) which, as v 21 shows, are bounded on the east and on the west by two remaining sections each measuring twenty-five thousand cubits from north to south, the east-west extent of which is not defined. In what follows, vv 10–12 deal with the priests' portion, vv 13–14 with the Levites' portion, vv 15–20 with the portion belonging to the city and vv 21–22 with the prince's land.

■ **48:10** V 10 sounds again like a superscription. We are now to be informed to whom the תרומת הקדש ("sacred area") (this designation occurs again in v 20) is to be allotted. Under this superscription the priests are cited first. These include, however, also the Levites mentioned in v 13. In v 14 it is affirmed, by way of conclusion, after the priestly and Levitical portion, that the land described in vv 10–14 is holy. V 15 then has the statement, by way of contrast, that the city land is profane. It should be observed here that the term אחזה ("possession") is not used in connection with the land of the priests and Levites. It is used in vv 20(21) for the "property" of the city. Priests and Levites alike stand side by side here as partners in the sacred תרומה ("consecrated area") under the "Levitical rule" of non-possession of property.[35] The sharp differentiation between the two, which was discernible in 45:1–8a and is present in an accentuated form in the tendentious alterations in the measurement of the sacred תרומה ("consecrated area") in 𝔐 45:1, 3f; 48:9, has not yet been achieved here. The priestly land is described here in detail in its dimensions in all four directions (twenty-five thousand cubits by ten thousand), and it is affirmed in particular of this land that Yahweh's sanctuary stands in the center of it. Since, according to v 8, the sanctuary is to be located not at the edge but in the center of the תרומה ("consecrated area") as a whole, this must suggest that the priests' portion lies between the Levites' portion and the city portion. The sequence of the enumeration from north to south, which predominated in the case of the tribes in vv 1–7, has thus been displaced in the description of the תרומה ("consecrated area") by enumeration in accordance with the degree of sanctity. Thus the assumption of Mackay that the temple mount is to be located at Shechem[36] is untenable.

In addition, the details about the priests again betray the hand of expanders who want to harmonize what is said about the priests here with the details about the priests and Levites in 44:6ff. These rules are thus to be located, from the point of view of time, later than the basic text of chapter 48.

■ **48:11** Thus v 11, entirely in accord with the ideology of 44:6ff, expands the statements about the priests, who are particularly set apart as "holy," by the reference to their obedience when Israel and the Levites went astray (see 44:15 and v 10).

■ **48:12** And v 12 adds to this the statement that the priests received their portion of land as a consecrated gift from the consecrated gift (on תרומיה "a particular consecrated part" cf. note a), and this is quite in line with the tithe which the Levites, according Nu 18:26, have to pay to the priests and which was also referred to in 44:30.[37] The Levites are thus removed from their position alongside the priests, which they occupy in the original text, and are set alongside the community who have to give gifts to the priests. The regulations about tithes in Nu 18 have here been transferred by analogy to the gift of land. The gift of land itself thus comes under the perspective of the gift to the priests. And in consequence the gift given to the priests is then qualified by the heightened holiness term קדש קדשים ("a most holy place").

■ **48:13–14** In the original text the statement about the Levites in v 13 followed immediately after v 10. The Levites' portion of the תרומה ("consecrated area") is also measured out, though here all four directions are not mentioned again. It corresponds to the priests' תרומה ("consecrated area") (twenty-five thousand by ten thousand cubits). The regulation which follows in v 14, about the inalienable nature of the land which is holy to Yahweh, again links priests and Levites together. At the same time it is made clear by this regulation, beyond all doubt,

35 See above p. 457.

36 See the map in Cameron M. Mackay, "Ezekiel's Division of Palestine among the Tribes," *PrincTR* 22 (1924): 29.

37 See above pp. 462f.

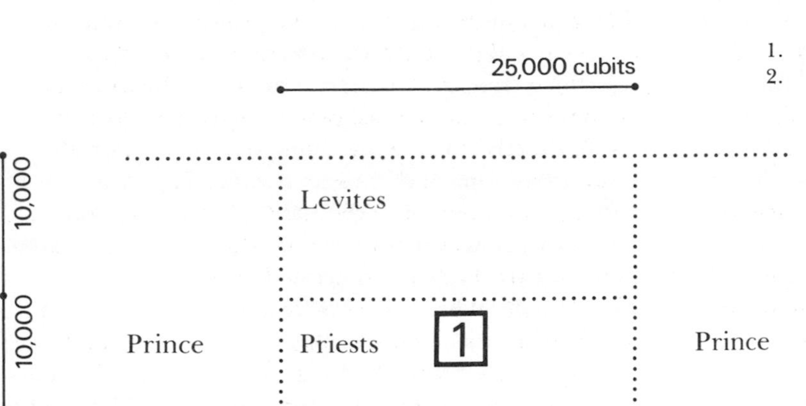

Fig. 7
The internal allocation of the תְּרוּמָה ("consecrated area") to the Priests, Levites and Prince and the position of temple and city

1. Temple precinct
2. City, including surrounding pasture ground

that Yahweh is the owner of the sacred תרומה ("consecrated area") and that neither priests nor (as in 45:1–8a) Levites have any "property" (אחזה) in it. The regulation recalls the ordinance for the prince's land in 46:16ff, but surpasses it to the extent that here it is not simply a question of the maintenance of the correct apportionment of land within the nation, but also of the preservation of Yahweh's sacred right of possession within the context of Israel's consecrated gift of land to him.

■ **48:15** When v 15 speaks of a "remainder" (נותר) which falls to the city, there stands behind that, as the "whole" against which the measurement is made, once again the wider concept of the תרומה ("consecrated area") contained v 8. The "sacred תרומה" of vv 9–14 has not yet been supplemented by the city portion described in v 15 to become the complete תרומה of v 8. But the city territory, which measures five thousand cubits by twenty-five thousand, serves to make up the sacred תרומה ("consecrated area") into a full square of twenty-five thousand cubits square. This remainder is now to serve the city as land for dwellings and for pasture. In contrast to the sacred תרומה ("consecrated area") of the priests and Levites, however, it is profane. In the formula חל הוא ("it is profane") can be discerned linguistically the form of the priest's declaratory judgment.[38] The concise observations about the city in v 15 make a few more specific remarks necessary.

■ **48:16** Once again a superscription introduces first of all the measurements for the city territory. In the same detailed fashion as in the case of the priestly land (v 10), it is measured in all four directions. Each "side" (פאה as in the case of the sides of the land as a whole, 47:15–20) measures four thousand five hundred cubits.

■ **48:17** With similar detail, the pasture land which encloses the city area on the four sides is also described, as a strip two hundred and fifty cubits broad, so that city and pasture land together cover an area five thousand cubits square—we are in the same system of measurement as in chapters 40–42. In 45:2 a similar (protective) zone of pasture land has been added secondarily, in a late addition, round about the sanctuary.[39] The square city area, if it is situated in the center of the total strip measured out in v 15, leaves free on both sides (west and east) an area of five thousand cubits by ten thousand.

■ **48:18** On these two remaining areas (הנותר "the remainder") the inhabitants of the city are to grow their food.

38 See 1,376 on 18:9. On חל cf. 22:26; 42:20; 44:23.

39 See above p. 468.

Here is to be located the city's arable land. Since only arable land is real "property," the אחזה of the city may then correctly be spoken of in v 20.

■ **48:19** Before that, however, v 19 tries to achieve clarity in a question which will emerge here. What is the relationship between the population of the city and the tribal portions? Must not the member of the individual tribe receive his portion of arable land in his tribal area? Here the rule is made that everyone who does his work in "the city" (Jerusalem) (v 18 note d), from whatever tribe he may come, receives a share in this arable land. Whether, as Ehrlich supposes, the thought of an incorporation of the kind which is found in Neh 11:1f and which brings men from the country to the city lies behind this cannot be decided with certainty.

■ **48:20** In v 20 everything described in vv 9–19 is summarized. The square which results from the union of תרומת הקדש ("the sacred area"), i.e. priests' and Levites' land, and the (profane) city property (אחזת העיר "the property of the city") is once again described with its measurements (twenty-five thousand cubits square). The fact that in v 21 reference has to be made once again to a "remaining area" (הנותר) shows that to achieve the complete תרומה ("consecrated area") of v 8, although v 20 had already referred to כל התרומה ("the whole consecrated area"), a remaining area must still be counted in, namely the land of the prince.

First of all, however, the question must be asked whether within the square תרומה ("consecrated area") described in v 20 a specific sequence of the three areas mentioned can be observed. More precisely the question narrows down to whether the Levites' land or the city territory is to be located north of the priests' territory, which undoubtedly lies in the center. Now historical recollection will clearly say that the city of David, which in chapters 40–42 was clearly marked off from the sanctuary, lay in the southern part of the temple mount. That surely permits the conclusion that the תרומה ("consecrated area")-strip where the city was is to be located south of the priests' land. The מנגב ("in the south") of 40:2 (note g), which was added by a glossator, at any rate seems to represent that point of view. In addition, one may wonder whether the location of Benjamin south of the תרומה ("consecrated area") directly next to the city territory—a location which contradicts every historical tradition—is not in fact trying to preserve the element of correct recollection that the city territory of Jerusalem once lay in Benjaminite tribal territory (Josh 18:11–28, especially v 28).

■ **48:21a** For the territory of the prince there remain those parts of the תרומה ("consecrated area")-strip stretching from the Mediterranean to the Jordan which lie to the west and the east of the square described in vv 9–20. Exactly as in the preceding section, the north-south measurement of these two remaining areas is given with figures (twenty-five thousand cubits). In great detail it is described that they border on the west and east sides of the square תרומה ("consecrated area").

■ **48:21b–22** What follows in vv 21b–22 is an addition, which, in its orientation, belongs with 45:1–8a. In it, once again the תרומת הקדש ("the sacred area"), with the sanctuary in its center, is limited to the priests' land. The Levites' portion is, like the city portion, designated as the אחזה ("property") of its inhabitants and thus deducted from the sacred consecrated area. In addition, v 22 is clearly anticipatory with the information that the prince's land, which flanks the square center to the west and to the east, lies between the tribal territories of Judah and Benjamin.

■ **48:23–29** The conclusion in vv 23–28(29) is once again introduced by a superscription, which connects with the superscription in v 1 and announces the enumeration of the remaining tribes. They are listed with a phraseology identical with that used with the first seven tribes, and the north-south direction is maintained. Benjamin is followed by Simeon, Issachar and Zebulun. Gad concludes the series. As was the case with the most northerly tribe, so too with the most southerly: its outer boundary is also described and this coincides with the southern boundary of the whole territory as described in 47:19. In the style of a tailpiece, in v 29, the statement of 47:21 which introduced the tribal enumeration is repeated, before a concluding final section, which is followed still by the formula for a divine saying, closes the list of portions. מחלקות is attested only here in the OT with the meaning "portion."

■ **48:1–29** As we look back on this great land allocation list there is still a series of questions which arise not least from a consideration of the varying use of the term תרומה ("consecrated area"). It is, first of all, quite clear that from the land of the twelve tribes a central area is to be set apart as something special. In this area that which

Fig. 8
The allocation of land to the tribes

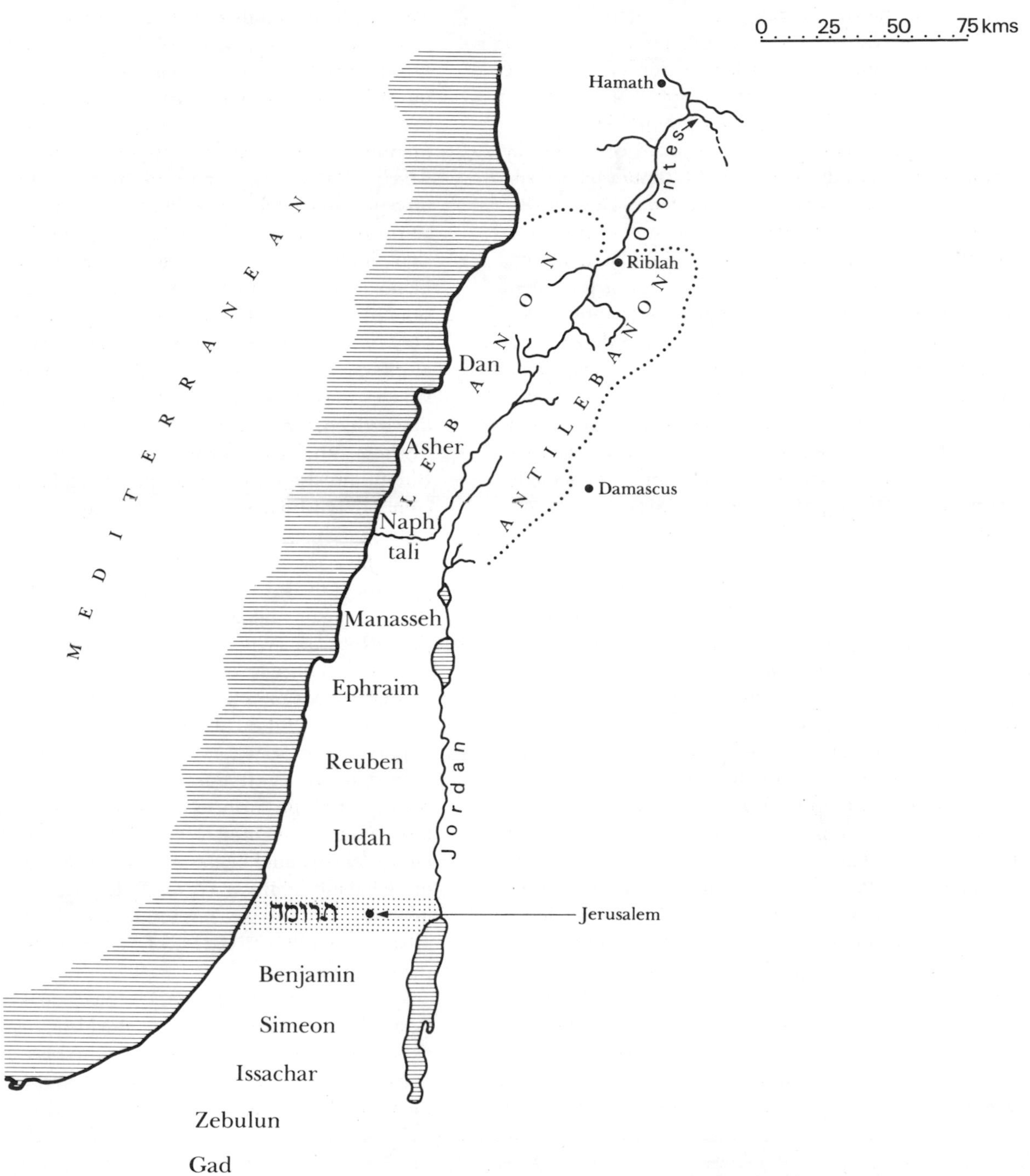

is holy predominates. But why then is not the whole separated area of the תרומה in its widest sense (v 8) declared to be the sacred area? The real intention of the dedication to Yahweh and his sanctuary of a portion of land corresponding to the tribal portions—an intention which cannot be ignored in the designation תרומה—would then acquire a much clearer expression.

This simple solution is quite obviously countered by elements in the tradition which also cannot be passed over in the bold programme contained in Ezekiel 48.

There is, on the one hand, the element of the *city* which is never named but is simply designated as העיר ("the city"). There can be no doubt that it is Jerusalem that is meant. In the whole blueprint of chapters 40–47, except in the addition in 45:1–8a which is dependent on chapter 48 (on 40:2 see above and note g there), this city has not figured at all. With the royal palace, it was banished far from the temple precinct. In a consideration of the land as a whole, however, it clearly cannot be passed over. And, equally clearly, it cannot simply be included in one of the tribal portions. Jerusalem is precisely too laden with tradition for Israel for that to happen. It is not a city like any other but is "the city." Thus, a particular area within the תרומה, which is, according to the primary intention, set apart for Yahweh and his servants, is specifically allocated to it, a remarkable, profane area within the sacred center of the new land. The significance of Jerusalem, which, as 5:5, e.g., would already show, is in reality more than any other profane area, can be discerned also in later tradition.[40] In Deutero-Isaiah and Trito-Isaiah it is not the temple but the city which stands in the center of expectations (see, e.g., Isaiah 60, where the temple is mentioned only incidentally in v 13). But even in Zechariah, who, traditio-historically, ought to stand closer to Ezekiel and who is one of the great driving forces in the building of the second temple, reference is made to Zion and Jerusalem as chosen anew by Yahweh (1:17; 2:16). There is no sign here of a breach between temple and city. Indeed, the book of Ezekiel itself, with its quite surprising conclusion in 48:30–35, where it is the city, not the temple which was separated from it according to 48:1–29, that acquires the name "Yahweh is there," testifies to the strength of the tradition of the holy city, which goes far beyond the mention of the profane Jerusalem within the area of the תרומה, which is all that 48:1–29 concedes.

The second is the figure of the *"prince"* (נשיא), who is removed rather further from the center of the תרומה but nevertheless is given his portion of land within it. The pre-exilic period had allocated to the kings, as was mentioned in connection with 46:16–18, royal property which will have been scattered throughout the land.[41] The plan in Ezekiel 48 no longer returns to this solution. In the new order it is to be that the prince too is given his share in the תרומה (in its widest sense 48:8). There can be no doubt that this portion of land too was not considered to be holy, but, like the city property, profane. Here too the phraseology in the regulation of the right of gift of the prince's land in 46:16–18 (and also 45:8), which speaks of the prince's אחוזה ("property"), is quite in line with chapter 48, even if the term is not used explicitly here. The prince's land is the prince's "property." But it is precisely also the property of a figure in the new community who has his particular rank and his significance for Israel.

So this is the place to reflect comprehensively on the position of the נשיא ("prince") in chapters 40–48. It has struck us again and again how different the figure of the prince looks in chapters 40–48 in comparison with chapters 1–39. There reference was made to "princes" of the Mediterranean area (26:16), of Arabia (27:21), of Egypt (30:13) and of Edom (32:29). Gog was described as a mighty prince (ראש נשיא "chief prince" 38:2f; 39:1). With regard to Israel, reference could be made in a polemical retrospect of the "princes (of Israel)" (7:27;[42] 22:6), their fate could be lamented (19:1; 21:17) or even the individual Zedekiah could be described by this title (12:10, 12) or be harshly addressed (21:30). In 34:24 and 37:25, however, נשיא ("prince") is found in the expectation of salvation as a title of David, whose return would usher in the era of salvation.

The references to the נשיא ("prince") in 44:3; 45f; 48 (apart from the invective in 45:8f which is clearly orientated towards the old polemic and is part of a later expansion) also obviously refer to the נשיא ("prince") in the sphere of the future realization of salvation. His

40 See 1, 174f.
41 See above p. 496.
42 See 1, 209.

description lacks, however, the glowing colors of the נשיא ("prince") of 34:24 and 37:25. There is no reference here to a definitive proclamation of salvation. With perceptible realism, there is projected the form of a new order of life in the newly gifted land and above all in the restored sanctuary. The hopes of chapters 34 and 37 ought certainly not simply to be buried. But they take a secondary place to the regulating of life in the land, which is envisaged as being for the near future, in view of the concrete tasks which then arise. What then is to be the position of the נשיא ("prince"), who in these texts is always an individual, "the" representative of the house of David on whom the promise lies? It has occasionally been asserted, in a somewhat devaluating fashion, that the prince here figures simply as an ecclesiastical patron.[43] To this extent the observation is correct that the regulations in 44:3; 45f consider the position of the נשיא ("prince") quite exclusively in connection with the cult in the new temple and endeavor to clarify his position there. The reform programme discernible in the temple statutes does not initially see beyond the sphere of cultic life. This may be connected with the fact that this planning takes place within the orbit of the major eastern power, whose obvious supremacy does not at all permit in the first place any further thinking out of political possibilities for a new "Israel." Just as judgment, according to 9:6, begins with the sanctuary and its ordinances, so too the new obedience is to begin with the sanctuary and its ordinances. In these ordinances the endeavor is made to determine the position of the prince.

When then, as in chapter 48 (45:1ff), the perspective passes beyond the sanctuary precinct and the new arrangements for the land are considered as the granting of the possibility of a completely new beginning, then the prince acquires, through the allocation of land given him within the תרומה, a clearly elevated position in contrast to the proprietary political circumstances of the pre-exilic period. Just as Jerusalem, as a city upon which lay ancient promises, cannot simply be incorporated into the tribal area but receives a share in the תרומה—even if it is a "profane" share—so too the prince, who appears before Yahweh, according to the cultic regulations of 45:21–46:12, as the true representative of the community, is not simply to be thrust back into a sphere of crown properties scattered about in the tribal portions but is to acquire his portion within the תרומה, clearly visible to the outside world. In this way he is also clearly set apart from the tribes as a whole as a special figure upon whom lies a special promise. What could have no place as yet in the land allocation of the Joshua period, however that was regarded by the later period, now exists among God's people as a phenomenon with a particular theological designation. And it is part of the new ordinance in this respect too, that it does not simply re-create the circumstances of the Joshua period, but, in the land allocation, clearly takes account of what has happened in the interval to Jerusalem and to the Davidic dynasty. The fact that in this context nothing is heard of continuing political expectations is connected with the place where this new planning arose and with the intention towards which it is orientated. We can certainly not assume that this realistic planning for the prince of the restoration period is still from the hand of the prophet Ezekiel himself, who, in the period of defeat and early exile, had first to build, through his message, the basis for new hopes among his people.

Here too the post-exilic period did not realize the plans of Ezekiel 40–48. Admittedly, at the giving back of the stolen temple vessels according to Ezr 1:8, there instantly appears, in the figure of the commissar Sheshbazzar who was entrusted with them, the expression הנשיא ליהודה ("the prince of Judah"). The Chronicler will have regarded him as a descendant of David. Since, however, the equation of Sheshbazzar with Shenazzar son of Jehoiachin (1 Chr 3:18) cannot be proved with certainty and since his function also remains remarkably obscure, not much can be deduced from this passage.[44] Sheshbazzar then disappears immediately again from the accounts. In the messianic expectations which then flare up immediately afterwards around Zerubbabel, as these can be discerned in the books of Haggai, Zechariach and Ezra, there are in the accounts no elements of the programme set forth in Ezekiel 40–48. In the Priestly writings, however, whose proximity to the Ezekiel tradition cannot be denied, in spite of the frequent occurrence of the title נשיא ("prince") for the tribal

43 See, e.g., Begrich, "Messiasbild," especially 454.

44 See also Noth, *History of Israel*, 309f; Kurt Galling, *Studien zur Geschichte Israels im persischen Zeitalter* (Tübingen: Mohr, 1964), 81.

princes of Israel (even Abraham, Gen 23:6) and Ishmael (Gen 25:16), there is only one passage, in Lev 4:22, which seems to envisage a נשיא ("prince") of Israel. It recalls the regulations of Ezek 45:21–46:12 when here for the sin offering of the נשיא ("prince") (admittedly without the article) a special ruling is laid down and a regulation for the עם הארץ ("people of the land") is at once added to it.[45] At the same time, however, this isolated mention may also reveal the concern for the significance of the נשיא ("prince") in the post-exilic community. In it there is no longer any room for the figure still envisaged by Ezekiel 40–48, the most prominent member of the community who represents his people and who is also set apart from all those who belong to tribe or city by an unusual allocation of land. Already Zechariah (particularly, e.g., in the secondary reworking of 6:9–15) shows how the figure of the high priest in the post-exilic period begins to attract to himself the most significant signs of dignity formerly characteristic of the prince of the house of David.[46]

The concentrated interest of those who planned the land arrangement is centered first of all on the sanctuary in the middle of the land and on the תרומה. Thus, then, the ordinances for priests and Levites are placed at the head of the discussion about the תרומה. For deciding the period of origin of this plan it is important to note that the land of both is described as "holy." Nothing is said in the basic text of chapter 48 about a differentiation between holy and most holy. A later hand felt obliged to add that in v 12. Thus, too, then the differentiation between *priests* and *Levites* is to be observed only in the fact that the sanctuary lies in the priests' portion. The negative emphases of 44:10ff, which defame the Levites by contrast with the Zadokites, have again been added only secondarily by a later hand in order to harmonize with chapter 44. Yet in the nomenclature priests and Levites are differentiated, and this goes beyond the phraseology of 40:45, 46a.

Here too, however, it can be seen that the plan which gives priests and Levites each a self-contained portion of land within the תרומה has not been carried through. In the legal section of P there is no further mention of this either. The regulation about the Levitical cities in Nu 35:2–8 (Joshua 21) reveals living and pasture areas for the Levites scattered throughout the land.[47]

As far as the *enumeration of the tribes* is concerned, the list which is contained here does not include Levi, but in its place the Joseph tribe appears in its two subdivisions of Manasseh and Ephraim.[48] The gloss in 47:13b (note d), which specifically attributes two sections to Joseph, presupposes the series of twelve in which Levi also figures and Joseph appears as a tribe, and aims by this means to create the compromise between Joseph and the two portions of land (to Ephraim and Manasseh).

Very remarkable is the geographical order of the tribes among whom the land on both sides of the תרומה as far as the northern and southern boundaries already described in 47:15ff is divided. In it, on the one hand, can clearly be discerned elements of already existing tradition. Thus the division of the twelve tribes into a group of seven in the north and a group of five in the south reflects the genuine recollection of the fact that the northern territory of Israel north of Jerusalem was larger than the southern territory. Yet the tribal division mentioned at the division of the kingdom of ten in the north and two for the south (1 Kgs 11:30f) has here been evened out almost to the point of complete equality of the two halves, without, however, the restoration of complete equality of the halves being hazarded.

The description of the boundaries of the land in 47:15–20 revealed that in the new arrangement the territory east of the Jordan was not included in Israel. The supposition has been expressed above that this is not simply the expression of a "policy of renunciation" forced on them from somewhere or other, but represents earlier tradition. For the establishment of a new division of the tribal portions there resulted from this the necessity of including the tribes which lived east of the Jordan in the monarchical period in the land west of the Jordan. In the course of this, Gad, with no support at all in the tradition, has been put right in the south, while the half-tribe of Manasseh enters in its correct position north of Ephraim united in a total Manasseh with that half of the tribe which lived west of the Jordan. The fact that Reuben is put immediately next to Judah may reflect its old pre-eminence as Jacob's eldest son (Gen 49:3). In

45 See Gese, 111.

46 See, e.g., Noth, "Office," 235–238.

47 On this see Haran.

48 On this see Noth, *System*, especially 3–28.

addition this may also have preserved a genuine recollection of a settlement of Reubenite groups in the area north of Jerusalem.[49]

A further principle which has led to the present sequence will have to be found in the differentiation between step-tribes and full tribes, i.e., according to Genesis 29f, between sons of principal wives and sons of secondary wives. The full tribes are given the more privileged places closer to the sanctuary. The step-tribes are on the periphery. Dan, for whom its relative position in the pre-exilic tribal settlement allocation is maintained, is in the furthest north and Asher and Naphtali adjoin it. In their case, too, this is not far from their former, actual dwelling place. We have already referred to the transfer of the step-tribe Gad to the furthest south. In the case of the four full tribes which now immediately surround the תרומה south and north, in order to preserve the intended division in the proportion of five to seven, the tribes of Issachar and Zebulun, which had settled in and to the north of the plain of Jezreel, had to be transferred to the south, where the remains of Simeon earlier had their settlements in the region of Beersheba (Josh 19:1–9). The fact that Judah and Benjamin, the actual representative tribes of pre-exilic Judah, are given the places immediately to the right and left of the תרומה is easily understood. What is remarkable here is the interchange between Judah and Benjamin in their geographical disposition. It has already been discussed above whether the old connection of Jerusalem with Benjamin, in whose territory Jerusalem lay, was not in fact still so strong in the consciousness of the exiled Jerusalemites that they were unable to sever Benjamin from "the city" by the intervention of another territorial portion. The disposition of the city territory south of the temple territory could not be altered either. On the other hand, however, the royal tribe of Judah could not be separated by the intervention of Benjamin from proximity to the תרומה or from the land of the נשיא ("prince"), who came from Judah. So, against every historical tradition, Judah was located immediately to the north. Whether the desire to establish an immediate proximity of the Leah tribe Judah with the Leah tribes Levi (in the south) and Reuben (in the north) also commended this location may be asked. The structure of this group of three in v 31 may nevertheless be noted. At any rate the position is reached that the תרומה is now immediately surrounded by the two principal tribes of the old southern kingdom of Judah, Judah and Benjamin, which was also commended for its southern location by its name בן ימין "son of the right hand, i.e. of the south."

Concerning the width of the individual tribal portions, apart from the תרומה, nothing certain can be said. If the איש כאחיו ("each . . . as the other") of 47:14 is to be understood in the strict sense so that each tribal portion is to be of equal size, then for the southern area (five tribes divided out along the distance from Jerusalem to Kadesh) a portion of about thirty kilometers width (north-south distance) could be calculated. The corresponding calculation for the northern area with its seven tribes would produce a northern boundary for the land somewhere on a level with Damascus and the southern part of the *beqāʿ*. But presumably the planners of Ezekiel 48 did not have at their disposal any very precise distance measurements for Syria-Palestine. Thus the measurements of width are missing, surely not unintentionally, for the measurement of the tribal portions. They are at any rate to be thought of as broader than the תרומה with its width of twenty-five thousand cubits (twelve and a half kilometers). In no case, however, do these considerations lead to any certain conclusion for the problems of the northern boundary.

Of this plan for the allocation of land, too, it must be stated that post-exilic reality reveals no sign of its having been carried out. The complete disappearance of the tribes of the former northern kingdom would certainly not lead us to expect anything else. The list of those returning from exile Ezra 2/Nehemiah 7 reveals no sign of any division into tribes. It speaks in comprehensive fashion of the "men of the people of Israel" (Ezr 2:2) or simply of "Israel" (Ezr 2:59). Nevertheless, here too, in the leading group of twelve men, it is possible to discern the "saving history aspect": "It is the leadership of Israel, the community which was once made up of twelve tribes."[50] One may ask how the originator of Ezekiel 48 envisaged the creation of the presuppositions for the new order of land allocation. It has been felt here that behind

49 See Noth, *History of Israel*, 63–65.
50 Galling (see fn. 44), 95.

the new allocation of land, soberly planned on the drawing board, there is encountered once again the expectation of a miraculous restoration of the nation of twelve tribes. This shows that the actualization of the arrangements for the new land cannot be separated from the expectation of the great gathering in, to be brought about by Yahweh alone, of the Israel that had been scattered through all lands (20:34). Here too the new order is planned against the background of divine miracle.

Setting

The detailed examination of 47:13–48:29 has made it clear that the basic text of the programme for land allocation that is developed here takes its specific place in the tradition structure of chapters 40–48. In its delimitation of the land to be allocated, in 47:15–20, it can only with difficulty be understood against a background of purely exilic considerations, but must go back to earlier land postulates. In the enumeration of boundary points it presupposes list-type material which has also been used in a different adaptation in the (later) section Numbers 34.

In the projected land allocation, on the other hand, one has the impression of coming upon a purely exilic programme precisely at the points where older elements (evaluation of the city, of the prince) made it necessary to make quite specific modifications and inconsequential changes in the plan. The actual circumstances of the restoration period are not yet discernible. Furthermore, a glance at the treatment of the sanctuary servants makes it clear that the distinction between priests and Levites has already been carried through in the terminology, which seems to suggest a period later than the state of affairs envisaged in 40:45, 46a. The strong interest in the נשׂיא ("prince") also shows that there is a concern to think in quite concrete terms of the position to be accorded to the representative of the Davidic dynasty in a post-exilic community which is assembled round the center formed by the temple. On the other hand, there is still no sign in the basic text of the devaluation of the Levites and of the view of history represented in 44:10ff. Only the secondary addition in 48:11 introduces the Zadokites along the lines of chapter 44. Also, only in the secondary v 12 is anything said about a differentiation between holy and most holy with regard to land portions within the תרומה ("consecrated area"). Thus chapter 48 is clearly earlier than the slightly re-emphasized presentation in 45:1–8a. It can, however, be said with certainty that 47:13–48:29 also emerges from priestly reflection. Here too we are dealing with the "school" which hands on Ezekiel's words.

Aim

In the present section we are dealing with a new relationship between the people of God and the land which their God has restored to them. In the background of the whole layout which is developed here there stands the oath mentioned in 47:14 which was sworn by God to the patriarchs and in which he promised them the land as the place where they could live in the presence of God. This land God's community lost through their straying from him. Now, through the prophetic promise, they are positioned anew on the threshold of this land, ready to enter it and there experience the faithfulness of God who wishes to adhere to his original promise.

What is now described here as a fairly sober, clearly presented project of land allocation is to be understood as the correct response of God's people to the gift of land, newly given by God and understood as the token of his mercy. It had been seen how God's people are brought again to that threshold over which it entered the land once in their early history. How are they correctly to honor God in the gift which they receive as a token of his mercy? That is the question which dominates the regulations laid down in 47:13–48:29.

The first aspect is clarified right at the beginning. It is not to be that everyone is now to rush on the land, seeking to snatch as his prize as much as he can snatch, in which process, as in that flock which no longer has a good shepherd (chapter 34), the strongest acquires the largest share and the weak falls under the feet of the strong. Although there is no reference here to a Joshua who would divide the land, any more than there is of the good shepherd who helps everyone to acquire what is his right, the just rule of allocation is made clear: each and every one alike is to receive his portion. The rule of the just portion is to prevail.

Still more clearly does the second aspect stand out. From the whole, newly bestowed gift, "the best of the land" (ראשית הארץ 48:14) is to be set apart. No human hand is to reach out for it as if it belonged to it. Rather, this "selected area" which lies around the (historical) center of the land is to be an area which is freed from the possession of the twelve tribes—the permanent reminder of the fact that the land is a gift. Such freedom to withdraw "the best" (ראשית) from their own use and hand it over to God occurs also in the way in which God is given the honor for a gift (Ex 23:19; 34:26; Lev 2:12 and elsewhere).

In the use of this gift, however, it should emerge in what way God has dealt with his people. The area around the place of God's proximity must not simply lie fallow. Priests and Levites are to receive their portion here. Those who serve in the holy place are not to go hungry. God feeds them from the best that is his own property (Psalm 84). The servant in the holy place, however, is not to feed on this best in such a way that he treats it insolently as his own rightful possession (1 Sam 2:12ff). He is not to sell it as his own property as if he were the owner of it, but he is to keep God's holy place holy and acknowledge it as God's property (48:14). At the same time, however, within the area of this gift of land that is set apart there is also room at the disposal of the city—the place which is set apart through God's history from all other cities. Still further, in this area land is also allocated to the prince, the descendant of David, land from which he can live. God has had special dealings wih David and has pronounced over the house of David the great promise for the future which gives hope to all Israel. Thus the delimited, consecrated area in its various parts, not all of them equally sacred, keeps alive the memory of God's way with his people. In submitting to this arrangement God's people honor the God who has come to them not directly from heaven without a history but in his activity on earth, in which activity Jerusalem and David became important.

It is a particular characteristic of humble care that in this arrangement of the correct allocation of God's gracious gift foreigners were also subsequently included (47:22f), those who are not already part of God's history through blood and descent, but who, through seeing God's activity with his people and overwhelmed by the resultant testimony (Is 45:14f, 22ff; Zech 2:15; 8:20ff), have come to him from outside. Alongside the word which has been added in 48:12 and which delimits still further the place of the divine presence and alongside the particular setting apart of the "sanctified" Zadokite priests which removes the holy still further, there is found in the later development of the text the invitation to those who are outside and their full participation in the possession of land. In this can surely be seen in outline something of the double way taken in the subsequent period by the encounter of God with his people—the duality which is reflected in the OT canon in the juxtaposition of Ezra and, for example, the instruction of the book of Jonah and to which a definitive answer is given by the parable of the great banquet (Lk 14:15–24) in the mouth of the Son.

3. The City and its Gates

Bibliograhy

Cameron M. Mackay
"The City of Ezekiel's Oblation," *PrincTR* 21 (1923): 372–388.

48

30 **These are the exits[a] of the city: From the**
north side[b] which measures[c] four thou-
sand five hundred (cubits) 31/—and the
gates of the city (are) named after the
tribes of Israel—[a], three gates[b] [facing
north][c]: the gate of Reuben: one, the gate
of Judah: one, the gate of Levi: one.

48:30 30a 𝔐 תוצאת. 𝔊 αἱ διεκβολαί ($\mathfrak{L}^{WC}$ *emissiones*), 𝔅 *egressus*, 𝔗 𝔖 מפקני[ה]. The word is attested only here in Ezekiel. In 42:11; 43:11; 44:5 מוצא was used. Is this simply different linguistic usage or is it a conscious differentiation between city and temple gates? Although תוצאת is not found elsewhere with the meaning "gates," but occurs frequently in Nu 34; Josh 15–19 referring to the offshoot, endpoint of a boundary line, we must not take it to mean "outskirts" here as Cooke does and have to refer it to the measuring of the outer wall.

b 𝔐 מפאת is clearly defined by the יצא in תוצאת and should not be emended without further consideration to (צפונ[ה]) פאת with which the list without a superscription would surely begin (so Bertholet, Fohrer, Gese, BH[3]). The imposition of strict uniformity on vv 30–34 is prohibited also by further observations on the text.

c 𝔐 מדה occurs again only in connection with the south side (v 33). 𝔅, which renders it freely in both places by *mensurabis* and *metieris* respectively, and 𝔗 correspond to 𝔐. 𝔊 offers in addition a μέτρῳ in connection with the west side too (v 34), while 𝔖, which as usual treats the text in the freest way, adds the משוחתא in the fourth place too where the measurement of the side is given, in v 32. This clearly looks like a secondary uniformity imposed on the text.

31 31a The sentence in v 31aα clearly breaks the connection bewteen v 30b and v 31aβ. It is usually transferred by commentators to after v 30a, but this, in view of the connection of מפאת with תוצאת, is scarcely admissible. It is, rather, an additional observation, inserted secondarily at an inappropriate point, which expresses explicitly what would also be clear from what follows.

b 𝔐 שערים is attested by the versions, even by 𝔊 𝔖, which like the syndetic connection, and should not be emended. There is nevertheless the possibility that the copula was omitted only after the insertion of the gloss v 31aα, since the asyndetic connection after the half verse which begins with שערי העיר is stylistically more correct.

c 𝔐 צפונה has been inserted after v 31aβ became separated from v 30b by the insertion of v 31aα.

32 **And on the east side[a] four thousand five hundred (cubits) and three gates: <>[b] the gate of Joseph: one, the gate of Benjamin: one, the gate of Dan: one.**
33 **And the south side, which measures[a] four thousand five hundred (cubits) and (has) three gates: the gate of Simeon: one, the gate of Issachar: one, the gate of Zebulun: one.**
34 **<And>[a] the west side four thousand five hundred (cubits) <and> three <gates>[b] the gate of Gad: one, the gate of Asher: one, the gate of Naphtali: one.**
35 **Round about, eighteen thousand (cubits). And the name of the city from now on shall be: Yahweh is there[a].**

32 32a 𝔐 ואל פאת קדימה does not necessarily need to be harmonized with פאת[ו] in vv 33, 34, cf. v 30 notes b and c.

b 𝔐 ושער. The copula, which is stylistically unusual at this point, should, with 11 MSS and the versions (even 𝔗), be deleted.

33 33a Cf. v 30 note c.

34 34a 𝔐 פאת. The versions (this time without 𝔗, which corresponds to 𝔐) presuppose the copula. It would be better to read it here.

b 𝔐 שעריהם. The suffix does not have an obvious antecedent. 𝔊 𝔖 attest the form ושערים, which should be restored here.

35 35a 𝔊 *καὶ τὸ ὄνομα τῆς πόλεως, ἀφ' ἧς ἂν ἡμέρας γένηται, ἔσται τὸ ὄνομα αὐτῆς* has misunderstood the final words of 𝔐 as יִהְיֶה שָׁמָּה and has referred the מיום, with a free expansion, to the future (?) new day of Jerusalem's formation. Here, in fact, we would have to find the day to which the vision of chapters 40–48 points, with its prospect of Yahweh's re-entry into his sanctuary. With sonorous phraseology (one cannot postulate a direction in שָׁמָּה, see also 23:3; 32:29f), expression is given to Yahweh's presence in Jerusalem, now valid for all time. So 𝔙 *ex illa die.* 𝔗 מיומא דישרי יהוה שכינתיה תמן "from the day on which Yahweh will make his שכינא to dwell there." 𝔖 changes the name to מריא שמהה "Lord is his name." See also Driver, "Ezekiel," 312.

Form

A superscription in the style of the superscriptions of 48:1, 16 is followed by a description of the city, visualized as a square, and its sides which face the four points of the compass. The structure recalls the description of the four national boundaries in 47:15–20. Still closer, however, is the description in 48:16, where the four outer sides of the city are measured with the same measurement. One can hear the double echo of the מדות ("measurements") of the superscription of v 16 in the affixed מדה ("measurement") in vv 30, 33. But the sequence of the points of the compass corresponds to neither of the two parallels. The (unrealistic) enumeration of the gates with final אחד ("one"), however, corresponds once again to the tribal enumeration in vv 1–7, 23–27. When, on each occasion, the reference to the direction is followed first by the measurement of the city wall and then by the list of the gates, this scarcely gives us the right, with Jahn and Hölscher, abruptly to abbreviate and critically eliminate the measurements of the city walls which are added together to give a total circumference in v 35a. Thus in the formal structure, the dependence on the pattern given in chapters 47f should not be overlooked. The conclusion of the whole in the giving of a name recalls the frequent occurence of this element of the new name in Trito-Isaiah (58:12; 60:14, 18; 61:3; 62:2, 4, 12).

Setting

The marked, formal dependence on elements in the preceding section shows that the author of vv 30–35 had that section before him when he wrote down his text. On the other hand, however, the content prevents us from assuming an identity of authors. While in 47:13–48:29, as in the preceding sections of chapter 40–48, the temple stands in the center, here, quite surprisingly, it is the city which is the place of Yahweh's presence. This is closer to what is said in Deutero- and Trito-Isaiah. Vv 30–35 will have to be regarded as a late expansion, which, from the point of view of subject matter, leaves the line of the previous statements in chapters 40–48 but is formally closely dependent on the immediately preceding section. The old tradition of the city of Jerusalem as the place of the divine presence finds expression here once more, unconcerned by all that has been stated earlier.

Interpretation

■ **48:30** With the unusual word תוצאת ("gates"), which is otherwise unknown in the book of Ezekiel, a superscription here at the beginning heralds the description of the gates. Somewhat surprisingly, there is then prefixed, after the mention of the gates, the measurement of the outer circumference of the four sides of the city, measurements already familiar from v 16. This is to be regarded as conscious dependence on v 16, where one would actually also normally expect a reference to the gates.

■ **48:31-34** Even the addition in v 31a*α*, appended secondarily by way of elucidation, is dependent on what has gone before (48:1) and is basically a gloss on the superscription in v 30a with the observation, which, in view of the following enumeration, is not at all necessary, to the effect that the gates are named after the tribes. The תוצאת ("gates") of v 30 are thus interpreted by the normal שׁערים ("gates").

Just as, according to Parrot, twelve entrances led into the sacred precinct of the Babylonian ziggurat Etemenanki,[1] so "the city," according to 48:30–35, has twelve exits, with, in Israel, the number twelve being referred to the twelve tribes. The gates are divided symmetrically among the four sides of the city, each of which measures four thousand five hundred cubits (not poles, so Mackay). While a Benjamin or Ephraim gate in pre-exilic Jerusalem (Jer 37:13; 2 Kgs 14:13) naturally took its name from the region reached by whoever went out through the gate in question, this natural connection cannot be maintained here in view of the fact that the sequence of tribes is along a north-south axis. The three gates leading west and the three leading east cannot be called after tribes which lay in that direction. Thus, other connections for the order of the gates must be found. Closer examination shows that their allocation must presuppose the order of tribes in vv 1–29, which once more attests the dependence of vv 30–35 on what precedes. In this way still closer regard is paid to the closer genealogical relationships.

In the enumeration of the names of the gates, following the order north-east-south-west, the system is used which still contains the name Levi and which groups the half tribes Ephraim and Manasseh under the name Joseph.[2] In contrast to vv 1–29, we are not dealing here with land allocation, which would prevent a reference to Levi. The discrepancy between the two tribal lists has contributed to the insertion of the gloss in 47:13b. In what follows the tribes are grouped in the following way. The northern gates are named after the two tribal territories which lie immediately to the north, Reuben and Judah. Alongside them there is mentioned Levi, whose portion in the תרומה ("consecrated area") lies in direct proximity to Judah. In this way the three more important Leah tribes are listed together. The remaining three Leah tribes, Simeon, Issachar and Zebulun, the last two of which were displaced in the land allocation (vv 25f) from their historical location in the north to the south for the reasons mentioned above,[3] give their names to the three southern gates. The arrangement on the significant east side is obviously also determined by a closer genealogical relationship. Benjamin and Joseph are sons of Rachel. Dan, which is brought down from the far north, is, according to Gen 30:5f, a son of Rachel's maid Bilhah. On the west side, on the other hand, the side which is least esteemed, are set the names of the three remaining step-tribes. Gad and Asher are sons of Leah's maid Zilpah and Naphtali is Bilhah's second son. Thus the distribution of the tribal names is clearly dominated by genealogical derivation. It appears here still more decisively than in the land allocation in vv 1–29, where the Rachel tribes were separated. In these principles of distribution, too, one can see a contrast with vv 1–29.

■ **48:35** While in vv 30–34 the measurement of the sides is followed by the tribal or gate names, in v 35 the total measurement is followed by the comprehensive name of the city. "Three are called by the name of the Holy One, blessed be He," says R. Samuel b. Nahmani in the name of R. Johanan,[4] "and they are the following: The righteous, the Messiah and Jerusalem. The righteous as we have already said (see Is 43:7). The Messiah, for it is written: And this is the name by which he will be called,

1 Parrot, *Babylon*, 45.
2 See Noth, *System*.
3 See above p. 541.
4 *b. B. Bat.* 75b.

The Lord (= יהוה) is our righteousness (Jer 23:6). Jerusalem, for it is written: Round about eighteen thousand, and the name of the city from then on shall be 'the Lord (יהוה) is there,' but do not read 'there' (שָׁמָּה) but 'its name' (שְׁמָהּ), i.e. its name is Yahweh." According to this we have represented here an interpretation which gives to the city the very name Yahweh. But 𝔐 on the other hand is surely correct with its reading. That Yahweh is in Jerusalem, so that the latter can in fact be called after him, links up with 43:1ff, where Jerusalem has taken the place of the temple. So, too, the Zion Psalms 46, 48, 76 celebrate Jerusalem, Zion, as Yahweh's dwelling place. It is over Jerusalem, too, according to Isaiah 60, that the glory of Yahweh rises. Thus it is given the name "city of Yahweh, the Zion of the Holy One of Israel" (60:14; see further 62:2, 4, 12 as well as 1:26). The last sentence of the book of Ezekiel shows how the old tradition of the city of God has forcefully obtained justice for itself against the priestly reform project, which, through the separation of city and temple, has robbed the city of much of its dignity.

Aim

It is the aim of this addition, which comes from a different hand but which emerges entirely from the information given in 48:16, to represent the glory of the city of Jerusalem, which in the exposition hitherto of chapters 40–48 has been, in the experience of the author, unjustifiably suppressed. It has twelve gates like that magnificent area around the ziggurat Etemenanki. In the names of the twelve gates, however, the totality of the nation of twelve tribes can be discerned. Admittedly, in contrast to Is 54:12, nothing is said of the magnificence of the gates adorned with precious stones, nor is the transformation of the city described any more as it is in Isaiah 60 with glowing colors such as is the case in the verses round about Rev 21:12f, where the present passage is cited in the description of Jerusalem coming down from heaven. The unique thing which still ensues here is the giving of the new name to the city which arises transformed. In this name there is included of course the greatest that can be said. What was reported in 43:1ff, the return of Yahweh to his temple, is here transferred to the city, which then once more, as in former times, is viewed in close relationship with the temple. Yahweh is there.

Herein, however, lies the fulfillment of the deepest expectation which, from chapters 8–11 onwards, has lain over the oracles of the prophetic book. God, who had to leave his people because of the abominations which had happened in its midst, will once again be with his people. It can now be once more that the members of God's people can come to the place where he declares himself to his people as the ever present one and find life in the presence of the holy and merciful one. The text does not attempt to anticipate rashly what men may not appropriate for themselves. "From now on" (מיום) "the city" will bear the new name. This "now," however, lies in the hands of the God who, according to the introductory statements of chapters 40–48, had revealed himself to his prophet as being imminently about to come.

Setting

The Literary Pre-History of Chapters 40–48. The detailed examination of chapters 40–48 has shown that this complex has arisen in the course of a lively history of growth. Now is the time to reflect on that history in its totality and to summarize what can be said about the "setting" of chapters 40–48. In this domain Gese has done valuable spadework.

The form of chapters 40–48 is that of a great account of a vision. The date and introductory superscription of the vision are thus indissolubly linked with the guidance vision which is found in 40:1–37, 47–49; 41:1–4 and in which the prophet is led to the goal of the holy of holies. This is to be regarded as the core of chapters 40–48. It was noted in that context that the vision, regardless of the elements of movement within it, guidance and measurement, revealed no awareness of the height of structures, but, in its omission of all references to heights, pointed to a ground sketch plan of the whole temple area, the measurements of which were then described.

The detailed examination also showed that the complex 41:5–15a, in spite of its quite different stylistic structure, is indispensable to the full understanding of the measurements imparted in the guidance vision. The juxtaposition of figure 5 and figure 6 makes clear the complementary character of the guidance vision and the description in 41:5–15a, which originally also must have lacked all height measurements.[5] In 41:5–15a we see the author poring over the same ground plan as in the guidance vision. To this there belongs also 42:15–20, which rounds off the total measurement of the temple area and stylistically cannot be separated from 41:13–15a. Thus the core of the guidance vision, which, form-critically and according to its inner structure, represents a self-contained section, must have been expanded soon after its composition, and by the hand of the same author, by the expansion represented by 41:5–15a.

In what follows, 43:1–11(12) could not be removed too far either from the basic element of guidance. Here the prophet envisages how the glory of Yahweh returning from the east to the temple takes possession of the latter. This report represents a much more lively "vision" than the preceding measuring of the temple. What is described here proves, when one looks at the book as a whole, to correspond to the great vision of the sin in the temple in chapters 8–11 and the departure of Yahweh's glory described there. Thus we have probably reached here the really definitive statement of the transportation vision of chapters 40ff, unmistakably understood as a counterpart to chapters 8–11. It comes about here, too, that Yahweh begins to speak, promising his eternal presence and proclaiming the new temple ordinance. The guidance vision, at the climax of which the guidance figure makes a designation statement, has, regarded on its own, something unsatisfactory about it. The separation of the (neutrally) holy awaits the speech of the one who is himself personally holy. Just as the vision of the temple abomination in chapter 8 was the presupposition for the proclamation of judgment that follows in chapter 9 and the subsequent departure of Yahweh from his sanctuary, so the description of the new sanctuary including the holy of holies is the presupposition for the renewed coming of Yahweh and the proclamation of his abiding presence with his people. In both passages, the one cannot be without the other. In addition, there is what was established in the course of the detailed exegesis, namely the strong inner relationship of the two units to each other. The polemic which can be heard in 43:7–9 against the connection of temple and palace provides the explanation, necessary for full comprehension, of the total layout of the temple precinct which was silently measured in chapters 40f. The return of 43:10f (12), thus providing a framework, to the demand, uttered at the beginning by the guidance figure, to proclaim what has been seen to the house of Israel (40:4) seems to commend the connection between 43:1–11(12) and the basic material plainly distinguished in chapters 40–42.

In this connection there may be posed the question of the temporal sequence of the composition of the individual sections. Did 43:1–11(12) originally follow directly on 40:1–37, 47–49; 41:1–4 so that the prophet saw the coming of Yahweh to the holy of holies immediately after he had been led there? One would then of course have to reckon with the idea that an original ויוצאני (or וישבני ?) had been replaced in 43:1, as a result of the והוציאני of 42:15 which has subsequently intervened, by the ויולכני of 𝔐. 43:1ff to begin with presupposes the prophet to be outside the temple area. Thus one is surely better to reckon, as has been done in the exposition, with the idea that the guidance vision has first had 41:5–15a and 42:15–20 added to it before 43:1–11(12) was added. In all this, however, the intention is to describe a single coherent vision.

In response to the question about the origin of the basic elements of the vision hitherto mentioned, it was stated above that their derivation from the prophet Ezekiel cannot conclusively be excluded.[6] 29:17–21, the latest dated oracle of the prophet, pointed to the twenty-seventh year after Jehoiachin's deportation. 29:21 stated that the imminently expected fall of Egypt would be for the house of Israel the "sprouting of a horn," i.e. imminent deliverance, and that the prophet himself would thereby gain new confidence. The vision of the new temple and of Yahweh's impending return, which is dated two years earlier in the twenty-fifth year, shows then how the prophet's outward looking has already begun to take shape in terms of very definite reflections on the layout of the new sanctuary.

It must now be asked whether there are not other elements of a visionary nature which should be included in the older basic content of chapters 40–48. Fohrer has followed this line and has put together 43:1–9; 44:1–3

5 See above p. 357; p. 376; pp. 375–380.

6 See above p. 345.

and 47:1–12 as an "Account of an Ecstatic Experience." Just as little as it is advisable, on the basis of our earlier arguments, to separate 43:1ff from the introductory measuring of the temple, so much must the connection suggested here with other elements of visionary material be along the right lines. 44:1–2 (on v 3 see below), the vision of the closed east gate, is, from the content point of view, closely connected with 43:1ff, the vision of the entry of Yahweh's glory into the temple. The next following element of visionary description in 44:4f has proved on detailed analysis to be a later, imprecise copy of 43:1ff and 40:4 (taking account of 44:1f). The section has the aim of introducing the complex 44:6ff, which begins here with completely new subject matter. A further section of visionary guidance description follows in 46:19–24. Yet this section was discernible from its content, which clearly presupposes 44:6ff (and 42:1–14), as a late element which is interested in further specialization and the exclusive nature of degrees of holiness. On the other hand, 47:1–12 stood out by reason of its easy omission of these concerns. Here the knowledge of Yahweh's saving presence in the sanctuary, of which 43:1ff had spoken, lies behind this as a major element when the subject matter is the river which runs from the sanctuary bringing wholeness to the land round about. At the same time it could be seen that 44:1f, the account of the closed east gate, was presupposed. For this reason the most likely assumption is that the visionary description, in an earlier stage of its development, continued in 44:1f and in 47:1–12 and reached its resounding conclusion in 47:12a.[7] In this connection, in view of the conclusion reached in 43:1–11(12), it is not improbable that the two last-mentioned sections also were added, for their part, in the course of a somewhat later expansion. Since Ezekiel's acquaintance with Isaianic preaching as well as with the paradise tradition is clearly discernible[8] and since he may well have encountered the phenomenon of the "closed gate" in the world of his Babylonian exile, here too one cannot strictly exclude the possibility that both sections originated with Ezekiel. At any rate the question must be asked here whether the school which passed on Ezekiel's oracles would have handed down on their own initiative such characteristic figurative elements of a visionary nature. Yet this counter possibility cannot be necessarily excluded either.

This expanded account of a vision has then subsequently been enriched by a wealth of further additions in which the recollection of the visionary structure of the basic material is completely forgotten. In these additional sections we felt that we could detect an increasing realism in the reflections in view of the imminent new beginning in the land.

More precisely, in the context of this expansion of the basic visionary material, it is clear that the account of the process of measuring the sanctuary, which is rounded off by 42:15–20, has proved to be the most inflexible with regard to these expansions. Its core, the guidance vision of 40:1–41:4, has been penetrated only in 40:38–46 by a double addition in the description of the inner north gate. While the first part (vv 38–43) refers strictly to the north gate and describes the equipment found there for the preparation of the offerings, the second part (vv 44–46) widens the viewpoint to include also the inner south gate, which had already been dealt with in 40:28–31. This imprecision might be an argument in favor of the suggestion that vv 44–46 have been appended only secondarily to vv 38–43. The exact locality in which precisely the guidance vision had found itself in vv 35–37 has more clearly disappeared from sight. While vv 38–43 offered little evidence for a relative dating, the designation of the two priestly groups in vv 45–46a shows that the terminological distinction between priests and Levites of 44:10ff has not yet asserted itself and that consequently vv 44–46a must reflect an earlier state of affairs than 44:6ff. On the other hand, the addition of the naming of the second-named group of priests in v 46b unmistakably represents a "metastasis" of the point of view of 44:6ff. It must have been added as a harmonizing observation when 44:6ff was worked in (see below).

A further expansion in 42:1–14 has disrupted the original connection between 41:5–15a and 42:15–20.[9] Since it has been felt that one can see in the priestly sacristies described here a "rebuilding," greatly extended, of the still very modestly designed chambers of 40:44–46 for the priests of both categories, i.e. the later priests and Levites, and since the context also reveals a

7 On v 12b see pp. 514f.

8 See 1,172; 1,463 and above pp. 300f and 90f respectively.

9 See above pp. 397f.

fairly strict observance of the differentiated degrees of holiness within the temple, we should regard 42:1–14 as having been composed later than 40:44–46a. 42:1–14 also shows an advanced precision in that the difference in height between the two courts, which was not observed in 40:44–46a, seems to be precisely observed here. Thus impressions of height play a part here (in contrast to the basic form of chapters 40–42).

Subsequently the direct connection of 42:1–14 with 41:5–15a has then been disrupted by the insertion of 41:15b–26. This section, as the garbled ending shows, has been taken from a larger context. The form of wall ornamentation, which is discernibly more modest than that of 1 Kings 6f, to which in many respects it is closely related, surely prevents us from regarding it as a description of the first temple. The carefree differentiation between the upper and lower parts of the wall also shows its distance from the basic text. Into this context then there has also been inserted secondarily the addition in 41:21b–22 about the table of the showbread, surprisingly still completely in the style of the full visionary description. It harshly disrupts the description of the door and must be an even later element.

No further elements of temple description, on the other hand, have succeeded in forcing their way into the complex of chapters 40–42. This is true of the description of the great altar (43:13–17), for which 40:47 would have afforded the appropriate point of connection. It is true also of the description of the sacrificial kitchens in 46:19–24. This is once more in the form of a visionary guidance experience. It could have been appropriately connected with 42:1–14. The impression given by chapters 40–42 of being definitively closed no longer allowed the inclusion of these portions of text.

All the livelier, by way of compensation, is the history of the development of the expanded basic vision of 43:1–11(12); 44:1–2; 47:1–12. While the element of the temple stream flowing out into the land has attracted to itself only the great programme of land allocation (47:13–48:29), with the element of the city found there experiencing a secondary, more detailed description (in 48:30–35), so to the element of the appearance and proclamation of God in the temple and to the vision of the closed east gate a wealth of more precise instructions for the temple precinct has accrued in a complex history of development.

A first level of expansion is concerned with the figure of the נשׂיא ("prince") in the newly erected temple and with his place in the community's cult. In this context the community is described as "people of the land."[10]

In the new building project, one of the radical, novel characteristics which struck us was the strict separation of the sanctuary from palace and city. The divine proclamation then let us hear the extent to which the geographical separation of the temple precinct and the royal precinct is raised with passionate vigor to a programmatic level. Hence, on the approach of the period of new beginnings in the land, the question must have arisen how the position of the Davidic ruler, over whom the divine promise still extended, was to be defined within the framework of temple life. A response to this is given by the group of regulations which is appended in 44:3; 46:1–12 (minus v 11) with regard to the vision of the closed outer east gate in the temple area. It must initially have been inserted as a self-contained stratum (Gese's נשׂיא "prince"-stratum) between the statement about the closed temple gate and the account of the temple stream. The rule about the closed gate (to the outer east gate of 44:1f there is added also, in 46:1, the inner one) and the regulation about the passage of the people through the gates play a decisive role here. To the prince is granted the privilege of using rooms inside the east gate structure. The distancing of the royal precinct from the temple is thus correctly compensated for by this granting of privilege to the prince in his people's cultic practice.

One can ask, though scarcely be able to answer conclusively, whether the gate and access regulations for prince and people were prefaced from the very beginning by the regulation for the prince to present the festival offerings[11] and whether the two ritual-type regulations in 45:18–20 (cleansing of the sanctuary at the beginning of the year) and 46:13–14(15) (*Tamid*), which do not mention the prince, originally preceded and followed this complex.

It can then, however, be clearly seen how into the complex of the נשׂיא ("prince")-regulations, a section of a

10 עם הארץ (see above pp. 484f).

11 On this see Gese.

quite different type, introduced by the introduction in 44:4f, could be inserted secondarily in such a way that the natural connection of 44:3 with the later regulations for the נשיא ("prince") is broken. This complex, which violently intervenes and is furnished with the strongest emphases, deals with the priesthood. There is still no sign of a high priest. All the emphasis is on the different qualifications of priests and Levites. The polemic tone does not at all match the surrounding regulations for the נשיא ("prince"). The original components of these priestly regulations were shown, on analysis, to be 44:6–16, 28–30a. To them the תרומה-regulation of 45:13–15 could just possibly belong. The regulation for the priests has then subsequently (perhaps successively) been enriched by the additions in 44:17–27, 30b–31.

The most difficult chapter to assess is chapter 45, which leads from the regulations for the priest back again to those for the נשיא ("prince"). In the first place, vv 1–8 have clearly proved to be an addition to the תרומה-regulation in 44:30, an addition which has before it the land allocation of 48:1–29 but the details of which have been slightly modified in dependence on the anti-Levitical regulations of 44:6ff. V 9, too, which also makes the transition with a strongly polemical emphasis to the topic of the prince, seems to come from the hand of the late author of vv 1–8, who has also given their present form to vv 10–17. The תרומה-ordinance in vv 13–15, which has been worked in by him too, could once have been directly linked to 44:30a. But where did the continuation of the נשיא ("prince") topic, which was broken off after 44:3, originally begin, if the polemical structuring of the present text, which passes to the topic "prince" in 45:9, cannot come from the hand of the author of 44:3? In vv 18–20 there is prefixed to vv 21–25, which reports the sacrificial duties of the prince at the great festivals, surely again from a later hand, the ritual of an expiatory custom at the beginning of the year in which the prince plays no part. Thus we might consider whether the original continuation of the נשיא ("prince")-statement of 44:3 is to be found in 45:21–25. The topic of the closed gate then reappears in 46:1ff.

Thus the literary growth of chapter 45 is to be described thus: the catchword תרומה in 44:30a (vv 30b–31 must have been added only later) seems to necessitate a reference at this point also to the land-תרומה and in 45:1–8 attracted an excerpt from 48:1–29 modified in terms of the Levitical theory of chapter 44. The reference to the prince's land in the תרומה gave the author an opportunity to admonish the princes. This immediately introduced, in formal dependence on 44:6, the renewed discussion of the duties of the נשיא ("prince"). In this discussion there was incorporated the תרומה-regulation for the people, which connects with 44:30a and was originally formulated with no thought for the prince. When it was thus incorporated, it was prefaced by a summons directed at the prince to insure correct weights and measures and followed by a regulation in vv 16–17 anticipating like a superscription the following sacrificial regulations for the prince. This also achieves the connection with the נשיא ("prince")-stratum, which, after the first break by the insertion of 44:4ff, had connected directly with 45:13–15.

The insertion of the expiation ritual for the start of the year in 45:18–20, a ritual which knows nothing of the נשיא ("prince") and which separates the superscription-like v 17 from the expected continuation in 45:21–46:12, then surely occurred at a late stage in the history of chapter 45. The relationship in respect of form and also to a certain extent of content between the new year expiation ritual and the dedication ritual for the altar in 43:18–27 raises the question whether the same hand has not composed two insertions and whether it is not it, too, which has prefaced the altar dedication ritual with the description of the altar (43:13–17). The insertion of 43:13–17 at any rate has happened at a time when chapters 40–42 were already felt to be a closed building description which could no longer be tampered with. As the best place for the introduction of the description of the altar and of the ritual for the dedication of the altar there commended itself in these circumstances the point immediately after the description of Yahweh's entry into the sanctuary. Here, too, then in 43:19 a harmonization was made with 44:6ff in that the priests were described as Zadokites.

Nothing certain can be said about the sequence of the expansions to which 46:1–12 has been subject. The regulation for the *Tamid* in 46:13–15 is unmistakably connected with the regulation for the prince's offering, even if the prince is no longer mentioned in it. The exposition has also shown that v 15 has been added secondarily as an appendix to vv 13f. The regulation in 46:16–18 about the inalienable nature of princely property also represents an addition. The formal proximity of its opening to v 12 raises the question whether it once followed directly on v 12 and is thus older than vv 13–15. Observations with regard to content have made it likely that it comes from the hand which added 45:1–9. It already presupposes the fixed regulation for the prince's land. And finally, the account of the visionary guidance to the sacrificial kitchens (46:19–24) is also an addition which presupposes 42:1–14 as a completed unit. It ought to be located earlier than the vision which leads out from the sanctuary into the land. The visionary style could have been chosen as a conscious preparation for 47:1–12.

The description and allocation of the land has then been connected to the description of the temple spring already at a relatively early date, at any rate before the insertion of 45:1ff. It certainly already presupposes the juxtaposition of priests and Levites, not, however, the disqualification of the Levites indicated in 44:6ff. The text has then been subject to a number of harmonizing additions. 48:11 qualifies the priests as Zadokites and is to be regarded, like 40:46b and 43:19a*, as a "metastasis" of 44:6ff.[12] V 12, which expresses the idea of a special portion set apart for the priests along the lines of 44:30a (and Nu 18:28), is also to be regarded as such. The same is true for the addition in 48:21b–22.[13] A quite different direction is taken by the addition in 47:22f, which demands the participation of resident aliens in the allocation of land.

In the addition in 48:30–35, finally, we seem to find ourselves in proximity to Deutero-Isaianic reflection on the form of the gates of the newly rebuilt city (Is 54:12), also precisely in the fact that here the city, which still in 48:15–20 had an existence on the edge of the תרומה, returns to the center of the expectation of Yahweh's new presence.

This leads, finally, to the question of the absolute dating of the various strata discernible in chapters 40–48.[14] While an approximate picture could be reached of the relative sequence of the principal strata, the absolute dating presents greater difficulties. If one may reckon with the authenticity of the dating of the basic stratum 40:1–37, 47–49; 41:1–4, this brings us to the year 573. Then with the expansions in 41:5–15a; 42:15–20, as well as with the continuations in 44:1–2 and 47:1–12, one would not wish to move too far from that date. The latest oracle of the prophet which is certainly dated, 29:17ff, gives for the period of Ezekiel's activity room at any rate down to the spring of 571.

The textual elements which were next incorporated are concerned with the position of the נשיא ("prince") in the new temple and of the community which worships there (44:3; 45:21–46:12). It seems possible to conclude from this that the (priestly-prophetic?) tradition circles in which Ezekiel's words were handed down among the exiles reflected in practical terms, when the possibility of return was imminent, in the first place on the position of the Davidic ruler in a reconstituted community. Since in the pre-exilic period the temple had been a "royal sanctuary," the priority given to a clarification of precisely this problem is easily understood. The fact that Cyrus, immediately after his restoration edict, entrusted the נשיא ("prince") Sheshbazzar with bringing back the temple vessels (Ezr 1:8; 5:14) has the effect of confirming and justifying this forward planning.[15] With Zerubbabel, the second member of the Davidic house sent by the Persians in a high office to Judah, the office of נשיא ("prince"), which was singled out by the Persian power even to begin with in political terms, seems to have reached a state of crisis. There is no further indication of any member of the Davidic house being entrusted with the office of נשיא ("prince"). The plans for the office of נשיא ("prince") in Ezek 40–48 give no sign of such a crisis. Thus they are best located in the exilic period of preparation for the first sending of a נשיא ("prince"), i.e. in the period between 571 and Cyrus's restoration edict of 538. Since in the blueprint for the allocation of land in 48:1–29, which seems to be presupposed by the reflec-

12 See above pp. 442f.
13 See above p. 536.
14 On this see also Gese, 108–123.
15 On the identity of Sheshbazzar with the Davidic Shenazzar mentioned in 1 Chr 3:18 and on the further history of the נשיא in the post-exilic community, see Gese, 116–120.

tions on the cultic status of the נשיא ("prince"), there is no sign either of a renewed contact with actual conditions in the country or of the crisis involving the office of נשיא ("prince"), one is inclined to set the beginning of the plan for the נשיא ("prince") nearer to the upper limit of the period mentioned. For even the ideal planning for the alloction of land in 48:1–29 reveals no sign of disturbance by harsh realities which might have been encountered. Since at the same time, when it mentions priests and Levites together, it knows nothing of any tension between these two groups, one should assign to approximately the same period the insertion in 40:44–46a, which mentions the "priests who see to the service in the temple" happily alongside the "priests who see to the service at the altar," and then perhaps also the regulation for the chamber at the north gate (40:38–43).

Does the great tension between (Levitical) Zadokites and Levites suggest the end of the exilic period in which the Jerusalem priesthood had to be newly constituted? Since there is no reference in chapter 44 to a high priest, one would be disinclined to go any further into the post-exilic period, when this figure emerges with increasing clarity, as Haggai and Zechariah show. The quarrel between the various groups must indeed have broken out most violently immediately before the reinstitution of the cult, when decisions were to be expected. In this era of heightened antagonisms one would best also locate those sections which differentiate within the sanctuary the various spheres of holiness more sharply from each other, i.e. the account of the great temple sacristies in 42:1–14 and the sacrificial kitchens of 46:19–24. That also the final section, 48:30–35, in which the reality of the city, which includes the place of the divine presence, once again gains full prominence, belongs to the end of the exilic period or the beginning of the period of the reconstitution of the Jerusalem community was already probable because of its proximity to Deutero-Isaiah. To the period of tension between priests and Levites, which is reflected in the lack of enthusiasm for the return on the part of the Levites compared with the priests (Ezr 2:36–40, later 8:15ff), belongs also the theologically "revised" programme of land allocation in 45:1–8 which in its appendix in 45:9 (46:16–18 is dependent on this), also strikes a sharper tone towards the prince.

The rituals for the dedication of the altar and the double day of expiation at the beginning of the year (43:18–27 with altar description; 45:18–20) could then very well reflect how in the post-exilic cult the thought of expiation begins to acquire its full significance.

The suggestion that in the description of the buildings "the first plan was continuously revised in the light of the historical structures of the second temple"[16] cannot be proved in view of the lack of any precise information about Zerubbabel's temple and is basically in any case not very probable. Only in the case of 42:1–14 and of the expansions within 41:5–15a, which add height measurements secondarily, would one ask whether the stricter observance of the topographical data of the temple area does not already begin to play a part. In reality, Zerubbabel's temple must have been built much more wretchedly than and not so extensively as the sketch in Ezekiel 40–48 plans. It remains open where 41:15b–26 comes from. In view of the fact that chapters 40–42 became a closed unit at a relatively early date, it is best not to date it too late.

Finally one may ask whether the regulation for the future land ownership by the גרים ("resident aliens") (47:22f) is not to be located in the period of immediate preparation for the return of exiles. At any rate it could have facilitated the participation in this return of non-Israelites who wished to be associated with it.

16 Gese, 108.

Appendices
Bibliography
Indices

1. The Divine Name in the Book of Ezekiel

A

The name Yahweh occurs in Ezekiel four hundred and thirty-four times, after making the correction in 21:14 a total of four hundred and thirty-five times. Only once in this book, which, with its message, is nevertheless directed so decisively at the "house of Israel,"[1] is it found in the full formulation of "Yahweh the God of Israel" (44:2). The abbreviated אֱלֹהֵי יִשְׂרָאֵל of 10:20 belongs, as do the four occurrences of the expressions כְּבוֹד אֱלֹהֵי יִשְׂרָאֵל (8:4; 9:3; 10:19; 11:22), to strata of secondary expansion.

1. The expanded form of the divine name which is, on the other hand, really characteristic of the book of Ezekiel is אֲדֹנָי יהוה. In half of the cases, namely two hundred and seventeen times, the divine name occurs in this expanded form. Close examination in this respect shows that the occurrence of by far the majority is in the introductory and final formulaic material for divine sayings: one hundred and twenty-two times the introductory messenger formula is כֹּה אָמַר אֲדֹנָי יהוה;[2] eighty-one times the formula for a divine saying is נְאֻם אֲדֹנָי יהוה.[3] All together two hundred and three of the two hundred and seventeen occurrences of אֲדֹנָי יהוה, i.e. over ninety per cent, are thus found in this area. Here the question at once arises whether the infinitely rare occurrences of the simple כֹּה אָמַר יהוה (three or possibly four times) and נְאֻם יהוה (four times) are original. Now, the כֹּה אָמַר יהוה of 11:5 in fact belongs to an expansion which presents other problems too.[4] The same is true of the complex 30:1–19, to which the passage 30:6 belongs.[5] 21:1–12, too, to which 21:8 belongs (cf. note a there), is in a section which gives rise to questions.[6] Finally, over the reading of 21:14 there lies the uncertainty of a textual alteration (cf. notes a and b there). Simple נְאֻם יהוה occurs in 13:6, 7 in a quotation of the language of the false prophets which cannot then be the language of the prophet himself. 16:58 belongs to an expansion which was formulated after 587, but which is not absolutely to be denied to the prophet himself. There is no reason to deny 37:14 to the prophet (cf. also note a there).

Among the remaining fourteen passages outside this fomulaic stock where אֲדֹנָי יהוה occurs there emerges a small, self-contained separate group 4:14; 9:8; 11:13; 21:5. The אֲדֹנָי יהוה here stands in a cry to Yahweh which is intensified by a preceding אֲהָהּ. To this context belongs also the vocative in 37:3 which lacks the introductory אֲהָהּ. Text-critically there are no objections to these verses.

On this basis one would like to ask whether the five cases of אֲדֹנָי יהוה in some recognition formulae in the proof saying (13:9; 23:49; 24:24; 28:24; 29:16) are also to be taken together as a self-contained group. But they are contrasted by an overwhelming majority of eighty-seven (including 20:5, 7, 19) recognition formulae which have simple יהוה. Of the five passages mentioned, 23:49 belongs to a section which, on the basis of both language and content, is certainly to be classed as not from Ezekiel.[7] This cannot be said of the other passages. But since the recognition formula of the proof-saying in its inner structure undoubtedly leads to the terse self-presentation of Yahweh in his proper name,[8] we will have to regard the formulation with אֲדֹנָי יהוה, form-critically at any rate, as a later degenerate form and seriously to ask the question whether here the text has not been secondarily expanded. The intrusion of אֲדֹנָי יהוה into textual contexts in which it originally did not stand is thus not impossible.

A secondary intrusion of אֲדֹנָי יהוה could also exist in 8:1. The six passages which refer to the יַד־יהוה (1:3; 3:14, 22; 33:22; 37:1; 40:1) are contrasted with the single occurrence in 8:1 of the fuller יַד אֲדֹנָי יהוה. Less unambiguous is the numerical relationship in the formulation of the summons to attention. Seven occurrences of the terse שִׁמְעוּ (אֶת) דְּבַר יהוה or similar wording (13:2; 16:35; 21:3; 34:7, 9; 36:1; 37:4) are countered by three occurrences of the fuller שִׁמְעוּ דְּבַר אֲדֹנָי יהוה (6:3; 25:3; 36:4). Must we reckon here too with the secondary intrusion of the אֲדֹנָי יהוה?

2. Among the remaining two hundred and seventeen (including 21:14, 218) passages where יהוה occurs without the addition of אֲדֹנָי, the recognition formulae in the proof-sayings with its eighty-seven instances had already stood out as a great complex on its own. To these may be added the total of fifty formulae for the receiving of God's word with the construct relationship דְּבַר יהוה, of which forty-one are expressed with a consecutive imperfect, the re-

1 See Appendix 2.
2 See 1,133.
3 Baumgärtel, "Formel."
4 See 1,231 and what is said in Appendix 3 about the occurrence of רוּחַ in this passage.
5 See above pp. 127f.
6 See 1,422.
7 See 1,491f.
8 See Introduction 1,36–40.

maining nine with the perfect (1:3; 24:20; 26:1; 29:1, 17; 30:20; 31:1; 32:1, 17).[9] In this group it is remarkable that in no passage is there an additional אֲדֹנָי. The formula has clearly been more resistant to such expansion than, for example, the recognition formula of the proof saying and the summons to attention, whose seven simple יהוה-passages have already been mentioned.

Of the other expressions which show the name Yahweh with a preceding noun in the construct (forty occurrences), יַד־יהוה has already been mentioned as a formulation possibly susceptible to the secondary intrusion of אֲדֹנָי יהוה (six occurrences of the short form) as are the occurrences of the short form נְאֻם יהוה, the originality of which is suspect. In addition there occurs in 11:25 the plural דִּבְרֵי יהוה, 13:5 יוֹם יהוה, 7:19 more fully יוֹם עֶבְרַת יהוה, 36:20 עַם־יהוה, six occurrences of בֵּית־יהוה (8:14, 16; 10:19; 11:1; 44:4, 5), two occurrences of הֵיכַל יהוה (8:16a, b), one occurrence of מִקְדַּשׁ־יהוה (48:10), two occurrences of רוּחַ יהוה (11:5; 37:1) alongside רוּחַ אֱלֹהִים in 11:24. In addition there are ten occurrences of כְּבוֹד יהוה. The expression כְּבוֹד אֱלֹהֵי יִשְׂרָאֵל which intrudes alongside that in later expansions has already been mentioned earlier. And finally one can mention in this context also the five passages in which יהוה follows לִפְנֵי, which is, of course, understood purely as a preposition (41:22; 43:24; 44:3; 46:3, 9). These all belong, characteristically, in the context of later, priestly cult regulations.

Alongside the occurrence of construct relationships there occur, finally, thirty-four occurrences of varied, freer usages of the name Yahweh. The unique designation of "God of Israel" was mentioned already, as were the occurrences (three or four) of simple כֹּה אָמַר יהוה which were of questionable originality. The הַדָּבָר הַיּוֹצֵא מֵאֵת יהוה of 33:30 is a paraphrase of the simple דְּבַר־יהוה. Alongside the construct formation יוֹם יהוה there occurs in 30:3 a יוֹם לַיהוה. וַיֹּאמֶר יהוה (4:13) and וַיֹּאמֶר יהוה אֵלַי (23:36) seem to belong to secondary passages. In 44:2, 5 יהוה is a secondary gloss on the verbal clause, similarly in 9:4 (cf. note a there). Use is made of simple יהוה five times in quotations of words from the prophet's surroundings (8:12bα,β; 9:9bα,β; 11:15). According to 20:1 men come to consult Yahweh through the prophet. In 13:6; 22:28; 35:10 יהוה is the subject of a verbal nominal sentence. The remaining thirteen passages belong without exception to the later sections in chapters 40–48 (40:46; 42:13; 43:24b; 45:1, 4, 23; 46:4, 12, 13, 14; 48:9, 14, 35), among which in 43:24b, 45:1, 23; 46:4, 12, 13, 14; 48:9, 14 the name Yahweh is connected with the ל of dedication.

3. Alongside the dominant divine name יהוה the other divine names occur with much less frequency. The four places where (apart from 21:14, see above) אֲדֹנָי occurs as an independent designation of God (18:25, 29; 33:17, 20) must depend on a secondary alteration of an original יהוה (cf. 18:25 note a). אֱלֹהִים is attested thirty-six times, but never appears absolutely, like a proper name, as a synonym for Yahweh. Closest to such usage doubtless comes the language of the presumptuous prince of Tyre who asserts of himself: אֱלֹהִים אָנִי (28:9), thus making his heart Godlike (כְּלֵב אֱלֹהִים 28:2, 6). It is, however, characteristic that in this speech of a foreign prince there is used instead in 28:2a (see also vv 2b, 9) the word אֵל, in which there is an echo of the old Canaanite king of the gods אֵל. This word is found otherwise only in the name אֵל שַׁדַּי (10:5), which appears in 1:24 in the abbreviated form שַׁדַּי and must in both places refer to Yahweh.[10]

The pre-Yahwistic pre-history of the term אֱלֹהִים is also clearly discernible in the references, deriving from the realm of mythical concepts, to the dwelling-place of the gods/God (מוֹשַׁב אֱלֹהִים 28:2), to the garden of the gods/God (גַּן־אֱלֹהִים 28:13; 31:8a and b, 9) and to the mountain of the gods/God (הַר אֱלֹהִים 28:16; הַר קֹדֶשׁ אֱלֹהִים 28:14, see note c). It is, on the other hand, significant that the sacred mountain of the God of Israel is never described by this word. It is called, rather, הַר מְרוֹם יִשְׂרָאֵל (see Appendix 2). Pre-Yahwistic linguistic usage is perhaps to be found in the רוּחַ אֱלֹהִים of 11:24, which occurs alongside the רוּחַ יהוה of 11:5; 37:1 (see Appendix 3), and in the מַרְאוֹת אֱלֹהִים of 1:1; 8:3; 40:2.

Alongside these, however, there occurs the clear evidence for the adaptation by Israel of the word אֱלֹהִים. This can come about in such a way that there is a specific reference to Yahweh the God of Israel (44:2), and this is abbreviated in 10:20 to the simple אֱלֹהֵי־יִשְׂרָאֵל. The fact that then on this basis there are references in later expansions also to כְּבוֹד אֱלֹהֵי יִשְׂרָאֵל (8:4; 9:3; 10:19; 11:22; 43:2) has already been mentioned. Above all, in this context, however, we must mention the explicit covenant formulations in which Yahweh promises to be God (לֵאלֹהִים) for Israel (11:20; 14:11; 34:24; 36:28; 37:23, 27). 20:5, 7 speak explicitly of an action in which Yahweh had sworn to be such on the day of his choosing of Israel. These places also make clear how this can be referred to by means of אֱלֹהִים with suffix, with the suffix

9 On the formula for the receiving of God's word see 1, 144f and Introduction 1, 25.

10 See 1, 254f.

referring to the chosen people (20:19; 34:30, 31; 39:22). So it can also intrude in later, debased expressions into the recognition formula of the proof-saying (28:26; 39:28; see also 20:20).

4. The clear picture afforded by 𝔐 in Ezekiel of the use of the divine name can be illuminated antithetically by means of a comparison. It is an acknowledged fact that Ezekiel is in many respects close to Jeremiah.[11] It is all the more remarkable that the designation of God as יהוה צְבָאוֹת, which occurs no fewer than eight-two times in the book of Jeremiah, cannot be found even a single time in Ezekiel, not even in its latest additions. This shows that the two books in their present form come from quite different tradition circles and, in spite of all the points of contact, are not to be attributed overhastily to related editing (cf. S. Herrmann).

B

The predominantly clear picture which has resulted from the preceding review will now have its originality questioned at a decisive point by the adducing of the oldest secondary tradition in 𝔊. The question concerns the double designation of God as אֲדֹנָי יהוה, a form which emerges so characteristically in 𝔐.

1. The text tradition in 𝔊 is represented on this point in the following way. 𝔊^{B} translates the אֲדֹנָי יהוה in the opening chapters, with the exception of a *κύριε Θεὲ τοῦ Ισραηλ* in 4:14, consistently by a simple *κύριος*. For the first time in 12:10, then in 13:20; 14:6 and somewhat more frequently from 20:39–23:46 and later again from 26:15 onwards as far as chapter 39, there appears also the double expression *κύριος κύριος*. In 36:33, 37 (𝔊$^{B\ ab\ mg.}$ already in v 32), a remarkable context even in the Hebrew text, there occurs *αδωναι κύριος*.[12] The most remarkable change occurs in the final section, chapters 40–48, where between 43:18 and 44:27 *κύριος ὁ θεός* (in 43:18 also with the addition of Ισραηλ) and from 45:9 onwards simple *κύριος Θεός* appear as the rendering of אֲדֹנָי יהוה. Only in 43:27 is this sequence interrupted by a simple *κύριος*. Thus of the two hundred and seventeen passages where אֲדֹנָי יהוה occurs, in 𝔊^{B} one hundred and forty are translated by simple *κύριος* (once with the addition of "God of Israel"), fifty-seven (or fifty-six) by *κύριος κύριος*, two (or three) by *αδωναι κύριος*, seven by *κύριος ὁ θεός* (once with the addition of "Israel") and nine by *κύριος θεός*. Two occurrences have nothing corresponding to them. The picture in 𝔊^{A} and 𝔊^{Q} is quite different. Here, first of all, in a few cases *κύριος κύριος* is found, but then it continues in a largely unbroken sequence as far as chapter 20 with *αδωναι κύριος*. From here on in 𝔊^{Q} as far as 45:9 the two forms intermingle. From 45:9 on there occurs here *κύριος ὁ θεός* which had appeared once before in a quite isolated occurrence in 20:5. In 𝔊^{A}, in addition, in 14:4 and more frequently from 20:5 on the inflated form *κύριος κύριος ὁ θεός* occurs, though simple *κύριος ὁ θεός* predominates here from 45:9 on, interrupted only in 46:16 by an isolated *αδωναι κύριος*. In addition in 𝔊^{A}, in 23:32, there occurs even the multiplication to *αδωναι κύριος κύριος ὁ θεός*, in 26:15 *αδωναι κύριος κύριος*, in 37:21 and 38:17 *αδωναι κύριος ὁ θεός*. A comparison with 𝔄 has nevertheless shown that the texts behind 𝔊^{A} could not, in their original form, be very far from the tradition of 𝔊^{Q}.[13] We certainly cannot, therefore, adduce this confused tradition directly in an assessment of a possible Hebrew original.

In recent times 𝔊^{967} has now also appeared to join the tradition known hitherto.[14] This oldest 𝔊 tradition so far seems to add further complication to the state of affairs regarding the divine name in 𝔊 of Ezekiel in that here it too goes its own way. Precisely in regard to the rendering of the divine name it reveals a particularly close connection with the Old Latin tradition, thus clearly belonging to the pre-Hexaplaric tradition. In the Chester Beatty Papyri a comparison may be made in twenty cases. There, simple *κύριος* occurs ten times, *κύριος ὁ θεός* seven times in the rendering of 𝔐 אֲדֹנָי יהוה. In three places the relevant passage is missing. In addition, in 16:62 *κύριος ὁ θεός* has intruded into the recognition formula of the proof-saying. In the case of the John Scheide Papyri, Kase confirms in the introduction to the edition of the text that in the eighty-two passages in which the equivalent of 𝔐 אֲדֹנָי יהוה can be made out there occurs in seventy-six cases simple *κύριος*, with *κύριος ὁ θεός* in only six places.[15] The examination of the Cologne fragments enables a comparison to be made in forty-one other places. With the exception of a single passage which is completely missing from 𝔊^{967}, there occurs everywhere here simple *κύριος* as the rendering of 𝔐 אֲדֹנָי יהוה. By contrast with 𝔊^{B} this is consistently the case also between 43:18 and 46:1. There are now in addition, the Madrid fragments which permit a comparison in another twenty passages. Here the אֲדֹנָי יהוה of 𝔐 is rendered sixteen times by simple *κύριος*. Again this is true also in chapters 46–48, where 𝔊^{B} has *κύριος θεός*. Instead, in 37:5, 9, where 𝔊^{B} has simple *κύριος*, we find here the compound expression *κύριος ὁ θεός*. On

11 See Introduction 1,44–46.

12 See above p. 245.

13 Baumgärtel.

14 See Introduction 1,76f.

15 Edmund Harris Kase, "The 'nomen sacrum' in Ezekiel" in Johnson-Gehman-Kase, *Ezekiel*, 48–51.

two occasions there is no corresponding passage at all.

Whatever may be the individual problems of this old tradition, $\mathfrak{G}^{967}$ is able to make two things quite clear: 1) This oldest Greek evidence, known to us in these old witnesses and the Old Latin tradition which confirms it, seems predominantly to have read simply *κύριος* where 𝔐 has the double form of the name. Those passages in which $\mathfrak{G}^{967}$ also reads a double form, but which, seen as a whole, are infinitely few in number, are early signs of the secondary intrusion of the double form into the Greek tradition. 2) The reading of simple *κύριος* occurs initially in $\mathfrak{G}^{967}$ also in chapters 40–48, where $\mathfrak{G}^{B}$, with the exception of a single occurrence, consistently has the double form of the name.

2. How, in view of this state of affairs in the ancient translations, are we now to judge the tradition of 𝔐? It is clear that this question would have to be dealt with by scholars as soon as they began to work intensively with the secondary attestation of the Ezekiel text.

Thus a scholar as early as Cornill, in his textual analysis of the book of Ezekiel of 1886, in an "Appendix" to the Prolegomena has a section entitled "The Divine Name in Ezekiel."[16] He feels that 𝔐, with its vacillation in placing אֲדֹנָי יהוה alongside simple יהוה, should be classified as "completely arbitrary."[17] This impression emerges for him really properly only in the Greek tradition: "The LXX, too, reveals in the divine name unlimited arbitrariness."[18] Nevertheless, he believes he can find in 𝔊 a certain assistance for the reconstruction of the original. He believes that on the basis of 𝔊 he can deduce that, in the first part of the book (as far as chapter 39), in the fifty-eight out of two hundred and one אֲדֹנָי יהוה passages in which $\mathfrak{G}^{B}$ confirms the reading of the double name, this was original in the text. Here the prophet wishes to emphasize the thought of Yahweh as "the Lord." Yahweh's relationship to Israel is here essentially a legal one. In chapters 40–48, however, where $\mathfrak{G}^{B}$ in the אֲדֹנָי יהוה passages reads a *κύριος* (ὁ) *θεός*, he feels himself led to a reading יהוה אֱלֹהִים in the basic text. Here Yahweh is "God, and his relationship to Israel is that of grace."[19] From the fact that the title יהוה אֱלֹהִים is found in the OT only in Genesis 2f in the paradise story he believes that he can draw the further conclusion that Ezekiel meant to make his vision of the new Jerusalem parallel to the old paradise story. The history of Yahweh with his people would thus lead to the paradisiacal end time of salvation. The expected salvation is to be for Israel a restoration of the original paradisiacal situation.

This thesis was rejected in 1913 by J. Herrmann in a minute examination of the Hebrew and Greek traditions and the counter thesis presented that 𝔐 is essentially to be trusted and that the 𝔊 tradition should be questioned.[20] In this connection he points, amongst others, to an unpublished piece of work by G. A. Daechsel which tries to show that the formula כֹּה אָמַר אֲדֹנָי יהוה "characterizes the prophetic utterance as an edict of the king and the lord Yahweh analogous to the use of the formula כה אמר המלך as an introduction to royal edicts as such."[21] Here and in the other complexes where אֲדֹנָי יהוה is used the prophet, according to Herrmann, means to describe Yahweh explicitly as the Lord. The apparently divergent state of the translation in 𝔊 Herrmann tries to explain, here and, more fully documented, at the beginning of the work jointly produced by him and F. Baumgärtel, by the assumption of three different translators in 𝔊.[22] There, too, Baumgärtel has endeavored to illuminate above all the tradition of $\mathfrak{G}^{A}$.[23]

Herrmann's theories subsequently failed to hold the field. Above all, W. W. Graf Baudissin came to quite different conclusions.[24] In the fifth chapter of the second section he deals with the "Lesung und Ausdruck der Septuaginta für masoretisches *ădonāj jhwh* in Ezechiel."[25] In the course of this he comes to the assumption of a reworking of 𝔐 in which the אֲדֹנָי יהוה, which must have had its original position in addresses to Yahweh, intruded secondarily also in places where Yahweh was introduced as the speaker.

16 Cornill, 172–175.
17 Cornill, 172.
18 Cornill, 173.
19 Cornill, 174.
20 Johannes Herrmann, "Die Gottesnamen im Ezechieltexte. Ein Studie zur Ezechielkritik und zur Septuagintawertung" in *Alttestamentliche Studien Rudolf Kittel zum 60. Geburtstag*, BWAT 13 (Leipzig: Hinrichs, 1913), 70–87.
21 Herrmann (see preceding fn.), 81.
22 Johannes Herrmann and Friedrich Baumgärtel, *Beiträge zur Entstehungsgeschichte der Septuaginta*, BWAT 5 (Berlin: Kohlhammer, 1923).
23 Herrmann-Baumgärtel (see preceding fn.), Appendix I (pp. 81–95): "Zu den אדני יהוה-Stellen bei Ezechiel."
24 Wolf Wilhelm Graf Baudissin, *Kyrios als Gottesname im Judentum und seine Stelle in der Religionsgeschichte.* Erster Teil: Der Gebrauch des Gottesnamens Kyrios in Septuaginta (Giessen: Töpelmann, 1929) (published posthumously by O. Eissfeldt).
25 Baudissin (see preceding fn.), 525–588.

The same conclusion is also reached by J. Battersby Harford with an examination, provided with numerous tables, of the tradition of the "Divine Names in Ezekiel."[26]

Then in 1961, F. Baumgärtel re-examined the question on a broader basis, especially also by a comparative examination of Jeremiah, and sought to confirm Herrmann's thesis of the originality of אֲדֹנָי יהוה in the main areas where it occurs.[27]

3. If now an attempt is to be made to reach a judgment in the controversial question of the originality of אֲדֹנָי יהוה in Ezekiel, the unfortunate fact must be stated right at the beginning that we do not possess Hebrew textual attestations from the earlier period which could lead to definite conclusions in the assessment of the whole question. So far Qumran has not provided any assistance in this very question. The few fragments of Ezekiel texts provide no material for the present question.[28] On the other hand, a series of unedited fragments from the Cairo Genizah, which are in Oxford and Cambridge and the readings of which have been made accessible to me by Dr. Rüger (Tübingen), reveal phenomena even for the Hebrew textual tradition which recall the later textual witnesses of 𝔊. Thus, e.g., MS Heb. d 80, fol. 7–14 of the Bodleian Library, Oxford, reads in Ezek 2:4 and 3:11 a יהוה אדני יהוה instead of the אֲדֹנָי יהוה of 𝔐.[29] In the Taylor-Schechter MSS of the University Library, Cambridge, A 15^{10} also reads the אֲדֹנָי יהוה of 2:4 as יהוה אדני יהוה, that of 11:8 as יהוה אלהים; A 31^{49} that of 3:27 as אדני אלהים; both read that of 25:3 as יהוה אדני. After all this, one is left for the evaluation of the original state of the Hebrew text with only indirect conclusions.

In this connection, there emerges, first of all, from the general examination of the transmission of the divine name in the OT in Greek-speaking Judaism, the fact that there was here a very lively development. For the following information I am indebted to letters from Dr. H. Stegemann, who in the near future will publish a comprehensive examination of this whole complex. With P. Kahle one must nowadays start from the fact that in Jewish Bible MSS in the pre-Christian and Christian period basically the divine name Yahweh was retained, to begin with in a phonetic transliteration as ΙΑΩ then in the form of the Tetragrammaton itself in Old Hebrew script and then also in Aramaic square script.[30] These written forms of the Hebrew divine name in the Jewish Bible MSS imply of necessity for oral delivery specific "substitute readings," amongst which in the Hellenistic synagogue from the outset (ὁ) κύριος must have been predominant. A Hebrew original אֲדֹנָי יהוה could therefore have appeared in writing as κύριος יהוה (sometimes written in Old Hebrew script), and this would be pronounced sometimes as κύριος κύριος, sometimes as κύριος ὁ θεός and surely sometimes also simply as κύριος.

Christian manuscripts have then taken up these various possibilities of pronunciation and have also fixed them in writing in Greek script, thus enabling the various possibilities of translation to exist side by side sometimes even within one and the same MS. The juxtaposition of 𝔊^{967}, 𝔊^{A} and 𝔊^{B} and, within 𝔊^{B}, the juxtaposition of the translations of the divine name in chapters 1–39 and chapters 40-48 in the Ezekiel tradition are thus illuminated from that standpoint. Thus Stegemann wishes to regard the Christian 𝔊 tradition as "essentially irrelevant" for the question of the divine name. The judgment of F. Delekat (again by letter) is not quite so harsh. He sees, e.g., in the writing of the divine name of Ezek 22:19 in 𝔊^{62} as αδωναι ΠΙΠΙ, as in other ΠΙΠΙ-passages, nevertheless the influence of Jewish-Hellenistic written tradition on the Christian tradition. For in ΠΙΠΙ there is undoubtedly to be seen the transmission (subsequently not understood) of יהוה in square script.[31]

For the further assessment of the situation, according to Stegemann, a second area of consideration cannot be completely without significance. It concerns the "substitute readings" in the context of the public reading of the Hebrew text in the synagogue. The אֲדֹנָי which is to be found in the later *Qere*

26 Harford, *Studies,* 102–162.

27 Friedrich Baumgärtel, "Zu den Gottesnamen in den Büchern Jeremia und Ezechiel" in *Verbannung und Heimkehr. Beiträge zur Geschichte und Theologie Israels im 6. und 5. Jahrhundert v. Chr., Wilhelm Rudolph zum 70. Geburtstage dargebracht* (Tübingen: Mohr [Siebeck], 1961), 1–29.

28 See Introduction 1,75.

29 See Adolf Neubauer and A. E. Cowley, *Catalogue of the Hebrew Manuscripts in the Bodleian Library, and in the college libraries of Oxford* 2 (Oxford, 1906).

30 The latter can now be seen very beautifully in Pa. Fuad 266, which comes from Jewish-Hellenistic circles. On this and on what follows see Françoise Dunand, *Papyrus grecs bibliques (Papyrus F. Inv. 266): volumina de la Genèse et du Deutéronome (introduction)* (Le Caire: Impr. de l'Institut français d'archéologie orientale, 1966), especially VII (pp. 39–50): "La transcription du tétragramme dans les traductions grecques de la bible," and VIII (pp. 50–55): "Le caractère ineffable du nom divin et l'interdit qui l'entoure."

31 In addition see F. Lienhard Delekat, "Elohim im 2. und 3. Psalmbuch" in *Asylie und Schutzorakel am Zion-*

perpetuum for the name Yahweh and which has possibly found its way, under the influence of the Hellenistic-Jewish diaspora readings, also into the Palestinian synagogue can certainly be attested in the first century A. D., but probably also existed in the first century B. C. But scarcely any earlier. This is ruled out above all by the Palestinian-Jewish substitute readings of the earlier period which can still be reconstructed and which seem to suggest an אֱלֹהִים or אֵל or the simple personal pronoun הוּא to suggest the omission of the divine name or reference to it by means of a suffix. אֲדֹנָי, on the other hand, has in the earlier period the status of an independent divine designation which does not simply have, as it does in the later "substitute designations," generic significance, but has something of the character of a proper name. "אדני יהוה would then have to be understood, so to speak, as a Yahwistic extension of an original simple אדני." Thus the occurrences of אֲדֹנָי יהוה which are reliably attested in the text would have to be regarded as divine designations of independent significance, which surely initially had their own *Sitz im Leben* but could then have found their way into certain formulae. At any rate Stegemann does not feel that he can find anywhere proof of the suggestion that there might have been a development from a simple יהוה to an אֲדֹנָי יהוה. In contrast, for example, to the elohistic redaction of Books II and III of the Psalms there is nowhere any sign of an analogous "adonistic" redaction.

Alongside these findings of Stegemann, the suggestions which were first made by Baumgärtel, "Gottesnamen," can be reiterated. These begin from a comparison of the divine name in Jeremiah and Ezekiel. As has already been mentioned in a earlier context, there are in Jeremiah eighty-two occurrences of the name יהוה צְבָאוֹת. Of these, no fewer than fifty-three are in the introductory messenger formula, another seven are in the formula for a divine saying, four in an address to Yahweh, eight in the formula which explicitly designates יהוה צְבָאוֹת as a name of Yahweh (יהוה צְבָאוֹת שְׁמוֹ). Only eight passages, all of which can be proved to belong to secondary material in the book of Jeremiah, reveal less stereotyped usage. Quite analogously, the survey of the book of Ezekiel had shown the אֲדֹנָי יהוה was to be found predominantly in the introductory messenger formula and in the formula for a divine saying. That the smaller group of five occurrences with vocative use of the double name with prefixed אֲהָהּ must belong to a fixed, formalized speech is shown by the fact that all the other passages in the OT where אֲהָהּ occurs with the divine name also contain the double designation אֲדֹנָי יהוה (Josh 7:7; Ju 6:22; Jer 1:6; 4:10; 14:13; 32:17). The fact that אֲדֹנָי יהוה belongs to a specific, fairly closely delimited formulaic stock is shown not only by Ezekiel but also by the other occurrences of it in the OT.[32] Over and above the statements just made, there emerges, however, also in connecion with יהוה צְבָאוֹת, the remarkable fact that 𝔊 in Jeremiah renders this divine designation in the great majority of cases with simple *κύριος*. One cannot overlook the fact that these observations of Baumgärtel are in complete agreement with the statements of Stegemann, who warns against relying on the translations of 𝔊. A kind of counter-text to these negative assertions is afforded by the observation that the exclamation introduced by אֲהָהּ, which in the OT, as already mentioned, is formulated without exception with אֲדֹנָי יהוה, is rendered by $𝔊^{B}$ in two places by *δέσποτα κύριε*, in two others by *κύριε (μου) κύριε* and in the other six by simple *κύριε*.[33] Baumgärtel also agrees with Stegemann in the concluding observations. In the case of the divine designation יהוה צְבָאוֹת it can scarcely be doubted that we are here dealing with a divine name which has its origin in the cult of a specific locality, namely that of the ark. Could the same not also be true of the origin of the double name אֲדֹנָי יהוה, which appears in remarkably analogous situations, has found its way into the same formulaic stock and which therefore could not be dismissed as a late redactional phenomenon? Baumgärtel himself supposes that Ezekiel, living in exile, has consciously replaced the cult name Yahweh Sabaoth, with its associations with the ark, by the irreproachable archaic name אֲדֹנָי יהוה which survived in the ancient cry אֲהָהּ אֲדֹנָי יהוה, since for him Yahweh was no longer enthroned above the ark.[34]

However much in this last discussion a great deal must of necessity remain hypothetical, we must nevertheless take seriously, in spite of the initially confusing rendering of the double divine name in 𝔊,

heiligtum (Leiden: Brill, 1967), 343–380.

32 Of the other sixty-six occurrences, nineteen are in Amos, thirteen in Is 40ff, eight in Jeremiah, the remainder scattered among other prophetic and narrative books and in the Psalms.

33 Baumgärtel, "Gottesnamen," 18.

34 On this turning away from the ark see the exposition of Ezek 43:7 (pp. 415f).

the possibility that אֲדֹנָי יהוה in the formulaic groups of the complaint to Yahweh, the introductory messenger formula and the formula for a divine saying could have its original home in the prophet's own word—whatever further judgment one may come to about the origin of the double designation. Against a secondary intrusion of this divine designation into the formula for a divine saying and the introductory messenger formula there is the very strong evidence of the observation that the formula for the receiving of God's word has remained completely free of such coloring. In that case we cannot simply be dealing with an indiscriminate use of the double designation. This conclusion cannot be weakened even by the observation that in other passages the double designation has clearly intruded only secondarily (in the recognition formula of the proof saying, the expression "hand of Yahweh," possibly even the summons to attention). It is indeed faced with the completely opposite phenomenon that אֲדֹנָי יהוה has also been able to disappear in later formulations from the two above mentioned introductory and concluding prophetic formulae.

The bracketing of אֲדֹנָי which has been consistently carried through in the commentary on the basis of 𝔊 (Ziegler) should thus probably be revised in the case of the three formulaic oracle complexes.

Postscript

After the conclusion of the typesetting of the Appendices I received the contribution of J. Lust.[35]

Lust, too, comes to the conclusion there that the double name אדני יהוה is original in the three groups כה אמר אדני יהוה, נאם אדני יהוה and אהה אדני יהוה.[36]

In contrast to 𝔐, however, Lust wishes to vocalize the אדני in the passages mentioned not as אֲדֹנָי "Lord" but as אֲדֹנִי "my Lord." In all the passages in question the designation is not to be found in the mouth of Yahweh but in the mouth of the prophet. This is in accordance with the thorough stylization of the book of Ezekiel in the first person.[37] According to Lust, however, it is also in accordance with the theological view of the prophet, according to which before the full arrival of judgment Israel no longer has the right to designate Yahweh as her God. Thus he understands the designation of Yahweh by Ezekiel as "Yahweh, my lord" as a conscious distancing from the expression frequent in Deuteronomy and Jeremiah, "Yahweh, (our) your God." In Ezekiel it is only in statements describing the post-exilic situation that the expression "my people" (עַמִּי) is found in the mouth of Yahweh as a designation of Israel.

In contrast to these at first impressive considerations, one is unable, however, to suppress the question whether one can really accept, in a prophet who in the indication of his own feelings is otherwise so extremely restrained,[38] precisely in regular formulaic language this personal designation of Yahweh as "my lord."[39] The stimulating theses of Lust demand, however, in any case further careful examination.

35 J. Lust, "'Mon Seigneur Jahweh' dans le texte hébreu d'Ézéchiel," *EThL* 44 (1968): 482–488.

36 Over and above the work of Herrmann (Baumgärtel is not mentioned) Lust refers especially to the following works of Lucien Cerfaux, all published in the *Revue des sciences philosophiques et théologiques,* who comes to this same conclusion: "Le titre 'Kyrios' et la dignité royale de Jésus," 11 (1922): 40–71; "Le nom divin 'Kyrios' dans la Bible grecque," 20 (1931): 27–51; "'Adonaï et Kyrios,'" 20 (1931): 417–452.

37 See Introduction 1,24.

38 Cf., e.g., Introduction, 1,20f.

39 Cf. the parallel of "my God" and see Otto Eissfeldt, "'Mein Gott' im Alten Testament," *ZAW* 61 (1945/48): 3–16.

2. "Israel" in the Book of Ezekiel

1. It is remarkable how emphatically in the book of the Judaean Ezekiel it is of "Israel" that is spoken. The total of one hundred and eighty-six occurrences of יִשְׂרָאֵל is contrasted with a total of fifteen occurrences of יְהוּדָה. This observation has led J. Smith to see in Ezekiel a prophet of the northern kingdom. A closer examination quickly shows, however, that that thesis cannot be sustained. Thus there occurs, to take only one example, in the scene in chapters 8f, which is undoubtedly to be located in the Jerusalem temple, alongside the reference to the abomination of the "house of Judah" in 8:17 also the reference to the elders of the house of Israel (8:11, 12), to the "idols of the house of Israel" (8:10) and to the "guilt of the house of Israel" (9:9). In 8:6 "house of Israel" has surely intruded only secondarily.[1]

When nevertheless V. Herntrich feels able to assert, "Ezekiel alternates fairly indiscriminately in the use of the expressions ישראל and יהודה,"[2] this is not an adequate description of the facts. The name of the recipients of his message which is actually characteristic of Ezekiel is "Israel." Of the fifteen Judah passages, 48:7, 8, 22 belong in the context of the enumeration of the twelve tribes, from which Judah could not of course be missing. So, too, according to 48:31 one of the twelve city gates is given the name Judah. As in the trading list inserted in chapter 27, which in v 17 mentions "Judah and the land of Israel," we are dealing with formulations from another hand. Of the remaining ten passages, two others (4:6 and 9:9) drop out as due to secondary school editing or glossing.[3] In 21:25, again, where Nebuchadnezzar's military decision is depicted at the crossroads between Rabbah and Jerusalem, the concrete geographical situation is obviously so vivid that with the "Rabbah of the Ammonites" there is contrasted "Judah which has its fortress in Jerusalem."[4] The same can also be said about the oracles against Judah's most immediate neighbors, the oracles against Ammon, Moab and Edom, with their reference to Judah in 25:3, 8, 12. Here, in addition, 25:3 with its parallelism of "sanctuary," "land of Israel" and "house of Judah" clearly shows that Jerusalem, Judah and the land of Israel are understood as concentric circles and that "Israel" is certainly not to be taken to refer to the northern kingdom in contrast to Judah. 25:14, too, in the continuation of the Edom oracle, which begins in v 12 with the "house of Judah," passes naturally into speaking of "my people Israel." In a different way this understanding of "Israel" is clear also in the sign-action with the two staffs. Here with the staff inscribed with "Judah and the Israelites connected with it" there is contrasted, for the representation of the northern kingdom, not, for example, a "staff of Israel," but there is chosen the inscription "for Joseph and the whole house of Israel connected with it" (37:16, see also v 19). Israel here includes Joseph and Judah. It is along similar lines that in chapter 23, where the story of the two separated kingdoms is told in the image of the two wanton sisters, in contrast to Jer 3:6–13, the model for this description,[5] it is not the מְשֻׁבָה יִשְׂרָאֵל (Jer 3:6, 11, 12) and the בָּגוֹדָה or בֹּגֵדָה יְהוּדָה (Jer 3:7f, 10f) which are contrasted but the women with the pseudonyms Oholah and Oholibah. 16:46ff contrasts Samaria as the representative of the northern kingdom with Jerusalem in the south. Thus in the original words of Ezekiel the antithetical contrast Israel-Judah is nowhere to be found. In the long run there remains as indications of a synonymous alternation, the reason for which is not entirely clear, of Israel and Judah only the passages 8:1 ("elders of Judah"—alongside "elders of Israel" in 14:1 and 20:1; see also 8:11f) and 8:17, where the reference is to the sinning of the "house of Judah" (alongside 8:10 and 9:9 original text, where in related statements it is the name Israel that appears).

It is, therefore, better not to speak of an "indiscriminate" alternation between the two descriptions.

In his work *Israel bei den Propheten* (1937) L. Rost has shown that the designation of Judah with the name "Israel" can be attested in the prophets from the end of the eighth century when the northern kingdom fell. In the case of Ezekiel one might ask further whether he is not in addition influenced by priestly tradition, which already from early times addressed Yahweh's covenant people as "Israel" and previously also in the period of the divided monarchy allowed the use of different names to fade into the background. Yet, in view of the lack of certain proof

1 For a refutation of the point of view of J. Smith see also Harford, *Studies,* especially the excursus "The House of Israel" (pp. 77–101).

2 Herntrich, *Ezechielprobleme,* 13.

3 On 4:6 see 1, 166–168. In 9:9 "Judah" gives the clear impression of being a late addition and is factually in conflict with the neighboring "house of Israel."

4 See 1, 442.

5 See 1, 482.

of the existence of older priestly texts, it is better not to make anything more than a supposition here.

In any case, however, it can be very clearly seen that in this regard Ezekiel differs markedly from Jeremiah, his older contemporary by whom he is nevertheless very strongly influenced. In the book of Jeremiah, alongside one hundred and twenty-five occurrences of "Israel" (forty-nine of them in Jeremiah 1–25) there are a total of one hundred and eighty-three occurrences of "Judah" (seventy-one of them in Jeremiah 1–25). In addition in Jeremiah the description of the southern kingdom is found very often in the double formulation "cities of Judah// Jerusalem" (7:17, 34; 11:6 and elsewhere) or "Judah// Jerusalem" (4:5; 13:9; 14:2 and elsewhere). This double formulation correctly expresses the constitutional situation according to which the government of the city of Jerusalem as the personal dynastic rule of the house of David was connected with the state of Judah, where, according to 2 Sam 2:4, David was elected king.[6] In Ezekiel there is no trace of such a description. Where Jerusalem appears it is as representative and center of Israel. When 9:9aβ actually on one occasion mentions land and city in juxtaposition, there is no sign of any constitutional dualism Judah/Jerusalem. The late representation of the allocation of land in Ezekiel 48, which makes the sanctuary with the city the center of the land and separates, in remarkable fashion, the tribal territory of Judah from the sanctuary, makes very clear once again this direct link between Jerusalem, for which in addition the name "Zion" is completely absent, and Israel. The fact that in 25:3 sanctuary, Judah and Israel are mentioned together is not to be understood as an attempt to mediate in the link between Jerusalem and Israel.

In all this it is quite clear that Ezekiel in his preaching over and over again sees the people of God as a whole, no matter whether he is turning in particular to his exilic surroundings or is envisaging Jerusalem and Judah or is letting us hear the history of the nation as a whole in all its breadth. The peculiar distance to which thus the immediate political realities and immediate constitutional relationships of the period before 587, even when he appears to address Jerusalem directly, fade, clearly sets him apart from Jeremiah. It also gives internal probability to the statement made in the book that Ezekiel is speaking from the distance of the exile.

2. If, then, we look in detail at the way in which the designation "Israel" is used, it strikes us first that the word is used in only twenty of the one hundred and eighty-six occurrences in other than a construct relationship. It is mostly oracles of the later stage of proclamation or secondary expansions which explicitly refer to עַמִּי יִשְׂרָאֵל (14:9; 25:14; 36:8, 12; 38:14, 16; 39:7). Only in 13:4 is the vocative address found with simple "Israel." 20:5 speaks of the election, 37:28 of the sanctification, 44:10 of the going astray of Israel. In all the other passages Israel is the sphere in which something happens or something is located. A saying (12:23; 18:3), the resident alien (14:7), Gog's grave (39:11), heritable property (44:28), devoted things (44:29), princely property (45:8), the prince (45:16) are בְּיִשְׂרָאֵל, indeed Yahweh himself is holy בְּיִשְׂרָאֵל (39:7).

Much more frequent, on the other hand, is the designation of the state of Israel as בֵּית יִשְׂרָאֵל (eighty-three times; בֵּית יְהוּדָה is found in six of the fifteen occurrences of Judah). Here there is expressed the family solidarity, the all-embracing total entity of this Israel. It can be specially emphasized as a totality by כָּל־בֵּית יִשְׂרָאֵל (5:4; 12:10; 20:40; 37:11[16]; 39:25; 45:6) or even intensified by כָּל־בֵּית יִשְׂרָאֵל כֻּלֹּה (11:15; 36:10). To this national entity the prophet is summoned with his preaching (3:1, 4f and elsewhere); it is to it that he is to proclaim his message (40:4; 43:10). What is spoken of are its guilt (עֲוֹן בֵּית־יִשְׂרָאֵל 4:4f; 9:9), it abominations (6:11), its idols (גִּלּוּלֵי בֵּית יִשְׂרָאֵל 8:10; 18:6, 15). What it says is heard by Yahweh (12:9, 27; 18:29). It is often addressed directly in the vocative (11:5; 18:25, 29–31; 20:31, 39, 44; 33:11, 20; 36:22, 32) when it is unwilling to hear (3:7). Ezekiel's activity serves as a sign to it (4:3); he is appointed as a watchman for it (3:17; 33:7). And once (13:9) reference is to the list (כְּתָב בֵּית־יִשְׂרָאֵל) in which Yahweh's community, to whom deliverance is promised, is recorded.

In contrast, the designation בְּנֵי יִשְׂרָאֵל is noticeably less frequent. Of the total of eleven occurrences in in the book of Ezekiel, 2:3 is surely to be emended to בֵּית יִשְׂרָאֵל. 4:13 and 6:5 are in later additions. This individualistic designation is not found again until 35:5; 37:16, 21: 43:7 (as a variant of the parallel בֵּית־יִשְׂרָאֵל) and in 44:9, 15; 47:22; 48:11, sections which certainly do not come from Ezekiel himself. The "God of Israel" is referred to seven times, mostly in later expansions (8:4; 9:3; 10:19, 20; 11:22; 43:2; 44:2).[7] The expressions גְּבוּל יִשְׂרָאֵל (11:10f), זִקְנֵי יִשְׂרָאֵל (14:1; 20:1, 3 alongside זִקְנֵי יְהוּדָה 8:1), עָרֵי יִשְׂרָאֵל (39:9), שְׁאֵרִית יִשְׂרָאֵל (9:8; 11:13), שִׁבְטֵי יִשְׂרָאֵל (37:19; 47:13, 21, 22; 48:19, 29, 31) are in no sense

6 On this see Albrecht Alt, "The Formation of the Israelite State in Palestine" in *Essays on Old Testament History and Religion,* tr. R. A. Wilson (Garden City, New York: Doubleday, 1967), 173–237.

7 On this see also Appendix 1.

specific. Of the three occurrences of אֶרֶץ יִשְׂרָאֵל (27:17; 40:2; 47:18), only in the case of 40:2 at the most can a derivation from the prophet himself be envisaged. In the list of trading goods, in 27:17, it designates, as does the בֵּית יִשְׂרָאֵל of the secondary expansion in 4:5, on the basis of which 4:4 has then be re-interpreted, the northern kingdom of Israel as opposed to Judah. It has been discussed above how "Israel" never has that sense in the genuine words of the prophet.

In addition it can be seen that Ezekiel, whose preaching is so fully directed at Yahweh's people Israel, from this point of view also comes to quite unique reformulations, which are completely absent from the rest of the OT. This may not signify very much in the case of the unusual expression, in the later passage 45:15, מַשְׁקֵה יִשְׂרָאֵל, which cannot be interpreted with certainty. But Ezekiel's special understanding emerges quite clearly, however, in the expression which is attested only in Ezekiel (seventeen times!) אַדְמַת יִשְׂרָאֵל, alongside which can be placed הָרֵי יִשְׂרָאֵל, which again occurs only in Ezekiel (no fewer than sixteen times).[8] To these may be added the specific expression הַר מְרוֹם יִשְׂרָאֵל (17:23; 20:40), which must refer to the hill of the city and temple of God.[9] 34:14 extends the designation in the plural to the whole land when the הָרֵי מְרוֹם־יִשְׂרָאֵל are referred to. In the expression נְבִיאֵי יִשְׂרָאֵל, which is attested three times and occurs only in Ezekiel, the phenomenon of prophecy is assigned, already through this nomenclature, to the people of God (13:2, 16; 38:17). If Ezekiel is quite alone in the OT with the singular נְשִׂיא יִשְׂרָאֵל (21:30), the plural נְשִׂיאֵי יִשְׂרָאֵל (19:1; 21:17; 22:6; 45:9) has links with the language of P (in the OT only in Nu 1:44; 4:46; 7:2, 84). Even the reference to the ר[וֹ]עֵי יִשְׂרָאֵל is unique to Ezekiel. Thus in this nomenclature the offices of prophets, princes and shepherds are, as are also arable land and mountains, referred to Yahweh's people. In this respect the concrete sociological components and the concrete politico-geographical aspects fade into the background in the face of the desire to give expression to theological content.[10]

8 See 1, 203 and 1, 185f.
9 See also Appendix 1 (p. 557).
10 On this whole subject see also Zimmerli, "Israel."

3. רוּחַ in the Book of Ezekiel

In the book of Ezekiel the noun רוּחַ occurs fifty-two times.[1]

1. רוּחַ means in the first instance quite objectively the wind (Johnson: "air in motion"). Its intensification to the storm which can destructively knock a wall down is expressed in 13:11, 13 by the construct formation רוּחַ סְעָרוֹת. When alongside that in 17:10; 19:12; 27:26 the destructive storm is described as רוּחַ הַקָּדִים, this does not, in the first place, refer to the historical enemy from the east (Lys). Rather, this expression in its original formation betrays local Palestinian coloring. What is referred to by it is the destructive, hot east wind from the Arabian desert, which is mentioned as רוּחַ קָדִים also in Ex 10:13; 14:21; Jer 18:17; Jon 4:8 and elsewhere.[2] The scorching effect of this desert wind is specifically referred to in 17:10 and 19:12. The fact that the originally feminine רוּחַ is treated as masculine in this context (19:12; 27:26) is explained as due to the influence of the associated קָדִים. This can even appear alone as the designation of the east wind (Gen 41:6, 23, 27) and is then taken as masculine.

In 1:4 there is no destructive effect inherent in רוּחַ סְעָרָה. Here, in dependence on Israel's ancient theophany narratives (Exodus 19; Psalm 18), it is the vehicle of Yahweh's appearing.[3]

In a derived usage רוּחַ can then refer to the wind direction. Thus the construct relationships of 42:16–19 connect רוּחַ in turn with the names of the four points of the compass, and 42:20 mentions in summary fashion the אַרְבַּע רוּחוֹת as does 37:9. It is on this basis that the abbreviated reference to scattering לְכָל־רוּחַ (5:10, 12; 12:14; 17:21) is to be understood, alongside which the even more severely curtailed statement of 5:2 about scattering לָרוּחַ must have the same sense. In contrast to the passages mentioned earlier, רוּחַ here (against Lys) is not meant at the same time to be an instrument of judgment.

2. From the sense of "air in motion" the transition to the concept of רוּחַ as "breath of life" is easy. In this context one is surprised by the section 37:1–14 with its unique amalgamation of the two senses, which can nevertheless factually be clearly differentiated. According to 37:9, the prophet is to summon "from the four winds" the רוּחַ which in vv 9f is addressed in the singulr with the definite article. But this רוּחַ gives life to the dead bodies, which according to 37:8 are still lying motionless (וְרוּחַ אֵין בָּהֶם), as was promised by the proclamation which Yahweh entrusted to the prophet: הִנֵּה אֲנִי מֵבִיא (וְנָתַתִּי) בָכֶם רוּחַ וִחְיִיתֶם (37:5, 6 and, on that basis, v 10). From the designation of the wind directions which derives from the phenomenon of the wind blowing outside in nature, the reference passes imperceptibly to that of the breath of human life which is to be found also in other statements in Ezekiel. Thus 21:12 speaks of the debilitating extinction (כהה) of the רוּחַ which is accompanied by the weakening of all limbs. 2:2 and 3:24 show how the prophet who is in a state of collapse is set on his feet again by the רוּחַ entering into him and is made capable of speech.

In 11:5 and 20:32 רוּחַ designates man's intellectual center from where his thoughts arise. 14:4, 7, in a parallel expression, speak of man's heart (לֵב). In the observation of 3:14 וָאֵלֵךְ בְּחֲמַת רוּחִי (cf. note a there), רוּחַ describes not so much an attitude of will as a state of mind. It is otherwise in 1:12, where it is stated that the creatures carrying the throne went "wherever the spirit (הָרוּחַ) would go." This is then taken up in the expansion in 1:15–21, which adds to the vision of a throne vehicle the wheels of a throne carriage in such a way that in vv 20f the רוּחַ הַחַיָּה gives to the wheels too the direction of their movement. On this basis also 10:17. Here again רוּחַ is the organ of the decision of the will about the way to be taken. The fact that רוּחַ is once again treated as masculine is here too to be understood on the basis of the word to which רוּחַ is in construct relationship. In רוּחַ we see the working of the "creature" (חַיָּה) which carries the throne and which is explicitly equated in 10:15 with the (masculine) כְּרוּב.

Lys wishes to find in 11:5 and 20:32 already a reference to the corrupt nature of the human רוּחַ. Certainly this emphasis on human arbitrariness can be perceived in the reading of 𝔐 in 13:3 when it is stated that the prophets "follow after their own spirit (אַחַר רוּחָם)—according to that which they have not seen" (But cf. note b there). Thus then at this point the call to repentance begins. "Make for yourselves a new heart and a new spirit (רוּחַ חֲדָשָׁה)" runs the ex-

1 See the mongraph of Daniel Lys, *"Rûach." Le Souffle dans l'Ancien Testament,* Études d'histoire et de philosophie religieuses 56 (Paris: Presses universitaires de France, 1962), especially 121–146. Among the older literature indicated there particular attention should be paid to Johnson, *Vitality,* especially 26–39.

2 See, e.g., Klein, "Klima," 322–325.

3 See 1, 119.

hortation of 18:31. As has been mentioned,[4] the wording of this is in conflict with the pure promise of salvation of 11:19 and 36:26, according to which Yahweh himself promises to effect this new character for man. In all three passages רוּחַ is parallel to לֵב. Inconsistency exists only in the fact that in 11:19 and 36:26 the "old heart" is explicitly qualified as a "stone heart," while such a qualification is absent in the case of the רוּחַ. Here the רוּחַ which is promised for the future is described simply as a "new spirit."

3. These last remarks already lead to the third, most frequent area of the use of רוּחַ in the book of Ezekiel—to the idea of the רוּחַ which comes from the world of the divine. Here we can ascertain, for the second time, the remarkable lack of clarity in some statements in the book of Ezekiel which prevents the clear differentiation of areas of meaning. When in 37:1–14 the prophetic word summons the רוּחַ from the four wind directions to the dead human corpses—is this simply a mixture of the natural understanding of רוּחַ (wind) with the anthropological (human life spirit)? Is there not an admixture of the third component of the life element coming from the world of the divine? A glance at the related presentation in Gen 2:7, according to which Yahweh breathes his spirit (נְשָׁמָה there but see also, e.g., Eccl 12:7) into man who has been formed from the earth, would at any rate prevent a round negative answer to that question. To this, however, must still be added the reference to 37:14. Here, surprisingly, after the restoration of life to the dead bones has been interpreted with regard to the process of the restoration of the house of Israel to the "land of Israel," there is added: "I shall put my spirit (רוּחִי) within you so that you may have life and I shall place you in your land." The breath of life (הָרוּחַ), which is summoned from the four winds (מֵאַרְבַּע רוּחוֹת), changes here imperceptibly into Yahweh's own spirit (רוּחִי), which Israel is to receive. Again, this is scarcely to be differentiated from the promise of the new spirit to man. So, then, we find the same transition again in chapter 36, where the promise of the new spirit (36:26) is continued in v 27 by the promise: "And my spirit (רוּחִי) I shall put within you and will insure that you walk in my statutes and observe my laws and do them." The same statement is transformed in the late redactional formulation of 39:29 to the more concrete image of the pouring out of the spirit by Yahweh (שָׁפַכְתִּי אֶת־רוּחִי עַל־בֵּית יִשְׂרָאֵל). This paves the way for the "more distended" statement of Joel 3:1ff.[5] The expression must envisage the concept of the fructifying, beneficent rain from heaven giving growth and nourishment. In 36:27, on the other hand, where (as in 37:14) the verb נתן is used, what is envisaged is clearly the inner transformation of man which enables him to keep the commandments.

4. There is still a final line of use of the concept רוּחַ in Ezekiel along which the prophet differs in a quite remarkable way from earlier writing prophets, going back, traditio-historically, to the tradition of pre-writing prophets. This is the רוּחַ of the specific, prophetic experience of a call, which can be observed in nine passages.

Terminologically it can first of all be ascertained that in this context on one occasion, 11:24, doubtless in continuation of pre-Israelite linguistic usage,[6] the reference is to the רוּחַ אֱלֹהִים, whereas in 11:5 and 37:1 it is to the רוּחַ יהוה. In the other passages we find, surprisingly, the use of simple רוּחַ without the article (3:12, 14, 24; 8:3; 11:1, 24a; 43:5). From this, it appears to be an almost independently effective power, however clear it also is that in its activity we are dealing with effects brought about by Yahweh.

Here we have already touched on the fact that in the "spirit" which encounters the prophet from the part of Yahweh we are dealing with an experience of the effect of power which is characterized by a particular force. This can be seen already in the description of the coming of the spirit in 11:5, which belongs to a later insertion. According to this the spirit "falls" (נפל) on the prophet in the way that can be said also of the "hand of Yahweh" in 8:1.[7] 3:24 speaks in a more restrained way simply of the entry of the spirit into the prophet (וַתָּבֹא־בִי רוּחַ). The dynamic character of the רוּחַ is clearer when reference is made to its subsequent effect on the prophet. Only in the section 11:1–13, which has been added secondarily, is it stated in 11:5 that the coming of the spirit leads to the prophetic word. No fewer than six times, on the other hand, is it stated in other passages that the רוּחַ "lifts up" the prophet (נשׂא 3:12, 14; 8:3; 11:1, 24a; 43:5). Connected with this, in 3:14, is the verb לקח "take, carry off."[8] In 8:3 this verb precedes in a somewhat different coordination. More frequently, נשׂא is followed by the simple hip'il of בוא (8:3; 11:1, 24a; 43:5) in order to describe the process of transportation to another place. 37:1 states that the process of transportation (וַיּוֹצִאֵנִי) takes place "in the spirit of Yahweh (בְּרוּחַ יהוה)." The same description of the enveloping sphere is used in 11:24, looking back on the fading experience of transportation and vision which took place בַּמַּרְאָה בְּרוּחַ אֱלֹהִים.

4 See 1,386.
5 Wolff, *Joel and Amos*, 60. See also the אֶצֹּק רוּחִי ("I will pour my spirit") of Is 44:3.
6 See Appendix 1 (p. 557).
7 See also 1,117f.
8 See 1,139.

Again it may be asked whether then the statements of 2:2 and 3:24, according to which רוּחַ enters the prophet, who had collapsed in the face of Yahweh's kingly majesty, and sets him on his feet again, would not also be better included here than simply there, where we were discussing human life power. Here too a line of demarcation is hazy and leaves open the question whether רוּחַ here is to be understood simply in anthropological terms or whether it is not also theological.

More important, however, than this detailed problem of the evaluation of the two passages is the observation that in all this talk of the "spirit" as the power which transports the prophet to distant places and allows him to see things afar off there emerges a manner of speech and of experience which was completely avoided in written prophecy before Ezekiel. As distant suggestions of this talk of the spirit as the prophet's special experience of power, we could mention at the most Mic 3:8, where, however, precisely this reference to the spirit must be a later addition, and the calling of the prophet Hosea an אִישׁ הָרוּחַ by the people (Hos 9:7). Instead, this manner of speaking is to be found in pre-written prophecy. The problem of the surprisingly "archaic" usage of the word in the book of Ezekiel, which is particularly clearly discernible in the references to the prophetic רוּחַ, has been discussed in the Introduction in a wider context.[9]

9 See Introduction 1, 42f.

1. Commentaries (listed in order of their publication)

Haevernick, H. A. C.
Commentar über den Propheten Ezechiel (1843).

Hitzig, F.
Der Prophet Ezechiel erklärt, KeH 8 (Leipzig, 1847).

Kliefoth, Th.
Das Buch Ezechiels übersetzt und erklärt (Rostock, 1864/65).

Ewald, Heinrich
Die Propheten des Alten Bundes erklärt, volume 2, "Jeremja und Hezeqiel" (Göttingen, [2]1868).

Smend, Rudolf
Der Prophet Ezechiel, KeH (Leipzig, [2]1880).

Cornill, Carl Heinrich
Das Buch des Propheten Ezechiel (Leipzig, 1886).

Knabenbauer, Joseph
Commentarius in Ezechielem prophetam, CSS (Paris, 1890).

Bertholet, Alfred
Das Buch Hesekiel erklärt, KHC 12 (Freiburg: Mohr, 1897).

Toy, C. H.
The Book of the Prophet Ezekiel, SBOT 12 (New York: Dodd, Mead, 1899).

Kraetzschmar, Richard
Das Buch Ezechiel, HKAT (Göttingen: Vandenhoeck & Ruprecht, 1900).

Breuer, Joseph
Das Buch Jecheskel übersetzt und erläutert (Frankfurt: Sänger and Friedburg, 1921).

Rothstein, J. W.
Das Buch Ezechiel, HSAT (Tübingen: [4]1922).

Heinisch, Paul
Das Buch Ezechiel übersetzt und erklärt, HSAT 8 (Bonn: Hanstein, 1923).

Herrmann, Johannes
Ezechiel, übersetzt und erklärt, KAT (Leipzig: Deichert, 1924).

Troelstra, A.
Ezechiel, 2 vols, TeU (Groningen: Wolters, 1931).

Bertholet, Alfred and Galling, Kurt
Hesekiel, HAT 13 (Tübingen: Mohr [Siebeck], 1936).

Cooke, G. A.
A Critical and Exegetical Commentary on the Book of Ezekiel ICC (Edinburgh: Clark, 1936).

Matthews, I. G.
Ezekiel. An American Commentary on the Old Testament (Philadelphia: Judson, 1939).

Schumpp, Meinrad
Das Buch Ezechiel übersetzt und erklärt, Herders Bibelkommentar (Freiburg: Herder, 1942).

Auvray, P.
Ezéchiel, Témoins de Dieu (1947).

Ziegler, Joseph
Ezechiel, Echter-B (Würzburg: Echter, 1948).

Fohrer, Georg and Galling, Kurt
Ezechiel, HAT 13 (Tübingen: Mohr [Siebeck], [2]1955).

Aalders, Gerhard Charles
Ezechiel, 2 volumes, COT (Kampen: Kok, 1955 and 1957).

May, Herbert G.
"The Book of Ezekiel" in *The Interpreter's Bible* 6 (Nashville: Abingdon, 1956), 41–338.

Howie, Carl Gordon
The Book of Ezekiel; The Book of Daniel, The Layman's Bible Commentary 13 (Richmond, Va.: John Knox, 1961).

Lamparter, H.
Zum Wächter bestellt. Der Prophet Ezechiel, Botschaft des Alten Testaments 21 (Stuttgart: Calwer, 1968).

Taylor, J. B.
Ezekiel, Tyndale Old Testament Commentaries (Downers Grove, Ill.: InterVarsity, 1969).

Wevers, John W.
Ezekiel, Cent-B (London: Nelson, 1969).

Eichrodt, Walther
Der Prophet Hesekiel, ATD (1970).

Asensio, F.
"Ezequiel" in *La sagrada ecritura* AT 5 (1970), 713–919.

Alonso-Schökel, L.
Ezequiel, Los Libros sagrados IV/8 (Madrid: Ediciones cristiandad, 1971).

Becker, J.
Der priesterliche Prophet. Das Buch Ezechiel, Stuttg. Kl. Komm. AT 12/1 and 2 (Stuttgart, 1971).

Carley, K. W.
The Book of the Prophet Ezekiel, The Cambridge Bible Commentary (Cambridge: University Press, 1974).

Cortese, E.
Ezechiele, Novissima Versione della Bibbia 27 (1974).

Mosis, R.
Das Buch Ezechiel 1, Geistliche Schriftlesung AT 8/1 (Düsseldorf: Patmos, 1978).

2. Select Books, Monographs, and Articles (alphabetically)

Aalders, Gerhard Charles
"Ezechiël's Herstellingsvisioen (Capp. 40–48)," *Gereformeerd theologisch tijdschrift* 13 (1912/13): 453–474, 509–532.

Aalders, J. G.
Gog en Magog in Ezechiël (Kampen: Kok, 1951).

Abba, R.
"Priests and Levites in Ezekiel," *VT* 28 (1978): 1–9.

Abel, Felix Marie
Une croisière autour de la mer Morte, 1911.

Idem
Géographie de la Palestine, 2 volumes (Paris: Gabalda, [2]1933–1938).

Idem
"Notes complémentaires sur la mer Morte," *RB* 38 (1929): 237–260.

Aberbach, M.
"Ezekiel," *Encyclopaedia judaica* 6, 1078–1098.

Abraham, A.
Die Schiffsterminologie des Alten Testaments kulturgeschichtlich und etymologisch untersucht, unpub. Diss. (Bern, 1914).

Aharoni, Y.
"Kadesh-Barnea and Mount Sinai" in *God's Wilderness; Discoveries in Sinai,* tr. Joseph Witriol (London: Thames and Hudson, 1961), 115–182.

Idem
"The Negeb of Judah," *IEJ* 8 (1958): 26–38.

Idem
"Tamar and the Roads to Elath," *IEJ* 13 (1963): 30–42.

Aistleitner, Joseph
Die mythologischen und kultischen Texte aus Ras Schamra (Budapest: Akadémie Kaidó, 1959).

Idem
Wörterbuch der ugaritischen Sprache (Berlin: Akademie, 1963).

Albrecht, Karl
"את vor dem Nominativ und beim Passiv," *ZAW* 47 (1929): 274–283.

Albright, W. F.
"An Aramaean Magical Text in Hebrew from the Seventh Century B. C.," *BASOR* 76 (1939): 5–11.

Idem
"Baal-Zephon" in *Festschrift Alfred Bertholet* (Tübingen: Mohr [Siebeck], 1950), 1–14.

Idem
"The Babylonian Temple-Tower and the Altar of Burnt-Offering," *JBL* 39 (1920): 137–142.

Idem
"Contributions to Biblical Archaeology and Philology," *JBL* 43 (1924): 363–393 (3. 'Gog and Magog,' 378–385).

Idem
"Dedan" in *Geschichte und Altes Testament; Festschrift für A. Alt* (Tübingen: Mohr, 1953), 1–12.

Idem
"The Early Alphabetic Inscriptions from Sinai and Their Decipherment," *BASOR* 110 (1948): 6–22.

Idem
"Mesopotamian Elements in Canaanite Eschatology" in *Oriental Studies published in Commemoration of the Fortieth Anniversary (1883–1923) of Paul Haupt as director of the Oriental Seminary of the Johns Hopkins University* (Baltimore: Johns Hopkins Press, 1926), 143–154.

Idem
"New Light on the Early History of Phoenician Colonization," *BASOR* 83 (1941): 14–22.

Idem
"Notes on Ammonite History" in *Miscellanea biblica B. Ubach* (Montserrat, 1954), 131–136.

Alt, Albrecht
"Aus der ʿAraba II–IV," *ZDPV* 58 (1935): 1–78.

Idem
"Befreiungsnacht und Krönungstag" in *Kleine Schriften zur Geschichte des Volkes Israel* 2 (München: Beck, 1953), 206–225.

Idem
"Die Deltaresidenz der Ramessiden" in *Kleine Schriften zur Geschichte des Volkes Israel* 3 (München: Beck, 1959), 176–185.

Idem
"The Formation of the Israelite State in Palestine" in *Essays on Old Testament History and Religion,* tr. R. A. Wilson (Garden City, New York: Doubleday, 1967), 173–237.

Idem
"Hosea 5:8–6:6. Ein Krieg und seine Folgen in prophetischer Beleuchtung" in *Kleine Schriften zur Geschichte des Volkes Israel* 2 (München: Beck, 1953), 163–187.

Idem
"Das Institut im Jahre 1933," *PJ* 30 (1934): 5–31.

Idem
"Israels Gaue unter Salomo" in *Kleine Schriften zur Geschichte des Volkes Israel* 2 (München: Beck, 1953), 76–89.

Idem
"Judas Nachbarn zur Zeit Nehemias" in *Kleine Schriften zur Geschichte des Volkes Israel* 2 (München: Beck, 1953), 338–345.

Idem
"Die Rolle Samarias bei der Entstehung des Judentums" in *Kleine Schriften zur Geschichte des Volkes Israel* 2 (München: Beck, 1953), 316–337.

Idem
"Das System der Stammesgrenzen im Buche Josua" in *Sellin-Festschrif. Beiträge zur Religionsgeschichte und Archäologie Palästinas* (Leipzig: A. Deichert, 1927), 13–24.

Idem
"Die Staatenbildung der Israeliten in Palästina" in *Kleine Schriften zur Geschichte des Volkes Israel* 2

(München: Beck, 1953), 1–65.

Idem
"Taphnaein und Taphnas," *ZDPV* 66 (1943): 64–68.

Idem
"Die Ursprünge des israelitischen Rechts" in *Kleine Schriften zur Geschichte des Volkes Israel* 1 (München: Beck, 1953), 278–332.

Idem
"Zelte und Hütten" in *Alttestamentliche Studien; Friedrich Nötscher zum sechzigsten Geburtstag,* eds. Hubert Junker and Johannes Botterweck, BBB 1 (Bonn: Hanstein, 1950) 15–25; reprinted in *idem, Kleine Schriften zur Geschichte des Volkes Israel* 3 (München: Beck, 1959), 233–242.

Anbar, Moshé
"Une nouvelle allusion à une tradition babylonienne dans Ézéchiel (XXII 24)," *VT* 29 (1979): 353f.

Anderson, Andrew Runni
Alexander's Gate, Gog and Magog, and the inclosed Nations (Cambridge, Mass.: The Mediaeval Academy of America, 1932).

Anderson, Bernhard W.
"The Place of Shechem in the Bible," *BA* 20 (1957): 10–19 (part 2 of "Shechem, the 'Navel of the Land,'" 2–32).

Andrew, M. E.
"Geschehnis-Reaktion-Anerkennung des Gerichts; der theologische Gedankengang von Ez 1–24," *ThLZ* 103 (1978): 477–484.

Astour, Michael C.
"Ezekiel's Prophecy of Gog and the Cuthean Legend of Naram-Sin," *JBL* 95 (1976): 567–579.

Auerbach, E.
"Die Herkunft der Ṣadoḳiden," *ZAW* 49 (1931): 327f.

Auvray, P.
"Ezéchiel," *Dictionnaire de la Bible, Supplément,* 759–791.

Avigad, N. and Yadin, Y.
A Genesis Apocryphon, tr. S. S. Nardi (Jerusalem: Magnes, 1956).

Baars, W.
"Peshiṭta Institute Communications IX. A Palimpsest of Ezekiel Reconstructed," *VT* 20 (1970): 527–536.

Bach, Robert
"Bauen und Pflanzen" in *Studien zur Theologie der alttestamentlichen Überlieferungen,* ed. R. Rendtorff and K. Koch (Neukirchen-Vluyn: Neukirchener, 1961), 7–32.

Baedeker, Karl
Ägypten und der Sûdan; Handbuch für Reisende (Leipzig: K. Baedeker, [8]1938).

Idem
Egypt and the Sûdân; Handbook for Travellers (New York: C. Scribner's Sons, [7] 1914).

Bagatti, B.
"La posizione del tempio erodiano di Gerusalemme," *Bibl* 46 (1965): 428–444.

Balmer-Rinck, J. J.
Des Propheten Ezechiel Gesicht vom Tempel. Für Verehrer und Forscher des Wortes Gottes und für Freunde religiöser Kunst übersichtlich dargestellt und architektonisch erläutert, 1858.

Baltzer, D.
Ezechiel und Deuterojesaja; Berührungen in der Heilserwartung der beiden grossen Exilspropheten, BZAW 121 (Berlin: deGruyter, 1971).

Baltzer, K.
Die Biographie der Propheten (Neukirchen-Vluyn: Neukirchener, 1975).

Bardtke, Hans
"Jeremia der Fremdvölkerprophet. II," *ZAW* 54 (1936): 240–262 (XI. 'Das Orakel wider Kedar und Hazor 49:28–33,' 255–256).

Idem
"Der Prophet Ezechiel in der modernen Forschung," *ThLZ* 96 (1971): 721–734.

Barnes, W. Emery
"Ezekiel's Denunciation of Tyre (Ezek 26–28)," *JTS* 35 (1934): 50–54.

Idem
"Ezekiel's Vision of a Resurrection (Ezekiel 37:1–14)," *The Expositor* 8th series 14 (1917): 290–297.

Idem
"Two Trees become One: Ezek 37:16–17," *JTS* 39 (1938): 391–393.

Barnett, R. D.
"Ezekiel and Tyre," *Eretz Israel* 9 (1969): 6–13.

Barth, C.
"Ezechiel 37 als Einheit" in *Beiträge zur alttestamentlichen Theologie; Festschrift für Walther Zimmerli* (Göttingen: Vandenhoeck & Ruprecht, 1977), 38–52.

Barth, Christoph
Die Errettung vom Tode in den individuellen Klage- und Dankliedern des Alten Testaments (Zollikon: Evangelischer, 1947).

Barth, Jakob
Die Nominalbildung in den semitischen Sprachen (Leipzig: Hinrichs, [2]1894).

Baudissin, Wolf Wilhelm Graf
Die Geschichte des alttestamentlichen Priesterthums (Leipzig: Hirzel, 1889).

Idem
Kyrios als Gottesname im Judentum und seine Stelle in der Religionsgeschichte. Erster Teil: Der Gebrauch des Gottesnamens Kyrios in Septuaginta (Giessen: Töpelmann, 1929).

Baumgärtel, Friedrich
"Zu den Gottesnamen in den Büchern Jeremia und Ezechiel" in *Verbannung und Heimkehr. Beiträge zur Geschichte und Theologie Israels im 6. und 5. Jahrhundert v. Chr.; Wilhelm Rudolph zum 70. Geburtstage dargebracht* (Tübingen: Mohr [Siebeck], 1961), 1–29.

Baumgartner, Walter
Zum Alten Testament und seiner Umwelt; ausgewählte Aufsätze (Leiden: Brill, 1959).
Idem
"Zur Etymologie von schᵉʾōl," *ThZ* 2 (1946): 233–235.
Beckerath, Jürgen von
Tanis und Theben; historische Grundlagen der Ramessidenzeit in Ägypten, Ägyptologische Forschungen 16 (Glückstadt, New York: Augustin, 1951).
Beentjes, P. C.
"Ezekiel 19: Motive und Struktur," *Bijdragen* 35 (1974): 357–371 (Dutch).
Begrich, Karl
"Das Messiasbild des Ezechiel," *ZWTh* 47 (1904): 433–461.
Bentzen, Aage
"Zur Geschichte der Ṣadoḳiden," *ZAW* 51 (1933): 173–176.
Idem
"Priesterschaft und Laien in der jüdischen Gemeinde des fünften Jahrhunderts," *AfO* 6 (1930/31): 280–286.
Idem
"The Ritual Background of Amos 1:2–2:16," *OTS* 8 (1950): 85–99.
Idem
Studier over det zadokidiske praesteskabs historie (København: Lunos, 1931).
Bernhardt, Karl Heinz
"Beobachtungen zur Identifizierung moabitischer Ortslagen," *ZDPV* 76 (1960): 136–158.
Idem
Das Problem der altorientalischen Königsideologie im Alten Testament, VT Suppl 8 (Leiden: Brill, 1961).
Berry, George Ricker
"The Authorship of Ezekiel 40–48," *JBL* 34 (1915): 17–40.
Idem
"The Date of Ezekiel 38:1–39:29," *JBL* 41 (1922): 224–232.
Idem
"The Date of Ezekiel 45:1–8a and 47:13–48:35," *JBL* 40 (1921): 70–75.
Idem
"The Glory of Yahweh and the Temple," *JBL* 56 (1937): 115–117.
Idem
"Priests and Levites," *JBL* 42 (1923): 227–238.
Bertholet, Alfred
Der Verfassungsentwurf des Hesekiel in seiner religionsgeschichtlichen Bedeutung (Freiburg i. B.: Mohr, 1896).
Bettenzoli, G.
Geist der Heiligkeit; Traditionsgeschichtliche Untersuchung des QDS-Begriffes im Buch Ezechiel, Quaderni di semitistica 8 (Rome: Herder, 1979).
Betz, Otto
"Die Proselytentaufe der Qumransekte und die Taufe im Neuen Testament," *RQ* 1 (1958/59): 213–234.
Beuken, W. A. M.
"Ez 20: Thematiek en literaire vormgeving in onderling verband," *Bijdragen* 33 (1972): 39–64.
Bevan, A. A.
"The King of Tyre in Ezekiel 28," *JTS* 4 (1903): 500–505.
Bewer, Julius A.
"Das Datum in Hes 33:21," *ZAW* 54 (1936): 114f.
Idem
"Das Tal der Wanderer in Hesekiel 39:11," *ZAW* 56 (1938): 123–125.
Bieling, Hugo
Zu den Sagen von Gog und Magog, Wissenschaftliche Beilage zum Programm der Sophien-Realschule. Ostern 1882 (Berlin: Weidmannsche Buchhandlung, 1882).
Bietenhard, Hans
Das tausendjährige Reich; eine biblisch-theologische Studie (Bern: Graf-Lehmann, 1944).
Bilabel, Friedrich
Geschichte Vorderasiens und Ägyptens vom 16.–11. Jahrhundert v. Chr. (Heidelberg: Winter, 1927).
Billerbeck, Adolf and Delitzsch, Friedrich
Die Palasttore Salmanassars II. von Balawat, Beiträge zur Assyriologie und semitischen Sprachwissenschaft 6,1 (Leipzig: Hinrichs, 1908).
Birkeland, Harris
"The Belief in the Resurrection of the Dead in the Old Testament," *Studia Theologica* 3 (1949): 60–78.
Bissing, Friedrich Wilhelm Freiherr von
"Pyrene (Punt) und die Seefahrten der Ägypter" in *Die Welt des Orients. Wissenschaftliche Beiträge zur Kunde des Morgenlandes,* ed. Ernst Michel (Wuppertal: Hans Putty Verlag, 1948), 146–157.
Blanckenhorn, Max
"Entstehung und Geschichte des Todten Meeres. Ein Beitrag zur Geologie Palästinas," *ZDPV* 19 (1896): 1–59.
Blau, Josia
"Gibt es ein emphatisches ʾēṯ im Bibelhebraeisch?" *VT* 6 (1956): 211f.
Blome, Friedrich
Die Opfermaterie in Babylonien und Israel 1 (Rome: Pontifical Biblical Institute, 1934).
Boadt, Lawrence
"The A:B:B:A Chiasm of Identical Roots in Ezekiel," *VT* 25 (1975): 693–699.
Idem
Ezekiel's Oracles against Egypt; a Literary and Philological Study of Ezekiel 29–32, Biblica et Orientalia 37 (Rome: Pontifical Biblical Institute, 1980).
Idem
"Textual Problems in Ezekiel and Poetic Analysis of Paired Words," *JBL* 97 (1978): 489–499.
Boehmer, Julius
"מלך und נשיא bei Ezechiel," *ThStKr* 73 (1900):

112–117.

Idem

"Die prophetische Heilspredigt Ezechiels," *ThStKr* 74 (1901): 173–228.

Idem

"Wer ist Gog von Magog? Ein Beitrag zur Auslegung des Buches Ezechiel," *ZWTh* 40 (1897): 321–355.

Boettcher, Julius Friedrich

Neue exegetisch-kritische Aehrenlese zum Alten Testamente, 2. Abtheilung ed. F. Mühlau (1864), 183–191.

Idem

Proben alttestamentlicher Schrifterklärung nach wissenschaftlicher Sprachforschung mit kritischen Versuchen über bisherige Exegese und Beiträgen zu Grammatik und Lexicon (1833), 218–365 (XII. "Exegetisch-kritischer Versuch über die ideale Beschreibung der Tempelgebäude Ezech. C. 40–42; 46:19–24").

Bogaert, P.-M.

"Le témoignage de la Vetus Latina dans l'étude de la tradition des Septants. Ézéchiel et Daniel dans le Papyrus 967," *Bibl* 59 (1978): 384–395.

Borger, Riekele

Die Inschriften Asarhaddons, Königs von Assyrien, Archiv für Orientforschung Beiheft 9 (Graz: Im Selbstverlag des Herausgebers, 1956).

van den Born, A.

"'De deur (?) der volken' in Ezek 26:2," *StC* 26 (1951): 320–322.

Idem

"Études sur quelques toponymes bibliques," *OTS* 10 (1954): 197–214 (l. 'Le pays du Magog,' 197–201).

Botterweck, G. Joh.

"Textkritische Bemerkungen zu Ezechiel 44:3a," *VT* 1 (1951): 145f.

Bowman, John

"Ezekiel and the Zadokite Priesthood," *Transactions of the Glasgow Univerity Oriental Society* 16 (1955/56): 1–14.

Boyd, James Oscar

"Ezekiel and the Modern Dating of the Pentateuch," *PrincTR* 6 (1908): 29–51.

Braslavy, J.

"The End of Pharaoh—the great Crocodile in the Light of the Worship of the Crocodile in Egypt," *Beth Miqra* 53 (1973): 143–149 (Hebrew).

Breasted, James Henry

A History of Egypt from the Earliest Times to the Persian Conquest (New York: C. Scribner's Sons, [2]1920).

Bréchet, Raymond

Ézéchiel aujourd'hui; Israel et les Chrétiens dans le monde (Geneva: Éditions du Tricorne, 1979).

Brekelmans, C. H. W.

De ḥerem in het Oude Testament (Nijmegen: Centrale drukkerij, 1959).

Brin, G.

Studies in the Book of Ezekiel (Tel Aviv, 1975) (Hebrew).

Brockelmann, C.

Lexicon syriacum (Halis Saxonum: Niemeyer, 1928).

Idem

"Die Objektkonstruktion der Passiva im Hebräischen," *ZAW* 49 (1931): 147–149.

Brock-Utne, Albert

Der Gottesgarten; eine vergleichende religionsgeschichtliche Studie (Oslo: Dybwad, 1936).

Bron, Bernhard

"Zur Psychopathologie und Verkündigung des Propheten Ezechiel; zum Phänomen der prophetischen Ekstase," *Schweizer Archiv für Neurologie, Neurochirurgie und Psychiatrie* 128/1 (1981).

Brooke, A. E.

"Review of F. G. Kenyon, *The Chester Beatty Biblical Papyri. Descriptions and texts of twelve manuscripts on papyrus of the Greek Bible.* Fasciculi V–VII," *JTS* 39 (1938): 167–169.

Brown, Theo.

"A Note on Gog," *Folk-lore* (London) 61 (1950): 98–103.

Brownlee, William Hugh

"The Aftermath of the Fall of Judah according to Ezekiel," *JBL* 89 (1970): 393–404.

Idem

"Ezekiel's Parable of the Watchman and the Editing of Ezekiel," *VT* 28 (1978): 392–408.

Idem

"Ezekiel's poetic Indictment of the Shepherds," *HTR* 51 (1958): 191–203.

Idem

"Two Elegies on the Fall of Judah (Ezekiel 19)" in *Ex orbe religionum; Studia Geo Widengren* 1 (Leiden: Brill, 1972), 93–103.

Buber, Martin

For the Sake of Heaven, tr. Ludwig Lewisohn (Philadelphia: Jewish Publication Society, 1945).

Buchanan, George Wesley

"Eschatology and the 'End of Days,'" *JNES* 20 (1961): 188–193.

Budde, Karl

"Die Herkunft Ṣadoḳ's," *ZAW* 52 (1934): 42–50.

Buhl, Frants Peter William

Geschichte der Edomiter (Leipzig: Edelmann, 1893).

Buis, Pierre

"Ézéchiel 16," *Études théologiques et religieuses* 53 (1978): 502–507.

Van Buren, E. D.

"The Rod and the Ring," *Archiv Orientální* 17,2 (1949): 434–450.

Burrows, Millar

"Orthography, Morphology, and Syntax of the St. Mark's Isaiah Manuscript," *JBL* 68 (1949): 195–211.

Cannon, William Walter
"Some Notes on Zechariah c. 11," *AfO* 4 (1927): 139–146.
Carley, K. W.
Ezekiel among the Prophets, Studies in Biblical Theology II/31 (London: SCM, 1975).
Carreira, J. N.
"Raizes da linguagem profética de Ezequiel; A propósito de Ez 18, 5–9," *Estudios bíblicos* 26 (1967): 275–286.
Caspari, Wilhelm
"*ṭabur* (Nabel)," *ZDMG* 86 (1932): 49–65.
Cassem, N. H.
"Ezekiel's Psychotic Personality: Reservations on the Use of the Couch for Biblical Personalities" in *The Word in the World; Essays in Honor of F. L. Moriarty,* ed. Richard J. Clifford and George W. MacRae (Cambridge, MA: Weston College Press, 1973), 59–70.
Castellino, G.
"Les origines de la civilisation selon les textes bibliques et les textes cunéiformes" in *Volume du Congrès, Strasbourg 1956,* VT Suppl 4 (Leiden: Brill, 1957), 116–137.
Cerfaux, Lucien
"'Adonaï et Kyrios,'" *Revue des sciences philosophiques et théologiques* 20 (1931): 417–452.
Idem
"Le nom divin 'Kyrios' dans la Bible grecque," *Revue des sciences philosophiques et théologiques* 20 (1931): 27–51.
Idem
"Le titre 'Kyrios' et la dignité royale de Jésus," *Revue des sciences philosophiques et théologiques* 11 (1922): 40–71.
Chajes, H. P.
"Ez. 27:4," *ZAW* 21 (1901): 79.
Cheminant, P.
Les prophéties d'Ezéchiel contre Tyr (26–28:19), 1912.
Childs, Brevard S.
"The Enemy From the North and the Chaos Tradition," *JBL* 78 (1959): 187–198.
Chipiez, C. and Perrot, G.
"Restitution du temple de Jérusalem d'après Ézéchiel," *RGATP* 4 ser. 12 (1885): 151–167, 193–233.
Clements, Ronald E.
Prophecy and Tradition (Atlanta: John Knox, 1975).
Cooke, G. A.
"The Paradise Story of Ezekiel 28," *Old Testament Essays* (London: Charles Griffin and Co., Ltd., 1927), 37–45.
Idem
"Some Considerations on the Text and Teaching of Ezekiel 40–48," *ZAW* 42 (1924): 105–115.
Idem
A Text-Book of north-Semitic Inscriptions (Oxford: Clarendon, 1903).
Correns, D.
Schebiit (Berlin: Töpelmann, 1961).
Craghan, J. F.
"Ezekiel: A pastoral Theologian," *American Ecclesiastical Review* 166 (1972): 22–33.
Crenshaw, J. L.
Prophetic Conflict. Its Effect Upon Israelite Religion, BZAW 124 (Berlin: deGruyter, 1971).
Criado, R.
"Messianismo en Ez 21, 32," *Semana Biblica Española* 30 (1972): 263–317.
Dahood, M.
"Ezekiel 19 and Relative *kî,*" *Bibl* 56 (1975): 96–99.
Dalman, Gustaf
"Die Wasserversorgung des ältesten Jerusalem," *PJ* 14 (1918): 47–72.
Idem
"Der zweite Tempel zu Jerusalem," *PJ* 5 (1909): 29–57.
Day, J.
"The Daniel of Ugarit and Ezekiel and the Hero of the book of Daniel," *VT* 30 (1980): 174–184.
Dean, J. E.
"The Date of Ezekiel 40–43," *AJSL* 43 (1927): 231–233.
Delekat, F. Lienhard
"Elohim im 2. und 3. Psalmbuch" in *Asylie und Schutzorakel am Zionheiligtum* (Leiden: Brill, 1967), 343–380.
Delitzsch, Friedrich
Wo lag das Paradies? Eine biblisch-assyriologische Studie (Leipzig: Hinrichs, 1881).
Dhorme, E.
"Abraham dans le Cadre de l'Histoire" in *Recueil Édouard Dhorme; Études bibliques et orientales* (Paris: Imprimerie nationale, 1951), 191–272.
Idem
"Les peuples issus de Japhet d'après le chapitre X de la Genèse" in *Recueil Édouard Dhorme; Études bibliques et orientales* (Paris: Imprimerie nationale, 1951), 167–189 (= *Syria* 13 [1932], 28–49).
Díaz, J. Alonso
"Ezequiel, el profeta de ruina y de esperanza," *Cultura bíblica* 222 (1968): 290–299.
Díez-Macho, A.
"Un segundo fragmento del Targum Palestinense a los Profetas," *Bibl* 39 (1958): 198–205.
van Dijk, J.
"Le motif cosmique dans la pensée sumérienne," *Archiv Orientální* 28 (1965): 1–59.
Doniach, N. S.
"Studies in Hebrew Philology: √ עתר," *AJSL* 50 (1934): 178.
Donner, H.
Studien zur Verfassungs- und Verwaltungsgeschichte der Reiche Israel und Juda, Unpub. Diss. (Leipzig, 1956).

Idem
"Neue Quellen zur Geschichte des Staates Moab in der Zweiten Hälfte des 8. Jahrh. v. Chr.," *Mitteilungen des Instituts für Orientforschung* 5 (1957): 155-184.

Donner, H. and Röllig, W.
Kanaanäische und aramäische Inschriften, 3 volumes (Wiesbaden: Harrassowitz, 1962–64).

Van Doorslaer, J.
"No Amon," *CBQ* 11 (1949): 280–295.

Douglas, George C. M.
"Ezekiel's Temple," *ET* 9 (1897/98): 365–367, 420–422, 468–470, 515–518.

Idem
"Ezekiel's Vision of the Temple," *ET* 14 (1902/03): 365–368, 424–427.

Dressler, Harold H. P.
"The Identification of the Ugaritic DNIL with the Daniel of Ezekiel," *VT* 29 (1979): 152–161.

Driver, G. R.
Problems of the Hebrew Verbal System (Edinburgh: Clark, 1936).

Idem
"Uncertain Hebrew Words," *JSS* 45 (1944): 13f.

Driver, G. R. and Miles, J. C.
The Babylonian Laws 2 (Oxford; Clarendon, 1955).

Driver, S. R.
A Treaties on the Use of the Tenses in Hebrew and Other Syntacical Questions (Oxford: At the Clarendon Press, 1874, [3]1892).

Dubarle, A. M.
"La mention de Judith dans la littérature ancienne, juive et chrétienne," *RB* 66 (1956): 514–549.

Dumermuth, Fritz
"Zur deuteronomischen Kulttheologie und ihren Voraussetzungen," *ZAW* 70 (1958): 59–98.

Dunand, Françoise
Papyrus grecs bibliques (Papyrus F. inv. 266): volumina de la Genèse et du Deutéronome (introduction) (Le Caire: Impr. de l'Institut français d'archéologie orientale, 1966).

Dupont-Sommer, A.
Les inscriptions araméennes de Sfiré, Mémoires présentés par divers savants à l'Académie des Inscriptions et Belles-Lettres 15 (Paris, 1958).

Dürr, L.
Ursprung und Ausbau der israelitisch-jüdischen Heilandserwartung; ein Beitrag zur Theologie des Alten Testamentes (Berlin: Schwetschke, 1925).

Dus, Jan
"Melek Ṣōr-Melqart? (Zur Interpretation von Ez 28:11–19)," *Archiv Orientální* 26 (1958): 179–185.

Dussaud, R.
"Byblos et la mention des Giblites dans l'Ancien Testament," *Syria* 4 (1923): 300–315; 5 (1924): 388.

Idem
"Deux stèles de Ras Shamra portant une dédicace au dieu Dagon," *Syria* 16 (1935): 177–180.

Idem
"Ile ou rivage dans l'Ancien Testament," *Anatolian Studies* 6 (1956): 63–65.

Idem
"Les Phéniciens au Négeb et en Arabie d'après un texte de Ras Shamra," *Revue de l'histoire des religions* 108 (1933): 5–49.

Eakins, J. K.
Ezekiel's Influence on the Exilic Isaiah, Unpub. Diss. (Southern Theological Seminary, 1970).

Ebach, J. H.
Kritik und Utopie. Untersuchungen zum Verhältnis von Volk und Herrscher im Verfassungsentwurf des Ezechiel, Unpub. Diss. (Hamburg, 1972).

Eerdmans, B. D.
Alttestamentliche Studien 4 (Giessen: Töpelmann, 1912).

Eichrodt, Walther
"Ez 22, 23–31. Du text au sermon," *Études théologiques et religieuses* 44 (1969): 79–88.

Idem
"Die Höllenfahrt der Meerbeherrscherin—zur Erklärung von Hes 26, 19–21" in *Festschrift für J. Asano,* ed. N. Tajima (Tokyo, 1964), 59–65.

Idem
"Land und Volk der Heilszeit nach Hes. 40–48," *Der Freund Israels* 71 (1944): 57–60, 82–88; 72 (1945): 17–22.

Idem
"Der neue Tempel in der Heilshoffnung Hesekiels" in *Das ferne und nahe Wort; Festschrift für Leonhard Rost,* BZAW 105 (Berlin: deGruyter, 1967), 37–48.

Idem
"Der Sabbat bei Hesekiel. Ein Beitrag zur Nachgeschichte des Prophetentextes" in *Lex tua veritas; Festschrift H. Junker* (1961), 65–74.

Eissfeldt, Otto
"Das Datum der Belagerung von Tyrus durch Nebukadnezar," *FuF* 9 (1933): 421f.

Idem
Erstlinge und Zehnten im Alten Testament; Ein Beitrag zur Geschichte des israelitisch-jüdischen Kultus, BWAT 22 (Leipzig: Hinrichs, 1917).

Idem
"'Mein Gott' im Alten Testament," *ZAW* 61 (1945/48): 3–16.

Idem
"Die Menetekel-Inschrift und ihre Deutung," *ZAW* 63 (1951): 105–114.

Idem
"Phoiniker," *PW* NB 1st series 20 (=40th half-volume) (1950), 350–380.

Idem
"Tyros," *PW* NB 2nd series 7 (1948), 1876–1908.

Eliade, M.
"Lebensbaum," *RGG*[3] 4,250f.

Elliger, K.
"Die grossen Tempelsakristeien im Verfassungsentwurf des Ezechiel (42:1ff)" in *Festschrift für A. Alt* (Tübingen: Mohr, 1953), 79–103.

Idem
"Liber Ezechiel" in *Biblia Hebraica Stuttgartensia*, ed. K. Elliger and W. Rudolph (Stuttgart: Deutsche Bibelstiftung, 1977).

Idem
"Die Nordgrenze des Reiches Davids," *PJ* 32 (1936): 34–73.

Idem
"Ein Zeugnis aus der jüdischen Gemeinde im Alexanderjahr 332 v. Chr. Eine territorialgeschichtliche Studie zu Sach 9:1–8," *ZAW* 62 (1950): 63–115.

Engnell, Ivan
Studies in Divine Kingship in the Ancient Near East (Uppsala: Almquist & Wiksell, 1943).

Erling, B.
"Ezekiel 38–39 and the Origins of Jewish Apocalyptic" in *Ex orbe religionum; Studia Geo Widengren* 1 (Leiden: Brill, 1972), 104–114.

Erman, Adolf
Die Literatur der Aegypter (Leipzig: Hinrichs, 1923).

Idem
The Literature of the Ancient Egyptians, tr. Aylward M. Blackman (London: Methuen, 1927).

Erman, Adolf and Grapow, Hermann
Wörterbuch der aegyptischen Sprache, 7 volumes (Leipzig: Hinrichs, 1926–1963).

Falk, Z.
"Merits of the Fathers in Ezekiel," *Beth Miqra* 17 (1972): 393–397 (Hebrew).

Farmer, William R.
"The Geography of Ezekiel's River of Life," *BA* 19 (1956): 17–22.

Farrar, F. W.
"The Last Nine Chapters of Ezekiel," *The Expositor* 3rd series 9 (1889): 1–15.

Fensham, F. Charles
"Thunder-Stones in Ugaritic," *JNES* 18 (1959): 273f.

Fernandez-Galiano, M.
"Nuevas páginas del códice 967 del A.T. Griego (Ez 28,19–43,9)," *Studia papyrologica* X/1 (1971).

Feuillet, A.
"La formule d'appartenance mutuelle (II, 16) et les interprétations divergentes du Cantique des Cantiques," *RB* 78 (1961): 5–38.

Février, J.-G.
"L'ancienne marine phénicienne et les découvertes récentes," *NC* 1 (1949): 128–143.

Fleming, Wallace B.
The History of Tyre, Columbia University Oriental Studies 10 (New York: Columbia University Press, 1915).

Fohrer, Georg
"Neue Literatur zur alttestamentlichen Prophetie (1961–1970)," *ThR* 45 (1980): 1–39, 109–132, 193–225.

Idem
"Neuere Literatur zur alttestamentlichen Prophetie (1961–1970)," *ThR* 40 (1975): 193–209, 337–377; 41 (1976): 1–12.

Idem
Die Propheten des Alten Testaments 3: *Die Propheten des frühen 6. Jahrhunderts* (1975), 12–219.

Idem
"Die Struktur der alttestamentlichen Eschatologie," *ThLZ* 85 (1960): 401–420.

Idem
"Über den Kurzvers," *ZAW* 25 (1954): 199–236.

Forbes, Robert James
Metallurgy in Antiquity; a Notebook for Archaeologists and Technologists (Leiden: Brill, 1950).

Forrer, Emil
Die Provinzeinteilung des assyrischen Reiches (Leipzig: Hinrichs, 1920).

Förster, G.
"Die Neumondfeier im Alten Testamente," *ZWTh* 49 (1906): 1–17.

de Fraine, Jean
L'aspect religieux de la royauté israélite; l'institution monarchique dans l'Ancien Testament et dans les textes mésopotamiens, Analecta biblica 3 (Rome: Pontifical Biblical Institute, 1954).

Frankenberg, W.
"Review of H. Gunkel, *Genesis übersetzt und erklärt,*" *Göttingische gelehrte Anzeigen* 163 (1901): 677–706.

Frankfort, H.
Kingship and the Gods (Chicago: University of Chicago Press, 1948).

Freedy, K. S.
"The Glosses in Ezekiel I–XXIV," *VT* 20 (1970): 129–152.

Idem
The Literary Relations of Ezekiel; a Historical Study of Chapters 1–24, Unpub. Diss. (University of Toronto, 1969).

Freedy, K. S. and Redford, D. B.
"The Dates in Ezekiel in Relation to Biblical, Babylonian and Egyptian Sources," *JAOS* 90 (1970): 462–485.

Friedrich, Johannes
Phönizisch-punische Grammatik (Rome: Pontifical Biblical Institute, 1951).

Fushita, S.
The Temple Theology of the Qumran Sect and the Book of Ezekiel: Their Relationship to Jewish Literature of the last two Centuries, Unpub. Diss. (Princeton Theological Seminary, 1970).

Galling, Kurt
"Die Ausrufung des Namens als Rechtsakt in Israel," *ThLZ* 81 (1956): 65–70.

Idem
"Das Gemeindegesetz in Deuteronomium 23" in *Festschrift Alfred Bertholet* (Tübingen: Mohr [Siebeck], 1950), 176–191.
Idem
"Von Naboned zu Darius. Studien zur chaldäischen und persischen Geschichte," *ZDPV* 70 (1954): 4–32.
Idem
"Die Nekropole von Jerusalem," *PJ* 32 (1936): 73–101.
Idem
"Serubbabel und der Hohepriester beim Wiederaufbau des Tempels in Jerusalem" in *Studien zur Geschichte Israels im persischen Zeitalter* (Tübingen: Mohr, 1964), 127–148.
Idem
"Serubbabel und der Wiederaufbau des Tempels in Jerusalem" in *Verbannung und Heimkehr. Beiträge zur Geschichte und Theologie Israels im 6. and 5. Jahrhundert v. Chr., Wilhelm Rudolph zum 70. Geburtstage dargebracht* (Tübingen: Mohr [Siebeck], 1961), 67–96.
Idem
"Ein Stück judäischen Bodenrechts in Jesaia 8," *ZDPV* 56 (1933): 209–218.
Idem
Studien zur Geschichte Israels im persischen Zeitalter (Tübingen: Mohr, 1964).
Idem
"Die syrisch-palästinische Küste nach der Beschreibung bei Pseudo-Skylax," *ZDPV* 61 (1938): 66–96.
Garbini, G.
"Sull' origine di Ez 28, 12–24" in *Studi G. Rinaldi* (Genova: Studio e vita, 1967), 311–315.
Garmus, L.
O juízo divino na história. A História de Israel em Ez 20, 1–44 (Editora Vozes Petrópolis, 1975), 7–105.
Garrett, J.
"A Geographical Commentary on Ezekiel XXVII," *Geography* 24 (1939): 240–249.
Garscha, Jörg
Studien zum Ezechielbuch. Eine redaktionskritische Untersuchung von Ez 1–39, Europäische Hochschulschriften XXIII/23 (Bern: Lang, 1974).
Gaster, Moses
The Samaritans: their History, Doctrines and Literature (London: Oxford University Press, 1925).
Gaster, Theodore
"Ezekiel 28:17," *ET* 62 (1950/51): 124.
Gerleman, Gillis
"Hesekielsbokens Gog," *Svensk exegetisk årsbok* 12 12 (1947): 132–146.
Gese, Hartmut
"Ezekiel 20, 25f und die Erstgeburtsopfer" in *Beiträge zur alttestamentlichen Theologie; Festschrift für Walther Zimmerli* (Göttingen: Vandenhoeck & Ruprecht, 1977), 140–151.
Idem
Der Verfassungsentwurf des Ezechiel (Kap. 40–48) traditionsgeschichtlich untersucht, BHTh 25 (Tübingen: Mohr, 1957).
Geyer, John B.
"Ezekiel 18 and a Hittite Treaty of Mursilis II," *Journal for the Study of the Old Testament* 12 (1979): 31–46.
Glueck, Nelson
"Explorations in Eastern Palestine, II," *Annual of the American Schools of Oriental Research* 15 (1935) and "IV," 25–28 (1951).
Idem
"Three Israelite Towns in the Jordan Valley: Zarethan, Succoth, Zaphon," *BASOR* 90 (1943): 2–23.
de Goeje, M. J.
De muur van Gog en Magog, 1888.
Goldmann, M. D.
"The Meaning of 'רגע,'" *Australian Biblical Review* 4 (1954/55): 7–16.
Good, E.
"Ezekiel's Ship. Some extended Metaphors in the Old Testament (Ez 27, 3–11. 25b–36)," *Semitics* 1 (1970): 79–103.
Gordis, Robert
"A Note on YAD," *JBL* 62 (1943): 341–344.
Gordon, Cyrus H.
Ugaritic Handbook (Rome: Pontifical Biblical Institute, 1947 [1948]).
Goshen-Gottstein, M. H.
"Ezechiel und Ijob; zur Problemgeschichte von Bundestheologie und Gott-Mensch-Verhältnis" in *Wort, Lied und Gottesspruch; Festschrift für Joseph Ziegler,* Forschung zur Bibel 2 (Würzburg: Echter, 1972), 155–170.
Grapow, Hermann
"Medizinische Literatur," *HO* 1/2 (Leiden: E. J. Brill, 1952), 181–187.
Idem
Über die anatomischen Kenntnisse der altägyptischen Ärzte Leipzig: Hinrichs, 1935).
Gray, George Buchanan
Sacrifice in the Old Testament, its Theory and Practice (Oxford: Clarendon, 1925).
Gray, John
"The kingship of God in the Prophets and Psalms," *VT* 11 (1961): 1–29.
Idem
The Legacy of Canaan, VT Suppl 5 (Leiden: Brill, ²1965).
Greenberg, Moshe
"The Citations in the Book of Ezekiel as a Background for the Prophecies," *Beth Miqra* 50 (1973): 273–278 (Hebrew).
Idem
"On Ezekiel's Dumbness," *JBL* 77 (1958): 101–105.

Idem
"The Use of the Ancient Versions for Interpreting the Hebrew Text. A Sampling from Ezekiel II 1—III 11" in *Congress Volume, Göttingen 1977,* VT Suppl 29 (Leiden: Brill, 1978), 131–148.
Idem
"The Vison of Jerusalem in Ezekiel 8–11: A Holistic Interpretation" in *The Divine Helmsman; Studies on God's Control of Human Events, Presented to Lou H. Silberman,* ed. James L. Crenshaw and Samuel Sandmel (New York: Ktav, 1980), 143–164.
Grelot, Pierre
"Jean VII, 38: Eau du rocher ou source du Temple?" *RB* 70 (1963): 43–51.
Grill, Severin
"Der Schlachttag Jahwes," *BZ* 2 (1958): 278–283.
Gronkowski, Witold
Le messianisme d'Ézékiel (Strasbourg, 1930).
Gross, Heinrich
Die Idee des ewigen und allgemeinen Weltfriedens im Alten Orient und im Alten Testament, Trierer theologische Studien 7 (Trier: Paulinus, 1956).
Gross, H.
"Umkehr im Alten Testament. In der Sicht der Propheten Jeremia und Ezechiel" in *Zeichen des Glaubens; Festschrift für B. Fischer* (Freiburg: Herder, 1972), 19–28.
Gunkel, Hermann
Genesis übersetzt und erklärt (Göttingen: Vandenhoeck & Ruprecht, 1922).
Idem
"Gog und Magog," *RGG*² 2, 1303.
Idem
Das Märchen im Alten Testament (Tübingen: Mohr, 1917).
Gunneweg, Antonius H. J.
Leviten und Priester, FRLANT 89 (Göttingen: Vandenhoeck & Ruprecht, 1965).
Idem
Mündliche und schriftliche Tradition der vorexilischen Prophetenbücher als Problem der neueren Prophetenforschung, FRLANT 55 (Göttingen: Vandenhoeck & Ruprecht, 1959).
Guthe, Hermann
Bibelatlas (Leipzig: Wagner & Debes, ²1926).
Haag, E.
"Ez 31 und die alttestamentliche Paradiesvorstellung" in *Wort, Lied und Gottesspruch; Festschrift für Joseph Ziegler,* Forschung zur Bibel 2 (Würzburg: Echter, 1972), 171–178.
Haag, Herbert
Bibel-Lexikon (Einsiedeln, ²1964).
Habel, N. C.
"Ezekiel 28 and the Fall of the First Man," *Concordia Theological Monthly* 38 (1967): 516–524.
Halévy, J.
"Gog et Magog," *Revue sémitique* 12 (1904): 370–375.
Idem
"Notes de M. J. Halévy," *Journal asiatique* 8e series 19 (1892): 371.
Halperin, D. J.
"The Exegetical Character of Ezek 10, 9–17," *VT* 26 (1976): 129–141.
Hammershaimb, Erling
"Ezekiel's View of the Monarchy" in *Studia orientalia Ioanni Pedersen . . . dicata* (Hauniae: Munksgaard, 1953), 130–140; reprinted in *idem, Some Aspects of Old Testament Prophecy from Isaiah to Malachi* (København: Rosenkilde og Bagger, 1966), 51–62.
Hamp, V.
"Das Hirtenmotiv im Alten Testament" in *Episcopus; Studien über das Bischofsamt. Festschrift seiner Eminenz Michael Kardinal von Faulhaber, Erzbischof von München-Freising zum 80. Geburtstag dargebracht* (Regensburg: Gregorius, 1959), 7–20.
Haran, Menaḥem
"Biblical Studies. Ezekiel's Code (Ez 40–48) and its Relation to the Priestly School," *Tarbiz* 44 (1974): 30–53 (Hebrew).
Idem
"The Law Code of Ezekiel XL—XLVIII and its Relation to the Priestly School," *HUCA* 50 (1979): 45–71.
Idem
"The Levitical Cities," *Tarbiz* 27 (1958): 421–439 (Hebrew, with English summary).
Idem
"Studies in the Account of the Levitical Cities," *JBL* 80 (1961): 45–54, 156–165.
Harmuth, Karl
Die verschlossene Pforte; eine Untersuchung zu Ez 44:1–3, partially published Diss. (Breslau, 1933).
Hattori, Y.
The Prophet Ezekiel and his Idea of the Remnant, Unpub. Diss. (Westminster Theological Seminary, 1968).
Haupt, Paul
"A New Hebrew Particle," *Johns Hopkins University Circulars* 13 no. 114 (July, 1894): 107f.
Idem
"Die Schlacht von Taanach" in *Studien zur semitischen Philologie und Religionsgeschichte Julius Wellhausen zum siebzigsten Geburtstag,* BZAW 27 (Giessen: Töpelmann, 1914), 191–225.
Heller, Bernhard
"Gog und Magog im jüdischen Schrifttum" in *Jewish Studies in Memory of George A. Kohut,* ed. Salo W. Baron and Alexander Marx (New York: The Alexander Kohut Memorial Foundation, 1935), 350–358.
Henniger, J.
"Zum Verbot des Knochenzerbrechens bei den Semiten" in *Studi orientalistici in onore di Giorgio Levi Della Vida* 1 (Rome: Istituto per l'Oriente, 1956), 448–458.

Hentschke, Richard
Satzung und Setzender, ein Beitrag zur israelitischen Rechtsterminologie, BWANT 5. F. 3 (Stuttgart: Kohlhammer, 1963).

Hermisson, Hans Jürgen
Sprache und Ritus im altisraelitischen Kult; zur "Spiritualisierung" der Kultbegriffe im Alten Testament, WMANT 19 (Neukirchen-Vluyn: Neukirchener, 1965).

Hernando (García), E.
"Aspectos pastorales en el ministerio profético de Ezequiel, Lumen," *Vitoria* 19 (1970): 412–437.

Herrmann, Johannes
"Die Gottesnamen im Ezechieltexte. Ein Studie zur Ezechielkritik und zur Septuagintawertung" in *Alttestamentliche Studien Rudolf Kittel zum 60. Geburtstag,* BWAT 13 (Leipzig: Hinrichs, 1913), 70–87.

Herrmann, Johannes and Baumgärtel, Friedrich
Beiträge zur Entstehungsgeschichte der Septuaginta, BWAT 5 (Berlin: Kohlhammer, 1923).

Herrmann, Siegfried
"Die Naturlehre des Schöpfungsberichtes; Erwägungen zur Vorgeschichte von Genesis 1," *ThLZ* 86 (1961): 413–424.

Hess, J. J.
"Beduinisches zum Alten und Neuen Testament," *ZAW* 35 (1915): 120–131 ('פַּרְעֹה,' 129f).

Höffken, P.
Untersuchungen zu den Begründungselementen der Völkerorakel des Alten Testaments (Bonn: Rheinische Friedrich-Wilhelms Universität, 1977).

Hoffman, Y.
"Ezekiel 20—its Structure and Meaning," *Beth Miqra* 63 (1975): 473–489 (Hebrew).

Hoffmann, G.
"Über einige phönikische Inschriften," *Abhandlungen der Akademie der Wissenschaften in Göttingen* 36 (1889): 47.

Holladay, William L.
"'On every high hill and under every green tree,'" *VT* 11 (1961): 170–176.

Holma, H.
"Zum 'Nabel der Erde,'" *OLZ* 18 (1915): 41–43.

Holmberg, U.
Der Baum des Lebens, Annales Academiae Scientiarum Fennicae 16 (Helsinki, 1922/23).

Hölscher, Gustav
Drei Erdkarten; ein Beitrag zur Erdkenntnis des hebräischen Altertums (Heidelberg: Winter, 1949).

Idem
"Levi," *PW* NB 1st series 12 (1925), 2155–2208.

Honigmann, Ernst
"Azalla," *RLA* 1, 325a.

Idem
"Historische Topographie von Nordsyrien im Altertum, I," *ZDPV* 46 (1923): 149–193; "II," 47 (1924): 1–64.

Idem
"Sidon," *PW* NB 2nd series 2 (1923), 2216–2229.

Hooke. S. H.
"Gog and Magog," *ET* 26 (1914/15): 317–319.

Idem
Myth and Ritual (London: Oxford University Press, 1933).

Idem
Myth, Ritual, and Kingship (Oxford: Clarendon, 1958).

Van Hoonacker, A.
"Ezekiel's Priests and Levites," *ET* 12 (1901): 383, 494–498.

Idem
"Les prêtres et les Lévites dans le livre d'Ézéchiël," *RB* 8 (1899): 177–205.

Horst, Friedrich
Hiob, BK 16 (Neukirchen-Vluyn: Neukirchener, 1968).

Idem
Das Privilegrecht Jahves; rechtsgeschichtliche Untersuchungen zum Deuteronomium, FRLANT 28 (Göttingen: Vandenhoeck & Ruprecht, 1930); reprinted in *idem, Gottes Recht,* ThB 12 (München: Kaiser, 1961).

Idem
"Zwei Begriffe für Eigentum (Besitz): נַחֲלָה und אֲחֻזָּה" in *Verbannung und Heimkehr. Beiträge zur Geschichte und Theologie Israels im 6. und 5. Jahrhundert v. Chr., Wilhelm Rudolph zum 70. Geburtstage dargebracht* (Tübingen: Mohr [Siebeck], 1961), 135–156.

Hossfeld, Frank
Untersuchungen zu Komposition und Theologie des Ezechielbuches, Forschung zur Bibel 20 (Würzburg: Echter, 1977).

Hossfeld, Frank and Meyer, I.
Prophet gegen Prophet. Eine Analyse der alttestamentlichen Texte zum Thema: Wahre und falsche Propheten, Biblische Beiträge 9 (1973).

Houk, C. B.
"*bn-'dm* Patterns as Literary Criteria in Ezekiel," *JBL* 88 (1969): 184–190.

Idem
"The Final Redaction of Ezekiel 10," *JBL* (1971): 42–54.

Howie, Carl Gordon
"The East Gate of Ezekiel's Temple Enclosure and the Solomic Gateway of Megiddo," *BASOR* 117 (1950): 13–19.

Humbert, Paul
"Démesure et chute dans l'Ancien Testament" in *maqqél shâqédh. La branche d'amandier. Hommage à Wilhelm Vischer* (Montpellier, 1960), 63–82.

Idem
"L'emploi du verbe *pā'al* et de ses dérivés substantifs en hébreu biblique," *ZAW* 65 (1953): 35–44.

Idem
"L'étymologie du substantif *to'ēbā*" in *Verbannung und Heimkehr. Beiträge zur Geschichte und Theologie Israels im 6. und 5. Jahrhundert v. Chr., Wilhelm Rudolph zum 70. Gebrutstage dargebracht* (Tübingen: Mohr [Siebeck], 1961), 157–160.

Hüsing, G.
"Gūgu (678–643)," *OLZ* 18 (1915): 299–303.

Jahn, L. G.
Der griechische Text des Buches Ezechiel nach dem Kölner Teil des Papyrus 967, Papyrologische Texte und Abhandlungen 15 (Bonn: Habelt, 1972).

Jean, Charles F. and Hoftijzer, Jacob
Dictionnaire des inscriptions sémitiques de l'ouest (Leiden: Brill, 1960–65).

Jeremias, F.
Tyrus bis zur Zeit Nebukadnezars. Geschichtliche Skizze mit besonderer Berücksichtigung der keilschriftlichen Quellen, Unpub. Diss. (Leipzig, 1891).

Jeremias, Joachim
Golgotha, ΑΓΓΕΛΟΣ Archiv für neutestamentliche Zeitgeschichte und Kulturkunde 1 (Leipzig: Pfeiffer, 1926).

Idem
"Hesekieltempel und Serubbabeltempel," *ZAW* 52 (1934): 109–112.

Idem
Jerusalem in the Time of Jesus, tr. F. H. and C. H. Cave (Philadelphia: Fortress, 1969).

Idem
"*ποιμήν*," *TDNT* 6, 485–502.

Johnson, Aubrey R.
Sacral Kingship in Ancient Israel (Cardiff: University of Wales Press, 1955).

Joüon, Paul
"יָד = *jet* (Nombres 35:17–18; Ez 39:9)," *Mélanges de la faculté orientale de l'université Saint Joseph. Beyrouth* 6 (1913): 166f.

Idem
"Notes philologiques sur le texte hébreu d'Ezéchiel," *Bibl* 10 (1929): 304–312.

Joyce, P. M.
"Individual Responsibility in Ezekiel 18" in *Studia Biblica: Papers on Old Testament and Related Themes* (Sixth International Congress on Biblical Studies, Oxford 3–7 April 1978), ed. E. A. Livingstone. JSOT Suppl 11 (Sheffield, 1979), 185–196.

Judge, G. H.
"Aaron, Zadok, and Abiathar," *JTS* 7 (1956): 70–74.

Ḳaddari, M. Z.
"Syntactic Features of the Verb *ntn* in Ezekiel," *Beth Miqra* 17 (1972): 493–497 (Hebrew).

Kaiser, Otto
Isaiah 1–12: a Commentary, tr. R. A. Wilson. The Old Testament Library (London: SCM, 1972).

Kapelrud, A. S.
Baal in the Ras Shamra Texts (Copenhagen: Gad, 1952).

Kassing, A.
"Das verschlossene Tor Ez 44:1–3. Heilsgeschichtliches Sinnverständnis als ekklesiologisch-mariologische Anregung," *Wort und Wahrheit* 16 (1953): 171–190.

Kaufmann, Yeḥezkel
The Biblical Account of the Conquest of Palestine, tr. M. Dagut (Jerusalem: Magnes, 1953).

Keel, Othmar
Jahwe-Visionen und Siegelkunst. Eine neue Deutung der Majestätsschilderungen in Jes 6, Ez 1 und 10, und Sach 4, Stuttgarter Bibelstudien 84/85 (Stuttgart: Katholisches Bibelwerk, 1977).

Kees, Hermann
"Ägypten," *RGL.*

Idem
Ägypten (München: Beck, 1933).

Idem
Das alte Ägypten; eine kleine Landeskunde (Berlin: Akademie, 1955).

Idem
Der Götterglaube im alten Ägypten, MVÄG 45 (Leipzig: Hinrichs, 1941).

Idem
"Pyramidentexte," *HO* 1/2 (Leiden: E. J. Brill, 1952), 30–38.

Idem
Totenglauben und Jenseitsvorstellung der alten Ägypter (Berlin: Akademie, [2]1956).

Keller, Bernard
"La terre dans le livre d'Ézéchiel," *RHPhR* 55 (1975): 481–490.

Keller, Carl A.
"Gog und Magog," *RGG*[3] 2, 1683f.

Kienitz, Friedrich Karl
Die politische Geschichte Aegyptens vom 7. bis zum 4. Jahrhundert vor der Zeitwende (Berlin: Akademie, 1953).

Kittel, Rudolf
Studien zur hebräischen Archäologie und Religionsgeschichte, BWAT 1 (Leipzig, 1908).

Klein, R. W.
"Yahweh Faithful and Free—A Study in Ezekiel," *Concordia Theological Monthly* 42 (1971): 493–501.

Knobel, A.
Die Völkertafel der Genesis. Ethnographische Untersuchungen (Giessen: Ricker, 1850).

Koch, Klaus
"Die Eigenart der priesterschriftlichen Sinaigesetzgebung," *ZThK* 55 (1958): 36–51.

Idem
Die Priesterschrift von Exodux 25 bis Leviticus 16; eine überlieferungsgeschichtliche und literarkritische Untersuchung, FRLANT 53 (Göttingen: Vandenhoeck & Ruprecht, 1959).

Idem
"Sühne und Sündenvergebung um die Wende von der exilischen zur nachexilischen Zeit," *EvTh* 26 (1966): 217–239.

Koehler, Ludwig
"Alttestamentliche Wortforschung: sch^{e}'ōl," *ThZ* 2 (1946): 71–74.
König, Ed.
"Die letzte Pentateuchschicht und Hesekiel," *ZAW* 28 (1908): 174–179.
Idem
"The priests and the Levites in Ezkiel 44:7–15," *ET* 12 (1901): 300–303.
König, E.
"Zur Vorgeschichte des Namen Russen," *ZDMG* 70 (1916): 92–96.
König. F. W.
"Elam (Geschichte)," *RLA* 2, 324-338.
Kopf, L.
"Arabische Etymologien und Parallelen zum Bibelwörterbuch," *VT* 9 (1959): 247–287.
Kornfeld, Walter
"Der Symbolismus der Tempelsäulen," *ZAW* 74 (1962): 50–57.
Köster, August
Das antike Seewesen (Berlin: 1923).
Kraeling, Carl H.
The Synagogue, The Yale University Excavations at Dura-Europos final report 8, part 1 (New Haven: Yale University Press, 1956).
Kraeling, Emil G.
"The Meaning of the Ezekiel Panel in the Synagogue at Dura," *BASOR* 78 (1940): 12–18.
Kramer, S. N.
Sumerian Mythology, Memoirs of the American Philosophical Society 21 (Philadelphia: The American Philosophical Society, 1944).
Krauss, S.
"Textkritik auf Grund des Wechsels von ה und ם," *ZAW* 48 (1930): 321–324.
Krinetzki, G.
"Tiefenpsychologie im Dienste der alttestamentlichen Exegese; zu Stil und Metaphorik von Ezechiel 27," *Tübinger Theologische Quartalschrift* 155 (1975): 132–143.
Krinetzki, Leo
"'Tal' und 'Ebene' im Alten Testament," *BZ* 5 (1961): 204–220.
Kroll, Josef
Gott und Hölle, der Mythus vom Descensuskampfe (Berlin: Teubner, 1932).
Küchler, Friedrich
"Das priesterliche Orakel in Israel und Juda" in *Abhandlungen zur semitischen Religionskunde und Sprachwissenschaft Wolf Wilhelm Grafen von Baudissin,* BZAW 33 (Giessen: Töpelmann, 1918), 285–301.
Kühn, Ernst
"Ezechiels Gesicht vom Tempel der Vollendungszeit. Kap. 40–42: 43:13–17; 46:19–24. In redivierter Übersetzung und mit kurzer Erläuterung," *ThStKr* 55 (1882): 601–688.
Kuhn, K. G.
"Γὼγ καὶ Μαγώγ," *TDNT* 1, 789–791.
Kümmel, Werner Georg
"Die älteste religiöse Kunst der Juden," *Judaica* 2 (1946): 29-56.
Kuschke, Arnulf
"Beiträge zur Siedlungsgeschichte der Biḳā'," *ZDPV* 74 (1958): 81–120.
Idem
"Jeremia 48:1–8. Zugleich ein Beitrag zur historischen Topographie Moabs" in *Verbannung und Heimkehr. Beiträge zur Geschichte und Theologie Israels im 6. und 5. Jahrhundert v. Chr., Wilhelm Rudolph zum 70. Geburtstage dargebracht* (Tübingen: Mohr [Siebeck], 1961), 181–196.
Idem
"Das Deutsche Evangelische Institut für Altertumswissenschaft des Heiligen Landes. Lehrkursus 1960," *ZDPV* 77 (1961): 1–37 ('Zweimal *ḳrjtn* a) Das *ḳrjtn* der Mesa-Stele,' 24–31).
Kutsch, Ernst
"Zur Chronologie der letzten judäischen Könige (Josia bis Zedekia)," *ZAW* 71 (1959): 270–274.
Idem
"Erwägungen zur Geschichte der Passafeier und des Masotfestes," *ZThK* 55 (1958): 1–35.
Idem
Das Herbstfest in Israel, Unpub. Diss. (Mainz, 1955).
Landsberger, Benno
Der kultische Kalender der Babylonier und Assyrer (Leipzig: Hinrichs, 1915).
Lang, Bernhard
"Erträge der Forschung: Ezechiel" in *Wissenschaftliche Buchgesellschaft* (Darmstadt, 1981).
Idem
Kein Aufstand in Jerusalem: Die Politik des Propheten Ezechiel, Stuttgarter biblische Beiträge (Stuttgart: Katholisches Bibelwerk, 1978, [2]1981).
Idem
"A Neglected Method in Ezekiel Research: Editorial Criticism," *VT* 29 (1979): 39–44.
Langdon, Stephen Herbert
Die neubabylonischen Königsinschriften (Leipzig: Hinrichs, 1912).
deLanghe, Robert
"L'autel d'or du temple de Jérusalem" in *Studia biblica et orientalia,* Analecta Biblica 10 (Rome: Pontifical Biblical Institute, 1959), 342–360.
Lasch, R.
"Das Pfeifen und seine Beziehung zu Dämonenglauben und Zauberei," *ARW* 18 (1915): 589–592.
Lebram, J. C. H.
Das hebräische Priestertum nach J und E, Unpub. Diss. (Heidelberg, 1943).
van der Leeuw, Gerardus
Phänomenologie der Religion (Tübingen: Mohr, [2]1956).

Lenzen, Heinrich J.
Die Entwicklung der Zikkurat von ihren Anfängen bis zur Zeit der III. Dynastie von Ur, Ausgrabungen der Deutschen Forschungsgemeinschaft in Uruk-Warka 4 (Leipzig: Harrassowitz, 1942).

Levey, Samson H.
"The Targum to Ezekiel," *HUCA* 46 (1975): 139–158.

Lindsay, J.
"The Babylonian Kings and Edom 605–550 B.C.," *PEQ* 108 (1976): 23–79.

Liwak, Rüdiger
Überlieferungsgeschichtliche Probleme des Ezechielbuches. Eine Studie zu postezechielischen Interpretationen und Kompositionen, Unpub. Diss. (Bochum, 1976).

Lods, A.
"Les cuisines du temple de Jérusalem," *Revue de l'histoire des religions* 127 (1944): 30–54.

Idem
"La 'mort des incirconcis'" in *Comptes rendus des séances de l'Académie des inscriptions et belles-lettres* (Paris, 1943), 271–283.

Lofthouse, W. F.
"The City and the Sanctuary," *ET* 34 (1922/23): 198–202.

Loretz, O.
"Der Sturz des Fürsten von Tyrus (Ez 28, 1–19)," *Ugarit-Forschungen* 8 (1976): 455–458.

Idem
"Eine sumerische Parallele zu Ez 23, 20," *BZ* 14 (1970): 126.

Luria, B. Z.
"The City Called 'God is there' (Ez 48, 35)," *Beth Miqra* 63 (1975): 443–456 (Hebrew).

Lust, J.
"'Mon Seigneur Jahweh' dans le texte hébreu d'Ézékiel," *EThL* 44 (1968): 482-488.

Idem
Traditie, Redactie en kerygma bij Ezechiel. Een analyse van Ez 20, 1–26 (Brussels: Paleis der Academiën, 1969).

Idem
"Een visioen voor volwassenen met voorbehoud (Ezechiël 1, 1–3) Collationes," *Vlaams Tijdschrift voor Theologie en Pastoral* 4 (1976): 433–448.

Lys, Daniel
"Rûach." Le souffle dans l'Ancien Testament, Études d'histoire et de philosophie religieuses 56 (Paris: Presses universitaires de France, 1962).

Macholz, G. C.
"Noch einmal: Planungen für den Wiederaufbau nach der Katastrophe von 587," *VT* 19 (1969): 322–352.

Mackay, Cameron M.
"The City and the Sanctuary," *ET* 34 (1922/23): 475f.

Idem
"The City and the Sanctuary. Ezekiel 48," *PrincTR* 20 (1922): 399–417.

Idem
"The City of Ezekiel's Oblation," *PrincTR* 21 (1923): 372–388.

Idem
"Ezekiel's Division of Palestine among the Tribes," *PrincTR* 22 (1924): 27–45.

Idem
"Ezekiel's Sanctuary and Wellhausen's Theory," *PrincTR* 20 (1922): 661–665.

Idem
"The Key of the Old Testament (Ezek 40–48)," *CQR* 119 (1935): 173–196.

Idem
"The King of Tyre," *CQR* 117 (1934): 239–258.

Idem
"The Land of the Lost Boundary," *CQR* 116 (1933): 1–23.

Idem
"The North Boundary of Palestine," *JTS* 35 (1934): 22–40.

Idem
"Prolegomena to Ezekiel 40–48," *ET* 55 (1943/44): 292–295.

Maisler, B.
"Lebo-Hamath and the Northern Boundary of Canaan," *Bulletin of the Jewish Palestine Exploration Society* 12 (1946): 91–102 (Hebrew, with English summary).

Idem
Untersuchungen zur alten Geschichte und Ethnographie Syriens und Palästinas 1, Arbeiten aus dem Orientalischen Seminar der Universität Giessen 2 (Giessen: Töpelmann, 1930).

Manchot, Carl Hermann
"Ezechiel's Weissagung wider Tyrus. Capitel 26.27.28," *JPTh* 14 (1888): 423–480.

Margalioth, E.
"Gerichtswort des Propheten Ezechiel und seine Zukunftsvision," *Beth Miqra* (1971): 181–192 (Hebrew).

Margolis, Max L.
"Hes 27:4," *ZAW* 31 (1911): 313f.

Markert, L.
Struktur und Bezeichnung des Scheltworts, BZAW 140 (Berlin: deGruyter, 1977).

Marti, Karl
"Die Spuren der sogenannten Grundschrift des Hexateuchs in den vorexilischen Propheten des Alten Testaments (Schluss)," *JPTh* 6 (1880): 308–354.

Martin-Achard, Robert
"Ezéchiel, témoin de l'honneur de YHWH" in *Mélanges André Neher* (Paris: Maisonneuve, 1975), 165–174.

Idem
De la mort à la résurrection d'après l'Ancien Testament (Neuchâtel: Delachaux & Niestlé, 1956).

Idem
"Quelques remarques sur la réunification du peuple de Dieu d'après Ezéchiel 37, 15ss" in *Wort-Gebot-Glaube; Festschrift für Walther Eichrodt,* ATANT 59 (Zürich: Zwingli, 1970), 67–76.

Masson, Denise
Le Coran et la révélation judéo-chrétienne; études comparées (Paris: Adrien-Maisonneuve, 1958).

May, Herbert Gordon
"Some Aspects of Solar Worship at Jerusalem," *ZAW* 55 (1937): 269–281.

Idem
"Some Cosmic Connotations of *Mayim Rabbîm,* 'Many Waters,'" *JBL* 74 (1955): 9–21.

Maynard, John A.
"The Rights and Revenues of the Tribe of Levi," *Journal of the Society of Oriental Research* 14 (1930): 11–17.

Mays, James L.
Ezekiel; Second Isaiah, Proclamation Series (Philadelphia: Fortress, 1978).

Mazar, B.
"The Campaign of Pharaoh Shishak to Palestine" in *Volume du Congrès, Strasbourg 1956,* VT Suppl 4 (Leiden: Brill, 1957), 57–66.

Mazar, B., Dothan Trude, and Dunayevsky, I.
En-Gedi. The First and Second Seasons of Excavations, 1961–62, *'Atiqot* English series 5 (Jerusalem, 1966).

MaKane, William
"A Note on 2 Kings 12:10 (Evv 12:9)," *ZAW* 71 (1959): 260–265.

Meek, Theophile James
"Aaronites and Zadokites," *AJSL* 45 (1929): 149–166.

Meulenbelt, Hendrik Huibrecht
De prediking van den profeet Ezechiël (Utrecht: Breijer, 1888).

Meyer, Eduard
Geschichte des Altertums 3 (Stuttgart und Berlin: J. G. Cotta'sche Buchhandlung Nachfolger, [3]1954).

Idem
Die Israeliten und ihre Nachbarstämme (Halle a. S.: Niemeyer, 1906).

Idem
Der Papyrusfund von Elephantine (Leipzig: Hinrichs, 1912).

Idem
"Untersuchungen zur phönikischen Religion. Die Inschriften von Ma'ṣûb und Umm el 'awâmîd und die Inschrift des Bodostor von Sidon," *ZAW* 49 (1931): 1–15.

Meyer, Rudolf
"Betrachtungen zu drei Fresken der Synagoge von Dura-Europos," *ThLZ* 74 (1949): 29–38.

Idem
"Der gegenwärtige Stand der Erforschung der in Palästina neu gefundenen hebräischen Handschriften. 14. Zur Sprache von 'Ain Feschcha," *ThLZ* 75 (1950): 721–726.

Idem
"Levitische Emanzipationsbestrebungen in nachexilischer Zeit," *OLZ* 41 (1938): 721–728.

Mez, A.
Geschichte der Stadt Ḥarrān in Mesopotamien bis zum Einfall der Araber, Unpub. Diss. (Strassburg, 1892).

Milik, J. T.
"Notes d'épigraphie et de topographie palestiniennes," *RB* 66 (1959): 550–575.

Möhlenbrink, Kurt
"Die levitischen Überlieferungen des Alten Testaments," *ZAW* 52 (1934): 184–231.

Idem
Der Tempel Salamos; eine Untersuchung seiner Stellung in der Sakralarchitektur des Alten Orients, BWANT 4 (Stuttgart: Kohlhammer, 1932).

Molin, G.
"*ḥalonoth 'aṭumoth* bei Ezechiel," *BZ* 15 (1971): 250–253.

Monloubou, L.
"Cahier du Bible: Pour un monde renouvelé une liturgie nouvelle. Ez 40–48," *Bible et vie chrétienne* 92 (1970): 43–61.

Idem
Un prêtre devient prophète: Ezéchiel, Lectio divina 73 (Paris: Éditions du Cerf, 1972).

Montet, Pierre
Géographie de l'Égypte ancienne. Première Partie: To-Mehou, La Basse Égypte (Paris: Imprimerie Nationale, 1957).

Morenz, Siegfried
"Joseph in Ägypten," *ThLZ* 84 (1959): 410–416.

Morgenstern, Julian
"A Chapter in the History of the High-Priesthood," *AJSL* 55 (1938): 1–24, 183–197, 360–377.

Idem
"The King-God among the Western Semites and the meaning of Epiphanes," *VT* 10 (1960): 138–197.

Idem
"The Rest of the Nations," *JSS* 2 (1957): 225–231.

Idem
"The Three Calendars of Ancient Israel," *HUCA* 1 (1924): 13–78.

Mosis, R.
"Ez 14, 1–11—ein Ruf zur Umkehr," *BZ* 19 (1975): 161–194.

Mowinckel, Sigmund
"Zu Deuteronomium 23:2–9," *Acta orientalia* 1 (1923): 81–104.

Idem
Zum israelitischen Neujahr und zur Deutung der Thronbesteigungspsalmen (Oslo: Dybwad, 1952).

Idem
Psalmenstudien. V. Segen und Fluch in Israels Kult und Psalmdichtung (Kristiania: Dybwad, 1924).

Idem
"Die vorderasiatischen Königs- und Fürsteninschriften. Eine stilistische Studie" in *Eucharisterion für H. Gunkel,* FRLANT 19 (Göttingen, 1923), 278–322.
Mulder, M. J.
"Ezekiel 20, 39 and the Pešiṭta Version," *VT* 25 (1975): 233–237.
Müller, David Heinrich
Biblische Studien 3: Komposition und Strophenbau (Wien: Hölder, 1907) ('Die Komposition von Ezechiel Kap. 25,' 40–45).
Müller, Dieter
"Der gute Hirte; Ein Beitrag zur Geschichte ägyptischer Bildrede," *Zeitschrift für ägyptische Sprache und Altertumskunde* 86 (1961): 126–144.
Munch, Peter Andreas
The Expression bajjôm hāhū'; is it an eschatological terminus technicus? (Oslo: Dybwad, 1936).
Münderlein, G.
Kriterien wahrer und falscher Prophetie. Entstehung und Bedeutung im Alten Testament, Europäische Hochschulschriften XXIII/33 (Bern: Lang, 1974).
Myers, J. M.
"Edom and Judah in the Sixth-Fifth Centuries B.C." in *Near Eastern Studies in Honor of William Foxwell Albright,* ed. Hans Goedicke (Baltimore: Johns Hopkins Press, 1971), 377–392.
Myres, John L.
"Gog and the Danger from the North in Ezekiel," *Palestine Exploration Fund, Quarterly Statement* (1932): 213–219.
Neher, André
"Ezéchiel, rédempteur de Sodome" in *Mélanges Edmond Jacob,* RHLR 59, (Paris, 1979) 483–490.
Idem
"A Reflection on the Silence of God: 'I will not be inquired of by you' (Ez 20, 3)," *Judaism* 16 (1967): 434–442.
Neiman, David
"*PGR:* A Canaanite Cult-Object in the Old Testament," *JBL* 67 (1948): 55–60.
Neubauer, Adolf and Cowley, A. E.
Catalogue of the Hebrew Manuscripts in the Bodleian Library, and in the college libraries of Oxford 2 (Oxford, 1906).
Nober, P. P.
"Sein Blut komme über uns und unsere Kinder!" *Freiburger Rundbrief* 11, Nummer 41/44 (1958/59): 73–77.
Nöldeke, Theodor
"Review of Friedrich Baethgen, *Sindban oder die sieben weisen Meister. Syrisch und deutsch,*" *ZDMG* 33 (1879): 513–536.
North, Francis Sparling
"Aaron's Rise in Prestige," *ZAW* 66 (1954): 191–199.
Noth, Martin
"Beiträge zur Geschichte des Ostjordanlandes: III 3. Ammon und Moab," *ZDPV* 68 (1946–51): 36–50.
Idem
"La Catastrophe de Jérusalem en l'an 587 avant Jésus-Christ et sa signification pour Israël," *RHPhR* 33 (1953): 81–102.
Idem
"David and Israel in II Samuel VII" in *The Laws in the Pentateuch and Other studies,* tr. D. R. Ap-Thomas (Philadelphia: Fortress, 1967), 250–259.
Idem
"Dura-Europos und seine Synagoge," *ZDPV* 75 (1959): 164–181.
Idem
Exodus; a Commentary, tr. J. S. Bowden. The Old Testament Library (Philadelphia: Westminster, 1962).
Idem
Das Buch Josua, HAT 7 (Tübingen: Mohr, ²1953).
Idem
Könige, BK 9 (Neukirchen-Vluyn: Neukirchener, 1964–1968).
Idem
"Das Krongut der israelitischen Könige und seine Verwaltung," *ZDPV* 50 (1927): 211–244.
Idem
Leviticus; a Commentary, tr. J. E. Anderson. The Old Testament Library (Philadelphia: Westminster, 1966).
Idem
"Old Testament Covenant-Making in the Light of a Text from Mari" in *The Laws in the Pentateuch and Other Studies,* tr. D. R. Ap-Thomas (Philadelphia: Fortress, 1967), 108–117.
Idem
"Studien zu den historisch-geographischen Dokumenten des Josuabuches," *ZDPV* 58 (1935): 185–255.
Idem
"Die Wege der Pharaonenheere in Palästina und Syrien," *ZDPV* 60 (1937): 183–239.
Nötscher, F.
"Sakrale Mahlzeiten vor Qumran" in *Lex tua veritas* (Festschrift H. Junker) (1961), 145–174.
Ohler, A.
"Die Gegenwart Gottes in der Ferne: Die Berufungsvision des Ezechiel," *Bibel und Leben* 11 (1970): 159–168.
Olmstead, A. T.
History of Palestine and Syria to the Macedonian Conquest (New York: C. Scribner's Sons, 1931).
de Orbisco, Teófilo
"El oráculo contra Tiro en Isaías 23 y Ezequiel 26–28," *Estudios biblicos* 1 (1941): 597–625.
Orelli, Conrad von
"Gog und Magog," *Realencyklopädie für protestantische Theologie und Kirche*³ 6, 761–763.

Otranto, G.
"Ez 37, 1–14 nel' esegesi patristica del secondo secolo," *Vetera Christianorum* 9 (1972): 55–76.

Pareira, B. A.
The Call to Conversion in Ezekiel; Exegesis and Biblical Theology, Unpub. Diss. (Rome, 1975).

Parker, Charles H.
The Tyrian Oracles in Ezekiel; A Study of Ezekiel 26, 1–28, 19, Unpub. Diss. (Columbia Universtiy, 1970).

Parrot, André
The Tower of Babel, tr. Edwin Hudson (New York: Philosophical Library, 1955).

Parunak, H. Van Dyke
"The Literary Architecture of Ezekiel's *Mar'ôt 'Ĕlōhîm,*" *JBL* 99 (1980): 61–74.

Pedersen, J.
Der Eid bei den Semiten, Studien zur Geschichte und Kultur des islamischen Orients 3 (Strassburg: Trübner, 1914).

Pennachini, B.
Temi mitici in Ezechiele 28, 1–19 (Assisi: Studio teologico "Porziuncola," 1973).

Perles, Felix
"'Gewebe' im Alten Testament," *OLZ* 12 (1909): 251f.

Peters, John P.
"Critical Notes," *JBL* 12 (1893): 47–60.

Piotrowicz, Louis
"L'invasion des Scythes en Asie Antérieure au VIIe siècle av. J.-C," *Eos* 32 (1929): 473–508.

Plessis, Joseph
Les Prophéties d'Ezéchiel contre l'Egypte, 1912.

Ploeg, J. van der
"Les chefs du peuple d'Israël et leurs titres," *RB* 57 (1950): 40–61.

Pohl, A.
"Das verschlossene Tor Ez 44:1–3," *Bibl* 13 (1932): 90–92.

Pope, Marvin H.
El in the Ugaritic Texts, VT Suppl 2 (Leiden: Brill, 1955).

Posener, Georges
Dictionary of Egyptian Civilization, tr. Alix McFarlane (New York: Tudor, 1962).

Idem
Princes et pays d'Asie et de Nubie (Bruxelles: Fondation égyptologique Reine Élisabeth, 1940).

Power, E.
"The shepherd's two rods in modern Palestine and in some passages of the Old Testament," *Bibl* 9 (1928): 434–442.

Prijs, Leo
"ṣll Hifil," *ThZ* 5 (1949): 152.

Procksch, O.
"Fürst und Priester bei Hesekiel," *ZAW* 58 (1940/41): 99–133.

Pythian-Adams, W. J.
"Israel in the Arabah (II)," *Palestine Exploration Fund, Quarterly Statement* (1934): 181–188.

Quell, Gottfried
"Jesaja 14:1–23" in *Festschrift Friedrich Baumgärtel zum 70. Geburtstag* (Erlangen: Universitätsbund Erlangen, 1959), 131–157.

Quiring, H.
"Die Edelsteine im Amtsschild des jüdischen Hohenpriesters und die Herkunft ihrer Namen," *Sudhoffs Archiv für Geschichte der Medizin und der Naturwissenschaften* 38 (1954): 193–213.

Rad, Gerhard von
Studies in Deuteronomy, Studies in Biblical Theology 9 (London: SCM, 1953).

Raitt, T. M.
A Theology of Exile: Judgement/Deliverance in Jeremiah and Ezekiel (Philadelphia: Fortress, 1977).

Rautenberg, Willy
"Zur Zukunftsthora des Hesekiel," *ZAW* 33 (1913): 92–115.

Rembry, Jean Gabriel
"Le Thème du berger dans l'oeuvre d'Ezekiel," *Studii biblici Franciscani* 11 (1960/61): 113–144.

Rendtorff, Rolf
"Botenformel und Botenspruch," *ZAW* 74 (1962): 165–177.

Idem
"Die Offenbarungsvorstellungen im alten Israel" in *Offenbarung als Geschichte,* ed. Wolfhart Pannenberg. Kerygma und Dogma 1 (Göttingen: Vandenhoeck & Ruprecht, 1961), 21–41.

Idem
Studien zur Geschichte des Opfers im alten Israel, WMANT 24 (Neukirchen-Vluyn: Neukirchener, 1967).

Reventlow, Henning Graf
"Sein Blut komme über sein Haupt," *BT* 10 (1960): 311–327.

Rice, Tamara Talbot
The Scythians (New York: Praeger, 1957).

Richter, Georg
Der ezechielische Tempel; eine exegetische Studie über Ezechiel 40ff, BFChrTh 16,2 (Gütersloh, 1912).

Riefstahl, Elizabeth
"Two Hairdressers of the Eleventh Dynasty," *JNES* 15 (1956): 10–17.

Riesenfeld, Harald
The Resurretion in Ezekiel XXXVII and in the Dura-Europos Paintings, UUÅ (Uppsala: Lundequists, 1948).

Ringgren, Helmer and Zimmerli, Walther
Sprüche, Prediger, ATD 16 (Göttingen: Vandenhoeck & Ruprecht, 1962).

Rivlin, A. E.
"The Parable of the Vine and the Fire; Structure, Rhythm and Diction in Ezekiel's Poetry," *Beth Miqra* 63 (1975): 562–566 (Hebrew).

Robinson, Edward
Biblical Researches in Palestine, Mount Sinai and

Arabia Petraea 3 (Boston: Crocker & Brewster, 1841).

Rohde, E.
Psyche (Freiburg i. B.: J. C. B. Mohr [Paul Siebeck], 1898).

Roscher, W. H.
Der Omphalosgedanke bei verschiedenen Völkern, besonders den semitischen. Ein Beitrag zur vergleichenden Religionswissenschaft, Volkskunde und Archäologie, 1918.

Rose, Martin
Der Ausschliesslichkeitsanspruch Jahwes, BWANT 106 (Stuttgart: Kohlhammer, 1975).

Rosenau, W.
"Harel und Ha-Ariel; Ezechiel 43:15–16," *MGWJ* 65 (1921): 350–356.

Rosenberg, H.
"Zum Geschlecht der hebräischen Hauptwörter," *ZAW* 25 (1905): 325–339.

Rost, Leonhard
"Alttestamentliche Wurzeln der ersten Auferstehung" in *In memoriam Ernst Lohmeyer* (Stuttgart: Evangelisches Verlagswerk, 1951), 67–72.

Idem
"Erwägungen zum israelitischen Brandopfer" in *Von Ugarit nach Qumran,* BZAW 77 (Berlin, 1958), 177–183; reprinted in *idem, Das kleine Credo und andere Studien zum Alten Testament* (Heidelberg: Quelle & Meyer, 1965), 112–119.

Idem
"Weidewechsel und alttestamentlicher Festkalender," *ZDPV* 66 (1943): 205–215; reprinted in *idem, Das kleine Credo und andere Studien zum Alten Testament* (Heidelberg: Quelle & Meyer, 1965), 101–112.

Idem
"Die Wohnstätte des Zeugnisses" in *Festschrift Friedrich Baumgärtel zum 70. Geburtstag* (Erlangen: Universitätsbund Erlangen, 1959), 158–165.

Rost, Paul
"Der Altar Ezechiels, Kap. 43:13–17" in *Altorientalische Studien Bruno Meissner zum 60. Geburtstag,* Mitteilungen der altorientalischen Gesellschaft 4 (Leipzig: Harrassowitz, 1928/29), 170–174.

Rowley, H. H.
"The Meaning of Scarifice in the Old Testament," *Bulletin of the John Rylands University Library of Manchester* 33 (1950): 74–110.

Idem
"Zadok and Nehustan," *JBL* 58 (1939): 113–141.

Rubinstein, Arie
"The anomalous Perfect with *Waw*-Conjunctive in Biblical Hebrew," *Bibl* 44 (1963): 62–69.

Rudolph, Wilhelm
Chronikbücher, HAT 21 (Tübingen: Mohr, 1955).

Rüger, Hans Peter
Das Tyrusorakel Ezek 27, Unpub. Diss. (Tübingen, 1961).

Ruthven, J.
"Ezekiel's Rosch and Russia: A Connection?" *BS* 500 (1968): 324–333.

Růžička, Rudolf
Konsonantische Dissimilation in den semitischen Sprachen, Beiträge zur Assyriologie und semitischen Sprachwissenschaft 6, 4 (Leipzig: Hinrichs, 1909).

Saggs, W. F.
"'External Souls' in the Old Testament," *JSS* 19 (1974): 1–12.

Sakenfeld, Katharine D.
"Ezekiel 18, 25–32," *Interpretation* 32 (1978): 295–300.

Sarsowsky, A.
"Notizen zu einigen biblischen geographischen und ethnographischen Namen," *ZAW* 32 (1912): 146–151 (II. חֵילֵךְ, גַּמָּדִים, 147f; V. סַבְרַיִם, 149f).

Sauer, Georg
Die Sprüche Agurs, BWANT 5, 4 (Stuttgart: Kohlhammer, 1963).

de Savignac, J.
"Note sur le sense du terme *ṣâphôn* dans quelques passages de la Bible," *VT* 3 (1953): 95f.

Savoca, G.
"Un profeta interroga la storia; Ezechiele e la teologia della storia," *Aloisiana* 11 (1976).

Sayce, A. H.
"Silsilis in Upper Egypt" in *Sardis,* Publications of the American Society for the Excavation of Sardis 6: Lydian Inscriptions part 2, ed. W. H. Buckler (Leiden: Brill, 1924), 66–68.

Schaeffer, C. F. A.
Enkomi-Alasia; nouvelles missions en Chypre, 1946–1950, Publications de la Mission archéologique française 1 (Paris: Klincksieck, 1952).

Scharbert, Josef
Solidarität in Segen und Fluch im Alten Testament und in seiner Umwelt, BBB 14 (Bonn: Hanstein, 1958).

Idem
"Das Verbum PQD in der Theologie des Alten Testaments," *BZ* 4 (1960): 209–226.

Schlesinger, K.
"Zum Wortfolge im Hebräischen Verbalsatz," *VT* 3 (1953): 381–390.

Schmid, Herbert
"Jahwe und die Kulttraditionen von Jerusalem," *ZAW* 67 (1955): 168–197.

Schmid, Rudolf
Das Bundesopfer in Israel; Wesen, Ursprung und Bedeutung der alttestamentlichen Schelamim (München: Kösel, 1964).

Schmidt, H.
Die Erzählung von Paradies und Sündenfall (Tübingen: J. C. B. Mohr [Paul Siebeck], 1931).

Idem
Der heilige Fels in Jerusalem (Tübingen: J. C. B. Mohr [Paul Siebeck], 1933).

Schmidt, Martin Anton
Prophet und Tempel; eine Studie zum Problem der

Gottesnähe im Alten Testament (Zollikon-Zürich: Evangelischer, 1948).

Schmidt, Werner
"מִשְׁכָּן als Ausdruck Jerusalemer Kultsprache," *ZAW* 75 (1963): 91f.

Schmökel, Hartmut
Geschichte des alten Vorderasien, HO II, 3 (Leiden: Brill, 1957).

Schoff, Wilfred Harvey
The Ship "Tyre"; a Symbol of the Fate of Conquerors as prophesied by Isaiah, Ezekiel and John and fulfilled at Nineveh, Babylon and Rome; a study in the Commerce of the Bible (New York: Longmans, Green, 1920).

Schoneveld, J.
"Ezekiel 14, 1–8," *OTS* 15 (1969): 193–204.

Schott, Albert
Die Vergleiche in den akkadischen Königsinschriften, MVÄG 30 (Leipzig: Hinrichs, 1925).

Schötz, Dionys
Schuld- und Sündopfer im Alten Testament, Breslauer Studien zur historischen Theologie 18 (Breslau: Müller & Seiffert, 1930).

Schreiner, J.
"Wort-Geist-Vision; Ezechiels prophetische Tätigkeit" in *Wort und Botschaft. Eine theologische und kritische Einführung in die Probleme des Alten Testaments* (Würzburg: Echter, 1967), 209–225.

Schult, Hermann
"Der Debir im salomonischen Tempel," *ZDPV* 80 (1964): 46–54.

Schulz, Hermann
Das Todesrecht im Alten Testament. Studien zur Rechtsform der Mot-Jumat-Sätze, BZAW 114 (Berlin: Töpelmann, 1969).

Scott, R. B. Y.
"The Hebrew Cubit," *JBL* 77 (1958): 205–214.

Idem
"Weights and Measures of the Bible," *BA* 22 (1959): 22–40.

Segal, Moses Hirsch
A Grammar of Mishnaic Hebrew (Oxford: Clarendon, 1958).

Seidel, H.
"Horn und Trompete im alten Israel unter Berücksichtigung der 'Kriegsrolle' von Qumran," *WZ* 6 (1956/57): 589–599.

Sellers, Ovid R.
"Musical Instruments of Israel," *BA* 4 (1941): 33–47.

Simian, Horacio
Die theologische Nachgeschichte der Prophetie Ezechiels. Form- und traditionskritische Untersuchung zu Ez 6; 35; 36, Forschung zur Bibel 14 (Würzburg: Echter, 1974).

Simon, Maurice
The Babylonian Talmud, ed. I. Epstein (London: Soncino, 1948).

Simons, Jan Jozef
The Geographical and Topographical Texts of the Old Testament (Leiden: Brill, 1959).

Smend, Rudolf
Die Bundesformel, ThSt 68 (Zürich: EVZ, 1963).

Idem
Die Weisheit des Jesus Sirach (Berlin: Reimer, 1906).

Smit, E. J.
"The Concepts of Obliteration in Ez 5, 1–4," *Journal of Northwest Semitic Languages* 1 (1971): 46–50.

Smith, J. M. Powis
"The Syntax and Significance of Genesis i.1–3,"in *Old Testament Essays* (London: Charles Griffin and Co., Ltd., 1927), 163–171.

Smith, K. F.
"The Tale of Gyges and the King of Lydia," *American Journal of Philology* 23 (1902): 261–282, 361–387.

Smith, M.
"The Veracity of Ezekiel, the Sins of Manasseh, and Jeremiah 44, 18," *ZAW* 87 (1975): 11–16.

Smith, Sidney
"The Ship Tyre," *PEQ* 85 (1953): 97–110.

Snaith, N. H.
The Jewish New Year Festival; its origins and development (London: S. P. C. K., 1947).

Idem
"Sacrifices in the Old Testament," *VT* 7 (1957): 308–317.

Soares, Theo. G.
"Ezekiel's Temple," *The Biblical World* 14 (1899): 93–103.

Soden, Wolfram von
"Akkadisch *ta'û* und hebräisch *tā'* als Raumbezeichnungen," *WO* 1, 5 (1950): 356–361.

Idem
Akkadiches Handwörterbuch (Wiesbaden: Harrassowitz, 1959–1979).

Idem
"Die Unterweltsvision eines assyrischen Kronprinzen," *Zeitschrift für Assyriologie* 43 (1936): 1–31.

Speiser, E. A.
"Background and Function of the Biblical *nāśi'*," *CBQ* 25 (1963): 111–117.

Spiegelberg, Wilhelm
"Der ägyptische Name von Pelusium," *Zeitschrift für Ägyptische Sprache und Altertumskunde* 49 (1911): 81–84.

Idem
Ägyptologische Randglossen zum Alten Testament, 1904.

Idem
"Augustus 'Ρωμαῖος,'" *Zeitschrift für Ägyptische Sprache und Altertumskunde* 49 (1911): 85–87.

Stade, Bernhard
"Anmerkungen zu 2 Kö. 10–14," *ZAW* 5 (1885): 275–297.

Staerk, W.
"Der Gebrauch der Wendung באחרית הימים im at.

Kanon," *ZAW* 11 (1891): 247–253.
Idem
"Zu Habakuk 1:5–11. Geschichte oder Mythos?" *ZAW* 51 (1933): 1–28.
Stamm, Johann Jakob
Die akkadische Namengebung, MVÄG 44 (Leipzig: Hinrichs, 1939).
Staudigel, H.
Die Begriffe Gerechtigkeit und Leben und das Problem der Gerechtigkeit Gottes bei Ezechiel, Unpub. Diss. (Rostock, 1957).
Stevenson, W. B.
"Hebrew 'Olah and Zebach Sacrifices" in *Festschrift Alfred Bertholet* (Tübingen: Mohr [Siebeck], 1950), 488–497.
Strauss, Hans
Untersuchungen zu den Überlieferungen der vorexilischen Leviten (Bonn: Rheinische-Friedrich-Wilhelms-Universität, 1960).
Streck, Maximilian
"Das Gebiet der heutigen Landschaften Armenien, Kurdistân und Westpersien nach den babylonisch-assyrischen Keilinschriften (Schluss)," *Zeitschrift für Assyriologie* 15 (1900): 257–382.
Te Stroete, G. A.
"Ezekiel 24, 15–27: The Meaning of a Symbolic Act," *Bijdragen* 38 (1977): 163–175.
Talmon, Shemaryahu
"Double Readings in the Massoretic Text," *Textus* (Annual of the Hebrew University Bible Project) 1 (1960): 144–184.
Talmon, S.
"Literary Structuring Techniques in the Book of Ezekiel," *Beth Miqra* 63 (1975): 315–327 (Hebrew).
Idem
"The Structuring of Biblical Books: Studies in the Book of Ezekiel," *Annual of the Swedish Theological Institute* 10 (1976): 129–153.
Talmon, S. and Fishbane, M.
"Aspects of the Literary Structure of the Book of Ezekiel," *Tarbiz* 42 (1972): 27–41.
Täubler, Eugen
Biblische Studien; die Epoche der Richter (Tübingen: Mohr, 1958).
Thackeray, H. St. J.
A Grammar of the Old Testament in Greek according to the Septuagint 1 (Cambridge: University Press, 1909).
Idem
The Septuagint and Jewish Worship; a Study in Origins, The Schweich Lectures 1920 (London: Oxford University Press, 1921).
Thomas, D. Winston
"Mount Tabor: The Meaning of the Name," *VT* 1 (1951): 229f.
Thomsen, Peter
"Untersuchungen zur älteren Palästinaliteratur," *ZDPV* 29 (1906): 101–132.
Torrey, C. C.
"Alexander the Great in the Old Testament Prophecies" in *Vom Alten Testament. Karl Marti zum 70. Geburtstage,* BZAW 41 (Giessen: Töpelmann, 1925), 281–286.
Uhlemann, Max
"Über Gog und Magog," *ZWTh* 5 (1862): 265–286.
Unger, Eckhard
"Der älteste Hof- und Staatskalender der Welt," *FuF* 3 (1927): 1f.
Idem
Babylon; die heilige Stadt nach der Beschreibung der Babylonier (Berlin and Leipzig: de Gruyter, 1931).
Idem
"Namen im Hofstaate Nebukadnezars II," *ThLZ* 50 (1925): 481–486.
Idem
"Nebukadnezar II. und sein Šandabakku (Oberkommissar) in Tyrus," *ZAW* 44 (1926): 314–317.
Vaccari, A.
"Le Versioni arabe dei Profeti," *Bibl* 2 (1921): 401–423.
Vanhoye, A.
"L'utilisation du livre d'Ezéchiel dans l'Apocalypse," *Bibl* 43 (1962): 436–472.
de Vaux, Roland
Ancient Israel, its Life and Institutions, tr. John McHugh (New York: McGraw-Hill, 1961).
Idem
"Magog-Hiérapolis (Histoire d'une fausse exégèse)," *RB* 43 (1934): 568–571.
Idem
Les sacrifices de l'Ancien Testament, Cahiers de la Revue biblique 1 (Paris: Gabalda, 1964).
Idem
Studies in Old Testament Sacrifice (Cardiff: University of Wales Press, 1964).
Verbeek, Albert
Schwarzrheindorf. Die Doppelkirche und ihre Wandgemälde, 1953.
Viganò, L.
"Quelques exemples du singulier féminin en -ôt en Ezéchiel," *Studii biblici Franciscani* 27 (1977): 239–245.
Vincent, Albert
"Le rites du balancement (tenoûphâh) et du prélèvement (teroûmâh) dans le sacrifice de communion de l'Ancien Testament" in *Mélanges syriens offerts à M. René Dussaud* 1 (Paris: Geuthner, 1939), 267–272.
Vincent, Hugues
"L'autel des holocaustes et le caractère du temple d'Ézéchiel," *Analecta Bollandiana* 67 (1949): 7–20.
Idem
"Le caractère du temple salomonien" in *Mélanges bibliques rédigés en l'honneur d'André Robert,* Travaux de l'Institut Catholique de Paris 4 (Paris, 1957), 137–148.

Vogels, W.
"Restauration de l'Egypte et universalisme en Ez 29, 13–16," *Bibl* 53 (1972): 473–494.

Vogelstein, M.
"Nebuchadnezzar's Reconquest of Phoenicia and Palestine and the Oracles of Ezekiel," *HUCA* 23 (1950/51): 197–229.

Vogt, E.
"Die Lähmung und Stummheit des Propheten Ezekiel" in *Wort-Gebot-Glaube; Festschrift für Walther Eichrodt,* ATANT 59 (Göttingen: Vandenhoeck & Ruprecht, 1970), 87–100.

Idem
"Der Sinn des Wortes 'Augen' in Ez 1, 18 und 10, 12," *Bibl* 59 (1978): 93–96.

Idem
"Die vier 'Gesichter' (pānīm) der Keruben in Ez," *Bibl* 60 (1979): 327–347.

Idem
Untersuchungen zum Buch Ezekiel, Analecta Biblica 95 (Rome: Biblical Institute, 1981).

Vulgata
Biblica sacra iuxta Vulgatam Versionem ad codicum fidem iussu Pauli PP. VI cura et studio, Monachorum Abbatiae Pontificiae Sancti Hieronymi in Urbe Ordinis Sancti Benedicti edita. XV Liber Hiezechielis ex interpretatione Sancti Hieronymi cum prologo eiusdem et variis capitulorum seriebus (Rome: Typis Polyglottis Vaticanis, 1978).

Vriezen, Theodorus Christiaan
Onderzoek naar de paradijsvoorstelling bij de oude semietische volken (Wageningen: Veenman, 1937).

Wahono, S. W.
The Interpretation of Israel's Past History in the Book of Ezekiel as it is exemplified in Chapters 16, 20 and 23, Unpub. Diss. (Edinburgh, 1974).

Waterman, Leroy
"The Damaged 'Blueprints' of the Temple of Solomon," *JNES* 2 (1943): 284–294.

Weill, Julien
"Les mots תֻּפֶּיךָ וּנְקָבֶיךָ dans la complainte d'Ezéchiel sur le roi de Tyr (28:11–19)," *Revue des études juives* 42 (1901): 7–13.

Weissbach, Franz Heinrich
Das Hauptheiligtum des Marduk in Babylon, Esagila und Etemananki, Wissenschaftliche Veröffentlichungen der Deutschen Orientgesellschaft 59 (Leipzig: Hinrichs, 1938).

Idem
"Izala," *PW* NB 1st series 10 (1919), 1390; *idem, AfO* 7 (1930/31): 43b.

Weitzmann, Michael
"The Dates in Ezekiel," *The Heythrop Journal* 17 (1976): 20–30.

Wellhausen, Julius
Prolegomena to the History of Ancient Israel (Edinburgh: Black, 1885).

Wendel, Adolf
Das Opfer in der altisraelitischen Religion (Leipzig: Pfeiffer, 1927).

Wensinck, Arent Jan
The Ideas of the Western Semites concerning the Navel of the Earth (Amsterdam: Müller, 1916).

Wernberg-Møller, P.
"Observations on the Hebrew Participle," *ZAW* 71 (1959): 54–67.

Widengren, Geo
The Ascension of the Apostle and the Heavenly Book: King and Saviour III, UUÅ (Uppsala: Lundequists, 1950).

Idem
"Early Hebrew Myths and their Interpretation" in *Myth, Ritual, and Kingship,* ed. S. H. Hooke (Oxford: Clarendon, 1958), 149–203.

Idem
The King and the Tree of Life in Ancient Near Eastern Religion: King and Saviour IV, UUÅ (Uppsala: Lundequists, 1951).

Wiener, Harold M.
"Ezekiel's Prophecy against Tyre," *Nieuwe theologische studien* 6 (1923): 7f.

Wildberger, Hans
"Die Thronnamen des Messias, Jes 9:5b," *ThZ* 16 (1960): 314–332.

Wilke, F.
"Das Neumondfest im israelitischen-jüdischen Altertum," *Jahrbuch der Gesellschaft für die Geschichte des Protestantismus in Österreich* 67 (Festschrift für Josef Bohatec) (1951): 171–185.

Williams, A. J.
"The Mythological Background of Ezekiel 28, 12–19," *Biblical Theology Bulletin* 6 (1976): 49–61.

Wilson, R. R.
"An Interpretation of Ezekiel's Dumbness," *VT* 22 (1972): 91–104.

Winckler, H.
"Gog" in *Altorientalische Forschungen* 2 (Leipzig: Pfeiffer, 1898), 160–171.

Wischnitzer-Bernstein, Rachel
"The Conception of the Resurrection in the Ezekiel Panel of the Dura Synagogue," *JBL* 60 (1941): 43–55.

von Wissmann, Hermann
"Geographische Grundlagen und Frühzeit der Geschichte Südarabiens," *Saeculum* 4 (1953): 51–114.

Wolff, Hans Walter
"Jahwe als Bundesvermittler," *VT* 6 (1956): 316–320.

Idem
Joel and Amos, tr. Waldemar Janzen, S. Dean McBride, Jr., and Charles A. Muenchow, ed. S. Dean McBride, Jr. Hermeneia (Philadelphia: Fortress, 1977).

Woolley, C. Leonard
"The Excavations at Ur, 1925–6," *The Antiquaries Journal* 6 (1926): 365–401.

Woude, A. S. van der
Die messianischen Vorstellungen der Gemeinde von Qumrân, Studia semitica neerlandica 3 (Assen: Van Gorcum, 1957).
Woudstra, M. H.
"Edom and Israel in Ezekiel," *Calvin Theological Journal* 3 (1968): 21–35.
Idem
"The Everlasting Covenant in Ezekiel 16, 59–63," *Calvin Theological Journal* 6 (1971): 22–48.
Wright, G. Ernest
"A Solomonic City Gate at Gezer," *BA* 21 (1958): 103f.
Wünsche, August
Die Sagen vom Lebensbaum und Lebenswasser; altorientalische Mythen, Ex Oriente lux 1 (Leipzig: Pfeifer, 1905).
Yadin, Yigael
"Expedition D—The Cave of the Letters," *IEJ* 12 (1962): 227–257.
Idem
"Solomon's City Wall and Gate at Gezer," *IEJ* 8 (1958): 80–86.
Yates, D. R.
The Eschatological Message Concerning Man in the Book of Ezekiel, Unpub. Diss. (Boston University, 1972).
Yeivin, S.
"Random Notes on the Book of Ezekiel," *Beth Miqra* 53 (1973): 164–175 (Hebrew).
York, A. D.
"Ezekiel 1: Inaugural and Restoration Visions?" *VT* 27 (1977): 82–98.
Yoyotte, J.
"Sur le voyage Asiatique de Psammétique II," *VT* 1 (1951): 140–144.
Ziegler, Joseph
Ezechiel, Septuaginta. Vetus Testamentum graecum 16, 1 (Göttingen: Vandenhoeck & Ruprecht, [2]1978, "Nachtrag" und "Corrigenda zur 1. Auflage" by D. Fraenkel).
Idem
Sylloge. Gesammelte Aufsätze zur Septuaginta, Mitteilungen des Septuaginta-Unternehmens (MSU) 10 (Göttingen: Vandenhoeck & Ruprecht, 1971).
Zimmerli, Walther
"Alttestamentliche Prophetie und Apokalyptik auf dem Wege zur 'Rechtfertigung des Gottlosen'" in *Rechtfertigung; Festschrift für E. Käsemann* (Tübingen: Mohr, 1976), 575–592.
Idem
"Bildverkleidete und bildlos erzählte Geschichte bei Ezechiel und Daniel" in *I. L. Seeligmann Anniversary Volume* (Jerusalem, forthcoming).
Idem
"Deutero-Ezechiel?" *ZAW* 84 (1972): 501–516.
Idem
Ezechiel. Gestalt und Botschaft, Biblische Studien 62 (Neukirchen-Vluyn: Neukirchener, 1972).
Idem
"Ezekiel," *The Interpreter's Dictionary of the Bible, Supplementary Volume,* 314–317.
Idem
"Ezechieltempel und Salomostadt" in *Hebräische Wortforschung; Festschrift zum 80. Geburtstag vom Walter Baumgartner,* VT Suppl 16 (Leiden: Brill, 1967), 389–414.
Idem
"Das 'Gnadenjahr des Herrn'; Archäologie und Altes Testament" in *Festschrift für Kurt Galling* (Tübingen: Mohr, 1970), 321–332.
Idem
"Israel im Buche Ezechiel," *VT* 8 (1958): 75–90.
Idem
"The Message of the Prophet Ezekiel," *Interpretation* 23 (1969): 131–157.
Idem
1. [i.e. Erstes Buch] Mose 1–11. Die Urgeschichte, Zürcher Bibelkommentare (Zürich: Zwingli, [3]1967).
Idem
"Le nouvel 'exode' dans le Message des deux grands Prophètes de l'Exil" in *maqqēl shâqēdh. La branche d'amandier. Hommage à Wilhelm Vischer* (Montpellier, 1960), 216–227.
Idem
"'Offenbarung' im Alten Testament (Ein Gespräch mit R. Rendtorff)," *EvTh* 22 (1962): 15–31.
Idem
"Das Phänomen der 'Fortschreibung' im Buche Ezechiel" in *Prophecy; Essays presented to Georg Fohrer,* ed. J. A. Emerton. BZAW 150 (Berlin: deGruyter, 1980), 174–191.
Idem
"Zur Sprache Tritojesajas" in *Gottes Offenbarung,* ThB 19 (München: Kaiser, 1963), 217–233.
Idem
"Zur Struktur der alttestamentlichen Weisheit," *ZAW* 51 (1933): 177–204.
Idem
"Der Wahrheitserweis Jahwes nach der Botschaft der beiden Exilspropheten" in *Tradition und Situation. Studien zur alttestamentlichen Prophetie Artur Weiser zum 70. Geburtstag dargebracht* (1963), 133–151.
Zimmerli, Walther and Jeremias, Joachim
"παῖς Θεοῦ," *TDNT* 5, 654–717 (Zimmerli, 654–677; Jeremias, 677–717).
Idem
The Servant of God, Studies in Biblical Theology 20 (Naperville, Ill.: Allenson, 1965).
Zirker, Hans
"דרך (derekh) = potentia?" *BZ* 2 (1958): 291–294.
van Zyl, A. H.
The Moabites, Pretoria Oriental Series 3 (Leiden: Brill, 1960). 1715 Brill, 1960).

1. Passages*

* Note: 'I' signifies Ezekiel Volume I; 'II' signifies Volume II. Volume I page numbers marked by (x) indicate that the biblical reference is misprinted in the first edition of Volume I and should be corrected to the form appearing here.

2. Hebrew Words

3. Names and Subjects